# The SAGE Handbook of Social Psychology

This book is dedicated to the memory of
Henri Tajfel and Edward E. Jones

# The SAGE Handbook of
# Social Psychology

Concise Student Edition

Edited by
Michael A. Hogg
and Joel Cooper

Los Angeles | London | New Delhi
Singapore | Washington DC

First published 2007
Reprinted 2009

SAGE Publications Ltd
1 Oliver's Yard
55 City Road
London EC1Y 1SP

SAGE Publications Inc.
2455 Teller Road
Thousand Oaks, California 91320

SAGE Publications India Pvt Ltd
B 1/I 1 Mohan Cooperative Industrial Area
Mathura Road
New Delhi 110 004

SAGE Publications Asia-Pacific Pte Ltd
33 Pekin Stree #02-01
Far East Square
Singapore 048763

**British Library Cataloguing in Publication data**
A catalogue record for this book is available from the British Library

ISBN 978-1-4129-4535-6

**Library of Congress Control Number: 2006936102**

Typeset by C&M Digitals (P) Ltd., Chennai, India
Printed in Great Britain by the MPG Books Group
Printed on paper from sustainable resources

# Contents

# Advisory Board

**Dominic Abrams** is Professor of Social Psychology and Director of the Centre for the Study of Group Processes at the University of Kent, England. He is also a Fellow of the Academy of the Learned Societies in the Social Sciences. His research on group processes, intergroup relations, social-identity and social cognition is closely associated with the development of the social-identity perspective, and he has published widely on these topics. He is co-editor with Michael A. Hogg of the journal *Group Processes and Intergroup Relations*, and recently edited, with Michael A. Hogg and Jose Marques, *The Social Psychology of Inclusion and Exclusion* (Psychology Press, 2005). His research focuses on social inclusion and exclusion, developmental aspects of intergroup relations, intergroup deviance, intergroup contact, leadership, subtle forms of sexism, and the impact of alcohol on group processes.

**Elliot Aronson** is Professor Emeritus at the University of California at Santa Cruz and Distinguished Visiting Professor at Stanford. He has published over 130 research articles and eighteen books, including the award-winning *The Social Animal*. His written work has been translated into sixteen foreign languages. He is the only person in the history of the American Psychological Association (APA) to have received all three of its major academic awards: The National Media Award for Books (1973); the Distinguished Teaching Award (1980); and the Distinguished Research Contribution Award (1999). He has served as President of the Western Psychological Association and President of the Society of Personality and Social Psychology (Division 8) of the APA.

**Shelley E. Taylor** is Professor of Psychology at the University of California, Los Angeles. Author of over 300 publications, Taylor's research interests centre chiefly on the contribution of socioemotional resources to mental and physical health. She especially studies 'positive illusions', namely exaggerated positive views about the self, the world and the future that are protective of health, especially in threatening times. Taylor received both the Early Career Award and the Distinguished Scientific Contribution Award from the APA. She was elected to the American Academy of Arts and Sciences and to the National Academy of Science's Institute of Medicine. She has served as President of the Western Psychological Association and President of the Society of Personality and Social Psychology.

# Contributors

**Michael A. Hogg** is Professor of Social Psychology at Claremont Graduate University, and Honorary Professor of Psychology at the University of Kent and the University of Queensland. He is also a fellow of the Society for Personality and Social Psychology, the Society for the Psychological Study of Social Issues, and the Academy of the Social Sciences in Australia. His research on group processes, intergroup relations, social identity and social cognition is closely associated with the development of social identity theory. He has published 240 scientific books, chapters and articles on these topics. He is an associate editor of the *Journal of Experimental Social Psychology*, co-editor with Dominic Abrams of the journal *Group Processes and Intergroup Relations*, and senior consulting editor for the *Sage Social Psychology Program*. Current research focuses on leadership, deviance, uncertainty reduction, vicarious dissonance, and subgroup relations.

**Joel Cooper** is Professor of Psychology at Princeton University. He has been on the Princeton faculty since receiving his Ph.D. from Duke University in 1969. His major area of interest is the study of cognitive dissonance theory, and he has contributed several dozen articles on this topic. Other research interests include the study of persuasion processes in courts of law and gender discrepancies in the use of computers. Curently Editor of the *Journal of Experimental Social Psychology*, he is co-author of a social psychology textbook, co-editor of *Attribution and Social Interaction: The Legacy of Edward E. Jones*, and author of *An Invitation to Cognitive Dissonance*.

**Nadia Ahmad** received her Ph.D. from the University of Kansas in 2005. Her research interests include prosocial behavior, stereotyping and prejudice, and emotion.

**Craig A. Anderson** is Distinguished Professor of Psychology at Iowa State University. He has authored over 120 professional research articles on a wide range of topics in social, personality and cognitive psychology, such as attribution theory, depression, human inference and social judgment, covariation detection, and aggression. His recent research centers on media violence and human aggression. His new book on *Violent Video Game Effects on Children and Adolescents* is published by Oxford University Press (2007).

**C. Daniel Batson** is a professor of psychology at the University of Kansas. His major area of interest is in the various forms of prosocial motivation. He has authored four books, including *The Altruism Question* (1991), and more than 100 research articles and chapters, many on helping behavior and the motivation for helping.

**Galen V. Bodenhausen** is Professor of Psychology at Northwestern University in Evanston, Illinois. He is the author of more than seventy scientific articles on the topics of social cognition, social attitudes and intergroup relations. He is the editor of *Personality and Social Psychology Review*.

**Matthew T. Crawford** is a lecturer in social psychology in the Department of Experimental Psychology at the University of Bristol (UK). He obtained his Ph.D. from Indiana University, Bloomington in 2002.

**Phoebe C. Ellsworth** is the Frank Murphy Distinguished University Professor of Law and Psychology at the University of Michigan. After receiving her PhD in social psychology from Stanford University in 1970, she taught at Yale and Stanford and has been at Michigan since 1987. Her major areas of interest are cognition and emotion, psychology and law, and research methods. She is a co-author of *Methods of Research in Social Psychology* (with Elliot Aronson, J. Merrill Carlsmith, and Marti Hope Gonzales), and is a fellow of APA, APS, and the American Academy of Arts and Sciences.

**Russell H. Fazio** received his PhD from Princeton University in 1978. He is currently the Harold E. Burtt Professor of Psychology at Ohio State University. Fazio's program of research focuses upon attitudes, their formation, accessibility from memory, functional value, and the processes by which they influence attention, categorization, judgment, and behavior. Much of his current research concerns the utility of implicit measures of attitudes and their appropriate interpretation. He served as Editor of the *Journal of Experimental Social Psychology* from 1999 to 2002.

**Julie Fitness** is Senior Lecturer in Psychology at Macquarie University, Sydney, Australia. Her primary research interests concern the functions and features of emotions such as love, hate, anger and jealousy within intimate relationships and the workplace. She has published widely on emotion and relationship-related topics and is currently an associate editor of the journal *Personal Relationships*. Her latest book, *From Mating to Mentality: Evaluating Evolutionary Psychology* (co-edited with Kim Sterelny), was published by Psychology Press in 2003.

**Garth Fletcher** is Professor of Psychology at the University of Canterbury, New Zealand. He has published many books, chapters and research articles concerned with the social psychology of intimate relationships, including *The New Science of Intimate Relationships* (2002). He is a fellow of the Royal Society of New Zealand, the Society of Personality and Social Psychology, and the American Psychological Society.

**Joseph P. Forgas** is Scientia Professor of Psychology at the University of New South Wales, Sydney, Australia. His research focuses on the influence of affective and cognitive processes on social judgments and interpersonal behavior. He has published eighteen books and over 160 journal articles and chapters. His work has received widespread international recognition, including a D.Sc. degree from Oxford, the Distinguished Scientific Contribution Award by the APS, the Alexander von Humboldt Research Prize, and election to fellowships by the Association for Psychological Science, the Hungarian Academy of Sciences, the Australian Academy of the Social Sciences, and the Society for Personality and Social Psychology. He is Associate Editor of the *Frontiers of Social Psychology* series (Psychology Press, New York) and serves on the editorial boards of several leading journals in the field.

**Leonel Garcia-Marques** is Professor in the Department of Psychology and Educational Sciences at the University of Lisbon. His main research areas are social cognition and cognitive psychology and include topics such as person memory, stereotypes, hypothesis testing, false memories and collaborative memory. His recent work has appeared in the *Journal of Personality and Social Psychology,* the *Journal of Experimental Social Psychology* and *Group Processes and Intergroup Relations*. He was an associate editor of the *European Journal of Social Psychology* from 1997 to 2001.

**Ruth Gaunt** is Head of the Social Psychology Program in the Department of Sociology at Bar-Ilan University. After receiving her PhD from Tel-Aviv University, she has been a post-doctoral fellow at Harvard University and at the Univeristy of Louvain-la-Neuve. Her research interests include attribution processes, social perception and intergroup relations.

**George R. Goethals** assumed the E. Claiborne Robbins Distinguished Professorship in Leadership Studies at the Jepson School of Leadership Studies at the University of Richmond, Richmond, Virginia, starting in 2006. Previously he was for many years Professor of Psychology at Williams College in Williamstown, Massachusetts, where he was Chair of the Department of Psychology and founding Chair of the Program in Leadership Studies. He has published numerous articles on attitude change, social perception and self-evaluation and has co-edited volumes on memory, the self, group behavior, and a general theory of leadership. His current research interests concern how college students educate each other, political debates, and perceptions of the presidential leadership of Ulysses S. Grant.

**Richard Gonzalez** is Professor of Psychology at the University of Michigan, Ann Arbor, Michigan. His main research area is judgment and decision-making, where he has made both theoretical and applied contributions. He also specializes in methodology and statistics, focusing in particular on data from social interaction.

**Aiden P. Gregg** is Lecturer in the School of Psychology at the University of Southampton, UK. His research interests lie at the interface of self and social cognition. He is co-author (with Robert P. Abelson and Kurt P. Frey) of *Experiments with People: Revelations from Social Psychology*.

**David L. Hamilton** is Professor in the Department of Psychology at the University of California, Santa Barbara, California. His research interests focus on cognitive and affective processes in social perception, and his work has investigated impression formation, stereotyping, attribution processes and the perception of groups. He has edited or co-edited four books, including *Person Memory* (1980), *Cognitive Processes in Stereotyping and Intergroup Behavior* (1981), *Affect, Cognition, and Stereotyping* (1993), and *Social Cognition: Impact on Social Psychology* (1994).

**Stephen G. Harkins** is Professor and Chair of the Department of Psychology of Northeastern University in Boston, Massachusetts. He has published over fifty articles on topics such as social loafing and social facilitation. He edited a volume entitled *Multiple Perspectives on the Effects of Evaluation on Performance: Toward an Integration* (2001).

**Miles Hewstone** is Professor of Social Psychology and Fellow of New College, Oxford University. He has published widely on the topics of attribution theory, social cognition, stereotyping and intergroup relations. His current research focuses on the reduction of intergroup conflict. He is co-founding Editor of the *European Review of Social Psychology*, and a former editor of the *British Journal of Social Psychology*. He is a fellow of the British Academy and an honorary fellow of the British Psychological Society. He was the recipient of the Kurt Lewin Award, for Distinguished Research Achievement, from the European Association for Experimental Social Psychology in 2005.

**L. Rowell Huesmann** is Professor of Psychology and Communication Studies at the University of Michigan and a Senior Research Scientist at the Institute for Social Research where he directs the Aggression Research Program. His research has focused on the psychological foundations of aggressive and antisocial behavior and social-cognitive models to explain aggression. He was the lead author on the 1997 Human Capital Initiative report on the causes of violence and is past President of the International Society for Research on Aggression.

**Steven J. Karau** is Associate Professor of Management at Southern Illinois University, Carbondale, Illinois. His research focuses on issues such as individual motivation within groups, temporal and situational influences on group interaction and performance, gender differences in leadership, top management team dynamics and firm performance, and ethical judgments of organizational change initiatives.

**Paul A.M. van Lange** is Professor in Social Psychology at the Free University at Amsterdam, the Netherlands, and director of the Kurt Lewin Institute, an interuniversity research school for social psychology and its applications. He also holds a professorship in social psychology at the University of Leiden and has been an associate editor for the *Journal of Personality and Social Psychology* and the *European Journal of Social Psychology*. His major research interests focus on social interaction and interdependence, examining cooperation and competition, self-enhancement, and prosocial motivation and behavior, including generosity, sacrifice, and forgiveness.

**David A. Lishner** received his Ph.D. from the University of Kansas in 2003 and was a post-doctoral fellow at Vanderbilt University from 2003 to 2005. He is now Assistant Professor of Psychology, University of Wisconsin Oshkosh. His research focuses on the emotional and motivational aspects of human altruism and on empathy-related processes, employing both self-report and psychophysiological measures.

**C. Neil Macrae** is Professor of Social Cognition at the University of Aberdeen in Scotland. Interested in most aspects of social cognition, his current research focuses on the neural substrates of social-cognitive functioning.

**Robin Martin** is Professor of Social and Organizational Psychology at Aston University, Birmingham, UK. He has served on the faculties of the Universities of Sheffield, Swansea, Cardiff, and Queensland, Australia. While at the University of Queensland he was the Director of the Centre for Organizational Psychology. He conducts research in both social and organizational psychology. His current research interests are in attitude change, majority and minority influence, work-place motivation, and leadership.

**Michael A. Olson** is an assistant professor of psychology at the University of Tennessee. He received his PhD from Indiana University in 2003. His research interests span from attitudes to implicit social cognition to intergroup relations. Currently he is engaged in research investigating implicit measures of attitudes, the processes underlying the formation of classically conditioned attitudes, and intergroup anxiety in simulated contact situations.

**Nickola Overall** is a lecturer in psychology at the University of Auckland, New Zealand. Her research interests include relationship maintenance and regulation, partner support, forgiveness, mate selection, self-perceptions of mate value, relationship attachment, and bias and accuracy. She has published several book chapters and articles on these topics.

**Kimberly A. Quinn** is currently a lecturer in the School of Psychology at the University of Birmingham, UK. She earned her PhD from the University of Western Ontario and then pursued postdoctoral research at Northwestern University and Dartmouth College. Her primary research interests concern the social-cognitive processes implicated in categorical person perception (with emphasis on attentional and memorial processes in face-processing and social categorization), and the mental representation of stereotypes.

**Constantine Sedikides** is Professor of Psychology, University of Southampton, UK. He has authored more than 130 articles and chapters on self and identity, affect and motivation, close relationships, intergroup perception, and self-perception and self-evaluation. He has also co-edited eight books or special journal issues on self and identity and intergroup perception. His most recent co-edited books include *Frontiers in Social Psychology: The Self* (with Steve Spencer), *Individual Self, Relational Self, Collective Self* (with Marilynn Brewer, 2001) and *Intergroup Cognition and Intergroup Behavior* (with John Schopler and Chet Insko, 1998).

**Steven J. Sherman** is Professor of Psychology at Indiana University, Bloomington. He has authored many journal articles and book chapters in various areas of social psychology, focusing on social cognition, impressions of individuals and groups, judgment and decision-making, attitude formation and change, counterfactual thinking, and teen and adult cigarette-smoking.

**Craig A. Smith** received his PhD from Stanford University in 1986, and is currently an associate professor of psychology and human development at Peabody College of Vanderbilt University, Nashville, Tennessee. His research interests concern appraisal, emotion, coping, and adaptation, broadly defined. Current research projects focus, respectively, on explicating the cognitive processes underlying emotion-eliciting appraisals, on documenting the organization of physiological activities in emotion, and on examining coping and adjustment in children with recurrent abdominal pain. He is a fellow of Division 38 (Health Psychology) of the American Psychological Association. He currently serves as Editor of the journal *Cognition and Emotion*.

**Donald M. Taylor** is a Professor of Psychology at McGill University. He has published extensively in the social psychology of intergroup relations. His particular focus is the plight of disadvantaged groups, involving projects in Aboriginal communities, South Africa, and Indonesia. His most recent book is entitled *The Quest for Identity* which is published by Praeger.

**Yaacov Trope** is a professor of psychology at New York University. He has co-edited two books and published numerous articles and chapters on topics that include person perception, motivation and cognition, self-control, and judgment and decision-making. He is co-editor of *Dual-Process Theories in Social Psychology*.

**Penny S. Visser** is an associate professor in the Department of Psychology at the University of Chicago. Her research focuses primarily on the structure and function of attitudes, including the dynamics of attitude formation and change, the impact of attitudes on thought and behavior, the antecedents and consequences of attitude strength, and issues associated with attitude measurement and research methodology.

**Kipling D. Williams** is Professor of Psychological Sciences at Purdue University. He has authored or edited eight books on topics that include social self, social motivation and social cognition, and psychology and law. He has published over eighty articles and chapters on topics in group performance, social influence, aggression, ostracism, psychology and law, and Internet research. His books include *The Social Outcast: Ostracism, Social Exclusion, Rejection, and Bullying* (2005), *Ostracism: The Power of Silence* (2001), and *Psychology and Law: An Empirical Perspective* (2005).

**Stephen C. Wright** is Professor and Canada Research Chair in Social Psychology at Simon Fraser University. He received his PhD from McGill University, and spent twelve years at the University of California, Santa Cruz, California. His research focus on intergroup relations, specifically the consequences of membership in stigmatized groups, antecedents and barriers to collective action, prejudice and its reduction, and minority languages and cultures. He has served as Associate Editor for *Personality and Social Psychology Bulletin* and is on the editorial boards of numerous scholarly journals. His work has been published widely in scholarly volumes and social, educational, and cross-cultural psychology journals.

# Preface and Introduction

MICHAEL A. HOGG AND JOEL COOPER

*The Sage Handbook of Social Psychology* was published in 2003. With twenty-three chapters it was primarily a resource for academic researchers and graduate student research. We decided to prepare this Concise Student Edition to cater more for upper division and graduate student courses – focusing in on a subset of sixteen of the original chapters that are most closely aligned to relevant upper division and graduate classes. To prepare this edition, and to make the text more accessible, we had our authors thoroughly update their references and prepare a short introduction and summary for their chapters.

Editing a handbook of social psychology is not for the fainthearted. This is something we have learned. It is an awesome enterprise, not only because it is such a big task but also because handbooks occupy such an influential role in the discipline. Handbooks describe the state of the art – they survey what we know about social psychology, and in so doing identify gaps in our knowledge, current foci of research activity, and future research directions.

There have been many handbooks of social psychology. The first, edited by Murchison, was published in 1935 – it was a weighty tome that signaled that social psychology was a discipline to be taken seriously. Seventy years on, two of the most recent handbooks are the two-volume *Handbook of Social Psychology*, which is now in its fourth edition (Gilbert et al., 1998), and the *Blackwell Handbook of Social Psychology*, which comes as four separately edited volumes (Tesser and Schwartz, Fletcher and Clark, Hogg and Tindale, and Brown and Gaertner, respectively), published in 2001 under Hewstone and Brewer's overarching editorship.

The reason we originally set out to edit our own handbook is that the field of social psychology moves very quickly. We wanted to produce an accessible survey of the state of the discipline at the dawn of the new millennium – what do we know about human social behavior and what are the current and future hot topics for research? Such a survey must be authoritative, and so we invited leading scholars from around the world to write about their fields. We felt that such a survey should not only cover the field in a scholarly manner but also be accessible to graduate students, senior undergraduates, and, to some extent, people in relevant neighboring disciplines, and so we configured the chapters to fit into a single volume.

We felt that such a volume should reflect the international nature of contemporary social psychology. Although most social psychological research is conducted in the world's wealthiest and English-speaking countries, most particularly the USA, there is significant cutting-edge research done by leading scholars from other parts of the globe. In this *Concise Student Edition* we have thirty-nine contributors, twenty-six of whom are from North America (twenty-four from the USA, two from Canada), nine from Europe (seven from the UK, one each from the Netherlands and Portugal), and four from Australasia (two from Australia and two from New Zealand).

We have structured the book in a systematic yet conventional way that we feel fits the intrinsic structure of social psychology and the way the subject is often taught or presented. The first chapter (Chapter 1, by George R. Goethals) provides a history of the development of social psychology. Such a history is important because it helps us understand the origins of social psychological ideas, priorities, and foci. History also provides a more meaningful context for understanding current social psychological research and its future trajectory. Chapter 2, by Phoebe C. Ellsworth and Richard Gonzalez, discusses how we do social psychology – it discusses the methods and techniques that are available to social psychologists and that are used by them to address research questions. Since social psychology is a science in which theories rest on empirical evidence, methodological choices and constraints influence the sorts of theories and understandings that are developed.

Chapters 3 through 8 focus on key issues in social cognition. They address a number of important phenomena from the perspective of the mental representations within the head of the individual. In Chapter 3, Steven J. Sherman, Matthew T. Crawford, David L. Hamilton, and Leonel Garcia-Marques review what we know about how people make inferences about other people and how these inferences are affected by the way that social information is stored in memory. In Chapter 4, Kimberly A. Quinn, C. Neil Macrae, and Galen V. Bodenhausen review how social memory and social inference are affected by social categorization and stereotyping. In Chapter 5, Constantine Sedikides and Aiden P. Gregg discuss the crucial role of the self in social cognition and social behavior, and in Chapter 6, Russell H. Fazio and Michael A. Olson discuss the equally central role of attitudes in how we represent the social world and how we subsequently behave. Joseph P. Forgas and Craig A. Smith, in Chapter 7, remind us that people are not all cold cognition. Forgas and Smith take a comprehensive look at the role played by affect and emotion. The final social-cognition chapter, Chapter 8, is by Yaacov Trope and Ruth Gaunt, who discuss the role of causal attribution processes in the way we construct a meaningful and stable representation of the world around us.

Chapters 9 through 12 focus mainly on what happens between individuals – social interaction. In Chapter 9, Penny S. Visser and Joel Cooper discuss how people's attitudes can change. They look at cognitive and motivational aspects of the ways that people are influenced to alter their attitudes. In Chapter 10, Julie Fitness, Garth Fletcher, and Nickola Overall focus on another critical aspect of social interaction. When we think of social interaction, we also think of social relations – acquaintances, friends, lovers, partners, and enemies. Indeed, personal relationships are, for most of us, often at the heart of life itself. Fitness and colleagues take us on a journey through the development, maintenance, and dissolution of attraction, friendships, and intimate relationships.

Chapters 11 and 12 contrast the good and the bad of humanity. In Chapter 11, C. Daniel Batson, Paul A.M. van Lange, Nadia Ahmad, and David A. Lishner discuss when and how people help other people even to the extent of suffering personal losses. They distinguish between egoism (benefiting another to benefit oneself), altruism (benefiting another as an end in itself), collectivism (benefiting another to benefit a group), and principlism (benefiting another to uphold a moral principle). In Chapter 12, Craig A. Anderson and L. Rowell Huesmann discuss the environmental and interpersonal roots of human aggression and emphasize social cognitive theories of aggression. They survey the forms that aggression can take, discuss the influence of age and gender on aggression and discuss the relationship between situational and biological correlates of aggression.

Chapters 13 and 14 focus on what happens among individuals in a group – that is, group processes. In Chapter 13, Kipling D. Williams, Stephen G. Harkins, and Steve J. Karau discuss the effect of being in a group on performance of a task – do we work better or harder in a group, or are we lazy and more inefficient? They discuss the specific conditions of group life that influence task performance. Groups actively, or more passively through norms, influence our feelings, attitudes, and behaviors. Robin Martin and Miles Hewstone, in Chapter 14, discuss how groups provide a context for us to obey commands, how groups produce norms that we conform to, and how minority groups or groups that we do not belong to can actually change our attitudes and behaviors and thus contribute to wider social change.

Chapters 15 and 16 focus on what happens among people who are in different social groups – intergroup relations. This final pair of chapters opens with a discussion by Michael A. Hogg and Dominic Abrams, in Chapter 15, of intergroup relations and how they influence and are influenced by collective self-conception and social identity. The theme is continued in Chapter 16 by Stephen C. Wright and Donald M. Taylor, who focus more closely on the important phenomena of discrimination and prejudice, and ways that they can be combated.

The sixteen chapters of this Concise Student Edition of the *Sage Handbook of Social Psychology* survey what we know about social psychology at the beginning of the third millennium. Although the social psychology research agenda tackles enduring questions about social life, it also responds to the more proximal common life experiences of the scientists who represent the field. The sociohistorical context of the discipline affects the research agenda. Although we certainly are not making predictions of future directions, it is possible to detect in the chapters some common themes and emphases which may give some direction to the field over the next few years. These include a focus on self – how is it formed and changed, what forms does it take, and how does it affect and how is it affected by social cognition and behavior? Affect and emotion form another focus, which is an attempt to shift attention from cold cognitive perceptual processes toward the strong feelings that underpin much of social life.

There is also a growing accent on intergroup relations – how do groups interact with and perceive one another, and how can different groups in society learn to live harmoniously together? Perhaps tied to some extent to recognition of the intergroup context of social life is a growing concern with understanding the social psychology of morality and justice – an emphasis which focuses on the absolutely central role of justice in social life but may also eventually confront tricky issues to do with moral relativism and moral absolutism.

Recent scientific and technical developments revolving around DNA sequencing, genome mapping, and fMRI (functional magnetic resonance imaging) have helped provide impetus to another strong new direction in social psychology, social cognitive neuroscience, which seeks to discover the role of brain function and structure in cognition and social behavior. In a related vein, there is a new focus on the evolutionary parameters of social behavior. Social psychologists are asking what adaptive function for the species is served by some general classes of social behavior.

The original handbook of social psychology had a long gestation. The idea was first explored at the annual meeting of the Society of Experimental Social Psychology in Toronto in October 1997. Planning was completed in Princeton during the summer of 1998, and Joel and Mike met up again in March 1999 in Sydney and June 1999 in Princeton. Joel was in Brisbane for sabbatical in 2001, when the final touches were given. Much of the work of liaising with authors and with each other was done by email, but Mike was able to meet fairly regularly with Sage in London, and also on one memorable occasion in San Sebastián in 2002. The idea for a concise student edition was first explored at the Palm Springs meeting of the Society for Personality and Social Psychology in January 2006, followed up in mid-2006 when Joel was once again visiting Mike in Brisbane for sabbatical. The edition was completed after Mike had left Australia and taken up his new position at Claremont Graduate University in Los Angeles.

Editing a handbook is a huge undertaking – we had absolutely no idea just how huge when we set out. We just thought it would be an exciting and scientifically valuable project. We are very grateful to Michael Carmichael, our editor at Sage in London, for keeping us motivated and task-focused and for being so cheerfully tolerant of the various delays that are inevitable in a project of this magnitude. Throughout, he was enthusiastic and efficient and helpful. We would like to thank Tali Klein and Robert Mirabile, in Princeton, for the invaluable practical help they gave us – they read, commented upon, and copy-edited many of the original chapters. The entire job of editing this book was also made much easier for us because of the people we were working with – a selection of the world's leading social psychologists. Our authors were a joy to work with, and produced chapters that were inspirational to read. Finally, we would like to thank our editorial advisers, Dominic Abrams, Elliot Aronson, and Shelley Taylor, who advised us on the configuration, content, and authorship of chapters and generally gave us encouragement and a sense of confidence in the enterprise.

October 2006
Michael Hogg, Los Angeles
Joel Cooper, Princeton

# PART ONE

# HISTORY AND NATURE OF SOCIAL PSYCHOLOGY

# 1
# A Century of Social Psychology: Individuals, Ideas, and Investigations

GEORGE R. GOETHALS

**INTRODUCTION**

This chapter tells an exciting story of intellectual discovery. At the start of the twentieth century, social psychology began addressing age-old philosophical questions using scientific methods. What was the nature of human nature, and did the human condition make it possible for people to work together for good rather than for evil? Social pschology first addressed these questions by looking at the overall impact of groups on individuals and then began to explore more refined questions about social influence and social perception. How do we understand persuasion, stereotypes and prejudice, differences between men and women, and how culture affects thoughts and behavior?

In 1954, in his classic chapter on the historical background of modern social psychology, Gordon Allport nominated Auguste Comte as the founder of social psychology as a science. He noted that Comte, the French philosopher and founder of positivism, had previously, in 1839, identified sociology as a separate discipline. In fact, sociology did not really exist, but Comte saw it coming. Allport notes that 'one might say that Comte christened sociology many years before it was born' (Allport, 1968: 6). In the 1850s, during the last years of his life, Comte argued that beyond sociology a 'true final science' would emerge. Comte called this science *la morale positive*, but it was clearly psychology. In fact, combined with sociology it would become social psychology. Social psychology has a history before and after Comte. But it is interesting to know that when it was first conceptualized as a discipline it was seen as being the ultimate one.

If not with Comte, where does social psychology begin? Clearly, ancient philosophers pondered the inherent nature of humankind, the way people interact and influence each other, and the way they govern themselves. In *The Republic,* Plato argued that men organize themselves and form governments because they cannot achieve all their goals as individuals. They are interdependent. Some kind of social organization is required. Various forms emerge, depending on the situation, including aristocracy, oligarchy, democracy, and tyranny. Plato clearly favored aristocracy, where the wise and just govern, and allow individuals to develop their full potential. Whatever the form, social organization and government develop to serve the interests of people in achieving various goals.

As on many other issues, Plato's younger colleague Aristotle had a different view. He held that people came together and organized groups from instinctual tendencies toward sociability, rather than utilitarian needs for a social contract. He was also more positively disposed toward democracy than Plato. Plato reasoned from his concept of the ideal state that a ruling elite, governed by dispassionate reason and intellect, would be the best form of government. Aristotle had more faith that the combined talents of different individuals, combined with their inherent propensities for positive affiliations, would produce the better state. Aristotle based his judgments on data, as he understood them. His idea that people naturally came together and that they could be trusted to use their varying talents to create the good society was based on a more generous view of human nature than Plato's. Thus, the differing perspectives of these Greek philosophers defined enduring arguments that have since guided inquiry in social psychology and many other intellectual disciplines. How much of human behavior, particularly social behavior, can be understood as deriving from external constraints and contingencies vs. internal drives and dispositions? How capable are people of using their intellectual capacities wisely and effectively? Are the basic instincts of human beings good or evil? How much of human behavior can we understand and predict from deductive theoretical reasoning, and how much more can we learn from careful observation and induction?

Nearly 2,000 years later, these issues became matters of sharp debate during the Renaissance and the Enlightenment. According to Allport (1954), one of the most enduring issues was whether human behavior was governed rationally or irrationally. And if irrationality was dominant, what were the qualities of the irrational forces which guided human behavior?

Among the philosophers who struggled with these questions were Niccolò Machiavelli (1469–1527), Thomas Hobbes (1588–1679), John Locke (1632–1704), and Jean-Jacques Rousseau (1712–1782). The earlier thinkers, Machiavelli and Hobbes, were much more pessimistic about the quality of human nature and argued that some kind of social order needed to be imposed simply to constrain human selfishness and aggressiveness. Locke and Rousseau were more optimistic. Locke was particularly influential, with a balanced view of human qualities, and a faith that people could be reasonable, moderate, and cooperative (Allport, 1968: 19). The debate between the optimists and pessimists informed debates between Thomas Jefferson and Alexander Hamilton at the founding of the American republic in the 1780s, and still persists in the present day.

## The emergence of psychology

Plato's and Aristotle's fundamental arguments about the nature of human beings, especially as they related to ideas about the best forms of social organization and government, continued for centuries. Alongside these debates were other philosophical inquiries, also tracing back to the ancients, particularly Socrates and Aristotle, about many other aspects of the human condition. Are people capable of free will, or is behavior determined? What is the nature of human thought and consciousness? Do individuals perceive reality accurately? At the same time, as Comte pointed out, the sciences were also developing. People studied medicine, astronomy, mathematics, physics, chemistry, and physiology, again, with roots dating back to the Greeks and beyond. The scientific method emphasized evaluating philosophical and theoretical propositions against data – data that could be collected by a variety of methods.

When philosophers and scientists both began to tackle the same questions in the late nineteenth century, the 'true final science' of psychology emerged. A pivotal figure in this development was the German neural scientist Hermann von Helmholtz (1821–1894). He conducted important early research on the nervous system and various aspects of vision, hearing, and perception. The application of long-standing scientific methods to age-old philosophical questions about human behavior and mental processes gave birth to psychology. The year 1875 saw one marker of its emergence, when Wilhelm Wundt established a laboratory in Leipzig, Germany. In the same year, William James, like Wundt, a physician, physiologist, and philosopher, established an informal laboratory in his basement in Cambridge, Massachusetts in the USA, and gave the first psychology course at Harvard University. James is said to have commented that the first lectures on psychology he heard, he gave himself.

Psychology blossomed under the leadership of Wundt, James, and then G. Stanley Hall, who founded the first formal American psychological laboratory at Johns Hopkins University in 1883. In 1890, James published his classic two-volume *Principles of Psychology*, followed in 1892 by a 'briefer course' version of the same work. He wrote on such topics as sensation, vision, hearing, habit, the brain and neural activity, the self, and the will. While much of the earliest psychology dealt with questions outside the domains of social psychology, it was not long before the scientific method was applied to social questions. For example, Hall (1891) made extensive use of questionnaires in his studies of children's social interaction. In fact, the emergence of modern social psychology is marked by the application of the scientific methods that defined psychology as a whole to questions about social influence and social interaction. Two milestones in the emergence took place before the century ended.

### 1895: the birth of social psychology

In 1895, Norman Triplett at Indiana University in the USA began his studies of how social forces affect bicycle racing. In the same year, in Paris, Gustave Le Bon published his analysis of group behavior in *Psychologie des foules*, translated in 1896 as *The Crowd*. Both of these highly influential works considered the impact of other people on the individual.

Norman Triplett was a cycling enthusiast who pored over statistics from the Racing Board of the League of American Wheelmen. He noticed that riders' times were faster when they were racing against other riders than when they were simply racing against the clock. From these observations he developed a 'theory of dynamogenesis' that held that the presence of competing others released energy in individuals that they could not release on their own. Triplett then proceeded to test his theory with a series of experiments in which participants wound fishing reels alone and in direct competition with others. Triplett (1897) found that participants wound reels faster when competing than when alone and concluded that his theory was supported.

Triplett's work raised more questions than it answered. Was it the mere presence of others that produced enhanced performance? Or was it competition, or perhaps being observed by others (Wheeler, 1970)?

These questions were studied vigorously in the twentieth century, beginning with Floyd Allport during World War I (Allport, 1924). Allport coined the term 'social facilitation' to refer to the observation that the presence of others, for some reason, produced enhanced performance in individuals. Thus, Triplett not only conducted what are regarded as the first experiments in social psychology, but also initiated a rich and enduring line of theoretical and empirical exploration. Interestingly, as with many other social phenomena, social facilitation findings became increasingly complex. Sometimes the presence of others led to poorer performance. The extremely varied empirical landscape in this domain provided a basis for decades of theory and research (Geen and Bushman, 1987; Zajonc, 1965).

Gustave Le Bon also dealt with the impact of the presence of others. His contribution was more sweeping theoretically, but tied to a different kind of data. Rather than conduct experimental laboratory research with quantitative measures, Le Bon simply observed groups of many kinds, particularly those that gather in crowds. He was stunned by the transformation that comes over individuals in a group situation. He held that in crowds people are more emotional, less rational, more prone to extreme behaviors, and easily stimulated by leaders from one kind of extreme feeling to another in short periods of time. Le Bon described a person in a crowd as someone who has lost his or her individuality, whose conscious personality is somehow stripped away, revealing an ugly, aggressive unconscious personality that is widely shared by other group members. As Le Bon tried to explain the transformation of people in crowds, especially the lowering of intellectual functioning and the willingness to follow others with great emotional intensity, he relied heavily on notions of contagion and suggestion. In crowds, he argued, people are highly suggestible and can be led easily by emotional appeals of leaders. Mark Antony's stunning manipulation of the crowd in Shakespeare's *Julius Caesar* provides a powerful literary example of a leader's manipulating the extreme emotions of a crowd, and dramatically redirecting them from sympathy with the assassin Brutus to outrage ('The noble Brutus hath told you Caesar was ambitious. If it were so, it was a grievous fault, and grievously hath Caesar answered it.').

Le Bon's explanation of suggestion was less compelling than his description of wild mob behavior, but his observations and ideas had a lasting impact. They figured prominently in Freud's volume (1921) on group behavior and have influenced subsequent work on groupthink, deindividuation, and leadership.

## Stirrings: the early twentieth century

The general development of psychology, fostered in great part by G. Stanley Hall, brought social psychology along with it, but the field of sociology also contributed to the emergence of social psychology, just as Comte had foreseen. Le Bon's work was perhaps more influential among sociologists and informed important turn-of-the-century work by Charles Horton Cooley, whose book *Human Nature and the Social Order* (1902) developed the idea of imitation, a concept closely related to Le Bon's concept of suggestion. Imitation is more concerned with behavior, suggestion with thought and cognition.

A few years later, in 1908, sociologically and psychologically oriented treatments of social psychology were represented in two textbooks that contained the phrase 'social psychology' in their titles. E.A. Ross's *Social Psychology*, like Cooley's book, emphasized the ideas of suggestion or imitation. Social interaction could be largely understood in terms of the basic phenomenon of people influencing the thoughts and actions of others. Ross's ideas were applied especially to issues such as crowds, social movements, social class, marriage, and religion (Pepitone, 1999). William McDougall's *Introduction to Social Psychology* held that there were many different explanations of social behavior, but that many of them could be subsumed under the general concept of instincts. Among others, McDougall (1908) considered 'the reproductive and the parental instinct', the instinct of pugnacity, the gregarious instinct, and 'instincts through which religious conceptions affect social life'. Clearly, scholars had developed a fertile field of study and many ways of trying to understand its varied phenomena.

Although social psychology gained momentun from Ross and McDougall, neither their specific concerns with particular societal phenomena nor their concern with instincts remained central in the work of later social psychologists. The field as we recognize it in the twenty-first century can be seen taking shape in Floyd Allport's influential textbook, *Social Psychology* (1924). Allport was heavily influenced by behavioristic methods and ideas, and he firmly grounded social psychology in scientific methods. Allport was particularly influenced by J.B. Watson and his provocative *Psychological Review* paper (1913), 'Psychology as the Behaviorist Views It.' Watson challenged Wilhelm Wundt's (1894) introspectionist approach to psychology, an approach which emphasized individual reports of consciousness and mental processes. Watson argued that the study of consciousness should be banished and that psychologists would make progress only by focusing on observable stimuli and responses. The behavioral perspective became highly influential within psychology for over fifty years and was clearly congenial to Floyd Allport.

Among the problems that Allport took on were those explored by Triplett and Le Bon in 1895. Nearly thirty years after the publication of their work, Allport found these topics worthy of study. In fact, as noted above, Allport had been conducting research on social facilitation since World War I and explained enhanced performance in the presence of others in behavioristic, stimulus–response terms. The sight and sounds of others were a stimulus to more intense responses. He used similar concepts in explaining extreme behavior in crowd situations. Dramatic action by one or more people in a crowd was a stimulus to similar behavior in others, which in turn stimulated or restimulated the original actors, or led to yet others being drawn in.

The status of social psychology as a scientific discipline was firmly established by the early 1930s. In 1931, Gardner Murphy and Lois Murphy of Columbia University published *Experimental Social Psychology*, a volume which reviewed over 800 studies of social processes. In 1937, the Murphys and Theodore Newcomb, a Columbia PhD, brought out the encyclopedic revised edition, which reviewed several hundred more studies. The influence of Gardner Murphy is often overlooked in the history of social psychology. Theodore Newcomb was a student of Murphy, as were Solomon Asch and Muzafer Sherif, whose important work will be considered below.

## Explorations in social influence: the 1920s and 1930s

It is obviously a matter of interest and taste to identify which of the hundreds of studies reviewed by Murphy et al. (1937) are of lasting importance in understanding the evolution of social psychology. But, surely, the study of social influence was a key line of work in the pre-World War II decades. One early study by H.T. Moore (1921) demonstrated the influence of a reported majority of peers and of experts on participants' preferences between two musical, ethical, and linguistic options. Moore found that their judgments were very frequently reversed in response to either kind of influence, particularly majority influence. To Moore, these findings made sense. In the tradition of Floyd Allport, he argued that the opinions of others serve as stimuli that elicit a conforming response. This interpretation resonated with Ross's earlier emphasis on suggestion and imitation and the views of philosophers who had been pointing for many years to human irrationality. A similar study by Lorge was published in 1936, and again highlighted the impact of prestige and suggestion. He asked students their reactions to the statement that 'a little rebellion now and then is a good thing, and as necessary in the political world as storms are in the physical'. The statement was attributed to either Thomas Jefferson, who actually made it, or Vladimir Lenin. Lorge found that participants were much more likely to agree with the statement when it was attributed to Jefferson. The explanation was Jefferson's greater prestige, among Americans, than Lenin's.

Later, as we shall see, Solomon Asch (1948) took issue with the Moore/Lorge interpretation. He argued that people have a completely different interpretation of what 'a little rebellion' means when mentioned by Lenin as opposed to Jefferson. What changes is the object of judgment, not the judgment of the object (Wheeler, 1970). This debate once again goes back to basic questions – perhaps unresolvable – of human motivation and rationality.

Another important series of studies of interpersonal influence – studies that have become classics in the field – was conducted in the 1930s by Muzafer Sherif to address in part questions debated by McDougall and Floyd Allport in earlier decades. In 1920, McDougall published his book *The Group Mind*. In it, he argued that certain ideas and feelings in groups have an existence independent of the individuals in the group. In the Watsonian tradition, Allport argued that the term 'group mind' should be banished forever. For him, the unit of analysis should be the individual. There was no sense in positing an unobservable, unverifiable, mystical, and confusing group mind. McDougall came to regret using the term, but the debate about the nature of groups, and what, if anything, exists in groups apart from individuals became contentious. Sherif quite deliberately stepped onto this battlefield.

In Sherif's classic experiments, groups of participants were seated in a totally dark room with a single point-source of light in front of them. Because there is no frame of reference for judging the location of the light, it appears to move. How much it appears to move varies considerably with individual judges. Sherif established that groups devise norms that govern the judgments of individuals in the group, that new entrants into the group adopt those norms, and that people take established norms into new groups. Thus, Sherif found that a set of norms that is characteristic of the group exists quite apart from any particular individual. The implications of this research for the group mind controversy aside, Sherif showed how hard people in ambiguous situations work to reduce confusion and define a frame of reference for making judgments. They look to other people for information about reality and, through a process of mutual influence, develop norms and frames of reference. Importantly, Sherif showed that thoughtful, careful laboratory experimentation with relatively small numbers of people could explore basic aspects of group functioning that characterize groups ranging in size from a few individuals to whole cultures.

Two other important studies of interpersonal influence were conducted in the 1930s, before the USA entered World War II. They both show continuing concern with the impact of the group on individuals. The first was conducted by Kurt Lewin and his colleagues, and was inspired by Lewin's experience as a refugee from Nazi Germany (Lewin et al., 1939). Kurt Lewin is a giant in the history of social psychology, even though he was not a social psychologist at the beginning of his career. Lewin started publishing his work in Germany in 1917 and made major contributions to understanding personality, child development, learning, memory, and perception. His work on conflict was particularly influential. Lewin developed what he called 'field theory'. In some ways, it was more a language than a set of theoretical propositions. Strongly influenced by physics and topology, Lewin used concepts such as the life space, vectors, region, force field, energy, need, tension system, and valence. Field theory emphasized the way internal and environmental forces combined to influence behavior as people negotiated their way through their perceived world, or 'life space.'

Lewin was renowned for this linking of theory and data. Deeply concerned with world problems, Lewin wanted to do research that had an impact on important real-world problems. He and his students called their work action research. But Lewin wanted to base applications on theory and data. He is often quoted as saying, 'there's nothing so practical as a good theory', and the definitive biography of Lewin, written by his close friend and collaborator Alfred Marrow, is called *The Practical Theorist*.

When Lewin came to the USA in 1933, in the first year of Hitler's 'Reich' in Germany, he left the prestigious Psychological Institute in Berlin for the Department of Home Economics at Cornell. Shortly thereafter, he took an appointment at the Iowa Child Welfare Research Station. It was there that Lewin and his colleagues conducted an important study on social climate and behavior in groups. Clubs composed of groups of eleven-year-old boys were supervised by adults who adopted one of three leadership styles: democratic, autocratic, or laissez-faire. The democratic style produced constructive and independent group norms, marked by focused and energetic work whether the leader was present or absent. Boys in the groups with laissez-faire leadership were generally passive, while groups with autocratic leaders were either aggressive or apathetic. Here was research with a social message. When large and dangerous countries led by authoritarian and totalitarian regimes were threatening world peace and democratic institutions, Lewin's 'action research' spoke to the quality of life in differing social systems.

Research on group norms by Theodore Newcomb (1943) at Bennington College in the late 1930s had less social relevance but dealt with perennial questions of the nature of social norms and social influence. In the 1930s, the newly founded Bennington College, an undergraduate school for women, was an interesting mix of mostly liberal faculty members and mostly conservative students – at least when the young women first enrolled. Newcomb showed that students became considerably more liberal over time, and that the more they were accepted and integrated into the college community, the more liberal they tended to be. Local norms exerted a strong influence on those who became engaged in the community. In a follow-up study nearly thirty years later, Newcomb (1963) showed that the Bennington women remained liberal, particularly when they married husbands who supported their new attitudes.

The work of Sherif and Newcomb clearly demonstrated the power of social norms. It did not answer age-old questions about the role of rational as opposed to irrational processes in producing such dramatic conformity to social norms. These enduring questions would await further research, after World War II.

### World War II and studies of group dynamics, attitudes, and person perception

The research by Sherif on group norms and Lewin and his colleagues on leadership showed that social psychology was alive to important social issues. Once the USA was drawn into World War II, social psychologists became engaged in questions prompted by the need to mobilize the nation for a long conflict. Kurt Lewin again was at the forefront. He was asked by the National Research Council to study ways of persuading women homemakers to serve animal viscera – heart, sweetbreads, and kidneys – to their families. Lewin continued to be interested in group forces and reasoned that influence through group norms would be more influential and more lasting than influence produced by a persuasive message presented in a lecture. Lewin (1943) and later researchers (Bennett, 1955; Radke and Klisurich, 1947) found that changes in attitude and behavioral commitmentproduced by perceptions of group norms were, in fact, the most dramatic.

At the same time, other psychologists, led by Carl Hovland of Yale University, began exploring attitudes more broadly, with special emphasis on US army propaganda, especially with regard to issues affecting troop morale. In the 1920s, attitude had been thought to be the central concept in the field of social psychology (McGuire, 1968; Thomas and Zaniecki, 1918–20; Watson, 1925). The bulk of Murphy and Murphy's (1931) *Experimental Social Psychology* concerned attitudes. But attitude research had crested and faded during much of the 1930s, as more work was done on group dynamics and interpersonal influence. Issues of troop morale during the war brought renewed urgency to understanding attitudes. Much of the work that Hovland and his colleagues conducted during the war was summarized in the book *Experiments on Mass Communication* (Hovland et al., 1949). Their work was focused on such questions as how long the war against Japan in the Pacific would last after the defeat of Nazi Germany in Europe. It explored a wide variety of independent variables, including whether to present information by lectures or films, and whether two-sided or one-sided messages produced more, and more lasting, persuasion.

After the war, Hovland and his colleagues at Yale continued to do groundbreaking research on attitudes. This work culminated in the classic volume, *Communication and Persuasion* (1953) by Hovland et al. This research studied in detail the paradigm, 'Who said what to whom?' How are different audiences affected by different messages from different communicators? Specific questions concerned the credibility of communicators, the organization and structure of messages, whether fear-arousing communications enhanced persuasion, and what audience personality variables affected the success of persuasive messages. The work of the Yale school was guided in part by a model of persuasion based on the theoretical work of the behaviorist Clark Hull, long a member of the Yale faculty, and a mentor of Carl Hovland. Hull had developed the formulation that behavior is a function of drive and habit, or that performance is a function of learning and motivation. Therefore, the key to producing attitude change was to teach an audience a new point of view (learning) and the motivation to accept it. Persuasion could also be seen as following the three steps of paying attention to the message, understanding it, and, finally, accepting or yielding to it. A great deal of creative research was done by focusing on the elements in this formula.

Interestingly, this work was not divorced from the work on group dynamics and group norms that had been so influential prior to World War II. One of the chapters in *Communication and Persuasion* was 'Group Membership and Resistance to Influence'. It reported a number of important studies by Harold Kelley on conformity to group norms, and summarized Kelley's seminal theoretical paper on the normative and comparison functions of reference groups.

After the war, at the same time that Hovland and his colleagues developed their highly creative work on communication and persuasion, Kurt Lewin and his successors continued their vigorous exploration of group dynamics. Lewin attracted a group of original and highly productive young scholars to the group dynamics enterprise. One of the most brilliant, Leon Festinger, completed his PhD under Lewin at the University of Iowa before the war. Festinger sought Lewin out for graduate work not because of an interest in social psychology, but because of the power of Lewinian ideas such as force fields, memory, and tension systems, and because of the excitement of tying theory closely to data. Festinger joined Lewin and Dorwin Cartwright in establishing the Research Center for Group Dynamics at the Massachusetts Institute of Technology (MIT) near the end of the war. Among the distinguished social psychologists working at the Center were Kurt Back, Morton Deutsch, Murray Horwitz, Harold Kelley, Albert Pepitone, Stanley Schachter, and John Thibaut (Jones, 1985). In the very early years, there was significant interchange between the MIT Center for Group Dynamics and the newly formed Department of Social Relations at nearby Harvard University (Festinger, 1980). Thus, Gordon Allport and Jerome Bruner were involved in the dynamic intellectual ferment of the immediate postwar period.

In just a few years, due to MIT's waning interest in supporting an endeavor somewhat peripheral to its main concerns, the Center began a move to the University of Michigan. In the midst of this transition, Kurt Lewin suddenly died, and his successors took the leadership role. Major works from the MIT years included Festinger et al.'s (1950) work on affiliation in housing complexes in postwar Cambridge, Massachusetts. Once again, the influence of Lewin in doing practical research was evident. A housing shortage needed attention.

In addition to the research centers at Yale and Michigan, exploring attitudes and group dynamics, respectively, another significant postwar development was taking place in response to the creative work of Fritz Heider. Heider came to the USA from Hamburg, Germany, in 1930, teaching for a time at Smith College and then moving to the University of Kansas in 1947. Heider was a major figure in the tradition of Gestalt psychology, a perspective that emphasized cognitive and perceptual organization. The term 'Gestalt' comes from the German and means 'shape or form'. Gestalt psychologists, such as Koffka, Kohler, and Wertheimer, emphasized the very active way people process information and organize perceptual elements into coherent wholes, particularly wholes that have 'good fit' and are pleasing (Koffka, 1935). One of its key principles is that the whole is different from the sum of its parts. The parts are integrated into a meaningful and satisfying form. For example, the individual notes in a musical chord combine to make an integrated sound that has its own integrity (Wheeler, 1970).

In the 1940s, Heider wrote two extremely influential papers that extended Gestalt principles into the realms of person perception, attitude organization, and interpersonal relations. In 1944, Heider published the paper 'Social Perception and Phenomenal Causality', the first systematic treatment of attribution processes. Heider argued that perceivers link people's actions to underlying motives or dispositions because there is a good Gestalt or perceptual 'fit' between the way people behave and the nature of their personal qualities. This basic insight into the ways people make causal attributions for personal behavior was more fully developed later in Heider's classic book *The Psychology of Interpersonal Relations* (1958). Heider's other paper from the 1940s had even more immediate impact (Jones, 1985). In 'Attitudes and Cognitive Organization', Heider developed balance theory. Again the emphasis, with some mathematical adornment, was on principles of good perceptual fit. People had both attitudes toward (sentiment relations) and connections to (unit relations) other people, objects, ideas, or events. The organization of these units could be in balance or out of balance. Balance prevails, for example, when person *P* is linked to an action and likes another person, *O*, who approves of that action. Imbalance exists when two people like each other but are linked in opposite ways to objects, actions, or ideas, or dislike each other but are similarly linked. Balance theory gave rise somewhat later to a strong focus on cognitive consistency.

Another enduring line of research in social psychology also developed in the immediate postwar years. Solomon Asch conducted several extremely important studies of person perception within the Gestalt tradition. Asch, like Heider, had been born in Europe, but moved to New York City when he was thirteen. Like Muzafer Sherif and Theodore Newcomb, he studied at Columbia with Gardner Murphy. Asch's paper 'Forming Impressions of Personality' (1946) highlighted two findings. The first was that perceivers given information about another individual's personal qualities organized that information into a coherent whole such that one critical piece of information could color the entire impression. People told to form an impression of a person who was 'intelligent, skillful, industrious, warm, determined, practical, and cautious' perceived that individual very differently from one described as 'intelligent, skillful, industrious, cold, determined, practical, and cautious'. The only difference, of course, is the substitution of the word 'cold' for the word 'warm'. But these two traits serve to organize the overall impression such that terms like 'determined' and 'industrious' have a somewhat different meaning. Again, the whole perception is important, and the whole is different from the sum of the parts. Second, the impressions people form are strongly affected by the order in which they receive different pieces of information. People learning that a person is 'intelligent, industrious, impulsive, critical, stubborn, and envious' form a more positive impression than those who learn about someone who is 'envious, stubborn, critical, impulsive, industrious, and intelligent'. The initial traits form the basis for an initial impression, and later information is made to fit that first impression.

Early research on impression formation and person perception explored questions such as the personal qualities of accurate judges of personality, but Asch's work and that of others (cf. Bruner and Tagiuri, 1954) stimulated a more general consideration of the processes underlying the perception of people.

## The 1950s: the era of Leon Festinger

There are a number of giants in the history of social psychology: Floyd Allport, Solomon Asch, Fritz Heider, Muzafer Sherif, and, perhaps most of all, Kurt Lewin. But, arguably, the work of Leon Festinger has stimulated more theory, research, and controversy than that of anyone else. Festinger graduated from the College of the City of New York at a young age and found Kurt Lewin in Iowa. His talent and his seniority among the many students of Lewin made him, along with Dorwin Cartwright, the leader of the Center for Group Dynamics after Lewin's death. Festinger was enormously energetic and original, and he produced highly creative and influential theory and research in a number of areas. While it is possible to follow the transitions from one domain of research to another, the sheer range and variety of Festinger's work is extremely impressive.

Festinger's (1950) book on housing and affiliation, with Schachter and Back, was fundamentally a study of 'social pressures in informal groups'. Not surprisingly, in the same year, Festinger (1950) published an important theoretical paper, 'Informal Social Communication'. Festinger argued that the need to define 'social reality' or to achieve 'group locomotion' (a classic Lewinian term meaning 'getting something accomplished') created pressures toward uniformity of opinion within groups. These pressures would be observed in informal social communication, or talk, among group members, and would tend to produce uniformity through opinion change or the rejection of people with deviant opinions from the group. Festinger's theory produced a great deal of research that he conducted with colleagues such as Gerard, Hymovitch, Kelley, Raven, and Schachter. Perhaps the most important study in this tradition was Schachter's (1951) experiment on deviation and rejection, showing that people expressing a deviant opinion in groups were subject to an enormous amount of social-influence pressure, seen in increased communication, until they are rejected by the group if they refuse to conform. Rejection is seen in cessation of communication – treating the deviant as a nonperson – and the assignment of unpleasant tasks to the deviant.

Four years later, Festinger published his highly original and highly influential paper 'A Theory of Social Comparison Processes'. In the Lewinian tradition, Festinger and his colleagues also published a number of empirical papers supporting the new theory, effectively commandeering an issue of *Human Relations*. Social-comparison theory can be viewed as an extension of the theory of informal social communication. It argues that people evaluate their abilities as well as their opinions through reference to a social reality. A key difference is that the new theory focused on the individual's need to evaluate opinions and abilities by comparison with similar others rather than the group's need to establish opinion uniformity. This change in focus is reminiscent of issues pertaining to the group mind and the existence of group phenomena independent of the individuals in the group. The shift located Festinger's concerns directly in the mind of the individual person, thereby sidestepping the old questions of the independent nature of groups.

It is of interest that in considering ability as well as opinion evaluation, Festinger returned to the topic of his first publication, in 1940, on level of aspiration. While the consideration of abilities, and the emphasis on individuals, are striking differences, the similarities between the theory of informal social communication and the theory of social-comparison processes are even more impressive. Both theories highlight the importance of similarities among groups of individuals, and the tendency to reject, or cease comparing with, others who cannot be made similar. Social-comparison theory essentially got lost for some time after its appearance, though it re-emerged sporadically during the 1960s and 1970s (Latané, 1966; Suls and Miller, 1977). Now that it is firmly re-established, there is today a varied and vigorous tradition of social comparison research, a tradition linking social-comparison processes to issues of self and social identity (Suls and Wheeler, 2000).

Despite the enduring importance of social comparison theory, and the vitality of research on comparison processes today, Festinger is best known for another contribution. Moving quickly and creatively after the publication of social comparison research, Festinger began studying rumor transmission. This seemed like a natural extension of his interest in communication. In studying rumors about natural disasters, such as earthquakes and floods, Festinger was struck by studies showing that people in areas outside sites of immediate destruction spread rumors about even worse calamities about to come (Festinger, 1975). Why would people be creating and spreading fear-arousing rumors? Why would they make themselves scared? Festinger had a transforming insight. The people were not making themselves scared. They were already scared, but had no clear justification for their anxious feelings. They had to make up a cognition that fit and justified their emotion. The thought that they were scared did not fit the thought that there was nothing to fear. When cognitions do not fit, there is pressure, Festinger reasoned, to make them fit. Thus was born the idea of cognitive dissonance.

Early research by Brehm (1956) on decision making, research by Festinger et al. (1956) on proselytizing after failed prophecies, and Festinger's (1957) book *A Theory of Cognitive Dissonance* began an extremely vigorous research tradition which is still active today. As for Festinger himself, after responding to a number of criticisms of dissonance theory, he once again moved on, physically and intellectually and, in 1964, began studying color vision at the New School for Social Research.

The most enduring line of research coming out of dissonance has examined the consequences of behaving inconsistently with attitudes. The classic experiment by Festinger and Carlsmith (1959) showed that when participants lied by telling a confederate that an extremely boring task was actually a lot of fun, they subsequently came to believe that the task really was fun to a greater degree if they were paid a smaller ($1) rather than larger ($20) amount of money for saying so. A small incentive provides insufficient justification for the counterattitudinal behavior. Attitude change is necessary to justify the behavior and reduce dissonance. This and other research provided strong evidence for dissonance theory, even though critics dubbed the original experiment 'the 20 dollar misunderstanding'.

One reason that this line of research was important and controversial was that it cut against the behaviorist tradition which suggested that people should believe what they say the more they are paid (reinforced) for saying it. Those in the behaviorist tradition (Rosenberg, 1965) attacked the empirical base of the dissonance claims, but eventually most social psychologists came to accept the basic finding: there is an inverse relationship between reward for counter-attitudinal behavior and subsequent self-justificatory attitude change. Later critics accepted the data but offered challenging alternative explanations. A self-perception account (Bem, 1972) held that no dissonance motivation was needed to account for the findings – people were merely inferring their attitude after considering their behavior and the situation in which they performed it. A self-presentation account (Tedeschi et al., 1971) argued that people need only to appear consistent, not feel consistent. And a more recent self-affirmation theory (Steele, 1988) holds that people simply need to affirm that they are good rather than feel consistent. In contrast to these challenges, a provocative paper by Cooper and Fazio (1984) has strengthened the basic arguments of dissonance theory, pointing to the role of physiological arousal stemming from aversive consequences. A great deal of research on when and why self-justificatory attitude change takes place has kept the cognitive dissonance tradition alive and well.

## The 1960s: the return of social influence

Thanks in part to the impact of Leon Festinger's own changes in direction, social-influence and group-dynamics research receded in prominence immediately after World War II. One extremely important exception was the work of Solomon Asch on prestige influence and conformity. As noted above, Asch was influenced by Gestalt principles and, in 1948, he took on the studies by Moore and Lorge from the 1920s and 1930s, arguing that people were not thoughtlessly influenced by majority or expert opinion. In the late 1940s Asch also began his extremely important and influential studies of conformity. Asch (1951) asked naive research participants to make judgments about the length of lines when a unanimous majority of their peers made obviously erroneous judgments about the lines in a face-to-face situation. The question was whether people would simply conform to others' judgments when it was entirely clear that their judgments were wrong. Asch was surprised by the extent to which people did indeed conform. They were much more influenced by majority opinion, even when it was obviously in error, than he thought they would be.

Asch distinguished three processes that might have produced the conformity he observed. First, there might simply be 'distortion of action'. People knew that the majority was wrong but simply went along with it anyway. Second, there might be 'distortion of judgment' whereby people knew that they did not see the lines as the majority did, but figured that the majority must be correct. Finally, in a few cases, there was 'distortion of perception' whereby participants craned their necks and squinted until they actually saw the wrong line as the right one.

Huge quantities of research have been done to explore the details of Asch-like conformity. One of the most important distinctions in this literature is the one between compliance and internalization, that is, simply going along with social pressure without believing what one is saying as opposed to actually coming to believe that others are correct. Herbert Kelman (1961) importantly added to the conceptual overview by suggesting that identification should be set alongside compliance and internalization as a process of opinion change. Sometimes people come to believe something because they identify with an attractive source. They do not fully internalize the opinion into their belief and value system but hold it so long as they are trying to be like the attractive communicator. Reintroducing identification brings back one of the original explanations in Le Bon's (1895) and Freud's (1921) account of leadership and group behavior.

Issues of conformity and blind social influence were put into sharp relief in the early 1960s by Stanley Milgram's (1963, 1965) well-known studies of obedience to authority. Adult, rather than student, research participants were drawn from the New Haven, Connecticut, area. Through strikingly clever experimental theatrics, including highly convincing experimenters and confederates, participants were urged by an experimenter to give what they believed were extremely painful and dangerous electric shocks to a 'learner' in the context of a study on punishment. Would subjects obey the experimenter ordering these shocks, or refuse to continue? Like Asch, Milgram found much more social influence than he, or almost anyone else, thought possible. Exactly why so many people were fully obedient to the experimenter, even though they believed that they might be very seriously harming another person, is still not entirely clear. Probably critical was the experiment's insisting that he was responsible for the outcome of the experiment. Milgram proposed an essentially Lewinian explanation. A series of studies suggested that subjects were caught in a conflicting force field, and that they responded to whichever source – the experimenter or the 'learner' – was closer. The closer the learner was to the participant, the more the participant could see or hear him, the less they obeyed directives to shock him. Moreover, when the experimenter was more distant, sometimes even phoning in his directives, obedience dropped. The face-to-face (some might say 'in your face') nature of the situation seems extremely important, although it is not really clear what elements of the situation create such power. It may be that the participant's inability to articulate reasons for disobeying are an important element in producing obedience.

The Milgram research had a profound impact on social psychology for reasons quite beyond its empirical or theoretical implications. Observers of, as well as some participants in, the social psychological scene were disquieted by the wide use of deception in many of the experiments. But Milgram's research set off a firestorm (Baumrind, 1964). Was it ethical to deceive research participants? Was it moral to put them in situations that they had not consented to be in, and to stress, coerce, or embarrass them? These controversies (Kelman, 1968) led to the formulation of strict review procedures endorsed by the APA and administered by the federal government. These review procedures are designed to protect human participants in psychological research. Yet some psychologists feel that they may have had a chilling impact on the whole research enterprise (Festinger, 1980).

One of the arguments psychologists have made in requesting latitude in the procedures they use to conduct research is that they must create situations of high impact in order to study important phenomena. A compelling example of the study of behavior in high-impact situations is the research on bystander intervention in emergencies, or helping behavior, initiated by John Darley and Bibb Latané in the 1960s (Darley and Latané, 1968; Latané and Darley, 1970). Darley and Latané were spurred by the famous case in 1964 of Kitty Genovese in New York City, where thirty-eight bystanders watched while Genovese was stabbed repeatedly and eventually killed in an incident that unfolded over a half-hour. Not one of the observers even called the police, although that would have been very simple. Why didn't people help?

Darley and Latané explored these questions in a series of experiments that generated a large and lively research tradition on helping and altruism. They suggested a five-step model whereby intervening was dependent on noticing the emergency, interpreting it as a situation where help was needed, accepting responsibility for intervening oneself, knowing the appropriate form of assistance, and, finally, taking action. Studies suggested that misinterpretation and diffusion of responsibility were important variables in affecting people's behavior in such situations. Importantly, the presence of more than one observer dramatically increased the chances of both those variables depressing the rate of helping.

Research by Jane and Irving Piliavin (Piliavin et al., 1969; Piliavin and Piliavin, 1972) approached helping behavior in terms of rewards and costs, once again bringing a reinforcement perspective to social psychology. Originally focusing on both the rewards and costs of both helping and not helping in various situations, the model evolved toward putting more emphasis on the costs of each course of action, especially helping. The latter variable seems to have most impact.

Research on bystander intervention and helping raised basic questions about human values and human morality once again, questions that have been around since the ancient Greeks. Do people care for their fellow human beings? Can they cooperate, or are they doomed to compete? What mix of altruism and hedonism, or cooperation and competition, can we expect in social interaction? Questions of altruism are alive and well right now (Batson, 1998; Cialdini et al., 1987; Krebs and Miller, 1985). Similarly, questions of cooperation and competition, and, more generally, social justice are alive and well at present, largely due to influential work in the 1960s by Deutsch and Krauss (1960) on threat and cooperation and Lerner on people's belief in a just world (Lerner and Simmons, 1966). Morton Deutsch was heavily influenced by his mentor Kurt Lewin and productively explored conflict, cooperation, and competition for much of his career. Melvin Lerner's work on justice helped nurture and develop a tradition of concern with relative deprivation and social justice that had begun with the pioneering work in the 1940s and 1950s of Herbert Hyman (1942) on status and reference groups, Samuel Stouffer and his colleagues on the experiences of the American soldier (Stouffer et al., 1949), and Robert Merton on reference groups and relative deprivation (Merton and Kitt, 1950; cf. Pettigrew, 1967).

Another line of social-influence research beginning in the 1960s concerned 'the risky shift' and group polarization. Le Bon long ago noted the extremes to which people in groups would go, partly as a result of anonymity and diffusion of responsibility to a prestigious leader. Festinger et al. (1952) published a paper showing the kinds of deindividuation in groups that can result from these forces (Pepitone, 1999). Then a series of studies by Wallach, Kogan, and others focused on groups' tendencies to take more risk than could be expected from the risk-taking propensities of the members of the group (cf. Brown, 1965, 1986). Wallach and Kogan (Wallach et al., 1962) initially favored a diffusion of responsibility explanation of these findings, thus highlighting the broad importance of this phenomenon, already implicated in studies of obedience to authority, and soon to be applied to understanding bystander intervention. Later work seemed to establish quite clearly that diffusion of responsibility was less important than the fact that risk is a value. As a result, people compete to be as risky as similar others, and they advance and respond to persuasive arguments toward risk-taking (Burnstein, 1982; Goethals and Zanna, 1979).

This line of research was entirely reconceptualized and redirected by an important study by Moscovici and Zavalloni (1969) at the end of the decade. Moscovici and Zavalloni argued that the risky shift was simply one manifestation of the general tendency, identified by Le Bon, for groups to become extreme. They argued that whenever a cultural value is relevant to a group discussion or group decision, whether that value be risk, democracy, favoring the in-group, or evaluating national icons, the views of group members will become more extreme. The group will polarize. They showed that high-school students in France discussing the French president, Charles de Gaulle, or American tourists produced polarized evaluations, positive in the case of de Gaulle, negative in the case of American tourists.

Thus, the work of the 1960s underscored the rather dramatic lengths to which people would go as a result of influence from others, or as a result of their own group dynamics. The group polarization literature is especially interesting in raising once again decades-old and even century-old questions as to whether people are primarily governed by more rational or less rational, versus more emotional and motivational, processes.

## The emergence of European social psychology

It is noteworthy that the Moscovici and Zavalloni (1969) study cited above was conducted in Paris and inaugurated a series of studies by Moscovici and others that became one of the central, distinctly European contributions to social psychology (Moscovici, 1985). These studies emphasized novel forms of social influence overlooked in the North American tradition, particularly minority influence and innovation in groups. In his chapter on the recent history of social psychology in the 1985 *Handbook of Social Psychology* (Lindsey and Aronson, 1985), Edward E. Jones characterized modern social psychology as largely a North American enterprise. However, starting in the 1960s, with the work of Moscovici, Michael Argyle, Henri Tajfel, and others, a distinctly European social psychology took shape. The year 1969 marked the publication of Argyle's social psychology textbook, *Social Interaction*, and Tajfel's (1969) chapter, 'Social and Cultural Factors in Perception', in the 1969 *Handbook of Social Psychology*. Argyle focused principally on interpersonal and small-group interaction, especially nonverbal communication (cf. Argyle and Dean, 1965), while Tajfel was beginning to develop the research that led to the creation of social identity theory (see below).

Interestingly, American social psychologists played a significant role in the development of European social psychology, just as Europeans such as Heider, Lewin, and Asch had played a critical role in developing social psychology in North America, starting in the 1930s. John Thibaut, Harold Kelley, and others maintained close contact with European social psychologists and encouraged them to develop relationships among themselves. Thibaut involved European social psychologists in the founding of the *Journal of Experimental Social Psychology* in 1965 and facilitated the founding of the European Association of Experimental Social Psychology (EAESP) in 1966, the year after the Society for Experimental Social Psychology was founded in the USA. In 1971, EAESP sponsored the establishment of the *European Journal of Experimental Social Psychology*. From then on, European social psychology became a force, doing leading research on intergroup relations, value orientations, and bargaining.

## The 1970s: the rise of attribution theories

Research and theory on attribution processes that had been germinating since Fritz Heider's (1944) important paper, 'Social Perception and Phenomenal Causality,' took hold strongly in the late 1960s and dominated much of the 1970s. Heider's book (1958) on interpersonal relations flushed out his ideas on attribution and inspired highly influential treatments of attribution by Jones and Davis (1965) and Kelley (1967). In 1972, a group of attribution theorists published *Attribution: Perceiving the Causes of Behavior*, an edited volume that outlined theoretical treatments of attribution processes that still dominate research on the perception of causality in interpersonal perception (Jones et al., 1972).

Heider's (1958) treatment discussed processes entailed in 'perceiving the other person' and then 'the other person as perceiver'. We perceive others, and they perceive us back. We, in turn, perceive their perceiving us to varying extents. Heider's treatment of the 'naive analysis of action' discussed the way perceivers think about other people's performances, and the ways those performances reflect internal causes, such as other people's motivations (Heider's *try* variable) and their abilities (his *can* variable), as opposed to external causes such as task difficulty or luck. This approach led to a general consideration of the processes involved in making internal as opposed to external attributions, and in inferring personal qualities from behavior.

Jones and Davis's paper, 'From Acts to Dispositions: The Attribution Process in Person Perception', developed Heider's formulations into what became known as 'correspondent-inference theory'. Jones and Davis considered the question of when a perceiver can attribute a behavior to an internal, personal cause. Such an attribution is called a correspondent inference. It holds that a behavior corresponds to an underlying, causal, personal disposition, such as an ability, attitude, or trait, as opposed to some external locus of causality, such as social norms. For example, if a person got angry, the perceiver might make the correspondent inference that he is an angry, hostile person. However, if social norms endorse anger in this situation (perhaps the actor was swindled), it is more difficult to make a correspondent inference.

Harold Kelley's (1967) covariation analysis of attribution processes extended Heider's and Jones and Davis's work to consider especially how perceivers make internal as opposed to external attributions when they have observed an actor's behavior over time. Actions are attributed to causes with which they covary. If something is present when the action is performed and absent when the action is not performed, that something and the action covary. If anger erupts whenever Hank is present but peace prevails when Hank is absent, we attribute the hostility to Hank. For example, if Hank gets mad at everyone and everything, no matter what the circumstances are in which he encounters them, and no one else gets mad in any of those circumstances, the anger is attributed to Hank. However, if Hank got mad in response to only one provocation, and he gets consistently mad when similarly provoked, and other people get mad in that instance too, then Hank's anger is attributed to the provocation. Research by Leslie Zebrowitz (McArthur, 1972) supported Kelley's model.

In a later paper, Kelley articulated the highly influential discounting and augmentation principles. Possible causes for an action are discounted if there are other plausible explanations for the action. Similar to the Jones and Davis analysis of correspondent inferences, causality is ambiguous when several possible explanations seem plausible. A student's indifference to a college course could not confidently be attributed to low motivation if the teacher is boring. In general, whenever there is some plausible external cause for a behavior, the role of internal personal causes should be discounted. The augmentation principle works in the opposite way. When external factors make a response less likely, personal factors are given more attributional weight.

Decades of research have shown that both discounting and augmentation do exist, as Kelley suggested, but even more impressive and intriguing are the scores, perhaps by now hundreds, of studies showing that people often fail to discount. The original study demonstrating the failure to discount was an attribution of attitudes study by Jones and Harris (1967), which showed that participants attributed pro-Castro attitudes to actors who were required to write pro-Castro essays, even though it was clear that the actors had no choice about the essay which they were to write. Jones and Harris explained this finding in terms of Heider's statement that 'behavior in particular has such salient properties it tends to engulf the total field' (Heider, 1958: 54). That is, we simply do not notice or weigh sufficiently situational forces when the behavior itself captures so much attention. A range of other explanations have been offered for the basic findings. The idea that we make attributions to salient plausible causes (Taylor and Fiske, 1975) and the idea that discounting happens more often when people are cognitively busy (Gilbert et al., 1988) have both gained considerable support. The research demonstrating failure to discount was called the 'fundamental attribution error' by Ross (1977). It is also widely known as the 'correspondence bias' (Gilbert and Jones, 1986; Gilbert and Malone, 1995), reflecting the correspondent inference theory formulation that people are biased toward attributing behaviors to corresponding personal dispositions. These attributions give people a sense that they can predict and control other people. Gilbert (1998) has written masterfully about the varied and complex sources of error that give rise to this bias.

Closely linked to the correspondence bias is another bias identified by Jones and Nisbett (1972), the actor–observer bias. While observers are prone toward making correspondent inferences, actors do not show a similar bias in interpreting their own behavior. Instead, actors are more apt to attribute their behavior to the external constraints inducing them to perform a particular behavior. Salience again seems to be an important part of the explanation. For observers, actors are salient, and they attribute behavior to dispositions of the actors. For actors, aspects of the environment or situation are salient, and they attribute their own actions to those attributes.

Another vigorous line of attribution research explored how people perceive the causes of success and failure (Weiner et al., 1972). Very much influenced by Heider, this line of research explored how people attribute performances to internal versus external, stable versus unstable, controllable versus uncontrollable, and specific versus global loci of causality.

Overall, attribution theories have generated a tremendous amount of research, and attribution studies are plentiful at this writing. In general, the work has outlined broad principles that people do or, in some cases, should follow in understanding causality, as well as the biases and errors that govern attribution processes. In addition to helping us understand social thinking, attribution work has also helped psychologists understand and, to some extent, treat psychological problems, such as depression (Abramson et al., 1986) and marital discord (Fincham, 1985).

## The 1980s: social cognition, social identity, and the elaboration-likelihood model

### *Social cognition*

The study of attribution in the late 1960s and 1970s can be seen as one part of a larger concern developing during the same time for returning to a detailed exploration of the role of cognitive processes in understanding attitudes, attributions, and intergroup processes. As noted above, questions concerning the human capacity to reason effectively and govern behavior rationally go back to ancient Greek times. They have dominated much of philosophical discourse since the Enlightenment. The two works we mark as the beginning of social psychology, Triplett's work on social facilitation and Le Bon's book on the crowd, paid little heed to the cognitive or rational side of human behavior. Instead they emphasized drives and unmediated stimulus–response contingencies. The same is true of the textbooks of 1908 by Ross and McDougall. The emphasis on stimulus–response contingencies gained more ground with Floyd Allport's *Social Psychology* textbook (1924). But during this time, the more cognitively oriented approach to social psychology was also alive and well, if pushed out of the spotlight. A major work appeared in 1932, Frederick Bartlett's *Remembering: A Study in Experimental and Social Psychology*. His book is perhaps best remembered for the studies of the 'ghost story' in which subjects read a somewhat obscure folk tale and reported to others what they read. Their accounts revealed active efforts to integrate the material into familiar ways of understanding the world that Bartlett called 'schemas'. Bartlett's work was important as an early example of experimental social psychology and as one which looked directly at cognitive processes in social communication and memory. It helped frame Allport and Postman's (1947) discussion of motivation and expectancy in perception, and students of Bartlett conducted studies of rumor transmission that were critical in the germination of cognitive-dissonance theory (Jones, 1985).

The cognitive perspective received a substantial boost from the work of Gestalt psychologists that strongly influenced Asch, Heider, Lewin, and Sherif. As noted earlier, the active organizing of perceptions into 'good fits' informed the way Asch understood conformity and Heider understood phenomenal causality. Lewin combined Gestalt principles with ideas from physics in developing field theory. At least some of the Yale-school attitude researchers emphasized the cognitive aspects of persuasion, often in combination with Hullian perspectives.

A highly influential paper by Miller and Ross reintroduced the cognitive perspective with great force in 1975. Miller and Ross took on the conventional wisdom that apparently self-serving biases in attributions about the self reflected motivational forces, such as the desire to see oneself in a positive light. Their review of the literature helped define opposing sides in a motivation versus cognition debate about understanding a range of social phenomena – for example, the question of whether dissonance findings should be understood in terms of drive or self-attribution (cf. Bem, 1972).

As research in social cognition took hold, a wide range of issues was explored, including person memory, schema development, the role of cognition in persuasion, and social inference. There was an overall focus on the active, but not always accurate, cognitive construction of the social world. The social-cognition perspective reached full flower in 1984 with the publication of Susan Fiske and Shelley Taylor's *Social Cognition*. Defining social cognition as 'the study of how people make sense of other people and themselves' (Fiske and Taylor, 1991: 1), this book and its second edition of 1991 are truly impressive accounts of the entire domain of research in social cognition. The second edition has nearly 150 pages of references. The first edition contrasted the 'naive scientist' with the 'cognitive miser' models of social cognition, the latter emphasizing people's frequent reluctance to employ fully their abilities to perceive others accurately. The second edition suggested a third model, the 'motivated tactician', a person who, when motivated, would be more energetic and effective in using his or her cognitive abilities. Fiske and Taylor argued that although people can seem lazy and gullible, when they have reason, they can be effective social thinkers: 'In short, people are no fools' (Fiske and Taylor, 1991: 136).

In addition to work on attribution, social-cognition researchers have studied social inference, schemas, person memory, and attention and consciousness. The overall importance of social cognition as a defining area of social psychology is signaled in the name of one of the two main social psychology sections of the *Journal of Personality and Social Psychology*, 'Attitudes and Social Cognition'.

### *Social-identity theory*

Another significant influence in the 1980s was the full flowering of social-identity theory, and its development into self-categorization theory (Hogg, 2001). Social-identity theory was rooted in a series of studies on social categorization, ethnocentrism, and intergroup relations by Henri Tajfel, conducted during the 1960s and 1970s (Hogg, 2000). Many of these studies explored behavior in the 'minimal social situation' in which groups of participants were arbitrarily divided into two groups and subsequently asked to allocate rewards to members of their own group and members of the other group, referred to as the in-group and the out-group. The basic finding was one of strong in-group favoritism. People allocated rewards in such a way that the difference between the outcomes for the in-group and outcomes for the out-group was maximized, in favor of the in-group. This occurred even if participants had to give lower absolute rewards to in-group members. For example, typically they would rather allocate 7 points to an in-group member and 1 point to an out-group member rather than 19 points to an in-group member and 25 to an out-group member (Tajfel et al., 1971). Grounded in these findings and other studies of in-group favoritism, Tajfel and his former student John Turner published two important papers which stated the basic tenets of social-identity theory (Tajfel and Turner, 1979, 1986).

Social-identity theory holds that self-esteem reflects both personal identity and social identity. The former is based on one's personal accomplishments while the latter is based on the groups to which one belongs and the value one attaches to those groups. People are motivated to maintain a positive self-evaluation and want to view their individual achievements and personal qualities as favorably as they can, and they similarly want to see the groups that they belong to in the most positive possible light. In addition, social-identity theory holds that people automatically categorize others into groups, and that on the basis of categorization the social world is divided into in-groups and out-groups. Furthermore, people tend to minimize the differences between people within groups, both in-group and out-groups, and accentuate or maximize the differences between individuals in different groups. Finally, people tend to maximize their social identity by doing all that they can, not only to view their own group positively, but also to view members of other groups relatively negatively. These tendencies produce in-group favoritism, as described above, behaviors designed to benefit the in-group and/or harm the out-group.

Later theorizing by Turner (1985) develops the closely related self-categorization theory, which emphasizes 'depersonalization', or the tendency to see people in groups in relation to a prototype, a fuzzy set of attributes that define the ideal thoughts, feelings, and behaviors of members of those groups. Individuals are not perceived for their unique qualities. Rather, they are assimilated to the prototype of the group to which they belong, and differences between prototypical members of different groups are accentuated, forming the basis for stereotypes (cf. Hogg, 2001).

Social-identity theory holds much in common with social-comparison theory. Social-identity theory focuses on how we evaluate the groups to which we belong. Social comparison focuses on how we evaluate ourselves as individuals within certain groups. Social-identity theory has a distinctly European flavor. Most modern social psychology is American, but the contributions of European, and then Australian, social psychologists, beginning with the work of Argyle, Moscovici, and Tajfel, has had an enormous impact on social psychology in recent years. At the turn of the century, the field of social psychology was becoming much more international.

### *The elaboration-likelihood model of persuasion*

After an enormously creative burst of research on communication and persuasion generated by the Yale school in the decade or so following World War II, attitude research became somewhat less prominent in the 1960s and 1970s. Still, important work was being done on resistance to influence, the role of cognitive consistency in attitudes and attitude change, and the role of situational factors in influencing how people processed or yielded to persuasive attempts. A powerful and highly influential theoretical framing of the persuasion process and persuasion research was developed in the 1980s by Richard Petty and John Cacioppo. Their elaboration-likelihood model (ELM) distinguishes two routes to persuasion. One is a 'central route' whereby persuasion is effected by thoughtful processing, or elaboration, of the content of a persuasive message. The other is a 'peripheral route' whereby persuasion is effected not by the content of arguments themselves but by other 'peripheral' cues that signal to an audience that a message should be yielded to. Similar to the ELM approach to persuasion is Chaiken's 'heuristic-processing model', which distinguishes systematic from heuristic processing, the latter marked by shortcuts and rules of thumb that guide a person toward judging the believability of a message.

For example, in the ELM, the expertise or trustworthiness of a communicator is a peripheral cue that the message should be accepted. Similarly, a high number of arguments in a message is a cue that there is lots of ammunition supporting the message and that it should be believed. Sometimes peripheral cues act independently to affect persuasion. Sometimes they affect how carefully an audience elaborates or processes the actual arguments contained in the message. Cacioppo and Petty (1982) introduced an influential individual difference 'need for cognition' measure to explore personal variations in how much people are motivated to think carefully about the arguments in a persuasive communication.

These models of attitude change wrestle with the questions of rationality as opposed to irrationality that have been around for centuries. Obviously, people are both rational and irrational, depending on a host of personal and situational variables. The ELM and the heuristic-processing model attempt to explore the way these diverse facets of the human condition combine to influence our responses to persuasive communications.

## Recent developments in social psychology, and the future

It is difficult to anticipate what is of lasting importance from the social psychology of the last decade of the second millennium, and what trends will remain most vigorous in the new century. A number of lines of work seem particularly energetic and creative. First, there has been an explosion of interesting work on the self, beginning perhaps with questions of self-attribution, and the return to the exploration of social-comparison processes. Second, research and theory on prejudice and stereotypes seems particularly vigorous at this writing. Supported by advances in social cognition and by a greater understanding of cognitive and motivational elements of intergroup conflict and ethnic hostility (cf. Brown, 1986: part VI), research on stereotypes and prejudice has mushroomed. The work on stereotypes has been greatly influenced by a third development, namely, methodological and conceptual advances in the study of automatic information processing and responding. Fourth, there has been a recent and somewhat controversial body of work on evolutionary influences on social behavior. Fifth, there has also been a good deal of recent work on cultural differences in fundamental social psychological processes, with particular emphasis on differences between Western and Eastern societies. Finally, there continues to be great interest in questions of gender similarities and differences. These appear to be the major foci of social psychology in the first decade of the twenty-first century.

### *The self*

The self is one of the oldest topics in social psychology. William James's classic (1890) chapter on 'Consciousness of Self' introduced several of the major issues in the study of the self, and his views remain vibrant and influential today. James dealt with issues of self-presentation, the unity as opposed to multiplicity of the self, self-esteem, and self-awareness. After World War II, important work on self-presentation appeared, notably the paper 'On Face Work' and the book *The Presentation of Self* by Erving Goffman (1955, 1959), and the book *Ingratiation* by Edward E. Jones (1964). Then the focus on self-attribution led to a resurgence of interest in the self. Important contributions included Wicklund's (1975) theory of objective self-awareness, the closely related work by Carver and Scheier (1981) on self-attention and self-regulation, and Higgins's (1987) work on self-discrepancy. All of these contributions focus on how people react to noting ways that they fall short of meeting ideal standards. Other important contributions include Tesser's (1988) self-evaluation maintenance model, exploring the divergent reactions of feeling threatened by or basking in the reflected glory of the achievements of those to whom we are close; Steele's (1988) self-affirmation theory, noted above, which offers a reinterpretation of cognitive-dissonance theory findings; and Linville's (1987) theory of the beneficial effects of self-complexity. Recent work on self-esteem and self-enhancement is particularly influential at this writing (Kernis and Waschull, 1995; Leary and Baumeister, 2000; Sedikides and Strube, 1997).

### *Prejudice and stereotypes*

Recently, social identity and self-categorization theories have contributed a great deal to understanding the dynamics of both intergroup perception and intergroup interaction. The concepts of categorization, assimilation of perceptions of individuals within groups to prototypes, and accentuation of intergroup differences (Turner, 1999) are powerful explanatory concepts. An important study by Devine (1989) focused attention on the extent to which people automatically and unconsciously categorize people and apply stereotypical thinking to them. She showed that even if people do not believe stereotypes, they affect their perceptions.

Devine's work dovetails with other work examining the automatic processing of information. For example, Uleman et al.'s (1996) work on spontaneous trait inferences shows that people make dispositional judgments about others immediately on observing their behavior, without a conscious and complex causal analysis. Their work connects once again with questions of rationality. In that vein, Fiske and Neuberg (1990) argue that sometimes people use handy cognitive shortcuts, specifically schemas, in judging others, but at times they pay close attention to the data, and process them carefully. In short, work on intergroup and also interpersonal perception is extremely vital, and it is examining more carefully than ever the relatively thoughtful as opposed to relatively effortless and unconscious contributions. Recent work has considered the role of language in prejudice and stereotypes (Maass, 1999; Ruscher, 1998), individual differences in prejudice (Duckitt, 2001), and the responses of targets of stereotypes (Steele et al., 2002).

### Evolutionary approaches

In *The Crowd*, Gustave Le Bon put forth the view that even though humans had evolved into a superior species they were still capable of revealing their less noble animal ancestry. However, until recently, comparatively little work in social psychology considered the impact of evolution on human social behavior in everyday life. Starting with the publication of E.O. Wilson's *Sociobiology* in 1975, social psychologists began considering evolutionary perspectives with great energy (cf. Buss and Kenrick, 1998; Kenrick, 1994). One prominent example is the work that David Buss and his colleagues have done on human mating strategies, summarized in Buss's *The Evolution of Desire* (1994). Buss has tested a range of theoretical derivations from evolutionary principles, including the ideas that men attach high importance to women's physical attractiveness, since that can be taken as a clue to her fertility, while women attach more importance to men's economic capacity, status, dependability, and commitment, as these are signs that they have the motive and capacity to invest in the women's children (see also Berry, 2000). Other hypotheses have been derived concerning jealousy, casual sex, and points of harmony and conflict between the sexes.

Critics of evolutionary social psychology abound. A basic criticism is that the approach is too deterministic and offers explanations that cannot be convincingly tested, or are better explained in terms of social forces, or both. Perhaps, for example, men attach high importance to physical attractiveness because they have power in nearly every society and do not need to be as pragmatic as women in their choice of mates. Evolutionary theorists argue that there is really no incompatibility between evolutionary and cultural approaches, but the critics disagree. Time will tell what kind of force this perspective remains or becomes in social psychology. At the moment, it appears to be thriving.

### The role of culture

The theme of cultural differences has been significant in social psychology at least since the work of Muzafer Sherif in the 1930s. As an immigrant from Turkey who had studied sociology and anthropology, Sherif was highly sensitive to the power of culture. This sensitivity informed his studies of group norm formation. Harry Triandis (1972) kept the concern with culture alive during much of the second half of the twentieth century. In recent years, a large number of social psychologists have studied cultural differences in basic social psychological processes, such as self-conception, emotion, and attribution, with particular emphasis on the differences between the individualistic, independent societies of North America and Europe and the interdependent societies of East Asia (Fiske et al., 1998; Kitayama and Markus, 2000). Intriguing findings include differences in the experience of emotions, with American participants experiencing emotions for a longer time and more intensely than their Japanese counterparts (Matsumoto et al., 1988), presumably due to American emphasis on themselves as individuals and their unique internal states. In addition, it appears that there are significant cultural differences in the correspondence bias. People in interdependent cultures are less prone to underestimate the force of situational contingencies on behavior (Fiske et al., 1998).

### Gender

Questions about sex or gender differences have been explored for some time. Two early publications by Eleanor Maccoby (1966; Maccoby and Jacklin, 1974) explored the existing literature in great depth and pointed to reliable differences in aggression, and in verbal, mathematical, and spatial abilities, but precious little else. An influential book by Kay Deaux (1976), *The Behavior of Women and Men*, discussed a variety of differences between the social behavior of women and men – for example, in attributions for success and failure (women are more apt than men to attribute their successes to nonability causal loci) – but emphasized contextual influences and the potential of both sexes to behave flexibly and responsively in different situations. This perspective has been further developed by Deaux and Major (1987) and is discussed in greater depth in the more recent treatment of gender by Deaux and LaFrance (1998). Their emphasis is explicitly not on sex or gender differences but on the interaction of a range of factors in influencing both men and women.

Another productive perspective on gender is the social-role theory of Alice Eagly (1987) and her colleagues. Combining this with meta-analytic techniques, they have explored questions such as gender differences in leadership effectiveness (overall, there are none) and highlighted the crucial role of gender expectations (sometimes called 'gender-role or sex-role spillover') in many domains (Eagly et al., 1995). It seems certain that gender will continue to be rich a field of study in the decades ahead, especially given the concerns of evolutionary social psychology and the study of 'the cultural matrix of social psychology' (Fiske et al., 1998).

## Conclusion

Basic questions about social behavior go back to the ancients. Are men and women capable of governing themselves? Is their behavior governed by internal dispositions or the requirements of society and culture? Should we be optimistic or pessimistic about human potential and human performance? Are people rational or irrational? What hope is there for independent thought and action in the face of group pressures?

In reviewing the development of social psychology over the past 100 years or more, we are struck with the tremendous gain in knowledge combined with the intractability of the basic questions of human nature. We have learned a great deal about how people respond to social influence, about group dynamics and intergroup relations, and about social thought. The promise of learning more of real value is great. Further nuances of social behavior will be discovered, and the power of our thinking and methodologies will continue to generate new findings and continue to fascinate. However, basic questions, such as whether we should be more impressed with the shortcomings or the capacities of human social thought, will almost certainly remain unanswered. They are probably unanswerable. But the hunt for answers itself will engage us and enlighten us, and perhaps uplift us, for, if we are lucky, another 100 years.

**SUMMARY**

This chapter shows how psychology as a whole and then social psychology as part of the whole took shape in the twentieth century as scientific disciplines addressing fundamental philosophical questions of human nature. The earliest work focused on how groups influence individual performance. Later research explored conformity, the formation of norms, and whether people are active and thoughtful or merely reactive to social influence. During World War II research concentrated on urgent problems of persuasion and the ways people perceive each other. In the second half of the century research began on cognitive dissonance and self-justification as well as some of the subtleties of social influence, including how minorities influence majorities. Asch's studies of conformity to unanimous majorities and Milgram's studies of obedience to authority made clear the importance of scientific research on human potential and human frailty. Much attention was given to attribution theory and the more general problems of human social thinking. By the end of the century theory and research focused more on gender, stereotypes, culture, and the self. New perspectives, such as evolutionary psychology, competed for attention with more traditional domains of investigation such as social cognition, attitudes, and group behavior.

## References

Abramson, L.Y., Alloy, L.B., and Metalsky, G.I. (1986) 'The Cognitive Diathesis-Stress Theories of Depression: Toward an Adequate Evaluation of the Theories Validity', in L.B. Alloy (ed.), *Cognitive Processes in Depression.* New York: Guilford.

Allport, F.H. (1924) *Social Psychology*. Boston, MA: Houghton Mifflin.

Allport, G.W. (1954/1968) 'The Historical Background of Modern Social Psychology', in G. Lindzey (ed.), *The Handbook of Social Psychology* (vol. 1). Cambridge, MA.: Addison-Wesley, pp. 3–56.

Allport, G.W. and Postman, L. (1947) *The Psychology of Rumor*. New York: Henry Holt.

Asch, S.E. (1946) 'Forming Impressions of Personality', *Journal of Abnormal and Social Psychology*, 41: 1230–40.

Argyle, M. and Dean, J. (1965) 'Eye-contact, distance and affiliation', *Sociometry*, 28: 289–304.

Asch, S.E. (1948) 'The Doctrine of Suggestion, Prestige, and Imitation in Social Psychology', *Psychological Review*, 55: 250–76.

Asch, S.E. (1951) 'Effects of Group Pressure upon the Modification and Distortion of Judgment', in G. Guetzkow (ed.), *Groups, Leadership, and Men.* Pittsburgh, PA: Carnegie Press, pp. 177–90.

Bartlett, F.A. (1932) *Remembering: A Study in Experimental and Social Psychology*. New York: Cambridge University Press.

Batson, C.D. (1998) 'Altruism and Prosocial Behavior', in D.T. Gilbert and S.T. Fiske (eds), *The Handbook of Social Psychology* 4th edn (vol. 2). New York: McGraw-Hill, pp. 282–316.

Baumrind, D. (1964) 'Some Thoughts on Ethics of Research: After Reading Milgram's "Behavioral Study of Obedience"', *American Psychologist*, 19: 421–3.

Bem, E. (1972) 'Self-Perception Theory', in L. Berkowitz (ed.), *Advances in Experimental Social Psychology* (vol. 6). New York: Academic Press, pp. 1–62.

Bennett E. (1955) 'Discussion, Decision, Commitment, and Consensus in "Group Decision"', *Human Relations*, 5 (4): 327–46.

Berry, D.S. (2000) 'Attractiveness, Attraction, and Sexual Selection: Evolutionary Perspectives on the Form and Function of Physical Attractiveness', in M.P Zanna (ed.), *Advances in Experimental Social Psychology* (vol. 32). San Diego, CA: Academic Press, pp. 273–342.

Brehm, J.W. (1956) 'Post Decision Changes in the Desirability of Alternatives', *Journal of Abnormal and Social Psychology*, 52: 384–9.

Brown, R. (1965) *Social Psychology*. New York: Free Press.

Brown, R. (1986) *Social Psychology*, 2nd edn. New York: Free Press.

Bruner, J.S. and Tagiuri, R. (1954) 'The Perception of People', in G. Lindzey (ed.), *The Handbook of Social Psychology* (vol. 2). Reading, MA: Addison-Wesley, pp. 634–54.

Burnstein, E. (1982) 'Persuasion as Argument Processing', in M. Brandstatter, J.M. Davis and G. Stocker-Kreichgauer (eds), *Group Decision Processes*. London: Academic Press, pp. 103–24.

Buss, D.M. (1994) *The Evolution of Desire: Strategies of Human Mating*. New York: Basic Books.

Buss D.M. and Kenrick, D.T. (1998) 'Evolutionary Social Psychology', in D.T. Gilbert, S.T. Fiske, and G. Lindzey (eds), *The Handbook of Social Psychology,* 4th edn. New York: Oxford University Press.

Cacioppo, J.T. and Petty, R.E. (1982) 'The Need for Cognition', *Journal of Personality and Social Psychology*, 42: 116–31.

Carver, C.S. and Scheier, M.F. (1981) *Attention and Self-Regulation: A Control Theory Approach to Human Behavior*. New York: Springer-Verlag.

Cialdini, R.B., Schaller, M., Houlihan, D., Arps, K., Fultz, J., and Beaman, A.L. (1987) 'Empathy-Based Helping: Is It Selflessly or Selfishly Motivated?', *Journal of Personality and Social Psychology*, 52: 749–58.

Cooley, C.H. (1902) *Human Nature and the Social Order*. New York: Scribner.

Cooper, J. and Fazio, R.H. (1984) 'A New Look at Dissonance Theory', in L. Berkowitz (ed.), *Advances in Experimental Social Psychology* (vol. 17). New York: Academic Press, pp. 229–62.

Darley, J.M. and Latané, B. (1968) 'Bystander Intervention in Emergencies: Diffusion of Responsibility', *Journal of Personality and Social Psychology*, 8: 377–83.

Deaux, K. (1976) *The Behavior of Women and Men*. Monterey, CA: Brooks/Cole.

Deaux, K. and LaFrance, M. (1998) 'Gender', in D.T. Gilbert, S.T. Fiske, and G. Lindzey (eds), *The Handbook of Social Psychology*, 4th edn. New York: Oxford University Press, pp. 788–827.

Deaux, K. and Major, B. (1987) 'Putting Gender into Context: An Interactive Model of Gender-Related Behavior', *Psychological Review*, 94: 369–89.

Deutsch, M. and Krauss, R. (1960) 'The Effect of Threat upon Interpersonal Bargaining', *Journal of Abnormal and Social Psychology*, 61: 181–9.

Devine, P.G. (1989) 'Stereotypes and Prejudice: Their Automatic and Controlled Components', *Journal of Personality and Social Psychology*, 56: 5–18.

Duckitt, J. (2001) 'A Dual-Process Cognitive-Motivational Theory of Ideology and Prejudice', in M.P. Zanna (ed.), *Advances in Experimental Social Psychology* (vol. 33). San Diego, CA: Academic Press, pp. 41–113.

Eagly, A.H. (1987) *Sex Differences in Social Behavior: A Social Role Interpretation*. Mahwah, NJ: Erlbaum.

Eagly, A.H., Karau, S.J., and Makhijani, M.G. (1995) 'Gender and Effectiveness of Leaders: A Meta-Analysis', *Psychological Bulletin*, 117: 125–45.

Festinger, L. (1950) 'Informal Social Communication', *Psychological Review*, 57: 271–82.

Festinger, L. (1954) 'A Theory of Social Comparison Processes', *Human Relations*, 7: 117–40.

Festinger, L. (1957) *A Theory of Cognitive Dissonance*. Palo Alto, CA: Stanford University Press.

Festinger, L. (1975) *An Interview with Leon Festinger*, Charles Harris (ed.) [Audio tape]. Scranton, PA: Harper & Row Media Program [Distributor].

Festinger, L. (1980) *Retrospections on Social Psychology*. New York: Oxford University Press.

Festinger, L. and Carlsmith, J.M. (1959) 'Cognitive Consequences of Forced Compliance', *Journal of Abnormal and Social Psychology*, 58: 203–11.

Festinger, L., Pepitone, A., and Newcomb, T. (1952) 'Some Consequences of De-individuation in a Group', *Journal of Abnormal and Social Psychology*, 47: 382–9.

Festinger, L., Riecken, H.W., and Schachter, S. (1956) *When Prophecy Fails*. Minneapolis, MN: University of Minnesota Press.

Festinger, L., Schachter, S., and Back, K. (1950) *Social Pressures in Informal Groups*. New York: Harper.

Fincham, F.D. (1985) 'Attribution Processes in Distressed and Non-distressed Couples. 2. Responsibility for Marital Problems', *Journal of Abnormal Psychology*, 94: 183–90.

Fiske, A.P., Kitayama, S., Markus, H.R., and Nisbett, R.E. (1998) 'The Cultural Matrix of Social Psychology', in D.T. Gilbert, S.T. Fiske, and G. Lindzey (eds), *The Handbook of Social Psychology*, 4th edn. New York: Oxford University Press, pp. 915–81.

Fiske, S.T. and Neuberg, S.L. (1990) 'A Continuum of Impression Formation, from Category-Based to Individuating Processes: Influences of Information and Motivation on Attention and Interpretation', in M.P. Zanna (ed.), *Advances in Experimental Social Psychology* (vol. 23). New York: Academic Press, pp. 1–74.

Fiske, S.T. and Taylor, S.E. (1984) *Social Cognition*. Reading, MA: Addison-Wesley.

Fiske, S.T. and Taylor, S.E. (1991) *Social Cognition*, 2nd edn. Reading, MA: Addison-Wesley.

Freud, S. (1921) *Group Psychology and the Analysis of the Ego*. Trans. by James Strachey. London: International Psycholanalytical Press, 1922.

Geen, R.G. and Bushman, B.J. (1987) 'Drive Theory: Effects of Socially Engendered Arousal', in B. Mullen and G.R. Goethals, *Theories of Group Behavior*. New York: Springer-Verlag, pp. 89–109.

Gilbert, D.T. (1998) 'Ordinary Personology', in D.T. Gilbert, S.T. Fiske, and Lindzey, G. (eds), *The Handbook of Social Psychology*. New York: McGraw Hill, pp. 89–150.

Gilbert, D.T. and Jones, E.E. (1986) 'Perceiver-Induced Constraint: Interpretations of Self-Generated Reality', *Journal of Personality and Social Psychology*, 50: 269–80.

Gilbert, D.T., Krull, D.S., and Pelham, B.W. (1988) 'Of Thoughts Unspoken: Social Inference and the Self-Regulation of Behavior', *Journal of Personality and Social Psychology*, 55: 685–94.

Gilbert, D.T. and Malone, P.S. (1995) 'The Correspondence Bias', *Psychological Bulletin*, 117: 21–38.

Goethals G.R. and Zanna, M.P. (1979) 'The Role of Social Comparison in Choice Shifts', *Journal of Personality and Social Psychology*, 37: 1469–76.

Goffman, E. (1955) 'On Face Work: An Analysis of Ritual Elements in Social Interaction', *Psychiatry*, 18: 213–31.

Goffman, E. (1959) *The Presentation of Self in Everyday Life*. New York: Doubleday Anchor.

Hall, G.S. (1891) 'The Contents of Children's Minds on Entering School', *Pediatric Seminars*, 1: 139–73.

Heider, F. (1944) 'Social Perception and Phenomenal Causality', *Psychological Review*, 51: 358–74.

Heider, F. (1958) *The Psychology of Interpersonal Relations*. New York: Wiley.

Higgins, E.T. (1987) 'Self-Discrepancy: A Theory Relating Self and Affect', *Psychological Review*, 94: 319–40.

Hogg, M.A. (2000) 'Social Identity and Social Comparison', in J. Suls and L. Wheeler (eds), *Handbook of Social Comparison: Theory and Research*. New York: Plenum Publishers, p. 401.

Hogg, M.A. (2001) 'A Social Identity Theory of Leadership', *Personality and Social Psychology Review*, 5 (3): 184–200.

Hovland, C.I., Janis, I.L., and Kelley, H.H. (1953) *Communication and Persuasion*. New Haven, CT: Yale University Press.

Hovland, C.I., Lumsdaine, A.A., and Sheffield, F.D. (1949) *Experiments on Mass Communications*. Princeton, NJ: Princeton University Press.

Hyman, H. (1942) 'The Psychology of Status', *Archives of Psychology*, (269).

James, W. (1890) *The Principles of Psychology*. New York: Henry Holt.

James, W. (1892) *Psychology: Briefer Course*. New York: Henry Holt.

Jones, E.E. (1964) *Ingratiation*. New York: Appleton-Century, Crofts.

Jones, E.E. (1985) 'Major Developments in Social Psychology During the Past Five Decades', in G. Lindzey and E. Aronson (eds), *Handbook of Social Psychology*, 3rd edn (vol. 1). New York: Random House, pp. 1–46.

Jones, E.E. and Davis, K.E. (1965) 'From Acts to Dispositions: The Attribution Process in Person Perception', in L. Berkowitz (ed.), *Advances in Experimental Social Psychology* (vol. 2). New York: Academic Press, pp. 220–66.

Jones, E.E. and Harris, V.A. (1967) 'The Attribution of Attitudes', *Journal of Experimental Social Psychology*, 3: 1–24.

Jones, E.E. and Nisbett, R.E. (1972) 'The Actor and the Observer: Divergent Perceptions of the Causes of Behavior', in E.E. Jones, D.E. Kanouse, H.H. Kelley, R.E. Nisbett, S. Valins, and B. Weiner (eds), *Attribution: Perceiving the Causes of Behavior.* Morristown, NJ: General Learning Press, pp. 79–94.

Jones, E.E., Kanouse, D.E., Kelley, H.H., Nisbett, R.E., Valins, S. and Weiner B. (eds.) (1972) *Attribution: Perceiving the Causes of Behavior*. Morristown, NJ: General Learning Press.

Kelley, H.H. (1967) 'Attribution Theory in Social Psychology', in D. Levine (ed.), *Nebraska Symposium on Motivation* (vol. 15). Lincoln, NE: University of Nebraska Press, pp. 192–240.

Kelley, H.H. (1972) 'Attribution in Social Interaction', in E.E. Jones, D.E. Kanouse, H.H. Kelley, R.E. Nisbett, S. Valins, and B. Weiner (eds), *Attribution: Perceiving the Causes of Behavior*. Morristown, NJ: General Learning Press, pp. 79–94.

Kelman, H.C. (1961) 'Processes of Opinion Change', *Public Opinion Quarterly*, 25: 57–78.

Kelman, H.C. (1968) '*A Time to Speak*', San Francisco, CA: Jossey-Bass.

Kenrick, D. (1994) 'Evolutionary Social Psychology: From Sexual Selection to Social Cognition', in M.P. Zanna (ed.), *Advances in Experimental Social Psychology* (vol. 26). San Diego, CA: Academic Press, pp. 75–121.

Kernis, M.H. and Waschull, S.B. (1995) 'The Interactive Roles of Stability and Level of Self-Esteem: Research and Theory', in M.P. Zanna (ed.), *Advances in Experimental Social Psychology* (vol. 27). San Diego, CA: Academic Press, pp. 94–141.

Kitayama, S. and Markus, H.R. (2000) 'The Pursuit of Happiness and the Realization of Sympathy: Cultural Patterns of Self, Social Relations, and Well-Being', in E. Deiner and E.M. Suh (eds), *Subjective Well-Being Across Cultures*. Cambridge, MA: MIT Press.

Koffka, K. (1935) *Principles of Gestalt Psychology*. New York: Harcourt, Brace.

Krebs, D.L. and Miller, D.T. (1985) 'Altruism and Aggression', in G. Lindzey and E. Aronson (eds), *The Handbook of Social Psychology*, 3rd edn. New York: Random House, pp. 1–71.

Latané, B. (1966) 'Studies in Social Comparison: Introduction and Overview', *Journal of Experimental Social Psychology, Supplement*, 1: 1–5.

Latané, B. and Darley, J.M. (1970) *The Unresponsive Bystander: Why Doesn't He Help?* New York: Appleton-Century-Crofts.

Leary, M.R. and Baumeister, R.F. (2000) 'The Nature and Function of Self-Esteem: Sociometer Theory', in M.P. Zanna (ed.), *Advances in Experimental Social Psychology* (vol. 32). San Diego, CA: Academic Press, pp. 1–62.

Le Bon, G. (1895) *The Crowd: A Study of the Popular Mind*. New York: Ballantine.

Lerner, M.J. and Simmons, C.H. (1966) 'Observers Reaction to the "Innocent Victim": Compassion or Rejection', *Journal of Personality and Social Psychology*, 4: 203–10.

Lewin, K. (1943) 'Forces Behind Food Habits and Methods of Change', *Bulletin of the National Research Council*, 108: 35–65.

Lewin, K., Lippitt, R. and White, R.K. (1939) 'Patterns of Aggressive Behavior in Experimentally Created "Social Climates"', *Journal of Social Psychology*, 10: 271–99.

Lindsey, G. and Aronson, E. (1985) *The Handbook of Social Psychology*, 3rd edn. New York: Random House.

Linville, P.W. (1987) 'Self-Complexity as a Cognitive Buffer Against Stress-Related Depression and Illness', *Journal of Personality and Social Psychology*, 52: 663–76.

Lorge, I. (1936) 'Prestige, Suggestion, and Attitudes', *Journal of Social Psychology*, 7: 386–402.

Maass, A. (1999) 'Linguistic Intergroup Bias: Stereotype Perpetuation Through Language', in M.P. Zanna (ed.), *Advances in Experimental Social Psychology* (vol. 31). San Diego, CA: Academic Press, pp. 79–121.

Maccoby, E.E. (1966) *The Development of Sex Differences*. Stanford, CA: Stanford University Press.

Maccoby, E.E. and Jacklin, C.N. (1974) *The Psychology of Sex Differences*. Palo Alto, CA: Stanford University Press.

Matsumoto, D., Kudoh, T., Scherer, K. and Wallbott, H. (1988) 'Antecedents and Reactions to Emotions in the United States and Japan', *Journal of Cross-Cultural Psychology*, 19: 267–86.

McArthur, L.Z. (1972) 'The How and What of Why: Some Determinants and Consequences of Causal Attribution', *Journal of Personality and Social Psychology*, 22: 171–93.

McDougall, W. (1908) *An Introduction to Social Psychology*. London: Methuen.

McDougall, W. (1920) *The Group Mind*. New York: Putnam.

McGuire, W.J. (1968) 'The Nature of Attitudes and Attitude Change', in G. Lindzey and E. Aronson (eds), *The Handbook of Social Psychology*, 2nd edn. London: Addison-Wesley, pp. 136–314.

Merton, R.K. and Kitt, A. (1950) 'Contributions to the Theory of Reference Group Behavior', in R.K. Merton and P.F. Lazarfield (eds), *Continuities in Social Research: Studies in the Scope and Method of 'The American Soldier'*. Glencoe, IL: Free Press, pp. 40–105.

Milgram, S. (1963) 'Behavioral Study of Obedience', *Journal of Abnormal and Social Psychology*, 67: 371–8.

Milgram, S. (1965) 'Some Conditions of Obedience and Disobedience to Authority', *Human Relations*, 18: 57–76.

Miller, E.T. and Ross, M. (1975) 'Self-Serving Biases in the Attribution of Causality: Fact or Fiction?', *Psychological Bulletin*, 82: 213–25.

Moore, H.T. (1921) 'The Comparative Influence of Majority and Expert Opinion', *Journal of Psychology*, 32: 16–20.

Moscovivi, S. (1985) 'Social Influence and Conformity', in G. Lindzey and E. Aronson (eds), *The Handbook of Social Psychology* 3rd edn (vol. 2). New York: Random House, pp. 347–412.

Moscovici, S. and Zavalloni, M. (1969) 'The Group as a Polarizer of Attitudes', *Journal of Personality and Social Psychology*, 12: 125–35.

Murphy, G. and Murphy, L.B. (1931) *Experimental Social Psychology*. New York: Harper.

Murphy, G., Murphy, L.B. and Newcomb, T.M. (1937) *Experimental Social Psychology*, rev. edn. New York: Harper.

Newcomb, T.M. (1943) *Personality and Social Change: Attitude Formation in the Student Community*. New York: Dryden Press.

Newcomb, T.M. (1963) 'Persistence and Regression of Changed Attitudes: Long-Range Studies', *Journal of Social Issues*, 19: 3–14.

Pepitone, A. (1999) 'Historical Sketches and Critical Commentary About Social Psychology in the Golden Age', in A. Rodrigues and R.V. Levine (eds), *Reflections on 100 Years of Experimental Social Psychology*. New York: Basic Books, pp. 170–9.

Pettigrew, A. (1967) 'Social Evaluation Theory', in D. Levine (ed.), *Nebraska Symposium on Motivation* (vol. 15). Lincoln, NE: University of Nebraska Press, pp. 241–315.

Petty, R.E. and Cacioppo, J.T. (1986) 'The Elaboration Likelihood Model of Persuasion', in L. Berkowitz (ed.), *Advances in Experimental Social Psychology* (vol. 19). New York: Academic Press, pp. 123–205.

Piliavin, J.A. and Piliavin, I.M. (1972) 'Effect of Blood on Reactions to a Victim', *Journal of Personality and Social Psychology*, 23: 353–62.

Piliavin, I.M., Rodin, J. and Piliavin, J.A. (1969) 'Good Samaritanism: An Underground Phenomenon', *Journal of Personality and Social Psychology*, 13: 289–99.

Radke and Klisurich (1947) 'Experiments in Changing Food Habits', *Journal of the American Dietetic Association*, 24: 403–9.

Rosenberg, M.J. (1965) 'When Dissonance Fails: On Eliminating Evaluation Apprehension from Attitude Measurement', *Journal of Personality and Social Psychology*, 1: 28–43.

Ross, E.A. (1908) *Social Psychology*. New York: Macmillan.

Ross, L. (1977) 'The Intuitive Psychologist and His Shortcomings: Distortions in the Attribution Process', in L. Berkowitz (ed.), *Advances in Experimental Social Psychology* (vol. 10). New York: Academic Press, pp. 174–220.

Ruscher, J.B. (1998) 'Prejudice and Stereotyping in Everyday Communication', in M.P. Zanna (ed.), *Advances in Experimental Social Psychology* (vol. 30). San Diego, CA: Academic Press, pp. 243–307.

Schachter, S. (1951) 'Deviation, Rejection, and Communication', *Journal of Abnormal and Social Psychology*, 46: 190–207.

Sedikides, C. and Strube, M.J. (1997) 'Self-Evaluation: To Thine Own Self Be Good, to Thine Own Self Be Sure, to Thine Own Self Be True, and to Thine Own Self Be Better', in M.P. Zanna (ed.), *Advances in Experimental Social Psychology* (vol. 29). San Diego, CA: Academic Press, pp. 209–69.

Sherif, M. (1936) *The Psychology of Social Norms*. New York: Harper.

Steele, C.M. (1988) 'The Psychology of Self-Affirmation: Sustaining the Integrity of the Self', in L. Berkowitz (ed.), *Advances in Experimental Psychology* (vol. 21). New York: Academic Press, pp. 261–302.

Steele, C.M., Spencer, S.J. and Aronson, J. (2002) 'Contending with Group Image: The Psychology of Stereotype and Social Identity Threat', in M.P. Zanna (ed.), *Advances in Experimental Social Psychology* (vol. 34). San Diego: Academic Press, pp. 379–440.

Stouffer, S.A., Suchman, E.A., DeVinney, L.C., Star, S.A., and Williams, R.M., Jr. (1949) *The American Soldier:* vol. 1. *Adjustment during Army Life*. Princeton, NJ: Princeton University Press.

Suls, J.M. and Miller, R.L. (1977) *Social Comparison Processes: Theoretical and Empirical Perspectives*. Washington, DC: Hemisphere.

Suls, J. and Wheeler, L. (eds) (2000) *Handbook of Social Comparison: Theory and Research*. New York: Plenum.

Tajfel, H. (1969) 'Social and cultural factors in perception', in G. Lindzey and E. Aronson (eds), *Handbook of Social Psychology* (Vol. 3, pp. 315–94). Reading MA: Addison-Wesley.

Tajfel, H., Billig, M., Bundy, R.P., and Flament, C. (1971) 'Social Categorization and Intergroup Behavior', *European Journal of Social Psychology*, 1: 149–77.

Tajfel, H. and Turner, J.C. (1979) 'An Integrative Theory of Intergroup Conflict', in W.G. Austin and S. Worchel (eds), *The Social Psychology of Intergroup Relations*. Monterey, CA: Brooks/Cole, pp. 33–47.

Tajfel, H. and Turner, J.C. (1986) 'The Social Identity Theory of Intergroup Behavior', in S. Worchel and W.G. Austin (eds), *The Psychology of Intergroup Relations*. Chicago, IL: Nelson-Hall, pp. 7–24.

Taylor, S.E. and Fiske, S.T. (1975) 'Point-of-View and Perceptions of Causality', *Journal of Personality and Social Psychology*, 32: 439–45.

Tedeschi, J.T., Schlenker, B.R. and Bonoma, T.V. (1971) 'Cognitive Dissonance: Private Ratiocination or Public Spectacle?', *American Psychologist*, 26: 685–95.

Tesser, A. (1988) 'Toward a Self-Evaluation Maintenance Model of Social Behavior', in L. Berkowitz (ed.), *Advances in Experimental Social Psychology* (vol. 21). New York: Academic Press, pp. 181–227.

Thomas, W.I. and Zaniecki, F. (1918–20) *The Polish Peasant in Europe and America* (5 vols). Boston, MA: Badger.

Triandis, H.C. (1972) *The Analysis of Subjective Culture*. New York: Wiley.

Triplett, N. (1897) 'The Dynamogenic Factors in Pacemaking and Competition', *American Journal of Psychology*, 9: 507–33.

Turner, J.C. (1985) 'Social Categorization and the Self-Concept: A Social Cognitive Theory of Group Behavior', in E.J. Lawler (ed.), *Advances in Group Processes* (vol. 2). Greenwich, CT: JAI Press, pp. 77–121.

Turner, J.C. (1999) 'Some Current Issues in Research on Social Identity and Self-Categorization Theories', in- N. Ellemers, R. Spears, and B. Doosje (eds), *Social Identity*. Oxford: Blackwell, pp. 6–34.

Uleman, J.S., Newman, L.S., and Moskowitz, G.B. (1996) 'People as Flexible Interpreters: Evidence and Issues Form Spontaneous Trait Inference', in M.P. Zanna (ed.), *Advances in Experimental Social Psychology* (vol. 28). Boston, MA: Academic Press, pp. 211–79.

Wallach, M.A., Kogan, N. and Bem, D.J. (1962) 'Group infivence on individual risk taking', *Journal of Abnormal and Social Psychology*, 65: 75–86.

Watson, J.B. (1913) *Psychology, from the Standpoint of a Behaviorist*. Philadelphia, PA: Lippincott.

Watson, J.B. (1925) *Behaviorism*. New York: Norton.

Weiner, B., Frieze, I., Kukla, A., Reed, L., Rest, S., and Rosenbaum, R.M. (1972) 'Perceiving the Causes of Success and Failure', in E.E. Jones, D.E. Kanouse, H.H. Kelley, R.E. Nisbett, S. Valins, and B. Weiner (eds), *Attribution: Perceiving the Causes of Behavior*. Morristown, NJ: General Learning Press, pp. 95–120.

Wheeler, L. (1970) *Interpersonal Influence*. Boston, MA: Allyn and Bacon.

Wicklund, R.A. (1975) 'Objective Self-Awareness', in L. Berkowitz (ed.), *Advances in Experimental Social Psychology* (vol. 8). New York: Academic Press, pp. 233–75.

Wilson, E.O. (1975) *Sociobiology: The New Synthesis*. Cambridge, MA: Harvard University Press.

Wundt, W. (1894) *Lectures on Human and Animal Psychology*. London: Sonnenschein.

Zajonc, R.B. (1965) 'Social Facilitation', *Science*, 149: 269–74.

# 2

# Questions and Comparisons: Methods of Research in Social Psychology

PHOEBE C. ELLSWORTH AND RICHARD GONZALEZ

## INTRODUCTION

One of the most interesting and challenging aspects of social psychology is figuring out how to turn an interesting idea into a research question, and then how to turn the question into an actual study that will add to our understanding of human behavior. Designing a good study involves a whole range of skills from creative imagination to cold logic to interpersonal intuition. The social psychologist tries to create a situation that not only captures the essence of the scientific question, but is also meaningful and involving for the participants. This chapter will help you to get started.

This chapter is based on two fundamental premises. The first premise is that the task of the researcher is to ask questions. It is said that in real estate there are three key features for success: location, location, and location. But in research the three key features are questions, questions, and questions. The researcher should constantly be asking questions. What is the phenomenon I want to capture; for example, is it marital satisfaction or marital dysfunction? What is the best way to test my idea? What is the best measure to use? How do I want to explain the findings? Does the research design provide a fair test of this explanation? What other explanations might account for the findings? How should I analyze the data? Are my analyses consistent with the design I used? Does my written description adequately explain the model, the design and procedure, the analysis?

Curiosity, excitement, and passion should drive the consideration of such questions. Simply consulting a checklist of standard questions for each new research project will not do. The researcher should play the role of the child at the Seder who asks the Four Questions (for example, 'On all other nights we eat herbs of every kind; on this night, why do we eat only bitter herbs?'). If the phenomenon really captures the researcher's interest, inquisitiveness comes naturally. Answers to questions lead to new questions, and one of the intellectual attractions of research is that often one cannot predict the next two or three questions down the line. The feeling that one does not know the answer to a research question (but knows how to design a study to find an answer) is exactly what makes empirical research interesting and stimulating. That feeling of uncertainty is sometimes an obstacle for new researchers, who must learn to channel their sense of confusion and vagueness into a workable plan. Indeed, the elimination of confusion is a key motivator for many successful researchers.

Of all the questions a researcher could ask, perhaps the most fundamental one is, 'What is the phenomenon I want to study?' Am I interested in willing compliance or in the failure to resist pressure to conform? Do I think that attitudes can fundamentally change after a persuasive message, or do I think that attitudes remain stable and only the overt response changes? Before the researcher can begin to think clearly about which measures to use, which control variables to include, what the design should look like, how many subjects should be included, what should be counterbalanced, and so on, it is necessary to be clear about what the research phenomenon is. For any new research project, the best way to define the phenomenon under investigation or to frame questions about it may not be obvious, so it is useful to revisit the fundamental research question frequently. The basic message here is know thy research question.

There is a legend among cognitive psychologists that Endel Tulving stumped first-year graduate students by asking them the question, 'How do you measure a potato?' Thinking this question was an opportunity to demonstrate their creativity, the students generated multiple answers: you can weigh the potato, you can compute the potato's volume, you can measure its luminosity, its water content, its chemical composition, and so on. The list would grow quite long, until someone finally realized the point of the exercise. How can you measure something without knowing what interests you about it? What is it that you want to know about the potato? Once you know what it is you want to know about a potato, you can figure out the best way to measure it.

This charming story makes a deep point. Students often ask us, 'What statistics should I use on my data?', 'What method should I use in my dissertation?', 'Which measure should I use in my next study?' These questions are difficult to answer without knowing the answer to the fundamental question: What is the research question you want to answer?

The second premise of this chapter is that *comparison* is essential in research and should be omnipresent. Our view of comparison is not limited to experimental designs, where, typically, one compares cell means to other cell means; the concept, as we use it, is more general. Predictions can be compared against a known or expected standard (such as Milgram's [1974] use of prediction by experts as a baseline comparison); hypotheses can be compared with each other (for example, Triplett's [1897] analysis of seven hypotheses that could account for social facilitation in bicycle racing); experimental conditions or interventions or subject groups can be compared; individuals can be compared across time; and measures of related/correlated concepts can be compared to each other. A single research design need not include all types of comparison: which comparisons matter depends on the question being asked, but some form of comparison should be present in every research project.

From the second premise (comparison is essential) follow two corollaries: (1) research should attempt to reduce the number of alternative explanations; (2) research programs should be based on multiple methods. We should *compare* possible explanations of research findings to see whether any of them can be ruled out. We should *compare* research methods to see whether analogous empirical findings emerge across different paradigms.

One goal of social psychological research is to offer explanations for phenomena under investigation; these explanations sometimes take the form of process models (for example, stimulus S triggers psychological process P, which elicits behavioral response B). A social psychological finding typically can be explained by more than one process. A dissonance finding can be interpreted with a motivational explanation (Festinger, 1957), a behavioral explanation (Bem, 1967), or a self-threat explanation (Aronson, 1969; Steele and Lin, 1983). The emotional reaction to a sad event can be interpreted in terms of primacy of emotion or primacy of cognition (Lazarus, 1982; Zajonc, 1980). Carefully designed studies allow one to compare different explanations and, with a little luck, to distinguish between them.

Studies that directly compare theoretical explanations by pitting one prediction against another are important for the advancement of theory in the field (Platt, 1964). Greenwald (2004) argues that comparing theoretical explanations has not managed to resolve many theoretical disputes, and suggests that the field should focus instead on establishing the boundary (limiting) conditions of phenomena. We agree that boundary conditions (for example, how 'low' does a low reward have to be in a dissonance paradigm) are important to know, but we also believe that theory has a role and that empirical research in social psychology should contribute to the development of theory (Kruglanski, 2001).

If we ask what value social psychological research adds to our understanding and appreciation of phenomena that artists and novelists have grappled with for centuries, perhaps the best answer is that social psychology can offer theories that work. A theory should provide insight into a phenomenon. It should organize apparently disparate research findings. It should reveal why the observed boundary conditions are the way they are. Although it is rare that one theory emerges intact as the definitive winner, that does not really matter. What matters is that the confrontation or comparison of theories refines and redefines the questions and generates fresh questions that we might otherwise have been unable to imagine. What matters is the process of creation.

In addition to alternative explanations of basic psychological processes, there are alternative explanations that arise merely because of limitations in a particular research design. Perhaps the reason that participants in the high-threat condition did not perform as well on a memory task as those in the low-threat condition was not because the two groups were differentially 'threatened', but because participants in the low-threat condition were bored and inattentive, or the high-threat participants were distracted. These types of alternative explanations are not as interesting as those that arise from alternative theories, but they can seriously limit the knowledge that emerges from a study. It is incumbent on the researcher to design a study that reduces the number of possible alternative explanations, both theoretical and methodological.

Multiple methods force a type of comparison that is often neglected in social psychological research. The researcher who uses only one method to tackle a problem introduces a confound because all conclusions are conditional on that particular research strategy. Our point is deeper than the issue of whether a finding is generalizable, or robust across research methods. Consider a physicist studying the effect of gravity on objects in free fall. The physicist chooses to study this problem in the context of a vacuum so that extraneous factors can be controlled and derives interesting mathematical relations between variables such as time and the distance traveled by the object in free fall. This strategy, however, does not allow for the discovery of the effects of friction on objects in free fall (because the study is performed in a vacuum, without friction). The point is not merely that conclusions will not generalize to settings outside the vacuum but that the understanding of the underlying physical laws that can emerge from a single research technique is limited. The physicist could not discover more general laws involving the conservation of energy.

One of the basic messages of social psychology is that the situation is a powerful determinant of behavior and that its influence usually is not salient to the perceiver. Like the ordinary perceiver who commits the fundamental attribution error (Ross, 1977) by not giving sufficient weight to situational factors, the researcher who holds the method constant (that is, the 'situation') will not be in a position to give sufficient weight to method. By using multiple methods, an investigator can detect these 'situational' factors and hopefully develop a deeper understanding of the phenomenon under investigation. Social psychologists tend to favor experiments because of their potential for high internal validity (that is, their capacity to determine cause–effect relations); however, as we argue below, internal validity is only one of many criteria that research should satisfy. Even if internal validity were the only desideratum of research, the example of the objects in free fall shows that the use of a single paradigm, no matter how 'clean' from an experimental view, precludes complete understanding of a phenomenon.

Regardless of the method chosen, there are certain issues that all researchers must deal with as they progress through the various stages of the research process from generating an idea to writing up the results. In the remainder of the chapter, we will discuss these issues, following the researcher step by step through the process, noting how the choices made at each step constrain other options and describing how the process itself may differ depending on the type of question and the basic method chosen.

## The life history of a research project in social psychology

### *Generating questions*

Courses and textbooks on methods rarely have much to say about finding good research questions, forming hypotheses, or, least of all, generating theory. William J. McGuire (1973, 1997, 1999) has been a tireless advocate of the importance of hypothesis generation and has even provided a comprehensive list of tactics designed to stimulate would-be researchers who are looking for ideas. But these exhortations have had little impact on our discussions of research methods, probably because most people *do* have ideas about what they want to study. Turning a general idea into a researchable question, however, is not usually a simple, straightforward task, and here also our courses and textbooks provide little guidance.

Most students begin their research careers in one of two ways (1) they work on a variation of a question that their adviser is studying, or (2) they discover a flaw in some study that they have read and design research to show that the conclusions of that study were wrong. Research usually leads to further research, and over the course of graduate school most students either find a topic that they care about or choose another career.

A topic is not identical to a researchable question, however. Different researchers tend to prefer topics at different levels of abstraction and to favor different approaches to formulating research questions. Some naturally think in terms of conceptual variables and abstract constructs: inconsistency creates dissonance (Festinger, 1957); comparative judgments are more rational than absolute judgments (Hsee et al., 1999). Others go around noticing behaviors that seem surprising, irrational, or simply interesting: some people use a lot of hand gestures, others do not (Krauss et al., 1996); people get more upset when they miss a plane by two minutes than when they miss it by two hours (Kahneman and Tversky, 1982); I get mad at the inattentive driver who does not move when the light changes and honk my horn, but I also get mad at the guy who honks his horn at me when I am slow off the mark at the green light (Jones and Nisbett, 1972). Still others want to understand some general domain of behavior: what are the causes of aggression? (Berkowitz, 1993); what makes people happy? (Kahneman et al., 1999); what makes a decision good? (Hammond et al., 1999). None of these approaches is the right approach; none is the wrong approach. The examples we have given should make it clear that all can advance the field. But each one raises a somewhat different set of methodological challenges (Brinberg and McGrath, 1985).

Whatever one's approach, an important first step is to find out what other people have said about the topic and whether a body of empirical research already exists. This will be relatively easy if one is interested in a topic that has already been defined by the field – stereotyping, aggression, or attitude change, for example – but rather more difficult if one thinks one is onto something new. Suppose a person wants to study 'betrayal'. A PsychInfo search reveals that there is next to nothing listed under that term, but it would be wrong to conclude that there is no pertinent research. It may be that the person has merely coined a new term for an old concept and is at risk of wasting a great deal of time rediscovering familiar ideas (Kruglanski, 2001; Miller and Pederson, 1999). It is important to explore related topics – trust, deception, honor, defection – maybe even anger or expectancy disconfirmation. Even at the literature-search stage, it is important to consider alternatives. Doing so can help to refine or redefine the concept and may often help to turn a vague idea into a set of concrete questions.

If it turns out that there really has not been much psychological research on a topic, the researcher in search of a question must try other strategies – broader reading (of philosophers, biologists, novelists, or news reporters, for example), observation, and thinking. Research on lay reasoning has been influenced by the work of Francis Bacon (Nisbett and Ross, 1980); research on bystander intervention, by news reports of 'urban apathy' (Latané and Darley, 1970). Anthropologists commonly go off to the field without a clear question in mind, allowing their questions to emerge from their observations on the scene. This is a strategy that makes sense at the initial stages of research about unfamiliar people or settings, since predetermined questions might turn out to be inappropriate in the new context. Focus groups and 'grounded theory' methods (Kreuger and Casey, 2000; Strauss and Corbin, 1998) are also strategies for deriving concepts from observation. Finally, sooner or later, most of us who are trying to come to grips with a new topic spend a lot of time in intense thinking, alone or in conversation with others, in the car, in the kitchen, in the shower.

In order to get on with the business of actually designing research, however, at some point our reading, observation, and thinking must coalesce into a manageable hypothesis or question. In some disciplines, a rich description is the end product; for social psychology, it is usually not; we are looking for meanings and ideas that can be tested with other methods and in other settings. A good question should be clear and comprehensible to ourselves and others. It should be neither intractable nor too easy: an answer should be *possible* but not self-evident. A good question should allow for several possible answers, whose relative correctness can be evaluated (Hastie, 2001; Hilbert, 1900).

### *Pilot testing*

The purpose of pilot testing is to capture the phenomenon embodied in your question – to measure what you intend to measure, and to find or create conditions that match your conceptual variables. The intricate business of pilot testing is not much emphasized in current discussions of research methods, which seem to devote more and more attention to the final stages of the research process – measurement and data analysis – and less and less to the initial planning stages, where the design and procedures are worked out (Aronson, 2002; Ellsworth and Gonzalez, 2001). This is unfortunate. If the design is missing crucial controls, if the treatments and measures do not capture the intended meaning of the conceptual variables, if the participants are bored, or confused, or suspicious, no amount of sophisticated post-hoc statistical repair work can rescue the study. In recent years we have read MA and Ph.D. theses in which the treatments failed to have the intended effect – the subjects did not believe that the 'race-neutral' intelligence test was really race neutral; people given a positive mood induction felt no better than those in the control group; the researcher's idea of a highly credible communicator did not match the ideas of the population being studied. We have seen theses where there were floor or ceiling effects on the crucial measure – everyone's test performance was excellent, almost everyone in all conditions thought the defendant was guilty. With careful pilot testing, none of these problems should occur in a completed study: they should have been discovered and corrected before the study was run. Pilot testing, like all fine craftsmanship, can be frustrating and time-consuming, but surely running an entire study that gets null results because of flaws that could have been corrected is an even more frustrating waste of time.

Pilot testing is not a matter of running the whole experiment through from beginning to end to see if it 'works.' It is an opportunity to test the separate components of a study to see whether they have the intended meaning. Brown and Steele (2001) discovered that it requires a fairly elaborate presentation to get African-American students to believe that an intellectual ability test is really race neutral: simply calling it an unbiased test is not enough. A mood indution used by another researcher, studying a different question in a different context, may not work for your question and your context. A heavy-handed prime – for example, showing people a series of blonde bimbos right before testing their feminist attitudes – may be easy for the participants to figure out: the technique designed to prime sexist attitudes may actually prime defensive self-presentation strategies. During pilot testing, it is possible to stop the study immediately after the treatment has been administered and assess its effects: what did the person being studied think of the race-neutral test? Has her mood improved? What does he think was the point of the bimbo pictures? What stands out about the study so far?

It is often impossible to get information about questions like these during the actual experiment, and the information usually comes too late to be useful. Moreover, so-called 'manipulation checks' can sometimes cause more problems than they solve. An immediate manipulation check can interfere with the psychological processes the researcher cares about; a delayed manipulation check may be so delayed that the effects it is designed to 'check' have changed or vanished. For example, a verbal manipulation check immediately after the treatment might draw people's attention to the treatment and alter their responses to it, so that the real independent variable is not the one intended, but a combination of the independent variable and the probe. If there are several independent variables, the participant's experience becomes cluttered with distractions. Waiting until the end of the study to check on the manipulations is also problematic: other events and measures have taken place, and people may not be able to disentangle their current feelings from their earlier responses.

Likewise, it is possible to pilot test possible measures, whether the research involves an experiment, a survey, or an open-ended interview study. Pilot-testing measures can accomplish several purposes. First, it is possible to test people's psychological reactions to the measures themselves. Do they understand the questions? Do they find them offensive? What do they think you are interested in? Second, it is possible to find out about baseline levels of response – are there floor or ceiling effects? Is this a measure that is likely to vary with other variables in a correlational study, or to respond to changes in the situation? You may find that a task you thought was highly demanding is in fact very easy, that the criminal case you planned to use is overwhelmingly one-sided. You may find that people consider some of your questions to be too personal, and give neutral safe answers that do not reflect their actual beliefs (Visser et al., 2000). You may find that they think the questionnaire or interview is much too long and tedious, so that their earlier answers are much more careful than their later ones.

People are unlikely to give you honest evaluations of your incomprehensible, offensive, or boring questions during the actual study, but during pilot testing, if you tell them (honestly, as it happens) that you are still developing the questionnaire and that you want their help in designing a measure that will be acceptable and meaningful to people like them, they may be more forthcoming. Often, they are eager to be involved in the design of new research and to make suggestions. All empirical research, even the most qualitative, involves measures, and pilot testing is the time to develop measures that are involving, that mean what we want them to mean, and that people will answer honestly.

Especially for studies with manipulated independent variables, a few run-throughs of the whole experiment from beginning to end are useful – not so much to find out whether the experiment is going to 'work,' but to find out whether we have successfully translated our conceptual question into a coherent set of procedures that makes sense to people and holds their attention, and to find out whether the separate components work together. The pictures of blonde bimbos, for example, might be a perfectly good prime for sexist sentiments in some contexts, but not when followed by a dependent measure that is obviously a test of feminist attitudes. Either a subtler treatment or a subtler measure may be necessary to keep the subject from figuring out what you are trying to test.

Pretest–posttest designs can raise similar issues: asking people how they feel about affirmative action at the beginning of the hour, and then presenting them with a communication designed to change their attitudes about affirmative action may be quite different from simply presenting the communication. The pretest may sensitize the subject to the communication (Smith, 2000), making its effects stronger or weaker, but in any case *different* than they would have been otherwise. If a pretest is necessary, it is generally better to administer it much earlier, in a context apparently unrelated to the research. Often, it is not necessary to pretest at all, since random assignment can be used to ensure equivalence among groups (Greenwald, 1976).

Pilot testing is also the best opportunity to discover whether a study accords with ethical standards for research. One can find out whether the actual experience of participating in a particular study is upsetting, painful, or humiliating in a carefully monitored context where the experimenter is prepared to stop everything and talk to the participant at the first sign of distress. If some people find some of the emotionally arousing pictures too disturbing, or the task too embarrassing, or our questions too personal, or the deception unjustifiable, we must make changes. We can look for different stimuli or measures that still get at what we are interested in but that are less upsetting. Or we may learn that we need to screen out certain people, people whose life experiences might make them especially sensitive to some aspect of the research procedure. Occasionally, we may have to try a whole different approach to studying our question.

Most human-subjects review boards emphasize informed consent and debriefing as the primary ethical requirements. Important as these are, they are brackets around the person's actual experience, far less important to the participants than what actually happens to them during the study. In order to write an honest informed consent request, it is necessary to know how real people have actually reacted to the procedures – that is what participants need to know in order to be accurately informed. Of course, just as people may be reluctant to admit that they did not understand the questions or thought the experiment was stupid or transparent, they may be reluctant to admit that they were upset. Again, one way to elicit honest responses is to tell them that you are still developing the experiment, and ask them whether they think *other* people like them might be disturbed about some aspect of the procedure.

### *Generating alternative hypotheses*

It is important to develop multiple working hypotheses early in the research process, (Platt, 1964). Sometimes, if the topic is very new, the very first study may be designed to discover whether the phenomenon exists: whether people conform to group pressure when it contradicts the evidence of their senses, whether people from different cultures agree on the meaning of emotional facial expressions, or whether people are more concerned about losses than gains. At this stage, a simple demonstration can be an important contribution. Even if the phenomenon is brand-new, the researcher still has to consider and rule out artifactual alternatives, as we will discuss below. Moreover, it is important to think carefully about how novel one's phenomenon actually is – to ask, 'What are the most closely related phenomena that *have* been studied, and how can I argue that mine is really distinct?' Or, 'What are the most closely related treatments (or definitions of the independent variable) that have been used, and can I differentiate my conceptual variable from the ones they were designed to study?'

If the researcher has gone beyond the simple demonstration of a phenomenon and is interested in causes, processes, moderators, or mediators, it is important to consider other possible causes, processes, moderators, or mediators. One technique is to imagine that we have already found the results that we expected, and consider other possible interpretations. If the researcher is invested in his or her own favorite hypothesis, it is often very hard to generate plausible alternatives (e.g., Griffin and Ross, 1991; Ross et al., 1977), but it is important to make a serious effort while there is still time to modify the design or procedures. Discussing the research with other people is a good way to get beyond one's own biases; for example, if you describe your study as though it were already finished and your hypothesis was confirmed, your colleagues, anticipating the responses of your reviewers, will often suggest numerous alternative explanations. These may not, at first blush, seem *at all* plausible to you, but they are worth considering because they are plausible to *someone*. McGuire's (1997) detailed advice on how to generate initial hypotheses is at least as useful for generating alternative hypotheses.

Although only you yourself, aided by colleagues with whom you share your initial ideas and an open-minded literature search, can really judge the plausibility of alternative answers to the specific question you are posing, there are some generic, formal alternatives that should be considered, regardless of your question (cf. Brewer, 2000; Ellsworth, 1977). If your hypothesis is that X causes Y, a common alternative is that Y causes X. Ordinarily, when random assignment is possible, this will not be a plausible alternative (although in other settings, without random assignment, it might). In a correlational study of chronic attributes, reverse causality can be a serious rival. Does attractiveness lead to perceptions of competence, or vice versa? Or both? It is important to find a setting in which you can be sure that one precedes the other, or where you can introduce one independently of the other.

A second common alternative is the familiar third-variable correlation: X and Y occur together because some third variable, Z, is responsible for both. If a study finds that boys who are heavily involved in sports cry less often than boys who are not, it would be wrong to conclude that sports lead to stoic behavior or to happiness; one (of many) possibilities is that parents who have strong beliefs about appropriate sex-role behavior push their sons into sports and punish crying. Again, this alternative is generally ruled out in settings where people can be randomly assigned to the X treatment, but can be a serious problem in quasi-experimental and correlational designs.

A third possibility is that X alone is not enough – that X interacts with some other variable Z; that is, Z *moderates* the effects of X. Looking people in the eye makes them like you, but only in social contexts that are already positive; otherwise, it can be threatening (Ellsworth and Carlsmith, 1968). This kind of alternative cannot be ruled out by random assignment in a laboratory experiment. Typically, many features of the situation in a laboratory experiment are *held constant*, meaning that any one of them could potentially interact with the intended independent variable, but the interaction would not be discovered. If the experimenter studies only positive social interactions, she will conclude that eye contact is a positive signal; if only women are studied, if the communicator is always credible, or if the experimenter is extremely attractive, results that apparently confirm the hypothesis could actually be due to a combination of these constant variables with the variable the experimenter cares about.

These are the most common formal alternatives, but they are not the only ones. For a more extensive discussion, see Cook and Campbell (1979) or Ellsworth (1977). In designing a study, it is useful to consider these various alternatives, substituting one's own variables for the Xs and Ys, thinking carefully about possible Zs, and building in controls (groups, measures, or occasions) to test any that seem to be plausible rivals. For any given question, some of the suggested rivals may be completely *implausible* – the investigator will not be able to think of any credible alternative that takes that particular form (West et al., 2000). If the hypothesis is that males are more assertive than females, the reverse-causality hypothesis that assertiveness causes gender can instantly be ruled out. Similarly, in a situation where random assignment is not possible, the addition of measurement occasions may make the alternative explanation of time implausible (for example, three observations before the naturally occurring 'treatment' followed by three observations afterwards help rule out alternative explanations if the only change seen in the dependent variable occurred between the third and fourth observations). Adding a second condition to a before/after design in which different participants respond to the pretest and posttest measures but do not experience the intervening intervention helps rule out alternative explanations such as the possibility that the effect is due to the same participants answering the same question twice.

In addition to alternative hypotheses about the relationship among variables, it is also important to consider alternative hypotheses about the *definition* of the variables. These are problems of *confounds* and *construct validity*. (Usually, the term *confound* is used for a correlated variable that is specific to the research environment and relatively trivial, while *construct validity* is implicated if important variables are correlated in a wide range of settings.) If males behave more assertively than females in a given setting, for example, it may be due not to their gender per se, but to their greater power. Females who have become accustomed to power may be as assertive as males. (If men were given more resources in the context of a particular experiment, this would be a confound; the more general problem of males' power in the wider society raises questions about the construct validity of the concept of gender in relation to assertiveness.) Both independent and dependent variables may be correlated with other variables besides the one we care about, and so efforts must be made to vary or measure them independently.

### *Dull but serious alternative explanations*

Finally, there is a set of boring but fatal alternatives that are a risk of the research process itself: methodological artifacts such as demand characteristics and experimenter bias. *Demand characteristics* are 'subtle or not-so-subtle cues in the experimental setting that influence subjects' perceptions of what is expected of them, and that might systematically influence their behavior' (Aronson et al., 1990: 347).

Research participants usually know that they are being observed and studied, and they try to figure out what the research is about and what is expected of them. They may not take our treatments and measures at face value, but may instead interpret them in the light of our imagined intentions, and adjust their behavior accordingly. We may *tell* participants that they are participating in two entirely different studies or that 'there are no right or wrong answers to these questions', but the fact that we have said it does not guarantee that they believe it. Research participants are interested, curious human beings. Most of them associate psychology with tests of mental health and mental abilities, and they may be apprehensive about appearing smart, or sensitive, or normal, or whatever they think we are concerned about ('evaluation apprehension'; Rosenberg, 1969). If we expect differences among different groups of participants (whether randomly assigned or 'natural' groups) and the demand characteristics are different across groups, we have no way of being sure that the results were due to our conceptual variables rather than to differences in demand characteristics. Demand characteristics can be discovered and remedied during pilot testing, when we can ask people what they think the questionnaire is getting at or what the treatment means, and how they think a normal, smart, successful person would respond.

*Experimenter bias* occurs when an experimenter unintentionally influences the participants to behave in a way that confirms the hypothesis. Neither the experimenter nor the subject has any awareness that this has taken place. Sometimes its causes can be easily identified – for example, videotapes of pilot testing showed that one of our research assistants, when presenting an array of faces for children to choose from, inadvertently (and consistently) pointed to the one we expected would be chosen. More often, such cues are subtle, and cannot be identified, even though the effects are strong (Rosenthal, 1969). Experimenter bias is a serious, pervasive alternative explanation (Rosenthal and Rubin, 1978) that can occur in any kind of research involving interaction with human beings – whether the research is qualitative or quantitative; observational, survey, or experimental – and has even been demonstrated in studies of rats (Rosenthal and Fode, 1963). In fact, the first famous demonstration of the phenomenon was Clever Hans, the arithmetically gifted horse who could solve numerical problems by tapping out the right answers with his hoof. It turned out that his gifts were psychological rather than mathematical – he was able to notice subtle changes in his trainer's posture and expression when he reached the right answer, and stopped tapping.

Pilot testing usually cannot diagnose experimenter bias. The design of the experiment must include controls to rule out this alternative explanation. A purely automated presentation of stimuli and measures can be effective, but it sacrifices the 'social' aspect of many social psychological questions (and in any case is not a guarantee, because differences in the printed or recorded words across conditions can also be a source of bias (Krauss and Chin, 1998).

Having experimenters or interviewers or observers who are unaware of which experimental condition the participant is in provides complete protection, although it is sometimes hard to achieve. For example, if the study concerns obvious visible characteristics such as race or gender, experimenters may communicate different expectations even if the researcher does not tell them that the study is about race. Keeping the experimenters blind to one of the variables in a study protects against bias on that variable and on interactions with that variable. Keeping the experimenters unaware of the hypothesis may seem like an effective solution, but it is not. First, since the experimenters run all of the conditions and can observe the differences among them, and know what is being measured, the hypothesis may be pretty easy to figure out; second, even if the researcher tries to keep the experimenters in the dark, they will inevitably develop their own hypotheses and communicate those to the participants. Like the people being studied, research assistants are sentient human beings who want to know what is going on. (Protection against experimenter bias, though difficult, is achievable: fuller discussion may be found in Aronson et al., 1990.)

### *The independent variable*

The term 'independent variable' is often used to refer to the cause in a hypothesized cause–effect relationship, but it can also refer to any variable that *predicts* another. One might ask, for example, whether high levels of education predict better health; whether low popularity or high popularity is correlated with being a bully; whether moral standards vary with social class.

Independent variables differ on how much latitude their definitions offer. Abstract conceptual variables, such as power, mood, or group cohesiveness, can carry several concrete representations. We could give participants descriptions of high- and low-power people, or bring them into the laboratory and assign some the role of boss and the others the role of subordinate, or go to actual workplaces and interview real bosses and subordinates, or do an observational study in a classroom to see who influences whom, or simply ask people how powerful they think they are. Each of these methods will raise a different set of alternative hypotheses, which must be ruled out in the design of the study. Using more than one definition over a series of studies greatly increases the researcher's confidence that the important variable is really power, and not some correlated variable, because the correlated variables are likely to be different for different operational izations of power. This provides convergent validity for the meaning of the independent variable.

Other independent variables offer less freedom in definition. A researcher interested in gender differences or other demographic variables, or interested in a particular educational method (such as small class size), legal reform (such as allowing jurors to take notes; providing legal aid), or other social policy (such as a tax cut) has far fewer choices. But these 'obvious' independent variables do not necessarily make the researcher's task easier. True, there is no question of how to operationalize the concept of 'woman' as opposed to 'man', but there is still work to be done before one can conclude that gender is really the variable that matters. If a psychologist had decided to use Harvard and Radcliffe undergraduates to study gender differences in the 1960s, aside from the obvious problem of generalizability to the population at large, there would be a serious selection problem affecting the comparability of men and women even within this elite population. Harvard was large; Radcliffe was small. Given the norms of the time and the size of the classes admitted, the Radcliffe students represented a much more highly selected group than the Harvard students. Differences that looked like gender differences could have been differences in qualifications. Whether this would be a *plausible* alternative, of course, depends on the hypothesis. A finding that women had superior verbal skills would be suspect; however, the women's higher qualification would not be a plausible alternative explanation for Matina Horner's (1972) finding that women demonstrated 'fear of success'.

Again, one goal in research is to reduce the number of alternative explanations that can be attributed to an independent variable. One technique to reduce the number of alternative explanations is to show convergent validity – show that you get qualitatively similar results under different definitions of the independent variable. Convergent validity is merely one criterion. The discussion of additional criteria requires a classification of predictor variables into those that can be manipulated, measured, or 'found'.

### *Independent variables that can be manipulated*

Traditionally, social psychologists have favored the manipulated independent variable with random assignment of participants to two or more conditions, and there are good reasons for this preference, especially if the researcher has a causal hypothesis. Random assignment of participants to conditions is an enormously powerful technique because it allows the researcher to rule out whole categories of alternative explanations at once and guarantees that, on average, all of the groups are the same before the treatment is given. If the researcher finds differences between the groups, these differences can be attributed to the independent variable the experimenter cares about, and not to differences in the participants' backgrounds, personalities, abilities, motivation, or anything else about themselves or their lives before the random assignment took place.

Random assignment does not solve all problems, however. First, any differences in the experiences of the experimental group and the control group(s) that occur *after* the participants have been randomly assigned and that are not an essential feature of the treatment are possible alternative explanations for the results. If the participants in the experimental group interact with different people, work on a more interesting task, or have experiences that make them more confused or more suspicious, any of these differences could account for the results, rather than the independent variable the experimenter has in mind. In the ideal random assignment experiment, the experimental and control participants are given the same information, spend the same amount of time in the study, interact with the same people, and engage in the same activities, except for the introduction of the treatment. If the manipulation varies on many dimensions, it is difficult to pin down what it is really manipulating.

Second, if participants are more likely to drop out of one condition than the other(s) after they have been randomly assigned, we can no longer be sure that the groups are equivalent. Suppose participants in the experimental group are to see a film of a rape trial and those in the control group a film of an assault trial involving two men, in a test of whether viewing violence against women affects feminist attitudes. If many more people withdraw from the study when they are told that the film involves a rape, one hypothesis is that these are the participants with the strongest attitudes about violence towards women. This means that even before the experimenter shows the films, the average feminist attitudes of the treatment group and the control group might already differ, and any differences on the dependent variable measure might not be due to the rape film at all but to prior group differences. Note that if a study involved showing *all* participants a film of a rape trial, a high dropout rate is a less serious problem: it can raise questions about the generalizability of the results to people who are unwilling to view rape films, but not about their validity among the people who are willing.

In a laboratory study, careful pilot testing can usually ensure that loss of participants is minimized and differential dropout is not a problem. In field studies, in those rare and precious instances where random assignment is possible, participant attrition or reassignment often poses a more serious threat. Parents may agitate to get their children moved out of racially integrated classrooms or into programs designed to improve school achievement, compromising the initial random assignment. Students or workers with weak skills may drop out of programs they find too challenging. The result is that the groups that are measured after the treatment are no longer the groups that were randomly assigned, and any differences found could be due to differences in the composition of the groups rather than to the intended independent variable (Cook and Campbell, 1979; West et al., 2000). Sometimes in field studies, random assignment may be undermined at the very outset, as when doctors surreptitiously assign their high-risk patients to a promising treatment group, perhaps furthering humanitarian goals, but invalidating the results of the study (Kopans, 1994). Unless the experimenter has full control over who *gets* into the various conditions of the experiment and who *stays* in them, random assignment may be an illusion, and it is important to keep track of the *actual* composition of the groups throughout the study.

The most common use of random assignment in social psychology is in the laboratory study. A consequence of this preference is that our independent variables are often weak, our dependent variables often inconsequential, and our effects inevitably short term. *This does not mean that our studies are invalid or unimportant.* The insights and theories tested in laboratory studies – about conformity, altruism, attitudes, expectancy effects, cognitive biases, and many other topics – have proven to be powerful and often generalizable to a wide range of nonlaboratory settings. Still, working within such narrow confines, it is almost impossible to test the boundary conditions of our findings. Consider the manipulation of letting one student boss another around for 45 minutes, giving some ego-bolstering praise. If we find that participants given this brief power manipulation are likely to take the credit for successes and deny blame for failures (Tiedens et al., 2000), can we conclude that this is also true of government officials or CEOs who have experienced power on a daily basis for years? What do a few moments of criticism have in common with chronic low self-esteem? If the only attitudes we study are the sort of trivial attitudes that can be changed within the course of an hour, what have we learned about deep-seated ideological convictions? In fact, we may have learned a great deal – it is as wrong to claim that laboratory results do not generalize to the real world as it is to claim that they do; as wrong to claim that short-term acute laboratory manipulations of variables are different from their real-world counterparts as it is to claim that they are the same. These are open questions, and only research that uses different methods in new settings can answer them.

### *Independent variables that are measured*

When the independent variable is a measured variable, new problems arise. For example, when using self-report, the researcher must consider whether people can give an accurate assessment (for example, people may not be good judges of how powerful they are), as self-report measures can be woefully inaccurate (Reis and Gable, 2000; Wentland, 1993). Self-report measures can also make the variable salient in people's minds and bias future responses: a person who has just described herself as powerful might be especially likely to feel a burst of high self-esteem. Reverse causality and third-variable causality are also problems with measured variables; for example, low self-esteem may cause people to see themselves as powerless (or is it that not having power causes low self-esteem?). Thus, the problems with *measured* variables are first, construct validity – are we really measuring the variable we care about and only that variable? – and second, reactivity – whenever people are aware that they are being measured and have any control over their responses, the measure can be affected by the image the participant wants to convey, rather than by the variable we care about. The techniques for dealing with construct validity and reactivity problems of measured predictor variables are the same techniques one uses with 'found'independent variables, so we will review the solutions together in the next subsection.

### *Independent variables that are 'found'*

But what if the researcher is really interested in a variable that cannot be manipulated at all – gender, for example, or social class, or culture. These are, by definition, 'found' variables, although one's degree of gender, class, or cultural *identification* might be measured and might be relevant to some questions. In these cases, the strategy is to identify correlated variables, such as wealth or power, and attempt to rule them out, or to look for a variety of measures that might reflect the processes one cares about but that would not be affected by plausible third variables.

A psychologist interested in the effects of power on self-esteem, for example, might go to the field and study high- and low-power people in a hierarchically organized workplace ('found' power). Studying people who occupy real positions of high and low power has an appealing real-world relevance, but there are many possible variables that could cause differences in self-esteem between people in real-world positions of power and their subordinates. People could have attained powerful positions because they are older, more skilled, more educated, richer, whiter, or male – or even, perhaps, because they had higher self-esteem to begin with. Without random assignment, the researcher has to consider each of the plausible alternative hypotheses one by one and find ways to rule them out – by finding an all-black female group; by comparing jury forepersons on juries where the role is randomly assigned to those on juries where the members elect the foreperson; by statistically controlling for age, income, education, and so on. Rarely are these co plete solutions. Thus, the problems with *found* variables are problems of non-random selection (self-selection or selection by others) and correlated variables – income is correlated with success, health, power, and SAT scores, so in comparing people on any of these dimensions we have to worry about whether we are really comparing them on income.

There are three common ways to rule out correlated variables. First, the researcher can use careful selection to make sure that the correlated variable does not vary. The third variable is 'held constant'. You may have the hypothesis that women are more prone to depression than men, but you also know that women earn less money. Thus, the depression that appears to be due to gender could actually be due to lower income. So you attempt to hold income constant by studying only people within a narrow economic range. You lose generality by this method (that is the gender effect you have demonstrated may be limited to people in that narrow income range), but you gain confidence that gender (or, alas, something else that is correlated with gender but not with income) plays a role indepression.

Second, the researcher can construct a model that includes both variables, not only the one he or she cares about, but also the troublesome correlated variable (or several hypothesized variables and several correlated variables). This makes it possible to examine the effects of both variables separately. In actually conducting the research, you would have to find people in each of the groups you want to compare; in this case, women and men who were characterized by different levels of the correlated variable – poor men and women, middle-income men and women, and rich men and women, for example. This is analogous to the technique of systematic variation in a random assignment study. If women are more depressed than men in all three income groups, you are more sure of your hypothesis; other patterns of results force you to consider new hypotheses. The main problem with this method is that it can be difficult to implement, especially if you want to rule out several correlated variables, as some combinations of variables may be quite rare (for example, very rich women). New statistical procedures based on 'propensity score' techniques help make this problem tractable (Rosenbaum and Rubin, 1984).

Third, the researcher can use statistical methods, such as analysis of covariance (ANCOVA), to control for correlated variables. These methods, as typically implemented, control for the linear association of the third variable or set of variables. In effect, a linear regression is computed where the linear effect of the third variable on the independent variable is subtracted from the independent variable, and the remainder – the residual – is used as the independent variable instead of the original independent variable. When using these techniques, the researcher must be careful not to to make general pronouncements, such as 'we controlled for the effect of income'. More precisely, what typically was controlled for is the linear effect of the covariate. The data may still contain nonlinear effects of the correlated variable or interactions between the third variable and the independent variable.

We conclude this section on independent variables with this point: as long as a variable has been studied with only a single set of procedures, it is impossible to distinguish the role of the variable from the role of the procedures (Campbell and Fiske, 1959). The procedures, or the-variable-in-the-context-of-these-procedures, constitute an alternative explanation of the results that ordinarily cannot be ruled out in a single study. In order to make real progress, sooner or later it is important to study the same question by a different method – to compare the measured version of a variable with the manipulated version, to use an entirely different manipulation, or to find an instance of the variable rather than creating one. If the results are different, the researcher is confronted with a whole new set of questions about *why* they are different, questions that can stimulate real theoretical progress and understanding that would otherwise be unlikely. For example, laboratory experiments on social comparison showed strong evidence that people tend to compare themselves to others who are slightly better than they are on whatever dimension they are concerned about (upward social comparison). However, in field research, Taylor (1983) found that breast-cancer patients tended to use downward social comparison, comparing themselves to patients who were not doing so well, with the result that almost all of the women thought that they were adjusting very well. These field data extended our understanding of social comparison processes in ways that were not suggested by the experimental research.

### *The dependent variable*

Measured outcome variables raise the same issues as measured predictor variables. It is important to consider what *else* the measure might be tapping besides one's intended variable (construct validity). It is important to find out during pilot testing what sorts of motivations and interpretations participants experience when they encounter the measure (reactivity). And it is important to consider alternative explanations of the whole process, and include measures designed to assess other possible outcomes that might address these alternatives (tests of multiple working hypotheses) (John and Benet-Martinez, 2000). Sometimes the actual variable captured by the measure may be broader than the construct the researcher has in mind; for example, the researcher may be interested in favorable attitudes toward an outgroup, but the measure might actually reflect global good mood, in which case the predicted outcome is just a byproduct of a more general phenomenon. This possibility can be addressed by adding additional measures that are unaffected by mood, or additional measures that have nothing to do with the particular outgroup (known in the statistics literature as an *instrumental variable*). Sometimes the actual variable may be narrower than the researcher's concept. For example, the researcher may be interested in individualism as opposed to collectivism, but the scale may reflect *only* differences on the collectivism items while the groups are identical on the individualism items (Oyserman et al., 2002). This possibility can be assessed by looking for patterns and discrepancies in the individual items, for example, with confirmatory factor analysis. Sometimes the measure may tap a different variable altogether. For example, if one wants to measure knowledge or accuracy of perception, it is important to create a measure that is not affected by attitudes: if most of the 'correct' answers on a person perception measure involve negative qualities, what looks like accuracy could actually just be simple dislike.

### *Reliability and validity*

The reliability of a measure refers to its consistency: consistency over time, consistency over observers, or consistency over components of an overall measure, such as items on a questionnaire. All three are essential if one is trying to measure a stable attribute such as a personality trait, as is often the case when one is interested in a measured predictor variable (Bakeman, 2000; John and Benet-Martinez, 2000). Consistency over observers and consistency over components or items are analogous, in that both involve multiple attempts to measure the same thing at a given point in time. A researcher may use two or more observers to score how aggressively a person is behaving, how often dispositionalattributions occur in a narrative or a conversation, or any number of other variables. Or a researcher may ask several different questions all designed to tap aggression, the tendency to make dispositional attributions, or any number of other variables. If observers or items disagree, the measure is unreliable, and needs to be modified. Observers or coders may need further training (Bartholomew et al., 2000); items or coding categories may need to be revised or discarded. Generally, the more open-ended or unstructured the behavioral or verbal responses, and the more abstract and inferential the coding categories, the more difficult it is to develop a reliable measure. It is easier, for example, to measure competitiveness reliably in a game-like situation where there are only a few response alternatives, some competitive and some cooperative, than it is when observing playground behavior.It is easier to achieve reliability if one is measuring concrete behaviors ('hits', 'kicks', or 'shoves') than more abstract categories ('shows aggression').

While consistency over observers and measures is always essential in social psychological research, consistency over time is often not relevant. Very often we are interested in people's responses to an immediate situational stimulus – a threat to self-esteem, a subliminal prime, or a persuasive argument. We do not expect lasting effects; in fact, we go out of our way to debrief the participants in order to make sure that the effects are undone.

A measure that is unreliable cannot be valid. If observers cannot agree on whether behaviors are aggressive or merely assertive, if the items on a test are uncorrelated, or if a person gets different scores from one day to the next on a measure of a supposedly stable trait such as IQ or extraversion, the measure is useless. (Of course, the fact that a construct we thought was coherent or stable turns out not to be so may lead us to new theoretical insights, but the measure is useless for its original purpose.) Thus, reliability must be established before a measure is used.

A measure is *valid* if it measures what it is supposed to measure and nothing else. A reliable measure is not necessarily valid. A blood test, for example, may be a highly reliable (and valid) measure of whether people are HIV positive, but an invalid measure of whether they are immoral or gay. Validity is not easy to establish in social psychology, because our conceptual variables – variables such as prejudice or anxiety – often represent families of related variables rather than pure states, so there is no gold standard by which to measure them. Certain cognitive biases may be rigorously demonstrated as departures from a statistically correct response (Kahneman et al., 1982), but interpersonal biases are not so easily verified. 'Criterion-related validity' often makes no sense for social psychological variables, at least at the current stage of development of the science, because there is no single criterion that definitively identifies most of our variables. A recent example is work attempting to develop a measure of attitude ambivalence (Breckler, 1994; Priester and Petty, 1996; Thompson et al., 1995). Researchers disagree about whether ambivalence should be measured from a structural point of view (that is, ambivalence as a combination of separately measured positive and negative attitudes) or from an experiential view (that is, the subjective phenomenology of attitude ambivalence). There is currently no clear criterion against which to assess the validity of the various proposed measures of ambivalence.

For many of our variables, validity must be established slowly, by triangulation. If we want to use frowning as a measure of anger, for example, we might look to see whether frowning occurs with other variables plausibly associated with anger: with independent variables such as being thwarted or insulted, with dependent variables such as yelling, threatening, and slamming doors. This is the process of establishing *convergent validity*: many other indicators of the conceptual variable 'anger' are associated with frowning. Just as important, we want to make sure that frowning is unique to anger, that it is not associated with other mental states. This is the process of establishing *discriminant validity*: demonstrating that a frown discriminates anger from other states such as fear or sorrow (Campbell and Fiske, 1959; Judd and McClelland, 1998). In fact, it does not; frowning is characteristic of various kinds of mental effort, uncertainty, and perceived obstacles. Thus, it would not be a very good measure of anger *unless* other supporting measures were included that were *not* related to mental effort, or *unless* the situation was structured so that none of the other mental states that go with frowning was plausible in context.

What have we just said? We have said that frowning lacks discriminant validity as a measure of anger, but that in a context that rules out other types of uncertainty or obstacles, it could be a valid measure. There is an important *general* message here: that in social psychology many of our measures are not valid or invalid per se, but are valid or invalid in a particular context. Personality psychologists generally look for measures that are stable across time and context, but this is far less true of social psychologists. We are generally interested in situational variables, we expect our measures to be responsive to the particular situation, and therefore we should not expect to find measures that are universally valid or applicable. Just as the answers to individual questions (for example, 'Overall, how satisfied are you with your life in general?') can have different meanings depending on the questions that preceded them (Schwarz et al., 1998; Tourangeau and Rasinski, 1988), so *any* measure might have different meanings in different contexts. Many social psychologists seem to have forgotten this important fact. Whenever a set of messages is sent out over the Social and Personality Psychology Listserver, for example, there are almost always some that ask whether anyone knows of a good off-the-shelf measure of some variable – regret, ormistrust of authority, or vengeance – as though any measure that someone used successfully in one context is a generally valid measure. Often, these are not intended to be used as measures of enduring traits, but as measures of responses to situational variables. Rarely do these questioners ask about the context in which the measure was used or describe the context in which they plan to use it. This is a serious mistake. First, the measure may not be appropriate in the new context; for example, questions about racial prejudice may elicit different answers in all-white groups than they do in mixed-race groups. Second, the researcher often has a wide range of measures to choose from, each appropriate to some contexts but not to others, and looking for a generic measure may prevent the researcher from finding or creating a measure that fits the particular context. Racial prejudice, for example, may be measured by questions about affirmative action, welfare mothers, or the guilt of a particular criminal defendant; or by eye contact, conformity, helping, or any number of behaviors that in other contexts might have nothing to do with racial prejudice.

The analogous argument can be made about reliability. Social and personality psychologists often report the reliability of a scale (such as Cronbach's $\alpha$) as though the value of the reliability measure is an inherent property of the scale. Our journal articles contain sentences such as 'Scale X has been shown to have acceptable reliability, $\alpha$=0.82', with a reference to another article. Typical measures of reliability are a function of error variance, so anything that changes the error structure of the data (change in subjects, change in experimenter, change in instructions, change in manipulation, change in task, change in length of the study, etc.) will change the reliability of the scale. Thus, the reliability of a scale should always be reported for that particular study; it is meaningless to claim that a scale is reliable in one context because it was found to be reliable in another.

Many of our measures are open to multiple interpretations. A direct gaze, for example, can imply liking, subordination, disapproval, or simple attention. This does not mean that gaze direction is a bad or invalid measure; it can be an excellent measure of any of these concepts provided that that is the only meaning that makes sense in the particular context, that precautions have been taken to rule out alternative explanations. Nonverbal, behavioral measures (and manipulations) often come in for criticism because their link to the intended concept is less transparent than that of verbal measures. A scale that asks people to rate their anxiety on a seven-point scale seems to be a more direct measure of anxiety than a measure of speech hesitations or fidgeting. But this advantage is often more apparent than real. Verbal measures almost always come with *built-in* alternative explanations such as reactivity, social desirability, and cultural stereotypes or folk theories. Nonverbal measures are relatively free of these problems, because they are usually under less conscious control than verbal reports, and because it is often possible to keep the participant unaware that a measure is even being taken. For nonverbal measures (and sometimes for verbal measures as well) alternative explanations usually have to be figured out on an ad-hoc basis in each context.

### Internal and external validity

If all of the procedures in this section are followed, an experiment should have high internal validity. *Internal validity* means that in this particular study, any differences observed between the participants in different conditions or groups are due to the treatment, not to any artifact or confounded variable: being given a high-status role caused participants to respond to failure with anger, and being given a low-status role caused participants to respond to failure with sadness. Of course, to make even this claim, we have to be sure that our status manipulation affected status and not some related construct, and our anger and sadness measures reflected anger and sadness, and not something else. If so, we know that our treatments were responsible for the outcomes.

*External validity* means that the results will generalize to other people and other settings (Brewer, 2000; Campbell, 1957). No single study can have external validity, since it is impossible to know whether the results will replicate in another context. The findings of a study using college students as participants may or may not generalize to senior citizens; the findings of a study using senior citizens may or may not generalize to college students. The results of a laboratory study of productivity may or may not generalize to telemarketers; the results of a study of telemarketers may or may not generalize to postal workers. External validity is always an empirical question, requiring further research. Thus, there is no 'trade-off' between internal and external validity. If a study lacks internal validity, nothing has been learned, so there is nothing to generalize. If a study has internal validity, its external validity is always an open question.

Social psychologists are sometimes criticized because they hardly ever bother to use truly representative samples in their research, and often just use whatever participants are most ready to hand – for many of us, this means college students who are taking a course in introductory psychology. There are serious costs to restricting our research to one small segment of the population, just as there are serious costs to relying on a single type of method. Any results we find could be peculiar to the college student population, or could represent an interaction between some feature of that population (youth, IQ, interest in psychology) and the variable we are interested in, rather than the variable itself (Sears, 1986). Ultimately, no result can be trusted as general – or even as real – until it has been tested on different kinds of people with different kinds of methods.

However, conducting research on a truly representative sample of almost any population is enormously expensive. For some kinds of question, a representative sample is necessary; for others, it is not. It is important to think carefully about the kinds of samples that are appropriate for your research question and the kinds that are not.

A representative sample – a sample in which every member of some population has an equal chance of being included – is imperative if you want to make valid statements about the absolute frequencies of various responses in that population. For example, in predicting the outcome of a national election, you want to make accurate estimates of how many people favor each candidate and how many are undecided. In order to do this, you must draw a representative sample of voters. Likewise, if you want to know how blacks, whites, Hispanics, and Asians feel about affirmative action, or how often men are victims of violent crime compared to women, you need a representative sample.

But often in social psychology, our hypotheses are not about base-rate differences among groups, and often we are not concerned with the absolute percentages or exact numerical levels of the variables we measure. We ask questions such as: 'Can information people learn after an event change their memory for the event?' (Loftus, 1979); 'Does sorrow lead to a perception that events in general are uncontrollable?' (Keltner et al., 1993); 'Is a person more likely to help another when alone or when there are other people around?' (Latané and Darley, 1970). We are interested in the effects of psychological variables on other psychological variables and behavior. We do not particularly want to make statements about the exact percentage of people whose memory will be distorted with and without new information, or the precise size of the decreases in perceived controllability caused by sorrow. To us, estimates like these do not even make sense – there *is* no exact number: it will vary depending on the type of event, the type of new information, and all sorts of other factors. Testing a large random sample of Americans in one particular experiment designed to ask one of these questions would be a huge waste of time and money. Vastly more could be learned by a judicious choice of small, nonrepresentative samples in a variety of experimental contexts.

This is not to say that college students are fine for all our questions. They are not. The examples described above were chosen partly because they were plausibly true of old and young people, rich and poor, male and female. For questions like these, there is no compelling reason *not* to start with college students, although later on in one's research program it is important to move on to other groups in order to test generality and boundary conditions.

But for other questions, any old sample will not do. The researcher needs to consider what kind of sample will most likely provide useful answers to the question. The sample need not be representative, but it must meet certain specifications. Rather than a sample of convenience, a *sample of forethought* is needed. Sometimes the sample specifications are obvious. In research on aging, college students can only aspire to be in the control group; in research on cultural differences, you need people of different cultural backgrounds. But, at least at the outset, when you are trying to establish the existence of a relation between variables, you do not need *representative* samples of old and young people, or members of the cultures you want to compare. You must make sure to choose samples that are uncontaminated by correlated variables that might be alternative explanations for your results (e.g., you would not go to a hospital if you want old people, because they would be not only old but also unhealthy), and eventually you must test your hypotheses on different samples, but you do not need a fully representative sample.

For these questions, the need for samples of forethought is obvious. For other questions, the need to seek out special samples may be important, but less obvious. College students have certain characteristics that make them a poor choice for some questions (Sears, 1986). Much social psychological research on racism and prejudice, for example, has shown surprisingly weak effects, at odds with what we know about pervasive racial segregation, poverty rates, and the racial populations of America's prisons. Some of this discrepancy is undoubtedly due to the fact that undergraduates in research universities are much less likely to express overt prejudice than are some other segments of the population (Sommers and Ellsworth, 2000). By sticking to the college student population, we have learned more about weak prejudice laced with liberal guilt than we have about the sort of strong prejudice that inspires hate crimes. Likewise, college students would not be a good population for a researcher interested in fundamentalist religious beliefs, or the joy, pain, and guilt that come with assuming a responsible adult position in society.

For other variables, college students may be a poor choice because there is so little variability among them: most college students are pretty high in self-esteem and pretty low in depression, for example, and show a highly restricted range on many other psychological variables that might interest us. A median split on a college student sample does not *really* yield high and low self-esteem groups, however the researcher labels them. Usually, the comparison is actually between a high self-esteem group and a moderately high self-esteem group.

The main reason we overuse introductory psychology students is convenience, a reason which is scientifically unsound. But although it is extremely difficult and expensive to use a truly representative sample, it is relatively easy to find alternative samples that lack the drawbacks of college students. Researchers have recruited participants in airport waiting areas, departments of motor vehicles, courthouses, malls, and science museums. Especially in contexts where they are just waiting, people are usually quite willing to participate. If the study can be administered by telephone, community members can be used instead of college students. Of course, none of these are 'representative samples' of anything except themselves (for example, airline passengers flying out of Detroit), but they are likely to be *more* representative of the general population than college students are, and to be relatively free of the particular problems with college students (politically correct attitudes, lack of serious responsibility, bright future, and many more).

### *Data analysis*

After formulating the research question; thinking of alternative explanations; designing the study; pilot testing the procedures and materials; thinking about reliability, internal validity, and external validity; and selecting an optimal sample, you proceed with data collection. Then comes the stage of analyzing the data and reporting the results. There are excellent books and chapters on data analysis, so we need not reiterate those techniques here (e.g., Cohen and Cohen, 1984; Judd, 2000; Maxwell and Delaney, 1999; McClelland, 2000). Instead of reviewing specific procedures in basic data analysis, we provide a few prescriptions for reporting results.

First, report descriptive statistics. The results of a study are not just a p-value. The most important purpose of data analysis is description. Simple summary scores such as measures of central tendency, measures of variability, measures of association, and plots are what should be highlighted in a results section. If a complicated statistical model is used, the parameters of that model should be emphasized and interpreted. Results sections should emphasize results, not statistical tests (the section is not called 'Statistical Tests'). Sentences should begin with the results themselves – 'Attitudes in the prime condition, $M=5.2$, $sd=1.1$, were more favorable than attitudes in the control condition, $M=4.4$, $sd=1.3$, $t(130)=3.82$, $p<0.05$' – rather than with the statistical test (for example, 'A two-sample t-test reveals that mean scores in the two conditions differed, $p<0.05$'). Use the test statistic (the $t$, the $F$, the chi-square) and its corresponding p-value as punctuation marks at the end of the sentence, giving the conventional 'stamp of approval' on the pattern you observed.

Second, be aware of the statistical assumptions you make when conducting a test and check that your data are consistent with those assumptions. All statistical tests invoke a model that makes assumptions. Social psychologists appear to ignore this fact and act as though their hypotheses are tested in some absolute Platonic sense. A significant two-sample t-test does not show that one mean differs from another; instead, it provides a criterion by which to compare the means of two distributions under the assumption of equal variances, independence, and normality, leading to a particularly defined type I error rate. In other words, the researcher never tests a research hypothesis in isolation, but tests the *conjunction* of the research hypothesis and the set of assumptions required by the statistical test. A test may fail to reach statistical significance not because the research hypothesis failed (or there was not sufficient power), but because the assumptions were violated. For a discussion of how to check statistical assumptions, see McClelland (2000). Inform the reader that you checked the statistical assumptions and explain how you dealt with any violations.

Third, discuss a result in a manner consistent with the way you modeled it. An illustration of the violation of this prescription is seen in social psychologists' typical discussion of the Pearson correlation coefficient. Their usual language conveys an ordinal relation, in as 'the correlation shows that as anxiety increases, so does susceptibility to context effects'. As the reader knows from introductory statistics, the actual model underlying the correlation is a straight line (linear) relation between two variables. Therefore, the Pearson correlation assesses the degree of fit (defined in a particular way) between one variable and a linear transformation of the other variable (for example, 'The high correlation supports the model that anxiety and depression are linearly related'). If an ordinal relation is what the researcher wants to test, a different measure of association, one that measures the monotonic relation between two variables, should be used (e.g., Gonzalez and Nelson, 1996). It is possible for a Pearson correlation to be 0, and yet for the relation between those two variables to be systematic (that is, a Pearson correlation of 0 does not imply independence).

Fourth, do not describe an effect size as a measure of the underlying relation between constructs. The effect size is a normalized descriptive statistic. For example, the difference between two means is a descriptive statistic. The effect-size measure normalizes that difference by dividing it by the standard deviation. The term 'effect size' tends to convey more than the computation implies. We have seen researchers discuss effect sizes in a manner that implies a deep, fundamental relation. For example, in an experiment examining the effects of reward on performance, a researcher can easily fall into the trap of claiming to demonstrate the 'effect size of reward on performance'. This language, which is at the level of constructs, suggests that the effect size has uncovered some underlying constant – reward influences performance (two abstract constructs) with an effect size of 0.2. Indeed, the use of meta-analysis connotes that multiple studies each provide estimates of this 'effect size' and that one can average over such studies to arrive at an even better estimate of effect size. In the physical sciences, there are examples of underlying constants that are invariant and can be estimated (for example, Planck's constant and the speed of light). Are there such constants in social psychology? We doubt it. So do not fall into the trap of reading more into an effect size than is warranted by the ingredients – the descriptive statistics – that created it.

Data analysis should stay as close to the data and as close to the research hypothesis as possible. Present data and test the hypotheses that you have made (that is, if you made an ordinal prediction, use a test designed for ordinal hypotheses). Students frequently ask us to evaluate the 'proposed analyses' section of their dissertation proposal to check whether they will be 'analyzing the data correctly'. Such an evaluation is impossible for us to make out of context – we need to see the introduction, the hypotheses, the materials, and the procedure before we can make an evaluation of the 'correctness' of the analysis section. For us, a data-analysis plan is correct if it addresses the research question being asked and is consistent with the research design. All too often, researchers focus on only one of the two (for example, my design is within-subjects so I need to run a repeated-measures ANOVA).

The great contribution of social psychology has been to illuminate the ways in which people's beliefs, values, emotions, and behaviors are affected by their social context. Statistical tests, on the other hand, are designed to be relatively context-free, widely applicable, and sensitive only to crude psychological differences (is the variable one of frequency in a population or degree within individuals? is it dichotomous or continuous?) or to peculiarities in the underlying distribution of variables in a sample (for example, various departures from normality). From a statistical point of view, a person's response – *any* response – is a data point, and the challenges of statistical analysis involve problematic data points, not problematic people.

Advances in statistical and computer methodology have benefitted our field enormously, but they have seriously skewed our recent writings on research methodology. We all know the old slogan of the computer analysts, 'Garbage in, garbage out', but, lately, we have said very little about what goes in. We seem to be impressed more with what we can now churn out of a fancy statistical package than in choosing our ingredients carefully.

## Conclusion

The purpose of this chapter has been to rectify the dominance of analysis over design and procedure in methodological discussions; to remind ourselves and our students of the importance of the stages before the data are analyzed, indeed, even of the stages before the study is actually run. The most important phases of research are formulating a research question, creating a design that includes the comparisons required to answer it fairly and the comparisons required to test alternative possibilities, and devising a procedure that will represent that question in a way that is meaningful and involving for the people we are studying. Social psychology demands not just one talent, but many: cold logic, the free-ranging ability to see a problem from multiple points of view, and sympathetic human understanding. It demands them anew and in a different form, every time we plan a new study. Hackneyed research makes for dry social psychology. Intuition is not enough; we have to try out our methodological ideas on real people like the ones we plan to study before we can be sure that the ideas make sense. Often we have to revise them. Our questions are deep and difficult, and we have to sneak up on them through triangulation and intelligent compromise. Always we have to consider what else our results might mean, and design our next study to figure out which explanation is best. It is this combination of skills that has made our research a part of Western culture (Milgram's work on obedience, Asch's on conformity) and our technical terms a part of everyday discourse (dissonance, self-fulfilling prophecy), and it is the challenge of using all these skills together that makes our research so exciting.

## Acknowledgments

We are grateful to Wendy Treynor and Alexandra Gross, who helped us to make the writing clearer, and to Barbara Zezulka Brown, who instantly incorporated our revisions, and made it possible to come close to meeting the deadline.

### SUMMARY

No method is right in itself; what matters is whether it is appropriate for the researcher's question. All research requires some sort of comparison, and research that employs multiple methods and considers multiple alternative hypotheses is preferable to research that relies on the same method to address the question, or that simply asks whether a hypothesis has been confirmed or disconfirmed. Comparison can be across groups of people, time, circumstances, but some comparison is essential.

We suggest ways to come up with researchable questions, and emphasize the importance of pilot testing in any kind of social psychological research – pilot testing the measures, the treatments, and the whole experimental procedure to make sure that they make sense to the participants and mean what you intend them to mean.

We discuss ways to create effective treatments when random assignment is possible, and what to do when it is not. Creative compromise and triangulation are usually essential, and the researcher who can represent the independent variable or the dependent variable in different ways (e.g., verbal, behavioral) can be much more confident that the findings are real and robust. All aspects of research (design, procedures, measure, and data analysis) have implications for each other and should be considered simultaneously.

## References

Aronson, E. (1969) 'A Theory of Cognitive Dissonance: A Current Perspective', in L. Berkowitz (ed.), *Advances in Experimental Social Psychology* (vol. 4). New York: Academic Press, pp. 1–34.

Aronson, E. (2002) 'Drifting My Own Way: Following My Nose and My Heart', in R. Sternberg (ed.), *Psychologists Defying the Crowd: Eminent Psychologists Describe How They Battled the Establishment and Won.* Washington, DC: APA Books, pp. 2–31.

Aronson, E., Ellsworth, P.C., Carlsmith, J.M., and Gonzales, M.H. (1990) *Methods of Research in Social Psychology*, 2nd edn. New York: MCGraw-Hill.

Bakeman, R. (2000) 'Behavioral Observation and Coding', in H.T. Reis and C.M. Judd (eds), *Handbook of Research Methods in Social and Personality Psychology*. Cambridge: Cambridge University Press, pp. 138–59.

Bartholomew, K., Henderson, A.J.Z., and Marcia, J.E. (2000) 'Coding Semistructured Interviews in Social Psychological Research', in H.T. Reis and C.M. Judd (eds), *Handbook of Research Methods in Social and Personality Psychology*. Cambridge: Cambridge University Press, pp. 286–312.

Bem, D.J. (1967) 'Self-Perception: An Alternative Explanation of Cognitive Dissonance Phenomena', *Psychological Review*, 74: 183–200.

Berkowitz, L. (1993) 'Aggression: Its Causes, Consequences, and Control', New York: MCGraw-Hill.

Breckler, S.J. (1994) 'A Comparison of Numerical Indices for Measuring Attitude Ambivalence', *Educational and Psychological Measurement*, 54: 350–65.

Brewer, M. (2000) 'Research Design and Issues of Validity', in H.T. Reis and C.M. Judd (eds), *Handbook of Research Methods in Social and Personality Psychology*, Cambridge: Cambridge University Press, pp. 3–16.

Brinberg, D. and McGrath, J. (1985) *Validity in the Research Process*. Beverly Hills, CA: Sage.

Brown, J.L. and Steele, C.M. (2001) 'Performance Expectations Are Not a Necessary Mediator of Stereotype Threat in African American Verbal Test Performance.' Unpublished manuscript, Stanford University.

Campbell, D.T. (1957) 'Factors Relevant to the Validity of Experiments in Social Settings', *Psychological Bulletin*, 54: 297–312.

Campbell, D.T. and Fiske, D.W. (1959) 'Convergent and Discriminant Validation by the Multitrait–Multimethod Matrix', *Psychological Bulletin*, 56: 81–105.

Cohen, J. and Cohen, P. (1984) *Applied Multiple Regression/Correlation Analysis for the Behavioral Sciences*, 2nd edn. Mahwah, NJ: Lawrence Erlbaum.

Cook, T.D. and Campbell, D.T. (1979) *Quasi-Experimentation: Design and Analysis Issues for Field Settings.* Boston, MA: Houghton Mifflin.

Ellsworth, P.C. (1977) 'From Abstract Ideas to Concrete Instances: Some Guidelines for Choosing Natural Research Settings', *American Psychologist*, 32: 604–15.

Ellsworth, P.C. and Carlsmith, J.M. (1968) Effects of Eye Contact and Verbal Content on Affective Response to a Dyadic Interaction', *Journal of Personality and Social Psychology*, 10: 15–20.

Ellsworth, P.C. and Gonzalez, R. (2001) '"*The Handbook of Research Methods in Social and Personality Psychology*": A Tool for Serious Researchers', *Psychological Science*, 12: 266–8.

Festinger, L. (1957) *A Theory of Cognitive Dissonance*. Stanford, CA: Stanford University Press.

Gonzalez, R. and Nelson, T. (1996) 'Measuring Ordinal Association in Situations that Contain Tied Scores', *Psychological Bulletin*, 119: 159–65.

Greenwald, A. (1976) 'Within-Subjects Designs: To Use or Not to Use?', *Psychological Bulletin*, 83: 314–20.

Greenwald, A. (2004) 'The Resting Parrot, the Dessert Stomach, and Other Perfectly Defensible Theories', in J.T. Jost, M.R. Banaji, and D. Prentice (eds), *Perspectivism in Social Psychology: The Yin and Yang of Scientific Progress*. Washington, DC: APA, pp. 275–85.

Griffin, D. and Ross, L. (1991) 'Subject Construal, Social Inference, and Human Misunderstanding', in M. Zanna (ed.), *Advances in Experimental Social Psychology* (vol. 24). San Diego, CA: Academic Press, pp. 319–59.

Hammond, J.S., Keeney, R.L., and Raiffa, H. (1999) *Smart Choices: A Practical Guide to Making Better Decisions*. Boston, MA: Harvard Business School Press.

Hastie, R. (2001) 'Problems for Judgment and Decision Making', *Annual Review of Psychology*, 52: 653–83.

Hilbert, D. (1900) 'Mathematische Probleme', *Goettinger Nachrichten*, 24: 253–97. (M.W. Newson [trans.] [1902] 'Mathematical Problems', *Bulletin of the American Mathematical Society*, 8: 437–79.)

Horner, M. (1972) 'Toward an Understanding of Achievement-Related Conflicts in Women', *Journal of Social Issues*, 28: 157–75.

Hsee, C., Bloundt, S., Loewenstein, G., and Bazerman, M. (1999) 'Preference Reversals Between Joint and Separate Evaluations of Options: A Review and Theoretical Analysis', *Psychological Bulletin*, 125: 576–90.

John, O.R. and Benet-Martinez, V. (2000) 'Measurement: Reliability, Construct Validation and Scale Construction', in H.T. Reis and C.M. Judd (eds), *Handbook of Research Methods in Social and Personality Psychology*. Cambridge: Cambridge University Press, pp. 339–69.

Jones, E.E. and Nisbett, R.E. (1972) 'The Actor and the Observer: Divergent Perceptions of the Causes of Behavior', in E.E. Jones, D. Kanouse, H.H. Kelley, R.E. Nisbett, S. Valins, and B. Weiner (eds), *Attribution: Perceiving the Causes of Behavior*. Morristown, NJ: General Learning Press, pp. 79–94.

Judd, C.M. (2000) 'Everyday Data Analysis in Social Psychology: Comparisons of Linear Models', in H.T. Reis and C.M. Judd (eds), *Handbook of Research Methods in Social and Personality Psychology*. Cambridge: Cambridge University Press, pp. 370–92.

Judd, C.M. and McClelland, G.H. (1998) 'Measurement', in D. Gilbert, S. Fiske, and G. Lindzey (eds), *Handbook of Social Psychology*, 4th edn. New York: MCGraw-Hill, pp. 180–232.

Kahneman, D. and Tversky, A. (1982) 'The Simulation Heuristic', in D. Kahneman, P. Slovic, and A. Tversky (eds), *Judgment under Uncertainty: Heuristics and Biases*. Cambridge: Cambridge University Press. pp. 201–8.

Kahneman, D., Diener, E., and Schwarz, N. (eds) (1999) *Well-Being: The Foundations of Hedonic Psychology*. New York: Russell Sage Foundation.

Kahneman, D., Slovic, P., and Tversky, A. (eds) (1982) *Judgment under Uncertainty: Heuristics and Biases*. Cambridge: Cambridge University Press.

Keltner, D., Ellsworth, P.C., and Edwards, K. (1993) 'Beyond Simple Pessimism: Effects of Sadness and Anger on Social Perception', *Journal of Personality and Social Psychology*, 64: 740–52.

Kopans, D.B. (1994) 'Screening for Breast Cancer and Mortality Reduction Among Women 40–49 Years of Age', *Cancer*, 74 (Suppl.): 311–22.

Krauss, R.M., Chen, Y., and Chawla, P. (1996) 'Nonverbal Behavior and Nonverbal Communication: What Do Conversational Hand Gestures Tell Us?', in M. Zanna (ed.), *Advances in Experimental Social Psychology*. San Diego, CA: Academic Press, pp. 389–450.

Krauss, R. and Chin, C. (1998) 'Language and Social Behavior', in D.T. Gilbert, S.T. Fiske, and G. Lindzey (eds), *The Handbook of Social Psychology*, 4th edn. Boston, MA: MCGraw-Hill, pp. 41–88.

Krueger, R. and Casey, M.A. (2000) *Focus Groups: A Practical Guide for Applied Research*. Thousand Oaks, CA: Sage.

Kruglanski, A. (2001) 'That "Vision Thing": The State of Theory in Social and Personality Psychology at the Edge of the New Millennium', *Journal of Personality and Social Psychology*, 80: 871–5.

Latané, B. and Darley, J.M. (1970) *The Unresponsive Bystander: Why Doesn't He Help?* New York: Appleton-Century-Crofts.

Lazarus, R. (1982) 'Thoughts on the Relationship Between Emotion and Cognition', *American Psycho logist*, 37: 1019–24.

Loftus, E.F. (1979). *Eyewitness Testimony*. Cambridge, MA: Harvard University Press.

Maxwell, S.E. and Delaney, H.D. (1999) *Designing Experiments and Analyzing Data: A Model Comparison Perspective*. Mahwah, NJ: Lawrence Erlbaum.

McClelland, G.H. (2000) 'Nasty Data: Unruly, Ill-Mannered Observations Can Ruin Your Analysis', in H.T. Reis and C.M. Judd (eds), *Handbook of Research Methods in Social and Personality Psychology*. Cambridge: Cambridge University Press, pp. 393–411.

McGuire, W.J. (1973) 'The Yin and Yang of Progress in Social Psychology: Seven Koan', *Journal of Personality and Social Psychology*, 26: 446–56.

McGuire, W.J. (1997) 'Creative Hypothesis Generating in Psychology: Some Useful Heuristics', *Annual Review of Psychology*, 48: 1–30.

McGuire, W.J. (1999) *Constructing Social Psychology: Creative and Critical Processes*. Cambridge: Cambridge University Press.

Milgram, S. (1974) *Obedience to Authority*. New York: Harper and Row.

Miller, N. and Pedersen, W.C. (1999) 'Assessing Process Distinctiveness', *Psychological Inquiry*, 10: 150–5.

Nisbett, R. and Ross, L. (1980) *Human Inference: Strategies and Shortcomings of Social Judgment*. Englewood Cliffs, NJ: Prentice-Hall.

Oyserman, D., Coon, H.M., and Kemmelmeier, M. (2002) 'Rethinking Individualism and Collectivism: Evaluation of Theoretical Assumptions and Meta-Analyses. *Psychological Bulletin*, 128: 3–72.

Platt, J.R. (1964) 'Strong Inference', *Science*, 146: 347–53.

Priester, J. and Petty, R. (1996) 'The Gradual Threshold Model of Ambivalence: Relating the Positive and Negative Bases of Attitudes to Subjective Ambivalence', *Journal of Personality and Social Psychology*, 71: 431–49.

Reis, H.T. and Gable, S.T. (2000) 'Event Sampling and Other Methods for Studying Everyday Experience', in H.T. Reis and C.M. Judd (eds), *Handbook of Research Methods in Social and Personality Psychology*. Cambridge: Cambridge University Press, pp. 190–222.

Rosenbaum, P. and Rubin, D. (1984) 'Reducing Bias in Observational Studies Using the Subclassification on the Propensity Score', *Journal of the American Statistical Association*, 79: 516–24.

Rosenberg, M.J. (1969), 'The Conditions and Consequences of Evaluation Apprehension', in R. Rosenthal and R. Rosnow (eds), *Artifact in Behavioral Research.* NY: Academic Press, pp. 279–349.

Rosenthal, R. (1969) 'Interpersonal Expectations: Effects of the Experimenter's Hypothesis', in R. Rosenthal and R. Rosnow (eds), *Artifact in Behavioral Reserach.* New York: Academic Press, pp. 181–277.

Rosenthal, R. and Fode, K.L. (1963) 'The Effect of Experimenter Bias on the Performance of the Albino Rat', *Behavioral Science*, 8: 183–9.

Rosenthal, R. and Rubin, D.B. (1978) 'Interpersonal Expectancy Effects: The First 345 Studies', *Behavioral and Brain Sciences*, 3: 148–57.

Ross, L. (1977) 'The Intuitive Psychologist and His Shortcomings', in L. Berkowitz (ed.), *Advances in Experimental Social Psychology* (vol. 10). New York: Academic Press, pp. 173–220.

Ross, L., Greene, D., and House, P. (1977) 'The False Consensus Effect: An Egocentric Bias in Social Perception and Attribution Process', *Journal of Experimental Social Psychology*, 13: 279–301.

Schwarz, N., Groves, R.M., and Schuman, H. (1998) 'Survey Methods', in D.T. Gilbert, S.T. Fiske, and G. Lindzey (eds), *The Handbook of Social Psychology*, 4th edn. Boston, MA: MCGraw-Hill, pp. 143–79.

Sears, D.O. (1986) 'College Sophomores in the Laboratory: Influences of a Narrow Data Base on Social Psychology's View of Human Nature', *Journal of Personality and Social Psychology*, 51: 515–30.

Smith, E.R. (2000) 'Research Design', in H.T. Reis and C.M. Judd (eds), *Handbook of Research Methods in Social and Personality Psychology*, Cambridge: Cambridge University Press, pp. 17–39.

Sommers, S. and Ellsworth, P.C. (2000) 'Race in the Courtroom: Perceptions of Guilt and Dispositional Attribution', *Personality and Social Psychology Bulletin*, 26: 1367–79.

Strauss, A.L. and Corbin, J.M. (1998) *Basics of Qualitative Research: Techniques and Procedures for Developing Grounded Theory*, 2nd edn. Thousand Oaks, CA: Sage.

Steele, C.M. and Lin, T.J. (1983) 'Dissonance Processes and Self-Affirmation', *Journal of Personality and Social Psychology*, 45: 5–19.

Taylor, S.E. (1983) 'Adjustment to Threatening Events: A Theory of Cognitive Adaptation', *American Psychologist*, 38: 1161–73.

Thompson, M., Zanna, M., and Griffin, D. (1995) 'Let's Not Be Indifferent about (Attitudinal) Ambivalence', in R. Petty and J. Krosnick (eds), *Attitude Strength: Antecedents and Consequences*. Hillsdale, NJ: Lawrence Erlbaum, pp. 361–86.

Tiedens, L.Z., Ellsworth, P.C., and Mesquita, B. (2000) 'Sentimental Stereotypes: Emotional Expectancies for High and Low Status Group Members', *Personality and Social Psychology Bulletin*, 26: 560–74.

Tourangeau, R. and Rasinski, K.A. (1988) 'Cognitive Processes Underlying Context Effects in Attitude Measurement', *Psychological Bulletin*, 103: 299–314.

Triplett, N. (1897) 'The Dynamogenic Factors in Pacemaking and Competition', *American Journal of Psychology*, 9: 507–33.

Visser, P.S., Krosnick, J.A., and Lavrakas, P.J. (2000) 'Survey Research', in H.T. Reis and C.M. Judd (eds), *Handbook of Research Methods in Social and Personality Psychology*. Cambridge: Cambridge University Press, pp. 223–52.

Wentland, E.J. (1993) *Survey Responses: An Evaluation of Their Validity*. New York: Academic Press.

West, S.G., Biesanz, J.C., and Pitts, S.C. (2000) 'Causal Inference and Generalization in Field Settings: Experimental and Quasi-Experimental Designs', in H.T. Reis and C.M. Judd (eds), *Handbook of Research Methods in Social and Personality Psychology*. Cambridge: Cambridge University Press, pp. 40–84.

Zajonc, R.B. (1980) 'Feeling and Thinking: Preferences Need No Inferences', *American Psychologist*, 35: 151–75.

# PART TWO

# INDIVIDUAL PROCESSES

3

# Social Inference and Social Memory: The Interplay Between Systems

STEVEN J. SHERMAN, MATTHEW T. CRAWFORD, DAVID L. HAMILTON, AND LEONEL GARCIA-MARQUES

## INTRODUCTION

How do you make predictions, judgments, or inferences about individuals that you know? About groups to which you do or do not belong? About yourself? Are these judgments always accurate? What things do you remember about other people? About groups? About yourself? Are these memories always accurate? This chapter is about the biases that enter into these kinds of judgments and memories. In addition, the judgments and memories affect each other. The judgments and inferences that you make affect your memories, and what you remember affects your judgments. This chapter explores the interplay between our social judgments and our memories.

Both social inference and social memory have a long history and tradition in social psychology. Early work in the area of social inferences focused on the taxonomy of inference types (see Hastie, 1983, for a review). In addition, the psychological processes underlying social inferences have been an important part of social psychological thinking and research since Anderson's (1968; 1981) early work. Newer information-processing models, many of which have been borrowed from cognitive psychology, have also been a recent focus of attention (Hastie and Park, 1986; Smith and DeCoster, 1998; Smith and Zárate, 1992; Wyer and Carlston, 1994).

Another focus of attention of theory and research in the area of social inference concerns the direction in which these inferences are made (e.g., from the group to the individual versus the individual to the group; from the self to others versus from others to the self). For example, Hastie (1983) discussed differences between member-to-category inferences and category-to-member inferences. Beike and Sherman (1994) separated inductive, deductive, and analogical inferences. Finally, the content of inferences has been a major concern of social psychology for many years. Probabilistic inferences, stereotypes, causal inferences, moral inferences, social structural inferences, and trait inference all have a rich tradition in social psychology.

Similarly, the study of social memory has blossomed during the past twenty years and has explored a variety of issues concerning how information from the social world is represented in memory and subsequently used in making judgments and guiding behavior. Research has investigated factors that influence the encoding and interpretation of information, attributions that are made as that information is processed, and how those processes influence the way that information is represented in memory (Wyer and Carlston, 1994). Several theories have been advanced regarding the way social information is represented as a mental structure, and these models have generated considerable research testing their implications (Carlston and Smith, 1996; Kihlstrom and Klein, 1994; Smith and Queller, 1999). Other research has investigated how these mental representations, once established, can guide the processing of new information. Finally, the question of how stored knowledge is retrieved from memory for later use has also been the focus of investigation (Hamilton and Sherman, 1994; Olson et al., 1996).

The purpose of this chapter is to review and discuss research that illuminates the interplay between these two systems. It is clear that the content and process of social inference have important effects on memory, with regard to both the accuracy of memory and biases in memory. It is equally clear that memory structure and process affect in major ways inferences that are drawn about the social targets involved. We both examine the directions of effects and extract general principles by which social inference and social memory are linked.

## Inference → memory

### *Inferences about individuals*

The area of individual person perception has a long history in social psychology. This literature has reported extensively on specific mechanisms underlying impression formation of individual targets, especially emphasizing the ways in which information is encoded, integrated, and represented in memory. It has generally been concluded that people integrate trait or behavioral information about an individual into a strong dispositional impression (Anderson, 1966, 1981; Asch, 1946; Burnstein and Schul, 1982; Hastie and Park, 1986).

In terms of the processes by which individual target information is encoded, Hastie and Park (1986) provide evidence that individual targets induce *online* information processing, in which early information serves as a basis of the impression and subsequently encountered information is assimilated to fit the impression. Because perceivers are integrating information into a coherent representation, information that is inconsistent with the overall impression receives greater attention as it is perceived, leading to a greater number of associative memory linkages. Consequently, these target-relevant inconsistencies show a greater likelihood of recall in a subsequent task (Lichtenstein and Srull, 1987; Srull et al., 1985; see discussion in a later section). Online processing is also associated with primacy effects in memory (Srull and Wyer, 1989) as well as generally low recall–judgment correlations, as the actual recall of information is unnecessary for making a judgment (Hastie and Park, 1986). Thus, it is clear that the process and outcome of individual impression formation are very much related to the amount and type of information that are retrieved about that individual. We now turn to an important kind of inference about individual social targets that has extensive effects on memory for facts about that individual, the inference about the traits of individuals.

### *Spontaneous trait inferences and memory*

Considerable research has been conducted examining whether trait inferences from behavior can occur without explicit impression-formation instructions. Researchers argue that inferring traits from behavior is so ubiquitous and routinized that perceivers are able to do so spontaneously. If trait inferences are derived from behavior in a spontaneous fashion, these inferences should have important effects on memory for the behavior. The behaviors most important for the spontaneous trait inference should have an advantage in memory, as the trait will serve as a cue for these behaviors.

Uleman and his colleagues (Newman and Uleman, 1989; Uleman et al., 1992; Winter and Uleman, 1984) provided initial evidence for the spontaneity of trait inferences. In a first task, these researchers presented trait-implicative behavioral statements (for example, 'The accountant takes the orphans to the circus.'). In a subsequent recall task, either a semantically related (such as 'numbers' or 'fun') or a dispositional (such as 'kindhearted') retrieval cue preceded recall. Results indicated that dispositional cues had a significant advantage over semantic cues, as well as other kinds of cues, in their ability to elicit the original behavior. Tulving's encoding-specificity principle (Tulving and Thomson, 1973) holds that a cue can elicit the original material to the extent that it is used as an organizing principle at the time the information is encoded. The fact that dispositional cues were able to elicit the original trait-implicative behaviors indicates that the trait was spontaneously inferred at encoding and was thus available as an effective memory-retrieval cue (though some have questioned these conclusions: Bassili, 1989; Higgins and Bargh, 1987). These results clearly indicate the importance of trait inferences for the memory of the behaviors that served as the bases for those inferences.

More recently, Carlston, Skowronski, and colleagues (Carlston and Skowronski, 1994; Carlston et al., 1995; Skowronski et al., 1998) have shown that the learning of a person–trait association is facilitated when that person was previously paired with a behavioral statement implying that same trait. Such enhanced learning supports the idea of spontaneous trait inference from behavior. Targets are first paired with self-descriptive behavioral statements that imply specific traits. In a later task, these same targets are paired with a single trait term, and participants must learn these target–trait pairings. Half of the trials constitute relearning trials, as the trait terms are the same as those implied by the original behaviors. The other half require the learning of a new target–trait association with a previously seen target.

If the trait is spontaneously abstracted from the behavior in the first task, facilitation on the relearning task should occur. As predicted, performance on relearning trials was much greater than on learning trials, indicating that traits are abstracted spontaneously during the initial encoding phase. The savings in relearning occurred strongly even when participants were not given impression-formation instructions during the initial phase that paired targets with behaviors. Interestingly, in a subsequent recognition task, participants were unable to recognize the specific behaviors that first elicited the traits. It seems that, in this paradigm, once a trait is abstracted from the behavior, the behavior is unavailable to memory. Thus, sometimes a spontaneous trait inference enhances memory for behavior (Newman and Uleman, 1989), and at other times the abstraction of a trait leads the perceiver to forget the specific behavior that served as the basis for the trait inference (Carlston and Skowronski, 1994). The fact that the inferred trait can alternately facilitate or inhibit memory about the behaviors that allowed the trait inference raises questions regarding how both the behavioral and the trait information are stored in memory. Research by both Lingle and Ostrom (1979) and Carlston and Skowronski (1986) has shown that, even when a trait inference has been made, either the trait or the behavior can be accessed and used in a subsequent judgment.

Another way in which trait inferences are linked to subsequent memory is that these inferences often require the initial retrieval of some information about the person. Imagine that you are given behavioral information about a person and are then asked to decide whether the person is introverted. According to Klein and Loftus (1993), this inference will require you to access some of the original behavioral information. If you are then asked to recall a specific incident in which the person behaved in a way relevant to introversion/extraversion, the latency for answering should be less than if the original question simply asked you to define the word 'introverted'. This is because answering the inference question required accessing times when the person behaved in an introversion-relevant way. Interestingly, if sufficient behavioral information is initially provided about the person so that traits are spontaneously ascribed to that person, the inference task will not require accessing of any of the original behaviors, and the recall of such information will not be facilitated (Sherman, 1996). In addition, even after enough behavioral information is initially presented to allow abstracted trait inferences to form, there is still a facilitation of memory for behavioral episodes that are inconsistent with the trait inference (Babey et al., 1998).

### Trait inferences and memory organization

In addition to affecting the memory for the behavioral indicators of an individual's traits, trait inferences also act to organize and integrate in memory target-relevant behaviors that are related to each other. Of the types of memory models proposed, those utilizing an associative-network approach (Collins and Quillian, 1969) have continued to exert the most influence on social- psychological research and thinking. In its most basic formulation, associative networks contain concepts represented as nodes and connections between concepts as links between nodes (see Smith and Queller, 1999, for review of person-memory models).

Research has attempted to clarify how the trait inferences and expectancies that one has about other people affect memory for information relevant to those inferences (Hastie, 1980; Srull, 1981, 1983; for a review, see Stangor and McMillan, 1992). One of the most common approaches to investigate inferences and social memory is the impression-formation paradigm in which participants are presented with behavioral information about a target and are asked to form an impression about that target. This experimental approach generally utilizes subsequent recall measures to examine the way that inferences lead perceivers to represent the target in memory.

Hamilton and colleagues (Hamilton, 1981; Hamilton et al., 1980) proposed a model that integrated the representation of behaviors and traits. Some of their participants were given instructions to form inferences about the target actors (impression set), whereas others were given instructions intended to interfere with inference-making (memory set). Results indicated both heightened recall for behavioral information as well as greater trait clustering for impression-set than memory-set participants. Hamilton proposed that these differences in memory organization resulted from the greater tendency of the impression-set participants to infer traits from the behaviors and to represent target-relevant information around these inferred trait categories.

Subsequent investigations have led to the development of associative-network models that further specify the manner in which traits and behaviors are represented in memory (Srull and Wyer, 1989; Wyer and Gordon, 1984; Wyer and Srull, 1989). These models all hold that the process of inferring traits from behavioral information establishes associations in memory between the inferred trait and the specific behavioral episode. Multiple behavioral episodes along the same trait dimension are linked in trait-behavior clusters so that behaviors are organized in memory according to the traits they exemplify. Thus, the inference of traits from behavior leads to greater organization in memory, resulting in overall greater recall as well as trait clustering in recall.

### Trait inferences and biases in memory

To this point, we have focused on the role that trait inferences play in increasing the accuracy of memory for trait-relevant information. However, there is another side to the effects of trait inferences on memory. In addition to increasing the accuracy of memory for certain kinds of information, these same trait inferences can also lead to large and predictable memory distortions and reconstructions.

Cantor and Mischel (1977) described targets in ways that were indicative of either extraversion or introversion. For some participants, the targets were also explicitly labeled as extraverted or introverted. For other participants, there was no explicit label, and they had to infer the traits from the information provided. Whether the trait label was provided or inferred, participants made a large number of trait-consistent errors in recognition. That is, a greater number of concept-consistent, but nonpresented, trait items were endorsed as being previously seen than concept-inconsistent or irrelevant items. According to these authors, the inference of the targets' level of extraversion or introversion served as a prototype and resulted in the activation of related trait associations. In subsequent research (Cantor and Mischel, 1979), these authors provided evidence that this effect depends, in part, on the perceived prototypicality of the target. That is, inferences of high prototypicality led to better overall recall as well as more conceptually related, but nonpresented, trait intrusions. Thus, the trait inference, as well as the inference of fit to prototype, serve to bias memory in a prototype-consistent manner. These findings have been used to support a schema model of encoding that assumes that expectations about social targets are represented in the form of schemata that then guide and bias the processing of subsequent social information.

The meta-analysis by Stangor and McMillan (1992) reveals similar biasing effects of trait expectancies on memory. In addition, response biases toward congruent information are greater to the extent that the expectancy is strong, to the extent that processing resources are depleted, and to the extent that impression-formation goals are present. It is thus clear that trait inferences have both advantages and disadvantages for memory. On the one hand, such inferences generally increase the total amount of material recalled and lead to accuracy in filling in gaps where information is missing. On the other hand, these inferences also lead to biases in recall, generally toward consistent information. In the case of social targets, these memory biases have the effect of making it difficult to change existing inferences and expectations.

### *Effects of inferences about group membership on memory*

Inferences about traits are perhaps the most studied of the inferences that social perceivers make about individual social targets. The fact that such inferences are made spontaneously and that they have such robust effects on memory and on judgments accounts for the central role of trait inferences in the social-psychology literature. However, there are also other kinds of inferences about social targets that have equally important and impressive effects on social memory. For example, one often makes inferences about the group memberships of individuals based on certain behavioral or featural information about them. Inferred memberships into broad social categories (such as, nationality, religion, or social class) are especially important in this regard. Such inferences might be based on physical appearance, behavioral mannerisms, or linguistic cues. For example, a social perceiver might infer that a young man is homosexual from certain behavioral mannerisms, that a woman is Italian from her accent, or that an older man is Muslim from his clothing.

Once such inferences are made, the effects on memory should be very similar to the effects already discussed for trait inferences. That is, because social-category memberships bring with them many expectancies, often in the form of stereotypes, and because such memberships operate as schematic representations, they should enhance memory for certain kinds of information and also should bias memory in a category-consistent direction. An excellent example of the biasing effects on memory of social-category inferences is a study by Slusher and Anderson (1987). Participants were presented with the social-category memberships of certain targets (such as lawyer or artist). They were also asked to read some facts about the targets and to imagine certain scenes. For example, they might be asked to imagine a lawyer standing in front of his house. Slusher and Anderson (1987) found that participants tended to imagine events that were consistent with the stereotype of the social-category membership of the target. Thus, they were likely to imagine the lawyer standing in front of an expensive home or the artist standing in front of a funky cottage.

Having incorporated stereotyped traits and situations into their imaginations, they then proceeded to confuse in memory what they had imagined with facts that they had actually been given about the social target. This failure of reality monitoring (Johnson and Raye, 1981) led participants to misremember the actual facts about the targets in a stereotype-confirming direction and to end up believing that reality matched their stereotypes (rather than recognizing that inferences based on their stereotypes created this reality in their memories). Such effects, of course, would help strengthen and maintain the very stereotypes that led to the biased memory effects. The imaginal confirmation of such social stereotypes thus contributes to the self-perpetuating nature of stereotypes.

Similar kinds of effects are likely for social-category memberships such as religion or nationality. The impact of initial inferences about category membership on memory and judgments can be powerful indeed. Such effects are particularly interesting when we consider the fact that all individuals are members of many different social categories. That is, we are all multiply categorizable. Thus, Mary may be at the same time a woman, a wife, a mother, a lawyer, a chess player, and a Catholic. The particular operative categorical inference for a social target at any point in time is likely to make more accessible in memory information that is related to and consistent with that categorical inference. Thus, when Mary is categorized as a lawyer, the facts that she was on the debate team in college and is argumentative would be highly accessible in memory. When she is momentarily categorized as a chess player, the fact that she has good spatial skills and is competitive would become highly accessible.

The categorization of a person into a particular role or identity depends on both cognitive and motivational factors. Contextual cues implying stereotypes (Macrae et al., 1995), recently activated attitudes (Smith et al., 1996), or chronically accessible attitudes (Fazio and Dunton, 1997; Stangor et al., 1992) lead to the categorization of a multiply categorizable target in line with the context or attitude. For example, Macrae et al. (1995) presented a video of an Asian female either putting on lipstick (to achieve categorization as a female) or eating with chopsticks (to achieve categorization as an Asian). Participants in these experiments then responded more quickly to words that were consistent with the stereotype of the primed category, but, more interestingly, they responded more slowly than baseline to the nonprimed category – evidence for the memorial inhibition of that alternative categorization. This indicates that the different possible categorizations of the same target can lead to quite different accessibilities of information about the target in memory.

Zárate and Smith (1990; Smith and Zárate, 1990; see also Stroessner, 1996) examined the effect of group memberships on the categorization of multiply categorizable targets and found that perceivers were more likely to categorize social targets along dimensions that differentiated them from the self. That is, targets were categorized by their nonshared group memberships, or by deviations from the societal 'norms'. This would then have the effect of making accessible in memory those features associated with the category. From a motivational perspective, goals also affect the categorization of an object that belongs to more than one category (Gollwitzer and Moskowitz, 1996).

In general, the activation of any schema, script, theme, or stereotype will lead to inferences about a person or event that go beyond the information given. These inferences will affect judgment, amount of recall and recognition, and memory biases in the manner discussed previously. Some of this work has focused on expectations of a person based on stereotypes. For example, Cohen (1981) categorized a target individual as either a waitress or a librarian. Features that were prototypic of the category activated were more accurately recognized than were inconsistent features. More recently, Skowronski et al. (1993) labeled a target as mentally retarded, and this overt labeling of the target led to enhanced recall of stimulus items incongruent with retardation. However, covert priming of retardation enhanced memory for items congruent with retardation.

Other work has shown the important effects of expectancies and schemas on memory. Anderson and Pichert (1978) had participants read about a house. They read a story either within the framework of a robber casing the house or a potential buyer of the house. This activation of different scripts very much affected memory for details. In the robber script, items such as jewelry, an expensive television, and a broken window were remembered well. In the buyer script, participants remembered items such as hardwood floors and beautiful landscaping. Similar effects of schema representation on memory have been reported by Alba and Hasher (1983) and by Zadny and Gerard (1974).

### *Framing effects on memory*

Framing refers to the idea that identical information can be presented in different ways such that there is a different focus or a different salience of certain aspects of the information (Tversky and Kahneman, 1981). Different framings lead to different interpretations of information and thus to different inferences about the value of certain decisions, the motives or goals of actors, and the attitudes or beliefs of those actors. Framing messages or events with a focus on gains versus losses (Tversky and Kahneman, 1981), as promoting or preventing certain outcomes (Higgins, 1998), or as focusing on the positive aspects of doing something versus the negative aspects of not doing something (Rothman and Salovey, 1997) have all been shown to have effects on subsequent judgments and decisions. Because different frames make salient certain aspects of the information presented, allowing for different inferences, memory for information can be facilitated or inhibited, and biases in memory in a direction consistent with the framing are to be expected.

Higgins and Tykocinski (1992) distinguished between people who chronically framed events in terms of the presence or absence of positive outcomes versus those who framed events in terms of the presence or absence of negative outcomes. They presented participants with a story in which the protagonist experienced or failed to experience various positive and negative events. The difference in chronic approaches to interpreting events led to significant differences in participants' memory for the events in the story. Events framed in ways consistent with chronic thinking were best recalled.

One way in which framing can be used to ensure different interpretations of and inferences from information is through language. One can present the same basic information with slightly different words, and this difference can have significant effects on inferences as well as on subsequent judgments and memory. Research on the use of leading questions in eyewitness testimony is an excellent example of the use of language in this way. Loftus (1975; Loftus and Hall, 1982) has shown in many experiments that the framing of a question after an event can very much affect both interpretations of the event and memory for specific aspects of the event. In one such study, Loftus and Palmer (1974) showed participants a video of an automobile accident. After seeing the accident, some participants were asked, 'How fast were the cars going when they bumped?' Other participants were asked 'How fast were the cars going when they smashed?' The slight difference in wording very much affected participants' judgments of the speed of the cars. In addition, the difference in framing led to important differences in memory for information about the accident. For example, participants in the 'smashed' condition remembered actually seeing shattered glass, although none had been present in the video.

There are other ways in which linguistic framing can alter the interpretation of events and the inferences that are drawn from social information. Again, these differences in interpretation and inference will have subsequent effects on how the information is organized and represented in memory and on the items of information that are remembered and misremembered. Fiedler and Semin (1988) distinguished between state verbs and interpretative action verbs. State verbs (such as 'love' or 'hate') tend to evoke object attributions of causality, whereas interpretive action verbs (such as 'help' or 'cheat') evoke subject causal attributions. Sentence-framing did indeed lead to differences in whether the object or subject of a sentence was perceived as causal. In another study, Semin and Fielder (1988) distinguished among descriptive action verbs, interpretive action verbs, state verbs, and adjectives. There was a clear relation between the linguistic frame and the temporal stability of the quality expressed in a sentence, the sentence's informativeness about the subject, and the sentence's verifiability.

All of these differences imply that linguistic framing would very much affect what was remembered and how well it was remembered. In support of this, Semin and Greenslade (1985) argue that these different linguistic forms fulfill different functions in the description of behaviors and persons. They found that, as a consequence, the different linguistic forms very much affected and distorted memory-based judgments.

In a similar vein, Maass et al. (1989) investigated how the type of language used to describe in-group and out-group behaviors contributes to the persistence of stereotypes (see Maass, 1999, for a review). Their participants encoded and communicated desirable in-group and undesirable out-group behaviors more abstractly than undesirable in-group and desirable out-group behaviors – the linguistic intergroup bias effect. Such abstract as opposed to concrete encoding and communication of events would play an important role in perpetuating stereotypes, in part by altering the memory for aspects of the events and the mental representation of those events.

### *Inferences about groups*

In the first section, we focused on inferences about individuals that are likely to have effects on several aspects of memory – content, organization, accuracy, and bias. We now turn to inferences about another important kind of social target, the group. As we outline the effects of inferences about groups on memory, we shall pay attention to the similarities with and differences from the effects of inferences about individuals.

Historically, processes and outcomes involving group perceptions and stereotypes have been studied independently of research on person perception. Group perception and stereotype researchers have focused on processes of categorization (Allport, 1954; Bruner, 1957; Tajfel, 1969), perceptions of group variability (Linville et al., 1989; Park and Hastie, 1987), mental representation of group-level information (Klein and Loftus, 1990; Smith and Zárate, 1990), and the information-processing and social-judgment consequences of stereotypes (e.g., Bodenhausen and Wyer, 1985). Until recently, few researchers have attempted to integrate person perception and group perception into a single, more coherent framework (Hamilton and Sherman, 1996; Wyer et al., 1984). It is important, however, to consider the major similarities and differences that exist between individual and group perception.

### *Individual impression formation versus perception of groups: inferences of entitativity and online versus memory-based processing*

One of the major points of demarcation between the areas of individual person perception and group perception involves the manner in which target information is processed (Hamilton and Sherman, 1996). As we discussed earlier, information about individual targets is processed in an *online* manner, in which later information is integrated into an abstracted initial impression (Hastie and Park, 1986). This integrative style of processing is associated with several memory effects that we have discussed, including primacy in recall (Srull and Wyer, 1989), the ability to make judgments without accessing behavioral exemplars (Hastie and Park, 1986), and greater attempts at resolving inconsistencies (Srull et al., 1985).

Impressions of members of a group, however, appear to be made in a *memory-based* fashion. This less integrative processing involves storing pieces of information as they are received, until they are needed for a later judgment. Information is not integrated to form a coherent impression immediately, but each piece of information is stored as an exemplar for later use. The attempted inconsistency resolution associated with online processing does not occur when judgments are memory based. Consequently, recall of target-relevant inconsistencies is less likely when the target is a group. Because judgment relies on the recall of behavioral exemplars, the correlation between recall and judgment tends to be high (Hastie and Park, 1986). Additionally, memory-based judgments generally reflect recency effects, as the most recently encountered information remains the most highly accessible (Lichtenstein and Srull, 1987). In a direct test of this individual/group difference in processing, Susskind et al. (1999) investigated impression formation for individual and group targets. For individual targets, judgments were made more quickly, more extremely, and with greater confidence than for group targets. In addition, expectancy-inconsistent behaviors spontaneously triggered causal attributions to resolve the inconsistency for individual, but not group, targets. These results support the online versus memory-based judgments for individuals and group targets, respectively.

In one series of experiments using a modified illusory correlation paradigm (Hamilton and Gifford, 1976), McConnell et al. (1994) found that perceivers tended to form online impressions of individuals but memory-based judgments of group targets. Individual targets resulted in better recall, especially for items presented early, and quicker recognition of statements associated with specific individual targets than did group targets. However, these findings were influenced by the processing goal of the perceiver. When instructions to form impressions increased integrative processing, perceivers showed evidence of online impression formation regardless of whether the target was an individual or a group. Memory-set instructions decreased integrative information-processing and led to memory-based judgments, again regardless of the target type.

Thus, perceptions of individuals and groups can be based on differing processing characteristics. In an attempt to integrate and reconcile these processing differences, Hamilton and Sherman (1996) reintroduced the concept of entitativity (Campbell, 1958), the degree to which aggregates of individuals are perceived as social entities. They proposed that, when the expectations of coherence, consistency, and unity are made equivalent between individual and group targets, the processing online versus memory-based differences should disappear. That is, inferences about the entitativity of a target drives the manner in which information about that target is encoded, stored, and retrieved, not the type of target (individual or group).

In order to support this contention, McConnell et al. (1997) presented individual and group targets that were described as being either relatively high or low in entitativity. As predicted, highly entitative targets, regardless of whether they were an individual or a group, resulted in better recall, primacy in recall, and low memory–judgment correlations, and a lack of the traditional illusory correlation effect. These effects are all indications of online, integrative information-processing. However, targets with low expectations of entitativity (both individual and group targets) showed the opposite pattern of results (poorer recall, recency effects in recall, high memory–judgment correlations, and the illusory correlation effect), indicating memory-based processing for these targets. Thus, McConnell et al. (1997) provided direct evidence that inferences about entitativity affect the manner in which information about social targets is processed and the way in which memory for target information is affected. As such, inferences about the degree of entitativity of group targets have clear implications for both memory and for social judgment.

The previously discussed research indicates *processing* differences as a result of an inference about the level of entitativity of a target, but this inference should also affect the final product of the impression-formation process. Welbourne (1999) presented equal numbers of intelligent, unintelligent, and neutral (or kind, unkind, and neutral) behaviors to examine the abstraction of a unified impression in the face of inconsistent information. As in the findings of Susskind et al. (1999), an individual–group difference was found, indicating that, in the absence of an inference of high entitativity for groups, perceivers were more likely to attempt to resolve inconsistencies for individual, but not group, targets. However, when the entitativity of the targets was manipulated, perceivers were equally likely to attempt inconsistency resolution for high-entitativity targets regardless of whether the target was an individual or a group. Conversely, low-entitativity targets (both individuals and groups) resulted in a decreased attempt to resolve inconsistencies.

### Inferences about group type and memory organization

In addition to inferences about the entitativity of groups, another important inference about groups that has effects on memory involves inferences about group type. In a recent paper, Lickel et al. (2000) had participants rate various groups on a wide variety of attributes that could be used to describe those groups (for example, entitativity, similarity of group members, amount of interaction, importance, duration, common goals and common fate, group size, and permeability of group boundaries). Results indicated the presence of three major, distinct group-type clusters: intimacy groups (such as friends and family), task-oriented groups (such as coworkers and sports teams), and social categories (such as gender, race, and nationality). These types of groups differed in the pattern of attributes that described them. Intimacy groups were rated higher in entitativity than task-oriented groups, which in turn were rated as more entitative than social categories. In addition, intimacy groups were perceived as showing high levels of interaction, similarity, and importance; shared goals; and low permeability. Task-oriented groups were seen as having small size, common goals, moderate entitativity, and high levels of importance, interaction, and permeability. Social categories were characterized as being rather low in entitativity, along with having low levels of importance, interaction, similarity, and common goals.

Sherman et al. (2002) investigated the extent to which perceivers spontaneously use these group types to organize information in memory about various groups. They examined the spontaneous organization and representation of groups in memory by looking at errors in recognition when groups of various types were presented (Taylor et al., 1978). In a first phase of their experiment, participants were shown a series of sixty faces in random order, and each face was paired with one of six possible group labels. Two of the six labels were intimacy groups (family member and friend), two were task groups (jury and coworker), and two signified social categories (French and Presbyterian). In the following phase, the faces from the first phase were presented without labels, and participants were asked to supply the correct group label.

If members of various groups are spontaneously classified according to their superordinate group typology, errors in recognition should reveal the use of these group types. Indeed, participants made significantly more within-group-type errors than between-groups-type errors. That is, confusions of members of different groups within the same type (for example, a face labeled as French in the first phase mislabeled as Presbyterian in the second phase) were more common than confusions of members of groups of different types (for example, a face labeled French in the first phase mislabeled as coworker, jury member, family member, or friend in the second phase).

In another study, participants were presented with behaviors and group labels (again two groups of each group type), and were subsequently given a surprise free-recall task. Participants were asked to recall as many of the previously presented behaviors as possible. Recall protocols were analyzed to assess the organization of recalled behaviors, specifically with regard to within-group-type versus between-groups-type transitions in the behaviors recalled. If behaviors are clustered in memory by group type, there should be more within-group-type transitions (that is, recalling behaviors performed by members of groups of a single type sequentially) than between-groups-type transitions (that is, transition from a behavior performed by a group member of one group type to a behavior performed by a group member of a different group type). As expected, within-group-type transitions occurred significantly more than between-groups-type transitions.

Taken together, the results of the Sherman et al. (2002) study provide compelling evidence that the mental representation of groups is organized by group type. Inferences about group type can very much affect the organization of information about the group in memory, the accuracy of memory, and the particular kinds of errors of recognition and recall that are likely to occur.

### Inferences about the self

We have now examined the ways in which and the conditions under which inferences about both individual and group targets affect accuracy and bias in recall as well as memory organization. We shall now consider the effects of inferences on memory for a third type of social target, the self. Of course, one can consider the self as just another case of an individual social target. The only difference is that, in the case of the self, the perceiver and the perceived target are in the same skin. Thus, our discussion and conclusions about inferences and memory for individual targets would apply for the most part to the self as well. However, the self is a rather special target in several ways. Obviously, the self is of special importance, with much emotion and motivation attached to self-knowledge. Moreover, because we are always with ourselves, we have more knowledge about the self than about any other individuals.

Even though theorists have at times presented the self concept as a stable and unified structure (Kihlstrom and Cantor, 1984; Lecky, 1945), it is also recognized that there are many different aspects of the self. The self is multiply categorizable in the same way that any other person is. In addition, the traits applied to the self are not necessarily applied in a hard and fast way. At certain times, we might feel successful in our work, energetic, and cooperative. At other times, based on the context and surrounding circumstances, we might feel like failures in our work, lazy, and competitive. As with the perception of other social targets, the inferences that we draw about ourselves at any given time will affect the things that we recall about our past behaviors and outcomes. When we feel successful, we are likely more easily to recall past success experiences. When we feel competitive, we will have accessible those times in our lives when we competed with others.

Klein and Loftus (1993) addressed the question of what factors determine the inferences that people make about themselves. More specifically, they were concerned with whether people answered questions about their own traits and attributes by accessing specific autobiographical memories of relevant behaviors or whether they accessed a summary abstract representation of the self without having to rely on specific episodes. The answers to their questions were important for specifying how the self is represented in memory. In addition, the process by which trait inferences about the self are made would affect the content and speed of memory for self-relevant events.

Klein and Loftus (1993) employed a task-facilitation paradigm to address these issues. Participants first answered a question about whether a certain trait described them, or they were asked to define the trait. Next, they were asked to recall a time when they behaved in a way that was indicative of that trait. If people access specific past episodes in order to make inferences about their traits, they would have to access such episodes to answer the describe question. This would then increase the speed at which they answered the next question about recalling a trait-supportive episode (relative to the speed of doing this after the define task). Klein and Loftus (1993) found no indication that, in general, people make self-inferences by accessing specific behaviors. Thus, making trait inferences did not affect memory for behavioral episodes. Interestingly, when making inferences about the traits of others, even well-known others, people *do* access specific behaviors. Thus, the initial describe task facilitates the speed at which behaviors of others are accessed.

The findings of Klein and Loftus (1993) are important in suggesting that autobiographical and abstract self-knowledge is stored and accessed independently. Thus, inferences about and memory for either of these have no effect on the other. This is very different from the way in which episodes and abstract knowledge about other individuals (and groups) are stored and accessed. The relation between inferences and memory for the self and for others reflects these differences in storage and access.

In addition to the effects of specific inferences in directing specific memories, there are also important general memory effects of making inferences about the self with regard to the presence or absence of traits and attributes. Rogers et al. (1977) had participants respond to a list of attributes. For each attribute, participants had to indicate either whether the attribute was true of some other person, was true of them, rhymed with a certain word, or was written in capital letters. In the next phase, participants were simply asked to recall all the words. When participants had made an inference about whether an attribute was true of the self, memory for the attribute was especially strong – far better than for any other kind of processing of the attribute. Rogers et al. (1977) suggested that this self-referent effect is probably due to the fact that the self is such a rich and complex representation that making each trait inference with respect to the self leads to many associative links to the attribute in memory. However, Klein and his colleagues (Klein and Kihlstrom, 1986; Klein and Loftus, 1988) argued for an organizational processing interpretation, in which participants think about the trait-inference words on the stimulus list in relation to one another. This process of organizing the words about which self-inferences are made enhances memory by establishing inter-item associative paths and category labels. Klein and Loftus (1988) found evidence for both elaborative and organizational processes.

Just as inferences and expectancies about other individuals and about groups can lead both to accurate memories and to biases and reconstructions in recall, the same effects can also occur for the self. In fact, given the importance and the amount of affect associated with the self, such biases may be even more prevalent. One line of work has focused especially on the general role of expectancies and inferences about the self on reconstructive memory. The bottom line of this work is that our remembered past is built on what we expect it must have been in light of our present beliefs. These current expectancies about the past are based on schemas about how events in our lives are supposed to unfold. These schemas inform us about the temporal flow of life's events. They thus both guide and bias our recall in line with the schema-driven expectancies and inferences.

Work by Ross and his colleagues (Conway and Ross, 1984; McFarland et al., 1989; Ross et al., 1981) empirically demonstrates that recall of one's past is to a large extent determined by one's expectancies about how change occurs. For example, people tend to recall past attitudes as being much closer to present attitudes than they actually are (Ross et al., 1981). This is because people infer that attitudes must be stable over time, and this inference guides their memory. In other cases, people hold inferences and expectancies that behaviors or abilities should change over time. For example, after taking a self-help course, participants reported that their past situations were much worse than they actually were (Conway and Ross, 1984). This allows them to perceive that they have improved over time, a perception which is consistent with their inference about what should have happened over time given that they have taken a self-help course. Such misrecall of the past is also based on a motivation to see the self as better now than in the past, and thus to downgrade in memory one's past behaviors and achievements (Wilson and Ross, 2000). By using one's current standing as a benchmark, one then makes inferences about temporal change or stability, and remembers a past that fits these inferences. Hirt's research and his model of reconstructive memory strongly support these ideas (Hirt, 1990; Hirt et al., 1993).

Finally, in recent years, there have been many instances of adults who claim to have recently experienced awakened memories of childhood sexual abuse. The claim is that these memories had been repressed for as long as twenty-five years or more. According to Loftus (1997a, 1997b), these represent false memories of events that had never actually occurred. She describes the process of false memory production as generally involving clients in therapy who are suffering from depression, anxiety, or some other psychological disorder. They are in pain and are searching for a causal explanation for that pain. If the client is led (usually by the therapist) to draw an inference that the cause of the pain must have been some traumatic event from childhood, this assumption leads quite smoothly to the development of false memories of early childhood abuse. The memories can often be very detailed and specific in nature. Loftus and Pickrell (1995) have succeeded in showing that false memories of childhood events can actually be implanted if certain interpretations of early life events are brought about.

### *Summary of principles involving the effects of social inference on memory*

1 For individual targets, inferences are made online as information about the individual is received. Such inferences can lead to good overall memory for the information, primacy effects in recall, low memory–judgment correlations, and heightened memory for information inconsistent with the overall impression.
2 For group targets, inferences are generally memory based, formed after the original information has been received and stored. This judgment process leads to poor overall memory, recency effects in recall, high memory–judgment correlations, and heightened memory for information consistent with the overall impression.
3 The key to differences in processes of inference and memory for social targets is the perceived entitativity of the target. When individuals and groups have the same degree of perceived entitativity, whether high or low, processes and outcomes for inference and memory are the same.
4 Trait inference for individuals is done spontaneously, and this process leads to enhanced recall for behaviors that led to the trait inferences as well as to clustering in memory for behaviors that afforded the same trait inferences.
5 Spontaneous trait inferences can also cause memory distortions and reconstructions such that behaviors consistent with the inferred traits are wrongly recalled.
6 Inferences about the group membership of individuals (especially for groups that are stereotyped) lead to schematic representation of the individuals and have effects on both accuracy for certain stereotype-relevant information and biases in memory in a stereotype-consistent direction.
7 The framing of information causes differential salience of information, affecting the content of inferences as well as the subsequent accuracy and biasing of memory.
8 Inferences about group types affect the organization of group-relevant information in memory. This organization in turn affects the kinds of errors of recall and recognition that are made.
9 The principles of inference and memory for the self follow very closely the principles for individual social targets. However, the greater knowledge about the self, the greater affect associated with the self, and the special motivations that are self-relevant lead to even stronger effects of inferences on both memory accuracy and memory biases.

## Memory → inference

Thus far, we have discussed a variety of ways in which social-inference processes can guide, influence, shape, and determine our memories for social information. This relationship between inference and memory, however, is a two-way street. In this section, we discuss several ways in which memory can guide and influence the inferences we make.

### *Accessibility of information in memory*

The knowledge stored in memory is one's cognitive representation of information that has been previously processed. That information can be represented in various ways (Carlston and Smith, 1996) and, due to aspects of the way it was processed, not all information is represented equally. As a consequence, some information is potentially more easily retrievable than other information. Obviously, information that is easily accessible can have greater impact on subsequent judgments, inferences, and decisions than information not easily accessible. Hence, the accessibility of information from memory is an important factor that guides subsequent inference processes. This general effect has been manifested in numerous ways in social-psychological research. What makes some information more accessible in memory? There are several answers to that question.

### *Stimulus salience*

As social cognizers, we process information that is available to us in the immediate social context. However, some aspects of that information capture our attention, engage our processing, or otherwise become highly salient to us. Information salience may be due to a stimulus being highly vivid, or it may achieve its salience simply as a function of the context in which it is encountered. Highly salient information not only is more likely to be attended to, processed, and stored than nonsalient aspects of the social situation, but also is likely to be easily accessible from memory at a later time. The enhanced accessibility of salient information has been shown to influence social inferences in a variety of contexts (e.g., McArthur and Post, 1977; Taylor and Fiske, 1978). Using a mock-jury paradigm, Reyes et al. (1980) manipulated the vividness of either the prosecution or defense evidence, and subsequently participants judged the defendant's guilt or innocence either immediately or 48 hours later. Because all of the evidential arguments were easily retrievable immediately following the presentation of evidence, there were no effects of salience on immediate judgments. However, after a 48-hour delay, judgments were biased by the greater availability of the more vivid evidential information. Participants had better recall for the vivid information, and their verdict judgments were consistent with those recall differences. Thus, with the passage of time, the salient information was more available and consequently had greater impact on judgments.

Stimuli that occur infrequently often become salient simply due to their infrequency. The distinctiveness-based illusory correlation effect (Hamilton and Gifford, 1976) demonstrated that infrequently occurring stimuli can have greater impact on subsequent judgments and inferences than information that is more frequent. Participants read a series of statements, each one describing a behaviorperformed by a member of one of two groups. Most behaviors were desirable in nature, but approximately one-third were undesirable. Similarly, behaviors by members of one of the groups occurred twice as often as behaviors by members of the other group in the stimulus sentences. However, the two groups were equivalent in the proportion of desirable and undesirable behaviors performed by their members. Nevertheless, Hamilton and Gifford found that the co-occurrence of infrequent stimulus properties (undesirable behaviors performed by members of the smaller group) biased subsequent judgments. Specifically, participants estimated that members of the smaller group had performed a higher proportion of undesirable behaviors than the larger group, and they made less desirable evaluative ratings of the smaller group. Hamilton and Gifford (1976) explained these effects as due to the distinctiveness of the infrequently occurring stimulus items, which therefore become more accessible in memory and hence more available for use in subsequent judgment and inference tasks. Subsequent research has directly demonstrated the increased accessibility of these items (for a review of the research evidence and discussion of alternative explanations, see Hamilton and Sherman, 1989; Stroessner and Plaks, 2001).

### *Priming*

The salience effects noted above are due to properties of the stimuli themselves within a particular context. Another factor that influences the accessibility of information in memory is priming. The activation of stored knowledge through experiences in the immediate context can make prime-relevant information more accessible in memory, and such recent construct activation can influence inferences, evaluations, and decisions on subsequent tasks (Bargh and Pietromonaco, 1982; Bargh et al., 1986; Devine, 1989; Higgins et al., 1977, 1985; Sherman et al., 1990; Srull and Wyer, 1979). A second factor that influences the accessibility of information in memory is the frequency with which a construct has been primed (Bargh and Pietromonaco, 1982; Srull and Wyer, 1979). Traits, attitudes, or stereotypes that have been frequently activated in past experience are more available in memory than those that have been less frequently primed. Such frequency of activation, if it occurs on a regular and continuing basis, can result in certain constructs becoming chronically accessible, such that no external priming in the immediate context is necessary to make them highly accessible (Higgins et al., 1982). Moreover, because people differ in the kinds of experiences they have that would generate such routine construct activation, individuals quite naturally differ in the particular constructs that are chronically accessible (Bargh et al., 1986; Markus, 1977). All of these factors increase the accessibility of information in memory, which in turn increases its availability for use in subsequent inference and judgment tasks (for a review of accessibility effects, see Higgins, 1996).

### *Beliefs and expectancies*

Greater accessibility in memory due to priming is often the result of recent or frequent experiences. In addition, the information that we acquire and represent in memory varies in its accessibility due to its relevance to prior beliefs and expectancies. That is, the social perceiver is not incorporating new information into a mental vacuum, but rather is assimilating that information into a rich foundation of knowledge and beliefs that represent the 'wisdom' that has accumulated from a lifetime of experiences. Those prior beliefs and expectancies can influence the processing of information in a variety of ways. For example, expectancies can influence the interpretation of new information, the inferences drawn from it, and the nature of attributions and descriptive judgments made about the target of that information (for a review, see Olson et al., 1996). One consequence of these effects on processing is that expectancy-relevant information can become more accessible for later use. However, that simple statement masks some complexities in what we have learned about this matter. Indeed, as we shall see, these effects of prior expectancies can be complex.

There is a considerable body of research documenting that information that confirms prior expectancies is processed more easily and is subsequently more readily accessible (e.g., Bodenhausen, 1988; Bodenhausen and Lichtenstein, 1987; Cohen, 1981; Rothbart et al., 1979; for a review, see Hamilton and Sherman, 1994). It therefore exerts greater influence on subsequent inference processes than information that is unrelated to those expectancies. Participants in a study by Hamilton and Rose (1980) read information about members of three occupational groups, and were later asked to estimate how frequently various descriptive terms had been applied to members of each group. Results showed that participants consistently overestimated the frequency with which each of the groups had been characterized by stereotype-confirming items, compared to nonstereotypic information that had described those groups equally often in the stimulus descriptions. Thus, accessibility had a direct bearing on inferences.

As discussed earlier, there is also a large body of evidence indicating that information that is incongruent with expectancies is better recalled than expectancy-congruent information, suggesting that such disconfirming information would have greater accessibility to influence subsequent judgments. Following a paradigm introduced by Hastie and Kumar (1979), an initial impression of a target person is established by providing participants with a set of trait-descriptive terms (such as 'friendly' and 'sociable'), and then presenting a series of sentences describing behaviors that are consistent or inconsistent with that impression. Numerous studies have found that, on a subsequent surprise recall task, expectancy-inconsistent behaviors are recalled with higher probability than expectancy-consistent or neutral behaviors (Bargh and Thein, 1985; Crocker et al., 1983; Hastie and Kumar, 1979; Srull, 1981; Srull et al., 1985; Wyer and Gordon, 1982; Wyer and Martin, 1986).

The dominant explanation for this incongruency effect (recall advantage for inconsistent over consistent or neutral behaviors) is derived from an associative network model of social memory (Hastie, 1980; Srull, 1981) in which the behavioral items become attached to a person node representing the target person. Once an impression that the target is 'friendly' has been formed, expectancy-consistent behaviors (for example, 'he gave directions to the visitors who were lost') are easily processed and represented in memory. In contrast, when an inconsistent behavior is encountered ('he lost his temper over a minor disagreement'), the perceiver attempts to understand this unexpected event by comparing it to other behavioral information previously learned about the target person. In doing so, these incongruent items form direct connections with those retrieved items in the network representation. These inter-item associations, all of which necessarily involve incongruent items, provide more retrieval routes leading to the incongruent items, therefore producing a greater likelihood of recalling those expectancy-inconsistent behaviors.

Research has provided considerable support for the network model (Srull and Wyer, 1989). Stern et al. (1984) found that participants had longer processing times for incongruent than congruent items in a self-paced impression-formation task, supporting the hypothesis that some form of 'extra' processing is triggered by expectancy-inconsistent information. What is the nature of that processing? Consistent with the model's assumptions, Sherman and Hamilton (1994) provided evidence that, as an incongruent item is processed, previously encountered information is activated and brought into working memory, thereby generating inter-item links. Moreover, evidence indicates that information that contradicts the existing impression spontaneously triggers the attribution process as the perceiver tries to understand the inconsistent behaviors (Clary and Tesser, 1983; Hastie, 1984; Susskind et al., 1999).

Although the Hastie–Srull associative-network model is supported by studies using single-trait representations, the incongruency effect does not occur with increasingly complex multitrait presentation. Hamilton et al. (1989) presented behavior-descriptive sentences about multiple-trait imensions and found that both congruent and incongruent items from the same trait dimension were stored together and were directly associated in memory. Because of these associations, both types of information were recalled equally well.

In addition, the effects of trait expectancies on memory depend on whether the dependent measure involves recognition or recall and on the cognitive resources available to the social perceiver. With adequate cognitive resources, for individual targets both recognition and recall show an advantage for incongruent behaviors. However, when cognitive load depletes the resources available, recognition-sensitivity measures continue to show an advantage for inconsistent behaviors whereas recall measures now show a memory advantage for consistent behaviors (Sherman and Frost, 2000; Stangor and McMillan, 1992).

As discussed earlier, compared to the effects of inferences about individuals, inconsistency resolution for groups (especially loosely associated groups) is less likely to occur because there is no global expectancy for consistency or stability of traits across the various members of a group. Thus, perceivers will not be motivated to resolve inconsistencies in the case of groups (Susskind et al., 1999) and will not spend a greater amount of time processing inconsistent as opposed to consistent information (Stern et al., 1984). Therefore, the memory advantage for inconsistent information observed with individual targets has been shown not to emerge in forming impressions of groups (Srull, 1981; Srull et al., 1985; Wyer et al., 1984). This conclusion has been supported in a meta-analysis (Stangor and McMillan, 1992).

### *Self-relevance*

If you watch sports often enough, you will notice that the way the coach accounts for success has mainly to do with the team's behavior, and the coach often cites episodes of the team's winning spirit. One might conjecture that the coach is simply trying to bolster the team's merits. However, the same own-team single-mindedness seems to occur when the team loses. The outcome is then often accounted for by the self-defeating performance of the team, and, again, instances of this self-defeating attitude are abundantly described. One possible explanation is that, during the game, the coach focused on his own team's behavior and has mainly retained episodes diagnostic of his own team's performance. With the heightened accessibility of his own team's behavior, the coach will mainly refer to such information when asked to account for the outcome. As a general rule, the more attention one pays to a given episode or a given episode facet, the better will this episode or facet be retained and, in turn, be more accessible to influence later judgments.

Research has provided evidence for this bias toward own or self-relevant behavior. For instance, each partner of a close relationship often attributes more credit to himself or herself for the events and activities in the relationship than the other partner is willing to grant. Ross and Sicoly (1979) indicated that these results could be due to (a) the informational disparity between partners, (b) the motivated or self-enhancing strategy of each partner, or (c) the greater accessibility of self-relevant information. Subsequent research favors the last account because this egocentric bias remains invariant across less visible, more stressful, and negative relationship domains or events (Thompson and Kelley, 1981).

### *Memory organization*

Tversky and Kahneman (1973) asked participants whether there are more words in the English language with the letter 'r' in the first position or the third position, and most people responded that there are more words beginning with 'r'. Tversky and Kahneman (1973) argued that, because alphabet order is a strong organizer for verbal memory, word instances that begin with an 'r' are more *available* in memory than instances of words with 'r' in the third position, although the latter are actually more frequent in English. Subsequent research that directly manipulated memory accessibility has supported the notion that memory accessibility has a strong impact on judgment (Gabrielcik and Fazio, 1984; Garcia-Marques et al., 2002). A clear example of the impact of memory organization on judgment can be found in research by Sherman et al. (1992). In their study, participants were asked, for instance, to estimate the percentage of men who prefer chocolate to anchovies or the percentage of people who are men who prefer chocolate to anchovies. Sherman et al. (1992) argued that memory is much more likely to be compartmentalized according to gender than to food preference and therefore that the appropriate sampling should be more easily formed in the former case. In fact, the results showed that judgments concerning the more natural sampling space are much less biased and more coherent. In sum, memory organization makes some types of information more available than other types. As a consequence, this greater accessibility can facilitate subsequent retrieval and facilitate judgments that depend upon the more available information, while it can hinder retrieval and impair judgments that depend upon the less available information.

### *Misattributed memories*

The effects of memory on judgment, inference, and decision are so pervasive that they often go unrecognized. Many authors have argued that the reprocessing of a given stimulus does not always result in recollection (Begg et al., 1992; Bornstein and D'Agostino, 1994; Jacoby and Dallas, 1981; Jacoby and Kelley, 1987; Jacoby et al., 1989b; Mandler et al., 1987). Often the enhanced processing fluency derived from stimulus familiarity is taken as a reflection of the objective nature of the stimulus, particularly when the occurrence of stimulus repetition is unnoticed (Bornstein, 1992). Repeated stimuli are thus often judged to have been presented for a longer duration (Witherspoon and Allan, 1985), in a less annoying context (Jacoby et al., 1988), or in more perceptively distinct manner (Mandler et al., 1987). Repeated names are often misjudged as famous (Jacoby et al., 1989a, 1989c), repeated sentences are taken to be more valid (Bacon, 1979; Begg et al., 1985), and repeated objects are considered more likeable (Bornstein, 1989; Zajonc, 1968). These results show that, although stimulus repetition has a considerable impact on judgment and inference, this impact is often unaccompanied by a corresponding recollective experience. This subtlety of the hidden influence of memory on judgment and inference makes it all the more easy to yield to.

### *Ease of retrieval*

We have argued that memory accessibility is a factor that strongly affects judgment because only memories retrieved at the time of judgment can directly affect judgment. But memory accessibility effects go beyond the impact of the content of retrieved memories. The process of memory search by itself can inform judgment in a number of ways. Both an observer and the respondent often take a rapid answer to a given query as an indication of the respondent's expertise. Easily accessed answers are perceived as correct answers. However, what is less obvious is that, even though more easily retrieved memories have a greater impact on memory-based judgments then less easily retrieved ones, things other than the truth value of an item can affect its retrievability. In fact, research that we cited under the rubric of the *availability heuristic* has provided convincing examples showing that accessibility is often independent of truth.

A good example of the effects of the ease of retrieval on judgments, independent of the content of retrieved memory, was reported by Schwarz et al. (1991). Participants recalled either six or twelve instances of their own assertive or unassertive behaviors. They then asked participants to rate themselves on assertiveness scales. Pretesting had revealed that generating six instances of such behaviors is generally easy, whereas retrieving twelve instances is generally difficult. Participants who had recalled six assertive (unassertive) instances rated themselves as more assertive (unassertive) than participants who had recalled twelve instances, even though the latter group had actually recalled a greater number of assertive (unassertive) behaviors. Thus, the ease of retrieving relevant instances (six versus twelve instances) was used as an indirect indication of the content of memory. In a related vein, other studies have demonstrated that easily retrieved (Lichtenstein et al., 1978) or easily imagined events are judged to be more frequent or more likely (Sherman et al., 1985).

### *Retrieval strategies*

In one way or another, making inferences almost invariably involves the *use* of the knowledge stored in memory. That is, some portion of the information in memory is accessed and becomes the basis for inferences, evaluations, and decisions. As we have just seen, certain properties of the information itself can make some items of information more accessible than others. In addition, the individual searches (consciously or unconsciously) through memory to retrieve information for various purposes. The retrieval processes engaged in by the individual will therefore influence the information available for use and hence can become an important determinant of the nature of the inferences and judgments made. One might prefer to view the individual as an impartial inquisitor searching through stored knowledge for the most reasonable basis for making judgments. However, although there may be times when this model is applicable (for example, when the decision is important), a number of factors can influence this process, making retrieval a less comprehensive and potentially more selective process. Consequently, when the retrieved information is used as the basis for subsequent processes (inferences, decisions), these aspects of the retrieval process can bias the resulting inferences. We have already discussed such biasing effects in research by McArthur and Post (1977), Taylor and Fiske (1978), Reyes et al. (1980), and Hamilton and Gifford (1976).

Earlier in the chapter, we saw how inferences and expectancies can bias memory in such a way as to render memory consistent with inferences. Here we suggest that memory can bias inferences in a way to render inferences consistent with what is remembered.

### *Exhaustive and heuristic retrieval strategies: the TRAP model*

We have discussed numerous factors that can influence and guide the search of memory in accordance with goals, contexts, and prior expectancies. These variables can have effects on both the amount of information retrieved and the content of that information. Of course, once memory is affected or certain aspects of memory become more accessible, the information retrieved will have important effects on subsequent inferences. We now turn to a somewhat different parameter in information retrieval, the strategy by which the individual searches memory for task-relevant information.

Garcia-Marques and Hamilton (1996; Garcia-Marques et al., 2002; Hamilton and Garcia-Marques, 2003) introduced a distinction between two strategies for retrieving information from memory, exhaustive and heuristic retrieval. Exhaustive retrieval refers to the typical conception of memory search, as in the standard recall of learned information from memory. It is an effortful search process that searches sequentially through associative memory, using each retrieved item as a cue for the retrieval of other items in the most thorough possible way. Its output consists of the retrieval of a series of specific episodic traces. In contrast, heuristic retrieval represents an indirect way of probing memory. It uses the degree of fit between available retrieval cues and the stored memory traces as a whole as a clue to some aspect of memory content (such as the frequency of a given episodic feature). Its output is typically an overall summary judgment, such as a frequency estimate. The retrieval output of these two modes depends upon different factors. Exhaustive retrieval is a resource-consuming process and therefore will be affected by cognitive load. Heuristic retrieval, however, is a relatively quick and low resource-demanding retrieval technique that will be affected by memory accessibility (that is, recent and frequent priming) and cue salience.

To investigate this distinction, Garcia-Marques and Hamilton (1996) combined the main features of the paradigms discussed previously – specifically, those used by Hastie and Kumar (1979) and Hamilton and Rose (1980). Participants were given impression-formation instructions and were then presented with a list of behaviors performed by two social targets. Expectancies were induced implicitly by providing the target's occupation, and the two targets had occupations that generated opposite trait expectancies (for example, librarian–cultured; waitress–uncultured). One-third of the behaviors were expectancy-congruent, another third were expectancy-incongruent, and the final third were expectancy-neutral. Following a distracter task, participants were asked to (a) free-recall all the behaviors, (b) estimate the frequency of occurrence of behaviors illustrative of each trait, and (c) judge the target on several trait-rating scales.

The results revealed the difference between the exhaustive strategy involved in free recall and the heuristic retrieval strategy that underlies frequency estimation and trait judgments. Incongruent behaviors were recalled better than congruent behaviors. In contrast, frequency estimates were higher for congruent behaviors than for incongruent behaviors, and trait judgments were more heavily influenced by the congruent information. Thus, the predicted dissociation between recall and judgment occurred. These results were interpreted as due to the different search processes engaged in free recall (exhaustive) and in frequency estimation and trait judgment (heuristic). These findings are particularly impressive in that these seemingly incompatible effects – better recall of incongruent items and overestimation of congruent items – were obtained on immediately successive tasks performed by the same participants.

As discussed earlier, the incongruency effect in free recall has been obtained in numerous studies. However, it does not always occur, and the TRAP model's distinction between exhaustive and heuristic retrieval provides a framework for understanding these outcomes. Research has shown that, because exhaustive retrieval is cognitively demanding, the incongruency effect occurs only when a number of favorable cognitive factors are met (Garcia-Marques et al., 2002; Hamilton et al., 1989). Specifically, the incongruency effect will be evident when all acquired information pertains to only one trait dimension, when no distractions are present and sufficient processing resources are available, and when one later tries to recall any and all information about the person, in any order, with no concern for content themes. However, when the information pertains to more than one trait, when the perceiver is under cognitive load, or when retrieval is selectively aimed at certain facets of the information, the incongruency effect does not occur.

These qualifications of the incongruency effect are important because impression formation typically occurs when the perceiver learns an array of information pertaining to several facets of the person's life. The perceiver is simultaneously coping with multiple demands on cognitive resources, and subsequent retrieval of specific information about the person will be for a given purpose that will guide the retrieval process to search for particular content. In other words, the conditions that limit the generality of the incongruency effect seem to be typical of many everyday social contexts. They also suggest the relative infrequency of exhaustive retrieval in day-to-day life. It seems likely that heuristic retrieval occurs much more commonly in everyday contexts, and therefore, that the corresponding procongruent memory and judgment effects will be more commonly observed (Hamilton and Garcia-Marques, 2003).

### *Relationship between memory and judgment*

When a given judgment is called for, the reported judgment can be either computed at that time or simply retrieved (if it has been previously computed). This simple distinction has a number of consequences for the nature of the judgment and for its relationship to the available relevant memory content.

Hastie and Park (1986) distinguished between online and memory-based judgments. Online judgments are computed at the time the relevant information is processed. Memory-based judgments are computed only after the relevant information has been processed and therefore are based on whatever relevant information is retrieved from memory at the time. Hastie and Park (1986) argued that memory-based judgments should be strongly correlated with the output of free recall because the retrieval of relevant information is a necessary precondition for memory-based judgments. In contrast, no such correlation is expected for online judgments because the factors that affected the online judgment are not necessarily those that moderate the later availability of the relevant information in memory.

Hastie and Park's (1986) distinction between online and memory-based judgments was a centrally important contribution. It has not only advanced our understanding of factors that govern the relationship between memory and judgment but has also broadened our perspective on what that relationship should look like, when, and why. The basic prediction from their analysis is clear-cut and important; in many cases, it represents a valid account of memory–judgment relationships. However, the TRAP model suggests that at least two amendments can be made.

First, the designation 'memory-based judgment' is a misnomer. Hastie and Park (1986) refer to free recall and not necessarily to 'memory'. As we argued earlier, there are search processes in memory that are very different from the retrieval processes in free recall (that is, heuristic retrieval processes). Moreover, with our increasingly extended knowledge about memory dissociations, it is difficult to speak about a judgment being correlated with 'memory'. There are a host of memory measures (for example, direct, indirect; implicit, explicit), and many of these memory indicators do not correlate well with each other (see Richardson-Klavehn and Bjork, 1988). For instance, Garcia-Marques and Hamilton (1996) found that, although impression judgments seldom correlated with the output of free recall (a memory measure), they were highly correlated with frequency estimation (another memory measure).

Second, according to the TRAP model, free recall and impression judgments commonly depend upon different retrieval search processes (exhaustive versus heuristic retrieval). However, the independence often observed between free recall and judgment derives, according to the TRAP model, from the fact that their respective underlying search processes explore different features of the relevant cognitive representation. Exhaustive retrieval searches through item-to-item associations, whereas heuristic search mainly explores the associations between items and referent nodes. Thus, for instance, in standard impression-formation conditions, associative density among items and the association strength between items and referent nodes generate opposite implications, in that the former benefits expectancy-incongruent retrieval and the latter benefits expectancy-congruent information. Under these conditions, impression judgments and free recall are independent. However, item-to-item associations are sometimes not developed at all (for example, when cognitive demands during encoding are high). Under other conditions, item-to-item associations are formed but they may not be explored during retrieval (for example, because of scarce resources, or because the recall goal is selective). In such cases, both exhaustive and heuristic retrieval are limited to searching via associations between items and referent nodes, and under these conditions high correlations between the output of free recall and impression judgments can emerge (Garcia-Marques and Hamilton, 1996; Garcia-Marques et al., 2002). In sum, the distinction put forth by Hastie and Park (1986) can be usefully deepened and extended if the diversity and complexity of retrieval processes are recognized.

### *Summary of principles involving the effects of memory on inference*

1 Information accessible in memory has greater influence on inferences and judgments. Among the factors that can heighten the accessibility in memory are stimulus salience, priming, prior beliefs and expectancies, memory organization, and the self-relevance of information.
2 Information in memory that is easily retrieved and events that are easily imagined influence inferences and judgments more than memories that are less easily retrieved.
3 The processing effects of memory can be misattributed to features of the stimulus or of the context. The fluency that derives from reprocessing a stimulus can be attributed to its perceptive or evaluative nature.

4 Memory retrieval can affect judgment by the relative ease or difficulty of the retrieval process itself. The relative ease of retrieving an episode is often taken as an indication of its prevalence in memory.
5 Information can be retrieved from memory in different ways. Use of different retrieval strategies or modes can influence what information is accessed, which in turn can provide differing bases for subsequent inferences.
6 Inferences and judgments are sometimes based directly on recalled information (memory-based judgments), producing a positive relation between recall and judgment. Alternatively, many social inferences and judgments are formed as information is initially processed (online judgments), and these have no necessary relation to recalled memories.

## Conclusion

We have reviewed and discussed a broad range of research and thinking concerning social inference and social memory. Most important, we have tried to demonstrate and clarify the interplay between the two. Just as the content and processes of social inference affect memory for social targets and events, memories of those targets and events have equally important effects on subsequent inferences.

Because of this complex interplay between inferences and memory, it is difficult to end with a simple, neat conclusion that captures a bottom line in a pithy phrase or paragraph. Perhaps the best way to conclude is by adopting one of Carlston and Smith's (1996) principles of mental representation: the mental mush principle. Within this principle, Carlston and Smith (1996) recognize that stored knowledge affects interpretation. Likewise, they recognize the impact of this stored knowledge on memory. In addition, they propose that there are multiple mental representations, each having effects on attributions in both perception and memory.

Rather than proposing a representational mental model that consists of each item represented in a separate file with independent access, they suggest that mental representations are superposed, so that accessing any item will access all items, and changing the representation of any item will change everything. Such a model forces one to exactly the conclusion that we have reached – our perceptions, inferences, judgments, and memories are all constructed from the same information contained in multiple mental representations. These perceptions, inferences, judgments, and memories are all intertwined and interconnected. In fact, labeling an event as an inference, a perception, or a memory may be somewhat arbitrary and depend only on the existing context. While we might prefer a simpler view where the processes and representations are discrete and independent, how much more exciting it is to recognize the complexity involved and to unravel the complexity.

## Acknowledgments

Preparation of this chapter was facilitated by National Institute of Mental Health Grant MH-40058 to S.J. Sherman and D.L. Hamilton, and by National Institute on Drug Abuse Grant K05DA00492 to S.J. Sherman.

### SUMMARY

Research and theory in the areas of social inference and social memory have played important roles in social psychology. In this chapter we discuss the ways in which these two systems interact. The content and process of social inference have significant effects on the content, accuracy, and biases of memory. Also, memory structure and process affect inferences about social targets. By examining both directions of effects, we extract general principles by which social inference and memory are linked.

Regarding the effects of social inference on memory, we discuss inferences about individuals, groups, and the self. The key factor in differences in inference and memory for social targets is the perceived coherence of the target. Individuals generally have higher coherence, and information is processed online. Information about groups, which have lower coherence, is processed in a memory-based fashion. The greater knowledge and affect associated with the self render this a unique case with especially significant effects of inferences on memory.

Regarding the effects of memory on inference, the key factors are the accessibility of information and the ease of the retrieval process itself. Different retrieval strategies have effects on the specific information that is retrieved as well as on subsequent inferences.

## References

Alba, J.W. and Hasher, L. (1983) 'Is Memory Schematic?', *Psychological Bulletin*, 93: 203–31.

Allport, G.W. (1954) *The Nature of Prejudice*. Cambridge, MA: Addison-Wesley.

Anderson, N.H. (1966) 'Component Ratings in Impression Formation', *Psychonomic Science*, 6: 179–80.

Anderson, N.H. (1968) 'Application of a Linear-Serial Model to a Personality-Impression Task Using Serial Presentation', *Journal of Personality and Social Psychology*, 10: 354–62.

Anderson, N.H. (1981) *Foundations of Information Integration Theory*. New York: Academic Press.

Anderson, R.C. and Pichert, J.W. (1978) 'Recall of Previously Unrecallable Information Following a Shift in Perspective', *Journal of Verbal Learning and Verbal Behavior*, 17: 1–12.

Asch, S.E. (1946) 'Forming Impressions of Personality', *Journal of Abnormal and Social Psychology*, 41: 258–90.

Babey, S.H., Queller, S., and Klein, S.B. (1998) 'The Role of Expectancy Violating Behaviors in the Representation of Trait Knowledge: A Summary-Plus-Exception Model of Social Memory', *Social Cognition*, 16: 287–339.

Bacon, F.T. (1979) 'Credibility of Repeated Statements: Memory for Trivia', *Journal of Experimental Psychology: Human Learning and Memory*, 5: 241–52.

Bargh, J.A. and Pietromonaco, P. (1982) 'Automatic Information Processing and Social Perception: The Influence of Trait Information Presented Outside of Consciousness in Impression Formation', *Journal of Personality and Social Psychology*, 43: 437–49.

Bargh, J.A. and Thein, R.D. (1985) 'Individual Construct Accessibility, Person Memory, and the Recall-Judgment Link: The Case of Information Overload', *Journal of Personality and Social Psychology*, 49: 1129–46.

Bargh, J.A., Bond, R.N., Lombardi, W.L., and Tota, M.E. (1986) 'The Additive Nature of Chronic and Temporary Sources of Construct Accessibility', *Journal of Personality and Social Psychology*, 50: 869–78.

Bassili, J.N. (1989) 'Trait Encoding in Behavior Identification and Dispositional Inference', *Personality and Social Psychology Bulletin*, 15: 285–96.

Begg, I., Anas, A., and Farinacci, S. (1992) 'Dissociation of Processes in Belief: Source Recollection, Statement Familiarity, and the Illusion of Truth', *Journal of Experimental Psychology: General*, 121: 446–58.

Begg, I., Armour, V., and Kerr, T. (1985) 'On Believing What We Remember', *Canadian Journal of Behavioral Science*, 17: 199–214.

Beike, D.R. and Sherman, S.J. (1994) 'Social Inference: Inductions, Deductions, and Analogies', in R.J. Wyer, Jr. and T.K. Srull (eds), *Handbook of Social Cognition, Vol. 1: Basic Processes*, 2nd edn. Hillsdale, NJ: Erlbaum, pp. 209–85.

Bodenhausen, G.V. (1988) 'Stereotypic Biases in Social Decision Making and Memory: Testing Process Models of Stereotype Use', *Journal of Personality and Social Psychology*, 55: 726–37.

Bodenhausen, G.V. and Lichtenstein, M. (1987) 'Social Stereotypes and Information Processing Strategies: The Impact of Task Complexity', *Journal of Personality and Social Psychology*, 52: 871–80.

Bodenhausen, G.V. and Wyer, R.S., Jr. (1985) 'Effects of Stereotypes in Decision Making and Information-Processing Strategies', *Journal of Personality and Social Psychology*, 48: 267–82.

Bornstein, R.F. (1989) 'Exposure and Affect: Overview and Meta-Analysis of Research, 1968–1978', *Psychological Bulletin*, 106: 265–89.

Bornstein, R.F. (1992) 'Inhibitory Effects of Awareness on Affective Responding: Implications for the Affect-Cognition Relationship', in M.S. Clark (ed.), *Review of Personality and Social Psychology* (vol. 13). Beverly Hills, CA: Sage, pp. 235–55.

Bornstein, R.F. and D'Agostino, P.R. (1994) 'The Attribution and Discounting of Perceptual Fluency: Preliminary Tests of a Perceptual Fluency/Attributional Model of the Mere Exposure Effect', *Social Cognition*, 12: 123–8.

Bruner, J.S. (1957) 'On Perceptual Readiness', *Psychological Review*, 64: 123–52.

Burnstein, E. and Schul, Y. (1982) 'The Informational Basis of Social Judgments: Operations in Forming an Impression of Another Person', *Journal of Experimental Social Psychology*, 18: 217–34.

Campbell, D.T. (1958) 'Common Fate, Similarity, and Other Indices of the Status of Aggregates of Persons as Social Entities', *Behavioral Science*, 3: 14–25.

Cantor, N. and Mischel, W. (1977) 'Traits as Prototypes: Effects on Recognition Memory', *Journal of Personality and Social Psychology*, 35: 38–48.

Cantor, N. and Mischel, W. (1979) 'Prototypicality and Personality: Effects on Free Recall and Personality Impressions', *Journal of Research in Personality*, 13: 187–205.

Carlston, D.E. and Skowronski, J.J. (1986) 'Trait Memory and Behavior Memory: The Effects of Alternative Pathways on Impression Judgment Response Times', *Journal of Personality and Social Psychology*, 50: 5–13.

Carlston, D.E. and Skowronski, J.J. (1994) 'Savings in the Relearning of Trait Information as Evidence for Spontaneous Inference Generation', *Journal of Personality and Social Psychology*, 66: 840–56.

Carlston, D.E., Skowronski, J.J., and Sparks, S. (1995) 'Savings in Relearning. II. On the Formation of Behavior-Based Trait Associations and Inferences', *Journal of Personality and Social Psychology*, 69: 429–36.

Carlston, D.E. and Smith, E.R. (1996) 'Principles of Mental Representation', in E.T. Higgins and A.W. Kruglanski (eds), *Social Psychology: Handbook of Basic Principles*. New York: Guilford Press, pp. 184–210.

Clary, E.G. and Tesser, A. (1983) 'Reactions to Unexpected Events: The Naïve Scientist and the

Interpretative Activity', *Personality and Social Psychology Bulletin*, 9: 609–20.

Cohen, C.E. (1981) 'Person Categories and Social Perception: Testing Some Boundaries of the Processing Effects of Prior Knowledge', *Journal of Personality and Social Psychology*, 40: 441–52.

Collins, A.M. and Quillian, M.R. (1969) 'Retrieval Time From Semantic Memory', *Journal of Verbal Learning and Verbal Behavior*, 8: 240–7.

Conway, M. and Ross, M. (1984) 'Getting What You Want by Revisiting What You Had', *Journal of Personality and Social Psychology*, 47: 738–48.

Crocker, J., Hannah, D.B., and Weber, R. (1983) 'Person Memory and Causal Attribution', *Journal of Personality and Social Psychology*, 44: 55–66.

Devine, P.G. (1989) 'Stereotypes and Prejudice: Their Automatic and Controlled Components', *Journal of Personality and Social Psychology*, 56: 5–18.

Fazio, R.H. and Dunton, B.C. (1997) 'Categorization by Race: The Impact of Automatic and Controlled Components of Racial Prejudice', *Journal of Experimental Social Psychology*, 33: 451–70.

Fiedler, K. and Semin, G.R. (1988) 'On the Causal Information Conveyed by Different Interpersonal Verbs: The Role of Implicit Sentence Context', *Social Cognition*, 6: 21–39.

Gabrielcik, A. and Fazio, R.H. (1984) 'Priming and Frequency Estimation: A Strict Test of the Availability Heuristic', *Personality and Social Psychology Bulletin*, 10: 85–9.

Garcia-Marques, L. and Hamilton, D.L. (1996) 'Resolving the Apparent Discrepancy Between the Incongruency Effect and the Expectancy-Based Illusory Correlation Effect: The TRAP Model', *Journal of Personality and Social Psychology*, 71: 845–60.

Garcia-Marques, L., Hamilton, D.L., and Maddox, K.B. (2002) 'Exhaustive and Heuristic Retrieval Processes in Person Cognition: Further Tests of the TRAP Model', *Journal of Personality and Social Psychology*, 82: 193–207.

Gollwitzer, P.M. and Moskowitz, G.B. (1996) 'Goal Effects on Action and Cognition', in E.T. Higgins and A.W. Kruglanski (eds), *Social Psychology: Handbook of Basic Principles*. New York: Guilford, pp. 361–99.

Hamilton, D.L. (1981) 'Cognitive Representations of Persons', in E.T. Higgins, C.P. Herman, and M.P. Zanna (eds), *Social Cognition: The Ontario Symposium* (vol. 1). Hillsdale, NJ: Erlbaum, pp. 135–60.

Hamilton, D.L., Driscoll, D.M., and Worth, L.T. (1989) 'Cognitive Organization of Impressions: Effects of Incongruency in Complex Representations', *Journal of Personality and Social Psychology*, 57: 925–39.

Hamilton, D.L. and Garcia-Marques, L. (2003) 'Effects of Expectancies on the Representation and Use of Social Information', in G.V. Bodenhausen and A.J. Lambert (eds), *Foundations of Social Cognition: A Festschrift in Honor of Robert S. Wyer, Jr.* Hillsdale, NJ: Erlbaum, pp. 25–50.

Hamilton, D.L. and Gifford, R.K. (1976) 'Illusory Correlation in Interpersonal Perception: A Cognitive Basis for Stereotypic Judgments', *Journal of Experimental Social Psychology*, 12: 392–407.

Hamilton, D.L., Katz, L.B., and Leirer, V. (1980) 'Organizational Processes in Impression Formation', in R. Hastie, T.M. Ostrom, E.B. Ebbesen, R.S. Wyer, Jr., D.L. Hamilton, and D.E. Carlston (eds), *Person Memory: The Cognitive Basis of Social Perception*. Hillsdale, NJ: Erlbaum, pp. 121–54.

Hamilton, D.L. and Rose, T.L. (1980) 'Illusory Correlation and the Maintenance of Stereotypic Beliefs', *Journal of Personality and Social Psychology*, 39: 832–45.

Hamilton, D.L. and Sherman, S.J. (1989) 'Illusory Correlations: Implications for Stereotype Theory and Research', in D. Bar-Tal, C.F. Graumann, A.W. Kruglanski, and W. Stroebe (eds), *Stereotypes and Prejudice: Changing Conceptions*. New York: Springer-Verlag. pp. 59–82.

Hamilton, D.L. and Sherman, J.W. (1994) 'Stereotypes', in R.S. Wyer, Jr. and T.K. Srull (eds), *Handbook of Social Cognition* (vol. 2). *Applications*, 2nd edn. Hillsdale, NJ: Erlbaum, pp. 1–68.

Hamilton, D.L. and Sherman, S.J. (1996) 'Perceiving Persons and Groups', *Psychological Review*, 103: 336–55.

Hastie, R. (1980) 'Memory for Behavioral Information that Confirms or Contradicts a Personality Information', in R. Hastie, T.M. Ostrom, E.B. Ebbesen, R.S. Wyer, Jr., D.L. Hamilton, and D.E. Carlston (eds), *Person Memory: The Cognitive Basis of Social Perception*. Hillsdale, NJ: Erlbaum, pp. 155–77.

Hastie, R. (1983) 'Social Inference', *Annual Review of Psychology*, 34: 511–42.

Hastie, R. (1984) 'Cause and Effects of Causal Attribution', *Journal of Personality and Social Psychology*, 46: 44–56.

Hastie, R. and Kumar, P.A. (1979) 'Person Memory: Personality Traits as Organizing Principles in Memory for Behaviors', *Journal of Personality and Social Psychology*, 37: 25–38.

Hastie, R. and Park, B. (1986) 'The Relationship Between Memory and Judgment Depends on Whether the Judgment Task is Memory-Based or On-line', *Psychological Review*, 93: 258–68.

Higgins, E.T. (1996) 'Knowledge Activation: Accessibility, Applicability and Salience', in E.T. Higgins and A.W. Kruglanski (eds), *Social Psychology: Handbook of Basic Principles*. New York: Guilford, pp. 133–67.

Higgins, E.T. (1998) 'The Aboutness Principle: A Pervasive Influence on Human Inference', *Social Cognition: Special Issue: Naïve Theories and Social Judgment*, 16: 173–98.

Higgins, E.T. and Bargh, J.A. (1987) 'Social Cognition and Social Perception', *Annual Review of Psychology*, 38: 369–425.

Higgins, E.T., Bargh, J.A., and Lombardi, W. (1985) 'The Nature of Priming Effects in Categorization', *Journal of Experimental Psychology: Learning, Memory and Cognition*, 11: 59–69.

Higgins, E.T., King, G.A., and Mavin, G.A. (1982) 'Individual Construct Accessibility and Subjective Impressions and Recall', *Journal of Personality and Social Psychology*, 43: 35–47.

Higgins, E.T., Rholes, W.S., and Jones, C.R. (1977) 'Category Accessibility and Impression Formation', *Journal of Experimental Social Psychology*, 13: 141–54.

Higgins, E.T. and Tykocinski, O. (1992) 'Self-Discrepancies and Biographical Memory: Personality and Cognition at the Level of Psychological Situation', *Personality and Social Psychology Bulletin*, 18: 527–35.

Hirt, E.R. (1990) 'Do I See Only What I Expect? Evidence for an Expectancy-Guided Retrieval Model', *Journal of Personality and Social Psychology*, 58: 937–51.

Hirt, E.R., Erickson, G.A., and McDonald, H.E. (1993) 'Role of Expectancy Timing and Outcome Consistency in Expectancy-Guided Retrieval', *Journal of Personality and Social Psychology*, 65: 640–56.

Jacoby, L.L., Allan, L.G., Collins, J.C., and Larwill, L.K. (1988) 'Memory Influences Subjective Experience: Noise Judgments', *Journal of Experimental Psychology: Learning, Memory and Cognition*, 14: 240–7.

Jacoby, L.L. and Dallas, M. (1981) 'On the Relation Between Autobiographical Memory and Perceptual Learning', *Journal of Experimental Psychology: General*, 3: 306–40.

Jacoby, L.L. and Kelley, C.M. (1987) 'Unconscious Influences of Memory for a Prior Event', *Personality and Social Psychology Bulletin*, 13: 314–36.

Jacoby, L.L., Kelley, C.M., Brown, J., and Jasechko, J. (1989a) 'Becoming Famous Overnight: Limits on the Ability to Avoid Unconscious Influences of the Past', *Journal of Personality and Social Psychology*, 56: 326–38.

Jacoby, L.L., Kelley, C.M., and Dywan, J. (1989b) 'Memory Attributions', in H.L. Roediger and F.I.M. Craik (eds), *Varieties of Memory and Consciousness: Essays in Honour of Endel Tulving*. Hillsdale, NJ: Erlbaum, pp. 391–422.

Jacoby, L.L., Woloshin, V., and Kelley, C.M. (1989c) 'Becoming Famous Without Being Recognized: Unconscious Influences of Memory Produced by Dividing Attention', *Journal of Experimental Psychology: General*, 118: 115–25.

Johnson, M.K. and Raye, C.L. (1981) 'Reality Monitoring', *Psychological Review*, 88: 67–85.

Kihlstrom, J.F. and Cantor, N. (1984) 'Mental Representations of the Self', in L. Berkowitz (ed.), *Advances in Experimental Social Psychology* (vol. 21). New York: Academic Press, pp. 145–80.

Kihlstrom, J.F. and Klein, S.B. (1994) 'The Self as a Knowledge Structure', in R.J. Wyer, Jr. and T.K.Srull (eds), *Handbook of Social Cognition* (vol. 1). *Basic Processes*, 2nd edn. Hillsdale, NJ: Erlbaum, pp. 153–208.

Klein, S.B. and Kihlstrom, J.F. (1986) 'Elaboration, Organization, and the Self-Reference Effect in Memory', *Journal of Experimental Psychology: General*, 115: 26–38.

Klein, S.B. and Loftus, J. (1988) 'The Nature of Self-Referent Encoding: The Contributions of Elaborative and Organizational Processes', *Journal of Personality and Social Psychology*, 55: 5–11.

Klein, S.B. and Loftus, J. (1990) 'Rethinking the Role of Organization in Person Memory: An Independent Trace Storage Model', *Journal of Personality and Social Psychology*, 59: 400–10.

Klein, S.B. and Loftus, J. (1993) 'The Mental Representation of Traits and Autobiographical Knowledge About the Self', in T.K. Srull and R.S. Wyer, Jr., *Advances in Social Cognition* (vol. 5). Hillsdale, NJ: Erlbaum, pp. 1–49.

Lecky, P. (1945) *Self-Consistency: A Theory of Personality*. Washington, DC: Island Press.

Lichtenstein, S., Slovic, P., Fischhoff, B., Layman, M., and Coombs, B. (1978) 'Judged Frequency of Lethal Events', *Journal of Experimental Psychology: Human Learning and Memory*, 4: 551–78.

Lichtenstein, M. and Srull, T.K. (1987) 'Processing Objectives as a Determinant of the Relationship Between Recall and Judgment', *Journal of Experimental Social Psychology*, 23: 93–118.

Lickel, B., Hamilton, D.L., Wieczorkowska, G., Lewis, A., Sherman, S.J., and Uhles, A.N. (2000) 'Varieties of Groups and the Perception of Group Entitativity', *Journal of Personality and Social Psychology*, 78: 223–46.

Lingle, J.H. and Ostrom, T.M. (1979) 'Retrieval Selectivity in Memory-Based Impression Judgments', *Journal of Personality and Social Psychology*, 37: 180–94.

Linville, P.W., Fischer, G.W., and Salovey, P. (1989) 'Perceived Distributions of the Characteristics of In-Group and Out-Group Members: Empirical Evidence and a Computer Simulation', *Journal of Personality and Social Psychology*, 57: 165–88.

Loftus, E.F. (1975) 'Leading Questions and the Eyewitness Report', *Cognitive Psychology*, 7: 560–72.

Loftus, E.F. (1997a) 'Memories for a Past That Never Was', *Current Directions in Psychological Science*, 6: 60–5.

Loftus, E.F. (1997b) 'Creating Childhood Memories', *Applied Cognitive Psychology*, 11 (Special Issue): S75–S86.

Loftus, E.F. and Hall, D.F. (1982) 'Memory Changes in Eyewitness Accounts', in A. Trankell (ed.), *Reconstructing the Past*. Stockholm: P.A. Norstedt, pp. 189–203.

Loftus, E.F. and Palmer, J.C. (1974) 'Reconstruction of Automobile Destruction: An Example of the Interaction Between Language and Memory', *Journal of Verbal Learning and Verbal Behavior*, 13: 585–9.

Loftus, E.F. and Pickrell, J.E. (1995) 'The Formation of False Memories', *Psychiatric Annals*, 25: 720–5.

Maass, A. (1999) 'Linguistic Intergroup Bias: Stereotype-Perpetuation through Language', in M.P. Zanna (ed.),

*Advances in Experimental Social Psychology* (vol. 31). San Diego, CA: Academic Press, pp. 79–121.

Maass, A., Salvi, D., Arcuri, L., and Semin, G.R. (1989) 'Language Use in Intergroup Contexts: The Linguistic Intergroup Bias', *Journal of Personality and Social Psychology*, 57: 981–93.

Macrae, C.N., Bodenhausen, G.V., and Milne, A.B. (1995) 'The Dissection of Selection in Person Perception: Inhibitory Processes in Social Stereotyping', *Journal of Personality and Social Psychology*, 69: 397–407.

Mandler, G., Nakamura, Y., and Van Zandt, B.J.S. (1987) 'Nonspecific Effects of Exposure on Stimuli That Cannot Be Recognized', *Journal of Experimental Psychology: Learning, Memory and Cognition*, 113: 646–48.

Markus, H. (1977) 'Self-Schemata and Processing Information About the Self', *Journal of Personality and Social Psychology*, 35: 63–78.

McArthur, L.Z. and Post, D.L. (1977) 'Figural Emphasis and Person Perception', *Journal of Experimental Social Psychology*, 13: 520–35.

McConnell, A.R., Sherman, S.J., and Hamilton, D.L. (1994) 'On-Line and Memory-Based Aspects of Individual and Group Target Judgments', *Journal of Personality and Social Psychology*, 67: 173–85.

McConnell, A.R., Sherman, S.J., and Hamilton, D.L. (1997) 'Target Entitativity: Implications for Information Processing About Individual and Group Targets', *Journal of Personality and Social Psychology*, 72: 750–62.

McFarland, C., Ross, M., and DeCourville, N. (1989) 'Women's Theories of Menstruation and Biases in Recall of Menstrual Symptoms', *Journal of Personality and Social Psychology*, 57: 522–31.

Newman, L.S. and Uleman, J.S. (1989) 'Spontaneous Trait Inference', in J.S. Uleman and J.A. Bargh (eds), *Unintended Thought*. New York: Guilford. pp. 155–88.

Olson, J.M., Roese, N.J., and Zanna, M.P. (1996) 'Expectancies', in E.T. Higgins and A.W. Kruglanski (eds), *Social Psychology: Handbook of Basic Principles*. New York: Guilford, pp. 211–38.

Park, B. and Hastie, R. (1987) 'Perception of Variability in Category Development: Instance- Versus Abstraction-Based Stereotypes', *Journal of Personality and Social Psychology*, 53: 621–35.

Reyes, R.M., Thompson, W.C., and Bower, G.H. (1980) 'Judgmental Biases Resulting from Differing Availabilities of Arguments', *Journal of Personality and Social Psychology*, 39: 2–12.

Richardson-Klavehn, A. and Bjork, R.A. (1988) 'Measures of Memory', *Annual Review of Psychology*, 39: 475–543.

Rogers, T.B., Kuiper, N.A. and Kirker, W.S. (1977) 'Self-Reference and the Encoding of Personal Information', *Journal of Personality and Social Psychology*, 35: 677–88.

Ross, L., Lepper, M.R., and Hubbard, M. (1975) 'Perseverance in Self-Perception and Social Perception: Biased Attributional Processes in the Debriefing Paradigm', *Journal of Personality and Social Psychology*, 32: 880–92.

Ross, M., McFarland, C., and Fletcher, G.J. (1981) 'The Effect of Attitude on the Recall of Personal Histories', *Journal of Personality and Social Psychology*, 40: 627–34.

Ross, M. and Sicoly, F. (1979) 'Egocentric Biases in Availability and Attribution', *Journal of Personality and Social Psychology*, 37: 322–37.

Rothbart, M., Evans, M., and Fulero, S. (1979) 'Recall for Confirming Events: Memory Processes and the Maintenance of Social Stereotypes', *Journal of Experimental Social Psychology*, 15: 343–55.

Rothman, A.J. and Salovey, P. (1997) 'Shaping Perceptions to Motivate Healthy Behavior: The Role of Message Framing', *Psychological Bulletin*, 121: 3–19.

Schwarz, N., Bless, H., Strack, F., Klumpp, G., Rittenauer-Achatka, H., and Simon, A. (1991) 'Ease of Retrieval as Information: Another Look at the Availability Heuristic', *Journal of Personality and Social Psychology*, 61: 195–202.

Semin, G.R. and Fiedler, K. (1988) 'The Cognitive Functions of Linguistic Categories in Describing Persons: Social Cognition and Language', *Journal of Personality and Social Psychology*, 54: 558–68.

Semin, G.R. and Greenslade, L. (1985) 'Differential Contributions of Linguistic Factors to Memory-Based Ratings: Systematizing the Systematic Distortion Hypothesis', *Journal of Personality and Social Psychology*, 49: 1713–23.

Sherman, J.W. (1996) 'Development and Mental Representation of Stereotypes', *Journal of Personality and Social Psychology*, 70: 1126–41.

Sherman, J.W. and Frost, L.A. (2000) 'On the Encoding of Stereotype-Relevant Information Under Cognitive Load', *Personality and Social Psychology Bulletin*, 26: 26–34.

Sherman, J.W. and Hamilton, D.L. (1994) 'On the Formation of Interitem Associative Links in Person Memory', *Journal of Experimental Social Psychology*, 30: 203–17.

Sherman, S.J., Castelli, L., and Hamilton, D.L. (2002) 'The Spontaneous Use of a Group Typology as an Organizing Principle in Memory', *Journal of Personality and Social Psychology*, 82: 328–42.

Sherman, S.J., Cialdini, R.B., Schwartzman, D.F., and Reynolds, K.D. (1985) 'Imagining Can Heighten or Lower the Perceived Likelihood of Contracting a Disease: The Mediating Effect of Ease of Imagery', *Personality and Social Psychology Bulletin*, 118–27.

Sherman, S.J., Mackie, D.M., and Driscoll, D.M. (1990) 'Priming and the Differential Use of Dimensions in Evaluation', *Personality and Social Psychological Bulletin*, 16: 405–18.

Sherman, S.J., McMullen, M.N., and Gavanski, I. (1992) 'Natural Sample Spaces and the Inversion of Conditional Judgments', *Journal of Experimental Social Psychology*, 28: 401–21.

Skowronski, J.J., Carlston, D.E., and Isham, J.T. (1993) 'Implicit Versus Explicit Impression Formation: The Differing Effects of Overt Labeling and Covert Priming on Memory and Impressions', *Journal of Experimental Social Psychology*, 29: 17–41.

Skowronski, J.J., Carlston, D.E., Mae, L., and Crawford, M.T. (1998) 'Spontaneous Trait Transference: Communicators Take on the Qualities They Describe in Others', *Journal of Personality and Social Psychology*, 74: 837–48.

Slusher, M.P. and Anderson, C.A. (1987) 'When Reality Monitoring Fails: The Role of Imagination in Stereotype Maintenance', *Journal of Personality and Social Psychology*, 52: 653–62.

Smith, E.R. and DeCoster, J. (1998) 'Person Perception and Stereotyping: Simulation Using Distributed Representations in a Recurrent Connectionist Network', in S.J. Read and L.C. Miller (eds), *Connectionist Models of Social Reasoning and Social Behavior*. Mahwah, NJ: Erlbaum, pp. 111–40.

Smith, E.R., Fazio, R.H., and Cejka, M.A. (1996) 'Accessible Attitudes Influence Categorization of Multiply Categorizable Objects', *Journal of Personality and Social Psychology*, 71: 888–98.

Smith, E.R. and Queller, S. (1999) 'Mental Representations', in G.J.O. Fletcher and M.S. Clark (eds), *Blackwell Handbook in Social Psychology* (vol. 1). *Intraindividual Processes*. Oxford: Blackwell.

Smith, E.R. and Zárate, M.A. (1990) 'Exemplar and Prototype Use in Social Categorization', *Social Cognition*, 8: 243–62.

Smith, E.R. and Zárate, M.A. (1992) 'Exemplar-Based Model of Social Judgment', *Psychological Review*, 99: 3–21.

Srull, T.K. (1981) 'Person Memory: Some Tests of Associative Storage and Retrieval Models', *Journal of Experimental Psychology: Human Learning and Cognition*, 7: 440–62.

Srull, T.K. (1983) 'Organizational and Retrieval Processes in Person Memory: An Examination of Processing Objectives, Presentation Format, and the Possible Role of Self-Generated Retrieval Cues', *Journal of Personality and Social Psychology*, 44: 1157–70.

Srull, T.K., Lichtenstein, M., and Rothbart, M. (1985) 'Associative Storage and Retrieval in Person Memory', *Journal of Experimental Psychology: Learning, Memory and Cognition*, 11: 316–45.

Srull, T.K. and Wyer, R.S., Jr. (1979) 'The Role of Category Accessibility in the Interpretation of Information about Persons: Some Determinants and Implications', *Journal of Personality and Social Psychology*, 37: 1660–72.

Srull, T.K. and Wyer, R.S., Jr. (1989) 'Person Memory and Judgment', *Psychological Review*, 96: 58–83.

Stangor, C., Lynch, L., Duan, C., and Glass, B. (1992) 'Categorization of Individuals on the Basis of Multiple Social Features', *Journal of Personality and Social Psychology*, 62: 207–18.

Stangor, C. and McMillan, D. (1992) 'Memory for Expectancy-Congruent and Expectancy-Incongruent Information: A Review of the Social and Social Developmental Literatures', *Psychological Bulletin*, 111: 42–61.

Stern, L., Marrs, S., Millar, M., and Cole, E. (1984) 'Processing Time and the Recall of Inconsistent and Consistent Behaviors of Individuals and Groups', *Journal of Personality and Social Psychology*, 47: 253–62.

Stroessner, S.J. (1996) 'Social Categorization by Race or Sex: Effects of Perceived Non-Normalcy on Response Times', *Social Cognition*, 14: 247–76.

Stroessner, S.J. and Plaks, J.E. (2001) 'Illusory Correlation and Stereotype Formation: Tracing the Arc of Research over a Quarter Century', in G.B. Moskowitz (ed.), *Cognitive Social Psychology: The Princeton Symposium on the Legacy and Future of Social Cognition*. Mahwah, NJ: Erlbaum, pp. 247–59.

Susskind, J., Maurer, K., Thakkar, V., Hamilton, D.L., and Sherman, J.W. (1999) 'Perceiving Individuals and Groups: Expectancies, Dispositional Inferences and Causal Attributions', *Journal of Personality and Social Psychology*, 76: 181–91.

Tajfel, H. (1969) 'Cognitive Aspects of Prejudice', *Journal of Social Issues*, 25: 79–97.

Taylor, S.E. and Fiske, S.T. (1978) 'Salience, Attention and Attribution: Top of the Head Phenomena', *Advances in Experimental Social Psychology*, 11: 249–88.

Taylor, S.E., Fiske, S.T., Etcoff, N.L., and Ruderman, A.J. (1978) 'Categorical and Contextual Bases of Person Memory and Stereotyping', *Journal of Personality and Social Psychology*, 36: 778–93.

Thompson, S.C. and Kelley, H.H. (1981) 'Judgments of Responsibility for Activities in Close Relationships', *Journal of Personality and Social Psychology*, 41: 469–77.

Tulving, E. and Thompson, D.M. (1973) 'Encoding Specificity and Retrieval Processes in Episodic Memory', *Psychological Review*, 80: 352–73.

Tversky, A. and Kahneman, D. (1973) 'Availability: A Heuristic for Judging Frequency and Probability', *Cognitive Psychology*, 5: 207–32.

Tversky, A. and Kahneman, D. (1981) 'The Framing of Decisions and the Psychology of Choice', *Science*, 211: 453–58.

Uleman, J.S., Newman, L., and Winter, L. (1992) 'Can Personality Traits Be Inferred Automatically? Spontaneous Inferences Require Cognitive Capacity at Encoding', *Consciousness and Cognition*, 1: 77–90.

Welbourne, J.L. (1999) 'The Impact of Perceived Entitivity on Inconsistency Resolution for Groups and Individuals', *Journal of Experimental Social Psychology*, 35: 481–508.

Wilson, A.E., and Ross, M. (2000) 'The Frequency of Temporal-Self and Social Comparisons in People's Personal Appraisals', *Journal of Personality and Social Psychology*, 78: 928–42.

Winter, L. and Uleman, J.S. (1984) 'When Are Social Judgments Made? Evidence for the Spontaneousness of Trait Inferences', *Journal of Personality and Social Psychology*, 47: 237–52.

Witherspoon, D. and Allan, L.G. (1985) 'Time Judgments and the Repetition Effect in Perceptual Identification', *Memory and Cognition*, 13: 101–11.

Wyer, R.S., Jr., Bodenhausen, G., and Srull, T.K. (1984) 'The Cognitive Representation of Persons and Groups and Its Effects on Recall and Recognition Memory', *Journal of Experimental Social Psychology*, 20: 445–69.

Wyer, R.S., Jr. and Carlston, D.E. (1994) 'The Cognitive Representation of Persons and Events', in R.J. Wyer, Jr. and T.K. Srull (eds), *Handbook of Social Cognition* (vol. 1). *Basic Processes*, 2nd edn. Hillsdale, NJ: Erlbaum, pp. 41–98.

Wyer, R.S., Jr. and Gordon, S.E. (1982) 'The Recall of Information about Persons and Groups', *Journal of Experimental Social Psychology*, 18: 128–64.

Wyer, R.S., Jr. and Gordon, S.E. (1984) 'The Effects of Predicting a Person's Behavior on Subsequent Trait Judgments', *Journal of Experimental Social Psychology*, 20: 29–46.

Wyer, R.S., Jr. and Martin, L.L. (1986) 'Person Memory: The Role of Traits, Group Stereotypes and Specific Behaviors in the Cognitive Representation of Persons', *Journal of Personality and Social Psychology*, 50: 661–75.

Wyer, R.S., Jr. and Srull, T.K. (1989) *Memory and Cognition in Its Social Context*. Hillsdale, NJ: Erlbaum.

Zadny, J. and Gerard, H.B. (1974) 'Attributed Intentions and Informational Selectivity', *Journal of Experimental Social Psychology*, 10: 34–52.

Zajonc, R.B. (1968) 'Attitudinal Effects of Mere Exposure', *Journal of Personality and Social Psychology*, 9: 1–27.

Zárate, M.A. and Smith, E.R. (1990) 'Person Categorization and Stereotyping', *Social Cognition*, 8: 161–85.

# 4

# Stereotyping and Impression Formation: How Categorical Thinking Shapes Person Perception

KIMBERLY A. QUINN, C. NEIL MACRAE, AND GALEN V. BODENHAUSEN

**INTRODUCTION**

To engage in successful social interaction, we must form impressions that capture other people's characteristics coherently and meaningfully. What is perhaps most remarkable about this process is the ease with which it is accomplished: Impressions often spring to mind so readily that they seem to directly reflect the immediately obvious, objective characteristics of the target person, without any active inferential construction or bias on our part. In reality, however, research on impression formation has revealed a complex series of mental processes – most notably, stereotyping – that are involved in construing the character of others and the meaning of their behavior.

In everyday life, we are repeatedly confronted with people with whom we must interact. In order to accomplish this goal, however, we must form an impression that captures the other person's characteristics in a coherent and meaningful manner. What is perhaps most remarkable about this process of impression formation is the ease and rapidity with which it is accomplished. Impressions often spring to mind so readily that it seems as though they directly reflect the immediately obvious, objective characteristics of the target person, without any active inferential construction of the impression on our part.

In reality, research on impression formation has revealed a complex series of mental processes that are involved in construing the character of others and the meaning of their behavior. Impression formation begins with the observation of a target person by the social perceiver. This observation leads to the identification and categorization of the target's behavior. Through a process of attribution, this behavioral categorization leads to a characterization or inference about the actor, and these inferences may or may not be moderated by a process of correction in which the perceiver considers other (perhaps situational) factors that might have produced the behavior. Through a process of integration, the various inferences that are drawn about the behavior are combined into a coherent, organized impression of the target.

Consider, for a moment, what kind of impression you may form of the first author's great aunt. She is an elderly woman, short, somewhat overweight, with stooped posture. She walks with a cane, wears thick-rimmed black glasses, and is soft-spoken. She never married, has no children, and has no family in the community in which she lives. She has very little money. Knowing all of this, you would probably expect her to be lonely and unhappy. As it turns out, however, Aunt Gertrude is a very caring, understanding individual who always appears to be satisfied. But how can this be? A brief interaction with

Aunt Gertrude may be sufficient to resolve this puzzle. Aunt Gertrude is a Catholic nun who has devoted her life to charity. The immediate visual evidence provided by her nun's habit is all that it would take to enable you to make sense of her various attributes and to form a coherent impression of her. But the story is more complex. Aunt Gertrude loves romance novels, even the very sexy ones, the ones with cover illustrations of handsome men, shirtless and flexing under the adoring gaze of semiclad women. She absolutely devours them (the novels, that is!). How, then, can this revealing bit of information be reconciled with your impression of sweet, chaste, elderly Sister Gertrude?

## Stereotypes and efficient person perception

Even simple examples such as the case of Aunt Gertrude underscore the complexity of the task facing social perceivers in considering the overwhelming amount of information that is available in our complex social world. In recognition of this complexity, recent approaches to impression formation have converged on a set of working assumptions, the most basic of which is that perceivers prefer simple, well-structured impressions (Bodenhausen and Macrae, 1994) and that they achieve this coherence by regularly constructing and using categorical representations (such as stereotypes) in their attempts to understand others. By construing others not in terms of their unique constellations of attributes and inclinations but, rather, on the basis of the social categories to which they belong (such as race, age, sex, or occupation), perceivers can make use of the wealth of related stereotype-based mateial that resides in long-term memory. As Gilbert and Hixon (1991: 509) have noted, 'the ability to understand new and unique individuals in terms of old and general beliefs is … among the handiest tools in the social perceiver's kit'.

A wealth of research has documented that when a particular categorization is made and associated stereotypes are activated, they influence impressions both directly and indirectly. The direct influences come from the activation of stereotypic beliefs themselves, which may be added (or averaged) into one's general impression of the target. More interesting, however, are the indirect effects that emerge when activated stereotypic concepts influence the selection and interpretation of other available information. Stereotypes appear to direct attention and influence which information gets encoded and how information is interpreted, such that people often notice instances that confirm their existing stereotype-based beliefs (Bodenhausen, 1988; Chapman and Chapman, 1967, 1969; Higgins and Bargh, 1987; Rothbart et al., 1979), interpret ambiguous information as confirming their stereotypes (Darley and Gross, 1983; Duncan, 1976; Jacobs and Eccles, 1992; Jones, 1990), and actively seek information that confirms their view of others (Snyder and Swann, 1978).

The guiding assumption of contemporary models of impression formation, then, is that whenever we encounter someone and categorize him or her as a member of a particular group, stereotypes about this group will exert an influence on the interpretive processes involved in forming an impression of the person (Bodenhausen and Macrae, 1998; Bodenhausen et al., 1997; Brewer, 1988, 1996; Fiske and Neuberg, 1990; Hamilton et al., 1990; Macrae and Bodenhausen, 2000). This categorical thinking is assumed to shape person perception in at least two important ways: categorical thinking enables perceivers, first, to use the activated knowledge structure to guide the processing (for example, encoding or representation) of any target-related information that is encountered and, second, to rely on the contents of the activated knowledge structure (for example, trait and behavioral expectancies) to derive evaluations and impressions of a target. Thus, at the categorization stage, stereotypes are assumed to be activated along with trait representations and situational scripts, enabling assimilative effects on attention and encoding. At the characterization stage, stereotypes are assumed to influence comprehension of the target's actions, producing assimilative influences on behavioral interpretation and inference generation, and permitting the selective processing of expectancy-consistent information. At the correction stage, it is assumed that social perceivers may attempt to take into account how stereotypes might be biasing their overall impressions. At each of these stages, stereotypes can have both facilitative and inhibitory influences on information processing, alternately enhancing or diminishing the stereotypicality of the system's outputs (Bodenhausen and Macrae, 1998).

## Categorization processes in impression formation: stereotype activation

Central to several influential models of person perception is the notion that the stereotypes associated with social categories are automatically activated in the mere presence of a triggering stimulus (e.g., Brewer, 1988; Fiske and Neuberg, 1990). The origins of this notion can be traced to Allport's (1954) seminal writings on the nature of prejudice. The message that Allport forwarded was straightforward and powerful: to simplify the demands of daily interaction, mere exposure of a stimulus target is sufficient to stimulate categorical thinking and promote the emergence of its associated judgmental, memorial, and behavioral products (that is, stereotyped reactions). According to this account, then, categorical thinking is an unavoidable aspect of the person-perception process. Allport's ideas have enjoyed a revival in recent decades, prompted largely by a landmark paper by Devine (1989). Devine proposed that racial stereotypes are indeed activated automatically upon detection of a person's group membership. She argued that because people are inevitably exposed to the cultural transmission of stereotypical ideas during childhood socialization, social-category membership comes to be inextricably associated with stereotypical notions that spring to mind without any conscious intention on the part of the perceiver.

Supporting this reasoning was work reported by Dovidio et al. (1986). In their research, they presented participants with a category label (such as 'Black' or 'White'), followed by a series of adjectives (such as 'musical' or 'metallic') that were either stereotypical or nonstereotypical with respect to the presented category label. The participants' task was simply to report, as quickly as possible, whether each item could ever be true of the primed category. As expected, participants responded more rapidly when stereotypic rather than nonstereotypical items followed the priming label, suggesting that the categorical representation of the group was activated during the task.

Nonetheless, because the participants' attention was directed toward the category label, this early demonstration failed to provide unequivocal evidence of automatic stereotype activation. However, in a series of more controlled tests of the automatic-activation hypothesis, Devine (1989) demonstrated that even preconscious presentation of racial material was sufficient to prompt the activation of stereotypical concepts. After exposure to preconscious primes pertaining to the category 'African-American', participants later judged an ambiguous target person in a decidedly stereotypical way. In more recent research, preconscious cues have also been shown to precipitate stereotype activation in the domains of sex, age, and occupation (Bargh, 1999).

Following these initial demonstrations, an abundance of experiments emerged in which researchers measured the accessibility of categorical contents (that is, stereotypic traits) after the presentation of priming stimuli, usually (though not always) verbal labels (such as 'Asian'). These subsequent investigations employed a variety of semantic priming techniques that attempted to obscure or conceal the relationship between the experimental primes and target stimuli. The logic of these studies is straightforward: if perceivers are unable to avoid stereotype activation when the triggering stimuli lie outside awareness or are seemingly irrelevant to the task at hand, then evidence of stereotype activation would corroborate the viewpoint that stereotype activation is unconditionally automatic. As it turns out, the available evidence tends to support this view (Bargh, 1999).

### *Conditional automaticity in categorization and stereotype activation*

But does this really signal that stereotype activation is unconditionally automatic in the sense proposed by Allport (1954)? The answer to this question remained unclear, for at least two reasons. First, many of the social stereotypes that had attracted empirical attention were those linked to group memberships that could be discerned from a rudimentary visual appraisal of a stimulus target: sex, ethnicity, and age group. It seemed quite reasonable that perceivers might automatically categorize others into groups on the basis of these readily discernible visual cues; indeed, they have often been referred to as the 'Big Three' in stereotyping (Fiske, 1998), and research on the 'white male norm' hypothesis and related effects does provide evidence that race and sex categorizations occur quickly and effortlessly (e.g., Stroessner, 1996; Zárate and Smith, 1990). Nonetheless, it was less clear whether categorizations based on less rudimentary cues would also elicit mental activation of the stereotypes associated with the group in question.

It was also unclear whether stereotypes were activated automatically by the strict definition of automaticity as involuntary, unintentional, effortless, and unconscious (Bargh, 1989). In fact, under empirical scrutiny, most mental operations fail to satisfy the multiple criteria required to specify a process as exclusively automatic in nature (Bargh, 1990, 1994, 1997; Kahneman and Treisman, 1984; Logan and Cowan, 1984); even prototypic examples of automatic mental processes fail in this respect. As Logan (1989: 70) has remarked, 'automatic reactions can be modulated by attention and intention; they can be inhibited and suppressed; and they can be coherent and planful'. Given this state of affairs, a revised conception of automaticity has emerged in recent years, a conception that emphasizes not the unitary nature of the concept but, rather, the extent to which its various components (that is, awareness, intention, efficiency, and control) are independently implicated in the execution of specific mental operations.

The possibility that stereotype activation is conditionally, rather than unconditionally, automatic has attracted considerable empirical attention in recent years and has engendered heated theoretical debate. Backed by a revised conception of automaticity, researchers have challenged the assumption that stereotypical representations are activated automatically in the presence of a stimulus target. As Bargh (199: 14) has argued, 'as with all preconscious processes, what determines whether the stereotype becomes automatically activated is whether it has been frequently and consistently active in the past in the presence of relevant social group features'. Thus, if there is meaningful variation in the frequency and consistency of people's exposure to stereotypes, there may also be variation in the automatic component of stereotype activation as well. Indeed, this is precisely the message that is beginning to emerge in the literature on the subject.

In one of the earliest challenges to Devine's (1989) argument, Lepore and Brown (1997) demonstrated that people high and low in prejudice respond similarly if stereotypes are activated, but that they respond differently to category activation. Although high- and low-prejudice participants demonstrated equivalent knowledge of the black stereotype and responded to stereotype activation with similarly negative impressions of the target individual, these similarities were not replicated when participants were primed subliminally with the category 'Black'. Following priming of the category label, high-prejudice people exhibited the same negative impression of the target, relative to a control condition; low-prejudice people did not, suggesting that priming 'Black' failed to lead to the activation of the black stereotype (see also Kawakami et al., 1998; Lepore and Brown, 2002; Locke et al., 1994; Moskowitz et al., 1999). More recently, Livingston and Brewer (2002) reported evidence to suggest that even the presentation of black faces, which are presumably more meaningfully linked to the black stereotype than is the label 'Black', do not lead inevitably to activation of the black stereotype.

Indeed, a host of variables have been shown to moderate the supposedly automatic nature of stereotype activation. Many of these variables reside within the social perceiver, influencing both the motivation and the ability to override stereotypical responding. Other variables, however, reside outside the perceiver, in the contextual constraints that make stereotypical information more or less relevant to the task at hand. (For a review, see Blair, 2002.)

### *Cognitive moderators of stereotype activation*

In addition to evidence that prejudice level may moderate the automaticity of stereotype activation, other research has suggested that stereotype activation may also be constrained by a number of cognitive, or capacity-related, factors. One such factor is the perceiver's level of attentional resources. Most notably, Gilbert and Hixon (1991) reported evidence to suggest that stereotype activation may not occur when perceivers are resource-depleted. In their experiments, participants viewed a video depicting an Asian woman turning over a series of cards on which word fragments were written. The participants' task was simply to complete each word fragment with the first word that came to mind. The results demonstrated that participants did indeed tend to choose stereotypical word completions for the fragments (for example, 'rice' rather than 'mice' for '——ice'), but only when they had sufficient attentional resources available to do so. Gilbert and Hixon concluded that stereotype activation is only conditionally automatic, in that its occurrence depends on the availability of attentional resources.

Physiological processes may also moderate stereotype activation through their impact on arousal level and resultant information-processing resources. For example, Macrae et al. (2002a; see also Johnston et al., 2003, 2005) recently provided evidence of hormonal influences on social-cognitive functioning. From evidence that women are more attracted to facial symmetry and masculinity during ovulation, Macrae et al. reasoned that women should similarly be sensitive to category-level (that is, stereotypical) information during periods of high conception risk because of the relevance of this information to potential reproductive success. Indeed, they demonstrated that during high conception risk, women categorized male faces more quickly than they categorized female faces (demonstrating hormonally moderated categorization) and classified male-stereotypical words more quickly than counterstereotypical words (demonstrating hormonally moderated stereotype activation).

### *Motivational moderators of stereotype activation*

Other research has suggested that stereotype activation may also be constrained by motivational concerns (e.g., Blair, et al. 2004; Hugenberg and Bodenhausen, 2004; Richeson and Trawalter, 2005). Several researchers have sought to demonstrate that perceivers' immediate processing goals may be a more potent determinant of stereotype activation than the availability of attentional resources per se. Spencer et al. (1998), for example, have proposed that sufficiently motivated perceivers might be able to activate social stereotypes even under conditions of resource depletion. That is, they have demonstrated that even resource-depleted perceivers are capable of activating stereotypes if such activation can enhance their feelings of self-worth. Participants who received negative feedback responded more quickly to words denoting evaluator-relevant stereotypes than did participants who did not receive negativefeedback, even when they were cognitively busy.

Further evidence for goal-directed stereotype activation can be found in a study by Pendry and Macrae (1996), who demonstrated that the extent of stereotype activation is moderated by perceivers' level of involvement with a target. When relatively uninvolving processing objectives are in place (for example, estimating a target's height), stereotype activation typically occurs at the broadest (that is, superordinate) level of categorization. However, when complex interactional goals are operating (for example, accountability and outcome dependence), a target is categorized both in terms of a higher-order representation (for example, 'woman') and a more differentiated category subtype (for example, 'business woman'). Stereotype activation thus appears to be goal-dependent, with its occurrence contingent on the interplay of both cognitive and motivational forces.

Perceiver goals may also determine the nature of the processing undertaken when a target is encountered, with implications for categorization and thus stereotype activation. Macrae et al. (1997b; see also Wheeler and Fiske, 2005) demonstrated that the encoding operation that is undertaken when a person is encountered is a critical determinant of stereotype activation. Specifically, only the semantic appraisal of a person prompts the relevant categorical knowledge structures; presemantic processing orientations (for example, perceptual goals) are not sufficient to elicit stereotype activation. Thus, participants who judged the animacy of visual targets, determined the presence or absence of a white dot on those targets, or simply reported the detection of the targets were all equally accurate in a subsequent face-recognition task. Nonetheless, only participants who made the semantic (that is, animate-inanimate) judgments displayed stereotype activation.

### *Contextual moderators of stereotype activation*

Stereotype activation is not moderated solely by the contents of the perceiver's mind. Contextual factors also play a role in determining whether stereotypes are activated in the presence of social category members (e.g., Castelli et al., 2004; Plant et al., 2005; Schaller et al., 2003). In particular, the situational context in which category members are encountered provides important input to the categorization process, as was demonstrated recently by Wittenbrink et al. (2001: Experiment 2). They used a sequential priming paradigm (following Fazio et al., 1995) in which participants responded to black and white face primes that were accompanied by positive or negative background scenes (a church interior or a street corner, respectively). The results indicated that in the negative context, black face primes produced disproportionately facilitated responses to negative items, particularly negative stereotypic items. In the positive context, however, there was no evidence of a prejudiced valence bias, suggesting that activation of the negative black stereotype was attenuated by its presentation in a negative-stereotype-incongruent context.

Work by Kurzban et al. (2001) also supports the role of contextual information in determining stereotype activation. Kurzban et al. sought to challenge race as one of the 'Big Three' in social categorization (Fiske, 1998) and to demonstrate that the propensity of social perceivers to categorize according to race is a byproduct of the tendency for race and coalitional friend/enemy status to becorrelated. Kurzban et al. employed the category confusion paradigm (Taylor et al., 1978), asking participants to form impressions of a series of individuals through a set of materials pairing faces (of black and white individuals) with opinions ostensibly expressed by the individuals. In one experiment, the expressed opinions provided cues to 'coalitions' and suggested two allegiances within the set of individuals. In a surprise recall test, participants continued to make more within-race errors than between-race errors, demonstrating a lack of differentiation among blacks and suggesting categorization on the basis of race. However, the same participants also exhibited category confusions on the basis of coalition, albeit less strongly. In a follow-up experiment, physical cues to allegiance were added to the verbal cues; in this case, there was a reversal in the importance of race versus coalition categorization such that race confusions decreased dramatically and coalition confusions increased just as dramatically.

In another examination of how factors outside the perceiver affect stereotype activation, Macrae et al. (2002b) adopted a functionalist approach and speculated that the direction of the target's eye gaze would moderate stereotype activation. They reasoned that eye gaze acted as a cue through which perceivers could assess the relevance of the target, such that eye gaze directed toward the perceiver would be particularly relevant and would impel the perceiver to discern the intentions of the target. Importantly, assessing these intentions would be facilitated to the extent that any relevant information could be accessed, and categorical (that is, stereotypical) information could provide intention-relevant information. Indeed, their research demonstrated that gender categorization was faster for direct-gaze faces than for faces with averted gaze or faces with closed eyes. Furthermore, lexical decisions were faster when gender-stereotypical words were preceded by direct-gaze faces than by laterally averted faces or faces with closed eyes, suggesting that gaze direction moderates both person categorization and stereotype activation. Other evidence also supports the role of target characteristics (e.g., Blair et al., 2002, 2004; Hugenberg and Bodenhausen, 2004; Locke et al., 2005; Maddox, 2004; Maddox and Gray, 2002).

### *Categorization and stereotype activation: the case of multiply categorizable targets*

But what of social categorization in the real world, where category labels are not provided by an experimenter or where the target's identity reflects multiple category memberships? Upon encountering an individual, perceivers must make their own cat-egorization, a categorization that can take many forms depending on the behaviors or features to which the social perceiver attends. Stereotypes will not influence thought or action if they are not activated, and they will not be activated if the target's membership in a stereotyped group is not detected, as may be the case when the target belongs to several groups (for example, gender, ethnic, occupational, and so on).

How does the mind deal with the problem of multiple category memberships? One possibility is that the target will be classified in all possible ways and that each of the applicable stereotypes will be activated simultaneously. Perhaps, then, all of the stereotypes that happen to be associated with these various categorizations will be activated, and from this assortment of associations the perceiver will attempt to produce a meaningful, coherent, and well-structured impression of the target. One recent model (Kunda and Thagard, 1996) suggests that these disparate categorizations, and indeed anything else that is known about the target (that is, individuating information) will be activated simultaneously and will mutually constrain each other's meanings, eventually converging on a summary impression that can best accommodate the various elements composing one's knowledge of the target. When perceivers encounter a multiply categorizable target, all applicable categories are believed to be activated in parallel and a competition for mental dominance then ensues. Contextual salience (e.g., Biernat and Vescio, 1993), chronic and temporary category accessibility (e.g., Smith et al., 1996), comparative and normative fit (Oakes et al., 1991), and temporary goal states (e.g., Pendry and Macrae, 1996) are all factors that are likely to confer an activation advantage to particular categories in such a competition.

This task could be daunting and counterproductive, however. Almost inevitably, some elements of the available information will work against these goals of simplicity and coherence, either by conflicting with other information (for example, the nun known to have taken the vow of chastity, but who was observed to spend many hours reading racy romance novels) or by distracting the perceiver from whatever dominant themes might emerge in her impressions (for example, the nun who displayed behaviors consistent with kindness and charity, but who was also seen to perform an interpretive belly dance). In light of this, recent approaches assume that the process of information selection in impression formation involves not only the facilitation of some information, but also the inhibition of interfering or irrelevant information. In this variation of the parallel-constraint-satisfaction view, 'mutual constraint' refers not only to the contextualization of an attribute's meaning, given other known attributes, but also (under some circumstances) to the active inhibition of some attributes by others. That is, category selection is assumed to be facilitated through the implementation of basic inhibitory processes, such that potentially distracting categorizations are removed from the cognitive landscape through a process of spreading inhibition. The result is an impression that is coherent and straightforward, undiluted by distracting and complicating elements.

Evidence for inhibitory processes in stereotype activation comes from Macrae et al. (1995; see also Dunn and Spellman, 2003). The studies involved the video presentation of an Asian woman who could be categorized in two salient ways (that is, on the basis of sex or ethnicity). In one study, prior to viewing the video and judging its edit quality, participants underwent a parafoveal priming manipulation in which either the category 'woman', the category 'Chinese', or no category was activated. After viewing the video, participants performed an allegedly unrelated lexical decision task in which the critical trials included words that were stereotypical of either women or Asians. With the control condition as a baseline, the data showed evidence of both activation of the primed stereotype and inhibition of the nonprimed stereotype: when the category 'woman' had been primed, participants were both significantly faster to verify stereotypical associates of 'woman' and significantly slower to verify stereotypical associates of 'Asian' than controls. Conversely, when the category 'Chinese' had been primed, participants were both significantly faster to verify stereotypic associates of 'Chinese' and significantly slower to verify stereotypical associates of 'woman' than controls. This basic pattern was replicated in a second experiment in which the salience of the particular categorization was manipulated with contextual cues rather than the parafoveal priming manipulation. (For evidence against category dominance, see Stroessner, 1996; Weeks and Lupfer 2004.)

Interestingly, perceivers' motivational states also seem to play an influential role in the active inhibition of competing social categories (e.g., Kunda et al., 2002). In a provocative demonstration, Sinclair and Kunda (1999; see also Kunda and Sinclair, 1999) demonstrated that after participants received favorable feedback from a black doctor, associates of the category 'black' became significantly less accessible, while associates of the category 'doctor' became significantly more accessible. In other words, when motivated to view the black doctor as competent, participants inhibited the category 'black' and activated the category 'doctor'. They did just the reverse, however, when the black doctor provided negative feedback and they were thus motivated to view him unfavorably, activating the category 'black' and inhibiting the category 'doctor'. Interestingly, a final experiment demonstrated that the tendency to inhibit the black stereotype following positive feedback was present only among high-prejudiced participants, who presumably had more reason than low-prejudice participants to avoid thinking positively of blacks. Motivational factors therefore appear to be as important in the inhibition as in the activation of stereotypes.

## Characterization processes in impression formation: stereotype application

Given the challenges of monitoring a multiplicity of information in the social environment, perceivers may need to be selective in allocating attention. In addition to the problem of allocating limited attentional resources to the range of environmental stimuli available (either in the context or in the multiply categorizable target herself), perceivers are also confronted with the task of disambiguating the stimuli to which they attend. Human behavior is often complex and ambiguous and, therefore, open to multiple plausible interpretations. Stereotypical expectancies provide one way of selecting among competing interpretations and, in so doing, have a number of intriguing effects.

Not surprisingly, when all one knows about an individual is that he or she belongs to a particular social category, the stereotype associated with that category can determine the perceiver's impression of that individual. Thus, a person described only by a male name may, when no other information is available, be viewed as more likely than a person described only by a female name to be characterized by a host of traits associated with masculinity (Heilman, 1984; Locksley et al., 1980). Students described by only their academic majors may be expected to behave differently in ways that are consistent with the stereotypes about their majors (Nisbett et al., 1981). Blacks portrayed only in photographs may be viewed as more superstitious, lazy, emotional, untidy, and immoral than whites portrayed in photographs (Secord et al., 1956).

Stereotypes also appear to influence the perceiver's interpretation of behavior (e.g., Cameron and Trope, 2004; Jones and Kaplan, 2003; Maass et al., 2005; Ottati et al., 2005). When a person known to belong to a particular social category performs an ambiguous behavior, the stereotype associated with that category influences the apparent meaning of the behavior. Thus, a shove may be viewed as more violent when performed by a black individual than by a white individual (Duncan, 1976; Sagar and Schofield, 1980), a mixed performance on an academic test may be considered better when performed by a child of a higher rather than lower socioeconomic background (Darley and Gross, 1983), and the behavior 'hit someone who annoyed him or her' may be interpreted as 'punched an adult' when performed by a construction worker but as 'spanked a child' when performed by a housewife (Kunda and Sherman-Williams, 1993). More recently, D'Agostino (2000) demonstrated that exposure to ambiguous sentences such as 'Some felt that the politician's statements were untrue' led participants later to manifest stereotypical (for example, politician–lied) than nonstereotypical (politician–erred) recall errors, suggesting that stereotypes had influenced the construal of the behaviors.

Stereotypes also influence the meaning that a perceiver assigns to a particular trait. When a trait is used to describe a member of a stereotyped group, its meaning can be influenced by the group's stereotype. That is, the same trait can imply different behaviors when applied to members of different groups. Kunda et al. (1995) found that perceivers rated lawyers and construction workers as equally aggressive but nevertheless held very different expectations about their likely aggressive behaviors: lawyers were viewed as more likely to argue and complain and less likely to punch and yell insults than were construction workers.

Several studies suggest that the assimilative effects of stereotyping extend even to situations in which apparently irrelevant information is available to supplement category membership information (e.g., Hilton and Fein, 1989; Krueger and Rothbart, 1988; Locksley et al., 1980; Raskinski et al., 1985). Darley and Gross (1983), for example, demonstrated that a child was viewed as possessing better liberal arts skills, cognitive ability, and emotional maturity when she was viewed on a brief video in a context implying high, rather than low, socioeconomic background (without the video evidence, however, these differential evaluations of the child did not emerge). Thus, ample evidence has accrued to demonstrate the effects of stereotypes on social judgment (e.g., Biernat et al., 1991; Duncan, 1976; Kunda and Sherman-Williams, 1993; Sagar and Schofield, 1980; Vallone et al., 1985). Similar outcomes have been observed in the context of jury decision-making (e.g., Bodenhausen and Wyer, 1985), and job-applicant evaluation studies (e.g., Heilman, 1984).

As in the case of stereotype activation, stereotype-application effects are moderated by a host of cognitive variables. Some conditions that exacerbate the impact of stereotypical knowledge on judgment and memory include mental busyness (e.g., Macrae et al., 1993; Pendry and Macrae, 1994), task complexity (e.g., Bodenhausen and Lichtenstein,

1987), information overload (e.g., Pratto and Bargh, 1991; Rothbart et al., 1978), time pressure (e.g., Kruglanski and Freund, 1983), and low levels of circadian arousal (Bodenhausen, 1990).

### *Affect and stereotype application*

In general, the cognitive moderators just discussed appear to confer greater importance to the activated stereotypical concepts in social judgment by undermining more evidence-based processing of the stimulus field. The impact of stereotypes on judgment and memory is also exacerbated by certain emotional states (for a review, see Bodenhausen et al., 2001). Initially, this work focused on valence-based mood effects in which the focal comparisons were on the differential effects of negative versus neutral versus positive affective states. An implicit assumption of this approach was the notion that different types of affect within a particular valence (for example, anger, sadness, and fear) produce functionally equivalent effects. Intuitively, one might expect to find that negative moods of any sort would be likely to promote greater use of negative stereotypes, whereas positive moods would have the opposite tendency. These common-sense intutitions, however, have proved to be incorrect.

In general, positive moods appear to increase reliance on heuristics and generic knowledge structures (e.g., Bless et al., 1996a; Isen and Daubman, 1984; Isen and Means, 1983; Ottati et al., 1997; Schwarz et al., 1991; Worth and Mackie, 1987). In contrast, sadness seems to be associated with the avoidance or minimization of the use of heuristics, schemas, and other simplified processing strategies (e.g., Bless et al., 1990; Weary and Gannon, 1996). These findings clearly imply that happiness will likely be associated with greater reliance on stereotypes, whereas sadness may be associated with reduced reliance on them.

Much evidence supports this expectation. In general, category information has been found to exert a stronger effect on the judgments of happy than sad or neutral perceivers in several studies (e.g., Abele et al., 1998; Bless et al., 1996c; Blessum et al., 1998). Bodenhausen et al. (1994a) reported several experiments in which individuals in a positive mood were more likely than their neutral-mood counterparts to judge individual targets in ways that were stereotypic of their social groups. Park and Banaji (2000) showed that happy people are less likely to discriminate accurately among different members of a stereotyped group. Instead, they tend to set a lower threshold for drawing stereotypical conclusions and, hence, are more likely to remember incorrectly that specific group members possessed stereotypical traits.

The fact that positive moods can increase perceivers' reliance on simplistic social stereotypes seems fairly counterintuitive. Closer examination of the relation between happiness and stereotyping, however, has provided some insight into these findings. Schwarz (1990) and Schwarz and Bless (1991) proposed that happy moods signal that everything is fine and that there is little need for careful analysis of the environment. Consequently, happy perceivers may generally prefer to conserve their mental resources rather than engaging in systematic thinking. This line of argument gains some support from evidence that the superficial forms of thinking observed among happy people can be readily eliminated when the situation provides other bases for effortful processing, such as relevance to personal outcomes (Forgas, 1989), accountability to a third party (Bodenhausen et al., 1994a), or task demands (Martin et al., 1993). Relatedly, Bless and colleagues (Bless and Fiedler, 1995; Bless et al., 1996a, 1996b, 1996c) suggested that happy perceivers are often content to rely on their general knowledge and to use it as a basis for constructive elaboration (Fiedler et al., 1991), but that they are reluctant to do so if it proves to be inadequate to make sense of the target (for example, when the available individuating information is unambiguously counterstereotypical, Bless et al., 1996c).

Greater stereotype application under conditions of positive affect has thus been attributed to distraction, a general lack of epistemic motivation, and a generally greater confidence in generic knowledge structures. Happy people are generally neither unwilling nor unable to engage in systematic thinking. Rather, happy people appear to be flexible in their information-processing strategies. Although often content to rely on efficient, simplified bases for judgment (such as stereotypes), they are quite capable of engaging in more detail-oriented processing if personally involved or otherwise motivated for more systematic thinking, or if simplified processing fails to provide a satisfactory basis for judgment.

With respect to sadness, there is less evidence, but the available studies are generally consistent with the idea that sad perceivers do not rely on generic knowledge (e.g., Edwards and Weary, 1993). Bodenhausen et al. (1994a), for example, demonstrated that sad participants did not differ from neutral participants in their tendency to rely on stereotypes. Park and Banaji (2000) found that sad participants were similar to neutral-mood participants in their sensitivity in distinguishing among category members and that they set a more stringent threshold for drawing stereotypic conclusions than did neutral-mood controls.

Complementing their functional analysis of happy moods, Schwarz (1990) and Schwarz and Bless (1991) argued that sad moods suggest to perceivers that their environment is problematic and thereby promote more detail-oriented, careful thinking. Research by Lambert et al. (1997) shows that the fact that sad perceivers are less likely to rely on stereotypes is attributable to their tendency to engage in stereotype correction. Drawing on Schwarz's (1990) analysis, Lambert et al. argued that sadness should induce perceivers to scrutinize the use of stereotypes in the judgment process. Specifically, they assumed that sad perceivers should use stereotypes only in cases in which their use seemed appropriate to the judgment. They found, for example, that sad perceivers were more likely than controls to correct for negative but not positive stereotypes. Presumably, positive stereotypes were not considered an inappropriate basis for judgment. This kind of finding is consistent with the general idea that sad perceivers are likely to be careful, systematic thinkers (e.g., Schwarz, 1990; Weary, 1990), applying stereotypes only when it seems appropriate to do so; otherwise, they seem to take pains to avoid letting such biases influence their judgments.

Importantly, the effects for sadness do not generalize to other negative moods: compared to neutral-mood controls, heightened stereotyping has been observed among both angry (Bodenhausen et al., 1994a; Keltner et al., 1993) and anxious (Baron et al., 1992; Raghunathan and Pham, 1999) individuals, presumably because the accompanying arousal levels interfere with processing capacity.

### *Motivation and stereotype application*

In addition to the role of cognitive and affective moderators of stereotype application, a variety of motivational states also seem to be important. It is fairly well established that epistemic motivation undermines the use of stereotypes. Holding perceivers accountable for their judgments (e.g., Bodenhausen et al., 1994a), placing perceivers in a position of interdependence with (or dependence on) the target (e.g., Fiske and Dépret, 1996), and making the judgment personally relevant or important to the perceiver (e.g., Kruglanski and Freund, 1983) also motivate perceivers to invest more effort in the judgmental process and lead to less stereotypical judgments. Causal uncertainty appears to have similar effects (Weary et al., 2001), as does experiencing a loss of control (Pittman and D'Agostino, 1989) and holding nonprejudiced attitudes (Wyer, 2004).

In contrast, other motivational states such as prescriptive norms (Gill, 2004), prejudice (Hugenberg and Bodenhausen, 2003; Kawakami et al., 2002), and the need for ego defense serve to enhance the use of stereotypes in judgment. Sinclair and Kunda (2000), for example, demonstrated that participants viewed women as less competent than men after receiving negative, but not positive, evaluations from them, suggesting that participants' motivation to protect their self-views led them to use an available stereotype that they would not have used in the absence of this motivation (for similar arguments, see also Fein and Spencer, 1997; Spencer et al., 1998).

'Social judgeability' concerns also moderate stereotype application: unless perceivers believe there is a legitimate informational basis for a stereotypical judgment (whether or not such a basis exists), they are unlikely to report category-based (that is, stereotypic) assessments. When the only information that is available to perceivers is the target's category membership or when the additional noncategorical information is deemed irrelevant to the judgment, perceivers are reluctant to rely on stereotypes. When additional pseudorelevant or subjectively individuating information is available, however, perceivers do allow stereotypic information to contribute to their judgments. Thus, perceivers render more stereotypical judgments only to the extent that their stereotypes are not perceived as being the main source of information for the judgments and to the extent that they feel entitled to judge the target (e.g., Yzerbyt et al., 1994, 1997, 1998).

Finally, implicit theories of personality influence stereotype application: people who hold an 'entity' theory of human nature (and believe that traits are fixed and enduring) are more likely to render stereotypical judgments than are people who hold an 'incremental' theory (and believe that traits are malleable, Levy and Dweck, 1999; Levy et al., 1998; see Bastian and Haslam, 2006, for an alternative perspective). Theories about particular stereotypes also have implications for the construal of social information. In three studies, Wittenbrink et al. (1997; see also Wittenbrink et al., 1998) demonstrated that specific causal assumptions about the underlying socioeconomic disadvantage among African-Americans (as either personal or structural) influenced participants' construal of causality in a situation that involved a black target and that interfering with participants' ability to integrate the available information into a coherent representation on encoding reduced substantially the stereotyping effects. In a trial simulation, ascriptions of personal (rather than structural) causality of black disadvantage led to more guilty verdicts, longer sentencing recommendations, and more stereotypical trait ratings of the black defendant – but only when participants were able to integrate the presented information.

### *Processes in stereotype application*

An expansive literature has thus confirmed Walter Lippmann's (1922) suggestion that stereotype application is likely to occur when a perceiver lacks the motivation, time, or cognitive capacity to think deeply (and accurately) about others. The general pattern is that judgment becomes more stereotypical when either motivation or capacity is depleted, as long as there is not a demonstrably poor fit between the stereotypical expectations and the available target information. But what is the mechanism or process underlying these effects? Certainly, much of the evidence reviewed here suggests that interpretation is biased in the direction of the available stereotype. However, work by Bodenhausen (1988) has demonstrated that selective processing also contributes to the apparent assimilative effects of stereotype activation. In a series of studies, Bodenhausen compared biased interpretation and selective processing accounts of stereotyping. The biased interpretation account implies that the activation of a stereotype may lead perceivers to interpret all newly encountered information in a more stereotypical manner than they otherwise would. The selective processing account, however, implies that the activation of a stereotype may lead to differential processing of newly encountered evidence, favoring information that is consistent (rather than inconsistent) with the implications of the stereotype.

In the context of a mock-jury decision-making task, participants read booklets containing information extracted from a hypothetical criminal trial in which the defendant was identified, either at the beginning or end of the transcript, as either Hispanic or ethnically nondescript. After considering the evidence, participants made judgments about the defendant's guilt and rated the relevance of each piece of evidence. After an intervening task, a surprise recall test was administered. Consistent with both the selective processing and the biased interpretation accounts, the results indicated that participants viewed the defendant as more likely to be guilty if he could be stereotyped. Results from the evidence-rating task indicated that participants viewed the evidence as more unfavorable when the defendant was Hispanic than when he was ethnically nondescript. This effect was not contingent on whether the stereotype was activated before or after the evidence was read, however, suggesting that biased interpretation of information as it is encountered could not account for the pattern of guilt judgments. Crucially, participants exhibited preferential recall of incriminating versus exculpating evidence – but only when the stereotype was activated before the evidence was considered, consistent with the selective processing account. A second experiment confirmed the superiority of the selective-processing account over the interpretation account by providing evidence that a manipulation preventing selective processing also eliminated biases in judgment and recall.

### *Processes underlying the functional efficiency of stereotype application*

Together, this abundance of research findings is suggestive of the basic benefits that a perceiver can accrue from the application of categorical thinking, especially during times of cognitive duress. Categorical thinking enables rapid inference generation and the efficient deployment of limited processes resources. But how is this efficiency achieved, and through which processing operations is it realized? According to the 'encoding flexibility model' of Sherman et al. (1998), categorical thinking is efficient because it facilitates the encoding of both stereotype-consistent and stereotype-inconsistent information, particularly when processing resources are limited. Following the activation of a categorical knowledge structure, expected material can be processed in a conceptually fluent manner, even when a perceiver's capacity is low. Any spare processing resources can therefore be directed toward unexpected material, material that is especially difficult to process and comprehend under conditions of attentional depletion. This encoding flexibility is functional because it promotes both stability and plasticity: categorical thinking allows expected information to be easily understood, thereby enabling perceivers to be alert to surprising events and facilitating the execution of an appropriate response.

The benefits of categorical thinking are thus twofold: first, expected material is processed in a relatively effortless manner; second, residual resources are redirected to any unexpected information that is present, enabling perceivers to process (and remember) this potentially important material. Indeed, Macrae et al. (1994c) demonstrated that category activation enables rapid and efficient processing of stereotypical information, relative to nonstereotypical information, and provided some evidence that the efficiency of stereotypes allowed perceivers to devote more attention to other tasks. Macrae et al. (1994b) similarly provided evidence that stereotypes function as resource-saving devices. In three experiments, they demonstrated that participants who were given concurrent goals of forming an impression of a target and completing an unrelated (and stereotype-irrelevant) task performed better on the concurrent task when a stereotype was available to facilitate the impression-formation task than when it was not. Sherman et al. (1998) extended these findings to demonstrate that the efficiency conferred by stereotypes facilitates the processing not only of stereotype-irrelevant information, but also stereotype-inconsistent information (see also Sherman et al., 2003, 2004, 2005; Sherman and Frost, 2000; von Hippel et al., 1993, 1995; Wigboldus et al., 2004).

If both stereotypical and counterstereotypical information is encountered, which kind of information will dominate the perceiver's reactions? In the domain of memory, at least, it is clear that counter-stereotypical information is most likely to dominate subsequent processing, particularly during impression formation (see Stangor and McMillan, 1992, for a meta-analysis, and Ehrenberg and Klauer, 2005, for a multinomial model). This is a benefit of the cognitive system: an ability to deal with the unexpected is conducive to successful social interaction (when Sister Gertrude is observed with one of her romance novels, successful social interaction entails not displaying shock or disapproval). Recognizing the inconsistency confronting them in such instances, social perceivers need to make sense of the situation by resolving the inconsistency between prior expectancies and current actualities. In other words, they must individuate the target, organizing their memories around the individual's personal identity rather than in terms of his or her group membership.

But how exactly do perceivers do this? Recent research has speculated that these two crucial processes in person perception (that is, inconsistency resolution and individuation) come under the purview of executive cognitive functioning, a raft of higher-order cognitive operations that are involved in the planning, execution, and regulation of behavior (Macrae et al., 1999b; Payne, 2005). Indeed, Macrae et al. (1999b) have demonstrated that under conditions of executive impairment, perceivers' recollective preference for unexpected information is eliminated, such that they are no longer able to organize their memories of others in an individuated manner, and they were unable to identify the source of their recollections, particularly when these recollections were counterstereotypical in implication. When attentional depletion did not obstruct executive functioning, however, none of these effects emerged. These findings are theoretically noteworthy because they confirm that it is not attentional depletion per se that obstructs inconsistency resolution and individuation; rather, it is executive dysfunction.

Mather et al. (1999) have also linked stereotyping to executive function, demonstrating that stereotype-related source confusions among elderly participants were correlated with processes based in brain regions typically associated with executive functioning. The finding that elderly perceivers are more prone to false stereotypical memories than are younger participants, and that this effect is mediated by executive function, was recently corroborated by Macrae et al. (2002d). This research demonstrated that when social perceivers 'remembered' information that they never encountered, the information was more likely to be stereotype-consistent than – inconsistent in nature. Importantly, results demonstrated that, among younger participants, this bias in recognition memory was exacerbated by 'executive dysfunction', leading them to exhibit similar memory confusions to those exhibited by older participants (for similar analyses, see Lenton et al., 2001; Sherman and Bessenoff, 1999).

Recently, von Hippel et al. (2000) have linked these memory failures among the elderly to a failure in inhibitory processes, also purportedly governed by executive function. Indeed, Dijksterhuis and van Knippenberg (1996) have provided evidence to suggest that efficient stereotype application does involve both facilitative and inhibitory processes. Specifically, when stereotypical attributes associated with a particular category become activated, it appears that stereotype-inconsistent attributes are actively inhibited. In one study, participants were primed either with a 'soccer hooligan' stereotype or no stereotype and then completed an ostensibly unrelated lexical decision task. In line with previous demonstrations, primed participants were significantly faster to verify stereotype-consistent words, relative to controls. Of greater interest, however, primed participants were also significantly slower to verify stereotype-inconsistent words than were controls. This pattern was replicated in two additional experiments using different procedures to assess trait accessibility. Thus, it appears that once specific stereotypes are activated, they inhibit the processing of inconsistent data (see also Dijksterhuis and van Knippenberg, 1995; van Knippenberg and Dijksterhuis, 1996; Wigboldus et al., 2003).

The application-memory relation, however, is not invariant. Research by Macrae et al. (2002c), for example, suggests that stereotypes do prompt facilitated processing of consistent information and inhibit processing of inconsistent information but that the extent of these effects depends on the strength of association between the categorical cue and its stereotypic associates. More specifically, Macrae et al. conducted research in which strength of association, as reflected in participants' subjective estimates of cue stereotypicality, was manipulated. These studies employed forenames as categorical cues; these names differed in the degree to which they were gender-typed (for example, 'Sarah' is a more familiar female name than is 'Glenda'). A semantic priming study demonstrated that, overall, participants responded more quickly to a stereotype-consistent target (for example, 'cosmetics') and less quickly to a stereotype-inconsistent target word (for example, 'hockey') when the target word was preceded by a gender-typed rather than neutral prime. Notably, however, the facilitation and inhibition effects were somewhat stronger when the primes were strongly, rather than weakly, associated gender-typed forenames. This demonstration underscores a further aspect of stereotype accessibility: not only are stereotypes only conditionally automatic, but they also vary in the extent to which they are activated by categorical cues, with resulting implications for the processing of consistent versus inconsistent information (for earlier evidence that exemplar typicality moderates stereotype activation, see Macrae et al., 1999a).

Evidence is emerging to suggest that the differential possessing of consistent and inconsistent information is also moderated by a host of individual difference variables. Individuals high in need of closure, for example, recall (Dijksterhuis et al., 1996) and draw more trait inferences from (Maass et al., 2005) stereotype-consistent versus stereotype-inconsistent information than do individuals low in need of closure, leading them to judge target groups in a more stereotypical fashion. Need for cognition has also been shown to moderate stereotypical memory and judgment (Crawford and Skowronski, 1998), such that ‘cognitively active’ individuals display enhanced memory for stereotype-consistent information but less evidence of stereotypical judgment than do ‘cognitively lazy’ individuals.

Motivational factors also appear to play a role. In particular, perceiver power leads to differential attention to stereotype-consistent and -inconsistent information, reflecting the differential concerns of the parties involved in the power relationship. More specifically, powerful perceivers attend to the stereotype-consistent (especially negative) attributes of the powerless, presumably to justify the power inequity, whereas powerless perceivers attend to the stereotype-inconsistent attributes of the powerful, presumably to enhance their perceptions of control (Rodriguez-Bailon et al., 2000). Related research has suggested that the stereotyping patterns of the powerful have two bases: a lack of perceived dependence on the powerless, which allows the powerful to ignore the stereotype-inconsistent attributes of the powerless; and a motivation for continued control, which allows them to attend to system-justifying, stereotype-consistent attributes (Goodwin et al., 1998, 2000). Target power also has implications for stereotype application (Sekaquaptewa and Espinoza, 2004).

Just as there are situations in which stereotype activation is likely to have a greater impact on construal processes, there may be a variety of circumstances under which the activation of stereotypical beliefs has little if any impact on construal. One limiting condition on stereotype activation is the presence of target information that is incompatible with stereotypical construals. When the target does not appear to fit the social category well, and this disconfirmatory information is not easily overlooked, he or she may not be subject to stereotypic impressions (for reviews, see Brewer, 1996; Fiske and Neuberg, 1990). Similarly, if diagnostic and nonstereotypical information about a target is readily available and perceivers are motivated and able to process this information, its influence may often dominate construals of the target, thereby minimizing stereotypical influences (for a review, see Kunda and Thagard, 1996). Another set of limiting conditions concerns the ways that perceivers may attempt to compensate for stereotypical biases, often in an explicit effort to avoid unfairly biased or discriminatory responses.

## Correction processes in impression formation: stereotype suppression

The activation and application of stereotypes in no way guarantee that impressions and judgments will themselves be stereotypical. There are various reasons why a person might have the goal of avoiding stereotype use. With the rise of liberal democratic values and awareness of civil-rights issues, there has been a dramatic increase in the endorsement of the principle of egalitarianism. This change in the nature of prejudice (or, at least, its expression) has been recognized within several more contemporary models of prejudice, including symbolic racism (Kinder and Sears, 1981), aversive racism (Dovidio and Gaertner, 1998; Gaertner and Dovidio, 1986), racial ambivalence (Katz and Hass, 1988; Katz et al., 1986), and ambivalent sexism (Glick and Fiske, 1996, 2001). Although these models differ in several respects (for example, in terms of whether perceivers have access to their ‘true’ attitudes), they all acknowledge that perceivers may attempt to prevent the expression of categorical thinking, either because legal sanctions may follow or because stereotyping violates their personal standards of fairness and equality. Whether the motivation arises from societal or personal sources, there may be many conditions in which perceivers desire to avoid the influence of activated stereotypes on their evaluations of others.

The most influential research program investigating the motivation to avoid stereotyping has been conducted by Devine, Monteith, and their associates. Their work proceeds from the assumption that stereotyping is a largely automatic, conditioned process, even in those who deny the veracity of the stereotypes, but that it can be overcome by effortful processes if people are sufficiently motivated. Monteith's (1993) analysis of the self-regulation of stereotyping suggests that when people are committed to egalitarian, nonprejudiced standards and their behavior appears to violate these standards, they experience guilt and compunction and direct their efforts toward reducing this discrepancy (see also Czopp et al., 2006; Peruche and Plant, 2006).

When people become cognizant of the potential for stereotypical bias in their reactions to others, a variety of regulatory procedures can be used. One possible strategy, for instance, is simply to make direct adjustments to social judgments in the direction opposite to that of the presumed bias. More ambitious, however, are self-regulatory strategies whereby perceivers actively attempt to prevent stereotypical thoughts from ever entering into their deliberations. Perceivers may attempt, for instance, to forget the stereotypical information that they believe confronts them. An example of this process comes from research using the directed-forgetting paradigm (Macrae et al., 1997a). In an adaptation of the procedure, participants who had been primed (or not) with a social category were presented with a list of words to learn; this list comprised words that were stereotypical of the social category. At the end of this task, participants were given a second list, comprised of stereotype-irrelevant words. Some participants were instructed that they should learn both lists. Other participants, however, learned that there had been a procedural error and that they should disregard the first list and learn the other.

The results demonstrated that the encoding and retention of stereotypical information are indeed facilitated by stereotype activation, leading to greater difficulty in forgetting the stereotypical materials and interference in remembering the nonstereotypical material. When participants were primed with the category label, they exhibited better recall of stereotypical items (compared to nonprimed participants), regardless of being told to forget them. Moreover, constraining their processing resources further undermined their ability to succeed in their efforts to forget the stereotypical material: contrary to the forgetting instructions, busy, primed participants actually recalled more of the to-be-disregarded stereotypical items than they recalled of the to-be-remembered nonstereotypical items.

These direct attempts at stereotype avoidance implicate the mechanisms of mental control identified by Wegner and his colleagues (e.g., Wegner, 1994; Wegner and Erber, 1992). Their model postulates that the goal of avoiding a certain type of thought (such as a stereotype) is realized by the joint operation of two cognitive processes. The first is a monitoring process that scans the mental environment looking for signs of the unwanted thought. If detected, a second operating process is initiated that directs consciousness away from the unwanted thought by focusing attention on a suitable distracter. Crucially, whereas the monitoring process is assumed to operate in a relatively automatic manner, the operating process is po tulated to be effortful and to require adequate cognitive resources for its successful execution. Thus, detecting the presence of stereotypical ideas is a task that can be accomplished with ease, independently of any other demands that are imposed on a perceiver's processing resources. Replacing these thoughts with suitable distracters, however, is an altogether more demanding affair that can happen only when sufficient attentional resources are available.

One of the ironic aspects of mental control that is specified within this theoretical perspective is that trying to avoid a particular thought may result in its hyperaccessibility. That is, the very act of trying not to think in stereotypical terms may actually increase the extent of stereotype activation. To detect unwanted thoughts, one must keep in mind what it is one is trying to avoid, and so the monitoring process must involve at some level the mental activation of the to-be-avoided material (otherwise there would be no criterion on which to conduct the search of consciousness). Of course, as long as perceivers have adequate resources and consistent motivation, the operating process may be able to keep the focus of attention away from the stereotypical material. But if a perceiver is cognitively busy, distracted, or under time pressure, or, indeed, if the motivation for suppression has been relaxed for any reason, the hyperaccessibility created by suppression efforts may not be checked by the operating process.

Several studies have documented the ironic consequences of stereotype suppression, as manifest in a perceiver's reactions (for example, evaluations, recollections, and behavior) toward stereotyped targets. Macrae et al. (1994a) provided the first demonstrations of stereotype rebound effects in social impressions. In each of a series of studies, participants were asked to view a picture of a target (who, on the basis of visual cues, could easily be categorized as a skinhead) and then write a passage about their impression of him. Half of the participants were instructed further not to rely on stereotypes. Consistent with the view that motivated perceivers with ample processing capacity can successfully regulate their impressions, the passages written by stereotype suppressors were significantly less stereotypical, as rated by independent coders, than those written by control participants. However, the same participants, when later asked to write about a second skinhead (this time without any suppression instructions), produced significantly more stereotypical descriptions of the second target than did control participants. Evidence for the role of stereotype hyperaccessibility came from another experiment (Macrae et al., 1994a: Experiment 3), in which participants completed an ostensibly unrelated lexical decision task following the passage-writing task. Although there was no difference between the control and suppression groups in verifying nonstereotypical words, the suppressors were significantly faster than the control group in verifying the stereotypical words.

Ironic effects of this kind also extend to a perceiver's recollections of stereotyped targets. In another set of studies (Macrae et al., 1996), participants were given an unexpected memory test for the nonstereotypical details of the target description. The results confirmed that following the cessation of a well-intentioned period of suppression, perceivers display a recollective preference (both in recall and recognition) for the stereotypical material they were formerly trying to dismiss, as well as impaired memory for nonstereotypical information.

As is the case with other mental contents, it would appear that an explicit instruction to suppress stereotypes can actually serve to enhance the accessibility of this material in memory, thereby setting the stage for postsuppression rebound effects.

The results of this research also support the assumption that thought suppression is effortful. In the Macrae et al. (1996) studies, participants performed a simultaneous probe-reaction task while listening to the audiotape. This task was designed to assess the attentional load imposed by suppression. In the task, participants were to hit the space bar on the computer keyboard every time an illuminated light bulb appeared on the computer screen; the speed of response on this task is an indicator of the amount of free processing resources available. Probe reaction times were significantly longer among suppressors than among control participants, particularly when the amount of stereotypical material to be suppressed was relatively high, suggesting that they were distracted by their thought-control attempts.

Inhibitory efficiency can also be undermined by such diverse factors as depressive affect and the cognitive changes associated with aging (von Hippel et al., 2000). If the inhibitory system is compromised, whatever the reason, the intention to avoid biased judgments and reactions may backfire, producing even more of the unwanted reaction than would otherwise have been the case. Thus, although the road to stereotype avoidance may be paved with good intentions, without consistent motivation and processing capacity, these laudable goals may be unsatisfied and, indeed, even reversed. With stereotypic concepts highly accessible and no operating process in place to direct attention elsewhere, construals of social targets are driven by stereotype-based preconceptions, often to a degree that is greater than if a perceiver had never sought to suppress the stereotype in the first place.

### *Moderators of stereotype suppression and rebound*

Although a compelling phenomenon with important implications, the generality of stereotype rebound has been questioned (for a review, see Monteith et al., 1998a). One limitation of early research on this topic was that it employed stereotypes that perceivers are not highly motivated to avoid (such as skinheads). Thus, the question remained as to whether rebound effects would emerge for groups where there are strong personal or societal prohibitions against stereotyping (for example, African-Americans, women, and homosexuals). As it turns out, the evidence on this issue is equivocal. Evidence that suppression can increase stereotyping for even socially sensitive groups can be garnered from recent work by Sherman et al. (1997) and Wyer et al. (1998). In each of these studies, racial stereotyping was exacerbated following a period of suppression. However, Monteith et al. (1998b) reported evidence that participants with low-prejudice attitudes toward gays were not susceptible to rebound effects (on either overt or covert measures of stereotyping) following a period of suppression. In contrast, suppression did prompt the hyperaccessibility of stereotypes among participants who were prejudiced toward gays. Moreover, recent work reported by Wyer et al. (2000) suggests that people may be more consistent in their efforts to avoid stereotyping highly sensitive social groups. Because consistency of suppression motivation is an important factor in the avoidance of ironic suppression effects, this work does suggest that rebound effects arising from the suspension of suppression motivation may indeed be less likely when a highly sensitive social category is involved.

Ambiguity also surrounds the conditions under which self-regulatory processes are initiated by perceivers. Despite growing interest in the topic of stereotype suppression, surprisingly little is known about how and when inhibitory processes are spontaneously implemented. A characteristic feature of much of the available research on this topic is that the intention to suppress a particular thought or impulse is provided to participants by the experimenter in the form of an explicit instruction not to think about a particular person in a stereotype-based manner. Although such a strategy offers obvious methodological advantages, it does sidestep a number of important theoretical questions, most notably the spontaneity issue. It is one thing to suppress stereotypes in response to an explicit experimental instruction, but it may be an entirely different matter to do so spontaneously.

So when, exactly, does a perceiver attempt to regulate the expression of stereotypical thinking? Insight into the determinants of uninstructed self-censorship can be gleaned from the work of Devine et al. (1991) and Monteith (1993). Monteith, for example, has shown that attempts at self-regulation are implemented when perceivers experience a discrepancy between their internalized standards and actual behavior. When people are committed to egalitarian, nonprejudiced standards and their behavior apparently violates these standards, they feel guilty, experience compunction, become self-focused, and direct their efforts at reducing this discrepancy. That is, having reacted in an ostensibly prejudiced manner, a perceiver implements self-regulatory procedures in an attempt to avoid a potential repetition of the action. Although this idea has yet to be tested directly, it also seems plausible that self-regulation of stereotyping is likely to be moderated in different ways by internal versus external motivation to respond without prejudice (Plant and Devine, 1998; Devine et al., 2002).

But is the commission of a prejudiced action, or, indeed, the belief that such an action has occurred, a necessary precursor of stereotype inhibition? Recent research would tend to suggest not. Wyer et al. (2000) have suggested that any cue that makes salient social norms (personal or societal) against stereotyping is likely to promote the spontaneous suppression of stereotypical thinking. Indeed, heightened self-focus (that is, self-directed attention) appears to be sufficient to trigger the spontaneous suppression of unwanted stereotypic thoughts. A common experimental finding is that when the self becomes the focus of attention, perceivers are especially likely to behave in accordance with internalized standards and norms; stereotype suppression has also been shown to operate in such a manner (Macrae et al., 1998). Thus, task context, the presence of others, and current information-processing goals are factors that are likely to moderate stereotype suppression (Wyer et al., 2000). Triggered by situational cues, stereotype suppression does not demand a conscious inhibitory intention on the part of a perceiver.

To date, much of the research on stereotype avoidance paints a picture of self-regulation that is disheartening. Wegner (1994), however, has suggested that mental control can improve with practice, whereby effortful processes gradually become more and more automatized and resource independent. Although little research exists to document this progression through the suppression paradigm, research by Kawakami et al. (2000) demonstrates that practice in negating (that is, saying 'no' to) stereotypes can lead to a subsequent decrease in stereotype accessibility. Although it is worth noting that the mechanism underlying Kawakami et al.'s effects is unknown, in that it remains unclear as to whether the negation training decreases the accessibility of the stereotype or (more likely) increases the accessibility of a non-stereotypical response, it is nonetheless encouraging to note that conscientious social perceivers can learn to control their stereotypical responding.

## Where do we go from here?

A fundamental set of questions in social psychology concerns how, why, and when stereotypes influence people's impressions of others. In this chapter, we have attempted to provide at least a partial account of the facilitative and inhibitory mechanisms associated with stereotyping and the conditions under which they influence each stage of the impression-formation process.

The picture is certainly not complete, however, and there is much to be learned about the intricacies of stereotyping and impression formation. The goal of future research in the field will undoubtedly be the accumulation of more detailed and specific knowledge about the boundary conditions and moderators of the various mechanisms reviewed in this chapter. What we are advocating is an integrative approach to these future investigations, one that encourages multiple levels of analysis and that involves a complete theoretical decomposition of stereotyping and the intergroup context.

### *Levels of analysis in stereotyping research*

In a recent review of the literature on stereotyping, prejudice, and discrimination, Fiske (1998) highlighted two levels of analyses that have been invoked to explain stereotyping and prejudice. As Fiske pointed out, many early approaches adopted either the individual or the society as the appropriate level of analysis, emphasizing personality differences (for example, authoritarianism; Adorno et al., 1950) or structural conditions (for example, intergroup contact; Amir, 1969), respectively, as the roots of prejudice and stereotype endorsement. Both of these levels of analysis yielded data that were compelling and informative regarding the motivational and situational concomitants of intergroup conflict. The advent of the cognitive evolution, however, and the motivated cognition approach that followed, both served to situate stereotyping and prejudice more firmly in the mind of the social perceiver. This newer level of analysis is more dynamic than the earlier approaches, in that it examines processes that vary both within and between individuals can account for the psychological underpinnings of responses arising from social, structural, and personality variables.

We advocate adding another level of analysis to our conceptualizations of categorical thinking and person perception: social neuroscience (Cacioppo and Berntson, 1992, 1996; Ochsner and Lieberman, 2001). Acknowledging the obvious necessity of studying overt behavioral and attitudinal responses to answer questions about complex behavior, we nonetheless believe that a complete understanding of the component processes of stereotyping requires the additional specification of how neural systems are organized. At the very least, social psychological theorizing can benefit from theory and findings from neuropsychology and cognitive neuroscience (e.g., Macrae et al., 2002d; von Hippel et al., 2000; Sanders et al., 2004; Zárate et al., 2000). That is, neuroscience data can provide valuable constraints on theory. The functional organization of the brain can suggest specific processes that are recruited by various social-cognitive activities, and the time course of activation patterns can suggest sequencing of those processes. The story of theoretical progress is always a story of establishing better empirical constraints, and this new level of analysis brings a new set of useful constraints to the table.

Adopting the techniques of neuroscience, such as split-brain studies (e.g., Mason and Macrae, 2004), event-related potentials (ERP; e.g., Ito et al., 2004) and functional magnetic resonance imaging (fMRI) may also provide social psychologists with more sensitive measures of constructs of interest. Examples of how research from neuroscientific methods can inform social psychological investigations of prejudice and stereotyping comes from recent studies using fMRI to examine brain activity in the amygdala. Hart et al. (2000), for example, found that white participants exhibited differential activation in the amygdala in response to white versus black faces such that, over time, amygdalar activation in response to white (in-group) faces was attenuated, whereas amygdalar activation in response to black (out-group) faces showed no change. Research by Phelps et al. (2000) demonstrated further that the extent of amygdalar activation exhibited by white participants viewing black versus white faces correlated with the extent to which these participants manifested implicit bias against black versus white stimuli on an implicit association test (Greenwald et al., 1998). Importantly, this correlation is attenuated when the black faces in question belonged to familiar and positively evaluated black celebrities (Phelps et al., 2000) and when perceivers have alternative processing goals (Wheeler and Fiske, 2005). Interestingly, the amygdala is a subcortical structure known to play a role in nonconscious emotional evaluation and learning, especially with regard to fear and threat (LeDoux, 2000). Although it may come as no surprise that implicit bias would be related to fear or threat appraisals, it is potentially more informative that conscious emotional learning does not necessarily implicate the amygdala; this knowledge, which could not be garnered without neuroscientific evidence and techniques, might be useful for understanding the boundary conditions on conscious strategies for stereotype control. (For a review of the social neuroscience of person construal, see Mitchell et al., 2006.)

### *Functional analyses of stereotyping and the intergroup context*

The use of neuroscientific evidence and techniques is but one avenue for future investigation. Advancing our understanding of the moderators of categorical thinking will also benefit from more careful theoretical decomposition of stereotyping and of the intergroup context itself. In an approach somewhat analogous to the components-of-processing approach to the study of memory (Moskovitch, 1994), in which memory tasks are decomposed into (and subsequently investigated according to) the various processes that are believed to be necessary for successful task completion, we advocate a more thorough analysis of the dynamics of social interaction to include not only an analysis of the social perceiver's expectancies and attitudes, but also analysis of the target of perception and of the context in which categorical thinking occurs.

Indeed, this 'component-processing' approach to categorical thinking is already taking hold in social cognition. As we have already reviewed, research by Wittenbrink et al. (2001), for example, has demonstrated the importance of considering the context in investigations of stereotype activation. Researchers have also begun to acknowledge the complexity of social stimuli, relying less on verbal labels and more on visual stimuli (e.g., Barden et al., 2004; Blair et al., 2002, 2004, 2005; Eberhardt et al., 2004; Hugenberg and Bodenhausen, 2003, 2004; Macrae et al., 2005; 2002; Maddox and Gray, Quinn and Macrae, 2005), in recognition that the mere perception of a stimulus person is not always sufficient to trigger a stereotype (Gilbert and Hixon, 1991; Macrae et al., 1995) and that a stimulus person can inevitably be categorized in many ways (Dunn and Spellman, 2003; Macrae and Bodenhausen, 2000; Macrae et al., 1995; Quinn and Macrae, 2005; Sinclair and Kunda, 1999; Smith et al., 1996).

What these examples suggest is encouraging: there is an increasing recognition that understanding the complexity of the social landscape is critical to understanding social cognition, and that empirical investigation should be sensitive to these complexities. Even these studies, however, relied on relatively impoverished stimuli and constrained the categorizations and responses that participants were able to make. As a result, the early evidence for category dominance and contextual variation in stereotype activation provides only a hint of how the informational processing unfolds to address the complexity of the social situation.

The issue goes beyond ecological validity. Social categorization develops in the real world, where the target can be viewed in many ways and where the significance of the target to the perceiver depends on a multitude of chronic and current factors. The component-process analysis that we advocate involves a dissection of the entire social interaction, including the significance of the target to the perceiver not only in general but also in the specific context in which the perceiver encounters the target.

This analysis of the entire context of impression formation may provide insight into many questions in social cognition, including the question of how the social perceiver forms an impression of a multiply categorizable target. Exactly how does the social perceiver cope with the multiplicity of identity? How do perceivers select relevant categories when any given target of perception could be categorized in seemingly infinite ways? How, or how efficiently, do perceivers identify the various features of the target and the various features of the context to their basic security and affiliation goals as well as to any other concurrently active epistemic or directional goals? And once these contextual or motivational factors have been identified, how are they evaluated and ranked?

Do perceivers routinely categorize people simultaneously along multiple dimensions, or does a single category tend to dominate perceptions in many everyday circumstances, as the early evidence suggests? And when a categorization is made – whether the individual is categorized according to one particular group membership or a conjunction of memberships – what happens to the information relevant to the nonchosen categorization?

And what of the role of the particular affect that is experienced during the interaction? Does the target or the context have a particular relation to the perceiver (for example, target as friend versus foe, context as familiar versus unfamiliar) that would elicit particular emotions with predictable cognitive and motivational implications for categorization and stereotype activation? Interestingly, analyses of mood and stereotyping have often been characterized by the type of functionalist analysis we advocate, with theory being derived from assumptions about what the particular emotional state in question would signal to the perceiver (e.g., Clore et al., 2001). The role of affect in categorical thinking can be clarified, however, by extending the analysis from incidental to integral affect; that is, from the impact of affective states that arise for reasons having nothing to do with the intergroup context itself to the impact of affective states that are elicited by the group itself and the social situations within which the group is encountered (Bodenhausen, 1993; see also Bodenhausen and Moreno, 2000; Moreno and Bodenhausen, 2001). Would the findings regarding incidental affect generalize to integral affect? Or are there aspects of integral affect that might augment or diminish the impact of stereotypes on social impressions and behavior? It seems reasonable to expect that the emotions that are experienced directly as a result of an intergroup encounter would be more focused than incidental affect would be and, thus, that integral emotion would be more likely to contribute to relevant appraisal and attribution processes. Would these supplemental processes lead simply to differences in the amount of stereotyping that would be observed? Or would the appraisal involve component processes – such as the alignment of the affective state with the emotional content of the group stereotype – that could change the apparent significance of the affective state and thus the apparent applicability of the stereotype in that context? Investigations of these issues will be important to theoretical progress.

## Conclusion

Although the processes involved in person perception may occasionally backfire, in that they sometimes lead to judgmental and memorial biases and errors, they nonetheless provide the social perceiver with a very handy set of tools for the construction of stable person impressions and the efficient navigation of social interaction. Social perceivers, with little or no effort, spontaneously categorize targets according to their social groups ('Aunt Gertrude is a Catholic nun'), activate relevant group stereotypes ('She's chaste and virtuous'), and use those stereotypes to provide working impressions of those targets. This sequence, however, is not invariant. As our review suggests, a host of variables – chronic and situational, cognitive and motivational – affect the output of person perception at all processing stages, alternately augmenting or reducing the stereotypicality of the final judgment ('But she's not as proper as I would have expected!'). The direction of future research in this area will be to place these various moderators into their functional context, in order to provide a complete account of how the social perceiver manages the myriad goals activated during social interaction.

**SUMMARY**

To facilitate social interaction, social perceivers prefer simple, well-structured impressions of others, and they achieve this coherence by regularly using categorical representations (that is, stereotypes) as a basis for their impressions. By construing others not in terms of their unique constellations of attributes and inclinations but, rather, on the basis of the social categories to which they belong (such as race, age, sex, or occupation), perceivers can make use of a wealth of stereotype-based information stored in long-term memory to guide processing and thus forgo the challenge of processing the full complexity of the social world. This chapter reviews the mental processes (automatic and controlled) that are involved in the categorical construal of others and their behavior, including identification and categorization of the target, reliance on activated stereotypes to guide attention to and comprehension of the target, and attempts to control stereotypes and their influence on impressions and judgment. We review evidence that stereotypes can have both facilitative and inhibitory influences on information processing at each of these stages, alternately enhancing or diminishing the stereotypicality of the system's outputs. In tandem with other cognitive, affective, motivational, and contextual factors, stereotype-based processing facilitates subjectively coherent and meaningful impressions of others.

## References

Abele, A., Gendolla, G.H.E., and Petzold, P. (1998) 'Positive Mood and In-Group-Out-Group Differentiation in a Minimal Group Setting', *Personality and Social Psychology Bulletin*, 24: 1343–57.

Adorno, T.W., Frenkel-Brunswik, E., Levinson, D.J., and Sanford, R.N. (1950) *The Authoritarian Personality.* New York: Harper.

Allport, G.W. (1954) *The Nature of Prejudice.* Cambridge, MA: Addison-Wesley.

Amir, Y. (1969) 'Contact Hypothesis in Ethnic Relations', *Psychological Bulletin*, 71: 319–42.

Barden, J., Maddux, W.W., Petty, R.E., and Brewer, M.B. (2004) 'Contextual Moderation of Racial Bias: The Impact of Social Roles on Controlled and Automatically Activated Attributes', *Journal of Personality and Social Psychology*, 87: 5–22.

Bargh, J.A. (1989) 'Conditional Automaticity: Varieties of Automatic Influence in Social Perception and Cognition', in J.S. Uleman and J.A. Bargh (eds), *Unintended Thought.* New York: Guilford, pp. 3–51.

Bargh, J.A. (1990) 'Automotives: Preconscious Determinants of Thought and Behavior', in E.T. Higgins and R.M. Sorrentino (eds), *Handbook of Motivation and Cognition* (vol. 2). New York: Guilford, pp. 93–130.

Bargh, J.A. (1994) 'The Four Horsemen of Automaticity: Awareness, Intention, Efficiency, and Control in Social Cognition', in R.S. Wyer, Jr. and T.K. Srull (eds), *Handbook of Social Cognition: Basic Processes*, 2nd edn (vol. 1). Hillsdale, NJ: Erlbaum, pp. 1–40.

Bargh, J.A. (1997) 'The Automaticity of Everyday Life', in R.S. Wyer, Jr. (ed.), *Advances in Social Cognition* (vol. 10). Mahwah, NJ: Erlbaum, pp. 1–61.

Bargh, J.A. (1999) 'The Cognitive Monster: The Case Against the Controllability of Automatic Stereotype Effects', in S. Chaiken and Y. Trope (eds), *Dual Process Theories in Social Psychology*. New York: Guilford, pp. 361–82.

Baron, R.S., Inman, M.L., Kao, C.F., and Logan, H. (1992) 'Negative Emotion and Superficial Social Processing', *Motivation and Emotion*, 16: 323–46.

Bastian, B. and Haslam, N. (2006) 'Psychological Essentialism and Stereotype Endorsement', *Journal of Experimental Social Psychology*, 42: 228–235.

Biernat, M., Manis, M., and Nelson, T.E. (1991) 'Stereotypes and Standards of Judgment', *Journal of Personality and Social Psychology*, 60: 485–99.

Biernat, M. and Vescio, T.K. (1993) 'Categorization and Stereotyping: Effects of Group Context on Memory and Social Judgment', *Journal of Experimental Social Psychology*, 29: 166–202.

Blair, I.V. (2002) 'The Malleability of Automatic Stereotypes and Prejudice', *Personality and Social Psychology Review*, 6: 242–261.

Blair, I.V., Chapleau, K.M., and Judd, C.M. (2005) 'The Use of Afrocentric Features as Cues for Judgment in the Presence of Diagnostic Information', *European Journal of Social Psychology*, 35: 59–68.

Blair, I.V., Judd, C.M., and Fallman, J.L. (2004) 'The Automaticity of Race and Afrocentric Facial Features in Social Judgments', *Journal of Personality and Social Psychology*, 87: 763–778.

Blair, I.V., Judd, C.M., Sadler, M.S., and Jenkins, C. (2002) 'The Role of Afrocentric Features in Person Perception: Judging by Features and Categories', *Journal of Personality and Social Psychology*, 83: 5–25.

Bless, H., Bohner, G., Schwarz, N., and Strack, F. (1990) 'Mood and Persuasion: A Cognitive Response Analysis', *Personality and Social Psychology Bulletin*, 16: 331–45.

Bless, H., Clore, G., Schwarz, N., Golisan, V., Rabe, C., and Wölk, M. (1996a) 'Mood and the Use of Scripts: Does a Happy Mood Really Lead to Mindlessness?', *Journal of Personality and Social Psychology*, 71: 665–79.

Bless, H. and Fiedler, K. (1995) 'Affective States and the Influence of Activated General Knowledge', *Personality and Social Psychology Bulletin*, 21: 766–78.

Bless, H., Schwarz, N., and Kemmelmeier, M. (1996b) 'Mood and Stereotyping: Affective States and the Use of General Knowledge Structures', in W. Stroebe and M. Hewstone (eds), *European Review of Social Psychology* (vol. 7). Chichester: Wiley, pp. 63–93.

Bless, H., Schwarz, N., and Wieland, R. (1996c) 'Mood and the Impact of Category Membership and Individuation Information', *European Journal of Social Psychology*, 26: 935–60.

Blessum, K.A., Lord, C.G., and Sia, T.L. (1998) 'Cognitive Load and Positive Mood Reduce Typicality Effects in Attitude-Behavior Consistency', *Personality and Social Psychology Bulletin*, 24: 496–504.

Bodenhausen, G.V. (1988) 'Stereotypic Biases in Social Decision Making and Memory: Testing Process Models of Stereotype Use', *Journal of Personality and Social Psychology*, 55: 726–37.

Bodenhausen, G.V. (1990) 'Stereotypes as Judgmental Heuristics: Evidence of Circadian Variation in Discrimination', *Psychological Science*, 1: 319–22.

Bodenhausen, G.V. (1993) 'Emotions, Arousal, and Stereotypic Judgment: A Heuristic Model of Affect and Stereotyping', in D.M. Mackie and D.L. Hamilton (eds), *Affect, Cognition, and Stereotyping: Interactive Processes in Group Perception.* San Diego, CA: Academic Press, pp. 13–37.

Bodenhausen, G.V., Kramer, G.P., and Süsser, K. (1994a) 'Happiness and Stereotypic Thinking in Social Judgment', *Journal of Personality and Social Psychology*, 66: 621–32.

Bodenhausen, G.V. and Lichtenstein, M. (1987) 'Social Stereotypes and Information-Processing Strategies: The Impact of Task Complexity', *Journal of Personality and Social Psychology*, 52: 871–80.

Bodenhausen, G.V. and Macrae, C.N. (1994) 'Coherence versus Ambivalence in Cognitive Representations of Persons', in R. S. Wyer (ed.), *Advances in Social Cognition: Associated Systems Theory: A Systematic Approach to Cognitive Representations of Persons* (vol. 7). Hillsdale, NJ: Erlbaum, pp. 149–56.

Bodenhausen, G.V. and Macrae, C.N. (1998) 'Stereotype Activation and Inhibition', in R.S. Wyer, Jr. (ed.), *Advances in Social Cognition* (vol. 11). Mahwah, NJ: Erlbaum, pp. 1–52.

Bodenhausen, G.V., Macrae, C.N., and Garst, J. (1997) 'Stereotypes in Thought and Deed: Social-Cognitive Origins of Intergroup Discrimination', in C. Sedikides, J. Schopler, and C.A. Insko (eds), *Intergroup Cognition and Intergroup Behavior*. Mahwah, NJ: Erlbaum, pp. 311–35.

Bodenhausen, G.V. and Moreno, K.N. (2000) 'How Do I Feel About Them? The Role of Affective Reactions in Intergroup Perception', in H. Bless and J.P. Forgas (eds), *The Message Within: The Role of Subjective Experience in Social Cognition and Behavior*. Philadelphia, PA: Psychology Press, pp. 283–303.

Bodenhausen, G.V., Mussweiler, T., Gabriel, S., and Moreno, K.N. (2001) 'Affective Influences on Stereotyping and Intergroup Relations', in J.P. Forgas (ed.), *Handbook of Affect and Social Cognition*. Mahwah, NJ: Erlbaum, pp. 319–43.

Bodenhausen, G.V., Sheppard, L., and Kramer, G.P. (1994b) 'Negative Affect and Social Judgment: The Differential Impact of Anger and Sadness', *European Journal of Social Psychology*, 24: 45–62.

Bodenhausen, G.V. and Wyer, R.S., Jr. (1985) 'Effects of Stereotypes on Decision Making and Information-Processing Strategies', *Journal of Personality and Social Psychology*, 48: 267–82.

Brewer, M.B. (1988) 'A Dual-Process Model of Impression Formation', in R.S. Wyer, Jr. and T.K. Srull (eds), *Advances in Social Cognition* (vol. 1). Hillsdale, NJ: Erlbaum, pp. 1–36.

Brewer, M.B. (1996) 'When Stereotypes Lead to Stereotyping: The Use of Stereotypes in Person Perception', in C.N. Macrae, C. Stangor, and M. Hewstone (eds), *Stereotypes and Stereotyping*. New York: Guilford, pp. 254–75.

Cacioppo, J.T. and Berntson, G.G. (1992) 'Social Psychological Contributions to the Decade of the Brain: Doctrine of Multilevel Analysis', *American Psychologist*, 47: 1019–28.

Cacioppo, J.T. and Berntson, G.G. (1996) 'Social Neuroscience: Principles of Psychophysiological Arousal and Response', in E.T. Higgins and A.W. Kruglanski (eds), *Social Psychology: Handbook of Basic Principles*. New York: Guilford, pp. 72–101.

Cameron, J.A. and Trope, Y. (2004) 'Stereotype-Biased Search and Processing of Information about Group Members', *Social Cognition*, 22: 650–672.

Castelli, L., Macrae, C.N., Zogmaister, C., and Arcuri, L. (2004) 'A Tale of Two Primes: Contextual Limits on Stereotype Activation', *Social Cognition*, 22: 233–247.

Chapman, L.J. and Chapman, J.P. (1967) 'Genesis of Popular but Erroneous Diagnostic Observations', *Journal of Abnormal Psychology*, 72: 193–204.

Chapman, L.J. and Chapman, J.P. (1969) 'Illusory Correlations as an Obstacle to the Use of Valid Psycho-Diagnostic Signs', *Journal of Abnormal Psychology*, 74: 272–80.

Clore, G.L., Gasper, K., and Garvin, K. (2001) 'Affect as Information', in J.P. Forgas (ed.), *Handbook of Affect and Social Cognition*. Mahwah, NJ: Erlbaum, pp. 121–44.

Crawford, M.T. and Skowronski, J.J. (1998) 'When Motivated Thought Leads to Heightened Bias: High Need for Cognition Can Enhance the Impact of Stereotypes on Memory', *Personality and Social Psychology Bulletin*, 24: 1075–88.

Czopp, A.M., Monteith, M.J., and Mark, A.Y. (2006) 'Standing Up for a Change: Reducing Bias through Interpersonal Confrontation', *Journal of Personality and Social Psychology*, 90: 784–803.

D'Agostino, P.R. (2000) 'The Encoding and Transfer of Stereotype-Driven Inferences', *Social Cognition*, 18: 281–91.

Darley, J.M. and Gross, P.H. (1983) 'A Hypothesis-Confirming Bias in Labeling Effects', *Journal of Personality and Social Psychology*, 44: 20–33.

Devine, P.G. (1989) 'Stereotypes and Prejudice: Their Automatic and Controlled Components', *Journal of Personality and Social Psychology*, 56: 5–18.

Devine, P.G., Monteith, M.J., Zuwerink, J.R., and Elliott, A.J. (1991) 'Prejudice With and Without Compunction', *Journal of Personality and Social Psychology*, 60: 817–30.

Devine, P.G., Plant, E.A., Amodio, D.M., Harmon-Jones, E., and Vance, S.L. (2002) 'The Regulation of Explicit and Implicit Race Bias: The Role of Motivations to Respond Without Prejudice', *Journal of Personality and Social Psychology*, 82: 835–48.

Dijksterhuis, A. and van Knippenberg, A. (1995) 'Timing of Schema-Activation and Memory: Inhibited Access to Inconsistent Information', *European Journal of Social Psychology*, 25: 383–90.

Dijksterhuis, A. and van Knippenberg, A. (1996) 'The Knife that Cuts Both Ways: Facilitated and Inhibited Access to Traits as a Result of Stereotype Activation', *Journal of Experimental Social Psychology*, 32: 271–88.

Dijksterhuis, A., van Knippenberg, A., Kruglanski, A.W. and Schaper, C. (1996) 'Motivated Social Cognition: Need for Closure Effects on Memory and Judgment', *Journal of Experimental Social Psychology*, 32: 254–70.

Dovidio, J.F., Evans, N., and Tyler, R.B. (1986) 'Racial Stereotypes: The Contents of their Cognitive Representations', *Journal of Experimental Social Psychology*, 22: 22–37.

Dovidio, J.F. and Gaertner, S.L. (1998) 'On the Nature of Contemporary Prejudice: The Causes, Consequences, and Challenges of Aversive Racism', in J.L. Eberhardt and S.T. Fiske (eds), *Confronting Racism: The Problem and the Response*. Thousand Oaks, CA: Sage, pp. 3–32.

Duncan, B.L. (1976) 'Differential Social Perception and Attribution of Intergroup Violence: Testing the Lower Limits of Stereotyping of Blacks', *Journal of Personality and Social Psychology*, 34: 590–8.

Dunn, E.W., and Spellman, B.A. (2003) 'Forgetting by Remembering: Stereotype Inhibition through Rehearsal of Alternative Aspects of Identity', *Journal of Experimental Social Psychology*, 39: 420–433.

Eberhardt, J.L., Goff, P.A., Purdie, V.J., and Davies, P.G. (2004) 'Seeing Black: Race, Crime, and Visual Processing', *Journal of Personality and Social Psychology*, 87: 876–893.

Edwards, J.A. and Weary, G. (1993) 'Depression and the Impression Formation Continuum: Piecemeal Processing Despite the Availability of Category Information', *Journal of Personality and Social Psychology*, 64: 636–45.

Ehrenberg, K. and Klauer, K.C. (2005) 'Flexible Use of Source Information: Processing Components of the Inconsistency Effect in Person Memory', *Journal of Experimental Social Psychology*, 41: 369–387.

Fazio, R.H., Jackson, J.R., Dunton, B.C., and Williams, C.J. (1995) 'Variability in Automatic Activation as an Unobtrusive Measure of Racial Attitudes: A Bona Fide Pipeline?', *Journal of Personality and Social Psychology*, 69: 1013–27.

Fein, S. and Spencer, S.J. (1997) 'Prejudice as Self-Image Maintenance: Affirming the Self through Derogating Others', *Journal of Personality and Social Psychology*, 73: 31–44.

Fiedler, K., Asbeck, J., and Nickel, S. (1991) 'Mood and Constructive Memory Effects on Social Judgement', *Cognition and Emotion*, 5: 363–78.

Fiske, S.T. (1998) 'Stereotyping, Prejudice, and Discrimination', in D.T. Gilbert, S.T. Fiske, and G. Lindzey (eds), *Handbook of Social Psychology*, 4th edn. Boston, MA: MCGraw-Hill, pp. 357–411.

Fiske, S.T. and Dépret, E. (1996) 'Control, Interdependence, and Power: Understanding Social Cognition in its Social Context', in W. Stroebe and M. Hewstone (eds), *European Review of Social Psychology* (vol. 7). New York: Wiley, pp. 31–61.

Fiske, S.T. and Neuberg, S.L. (1990) 'A Continuum Model of Impression Formation from Category-Based to Individuated Processes: Influences of Information and Motivation on Attention and Interpretation', in M.P. Zanna (ed.), *Advances in Experimental Social Psychology* (vol. 3). New York: Academic Press, pp. 1–74.

Forgas, J.P. (1989) 'Mood Effects on Decision Making Strategies', *Australian Journal of Psychology*, 41: 197–214.

Gaertner, S.L. and Dovidio, J.F. (1986) 'The Aversive Form of Racism', in J.F. Dovidio and S.L. Gaertner (eds), *Prejudice, Discrimination, and Racism*. San Diego, CA: Academic Press, pp. 61–89.

Gilbert, D.T. and Hixon, J.G. (1991) 'The Trouble of Thinking: Activation and Application of Stereotypic Beliefs', *Journal of Personality and Social Psychology*, 60: 509–17.

Gill, M.J. (2004) 'When Information Does Not Deter Stereotyping: Prescriptive Stereotyping Can Foster Bias under Conditions that Deter Descriptive Stereotyping', *Journal of Experimental Social Psychology*, 40: 619–32.

Glick, P. and Fiske, S.T. (1996) 'The Ambivalent Sexism Inventory: Differentiating Hostile and Benevolent Sexism', *Journal of Personality and Social Psychology*, 70: 491–512.

Glick, P. and Fiske, S.T. (2001) 'Ambivalent sexism', in M.P. Zanna (ed.), *Advances in Experimental Social Psychology* (vol. 33). San Diego, CA: Academic Press, pp. 115–88.

Goodwin, S.A., Gubin, A., Fiske, S.T., and Yzerbyt, V.Y. (2000) 'Power Can Bias Impression Processes: Stereotyping Subordinates by Default and by Design', *Group Processes and Intergroup Relations*, 3: 227–56.

Goodwin, S.A., Operario, D., and Fiske, S.T. (1998) 'Situational Power and Interpersonal Dominance Facilitate Bias and Inequality', *Journal of Social Issues*, 54: 677–98.

Greenwald, A.G., McGhee, D.E., and Schwartz, J.L.K. (1998) 'Measuring Individual Differences in Implicit Cognition: The Implicit Association Test', *Journal of Personality and Social Psychology*, 74: 1464–80.

Hamilton, D.L., Sherman, S.J., and Ruvolo, C.M. (1990) 'Stereotype-Based Expectancies: Effects on Information Processing and Social Behavior', *Journal of Social Issues*, 46 (2): 35–60.

Hart, A.J., Whalen, P.J., Shin, L.M., McInerney, S.C, Fischer, H., and Rauch, S.L. (2000) 'Differential Response in the Human Amygdala to Racial Outgroup vs Ingroup Face Stimuli', *Brain Imaging*, 11: 2351–5.

Heilman, M.E. (1984) 'Information as a Deterrent Against Sex Discrimination: The Effects of Applicant Sex and Information Type on Preliminary Employment Decisions', *Organizational Behavior and Human Decision Processes*, 33: 174–86.

Higgins, E.T. and Bargh, J.A. (1987) 'Social Cognition and Social Perception', *Annual Review of Psychology*, 38: 369–425.

Hilton, J.L. and Fein, S. (1989) 'The Role of Typical Diagnosticity in Stereotype-Based Judgments', *Journal of Personality and Social Psychology*, 57: 201–11.

Hugenberg, K. and Bodenhausen, G.V. (2003) 'Facing Prejudice: Implicit Prejudice and the Perception of Facial Threat', *Psychological Science*, 14: 640–3.

Hugenberg, K. and Bodenhausen, G.V. (2004) 'Ambiguity in Social Categorization: The Role of Prejudice and Facial Affect in Race Categorization', *Psychological Science*, 15: 342–5.

Isen, A.M. and Daubman, K.A. (1984) 'The Influence of Affect on Categorization', *Journal of Personality and Social Psychology*, 47: 1206–17.

Isen, A.M. and Means, B. (1983) 'The Influence of Positive Affect on Decision-Making Strategy', *Social Cognition*, 2: 18–31.

Ito, T.A., Thompson, E., and Cacioppo, J.T. (2004) 'Tracking the Timecourse of Social Perception: The Effects of Racial Cues on Event-Related Brain Potentials', *Personality and Social Psychology Bulletin*, 30: 1267–80.

Jacobs, J.E. and Eccles, J.S. (1992) 'The Impact of Mothers' Gender-Role Stereotypic Beliefs on Mothers' and Children's Ability Perceptions', *Journal of Personality and Social Psychology*, 63: 932–44.

Johnston, L., Arden, K., Macrae, C.N., and Grace, R.C. (2003) 'The Need for Speed: The Menstrual Cycle and Person Construal', *Social Cognition*, 21: 89–100.

Johnston, L., Miles, L., Carter, C., and Macrae, C.N. (2005) 'Menstrual Influences on Person Perception: Male Sensitivity to Fluctuating Female Fertility', *Social Cognition*, 23: 279–90.

Jones, C.S. and Kaplan, M.F. (2003) 'The Effects of Racially Stereotypical Crimes on Juror Decision-Making and Information-Processing Strategies', *Basic and Applied Social Psychology*, 25: 1–13.

Jones, E.E. (1990) *Interpersonal Perception*. New York: W.H. Freeman.

Kahneman, D. and Treisman, A. (1984) 'Changing Views of Attention and Automaticity', in R. Parasuraman and D.R. Davies (eds), *Varieties of Attention*. San Diego, CA: Academic Press, pp. 29–61.

Katz, I. and Hass, R.G. (1988) 'Racial Ambivalence and American Value Conflict: Correlational and Priming Studies of Dual Cognitive Structures', *Journal of Personality and Social Psychology*, 55: 893–905.

Katz, I., Wackenhut, J., and Hass, R.G. (1986) 'Racial Ambivalence, Value Duality, and Behavior', in J.F. Dovidio and S.L. Gaertner (eds), *Prejudice, Discrimination, and Racism*. San Diego, CA: Academic Press, pp. 35–59.

Kawakami, K., Dion, K.L., and Dovidio, J.F. (1998) 'Racial Prejudice and Stereotype Activation', *Personality and Social Psychology Bulletin*, 24: 407–16.

Kawakami, K., Dovidio, J.F., Mall, J., Hermsen, S., and Russin, A. (2000) 'Just Say No (to Stereotyping): Effects of Training in the Negation of Stereotypic Associations on Stereotype Activation', *Journal of Personality and Social Psychology*, 78: 871–88.

Kawakami, K., Spears, R., and Dovidio, J.F. (2002) 'Disinhibition of Stereotyping: Context, Prejudice, and Target Characteristics', *European Journal of Social Psychology*, 32: 517–530.

Keltner, D., Ellsworth, P.C., and Edwards, K. (1993) 'Beyond Simple Pessimism: Effects of Sadness and Anger on Social Judgment', *Journal of Personality and Social Psychology*, 64: 740–52.

Kinder, D.R. and Sears, D.O. (1981) 'Prejudice and Politics: Symbolic Racism Versus Racial Threats to the Good Life', *Journal of Personality and Social Psychology*, 40: 414–31.

Krueger, J. and Rothbart, M. (1988) 'Use of Categorical and Individuating Information in Making Inferences about Personality', *Journal of Personality and Social Psychology*, 55: 187–95.

Kruglanski, A.W. and Freund, T. (1983) 'The Freezing and Unfreezing of Lay-Inferences: Effects on Impressional Primacy, Ethnic Stereotyping, and Numerical Anchoring', *Journal of Experimental Social Psychology*, 19: 448–68.

Kunda, Z., Davies, P.G., Adams, B.D., and Spencer, S.J. (2002) 'The Dynamic Time Course of Stereotype ctivation: Activation, Dissipation, and Resurrection', *Journal of Personality and Social Psychology*, 82: 283–99.

Kunda, Z. and Sherman-Williams, B. (1993) 'Stereotypes and the Construal of Individuating Information', *Personality and Social Psychology Bulletin*, 19: 90–9.

Kunda, Z., Sinclair, L., and Griffin, D. (1997) 'Equal Ratings but Separate Meanings: Stereotypes and the Construal of Traits', *Journal of Personality and Social Psychology*, 72: 720–34.

Kunda, Z. and Sinclair, L. (1999) 'Motivated Reasoning with Stereotypes: Activation, Application, and Inhibition', *Psychological Inquiry*, 10: 12–22.

Kunda, Z., Sinclair, L., and Griffin, D. (1995) 'Equal Ratings but Separate Meanings: Stereotypes and the Construal of Traits', *Journal of Personality and Social Psychology*, 72: 720–34.

Kunda, Z. and Thagard, P. (1996) 'Forming Impressions from Stereotypes, Traits, and Behaviors: A Parallel Constraint Satisfaction Theory', *Psychological Review*, 103: 284–308.

Kurzban, R., Tooby, J., and Cosmides, L. (2001) 'Can Race Be Erased? Coalitional Computation and Social Categorization', *Proceedings of the National Academy of Sciences of the United States of America*, 98: 15387–92.

Lambert, A.J., Khan, S., Lickel, B., and Fricke, K. (1997) 'Mood and the Correction of Positive Versus Negative Stereotypes', *Journal of Personality and Social Psychology*, 72: 1002–26.

LeDoux, J.E. (2000) 'Emotion Circuits in the Brain', *Annual Review of Neuroscience*, 23: 155–84.

Lenton, A.P., Blair, I.V., and Hastie, R. (2001) 'Illusions of Gender: Stereotypes Evoke False Memories', *Journal of Experimental Social Psychology*, 37: 3–14.

Lepore, L. and Brown, R. (1997) 'Category and Stereotype Activation: Is Prejudice Inevitable?', *Journal of Personality and Social Psychology*, 72: 275–87.

Lepore, L. and Brown, R. (2002) 'The Role of Awareness: Divergent Automatic Stereotype Activation and Implicit Judgment Correction', *Social Cognition*, 20: 321–51.

Levy, S.R. and Dweck, C.S. (1999) 'The Impact of Children's Static Versus Dynamic Conceptions of People on Stereotype Formation', *Child Development*, 70: 1163–80.

Levy, S.R., Stroessner, S.J., and Dweck, C.S. (1998) 'Stereotype Formation and Endorsement: The Role of Implicit Theories', *Journal of Personality and Social Psychology*, 74: 1421–37.

Leyens, J.-P., Yzerbyt, V.Y., and Schadron, G. (1992) 'The Social Judgeability Approach to Stereotypes', in W. Stroebe and M. Hewstone (eds), *European Review of Social Psychology* (vol. 3). New York: Wiley, pp. 91–120.

Lippmann, W. (1922) *Public Opinion*. New York: Harcourt Brace.

Livingston, R.W. and Brewer, M.B. (2002) 'What Are We Really Priming? Cue-Based Versus Category-Based

Processing of Facial Stimuli', *Journal of Personality and Social Psychology*, 82: 5–18.

Locke, V., MacLeod, C., and Walker, I. (1994) 'Automatic and Controlled Activation of Stereotypes: Individual Differences Associated with Prejudice', *British Journal of Social Psychology*, 33: 29–46.

Locke, V., Macrae, C.N., and Eaton, J.L. (2005) 'Is Person Categorization Modulated by Exemplar Typicality', *Social Cognition*, 23: 417–28.

Locksley, A., Borgida, E., Brekke, N., and Hepburn, C. (1980) 'Sex Stereotypes and Social Judgment', *Journal of Personality and Social Psychology*, 39: 821–31.

Logan, G.D. (1989) 'Automaticity and Cognitive Control', in J.S. Uleman and J.A. Bargh (eds), *Unintended Thought*. New York: Guilford, pp. 52–74.

Logan, G.D. and Cowan, W.B. (1984) 'On the Ability to Inhibit Thought and Action: A Theory of an Act of Control', *Psychological Review*, 91: 295–327.

Maass, A., Cadinu, M., Boni, M., and Borini, C. (2005) 'Converting Verbs into Adjectives: Asymmetrical Memory Distortions for Stereotypic and Counterstereotypic Information', *Group Processes and Intergroup Relations*, 8: 271–290.

Macrae, C.N., Alnwick, K.A., Milne, A.B., and Schloerscheidt, A.M. (2002a) 'Person Perception Across the Menstrual Cycle: Hormonal Influences on Social Cognitive Functioning', *Psychological Science*, 13: 532–6.

Macrae, C.N. and Bodenhausen, G.V. (2000) 'Social Cognition: Thinking Categorically About Others', *Annual Review of Psychology*, 51: 93–120.

Macrae, C.N., Bodenhausen, G.V., and Milne, A.B. (1995) 'The Dissection of Selection in Person Perception: Inhibitory Processes in Social Stereotyping', *Journal of Personality and Social Psychology*, 69: 397–407.

Macrae, C.N., Bodenhausen, G.V., and Milne, A.B. (1998) 'Saying No to Unwanted Thoughts: Self-Focus and the Regulation of Mental Life', *Journal of Personality and Social Psychology*, 74: 578–89.

Macrae, C.N., Bodenhausen, G.V., Milne, A.B., and Castelli, L. (1999a) 'On Disregarding Deviants: Exemplar Typicality and Person Perception', *Current Psychology*, 18: 47–70.

Macrae, C.N., Bodenhausen, G.V., Milne, A.B., and Ford, R.L. (1997a) 'On the Regulation of Recollection: The Intentional Forgetting of Stereotypical Memories', *Journal of Personality and Social Psychology*, 72: 709–19.

Macrae, C.N., Bodenhausen, G.V., Milne, A.B., and Jetten, J. (1994a) 'Out of Mind but Back in Sight: Stereotypes on the Rebound', *Journal of Personality and Social Psychology*, 67: 808–17.

Macrae, C.N., Bodenhausen, G.V., Milne, A.B., Thorn, T.M.J., and Castelli, L. (1997b) 'On the Activation of Social Stereotypes: The Moderating Role of Processing Objectives', *Journal of Experimental Social Psychology*, 33: 471–89.

Macrae, C.N., Bodenhausen, G.V., Milne, A.B., and Wheeler, V. (1996) 'On Resisting the Temptation for Simplification: Counterintentional Effects of Stereotype Suppression on Social Memory', *Social Cognition*, 14: 1–20.

Macrae, C.N., Bodenhausen, G.V., Schloerscheidt, A.M., and Milne, A.B. (1999b) 'Tales of the Unexpected: Executive Function and Person Perception', *Journal of Personality and Social Psychology*, 76: 200–13.

Macrae, C.N., Hewstone, M., and Griffiths, R.J. (1993) 'Processing Load and Memory for Stereotype-Based Information', *European Journal of Social Psychology*, 23: 77–87.

Macrae, C.N., Hood, B.M., Milne, A.B., Rowe, A.C., and Mason, M.F. (2002b) 'Are You Looking at Me? Eye Gaze and Person Perception', *Psychological Science*, 13: 460–4.

Macrae, C.N., Milne, A.B., and Bodenhausen, G.V. (1994b) 'Stereotypes as Energy-Saving Devices: A Peek Inside the Cognitive Toolbox', *Journal of Personality and Social Psychology*, 66: 37–47.

Macrae, C.N., Mitchell, J.P., and Pendry, L.F. (2002c) 'What's in a Forename: Cue Familiarity and Stereotypical Thinking', *Journal of Experimental Social Psychology*, 38: 186–93.

Macrae, C.N., Quinn, K.A., Mason, M.F., and Quadflieg, S. (2005) 'Understanding Others: The Face and Person Construal', *Journal of Personality and Social Psychology*, 89: 686–95.

Macrae, C.N., Schloerscheidt, A.M., Bodenhausen, G.V., and Milne, A.B. (2002d) 'Creating Memory Illusions: Expectancy-Based Processing and the Generation of False Memories', *Memory*, 10: 63–80.

Macrae, C.N., Stangor, C., and Milne, A.B. (1994c) 'Activating Social Stereotypes: A Functional Analysis', *Journal of Experimental Social Psychology*, 30: 370–89.

Maddox, K.B. (2004) 'Perspectives on Racial Phenotypicality Bias', *Personality and Social Psychology Review*, 8: 383–401.

Maddox, K.B. and Gray, S.A. (2002) 'Cognitive Representations of Black Americans: Reexploring the Role of Skin Tone', *Personality and Social Psychology Bulletin*, 28: 250–9.

Martin, L.L., Ward, D.W., Achee, J.W., and Wyer, R.S., Jr. (1993) 'Mood as Input: People Have to Interpret the Motivational Implications of Their Moods', *Journal of Personality and Social Psychology*, 64: 317–26.

Mason, M.F. and Macrae, C.N. (2004) 'Categorizing and Individuating Others: The Neural Substrates of Person Perception', *Journal of Cognitive Neuroscience*, 16: 1785–95.

Mather, M., Johnson, M.K., and De Leonardis, D.M. (1999) 'Stereotype Reliance in Source Monitoring: Age Differences and Neuropsychological Test Correlates', *Cognitive Neuropsychology*, 16: 437–58.

Mitchell, J.P., Mason, M.F., Macrae, C.N., and Banaji, M.R. (2006) 'Thinking about Others: The Neural Substrates of Social Cognition', in J.T. Cacioppo, P.S. Visser, and C.L. Pickett (eds), *Social Neuroscience: People Thinking about People*. Cambridge, MA: MIT Press, pp. 63–82.

Monteith, M.J. (1993) 'Self-Regulation of Prejudiced Responses: Implications for Progress in Prejudice Reduction', *Journal of Personality and Social Psychology*, 65: 469–85.

Monteith, M.J., Sherman, J.W. and Devine, P.G. (1998a) 'Suppression as a Stereotype Control Strategy', *Personality and Social Psychology Review*, 2: 63–82.

Monteith, M.J., Spicer, C.V., and Tooman, G.D. (1998b) 'Consequences of Stereotype Suppression: Stereotypes on and Not on the Rebound', *Journal of Experimental Social Psychology*, 34: 355–77.

Moreno, K.N. and Bodenhausen, G.V. (2001) 'Intergroup Affect and Social Judgement: Feelings as Inadmissible Information', *Group Processes and Intergroup Relations*, 4: 21–9.

Moscovitch, M. (1994) 'Memory and Working with Memory: Evaluation of a Component Process Model and Comparisons with Other Models', in D.L. Schacter and E. Tulving (eds), *Memory Systems 1994*. Cambridge, MA: MIT Press, pp. 269–310.

Moskowitz, G.B., Gollwitzer, P.M., Wasel, W., and Schaal, B. (1999) 'Preconscious Control of Stereotype Activation through Chronic Egalitarian Goals', *Journal of Personality and Social Psychology*, 77: 167–84.

Nisbett, R.E., Zukier, H., and Lemley, R.E. (1981) 'The Dilution Effect: Nondiagnostic Information Weakens the Implications of Diagnostic Information', *Cognitive Psychology*, 13: 248–77.

Oakes, P.J., Turner, J.C., and Haslam, S.A. (1991) 'Perceiving People as Group Members: The Role of Fit in the Salience of Social Categorization', *British Journal of Social Psychology*, 30: 125–44.

Ochsner, K.N. and Lieberman, M.D. (2001) 'The Emergence of Social Cognitive Neuroscience', *American Psychologist*, 56: 717–34.

Ottati, V., Claypool, H.M., and Gingrich, B. (2005) 'Effects of a Group Stereotype on Memory for Behaviors Performed by a Group Member', *European Journal of Social Psychology*, 35: 797–808.

Ottati, V., Terkildsen, N., and Hubbard, C. (1997) 'Happy Faces Elicit Heuristic Processing in a Televised Impression Formation Task: A Cognitive Tuning Account', *Personality and Social Psychology Bulletin*, 23: 1144–56.

Park, J. and Banaji, M.R. (2000) 'Mood and Heuristics: The Influence of Happy and Sad States on Sensitivity and Bias in Stereotyping', *Journal of Personality and Social Psychology*, 78: 1005–23.

Payne, B.K. (2005) 'Conceptualizing Control in Social Cognition: How Executive Functioning Modulates the Expression of Automatic Stereotyping', *Journal of Personality and Social Psychology*, 89: 488–503.

Pendry, L.F. and Macrae, C.N. (1994) 'Stereotypes and Mental Life: The Case of the Motivated but Thwarted Tactician', *Journal of Experimental Social Psychology*, 30: 303–25.

Pendry, L.F. and Macrae, C.N. (1996) 'What the Disinterested Perceiver Overlooks: Goal-Directed Social Categorization', *Personality and Social Psychology Bulletin*, 3: 250–7.

Peruche, B.M. and Plant, E.A. (2006) 'Racial Bias in Perceptions of Athleticism: The Role of Motivation in the Elimination of Bias', *Social Cognition*, 24: 438–52.

Phelps, E.A., O'Connor, K.J., Cunningham, W.A., Funayama, E.S., Gatenby, J.C., Gore, J.C., and Banaji, M.R. (2000) 'Performance on Indirect Measures of Race Evaluation Predicts Amygdala Activation', *Journal of Cognitive Neuroscience*, 12: 729–38.

Pittman, T.S. and D'Agostino, P.R. (1989) 'Motivation and Cognition: Control Deprivation and the Nature of Subsequent Information Processing', *Journal of Experimental Social Psychology*, 25: 465–80.

Plant, E.A. and Devine, P.G. (1998) 'Internal and External Motivation to Respond Without Prejudice', *Journal of Personality and Social Psychology*, 75: 811–32.

Plant, E.A., Peruche, B.M., and Butz, D.A. (2005) 'Eliminating Automatic Racial Bias: Making Race Non-Diagnostic for Responses to Criminal Suspects', *Journal of Experimental Social Psychology*, 41: 141–56.

Pratto, F. and Bargh, J.A. (1991) 'Stereotyping Based upon Apparently Individuating Information: Trait and Global Components of Sex Stereotypes Under Attention Overload', *Journal of Experimental Social Psychology*, 27: 26–47.

Quinn, K.A. and Macrae, C.N. (2005) 'Categorizing Others: The Dynamics of Person Construal', *Journal of Personality and Social Psychology*, 88: 467–79.

Raghunathan, R. and Pham, M.T. (1999) 'All Negative Moods Are Not Equal: Motivational Influences of Anxiety and Sadness on Decision Making', *Organizational Behavior and Human Decision Processes*, 79: 56–77.

Raskinski, K.A., Crocker, J., and Hastie, R. (1985) 'Another Look at Sex Stereotypes and Social Judgments: An Analysis of the Social Perceiver's Use of Subjective Probabilities', *Journal of Personality and Social Psychology*, 49: 317–26.

Richeson, J.A., and Trawalter, S. (2005) 'On the Categorization of Admired and Disliked Exemplars of Admired and Disliked Racial Groups', *Journal of Personality and Social Psychology*, 89: 517–30.

Rodriguez-Bailon, R., Moya, M., and Yzerbyt, V. (2000) 'Why Do Superiors Attend to Negative Stereotypic Information about Their Subordinates? Effects of Power Legitimacy on Social Perception', *European Journal of Social Psychology*, 30: 651–71.

Rothbart, M., Evans, M., and Fulero, S. (1979) 'Recall for Confirming Events: Memory Processes and the Maintenance of Social Stereotypes', *Journal of Experimental Social Psychology*, 15: 343–55.

Rothbart, M., Fulero, S., Jenson, C., Howard, J., and Birrell, B. (1978) 'From Individual to Group Impressions: Availability Heuristics in Stereotype Formation', *Journal of Experimental Social Psychology*, 14: 237–55.

Sagar, H.A. and Schofield, J.W. (1980) 'Racial and Behavioral Cues in Black and White Children's Perceptions of Ambiguously Aggressive Acts', *Journal of Personality and Social Psychology*, 39: 590–8.

Sanders, J.D., McClure, K.A., and Zárate, M.A. (2004) 'Cerebral Hemisphere Asymmetries in Social Perception: Perceiving and Responding to the Individual and the Group', *Social Cognition*, 22: 279–91.

Schaller, M., Park, J.H., and Mueller, A. (2003) 'Fear of the Dark: Interactive Effects of Beliefs about Danger and Ambient Darkness on Ethnic Stereotypes', *Personality and Social Psychology Bulletin*, 29: 637–49.

Schwarz, N. (1990) 'Feelings as Information: Informational and Motivational Functions of Affective States', in E.T. Higgins and R.M. Sorrentino (eds), *Handbook of Motivation and Cognition: Foundations of Social Behavior* (vol. 2). New York: Guilford, pp. 527–61.

Schwarz, N. and Bless, H. (1991) 'Happy and Mindless, but Sad and Smart? The Impact of Affective States on Analytical Reasoning', in J.P. Forgas (ed.), *Emotion and Social Judgments*. Oxford: Pergamon Press, pp. 55–71.

Schwarz, N., Bless, H., and Bohner, G. (1991) 'Mood and Persuasion: Affective States Influence the Processing of Persuasive Communications', in M.P. Zanna (ed.), *Advances in Experimental Social Psychology* (vol. 24). Orlando, FL: Academic Press, pp. 161–99.

Secord, P.F., Bevan, W., and Katz, B. (1956) 'The Negro Stereotype and Perceptual Accentuation', *Journal of Abnormal and Social Psychology*, 53: 78–83.

Sekaquaptewa, D. and Espinoza, P. (2004) 'Biased Processing of Stereotype Incongruency Is Greater for Low than High Status Groups', *Journal of Experimental Social Psychology*, 40: 128–35.

Sherman, J.W. and Bessenoff, G.R. (1999) 'Stereotypes as Source-Monitoring Cues: On the Interaction between Episodic and Semantic Memory', *Psychological Science*, 10: 106–10.

Sherman, J.W., Conrey, F.R., and Azam, O.A. (2005) 'Prejudice and Stereotype Maintenance Processes: Attention, Attribution, and Individuation', *Journal of Personality and Social Psychology*, 89: 607–22.

Sherman, J.W., Conrey, F.R., and Groom, C.J. (2004) 'Encoding Flexibility Revisited: Evidence for Enhanced Encoding of Stereotype-Inconsistent Information under Cognitive Load', *Social Cognition*, 22: 214–32.

Sherman, J.W. and Frost, L.A. (2000) 'On the Encoding of Stereotype-Relevant Information under Cognitive Load', *Personality and Social Psychology Bulletin*, 26: 26–34.

Sherman, J.W., Groom, C.J., Ehrenberg, K., and Klauer, K.C. (2003) 'Bearing False Witness under Pressure: Implicit and Explicit Components of Stereotype-Driven Memory Distortions', *Social Cognition*, 23: 213–46.

Sherman, J.W., Lee, A.Y., Bessenoff, G.R., and Frost, L.A. (1998) 'Stereotype Efficiency Reconsidered: Encoding Flexibility under Cognitive Load', *Journal of Personality and Social Psychology*, 75: 589–606.

Sherman, J.W., Stroessner, S.J., Loftus, S.T., and DeGuzman, G. (1997) 'Stereotype Suppression and Recognition Memory for Stereotypical and Non-Stereotypical Information', *Social Cognition*, 15: 205–15.

Sinclair, L. and Kunda, Z. (1999) 'Reactions to a Black Professional: Motivated Inhibition and Activation of Conflicting Stereotypes', *Journal of Personality and Social Psychology*, 77: 885–904.

Sinclair, L. and Kunda, Z. (2000) 'Motivated Stereotyping of Women: She's Fine if She Praised Me but Incompetent if She Criticized Me', *Personality and Social Psychology Bulletin*, 26: 1329–42.

Smith, E.R., Fazio, R.H., and Cejka, M.A. (1996) 'Accessible Attitudes Influence Categorization of Multiply Categorizable Objects', *Journal of Personality and Social Psychology*, 71: 888–98.

Snyder, M. and Swann, W.B., Jr. (1978) 'Behavioral Confirmation in Social Interaction: From Social Perception to Social Reality', *Journal of Experimental Social Psychology*, 14: 148–62.

Spencer, S.J., Fein, S., Wolfe, C.T., Fong, C., and Dunn, M. (1998) 'Automatic Activation of Stereotypes: The Role of Self-Image Threat', *Personality and Social Psychology Bulletin*, 24: 1139–52.

Stangor, C. and McMillan, D. (1992) 'Memory for Expectancy-Congruent and Expectancy-Incongruent Information: A Review of the Social and Social Developmental Literatures', *Psychological Bulletin*, 111: 42–61.

Stroessner, S.J. (1996) 'Social Categorization by Race or Sex: Effects of Perceived Non-Normalcy on Response Times', *Social Cognition*, 14: 247–76.

Taylor, S.E., Fiske, S.T., Etcoff, N.L., and Ruderman, A.J. (1978) 'Categorical and Contextual Bases of Person Memory and Stereotyping', *Journal of Personality and Social Psychology*, 36: 778–93.

Vallone, R.P., Ross, L., and Lepper, M.R. (1985) 'The Hostile Media Phenomenon: Biased Perception and Perceptions of Media Bias in Coverage of the Beirut Massacre', *Journal of Personality and Social Psychology*, 49: 577–85.

van Knippenberg, A. and Dijksterhuis, A. (1996) 'A Posteriori Stereotype Activation: The Preservation of Stereotypes through Memory Distortion', *Social Cognition*, 14: 21–53.

von Hippel, W., Jonides, J., Hilton, J.L., and Narayan, S. (1993) 'Inhibitory Effect of Schematic Processing on Perceptual Encoding', *Journal of Personality and Social Psychology*, 64: 921–35.

von Hippel, W., Sekaquaptewa, D., and Vargas, P. (1995) 'On the Role of Encoding Processes in Stereotype Maintenance', in M.P. Zanna (ed.), *Advances in Experimental Social Psychology* (vol. 27). New York: Academic Press, pp. 177–254.

von Hippel, W., Silver, L.A., and Lynch, M.E. (2000) 'Stereotyping against Your Will: The Role of Inhibitory Ability in Stereotyping and Prejudice Among the Elderly', *Personality and Social Psychology Bulletin*, 26: 523–32.

Vonk, R. (2002) 'Effects of Stereotypes on Attitude Inference: Outgroups Are Black and White, Ingroups Are Shaded', *British Journal of Social Psychology*, 41: 157–67.

Weary, G. (1990) 'Depression and Sensitivity to Social Information', in B.S. Moore and A.M. Isen (eds), *Affect and Social Behavior*. Cambridge: Cambridge University Press, pp. 207–30.

Weary, G. and Gannon, K. (1996) 'Depression, Control Motivation, and Person Perception', in P.M. Gollwitzer and J.A. Bargh (eds), *The Psychology of Action: Linking Cognition and Motivation to Behavior*. New York: Guilford, pp. 146–67.

Weary, G., Jacobson, J.A., Edwards, J.A., and Tobin, S.J. (2001) 'Chronic and Temporarily Activated Causal Uncertainty Beliefs and Stereotype Usage', *Journal of Personality and Social Psychology*, 81: 206–19.

Weeks, M. and Lupfer, M.B. (2004) 'Complicating Race: The Relationship between Prejudice, Race, and Social Class Categorizations', *Personality and Social Psychology Bulletin*, 30: 972–84.

Wegner, D.M. (1994) 'Ironic Processes of Mental Control', *Psychological Review*, 101: 34–52.

Wegner, D.M. and Erber, R. (1992) 'The Hyperaccessibility of Suppressed Thoughts', *Journal of Personality and Social Psychology*, 63: 903–12.

Wheeler, M.E. and Fiske, S.T. (2005) 'Controlling Racial Prejudice: Social-Cognitive Goals Affect Amygdala and Stereotype Activation', *Psychological Science*, 16: 56–63.

Wigboldus, D.H.J., Dijksterhuis, A., and van Knippenberg, A. (2003) 'When Stereotypes Get in the Way: Stereotypes Obstruct Stereotype-Inconsistent Trait Inferences', *Journal of Personality and Social Psychology*, 84: 470–84.

Wigboldus, D.H.J., Sherman, J.W., Franzese, H.L., and van Knippenberg, A. (2004) 'Capacity and Comprehension: Spontaneous Stereotyping Under Cognitive Load', *Social Cognition*, 22: 292–309.

Wittenbrink, B., Gist, P.L., and Hilton, J.L. (1997) 'Structural Properties of Stereotypic Knowledge and Their Influences on the Construal of Social Situations', *Journal of Personality and Social Psychology*, 72: 526–43.

Wittenbrink, B., Hilton, J.L., and Gist, P.L. (1998) 'In Search of Similarity: Stereotypes as Naïve Theories in Social Categorization', *Social Cognition*, 16: 31–55.

Wittenbrink, B., Judd, C.M., and Park, B. (2001) 'Spontaneous Prejudice in Context: Variability in Automatically Activated Attitudes', *Journal of Personality and Social Psychology*, 81: 815–27.

Worth, L.T. and Mackie, D.M. (1987) 'Cognitive Mediation of Positive Affect in Persuasion', *Social Cognition*, 5: 76–94.

Wyer, N.A. (2004) 'Not All Stereotypic Biases Are Created Equal: Evidence for a Stereotype-Disconfirming Bias', *Personality and Social Psychology Bulletin*, 30: 706–20.

Wyer, N.A., Sherman, J.W., and Stroessner, S.J. (1998) 'The Spontaneous Suppression of Racial Stereotypes', *Social Cognition*, 16: 340–52.

Wyer, N.A., Sherman, J.W. and Stroessner, S.J. (2000) 'The Roles of Motivation and Ability in Controlling the Consequences of Stereotype Suppression', *Personality and Social Psychology Bulletin*, 26: 13–25.

Yzerbyt, V.Y., Leyens, J.-P., and Corneille, O. (1998) 'The Role of Naïve Theories of Judgment in Impression Formation', *Social Cognition*, 16: 56–77.

Yzerbyt, V.Y., Leyens, J.-P., and Schadron, G. (1997) 'Stereotypes as Explanations: A Subjective Essentialist View of Group Perception', in R. Spears, P.J. Oakes, N. Ellemers, and S.A. Haslam (eds), *The Social Psychology of Stereotyping and Group Life*. Cambridge, MA: Blackwell, pp. 20–50.

Yzerbyt, V.Y., Leyens, J.-P., Schadron, G., and Rocher, S. (1994) 'Social Judgeability: The Impact of Meta-Informational Cues on the Use of Stereotypes', *Journal of Personality and Society Psychology*, 66: 46–55.

Zárate, M.A. and Smith, E.R. (1990) 'Person Categorization and Stereotyping', *Social Cognition*, 8: 161–85.

Zárate, M.A. Sanders, J.D., and Garza, A.A. (2000) 'Neurological Disassociations of Social Perception Processes', *Social Cognition*, 18: 223–51.

# 5
# Portraits of the Self

CONSTANTINE SEDIKIDES AND
AIDEN P. GREGG

**INTRODUCTION**

The self has long fascinated writers, poets, and philosophers. More recently, scientists have begun to investigate it empirically, using rigorous and inventive methodologies. The focus here is on the motivational and affective components of selfhood. In general, the evidence suggests that people regard the self as their most prized possession: they go to great lengths to protect and promote it, playing up personal strengths and playing down personal weaknesses. However, some people are better at this than others. The result is differences in self-esteem. Having high self-esteem feels good; however, contrary to popular belief, it also has some definite drawbacks.

The *self* manages to be wholly familiar and frustratingly elusive at the same time. At first blush, it appears that, if I know anything at all, then I know that I am a self-aware being, an 'I' that not only thinks, as Descartes famously asserted, but that also senses, feels, desires, intends, and acts. Yet, establishing exactly what this 'I' is, and how it manages to do what it does, is an excellent way to pass an otherwise interminable journey on British Rail. Indeed, so slippery has the self seemed to some that they have concluded it is merely a grammatical fiction or a cultural artifact (Gergen, 1991; Wittgenstein, 1953). An insubstantial self of this sort could never be the object of scientific scrutiny: it could only be an empty construct for linguists to parse or for postmodernists to critique. Social psychologists who study the self reject such deflationary interpretations, however. They start from the full-blooded assumption that the self is real (Baumeister, 1998; Sedikides and Brewer, 2001; Tesser, 2001) and that, although it may contain an element of subjectivity liable to awe and mystify (Nagel, 1974; Tallis, 1999), it nonetheless lends itself to objective empirical investigation.

This being the case, we define the self as *the totality of interrelated yet distinct psychological phenomena that either underlie, causally interact with, or depend upon reflexive consciousness*. The merit of this inclusive, if somewhat wordy, definition is that it does not describe the self as some arcane unity about which nothing further can be said. Rather, it describes the self as a set of properties and processes, each of which can be conceptually defined and empirically indexed. This opens the door to scientific progress: social psychologists can seek greater insight into the nature of selfhood by studying particular manifestations of the self, as well as their correlates, causes, and consequences. They can come up with testable theories that link self-related phenomena to one another and to phenomena beyond the self.

Two brief refinements of this definition are nonetheless in order. First, the properties and processes that collectively compose the self are themselves fairly *complex*. Although more primitive aspects of mental functioning may distantly affect or be affected by reflexive consciousness, the psychology of the self is typically pitched at a molar rather than at a molecular level of analysis. Second, the self operates predominantly *within the social world*. This means that the psychological phenomena that fall under its umbrella typically arise in interaction with others, real or imagined. Consequently, the self, though rooted in an individual brain, is dynamically responsive to social context.

Having sketched out what we think the self is, that is, the psychological domains that it covers, we aim to provide a taste of what empirical research has revealed about it. Unfortunately, this can be only a taste, given the sheer breadth of the literature and the space limitations imposed by a volume of this sort. Hence, we will concentrate on two heavily researched topics: the *motivational* and *affective* aspects of the self – specifically, *self-motives* and *self-esteem*. As we describe the cardinal findings in the area, and the theories put forward to explain them, we hope to show compellingly that the scientific study of the self substantially illuminates our understanding of human beings.

## Self-motives

If humans entirely lacked emotion, like the perfectly rational android Data on *Star Trek*, selfhood would involve little more than the disinterested encoding, storage, and retrieval of self-related information, either as a means of acquiring accurate knowledge or of carrying out effective action. However, as anyone who has never been an android knows, selfhood is a far more colorful, visceral affair.

Motivation is a case in point: the self is immersed in a variety of motives. Indeed, several taxonomies of *self-motives* have been proposed by social psychologists (Deci and Ryan, 2000; Epstein and Morling, 1995; Sedikides and Strube, 1997). We start with the *self-enhancement motive*, as it is arguably the pre-eminent one (Sedikides, 1993). Next, we move on to discussing various other self-motives in the light of it, either as notable instances where it has been subverted, or as tactical means of satisfying it. Finally, we consider the correlates and consequences of *self-esteem*, a psychological attribute that, in its abundance or shortage, can be understood as the habitual ability or inability to satisfy the key self-motive for *self-enhancement*.

### *Self-enhancement*

*Self-enhancement* denotes the drive to *affirm* the self (Steele, 1988), that is, to convince ourselves, and any significant others in the vicinity, that we are intrinsically meritorious persons: worthwhile, attractive, competent, lovable, and moral. Although the term 'self-enhancement' suggests the pursuit of a more positive self-view (*self-promotion*), it is also understood technically as covering attempts to maintain or defend an already positive self-view (*self-protection*) (Sedikides and Strube, 1997).

Research amply bears out what astute observers have long suspected: that people self-enhance with enthusiasm and ingenuity (Brown and Dutton, 1995; Greenwald, 1980; Taylor and Brown, 1988). Indeed, the manifestations of self-enhancement are so manifold that the label 'zoo' has been drolly applied to them (Tesser et al., 1996). A brief inventory of the inmates of this 'zoo', some familiar, others exotic, is in order.

#### The self-enhancing triad: the above-average effect, illusions of control, and unrealistic optimism

By and large, people hold flattering views of their own attributes. Most university students, for example, regard themselves as well above the fiftieth percentile in the degree to which they exhibit such sought-after attributes as social grace, athletic prowess, and leadership ability (Alicke, 1985; College Board, 1976–7; Dunning et al., 1989). Even conspicuously low (twelfth percentile) achievers in such domains as grammar and logic consider themselves to be relatively high (sixty-second percentile) achievers (Kruger and Dunning, 1999). No less immune to vanity, 94 percent of university professors regard their teaching ability as above average (Cross, 1977). Such self-ascriptions must, at least for a subset of respondents, be false, assuming that the sample tested is representative of the sample that respondents broadly envisage and that 'average' is taken to imply either the mean of a symmetric distribution or the median of a nonsymmetric one (Brown, 1998). The robustness of the *above-average effect* is borne out by the fact that, even when the criteria on which people base judgments of self and others are made identical, they still rate themselves more favorably (Alicke et al., 2001). All the more ironic, then, that people should consider themselves less susceptible to motivational and cognitive biases than their peers, even when explicitly informed about them (Pronin et al., 2002). Finally, anything close to the self basks in the glow of this perceived superiority: people value their close relationships (Murray, 1999; Rusbult et al., 2000) and their personal possessions (Nesselroade et al., 1999) above those of others.

People also overestimate their degree of control over outcomes and contingencies. Such *illusions of control* (Langer, 1975) are apparent in people's conviction that they can influence the outcome of inherently random systems such as lotteries, card-drawings, and dice-throws, especially when such systems are accompanied by features conventionally associated with skill-based tasks (for example, choosing one's own lottery number, practicing guessing the outcome of a dice throw, or competing against a nervous opponent). Even when a degree of contingency does exist between actions and outcomes, people still overestimate the strength of that contingency (Jenkins and Ward, 1965).

Moreover, people think that fate will smile upon them. They believe, in particular, that a greater number of positive life experiences (such as having a gifted child or living to a ripe old age) and a lesser number of negative life experiences (such as being a victim of crime or falling ill) lie in store for them than for similar others (Helweg-Larsen and Shepperd, 2001; Weinstein, 1980; Weinstein and Klein, 1995). Such *unrealistic optimism* is extended, albeit to a lesser degree, to others closely linked to the self, such as friends (Regan et al., 1995). In addition, people both overestimate their ability to predict the future (Vallone et al., 1990) and underestimate how long it will take to complete a variety of tasks (Buelher et al., 1994). As if that were not enough, people also overestimate the accuracy of their social predictions (Dunning et al., 1990).

### The self-serving bias in attribution

Self-enhancement infects not only comparative judgments but also causal explanations for social outcomes, in that people manifest a *self-serving bias* when they explain the origin of events in which they personally had a hand or a stake (Campbell and Sedikides, 1999; Zuckerman, 1979). Specifically, they attribute *positive* outcomes *internally* to themselves, but *negative* outcomes *externally* to others (or to circumstance), thus making it possible to claim credit for successes but to disclaim responsibility for failures. The self-serving bias is a robust phenomenon, occurring in private as well as public (Greenberg et al., 1982; Schlenker and Miller, 1977), and even when a premium is placed on honesty (Riess et al., 1981). People's explanations for moral transgressions follow a similar self-serving pattern (Baumeister et al., 1990; Gonzales et al., 1990). Perhaps even the *ultimate attribution error* (Pettigrew, 2001), the tendency to regard negative acts by the outgroup and positive acts by the ingroup as essential to their nature, may simply reflect the operation of the self-serving bias refracted through the prism of social identification (Cialdini et al., 1976; Gramzow et al., 2001).

### Mnemic neglect, selective attention, and selective exposure

People sometimes self-enhance by expediently remembering their strengths better than their weaknesses. For example, Sedikides and Green (2000) found that, following false feedback in the form of behaviors of mixed valence allegedly predicted by a bogus personality test, participants recalled more positive behaviors than negative ones, but only when those behaviors exemplified central traits, not peripheral ones, and only when the feedback pertained to themselves, not to other people. We label this pattern of selective forgetting *mnemic neglect*. Broadly similar findings have emerged when the to-be-recalled information takes the form of personaity traits (Mischel et al.,1976), relationship-promoting or relationship-undermining behaviors (van Lange et al., 1999), frequencies of social acts (Gosling et al., 1998), and autobiographical memories (Skowronski et al., 1991).

The processing mechanisms underlying mnemic neglect may involve bias at encoding, retrieval, or retention. First, at encoding, people conveniently avoid attending to unflattering information (Baumeister and Cairns, 1982; Sedikides and Green, 2000: Experiment 3), thereby impeding its registration. The pattern of *selective attention* exhibited often follows a mobilization-minimization trajectory: a brief initial orientation towards the threat followed by a more prolonged evasion of it (Taylor, 1991). In addition, such selective attention manifests itself in overt behavior. For example, people *selectively expose* themselves to information that justifies important prior decisions (Festinger, 1957), at least when this information is perceived to be valid, and the decision freely made and irreversible (Frey, 1986). Moreover, when people suspect that they might possess characteristics of which they disapprove, they strive to avoid those who exhibit them (Schimel et al., 2000).

Second, at retrieval, people bring to mind a biased sample of congenial memories. Such selective recall has been found for behaviors that exemplify desirable personality traits (Sanitioso et al., 1990), harmonious interpersonal relationships (Murray and Holmes, 1993), or health-enhancing habits (Ross et al., 1981). Finally, affect associated with unpleasant memories fades faster than affect associated with pleasant memories (Walker et al., 2003), possibly due to the various behind-the-scenes activities of the psychological immune system (Gilbert et al., 1998).

### Selective acceptance and refutation

Where the ego-threatening information cannot be easily ignored, or where it looks open to challenge, people will spend time and psychological resources trying to refute it. This is evident in the adoption of a more critical attitude towards blame and a more lenient one towards praise (Ditto and Boardman, 1995; Pyszczynski and Greenberg, 1987), and in the tendency to counterargue uncongenial information energetically but to accept congenial information at face value (Ditto and Lopez, 1992; Ditto et al., 1998). A familiar example is of the student who unthinkingly accepts as valid an examination on which he performed well (*selective acceptance*) but mindfully searches for reasons to reject as invalid an examination on which he performed poorly (*selective refutation*) (Arkin and Maruyama, 1979; Greenwald, 2002). Often, selective refutation involves generating serviceable theories that enable criticism to be credibly defused. For example, members of stigmatized groups can, by imputing prejudice to those who derogate either them or their group, maintain high levels of self-esteem (Crocker and Major, 1989).

### Strategic social comparison

Self-evaluation is a comparative rather than absolute affair: it takes place not in a self-contained psyche but in the social world thronged with individuals of varying merit. Consequently, although many social comparisons may be objectively forced upon people by circumstance, their minds can nonetheless exploit whatever subjective leeway remains to satisfy the self-enhancement motive. Most notably, despite a well-documented tendency to compare themselves to roughly similar or slightly superior others (Gruder, 1971; Miller et al., 1988), people are often disposed to *downwardly compare* themselves to relevantly inferior others, in order to capitalize upon an ego-defensive *contrast effect* (Biernat and Billings, 2001; Suls and Wills, 1991).

Notably, even *lateral comparisons* and *upward comparisons* can further self-enhancement goals. For example, lateral ingroup comparisons, especially among members of disadvantaged groups, can protect self-esteem (Crocker et al., 1991). Moreover, upward comparison to superior others with whom one feels affinity can prompt self-enhancement through *assimilation* (Collins, 1996), at least where the gap is not unduly or unexpectedly large (Wheeler, 1966), the target's skill or successes are seen as attainable (Lockwood and Kunda, 1997), and the target is not viewed as a competitor (Wood, 1989). Indeed, self-esteem moderates the beneficial evaluative consequences of comparisons to *both* inferior and superior others. This is possibly because people with higher self-esteem are more optimistic about both evading the failures and misfortunes of their inferiors, and about securing the success and good fortune of their superiors (Buunk et al., 1990).

### Strategic construal

The concepts that people use to understand themselves and their social world are characteristically loose and fuzzy, lacking necessary and sufficient defining conditions (Cantor and Mischel, 1979). Consequently, people can, when making social comparisons or estimations, subtly shift their construal of the meaning of those concepts in order to self-enhance. For example, people's interpretation of what counts as virtue or talent is slanted in favor of attributes they possess, and of what counts as vice or deficiency, in favor of attributes they lack (Dunning et al., 1991). Such *strategic construal*, affirming the self by semantic adjustment, is exacerbated following negative feedback, thereby implicating the ego in its genesis (Dunning et al., 1995). Thematic variations of the phenomenon include playing up the importance of skills in domains of competence (Story and Dunning, 1998) while downplaying those in domains of incompetence (Tesser and Paulhus, 1983). Though psychically soothing (Simon et al., 1995), such strategies may sometimes prove materially counterproductive. For example, members of minority groups, who, due to an inhospitable cultural climate, perform poorly in academic settings, subsequently disengage psychologically from, and disidentify with, academic pursuits in general, thereby safeguarding their self-esteem but imperilling their socioeconomic prospects (Crocker et al., 1998).

Strategic construal can operate in a more devious manner still: people make self-aggrandizing interpretations, not only of their own attributes, but also of *others*, in order to cast themselves in a comparatively favorable light. For example, couch potatoes construe everyone as fairly athletic, whereas *gym gerbils* see athleticism as a singular attribute (Dunning and Cohen, 1992). In addition, low achievers in a domain are liable to regard the accomplishments of high achievers as exceptional, thereby lessening the shame of their own ineptitude (Alicke et al., 1997). In experimental settings, too, after positive or negative feedback, people with high, but not low, self-esteem, conveniently adjust their perceptions of others, of varying ability and performance, in a self-enhancing direction (Dunning and Beauregard, 2000). Moreover, not only is the meaning of categories subject to strategic construal, but also the degree to which they are believed to characterize other people. Over and above the general tendency to assume that others share their characteristics (Ross et al., 1977), people overestimate the prevalence of their shortcomings (for example, show an enhanced *false consensus effect*) and underestimate the prevalence of their strengths (for example, show a contrary *false uniqueness effect*) (Mullen and Goethals, 1990).

In summary, people's representations of self and others are not determined merely by impartial computation. Instead, they are transformed, in idio-syncratic ways, to satisfy self-enhancing prerogatives.

## *Behavioral implications of self-enhancement*

Self-enhancement is not just confined to the intrapsychic sphere: it also has ramifications for how people behave. We outline below how self-enhancement influences behavior in two important ways.

### Self-evaluation maintenance

Self-evaluation maintenance theory specifies how self-enhancement waxes and wanes as a function of one's ability level in the context of interpersonal relationships, and how this, in turn, influences interpersonal attitudes and behavior (Tesser, 1988). The theory specifies three relevant factors: the *closeness* of a relationship, the personal *relevance* of a particular ability, and one's level of performance in that ability domain. First, comparisons of one's own *performance* with that of others are more likely to occur, and, when they occur, are more consequential in cases where others are close rather than distant. Second, the nature of that comparison will differ depending on whether others' performance is or is not in an ability domain relevant to oneself. When the ability domain is *not* personally relevant, *reflection* will occur: one will undergo self-enhancement (pride) if others perform well but self-derogation (shame) if others perform poorly. However, when the ability domain is personally relevant, *comparison* will occur: one will undergo self-derogation (humiliation) if others perform poorly but self-enhancement (triumph) if others perform well.

As a consequence of interpersonal self-enhancement or self-derogation, and the affective correlates, people adopt a variety of coping strategies. They choose as associates, friends, and partners those who excel, but not in the same domains as they do (Beach and Tesser, 1993); they withhold information that is likely to improve the performance of close others on personally relevant domains (Pemberton and Sedikides, 2001); they alter the relevance of the performance domain by changing their self-concept, thereby moderating the impact of the reflection and comparison processes (Tesser and Paulhus, 1983); and they broaden or narrow the gap between themselves and others, even by deliberately altering the difficulty of domain-relevant tasks (Tesser and Smith, 1980).

### Behavioral self-handicapping

*Behavioral self-handicapping* refers to the act of erecting obstacles to task success in order to deflect the evaluative implications of unhindered task performance (Jones and Berglas, 1978). Self-handicapping permits self-enhancement to occur in two ways (Feick and Rhodewalt, 1997). First, in the case of failure, one can protect one's self-esteem by attributing failure to the obstacle that one has erected (*discounting*); second, in the case of success, one can promote one's self-esteem by attributing that success to oneself *despite* the obstacle erected (*augmenting*). People low in self-esteem opt for the former self-protective route, to avoid being perceived as incompetent, whereas people high in self-esteem preferentially select the latter self-promoting route, to enhance perceptions of competence (Rhodewalt et al., 1991; Tice, 1991). The word 'perceptions' is important, as self-handicapping, though still present when task performance is private (Rhodewalt and Fairfield, 1991), is magnified by public scrutiny (Tice and Baumeister, 1990). Yet, from a self-presentational point of view, self-handicapping is also a risky strategy: if found out, those who use it face the censure of others (Rhodewalt et al., 1995).

What factors prompt self-handicapping? One is a sense of uncertainty over whether good performance can be attained, due to limited control over similar task outcomes, or an insecure sense of self generally (Arkin and Oleson, 1998). Another is the tendency to hold *fixed-entity* as opposed to *incremental* theories of domain competency (Dweck, 1999): believing that improvement is impossible prompts evasive self-enhancing maneuvers. Third, self-handicapping occurs only when a task or evaluation is important (Shepperd and Arkin, 1991). Finally, negative feedback makes self-handicapping more likely, allowing the wounded ego the chance to protect or promote itself (Rhodewalt and Tragakis, 2002). Regardless, whatever the antecedents of self-handicapping, the self-defeating end result is the same: outcome quality is compromised in order to make the meaning of that outcome more palatable. Indeed, students who report a proneness to use self-handicapping strategies also underperform relative to their aptitude, with poor examination preparation mediating the effect (Zuckerman et al., 1998).

### *Constraints on self-enhancement*

Self-enhancement comes in many shapes and forms. However, it would be an exaggeration to say that self-enhancement is *always* the dominant self-motive, that mental life is ruled by nothing else. Indeed, there are identifiable conditions under which self-enhancement is contained or in which other motives assume priority. Competing motives involved in self-evaluation include *self-assessment* (the desire to know the truth about oneself), *self-verification* (the desire to confirm pre-existing views about oneself), and *self-improvement* (the desire to expand one's abilities and become a better person) (Sedikides and Strube, 1997). We will begin by discussing specific factors that constrain self-enhancement and gradually move into a discussion of how these other motives are implicated in such constraints.

### Plausibility constraints

Much self-enhancement thrives upon the *vagueness* or *ambiguity* of the evidence. For example, the above-average effect subsides when the trait being judged is clearly defined and easily verified (for example, 'punctual' as opposed to 'sensitive') (van Lange and Sedikides, 1998). In addition, the tendency to selectively recall instances of desirable traits is held in check by one's actual standing on those traits (Sanitioso et al., 1990). Finally, unpalatable evidence is reluctantly taken on board when there is no room for interpretative maneuver (Doosje et al., 1995).

Such deference to reality is advantageous. Unqualified self-aggrandizement would preclude any informed assessment of one's strengths and weakness, a deficit that would hamstring effective social functioning – as the interpersonal abrasiveness of narcissists attests (Morf and Rhodewalt, 2001). Unless one is minimally committed to the facts at hand, which occasionally imply ugly truths about the self, one cannot exploit self-enhancing biases. This is because such biases operate effectively only under the veneer of rationality: to own up to a bias is to undermine any grounds for believing in the comforting conclusions it implies (Gilbert et al., 1998). Self-presentation is characterized by similar favorability/plausibility tradeoffs: people self-enhance to the degree that they believe they can get away with it (Sedikides et al., 2002; Tice et al., 1995).

Another relevant finding in this connection is that *ambicausal* introspection, namely, the deliberate attempt to generate possible reasons for why one might either possess or lack a personality trait, attenuates self-enhancement, especially when people commit those reasons to paper (Horton and Sedikides, 2002). Ambicausal introspection works by undermining the certainty that one possesses positive traits and lacks negative traits.

Of course, people are sometimes motivated to seek out accurate, diagnostic information about themselves (Trope, 1986). Such unbiased *self-assessment* has obvious advantages. Knowing one's objective strengths and limitations, one's likes and dislikes, allows one to set and pursue personal goals that are both realistically achievable and personally beneficial (Oettingen and Gollwitzer, 2001). Unsurprisingly, then, people sometimes choose tasks believed to provide diagnostic information about the self, even when these tasks are difficult (Trope, 1979) or the information they transmit unflattering (Trope, 1980). Indeed, people invest effort in tasks to the extent that they believe those tasks will yield diagnostic information. This tendency is furthermore exacerbated by prior manipulations that increase uncertainty about the self, showing that it is the thirst for self-knowledge that underlies it (Trope, 1982).

### Mood

This brings us neatly to mood as a moderator of self-enhancement. The initial experience of success, or the induction of a positive mood, will make people even more receptive to negative diagnostic feedback. Indeed, people will review their past successes in expectation of receiving such feedback, presumably to shore up their mood (Trope and Neter, 1994). Such findings suggest that state self-esteem, or the mood that accompanies it, serves as a *resource* that can be deployed to cope with ego threat (Pyszczynski et al., 1997; Steele, 1988).

If positive mood curtails self-enhancement, then, ironically, so does *negative* mood. For example, although immodesty is usually evident in discrepancies between people's estimates of their own virtues and the estimates of neutral observers, a depressive disposition decreases the discrepancy (Campbell and Fehr, 1990; Lewinsohn et al., 1980). In addition, illusions of control are moderated by melancholy (Alloy and Abramson, 1988), and Pollyannaish prognostications are diluted by dysphoria (Pyszczynski et al., 1987). Finally, depressives seem to be less resolute self-enhancers in response to negative feedback than do normals (Blaine and Crocker, 1993; Kuiper, 1978). The divergent effects of mood may be best explained by negative mood making one less *able* to deploy self-enhancing tactics, and positive mood making their deployment less *necessary*. This raises the interesting possibility that not all manifestations of self-enhancement will positively correlate with one another.

However, contrary to some early suggestions (Alloy and Abramson, 1979), sadder does not always mean wiser (Dunning and Story, 1991; Ruehlman et al., 1985). For example, although the self-ratings of depressives are more in line with those of neutral observers than the self-ratings of normals, the self-ratings of normals are nonetheless more in line with those of friends and family than the self-ratings of depressives (Campbell and Fehr, 1990). Hence, so-called *depressive realism* may merely be the inadvertent consequence of viewing life through blue-tinted spectacles rather than the reliable result of greater self-insight (Shrauger et al., 1998; Wood et al., 1998).

### Social context

When people interact with close others, the self-enhancement motive appears to be enfeebled. For example, when friends, or previous strangers whose intimacy levels have been experimentally enhanced, cooperate on a joint task, they do not manifest the self-serving bias, unlike casual acquaintances or continued strangers who do (Sedikides et al., 2002).

People's graciousness in the presence of close others appears to be mediated by mutual liking and expectations of reciprocity, reflecting a communal rather than an exchange orientation (Clark and Mills, 1979). Indeed, a betrayal of trust reinstates the self-serving bias, which tallies with the real-world finding that relationship satisfaction is inversely correlated with such betrayal (Fincham and Bradbury, 1989). In addition, although people are inclined to self-present boastfully in front of strangers, they curtail their conceit in front of friends (Tice et al., 1995). Finally, others close to the self tend to be more highly evaluated than distant others (Murray et al., 1996a), a state of affairs that can be interpreted as the concept of the other being subsumed under the self-concept (Aron et al., 1991).

## Culture

It has become a virtual truism that psychological functioning is moderated by the influence of culture (Fiske et al., 1998; Markus and Kitayama, 1991; Triandis and Suh, 2002). Principal among the claims made has been that Eastern and Western cultures fundamentally diverge, in that the former, being more collectivistic prioritizes *interdependence* (interpersonal harmony, group cohesion, and social duty), whereas the latter, being more individualistic prioritizes *independence* (separate identity, private fulfillment, and greater autonomy). It has further been claimed that, due to the greater emphasis laid on internal attributes in the West, self-enhancement tends to overshadow self-criticism, where as the opposite tends to happen, due to the greater emphasis laid on relational attributes, in the East (Kitayama et al., 1995a). In other words, self-enhancement, for all its manifold manifestations, is a phenomenon largely limited to the West, where social ties are looser. Indeed, this would be roughly consistent with experimental findings showing that relationship closeness constrains self-enhancement (Sedikides et al., 2002).

Taken at face value, there is much evidence to support this culture-specific view of self-enhancement. For example, when describing themselves, Easterners spontaneously use more negative terms than Westerners do (Kanagawa et al., 2001), and provide less inflated ratings of their own merits (Kitayama et al., 1997). In addition, Easterners indulge in self-deprecatory social comparisons (Takata, 1987), entertain less unrealistically optimistic visions of the future (Heine and Lehman, 1995), and show a self-serving attributional bias that is attenuated, absent and even reversed, (Kitayama et al., 1995b).

It also seems that East Asians manifest a greater desire for *self-improvement* through self-criticism than Westerners do (Heine et al., 1999). They are reluctant, rather than eager, to conclude that they have performed better than an average classmate (Heine et al., 2000) and readily acknowledge, rather than reflexively discount, negative feedback (Heine et al., 2001a). They also persist more after initial failure than success, rather than vice versa, and consider tasks on which they fail to be more diagnostic of merit, not less (Heine et al., 2001b). More generally, the self-improvement motive, as an aspiration towards a possible self (Markus and Nurius, 1986), may moderate a variety of psychological processes, in both independent and inter-dependent cultures (Sedikides, 1999).

Yet, there are signs that self-enhancement is not altogether absent from interdependent cultures. Easterners self-efface on only some personality dimensions, not others (Yik et al., 1998). For example, Chinese schoolchildren rate themselves highly on the dimension of competence (Falbo et al., 1997) and Taiwanese employees rate themselves more favorably than their employers do (Fahr et al., 1991). On a more profound level, it may be that cultural differences in self-enhancement phenomena stem not from variations in the *strength* of the underlying motive, but rather from differences in how *candidly* or *tactically* that motive is acted upon (Sedikides and Strube, 1997), and in terms of what characteristics are deemed *important* by individuals as they strive to fulfill the roles that their culture prescribes. There is evidence, for example, that Westerners self-enhance on individualistic attributes while Easterners self-enhance on collectivistic attributes (Kurman, 2001; Sedikides et al., 2003), and that this difference is explained at least partly in terms of the relative importance that members of each culture place on these attributes (Sedikides et al., 2003).

## Self-verification

It has been argued that people desire not merely to know how great they are (self-enhancement), or what they are really like (self-assessment), but also to confirm that they are the type of people they already thought they were. In other words, people seek to *self-verify* (Swann, 1987, 1990). The idea is that self-verification serves to stabilize self-views, and that stable self-views, in turn, increase the predictability and controllability of future events in the social world. More specifically, self-verification may be pursued for one of two reasons: epistemic, to induce or preserve a sense of cognitive coherence; and pragmatic, to allow interpersonal interactions to proceed smoothly. So, if people's sense of identity is undermined, or society takes a view of them discordant with their own, their psychological functioning will be impaired. Hence, people will be motivated to seek information that confirms their pre-existing self-views, as well as the company of other people who will provide them with such self-confirmatory information. For self-views of neutral valence, there is some evidence that this is true, particularly when those self-views are confidently held (Pelham and Swann, 1994).

Note that, because people are already inclined to believe that they possess positive traits (Alicke, 1985), they could prefer to receive (or actively seek) positive feedback (or individuals likely to provide it) either to self-enhance or to self-verify. For example, if people already believed that they were extraverted, a normatively positive trait, the observation that they sought to confirm this fact, say, by correcting evaluators' misperceptions, would not by itself furnish evidence of self-verification (Swann and Ely, 1984; see McNulty and Swann, 1994, and Swann et al., 2000, for similarly ambiguous findings). The acid test for self-verification is whether people will prefer and seek negative feedback, or the people who provide it, when such feedback is consistent with a *negative* view of self.

Much research appears to pass this acid test. For example, people choose to interact with evaluators who give them confirmatory feedback about their 'worst' attribute (Swann et al., 1989), or about their negative self-views in general (Swann et al., 1992a), even when they have the twin alternatives of either interacting with an evaluator who will provide them with positive information, or opting out of the study altogether (Swann et al., 1992d). In addition, people are prepared to act in such a way as to confirm existing self-perceptions. Those who regard themselves as dislikable will strive to disabuse an evaluator who likes them of his flattering misconceptions (Swann and Read, 1981). Married people, when provided with bogus evaluations supposedly from their spouses, reject those evaluations when they clash with others obtained from a previous session, even when the new evaluation is comparatively positive (that is, more favorable than the previous ratings implied) (De La Ronde and Swann, 1998). There is even a suggestion that spouses (but not dating partners) who confirm each other's self-views are more intimate with one another (Swann et al., 1994; though see Murray et al., 1996a). Finally, people with negative self-views seem to gravitate towards those who view them negatively (Swann et al., 1992c).

Although these results show that people may opt to receive information congruent with negative self-views, and opt to interact with those who provide it, they do not in themselves establish the *motivation* that underlies the choosing of that option. People self-verify, certainly. But do they *want* to self-verify? Some light is shed on the matter by the think-aloud protocols of participants deliberating over which interaction partner to choose. In one study (Swann et al., 1992a), participants mostly mentioned that having a partner who agreed with them was important, a response which the researchers classified as an epistemic reason for making a choice; next, they mentioned being concerned that the interaction would take place smoothly (classified as a pragmatic reason); finally, they noted that a perceptive partner would be most desirable (classified as a concern with accuracy). Unfortunately, the most often mentioned reason leaves moot the underlying motivation (participants' noted agreement was crucial, but why?), and the last reason could have more to do with wanting a competent interaction partner than obtaining additional accurate self-assessment. Moreover, self-reports of motivations are suspect, as they may reflect a lack of introspective access (Nisbett and Wilson, 1977), expectancy effects (Rosenthal and Rubin, 1978), and self-presentation or self-deception (Paulhus, 1991).

Furthermore, there are at least two credible explanations, apart from bolstering a pre-existing view of self, for why people might prefer interaction partners who concur with their negative view of self. First, people like, and are drawn to, others who are similar to them and who share their views (Byrne, 1997). Although one might explain the effects of similarity in terms of a desire for verification, it cannot be ruled out, a priori, that other factors, such as an inchoate sense of familiarity (Bornstein, 1989), or a generalization of response from related past examples of attitude similarity, could also be responsible. Second, people with negative self-views who are glowingly evaluated by imminent interaction partners are likely to chafe at the prospect of disappointing those partners' upbeat expectations. They may react in this way because they are risk-averse in general (Baumeister et al., 1989) and are most upset by patterns of feedback that start out positive but then turn negative (Brown et al., 2002).

This, of course, still does not explain why participants would seek out negative information in the absence of any future interaction (Giesler et al., 1996; Swann et al., 1990). However, even here, the evidence clearly points to the fact that people with negative self-views do not *want* negative feedback. Much has been made of the assertion that affective responses to feedback are governed by self-enhancement whereas cognitive responses to feedback are governed by self-verification (or self-consistency) (McFarlin and Blascovich, 1981; Shrauger, 1975; Swann et al., 1987). However, this boils down to claiming that when people think about it, they generally cannot find sufficient *reason* to dispute the accuracy of feedback consistent with their self-view, positive or negative, although they still would *prefer* to receive positive feedback. A further elegant confirmation of this is that when people's cognitive resources are taxed, and their rational thought disrupted, they choose interaction partners on the basis of congeniality alone (Swann et al., 1990). But if people regard information consistent with their self-view as more credible, is it any surprise that they choose it in preference to information inconsistent with their self-view that they consider less credible? Why would they opt for positive information, or choose interaction partners who provide it, if they are incapable of believing it? Self-verification effects may simply be due to ubiquitous plausibility constraints. It is therefore a challenge for future research to implicate directly a drive for cognitive coherence in self-verification effects, an enterprise that would be aided by the development of specific measures and manipulations of such coherence.

### *Relative self-motive strength*

In our discussion so far, some reference has been made to how the self-evaluation motives – self-enhancement, self-assessment, self-verification, and self-improvement – vie with one another, although the evidence is sometimes open to different interpretations. In one study, however, a direct attempt was made to compare the relative strength of various motives (excluding self-improvement) in the neutral context of a self-reflection task (Sedikides, 1993). Participants chose the question that they would be most likely to ask themselves in order to determine whether or not they possessed a particular type of personality trait. Questions varied in terms of the valence (positive/negative), diagnosticity (high/low), and importance (central/peripheral) of the answers they elicited. Participants' yes/no answers to the questions were also noted. It turned out that, on the whole, participants self-enhanced more than they self-assessed or self-verified. For example, they chose higher diagnosticity questions concerning central positive traits than central negative ones and answered 'yes' more often to central positive questions than central negative questions. However, participants also self-verified more than they self-assessed, in that they chose more questions overall concerning (relatively certain) central traits than (relatively uncertain) peripheral traits.

Nonetheless, the strength of activation of particular motives, and hence their relative strength, is likely to be situation- or state-specific. It has already been mentioned how an acutely positive mood makes people more capable of taking on board negative information, thereby facilitating even-handed self-assessment (Trope and Neter, 1994). Another factor that matters is *timing*. Prior to having made a decision, people may impartially muse upon the merits of deciding either way, but once they have made up their minds, and start acting accordingly, they move from a *deliberative* to an *implementational* mindset (Gollwizer and Kinney, 1989) and are likely to prefer self-enhancing information that justifies their prior decision. The classical research literature is peppered with examples of post-choice rationalization (Aronson and Mills, 1959; Brehm, 1956; Staw, 1976). Of course, having made a decision, one no longer has *control* over whether or not to make it. To the extent that one retains control over outcome, one may be less inclined to self-enhance. This is illustrated with regard to people's theories with respect to whether a particular characteristic is malleable or fixed (Dauenheimer et al., 2002). For example, if people believe that an important personality trait cannot be altered, they show a self-enhancing pattern, welcoming feedback on that trait after initial success, but not failure at displaying it. However, if people believe that this trait can be altered (that is, that it is partly under their control), they show a self-assessment pattern, welcoming feedback regardless of initial success or failure (Dunning, 1995). Similarly, the controllability of trait is one factor that attenuates the above-average effect (van Lange and Sedikides, 1998).

It should not be assumed, however, that the different self-motives are implacably opposed to one another. For example, it could be argued that self-assessment and self-improvement can be classified as different manifestations of a single learning motive (Sedikides and Skowronski, 2000). In addition, it has been proposed that self-enhancement is the master motive and that all the others represent tactical as opposed to candid ways of satisfying it (Sedikides and Strube, 1997). On this view, all the motives are ultimately 'on the same team'.

## **Self-esteem**

Some people are more successful at self-enhancing than others; the affective correlate (and potential cause or effect) is level of *self-esteem*. Self-esteem can be manifest either as an underlying dispositional tendency (*trait self-esteem*) or as a transient psychological condition (*state self-esteem*). As the former, it is typically measured by self-report scales (Fleming and Courtney, 1984; Rosenberg, 1965), whereas, as the latter, it is typically induced by administering favorable or unfavorable feedback (Brown, 1993; Tesser, 1988), although reliable measures of state self-esteem also exist (Heatherton and Polivy, 1991). Trait and state self-esteem correlate substantially with one another (Heatherton and Ambady, 1993), and the latter can be construed as a temporary positive or negative departure from the former.

Although self-esteem occupies a privileged position in popular psychological discourse, social psychologists have long debated, and continue to debate, its meaning, origin, and implications. Nonetheless, few theorists would dispute that self-esteem involves something akin to an *attitude towards oneself* (Banaji and Prentice, 1994). As an attitude, self-esteem is associated with numerous *self-beliefs* (Markus and Wurf, 1987) that pertain either to the self as a whole ('I am likable') or to its particular attributes ('I make people laugh'). Importantly, such self-beliefs are *evaluative* in nature (for example, being likable, or making people laugh, is *good*); that is, self-knowledge is experienced, not dispassionately, but as intrinsically positive or negative. Moreover, self-esteem is associated with *feelings* about oneself (Brown, 1998), again pertaining either globally to the self ('I am fabulous') or locally to certain attributes ('I like my elegant sense of dressing'). In the general population, feelings about the global self are positively biased and rarely blatantly negative (Baumeister et al., 1989; Brown, 1986), an unsurprising state of affairs given the strength of the self-enhancement motive. Although such feelings might appear to be entirely a function of evaluative self-beliefs, the effect is probably bidirectional, given that people believe what they desire to be true (McGuire, 1990), and exploit semantic ambiguity to do so (Dunning, 1999; Kunda, 1990).

Opinion is divided on the subject of whether global self-beliefs and feelings derive, *bottom-up*, from local ones (Marsh, 1990; Pelham and Swann, 1989) or whether local self-beliefs and feelings derive, *top-down*, from global ones (Baumeister et al., 2002; Brown et al., 2001). Conceivably, the causality involved could again be bidirectional. However, bottom-up models that weight self-attributes by their idiosyncratic importance oddly fail to predict global self-esteem any better than models that do without such weighting (Marsh, 1995; Pelham, 1995). There are several possible explanations for this oddity, including the inaccuracy of self-reported importance ratings (Brown, 1998), but if a globally positive self-view promotes above-average perceptions across the board, then ratings of peripheral traits should mirror that self-view and, therefore, correlate with global self-ratings. Also relevant to this connection is the fact that the higher their self-esteem, the more people regard themselves as possessing flattering attributes to an illusory degree (Baumeister et al., 2002). Given that 'illusory' is here defined in terms of disagreement with peers, there would seem to be no basis for self-ascribing such attributes apart from a subjective sense of overall merit (Brown, 1998). That said, people do differ measurably in terms of their preconditions for feeling good about themselves, and feedback affects them profoundly depending on whether it does or does not pertain to such preconditions (Crocker and Wolfe, 2001).

### *High self-esteem: correlates,benefits, and drawbacks*

In modern Western culture, global self-esteem has been regarded as a psychological attribute of cardinal importance. In abundance, it is hailed as a panacea for psychosocial ills such as bullying, delinquency, and neurosis; in dearth, it is derided as a prescription for them (Branden, 1988; Mackay and Fanning, 2000; Mruk, 1999; National Association for Self-Esteem, 2002). Yet the argument has been made that this view may generalize neither culturally (Heine et al., 1999; but see Sedikides et al., 2003) nor historically (Baumeister, 1987; Exline et al., 2002; Twenge and Campbell, 2001; but see Sedikides and Skowronski, 1997, 2002). Moreover, academic skepticism regarding the validity of self-esteem has increased as research findings have accumulated (Baumeister et al., 2002; Dawes, 1994).

#### Methodological issues

Drawing summary conclusions about the correlates and alleged benefits of self-esteem poses problems. Care is needed to distill reality from perception, because self-esteem distorts the outlook on life in general, and many studies rely on subjective perceptions and verbal reports. Thus, an artifactual relation between self-esteem and, say, toe-tapping ability, might emerge simply because people with high self-esteem, seeing themselves through rose-tinted spectacles, conclude that they are talented toe-tappers, whereas people with low self-esteem, seeing themselves through blue- or nontinted spectacles, conclude that their toe-tapping ability leaves a lot to be desired. When objective measures of predicted outcomes are used, correlations with self-esteem decline dramatically or vanish altogether (Gabriel et al., 1994; Miller and Downey, 1999). For example, although self-reported physical attractiveness correlates substantially (r=.59) with self-esteem, observer-rated physical attractiveness correlates with it hardly at all ($r_5$=.00 to .14, depending on the aspect of appearance in question) (Diener et al., 1995).

Moreover, even if a genuine correlation obtains between self-esteem and a variable of interest, in the absence of further experimentation, longitudinal prediction, or structural equation analysis, the direction of causation remains unclear. From an a-priori standpoint, it is at least as plausible that possessing a characteristic of objective significance will boost self-esteem as that high self-esteem will promote the development of such a characteristic. Take extraversion, for instance: although it reliably accompanies self-esteem (Robins et al., 2002), it is not clear which (if either) is the antecedent of the other.

Furthermore, even if it is established that self-esteem is the antecedent rather than the consequence of some variable of interest, another background factor might still account, either statistically or causally, for self-esteem's predictive capacity. For example, suppose that self-esteem predicted extraversion over time but that the inverse prediction was not observed. Self-esteem might nonetheless fail to predict over time any extraversion that was not *also* predicted over time by, say, social inclusion. Considerations like these act as salutary checks on overzealous interpretations of correlations between measures of self-esteem and desirable outcome variables.

## Achievement and performance

The cautionary preamble out of the way, we can now inquire what self-esteem relates to (causally or otherwise) and whether it lives up to its sterling reputation. For starters, the evidence that self-esteem improves performance in academic settings is weak. Correlations are typically variable and exceedingly modest on average (Davies and Brember, 1999; Robins and Beer, 2001; Ross and Broh, 2000). Moreover, self-esteem seems to be an effect rather than a cause and explains little beyond what other background variables do (Bachman and O'Malley, 1986; Midgett et al., 2002; Pottebaum et al., 1986). Furthermore, interventions designed to raise self-esteem may either fail to influence academic performance (Scheirer and Kraut, 1979) or actually undermine it, by encouraging complacency (Forsyth and Kerr, 1999). The general picture is not different for performance in other domains (Judge and Bono, 2001; Wallace and Baumeister, 2002), although differences between people with high and low self-esteem may become apparent only as time goes by (Di Paula and Campbell, 2001) or in the wake of ego threat (Brockner et al., 1983; Campbell and Fairey, 1989). High self-esteem people do spontaneously show greater persistence (McFarlin, 1985; McFarlin et al., 1984; Shrauger and Sorman, 1977) and, importantly, more *judicious* persistence (Di Paula and Campbell, 2001; Sandelands et al., 1998) in the face of adversity than people with low self-esteem. However, ego threat can also goad people with high (but not low) self-esteem into persisting overoptimistically and fruitlessly (Baumeister et al., 1993).

One might expect self-esteem to be an important predictor of leadership ability, given the initiative and confidence that leadership requires. Although significant correlations do emerge – for example, in studies of military recruits incorporating multiple and objective dependent measures (Chemers et al., 2000) – these correlations mostly dwindle into insignificance when placed in statistical competition with other predictors. Nevertheless, some evidence does suggest that high self-esteem is associated with willingness to speak out critically in a variety of occupational groups (LePine and Van Dyne, 1998) and that people with high (though not grandiose) self-esteem are valued as work-group contributors (Paulhus, 1998). It may also be the case that, being such a nonspecific variable, self-esteem predicts overall success in life better than success in any particular domain. We could find no pertinent data addressing this issue, however.

## Physical health

If self-esteem does not seem to propel forcefully achievement or performance, might it nonetheless promote physical health? The existing evidence does support the hypothesis, both directly for overall health (Forthofer et al., 2001; Nirkko et al., 1982) and indirectly for biological predictors of health (Prussner et al., 1998; Seeman et al., 1995). Moreover, although positive life events improve the overall health (both self-reported and objectively measured) of people with high self-esteem, they paradoxically impair the health of people with low self-esteem, possibly by disrupting their fragile identity (Brown and McGill, 1989).

With regard to specific health behaviors, however, the picture is less clear. On the one hand, low self-esteem features as a prominent clinical correlate of anorexia (Bers and Quinlan, 1992), bulimia (Mintz and Betz, 1988) or eating disorders generally (French et al., 2001; Williams et al., 1993), and longitudinal data suggest that it may play a causal role (Button et al., 1996; van der Ham et al., 1998), although the bidirectional effects of disordered eating and self-esteem on each other may also be responsible for spiraling symptoms (Heatherton and Polivy, 1992). In addition, low self-esteem may exert its effects only in complex interaction with other risk factors, such as perfectionism and body dissatisfaction (Vohs et al., 1999, 2001).

However, several large studies, both cross-sectional and prospective in design, find neither a simple nor a complex relation between self-esteem and smoking (Glendinning and Inglis, 1999; Koval and Pederson, 1999; McGee and Williams, 2000), except perhaps for females (Abernathy et al., 1995; Lewis et al., 2001). Comparable studies examining the link between self-esteem and alcohol consumption find either no effect (Hill et al., 2000; McGee and Williams, 2000; Poikolainen et al., 2001) or only complex and equivocal effects (Jackson et al., 1997; Scheirer et al., 2000). The same goes for sexual behavior: self-esteem does not reliably predict pregnancy or early sexual activity (Berry et al., 2000; McGee and Williams, 2000; Paul et al., 2000) and its relation to safer-sex activities is far from proven (Hollar and Snizek, 1996; Langer and Tubman, 1997). High self-esteem may simply dispose one to *more* sex of whatever type (Herold and Way, 1993).

Part of the reason for the lack of clear findings for sex and drugs may be that self-esteem exerts contrary effects, on the one hand, affording people the self-confidence to resist social pressure (Brockner, 1984) or escapist temptations (Baumeister, 1991), but, on the other hand, affording them the initiative to try more risky or forbidden activities (Brockner and Elkind, 1985) under self-serving illusions of invulnerability (Gerrard et al., 2000). Indeed, people with high self-esteem who relapse into smoking after a period of abstention are more adept at rationalizing their relapse (Gibbons et al., 1997).

### Psychological health

The clearest correlate of self-esteem is *subjective well-being*. Self-esteem strongly and consistently predicts self-reported life satisfaction and assorted measures of happiness (Diener and Diener, 1995; Furnham and Cheng, 2000; Lyubomirsky and Lepper, 1995; Shackleford, 2001). Admittedly, such data remain to be supplemented by others based on more objective indices (such as peer ratings) and on designs capable of disambiguating causal links. Nonetheless, diverging patterns of correlation with other variables already indicate that happiness and self-esteem are not merely redundant constructs.

Self-esteem also strongly and consistently predicts, in a negative direction, various manifestations of psychological distress, such as anxiety (Greenberg et al., 1992; Leary and Kowalski, 1995), depression (Tennen and Affleck, 1993; Tennen and Herzberger, 1987), hopelessness (Crocker et al., 1994), and neuroticism (Horner, 2001), although variance shared with neuroticism may account, in part, for self-esteem's predictive power (Judge and Bono, 2001; Neiss et al., 2002). In addition, levels of self-esteem are associated with greater positive affect, and less variable affect, in the course of everyday life, and in reaction to much the same external events (Campbell et al., 1991).

Longitudinal and experimental studies also suggest that self-esteem promotes coping. Some studies find a simple adaptive benefit (Murrell et al., 1991; Robinson et al., 1995), others that high self-esteem acts as a buffer in times of high stress (Bonanno et al., 2002; Corning, 2002), and still others that low self-esteem acts as a spoiler in times of low stress (Ralph and Mineka, 1998; Whisman and Kwon, 1993). Despite the complexity of these findings, they are unanimous that high self-esteem is adaptive.

One reason why coping may be difficult for people with low self-esteem is that they are more prone to demoralization as a result of inauspicious feedback. Whereas people, regardless of their level of self-esteem, feel elated by success and saddened by failure, only those with low self-esteem experience substantial fluctuations in their underlying sense of self-worth (Brown and Dutton, 1995). Such fluctuations may be due to a greater tendency to see a specific poor performance as a reflection of general underlying ability: people low in self-esteem show less pronounced self-serving attributional biases (Blaine and Crocker, 1993) and indeed regard positive and negative feedback as equally credible (Shrauger, 1975). For people low in self-esteem, failure in a specific domain has wide psychological implications (Epstein, 1992; Heyman et al., 1992). It prompts them to lower their estimates of ability in unrelated domains, whereas their high self-esteem counterparts are prompted to raise their estimates by way of compensation (Brown et al., 2001; Rhodewalt and Eddings, 2002).

The above divergent pattern emerges elsewhere. With regard to expectations of future performance, people with low self-esteem, following failure, expect to fail again, whereas people with high self-esteem become paradoxically more optimistic about success (McFarlin and Blascovich, 1981). Moreover, following the activation of *self*-doubt, people with low self-esteem perceive their relationship partners as less fond and forgiving and report needing the relationship less, whereas people with high self-esteem perceive their partners as more fond and forgiving and report needing the relationship more (Murray et al., 1998). It seems that, because such individuals strongly link personal faults and failings to rejection, they are unable to use intimate relationships as a self-affirmational resource (Murray et al., 2001a). One final consequence of their demoralization may be self-regulatory paralysis: people with low self-esteem seem relatively less likely to deploy mood-repair tactics, even when they know that they would be effective (Heimpel et al., 2002).

The greater affective vulnerability of people with low self-esteem is accompanied by, and possibly stems from, self-conceptions that are more tentative and less coherent (Baumeister, 1993; Baumgardner, 1990; Campbell, 1990; Campbell and Lavallee, 1993; Greenwald et al., 1988). Relative to those with low self-esteem, people with high self-esteem: (i) rate themselves faster and more extremely; (ii) give more definite ratings; (that is, report narrower confidence intervals) and express more confidence in the accuracy of these ratings; (iii) provide ratings that are internally consistent (that is, respond identically to synonyms) and also consistent over time; (iv) behave more consistently with those ratings; and (v) furnish more detailed and extensive open-ended self-reports. All this suggests more certain, accurate, and thorough self-knowledge. Hence, it is not so much that people low in self-esteem despise themselves – in fact, they give intermediate and even sporadically favorable ratings of themselves (Baumeister et al., 1989; Pelham, 1993) – but rather that they lack the enduring, firmly held, and richly supported positive identities that people high in self-esteem have.

Given the greater affective vulnerability and cognitive irresolution of people with low self-esteem, it is unsurprising that they prefer to proceed with *caution*, conserving their precious reserves of self-worth and safeguarding their fragile identity, whereas people with high *self-esteem*, being psychologically robust, prefer to court risk, their ego being able to stomach some minor devaluation and their identity some light revision. Another way of putting this is to say that, whereas people with low self-esteem seek to affirm the self by using subtle, *self-protective* strategies, people with high self-esteem seek to affirm the self by using overt, *self-promoting* strategies (Baumeister et al., 1989; Tice, 1993; Wolfe et al., 1986), the difference being mediated by the availability of self-affirmatory resources (Spencer et al., 1993).

Examples of this principle abound. People with low self-esteem make decisions carefully in order to minimize the possibility of future regret and embarrassment, whereas those with high self-esteem are prepared to carelessly spin the wheel (Josephs et al., 1992). Additionally, people with high self-esteem have fewer qualms about openly declaring their positive qualities to an audience (Baumeister, 1982), whereas their low-esteem counterparts prefer to self-enhance more indirectly, through association rather than competition (Schuetz and Tice, 1997). Indeed, assertive self-presentation comes so naturally to people with high self-esteem, and modest self-presentation so naturally to those with low, that instructing either to go against their inclination impairs their memory for the relevant social interaction (Baumeister et al., 1989).

In addition, people behaviorally self-handicap only when the advantages of doing so match their preferred risk-orientation (Rhodewalt et al., 1991). For example, people with low self-esteem refrain from practicing for a test if that test is described as indexing only stupidity, whereas people with high self-esteem refrain from practicing for it if it is described as indexing only genius (Tice, 1991). Moreover, how people act after success or failure reflects their risk-orientation: people high in self-esteem persist after success and desist after failure (going for glory and hiding from shame) whereas those low in self-esteem desist after success and persist after failure (fearing to jeopardize success and striving to remedy deficiencies) (Baumeister and Tice, 1985). This finding also squares with another one: high self-esteem people are most upset by repeated failure and low self-esteem people by failure that follows initial success (Brown et al., 2002).

## Interpersonal behavior

Clearly, self-esteem is beneficial for an individual insofar as it *feels* good to have it. But what are its social implications? Is the oft-repeated popular psychological shibboleth true, namely, that, in order to love other people (for example, live in harmony with them), one must first love oneself? The evidence suggests not.

People with high self-esteem consider themselves to be more popular (Battistich et al., 1993), to have superior friendships (Keefe and Berndt, 1996), to get along better with workmates (Frone, 2000), to enjoy more pleasant social interactions and to experience greater social support. But are such benefits merely in the eye of the beholder? Apparently so, given that both sociometric studies, in which all participants systematically rate both themselves and one another (Bishop and Inderbitzen, 1995; Dolcini and Adler, 1994), and independent criterion studies, in which ratings are provided by observers such as teachers and peers (Adams et al., 2000; Buhrmester et al., 1988), show no evidence of such benefits. The results of 'get-acquainted' studies in the laboratory only confirm that people high in self-esteem, despite their pretensions, are not better liked than people low in it (Brockner and Lloyd, 1986; Campbell and Fehr, 1990) and, after ego threat, are actually disliked more, because they compensate by assertively de-emphasizing their interdependence with others (Vohs and Heatherton, 2001).

There is little direct evidence that high self-esteem promotes the quality or durability of intimate relationships, and, theoretically, matters would work both ways. On the one hand, low self-esteem contaminates regard for one's partner and the partner's views of self (Murray et al., 2001b), thereby acting as a midwife for unmerited distrust, excessive reassurance-seeking, and relational conflict (Murray et al., 1996b), all of which are likely to lower relationship satisfaction and increase the likelihood of relationship dissolution (Hendrick et al., 1988). On the other hand, people with high self-esteem are more likely to opt for 'exit' responses to relationship problems, by deciding to leave, seek other partners, and otherwise eschew constructive attempts to solve relationship problems (Rusbult et al., 1987). Perhaps lacking initiative and confidence, low self-esteem persons are more willing to passively endure relationship problems.

## Aggression and violence

Conventional wisdom, rooted in clinical impressions, had it that low self-esteem was a key cause of aggression and violence, though the underlying psychological mechanism was left unspecified. However, the weight of the evidence suggests that those who perpetrate aggression – delinquents, spouse-beaters, child-beaters, murderers, assaulters, rapists, torturers, psychopaths, and warriors – are in fact rather fond of themselves (Baumeister et al., 1996). Such a correlation makes sense, for two reasons. First, people with high self-esteem, in view of their habitually positive self-appraisals, are more likely to perceive a discrepancy when others appraise them negatively. Second, people with high self-esteem, given the choice between shamefully accepting or angrily rejecting those negative appraisals, will opt for the latter course of action, given their greater self-confidence and initiative. However, this *threatened egoism* model may apply only to people whose self-esteem, as well as being high, is at the same time *fragile* (Kernis, 2003). That is, although aggressive and violent people have high rather than low self-esteem, people with high self-esteem are not necessarily aggressive and violent. This conclusion is supported by studies showing that self-esteem, on its own, does not predict aggression or defensiveness in response to insults or ego threat: narcissism (Bushman and Baumeister, 1998) or self-esteem instability (Kernis et al., 1989) must also be present. In fact, people with high self-esteem may show the *least* aggression and defensiveness when their self-esteem is *not* fragile.

This conclusion is further supported by nonexperimental evidence from several domains. For example, there is no simple link between self-esteem and bullying (Olweus, 1991; Slee and Rigby, 1993). However, one large sociometric study, featuring measures of self-esteem, peer-rated self-esteem, and defensive self-esteem (a combination of high scores on the first two measures combined with high scores on a separate defensive egoism scale) found that bullies had high defensive self-esteem, those who thwarted their bullying had high nondefensive self-esteem, and the bullied themselves had low self-esteem (Salmivalli et al., 1999). As for delinquency, the evidence is equally mixed. Some studies find no link (Joon and Thornberry, 1998), others find a link explained away by background variables (Neumark-Sztainer et al., 1997), and still others find an independent link (Trzesniewski et al., 2002: Study 1). Complicating factors include the possibility that becoming delinquent may raise previously low levels of self-esteem (Rosenberg et al., 1989) and that elinquency is mostly measured by self-reports. However, one longitudinal study using objective measures does suggest that self-esteem offers causal protection against the development of delinquency (Trzesniewski et al., 2002: Study 2).

### Summary

The correlates, benefits, and drawbacks of self-esteem can be succinctly summarized. First, self-esteem is only tangentially related to many of the objective benefits it has traditionally been held to cause. Second, self-esteem is, nonetheless, strongly correlated with subjective well-being. Third, high self-esteem, particularly when fragile or extreme, can be socially disruptive.

Given these findings, why has self-esteem been ballyhooed as an *unqualified* good for so many years, at least in Western societies? It may partly be historical accident, an offshoot of twentieth-century social and economic individualism (Baumeister, 1986). Alternatively, the fact that self-esteem feels so good and prompts the self-ascription of illusory virtues (Brown, 1991) may have contributed to an overestimation of its objective merit, even among the psychological community.

## *Beyond self-esteem*

Research suggests, then, that high self-reported self-esteem does not quite merit its traditionally sterling reputation. Might it be possible to go beyond traditional measures of self-esteem to distinguish between individuals with fragile and secure self-esteem? We will focus here on three relevant lines of inquiry: *implicit* self-esteem, *contingent* self-esteem, and self-esteem *stability*.

### Implicit self-esteem

Awareness has grown about the limitations and pitfalls of self-report instruments (Paulhus, 2002). In particular, self-report measures of self-esteem are biased by self-presentation (Schlenker, 1980), self-deception (Paulhus, 1984), and self-ignorance (Wilson et al., 2000).

Regarding self-presentation, people self-aggrandize in front of strangers but self-efface in front of friends (Tice et al., 1995). Regarding self-deception, people may be reluctant to admit to themselves that they harbor self-doubt, a reluctance they can express in *socially desirable* responses (Crowne and Marlowe, 1960). Indeed, people who are, on an anonymous questionnaire, loath to self-ascribe common vices but keen to self-ascribe uncommon virtues, are more likely, following subsequent failure feedback, to present themselves in glowing terms to an audience, presumably in an attempt to affirm publicly a shaky self-image (Schneider and Turkat, 1975). Regarding self-ignorance, a theoretical distinction can be drawn between *explicit* self-esteem, rooted in the *rational* mind (that is, conscious, controlled, intentional, effortful, verbal, rule-based, slow-processing, and fast-changing), and *implicit* self-esteem, rooted in the *experiential* mind (that is, unconscious, automatic, unintentional, effortless, nonverbal, associationist, fast-processing, and slow-changing) (Smith and DeCoster, 2000).

Explicit self-esteem has been all but equated with responses to traditional self-report measures, and implicit self-esteem with responses to one of several indirect, subtle, and unobtrusive measures. The latter include the Implicit Association Test (IAT; Greenwald et al., 1998), the Go No-Go Association Test (GNAT; Nosek and Banaji, 2001), the Extrinsic Affective Simon Task (EAST; De Houwer, 2002), the Name Letter Task (NLT; Koole et al., 2001), the Self-Apperception Test (SAT; Aidman, 1999), evaluative priming paradigms (Fazio, 2001), and word-fragment completion tasks (Hetts et al., 1999). Yet, for all their diversity, implicit measures of self-esteem operate on the premise that stimuli intimately associated with the self (for example, first and last names, reflexive pronouns) reflect the valence of the self (Beggan, 1992; Hoorens and Nuttin, 1993). Hence, by assessing the valence of self-related stimuli, the underlying valence of the self can be inferred, free from the distortions of self-presentation, self-deception, and self-ignorance.

What, then, do implicit measures reveal? The matter remains controversial. Certainly, implicit measures readily replicate, at a mean level, preferences for self shown on explicit measures. At the same time, implicit measures either show no, or only modest, correlations with explicit measures (Bosson et al., 2000; Jordan et al., 2001). This finding could indicate, significantly, that explicit and implicit measures of self-esteem tap into different underlying constructs, or, mundanely, that the reliability of the latter is poor (Cunningham et al., 2001; Lane et al., 2001).

Nonetheless, consistent with theoretical expectation, the correspondence between explicit and implicit measures is increased if cognitive resources are made scarce during explicit responding (Koole et al., 2001; Wilson et al., 2000). Unfortunately, simply presenting explicit measures first also has the same effect (Bosson et al., 2000), calling into question the autonomy of implicit measures. Also problematic is the fact that implicit measures of self-esteem habitually fail to intercorrelate (Bosson et al., 2000; Jordan et al., 2001), again perhaps due to low reliability, but also perhaps to meaningful structural differences between tasks, the precise modus operandi of which remains under debate (De Houwer, 2000; Gregg, 2003; Klinger et al., 2000). The generic label 'implicit' may hide substantial heterogeneity. Nevertheless, the IAT does appear to index automatic associations between self, valence, and social identity that bear out the predictions of classical balance theory (Heider, 1958) better than explicit measures of the same constructs, suggesting that implicit measures may yet prove to be useful windows on the soul (Greenwald et al., 2002).

As regards the predictive validity of implicit self-esteem, the findings are promising but mixed. On the one hand, implicit self-esteem has failed to predict reasonable validity criteria. These include independent ratings of self-esteem and interpretations of ambiguous statements (Bosson et al., 2000), as well as a wide array of self-related constructs, including well-being, psychiatric symptoms, loneliness, self-construal, and personality traits (Gregg and Sedikides, 2002). On the other hand, implicit self-esteem has predicted nonverbal anxiety in an interview situation where explicit self-esteem proved unsuccessful (Spalding and Hardin, 1999). In addition, an IAT measure of implicit self-esteem has independently predicted greater psychological robustness in the face of failure (Jordan et al., 2001), suggesting that the IAT is diagnostic of fragile self-esteem. Perhaps the most striking predictive findings to date pertain to the name–letter effect (the preference for letters in one's name over letters not in it, controlling for normative letter–liking; Nuttin, 1987). A person (for example, Scott) is disproportionately likely to reside in or move to a location (for example, Scotland) and to hold or pursue an occupation (for example, scoutmaster) whose name resembles his or her own (Pelham et al., 2002).

In summary, research on implicit self-esteem has yielded some promising findings consistent with its reflecting secure self-esteem. However, issues involving both the coherence and interpretation of these findings persist. Future research incorporating manipulations as well as measures of explicit and implicit self-esteem may help clarify such issues. It has already been found that explicit and implicit factors combine in interesting ways to predict defensiveness (Jones et al., 2002) and self-serving biases (Kernis et al., 2000).

## Contingent self-esteem

A distinction can be drawn between whether self-esteem is high or low and the extent to which self-esteem depends on particular conditions being met. In other words, self-esteem can vary not only in level but also in how *contingent* it is. When people with dispositionally contingent self-esteem do not meet specific standards and expectations, their sense of self-worth suffers, and feelings of shame result. Such people, therefore, require continual validation and spend a great deal of time defending their frail egos against looming threats. In contrast, people with noncontingent self-esteem, though they certainly savor successes and lament failures, do not undergo comparable fluctuations in their sense of self-worth. Their core attitude towards themselves remains stable and positive (Deci and Ryan, 1995).

It has been theorized that such stable positive self-regard derives from the satisfaction of people's fundamental needs for *autonomy*, *competence*, and *relatedness* (Deci and Ryan, 2000). This happens when their actions spring from intrinsic desires rather than extrinsic demands, when their actions prove to be habitually efficacious, and where they manage to forge and maintain meaningful and harmonious relationships. Sure enough, studies find that intrinsic aspirations (personal growth, meaningful relationships, and community aspirations) predict several dimensions of well-being, whereas extrinsic motivations (money, fame, and wealth) predict several dimensions of ill-being (Kasser and Ryan, 1996).

Along with an effort to identify the bases of contingent self-esteem, relevant research has progressed along three directions. First, an attempt has been made to characterize, as an individual difference, the degree to which one's self-esteem is contingent or noncontingent (Paradise and Kernis, 1999). When we control for level of trait self-esteem, contingent self-esteem, as expected, predicts less anger and hostility in response to insulting feedback, as well as the choice of better anger-management strategies in hypothetical scenarios (Kernis, 2003).

Second, an attempt has been made to locate the various dimensions on which self-esteem is contingent (Crocker and Wolfe, 2001). These dimensions include approval, acceptance, family, God, power, self-reliance, identity, morality, appearance, and academic ability (Crocker et al., 1999). As predicted, state self-esteem fluctuates to a greater or less extent depending on whether an important or unimportant contingency of self-worth has been targeted by feedback (Crocker et al., 2000; Lun and Wolfe, 1999). Interestingly, however, basing one's self-esteem on dimensions such as God, family, and morality is associated with greater noncontingency of self-esteem overall (Jordan et al., 2001).

Finally, researchers have attempted to qualify the extent to which interpersonal acceptance and rejection (closely linked to self-esteem; Leary and Baumeister, 2000) are considered to be contingent upon success and failure (Baldwin and Sinclair, 1996). High trait self-esteem is associated with weaker 'if–then' contingencies of this sort, as assessed by priming paradigms. The strength of such contingencies can be acutely reinforced or weakened by cuing people with thoughts of relationships in which another person's esteem for the self is contingent, so-called *relationship schemas*, or by having them experience success and failure experiences directly (Baldwin and Meunier, 1999; Baldwin and Sinclair, 1996). Although research on 'if–then' contingencies has not been expressly conducted with a view to going beyond self-reported self-esteem, it could be used for that purpose. What complicates the picture somewhat is that, like self-esteem, contingencies of self-worth also fluctuate with external events.

### Self-esteem stability

Self-esteem stability can be defined as the absence of variation in self-reported self-esteem over either the short term or the long term; alternatively, it can be defined as the absence of variation in departures of momentary state self-esteem from resting levels of trait self-esteem. Either way, self-esteem stability has been typically indexed by the standard deviation of scores across multiple modified measures of self-esteem over several days (Kernis et al., 1992). Self-esteem stability correlates moderately, but not redundantly, with self-esteem level.

Theoretically, one might expect self-esteem instability to be the result of contingent self-esteem: to the extent that one's sense of self-worth is precarious, it is liable to wax and wane with everyday triumphs and disappointments. Indeed, there is evidence that unstable self-esteem is linked to the placing of greater importance upon particular sources of self-esteem (Kernis et al., 1993) and to fears of social rejection (Greenier et al., 1999). Furthermore, unstable self-esteem predisposes people to react antisocially in a manner indicative of psychological fragility. For example, self-esteem level and self-esteem stability interact in an interesting way to predict self-reported proneness to anger and hostility: people with high and unstable self-esteem report the greatest proneness, and people with high and stable self-esteem, the least (Kernis et al., 1989).

A similar pattern of interaction characterizes psychological reactions to valenced feedback and mental simulations of doing well or poorly. Specifically, people whose self-esteem is both high and stable are relatively unaffected, whereas those whose self-esteem is high but unstable become self-aggrandizing or self-defensive (Kernis et al., 1997). For people low in self-esteem, the pattern is less clear-cut, though instability may be predictive of *reduced* defensiveness. In other words, self-esteem instability may not be wholly negative when self-esteem is low. Indeed, although self-esteem instability is concurrently associated with greater depression among people with high self-esteem, it is associated with *less* depression among those with low (Kernis et al., 1991). Perhaps people with low/unstable self-esteem are better able to mobilize self-protective strategies than those with low/stable self-esteem. One study (Kernis et al., 1992) found that the former were more likely than the latter to use excuses to mitigate negative feedback, a practice which could guard against persistent dysphoria. In contrast, people with high/unstable self-esteem were more likely than those with high/stable self-esteem to use excuses to magnify positive feedback. This discrepancy suggests that self-esteem instability drives some of the self-protection/self-enhancement discrepancies usually attributed to levels of self-esteem per se (Tice, 1993).

However, self-esteem instability is hardly a blessing. Over and above self-esteem level, it correlates with deficits in intrinsic motivation and self-determination (Kernis et al., 2000), predicts depression longitudinally in interaction with daily hassles (Kernis et al., 1998), and predicts more extreme reactions to negative events (Greenier et al., 1999). Explorations of the links between self-esteem instability and other indices of fragile self-esteem stability will prove a fertile area of future research.

## Epilogue

The self is a key locus of motivation and affect (Gaertner et al., 2002; Sedikides and Brewer, 2001). Our intent in this chapter has been to document some interesting ways in which social psychology has shown this to be so and, thereby, to highlight the value of empirical forays into the nature of the self. Unfortunately, we had no space even to summarize, much less scrutinize, the equally wide-ranging and intriguing research literatures, both classic and contemporary, on the semantic/representational and the executive/self-regulatory aspects of self (see Baumeister, 1998, 2000). We nonetheless hope to have conveyed to our readers a vibrant sense of what social psychology has told us about selfhood and of its potential to tell us ever more about it in the years ahead.

**SUMMARY**

Selfhood in self-conscious human beings can be divided into three main components: *self-concept, self-evaluation*, and *self-regulation*. The second component is of primary interest here. Although people are motivated to discover the facts about themselves – to self-assess – they are also motivated to discover that those facts are positive – to *self-enhance*. Flattering self-evaluations feel good and critical self-evaluations feel bad. Hence, within the constraints of plausibility (and some other constraints), people's minds work unconsciously to generate flattering self-evaluations, processing social information in various biased ways. For instance, people generally regard themselves as above average, attribute successes to themselves and failures to chance, and preferentially forget negative feedback. However, people also differ in how successfully they self-enhance: some are more able to do so than others. The upshot is differences in self-esteem. In general, having high self-esteem yields subjective benefits, including greater well-being and mental health. However, having high self-esteem yields a mixture of objective benefits and costs. So, although people with high self-esteem are, say, healthier, they are also, say, more prone to aggression. Recent research has shifted from studying sheer quantity of self-esteem towards studying its underlying quality, exploring how it varies, what it depends on, and whether it is automatic.

## References

Abernathy, T.J., Massad, L., and Romano-Dwyer, L. (1995) 'The Relationship between Smoking and Self-Esteem', *Adolescence*, 30: 899–907.

Adams, G.R., Ryan, B.A., Ketsetzis, M., and Keating L. (2000) 'Rule Compliance and Peer Sociability: A Study of Family Process, School-Forced Parent–Child Interactions, and Children's Classroom Behavior', *Journal of Family Psychology*, 14: 237–50.

Aidman, E.V. (1999) 'Measuring Individual Differences in Implicit Self-Concept: Initial Validation of the Self-Apperception Test', *Personality and Individual Differences*, 27: 211–28.

Alicke, M.D. (1985) 'Global Self-Evaluation as Determined by the Desirability and Controllability of Trait Adjectives', *Journal of Personality and Social Psychology*, 49: 1621–30.

Alicke, M.D., LoSchiavo, F.M., Zerbst, J., and Zhang, S. (1997) 'The Person Who Outperforms Me Is a Genius: Maintaining Perceived Competence in Upward Social Comparison', *Journal of Personality and Social Psychology*, 73: 781–9.

Alicke, M.D., Vredenburg, D.S., Hiatt, M., and Govorun, O. (2001) 'The "Better than Myself Effect"', *Motivation and Emotion*, 25: 7–22.

Alloy, L.B. and Abramson, L.Y. (1979) 'Judgment of Contingency in Depressed and Non-Depressed Students: Sadder but Wiser?', *Journal of Experimental Psychology: General*, 108: 441–85.

Alloy, L.B. and Abramson, L.Y. (1988) 'Depressive Realism: Four Theoretical Perspectives', in L.B. Alloy (ed.), *Cognitive Processes in Depression*. New York: Guilford Press, pp. 223–65.

Arkin, R.M. and Maruyama, G.M. (1979) 'Attribution, Affect, and College Exam Performance', *Journal of Educational Psychology*, 71: 85–93.

Arkin, R.M. and Oleson, K.C. (1998) 'Self-Handicapping', in J. Darley and J. Cooper (eds), *Attribution and Social Interaction: The Legacy of Edward E. Jones*. Washington, DC: American Psychological Association, pp. 313–48.

Aron, A., Aron, E.N., Tudor, M., and Nelson, G. (1991) 'Close Relationships as Including Other in the Self', *Journal of Personality and Social Psychology*, 60: 241–53.
Aronson, E. and Mills, J. (1959) 'The Effect of Severity of Initiation on Liking for a Group', *Journal of Abnormal and Social Psychology*, 59: 177–81.
Bachman, J. and Malley, P. (1986) 'Self-Concepts, Self-Esteem, and Educational Experiences: The Frog Pond Revisited (Again)', *Journal of Personality and Social Psychology*, 50: 35–46.
Baldwin, M.W. and Meunier, J. (1999) 'The Cued Activation of Attachment Relational Schemas', *Social Cognition*, 17: 209–27.
Baldwin, M.W. and Sinclair, L. (1996) 'Self-Esteem and "If ... Then" Contingencies of Interpersonal Acceptance', *Journal of Personality and Social Psychology*, 71: 1130–41.
Banaji, M.R. and Prentice, D.A. (1994) 'The Self in Social Contexts', in L. Porter and M. Rosenweig (eds), *Annual Review of Psychology* (vol. 45). Palo Alto, CA: Annual Reviews, Inc, pp. 297–332.
Bartlett, S.J., Wadden, T.A., and Vogt, R.A. (1996) 'Psychosocial Consequences of Weight Cycling', *Journal of Consulting and Clinical Psychology,* 64: 587–92.
Battistich, V., Solomon, D., and Delucchi, K. (1993) 'Interaction Processes and Student Outcomes in Cooperative Learning Groups'. *Elementary School, Journal*, 94: 19–32.
Baumeister, R.F. (1982) 'Self-Esteem, Self-Presentation, and Future Interaction: A Dilemma of Reputation', *Journal of Personality*, 50: 29–45.
Baumeister, R.F. (1986) *Identity: Cultural Change and the Struggle for Self.* New York: Oxford University Press.
Baumeister, R.F. (1987) 'How the Self Became a Problem: A Psychological Review of Historical Research', *Journal of Personality and Social Psychology*, 52: 163–76.
Baumeister, R.F. (1991) *Escaping the Self: Alcoholism, Spirituality, Masochism, and Other Flights from the Burden of Selfhood.* New York: Basic Books.
Baumeister, R.F. (1993) *Self-Esteem: The Puzzle of Low Self-Regard.* New York: Plenum Press.
Baumeister, R.F. (1998) 'The Self', in D.T. Gilbert, S.T. Fiske, and G. Lindzey (eds), *Handbook of Social Psychology*, 4th edn (vol. 1). New York: MCGraw-Hill, pp. 680–740.
Baumeister, R.F. (2000) 'Ego Depletion and the Self's Executive Function', in A. Tesser, R.B. Felson, and J.M. Suls (eds), *Psychological Perspectives on Self and Identity.* Washington, DC: American Psychological Association, pp. 9–33.
Baumeister, R.F. and Cairns, K.J. (1982) 'Repression and Self-Presentation: When Audiences Interfere with Self-Deceptive Strategies', *Journal of Personality and Social Psychology*, 62: 851–62.
Baumeister, R.F., Campbell, J., and Krueger, J.I. (2002) 'Does High Self-Esteem Cause Better Performance, Interpersonal Success, Happiness, or Healthier Lifestyles?' Unpublished Manuscript. Case Western Reserve University, Cleveland, OH.
Baumeister, R.F., Heatherton, T.F., and Tice, D.M. (1993) 'When Ego Threats Lead to Self-Regulation Failure: Negative Consequences of High Self-Esteem', *Journal of Personality and Social Psychology*, 64: 141–56.
Baumeister, R.F., Smart, L., and Boden, J.M. (1996) 'Relation of Threatened Egotism to Violence and Aggression: The Dark Side of High Self-Esteem', *Psychological Review*, 103: 5–33.
Baumeister, R.F., Stillwell, A., and Wotman, S.R. (1990) 'Victim and Perpetrator Accounts of Interpersonal Conflict: Autobiographical Narratives about Anger', *Journal of Personality and Social Psychology*, 59: 994–1005.
Baumeister, R.F. and Tice, D.M. (1985) 'Self-Esteem and Responses to Success and Failure: Subsequent Performance and Intrinsic Motivation', *Journal of Personality*, 53: 450–67.
Baumeister, R.F., Tice, D.M., and Hutton, D.G. (1989) 'Self-Presentational Motivations and Personality Differences in Self-Esteem', *Journal of Personality*, 57: 547–79.
Baumgardner, A.H. (1990) 'To Know Oneself Is to Like Oneself: Self-Certainty and Self-Affect', *Journal of Personality and Social Psychology*, 58: 1062–72.
Beach, S.R.H. and Tesser, A. (1993) 'Decision Making Power and Marital Satisfaction: A Self-Evaluation Maintenance Perspective', *Journal of Social and Clinical Psychology*, 12: 471–94.
Beggan, J.K. (1992) 'On the Social Nature of Non-Social Perception: The Mere Ownership Effect', *Journal of Personality and Social Psychology*, 62: 229–37.
Berry, E.H., Shillington, A.M., Peak, T., and Hohman, M.M. (2000) 'Multi-Ethnic Comparison of Risk and Protective Factors for Adolescent Pregnancy', *Child and Adolescent Social Work Journal*, 17: 79–96.
Bers, S.A. and Quinlan, D.M. (1992) 'Perceived Competence Deficit in Anorexia Nervosa', *Journal of Abnormal Psychology*, 101: 423–31.
Biernat, M. and Billings, L.S. (2001) 'Standards, Expectancies, and Social Comparison', in A. Tesser and N. Schwartz (eds), *Blackwell Handbook of Social Psychology: Intraindividual Processes.* Oxford: Blackwell, pp. 257–83.
Bishop, J.A. and Inderbitzen, H.M. (1995) 'Peer Acceptance and Friendship: An Investigation of Their Relation to Self-Esteem', *Journal of Early Adolescence*, 15: 476–89.
Blaine, B. and Crocker, J. (1993) 'Self-Esteem and Self-Serving Biases in Reactions to Positive and Negative Events: An Integrative Review', in R.F. Baumeister (ed.), *Self-Esteem: The Puzzle of Low Self-Regard.* New York: Plenum Press, pp. 55–85.
Bonanno, G.A., Field, N.P., Kovacevic, A., and Kaltman, S. (2002) 'Self-Enhancement as a Buffer against Extreme Adversity: Civil War in Bosnia and Traumatic Loss in the United States', *Personality and Social Psychology Bulletin*, 28: 184–96.

Bornstein, R.F. (1989) 'Exposure and Affect: Overview and Meta-Analysis of Research, 1968–1987', *Psychological Bulletin*, 106: 265–89.

Bosson, J.K., Swann, W.B., and Pennebaker, J.W. (2000) 'Stalking the Perfect Measure of Implicit Self-Esteem: The Blind Men and the Elephant Revisited?', *Journal of Personality and Social Psychology*, 79: 631–43.

Branden, N. (1988) *How to Raise Your Self-Esteem*. New York: Bantam Books.

Brehm, J.W. (1956) 'Post-Decision Changes in Desirability of Alternatives', *Journal of Abnormal and Social Psychology*, 52: 384–9.

Brockner, J. (1984) 'Low Self-Esteem and Behavioural Plasticity: Some Implications for Personality and Social Psychology', in L. Wheeler (ed.), *Review of Personality and Social Psychology* (vol. 4). Beverly Hills, CA: Sage, pp. 237–71.

Brockner, J. and Elkind, M. (1985) 'Self-Esteem and Reactance: Further Evidence of Attitudinal and Motivational Consequences', *Journal of Experimental Social Psychology*, 21: 346–61.

Brockner, J., Gardner, M., Bierman, J., Mahan, T., Thomas, B., Weiss, W., Winters, L., and Mitchell, A. (1983) 'The Roles of Self-Esteem and Self-Consciousness in the Wortman–Brehm Model of Reactance and Learned Helplessness', *Journal of Personality and Social Psychology*, 45: 199–209.

Brockner, J. and Lloyd, K. (1986) 'Self-Esteem and Likability: Separating Fact from Fantasy', *Journal of Research in Personality*, 20: 496–508.

Brown, J.D. (1986) 'Evaluations of Self and Others: Self-Enhancement Biases in Social Judgments', *Social Cognition*, 4: 353–76.

Brown, J.D. (1991) 'Accuracy and Bias in Self-Knowledge', in C.R. Snyder and D.R. Forsyth (eds), *Handbook of Social and Clinical Psychology: The Health Perspective*. Elmsford, NY: Pergamon Press, pp. 158–78.

Brown, J.D. (1993) 'Self-Esteem and Self-Evaluation: Feeling Is Believing', in J. Suls (ed.), *Psychological Perspectives on the Self*. Hillsdale, NJ: Erlbaum, pp. 27–58.

Brown, J. (1998) *The Self*. New York: MCGraw-Hill.

Brown, J.D., Dutton, K.A., and Cook, K.E. (2001) 'From the Top Down: Self-Esteem and Self-Evaluation', *Cognition and Emotion*, 15: 615–31.

Brown, J.D. and Dutton, K.A. (1995) 'Truth and Consequences: The Costs and Benefits of Accurate Self-Knowledge', *Personality and Social Psychology Bulletin*, 21: 1288–96.

Brown, J.D., Farnham, S.D., and Cook, K.E. (2002) 'Emotional Responses to Changing Feedback: Is It Better to Have Won and Lost Than Never to Have Won at All?', *Journal of Personality*, 70: 127–41.

Brown, J.D. and McGill, K.L. (1989) 'The Cost of Good Fortune: When Positive Life Events Produce Negative Health Consequences', *Journal of Personality and Social Psychology*, 57: 1103–10.

Buehler, R., Griffin, D., and Ross, M. (1994) 'Exploring the "Planning Fallacy": Why People Underestimate Their Task Completion Times', *Journal of Personality and Social Psychology*, 67: 366–81.

Buhrmester, D., Furman, W., Wittenberg, M.T., and Reis, H.T. (1988) 'Five Domains of Interpersonal Competence in Peer Relationships', *Journal of Personality and Social Psychology*, 55: 991–1008.

Bushman, B.J. and Baumeister, R.F. (1998) 'Threatened Egotism, Narcissism, Self-Esteem, and Direct and Displaced Aggression: Does Self-Love or Self-Hate Lead to Violence?', *Journal of Personality and Social Psychology*, 75: 219–29.

Buunk, B.P., Collins, R.L., Taylor, S.E., Van Yperen, N.W., and Dakof, G.A. (1990) 'The Affective Consequences of Social Comparison: Either Direction Has Its Ups and Downs', *Journal of Personality and Social Psychology*, 59: 1238–49.

Button, E.J., Sonuga-Barke, E.J.S., Davies, J., and Thompson, M. (1996) 'A Prospective Study of Self-Esteem in the Prediction of Eating Problems in Adolescent Schoolgirls: Questionnaire Findings', *British Journal of Clinical Psychology,* 35: 193–203.

Byrne, D. (1997) 'An Overview (and Underview) of Research and Theory within the Attraction Paradigm', *Journal of Social and Personal Relationships*, 14: 417–31.

Campbell, J.D. (1990) 'Self-Esteem and Clarity of the Self-Concept', *Journal of Personality and Social Psychology*, 59: 538–49.

Campbell, J.D., Chew, B., and Scratchley, L.S. (1991) 'Cognitive and Emotional Reactions to Daily Events: The Effects of Self-Esteem and Self-Complexity', *Journal of Personality*, 59: 473–505.

Campbell, J.D. and Fairey, P.J. (1989) 'Informational and Normative Routes to Conformity: The Effect of Faction Size as a Function of Norm Extremity and Attention to the Stimulus', *Journal of Personality and Social Psychology*, 57: 457–68.

Campbell, J.D. and Fehr, B.A. (1990) 'Self-Esteem and Perceptions of Conveyed Impressions: Is Negative Affectivity Associated with Greater Realism?', *Journal of Personality and Social Psychology*, 58: 122–33.

Campbell, J.D. and Lavallee, L.F. (1993) 'Who Am I? The Role of Self-Concept Confusion in Understanding the Behavior of People with Low Self-Esteem', in R.F. Baumeister (ed.), *Self-Esteem: The Puzzle of Low Self-Regard*. New York: Plenum Press, pp. 3–20.

Campbell, K.W. and Sedikides, C. (1999) 'Self-Threat Magnifies the Self-Serving Bias: A Meta-Analytic Integration', *Review of General Psychology*, 3: 23–43.

Cantor, N. and Mischel, W. (1979) 'Prototypicality and Personality: Effects on Free Recall and Personality Impressions', *Journal of Research in Personality*, 13: 187–205.

Chemers, M.M., Watson, C.B., May, S.T. (2000) 'Dispositional Affect and Leadership Effectiveness: A Comparison of Self-Esteem, Optimism, and Efficacy', *Personality and Social Psychology Bulletin*, 26: 267–77.

Cialdini, R.B., Borden, R.J., Thorne, A., Walker, M.R., Freeman, S., and Sloan, L.R. (1976) 'Basking in

Reflected Glory: Three (Football) Field Studies', *Journal of Personality and Social Psychology*, 34: 366–75.

Clark, M.S. and Mills, J. (1979) 'Interpersonal Attraction in Exchange and Communal Relationships', *Journal of Personality and Social Psychology*, 37: 12–24.

College Board (1976–7) '*Student Descriptive Questionnaire*. Princeton, NJ: Educational Testing Service.

Collins, R.L. (1996) 'For Better for Worse: The Impact of Upward Social Comparison on Self-Evaluation', *Psychological Bulletin*, 119: 51–69.

Corning, A.F. (2002) 'Self-Esteem as a Moderator between Perceived Discrimination and Psychological Distress among Women'. *Journal of Counselling Psychology*, 49: 117–26.

Crocker, J., Luhtanen, R., Blaine, B., and Broadnax, S. (1994) 'Collective Self-Esteem and Psychological Well-Being among White, Black, and Asian College Students', *Personality and Social Psychological Bulletin*, 20: 503–13.

Crocker, J., Luhtanen, R.K., Wolfe, C., and Bouvrette, S. (1999) 'Determining the Sources of Self-Esteem: The Contingencies of Self-Esteem Scale'. Unpublished Manuscript. University of Michigan, Ann Arbor, MI.

Crocker, J. and Major, B. (1989) 'Social Stigma and Self-Esteem: The Self-Protective Properties of Stigma', *Psychological Review*, 96: 608–30.

Crocker, J., Major, B., and Steele, C. (1998) 'Social Stigma', in D.T. Gilbert, S.T. Fiske, and G. Lindzey (eds), *The Handbook of Social Psychology*, 4th edn. New York: MCGraw-Hill, pp. 504–53.

Crocker, J., Sommers, S.R., and Luhtanen, R.K. (2000) 'Hopes Dashed and Dreams Fulfilled: Contingencies of Self-Esteem and the Graduate School Admissions Process'. Unpublished manuscript. University of Michigan, Ann Arbor, MI.

Crocker, J., Voelkl, K., Testa, M., and Major, B. (1991) 'Social Stigma: The Affective Consequences of Attributional Ambiguity', *Journal of Personality and Social Psychology*, 60: 218–28.

Crocker, J. and Wolfe, C.T. (2001) 'Contingencies of Self-Worth', *Psychological Review*, 108: 593–623.

Cross, P. (1977) 'Not Can but Will College Teaching Be Improved?', *New Directions for Higher Education*, 17: 1–15.

Crowne, D.P. and Marlowe, D. (1960) 'A New Scale of Social Desirability Independent of Psychopathology', *Journal of Consulting Psychology*, 24: 349–54.

Cunningham, W.A., Preacher, K.J., and Banaji, M.R. (2001) 'Implicit Attitude Measures: Consistency, Stability, and Convergent Validity', *Psychological Science*, 121: 163–70.

Dauenheimer, D.G., Stahlberg, D., Spreeman, S., and Sedikides, C. (2002) 'Self-Enhancement, Self-Assessment, or Self-Verification? The Intricate Role of Trait Modifiability in the Self-Evaluation Process', *Revue Internationale de Psychologie Sociale*, 15: 89–112.

Davies, J. and Brember, I. (1999) 'Self-Esteem and National Tests in Years 2 and 6: A 4–Year Longitudinal Study', *Educational Psychology*, 19: 337–45.

Dawes, R. (1994) *House of Cards: Psychology and Psychotherapy Built on Myth*. New York: Free Press.

Deci, E.L. and Ryan, R.M. (1995) 'Human Agency: The Basis for True Self-Esteem', in M.H. Kernis (ed.), *Efficacy, Agency, and Self-Esteem*. New York: Plenum Press, pp. 31–50.

Deci, E.L. and Ryan, R.M. (2000) 'The "What" and "Why" of Goal Pursuits: Human Needs and the Self-Determination of Behavior', *Psychological Inquiry*, 11: 227–68.

De Houwer, J. (2001) 'A Structural and Process Analysis of the Implicit Association Test', *Journal of Experimental Social Psychology*, 37: 443–51.

De Houwer, J. (2002) 'The Extrinsic Affective Simon Task'. Unpublished manuscript. University of Ghent, Ghent, Belgium.

De La Ronde, C. and Swann, W.B. (1998) 'Partner Verification: Restoring Shattered Images of Our Intimates', *Journal of Personality and Social Psychology*, 75: 374–82.

Diener, E. and Diener, M. (1995) 'Cross-Cultural Correlates of Life Satisfaction and Self-Esteem', *Journal of Personality and Social Psychology*, 68: 653–63.

Diener, E., Wolsic, B., and Fujita, F. (1995) 'Physical Attractiveness and Subjective Well-Being', *Journal of Personality and Social Psychology*, 69: 120–9.

Di Paula, A. and Campbell, J.D. (2001) 'Self-Esteem and Persistence in the Face of Failure'. Unpublished manuscript. University of British Columbia, Vancouver, Canada.

Ditto, P.H. and Boardman, A.F. (1995) 'Perceived Accuracy of Favorable and Unfavorable Psychological Feedback', *Basic and Applied Social Psychology*, 16: 137–57.

Ditto, P.H. and Lopez, D.F. (1992) 'Motivated Skepticism: Use of Differential Decision Criteria for Preferred and Nonpreferred Conclusions', *Journal of Personality and Social Psychology*, 63: 568–84.

Ditto, P.H., Scepansky, J.A., Munro, G.D., Apanovitch, A., and Lockhart, L.K. (1998) 'Motivated Sensitivity to Preference-Inconsistent Information', *Journal of Personality and Social Psychology*, 75: 53–69.

Dolcini, M.M. and Adler, N.E. (1994) 'Perceived Competencies, Peer Group Affiliation, and Risk Behavior among Early Adolescents', *Health Psychology*, 13: 496–506.

Doosje, B., Spears, R., and Koomen, W. (1995) 'When Bad Isn't All Bad: Strategic Use of Sample Information in Generalization and Stereotyping', *Journal of Personality and Social Psychology*, 69: 642–55.

Dunning, D. (1995) 'Trait Importance and Modifiability as Factors Influencing Self-Assessment and Self-Enhancement Motives', *Personality and Psychology Bulletin*, 21: 1297–306.

Dunning, D.A. (1999) 'A Newer Look: Motivated Social Cognition and the Schematic Representation of Social Concepts', *Psychological Inquiry*, 10: 1–11.

Dunning, D. and Beauregard, K.S. (2000) 'Regulating Impressions of Others to Affirm Images of the Self', *Social Cognition*, 18: 198–222.

Dunning, D. and Cohen, G.L. (1992) 'Egocentric Definitions of Traits and Abilities in Social Judgment', *Journal of Personality and Social Psychology*, 63: 341–55.

Dunning, D., Griffin, D.W., Milojkovic, J.D., and Ross, L. (1990) 'The Overconfidence Effect in Social Prediction', *Journal of Personality and Social Psychology*, 58: 568–81.

Dunning, D., Leuenberger, A., and Sherman, D.A. (1995) 'A New Look at Motivated Inference: Are Self-Serving Theories of Success a Product of Motivational Forces?', *Journal of Personality and Social Psychology*, 69: 58–68.

Dunning, D., Meyerowitz, J.A., and Holzberg, A.D. (1989) 'Ambiguity and Self-Evaluation: The Role of Idiosyncratic Trait Definitions in Self-Serving Assessments of Ability', *Journal of Personality and Social Psychology*, 57: 1082–90.

Dunning, D., Perie, M., and Story, A.L. (1991) 'Self-Serving Prototypes of Social Categories', *Journal of Personality and Social Psychology*, 61: 957–68.

Dunning, D. and Story, A.L. (1991) 'Depression, Realism, and the Overconfidence Effect: Are the Sadder Wiser when Predicting Future Actions and Events?', *Journal of Personality and Social Psychology*, 61: 521–32.

Dweck, C.S. (1999) *Self-Theories: Their Role in Motivation, Personality, and Development*. Philadelphia, PA: Psychology Press.

Epstein, S. (1992) 'Coping Ability, Negative Self-Evaluation, and Overgeneralization: Experiment and Theory'. *Journal of Personality and Social Psychology*, 62: 826–36.

Epstein, S. and Morling, B. (1995) 'Is the Self Motivated to Do More than Enhance and/or Verify Itself?', in M.H. Kernis (ed.), *Efficacy, Agency, and Self-Esteem*. New York: Plenum Press, pp. 9–29.

Fahr, J., Dobbins, G.H., and Cheng, B. (1991) 'Cultural Relativity in Action: A Comparison of Self-Ratings Made by Chinese and U.S. Workers', *Personnel Psychology*, 44: 129–47.

Falbo, T., Poston, D.L., Jr., Triscari, R.S., and Zhang, X. (1997) 'Self-Enhancing Illusions among Chinese Schoolchildren', *Journal of Cross-Cultural Psychology*, 28: 172–91.

Fazio, R.H. (2001) 'On the Automatic Activation of Associated Evaluations: An Overview', *Cognition and Emotion*, 15: 115–41.

Feick, D.L. and Rhodewalt, F. (1997) 'The Double-Edged Sword of Self-Handicapping: Discounting, Augmentation, and the Protection and Enhancement of Self-Esteem', *Motivation and Emotion*, 21: 147–63.

Festinger, L. (1957). *A Theory of Cognitive Dissonance*. Stanford, CA: Stanford University Press.

Fincham, F.D. and Bradbury, T.N. (1989) 'The Impact of Attributions in Marriage: An Individual Difference Analysis', *Journal of Social and Personal Relationships*, 6: 69–85.

Fiske, A.P., Kitayama, S., Markus, H.R., and Nisbett, R.E. (1998) 'The Cultural Matrix of Social Psychology', in D.T. Gilbert, S.T. Fiske, and G. Lindzey (eds), *The Handbook of Social Psychology*, 4th edn. Boston, MA: MCGraw-Hill, pp. 915–81.

Fleming, J.S. and Courtney, B.E. (1984) 'The Dimensionality of Self-Esteem. II. Hierarchical Facet Model for Revised Measurement Scales', *Journal of Personality and Social Psychology*, 46: 404–21.

Forsyth, D.R. and Kerr, N.A. (1999) *Are Adaptive Illusions Adaptive?* Poster presented at the Annual Meeting of the American Psychological Association, Boston, MA, August.

Forthofer, M.S., Janz, N.K., Dodge, J.A., and Clark, N.M. (2001) 'Gender Differences in the Associations of Self-Esteem, Stress and Social Support with Functional Health Status among Older Adults with Heart Disease', *Journal of Women and Aging*, 31: 19–37.

French, S.A., Leffert, N., Story, M., Neumark-Sztainer, D., Hannan, P., and Senson, P.L. (2001) 'Adolescent Binge/ Purge and Weight Loss Behaviors: Associations with Developmental Assets', *Journal of Adolescent Health*, 28: 211–21.

Frey, D. (1986) 'Recent Research on Selective Exposure to Information', in L. Bercowitz (ed.), *Advances in Experimental Social Psychology* (vol. 19). New York: Academic Press, pp. 41–80.

Frone, M.R. (2000) 'Interpersonal Conflict at Work and Psychological Outcomes: Testing a Model among Young Workers', *Journal of Occupational Health Psychology*, 5: 246–55.

Furnham, A. and Cheng, H. (2000) 'Lay Theories of Happiness', *Journal of Happiness Studies*, 1: 227–46.

Gabriel, M.T., Critelli, J.W., and Ee, J.S. (1994) 'Narcissistic Illusions in Self-Evaluations of Intelligence and Attractiveness', *Journal of Personality*, 62: 143–55.

Gaertner, L., Sedikides, C., Vevea, J., and Iuzzini, J. (2002) 'The "I", the "We", and the "When": A Meta-Analysis of Motivational Primacy in Self-Definition', *Journal of Personality and Social Psychology*, 83: 574–91.

Gaertner, L., Sedikides, C., and Graetz, K. (1999) 'In Search of Self-Definition: Motivational Primacy of the Individual Self, Motivational Primacy of the Collective Self, or Contextual Primacy?', *Journal of Personality and Social Psychology*, 76: 5–18.

Gergen, K.J. (1991) *The Saturated Self: Dilemmas of Identity in Contemporary Life*. New York: Basic Books.

Gerrard, M., Gibbons, F.X., Reis-Bergan, M., and Russell, D.W. (2000) 'Self-Esteem, Self-Serving Cognitions, and Health Risk Behavior', *Journal of Personality*, 68: 1177–201.

Gibbons, F.X., Eggleston, T.J., and Benthin, A.C. (1997) 'Cognitive Reactions to Smoking Relapse: The Reciprocal Relation Between Dissonance and Self-Esteem', *Journal of Personality and Social Psychology*, 72: 184–95.

Giesler, R.B., Josephs, R.A., and Swann, W.B. (1996) 'Self Verification in Clinical Depression: The Desire for

Negative Evaluation', *Journal of Abnormal Psychology*, 105: 358–68.

Gilbert, D.T., Pinel, E.C., Wilson, T.D., Blumberg, S.J., and Wheatley, T.P. (1998) 'Immune Neglect: A Source of Durability Bias in Affective Forecasting', *Journal of Personality and Social Psychology*, 73: 617–38.

Glendinning, A. and Ingus, D. (1999) 'Smoking Behaviour in Youth: The Problem of Low Self-Esteem?', *Journal of Adolescence*, 22: 673–82.

Gollwitzer, P.M. and Kinney, R.F. (1989) 'Effects of Deliberative and Implemental Mind-Sets on Illusion of Control', *Journal of Personality and Social Psychology*, 56: 531–42.

Gonzales, M.H., Pederson, J.H., Manning, D.J., and Wetter, D.W. (1990) 'Pardon My Gaffe: Effects of Sex, Status, and Consequence Severity on Accounts', *Journal of Personality and Social Psychology*, 58: 610–21.

Gosling, S.D., John, O.P., Craik, K.H., and Robins, R.W. (1998) 'Do People Know How They Behave? Self-Reported Act Frequencies Compared with On-line Codings by Observers', *Journal of Personality and Social Psychology*, 74: 1337–49.

Gramzow, R.H., Gaertner, L., and Sedikides, C. (2001) 'Memory for Ingroup and Outgroup Information in a Minimal Group Context: The Self as an Informational Base', *Journal of Personality and Social Psychology*, 80: 188–205.

Greenberg, J., Pyszczynski, T.A., and Solomon, S. (1982) 'The Self-Serving Attributional Bias: Beyond Self-Presentation', *Journal of Experimental Social Psychology*, 18: 56–67.

Greenberg, J., Solomon, S., Pyszczynski, T., Rosenblatt, A., Burling, J., Lyon, D., Simon, L., and Pinel, E. (1992) 'Why Do People Need Self-Esteem? Converging Evidence that Self-Esteem Serves an Anxiety-Buffering Function', *Journal of Personality and Social Psychology*, 63: 913–22.

Greenier, K.D., Kernis, M.H., McNamara, C.W., Waschull, S.B., Berry, A.J., Herlocker, C.E., and Abend, T.A. (1999) 'Individual Differences in Reactivity to Daily Events: Examining the Roles of Stability and Level of Self-Esteem', *Journal of Personality*, 67: 185–208.

Greenwald, A.G. (1980) 'The Totalitarian Ego: Fabrication and Revision of Personal History', *American Psychologist*, 35: 603–18.

Greenwald, A.G. (2002) 'Constructs in Student Ratings of Instructors', in H.I. Braun and D.N. Douglas (eds), *The Role of Constructs in Psychological and Educational Measurement*. Mahwah, NJ: Lawrence Erlbaum, pp. 277–97.

Greenwald, A.G., Banaji, M.R., Rudman, L.A., Farnham, S.D., Nosek, B.A., and Mellott, D.S. (2002) 'A Unified Theory of Implicit Attitudes, Stereotypes, Self-Esteem, and Self-Concept', *Psychological Review*, 109: 3–25.

Greenwald, A.G., Bellezza, F.S., and Banaji, M.R. (1988) 'Is Self-Esteem a Central Ingredient of the Self-Concept?', *Personality and Social Psychology Bulletin*, 14: 34–45.

Greenwald, A.G., McGhee, D.E., and Schwartz, J.L.K. (1998) 'Measuring Individual Differences in Implicit Cognition: The Implicit Association Test', *Journal of Personality and Social Psychology*, 74: 1464–80.

Gregg, A.P. (2003) 'Optimally Conceptualizing Implicit Self-Esteem', *Psychological Inquiry*, 14: 35–37.

Gregg, A.P. and Sedikides, C. (2002) 'Explicit Self-Esteem, Implicit Self-Esteem, and Self-Related Constructs'. Unpublished data.

Gruder, C.L. (1971) 'Determinants of Social Comparison Choices', *Journal of Experimental Social Psychology*, 7: 473–89.

Heatherton, T.F. and Ambady, N. (1993) 'Self-Esteem, Self-Prediction, and Living up to Commitments', in R.F. Baumeister (ed.), *Self-Esteem: The Puzzle of Low Self-Regard*. New York: Plenum Press, pp. 131–45.

Heatherton, T.F. and Polivy, J. (1991) 'Development and Validation of a Scale for Measuring State Self-Esteem', *Journal of Personality and Social Psychology*, 60: 895–910.

Heatherton, T.F. and Polivy, J. (1992) 'Chronic Dieting and Eating Disorders: A Spiral Model', in J.H. Crowther and D.L. Tennenbaum (eds), *The Etiology of Bulimia Nervosa: The Individual and Familial Context*. Washington, DC: Hemisphere, pp. 133–55.

Heider, F. (1958) *The Psychology of Interpersonal Relations*. New York: Wiley.

Heimpel, S.A., Wood, J.V., Marshall, M.A. and Brown, J. (2002) 'Do People with Low Self-Esteem Really Want to Feel Better? Self-Esteem Differences in Motivation to Repair Negative Moods', *Journal of Personality and Social Psychology*, 82: 128–47.

Heine, S.J., Kitayama, S., and Lehman, D.R. (2001a). 'Cultural Differences in Self-Evaluation: Japanese Readily Accept Negative Self-Relevant Information', *Journal of Cross Cultural Psychology*, 32: 434–43.

Heine, S.J., Kitayama, S., Lehman, D.R., Takata, T., Ide, E., Leung, C., and Matsumoto, H. (2001b) 'Divergent Consequences of Success and Failure in Japan and North America: An Investigation of Self-Improving Motivations and Malleable Selves', *Journal of Personality and Social Psychology*, 81: 599–615.

Heine, S.J. and Lehman, D.R. (1995) 'Cultural Variation in Unrealistic Optimism: Does the West Feel More Invulnerable than the East?' *Journal of Personality and Social Psychology*, 68: 595–607.

Heine, S.H., Lehman, D.R., Markus, H.R., and Kitayama, S. (1999) 'Is There a Universal Need for Positive Self-Regard?', *Psychological Review*, 106: 766–94.

Heine, S.J., Takata, T., and Lehman, D.R. (2000) 'Beyond Self-Presentation: Evidence for Self-Criticism among Japanese', *Personality and Social Psychology Bulletin*, 26: 71–8.

Helweg-Larsen, M. and Sheppard, J.A. (2001) 'Do Moderators of the Optimistic Bias Affect Personal or Target Risk Estimates? A Review of the Literature', *Personality and Social Psychology Review*, 5: 74–95.

Hendrick, S.S., Hendrick, C., and Adler, N.L. (1988) 'Romantic Relationships: Love, Satisfaction, and

Staying Together', *Journal of Personality and Social Psychology*, 54: 980–8.

Herold, E.S. and Goodwin, M.S. (1979) 'Self-Esteem and Sexual Permissiveness', *Journal of Clinical Psychology*, 35: 908–12.

Herold, E.S. and Way, L. (1983) 'Oral-Genital Sexual Behaviour in a Sample of University Females', *Journal of Sex Research*, 19: 327–38.

Hetts, J.J., Sakuma, M., and Pelham, B.W. (1999) 'Two Roads to Positive Regard: Implicit and Explicit Self-Evaluation and Culture', *Journal of Experimental Social Psychology*, 35: 512–59.

Heyman, G.D., Dweck, C.S., and Cain, K.M. (1992) 'Young Children's Vulnerability to Self-Blame and Helplessness: Relationship to Beliefs About Goodness', *Child-Development*, 63: 401–15.

Hill, S.Y., Shen, S., Lowers, L., and Locke, J. (2000) 'Factors Predicting the Onset of Adolescent Drinking in Families at High Risk for Developing Alcoholism', *Biological Psychiatry*, 48: 265–75.

Hollar, D.S. and Snizek, W.E. (1996) 'The Influences of Knowledge of HIV/AIDS and Self-Esteem on the Sexual Practices of College Students', *Social Behavior and Personality*, 24: 75–86.

Hoorens, V. and Nuttin, J.M. (1993) 'Overvaluation of Own Attributes: Mere Ownership or Subjective Frequency?', *Social Cognition*, 11: 177–200.

Horner, K.L. (2001) 'Personality and Intimate Support Influences on Prospective Health Status', *Psychology, Health, and Medicine*, 6: 473–9.

Horton, R.S. and Sedikides, C. (2002) 'Introspection and Self-Evaluation: Does Introspection Put the Brakes on Self-Enhancement?' Unpublished manuscript. University of Southampton, Southampton, UK.

Jackson, C., Henriksen, L., Dickinson, D., and Levine, D.W. (1997) 'The Early Use of Alcohol and Tobacco: Its Relation to Children's Competence and Parents' Behavior', *American Journal of Public Health*, 87: 359–64.

Jenkins, H.M. and Ward, W.C. (1965) 'Judgments of Contingency Between Response and Outcome', *Psychological Monographs*, 79: (1, Whole No. 594).

Jones, E.E. and Berglas, S. (1978) 'Control of Attributions about the Self through Self-Handicapping Strategies: The Appeal of Alcohol and Underachievement', *Personality and Social Psychology Bulletin*, 4: 200–6.

Jones, J., Pelham, B., Mirenberg, M., and Hetts, J. (2002) 'Name Letter Preferences Are Not Merely Mere Exposure: Implicit Egotism as Self-Regulation', *Journal of Experimental Social Psychology*, 38: 170–7.

Joon, S.J. and Thornberry, T.P. (1998) 'Self-Esteem, Delinquent Peers, and Delinquency: A Test of the Self-Enhancement Hypothesis', *American Sociological Review*, 63: 586–98.

Jordan, C.H., Spencer, S.J., and Zanna, M.P. (2001) '"I Love Me ... I Love Me Not": Implicit Self-Esteem, Explicit Self-Esteem, and Defensiveness'. Unpublished manuscript. University of Waterloo, Toronto, Canada.

Josephs, R.A., Larrick, R.P., Steele, C.M., and Nisbett, R.E. (1992) 'Protecting the Self from the Negative Consequences of Risky Decisions', *Journal of Personality and Social Psychology*, 62: 26–37.

Judge, T.A. and Bono, J.E. (2001) 'A Rose by any Other Name: Are Self-Esteem, Generalized Self-Efficacy, Neuroticism, and Locus of Control Indicators of a Common Construct?', in B.W. Roberts and R. Hogan (eds), *Personality Psychology in the Workplace*. Washington, DC: American Psychological Association, pp. 93–118.

Kanagawa, C., Cross, S.E., and Markus, H.R. (2001) '"Who Am I?": The Cultural Psychology of the Conceptual Self', *Personality and Social Psychology Bulletin*, 27: 90–103.

Kasser, T. and Ryan, R.M. (1996) 'Further Examining the American Dream: Differential Correlates of Intrinsic and Extrinsic Goals', *Personality and Social Psychology Bulletin*, 22: 280–7.

Keefe, K. and Berndt, T.J. (1996) 'Relations of Friendship Quality to Self-Esteem in Early Adolescence', *Journal of Early Adolescence*, 16: 110–29.

Kernis, M.H. (2003) 'Toward a Conceptualization of Optimal Self-Esteem', *Psychological Inquiry*, 14: 1–26.

Kernis, M.H., Cornell, D.P., Sun, C.R., Berry, A.J., and Harlow, T. (1993) 'There's More to Self-Esteem Than Whether It Is High or Low: The Importance of Stability of Self-Esteem', *Journal of Personality and Social Psychology*, 65: 1190–204.

Kernis, M.H., Goldman, B.N., Shrira, I., and Paradise, A.W. (2000) 'Discrepancies between Implicit and Explicit Self-Esteem and Outgroup Derogation'. Unpublished manuscript. University of Georgia, Athens, GA.

Kernis, M.H., Grannemann, B.D., and Barclay, L.C. (1989) 'Stability and Level of Self-Esteem as Predictors of Anger Arousal and Hostility', *Journal of Personality and Social Psychology*, 56: 1013–23.

Kernis, M.H., Grannemann, B.D., and Barclay, L.C. (1992) 'Stability of Self-Esteem: Assessment, Correlates, and Excuse Making', *Journal of Personality*, 60: 621–44.

Kernis, M.H., Grannemann, B.D., and Mathis, L.C. (1991) 'Stability of Self-Esteem as a Moderator of the Relation between Level of Self-Esteem and Depression', *Journal of Personality and Social Psychology*, 61: 80–4.

Kernis, M.H., Greenier, K.D., Herlocker, C.E., Whisenhunt, C.W., and Abend, T. (1997) 'Self-Perceptions of Reactions to Positive and Negative Outcomes: The Roles of Stability and Level of Self-Esteem', *Personality and Individual Differences*, 22: 846–54.

Kitayama, S., Markus, H.R., and Lieberman, C. (1995a). 'The Collective Construction of Self-Esteem: Implications for Culture, Self, and Emotion', in R. Russell, J. Fernandez-Dols, T. Manstead, and J. Wellenkamp (eds), *Everyday Conceptions of Emotion: An Introduction to the Psychology, Anthropology, and Linguistics of Emotion*. Dordrecht, The Netherlands: Kluwer Academic, pp. 523–50.

Kitayama, S., Markus, H.R., Matsumoto, H., and Norasakkunkit, V. (1997) 'Individual and Collective

Processes in the Construction of the Self: Self-Enhancement in the United States and Self-Criticism in Japan', *Journal of Personality and Social Psychology*, 72: 1245–67.

Kitayama, S., Takagi, H., and Matsumoto, H. (1995b) 'Seiko to shippai no kiin: Nihonteki jiko no bunka-shinrigaku' ('Causal Attributions of Success and Failure: Cultural Psychology of Japanese Selves'), *Japanese Psychological Review*, 38: 247–80.

Klinger, M.R., Burton, P.C., and Pitts, G.S. (2000) 'Mechanisms of Unconscious Priming. I. Response Competition, Not Spreading Activation', *Journal of Experimental Psychology: Learning, Memory, and Cognition*, 26: 441–55.

Koole, S.L., Dijksterhuis, A., and van Knippenberg, A. (2001) 'What's in a Name: Implicit Self-Esteem and the Automatic Self', *Journal of Personality and Social Psychology*, 80: 669–85.

Koval, J.J. and Pederson, L.L. (1999) 'Stress-Coping and Other Psychosocial Risk Factors: A Model for Smoking in Grade 6 Students', *Addictive Behaviors*, 24: 207–18.

Kruger, J. and Dunning, D. (1999) 'Unskilled and Unaware of It: How Difficulties in Recognizing One's Own Incompetence Lead to Inflated Self-Assessments', *Journal of Personality and Social Psychology*, 77: 1121–34.

Kuiper, N.A. (1978) 'Depression and Causal Attributions for Success and Failure', *Journal of Personality and Social Psychology*, 36: 236–46.

Kunda, Z. (1990) 'The Case for Motivated Reasoning', *Psychological Bulletin*, 108: 480–98.

Kurman, J. (2001) 'Self-Enhancement: Is It Restricted to Individualistic Cultures?', *Personality and Social Psychology Bulletin*, 12: 1705–16.

Lakey, B., Tarcliff, T.A., and Drew, J.B. (1994) 'Negative Social Interactions: Assessment and Relations to Social Support, Cognition and Psychological Distress', *Journal of Social and Clinical Psychology*, 13: 42–62.

Lane, K., Brescoll, V., and Bosson, J. (2002) 'Relationship between Implicit and Explicit Measures of Self-Esteem'. Unpublished manuscript. Yale University, New Haven, CT.

Langer, E.J. (1975) 'The Illusion of Control', *Journal of Personality and Social Psychology*, 32: 311–28.

Langer, L.M. and Tubman, J.G. (1997) 'Risky Sexual Behavior among Substance-Abusing Adolescents: Psychosocial and Contextual Factors', *American Journal of Orthopsychiatry*, 67: 315–22.

Leary, M.R. and Baumeister, R.F. (2000) 'The Nature and Function of Self-Esteem: Sociometer Theory', in M. Zanna (ed.), *Advances in Experimental Social Psychology* (vol. 32). San Diego, CA: Academic Press, pp. 1–62.

Leary, M.R. and Kowalski, R.M. (1995) *Social Anxiety*. New York: Guilford Press.

LePine, J.A. and Van Dyne, L. (1998) 'Predicting Voice Behavior in Work Groups', *Journal of Applied Psychology*, 83: 853–68.

Lewinsohn, P.M., Mischel, W., Chaplin, W., and Barton, R. (1980) 'Social Competence and Depression: The Role of Illusory Self-Perceptions', *Journal of Abnormal Psychology*, 89: 203–12.

Lewis, P.C., Harrell, J.S., Bradley, C., and Deng, S. (2001) 'Cigarette Use in Adolescents: The Cardiovascular Health in Children and Youth Study', *Research in Nursing and Health*, 24: 27–37.

Lockwood, P. and Kunda, Z. (1997) 'Superstars and Me: Predicting the Impact of Role Models on Self', *Journal of Personality and Social Psychology*, 73: 91–103.

Lun, J. and Wolfe, C. (1999) 'Power as a Basis of Self-Esteem: The Effects on Stereotyping and Self-Affirmation'. Unpublished senior thesis. University of Michigan, Ann Arbor, MI.

Lyubomirsky, S. and Lepper, H.S. (2002) 'What Are the Differences between Happiness and Self-Esteem?' Unpublished manuscript. University of California, Riverside, CA.

Markus, H.R. and Kitayama, S. (1991) 'Culture and the Self: Implications for Cognition, Emotion, and Motivation', *Psychological Review,* 98: 224–53.

Markus, H.R. and Nurius, P. (1986) 'Possible Selves', *American Psychologist*, 41: 954–69.

Markus, H.R. and Wurf, E. (1987) 'The Dynamic Self-Concept: A Social Psychological Analysis', *Annual Review of Psychology*, 38: 299–337.

Marsh, H.W. (1990) 'A Multidimensional, Hierarchical Model of Self-Concept: Theoretical and Empirical Justification', *Educational Psychological Review*, 2: 70–172.

Marsh, H.W. (1995) 'A Jamesian Model of Self-Investment and Self-Esteem: Comment on Pelham (1995)', *Journal of Personality and Social Psychology*, 69: 1151–60.

McFarlin, D.B. (1985) 'Persistence in the Face of Failure: The Impact of Self-Esteem and Contingency Information', *Personality and Social Psychology Bulletin*, 11: 153–63.

McFarlin, D.B. and Blascovich, J. (1981) 'Effects of Self-Esteem and Performance Feedback on Future Affective Preferences and Cognitive Expectations', *Journal of Personality and Social Psychology*, 40: 521–31.

McFarlin, D.B., Baumeister, R.F., and Blascovich J. (1984) 'On Knowing When to Quit: Task Failure, Self-Esteem, Advice, and Nonproductive Persistence', *Journal of Personality*, 52: 138–55.

McGee, R. and Williams, S. (2000) 'Does Low Self-Esteem Predict Health Compromising Behaviours among Adolescents?', *Journal of Adolescence*, 23: 569–82.

McGuire, W.J. (1990) 'Dynamic Operations of Thought Systems', *American Psychologist*, 45: 504–12.

McKay, M. and Fanning, P. (2000) *Self-Esteem,* 3rd edn. Oakland, CA: New Harbinger Publications.

McNulty, S.E. and Swann, W.B. (1994) 'Identity Negotiation in Roommate Relationships: The Self as Architect and Consequence of Social Reality', *Journal of Personality and Social Psychology*, 67: 1012–23.

Midgett, J., Ryan, B.A., Adams, G.R., and Corville-Smith, J. (2002) 'Complicating Achievement and Self-Esteem:

Considering the Joint Effects of Child Characteristics and Parent–Child Interactions', *Contemporary Educational Psychology*, 27: 132–43.

Miller, C.T. and Downey, K.T. (1999) 'A Meta-analysis of Heavy Weight and Self-Esteem', *Personality and Social Psychology Review*, 3: 68–84.

Miller, D.T., Trunbull, W., and McFarland, C. (1988) 'Particularistic and Universalistic Evaluation in the Social Comparison Process', *Journal of Personality and Social Psychology*, 55: 908–17.

Mintz, L.B. and Betz, N.E. (1988) 'Prevalence and Correlates of Eating Disordered Behaviours among Undergraduate Women', *Journal of Counseling Psychology*, 35: 463–71.

Mischel, W., Ebbesen, E.B., and Zeiss, A.R. (1976) 'Determinants of Selective Memory about the Self', *Journal of Consulting and Clinical Psychology*, 44: 92–103.

Morf, C.C. and Rhodewalt, F. (2001) 'Unraveling the Paradoxes of Narcissism: A Dynamic Self-Regulatory Processing Model', *Psychological Inquiry*, 12: 177–96.

Mruk, C.J. (1999) *Self-Esteem: Research, Theory, and Practice*. New York: Springer.

Mullen, B. and Goethals, G.R. (1990) 'Social Projection, Actual Consensus, and Valence', *British Journal of Social Psychology*, 29: 279–82.

Murray, S.L. (1999) 'The Quest for Conviction: Motivated Cognition in Romantic Relationships', *Psychological Inquiry*, 10: 23–34.

Murray, S.L., Bellavia, G., Feeney, B., Holmes, J.G., and Rose, P. (2001a) 'The Contingencies of Interpersonal Acceptance: When Romantic Relationships Function as a Self-Affirmational Resource', *Motivation and Emotion*, 25: 163–89.

Murray, S.L. and Holmes, J.G. (1993) 'Seeing Virtues in Faults: Negativity and the Transformation of Interpersonal Narratives in Close Relationships', *Journal of Personality and Social Psychology*, 65: 707–22.

Murray, S.L., Holmes, J.G., and Griffin, D.W. (1996a) 'The Benefits of Positive Illusions: Idealization and the Construction of Satisfaction in Close Relationships', *Journal of Personality and Social Psychology*, 70: 79–98.

Murray, S.L., Holmes, J.G., and Griffin, D.W. (1996b) 'Self-Esteem and the Quest for Felt Security: How Perceived Regard Regulates Attachment Processes', *Journal of Personality and Social Psychology*, 71: 1155–80.

Murray, S.L., Holmes, J.G., and Griffin, D.W., Bellavia, G. and Rose, P. (2001b) 'The Mismeasure of Love: How Self-Doubt Contaminates Relationship Beliefs', *Personality and Social Psychology Bulletin*, 27: 423–36.

Murray, S.L., Holmes, J.G., MacDonald, G., and Ellsworth, P. (1998) 'Through the Looking-Glass Darkly? When Self-Doubts Turn into Relationship Insecurities', *Journal of Personality and Social Psychology*, 75: 1459–80.

Murrell, S.A., Meeks, S. and Walker, J. (1991) 'Protective Functions of Health and Self-Esteem against Depression in Older Adults Facing Illness or Bereavement', *Psychology and Aging*, 6: 352–60.

Nagel, T. (1974) 'What Is It Like to Be a Bat?', *Philosophical Review*, 4: 435–50.

National Association for Self-Esteem (2002) *Masters Coalition – A Work in Progress*, http://www.self-esteem-nase. org.

Neiss, M.B., Sedikides, C., and Stevenson, J. (2002) 'Self-Esteem: A Behavioural Genetics Perspective', *European Journal of Personality*, 16: 1–17.

Nesselroade, K.P., Beggan, J.K., and Allison, S.T. (1999) 'Possession Enhancement in an Interpersonal Context: An Extension of the Mere Ownership Effect', *Psychology and Marketing*, 16: 21–34.

Neumark-Sztainer, D., Story, M., French, S.A., and Resnick, M.D. (1997) 'Psychosocial Correlates of Health Compromising Behaviors among Adolescents', *Health Education Research*, 12: 37–52.

Nirkko., O., Lauroma, H.J., Siltanen, P., Tuominen, H., and Vanhala, K. (1982) 'Psychological Risk Factors Related to Coronary Heart Disease. Prospective Studies among Policemen in Helsinki', *Acta Medica Scandinavica (Supplementum)*, 660: 137–46.

Nisbett, R.E. and Wilson, T.D. (1977) 'Telling More Than We Can Know: Verbal Reports on Psychological Processes', *Psychological Review*, 84: 231–59.

Nosek, B.A. and Banaji, M.R. (2001) 'The Go/No-Go Association Task', *Social Cognition*, 19: 625–66.

Nuttin, J.M. (1987) 'Affective Consequences of Mere Ownership: The Name Letter Effect in Twelve European Languages', *European Journal of Social Psychology*, 52: 245–59.

Oettingen, G. and Gollwitzer, P.M. (2001) 'Goal Setting and Goal Striving', in A. Tesser and N. Schwarz (eds), *Intraindividual Processes: Blackwell Handbook of Psychology*. Malden, MA: Blackwell, pp. 329–47.

Olweus, D. (1991) 'Victimization among Schoolchildren', in R. Baenninger (ed.), 'Targets of Violence and Aggression', *Advances in Psychology*, 76: 45–102.

Paradise, A.W. and Kernis, M.H. (1999) 'Development of the Contingent Self-Esteem Scale', unpublished data. University of Georgia, Athens, GA.

Paul, C., Fitzjohn, J., Herbison, P., and Dickson, N. (2000) 'The Determinants of Sexual Intercourse before Age 16', *Journal of Adolescent Health*, 27: 136–47.

Paulhus, D.L. (1984) 'Two-Component Models of Socially Desirable Responding', *Journal of Personality and Social Psychology*, 46: 598–609.

Paulhus, D.L. (1991), 'Measurement and Control of Response Bias', In J.P. Robinson and P.R. Shaver (eds), *Measures of Personality and Social Psychological Attitudes. Measures of Social Psychological Attitudes* (vol. 1). San Diego, CA: Academic Press, pp. 17–59.

Paulhus, D.L. (1998) 'Interpersonal and Intrapsychic Adaptiveness of Trait Self-Enhancement: A Mixed Blessing?', *Journal of Personality and Social Psychology*, 74: 1197–208.

Paulhus, D.L. (2002) 'Socially Desirable Responding: The Evolution of a Construct', in H.I. Braun and D.N. Jackson (eds), *The Role of Constructs in Psychological and Educational Measurement*. Mahwah, NJ: Erlbaum, pp. 37–48.

Pelham, B.W. (1993) 'On the Highly Positive Thoughts of the Highly Depressed', in R.F. Baumeister (ed.), *Self-Esteem: The Puzzle of Low Self-Regard*. New York: Plenum Press, pp. 183–99.

Pelham, B.W. (1995) 'Further Evidence for a Jamesian Model of Self-Worth: Reply to Marsh (1995)', *Journal of Personality and Social Psychology*, 69: 1161–5.

Pelham, B.W. and Hetts, J.J. (1999) 'Implicit and Explicit Personal and Social Identity: Toward a More Complete Understanding of the Social Self', in T. Tyler and R. Kramer (eds), *The Psychology of the Social Self*. Mahwah, NJ: Erlbaum, pp. 115–43.

Pelham, B.W., Mirenberg, M.C., and Jones, J.T. (2002) 'Why Susie Sells Seashells by the Seashore: Implicit Egotism and Major Life Decisions', *Journal of Personality and Social Psychology*, 82: 469–87.

Pelham, B.W. and Swann, W.B. (1989) 'From Self-Conceptions to Self-Worth: On the Sources and Structure of Global Self-Esteem', *Journal of Personality and Social Psychology*, 57: 672–80.

Pelham, B.W. and Swann, W.B. (1994) 'The Juncture of Intrapersonal and Interpersonal Knowledge: Self Certainty and Interpersonal Congruence', *Personality and Social Psychology Bulletin*, 20: 349–57.

Pemberton, M. and Sedikides, C. (2001) 'When Do Individuals Help Close Others Improve?: Extending the Self-Evaluation Maintenance Model to Future Comparisons', *Journal of Personality and Social Psychology*, 81: 234–46.

Pettigrew, T.F. (2001) 'The Ultimate Attribution Error: Extending Allport's Cognitive Analysis of Prejudice', in M.A. Hogg and D. Abrams (eds), *Intergroup Relations: Essential Readings*. Philadelphia, PA: Psychology Press/Taylor & Francis, pp. 162–73.

Poikolainen, K., Tuulio-Henriksson, A., Aalto-Setala, T., Marttunen, M., and Lonnqvist, J. (2001) 'Predictors of Alcohol Intake and Heavy Drinking in Early Adulthood: A 5-Year Follow-Up of 15–19 Year Old Finnish Adolescents', *Alcohol and Alcoholism*, 36: 85–8.

Pottebaum, S.M., Keith, T.Z., and Ehly, S.W. (1986) 'Is There a Causal Relation between Self-Concept and Academic Achievement?', *Journal of Education Research*, 79: 140–4.

Pronin, E., Yin, D.Y., and Ross, L. (2002) 'The Bias Blind Spot: Perceptions of Bias in Self Versus Others', *Personality and Social Psychology Bulletin*, 3: 369–81.

Prussner, J.C., Hellhammer, D.H., and Kirschbaum, D. (1998) 'Low Self-Esteem, Induced Failure and the Adrenocortical Stress Response', *Personality and Individual Differences*, 27: 477–89.

Pyszczynski, T. and Greenberg, J. (1987) 'Toward an Integration of Cognitive and Motivational Perspectives on Social Inference: A Biased Hypothesis-Testing Model', *Advances in Experimental Social Psychology*, 20: 297–341.

Pyszczynski, T., Greenberg, J., and Solomon, S. (1997) 'Why Do We Need What We Need?: A Terror Management Perspective on the Roots of Human Social Motivation', *Psychological Inquiry*, 8: 1–20.

Pyszczynski, T., Holt, K., and Greenberg, J. (1987) 'Depression, Self-Focused Attention, and Expectancies for Positive and Negative Future Life Events for Self and Others', *Journal of Personality and Social Psychology*, 52: 994–1001.

Ralph, J.A. and Mineka, S. (1998) 'Attributional Style and Self-Esteem: The Prediction of Emotional Distress Following a Midterm Exam', *Journal of Abnormal Psychology*, 107: 203–15.

Regan, P.C., Snyder, M., and Kassin, S.M. (1995) 'Unrealistic Optimism: Self-Enhancement or Person Positivity?', *Personality and Social Psychology Bulletin*, 21: 1073–82.

Rhodewalt F. and Eddings, S.K. (2002) 'Narcissus Reflects: Memory Distortion in Response to Ego-Relevant Feedback among High- and Low-Narcissistic Men', *Journal of Research in Personality*, 36: 97–116.

Rhodewalt, F. and Fairfield, M. (1991) 'Claimed Self-Handicaps and the Self-Handicapper: The Relation of Reduction in Intended Effort to Performance', *Journal of Research in Personality*, 25: 402–17.

Rhodewalt, F., Morf, C., Hazlett, S., and Fairfield, M. (1991) 'Self-Handicapping: The Role of Discounting and Augmentation in the Preservation of Self-Esteem', *Journal of Personality and Social Psychology*, 61: 122–31.

Rhodewalt, F., Sanbonmatsu, D.M., Tschanz, B., and Feick, D.L. (1995) 'Self-Handicapping and Inter-Personal Trade-Offs: The Effects of Claimed Self-Handicaps on Observers' Performance Evaluations and Feedback', *Personality and Social Psychology Bulletin*, 21: 1042–50.

Rhodewalt, F. and Tragakis, M. (2002) 'Self-Handicapping and the Social Self: The Cost and Reward of Interpersonal Self-Construction', in J. Forgas and K. Williams (eds), *The Social Self: Cognitive, Interpersonal, and Intergroup Perspectives*. Philadelphia, PA: Psychology Press, pp. 121–43.

Riess, M., Rosenfeld, P., Melburg, V., and Tedeschi, J.T. (1981) 'Self-Serving Attributions: Biased Private Perceptions and Distorted Public Descriptions', *Journal of Personality and Social Psychology*, 41: 224–31.

Robins, R.W. and Beer, J.S. (2001) 'Positive Illusions about the Self: Short-Term Benefits and Long-Term Costs', *Journal of Personality and Social Psychology*, 80: 340–52.

Robins, R.W., Trzesniewski, K., Potter, J., Gosling, S.D., and Tracy, J.L. (2002) 'Personality Correlates of Self-Esteem', *Journal of Research in Personality*, 35: 2001.

Robinson, N.S., Garber, J., and Hilsman, R. (1995) 'Cognitions and Stress: Direct and Moderating Effects on Depressive Versus Externalizing Symptoms during the Junior High School Transition', *Journal of Abnormal Psychology*, 104: 453–63.

Rosenberg, M. (1965) *Society and the Adolescent Self-Image*. Princeton, NJ: Princeton University Press.

Rosenberg, M., Schooler, C. and Schoenbach, C. (1989) 'Self-Esteem and Adolescent Problems: Modeling Reciprocal Effects', *American Sociological Review*, 54: 1004–18.

Rosenthal, R. and Rubin, R.L. (1978) 'Interpersonal Expectancy Effects: The First 345 Studies', *Behavioral and Brain Sciences*, 3: 377–86.

Ross, C.E. and Broh, B.A. (2000) 'The Role of Self-Esteem and the Sense of Personal Control in the Academic Achievement Process', *Sociology of Education*, 73: 270–84.

Ross, L., Greene, D., and House, P. (1977) 'The False Consensus Effect: An Attributional Bias in Self-Perception and Social Perception Processes', *Journal of Experimental Social Psychology*, 13: 279–301.

Ross, M., McFarland, C., and Fletcher, G.J. (1981) 'The Effect of Attitude on the Recall of Personal Histories'. *Journal of Personality and Social Psychology*, 40: 627–34.

Ruehlam, L.S., West, S.G., and Pasahow, R.J. (1985) 'Depression and Evaluative Schemata', *Journal of Personality*, 53: 46–92.

Rusbult, C.E., Morrow, G.D., and Johnson, D.J. (1987) 'Self-Esteem and Problem-Solving Behaviour in Close Relationships', *British Journal of Social Psychology*, 26: 293–303.

Rusbult, C.E., van Lange, P.A.M., Wildschut, T., and Yovetich, N.A. and Verette, J. (2000) 'Perceived Superiority in Close Relationships: Why It Exists and Persists', *Journal of Personality and Social Psychology*, 79: 521–45.

Salmivalli, C., Kaukiainen, A., Kaistaniemi, L., and Lagerspetz, K.M.J. (1999) 'Self-Evaluated Self-Esteem, Peer-Evaluated Self-Esteem, and Defensive Egotism as Predictors of Adolescents' Participation in Bullying Situations', *Personality and Social Psychology Bulletin*, 25: 1268–78.

Sandelands, L.E., Brocker, J., and Blynn, M.A. (1988) 'If at First You Don't Succeed, Try, Try Again: Effects of Persistence-Performance Contingencies, Ego Involvement, and Self-Esteem on Task Persistence', *Journal of Applied Psychology*, 73: 208–16.

Sanitioso, R., Kunda, Z., and Fong, G.T. (1990) 'Motivated Recruitment of Autobiographical Memories', *Journal of Personality and Social Psychology*, 59: 229–41.

Scheier, L.M., Botvin, G.J., Griffin, K.W., and Diaz, T. (2000) 'Dynamic Growth Models of Self-Esteem and Adolescent Alcohol Use', *Journal of Early Adolescence*, 20: 178–209.

Scheirer, M.A. and Kraut, R.E. (1979) 'Increased Educational Achievement Via Self-Concept Change', *Review of Educational Research*, 49: 131–50.

Schimel, J., Pyszczynski, T., Greenberg, J., O'Mahen, H., and Arndt, J. (2000) 'Running from the Shadow: Psychological Distancing from Others to Deny Characteristics People Fear in Themselves', *Journal of Personality and Social Psychology*, 78: 446–62.

Schlenker, B.R. (1980) *Impression Management: The Self-Concept, Social Identity, and Interpersonal Relations*. Monterey, CA: Brooks/Cole.

Schlenker, B.R. and Miller. R.S. (1977) 'Egocentrism in groups: Self-serving biases or logical information processing?', *Journal of Personality and Social Psychology*, 35: 755–64.

Schneider, D.J. and Turkat, D. (1975) 'Self-Presentation Following Success and Failure: Defensive Self-Esteem Models', *Journal of Personality*, 43: 127–35.

Schuetz, A. and Tice, D.M. (1997) 'Associative and Competitive Indirect Self-Enhancement in Close Relationships Moderated by Trait Self-Esteem', *European Journal of Social Psychology*, 27: 257–73.

Sedikides, C. (1993) 'Assessment, Enhancement, and Verification Determinants of the Self-Evaluation Process', *Journal of Personality and Social Psychology*, 65: 317–38.

Sedikides, C. (1999) 'A Multiplicity of Motives: The Case of Self-Improvement', *Psychological Inquiry*, 9: 64–5.

Sedikides, C. and Gaertner, L. (2001) 'A Homecoming to the Individual Self: Emotional and Motivational Primacy', in C. Sedikides and M.F. Brewer (eds), *Individual Self, Relational Self, Collective Self* Philadelphia, PA: Psychology Press, pp. 7–23.

Sedikides, C. and Brewer, M.B. (2001) *Individual Self, Relational Self, Collective Self*. Philadelphia, PA: Psychology Press.

Sedikides, C., Campbell, W.K., Reeder, G., and Elliot, A.J. (2002) 'The Self in Relationships: Whether, How, and When Close Others Put the Self "in its Place"', *European Review of Social Psychology,* 12: 237–65.

Sedikides, C., Gaertner, L., and Toguchi, Y. (2003) 'Pancultural Self-Enhancement', *Journal of Person ality and Social Psychology*, 84: 60–79.

Sedikides, C. and Green, J.D. (2000) 'On the Self-Protective Nature of Inconsistency/Negativity Management: Using the Person Memory Paradigm to Examine Self-Referent Memory', *Journal of Personality and Social Psychology*, 79: 906–22.

Sedikides, C., Herbst, K.C., Hardin, D.P., and Dardis, G.J. (2002) 'Accountability as a Deterrent to Self-Enhancement: The Search for Mechanisms', *Journal of Personality and Social Psychology*, 83: 592–605.

Sedikides, C. and Skowronski, J.A. (1997) 'The Symbolic Self in Evolutionary Context', *Personality and Social Psychology Review*, 1: 80–102.

Sedikides, C. and Skowronski, J.J. (2000) 'On the Evolutionary Functions of the Symbolic Self: The Emergence of Self-Evaluation Motives', in A. Tesser, R. Felson, and J. Suls (eds), *Psychological Perspectives on Self and Identity*. Washington, DC: APA Books, pp. 91–117.

Sedikides, C. and Skowronski, J.J. (2002) 'Evolution of the Self: Issues and Prospects', in M.R. Leary and J.P. Tangney (eds), *Handbook of Self and Identity* New York: Guilford, pp. 1310–42.

Sedikides, C. and Strube, M.J. (1997) 'Self-Evaluation: To Thine Own Self Be Good, to Thine Own Self Be Sure, to Thine Own Self Be True, and to Thine Own Self Be Better', in M.P. Zanna (ed.), *Advances in Experimental*

*Social Psychology* (vol. 29). New York: Academic Press, pp. 209–69.

Seeman, T.E., Berkman, L.F., Gulanski, B.I., Robbins, R.J., Greenspan, S.L., Charpentier, P.A., and Rowe, J.W. (1995) 'Self-Esteem and Neuroendocrine Response to Challenge: MacArthur Studies of Successful Aging', *Journal of Psychosomatic Research*, 39: 69–84.

Shackelford, T.K. (2001) 'Self-Esteem in Marriage', *Personality and Individual Differences*, 30: 71–90.

Shepperd, J.A. and Arkin, R.M. (1991) 'Behavioral Other-Enhancement: Strategically Obscuring the Link between Performance and Evaluation', *Journal of Personality and Social Psychology*, 60: 79–88.

Shrauger, J.S. (1975) 'Response to Evaluation as a Function of Initial Self-Perceptions', *Psychological Bulletin*, 82: 581–96.

Shrauger, J.S., Mariano, E., and Walter, T.J. (1998) 'Depressive Symptoms and Accuracy in the Prediction of Future Events', *Personality and Social Psychology Bulletin*, 24: 880–92.

Shrauger, J.S. and Sorman, P.B. (1977) 'Self-Evaluations, Initial Success and Failure, and Improvement as Determinants of Persistence', *Journal of Consulting and Clinical Psychology*, 45: 784–95.

Simon, L., Greenberg, J., and Brehm, J. (1995) 'Trivialization: The Forgotten Mode of Dissonance Reduction', *Journal of Personality and Social Psychology*, 68: 247–60.

Skowronski. J.J., Betz, A.L., Thompson, C.P., and Shannon, L. (1991) 'Social Memory in Everyday Life: Recall of Self-Events and Other-Events', *Journal of Personality and Social Psychology*, 60: 831–43.

Slee, P.T. and Rigby, K. (1993) 'The Relationship of Eysenck's Personality Factors and Self-Esteem to Bully/Victim Behaviour in Australian Schoolboys', *Personality and Individual Differences*, 14: 371–3.

Smith, E.R. and Decoster, J. (2000) 'Dual-Process Models in Social and Cognitive Psychology: Conceptual Integration and Links to Underlying Memory Systems', *Personality and Social Psychological Review*, 4: 108–31.

Spalding, L.R. and Hardin, C.D. (1999) 'Unconscious Unease and Self-Handicapping: Behavioral Consequences of Individual Differences in Implicit and Explicit Self-Esteem', *Psychological Science*, 10: 535–9.

Spencer, S.J., Josephs, R.A., and Steele, C.M. (1993) 'Low Self-Esteem: The Uphill Struggle for Self-Integrity', in R.F. Baumeister (ed.) *Self-Esteem: The Puzzle of Low Self-Regard*. New York: Plenum Press, pp. 21–36.

Staw, B.M. (1976) 'Knee-Deep in the Big Muddy: A Study of Escalating Commitment to a Chosen Course of Action', *Organizational Behavior and Human Performance*, 16: 27–44.

Steele, C.M. (1988) 'The Psychology of Self-Affirmation: Sustaining the Integrity of the Self', in L. Berkowitz (ed.), *Advances in Experimental Social Psychology*. Hillsdale, NJ: Erlbaum, pp. 261–302.

Story, A.L. and Dunning, D. (1998) 'The More Rational Side of Self-Serving Prototypes: The Effects of Success and Failure Performance Feedback', *Journal of Experimental Social Psychology*, 34: 513–29.

Suls, J. and Wills, T.A. (eds) (1991) *Social Comparison: Contemporary Theory and Research*. Hillsdale, NJ: Erlbaum.

Swann, W.B., Jr. (1987) 'Identity Negotiation: Where Two Roads Meet', *Journal of Personality and Social Psychology*, 53: 1038–51.

Swann, W.B. (1990) 'To Be Adored or to Be Known? The Interplay of Self-Enhancement and Self-Verification', in E.T. Higgins and R.M. Sorrentino (eds), *Handbook of Motivation and Cognition: Foundations of Social Behaviour*. New York: Guilford Press, pp. 408–48.

Swann, W.B., De La Ronde, C., and Hixon, J.G. (1994) 'Authenticity and Positivity Strivings in Marriage and Courtship', *Journal of Personality and Social Psychology*, 66: 857–69.

Swann, W.B. and Ely, R.J. (1984) 'A Battle of Wills: Self-Verification Versus Behavioural Confirmation', *Journal of Personality and Social Psychology*, 46: 1287–302.

Swann, W.B., Griffin, J.J., Predmore, S.C., and Gaines, B. (1987) 'The Cognitive-Affective Crossfire: When Self-Consistency Confronts Self-Enhancement', *Journal of Personality and Social Psychology*, 52: 881–9.

Swann, W.B., Jr., Hixon, J.G., Stein-Seroussi, A., and Gilbert, D.T. (1990) 'The Fleeting Gleam of Praise: Cognitive Processes Underlying Behavioral Reactions to Self-Relevant Feedback', *Journal of Personality and Social Psychology*, 59: 17–26.

Swann, W.B., Milton, L.P., and Polzer, J.T. (2000) 'Should We Create a Niche or Fall in Line?: Identity Negotiation and Small Group Effectiveness', *Journal of Personality and Social Psychology*, 79: 238–50.

Swann, W.B. Jr., Pelham, B.W., and Krull, D.S. (1989) 'Agreeable Fancy or Disagreeable Truth?: Reconciling Self-Enhancement and Self-Verification', *Journal of Personality and Social Psychology*, 57: 782–91.

Swann, W.B. and Read, S.J. (1981) 'Acquiring Self-Knowledge: The Search for Feedback that Fits', *Journal of Personality and Social Psychology*, 41: 1119–28.

Swann, W.B., Stein-Seroussi, A., and Giesler, R.B. (1992a). 'Why People Self-Verify', *Journal of Personality and Social Psychology*, 62: 392–401.

Swann, W.B., Stein-Seroussi, A., and McNulty, S.E. (1992b) 'Outcasts in a White-Lie Society: The Enigmatic Worlds of People with Negative Self-Conceptions', *Journal of Personality and Social Psychology*, 62: 618–24.

Swann, W.B., Wenzlaff, R.M., Krull, D.S., and Pelham, B.W. (1992c) 'Allure of Negative Feedback: Self-Verification Strivings among Depressed Persons', *Journal of Abnormal Psychology*, 101: 293–306.

Swann, W.B., Wenzlaff, Richard, M., and Tafarodi, R.W. (1992d) 'Depression and the Search for Negative Evaluations: More Evidence of the Role of Self-Verification Strivings', *Journal of Abnormal Psychology*, 101: 314–17.

Takata, T. (1987) 'Self-Depreciative Tendencies in Self-Evaluation through Social Comparison', *Japanese Journal of Experimental Social Psychology*, 27: 27–36.

Tallis, R. (1999) *The Explicit Animal*. Basingstoke: Macmillan.

Taylor, S.E. (1991) 'Asymmetrical Effects of Positive and Negative Events: The Mobilization-Minimization Hypothesis', *Psychological Bulletin*, 110: 67–85.

Taylor, S.E. and Brown, J.D. (1988) 'Illusion and Well-Being: A Social Psychological Perspective on Mental Health', *Psychological Bulletin*, 103: 193–210.

Tennen, H. and Affleck, G. (1993) 'The Puzzles of Self-Esteem: A Clinical Perspective', in R.F. Baumeister (ed.), *Self-Esteem: The Puzzle of Low Self-Regard*. New York: Plenum Press, pp. 241–62.

Tennen, H. and Herzberger, S. (1987) 'Depression, Self-Esteem, and the Absence of Self-Protective Attributional Biases', *Journal of Personality and Social Psychology*, 52: 72–80.

Tesser, A. (1988) 'Towards a Self-Evaluation Maintenance Model of Social Behavior', in L. Berkowitz (ed.), *Advances in Experimental Social Psychology* (vol. 21). New York: Academic Press, pp. 181–227.

Tesser, A. (2001) 'Self-Esteem', in A. Tesser and N. Schwarz (eds), *Blackwell Handbook of Social Psychology: Intraindividual Processes*. Malden, MA: Blackwell, pp. 479–98.

Tesser, A., Martin, L.L., and Cornell, D.P. (1996) 'On the Substitutability of Self-Protective Mechanisms', in P.M. Gollwitzer and J.A. Bargh, (eds), *The Psychology of Action: Linking Cognition and Motivation to Behavior*. New York: Guilford, pp. 48–68.

Tesser, A. and Paulhus, D. (1983) 'The Definition of Self: Private and Public Self-Evaluation Management Strategies', *Journal of Personality and Social Psychology*, 44: 672–82.

Tesser, A. and Smith, J. (1980) 'Some Effects of Task Relevance and Friendship on Helping: You Don't Always Help the One You Like', *Journal of Experimental Social Psychology*, 16: 582–90.

Tice, D.M. (1991) 'Esteem Protection or Enhancement? Self-Handicapping Motives and Attributions Differ by Trait Self-Esteem', *Journal of Personality and Social Psychology*, 60: 711–25.

Tice, D.M. (1993) 'The Social Motivations of People with Low Self-Esteem', in R.F. Baumeister (ed.), *Self-Esteem: The Puzzle of Low Self-Regard*. New York: Plenum, pp. 37–53.

Tice, D.M. and Baumeister, R.F. (1990) 'Self-Esteem, Self-Handicapping, and Self-Presentation: The Strategy of Inadequate Practice', *Journal of Personality*, 58: 443–64.

Tice, D.M., Butler, J.L., Muraven, M.B., and Stillwell, A.M. (1995) 'When Modesty Prevails: Differential Favorability of Self-Presentation to Friends and Strangers', *Journal of Personality and Social Psychology*, 69: 1120–38.

Triandis, H.C. and Suh, E.M. (2002) 'Cultural Influences on Personality', *Annual Review of Psychology*, 53: 133–60.

Trope, Y. (1979) 'Uncertainty-Reducing Properties of Achievement Tasks', *Journal of Personality and Social Psychology*, 37: 1505–18.

Trope, Y. (1980) 'Self-Assessment, Self-Enhancement, and Task Preference', *Journal of Experimental Social Psychology*, 16: 116–29.

Trope, Y. (1982) 'Self-Assessment and Task Performance', *Journal of Experimental Social Psychology*, 18: 201–15.

Trope, Y. (1986) 'Self-Enhancement and Self-Assessment in Achievement Behavior', in R.M. Sorrentino and E.T. Higgins (eds), *Handbook of Motivation and Cognition: Foundations of Social Behavior*. New York: Guilford, pp. 350–78.

Trope, Y. and Neter, E. (1994) 'Reconciling Competing Motives in Self-Evaluation: The Role of Self-Control in Feedback Seeking', *Journal of Personality and Social Psychology*, 66: 646–57.

Trzesniewski, K.H., Donnellan, M.B., Robins, R.W., Moffitt, T.E., and Caspi, A. (2002) 'Do Juvenile Delinquents Have High or Low Self-Esteem?', paper presented at the annual meeting of the Society for Personality and Social Psychology, February, Savannah, GA.

Twenge, J.M. and Campbell, W.K. (2001) 'Age and Birth Cohort Differences in Self-Esteem: A Cross-Temporal Meta-Analysis', *Personality and Social Psychology Review*, 5: 321–44.

Vallone, R.P., Griffin, D.W., Lin, S., and Ross, L. (1990) 'Overconfident Prediction of Future Actions and Outcomes by Self and Others', *Journal of Personality and Social Psychology*, 58: 582–92.

van der Ham, T., van Strien, D.C., and van Engeland, H. (1998) 'Personality Characteristics Predict Outcomes of Eating Disorders in Adolescents: A 4–Year Prospective Study', *European Child and Adolescent Psychiatry*, 7: 79–84.

van Lange, P.A.M., Rusbult, C.E., Semin-Goossens, A., Goerts, C.A., and Stalpers, M. (1999) 'Being Better than Others but Otherwise Perfectly Normal: Perceptions of Uniqueness and Similarity in Close Relationships', *Personal Relationships*, 6: 269–89.

van Lange, P.A.M. and Sedikides, C. (1998) 'Being More Honest but Not Necessarily More Intelligent than Others: Generality and Explanations for the Muhammad Ali Effect', *European Journal of Social Psychology*, 28: 675–80.

Vohs, K.D., Bardone, A.M., Joiner, T.E., Jr., Abramson, L.Y., and Heatherton, T.F. (1999) 'Perfectionism, Perceived Weight Status, and Self-Esteem Interact to Predict Bulimic Symptoms: A Model of Bulimic Symptom Development', *Journal of Abnormal Psychology*, 108: 695–700.

Vohs, K.D. and Heatherton, T.D. (2001) 'Self Esteem and Threats to Self: Implications for Self Construals and Interpersonal Perceptions', *Journal of Personality and Social Psychology*, 8: 1103–18.

Vohs, K.D., Voelz, Z.R., Pettit, J.W., Bardone, A.M., Katz, J., Abramson, L.Y., Heatherton, T.F., and Joiner, T.E., Jr. (2001) 'Perfectionism, Body Dissatisfaction, and Self-Esteem: An Interactive Model of Bulimic Symptom Development', *Journal of Social and Clinical Psychology*, 20: 476–96.

Walker, W.R., Skowronski, J.J., and Thompson, C.P. (2003) 'Life is Pleasant – and Memory Helps to Keep

It That Way!', *Review of General Psychology*, 7: 203–210.

Wallace H.M. and Baumeister, B.F. (2002) 'The Performance of Narcissists Rises and Falls with the Opportunity for Glory', *Journal of Personality and Social Psychology*, 82: 819–34.

Weinstein. N.D. (1980) 'Unrealistic Optimism about Future Events', *Journal of Personality and Social Psychology*, 39: 806–29.

Weinstein, N.D. and Klein, W.M. (1995) 'Resistance of Personal Risk Perceptions to Debiasing Manipulation', *Health Psychology*, 14: 132–40.

Wheeler, L. (1966) 'Motivation as a Determinant of Upward Social Comparison', *Journal of Experimental Social Psychology*, 2 (Suppl. 1): 27–31.

Whisman, M.A. and Kwon, P. (1993) 'Life Stress and Dysphoria: The Role of Self-Esteem and Hopelessness', *Journal of Personality and Social Psychology*, 65: 1054–60.

Williams, G.J., Power, K.G., Millar, H.R., Freeman, C.P., Yellowlees, A., Dowds, T., Walker, M., Campsie, L., MacPherson, F., and Jackson, M.A. (1993) 'Comparison of Eating Disorders and Other Dietary/Weight Groups on Measures of Perceived Control, Assertiveness, Self-Esteem, and Self-Directed Hostility', *International Journal of Eating Disorders*, 14: 27–32.

Wilson, T.D., Lindsey, S. and Schooler, T.Y. (2000) 'A Model of Dual Attitudes', *Psychological Review*, 107: 101–26.

Wittgenstein, L. (1953) *Philosophical Investigations* (trans. G.E.M. Anscambe). Oxford: Basil Blackwell.

Wolfe, R.N., Lennox, R.D., and Cutler, B.L. (1986) 'Getting Along and Getting Ahead: Empirical Support for a Theory of Protective and Acquisitive Self-Presentation', *Journal of Personality and Social Psychology*, 50: 356–61.

Wood, J.V. (1989) 'Theory and Research Concerning Social Comparison of Personality Attributes', *Psychological Bulletin*, 106: 231–48.

Wood, J., Moffoot, A.P.R., and O'Carroll, R.E. (1998) '"Depressive Realism" Revisited: Depressed Patients Are Realistic when They Are Wrong but Are Unrealistic when They Are Right', *Cognitive Neuropsychiatry*, 3: 119–26.

Yik, M.S.M., Bond, M.H., and Paulhus, D.L. (1998) 'Do Chinese Self-Enhance or Self-Efface? It's a Matter of Domain', *Personality and Social Psychology Bulletin*, 24: 399–406.

Zuckerman, M. (1979) 'Attribution of Success and Failure Revisited, or: The Motivational Bias Is Alive and Well in Attribution Theory', *Journal or Personality*, 47: 245–87.

Zuckerman, M., Kieffer, S.C., and Knee, C.R. (1998) 'Consequences of Self-Handicapping: Effects on Coping, Academic Performance, and Adjustment', *Journal of Personality and Social Psychology*, 74: 1619–28.

# 6
# Attitudes: Foundations, Functions, and Consequences

RUSSELL H. FAZIO AND MICHAEL A. OLSON

**INTRODUCTION**

Likes and dislikes form an integral part of daily life. For this very reason, attitudes have long been one of the major domains of inquiry in the field of social psychology. This chapter discusses classic and current conceptualizations of the attitude construct. Theory and research concerning the cognitive, affective, and/or behavioral bases of attitudes are reviewed, as well as ways in which attitudes can vary in their strength. We then turn to various functions that attitudes have been posited to serve, emphasizing their value as tools for quick and efficient object appraisal. Finally, we consider the multiple processes by which attitudes can influence judgments and behavior.

It is difficult to imagine a psychological world without attitudes. One would go about daily life without the ability to think in terms of 'good' and 'bad', 'desirable' and 'undesirable', or 'approach' and 'avoid'. There would be no activation of positivity or approach tendencies upon encountering objects that would engender positive outcomes, but, perhaps more seriously, there would also be no mental faculty for avoiding negative objects in one's environment. Our environment would make little sense to us; the world would be a cacophony of meaningless blessings and curses. Existence would be truly chaotic, and probably quite short.

For these reasons, the attitude construct has proven indispensable in social psychology's understanding of why we think, feel, and do the things we do. Indeed, the field of social psychology was once defined as the study of attitudes (Thomas and Znaniecki, 1918). Even a quick perusal of the various books and review chapters on the attitude construct reveals that virtually everyone begins with broad assertions about how pervasive evaluation is in everyday life (e.g., Fazio, 2001; Petty and Cacioppo, 1981). Osgood et al. (1957) showed that most of the meaning in language comes from evaluation. Certainly, attitudes have occupied a central position in social psychology for decades (Allport, 1935; Doob, 1947; McGuire, 1985).

How do we come to evaluate objects in our environment as positive or negative? What are the functions of these evaluations? How are they represented in memory, and how does this representation affect the ways they operate in predicting behavior? History has proven these questions to be some of the most important, and challenging, of social psychology. Our goal in this chapter is to describe some of the ways in which researchers have approached these questions about the nature of attitudes and to relate some of the insights that the field has collected in nearly 100 years. We do not aspire to be exhaustive. But we do hope to provide a broad coverage of attitude function and consequences, enough to stimulate the reader's thinking in ways that might later prove useful in filling some of the gaps of understanding that challenge the field. We discuss the classic tripartite view of attitudes and some more recent developments concerning how attitudes might be conceptualized. Next, some important qualities of attitudes, including various indices of attitude strength, are covered. We then turn to the question of why people form and hold attitudes; that is, what functions attitudes serve. Finally, we address the attitude–behavior relation and provide a framework for thinking about the conditions under which attitudes are more likely to guide behavior.

## The classic three-component view

Historically, the most prominent framework for the study of attitudes has been the tripartite, or three-component model (Katz and Stotland, 1959; Rosenberg and Hovland, 1960). In this view, the attitude is an unobservable psychological construct which can manifest itself in relevant beliefs, feelings, and behavioral components (Eagly and Chaiken, 1993). Because the attitude exists only within the mind of the person, one must look for it in more observable realms (MacCorquodale and Meehl, 1948). So, for example, one's positive attitude toward chocolate might appear in favorable beliefs ('A good piece of chocolate really improves my day'), feelings ('Chocolate melting in my mouth brings me such a tranquil feeling'), and behavior ('I'm eating chocolate now').

At first glance, the tripartite view seems to be a foregone conclusion for several reasons. First, it provides a way of cataloguing various attitudinal responses and a framework for their study (e.g., Breckler, 1984). Second, it has served as a road map for guiding research on attitude formation and change (see Eagly and Chaiken, 1993, for a review). Third, it matches fairly well the intuitive distinction between the components. Indeed, the heart–head dichotomy has roots as far back as Plato and has enjoyed privileged status in many popular psychological theories (McGuire, 1969, 1985). It also seems to exhaust the universe of possibilities of attitudinal responses (one would be hard pressed to invent a response that could not fit somewhere in one of the three categories). However, the tripartite view includes several assumptions about the nature of attitudes that might better be left unmade (Zanna and Rempel, 1988). Indeed, these questions should remain open as empirical questions worthy of investigation.

Specifically, the tripartite view suggests that while one cannot get into the head of the attitude-holder to study his or her attitude toward, say, abortion, that attitude should be observable in reported thoughts, feelings, and behavior toward the topic of abortion. That is, the attitude should manifest in all three ways (Rosenberg and Hovland, 1960). By this definition, all three components must be present for an evaluative tendency to exist. However, research suggests that attitudes can form as a result of any one (or combination) of the three components, and, moreover, that which forms the roots of the attitude has implications for the strength and persistence of the attitude (e.g., Abelson et al., 1982; Bem, 1972; Chaiken et al., 1995; Fazio and Zanna, 1981; Fishbein and Ajzen, 1975; Tyler and Rasinski, 1984; van den Berg et al., 2006).

The tripartite view also makes the dubious assumption that the three classes of evaluative responding must be consistent with each other, given their common dependency on an underlying construct. However, it is easy to imagine someone who believes that reproductive rights should be protected but whose emotional reactions to the issue of abortion are quite negative (Breckler and Wiggins, 1989; Rosenberg, 1968). Such inconsistencies between affective and cognitive responses to an attitude object have important implications (which we discuss later), but they risk being overlooked (or the attitude would not really be considered an attitude) within a traditional tripartite model. Finally, and perhaps most problematic, is the assumption of attitude–behavior consistency. The assumption that attitudes always guide behavior not only rails against common sense, but also inhibits some important questions from being asked regarding the conditions under which attitudes might best predict behavior, as we shall see later in the section on attitude–behavior relation.

With such ambiguity surrounding the tripartite model, it is not surprising that several researchers have attempted to reduce the number of components to two or even one. For example, some advocates of a one-component view argue that cognition forms the foundation of all attitudes, and that feelings and behaviors toward the attitude object simply derive from beliefs, as when, on the basis of cool-headed hard evidence, one decides to prefer Macintosh to Windows computer operating systems (e.g., Fishbein and Ajzen, 1975; Fishbein and Middlestadt, 1995). Others have insisted that 'feelings need no inferences', and that one's affective reactions to an object can precede any beliefs about it, as when one has a 'bad feeling' about a new acquaintance but cannot seem to say why (e.g., Monahan et al., 2000; Zajonc, 1980). Finally, evidence exists that, in the absence of either beliefs or feelings about the attitude object, one can infer an attitude into existence from past behavior toward the attitude object, as when one author of this chapter noticed that he consistently bought olive-colored shirts and, therefore, must like the color olive (e.g., Bem, 1972; Fazio, 1987). In any case, in light of several decades of evidence to the contrary, the assumption that all three components must be present and in agreement seems dubious indeed.

Zanna and Rempel (1988) re-examined some of the assumptions of earlier models of attitudes, including the tripartite view, and arrived at a less presumptuous formulation of the attitude construct. First, they regard attitudes simply as categorizations of an object or issue along an evaluative dimension. Essentially, this definition accords with Thurstone's

(1946: 39) classic, single-factor view of attitudes as 'the intensity of positive or negative affect for or against a psychological object'. Second, Zanna and Rempel (1988) retain the notion that attitudes can form and manifest themselves from beliefs, feelings, and behavior but strip away with the problematic assumptions of the traditional tripartite model. In their view, attitudes can be based on any combination of the three components, and they leave the issue of agreement between the three components as an empirical question. Thus, an attitude might develop through cognitive, affective, or behavioral processes, and no assumptions are made about which component might predominate, how the components interact in determining an overall evaluation of an attitude object, or how the components might affect one another.

A similar approach is evident in the view of attitudes proposed by Fazio and his colleagues (Fazio, 1990, 1995; Fazio et al., 1982). Here, attitudes are viewed as associations in memory between attitude objects and their evaluation (Fazio, 1990, 1995). These associations are based on cognitive, affective, and/or behavioral knowledge of the attitude object, from which is derived a 'summary' evaluation. The strength of the association between an attitude object and its evaluation becomes an important quality of the attitude, one that will be discussed later (Fazio, 1995).

## Cognitive, affective, and behavioral processes of attitude formation

Newer conceptualizations of the attitude construct advance the possibility that attitudes can form in multiple ways. The three key means of attitude formation we discuss implicate cognitive, affective, or behavioral processes.

### *Cognitive routes*

An attitude is formed on the basis of cognitions when one comes to believe either that the attitude object possesses (un)desirable attributes, or that the attitude object will bring about (un)desired outcomes. Like the example of computer operating systems mentioned earlier, such an attitude is marked by an emphasis on beliefs about the attitude object. Perhaps the best known cognitive model is Fishbein and Ajzen's (1975) expectancy-value model. They argue that an attitude toward a given object is the sum of the expected value of the attributes of the object. Expectancy is defined as the estimate of the probability that the object has a given attribute, and the value of an attribute is simply one's evaluation of it. For each attribute, an expected value is computed by multiplying the expectancy and the value of the attribute. An overall attitude toward the object is reached by taking the sum of the expected values of all the attributes an attitude object is thought to have (e.g., Smith and Clark, 1973). Other models, such as Anderson's (1991) information-integration theory, also describe attitude formation as a function of combinations of various beliefs and their evaluative implications (e.g., Anderson, 1981, 1982).

This all sounds very cerebral, and indeed it is. Surprisingly, Fishbein and Ajzen (1975) make the claim that all attitudes are based on beliefs about the attitude object, and that all attitudes are formed via the summation of subjective probabilities and values (see Fishbein and Middlestadt, 1995, for a recent argument to this effect). But while beliefs about attitude objects certainly contribute to our evaluations of them, and while some evidence supports the model's account of how beliefs about attitude objects combine (e.g., Cronen and Conville, 1975), the model fails to address some important issues. Correspondence between the model's predictions and empirical data implies nothing about the process by which those attitudes are derived. Whether people actually engage in the probability assessment and summation processes these theorists describe is another question, and there are certainly ways other than their expected value equation that people arrive at the same attitude (see Eagly and Chaiken, 1993, for a critique of the model). Moreover, as evidence we will discuss below indicates, evaluations can form in the absence of beliefs about the object.

Other cognitive models focus more on the qualitative aspects of belief-based attitude change. The 'cognitive-response' model addresses questions of how perceivers react to and elaborate on information (in the form of persuasive arguments) relating to an attitude object (Greenwald, 1981; Petty et al., 1981). Such models lack the precision of the mathematical models, but address some of the person, situation, and message variables that affect attitude development and change (for a review, see Petty and Cacioppo, 1986). Cognitive-response models have been studied mostly within persuasion settings, and so the reader is referred to Chapter 9 to read more about this and its more modern descendants.

### *Affective routes*

Attitudes formed from affect stem from emotional reactions to the attitude object. Like the example of chocolate mentioned earlier, one can be said to have an affectively based attitude when either positive or negative feelings are evoked when considering the attitude object. Social psychologists have uncovered three primary ways in which attitudes might be formed on the basis of affect: operant conditioning, classical conditioning, and mere exposure. Traditionally, operant conditioning has been used by experimental psychologists interested in basic learning principles, and is typically defined by the frequency of a response – positive outcomes increase the rate of response, and negative outcomes decrease it (e.g., Hull, 1951; Thorndike, 1932). Attitudes can be learned in a similar way when considered as a response. Attitudinal responses that lead to positive outcomes are more likely to occur again in the future, and attitudinal responses that lead to negative outcomes are less likely to occur. In a classic example, Hildum and Brown (1956) telephoned university students and acted as survey researchers interested in attitudes toward policies at their school. Some students' responses were answered with a 'good!' by the surveyors (responses that suggested a positive attitude toward a university policy). These researchers found that positively reinforced responses were more likely to occur later – students whose positive responses toward a university policy were reinforced voiced more positive responses to university policies later. Insko (1965) found that reinforced responses were more likely to occur even when tested a week later in a different setting.

Classical conditioning is similar to operant conditioning, but the response emitted is thought to be internal. That is, no overt response is necessary to learn through classical conditioning; one need only attend to covariations between objects in one's environment. Through repeated pairings of some attitude object (such as a new beverage) and other clearly positive or negative objects (such as a sexy model), the affect associated with the second object comes to be associated with the attitude object. For example, Staats and Staats (1958) paired national names (such as 'Swedish') with positive or negative words and found that the nation paired with positive words was evaluated more positively than the nation paired with negative words. Others have paired the onset or offset of shock with other words and have shown similar effects (Zanna et al., 1970). While some researchers have questioned whether this 'evaluative conditioning' can occur in the absence of awareness of the between the conditioned and unconditioned stimuli contingencies (e.g., Field, 2000), there is now evidence to suggest that people are quite good at encoding environmental covariations in memory even if they never consciously 'notice' them (for a review, see Seger, 1994). For example, Olson and Fazio (2001), in the context of a study about 'attention and surveillance', told participants that they would see a variety of 'random' words and images on the computer screen and that they should press a response button whenever they saw a predetermined target item appear. While they were being vigilant for the target items, several other words and images were presented, supposedly as distracters to make the task more challenging. Embedded in this stream of random images were critical pairings of novel objects (Pokemon cartoon creatures) with either positive or negative words and images. Tests of explicit memory indicated that participants were completely unaware of the systematic pairings, but a surprise evaluation task indicated that they found the Pokemon creature paired with positive items more pleasant than the Pokemon creature paired with negative items (see also Olson and Fazio, 2002, 2006). Because these attitudes can form in the absence of conscious beliefs about the attitude object, classical conditioning stands to be a potentially ubiquitous form of attitudes in the real world (for a review, see De Houwer et al., 2001).

The evidence regarding operant and classical conditioning argues for the existence of attitudes on the basis of only affect. So does research concerning the mere exposure effect. The underlying premise of the effect is that simply making an object 'accessible to the individual's perception' increases liking for it (Zajonc, 1968: 1). In a now classic experiment, Zajonc presented nonsense words (which he presented as Turkish words; for example, 'biweejni'), Chinese ideographs, or yearbook photos, to participants in varying numbers of repetitions. Participants were then asked to guess the meaning of the Turkish/nonsense words or Chinese ideographs, or to estimate how much they might like a person in one of the yearbook photos. His simple finding was that the more participants were exposed to a given item, the more favorably they evaluated it. Later researchers found that the effect generalized to many other attitude objects, and that it is most robust when the exposure is subliminal (Harmon-Jones and Allen, 2001; Monahan et al., 2000; see Bornstein, 1989; Zajonc, 2001, for reviews). Thus, short of the minimal amount of (probably nonconscious) cognitive work required to categorize the repeatedly presented items as familiar, familiarity appears to breed liking even in the absence of beliefs about the object.

### *Behavioral routes*

Without either clear feelings or beliefs about a potential attitude object, one may have still had past experience with it, as in the example mentioned earlier of one author's tendency to purchase olive-colored clothing. Bem (1972) claimed that this past behavior can be used to infer an attitude toward an object through self-perception. For example, Bandler et al. (1968) exposed participants to electric shocks and induced them to either escape (that is, terminate) the shock or not. Although the shocks were of equal intensity, participants reported the shocks from which they had escaped to be more painful. Presumably, they inferred from their termination of the shocks that they must have been painful. Self-perception can also lead one to discount one's behavior as a source of information about one's attitudes, as when an intrinsically rewarding behavior comes to be associated with external rewards. For example, Lepper et al. (1973) found that children who had earlier freely engaged in an enjoyable activity enjoyed it less after having experienced an event in which they engaged in the activity in order to receive a reward (see Chapter 10, this volume, for a more in-depth discussion of self-perception and related processes).

In summary, attitudes can be based on either affect, cognition, or behavior, and the existence of an evaluation based on one of the elements need not imply the existence of the other two elements. Attitude researchers have taken Zanna and Rempel's advice and have spent a good deal of energy in exploring the complex structural relationships between the three bases of attitudes and how these bases affect the nature and behavior of attitudes (e.g., Edwards, 1990; Fabrigar and Petty, 1999; Millar and Millar, 1990; van den Berg et al., 2006). In fact, some of the most exciting work on attitudes premises itself on the often conflictual relationships between the elements. We describe some of these dynamics below in our discussion of the structural qualities of attitudes.

## Qualities of attitudes

When prompted with a political survey question, two individuals might both rate George W. Bush as a '–2' on a –3-to-+3 scale. However, even though their *reported* attitudes might look the same, their underlying evaluations may be very different. For example, one individual might have to think about it for a while before settling on an answer, whereas the other might explode with a vehement '–2!' immediately after being asked. For one individual, the attitude may stem primarily from affect, whereas for the other it may involve a thoughtful consideration of Bush's stands on important national issues. Such differences in the underlying qualities may have important implications for attitude function. Despite their numeric equivalence, one person's attitude might be stronger than the other's.

Many indices of attitude strength have been proposed. Among them are attitude certainty, importance, and centrality, as well as ego involvement, knowledge, commitment, and conviction. There is certainly overlap between the various strength measures, but, as of yet, there is little consensus on whether the many measures might be reduced to a simple few (see Bassili, 1996; Petty and Krosnick, 1995, Visser et al., 2003). In the interest of brevity, we will focus on only a few of these measures, beginning with attitude accessibility.

### *Attitude accessibility*

Recall that in the framework described by Fazio et al. (1982), an attitude is seen as an association in memory between an attitude object and its summary evaluation. The strength of that association can vary, and all attitudes are thought to exist somewhere along this strength continuum (Fazio, 1990, 1995). One end of the continuum is marked by nonattitudes (Converse, 1970); these are evaluations that simply are not available in memory. When prompted to make an attitudinal response, someone with a nonattitude toward a given object must construct one based on any currently known or observable attributes of the object. The other end of the continuum is characterized by strong associations in memory between attitude objects and their respective evaluations. Such attitudes are capable of being automatically activated upon encountering the attitude object (Fazio, 1995). So, whereas the sight of an obscure brand of juice activates little from memory, and an evaluation of that juice must be based on whatever is known or might be learned about it at the time, the mere sight or aroma of coffee activates an impressive rush of positivity in many a coffee drinker.

This reasoning underlies a common measurement of associative strength, latency to respond to attitudinal inquiries, or 'attitude accessibility' (e.g., Powell and Fazio, 1984). In this procedure, participants are presented with labels or images of several attitude objects and are asked to indicate, as each object is presented, whether they like or dislike the attitude object by pressing one of two response keys as quickly as possible. Because strong attitudes require less cognitive work to report, they are responded to much more quickly than weaker ones. Thus, response latencies to attitudinal judgments serve as an indicator of associative strength.

Because strong attitudes are capable of automatic activation, the mere presentation of the attitude object can activate positivity or negativity, depending on the attitude. Borrowing from work in cognitive psychology on automatic activation (e.g., Schneider and Shiffrin, 1977), Fazio and colleagues (e.g., Fazio et al., 1986) reasoned that if an attitude object's presentation automatically activates, say, positivity, responses to other positive items should be facilitated. Measurement of the activation of some other positive item in memory after presentation of the first positive item could then serve as an indirect indicator of the extent to which positivity is automatically activated in response to the first item (Fazio et al., 1986, 1995). In this paradigm, an attitude object, say, 'coffee', is presented for a short duration (usually 100–300 milliseconds), and it is followed by either a positive or a negative adjective. The participant's task is to indicate whether the adjective means 'good' or 'bad' by pressing one of two corresponding response keys. If the attitude toward coffee is sufficiently strong (and positive), and is followed by the word 'awesome', one should be quicker to identify 'awesome' as a positive word. Analogously, one should be slower to identify a negative word, say, 'horrible', as negative.

In their first demonstration of the paradigm, Fazio et al. (1986) presented attitude objects as primes that had been idiosyncratically selected for each participant as strong and weak. In a later experiment, accessibility was manipulated by having participants repeatedly express their evaluations of some attitude objects in an earlier phase of the procedure. In both cases, attitudes characterized by stronger object–evaluation associations were relatively more capable of automatic activation. For these relatively accessible attitudes, participants were quicker to identify evaluatively congruent target adjectives that followed the presentation of the attitude object (see Fazio, 2001, for a review of recent developments concerning the affective priming paradigm and automatic attitude activation). These relatively strong attitudes are then more likely to direct attention to the attitude object, affect perceptions of it, and guide behavior toward it, as we shall see later.

### Ambivalence

Any given attitude object may be characterized by both positive and negative qualities. To the extent that such inconsistencies are unresolved, an individual may possess both positive and negative evaluations of the attitude object. In other words, the individual's attitude can be viewed as 'ambivalent' (Kaplan, 1972).

Traditional measures of attitudes assume that attitudes exist somewhere between absolutely negative and absolutely positive and require respondents to place their attitude toward a given object somewhere on a single dimension scale, typically anchored at one end with 'dislike', and at the other end with 'like' (Himmelfarb, 1993; Thurstone, 1928; see Cacioppo et al., 1997, for a bidimensional conception of attitudes). Such scales deny the possibility that someone might feel *both* positively and negatively toward a given object (that is, ambivalent), or *neither* positively nor negatively toward a given object (that is, indifferent). The meaning of the zero or neutral point on the scale then becomes questionable, because, presumably, respondents would respond somewhere near the zero or neutral point whether they feel both positivity and negativity, or neither (Converse, 1970; Kaplan, 1972). As one might suspect, there are important differences between the two cases that we will discuss below. Researchers interested in ambivalence have circumvented this problem by requiring respondents to make two estimates toward a given object – one with regard to the positivity they feel toward the object, and another with regard to the negativity they feel toward the object. A variety of methods exists for computing indices of ambivalence based on these responses, but all agree that ambivalence exists to the extent that respondents indicate feeling some degree of both positivity and negativity toward the object (Kaplan, 1972; Priester and Petty, 1996; Thompson et al., 1995).

Many researchers would argue that ambivalence is an unstable and subjectively uncomfortable state (e.g., Newby-Clark et al., 2002), and some of the consequences of ambivalence are based on this premise (Katz, 1981; Katz and Hass, 1988). One such consequence is 'ambivalence amplification', which is the notion that behavior toward the attitude object is amplified, or extremitized, in either the positive or negative direction, in an effort to reduce ambivalence (e.g., Hass et al., 1994). For example, Katz and Hass (1988) argue that many whites hold ambivalent attitudes toward blacks – they believe that blacks deserve egalitarian treatment and respect as individuals, but they simultaneously believe that blacks violate the American values of hard work and independence. The result is often exaggeratedly positive or negative treatment of blacks.

Ambivalent attitudes are marked by other important qualities as well. Because ambivalence is thought to be an unstable state, ambivalent attitudes are prone to change (Bargh et al., 1992; Bassili, 1996) and are relatively less predictive of behavior (Armitage and Conner, 2000). They are also more context dependent, meaning that whether the positive or the negative component is activated depends on the particular situation (Moore, 1980).

### Evaluative-cognitive consistency

As Zanna and Rempel (1988) note, numerous permutations of agreement or disagreement between affect, cognition, and behavior, as well as the overall summary attitude, are theoretically possible and interesting. For example, the 'heart' (affect) and 'mind' (cognition) may not cohere perfectly, or the summary evaluation may correspond more closely to affect than to cognition, or vice versa.

One such form of potential inconsistency within the structure of an attitude has received much more attention than others. Although originally labeled affective-cognitive consistency, the research is more appropriately referred to as involving evaluative-cognitive consistency, as Chaiken et al. (1995) have argued. The research concerns the degree of consistency between an individual's overall evaluation of an attitude object and the evaluative implications of his or her beliefs about the object. Beginning with the work of Rosenberg (1960, 1968), interesting relations have been observed between the extent of such correspondence and indications of attitude strength. Chaiken and Baldwin (1981) found that individuals whose attitudes were characterized by greater evaluative-cognitive consistency were less influenced by the implications of a linguistically biased questionnaire that made salient either their pro- or antienvironment behaviors. Whereas participants with initial attitudes characterized by low consistency displayed attitude change in the direction of the salient behavioral information, those with higher evaluative-cognitive consistency were unaffected. Their attitudes remained stable. In a parallel manner, Rosenberg (1968) obtained evidence that greater evaluative-cognitive consistency was associated with greater resistance to counterpersuasion, and Norman (1975) found such intra-attitudinal correspondence to be associated with greater consistency between attitudes and subsequent behavior. Chaiken et al. (1995) provide a more detailed and comprehensive review of research concerning such measures of structural consistency and their relation to attitude strength.

We have reviewed a few important qualities of attitudes: attitude accessibility, ambivalence, and evaluative-cognitive consistency. Much more work has been done on these and other qualities of attitudes, and, more generally, on various indices of attitude strength (Petty and Krosnick, 1995). Likewise, ambivalence can take additional forms beyond those mentioned here (Zanna and Rempel, 1988). Our review has been necessarily selective, but we hope we have succeeded in communicating at least some of the important complexities of attitude structure. Next we address the functions that attitudes serve; that is, why we evaluate.

## Attitude function: then and now

In the late nineteenth and early twentieth centuries, psychologists divided themselves rather decisively into two camps: structuralists and functionalists. Structuralists believed that psychology's purpose should be merely to describe the phenomena of the human mind and not speculate why these phenomena exist (e.g., Titchener, 1910). Functionalists, however, were interested in the adaptive significance of psychological phenomena and held that understanding human psychology required an appreciation of the premise that the human mind has evolved to solve certain adaptive problems – that psychological phenomena have specific functions (e.g., James, 1952). We would agree that, in the case of attitudes, understanding why we evalute is a crucial component to understanding attitudes more generally.

### *Theoretical perspectives*

Consideration of the functions served by attitudes began in the 1950s. Smith et al. (1956) and Katz (1960) each proposed a series of attitudinal functions aimed at covering the various reasons why people evaluate objects in their environment. Katz's taxonomy included a utilitarian, knowledge, ego-defensive, and value-expressive function. The utilitarian function is premised in the behaviorist principle of seeking rewards and avoiding punishment in one's environment. In this sense, attitudes help to ensure the organism's survival, but, more broadly, any attitude based on an interest in maximizing pleasure and minimizing pain for oneself can be considered utilitarian (Green and Gerken, 1989). The knowledge function is related to the utilitarian function in that it helps in navigating one's environment, but, according to Katz, it also fulfills a specific need to organize one's world and make sense of an otherwise daunting information environment (see also Allport, 1935). Dividing the world into likes and dislikes provides the kind of order and predictability that, according to Katz, we all crave. Smith et al. (1956) proposed an 'object-appraisal' function, which can be thought of as a combination of Katz's utilitarian and knowledge functions. They argue that such an attitude provides a way of 'sizing up' objects in one's environment, saving the time and energy that would be required constantly to compute new attitudes toward objects. Such 'ready-aids' allow organisms to navigate more efficiently their environment and quickly decide whether an object should be approached or avoided. We have more to say about this particular function later.

Katz's ego-defensive function and what Smith et al. called the 'externalization' function are quite similar. Both are rooted in psychoanalytic defense mechanisms such as repression and projection, which are argued to provide a means of preserving the self-concept in the face of some threat. For example, Katz (1960) argued that prejudice is often the result of one's own feelings of inferiority and that derogating an out-group can make the individual feel better by comparison. Beyond prejudice, ego-defensive attitudes can serve to protect the self under conditions of any threat (such as economic depression and health risks; Eagly and Chaiken, 1993).

'Value-expressive' attitudes are thought to affirm the self and one's identity. Katz and others (e.g., McGuire, 1985; Steele, 1988) propose that people have an inherent need to solidify their beliefs about who they are, and that expressing important aspects of the self verifies one's identity. Some attitudes – ones of great importance to the individual – become a kind of realization of one's identity when expressed. A firmly held conviction, such as opposing all forms of war, should lead one to adopt proattitudinal positions and perform proattitudinal behaviors for the purpose of affirming the self. But while value-expressive attitudes perform important functions at an individual level, we would say that the attitude is performing what Smith et al. (1956) termed the 'social adjustive' function when one's antiwar stance wins praise and promotes friendship with like-minded others. Such attitudes can influence relationships and fulfill the need to relate to others.

### *Empirical progress*

Perhaps owing to its intuitive appeal, functional theory was readily accepted by researchers interested in attitudes. However, the theory actually stimulated surprisingly little research (Eagly and Chaiken, 1993). Indeed, until recently, there was little experimental evidence to support some of the fundamental tenets of functional theory. This lack of empirical progress may have been due to a lack of adequate measures and operationalizations of function. Without some means of assessing the function that was being served by a given attitude, little could be decided either way on the merits of functional theory (Herek, 1986). Fortunately, progress is apparent in more recent work. Some of these advances include approaches to the assessment of attitude functions (e.g., Herek, 1987), consideration of individual differences concerning attitude functions (e.g., Snyder and DeBono, 1987), and examination of the ego-defensive (e.g., Fein and Spencer, 1997) and object-appraisal (e.g., Fazio, 2000) functions in particular. Each will be reviewed in turn.

Herek (1987) derived an open-ended measure of assessing attitude function. Essays that participants wrote about their attitudes were content-analyzed for their functional themes. Although Herek's original formulation was aimed at assessing the functional orientations of attitudes toward stigmatized groups, theoretically, it could be applied to other attitude objects as well (Eagly and Chaiken, 1993). Indeed, related open-ended, thought-listing measures of function have been fruitfully employed to study a wide array of attitude objects (e.g., Prentice, 1987; Shavitt, 1990).

Others have taken an individual-difference approach to the study of attitude function. Snyder and colleagues argue that self-monitoring, the extent to which one is concerned with how appropriate his or her behavior is in others' presence, has implications for attitude function (Lavine and Snyder, 2000; Snyder, 1974, Snyder and DeBono, 1987). They argue that high self-monitors' attitudes are more likely to serve a social adjustive function, and that low self-monitors' attitudes are more likely to serve a value-expressive function. As evidence for this assertion, DeBono (1987) presented arguments against the deinstitutionalization of mentally ill patients to high and low self-monitoring college students who were in favor of deinstitutionalization. One set of statements emphasized that most students were opposed to deinstitutionalization (thus appealing to the social adjustive function), while another set emphasized that opposing deinstitutionalization was consistent with important personal values (thus appealing to the value-expressive function). The intent of this design was to test an idea that came from early theorizing on attitude function and persuasion: the functional matching hypothesis – the idea that persuasive arguments will lead to greater attitude change if they match the functional basis of the attitude. Consistent with this hypothesis, high self-monitors were more swayed by the social adjustive statements, and low self-monitors were more convinced by the value-expressive arguments. Petty and Wegener (1998) later showed that this effect of functional matching was the result of greater scrutiny of arguments that match the function of the attitude, and, hence, is limited to messages employing strong arguments.

In a different twist on the individual difference approach, Prentice (1987) argues that people differ in their functional orientations in general – specifically, that functional orientations toward their valued possessions indicate functional orientations of their attitudes more generally. She derived participants' functional orientations through their open-ended descriptions of why they valued their favorite possessions and was able to determine the degree to which a given individual was 'symbolic' (that is, value-oriented) or 'instrumental' in orientation. For example, some people may say that they love their car because it symbolizes their freedom, and others may simply appreciate its performance or reliability. Knowing their functional orientations, Prentice then presented people with different arguments about a variety of attitudinal issues. Consistent with the functional matching hypothesis, symbolically oriented individuals were more receptive of symbolic arguments, and instrumentally oriented individuals were more receptive of instrumental arguments.

However, Shavitt (1990) has shown that attitude objects themselves promote different kinds of functions. Using thought-listing procedures, she identified attitude objects for which attitude function inhered to the object. For example, attitudes toward perfume and greeting cards usually serve a social-adjustive, or what Shavitt refers to as a 'social-identity', function, whereas attitudes toward air conditioners and coffee are utilitarian in nature. Persuasive messages that matched the typical function of the attitude object proved more effective than mismatched arguments did. Thus, not only can specific attitudes differ in their symbolic or instrumental functions, but people differ in their symbolic or instrumental orientations toward objects in general, and objects themselves can lend themselves to different attitude functions.

Other recent advances concerning attitude function come from work on the ego-defensive function of prejudice. Fein and Spencer (1997) argue that derogating a member of an out-group can provide a boost to the self-image after it has been threatened, but is less likely if one has recently experienced self-affirmation. Participants who had been given self-esteem-damaging feedback regarding their performance on an intelligence test were more likely to derogate a job candidate in a later task. Moreover, mediational analyses indicated that to the extent that these threatened participants derogated the candidate, their self-esteem improved. Fein and Spencer (1997) also found that participants who had recently affirmed their core values were less likely to derogate a job candidate on the basis of ethnicity or sexual orientation.

More recently, these authors have shown that the automatic activation of negativity toward a member of a stereotyped group can be mediated by threats to the self (Spencer et al., 1998). Several studies in social cognition suggest that stereotypes of out-groups can be activated automatically, but only in cases where participants are not under 'cognitive load', that is, distracted by some additional task. Spencer et al. (1998) exposed participants to either an Asian-American (Experiment 1) or an African-American (Experiments 2 and 3) while under cognitive load and assessed the degree to which negative stereotypes were activated, using a word fragment completion task (for example, 's–y' might be completed as 'shy', showing activation of the Asian stereotype). Earlier, participants had completed an intelligence test, and half were told that they performed poorly on it (thus evoking a self-image threat), while the other half were told that they performed relatively well. Only the participants who had received negative feedback showed evidence of stereotype activation, suggesting that they were prepared to apply their stereotypes to the Asian- and African-American targets in ego defense.

These studies by Fein and Spencer (1997) and Spencer et al. (1997) provide strong evidence that negative evaluations of members of out-groups can serve an ego-defensive function. Interestingly, very recent work suggests that evaluations of out-group members can be positive in cases where the out-group member reacts favorably to the perceiver, and negative in cases where the out-group members reacts negatively to the perceiver (Sinclair and Kunda, 1999). Thus, it appears that evaluations of out-group members might be used flexibly to arrive at whatever best suits the ego in a given situation.

### The object-appraisal function

So far we have shown evidence that liking or disliking a given attitude object can serve one of several psychological functions, and that function drives the direction of the attitude, whether the attitude assumes a positive or negative valence. That is, the function served by a given object for a given individual forms the basis of the attitude. The object-appraisal function, however, is unique in that it implies that merely having an attitude, regardless of its valence, is functional for the individual (Fazio, 1995; Fazio et al., 1992; for a more extensive review, see Fazio, 2000). As suggested in the opening of this chapter, having precomputed evaluations allows one to navigate one's environment efficiently, without being forced to decide, upon encountering each new object, whether it should be approached or avoided. Indeed, object appraisal is the most primary and widely applicable of the attitude functions.

Accessible attitudes in particular are likely to serve this object-appraisal function (Fazio, 2000). Recall that these attitudes are characterized by strong object-evaluation associations and, hence, are most easily brought to mind in the presence of the attitude object. The stronger the object-evaluation association is for a given object, the less work one must do in 'sizing up' the object when presented with it. As we shall see, the functional benefits of accessible attitudes span from guiding attention to important objects in one's environment to arriving at better-quality decisions and to free up resources to deal with other environmental stimuli.

#### *Visual attention*

Considering the number of objects in one's visual environment at any given time, some items must be filtered out of perception as unimportant, and others must be focused on because of their hedonic value. Roskos-Ewoldsen and Fazio (1992) hypothesized that attitude objects toward which people hold accessible attitudes perform this basic perceptual function by guiding attention toward hedonically relevant stimuli in the environment. They either measured attitude accessibility (using the response latency technique mentioned earlier) or increased the accessibility of attitudes with a manipulation whereby participants were induced to rehearse their attitudes repeatedly. The attitude objects used were simple line drawings of objects, and participants were shown several such drawings in a visual array (some of which included the drawings toward which attitudes were highly accessible). Whether attitude accessibility was measured or manipulated, participants were quicker to notice objects toward which they had accessible attitudes. These attitude objects were more likely to attract attention even when they were presented as distracters in a task where their presence was completely irrelevant. Thus, objects toward which people have accessible attitudes are at an advantage to be noticed (much like when a coffee drinker is quick to notice the aroma of coffee in the air). These attitudes simply affect what we see, and such a function is valuable in a world filled with distractions. Objects that have been associated with positive or negative outcomes in the past are important to attend to in order to ready approach or avoidance responses, and accessible attitudes fulfill this attentional function.

### *Categorization*

Objects can be categorized in multiple ways, and the categories into which they fall can affect further information-processing and behavior. For example, a cigarette can be thought of as a much needed 'fix' to a smoker, an annoyance to a nonsmoker, or a serious health hazard to an asthmatic. How an object is categorized can depend on one's attitudes. Smith et al. (1996) reasoned that the presentation of an attitude object activates, at least to some extent, each category into which it might be placed, and that which category predominates depends on the attitudes one has toward the categories. The category associated with the most accessible attitude toward it is likely to guide attention toward the relevant aspects of the stimulus and encourage categorization of the object into that category. So in the same way that attitude-evoking objects attract attention, attitude-evoking categories increase the likelihood that they will be used to categorize objects that may fit into them.

Smith et al.'s (1996) experiments focused on a given attitude object and two potential categories into which it might fit (for example, 'yogurt' might be a dairy product or a health food). Attitudes were rehearsed for one category (say, health foods) through repeated expression to increase their accessibility, and judgments of whether the category was animate or inanimate were made for the other category (say, dairy products). Participants performed this task for several categories. Later in the experiment, participants were presented with the attitude object (yogurt) for the first time and were instructed to use it as a cue to remember the earlier items. Recall the earlier reasoning that each category into which an object might be placed should receive some activation. If the attitude toward the category 'health food' was made more accessible, greater attention should be drawn to the health-food-relevant attributes of yogurt. The result would be a greater tendency to categorize yogurt as a health food, which would then serve as a recall cue for the earlier rehearsed items. This is exactly what Smith et al., found – categories toward which participants had more accessible attitudes were more effectively cued by attitude objects that could be members of the category. Analogous results were found even when there was a one-week delay between the attitude-rehearsal phase and the cued recall phase. Thus, accessible attitudes promote the construal of objects in a manner that is hedonically meaningful for the perceiver.

A similar study replicated these same basic results using people of various races as attitude objects (Fazio and Dunton, 1997). To assess the extent to which race was attitude-evoking, Fazio and Dunton (1997) adapted the priming measure of attitudes mentioned earlier, using black and white faces as primes (Fazio et al., 1995). Participants then took part in a 'second experiment', where they made similarity judgments about many combinations of pairs of individual photos that varied on a number of dimensions, including race. Fazio and Dunton found that the attention of participants for whom race was attitude-evoking (whether it was a positive or a negative attitude) was drawn to the races of the photo pairs, which led them to use race to categorize the faces and make their similarity estimates. Arguably, that act of categorizing the faces by their race could then affect perceptions, judgments, and later behavior toward the targets.

### *Decision-making*

Perhaps the most direct evidence that accessible attitudes satisfy the object-appraisal function would be a demonstration that decision-making that allows for the use of accessible attitudes is less effortful than decision-making that does not. Fazio et al. (1992) did this by measuring participants' blood pressure while they were forced to make pair-wise preference ratings in a rapidly presented series of abstract paintings. Some participants had rehearsed their attitudes toward the individual paintings before the preference task, thus increasing the accessibility of their attitudes toward the paintings. The task was much easier for these participants, as indicated by their lower blood pressure while performing it, as compared to those who did not rehearse their attitudes (see also Blascovich et al., 1993).

This research not only indicated that accessible attitudes ease decision-making but also provided evidence that they increase the *quality* of decision-making. After completing the pair-wise preference task, participants were asked to rank order the paintings at their leisure (providing unlimited time to offer their evaluations of the paintings presumably allowed participants to be more accurate). Their rank orderings were then compared to the preferences reported in the speeded pair-wise preference task. Greater correspondence between the preferences reported in the pair-wise task and the ranking task was found for those whoseattitudes had been made more accessible. So, when the environment demands rapid reactions, accessible attitudes not only reduce the stress of decision-making but also enhance the quality of the decisions.

### *Freeing resources for coping with other stressors*

These findings illustrate the various ways in which accessible attitudes make navigating one's environment an easier task. But, more broadly, having accessible attitudes toward a variety of objects can free up one's cognitive resources considerably – resources that may then be used to deal with other environmental stressors. One's first semester incollege is filled with stressors, and Fazio and Powell (1997) investigated whether entering college with accessible attitudes towards college-related activities helped reduce the impact of these stressors. They measured the accessibility of a variety of college-related attitudes (such as studying in the library, pulling an all-nighter, and potential majors) of incoming freshmen, using the latency to respond to attitudinal inquiries measure. Comparing students' response latencies to items concerning college activities to other filler issues, they were able to derive a general estimate of the extent to which each student arrived at college 'pre-equipped' with accessible attitudes toward a variety of stressors they were soon to face. Students also reported a wealth of information about their current levels of stress, depression, and other mental-health-related states, as well as information about their current physical health. Two months later, they returned and completed the same mental and physical health measures. The relationship between these measures from time 1 and time 2 varied as a function of having accessible attitudes. For those students who began college with relatively poor health, the number of stressors they were experiencing affected their recovery in that fewer stressors at time 1 led to better health at time 2. However, the relationship between stressors and improved health was moderated by attitude accessibility – those students with accessible college-related attitudes and fewer stressors at time 1 improved more. For students who began college in relatively good health, more stressors at time 1 led to poorer health later. But for those who had accessible attitudes, the negative effect of stressors on later health was diminished. Thus, having a reservoir of accessible attitudes to draw from frees one's energies for dealing with other stressors, and the deeper the reservoir, the more energy one will have for dealing with whatever life might present.

### *Costs of accessible attitudes*

So far, we have seen that attitudes perform important functions for the perceiver, and that accessible attitudes in particular are well suited to serve the object-appraisal function. However, recent research suggests that the efficiency with which accessible attitudes allow one to navigate the environment might come at some cost. For example, the generally adaptive ability of accessible attitudes to guide one's attention to the attitude object (Roskos-Ewoldsen and Fazio, 1992) presumably cannot be 'turned off' in situations where attending to the object distracts one from more pressing tasks. Such might be the case when the proverbial male driver runs into a parked car after his attention is automatically drawn to an attractive female pedestrian. Thus, the relevance of the attitude object to the immediate task concerns is critical as to whether possession of the attitude proves beneficial or costly. If the objects to which they pertain are relevant to the immediate task goal, accessible attitudes may facilitate performance. If irrelevant, they may impair task performance. If no pressing task demands are occupying the perceiver, having attention automatically drawn to attitude-evoking objects can orient the individual to objects in the immediate environment that are potentially rewarding or harmful.

A somewhat different cost of accessible attitudes may arise in some special circumstances. Accessible attitudes may color one's perceptions at a very fundamental level, such that the world is forced to fit the view implied by the attitudes. At the level of a specific attitude object, a strong attitude might 'do the work' of perception such that the perceiver is unable to notice new qualities of the object. Fazio et al. (2000) investigated this possibility in a series of experiments in which participants viewed several photographs of faces while either rehearsing their attitudes toward the faces (and thus making the attitudes more accessible) or performing a control task. In a later detection phase, they were shown a variety of faces and were asked to indicate whether each face they saw was the same or different in some way from a face they had seen earlier. Some of the faces were, in fact, exactly the same as those they had seen earlier. Some, however, were 'morphs' of earlier faces with other faces they had not seen. Some of the morphs were relatively close to the original (for example, a composite of 63 percent of the original face and 37 percent of a new face), while others were quite different from the originals (for example, 13 percent original and 87 percent new). Participants naturally found it more difficult to identify morphs that most closely resembled the original photos. However, for those who had rehearsed their attitudes toward the original photos, the task was apparently much more difficult. These participants took much longer to identify a morphed face as different from the original, and took especially long to perform the task in cases where the morph was close to the original. Apparently, their accessible attitudes interfered with their ability to perceive accurately whether the faces had changed or not. In subsequent experiments, participants with relatively accessible attitudes toward the faces made more errors in identifying the morphs, and, perhaps most telling, perceived less change in the morphed images than did control participants. The former were more likely to view a morphed image as a different photo of a person they had seen earlier than as a photo of a new person. Thus, like lenses designed to view particular objects, accessible attitudes have the tendency to color one's perceptions and decrease the likelihood of noticing changes in the objects. To the extent that an object remains relatively stable over time, this potential cost should be minimal and well offset by the many functional benefits of attitudes we have already discussed. However, in cases where the object has undergone some change since the time that the attitudes were formed, our attitudes risk leading us astray.

In summary, we have seen that attitudes can serve a variety of functions, from affirming and protecting the self (the value-expressive and ego-defensive functions), to securing relationships with others (the social-adjustive function). We have spent considerable time on the object-appraisal function, for this function is the most basic and adaptive. We have seen how attitudes, especially accessible ones, can guide attention and categorization, ease and improve decision-making, and facilitate the navigation of a novel environment – but that these functions can come at a cost. The field has seen advances in function measurement and identifying functions in individuals, as well as in our understanding of the functional matching hypothesis. We have also seen how functions vary by individual, attitude object, and situation. For a much more extensive treatment of the functions served by attitudes, see Maio and Olson (2000).

## The attitude–behavior relation

It's fitting that the final section of our chapter addresses the end product of attitudes: behavior. The two have suffered a troubled history together, and their relation can be a tenuous one (see McGuire, 1985, for a review). For a long time, and in no small part due to the very definition of attitudes, it had been assumed that attitudes predict subsequent behavior. Indeed, the very value of the attitude construct would be called into question if this were not the case. However, coffee drinkers often say 'no' to a cup of coffee, staunch Democrats sometimes vote Republican, and social psychologists have been known to get people to eat worms (e.g., Comer and Laird, 1975). That is, attitudes sometimes do not predict behavior.

When the assumption of attitude–behavior correspondence began to receive serious scrutiny in the late 1960s and early 1970s, such instances of low attitude–behavior correlations were regarded as very problematic. In fact, some advocated abandoning the attitude construct altogether (LaPiere, 1934; Wicker, 1971). However, while it may be the case that attitudes often do not predict behavior, there is ample evidence that they sometimes do. Eventually, researchers (e.g., Regan and Fazio, 1977; Zanna and Fazio, 1982) began calling for research asking not *whether* attitudes predict behavior, but, rather, *when* attitudes predict behavior. That is, under what conditions might we expect an attitude–behavior relation? This question has occupied a sizable chunk of the attitude literature and has been addressed from a variety of angles, including characteristics of the individual, the situation, and the attitude itself.

Characteristics of the individual have probably been the least studied approach to the question of attitude–behavior consistency, so we will just briefly touch on some examples. Self-monitoring, mentioned earlier with respect to its relationship to attitude functions, also can affect the attitude–behavior relation. Evidence suggests that because high self-monitors are more sensitive to their social situation, they are more affected by it. Hence, they are more likely to be influenced more by situational pressures than their own attitudes (Snyder, 1974). Low self-monitors, however, display greater attitude–behavior consistency (e.g., Snyder and Swann, 1976; Zanna et al., 1980). Self-awareness has a kind of opposite affect – people who are more self-aware are more attuned to their internal states, including their own attitudes. Thus, greater self-awareness has been shown to lead to greater attitude–behavior consistency (Carver, 1975).

Some of the poor predictive power of attitudes on behavior can be accounted for by a lack of correspondence in specificity between the two. Most research has attempted to predict a specific behavior, say, consuming chocolate today, based on a global attitude, say, toward chocolate. However, a number of influences other than attitudes might affect chocolate consumption today, and Ajzen and Fishbein (1977) made just this point when they advocated what they called the 'correspondence principle'. According to the principle, attitudes and behavior correspond when their degree of specificity corresponds. For example, if we were interested in predicting whether or not someone might consume chocolate today, we should ask about his or her attitude toward consuming chocolate today. Consistent with this reasoning, reviews of the literature have shown that the predictive power of attitudes is greater when the level of specificity between attitudes and the behavior they purport to predict are better matched (e.g., Ajzen and Fishbein, 1977; Davidson and Jaccard, 1979; Kraus, 1995). Another approach has been to look at behavior aggregated across several instances. Thus, in order best to predict our chocolate consumer's behavior from his or her attitude, we should use his or her global attitude toward chocolate to predict behavior not only today but across a longer time span. Improved predictive power comes from this aggregation approach as well (Fishbein and Ajzen, 1974; Weigel and Newman, 1976).

Fishbein and Ajzen's (1975) 'theory of reasoned action' takes into account the correspondence principle and contextual influences on behavior. In their model, behavior is proximally determined by 'behavioral intentions', and these behavioral intentions are, in turn, determined by two families of variables, attitudes toward the behavior and subjective norms. The attitude toward the behavior is the product of the expectancy-value equation mentioned earlier. Subjective norms are similarly computed, based upon the expected value of the perceived social consequences of performing the behavior. The values of both attitudes toward the behavior and subjective norms can be either positive or negative, increasing or decreasing, respectively, the likelihood of forming a behavioral intention. In sum, the model proposes that attitudes toward the behavior and subjective norms cause the formation of a behavioral intention. The behavioral intention then determines the behavior to be performed.

Ajzen (1991) later added the notion of 'perceived behavioral control', the extent to which people believe they *could* perform the behavior. This variable is argued to affect attitudes toward the behavior and perceived subjective norms, as well as have a direct effect on both behavioral intentions and the behavior itself. For example, if one is too busy or lacks the money to buy chocolate, a positive attitude toward the behavior is less likely to develop, a behavioral intention is less likely to form, and the behavior itself is less likely to occur. Especially with respect to challenging behaviors, the inclusion of perceived behavioral control has been found to increase the predictive power of the model (e.g., Ajzen and Madden, 1986; Kelly and Breinlinger, 1995; see Bandura, 1982, for a related discussion on self-efficacy).

Although these models have received considerable empirical support, they suffer from some shortcomings. At the definitional level, attitudes become increasingly specific in these models, a feature which risks turning the attitude–behavior relation into a tautology. For example, it would be rather unimpressive to demonstrate that an attitude 'toward eating the chocolate on the counter within the next two minutes' could reliably predict such a behavior. In these models, attitudes risk becoming temporary constructions, mere layovers on the flight to behavior, and general, enduring attitudes are relatively ignored.

The most problematic assumption of these models, however, is that behavior is treated as intentional, thoughtful, and based on the output of deliberate consideration of expected values of the behavior. Certainly, this is not always, and perhaps not even usually, the case. In fact, we have already seen evidence that attitudes can exert a direct impact on judgments and behavior, unmediated by thought, let alone intentions. In our section on attitude function, we saw how attitudes can affect fundamental processes such as visual attention and categorization. Accessible attitudes in particular are thought to affect judgments and behaviors through a spontaneous process.

This is not to say that attitudes do not often exert their influence via the deliberative route described earlier. Indeed, the literature on judgment and decision-making provides a host of examples of very thoughtful, deliberate judgment and behavior processes, characterized by weighing of decision alternatives, attention to the self and social implications of a particular act and attention to the attributes of the attitude object (e.g., Einhorn and Hogarth, 1981). Clearly, people sometimes make deliberate decisions, but often their judgments and behaviors flow more spontaneously from their attitudes. The critical distinction between these two processes is whether decisions are 'data-driven', where the perceiver goes through the effortful process of attending to, analyzing, and interpreting relevant information, or relatively more 'theory-driven' and spontaneous, where the perceiver's decision is more directly based on the attitude that is automatically activated from memory. The model we describe next addresses the issue of whether and when one process or the other is likely to occur.

## The MODE model

'MODE' is an acronym based on *M*otivation and *O*pportunity as *DE*terminants of the attitude–behavior relation – these are the two variables argued to determine whether a spontaneous or deliberate attitude–behavior process might occur. The basic premise is that when both are adequately present, behavior will be driven by deliberative processes, but when either is absent, any impact of attitudes on behavior will occur via a more spontaneous process (for more extensive reviews, see Fazio, 1990; Fazio and Towles-Schwen, 2000).

Motivation can mean a variety of things, but integral to its definition is the exertion of effort. This effort can be focused on making the best, most accurate decision, or a fear of coming to an invalid conclusion, and would be reflected in a thorough consideration of the behavior's potential consequences (e.g., Kruglanski and Webster, 1996). For example, our chocolate lover might have the rare opportunity to visit an exclusive candy store in another country and, on this special occasion, engage in a systematic appraisal of each potential purchase before making a decision. Here, the motivation to make the best choice is high, suggesting that greater attention will be given to the attributes of each potential purchase. However, our chocolate lover must have ample time to peruse each item before making a selection. That is, there must be enough opportunity to engage in the deliberative decision-making process. If either motivation or opportunity is lacking, the decision will more likely be based on whatever attitude is activated from memory. So if our chocolate lover is tired and unmotivated to investigate systematically each selection, or is in a hurry, it is likely that whatever attitude is activated will guide behavior spontaneously. For example, the first chocolate bar encountered might activate positivity, and then be purchased.

Several studies provide evidence of the MODE model's assumptions. Sanbonmatsu and Fazio (1990) presented participants with information on two department stores, and participants were asked to decide on which they would go to buy a camera. One store was good in all respects but one – the camera department. The other store had a good camera department, but was of poor quality overall. Whether participants chose the first or the second store provided an indicator of whether they were using their global attitudes toward the store as the basis for their decision (if they chose the first one) or were focusing on the relevant attributes of the store (if they chose the second). To manipulate motivation, some participants were provided with an extra incentive to be accurate – they were told that they would have to justify their answers to the experimenter and other participants later. Others were not given these instructions. To manipulate opportunity, some participants were given a short time limit to reach a conclusion, while others had ample opportunity to investigate each department store. The MODE model's predictions were confirmed in that only participants in the high-motivation, high-opportunity condition chose the department store with the better camera department. In other words, only with both motivation and opportunity did a deliberative decision-making process ensue, one that involved effortfully retrieving the specific attributes of each department store from memory. Participants without motivation or opportunity relied on their global attitudes toward the stores (see Fabrigar et al., 2006, for related findings).

Earlier, we discussed the tendency to judge information consistent with one's attitude more favorably. Schuette and Fazio (1995) investigated this effect within the context of the MODE model. Using a paradigm developed by Lord et al. (1979), they provided participants with information on two empirical studies that were supposedly conducted to investigate whether capital punishment was an effective deterrent, one that supported the death penalty, and one that opposed it. After reading about the studies, participants were asked to judge their quality. Motivation was manipulated similarly to the Sanbonmatsu and Fazio (1990) study. Attitude accessibility was also manipulated in Schuette and Fazio's experiment through the repeated expression manipulation mentioned earlier. They found that participants' judgments were biased by their attitudes – studies that were consistent with their attitudes were seen as higher in quality. However, this effect occurred only for those with low motivation and more accessible attitudes. More motivated participants, and those with less accessible attitudes, presumably attended more to the specific features of the studies, as opposed to their conclusions, when judging the quality of the research.

That attitude accessibility played a role in this study is an important point. Recall that accessible attitudes are more likely to be activated in the presence of the attitude object and more likely to have a host of influences on perception, categorization, and so on. Indeed, as we have argued, the less accessible the attitude is toward a given object, the more the individual will be forced to follow a more deliberative process of evaluating it. It is this interplay – between the relatively automatic processes associated with a spontaneous decision route, and the more deliberative, attribute-based decision route – that is at the center of the MODE model. Without an accessible attitude, a deliberative decision-making process is the only alternative. With it, it is a matter of whether motivation and opportunity are present as to which process will occur. Given sufficient motivation and opportunity, individuals can overcome the effects of an accessible attitude.

This latter point is relevant to a postulate of the MODE model. The model argues that many decisions are based on 'mixed' processes, those that include both automatic and deliberative components. Take, for example, an attitude that has been automatically activated in the face of the attitude object. If motivated and able, the individual may try to 'correct' for the influence of the attitude and reach a less biased conclusion (see Wegener and Petty, 1995). Such a process may have occurred in Schuette and Fazio's study (1995) for those participants whose attitudes toward the death penalty were made more accessible but who had the motivation to be accurate. Their attitudes were probably activated when presented with the death-penalty studies. However, their motivation to be accurate may have led them to consider more carefully the features of the studies they were judging and to attempt to curb the influence of their attitudes while doing so.

Racial prejudice is a domain where the interplay of automatically activated attitudes and motivation to avoid their biasing effects is particularly applicable. For example, many white Americans feel negativity toward blacks but are motivated to avoid being biased by race. The interaction between attitudes and motivation in this case stands to be particularly informative as to when and how racial prejudice appears in society. Research testing the MODE model's predictions in the domain of racial prejudice has utilized a priming measure of racial attitudes (Fazio et al., 1995). In this version of the priming task, photos of faces of various races serve as potential primes, and response latencies to identify the connotation of positive and negative adjectives serve as a measure of activation of either positivity or negativity. For example, on a given trial, a black face might appear on the screen, followed by the adjective 'awful'. If negativity is activated in response to the black prime, identifying 'awful' as a negative word should occur relatively quickly. An overall attitude estimate can be derived toward blacks and whites by comparing response latencies to positive and negative adjectives following black primes to those following white primes. The benefits of this method of attitude measurement over traditional paper-pencil measures are several. First, the priming measure is unobtrusive, which allows the measurement of attitudes participants may be unwilling to report honestly. Moreover, the strength of evaluative associations is being measured in this procedure, not merely the valence of the attitude (see Fazio and Olson, 2003, for a review).

The priming measure is also well suited to test whether race-related judgments can be driven by the spontaneous attitude-to-behavior process posited by the MODE model. Evidence for this assertion comes from several relevant studies. For example, after completing the measure, participants in one study were given a mock 'debriefing' by a black experimenter, who then completed friendliness ratings for each participant (Fazio et al., 1995). The ratings were related to attitude estimates derived from the priming measure – those with more negative automatically activated attitudes were seen as less friendly toward the black experimenter. In another study (Jackson, 1997), these attitude estimates were reflected in judgments of the quality of an essay purportedly written by a black undergraduate. Similarly, they also predicted participants' ratings of a black relative to a white applicant for a volunteer position in the Peace Corps (Olson and Fazio, 1999).

So far we have evidence of the priming measure's predictive validity, and, consequently, that race-related judgments can be influenced by relatively spontaneous processes, largely driven by the attitude that is automatically activated. But according to the MODE model, such attitudes should have less influence on judgments and behaviors when there is adequate motivation and opportunity. Regarding motivation, Dunton and Fazio (1997) developed a measure of motivation to control prejudiced reactions, a seventeen-item scale that contains items such as, 'I feel guilty when I have a negative thought or feeling about a black person' and, 'In today's society, it is important that one not be perceived as prejudiced in any manner.' By assessing racial attitudes with the priming measure, and motivation to control prejudiced reactions, both automatic and deliberate contributions to race-related judgments and behaviors can be examined.

Evaluations of a 'typical black male undergraduate' were collected in Dunton and Fazio's (1997) study, and attitude estimates and motivation scores were jointly used to predict them. Confirming the MODE model's predictions, racial attitudes and motivation to control prejudice interacted to predict the evaluations. For participants with little motivation, racial attitude estimates predicted evaluations such that more negative evaluations of the 'typical black male undergraduate' were found for those with negative attitude estimates. This relation was attenuated, and eventually reversed, as motivation increased. Motivated individuals with negative automatically activated racial attitudes exhibited positive evaluations of the black man, indicating that participants with negative attitudes were able to overcome the influence of their attitudes if properly motivated. Similar evidence for correction of automatically activated attitudes was found by Olson and Fazio (2004), where the targets about which participants formed impressions consisted of a variety of photos of people of various races in various occupational roles. Automatically activated racial attitudes predicted the impressions of black relative to white targets made by low-motivation participants, suggesting a spontaneous attitude-to-behavior process. The more positive the attitude, the more favorable the impression. However, more motivated participants for whom negativity was automatically activated expressed relatively favorable evaluations of the black targets.

In sum, sometimes judgments and behavior appear to be driven by relatively automatic attitude-to-behavior processes. Nevertheless, given proper motivation and opportunity, people are able to overcome their attitudes in the judgments they make. We have not, however, addressed the role of opportunity in this domain of race. While there is little research that systematically investigates the role of opportunity with respect to racial prejudice, there is evidence to suggest that some behaviors are more controllable than others. Nonverbal behavior, such as eye contact, smiling, and shoulder orientation, can be difficult to control (for a review, see DePaulo and Friedman, 1998). In the MODE model's terms, the lack of control that people have over their nonverbal behavior can be characterized as a lack of opportunity – if negativity is automatically activated, it may appear in behavior despite one's intentions. Recent research has indicated that these less controllable behaviors do relate more strongly to automatically activated racial attitudes than do more controllable verbal responses (e.g., Bessenoff and Sherman, 2000; Dovidio et al., 1997, 2002).

## Closing commentary: attitudes as stable entities versus momentary constructions

We have reviewed a considerable amount of evidence illustrating that not all attitudes are equal. Both the functional value of attitudes and the influence that they exert on judgments and behavior can vary. In particular, the evidence indicates that attitudes characterized by stronger object–evaluation associations in memory and, hence, greater accessibility, are relatively more functional, in the sense that they ease decision-making, orient visual attention and categorization processes in a useful manner, and free resources for coping with stressors. Likewise, such attitudes are relatively more powerful in terms of the influence that they have on information-processing and, ultimately, behavior.

Recently, some scientists have proposed a view of attitudes as momentary constructions (Schwarz and Bohner, 2001; see also Wilson and Hodges, 1992, and Zaller and Feldman, 1992). These formulations contrast with Allport's (1935) classic view of attitudes as enduring entities that determine behavioral responses. Instead, attitudes are viewed as evaluative judgments that are always computed from scratch on the basis of information accessible at that moment. Indeed, the dependence of verbal self-reports of attitude on context is cited as evidence for the theoretical perspective.

As an example of such contextual dependence, we can consider Stapel and Schwarz's (1998) research concerning General Colin Powell's decision in 1995 to join the Republican Party but not seek the party's presidential nomination. By asking participants to indicate either which political party Powell had recently joined, or which party's overtures that he run as a candidate he had rejected, the researchers induced participants to include or exclude the highly respected Colin Powell in their mental representation of the Republican Party. The respondents evaluated the Republican Party more favorably when the preceding question invited Powell's inclusion rather than exclusion from the representation of the party. Such evidence is cited as support for the idea that attitudes are momentary constructions.

While it is unquestionably provocative, we think the constructionist viewpoint is at variance with the accumulation of evidence that we summarized earlier. Although attitudinal reports certainly are dependent on context, findings such as Stapel and Schwarz's (1998) do not rule out the possibility that pre-existing memorial associations influence the production of these reports. Verbal *reports* of one's attitude are always constructions in that they involve, as Schwarz and Bohner (2001) articulate, issues of question comprehension, scale interpretation, and the identification and employment of appropriate standards of comparison. However, our theoretical perspective is that such reports can be influenced by previously formed attitudinal judgments, and the extent to which this occurs will vary as a function of the accessibility of the attitude from memory. Is it at all plausible to expect the attitude of a die-hard Republican, one who has voted Republican his or her entire life and donated time and money to party activities, to change as a function of whether Colin Powell is or is not momentarily construed as a loyal party member? Is there any reason to believe that an individual with an allergy to peanuts would need to construct anew a negative attitude toward peanut butter each time a judgment is called for? Much like the attitude of the infamous Dr Seuss character describing green eggs and ham, attitudes are sometimes remarkably unaffected by context: 'I would not like them here or there. I would not like them anywhere. I do not like green eggs and ham. I do not like them, Sam-I-am … I would not, could not, in the rain. Not in the dark. Not on a train. Not in a car. Not in a tree. I do not like them, Sam, you see.'

In fact, the influence of momentarily salient contextual features on attitude reports has been found to vary as a function of the degree to which individuals' attitudes are accessible from memory (Hodges and Wilson, 1993). Verbal reports are less influenced by momentarily salient information when attitudes are relatively more accessible from memory (see Chaiken and Baldwin, 1981, for similar evidence regarding the moderating effects of evaluative-cognitive consistency on attitude reports). The same is true for behavioral decisions (Fazio et al., 1989, 1992). Relatedly, the stability and persistence of attitudes over time and/or in resistance to counterinformation has been found to increase as attitude accessibility increases (Bassili, 1996; Bassili and Fletcher, 1991; Fazio and Williams, 1986; Zanna et al., 1994).

Finally, a logical problem inherent to the constructionist perspective should be noted. Consider again the influence of Colin Powell's inclusion or exclusion from the mental representation of the Republican Party on evaluations of the party. The phenomenon hinges on Powell himself being positively evaluated. Were the positive attitudes toward Powell not themselves a pre-existing evaluative association in memory? If so, then some attitudes clearly are not constructed anew each time the object is encountered. If not, then the attitudes toward Powell, as well as the Republican Party, needed to be constructed on the spot, a fact which opens the entire formulation to a problem of infinite regress. Ultimately, some relevant evaluation has itself to be represented in memory.

From our theoretical perspective, the constructionist view of attitudes is just as implausibly extreme as the classic, but now outdated, view of attitudes as omnipotent determinants of perception, judgment, and behavior. Clearly, an adequate resolution has to lie somewhere between these two extremes. Attitudes vary in terms of the strength of their object–evaluation associations in memory. The resultant accessibility of the attitude from memory determines not only the power and functionality of the attitude, but also the extent to which construction processes are involved in response to any situational need to evaluate the object in question.

## Conclusion

We have spanned a wide range of attitude phenomena in this chapter. From how we define attitudes, to their origins, to their functions and consequences, we hope to have communicated an appreciation of what has become a vast literature, capable of occupying at least these authors' careers. To the question, 'How much have we learned about attitudes over the years?', the answer is an emphatic, 'a lot'. To the question, 'How much about attitudes is still unknown?', the answer is also an emphatic, 'a lot'. Attitudes have been viewed as the shining star of social psychology, as well as its problem child. Time has told, however, that the attitude construct is indispensable to social psychology and an essential variable in understanding human behavior.

## Acknowledgements

Preparation of this chapter was facilitated by Senior Scientist Award MH01646 and Grant MH38832 from the National Institute of Mental Health. The authors thank Julie Brown and Suzanne Miller for valuable feedback on earlier drafts of this chapter.

### SUMMARY

Largely out of concern about some dubious assumptions made by the classic three-component framework, most current researchers have adopted a view of attitudes as overall evaluations of some object, person, or issue. These evaluations may stem from a consideration of the attributes of the object (as in the expectancy-value framework), from the emotional reactions the object evokes, or from inferences regard in one's freely chosen behavior. Attitudes also can vary in their strength, including their accessibility in memory and the extent to which they are characterized by some form of ambivalence.

Attitudes have been shown to serve a variety of functions, including affirming and protecting the self. However, their most pervasive function is as efficient tools for object appraisal. To the extent that they are readily accessible from memory, attitudes orient visual attention and categorization processes in a functional manner, ease decision-making, and free resources for coping with other stressors that one is experiencing. Finally, attitudes have the potential to influence judgments and behavior via multiple processes, varying from the relatively spontaneous to the very deliberative. Whereas the former involve no effortful reflection, the latter require that the individual be both motivated to deliberate and have the opportunity to do so.

## References

Abelson, R.P., Kinder, D.R., Peters, M.D., and Fiske, S.T. (1982) 'Affective and Semantic Components in Political Person Perception', *Journal of Personality and Social Psychology*, 42: 619–30.

Ajzen, I. (1991) 'The Theory of Planned Behavior', *Organizational Behavior and Human Decision Processes*, 50: 179–210.

Ajzen, I. and Fishbein, M. (1977) 'Attitude–Behavior Relations: A Theoretical Analysis and Review of Empirical Research', *Psychological Bulletin*, 84: 888–918.

Ajzen, I. and Madden, T.J. (1986) 'Prediction of Goal-Directed Behavior: Attitudes, Intentions and Perceived Behavioral Control', *Journal of Experimental Social Psychology*, 22: 453–74.

Allport, G.W. (1935) 'Attitudes', in C. Murchison (ed.), *Handbook of Social Psychology*. Worcester, MA: Clark University Press, pp. 798–844.

Anderson, N.H. (1981) 'Integration Theory Applied to Cognitive Responses and Attitudes', in R.E. Petty, T.M. Ostrom, and T.C. Brock (eds), *Cognitive Responses in Persuasion*. Hillsdale, NJ: Erlbaum. pp. 361–97.

Anderson, N.H. (1982) *Methods of Information Integration Theory*. San Diego, CA: Academic Press.

Anderson, N.H. (ed.) (1991) *Contributions to Information Integration Theory* (vols 1, 2, and 3). Hillsdale, NJ: Erlbaum.

Armitage, C.J. and Conner, M. (2000) 'Attitude Ambivalence: A Test of Three Key Hypotheses', *Personality and Social Psychology Bulletin*, 26: 1421–32.

Bandler, R.J., Madaras, G.R., and Bem D.J. (1968) 'Self-Observation as a Source of Pain Perception', *Journal of Personality and Social Psychology*, 9: 205–9.

Bandura, A. (1982) 'Self-Efficacy Mechanism in Human Agency', *American Psychologist*, 37: 122–47.

Bargh, J.A., Chaiken, S., Govender, R., and Pratto, F. (1992) 'The Generality of the Automatic Attitude Activation Effect', *Journal of Personality and Social Psychology*, 62: 893–912.

Bassili, J.N. (1996) 'Meta-Judgmental Versus Operative Indexes of Psychological Attributes: The Case of Measure of Attitude Strength', *Journal of Personality and Social Psychology*, 71: 637–53.

Bassili, J.N. and Fletcher, J.F. (1991) 'Response-Time Measurement in Survey Research: A Method for CATI and a New Look at Nonattitudes', *Public Opinion Quarterly*, 55: 331–46.

Bem, D.J. (1972) 'Self-Perception Theory', in L. Berkowitz (ed.), *Advances in Experimental Social Psychology* (vol. 6). San Diego, CA: Academic Press, pp. 1–62.

Bessenoff, G.R. and Sherman, J.W. (2000) 'Automatic and Controlled Components of Prejudice toward Fat People: Evaluation versus Stereotype Activation', *Social Cognition*, 18: 329–53.

Blascovich, J., Ernst, J.M., Tomaka, J., Kelsey, R.M., Salomon, K.L., and Fazio, R.H. (1993) 'Attitude Accessibility as a Moderator of Autonomic Reactivity During Decision Making', *Journal of Personality and Social Psychology*, 64: 165–76.

Bornstein, R.F. (1989) 'Exposure and Affect: Overview and Meta-Analysis of Research, 1968–1987', *Psychological Bulletin*, 106: 265–89.

Breckler, S.J. (1984) 'Empirical Validation of Affect, Behavior, and Cognition as District Components of Attitude', *Journal of Personality and Social Psychology*, 47: 1191–205.

Breckler, S.J. and Wiggins, E.C. (1989) 'Affect Versus Evaluation in the Structure of Attitudes', *Journal of Experimental Social Psychology*, 25: 253–71.

Cacioppo, J.T., Gardner, W.L., and Bernston, G.G. (1997) 'Beyond Bipolar Conceptualizations and Easures: The Case of Attitudes and Evaluative Space', *Personality and Social Psychology Review*, 1: 3–25.

Carver, C.S. (1975) 'Physical Aggression as a Function of Objective Self-Awareness and Attitudes Toward Punishment', *Journal of Experimental Social Psychology*, 11: 510–19.

Chaiken, S. and Baldwin, M.W. (1981) 'Affective-Cognitive Consistency and the Effect of Salient Behavioral Information on the Self-Perception of Attitudes', *Journal of Personality and Social Psychology*, 41: 1–12.

Chaiken, S., Pomerantz, E.M., and Giner-Sorolla, R. (1995) 'Structural Consistency and Attitude Strength', in R.E. Petty and J.A. Krosnick (eds), *Attitude Strength: Antecedents and Consequences*. Hillsdale, NJ: Erlbaum, pp. 387–412.

Comer, R. and Laird, J.D. (1975) 'Choosing to Suffer as a Consequence of Expecting to Suffer: Why Do People Do It?', *Journal of Personality and Social Psychology*, 32: 92–101.

Converse, P.E. (1970) 'Attitudes and Non-Attitudes: Continuation of a Dialogue', in E.R. Tufte (ed.), *The Quantitative Analysis of Social Problems*. Reading, MA: Addison-Wesley, pp. 168–89.

Cooper, J. and Fazio, R.H. (1984) 'A New Look at Dissonance Theory', in L. Berkowitz (ed.), *Advances in Experimental Social Psychology* (vol. 17). San Diego, CA: Academic Press, pp. 229–66.

Cronen, V.E. and Conville, R.L. (1975) 'Summation Theory and the Predictive Power of Subjects' Own Salient Beliefs', *Journal of Social Psychology*, 97: 47–52.

Davidson, A.R. and Jaccard, J.J. (1979) 'Variables that Moderate the Attitude–Behavior Relation: Results of a Longitudinal Survey', *Journal of Personality and Social Psychology*, 37: 1364–76.

DeBono, K.G. (1987) 'Investigating the Social-Adjustive and Value-Expressive Functions of Attitudes: Implications for Persuasion Processes', *Journal of Personality and Social Psychology*, 52: 279–87.

De Houwer, J., Thomas, S., and Baeyens, F. (2001) 'Associative Learning of Likes and Dislikes: A Review of 25 Years of Research on Human Evaluative Conditioning', *Psychological Bulletin*, 127: 853–69.

DePaulo, B.M. and Friedman, H.S. (1998) 'Nonverbal Communication', in D.T. Gilbert, S.T. Fiske, and G. Lindzey (eds), *The Handbook of Social Psychology,* 4th edn (vol. 2). New York: McGraw-Hill, pp. 3–40.

Doob, L.W. (1947) 'The Behavior of Attitudes', *Psychological Review*, 54: 135–56.

Dovidio, J.F., Kawakami, K., and Gaertner, S.L. (2002) 'Implicit and Explicit Prejudice and Interracial Interactions', *Journal of Personality and Social Psychology*, 82: 62–8.

Dovidio, J.F., Kawakami, K., Johnson, C., Johnson, B., and Howard, A. (1997) 'On the Nature of Prejudice: Automatic and Controlled Processes', *Journal of Experimental Social Psychology*, 33: 510–40.

Dunton, B.C. and Fazio, R.H. (1997) 'An Individual Difference Measure of Motivation to Control Prejudiced Reactions', *Personality and Social Psychology Bulletin*, 23: 316–26.

Eagly, A.H. and Chaiken, S. (1993) *The Psychology of Attitudes.* New York: Harcourt Brace Jovanovich.

Edwards, K. (1990) 'The Interplay of Affect and Cognition in Attitude Formation and Change', *Journal of Personality and Social Psychology*, 59: 202–16.

Einhorn, H.J. and Hogarth, R.M. (1981) 'Behavioral Decision Theory: Processes of Judgment and Choice', *Annual Review of Psychology*, 32: 52–88.

'Fabrigar, L.R., and Petty, R.E. (1999) 'The Role of the Affective and Cognitive Bases of Attitudes in Susceptibility to Affectively and Cognitively Based Persuasion', *Personality and Social Psychology Bulletin*, 25: 363–81.

Fabrigar, L., Petty, R.E., Smith, S.M., and Crites, S.L. (2006) Understanding Knowledge Effects on Attitude-Behavior Consistency: The Role of Relevance, Complexity, and Amount of Knowledge', *Journal of Personality and Social Psychology*, 90: 556–577.

Fazio, R.H. (1987) 'Self-Perception Theory: A Current Perspective', in M.P. Zanna, J.M. Olson, and C.P. Herman (eds), *Social Influence: The Ontario Symposium* (vol. 5). Hillsdale, NJ: Erlbaum pp. 129–50.

Fazio, R.H. (1990) 'Multiple Processes by Which Attitudes Guide Behavior: The MODE Model as an Integrative Framework', in M.P. Zanna (ed.), *Advances in Experimental Social Psychology* (vol. 23). San Diego, CA: Academic Press, pp. 75–109.

Fazio, R.H. (1995) 'Attitudes as Object-Evaluation Associations: Determinants, Consequences and Correlates of Attitude Accessibility', in R.E. Petty and J.A. Krosnick (eds), *Attitude Strength: Antecedents and Consequences.* Hillsdale, NJ: Erlbaum. pp. 247–82.

Fazio, R.H. (2000) 'Accessible Attitudes as Tools for Object Appraisal: Their Costs and Benefits', in G.R. Maio and J.M. Olson (eds), *Why We Evaluate: Functions of Attitudes.* Mahwah, NJ: Erlbaum. pp. 1–36.

Fazio, R.H. (2001) 'On the Automatic Activation of Associated Evaluations: An Overview', *Cognition and Emotion*, 15: 115–41.

Fazio, R.H., Blascovich, J., and Driscoll, D.M. (1992) 'On the Functional Value of Attitudes: The Influence of Accessible Attitudes Upon the Ease and Quality of Decision Making', *Personality and Social Psychology Bulletin*, 18: 388–401.

Fazio, R.H., Chen, J., McDonel, E.C., and Sherman, S.J. (1982) 'Attitude Accessibility, Attitude-Behavior Consistency and the Strength of the Object-Evaluation Association', *Journal of Experimental Social Psychology*, 18: 339–57.

Fazio, R.H. and Dunton, B.C. (1997) 'Categorization by Race: The Impact of Automatic and Controlled Components of Racial Prejudice', *Journal of Experimental Social Psychology*, 33: 451–70.

Fazio, R.H., Jackson, J.R., Dunton, B.C., and Williams, C.J. (1995) 'Variability in Automatic Activation as an Unobtrusive Measure of Racial Attitudes: A Bona Fide Pipeline?', *Journal of Personality and Social Psychology*, 69: 1013–27.

Fazio, R.H., Ledbetter, J.E., and Towles-Schwen, T. (2000) 'On the Costs of Accessible Attitudes: Detecting that the Attitude Object Has Changed', *Journal of Personality and Social Psychology*, 78: 197–210.

Fazio, R.H. and Olson, M.A. (2003) 'Implicit Measures in Social Cognition Research: Their Meaning and Use', *Annual Review of Psychology*, 54: 297–327. Palo Alto, CA: Annual Reviews, Inc.

Fazio, R.H. and Powell, M.C. (1997) 'On the Value of Knowing One's Likes and Dislikes: Attitude Accessibility, Stress and Health in College', *Psychological Science*, 8: 430–6.

Fazio, R.H., Powell, M.C., and Williams, C.J. (1989) 'The Role of Attitude Accessibility in the Attitude-to-Behavior Process', *Journal of Consumer Research*, 16: 280–8.

Fazio, R.H., Sanbonmatsu, D.M., Powell, M.C., and Kardes, F.R. (1986) 'On the Automatic Activation of Attitudes', *Journal of Personality and Social Psychology*, 50: 229–38.

Fazio, R.H. and Towles-Schwen, T. (2000) 'The MODE Model of Attitude–Behavior Processes', in S. Chaiken and Y. Trope (eds), *Dual Process Theories in Social Psychology*. New York: Guilford Press, pp. 97–116.

Fazio, R.H. and Williams, C.J. (1986) 'Attitude Accessibility as a Moderator of the Attitude–Perception and Attitude–Behavior Relations: An Investigation of the 1984 Presidential Election', *Journal of Personality and Social Psychology*, 51: 505–14.

Fazio, R.H. and Zanna, M.P. (1981) 'Direct Experience and Attitude-Behavior Consistency', in L. Berkowitz (ed.), *Advances in Experimental Social Psychology* (vol. 14). New York: Academic Press, pp. 161–202.

Fein, S. and Spencer, S.J. (1997) 'Prejudice as Self-Image Maintenance: Affirming the Self through Derogating Others', *Journal of Personality and Social Psychology*, 73: 31–44.

Field, A.P. (2000) 'I Like It, but I'm Not Sure Why: Can Evaluative Conditioning Occur Without Conscious Awareness?', *Consciousness and Cognition*, 9: 13–36.

Fishbein, M. and Ajzen, I. (1974) 'Attitudes Toward Objects as Predictors of Single and Multiple Behavioral Criteria', *Psychological Review*, 81: 59–74.

Fishbein, M. and Ajzen, I. (1975) *Belief, Attitude, Intention, and Behavior: An Introduction to Theory and Research.* Reading, MA: Addison-Wesley.

Fishbein, M. and Middlestadt, S. (1995) 'Noncognitive Effects on Attitude Formation and Change: Factor Artifact?' *Journal of Consumer Psychology*, 4: 181–202.

Green, D.P. and Gerken, A.E. (1989) 'Self-Interest and Public Opinion Toward Smoking Restrictions and Cigarette Taxes', *Public Opinion Quarterly*, 53: 1–16.

Greenwald, A.G. (1981) 'Cognitive Response Analysis: An Appraisal', in R.E. Petty, T.M. Ostrom, and T.C. Brock (eds), *Cognitive Responses in Persuasion.* Hillsdale, NJ: Erlbaum, pp. 127–33.

Harmon-Jones, E. and Allen, J.J.B. (2001) 'The Role of Affect in the Mere Exposure Effect: Evidence from Psychophysiological and Individual Differences Approaches', *Personality and Social Psychology Bulletin*, 27: 889–98.

Hass, R.G., Katz, I., Rizzo, N., Bailey, J., and Moore, L. (1994) 'When Racial Ambivalence Evokes Negative Affect, Using a Disguised Measure of Mood', *Personality and Social Psychology Bulletin*, 18: 786–97.

Herek, G.M. (1986) 'The Instrumentality of Attitudes: Toward a Neofunctional Theory', *Journal of Social Issues*, 42: 99–114.

Herek, G.M. (1987) 'Can Functions Be Measured? A New Perspective on the Functional Approach to Attitudes', *Social Psychology Quarterly*, 50: 285–303.

Hildum, D.C. and Brown, R.W. (1956) 'Verbal Reinforcement and Interviewer Bias', *Journal of Abnormal and Social Psychology*, 53: 108–11.

Himmelfarb, S. (1993) 'The Measurement of Attitudes', in A.H. Eagly and S. Chaiken, *The Psychology of Attitudes.* New York: Harcourt Brace Jovanovich. pp. 23–88.

Hodges, S.D. and Wilson, T.D. (1994) 'Effects of Analyzing Reasons on Attitude Change: The Moderating Role of Attitude Accessibility', *Social Cognition*, 11: 353–66.

Hodges, S.D. and Wilson, T.D. (1993) 'Effects of Analyzing Reasons on Attitude Change: The Moderating Role of Attitude Accessibility', *Social Cognition*, 11: 353–66.

Hull, C.H. (1951) *Essentials of Behavior.* New Haven, CT: Yale University Press.

Insko, C.A. (1965) 'Verbal Reinforcement of Attitude', *Journal of Personality and Social Psychology*, 2: 621–3.

Jackson, J.R. (1997) 'Automatically Activated Racial Attitudes'. Unpublished doctoral dissertation, Indiana University.

James, W. (1952) *The Principles of Psychology.* Chicago, IL: Encyclopaedia Britannica (original work published 1890).

Kaplan, K.J. (1972) 'On the Ambivalence-Indifference Problem in Attitude Theory and Measurement: A Suggested Modification of the Semantic Differential Technique', *Psychological Bulletin*, 77: 361–72.

Katz, D. (1960) 'The Functional Approach to the Study of Attitudes', *Public Opinion Quarterly*, 24: 163–204.

Katz, I. (1981) *Stigma: A Social Psychological Analysis.* Hillsdale, NJ: Erlbaum.

Katz, I. and Hass, R.G. (1988) 'Racial Ambivalence and American Value Conflict: Correlation and Priming Studies of Dual Cognitive Structures', *Journal of Personality and Social Psychology*, 55: 893–905.

Katz, I. and Stotland, E. (1959) 'A Preliminary Statement to a Theory of Attitude Structure and Change', in S. Koch (ed.), *Psychology: A Study of a Science* (vol. 3). New York: McGraw-Hill, pp. 423–75.

Kelly, C. and Breinlinger, S. (1995) 'Attitudes, Intentions, and Behavior: A Study of Women's Participation in Collective Action', *Journal of Applied Social Psychology*, 25: 1430–45.

Kraus, S.J. (1995) 'Attitudes and the Prediction of Behavior: A Meta-Analysis of the Empirical Literature', *Personality and Social Psychology Bulletin*, 21: 58–75.

Kruglanski, A.W. and Webster, D.M. (1996) 'Motivated Closing of the Mind: "Seizing" and "Freezing"', *Psychological Review*, 103: 263–83.

LaPiere, R.T. (1934) 'Attitudes vs. Actions', *Social Forces*, 13: 230–7.

Lavine, H. and Snyder, M. (2000) 'Cognitive Processes and the Functional Matching Affect in Persuasion: Studies of Personality and Political Behavior', in G.R. Maio and J.M. Olson (eds), *Why We Evaluate: Functions of Attitudes.* Mahwah, NJ: Erlbaum. pp. 97–132.

Lepper, M.R., Greene, D., and Nisbett, R.E. (1973) 'Undermining Children's Intrinsic Interest with Extrinsic Reward: A Test of the "Overjustification" Hypothesis', *Journal of Personality and Social Psychology*, 28: 129–37.

Lord, C.G., Ross, L., and Lepper, M.R. (1979) 'Biased Assimilation and Attitude Polarization: The Effects of Prior Theories on Subsequently Considered Evidence', *Journal of Personality and Social Psychology*, 37: 2098–109.

MacCorquodale, K. and Meehl, P.E. (1948) 'On a Distinction between Hypothetical Constructs and Intervening Variables', *Psychology Review*, 55: 95–107.

Maio, G.R. and Olson, J.M. (eds) (2000) *Why We Evaluate: Functions of Attitudes.* Mahwah, NJ: Erlbaum.

McGuire, W.J. (1969) 'The Nature of Attitudes and Attitude Change', in G. Lindzey and E. Aronson (eds), *Handbook of Social Psychology* 2nd edn (vol. 3). Reading, MA: Addison-Wesley, pp. 136–314.

McGuire, W.J. (1985) 'Attitudes and Attitude Change', in G. Lindzey and E. Aronson (eds), *Handbook of Social Psychology*, 3rd edn (vol. 2). New York: Random House, pp. 233–346.

Millar M.G. and Millar, K.U. (1990) 'Attitude Change as a Function of Attitude Type and Argument Type', *Journal of Personality and Social Psychology*, 59: 217–28.

Monahan, J.L., Murphy, S.T., and Zajonc, R.B. (2000) 'Subliminal Mere Exposure: Specific, General, and Diffuse Effects', *Psychological Science*, 11: 462–6.

Moore, M. (1980) 'Validation of the Attitude toward Any Practice Scale through the Use of Ambivalence as a Moderator Variable', *Educational and Psychological Measurement*, 40: 205–8.

Newby-Clark, I.R., McGregor, I., and Zanna, M.P. (2002) 'Thinking and Caring about Cognitive Inconsistency: When and for Whom Does Attitudinal Ambivalence Feel Uncomfortable?', *Journal of Personality and Social Psychology*, 82: 157–66.

Norman, R. (1975) 'Affective-Cognitive Consistency, Attitudes, Conformity, and Behavior', *Journal of Personality and Social Psychology*, 32: 83–91.

Olson, M.A. and Fazio, R.H. (2002) 'Implicit Acquisition and Manifestation of Classically Conditioned Attitudes', *Social Cognition*, 20: 89–104.

Olson, M. A., and Fazio, R. H. (2006) 'Reducing Automatically-Activated Racial Prejudice through Implicit Evaluative Conditioning', *Personality and Social Psychology Bulletin*', 32: 421–433.

Olson, M.A. and Fazio, R.H. (1999, April) 'Nonverbal Leakage during Public Evaluations of Black Candidates: The Roles of Automatically-Activated Racial Attitudes and Motivation to Control Prejudiced Reactions'. Paper presented at the annual meeting of the Midwestern Psychological Association, Chicago, IL.

Olson, M.A. and Fazio, R.H. (2001) 'Implicit Attitude Formation through Classical Conditioning', *Psychological Science*, 12: 413–17.

Olson, M.A. and Fazio, R.H. (2004) 'Trait Inferences as a Function of Automatically-Activated Attitudes and Motivation to Control Prejudiced Reactions', *Basic and Applied Social Psychology*, 26, 1–11.

Osgood, C.E., Suci, G.J., and Tannenbaum, P.H. (1957) *The Measurement of Meaning*. Urbana, IL: University of Illinois Press.

Petty, R.E. and Cacioppo, J.T. (1981) *Attitudes and Persuasion: Classic and Contemporary Approaches*. Dubuque, IA: Wm. C. Brown.

Petty, R.E. and Cacioppo, J.T. (1986) 'The Elaboration Likelihood Model of Persuasion', in L. Berkowitz (ed.), *Advances in Experimental Social Psychology* (vol. 19). San Diego, CA: Academic Press, pp.123–205.

Petty, R.E. and Krosnick, J.A. (1995) *Attitudes Strength: Antecedents and Consequences*. Hillsdale, NJ: Erlbaum.

Petty, R.E., Ostrom, T.M., and Brock, T.C. (1981) 'Historical Foundations of the Cognitive Response Approach to Attitudes and Persuasion', in R.E. Petty, T.M. Ostrom, and T.C. Brock (eds), *Cognitive Responses in Persuasion*. Hillsdale, NJ: Erlbaum, pp. 5–29.

Petty, R.E and Wegener, D.T. (1998) 'Matching versus Mismatching Attitude Functions: Implications for Scrutiny of Persuasive Messages', *Personality and Social Psychology Bulletin*, 24: 227–40.

Powell, M.C. and Fazio, R.H. (1984) 'Attitude Accessibility as a Function of Repeated Attitudinal Expression', *Personality and Social Psychology Bulletin*, 10: 139–48.

Prentice, D.A. (1987) 'Psychological Correspondence of Possessions, Attitudes, and Values', *Journal of Personality and Social Psychology*, 53: 993–1003.

Priester, J.R. and Petty, R.E. (1996) 'The Gradual Threshold Model of Ambivalence: Relating the Positive and Negative Bases of Attitudes to Subjective Ambivalence', *Journal of Personality and Social Psychology*, 71: 431–49.

Regan, D.T. and Fazio, R.H. (1977) 'On the Consistency between Attitudes and Behavior: Look to the Method of Attitude Formation', *Journal of Experimental Social Psychology*, 13: 28–45.

Roskos-Ewoldsen, D.R. and Fazio, R.H. (1992) 'On the Orienting Value of Attitudes: Attitude Accessibility as a Determinant of an Object's Attraction of Visual Attention', *Journal of Personality and Social Psychology*, 63: 198–211.

Rosenberg, M.J. (1960) 'An Analysis of Affective-Cognitive Consistency', in M.J. Rosenberg, C.I. Hovland, W.J. McGuire, R.P. Abelson, and J.W. Brehm (eds), *Attitude Organization and Change: An Analysis of Consistency among Attitude Components*. New Haven, CT: Yale University Press, pp. 15–64.

Rosenberg, M.J. (1968) 'Hedonism, Inauthenticity, and Other Goals toward Expansion of a Consistency Theory', in R.P. Abelson, E. Aronson, W.J. McGuire, T.M. Newcomb, M.J. Rosenberg, and P.H. Tannenbaum (eds), *Theories of Cognitive Consistency: A Sourcebook*. Chicago, IL: Rand McNally, pp. 73–111.

Rosenberg, M.J. and Hovland, C.I. (1960) 'Cognitive, Affective, and Behavioral Components of Attitudes', in C.I. Hovland and M.J. Rosenberg (eds), *Attitude Organization and Change: An Analysis of Consistency among Attitude Components*. New Haven, CT: Yale University Press, pp. 1–14.

Sanbonmatsu, D.M. and Fazio, R.H. (1990) 'The Role of Attitudes in Memory-Based Decision Making', *Journal of Personality and Social Psychology*, 59: 614–22.

Schneider, W. and Shiffrin, R.M. (1977) 'Controlled and Automatic Human Information Processing. I. Detection, Search, and Attention', *Psychological Review*, 84: 1–66.

Schuette, R.A. and Fazio, R.H. (1995) 'Attitude Accessibility and Motivation as Determinants of Biased Processing: A Test of the MODE Model', *Personality and Social Psychology Bulletin*, 21: 704–10.

Schwarz, N. and Bohner, G. (2001) 'The Construction of Attitudes', in A. Tesser and N. Schwarz (eds), *Blackwell Handbook of Social Psychology: Intraindividual Processes*. Malden, MA: Blackwell, pp. 436–57.

Seger, C.A. (1994) 'Implicit Learning', *Psychological Bulletin*, 115: 163–96.

Shavitt, S. (1990) 'The Role of Attitude Objects in Attitude Functions', *Journal of Experimental Social Psychology*, 26: 124–48.

Sinclair, L. and Kunda, Z. (1999) 'Reactions to a Black Professional: Motivated Inhibition and Activation of Conflicting Stereotypes', *Journal of Personality and Social Psychology*, 77: 885–904.

Smith, M.B., Bruner, J.S., and White, R.W. (1956) *Opinions and Personality*. New York: Wiley.

Smith, E.R., Fazio, R.H., and Cejka, M.A. (1996) 'Accessible Attitudes Influence Categorization of Multiply Categorizable Objects', *Journal of Personality and Social Psychology*, 71: 888–98.

Smith, A.J. and Clark, R.D. (1973) 'The Relationship between Attitudes and Beliefs', *Journal of Personality and Social Psychology*, 26: 321–6.

Snyder, M. (1974) 'Self-Monitoring of Expressive Behavior', *Journal of Personality and Social Psychology*, 30: 526–37.

Snyder, M. and DeBono, K.G. (1987) 'A Functional Approach to Attitudes and Persuasion', in M.P. Zanna, J.M. Olson, and C.P. Herman (eds), *Social Influence: The Ontario Symposium* (vol. 5). Hillsdale, NJ: Erlbaum, pp. 107–25.

Snyder, M. and Swann, W.B. (1976) 'When Actions Reflect Attitudes: The Politics of Impression Management', *Journal of Personality and Social Psychology*, *34*: 1034–42.

Spencer, S.J., Fein, S., Wolfe, C.T., Fong, C., and Dunn M.A. (1998) 'Automatic Activation of Stereotypes: The Role of Self-Image Threat', *Personality and Social Psychology Bulletin*, 24: 1139–52.

Staats, A.W. and Staats, C.K. (1958) 'Attitudes Established by Classical Conditioning', *Journal of Abnormal and Social Psychology*, 11: 187–92.

Stapel, D.A. and Schwarz, N. (1998) 'The Republican Who Did Not Want to Become President: An Inclusion/Exclusion Analysis of Colin Powell's Impact on Evaluations of the Republican Party and Bob Dole', *Personality and Social Psychology Bulletin*, 24: 690–8.

Steele, C.M. (1988) 'The Psychology of Self-Affirmation: Sustaining the Integrity of the Self', in L. Berkowitz (ed.), *Advances in Experimental Social Psychology* (vol. 21). San Diego, CA: Academic Press. pp. 261–302.

Thomas, W.I. and Znaniecki, F. (1918) *The Polish Peasant in Europe and America* (vol. 1). Boston, MA: Badger.

Thompson, M.M., Zanna, M.P., and Griffin, D.W. (1995) 'Let's Not be Indifferent about (Attitudinal) Ambivalence', in R.E. Petty and J.A. Krosnick (eds), *Attitude Strength: Antecedents and Consequences*. Hillsdale, NJ: Erlbaum, pp. 361–86.

Thorndike, E.L. (1932) *The Fundamentals of Learning*. New York: Teachers College.

Thurstone, L.L. (1928) 'Attitudes Can Be Measured', *American Journal of Sociology*, 33: 529–54.

Thurstone, L.L. (1946) 'Comment', *American Journal of Sociology*, 52: 39–40.

Titchener, E.B. (1910) *A Textbook of Psychology* (rev. edn). New York: Macmillan.

Tyler, T.R. and Rasinski, K. (1984) 'Comparing Psychological Images of the Social Perceiver: Role of Perceived Informativeness, Memorability, and Affect in Mediating the Impact of Crime Victimization', *Journal of Personality and Social Psychology*, 46: 308–29.

van den Berg, H., Manstead, A. S. R., van der Pligt, J., and Wigboldus, D. H. J. (2006) 'The Impact of Affective and Cognitive Focus on Attitude Formation', *Journal of Experimental Social Psychology*, 42: 373–379.

Visser, P.S., Krosnick, J.A., and Simmons, J.P. (2003) 'Distinguishing the Cognitive and Behavioral Consequences of Attitude Importance and Certainty: A New Approach to Testing the Common-Factor Hypothesis', *Journal of Experimental Social Psychology*, 39, 118–41.

Wegener, D.T. and Petty, R.E. (1995) 'Flexible Correction Processes in Social Judgment: The Role of Naive Theories in Corrections for Perceived Bias', *Journal of Personality and Social Psychology*, 68: 36–51.

Weigel, R.H. and Newman, L.S. (1976) 'Increasing Attitude–Behavior Correspondence by Broadening the Scope of the Behavioral Measures, *Journal of Personality and Social Psychology*, 33: 793–802.

Wicker, A.W. (1971) 'An Examination of the "Other Variables" Explanation of Attitude–Behavior Inconsistency', *Journal of Personality and Social Psychology*, 19: 18–30.

Wilson, T.D. and Hodges, S.D. (1992) 'Attitudes as Temporary Constructions', in L.L. Martin and A.Tesser (eds), *The Construction of Social Judgments*. Hillsdale, NJ: Erlbaum, pp. 37–65.

Zajonc, R.B. (1968) 'Attitudinal Effects of Mere Exposure', *Journal of Personality and Social Psychology*, 9: 1–27.

Zajonc, R.B. (1980) 'Feeling and Thinking: Preferences Need No Inferences', *American Psychologist*, 35: 151–75.

Zajonc, R.B. (2001) 'Mere Exposure: A Gateway to the Subliminal', *Current Directions in Psychological Science*, 10: 224–8.

Zaller, J. and Feldman, S. (1992) 'A Simple Theory of the Survey Response: Answering Questions Versus Revealing Preferences', *American Journal of Political Science*, 36: 579–616.

Zanna, M.P. and Fazio, R.H. (1982) 'The Attitude–Behavior Relation: Moving toward a third Generation of Research', in M.P. Zanna, E.T. Higgins, and C.P. Herman (eds), *Consistency in Social Behavior: The Ontario Symposium* (vol. 2). Hillsdale, NJ: Erlbaum, pp. 283–301.

Zanna, M.P., Fazio, R.H., and Ross, M. (1994) 'The Persistence of Persuasion', in R.C. Schank and E. Langer (eds), *Beliefs, Reasoning, and Decision Making: Psycho-Logic in Honor of Bob Abelson*. Hillsdale, NJ: Erlbaum, pp. 347–62.

Zanna, M.P., Kiesler, C.A., and Pilkonis, P.A. (1970) 'Positive and Negative Attitudinal Affect Established by Classical Conditioning', *Journal of Personality and Social Psychology*, 14: 321–8.

Zanna, M.P., Olson, J.M., and Fazio, R.H. (1980) 'Attitude–Behavior Consistency: An Individual Difference Perspective', *Journal of Personality and Social Psychology*, *38*: 432–40.

Zanna, M.P. and Rempel, J.K. (1988) 'Attitudes: A New Look at an Old Concept', in D. Bar-Tal and A.W. Kruglanski (eds), *The Social Psychology of Knowledge*. Cambridge: Cambridge University Press, pp. 315–34.

# 7
# Affect and Emotion

JOSEPH P. FORGAS AND CRAIG A. SMITH

### INTRODUCTION

Since time immemorial, people have been fascinated by the strange duality of human nature. On the one hand we are rational, logical creatures capable of impressive analytic thinking, yet many of our everyday judgments and behaviors seem to be driven by subconscious affective impulses that are still poorly understood. The past twenty years have produced an impressive expansion in our knowledge of affectivity. This chapter surveys some of the most recent achievements in experimental research on affect and demonstrates how affective states have a subtle yet significant influence on both the content and the process of everyday thinking and behavior.

Social life is imbued with affect. Every interaction with others can influence our emotional state, and affect, in turn, plays an important role in the way we form judgments and behave in strategic social situations. Yet social psychologists have, until quite recently, remained surprisingly ignorant about the widespread role that affective states play in interpersonal behavior. It was not until the early 1980s that affect was rediscovered in social psychology (Zajonc, 1980), partly as a result of renewed interest in affect by cognitive psychologists (Bower, 1981). The past two decades saw a dramatic increase in research on affect by social psychologists. This progress has been achieved against considerable odds. The very definition of what we mean by 'affect' and 'emotion' remains problematic, and the relationship between affect and cognition continues to be the subject of debate (Zajonc, 1998).

Why has affect been neglected for so long? One explanation offered by Hilgard (1980) is that affect remained the most neglected member of the historical tripartite division of the human mind into cognition, affect, and conation, due to the dominance of first the behaviorist and later the cognitivist paradigms in psychology. A contributing factor may have been the long-dominant view that affect was a dangerous, invasive force that subverts rational thinking and behavior. This idea has a long history in Western philosophy, going back to the works of Plato, who saw emotions as characteristic of a more primitive, subhuman way of functioning. Freud's psychoanalytic theories further emphasized this view of affect as a subconscious, invasive force that needs to be controlled and subjugated. Fortunately, the past few decades saw a radical change in our view of affect. As a result of advances in physiology and neuroanatomy, several lines of evidence now indicate that affect is often an essential and adaptive component of response to social situations (Adolphs and Damasio, 2001; Forgas, 1995a, 2002; Ito and Cacioppo, 2001; Zajonc, 2000).

Thus, the past two decades saw an 'affective revolution' in social-psychological research, as investigators explored both the antecedents (Smith and Kirby, 2000) and the consequences (Forgas, 2002) of affective states in social life. However, there remains a fundamental division in the literature. On the one hand, some researchers are interested in discovering the cognitive appraisals social actors engage in to understand the emotional significance of social situations; their focus is on the cognitive *antecedents of emotions* (e.g., Smith and Kirby, 2000). On the other hand, other researchers ask a complementary question: once affect is experienced, what will be the cognitive and behavioral consequences? Their focus is on the *consequences of affect*, often quite mild moods (e.g., Eich et al., 2001; Forgas, 2001). This review seeks to summarize what we now know about both the antecedents and the consequences of affect for social thinking and behavior. Ultimately, these two orientations should converge and so help answer one of the most intriguing questions about our species: what is the relationship between the rational and the emotional aspects of human nature (Hilgard, 1980)?

This review begins with an historical overview of research on affect and social behavior, followed by a summary of contemporary theories about how affective states are appraised and elicited. We then review research on the consequences of affective states for social judgments and behaviors, including effects on social memory, self-perception, intergroup relations and stereotyping, and attitudes and attitude change. The role of different information-processing strategies in mediating these effects receives special attention.

## Historical background and antecedents

Few theories had such a stultifying influence on psychology for so long, and for so little ultimate gain, as behaviorism. Radical behaviorism explicitly excluded the study of mental phenomena such as affect from psychology. Affectivity, if studied at all, was often equated with fundamental drive states, crudely manipulated through electric shocks and food or drink deprivation. Measuring the amount of feces deposited by a scared rat was a standard method for assessing 'emotionality' in the animal. Not surprisingly, radical behaviorists contributed relatively little to our understanding of the everyday role of affect in social judgments and behaviors.

Unfortunately, as Hilgard (1980) argued, the emergence of the cognitive paradigm in the 1960s produced little improvement. Most information-processing theories, until quite recently, assumed that the proper objective of cognitive research was to study cold, affectless thinking. From the cognitivist perspective, affect was mostly seen as a source of disruption and noise until the early 1980s (Bower, 1981; Neisser, 1982; Zajonc, 1980). Most research on social thinking, judgments, impression formation, and attributions also emphasized the rational, logical aspects of responding to the social world to the exclusion of affective influences. Surprisingly, even Heider's (1958) phenomenological analysis of interpersonal behavior largely ignored affectivity and focused on a logical-scientific model of attributions instead. Despite decades of research, until very recently, few studies looked at the role of feelings, emotions, and moods in causal attributions (Forgas et al., 1990, 1994).

The change in social psychology's approach to affect came in the early 1980s, due to several developments. Zajonc (1980) was among the first to argue that affective reactions often constitute the primary response to social stimuli, requiring no prior inferential processing as suggested by Schachter and Singer (1962). Twenty years later, Zajonc (2000) concluded that affect indeed functions as an independent, primary, and often dominant force in how people respond to social situations. What evidence supports this conclusion? First, people may readily and rapidly acquire an affective response towards social stimuli even when they have little time to process information and have little awareness of having encountered it at all (Zajonc, 1980, 2000). Second, such evaluative preferences often leave an enduring trace, influencing subsequent responses. Does this mean that affect constitutes a separate and primary mode of responding to the social world, independent of cognitive appraisals? Not necessarily. As Lazarus (1984) pointed out, some low-level cognitive processing is necessary just to identify correctly stimulus objects, before any affective response can occur. Affect is a critically important component of reactions to social stimuli; however, it typically operates in conjunction with other cognitive processes (Niedenthal and Halberstadt, 2000).

### *Affect and mental representations*

The uniquely human ability to represent symbolically social events lies at the heart of social behaviour (Forgas et al., 2001; Mead, 1934), and affect appears to play a major role in how people represent and structure their social experiences (Forgas, 1979, 1982). For example, in several investigations, groups of students, housewives, sports teams, or workers recorded their daily interactions in a diary. Subsequently people's implicit representations of these episodes were assessed by analyzing their ratings of the perceived similarity between their interactions. Affective reactions such as feelings of anxiety, confidence, intimacy, pleasure, or discomfort were primary in determining cognitive representation of social episodes. Thus, completely different events (such as visiting a dentist and attending a tutorial) often were mentally represented by people as highly similar because of the similar affective responses they elicited.

Recently, the role of affect in mental representations was further confirmed by Niedenthal and Halberstadt (2000: 381), who argue that 'stimuli can cohere as a category even when they have nothing in common other than the emotional responses they elicit'. Similar ideas were proposed several decades ago by Pervin (1976: 471), who pointed out that 'what is striking is the extent to which situations are described in terms of affects (e.g., threatening, warm, interesting, dull, tense, calm, rejecting) and organized in terms of similarity of affects aroused by them'. Thus, affective responses play a critical role in determining how mental representations about the social world are created and maintained in memory.

The close interdependence between the affective and cognitive domains is well illustrated by the extensive literature on emotion-appraisal processes. Attempts to understand the range and variety of affective experiences have focused on the subtle cognitive strategies people use in order to identify the appropriateness of various emotional reactions to complex social situations (Ortony et al., 1988). Next, we will review the current status of this major area of affect research.

## On the antecedents of emotion: the appraisal approach

The appraisal approach to emotion addresses the fundamental issue of how specific emotions such as anger, sadness, and fear are elicited, and the motivational functions they serve in particular social situations (see also Roseman and Smith, 2001). For example, anger is elicited under conditions in which someone or something is thwarting one's goals; people respond with fear under conditions of danger; sadness arises under conditions involving irreparable harm; and so on.

Understanding how emotions are elicited has been complicated by the fact that emotions are not simple, reflexive responses to a stimulus situation (but see Zajonc, 2000, for a contrary view). It is relatively easy to show that the same objective circumstances can evoke very different emotions across individuals. Thus, an upcoming examination that produces anxiety in a weak student might be a welcome challenge to a competent one, or may elicit indifference in one who is about to quit school. Depending on such appraisals, different affective reactions and different physiological responses will follow (Blascovich and Mendes, 2000). Such heterogeneity of response does not reflect a disorganized or chaotic system. Appraisal theorists assume that emotional reactions are *relational* and reflect what the circumstances that confront an individual *imply* given his or her personal hopes, desires, and abilities. The elicitation mechanism that gives emotion this relational character is one of 'appraisal', originally defined by Arnold (1960) as an evaluation of the potential harms or benefits presented in any given situation.

Beyond being relational, appraisal is also *meaning-based*, and *evaluative*. Because appraisal combines properties of the stimulus situation with those of the person, it cannot be a simple or reflexive response. Instead, appraisal reflects what the stimulus *means* to the individual. Appraisal is also evaluative. It is not a cold analysis of the situation. Rather, it is a personal assessment of whether the situation is good or bad, beneficial or harmful. That this evaluation is meaning-based provides the emotion-appraisal system with considerable flexibility and adaptational power. Not only will different individuals react to very similar situations with different emotions, but objectively different situations can elicit the same emotions if they imply the same meaning to the individuals appraising them. For example, research on perceptions of social situations showed that people will classify very different social situations as similar if they are appraised as having a similar emotional impact (Forgas, 1979, 1982). Additionally, an individual can react differently to the same situation over time if changes in desires and abilities alter the implications of that situation for his or her well-being.

A further assumption is that appraisal occurs continuously. That is, humans constantly engage in a *meaning analysis* in which the adaptational significance of their relationship to the social environment is appraised (see also Leary, 2000). The goal is to avoid or alleviate actual or potential harm, or to seek or maximize actual or potential benefit (e.g., Smith and Ellsworth, 1987; Smith and Lazarus, 1990). Emotional responses are part of an important motivational system that has evolved to alert the individual when he or she is confronted by adaptationally relevant circumstances. To serve this alerting function, the emotion-elicitation mechanism must be constantly 'on guard' to be able to signal such circumstances whenever they arise. It is important to note that appraisal theorists do not assert that this continuous appraisal process need be conscious or deliberate; instead, they have consistently maintained that appraisal can occur automatically outside awareness (e.g., Arnold, 1960; Lazarus, 1968; Leventhal and Scherer, 1987; Smith and Lazarus, 1990).

A final assumption is that the emotion system is *highly organized and differentiated*. Appraisal theorists recognize that the same basic approach/avoid dichotomy that characterizes drives and reflexes (Cannon, 1929) is fundamental to emotional responses. However, they emphasize that emotion is far more differentiated than a simple view of this dichotomy would allow. There are different types of harm and benefit, each having different implications for how one might best contend with it. This is especially true for actual and potential harms, where, depending on the circumstances, the most adaptive course might be to avoid the situation, but also could include active attack, reprimanding oneself, or accepting and enduring the harm. Appraisal theorists tend to conceptualize different emotions as different 'modes of action readiness' (Frijda, 1986), each of which is a response to a particular type of adaptationally relevant situation, and each of which physically and motivationally prepares the individual to contend with those circumstances in a certain way (for example, to attack in anger, to avoid or flee in fear, to accept and heal in sadness, and so on; cf. Frijda, 1986; Izard, 1977). Within this differentiated system, the fundamental role of appraisal, again, is to call forth the appropriate emotion(s) when the individual is confronted with personally adaptationally relevant circumstances.

The construct of appraisal, as outlined above, has considerable power and appeal when it comes to understanding affective responses to social situations. It has the power to drive a highly flexible and adaptive emotion system. However, to be of practical and theoretical utility, the construct needs to be fleshed out in at least two ways. First, the *contents* of appraisal need to be described. Specific models need to be developed to detail the appraisals responsible for the elicitation of the different emotions. Second, the cognitive processes underlying appraisal need to be described. This is especially important, since these processes are not necessarily conscious or deliberate, as critics of appraisal theory (e.g., Izard, 1993; Zajonc, 1980) have often assumed. Considerable effort has been devoted to the first issue, leading to the development and testing of several different *structural models* of appraisal. In addition, relatively recently, some appraisal theorists (e.g., Leventhal and Scherer, 1987; Smith and Kirby, 2000) have begun to develop *process models* of appraisal. Below we discuss developments along both of these fronts in turn.

### *Structural models of appraisal*

Several models have been proposed to identify the dimensions of appraisal and to describe how evaluations along these dimensions distinguish among distinct emotional experiences (e.g., Roseman, 1984, 1991; Scherer, 1984; Smith and Ellsworth, 1985; Smith and Lazarus, 1990). Many studies have now asked subjects to report on both their appraisals and a wide array of emotions across a variety of contexts, including diverse retrospectively remembered experiences (Ellsworth and Smith, 1988a, 1988b; Frijda et al., 1989; Scherer, 1997; Smith and Ellsworth, 1985), hypothetical vignettes (e.g., Roseman, 1991; Smith and Lazarus, 1993), and even ongoing meaningful experiences (e.g., Griner and Smith, 2000; Smith and Ellsworth, 1987; Smith and Kirby, 2001). In these studies, experiences of different emotions have been consistently found to be reliably and systematically associated with different appraisals, and the specific relations observed have largely been in line with the theoretical predictions of the models.

Although the various structural appraisal models differ in a number of respects (e.g., Lazarus, 1991; Ortony et al., 1988; Roseman, 1984; Scherer, 1984; Smith and Ellsworth, 1985; Smith and Lazarus, 1990; see also Scherer, 1988, for a comparison of these models), far more telling is the fact that, overall, they are highly similar in the appraisal dimensions they propose. These similarities reflect the fact that all appraisal theories seek to solve a common problem – to identify the evaluations that link the various modes of action readiness, serving different adaptational functions, to the circumstances in which those functions were called for. It is not so surprising, then, that they happened to hit upon similar solutions to that problem.

Thus, existing appraisal models generally include an evaluation of how important or relevant the stimulus situation is to the person, whether it is desirable or undesirable, whether and to what degree the person is able to cope with the situation, and who or what caused or is responsible for the situation. Different patterns of outcomes along such dimensions are hypothesized to result in different emotions. Moreover, the pattern of appraisal that produces a given emotion is conceptually closely linked to the functions served by that emotion. The model of Smith and Lazarus (1990) can be used to illustrate how these models are organized.

According to this model, situations are evaluated along seven dimensions: motivational relevance, motivational congruence, problem-focused coping potential, emotion-focused coping potential, self-accountability, other-accountability, and future expectancy. Each of these dimensions can be thought of as a question that the person evaluates in determining the affective significance of his or her circumstances. The major questions represented by the appraisal dimensions are depicted in Table 7.1. According to the model, different patterns of outcomes along these dimensions (having different adaptational implications) result in the experience of different emotions (serving different adaptational functions). Thus, these appraisal dimensions are held to be responsible for the differentiation of emotional experience.

The first two dimensions, motivational relevance and motivational congruence, are relevant to every emotional encounter and are sometimes referred to as dimensions of 'primary appraisal' (e.g., Lazarus,

Table 7.1 *Issues evaluated by the seven appraisal dimensions in the Smith and Lazarus (1990) model*

**Primary appraisal**

1 *Motivational relevance* – How relevant (important) is what is happening in this situation to my needs and goals?
2 *Motivational congruence* – Is this congruent with my goals (good)? Or is it incongruent with them (bad)?

**Secondary appraisal**

3 *Self-accountability* – To what extent am I responsible for what is happening in this situation?
4 *Other-accountability* – To what extent is someone or something else responsible for what is happening in this situation?
5 *Problem-focused coping potential* – To what extent can I act on this situation to make (or keep) it more like what I want?
6 *Emotion-focused coping potential* – To what extent can I handle and adjust to this situation however it might turn out?
7 *Future expectancy* – To what extent do I expect this situation to improve, or get worse, for any reason?

1991; Smith and Lazarus, 1990). By themselves, they can distinguish between situations that are irrelevant to well-being (low motivational relevance), and thus are not emotionally evocative, and those that are either beneficial (high motivational relevance and motivational congruence) or stressful (high motivational relevance and motivational incongruence). The additional appraisal dimensions concerning accountability and coping potential (often referred to as 'secondary appraisals' in the terminology of Lazarus [1991] and colleagues) give appraisal theory the power to account for considerable further differentiation among emotional states, particularly in the case of stressful situations (that is, those appraised as both motivationally relevant and motivationally incongruent; see also Blascovich and Mendes, 2000; Smith, 1991; Smith and Lazarus, 1990).

Thus, if a stressful situation is appraised as being caused by someone else (other-accountability) anger will result, motivating the person to act toward the perceived cause to fix the situation. If, however, the situation is appraised as being caused by oneself (self-accountability), shame or guilt results, motivating the person to make amends for the bad situation and to prevent the situation from happening again. If the situation is one that the person is unsure he or she can handle (low emotion-focused coping potential), fear or anxiety results, motivating the person to be cautious and to get rid of or avoid the potential harm. If the stressful situation is one in which the harm is perceived as unavoidable and irreparable (low problem-focused coping potential), sadness results, motivating the person to seek help and to adapt to the inevitable harm. Finally, the emotions associated with primary appraisals of stress are not always unpleasant or negative. If one is in a stressful situation where one does not have something one wants but perceives that with effort one can achieve one's goals (high coping potential), a state of challenge will result that motivates the person to stay engaged and to persevere to achieve his or her goals. As Blascovich and Mendes (2000) have shown, such challenge appraisals can automatically trigger appropriate physiological responses, preparing the organism for action. Even if problem-focused coping potential is low, hope might result if the person believes that, somehow, things might work out in the end (high future expectancy). In sum, different components of secondary appraisal combine with the same stress-related components of primary appraisal to yield a range of distinct emotional reactions that differ dramatically in their subjective and motivational properties. Furthermore, secondary appraisals can also mediate adaptive physiological responses to emotional situations (Blascovich and Mendes, 2000).

Structural models can contribute much to our understanding of emotional experiences in social life by linking specific patterns of appraisal to different emotions and the adaptational functions they serve. However, structural models have been largely silent with respect to the cognitive processes responsible for producing the appraisals. We now turn our attention to the nature of these cognitive processes.

### *Process considerations*

Although structural appraisal models have been quite successful in describing cognitive antecedents of emotion, taken by themselves they create a potential problem for appraisal theory. By emphasizing the complex relational information, this work could give the impression that appraisal is ponderous and slow.

In fact, appraisal theory has often been criticized on the grounds that the structural descriptions of appraisal imply that the process of appraisal is deliberate, slow, inferential, and verbally mediated. Such a mechanism would fly in the face of common observations that emotions can be elicited very quickly, unbidden, often with a minimum of cognitive effort, and sometimes with little or no awareness of the nature of the emotion-eliciting stimulus (e.g., Izard, 1993; Zajonc, 1980, 2000).

Appraisal theorists have been aware of this difficulty, and, to our knowledge, none have claimed that appraisal need be performed consciously or that the information evaluated in appraisal need be represented verbally. On the contrary, beginning with Magda Arnold (1960: 173), for whom appraisal was 'direct, immediate, [and] intuitive', most appraisal theorists have explicitly maintained that appraisal can occur automatically and outside focal awareness (e.g., Lazarus, 1968; Leventhal and Scherer, 1987; Smith and Lazarus, 1990). Only recently, however, have there been attempts to develop explicit process models of appraisal that would explain how appraisals can occur in this manner (e.g., Lazarus, 1991: ch. 4; Leventhal and Scherer, 1987; Robinson, 1998; Smith and Kirby, 2000). These models are still in their infancy, and there are few studies to address their validity. Nonetheless, we provide a brief overview of one such model (that of Smith and Kirby, 2000) because it illustrates how appraisal might occur continuously and automatically.

Instead of conceptualizing appraisal as a single process, this model draws upon current cognitive theories and posits multiple appraisal processes that can occur in parallel and involve distinct cognitive mechanisms. Two distinct modes of cognitive processing have been emphasized – *associative processing*, which involves priming and the activation of memories that can occur quickly and automatically, and *reasoning*, which involves a more controlled and deliberate thinking process that is more flexible than associative processing, but is relatively slow and attention intensive. The distinction between these modes of processing is quite common in the cognitive psychological literature (cf. Sloman, 1996; Smith and DeCoster, 2000). According to the model, appraisals produced by both of these types of cognitive processes can elicit emotions.

Associative processing is a fast, automatic, memory-based mode of processing that involves priming and spreading activation (Bargh, 1989; Bower, 1981). Based on perceptual or conceptual similarities with one's current circumstances, or due to associations with other memories that are already activated, memories of prior experiences can become activated quickly, automatically, in parallel, outside focal awareness, and with a minimum of attentional resources. As these memories are activated, any appraised meanings associated with them are also activated, and can influence the person's emotional state.

Several assumptions concerning associative processing should be emphasized. First, it is assumed that anything that can be represented in memory, ranging from concrete representations of physical sensations, sounds, smells, tastes, and images to representations of highly abstract concepts, is subject to this form of processing. Thus, cues that can activate appraisal-laden memories include not only concrete stimuli, such as sensations, images, and sounds, but also highly conceptual stimuli, such as abstract ideas or the appraisal meanings themselves. Second, it is assumed that through principles of priming and spreading activation, full-blown appraisals associated with prior experiences can be activated very quickly and automatically. Therefore, highly differentiated emotional reactions can be elicited almost instantaneously. Third, it is assumed that the activation threshold at which appraisal information starts to produce emotional feelings is somewhat less than the threshold at which the appraisal information and its associated memories become accessible to focal awareness and/or working memory. Through this assumption, it becomes possible that adaptationally relevant circumstances in one's environment, of which one is focally unaware, can activate memories and produce a rapid emotional reaction. In this way, the first conscious indication to the person that he or she might be in an adaptationally relevant situation can be the perception of the subjective feeling state associated with the associatively elicited emotional reaction. Finally, we assume that the processes of memory activation, priming, and spreading activation occur continuously and automatically. Thus, the person can be characterized as continuously appraising his or her circumstances for their implications for well-being, albeit not in a conscious, attention-intensive manner.

In contrast, reasoning is a relatively slow, controlled process that is effortful, requires considerable attention and focal awareness, and is largely verbally mediated. Moreover, whereas associative processing is largely passive, reasoning is much more constructive, whereby the contents of focal awareness are actively operated on and transformed to produce the appraisal meanings. Thus, reasoning corresponds closely to the active posing and evaluating of appraisal questions that have sometimes incorrectly been assumed to encompass all of appraisal.

Because reasoning is active and highly resource-intensive, it comes at a price. In addition to being relatively slow, this mode of processing is somewhat limited in the forms of information it can access. In contrast to associative processing, which can operate on any form of information stored in memory, only semantically encoded information is readily accessible to reasoning (Anderson, 1983; Paivio, 1971). That is, sensations, images, sounds, and so on, are relatively inaccessible to reasoning unless and until they have been associated with some sort of semantic meaning. This means that while associative processing has access to all of the information available to the reasoning process, the reverse is not true.

Despite these limitations, reasoning is extremely important because it enables the emotion system to utilize the full power of our highly developed and abstract thinking abilities. Emotion-eliciting situations can be thoroughly analyzed and their meanings reappraised (Lazarus, 1968, 1991). Initial associatively elicited appraisals that might not fully fit the current circumstances can be modified to provide a more appropriate evaluation and emotional response. New connections can be forged between one's present circumstances and past experiences. It is even possible that appraisal meanings associated with past experiences in memory can be re-evaluated and changed. In addition, the 'cognitive work' represented by reasoning – the results of the interpretation and reinterpretation of the emotion-eliciting situation – can be stored in memory as part of the emotion-eliciting event and thus become available for subsequent associative processing. This last fact is vital, as it provides a mechanism by which the emotion system can 'learn' and, through associative processing, can quickly and automatically produce the highly differentiated, information-rich signals that the motivational functions served by emotion seem to require.

So far, we have seen that emotional responses to social situations seem to be the product of the continuous monitoring of the environment and the rapid, automatic or slow, inferential appraisal of the available cues for their significance for our safety and well-being. Clearly, appraisal research represents a very promising framework for understanding the subtle social origins and *antecedents* of affective experiences. An equally interesting and complementary question has occupied researchers for several decades now: once an affective state is elicited, what are its *consequences* for the way people think, form judgments, and behave in social situations? We shall now turn to reviewing this complementary research tradition.

## Early explanations of affective influences on thinking and behavior

The idea that affect may influence the online perception and interpretation of logically unrelated social information has been around for a long time. Several early studies suggested that positive and negative moods often produce affect-congruent responses in unrelated judgments. For example, feeling good might make our judgments more positive, and feeling bad may distort the evaluation of neutral social stimuli in a negative direction (Feshbach and Singer, 1957; Razran, 1940). How and why does such 'affect infusion' occur, and what are the psychological mechanisms that facilitate or inhibit its occurrence? We shall next survey traditional and contemporary theoretical explanations of affective influences on thinking and behavior and, subsequently, discuss the empirical evidence for these effects. The earliest psychological explanations of affective influences on judgments and behavior relied on either psychoanalytic, or conditioning theories.

### *The psychoanalytic account of affect infusion*

The psychoanalytic speculations of Freud were influential in suggesting that affect has a dynamic quality and can 'invade' people's thinking and judgments unless psychological resources are deployed by the individual to control these impulses. In one early study, Feshbach and Singer (1957) relied on psychoanalytic theories to predict that attempts to suppress affect should paradoxically increase the 'pressure' for affect to infuse unrelated attitudes and judgments. They induced affect (fear) through electric shocks, and some participants were later instructed to suppress their fear. Interpersonal judgments after this manipulation were significantly influenced by affect. Fearful persons were more likely to see 'another person as fearful and anxious' (Feshbach abd Singer 1957: 286), and this pattern was greater when judges were trying to suppress their fear. This, according to Feshbach and Singer (1957: 286), can be explained in terms of the infusion of temporary affect into an unrelated judgment, because 'suppression of fear facilitates the tendency to project fear onto another social object'.

### *The conditioning account of affect infusion*

An alternative explanation for affect infusion was provided by conditioning theories. Although radical behaviorism denied the value of studying internal mental phenomena such as affect, the associationist approach nevertheless exerted an important influence on subsequent research. Watson's 'little Albert' studies were among the first to show that attitudes towards a previously neutral object, such as a furry rabbit, can be rapidly influenced by associating fear-arousing stimuli, such as a loud noise, with it (Watson and Rayner, 1920). Such patterns of cumulative associations are responsible for all our acquired affective reactions throughout life, according to Watson. Several experiments found some support for this associationist account of affect infusion. Some sixty years ago, Razran (1940) found that people who were made to feel bad or good (being exposed to highly aversive smells, or receiving a free lunch) spontaneously reported significantly more negative or positive attitudes towards sociopolitical slogans. A similar conditioning approach to understanding affective influences on attitudes and judgments was later used by Byrne and Clore (1970) and Clore and Byrne (1974) to account for affect infusion into interpersonal attitudes.

Within a classical conditioning framework, researchers argued that when people encounter a neutral attitude object, the affective reaction elicited by the environment will become associated with the new target and will influence attitudes and evaluations (a conditioned response). According to this view, simple temporal and spatial contiguity is enough to link an affective state and an incidentally encountered stimulus. Several studies demonstrated just such a conditioning effect (Gouaux, 1971; Gouaux and Summers, 1973; Griffitt, 1970). More recently, Berkowitz and his colleagues (Berkowitz et al., 2000) have reached back to early associationist theories and proposed a neoassociationist account of affective influences on attitudes and judgments. Thus, the idea that incidentally elicited affective states can coincidentally influence evaluative responses remains an important influence on some contemporary affect theories (Clore et al., 2001; Eich et al., 2001).

## Contemporary cognitive theories of affective influences

In contrast to traditional conditioning and psychoanalytic explanations, contemporary cognitive theories offer a more finely grained account of the mechanisms responsible for the infusion of affect into thinking, judgments, and behaviors. Two different kinds of cognitive mechanisms have been proposed to explain affect infusion. According to the inferential *affect-as-information* model, people may mistakenly rely on their prevailing affective state as a relevant cue to infer their evaluative reactions to ambiguous, neutral, or indeterminate social situations (e.g., Clore et al., 1994). Alternatively, *memory-based* accounts posit an automatic, subconscious process whereby affective states can influence unrelated thoughts and judgments (for example, the affect priming model; see Bower and Forgas, 2001). We should note that there is a direct parallel between these two processes of affect infusion and the two processes of affect appraisal (associative priming, and reasoning) discussed above. In addition to models that deal with how affect informs the content of cognition, several theories also emphasize the influence of affect on how social information is *processed*. We briefly review each of these three theoretical frameworks below.

### *Inferential accounts*

Certain kinds of affective influences on judgments may occur because 'rather than computing a judgment on the basis of recalled features of a target, individuals may [...] ask themselves: "How do I feel about it?" and in doing so, they may mistake feelings due to a pre-existing state as a reaction to the target' (Schwarz, 1990: 529) This 'how-do-I-feel-about-it?' model suggests that affective states can influence evaluations and judgments because of an inferential error: people 'misread' their affective states as informative about their reactions to an unrelated target. This idea has its roots in at least three different research traditions. Earlier conditioning theories already suggested that unrelated affective states can become linked to new stimuli (Clore and Byrne, 1974). Whereas conditioning explanation emphasized a direct associative link between affect and judgments, the affect-as-information model – rather less parsimoniously – relies on an internal inferential process to produce this effect (cf. Berkowitz et al., 2000). A second source of the affect-as-information model is research on misattribution and self-attribution processes. According to this view, people have no privileged access to internal reactions and so need to infer responses based on salient but often irrelevant cues – such as their prevailing affective state. Thus, only previously unattributed affective states can inform subsequent judgments. Finally, this model also shows some affinity with research on judgmental heuristics, in the sense that a temporary affective state functions as a heuristic cue in informing judgments.

Evidence suggests that people seem to rely on their affective state as a heuristic cue only in special circumstances. This is most likely when the judgmental target is unfamiliar or unimportant, there is no prior evaluation to fall back on, personal involvement is low, and cognitive resources are limited. Just such a situation was created in an experiment by Schwarz and Clore (1983), who telephoned strangers and asked them unexpected and unfamiliar questions. As respondents presumably had little personal involvement and lacked motivation, time, or cognitive resources to engage in extensive processing, they may well have relied on their temporary mood to inform their responses.

Other studies also found significant affect infusion into social judgments in similar circumstances. In one study, almost 1,000 people who were feeling good or bad after seeing happy or sad films were asked to complete a series of judgments after leaving a movie theater (Forgas and Moylan, 1987). Again, involvement and motivation were low, and subjects did seem to rely on their temporary affect as a heuristic cue to infer a judgment.

There are several issues to consider in evaluating this theory. First, it is not clear whether the 'how do I feel about it?' process implies a conscious, inferential search for a response, or an implicit, automatic mechanism. Another conceptual problem is that the model says nothing about how cues other than affect, such as the available external stimulus information, and internal knowledge structures are combined in producing a response. Thus, this is really a theory of misjudgment, or nonjudgment, or aborted judgment rather than a genuine theory of judgment.

Schwarz and Clore (1983, 1988; Clore et al., 1994) also claim that their model is falsifiable because it asserts the *absence* of affect congruence in judgments when the affective state is already attributed. Indeed, several studies found that when people's attention is called to the source of their affect, affect congruence is reduced or eliminated (Berkowitz et al., 2000; Clore et al., 1994; Schwarz and Clore, 1983, 1988). However, such findings do not provide support for the theory, as is often claimed. Logically, the fact that an effect can be eliminated by additional manipulations (such as emphasizing the correct source of their affect) says nothing about how the effect is produced in the first place in the absence of the manipulation. Focusing people's attention on their internal states can also reverse affect congruence when caused by affect priming effects (Berkowitz et al., 2000). Furthermore, affect congruence is not always eliminated just because the correct source of affect is known, as found in many experiments that use transparent and obvious mood manipulations (autobiographical recall and false feedback; see Forgas, 1995a, 2002, for reviews).

Several critics of the affect-as-information model, such as Abele and Petzold (1994), also argue that affect is just one among many information inputs that must be integrated in order to produce a judgment. A similar point is made by Martin (2000), who argued that the informational value of an affective state is unlikely to be constant. The same affective state can mean different things in different contexts. If the informational value of affect is not given, it can hardly be the source of invariant information as the model assumes. For example, a positive mood may inform us that a positive response is appropriate (if the setting happens to be a cabaret), but the same mood may send the opposite informational signal in a different setting, such as a funeral. It now appears that realistic responses which require some degree of elaboration and processing are more likely to be influenced by affect priming than the affect-as-information process.

### *The memory-based account: the affect-priming model*

Affect may influence thought, judgments, and behavior through selectively facilitating access to, and the use of, affect-congruent memory structures that people rely on when constructively interpreting social information. The most influential memory-based account was put forward by Bower (1981), who proposed that affect, cognition, and attitudes are linked within an associative network of mental representations. Experiencing an affective state should selectively and automatically prime associated thoughts and representations which are more likely to be used in constructive cognitive tasks. Such tasks involve the active elaboration and transformation of the available stimulus information, require the activation and use of previous knowledge structures, and result in the creation of new knowledge from the combination of stored information and new stimulus details. Early experiments provided encouraging evidence for mood-congruent effects in a number of situations, as predicted by associative network theories (Bower, 1981; Clark and Isen, 1982; Fiedler and Stroehm, 1986; Forgas and Bower, 1987; Isen, 1984, 1987).

Subsequent research showed, however, that affect priming and affect-congruent judgments are subject to important boundary conditions (Eich and Macauley, 2000; Forgas, 1995a). In their experiments exploring mood effects on memory, Eric Eich and his collaborators (Eich and Forgas, 2003; Eich and Macauley, 2000) demonstrated that mood-state dependence in memory is more likely in circumstances when the affective state induced is strong, salient, and self-relevant. Furthermore, these effects are stronger when the task requires the active generation and elaboration of information rather than mere reproduction of stimulus details. It is probably for this reason that mood-state dependence has been more difficult to demonstrate with tasks that are abstract and uninvolving, such as the word-list-learning experiments often preferred by cognitive researchers (Eich and Macauley, 2000). However, affect congruence in memory, judgments, and behaviors has been reliably found in social cognitive experiments where the task and information to be processed are more complex, realistic, and involving (Forgas, 1994; Forgas and Bower, 1987; Sedikides, 1995).

A similar point was made by Fiedler (1991, 2001), who distinguished between constructive and reconstructive cognitive processes and argued that affect congruence should be most likely when a task requires open, constructive elaboration of stimulus details and the combination of new information with stored knowledge structures. Tasks that require recognizing a stimulus or retrieving a prestructured response involve no constructive thinking, so there is little opportunity to use affectively primed information, and we should find little affect congruence. For example, recognition memory is typically far less influenced by a person's affective state than recall memory which requires more constructive processing.

Thus, the nature and extent of affective influences on thinking and judgments should depend on the information-processing strategy people employ in a particular situation. The consequence of affect priming is affect infusion, as long as an open, elaborate information-processing strategy is used that promotes the incidental use of affectively primed information (Fiedler, 1991, 2000; Forgas, 1995a, 2002a; Sedikides, 1995). Affect priming, rather than affect-as-information mechanisms, is largely responsible for affect infusion in most realistic tasks that require some degree of involvement and elaborate processing. There is now much empirical evidence for this prediction, and recent integrative theories explicitly focus on the role of different information-processing strategies in moderating affect congruence (Forgas, 1995a, 2002a).

### *Affective influences on information-processing strategies*

In addition to having an informational effect (influencing *what* people think), affect may also influence the *process* of cognition, or *how* people think (Clark and Isen, 1982; Fiedler and Forgas, 1988; Forgas, 2000, 2001a). Early evidence indicated that people in a positive mood seemed to reach decisions faster, used less information, avoided demanding, systematic thinking, and showed greater confidence in their decisions, suggesting that positive affect might produce a more superficial, less systematic, and less effortful processing style. In contrast, negative affect seemed to trigger a more effortful, systematic, analytic, and vigilant processing style (Clark and Isen, 1982; Isen, 1984, 1987; Mackie and Worth, 1989; Schwarz, 1990).

These processing differences were explained in terms of three alternative theories. One early idea emphasized affective influences on *processing capacity*. Ellis and his colleagues suggested, for example, that negative affect reduces attentional resources and processing capacity (Ellis and Ashbrook, 1988). In contrast, Mackie and Worth (1989) proposed that it is positive affect that sometimes reduces information-processing capacity. As the processing consequences of affect are clearly asymmetrical – positive and negative affect reliably promote very different thinking styles – it is unlikely that the explanations put forward by Ellis and Ashbrook (1988) and Mackie and Worth (1989) could both be correct. It remains unclear when and how cognitive capacity might play an role in mediating affective influences on information processing.

An alternative explanation emphasized the motivational consequences of positive and negative affect. According to some versions of this view (Clark and Isen, 1982; Isen, 1984, 1987), people in a positive mood may try to maintain this pleasant state by refraining from effortful activity. Negative affect in turn should motivate people to engage in vigilant, effortful processing as an adaptive response to improve an aversive state. Schwarz (1990) offered a slightly different account, suggesting that positive and negative affects have a signaling/tuning function, and their role is to automatically inform the person of whether a relaxed, effort-minimizing (positive affect) or a vigilant, effortful (negative affect) processing style is appropriate.

In recent years, a more differentiated picture began to emerge. Several experiments found that positive affect may have distinct processing advantages (Bless, 2000; Fiedler, 2001). People in a positive mood often adopt more creative, flexible, open, and inclusive thinking styles and perform more effectively on secondary tasks (Bless, 2000; Fiedler, 2000; Hertel and Fiedler, 1994). Affective influences on processing are thus not simply a matter of increasing or decreasing the effort, vigilance, and elaborateness of information-processing. Rather, as Bless (2000) and Fiedler (2000) showed, the fundamental evolutionary significance of positive and negative affective states is not simply to influence processing effort but to recruit more internally driven, top-down (positive affect), or externally oriented, bottom-up processing styles (Bless and Fiedler, 2006).

### *Integrative theories*

Affective states can have an informational, and a processing influence on the way people remember, interpret, judge, and respond to social information. However, these effects are context sensitive and often depend on the particular task or judgment to be performed. A more comprehensive explanation of these effects needs to specify the circumstances that promote or inhibit affect congruence and should define the conditions that lead to affect priming, or the affect-as-information mechanisms. Several attempts were made in recent years to propose such integrative theories (Fiedler, 2001; Martin, 2000). We will describe one such comprehensive theory, the affect infusion model (AIM) (Forgas, 1995a, 2002). This theory predicts that affect infusion should occur only in circumstances that promote open, constructive processing that involves active elaboration of the available stimulus details and use of memory-based information in this process.

The AIM assumes that affect infusion should be dependent on the kind of processing strategy that is used and identifies four alternative processing strategies: *direct access*, *motivated*, *heuristic*, and *substantive* processing. The first two strategies, direct access and motivated processing, call for highly targeted and predetermined patterns of information search and selection, which limit the scope for incidental affect infusion. In contrast, heuristic and substantive processing are more open, involve some constructive thinking and may thus produce affect infusion. These four strategies also differ in terms of two basic dimensions: the degree of *effort* exerted in seeking a solution, and the degree of *openness* and constructiveness of the information-search strategy. Thus, *substantive processing* involves high effort and open, constructive thinking, *motivated processing* involves high effort but closed, predetermined information search, *heuristic processing* is characterized by low effort but open, constructive thinking, and *direct access processing* represents low processing effort and closed information search.

The model also predicts that the use of these processing strategies is triggered by contextual variables related to the *task,* the *person,* and the *situation* that jointly influence processing choices. For example, the *direct access strategy* involves the direct retrieval of a pre-existing response and is most likely when the task is highly familiar, and when no strong cognitive, affective, situational, or motivational cues call for elaborate processing. Thus, when asked to produce a judgment about a well-known person, a previous response can be readily retrieved and used. Most of us possess a rich store of such pre-formed judgments. As such standard responses require no constructive processing, affect infusion should be absent, as found in a number of experiments (Sedikides, 1995). The *motivated processing strategy* involves highly selective and targeted thinking that is dominated by a particular motivational objective that precludes open information search, limiting affect infusion (Clark and Isen, 1982). For example, if during a job interview you are asked about your attitude towards the company you want to join, the response will be dominated by the motivation to produce an acceptable response rather than genuinely open and constructive thinking. Motivated processing may also produce a reversal of affect infusion and lead to mood-incongruent outcomes, when people wish to control or reverse their moods (Berkowitz et al., 2000; Forgas, 1991; Forgas and Ciarrochi, 2002; Forgas and Fiedler, 1996).

The other two processing strategies identified by the AIM, *heuristic* and *substantive* processing, require more constructive and open-ended information search strategies and can thus produce affect infusion. *Heuristic processing* is most likely when the task is simple, familiar, and of little personal relevance; cognitive capacity is limited; and there are no motivational pressures. In such cases, people may rely on simplifying heuristics like their mood to infer a response. For example, when people are asked to respond to a telephone survey (Clore et al., 1994), or asked to reply to a questionnaire on the street (Forgas and Moylan, 1987), heuristic processing can lead to affect infusion if respondents rely on the 'how do I feel about it?' heuristic. Finally, *substantive processing* should be adopted when the task is demanding, atypical, complex, novel, or personally relevant; there are no direct access responses available; there are no clear motivational goals to guide processing; and there is adequate time and other processing resources available to engage in elaborate processing.

Substantive processing is an open and constructive strategy, and affect may selectively prime access to, and facilitate the use of, related thoughts, ideas, memories, and interpretations. The AIM makes the interesting and counterintuitive prediction that affect infusion (and mood congruence) should be increased when more extensive and elaborate processing is required to deal with more complex, demanding, or novel tasks, a pattern that has been confirmed in several experiments (Fiedler and Stroehm, 1986; Forgas, 1992b, 1993, 1995b, 1998a, 1998b; Forgas and Bower, 1987; Sedikides, 1995). An important feature of the AIM is that it recognizes that affect itself can also influence processing choices. As we have seen before (e.g., Bless, 2000; Fiedler, 2000; Bless and Fiedler, 2006), positive affect typically generates a more top-down, schema-driven processing style, and negative affect often triggers piecemeal, bottom-up processing strategies focusing attention on external details. The key contribution of integrative models such as the AIM is that they can predict the *absence* of affect infusion when direct access or motivated processing is used, and the *presence* of affect infusion during heuristic and substantive processing. The implications of this model have been supported in a number of the experiments, some of which will be considered below.

## The empirical evidence

There are thus good theoretical reasons to expect that affect has a significant influence on how people represent the social world and the memories and constructs they use to interpret complex information. Typically, experiments in this field involve a two-stage procedure. Participants are first induced to experience an affective state by methods such as hypnotic suggestions, exposure to happy or sad movies, music, autobiographic memories, or positive or negative feedback about performance. After mood induction, judgments, memories, and behaviors are assessed in what participants believe is a separate, unrelated experiment (Bower, 1981; Forgas, 1992a, 1995a). In some field experiments, naturally occurring moods elicited by the weather, movies, sports events, and the like can be used to study mood effects on cognition and behavior (Forgas and Moylan, 1987; Mayer et al., 1992).

In this section, we will review a range of empirical studies demonstrating affective influences on social cognition and behavior. The review will focus on several areas where the role of affect on judgments and behavior has been demonstrated, including affective influences on (a) social memory, (b) social judgments, (c) self-perception, (d) stereotyping and intergroup judgments, (e) attitudes and persuasion, and (f) interpersonal behaviors.

### *Affective influences on social memory*

*Mood-state-dependent retrieval* is one of the key mechanisms responsible for affective influences on social memory, suggesting that memory should be enhanced whenever retrieval mood matches the original encoding mood, consistent with the encoding specificity principle proposed by Tulving (1983). Several experiments found that people are better at remembering social events and autobiographical memories when their recall mood matches the mood they experienced when the event occurred. For example, people in a positive mood recall more happy events from their childhood, and those in a bad mood remember more negative episodes (Bower, 1981). In another study, participants remembered significantly more mood-consistent than -inconsistent episodes from the events they recorded in their diary the previous week, as predicted by the affect priming model (Bower, 1981; Bower and Forgas, 2001). Depressed people show a similar pattern, preferentially remembering aversive childhood experiences, a memory bias that disappears once depression is brought under control. However, these mood-state-dependent memory effects are less reliable when the material to be remembered is abstract and uninvolving, such as word lists (Bower and Mayer, 1989). Studies that used more complex and relevant social stimuli presented in more realistic encoding and recall contexts have most reliably produced mood-state-dependent retrieval (Fiedler, 1990, 1991; Forgas, 1991a, 1992b, 1993; Forgas and Bower, 1987). It is these studies that are most likely to allow affective cues to function as a differentiating context in learning and recall, as originally suggested by Bower (1981).

*Mood-congruent retrieval* is a related memory effect that occurs when an affective state facilitates the recall of affectively congruent material from memory, irrespective of encoding mood. For example, depressed subjects take less time to retrieve unpleasant rather than pleasant memories, while nondepressed subjects show the opposite pattern (Lloyd and Lishman, 1975; Teasdale and Fogarty, 1979). However, some of these studies may confound mood-state-dependent retrieval with mood-congruent retrieval, as encoding mood is not always controlled for. A more convincing demonstration of mood-congruent retrieval requires that subjects experience no specific affect during encoding, yet still show better recall for mood-congruent information. Such results were obtained, for example, by Teasdale and Russell (1983), consistent with affect-priming predictions. Research using implicit memory tasks provides particularly clear support for affective influences on memory. For example, depressed people tend to complete word stems to produce negative rather than positive words they have seen before (Ruiz-Caballero and Gonzalez, 1994). Stem-completion and sentence-completion tasks were also found to indicate an implicit memory bias by Tobias and Kihlstrom (1992). However, mood-priming effects often seem difficult to demonstrate in word-recognition tasks (but see Niedenthal and Setterlund, 1994).

### Mood effects on learning and selective attention

Many social tasks involve information overload, when people need to select a small sample of information for further processing (Heider, 1958). Affect should have an influence on what people will pay attention to, according to affect-priming theories (Niedenthal and Setterlund, 1994). Due to the activation of a mood-related associative base, affect-congruent social information should receive greater attention and deeper processing (Bower, 1981; Forgas and Bower, 1987). Several experiments found that people spend longer reading affect-congruent social information, linking it into a richer network of primed associations, and, as a result, are better at remembering such information (Bower, 1981; Forgas, 1992b; Forgas and Bower, 1987). These effects occur because 'concepts, words, themes, and rules of inference that are associated with that emotion will become primed and highly available for use/in/top-down or expectation-driven processing/acting/as interpretive filters of reality' (Bower, 1983: 395).

Thus, people often process mood-congruent material more deeply, with greater associative elaboration and, thus, learn it better (Forgas and Bower, 1987). These experiments suggest that information that is congruent with prevailing affect is easier to access and use in social tasks (Anderson, 1983; Forgas, 1992a). Depressed psychiatric patients, for example, tend to show better learning and memory for negative information (Watkins et al., 1992), a bias that disappears once the depressive episode is over (Bradley and Mathews, 1983). However, mood-congruent learning seems a less robust phenomenon in patients suffering from anxiety (Burke and Mathews, 1992; Watts and Dalgleish, 1991), perhaps because anxious patients use particularly vigilant processing strategies to defend against anxiety-arousing information (Mathews and McLeod, 1994). Thus, processing strategies could play a crucial role in mediating affect-priming processes, as suggested by the affect infusion model (AIM) (Forgas, 1995a).

#### Mood effects on associations and interpretations

Interpersonal behavior often requires us to 'go beyond the information given', and rely on memories, associations, and inferences to make sense of complex and ambiguous social information (Heider, 1958). Affect can prime the kind of associations we rely on. For example, in word associations to an ambiguous word such as 'life', happy subjects think of more positive associations ('love' and 'freedom'), while sad subjects produce words such as 'struggle' and 'death' (Bower, 1981). Mood-congruent associations also emerge when emotional subjects daydream or make up stories about fictional characters on the Thematic Apperception Test (Bower, 1981). These associative effects also produce affect-congruent distortions in many real-life situations due to naturally occurring moods (Mayer and Volanth, 1985; Mayer et al., 1992).

Associative mood effects can also affect various social judgments, such as perceptions of human faces (Schiffenbauer, 1974), impressions about people (Forgas et al., 1984; Forgas and Bower, 1987), and self-perceptions (Sedikides, 1995). However, some recent experiments suggest that this associative effect is diminished as targets to be judged become more clear-cut and require less constructive processing (Forgas, 1994b, 1995b, 1997b, 1997c). This diminution in the associative consequences of mood with increasing stimulus clarity again suggests that open, constructive processing is an important prerequisite for affect-priming effects to occur (Fiedler, 1991, 2001).

#### Affective influences on eyewitness memory

Recent evidence suggests that affective influences on memory may have important practical consequences, for example in the area of eyewitness memory. To evaluate the role of affect in eyewitness memory, we asked people to witness complex social events presented on videotapes (such as a wedding scene or a robbery). A week later, good or bad mood was induced by films, and 'witnesses' were then questioned about what they saw. The questions either included or did not include 'planted', misleading information about the scenes (Forgas, 2001c). When eyewitness memory for the incidents was later tested, misleading information was more likely to be incorporated in the event and mistaken for a 'real' experience by those who were in a positive mood when the false information was presented. Negative mood reduced this memory distortion. The same effects were also observed in a field study, where students witnessed and later recalled a staged incident during a lecture (Forgas, 2001c).

### *Affective influences on social judgments*

Forming accurate judgments about others is an important prerequisite for successful interpersonal behavior (Forgas, 1985). Early experiments suggested that temporary moods might have a simple, mood-congruent influence on social judgments, an effect initially explained by psychoanalytic or conditioning principles (Clore and Byrne, 1974; Feshbach and Singer, 1957; Griffitt, 1970). Recent studies based on cognitive principles were also able to explore the boundary conditions for these effects.

#### Affective influences on making sense of observed behaviors

Interpreting ongoing social behaviors is perhaps the most fundamental judgment people make in everyday life. Such judgments typically require inferential processing and should be open to affect-infusion effects. This prediction was first evaluated by asking participants who were feeling happy or sad after a hypnotic mood induction to watch a videotape of their own social interactions with a partner from the previous day (Forgas et al., 1984). Participants were asked to make a series of rapid, online judgments evaluating the behaviours of themselves and their partner's as 'skilled, positive' or 'unskilled, negative'. Affect had a highly significant influence on judgments. Happy persons saw more positive, skilled and fewer negative, unskilled behaviors in both themselves and their partners than did sad subjects. Objective observers who received no mood induction showed no such affective biases.

Thus, even mild affective states can have a strong influence on the way complex and ambiguous interpersonal behaviors are interpreted, even when judgments are based on objective, videotaped evidence. These effects are most likely to occur because affect priming influences the kinds of memory-based interpretations, constructs, and associations people use as they interpret complex social behaviors. For example, the same smile seen as 'friendly' by a happy person could be judged as 'awkward' or 'condescending' when the observer experiences negative affect.

In subsequent experiments, happy or sad people were asked to form attitudes about target persons who possessed a number of positive and negative qualities presented on a computer screen, so reading and judgmental latencies could be recorded (Forgas and Bower, 1987). Again, there was strong evidence for an affect-congruent bias: happy judges formed more positive judgments, and sad judges were more critical. Analysis of processing latencies produced a pattern consistent with the affect-priming explanation. Judges spent more time reading, thinking about, and encoding information that was congruent with their affective state. This is consistent with the affect-priming account that predicts that when people *learn* new information, affect priming produces a richer activated knowledge base and, thus, increases the time taken to link new information to this more elaborate memory structure. In contrast, people took less time when *producing* affect-congruent judgments, because the relevant response is already primed by the affective state.

## Does elaborate processing increase affect infusion in judgments?

If affect infusion requires more substantive processing, then the more people need to think in order to compute a judgment, the greater the likelihood that affectively primed thoughts and associations will influence their judgments. Several experiments tested this paradoxical prediction by manipulating the complexity of the judgmental task to create more or less demand for extensive, elaborate processing (Forgas, 1993, 1994, 1995b). In one set of experiments (Forgas, 1993, 1995b), happy or sad participants were asked to form impressions about couples presented in pictures who were either highly typical and well-matched or atypical and badly matched for physical attractiveness. As expected, there was an affect-congruent influence on judgments, as happy participants formed more positive, lenient, and generous impressions than did sad participants. These mood effects were significantly greater when the couples were unusual and badly matched, so that forming a judgment required more extensive processing. Similar results were obtained when judges were asked to form judgments based on verbal descriptions (Forgas, 1992b). Furthermore, an analysis of processing latency and recall memory data confirmed that unusual, atypical persons took longer to process, and there was greater affect infusion into these elaborate judgments.

To what extent does affect infusion also occur in realistic interpersonal judgments? Several experiments evaluated the effects of mood on judgments about people's real-life relationships (Forgas, 1994). Results showed that people made more mood-congruent judgments about their intimate partners and about events in their long-term intimate relationships. Again, these mood effects were consistently greater when the events judged were more complex and serious and required more elaborate, constructive processing. This evidence suggests that judgments about highly familiar people are also prone to affect infusion, and these effects are magnified when more elaborate processing strategies are used.

## Affective influences on judgmental biases

As feeling good seems to produce a thinking style that relies more heavily on internal thoughts and dispositions, happy people may pay less attention to external information and be more prone to certain judgmental errors (Bless, 2000; Bless and Fiedler, 2006; Fiedler, 2001), such as the 'fundamental attribution error' (FAE) that occurs when people ignore external influences on behavior (Forgas, 1998c). In several studies, happy or sad people read essays that were freely chosen or coerced and then judged the underlying attitudes of the writers (Forgas, 1998c). Happy persons largely assumed that the essay reflected the writer's attitudes, thus committing the FAE. Those in a negative mood showed reduced bias and paid better attention to the available information and tended to discount coerced essays as indicative of the writer's real views. Many important decisions in everyday life require similar attention to situational details. For example, in a series of recent studies, Moylan (2001) showed that positive mood tends to increase, and negative mood tends to decrease, the incidence of a variety of errors and distortions in performance assessments in organizations.

More generally, mood may also influence the use of various judgemental heuristics, such as anchoring, availability, and representativeness (Tversky and Kahneman, 1974). Recent research provides partial support for this hypothesis (Chan and Forgas, 2001). People in a positive and negative mood were asked to make judgments about acceptable levels of risk in a variety of scenarios and were also provided with heuristic cues, such as anchors, before performing the judgment. Happy judges tended to rely more on the anchoring heuristic when the situation was 'hypothetical' and relatively unfamiliar. When the situation at hand was more personally relevant, it was people in a negative mood who were more susceptible to judgmental heuristics. It seems that the nature and familiarity of the task mediates mood effects on heuristic use, so, it appears that the processing strategy recruited by a situation has a large influence on the nature and extent of affective influences (Forgas, 2002; Forgas et al., 2005).

### *Affective influences on self-perception*

The self represents a particularly complex and elaborate cognitive schema incorporating rich information accumulated throughout a lifetime about our positive and negative social experiences. Affect should thus have a strong influence on self-related judgments whenever constructive, substantive processing is adopted (Forgas, 1995a, 2001a; Sedikides, 1992, 1995). Most research suggests a fundamental affect-congruent pattern: positive affect improves and negative affect impairs the valence of self-conceptions (Abele-Brehm and Hermer, 1993; Nasby, 1994, 1996). For example, when students were asked to make judgments about their success or failure on a recent examination, induced positive or negative mood had a significant mood-congruent influence. Those in a negative mood blamed themselves more when failing, and took less credit for their successes, whereas those in a positive mood claimed credit for success but refused to accept responsibility for their failures (Forgas et al., 1990).

However, recent studies indicate a more complex picture, suggesting that the nature of the judgmental task moderates mood effects on self-judgments. For example, Nasby (1994) asked participants to make affirmative or nonaffirmative judgments about how a series of trait adjectives applied to them. Later, recall memory for these self-descriptions was tested. Happy persons remembered more positive and sad persons remembered more negative self-traits, but only when prior ratings required an affirmative format. This result indicates that the different processing strategies required by affirmative and nonaffirmative trait judgments mediate the effect. Rejecting a trait as not applicable to ourselves may be a simple and direct process that requires no elaborate thinking. In contrast, affirming that a trait does apply to the self requires more elaborate thinking, enhancing the likelihood of affective influences.

It also appears that central and peripheral aspects of the self are differentially sensitive to affective influences (Sedikides, 1995). People's central self-conceptions are more salient, detailed and certain, representing the core of what people believe is their 'true' self, and are affirmed more strongly than peripheral features (Markus, 1977; Pelham, 1991; Sedikides, 1995; Sedikides and Strube, 1997; Swann, 1990). Judgments about the 'central' self should require less online elaboration and should be less open to affect infusion. Sedikides (1995) confirmed this pattern, finding that affect had no influence on judgments related to central traits, but had a significant mood-congruent influence on judgments related to peripheral traits. Later experiments showed that encouraging people to think more extensively about peripheral self-conceptions further increased affective influences on these judgments.

#### Self-esteem

Individual traits such as self-esteem also mediate mood effects on self-judgments (Baumeister, 1993, 1998; Rusting, 1998, 2001). People with low self-esteem generally have less certain and stable self-conceptions (Campbell et al., 1996; Kernis and Waschull, 1996). Affect may thus have a greater influence on the self-judgments of low self-esteem individuals, as found by Brown and Mankowski (1993). In another study, Smith and Petty (1995) induced happy and sad mood in high and low self-esteem participants, who were then asked to report on memories from their school years. Mood influenced the quantity and quality of responses by the low, but not by the high, self-esteem group. It seems that people with high self-esteem have a more stable self-concept and respond to self-related questions by directly accessing this stable knowledge, thus inhibiting the incidental infusion of affect into judgments. Affect intensity may be another individual difference variable that influences mood congruency effects on self-judgments (Larsen and Diener, 1987). Mood congruency may be stronger among high affect-intensity persons (Haddock et al., 1994) and among people who score higher on measures assessing openness to feelings as a personality trait (Ciarrochi and Forgas, 2000).

In some instances, negative affect infusion can have a debilitating and self-perpetuating influence on self-judgments. Extreme stress and anxiety can produce a dangerous 'neurotic cascade' of reverberating negative affect and negative thinking (Suls, 2001). In this state, minor problems may be magnified out of all proportion so that people sometimes set unreasonable targets, show decreased flexibility in adjusting their goals, and inadvertently produce more negative experiences. To break this cycle of negative affectivity, a conscious effort is often required.

Motivational variables may also influence self-judgments. For example, Cervone et al. (1994) found a mood-congruent pattern in performance ratings: sad participants were more critical of the same level of performance than neutral participants. However, the opposite effect occurred on judgments of performance standards: sad participants now expressed *higher* personal standards than neutral-mood participants, perhaps as a motivated, defensive strategy to justify their expected failure, in a process somewhat similar to self-handicapping attributions.

Motivational processes may also limit the negativity of self-judgments. In one study by Sedikides (1994), happy, neutral, or sad participants wrote a series of self-descriptive statements. Initially, judgments were affect congruent, but with the passage of time, negative self-judgments were spontaneously reversed, suggesting something like automatic mood-management strategy. We further investigated this 'spontaneous mood management' hypothesis (Forgas and Ciarrochi, 2002; Forgas et al., 2000) and also found that negative-mood effects on self-descriptions were spontaneously reversed over time. People who scored high on self-esteem were able to eliminate the negativity of their self-judgments very rapidly, while low self-esteem individuals continued to persevere with negative self-descriptions longer. It seems that there are automatic cognitive strategies people use to manage everyday mood fluctuations, spontaneously reversing affect congruence once a threshold value of affectivity is reached (Forgas and Ciarrochi, 2002).

### Affect as a resource

Interestingly, positive affect may serve as an important resource when people deal with aversive information about themselves. Feeling good may allow people to overcome defensiveness when dealing with potentially threatening information (Trope et al., 2001). Facing negative feedback often produces conflict, as we need to balance the cost of facing criticism with the benefits of acquiring useful feedback (Leary, 2000; Trope, 1986). Trope and Neter (1994) found that mood influences the relative weight people assign to the costs versus benefits of receiving negative feedback. Feeling good makes it easier to deal with threatening but diagnostic information, suggesting that positive mood functions as a resource. Additional experiments by Trope and Pomerantz (1998) and by Aspinwall (1998; Reed and Aspinwall, 1998) further confirmed that positive mood plays a role in facilitating the acquisition of useful self-knowledge.

However, it is only when the negative feedback is seen as potentially useful and constructive that people willingly undergo the emotional cost of acquiring it (Trope and Gervey, 1998). These effects may have important applied consequences, for example, when it comes to dealing with unwelcome but useful health-related messages (Raghunathan and Trope, 1999). It turns out that people in a positive mood not only selectively sought but also processed in greater detail and remembered better negatively valenced arguments about potential health risks.

### Some applied consequences: affect and health-related judgments

Affective influences on self-judgments can be especially important when it comes to health-related judgments (Salovey et al., 2001). Positive affect may promote more optimistic and adaptive attitudes, reduce the perceived severity of symptoms and also influence physical well-being (Salovey and Birnbaum, 1989). In contrast, illness is typically associated with more negative moods, thoughts, and judgments. Individuals experiencing negative affect also report more severe physical symptoms (Abele and Hermer, 1993; Croyle and Uretsky, 1987). Salovey and Birnbaum (1989) found that students who were suffering from cold or flu reported more severe symptoms and nearly twice as many aches and pains when made to feel sad than those made to feel happy – even though there were no differences between the two groups before the mood induction.

Happy persons typically judge themselves as better able to carry out health-promoting behaviors (Salovey and Birnbaum, 1989) and form more optimistic expectations (Forgas and Moylan, 1987; Mayer et al., 1992). Affective states may also influence the immune system and susceptibility to disease.

In conclusion, affect may have a strong mood-congruent influence on many self-related judgments, but these effects occur only when a degree of open and constructive processing is required, and there are no motivational forces to override affect congruence. Affect infusion seems to be greater in people who have low self-esteem, when judgments are related to peripheral rather than central self-conceptions, and when judgments require elaborate rather than simple processing. In addition to its dynamic influence on self-judgments, affect also plays an important role in the structure and organization of the self-concept (Deseno and Salovey, 1997; Niedenthal and Halberstadt, 2000) and people's ability to cope with adverse information (Trope et al., 2001).

### *Affective influences on intergroup judgments and stereotyping*

It has long been assumed that affect plays an important role in stereotyping and prejudice (for reviews, see Cooper, 1959; Haddock et al., 1993; Stangor et al., 1991). From psychoanalytic ideas and the frustration-aggression hypothesis, it was assumed that negative affect might contribute to intergroup discrimination and prejudice. Conditioning processes may also play a role in explaining how regularly encountering and associating certain groups in aversive situations can elicit negative emotions such as anger and resentment (Gaertner and Dovidio, 1986; Katz, 1976), just as evaluative reactions to individuals can be influenced by conditioning (Clore and Byrne, 1974; Griffitt, 1970; Zanna et al., 1970). Recently, cognitive theories have been invoked to explain similar effects. For example, Fiske and Pavelchak (1986) proposed that it is 'affective tags' linked to group representations that trigger an emotional response.

In turn, linking contact with out-group members to positive feelings may reduce negative attitudes and improve intergroup relations, according to the 'contact hypothesis' (Allport, 1954; Amir, 1969; Brewer and Miller, 1996; Jones, 1997; Stephan and Stephan, 1996). Furthermore, positive affect may also promote more inclusive cognitive categorizations, thus reducing intergroup distinctions (Dovidio et al., 1998; Isen et al., 1992). However, whether this effect is beneficial depends on whether the categories used are positive or negative and whether they are used to discriminate between or unify out-groups and in-groups. According to some recent studies, when group membership is of low relevance, positive mood may facilitate the use of in-group as opposed to out-group categories and increase intergroup discrimination (Forgas and Fiedler, 1996). The experience of anxiety may also amplify reliance on stereotypes, increasing the tendency to see out-groups in stereotypic ways (Stephan and Stephan, 1985, Wilder and Shapiro, 1989).

Recent experiments also found that trait anxiety can moderate the influence of negative affect on intergroup judgments (Ciarrochi and Forgas, 1999). Low trait-anxious whites in the USA reacted more negatively to a threatening black out-group when experiencing aversive mood. However, high trait-anxious individuals produced more positive judgments, suggesting that the combination of trait anxiety and negative affect triggered a more controlled, motivated processing strategy, leading to the reversal of socially undesirable intergroup judgments.

Different negative affective states have different effects on intergroup judgments. For example, sadness reduces, but anger and anxiety may increase, reliance on stereotypes (Bodenhausen et al., 1994b; Keltner et al., 1993; Raghunathan and Pham, 1999). The process of 'stereotyping' itself may involve at least four distinct cognitive operations (Gilbert and Hixon, 1991): the identification of the applicable category, activation of its contents, applying stereotyped features to the target, and correcting for stereotyping. Affect may influence stereotyping at each of the four stages of the stereotyping process.

For example, since positive moods often facilitate top-down, schematic processing (Bless, 2000; Bless and Fiedler, 2006; Fiedler, 2000), happy persons may produce less accurate social judgments (Forgas, 1998c; Sinclair and Mark, 1995) and are more likely to rely on stereotype information (Abele et al., 1998; Bless et al., 1996; Bodenhausen et al., 1994a; Forgas and Fiedler, 1996: Experiment 1; Park and Banaji, 1999). However, negative states other than sadness, such as anger or anxiety, may also increase reliance on stereotyping, according to evidence from several experiments (e.g., Bodenhausen et al., 1994b). Once a category is activated, affect may also influence the amount of stereotyped information people *access*. If processing resources are limited, fewer stereotyped details may be retrieved (Gilbert and Hixson, 1991). Given the highly prepared and automatic activation of stereotyped knowledge, affect may have only a limited influence on the amount of stereotyped knowledge activated. In the simplest instance, once activated, stereotypic beliefs can be directly used as the basis for a judgment, by functioning as a heuristic cue that eliminates the need for further processing. For example, we found that positive mood increased reliance on simple group stereotypes when making reward allocation judgments, but only when group membership was of low relevance (Forgas and Fiedler, 1996). At other times, stereotyped knowledge provides an initial influence on judgments that are likely to be supplemented and modified by other information (Bodenhausen et al., 1999; Chaiken and Maheswaran, 1994; Duncan, 1976).

Ultimately, a motivated tendency to *correct* judgments also influences stereotyping (Bodenhausen et al., 1998), as people correct or recompute what appears to be an undesirable judgment (Strack, 1992). Negative affect may facilitate a cautious, defensive interpersonal style (Forgas, 1999a, 1999b), and persons feeling sad, guilty or anxious seem to be more likely to engage in stereotype correction (Devine and Monteith, 1993; Lambert et al., 1997). Thus, negative affect sometimes functions as a warning, indicating the need for a motivated reassessment of potentially undesirable responses (Monteith, 1993). This alerting effect of negative mood is particularly strong for individuals high on trait anxiety (Ciarrochi and Forgas, 1999). Thus, affect plays a complex role in intergroup judgments, potentially influencing every stage of the stereotyping process. Contextual and situational factors again play a critical role in mediating these effects (Forgas, 1995a; 2002; Forgas et al., 2005; Martin, 2000).

### *Affect and attitudes*

Attitudes have long been regarded as a key construct in social psychology (Allport, 1954), comprising distinct cognitive, affective, and conative (behavioral) components (Eagly and Chaiken, 1993; see Chapter 7, this volume). Despite the affective character of attitudes, not enough is known about how affective states influence the generation, maintainance, organization, and expression of attitudes. Affective influences on attitude change and responses to persuasion received more attention (Petty et al., 2001) following early interest in the effectiveness of fear-arousing messages in producing attitude change (Boster and Mongeau, 1984; Ditto and Lopez, 1992; Janis and Feshbach, 1953).

Practitioners of rhetoric and persuasion have long believed that inducing an affective response is helpful in achieving attitude change. Studies confirmed that inducing positive affect promotes a positive response to persuasive messages (McGuire, 1985; Petty et al., 1991; Razran, 1940), although this effect is subject to important limitations (Bless et al., 1990; Mackie and Worth, 1989; Wegener et al., 1995). Affective influences on reactions to persuasion largely depend on how the message is processed (Petty et al., 1991, 2001). When people rely on superficial processing, affect might function as a heuristic cue and produce a mood-congruent response to the message.

Such predictions can be derived either from conditioning theories (Clore and Byrne, 1974; Griffitt, 1970; Razran, 1940), or from the affect-as-information model proposed by Clore et al. (1994, 2001) and others. Sinclair and Mark (1995) found that students were more likely to agree with a persuasive message about comprehensive examinations when they were feeling good (on a pleasant, sunny day) rather than feeling bad (asked on an unpleasant, rainy day). However, when people think more carefully about the message (for example, because the topic is involving), their reactions may be influenced by memory-based mechanisms. Petty et al. (1993) found that persuasive messages about a pen produced a more positive response when the audience was happy. However, when people were highly involved because they expected to choose and keep a pen, the effect was linked to more affect-congruent thoughts primed by the mood induction instead of heuristic thinking.

Individual differences are also important; people who habitually adopt elaborate thinking styles (they score high on need for cognition; Cacioppo and Petty, 1982) may be particularly prone to affect infusion when responding to persuasive arguments. The consequences of affective states may also be modified as a result of motivational factors. Theories such as the flexible correction model (FCM) proposed by Petty and Wegener (1993; Wegener and Petty, 1997) and integrative theories such as the affect-infusion model (Forgas, 2001a, 2001b) seek to explain the circumstances when motivated processing is likely to occur.

Perceived discrepancy or dissonance between attitudes and behaviors is another source of attitude change (Cooper and Fazio, 1984; Festinger, 1957; Harmon-Jones, 2001; Zanna and Cooper, 1974; see Chapter 10, this volume). Dissonance usually involves feelings of arousal and aversive affect, as discrepancy indicates uncertainty about the world (Harmon-Jones, 1999a, 2001; Harmon-Jones et al., 1996). Some versions of dissonance theory suggest that all dissonance is aversive; others suggest that dissonance is aversive only when consequences are 'real' and there is personal involvement (Cooper and Fazio, 1984). Evidence from appraisal research suggests that imagined consequences are often sufficient to trigger an affective reaction (Scherer, 1999). Other studies also found that negative affect increases dissonance reduction and attitude change even if the source of affect is unrelated (Kidd and Berkowitz, 1976; Rhodewalt and Comer, 1979). Once consonance is restored, the affective state also tends to improve (Burris et al., 1997; Elliot and Devine, 1994).

High self-esteem individuals seem better able to handle aversive affective states (Forgas et al., 2000; Harmon-Jones, 2001). We also know from self-discrepancy theory that different kinds of self-discrepancies evoke qualitatively distinct affective reactions (Higgins, 1989, 2001). Some studies suggest a direct link between discrepancy-produced negative affect and subsequent attitude change (Zanna and Cooper, 1974). Others, however, failed to find such a link (Elliot and Devine, 1994; Higgins et al., 1979), and even measures of arousal are not necessarily indicative of dissonance and attitude change (Elkin and Leippe, 1986; Harmon-Jones et al., 1996; Losch and Cacioppo, 1990). In conclusion, affect plays an important role in attitude change, influencing how people respond to persuasive messages, and how they resolve attitude–behaviour discrepancies, but these effects are again highly context sensitive.

### *Affective influences on interpersonal behaviors*

Humans are a gregarious species, and coordinating our interpersonal behaviors can be a demanding cognitive task (Heider, 1958; Pinker, 1997). As social interaction often demands open, constructive thinking, affective states may infuse our thoughts, plans, and, ultimately, behaviors. Positive affect may prime positive interpretations and produce more confident, friendly, and cooperative approach' behaviors, whereas negative affect may facilitate access to negative memories and produce more avoidant, defensive, or unfriendly attitudes and behaviors (Bower and Forgas, 2001; Eich and Macauley, 2000; Forgas, 1995a). The behavioral consequences of affect are now receiving increasing attention (Forgas, 2002). It seems that it is the very complexity and indeterminacy of many social situations that facilitate open, elaborate thinking, and promote the use of affectively primed interpretations in producing a response (Forgas, 2002).

We found, for example (Forgas and Gunawardena, 2001), that female undergraduates who were feeling good after watching a film behaved in a much more positive manner in a subsequent, unrelated interaction. They smiled more, communicated more effectively, disclosed more personal information, and generally behaved in a more poised, skilled, and rewarding manner, according to raters blind to the affect condition. Sad participants were rated as being less friendly, confident, relaxed, comfortable, active, interested, and competent than were happy participants. In other words, the mild affective consequences of watching a brief film seemed to have a significant subsequent influence on interpersonal behaviors that was readily detectable by observers.

### Requesting

How does affect influence strategic interpersonal behaviors, such as making a request? Requesting is a complex interpersonal task characterized by uncertainty and should thus require open, elaborate processing. Positive mood should prime a more confident, direct requesting style, and negative mood should lead to more cautious, polite requests (Forgas, 1999a). When happy or sad persons were asked to select among more or less polite requests they would use in easy or difficult social situations (Forgas, 1999a: Experiment 1), happy participants preferred more direct, impolite requests, while sad persons preferred more cautious and polite requests. Furthermore, mood effects on requesting were much stronger when the request situation was difficult and thus required more extensive, substantive processing. Mood had the same effect on open-ended requests (Forgas, 1999a: Experiment 2).

Do these mood effects also occur in real-life interactions? In an unobtrusive experiment (Forgas, 1999b: Experiment 2), participants first viewed happy or sad films. Next, in an apparently impromptu development, the experimenter casually asked them to get a file from a neighboring office. Their words in making the request were recorded by a concealed tape recorder, and the requests were subsequently analyzed for politeness and other qualities. Negative mood resulted in significantly more polite, elaborate, and hedging requests, whereas those in a positive mood used more direct and less polite strategies. An analysis of participants' later recall memory for the requests (indicating the extent of elaborate processing) showed that more elaborately processed requests were remembered better and were also more influenced by mood as predicted by models such as the AIM (Forgas, 2002).

### Responding to others

Spontaneous, impromptu reactions to social events also require constructive processing and should also be subject to affect infusion. For example, people are more willing to help others when feeling good after finding a coin in a telephone booth (Isen, 1984). Several recent field experiments carried out in a university library confirmed this prediction (Forgas, 1998b). Affect was induced by leaving folders containing funny or sad pictures (or text) on some unoccupied library desks. Students occupying the desks were surreptitiously observed as they exposed themselves to the mood induction. A few minutes later, another student (a confederate) made an unexpected polite or impolite request for several sheets of paper. Their responses were noted, and soon after, a second confederate asked them to complete a brief questionnaire assessing their perception and memory of the request and the requester. There was a clear mood-congruent pattern in responses. Sad people were less inclined to help, and evaluated the request and the requester more negatively. These mood effects were greater when the request was impolite and unconventional and thus required more elaborate and substantive processing. These results confirm that affect infusion into interpersonal behaviors is a real phenomenon that depends on how much constructive processing is required, in this case, to respond to more or less unusual, unconventional request forms.

### Negotiation

Even carefully planned social encounters such as negotiations may be open to affect infusion (Forgas, 1998a). In a series of studies, mood was induced before participants engaged in highly realistic interpersonal and intergroup negotiation. Happy participants were more confident, formed higher expectations about their success and made more optimistic and cooperative plans than did control or negative-mood participants. Furthermore, happy participants also achieved better outcomes. Interestingly, individuals who scored high on measures such as Machiavellianism and need for approval were less influenced by mood. It seems that affect infusion into interpersonal behaviors is reduced for individuals who habitually approach interpersonal tasks from a motivated, predetermined perspective that limits the degree of open, constructive thinking they employ. These findings support the principle that mood effects on social behaviors are dependent on processing strategies, often linked to enduring personality traits (Ciarrochi and Forgas, 1999, 2000; Ciarrochi et al., 2001).

### Being persuasive

Producing effective persuasive arguments is an important everyday task. We know that affect can influence information-processing strategies (Bless, 2000; Fiedler, 2000; Forgas, 1998a, 1998b), and it may be that negative affect may improve the quality of persuasive messages by focusing attention on situational details (Forgas et al., 2001). When we asked students feeling happy or sad to produce persuasive arguments either for or against popular or unpopular positions, mood had a significant influence on argument quality, as rated by observers. Negative mood produced higher quality and more persuasive arguments, consistent with the expected more externally oriented and bottom-up processing style associated with negative affect (Bless, 2000; Fiedler, 2001).

In another experiment, participants produced persuasive arguments in an interactive situation, writing their messages on a computer keyboard as if exchanging emails (Forgas, in press). Motivation was also manipulated, by offering some participants a significant reward for doing well (the chance to win highly desired movie passes). The persuasion task involved convincing the partner to participate in a boring experiment. Those in a negative mood again generated significantly higher quality arguments than the positive group. However, the provision of a reward reduced the size of mood effects on argument quality by imposing a strong motivational influence on how the task was approached.

### Self-disclosure

Self-disclosure is a critical aspect of skilled interpersonal behavior and essential for the development of rewarding intimate relationships (Forgas, 1985). Affective influences on self-disclosure were demonstrated in several experiments (Forgas, 2001b), when happy or sad participants indicated the order in which they would feel comfortable disclosing increasingly intimate information about themselves to a person they have just met. Happy people preferred more intimate disclosure topics, suggesting a generally more confident and optimistic interpersonal style. In subsequent experiments, participants interacted with another person in a neighboring room through a computer keyboard, as if exchanging emails. Using this 'bogus partner' method, the computer was preprogrammed to respond in ways that indicated either consistently high or low levels of self-disclosure. Individuals in a positive mood produced more intimate disclosure, revealed more positive information about themselves, and formed more positive impressions about the 'partner', but only when the 'partner' was also disclosing. Positive mood did not increase the intimacy of self-disclosure when the partner was not disclosing.

Why do these effects occur? In uncertain and unpredictable social encounters, we need to rely on open, constructive thinking to formulate our plans and guide their interpersonal behaviors. Affect can prime access to more affect-congruent thoughts, and these ideas should ultimately influence plans and behaviors. Thus, affective influences on social behaviors depend on how much open, constructive processing is required to deal with a demanding interpersonal task. Whenever motivated, closed information processing is used, mood effects are reduced. The same mechanisms of affect infusion seem to influence the way people formulate personal requests, the way they respond to approaches by others, the way they plan and execute negotiations, and the way they produce persuasive messages and self-disclose (Forgas, 1998b, 1998c, 1999a, 1999b).

## Summary and conclusions

This chapter reviewed evidence for the critical role that affective states play in social thinking and behavior. We considered both the cognitive *antecedents* and the *consequences* of affect in social situations. Many social encounters elicit powerful emotional responses, and we reviewed the role of appraisal processes in producing affective reactions. Affective states also have a significant influence on how people perceive and interpret social situations, the judgments they form, and how they plan and execute strategic interpersonal behaviors. Many of these effects are highly context sensitive, and there is also growing evidence that different information-processing strategies play a critical role in explaining the presence or absence of affect infusion into social thinking and behavior. Integrative theories, such as the affect-infusion model (Forgas, 1995a), offer a process-based explanation of when, how, and why affect infusion occurs.

A number of the studies indicate that, surprisingly, more extensive, substantive processing often enhances mood congruity effects (Forgas, 1992b, 1994, 1995b; Nasby, 1994, 1996; Sedikides, 1995). However, affect infusion is often absent when a social task can be performed by either a direct-access or a motivated-processing strategy that limits the use of affectively primed information in producing a response (Fiedler, 1991; Forgas,

1995a). These effects are not limited to controlled laboratory environments, as unobtrusive field experiments showed that affect infusion occurs in many real-life situations.

Most investigations of the cognitive and behavioral consequences of affect looked at mild, undifferentiated mood states, whereas research on the antecedents of emotion covers a wide variety of specific affective states beyond positivity and negativity. We believe that an important direction for future research is to integrate more explicitly research on the elicitation of emotion into the study of the influences of emotion on social-cognitive processes. Research on the social antecedents of emotion highlighted the distinctive motivational functions that discrete emotional states may serve. However, the judgmental and behavioral consequences of specific appraised emotions received far less attention. When different emotions of the same valence (for example, anger versus sadness versus fear) have been compared (e.g., Bodenhausen et al., 1994a; Keltner et al., 1993; Raghunathan and Pham, 1999), the results show that they produce different cognitive consequences, just as discrete-emotion theorists assumed (e.g., Frijda, 1986; Izard, 1977). Integrative models such as the AIM (e.g., Forgas, 1995a, 2002) can handle the subtlety and context dependence of affective influences on social cognition and behavior. An extension of such models to incorporate our growing understanding of the motivational properties of distinct emotional states should produce a welcome integration across these two branches of affect research.

In conclusion, evidence suggests a closely interactive relationship between affective states and information-processing strategies as the key to understanding affective influences on thinking, judgments, and interpersonal behavior. Cognitive processes are intimately involved in the generation of affective responses (Smith and Kirby, 2000), and the production of affective influences on judgments and behavior (Forgas, 2002). A number of contextual influences mediate and moderate these effects. In view of the fact that most of the research on affect in social psychology is less than twenty years old, a great deal has been achieved. However, we are still far from fully understanding the multifaceted influences that affect has on social thinking, judgments, and interpersonal behavior. Hopefully, this handbook, and the present chapter in particular, will stimulate further interest in this fascinating and rapidly developing area of inquiry.

## Acknowledgments

This work was supported by a Special Investigator award from the Australian Research Council, and the Research Prize by the Alexander von Humboldt Foundation to Joseph P. Forgas. For further information on this research project, see also website at www.psy.unsw.edu.au/~joef/jforgas.htm.

### SUMMARY

This chapter reviewed the most recent developments in research of affectivity and how affect influences everyday thinking and behavior. We saw that the interpretation and appraisal of affective states involves complex cognitive processes, and that the experience of affective states is closely linked to the social situations in which they arise. We have also surveyed historical approaches to studying affect, including the psychoanalytic, conditioning, and cognitive frameworks. We have seen that even mild and unconscious affective states, such as moods, can have a significant and predictable influence on the content of people's thinking and judgments (*what* they think), as well as the process of how they deal with social information (*how* they think). We have seen that mood states can influence the content of people's memories, associations and judgments, and the way they evaluate themselves and their social relationships. In the second half of the chapter, we surveyed a number of experiments showing that mood states also influence strategic interpersonal behaviors, such as the way people communicate with each other, make requests, use bargaining strategies, and disclose personal information to others. These effects can have a major influence on social behavior, both in our working and in our private lives.

## References

Abele, A., Gendolla, G.H.E., and Petzold, P. (1998) 'Positive Mood and In-Group-Out-Group Differentiation in a Minimal Group Setting', *Personality and Social Psychology Bulletin*, 24: 1343–57.

Abele, A. and Hermer, P. (1993) 'Mood Influences on Health-Related Judgments: Appraisal of Own Health versus Appraisal of Unhealthy Behaviours', *European Journal of Social Psychology*, 23: 613–25.

Abele, A. and Petzold, P. (1994) 'How Does Mood Operate in an Impression Formation Task? An Information

Integration Approach', *European Journal of Social Psychology*, 24: 173–88.

Adolphs, R. and Damasio, A. (2001) 'The Interaction of Affect and Cognition: A Neurobiological Perspective', in J.P. Forgas (ed.), *The Handbook of Affect and Social Cognition*. Mahwah, NJ: Erlbaum, pp. 27–49.

Allport, G.W. (1954) *The Nature of Prejudice*. Reading, MA: Addison Wesley.

Amir, Y. (1969) 'Contact Hypothesis in Ethnic Relations', *Psychological Bulletin*, 71: 319–42.

Anderson, J.R. (1983) *The Architecture of Cognition*. Cambridge, MA: Harvard University Press.

Arnold, M.B. (1960) *Emotion and Personality* (2 vols). New York: Columbia University Press.

Aspinwall, L.G. (1998) 'Rethinking the Role of Positive Affect in Self-Regulation', *Motivation and Emotion*, 22: 1–32.

Bargh, J.A. (1989) 'Conditional Automaticity: Varieties of Automatic Influence in Social Perception and Cognition', in J.S. Uleman and J.A. Bargh (eds), *Unintended Thought*. New York: The Guilford Press, pp. 3–51.

Baumeister, R.F. (1993) *Self-Esteem: The Puzzle of Low Self-Regard*. New York: Plenum Press.

Baumeister, R.F. (1998) 'The Self', in D.T. Gilbert, S.T. Fiske, and G. Lindzey (eds), *The Handbook of Social Psychology*. New York: Oxford University Press, pp. 680–740.

Berkowitz, L., Jaffee, S., Jo, E., and Troccoli, B.T. (2000) 'On the Correction of Feeling-Induced Judgmental Biases', in J.P. Forgas (ed.), *Feeling and Thinking: The Role of Affect in Social Cognition*. New York: Cambridge University Press, pp. 131–52.

Blascovich, J. and Mendes, W.B. (2000) 'Challenge and Threat Appraisals: The Role of Affective Cues', in J.P. Forgas (ed.), *Feeling and Thinking: The Role of Affect in Social Cognition*. New York: Cambridge University Press, pp. 59–82.

Bless, H. and Fiedler, K. (2006) 'Mood and the Regulation of Information Processing and Behavior', in: J.P. Forgas (ed.), *Affect in Social Thinking and Behavior*. New York: Psychology Press, pp. 78–86.

Bless, H. (2000) 'The Interplay of Affect and Cognition: The Mediating Role of General Knowledge Structures', in J.P. Forgas (ed.), *Feeling and Thinking: The Role of Affect in Social Cognition*. New York: Cambridge University Press, pp. 201–22.

Bless, H., Bohner, G., Schwarz, N., and Strack, F. (1990) 'Mood and Persuasion: A Cognitive Response Analysis', *Personality and Social Psychology Bulletin*, 16: 331–45.

Bless, H., Schwarz, N., and Wieland, R. (1996) 'Mood and the Impact of Category Membership and Individuating Information', *European Journal of Social Psychology*, 26: 935–59.

Bodenhausen, G.V. (1993) 'Emotions, Arousal, and Stereotypic Judgments: A Heuristic Model of Affect and Stereotyping', in D.M. Mackie and D.L. Hamilton (eds), *Affect, Cognition, and Stereotyping*. San Diego, CA: Academic Press, pp. 13–37.

Bodenhausen, G.V., Mussweiler, T., Gabriel, S., and Moreno, K.N. (2001) 'Affective Influences on Stereotyping and Intergroup Relations', in J.P. Forgas (ed.), *The Handbook of Affect and Social Cognition*. Mahwah, NJ: Erlbaum, pp. 147–72.

Bodenhausen, G.V. and Macrae, C.N. (1998) 'Stereotype Activation and Inhibition', in R.S. Wyer, Jr. (ed.), *Stereotype Activation and Inhibition: Advances in Social Cognition* (vol. 11). Mahwah, NJ: Erlbaum. pp. 1–52.

Bodenhausen, G.V. and Moreno, K.N. (2000) 'How Do I Feel about Them? The Role of Affective Reactions in Intergroup Perception', in H. Bless and J.P. Forgas (eds), *The Role of Subjective States in Social Cognition and Behavior*. Philadelphia, PA: Psychology Press. pp. 283–303.

Bodenhausen, GV., Kramer, G.P., and Süsser, K. (1994a) 'Happiness and Stereotypic Thinking in Social Judgment', *Journal of Personality and Social Psychology*, 66: 621–32.

Bodenhausen, G.V., Macrae, C.N., and Milne, A.B. (1998) 'Disregarding Social Stereotypes: Implications for Memory, Judgment, and Behavior', in J.M. Golding and C.M. MacLeod (eds), *Intenational Forgetting: Interdisciplinary Approaches*. Mahwah, NJ: Erlbaum, pp. 349–68.

Bodenhausen, G.V., Macrae, C.N., and Sherman, J.W. (1999) 'On the Dialectics of Discrimination: Dual Processes in Social Stereotyping', in S. Chaiken and Y. Trope (eds), *Dual-Process Theories in Social Psychology*. New York: Guilford, pp. 271–90.

Bodenhausen, G.V., Sheppard, L.A., and Kramer, G.P. (1994b) 'Negative Affect and Social Judgment: The Differential Impact of Anger and Sadness', *European Journal of Social Psychology*, 24: 45–62.

Boster, F.J. and Mongeau, P. (1984) 'Fear-Arousing Persuasive Messages', in R.N. Bostrom (ed.), *Communication Yearbook* (vol. 8). Beverly Hills, CA: Sage, pp. 330–75.

Bower, G.H. (1981) 'Mood and Memory', *American Psychologist*, 36: 129–48.

Bower, G.H. (1983) 'Affect and Cognition', *Philosophical Transactions of the Royal Society of London B*, 302: 387–402.

Bower, G.H. and Forgas, J.P. (2001) 'Mood and Social Memory', in J.P. Forgas (ed.), *The Handbook of Affect and Social Cognition*. Mahwah, NJ: Erlbaum. pp. 95–120.

Bower, G.H. and Mayer, J.D. (1989) 'In Search of Mood-dependent Retrieval', *Journal of Social Behavior and Personality*, 4: 121–56.

Bradley, P.P. and Mathews, A.M. (1983) 'Negative Self Schemata in Clinical Depression', *British Journal of Clinical Psychology*, 22: 173–81.

Brewer, M.B. and Miller, N. (1996) *Intergroup Relations*. Pacific Grove, CA: Brooks/Cole.

Brown, J.D. and Mankowski, T.A. (1993) 'Self-Esteem, Mood, and Self-Evaluation: Changes in the Mood and the Way You See You', *Journal of Personality and Social Psychology*, 64: 421–30.

Burke, M. and Mathews, A.M. (1992) 'Autobiographical Memory and Clinical Anxiety', *Cognition and Emotion*, 6: 23–35.

Burris, C.T., Harmon-Jones, E., and Tarpley, W.R. (1997) '"By Faith Alone": Religious Agitation and Cognitive Dissonance', *Basic and Applied Social Psychology*, 19: 17–31.

Byrne, D. and Clore, G.L. (1970) 'A Reinforcement Model of Evaluation Responses', *Personality: An International Journal*, 1: 103–28.

Cacioppo, J.T. and Petty, R.E. (1982) 'The Need for Cognition', *Journal of Personality and Social Psychology*, 42: 116–31.

Campbell, J.D., Trapnell, P.D., Heine, S.J., Katz, I.M., Lavallee, L.F., and Lehman, D.R. (1996) 'Self-Concept Clarity: Measurement, Personality Correlates, and Cultural Boundaries', *Journal of Personality and Social Psychology*, 70: 141–56.

Cannon, W.B. (1929) *Bodily Changes in Pain, Hunger, Fear, and Rage*, 2nd edn. New York: Appleton-Century.

Cervone, D., Kopp, D.A., Schaumann, L., and Scott, W.D. (1994) 'Mood, Self-Efficacy, and Performance Standards: Lower Moods Induce Higher Standards for Performance', *Journal of Personality and Social Psychology*, 67: 499–512.

Chaiken, S. and Maheswaran, D. (1994) 'Heuristic Processing Can Bias Systematic Processing: Effects of Source Credibility, Argument Ambiguity, and Task Importance on Attitude Judgment', *Journal of Personality and Social Psychology*, 66: 460–73.

Chan, N.Y.M. and Forgas, J.P. (2001) 'Affective Influences on Judgmental Heuristics'. Unpublished manuscript, University of New South Wales, Sydney, Australia.

Ciarrochi, J.V. and Forgas, J.P. (1999) 'On Being Tense Yet Tolerant: The Paradoxical Effects of Trait Anxiety and Aversive Mood on Intergroup Judgments', *Group Dynamics: Theory, Research and Practice*, 3: 227–38.

Ciarrochi, J.V. and Forgas, J.P. (2000) 'The Pleasure of Possessions: Affect and Consumer Judgments', *European Journal of Social Psychology*, 30: 631–49.

Ciarrochi, J.V. Forgas, J.P., and Mayer, J. (eds) (2001) *Emotional Intelligence: A Scientific Approach*. Philadelphia, PA: Psychology Press.

Clark, M.S. and Isen, A.M. (1982) 'Towards Understanding the Relationship between Feeling States and Social Behavior', in A.H. Hastorf and A.M. Isen (eds), *Cognitive Social Psychology*. New York: Elsevier-North Holland, pp. 73–108.

Clore, G.L. and Byrne, D. (1974) 'The Reinforcement Affect Model of Attraction', in T.L. Huston (ed.), *Foundations of Interpersonal Attraction*. New York, NY: Academic Press, pp. 143–70

Clore, G.L. Gasper, K., and Garvin, E. (2001) 'Affect as Information', in J.P. Forgas (ed.), *The Handbook of Affect and Social Cognition*. Mahwah, NJ: Erlbaum, pp. 95–120.

Clore, G.L., Schwarz, N., and Conway, M. (1994) 'Affective Causes and Consequences of Social Information Processing', in R.S. Wyer and T.K. Srull (eds), *Handbook of Social Cognition*, 2nd edn. Mahwah, NJ: Erlbaum.

Clore, G.L. and Tamir, M. (2002) 'Affect as Embodied Information', *Psychological Inquiry*, 13: 37–44.

Cooper, J.B. (1959) 'Emotion in Prejudice', *Science*, 130, 314–18.

Cooper, J. and Fazio, R.H. (1984) 'A New Look at Dissonance Theory', in L. Berkowitz (ed.), *Advances in Experimental Social Psychology* (vol. 17). San Diego, CA: Academic Press, pp. 229–66.

Croyle, R.T. and Uretsky, M.D. (1987) 'Effects of Mood on Self-Appraisal of Health Status', *Health Psychology*, 6: 239–53.

Damasio, A.R. (1994) *Descartes' Error*. New York: Grosste/Putnam.

Darwin, C. (1965) *The Expression of Emotions in Man and Animals*. Chicago, IL: University of Chicago Press (original work published in 1872).

DeSteno, D.A. and Salovey, P. (1997) 'The Effects of Mood on the Structure of the Self-Concept', *Cognition and Emotion*, 11: 351–72.

Devine, P.G. and Monteith, M.J. (1993) 'The Role of Discrepancy-Associated Affect in Prejudice Reduction', in D.M. Mackie and D.L. Hamilton (eds), *Affect, Cognition, and Stereotyping: Interactive Processes in Group Perception*. San Diego, CA: Academic Press, pp. 317–44.

Ditto, P.H. and Lopez, D.F. (1992) 'Motivated Skepticism: Use of Differential Decision Criteria for Preferred and Nonpreferred Conclusions', *Journal of Personality and Social Psychology*, 63: 568–84.

Dovidio, J.F., Gaertner, S.L., Isen, A.M., and Lowrance, R. (1995) 'Group Representations and Intergroup Bias: Positive Affect, Similarity, and Group Size', *Personality and Social Psychology Bulletin*, 18: 856–65.

Dovidio, J.F., Gaertner, S.L., Isen, A.M., Rust, M., and Guerra, P. (1998) 'Positive Affect, Cognition, and the Reduction of Intergroup Bias', in C. Sedikides, J. Schopler, and C.A. Insko (eds), *Intergroup Cognition and Intergroup Behavior*. Mahwah, NJ: Erlbaum. pp. 337–66.

Duncan, B.L. (1976) 'Differential Social Perception and Attribution of Intergroup Violence: Testing the Lower Limits of Stereotyping of Blacks', *Journal of Personality and Social Psychology*, 34: 590–8.

Eagly, A.H. and Chaiken, S. (1993) *The Psychology of Attitudes*. New York: Harcourt Brace Jovanovich.

Eich, E. and Forgas, J.P. (2003) 'Mood Congruence and Mood Dependence in Cognition and Memory', in I.B. Weiner (ed.), *Comprehensive Handbook of Psychology* (vol. 3), *Experimental Psychology* (A.F. Healy and R.W. Proctor, eds). New York: John Wiley.

Eich, E. and Macauley, D. (2000) 'Fundamental Factors in Mood-Dependent Memory', in J.P. Forgas (ed.), *Feeling and Thinking: The Role of Affect in Social Cognition*. New York: Cambridge University Press. pp. 109–30.

Eich, E., Kihlstrom, J.F., Bower, G.H., Forgas, J.P., and Niedenthal, P. (2001) *Cognition and Emotion*. New York: Oxford University Press.

Elkin, R.A. and Leippe, M.R. (1986) 'Physiological Arousal, Dissonance, and Attitude Change: Evidence for a Dissonance–Arousal Link and a "Don't Remind Me" Effect', *Journal of Personality and Social Psychology*, 51: 55–65.

Elliot, A.J. and Devine, P.G. (1994) 'On the Motivation Nature of Cognitive Dissonance: Dissonance as Psychological Discomfort', *Journal of Personality and Social Psychology*, 67: 382–94.

Ellis, H.C. and Ashbrook, T.W. (1988) 'Resource Allocation Model of the Effects of Depressed Mood State on Memory', in K. Fiedler and J.P. Forgas (eds), *Affect, Cognition and Social Behaviour*. Toronto: Hogrefe, pp. 25–43.

Ellsworth, P.C. and Smith, C.A. (1988a) 'From Appraisal to Emotion: Differences among Unpleasant Feelings', *Motivation and Emotion*, 12: 271–302.

Ellsworth, P.C. and Smith, C.A. (1988b) 'Shades of Joy: Patterns of Appraisal Differentiating Pleasant Emotions', *Cognition and Emotion*, 2: 301–31.

Esses, V.M. and Zanna, M.P. (1995) 'Mood and the Expression of Ethnic Stereotypes', *Journal of Personality and Social Psychology*, 69: 1052–68.

Feshbach, S. and Singer, R.D. (1957) 'The Effects of Fear Arousal and Suppression of Fear upon Social Perception', *Journal of Abnormal and Social Psychology*, 55: 283–8.

Festinger, L. (1957) *A Theory of Cognitive Dissonance*. Palo Alto, CA: Stanford University Press.

Fiedler, K. (1990) 'Mood-Dependent Selectivity in Social Cognition', in W. Stroebe and M. Hewstone (eds), *European Review of Social Psychology* (vol. 1). New York: Wiley, pp. 1–32.

Fiedler, K. (1991) 'On the Task, the Measures and the Mood in Research on Affect and Social Cognition', in J.P. Forgas (ed.), *Emotion and Social Judgments*. Oxford: Pergamon, pp. 83–104.

Fiedler, K. (2000) 'Towards an Integrative Account of Affect and Cognition Phenomena Using the BIAS Computer Algorithm', in J.P. Forgas (ed.), *Feeling and Thinking: The Role of Affect in Social Cognition*. New York: Cambridge University Press, pp. 223–52.

Fiedler, K. (2001) 'Affective Influences on Social Information Processing', in J.P. Forgas (ed.), *The Handbook of Affect and Social Cognition*. Mahwah, NJ: Erlbaum, pp. 163–85.

Fiedler, K. (2002) 'Mood-Dependent Processing Strategies from a Meta-Theoretical Perspective', *Psychological Inquiry*, 13: 49–53.

Fiedler, K. and Bless, H. (2001) 'The Formation of Beliefs in the Interface of Affective and Cognitive Processes', in N. Frijda, A. Manstead and S. Bem (eds), *The Influence of Emotions on Beliefs*. New York, NY: Cambridge University Press, pp.

Fiedler, K. and Forgas, J.P. (eds) (1988) *Affect, Cognition and Social Behavior*. Toronto: Hogrefe International.

Fiedler, K. and Forgas, J.P. (eds) (1988) *Affect, Cognition, and Social Behavior: New Evidence and Integrative Attempts*. Toronto: Hogrefe.

Fiedler, K. and Stroehm, W. (1986) 'What Kind of Mood Influences What Kind of Memory: The Role of Arousal and Information Structure', *Memory and Cognition*, 14: 181–8.

Fiske, S.T. and Pavelchak, M.A. (1986) 'Category-Based versus Piecemeal-Based Affective Responses: Developments in Schema-Triggered Affect', in R.M. Sorrentino and E.T. Higgins (eds), *Handbook of Motivation and Cognition* (vol. 1). New York: Guilford, pp. 167–203.

Forgas, J.P. (1979) *Social Episodes: The Study of Interaction Routines*. London: Academic Press.

Forgas, J.P. (1982) 'Episode Cognition: Internal Representations of Interaction Routines', in L. Berkowitz (ed.), *Advances in Experimental Social Psychology*. New York: Academic Press, pp. 59–104.

Forgas, J.P. (1985) *Interpersonal Behaviour: The Psychology of Social Interaction*. Sydney and Oxford: Pergamon Press.

Forgas, J.P. (1989) 'Mood Effects on Decision Making Strategies', *Australian Journal of Psychology*, 41: 197–214.

Forgas, J.P. (1990) 'Affective Influences on Individual and Group Judgments', *European Journal of Social Psychology*, 20: 441–53.

Forgas, J.P. (ed.) (1991a) *Emotion and Social Judgments*. Oxford: Pergamon.

Forgas, J.P. (1991b) 'Mood Effects on Partner Choice: Role of Affect in Social Decisions', *Journal of Personality and Social Psychology*, 61: 708–20.

Forgas, J.P. (1992a) Affect in Social Judgments and Decisions: A Multi-Process Model', in M. Zanna (ed.), *Advances in Experimental Social Psychology* (vol. 25). New York: Academic Press, pp. 227–75.

Forgas, J.P. (1992b) 'On Bad Mood and Peculiar People: Affect and Person Typicality in Impression Formation', *Journal of Personality and Social Psychology*, 62: 863–75.

Forgas, J.P. (1993) 'On Making Sense of Odd Couples: Mood Effects on the Perception of Mismatched Relationships', *Personality and Social Psychology Bulletin*, 19: 59–71.

Forgas, J.P. (1994) 'Sad and Guilty? Affective Influences on the Explanation of Conflict Episodes', *Journal of Personality and Social Psychology*, 66: 56–68.

Forgas, J.P. (1995a) 'Mood and Judgment: The Affect Infusion Model (AIM)', *Psychological Bulletin*, 117 (1): 39–66.

Forgas, J.P. (1995b) 'Strange Couples: Mood Effects on Judgments and Memory about Prototypical and Atypical Targets', *Personality and Social Psychology Bulletin*, 21: 747–65.

Forgas, J.P. (1998a) 'On Feeling Good and Getting Your Way: Mood Effects on Negotiation Strategies and Outcomes', *Journal of Personality and Social Psychology*, 74: 565–77.

Forgas, J.P. (1998b) 'Asking Nicely? Mood Effects on Responding to More or Less Polite Requests', *Personality and Social Psychology Bulletin*, 24: 173–85.

Forgas, J.P. (1998c) 'Happy and Mistaken? Mood Effects on the Fundamental Attribution Error', *Journal of Personality and Social Psychology*, 75: 318–31.

Forgas, J.P. (1999a) 'On Feeling Good and Being Rude: Affective Influences on Language Use and Request Formulations', *Journal of Personality and Social Psychology*, 76: 928–39.

Forgas, J.P. (1999b) 'Feeling and Speaking: Mood Effects on Verbal Communication Strategies', *Personality and Social Psychology Bulletin*, 25: 850–63.

Forgas, J.P. (ed.) (2000) *Feeling and Thinking: The Role of Affect in Social Cognition.* New York: Cambridge University Press.

Forgas, J.P. (ed.) (2001a) *The Handbook of Affect and Social Cognition.* Mahwah, NJ: Erlbaum.

Forgas, J.P. (2001b) 'Mood Effects on Self-Disclosure Strategies'. Unpublished manuscript, University of New South Wales, Sydney, Australia.

Forgas, J.P. (2001c) 'Feeling Good but Getting It Wrong? Affective Influences on the Accuracy of Eyewitness Memories'. Unpublished manuscript, University of New South Wales, Australia.

Forgas, J.P. (2002) 'Feeling and Doing: Affective Influences on Interpersonal Behavior', *Psychological Inquiry*, 13: 1–28.

Forgas, J.P. (in press) 'When Sad is Better than Happy: The Benefits of Mild Dysphoria in Interpersonal Situations', *Journal of Experimental Social Psychology.*

Forgas, J.P. and Bower, G.H. (1987) 'Mood Effects on Person Perception Judgements', *Journal of Personality and Social Psychology*, 53: 53–60.

Forgas, J.P., Bower, G.H., and Krantz, S. (1984) 'The Influence of Mood on Perceptions of Social Interactions', *Journal of Experimental Social Psychology*, 20: 497–513.

Forgas, J.P. Bower, G.H., and Moylan, S.J. (1990) 'Praise or Blame? Affective Influences on Attributions for Achievement', *Journal of Personality and Social Psychology*, 59: 809–18.

Forgas, J.P. and Ciarrochi, J. (2000) 'Affect Infusion and Affect Control: The Interactive Role of Conscious and Unconscious Processing Strategies in Mood Management', in Y. Rossetti and Antti Revonsuo (eds), *Beyond Dissociation: Interaction between Dissociated Implicit and Explicit Processing.* Amsterdam: John Benjamins, pp. 243–71.

Forgas, J.P. and Ciarrochi, J.V. (2002) 'On Managing Moods: Evidence for the Role of Homeostatic Cognitive Strategies in Affect Regulation', *Personality and Social Psychology Bulletin*, 28: 336–45.

Forgas, J.P., Ciarrochi, J.V., and Moylan, S.J. (2000) 'Subjective Experience and Mood Regulation: The Role of Information Processing Strategies', in H. Bless and J.P. Forgas (eds), *The Message Within: The Role of Subjective Experience in Social Cognition.* Philadelphia, PA: Psychology Press.

Forgas, J.P. Ciarrochi, J.V., and Moylan, S.J. (2001) 'Affective Influences on the Production of Persuasive Messages'. Unpublished manuscript, University of New South Wales, Sydney, Australia.

Forgas, J.P. and Fiedler, K. (1996) 'Us and Them: Mood Effects on Intergroup Discrimination', *Journal of Personality and Social Psychology*, 70: 36–52.

Forgas, J.P. and George, J.M. (2001) 'Affective Influences on Judgments and Behavior in Organizations: An Information Processing Perspective', *Organizational Behavior and Human Decision Processes*, 86*:* 3–34.

Forgas, J.P. and Gunawardena, A. (2001) 'Affective Influences on Spontaneous Interpersonal Behaviors'. Unpublished manuscript, University of New South Wales, Sydney, Australia.

Forgas, J.P., Levinger, G., and Moylan, S. (1994) 'Feeling Good and Feeling Close: The Effects of Mood on Relationship Perception', *Personal Relationships*, 2: 165–84.

Forgas, J.P. and Moylan, S.J. (1987) 'After the Movies: The Effects of Transient Mood States on Social Judgments', *Personality and Social Psychology Bulletin*, 13: 478–89.

Forgas, J.P. and Moylan, S.J. (1991) 'Affective Influences on Stereotype Judgments', *Cognition and Emotion*, 5: 379–97.

Forgas, J.P. Vargas, P. and Laham, S. (2005) 'Mood Effects on Eyewitness Memory: Affective Influences on Susceptibility to Misinformation', *Journal of Experimental Social Psychology*, 41: 574–588.

Frijda, N. (1986) *The Emotions*. Cambridge: Cambridge University Press.

Frijda, N.H., Kuipers, P., and ter Schure, E. (1989) 'Relations among Emotion, Appraisal, and Emotional Action Readiness', *Journal of Personality and Social Psychology*, 57: 212–28.

Gaertner, S.L. and Dovidio, J.F. (1986) 'The Aversive Form of Racism', in J.F. Dovidio and S.L. Gaertner (eds), *Prejudice, Discrimination, and Racism.* San Diego, CA: Academic Press, pp. 91–125.

Gilbert, D.T. and Hixon, J.G. (1991) 'The Trouble of Thinking: Activation and Application of Stereotypic Beliefs', *Journal of Personality and Social Psychology*, 60: 509–17.

Gilbert, D.T. and Wilson, T.D. (2000) 'Miswanting: Some Problems in the Forecasting of Future Affective States', in J.P. Forgas (ed.), *Feeling and Thinking: The Role of Affect in Social Cognition.* New York: Cambridge University Press, pp. 178–200.

Gouaux, C. (1971) 'Induced Affective States and Interpersonal Attraction', *Journal of Personality and Social Psychology*, 20: 37–43.

Gouaux, C. and Summers, K. (1973) 'Interpersonal Attraction as a Function of Affective States and Affective Change', *Journal of Research in Personality*, 7: 254–60.

Griffitt, W. (1970) 'Environmental Effects on Interpersonal Behavior: Ambient Effective Temperature and Attraction', *Journal of Personality and Social Psychology*, 15: 240–4.

Griner, L.A. and Smith, C.A. (2000) 'Contributions of Motivational Orientation to Appraisal and Emotion', *Personality and Social Psychology Bulletin*, 26: 727–40.

Haddock, G., Zanna, M.P., and Esses, V. (1994) 'Mood and the Expression of Intergroup Attitudes: The Moderating Role of Affect Intensity', *European Journal of Social Psychology*, 24: 189–205.

Haddock, G., Zanna, M.P., and Esses, V.M. (1993) 'Assessing the Structure of Prejudicial Attitudes: The Case of Attitudes toward Homosexuals', *Journal of Personality and Social Psychology*, 65: 1105–18.

Haidt, J. (2002) '"Dialogue between My Head and My Heart': Affective Influences on Moral Judgment', *Psychological Inquiry*, 13: 54–6.

Harmon-Jones, E. (1999) 'Toward an Understanding of the Motivation Underlying Dissonance Effects: Is the Production of Aversive Consequences Necessary?', in E. Harmon-Jones and J. Mills, *Cognitive Dissonance: Progress on a Pivotal Theory in Social Psychology*. Washington, DC: American Psychological Association, pp. 71–99.

Harmon-Jones, E. (2001) 'The Role of Affect in Cognitive Dissonance Processes', in J.P. Forgas (ed.), *The Handbook of Affect and Social Cognition*. Mahwah, NJ: Erlbaum, pp. 237–55.

Harmon-Jones, E., Brehm, J.W., Greenberg, J., Simon, L., and Nelson, D.E. (1996) 'Evidence that the Production of Aversive Consequences Is Not Necessary to Create Cognitive Dissonance', *Journal of Personality and Social Psychology*, 70: 5–16.

Heider, F. (1958) *The Psychology of Interpersonal Relations*. New York: Wiley.

Hertel, G. and Fiedler, K. (1994) 'Affective and Cognitive Influences in a Social Dilemma Game', *European Journal of Social Psychology*, 24: 131–45.

Higgins, E.T. (1989) 'Self-Discrepancy Theory: What Patterns of Self-Beliefs Cause People to Suffer?', in L. Berkowitz (ed.), *Advances in Experimental Social Psychology*, 22: 93–136.

Higgins, E.T. (2001) 'Promotion and Prevention Experiences: Relating Emotions to Non-Emotional Motivational States', in Forgas, J.P. (ed.), *The Handbook of Affect and Social Cognition*. Mahwah, NJ: Erlbaum, pp. 186–211.

Higgins, E.T., Rhodewalt, F., and Zanna, M.P. (1979) 'Dissonance Motivation: Its Nature, Persistence, and Reinstatement', *Journal of Experimental Social Psychology*, 15: 16–34.

Hilgard, E.R. (1980) 'The Trilogy of Mind: Cognition, Affection, and Conation', *Journal of the History of the Behavioral Sciences*, 16: 107–17.

Isen, A.M. (1984) 'Towards Understanding the Role of Affect in Cognition', in R.S. Wyer and T.K. Srull (eds), *Handbook of Social Cognition* (vol. 3). Hillsdale, NJ: Erlbaum, pp. 179–236.

Isen, A.M. (1987) 'Positive Affect, Cognitive Processes and Social Behaviour', in L. Berkowitz (ed.), *Advances in Experimental Social Psychology* (vol. 20). New York: Academic Press, pp. 203–53.

Isen, A.M., Niedenthal, P. and Cantor, N. (1992) 'An Influence of Positive Affect on Social Categorization', *Motivation and Emotion*, 16: 65–78.

Isen, A.M. and Daubman, K.A. (1984) 'The Influence of Affect on Categorization', *Journal of Personality and Social Psychology*, 47: 1206–17.

Ito, T. and Cacioppo, J. (2001) 'Affect and Attitudes: A Social Neuroscience Approach', in J.P. Forgas (ed.), *The Handbook of Affect and Social Cognition*. Mahwah, NJ: Erlbaum, pp. 50–74.

Izard, C.E. (1977) *Human Emotions*. New York: Plenum Press.

Izard, C.E. (1993) 'Four Systems for Emotion Activation: Cognitive and Noncognitive Processes', *Psychological Review*, 100: 68–90.

Janis, I.L. and Feshbach, S. (1953) Effects of Fear-Arousing Communications', *Journal of Abnormal and Social Psychology*, 48: 78–92.

Jones, J.M. (1997) *Prejudice and Racism*, 2nd edn. New York: MCGraw-Hill.

Katz, P.A. (1976) *Towards the Elimination of Racism*. Elmsford, NY: Pergamon Press.

Keltner, D., Ellsworth, P.C., and Edwards, K. (1993) 'Beyond Simple Pessimism: Effects of Sadness and Anger on Social Judgment', *Journal of Personality and Social Psychology*, 64: 740–52.

Kernis, M.H. and Waschull, S.B. (1996) 'The Interactive Roles of Stability and Level of Self-Esteem: Research and Theory', in M.P. Zanna (ed.), *Advances in Experimental Social Psychology*, 27: 93–141.

Kidd, R.F. and Berkowitz, L. (1976) 'Effect of Dissonance Arousal on Helpfulness', *Journal of Personality and Social Psychology*, 33: 613–22.

Koestler, A. (1978) *Janus: A Summing Up*. London: Hutchinson.

Labott, S.M. and Martin, R.B. (1990) 'Emotional Coping, Age, and Physical Disorder', *Behavioral Medicine*, 16: 53–61.

Lambert, A.J., Khan, S.R., Lickel, B.A., and Fricke, K. (1997) 'Mood and the Correction of Positive Versus Negative Stereotypes', *Journal of Personality and Social Psychology*, 72: 1002–16.

Larsen, R.J. and Diener, E. (1987) 'Affect Intensity as an Individual Difference Characteristic: A Review', *Journal of Research in Personality*, 21: 1–39.

Lazarus, R.S. (1968) 'Emotions and Adaptation: Conceptual and Empirical Relations', in W.J. Arnold (ed.), *Nebraska Symposium on Motivation* (vol. 16). Lincoln, NE: University of Nebraska Press, pp. 175–266.

Lazarus, R.S. (1984) 'On the Primary of Cognition', *American Psychologist*, 39: 124–9.

Lazarus, R.S. (1991) *Emotion and Adaptation*. New York: Oxford University Press.

Lazarus, R.S. and Launier, R. (1978) 'Stress-Related Transactions between Person and Environment', in L.A. Pervin (ed.), *Perspectives in Interactional Psychology*. New York: Plenum, pp. 287–327.

Leary, M.R. (2000) 'Affect, Cognition, and the Social Emotions', in J.P. Forgas (ed.), *Feeling and Thinking:*

*The Role of Affect in Social Cognition.* New York: Cambridge University Press, pp. 331–56.

Leventhal, H. and Scherer, K. (1987) 'The Relationship of Emotion to Cognition: A Functional Approach to a Semantic Controversy', *Cognition and Emotion*, 1: 3–28.

Lloyd, G.G. and Lishman, W.A. (1975) 'Effect of Depression on the Speed of Recall of Pleasant and Unpleasant Experiences', *Psychological Medicine*, 5: 173–80.

Losch, M.E. and Cacioppo, J.T. (1990) 'Cognitive Dissonance May Enhance Sympathetic Tonus, but Attitudes Are Changed to Reduce Negative Affect Rather than Arousal', *Journal of Experimental Social Psychology*, 26: 289–304.

Mackie, D.M. and Worth, L.T. (1989) 'Processing Deficits and the Mediation of Positive Affect in Persuasion', *Journal of Personality and Social Psychology*, 57: 27–40.

Markus, H. (1977) 'Self-Schemata and Processing Information about the Self', *Journal of Personality and Social Psychology*, 35: 63–78.

Martin, L.L. (2000) 'Moods Don't Convey Information: Moods in Context Do', in J.P. Forgas (ed.), *Feeling and Thinking: The Role of Affect in Social Cognition.* New York: Cambridge University Press, pp. 153–77.

Mathews, A.M. and McLeod, C. (1994) 'Cognitive Approaches to Emotion and Emotional Disorders', *Annual Review of Psychology*, 45: 25–50.

Mayer, J.D. and Volanth, A.J. (1985) 'Cognitive Involvement in the Emotional Response System', *Motivation and Emotion*, 9: 261–75.

Mayer, J.D., Gaschke, Y.N., Braverman, D.L., and Evans, T.W. (1992) 'Mood-Congruent Judgment Is a General Effect', *Journal of Personality and Social Psychology*, 63: 119–32.

McGuire, W.J. (1985) 'Attitudes and Attitude Change', in G. Lindzey and E. Aronson (eds), *The Handbook of Social Psychology*, 3rd edn (vol. 2). New York: Random House, pp. 233–346.

Mead, G.H. (1934) *Mind, Self and Society*. Chicago, IL: University of Chicago Press.

Monteith, M.J. (1993) 'Self-Regulation of Prejudiced Responses: Implications for Progress in Prejudice-Reduction Efforts', *Journal of Personality and Social Psychology*, 65: 469–85.

Moylan, S.J. (2001) 'Mood Effects on Appraisal Judgments'. Unpublished Ph.D. thesis, University of New South Wales, Sydney, Australia.

Nasby, W. (1994) 'Moderators of Mood-Congruent Encoding: Self-/Other-Reference and Affirmative/Nonaffirmative Judgement', *Cognition and Emotion*, 8: 259–78.

Nasby, W. (1996) 'Moderators of Mood-Congruent Encoding and Judgment: Evidence that Elated and Depressed Moods Implicate Distinct Processes', *Cognition and Emotion*, 10: 361–77.

Neisser, U. (1982) *Memory Observed.* San Francisco, CA: Freeman.

Niedenthal, P. and Halberstadt, J. (2000) 'Grounding Categories in Emotional Response', in J.P. Forgas (ed.), *Feeling and Thinking: The Role of Affect in Social Cognition.* New York: Cambridge University Press, pp. 357–86.

Niedenthal, P.M. and Setterlund, M.B. (1994) 'Emotion Congruence in Perception', *Personality and Social Psychology Bulletin*, 20: 401–11.

Ortony, A., Clore, G.L., and Collins, A. (1988) *The Cognitive Structure of Emotions*. New York: Cambridge University Press.

Paivio, A. (1971) *Imagery and Verbal Processes.* New York: Holt, Rinehart, and Winston.

Parrott, W.G. and Sabini, J. (1990) 'Mood and Memory Under Natural Conditions: Evidence for Mood Incongruent Recall', *Journal of Personality and Social Psychology*, 59: 321–36.

Pelham, B.W. (1991) 'On Confidence and Consequences: The Certainty and Importance of Self-Knowledge', *Journal of Personality and Social Psychology*, 60: 518–30.

Pervin, L.A. (1976) 'A Free-Response Description Approach to the Analysis of Person–Situation Inter-action', *Journal of Personality and Social Psychology*, 34: 465–74.

Petty, R.E. and Cacioppo, J.T. (1986) 'The Elaboration Likelihood Model of Persuasion', in L. Berkowitz (ed.), *Advances in Experimental Social Psychology* (vol. 19). New York: Academic Press, pp. 123–205.

Petty, R.E., DeSteno, D., and Rucker, D. (2001) 'The Role of Affect in Attitude Change', in J.P. Forgas (ed.), *The Handbook of Affect and Social Cognition.* Mahwah, NJ: Erlbaum, pp. 212–36.

Petty, R.E., Gleicher, F., and Baker, S.M. (1991) 'Multiple Roles for Affect in Persuasion', in J.P. Forgas (ed.), *Emotion and Social Judgments.* Oxford: Pergamon Press, pp. 181–200.

Petty, R.E., Schumann, D.W., Richman, S.A., and Strathman, A.J. (1993) 'Positive Mood and Persuasion: Different Roles for Affect under High- and Low-Elaboration Conditions', *Journal of Personality and Social Psychology*, 64: 5–20.

Petty, R.E. and Wegener, D.T. (1993) 'Flexible Correction Processes in Social Judgment: Correcting for Context-Induced Contrast', *Journal of Experimental Social Psychology*, 29: 137–65.

Raghunathan, R. and Trope, Y. (1999) 'Mood-as-a-Resource in Processing Persuasive Messages'. Unpublished manuscript.

Raghunathan, R. and Pham, M.T. (1999) 'All Negative Moods Are Not Equal: Motivational Influences of Anxiety and Sadness on Decision Making', *Organizational Behavior and Human Decision Processes*, 79: 56–77.

Razran, G.H.S. (1940) 'Conditioned Response Changes in Rating and Appraising Sociopolitical Slogans', *Psychological Bulletin*, 37: 481.

Reed, M.B. and Aspinwall, L.G. (1998) 'Self-Affirmation Reduces Biased Processing of Health-Risk Information', *Motivation and Emotion*, 22: 99–132.

Rhodewalt, F. and Comer, R. (1979) 'Induced-Compliance Attitude Change: Once More with Feeling', *Journal of Experimental Social Psychology*, 15: 35–47.

Robinson, M.D. (1998) 'Running from William James' Bear: A Review of Preattentive Mechanisms and Their Contributions to Emotional Experience', *Cognition and Emotion*, 12: 667–96.

Roseman, I.J. (1984) 'Cognitive Determinants of Emotions: A Structural Theory', in P. Shaver (ed.), *Review of Personality and Social Psychology* (vol. 5). Newbury Park, CA: Sage, pp. 11–36.

Roseman, I.J. (1991) 'Appraisal Determinants of Discrete Emotions', *Cognition and Emotion*, 5: 161–200.

Roseman, I.J. and Smith, C.A. (2001) 'Appraisal Theory: Overview, Assumptions, Varieties, Controversies', in K.R. Scherer, A. Schorr, and T. Johnstone (eds), *Appraisal Processes in Emotion: Theory, Methods, Research*. New York: Oxford University Press. pp. 3–19.

Ruiz-Caballero, J.A. and Gonzalez, P. (1994) 'Implicit and Explicit Memory Bias in Depressed and Non-Depressed Subjects', *Cognition and Emotion*, 8: 555–70.

Russell, J.A. (1980) 'A Circumplex Model of Affect', *Journal of Personality and Social Psychology*, 39: 1161–78.

Rusting, C.L. (1998) 'Personality, Mood, and Cognitive Processing of Emotional Information: Three Conceptual Frameworks', *Psychological Bulletin*, 124 (2): 165–96.

Rusting, C. (2001) 'Personality as a Mediator of Affective Influences on Social Cognition', in J.P. Forgas (ed.), *The Handbook of Affect amd Social Cognition*. Mahwah, NJ: Erlbaum, pp. 371–91.

Salovey, P. and Birnbaum, D. (1989) 'Influence of Mood on Health-Relevant Cognitions', *Journal of Personality and Social Psychology*, 57: 539–51.

Salovey, P., Detweiler, J.B., Steward, W.T., and Bedell, B.T. (2001) 'Affect and Health-Relevant Cognition', in J. Forgas (ed.), *Handbook of Affect and Social Cognition*. Mahwah, NJ: Erlbaum, pp. 344–70.

Salovey, P., Rothman, A.J., and Rodin, J. (1998) 'Health Behavior', in D.T. Gilbert, S.T. Fiske, and G. Lindzey (eds), *The Handbook of Social Psychology*, 4th edn (vol. 2). New York: MCGraw-Hill, pp. 633–83.

Schachter, S. and Singer, J.E. (1962) 'Cognitive, Social and Psysiological Determinants of Emotional State', *Physiological Review*, 69: 379–99.

Scherer, K.R. (1984) 'On the Nature and Function of Emotion: A Component Process Approach', in K.R. Scherer and P. Ekman (eds), *Approaches to Emotion*. Hillsdale, NJ: Erlbaum, pp. 293–317.

Scherer, K.R. (1997) 'Profiles of Emotion-Antecedent Appraisal: Testing Theoretical Predictions Across Cultures', *Cognition and Emotion*, 11: 113–50.

Scherer, K.R. (1988) 'Criteria for Emotion-Antecedent Appraisal: A Review', in V. Hamilton, G.H. Bower, and N.H. Frijda (eds), *Cognitive Perspectives on Emotion and Motivation*. Boston, MA: Kluwer Academic, pp. 89–126.

Scherer, K.R. (1999) 'Appraisal Theory', in T. Dalgleish and M. Power (eds), *Handbook of Cognition and Emotion*. Chichester: John Wiley, pp. 411–43.

Schiffenbauer, A.I. (1974) 'Effect of Observer's Emotional State on Judgments of the Emotional State of Others', *Journal of Personality and Social Psychology*, 30 (1): 31–5.

Schwarz, N. (1990) 'Feelings as Information: Informational and Motivational Functions of Affective States', in E.T. Higgins and R. Sorrentino (eds), *Handbook of Motivation and Cognition: Foundations of Social Behaviour* (vol. 2). New York: Guilford, pp. 527–61.

Schwarz, N. and Clore, G.L. (1983) 'Mood, Misattribution and Judgments of Well-Being: Informative and Directive Functions of Affective States', *Journal of Personality and Social Psychology*, 45: 513–23.

Schwarz, N. and Clore, G.L. (1988) 'How Do I Feel About It? The Informative Function of Affective States', in K. Fiedler and J.P. Forgas (eds), *Affect, Cognition, and Social Behavior.* Toronto: Hogrefe, pp. 44–62.

Sedikides, C. (1994) 'Incongruent Effects of Sad Mood on Self-Conception Valence: It's a Matter of Time', *European Journal of Social Psychology*, 24: 161–72.

Sedikides, C. (1995) 'Central and Peripheral Self-Conceptions Are Differentially Influenced by Mood: Tests of the Differential Sensitivity Hypothesis', *Journal of Personality and Social Psychology*, 69 (4): 759–77.

Sedikides, C. and Strube, M.J. (1997) 'Self-Evaluation: To Thine Own Self Be Good, to Thine Own Self Be Sure, to Thine Own Self Be True, and to Thine Own Self Be Better', in M.P. Zanna (ed.), *Advances in Experimental Social Psychology* (vol. 29). New York: Academic Press, pp. 209–70.

Sinclair, R.C. and Mark, M.M. (1995) 'The Effects of Mood State on Judgmental Accuracy: Processing Strategy as a Mechanism', *Cognition and Emotion*, 9: 417–38.

Sloman, S.A. (1996) 'The Empirical Case for Two Systems of Reasoning', *Psychological Bulletin*, 119: 3–22.

Smith, C.A. and Kirby, L.D. (2000) 'Consequences Require Antecedents: Toward a Process Model of Emotion Elicitation', in J. Forgas (ed.), *Feeling and Thinking: The Role of Affect in Social Cognition*. New York: Cambridge University Press, pp. 83–106.

Smith, C.A. and Kirby, L.D. (2001) 'Toward Delivering on the Promise of Appraisal Theory', in K.R. Scherer, A. Schorr, and T. Johnstone (eds), *Appraisal Processes in Emotion: Theory, Methods, Research*. New York: Oxford University Press, pp. 121–38.

Smith, C.A. (1991) 'The Self, Appraisal, and Coping', in C.R. Snyder and D.R. Forsyth (eds), *Handbook of Social and Clinical Psychology: The Health Perspective*. New York: Pergamon, pp. 116–37.

Smith, C.A. and Ellsworth, P.C. (1985) 'Patterns of Cognitive Appraisal in Emotion', *Journal of Personality and Social Psychology*, 48: 813–38.

Smith, C.A. and Ellsworth, P.C. (1987) 'Patterns of Appraisal and Emotion Related to Taking an Exam', *Journal of Personality and Social Psychology*, 52: 475–88.

Smith, C.A. and Lazarus, R.S. (1990) 'Emotion and Adaptation', in L.A. Pervin (ed.), *Handbook of Personality: Theory and Research*. New York: Guilford, pp. 609–37.

Smith, C.A. and Lazarus, R.S. (1993) 'Appraisal Components, Core Relational Themes, and the Emotions', *Cognition and Emotion*, 7: 233–69.

Smith, C.A., Griner, L.A., Kirby, L.D., and Scott, H.S. (1996) 'Toward a Process Model of Appraisal in Emotion', *Proceedings of the Ninth Conference of the International Society for Research on Emotions*. International Society for Research on Emotions: Toronto, Ontario, Canada, pp. 101–5.

Smith, E.R. and DeCoster, J. (2000) 'Dual-Process Models in Social and Cognitive Psychology: Conceptual integration and Links to Underlying Memory Systems', *Personality and Social Psychology Review*, 4: 108–31.

Smith, S.M. and Petty, R.E. (1995) 'Personality Moderators of Mood Congruency Effects on Cognition: The Role of Self-Esteem and Negative Mood Regulation', *Journal of Personality and Social Psychology*, 68: 1092–1107.

Snyder, C.R. (1994) *The Psychology of Hope: You Can Get There from Here*. New York: Free Press.

Stangor, C., Sullivan, L.A., and Ford, T.E. (1991) 'Affective and Cognitive Determinants of Prejudice', *Social Cognition*, 9: 359–80.

Stephan, W.G. and Stephan, C.W. (1985) 'Intergroup Anxiety', *Journal of Social Issues*, 41 (3): 157–75.

Stephan, W.G. and Stephan, C.W. (1996) *Intergroup Relations*. Boulder, CO: Westview Press.

Strack, F. (1992) 'The Different Routes to Social Judgments: Experiential Versus Informational Strategies', in L.L. Martin and A. Tesser (eds), *The Construction of Social Judgments*. Hillsdale, NJ: Erlbaum. pp. 249–75.

Suls, J. (2001) 'Affect, Stress and Personality', in J. Forgas (ed.), *Handbook of Affect and Social Cognition*. Mahwah, NJ: Erlbaum, pp. 392–409.

Swann, W.B. Jr. (1990) 'To Be Adored or to Be Known? The Interplay of Self-Enhancement and Self-Verification', in E.T. Higgins and R.M. Sorrentino (eds), *Handbook of Motivation and Cognition: Foundations of Social Behavior* (vol. 2). New York: Guilford, pp. 408–48.

Teasdale, J.D. and Forgarty, S.J. (1979) 'Differential Effects on Induced Mood on Retrieval of Pleasant and Unpleasant Events from Episodic Memory', *Journal of Abnormal Psychology*, 88: 248–57.

Teasdale, J.D. and Russell, M.L. (1983) 'Differential Effects of Induced Mood on the Recall of Positive, Negative and Neutral Words', *British Journal of Clinical Psychology*, 22: 163–71.

Thomas, W.I. and Znaniecki, F. (1928) *The Polish Peasant in Europe and America*. Boston, MA: Badger.

Tobias, B.A. and Kihlstrom, J.F. (1992) 'Emotion and Implicit Memory', in S. Christianson (ed.), *The Handbook of Emotion and Memory: Research and Theory*. Hillsdale, NJ: Erlbaum, pp. 265–89.

Trope, Y., Ferguson, M., and Raghunanthan, R. (2001) 'Mood as a Resource in Processing Self-Relevant Information', in J.P. Forgas (ed.), *The Handbook of Affect and Social Cognition*. Mahwah, NJ: Erlbaum, pp. 256–74.

Trope, Y. and Gervey, B. (1998) 'Resolving Conflicts among Self-Evaluative Motives', paper presented at the Annual Convention of Workshop of Achievement and Task Motivation, Thessaloniki, Greece.

Trope, Y. and Neter, E. (1994) 'Reconciling Competing Motives in Self-Evaluation: The Role of Self-Control in Feedback Seeking', *Journal of Personality and Social Psychology*, 66: 646–57.

Trope, Y. and Pomerantz, E.M. (1998) 'Resolving Conflicts among Self-Evaluative Motives: Positive Experiences as a Resource for Overcoming Defensiveness', *Motivation and Emotion*, 22: 53–72.

Tulring, E. (1983) *Elements of Episodic Memory*. Oxford: Oxford University Press.

Tversky, A. and Kahneman, D. (1974) 'Judgment under Uncertainty: Heuristics and Biases', *Science*, 185: 1124–31.

Velten, E. (1968) 'A Laboratory Task for Induction of Mood States', *Advances in Behavior Research and Therapy*, 6: 473–82.

Watkins, T., Mathews, A.M., Williamson, D.A., and Fuller, R. (1992) 'Mood Congruent Memory in Depression: Emotional Priming or Elaboration', *Journal of Abnormal Psychology*, 101: 581–6.

Watson, D. and Tellegen, A. (1985) 'Toward a Consensual Structure of Mood', *Psychological Bulletin*, 98: 219–35.

Watson, J.B. and Rayner, R. (1920) 'Conditioned Emotional Reactions', *Journal of Experimental Psychology*, 3: 1–14.

Watts, F.N. and Dalgleish, T. (1991) 'Memory for Phobia-Related Words in Spider Phobics', *Cognition and Emotion*, 5: 313–29.

Wegener, D.T., and Petty, R.E. (1997) 'The Flexible Correction Model: The Role of Naïve Theories of Bias in Bias Correction', in M.P. Zanna (ed.), *Advances in Experimental Social Psychology* (vol. 29). New York: Academic Press, pp. 141–208.

Wegener, D.T., Petty, R.E., and Smith, S.M. (1995) 'Positive Mood Can Increase or Decrease Message Scrutiny: The Hedonic Contingency View of Mood and Message Processing', *Journal of Personality and Social Psychology*, 69: 5–15.

Wegener, D.T., Petty, R.E., and Klein, D.J. (1994) 'Effects of Mood on High Elaboration Attitude Change: The Mediating Role of Likelihood Judgments', *European Journal of Social Psychology*, 24: 25–43.

Wilder, D.A. and Shapiro, P.N. (1989) 'Role of Competition-Induced Anxiety in Limiting the Beneficial Impact of Positive Behavior by an Outgroup Member', *Journal of Personality and Social Psychology*, 56: 60–9.

Wyer, R.S. and Srull, T.K. (1989) *Memory and Cognition in Its Social Context.* Hillsdale, NJ: Erlbaum.

Zajonc, R.B. (1980) 'Feeling and Thinking: Preferences Need No Inferences', *American Psychologist*, 35: 151–75.

Zajonc, R.B. (2000) 'Feeling and Thinking: Closing the Debate over the Independence of Affect', in J.P. Forgas (ed.), *Feeling and Thinking: The Role of Affect in Social Cognition.* New York: Cambridge University Press, pp. 31–58.

Zanna, M.P. and Cooper, J. (1974) 'Dissonance and the Pill: An Attribution Approach to studying the Arousal Properties of Dissonance', *Journal of Personality and Social Psychology*, 29: 703–9.

Zanna, M.P., Kiesler, C.A., and Pilkonis, P.A. (1970) 'Positive and Negative Attitudinal Affect Established by Classical Conditioning', *Journal of Personality and Social Psychology*, 14: 321–8.

# 8
# Attribution and Person Perception

YAACOV TROPE AND RUTH GAUNT

**INTRODUCTION**

In everyday interaction with other people, we often try to figure out what kind of people they are, what they want, and what they intend to do. The various types of relationship we eventually form with other people – close or distant, cooperative or competitive – depends on how we perceive them. A great deal of social-psychological research has examined how we form impressions of other people and read their mind. This chapter reviews what we have learned from this research about the cognitive and motivational mechanisms that underlie the perception of people and the explanation of their behavior.

A great deal of social-psychological research is based on the assumption that interpersonal relations depend on how people mentally construe each other's behavior. Indeed, socially significant types of interaction, such as cooperation, competition, helping, and aggression, have been found to depend on how people perceive others' goals, traits, and abilities. For example, people are more likely to cooperate when they perceive the other person as trustworthy, to help when they perceive the other person as unable to achieve her goal by herself, and to act aggressively when they perceive the other person as hostile. Attribution research investigates the process of forming such mental construals on the basis of observed behavior and, once formed, how they influence emotion, motivation, and behavior.

In his *Psychology of Interpersonal Relations*, Heider (1958) assumed that attributions are abstract, unambiguous, and normative. Classic attribution theories (Jones and Davis, 1965; Kelley, 1967) adopted these assumptions. The first assumption states that attribution is a process of *mental abstraction*, namely, that attributional inferences proceed from representation of concrete, contextualized features to representation of more general, invariant properties. The process uses surface features of objects – the phenotype – to infer underlying causal properties – the genotype. Object perception extracts distal, stable properties of objects, such as size, shape, and color, from proximal, perspective-dependent visual data. Similarly, person perception extracts psychological dispositions of people from their concrete behavioral information. Through this process, the complex information contained in a behavioral episode is represented more simply and abstractly in terms of goals, traits, or competencies (Semin and Fiedler, 1988). For example, the complex sequence of events comprising the episode of Bill's helping Jim finish his homework may be represented as an expression of Bill's helpfulness.

Related to the first assumption, the second assumption states that attributional inference is a process of *uncertainty reduction*. Concrete representations of behavior are inherently ambiguous because they lend themselves to multiple more abstract representations. For example, perceivers may infer that Bill helped Jim because Bill is helpful, because he hoped to get a favor in return, because he wanted to show off his ability, etc. Moving from a concrete to an abstract representation, attributional inference involves deciding on one of the alternative abstract representations. This, in turn, means omitting the features that are perceived to be less important and inconsistent while retaining those considered more important to the representation. For example, the representation of Bill's behavior as helpful may retain the costs but not the benefits of helping Jim. Thus, because attributions necessarily impose one of many possible interpretations and because irrelevant or inconsistent details are omitted, attributional inferences are simpler and less ambiguous than the concrete representations on which they are based (Fiske and Taylor, 1991: 98; Smith, 1998).

The third assumption, *normativeness*, concerns the way in which alternative attributional hypotheses are evaluated. Like Heider, classic attribution theorists (Jones and Davis, 1965; Kelley, 1967) assume that perceivers are motivated to understand, predict, and control their environment. Moreover, these theorists assume that people achieve these goals by engaging in attributional inferences that follow the basic rules of scientific hypothesis testing. Normative statistical methods used in scientific inquiry, such as covariation analysis (Kelley, 1967), information theory (Jones and Davis, 1965), and Bayesian updating (Ajzen and Fishbein, 1975; Trope, 1974), have been proposed as models of everyday attributional inferences.

Normative models of attribution were highly influential and generated a great deal of research comparing people's attributional inferences to normative inferences (see reviews by Gilbert, 1998; Kelley and Michela, 1980; Ross, 1977; Trope and Liberman, 1993). However, these comparisons revealed systematic violations of normative models. This research found that attributional inferences are biased by perceivers' self-esteem and social identity (Miller and Ross, 1975), that they are insensitive to statistical information (Nisbett and Ross, 1980), and that they depend on perceivers' attentional focus and perspective (Ross, 1977). Most important here was research demonstrating what Heider (1958) called the fundamental attribution error and Jones (1979) called the correspondence bias, namely, the tendency to attribute behavior to the actor's dispositions even when the actor is under situational pressure to produce the behavior (Gilbert and Malone, 1995). The correspondence bias is particularly problematic for normative models because it seems to violate the requirement to discount the validity of any given attributional hypothesis when there are alternative plausible hypotheses.

These systematic errors and biases cast doubt on the value of normative models as descriptive of attribution processes. It became increasingly clear that while purely normative models are elegant and precise, they do not fully capture the richness of attributional phenomena. Attribution researchers have therefore abandoned the assumption that attributions necessarily follow normative rules. Instead, they have attempted to develop more comprehensive accounts of attribution phenomena by incorporating into their theorizing factors that have been neglected by earlier normative models. Two broad sets of such factors can be distinguished: one concerns the content of perceivers' a-priori causal models of behavior, and the other concerns how perceivers use these a-priori models in processing the information contained in an immediate behavioral episode.

This chapter reviews research on these two sets of factors. The first section reviews research on perceivers' a-priori causal models of behavior. These models specify how personal and situational forces combine to determine behavior. We review research on variation in causal models of behavior as a function of type of behavior, type of perceiver, and type of target. The second section reviews research on the use of a-priori causal models in processing an immediate behavioral episode. This section describes research on how perceivers (a) identify the behavioral and situational information contained in a behavioral episode and (b) utilize these identifications as evidence in heuristic or systematic testing of attributional hypotheses. We conclude that taking into account perceivers' a-priori causal models, identification of attribution-relevant data, and testing of attributional hypotheses can help explain a wide range of empirical findings and suggest new directions for future research on the nature of attribution and person perception.

## A-priori causal models of behavior

Perceivers' a-priori causal models are organized sets of pre-existing beliefs regarding how various factors combine to determine behavior in specific domains such as aggressiveness, friendliness, and helpfulness (see Reeder, 1993; Shoda and Mischel, 1993; Trope and Liberman, 1993). Dispositions in these models are relatively general personal characteristics such as personality traits, values, and abilities. They represent an enduring propensity to experience certain momentary states (feelings, wishes, and goals) in the presence of appropriate situational inducements (Idson and Mischel, 2001; Mischel and Shoda, 1995). The models specify how situational inducements (incentives, demands, and opportunities) actually elicit these internal states and how these states, in turn, are expressed in behavior. For example, perceivers' a-priori model of aggressive behavior may specify the likelihood that situational provocation (for example, being teased or criticized) will elicit aggressive feelings or wishes (such as anger and hostility) in aggressive and nonaggressive individuals, and the likelihood that these feelings will be expressed in aggressive behavior (hitting or insulting somebody).

Situational inducements differ in how they are believed to affect behavior. Some situational inducements may affect behavior by eliciting the corresponding internal state. These situational inducements are intrinsic to the behavior. Other situational inducements may affect behavior without eliciting the corresponding internal state. These situational inducements are extrinsic (see Trope, 1989). For example, situational provocation is intrinsic to aggressiveness because it may lead to aggressive behavior by eliciting aggression-related states in the actor. Similarly, task difficulty is intrinsic to achievement behavior because it may promote achievement endeavors by eliciting a wish to excel. Social norms, role requirements, and commands are extrinsic to aggressive or achievement behavior because they may induce these behaviors without eliciting aggressive or achievement wishes. Instead, extrinsic inducements may induce these and other kinds of behavior by eliciting unrelated wishes to obey or secure some social or material gains.

A-priori causal models are important because they guide inference of dispositions from behavior. Regardless of how perceivers process the information contained in an immediate behavior episode, the impact of this information will depend on perceivers' a-priori beliefs regarding potential dispositional and situational causes of such behavior. Perceivers may use optimal strategies to draw inferences from immediate behavior. Nevertheless, situational inducements will have little or no effect on their judgments if they believe that this kind of behavior is fully determined by the corresponding personality trait. For example, situational provocation or group pressure to act aggressively will have little impact on inferences from an instance of aggressive behavior if this type of behavior is believed to be fully determined by the actor's dispositional aggressiveness. The question, then, is what is the weight of dispositional and situational factors as potential causes in people's a-priori models of behavior. Recent theoretical and empirical work suggests that there are marked variations in these weights across types of behavior, perceivers, and target persons. Below we review research on how a-priori causal models of behavior differ depending on behavioral domain, target person, and perceivers' characteristics.

### *Type of behavior*

The weight of personal dispositions and situational inducements in perceivers' causal models varies across the behavioral domain. Some behaviors are conceived of as primarily determined by personal dispositions, others as primarily determined by situational inducements, and still others are conceived as equally determined by both types of factors. Research by Reeder and his colleagues has found that people believe that certain types of behavior are unlikely to occur unless the target possesses the corresponding trait (Reeder, 1985, 1993, 1997; Reeder and Brewer, 1979; see also Trope, 1974; Trope and Burnstein, 1975). In these domains, traits are seen as necessary conditions for performing the corresponding behavior. For example, people assume immoral dispositions are necessary for committing immoral behaviors and certain competencies are necessary for succeeding. People's a-priori models in such cases assume that situational inducements are weak potential causes of behavior. Incompetent people are seen as unlikely to excel and moral people as unlikely to commit immoral acts regardless of situational incentives. In contrast, unsuccessful performance and moral and socially desirable behaviors are believed to depend on situational factors. A competent person may fail in the absence of incentives and an immoral person may act morally if appropriately rewarded.

Such a-priori assumptions permit and actually prescribe correspondent dispositional inferences from successful performance and immoral behavior with little adjustment for situational inducements. Indeed, a number of studies have shown that situational inducements affect dispositional inferences from failure and moral behaviors, but not dispositional inferences from success or immoral behaviors (see Devine et al., 1990; Evett et al., 1994; Reeder, 1993; Reeder and Spores, 1983; Skowronski and Carlston, 1989). Moreover, a-priori models have implications for the amount of behavioral evidence perceivers will need before concluding that the target possesses the corresponding disposition. If perceivers assume that situational inducements have little influence on successful or immoral behavior, then relatively few instances of such behavior should enable perceivers to draw correspondent dispositional inferences. Research by Gidron et al. (1993) and Rothbart and Park (1986) actually found that perceivers need a relatively small number of successful performances, immoral acts, and socially undesirable behaviors to conclude that a target possesses the corresponding personality traits.

Ybarra and Stephan (1996, 1999; Ybarra, 1999) proposed that people's causal models associate negative behavior with dispositional factors and positive behavior with situational factors. Consistent with this proposal, these researchers found that perceivers who were primed to think in terms of dispositional causes expected that a target person will enact more negative behaviors, whereas perceivers who were primed to think in terms of situational causes expected more positive behaviors (Ybarra and Stephan, 1999). Other researchers showed that perceivers more readily make dispositional inferences from negative behaviors than from positive behaviors (e.g., Reeder and Spores, 1983; Wyer and Gordon, 1982) and are more sensitive to situational factors when judging positive behaviors than negative behaviors (e.g., Lee and Hallahan, 1998; Vonk and van Knippenberg, 1994).

### *Perceivers' conception of personal dispositions*

Dweck and her colleagues proposed that perceivers differ in their conception of people as possessing invariant or malleable dispositions (Dweck et al., 1993; Dweck and Leggett, 1988; Levy et al., 1999). According to this proposal, some perceivers, called 'theorists', believe that dispositions, such as personality traits, intelligence, and moral character, are fixed. Other perceivers, 'incremental theorists', believe that dispositions are flexible and malleable. Global dispositions, compared to situational factors, may therefore have a greater weight in entity theorists' causal models of behavior than in incremental theorists' causal models of behavior. On the basis of these causal models, entity theorists (compared to incremental theorists) should see behavior as more diagnostic of underlying dispositions.

Supporting this prediction, Dweck and her colleagues demonstrated that entity theorists are more likely than incremental theorists to infer global dispositions from small and unreliable samples of behavior and to rely on such dispositions in making judgements and predictions about others' behavior (Chiu et al., 1997; Dweck et al., 1995). Incremental theorists are more likely than entity theorists to explain behavior in terms situationally activated goals, strategies, and expectancies, and draw inferences that are more specific, provisional, and dependent on circumstances (Chiu et al., 1997; Dweck et al., 1995). In achievement settings, entity theorists are oriented to demonstrating their general ability, whereas incremental theorists are oriented to acquiring and developing their task-specific skills (Dweck and Leggett, 1988). Entity theorists perceive initial performance as diagnostic of 'true' ability and infer higher ability in the case of declining performance, while incremental theorists base their inferences on the degree to which ability was acquired over time, and infer higher ability in the case of ascending performance (Butler, 2000).

### *Developmental stage*

Research on children's models of behavior has found important developmental changes in the way dispositions are understood (Rholes et al., 1990). This research suggests that during early and middle-childhood children gradually come to understand dispositions as constant aspects of persons that exert a consistent influence on behavior across situations and time. Dispositions should therefore have a more important role in older children's causal models of behavior and should be more readily utilized in these children's prediction of and inference from behavior.

To test this prediction, several studies presented children with a trait-implying behavior and asked them to predict how the actor would behave in a new situation that is relevant to this trait (e.g., Ferguson et al., 1986; Rholes and Ruble, 1984). These studies found that although younger children (five to six years old) can label behaviors in dispositional terms, they are less likely than older children (nine to ten years old) to expect cross-situationally consistent patterns of behavior. Thus, younger children seem to use dispositions primarily to describe behavior without inferring an underlying quality of the person. Consistent with these results, Ruble and her colleagues (Ruble et al., 1979) found that younger children are biased toward explaining behavior in terms of nondispositional, contextual factors. Similarly, compared to older children, younger children's (five years old) predictions for behavior are primarily based on situational information and neglect information about the actor's past trait-relevant behavior (Josephson, 1977). Interestingly, older children (eight to eleven years old) show the opposite tendency, that is, a tendency to make behavior predictions that are primarily based on disposition-relevant information. Adolescents and young adults (fifteen and twenty years old) use both situational and dispositional information to predict future behavior (Josephson, 1977). This research suggests that children's models of behavior change from emphasizing situational factors to emphasizing dispositional factors, before reaching a more interactionist conception of behavior. The perceived link between dispositions and behaviors reaches its peak during middle childhood and results in overreliance on the predictive capacity of dispositions.

### *Culture*

A considerable amount of research suggests cross-cultural differences in perceivers' beliefs regarding dispositional and situational influences on behavior (Choi et al., 1999; Cousins, 1989; Markus and Kitayama, 1991; Triandis, 1989). The typical finding is that Americans explain behaviors and events in terms of personality traits, whereas East Asians prefer contextual explanations that emphasize social roles, obligations, and specific situational factors (Choi and Markus, 1998; Miller, 1984; Morris and Peng, 1994). This difference emerges gradually through socialization. In a study that compared social explanations of children and adults, Western and Eastern children made much more similar causal attributions than Western and Eastern adults (Miller, 1984). Dispositional attributions increased with age for Westerns but not for Easterns.

Cultural differences in the perceived importance of dispositional and situational factors should also produce differences in behavior predictions. Ybarra and Stephan (1999) specifically argued that because dispositional causes are linked to negative behaviors and situational causes to positive behaviors, people who think more about dispositional causes should regard negative behaviors as being more likely than people who think more about situational causes. Indeed, Ybarra and Stephan (1999) found that, compared to Westerns, East Asians expected a target person to enact more positive behaviors and fewer negative behaviors.

### *Type of target*

Perceivers may have different a-priori models for different types of targets. Perceivers may believe that their own behavior is primarily determined by situational contingencies, whereas others' behavior is primarily determined by their personality traits (see Jones and Nisbett, 1971). Similarly, perceivers may think that personality traits are more influential in in-group behavior than in out-group behavior (Tajfel, 1982).

Idson and Mischel (2001) showed that perceivers tend to infer relatively fewer broad, uncontextualized traits (such as aggressive or friendly), and relatively more psychological mediating variables (for example, goals, affects, construals, and beliefs), when the target is someone they know very well, compared with a casual acquaintance. Presumably, the longer perceivers have known the target, the more opportunities they have had to observe the target's behavior in different situations. In this way, familiarity provides the information for inferring a person's psychological mediating variables. Moreover, this effect of familiarity was mediated by another target-factor – his or her importance to the perceiver (Idson and Mischel, 2001). That is, perceivers inferred more mediating variables and fewer traits as the target became more familiar, only if the target played an important role in their lives. Thus, while familiarity provides the information for inferring a person's psychological mediating variables, perceivers are motivated to process this information only if the target is important to them.

Shoda and Mischel (1993) suggest that perceivers may believe that for different kinds of people different kinds of situations elicit the same behavior. For example, our stereotypes may lead us to believe that African-Americans are motivated to perform well in athletic tasks, whereas Asian-Americans are motivated to perform well in academic tasks (Mischel et al., 2002). Perceivers, then, may use athletic challenges to assess the achievement needs of African-Americans and academic challenges to assess the achievement needs of Asian-Americans. In general, situationalinducements are unlikely to moderate inferences about individuals for whom these inducements are believed to be ineffective.

In sum, the research reviewed in this section suggests that the inferences perceivers draw from observed behavior are guided by their a-priori models of the potential causes of this kind of behavior. The roles of dispositional and situational causes in these models systematically vary as a function of behavioral domain, target person, and perceivers' characteristics. Depending on the type of behavior, target, and perceiver, a-priori models of behavior may thus lead one to assign equal or unequal weights to dispositional and situational causes in explaining observed behavior.

## Attributional processing

Attributional processing can be partitioned into two stages, identification and attributional inference (Trope, 1986). In the identification stage, perceivers categorize the behavioral and situational information contained in a behavioral episode (for example, 'This is a cheerful party' and 'Lisa acts cheerfully'). In this stage, the representations of the situation and the behavior and other representations that are activated by the behavioral episode (for example, prior knowledge about the actor) implicitly influence each other in determining the final identifications. In the subsequent attributional inference stage, perceivers use these identifications to evaluate an attributional hypothesis about the actor's momentary state (intention, feeling, or goal), his or her enduring dispositions, or the situational forces. For example, perceivers may want to know whether an actor's cheerful behavior results from a momentary good mood ('Does Lisa really feel cheerful?'), dispositional happiness ('Is Lisa a happy person?'), or a strong situational norm ('Does Lisa act cheerfully because she is expected to look happy in this party?'). In evaluating their hypothesis, perceivers may take into account the situational circumstances in which the behavior occurred as well as any stored knowledge about the target (for a cognitive-neuroscience perspective on the distinction between identification and attributional inference processes, see Lieberman et al., 2002).

### *Identification processes*

As part of the identification stage, perceivers categorize behavior in attribution-relevant terms (such as 'aggressive', 'helpful', and 'shy'). Uleman and his colleagues' research on spontaneous trait inference provides considerable evidence for this proposal (Newman and Uleman, 1989, 1993;

Uleman, 1987; Uleman et al., 1996; Winter et al., 1985). In their studies, participants are typically presented with a series of sentences for a subsequent memory test. Each sentence describes an actor performing a behavior that implies a trait (for example, 'The accountant takes the orphans to the circus'). Participants' recall is then tested, using either semantic cues (for example, 'enjoyable outing'), implied-trait cues (for example, 'kindhearted'), or no recall cues. Many studies in this paradigm have found that trait cues are more effective for sentence recall than no cues, and at least as effective as strong semantic cues, without being strong associates themselves (for a review, see Uleman, 1999). This finding indicates that the trait cues' effectiveness is based on identifications made at encoding, rather than on general semantic knowledge. It seems, then, that people unintentionally encode behaviors in terms of personality traits without conscious awareness and without any explicit instructions to do so.

Adopting Uleman's paradigm of spontaneous inference (e.g., Winter et al., 1985), Lupfer and his colleagues (Lupfer et al., 1990) have demonstrated context effects on the identification of behavior in situational and dispositional terms. In their study, participants were first provided with a short paragraph of background information, before being exposed to an actor's behavior. The background information created a dispositional or situational context for behavior. Participants' memory of the behavior was later tested by trait-cued or situational- cued recall. The results showed that dispositional context facilitated identification of behavior in trait terms, while situational context facilitated identification in situational terms (Lupfer et al., 1990). Presumably, contextual information elicits a certain a-priori model, which, in turn, determines the identification of behavior. Embedded in a situational context, behavior is then better recalled in the presence of a situational cue than in its absence, while dispositional context makes recall easier in the presence of trait cue.

### *Context-dependent identification*

The information contained in a behavioral episode is often ambiguous; that is, it is associated with multiple categories. For example, a silent response may be interpreted as empathic, submissive, or hostile. The choice of one interpretation may be implicitly influenced by context, namely, representations of information about the situation and the actor (Higgins, 1996; Higgins and Stangor, 1988; Trope, 1989; Wyer and Srull, 1981). For example, in the context of a friendly meeting, perceivers are likely to identify a slap on the back as a friendly gesture, whereas in the context of a provocation, perceivers are likely to interpret a slap on the back as an aggressive act. Similarly, prior information about the target person and stereotypic beliefs about the target's group membership suggesting that the target is a friendly or aggressive person may bias the identification of a slap on the back as friendly or aggressive.

A number of studies have investigated the influence of context on the identification of behavioral information. This research has shown that when the behavioral input is ambiguous, its identification depends on the context in which it is processed (see Trope, 1986; Trope and Alfieri, 1997; Trope et al., 1988, 1991). Context presumably determines which one of the alternative categorizations of the behavioral input will be sufficiently activated to reach conscious awareness, thus resolving the ambiguity of the input. Perceivers may be unaware of the alternative meanings of the behavioral input and the fact that contextual inducements determined which one was selected. As a result, they may treat their identifications as *independent* behavioral evidence rather than as *context produced.* Context may thus act as an implicit disambiguator of behavioral information. For example, in conflict situations, direct eye contact, close physical proximity, silence, and even a smile are likely to be perceived as hostile responses. Identifications of these same responses as sympathetic or cooperative are unlikely to be consciously considered. As a result, the identification of these responses as hostile is likely to be used as evidence for the target's dispositional hostility.

Kunda and Thagard's (1996) parallel-constraint-satisfaction model of impression formation describes the mechanism that might produce these contextual identifications. According to this model, behaviors, dispositions, and stereotypes can be represented as interconnected nodes in a spreading activation network. The spread of activation between nodes is constrained by positive and negative associations. The meaning of behavior emerges from the network of associates that is activated at the time of use of behavioral information. These associates may include related dispositions, situations, other behaviors, stereotypes, goals, and any other cognitive and affective units that are associated with the behavior. The associates are activated and deactivated simultaneously and jointly constrain behavior identification. For example, a slap on the back may activate both friendly and aggressive associates. The context in which the slap on the back is activated may serve to narrow its meaning. Thus, a friendly meeting may activate 'friendly' while deactivating 'aggressive'. In this manner, the contents of concepts representing behaviors vary from one context to another, depending on the activated associates.

Read and his colleagues (Read and Marcus-Newhall, 1993; Read and Miller, 1998; Read and Montoya, 1999; Read et al., 1997) have further elaborated the conceptualization of a parallel constraint satisfaction system. In their autoassociative model of causal reasoning, Read and Montoya (1999) suggest a single-layer network with a set of units that are completely interconnected. The connections in this network are bidirectional. Each pair of nodes is connected by two links, one running in each direction. Each of these links can be modified by learning, and each link in a pair can end up with a different weight. As a result, this network can learn asymmetric relations between causes and effects, an ability that captures the important distinction between necessary and sufficient causes. In addition, the autoassociative network is able to learn associations among all the elements that co-occur in an input, and, thus, it is able to learn not only the relationship between the effect and its potential causes but also the association between the potential causes themselves. Thus, it captures the learning of the relations among alternative causes that is an important part of both discounting and augmentation. Read and Montoya (1999) simulated the work of the autoassociative network with a computer program that modeled the principles of this network. In their simulations, the programmed network was first trained with a set of external input patterns that produced activations of causes and their corresponding effects. The researchers then turned on various possible effects and looked at the resulting activation of the various causes. These simulations were able to capture important principles in the causal reasoning literature such as the discounting of competing explanations and the distinction between necessary and sufficient causes.

### *Group membership as contextual information*

One important source of contextual information about a target person is the person's group membership. For example, knowing that the target person is African-American may activate the concept of aggressiveness, and thus lead to the identification of a slap on the back as aggressive behavior. Consistent with this proposal, Kunda and her colleagues' research (Kunda et al., 1997) showed that when informed of a target's disposition, perceivers expect this disposition to result in different behaviors according to the targets' group membership. Thus, while an aggressive construction worker is expected to exhibit physical violence, an aggressive lawyer is expected to show verbal abuse (Kunda et al., 1997).

In a study that directly tested the influence of stereotypes on behavior identification, Dunning and Sherman (1997: Experiment 1) presented participants with descriptions of ambiguous behaviors performed by stereotyped individuals (for example, 'After a few drinks, the two marriage counselors [lumberjacks] had a fight in the restaurant'). Participants were then given a recognition memory test in which the description was slightly modified in a way that was consistent or inconsistent with the stereotypic belief ('After a few drinks, the two marriage counselors [lumberjacks] had a quarrel [a fist fight] in the restaurant'). Results showed that participants were more likely to recognize falsely the modified description as previously presented when it was consistent with the stereotype than when it was inconsistent with the stereotype. In another experiment that used a free recall memory test (Dunning and Sherman, 1997; Experiment 4), providing participants with stereotype-consistent cues at the time of recall facilitated memory of the original description. This finding provides evidence that the influence of stereotypes on behavior identification occurs when behavioral information is encoded.

### *The determinants of assimilative identification*

A series of studies by Trope and his colleagues investigated the role of ambiguity of behavior and the order of behavioral and contextual information in producing assimilative identification (see Trope, 1986; Trope and Alfieri, 1997; Trope et al., 1988, 1991). It was predicted that contextual information is likely to produce assimilative identification when behavior is ambiguous and preceded by contextual information. For example, in a study by Trope et al. (1991), participants heard an evaluator present an ambiguous or unambiguous evaluation of another person. The contextual information in this study was a situational demand to present either a positive or a negative evaluation. The evaluator described the other person in either unambiguously positive terms (serious and persevering), unambiguously negative terms (gloomy and stubborn), or ambiguously, namely, in a way that could be identified as either positive or negative. It was found that participants' judgments of the favorability of the evaluation (that is, participants' behavior identifications) were influenced by the situational demands only when behavior was ambiguous and preceded by the situational information.

How does behavior ambiguity determine assimilative identification? Presumably, ambiguity allows perceivers to identify the behavior in terms of the contextually activated behavioral category, without being aware of alternative interpretations of behavior. This implies that activation of the alternative meanings of an ambiguous behavior should reduce assimilative identification. Trope and Sikron (1992) sought to test this hypothesis in a study that presented participants with a target person giving an evaluation of another person. Two different methods were used to activate the alternative meanings of behavior. In one method, both the positive and negative meanings of the ambiguous evaluation (for example, superficial and efficient) were primed before hearing the evaluation, as part of a supposedly unrelated experiment. In a second method, mixed evaluations were used. That is, unlike the ambiguous evaluations that consisted of statements which had both a positive and negative meaning, the mixed evaluations were combined of some unambiguously positive and some unambiguously negative statements. As expected, increasing perceivers' awareness of the alternative meanings of behavior by both methods resulted in reduced assimilative effects of contextual information on behavior identification. In other words, when the alternative meanings of the ambiguous evaluation were primed, or when the evaluation itself was mixed, situational demands no longer affected perception of the ambiguous evaluation. These findings demonstrate that contextual information affects behavior identification only when the behavioral evidence is ambiguous and perceivers are unaware of its alternative identifications.

In sum, research on identification processes suggests that the attribution process starts with a spontaneous process of representing the information contained in a behavior episode in attribution-relevant terms (for example, 'John is teased' and 'John is angry'). Perceivers treat their identifications as perceptual givens, as reflecting the properties of the behavioral episode. However, a considerable amount of research shows that under specifiable conditions the identifications are determined by contextual information. Information about the actor and the immediate situation influences the identification of behavioral information (e.g., Trope and Alfieri, 1997), and behavioral information may influence the identification of information about the actor and the situation (see Trope and Cohen, 1989).

### *Attributional inference processes*

The results of the identification process are used for evaluating an attributional hypothesis. The hypothesis may concern any plausible explanation of behavior, such as the target person's current motives, his or her enduring disposition, or the situation in which the behavior occurred. For example, seeing someone act nervously during an interview, perceivers may generate hypotheses concerning the actor's feelings (for example, 'Is she experiencing anxiety?'), her personality (for example, 'Is she an anxious person?'), or the interview situation (for example, 'Is this an anxiety-provoking interview?'). The evaluation of such attributional hypotheses is performed either heuristically or systematically. As described below, the use of a heuristic or systematic strategy depends on processing resources.

### *The role of perceivers' processing goals*

Perceivers' processing goals may determine which attributional hypothesis will become focal and therefore have an advantage under limited processing resources. To test this idea, Krull (1993) and Krull and Erickson (1995) manipulated the goal of observing a behavioral episode. In one condition, perceivers were instructed to assess the target person's characteristics, whereas in the other condition perceivers were instructed to assess situational characteristics. This research showed that participants who were instructed to assess the target's characteristics tended to overattribute her behavior to corresponding personality dispositions, especially when their cognitive resources were depleted. Conversely, participants who were instructed to assess the situation's characteristics tended to overattribute the target's behavior to the situation, especially when their cognitive resources were depleted.

Research by Uleman and Moskowitz (1994: Experiment 3) showed that perceivers are more likely to engage in dispositional inferences when their goal is to assess the actor's personality characteristics. These researchers presented participants with a set of trait-implying sentences and manipulated their processing goals. In one condition, participants were asked to estimate how likely they were to perform a behavior similar to that of the actor, if they were in the same situation. In a second condition, participants were asked to estimate how similar they were to the actor. In a third condition, participants were required to form an impression of the actor's personality traits. Using the cued-recall method, the explicit memory links between the actor and the implied traits were measured. The results showed that these links were influenced by participants' inferential goal. Specifically, when participants judged the actor's similarity to themselves, they did not form any explicit link from actor to traits. When they judged the likelihood that they would perform the behavior, they formed marginal links. Only when participants had the goal of forming an impression of the actor in trait terms, were these traits explicitly linked to the actor (see, however, Todorov and Uleman, 2002).

### *Systematic attributional inference*

Systematic inference is a diagnostic evaluation of the validity of an attributional hypothesis in light of behavioral evidence. This evaluation is based on perceivers' a-priori models of situational and dispositional determinants of behavior. For example, when the focal hypothesis is a personal disposition, perceivers use their models to assess systematically the probability of the observed behavior given that the target possesses the corresponding disposition (that is, the sufficiency of the hypothesized disposition) as well as the probability of the behavior given that the target does not possess the corresponding disposition (that is, the necessity of the hypothesized disposition). Behavior is taken as implying the corresponding disposition to the extent that it is more probable given that the target possesses the corresponding disposition than given that the target does not possess the corresponding disposition. The implications of the immediate behavior are integrated with any prior knowledge about the target to form a final judgment about the target's dispositions.

Sometimes, perceivers' causal models of behavior imply that situational inducements are sufficient to produce the behavior. In these cases, the presence of situational inducements will make behavior seem probable regardless of whether the target possesses the correspondent disposition. For example, the fact that a person acts anxiously when waiting for an important job interview would seem probable independent of whether the target person is dispositionally anxious. Anxious behavior in such a situation would therefore leave perceivers uncertain as to whether the target person is a dispositionally nervous person. Thus, by the diagnostic method, a dispositional hypothesis would be discounted in the presence of alternative hypotheses (see Trope, 1974; Trope and Liberman, 1993).

It is important to point out, however, that the presence of alternative potential causes of behavior does not always imply that the inference of a focal cause should be discounted. As discussed above under the heading 'A-priori causal models of behavior', this depends on perceivers' causal models of behavior. Indeed, in their analysis of perceivers' mental models as sets of probabilistic assumptions, Morris and Larrick (1995) showed that discounting is a normative inference from most, but not all, possible mental models of cause–effect relations. Specifically, their normative analysis suggests that discounting is implied by a mental model of multiple sufficient causes but not of multiple necessary conditions. This suggestion was tested in a study in which participants inferred the pro-Castro attitude of a writer from a pro-Castro essay (Morris and Larrick, 1995). Before asking participants for their attitude inferences, these researchers measured participants' a-priori assumptions concerning the relations between the situational constraints, attitude, and behavior. This study found that participants' perceptions of the sufficiency of causes were a key determinant of discounting. That is, incomplete discounting of attitudes reflected perceptions of the situational inducements as insufficient cause for behavior, rather than a failure to take into account these inducements. In a second study, the target's likely attitudes and the situational constraints were manipulated so that they were either positively or negatively associated. The results showed that when attitudes and situational constraints were positively associated, the situation produced little discounting of the attitudes, whereas when the two causes were negatively associated, discounting occurred. Thus, in this case, discounting occurred only when the situation and the target's attitudes had opposite effects on behavior.

Consistent with these findings, McClure's (1998) analysis of discounting effects suggests that an undiscounted inference may reflect a perception of multiple causes for behavior. In such cases, the degree of discounting is determined by the perceived necessity and sufficiency of the causes. People may perceive situational inducements as insufficient to produce the behavior, or they may perceive dispositional causes as necessary for the occurrence of behavior. In both cases, the causal model of behavior would not imply discounting of the dispositional inference in the presence of situational inducements. Very often, however, situational constraints are perceived as sufficient causes and thus render the behavior probable even in the absence of correspondent disposition. In these cases, perceivers' diagnostic evaluations result in discounted inferences.

### *Heuristic attributional inference*

Diagnostic inference is an effortful process, requiring assessment of the probability of the behavior under the focal attributional hypothesis and under alternative hypotheses. The likelihood of engaging in diagnostic inference may therefore depend on perceivers' motivation to reach an accurate conclusion and on the availability of attentional resources. Under limited motivational and cognitive resources, perceivers are likely to resort to a heuristic strategy of hypothesis evaluation. Pseudodiagnostic inference is such a strategy (see Trope and Liberman, 1993, 1996). In evaluating a dispositional hypothesis, this strategy focuses on the probability of the behavior given the corresponding disposition (that is, the disposition's sufficiency). The probability of the behavior under alternative hypotheses (that is, the disposition's necessity) is given little or no consideration. For example, an anxious response will be attributed to the target's dispositional anxiety to the extent that this response is believed to be probable for someone who is dispositionally nervous.

Thus, pseudodiagnostic inference is primarily based on the association between the observed behavior and the hypothesized cause. As such, it is simple and fast and demands little conscious attention. Moreover, pseudodiagnostic inference is also efficient because it often results in a similar conclusion to that of the diagnostic strategy. This is because when a cause is believed to be sufficient to produce a behavior, it is often also believed to be a necessary cause of that behavior. For example, aggressive behavior is seen as likely for aggressive people, but also as unlikely for nonaggressive people (see Trope and Liberman, 1993, 1996; Trope and Mackie, 1987). Hence, in many cases, evaluating a hypothesis leads to the same inference whether or not perceivers take into account alternative hypotheses.

However, when the sufficiency of a hypothesis for behavior is not correlated with its necessity, pseudodiagnostic inference may produce unwarranted attributions. When the focal hypothesis is a disposition, pseudodiagnostic inference focuses only on the probability of behavior given the disposition and ignores alternative potential causes of the behavior. Pseudodiagnostic inference is therefore insensitive to situational inducements and results in situationally undiscounted inferences. For example, knowing that a person is waiting for an important job interview will not lead perceivers who use the pseudodiagnostic heuristic to attenuate their attributions of a nervous reaction to a dispositional nervousness. This is because pseudodiagnostic inference gives little weight to the possibility that most people, not only dispositionally nervous people, would have reacted nervously to this situation.

### *The determinants of heuristic versus systematic attributional inference*

Diagnostic inference is a systematic but effortful process. Perceivers may engage in diagnostic evaluation of their hypothesis when their motivation to draw an accurate conclusion is high, when their processing resources are unimpaired by competing tasks, and when the alternative hypotheses are salient (see Ginossar and Trope, 1987; Harkness et al., 1985; Kruglanski and Mayseless, 1988; Trope, 1998; Trope and Gaunt, 2000). Under less favorable conditions, perceivers are likely to use the simpler pseudodiagnostic strategy.

#### Motivational resources

A series of studies by Tetlock (1985) investigated the effect of accountability on attitude inferences. Participants read an essay and were asked to infer the true attitude of the writer who was said to have either choice or no choice as to what position to advocate. Presumably, accountable participants were more motivated to make an accurate inference and therefore considered dispositional as well as situational explanations of the position the writer expressed. Consistent with this interpretation, accountable participants showed greater situational discounting, namely, weaker attitude inferences from an essay written under no choice than under choice conditions (Tetlock, 1992; see also Corneille et al., 1999).

Webster (1993) manipulated accuracy motivation by varying the attractiveness of the inference task. This researcher reasoned that an attractive inference task is intrinsically motivating and increases the perceiver's efforts, while an unattractive inference task is extrinsically motivating and leads perceivers to look for a quick answer and get the reward. Participants watched a target making a speech on a student-exchange program under free-choice or no-choice conditions. Task attractiveness was manipulated through a contrast with the task participants expected to perform subsequently, which was either promised to be particularly attractive (watching comedy videos) or unattractive (watching a video of a statistics lecture). This was assumed to render the current task relatively unappealing or appealing, respectively. Results showed that an attractive inference task increased participants' sensitivity to situational constraints and led them to attenuate their inference of the speaker's attitude. In the unattractive task condition, however, participants underused the situational information and drew correspondent attitude inference. In another experiment (Webster, 1993: Experiment 3), participants received information on the target's attitude and drew inferences about the situation. Here again, highly motivated participants showed a reduced tendency to over-attribute the behavior to the situation. This research suggests that accuracy motivation leads perceivers to take into account alternative explanations of behavior, as prescribed by diagnostic inference.

#### Cognitive resources

Gilbert and his colleagues (Gilbert et al., 1988a, 1988b, 1992; Gilbert and Osborne, 1989) studied the effect of cognitive resources by comparing inferences by perceivers who were free to devote their full attention to the inference task (no-load condition) and perceivers who were distracted by a secondary task, such as keeping in memory an eight-digit number (load condition). Perceivers watched an interviewee responding nervously to questions that were either anxiety-provoking ('Discuss your most intimate sexual fantasies') or neutral ('Discuss your view on home gardening'). These studies found that nondistracted perceivers were sensitive to the anxiety-provoking questions and discounted their attribution of dispositional nervousness. In contrast, perceivers under cognitive load failed to take the situational inducements into account and drew undiscounted dispositional inferences. Other studies manipulated cognitive resources using various distracting activities (such as word rehearsal, visual search task, gaze fixation, etc.) and showed that distracted perceivers fail to discount their dispositional inference for the influence of situational inducements (Gilbert et al., 1988a, 1992; Gilbert and Osborne, 1989; Osborne and Gilbert, 1992). This line of research also showed that social interaction is in itself a distracting task that leads perceivers to focus on the regulation of their own behavior and makes them less sensitive to situational constraints on the target's behavior (Gilbert et al., 1988a).

### Properties of alternative explanations

The use of information suggesting alternative explanations, like the use of any information, should depend on the salience, accessibility, and applicability of the information. For instance, when they are watching a nervous interviewee, the increased salience of the anxiety-provoking interviewer may draw perceivers' attention to the possibility that the anxious behavior was caused by the situation, and thus lead them to attenuate their dispositional attribution. Very often, situational explanations for behavior are low in salience and, thus, are likely to be underweighted in the inference.

Considerable support for this proposal comes from research that directly manipulated the perceptual salience of situational information (Arkin and Duval, 1975; McArthur and Post, 1977; Storms, 1973; Taylor and Fiske, 1978). This research shows that increasing the perceptual salience of situational inducements causes perceivers to give more weight to the situation in their inferences from behavior. More recently, a series of studies by Trope and Gaunt (2000) has suggested that the increased salience of the situation may compensate for the effect of depleted cognitive resources. This research examined the effect of cognitive load on situational discounting as a function of the perceptual salience, accessibility (priming), or applicability of situational inducements. Using Jones and Harris's (1967) attitude-inference paradigm, this research assessed attitude inferences from an essay written under choice or no-choice conditions. The salience of the situational demands on the writer was manipulated by presenting the demands either in a written form (low salience) or in an auditory form (high salience). Accessibility was manipulated by priming either situational explanations or irrelevant concepts before observing the behavior at hand. Specifically, in the situational priming condition, participants read and answered questions regarding proverbs that have to do with the influence of situational forces on people's behavior (for example, 'When in Rome, do as the Romans do'). In the neutral priming condition, participants read and answered questions regarding proverbs which are unrelated to situational influences on behavior (for example, 'Better late than never'). Applicability was manipulated by presenting the situational pressure either as directed individually to the actor or as directed to a large group of actors.

The findings showed that cognitive load eliminated perceivers' use of situational information when this information was low in salience, accessibility, or applicability. This finding replicated earlier results by Gilbert and his colleagues (Gilbert et al., 1988a, 1992; Gilbert and Osborne, 1989; Osborne and Gilbert, 1992). However, when situational information was more salient, accessible, or applicable, perceivers used it to discount their dispositional inferences even when they were under cognitive load.

Finally, in the same way that the increased salience, accessibility, or applicability of situational information results in discounted dispositional inference, Leyens et al. (1996) suggested that the increased accessibility of dispositional explanation results in undiscounted dispositional inference. Their studies assessed attitude inferences from an essay in favor or against euthanasia that was written under choice or no-choice conditions. Accessibility of dispositional explanation was manipulated by priming either personality concepts or irrelevant concepts of formal education. Specifically, in the dispositional priming condition, participants learned that the essay was written as part of a personality examination. They were presented with several other personality questionnaires that the writer was ostensibly required to fill out. In the formal education priming condition, participants learned that the essay was written as part of a university admission examination. They were then presented with several other forms that the writer was ostensibly required to fill out. The results showed that participants failed to discount their inference for the situational demands only when personality concepts were primed (Leyens et al., 1996). Presumably, an accessible dispositional explanation decreases perceivers' tendency to take into account situational information.

Moreover, Corneille and his colleagues (Corneille et al., 1999) suggested that accessibility of a dispositional hypothesis may compensate for the effect of increased motivational resources. Their studies examined the effect of accountability on situational discounting as a function of the accessibility of dispositional explanation. With a paradigm similar to Leyens et al.'s (1996), accountable or unaccountable participants were primed with dispositional or irrelevant prime. The results showed that accountable participants used situational information to discount their dispositional inference only when an irrelevant concept was primed. In the dispositional priming condition, however, even accountable perceivers underused situational information and drew undiscounted dispositional inference (Corneille et al., 1999: Experiment 3). Thus, increased accessibility of dispositional explanations can compensate for the effects of perceivers' feeling of accountability.

### *Identification and inference determinants of discounting*

Situational information may influence the inference process in two opposite directions. In the identification stage, situational inducements act as a context that disambiguates behavioral information. The identified behavior then serves as evidence for the correspondent disposition. In contrast, in the attributional inference stage, situational inducements act as a alternative explanations for an identified behavior, thus attenuating dispositional inferences. Thus, as a disambiguator of behavior, situational inducements enhance dispositional inference, but as alternative explanations of the identified behavior, situational inducements produce discounted dispositional inference. The observed effect of situational inducements on dispositional inference results from the combination of these two processes, which may take one of the four possible forms described below (see Table 8.1).

When perceivers use situational inducements as an alternative explanation, but not as a behavior disambiguator, discounting effects obtain (see Table 8.1, quadrant A). The requirements for discounting effects are likely to be met when the observed behavior is sufficiently unambiguous to prevent assimilative identification (that is, the use of the situation as a disambiguator of behavior) and perceivers possess sufficient cognitive and motivational resources to reason in a diagnostic manner, namely, to consider alternative causes for the identified behavior. When either one of these two requirements is not met, a null effect results. There are two possible types of null effects. One type of null effect results from failure to perform diagnostic inference (quadrant B). This is likely to occur when perceivers lack the motivational or processing resources needed to use situational inducements as alternative explanations of behavior. The other type of null effect results from the use of the situation as a disambiguator of behavior (quadrant C). Here, the disambiguated behavior is used as evidence for the hypothesized disposition, thus offsetting the use of situational inducements as alternative hypotheses. Finally, the fourth type of situational effect on dispositional inference is discounting reversal (quadrant D). In this case, situational inducements increase rather than decrease dispositional inference. Discounting reversals are likely to occur when perceivers use the situation as a disambiguator of behavior, but not as an alternative explanation of the disambiguated behavior.

In terms of Table 8.1, some of the studies reviewed earlier manipulated the determinants of the use of situational inducements as a behavior disambiguator, thus comparing quadrants A and B (e.g., Trope et al., 1991). Other studies manipulated the determinants of the use of situational inducements as alternative explanations, thus comparing quadrants A and C (e.g., Gilbert et al., 1988b; Trope and Gaunt, 2000). Two studies conducted by Trope and Alfieri (1997) compared all four quadrants within one experimental design. One study focused on the effortfulness of using the situation as a disambiguator of behavior and as an alternative interpretation. The other study focused on the flexibility of these two uses of situational inducements.

### *The effortfulness of using situational information*

Trope and Alfieri's first study manipulated the use of situational information as a disambiguator (by presenting ambiguous or unambiguous behavior)

Table 8.1 *The combined effect of situational inducements as behavior disambiguators and alternative explanations*

| | Attributional inference | |
|---|---|---|
| Behavior identification | Diagnostic | Pseudodiagnostic |
| Non-assimilative | A<br>Discounting effect | B<br>Null |
| Assimilative | C<br>Null | D<br>Discounting reversal |

and as an alternative explanation (by presenting the information under cognitive load or no cognitive load). Participants heard an evaluator describing another person, John, to their supervisor, who either liked or disliked John. The supervisor's opinion about John created a situational demand on the evaluator to present a positive or negative evaluation of John. The evaluation was either ambiguous or unambiguous, and the information was presented under cognitive load or no cognitive load. From this information, participants judged the favorability of the evaluation (behavior identification) and the evaluator's true attitude toward John (dispositional inference).

The behavior identifications were used as a mediator in the analysis of the attitude attributions. This analysis decomposed the effect of situational demands on attitude attribution into an indirect effect, as a behavior disambiguator, and a direct effect, as an alternative explanation. As expected, the indirect effect of situational demands increased with behavioral ambiguity and was independent of cognitive load. In contrast, the direct effect of situational demands on attitude attribution depended on cognitive load and was independent of behavioral ambiguity. Thus, ambiguity determined whether situational demands were used as context for disambiguating the content of the evaluation, whereas cognitive load determined whether demands were used as an alternative explanation of the evaluation.

Reflecting these underlying effects, the pattern of overall situational effects on attitude attributions was consistent with Table 8.1. First, situational demands produced a discounting effect only when participants were under no load and behavior was unambiguous (quadrant A). In this condition, participants used the situation as an alternative explanation, but not as a behavior disambiguator. Second, situational demands failed to produce discounting effects when either the participants were under load or the behavior was ambiguous (quadrants B and C). Specifically, when participants were under cognitive load, discounting failure was due to a failure to use the situation as an alternative explanation (quadrant B). When the behavior was ambiguous, discounting failure was due to the use of the situation as a behavior disambiguator (quadrant C). Finally, situational demands produced reversed discounting effects, enhancing rather than attenuating attitude attributions, when participants were under load and the behavior was ambiguous (quadrant D). In this condition, participants used the situation as a behavior disambiguator but not as an alternative explanation.

This study demonstrates all three possible effects of situational inducements: discounting effects, null effects, and reversed discounting effects. Moreover, the study demonstrated that these effects are predictable consequences of the use of the situation as context for behavior identification and as an alternative interpretation of the identified behavior.

### *The flexibility of using situational information*

Is dispositional inference a flexible process? Can perceivers with ample cognitive and motivational resources undo the discounting effects of situational information that turns out to be invalid? For example, if perceivers initially think an evaluator was expected to present a positive evaluation but then learn that the evaluator was unaware of these demands, could they undo the effects of the situational demands on their inference? From the present perspective, the use of the situation as a behavior disambiguator and as an alternative explanation should differ in this respect. Specifically, the use of the situation as an alternative explanation is presumably a deliberate process and should, therefore, be reversible. The use of the situational inducements as a disambiguator, however, is an implicit process and may, therefore, be irreversible. Perceivers may see their behavior identifications as perceptual givens rather than as context-derived and may, therefore, fail to change them when the original situational information is invalidated.

Trope and Alfieri's (1997) second experiment tested these predictions. Participants heard an evaluator describing another person, John, to their supervisor, who either liked or disliked John. The description strongly implied, but did not explicitly state, that the evaluator knew the supervisor's opinion about John and thus was under demand to present a positive or negative evaluation. Before making their judgments, some of the participants were told that this assumption was valid (validation condition), whereas others were told that this assumption was invalid, that is, that the evaluator was actually unaware of the supervisor's opinions about John (invalidation condition). As in the first study, the evaluation was either unambiguous or ambiguous, and participants judged the favorability of the evaluation (behavior identification) and the evaluator's true attitude toward John (dispositional inference).

Mediation analysis decomposed the effect of situational demands on attitude attribution into an indirect effect, as a behavior disambiguator, and a direct effect, as an alternative explanation. The indirect effect of situational demands depended on the ambiguity of the behavior but not on the validity of situational demands. That is, situational demands continued to affect identification of the ambiguous evaluation even when the demands were invalidated. In contrast, the direct effect of situational demands through their use as an alternative explanation depended on the validity of situational demands but not on ambiguity of the behavior. That is, the direct effect was significant when situational demands were validated, but it was negligible when these demands were invalidated.

The overall pattern of situational effects on attitude attribution reflected these underlying effects. First, when behavior was unambiguous and the demands were validated, a discounting effect was obtained. In this condition, situational demands were used only as an alternative explanation of the evaluation, producing discounted attitude attributions. Second, the overall effect of situational demands was nullified when either the behavior was ambiguous or situational demands were invalidated. Specifically, when behavior was ambiguous, situational demands produced two opposite effects on attributions. As disamabiguators of behavior, situational demands increased attitude attributions, but, as alternative explanations, situational demands attenuated attitude attributions. These two effects canceled each other, resulting in an overall null effect of situational demands. When situational demands were invalidated, the null effect simply reflected the fact that participants undid their initial use of the situation as an alternative explanation of the evaluation. Finally, situational demands produced a reverse discounting effect on attitude attribution when the behavior was ambiguous and the demands were invalidated. In this condition, participants undid their initial use of situational demands as an alternative explanation, but not the biasing influence of these demands on behavior identification.

The results of this study support the assumption that the use of situational information for identifying behavior is implicit and, therefore, more difficult to reverse than the use of this information for discounting inferences regarding the target's dispositions. Perceivers who learn that the information they have about the situation is false may be able to reverse their use of situational inducements as alternative explanations of behavior, but not their use of situational inducements as disambiguators of behavior.

### *Situational explanations*

In much of the research described above, participants were instructed to assess the target's traits, attitudes, or abilities. Participants' focal hypothesis was therefore a dispositional explanation of behavior, and the processes of behavior disambiguation and pseudodiagnostic inference favored confirmation of the dispositional hypothesis. It is important to point out, however, that the same processes may favor a situational explanation of behavior when this explanation is the focal hypothesis and dispositional hypotheses are alternatives to a situational hypothesis (see Trope and Gaunt, 1999). In evaluation of a situational hypothesis, disambiguated behavior identification is taken as evidence for the power of the situation. A gaze, a silent response, or a slap on the back in a hostile context is likely to be identified as an aggressive response, and these identifications may be then used as evidence for the hypothesis that the actor was provoked.

Diagnostic inference compares the focal situational explanation to alternative dispositional explanations. Information regarding the target's personal dispositions may thus discount situational inferences. For example, any information suggesting that the target is hostile may lead diagnostic perceivers to discount attributions of the aggressive response to situational provocation. However, under suboptimal processing conditions – when attentional or motivational resources for diagnostic processing are depleted – perceivers may resort to pseudodiagnostic inference. Under these conditions, perceivers are likely to focus on the situational hypothesis and give little or no weight to alternative dispositional hypotheses. Research on processing goals (Krull, 1993; Krull and Erickson, 1995) supports this analysis. When testing a dispositional hypothesis, cognitively distracted perceivers failed to discount their dispositional inferences for situational influences on behavior. Similarly, when testing a situational hypothesis, cognitively distracted perceivers failed to discount their situational inferences for the influence of the target's personality on behavior.

Thus, the same identification processes (behavior disambiguation) and inference processes (heuristic hypothesis evaluation) that favor dispositional explanations of behavior may also favor situational explanations of behavior when these latter explanations are part of a perceiver's focal hypothesis.

## Conclusions

The research reviewed in this chapter suggests that to understand attributional inferences we need to take into account (1) perceivers' a-priori causal models of behavior, (2) the identification of attribution-relevant evidence, and (3) heuristic and systematic modes of attributional inferences from the identified evidence.

The inferences perceivers draw from a behavioral episode depend on their a-priori causal models of behavior. These models specify how personal and situational factors combine to produce behavior in different domains. Behavior is likely to be seen as indicative of a situational or personal factor to the extent that this factor is a necessary cause of the behavior in the perceiver's causal model of the behavior. The role of situations and dispositions in perceivers' causal models of behavior may vary across different types of perceivers, behaviors, and targets. Perceivers from Western (rather than Eastern) cultures, and perceivers who see traits as fixed entities (rather than as malleable qualities) are likely to see dispositions as the prime potential causes of behavior (see Dweck et al., 1993; Markus and Kitiyama, 1991). For certain types of behavior (for example, immoral, successful, or extraverted behaviors), dispositional factors may be seen as primary potential causes, whereas for other behaviors (for example, moderate, moral, unsuccessful, or introverted behaviors), situational factors may be seen as primary (see Gidron et al., 1993; Reeder, 1993). Finally, perceivers may have different models for different targets. For some targets (for example, others, and out-group members), dispositional factors may be seen as primary potential causes, whereas for other targets (for example, self and in-group members), situational factors may be seen as primary.

Attributional processing starts with the identification of the behavioral and situational information contained in an immediate behavioral episode. In this identification process, the representations of the behavior, situation, and past information about the actor implicitly influence each other. Initially, ambiguous information may be disambiguated and subsequently used as unambiguous evidence for attributional inferences. For example, situational information may disambiguate behavior information, and the disambiguated behavior identification may then be used as evidence for the target person's dispositions (e.g., Trope, 1986; Trope and Alfieri, 1997).

Inferential processing of the identified evidence may be performed in a systematic, diagnostic manner or in a heuristic, pseudodiagnostic manner. The stronger the motivation to reach an accurate conclusion and the more abundant the attentional resources, the more likely are perceivers to engage in diagnostic rather than heuristic processing. Both processing modes are based on perceivers' a-priori models of behavior. However, whereas diagnostic inference relates behavior to multiple potential causes, pseudodiagnostic inference relates behavior to one focal cause. Together, the heuristic focus on one cause and the use of disambiguated behavior as evidence for this cause contribute to the tendency to draw overconfident attributional inferences. When a dispositional hypothesis is focal, biased identifications and heuristic inferences favor confirmation of a dispositional explanation of behavior. But when a situational hypothesis is the focal hypothesis, the same biased identifications and heuristic inferences favor confirmation of a situational explanation of behavior (Krull, 1993; Krull and Erickson, 1995).

Classical attribution theories (Heider, 1958; Jones and Davis, 1965; Kelley, 1967) assume that the attribution process aims at forming unambiguous and abstract construals of one's social world. Three decades of attribution research have provided ample support for this assumption by repeatedly showing that perceivers go beyond registering concrete features of behavioral episodes to inferring general underlying causes. At the same time, attribution research has challenged the assumption of classical theories that the attribution process simply follows normative rules of inductive inference. A rich array of cultural, motivational, and cognitive factors have been found to determine perceivers' causal theories of behavior and how these theories are used in processing immediate behavior. Developing a theoretical framework that is general enough to integrate these rich findings without losing the parsimony of classical theories remains a challenge for current and future attribution research.

## Acknowledgments

Preparation of this chapter was supported by NIMH Grant no. 1R01MH59030-01A1 and NSF Grant no. SBR-9808675 to Yaacov Trope.

### SUMMARY

This chapter examines how people perceive and explain their own and others' behavior. The first section reviews research on perceivers' mental models of behavior. These models specify how personal forces (abilities, traits) and situational forces (task difficulty, incentives) combine to determine behavior. Research has found that these models depend on the culture, developmental stage, and the personality of the perceiver. For example, in some cultures, personal traits are believed to be the primary determinant of the behavior, whereas, in other cultures, situational contingencies are believed to be the primary determinants of behavior. The second section reviews research on how these mental models guide the processing of information about self and others. Two processing modes, associative and analytic, are distinguished. The associative mode is fast, effortless, and uncontrollable, whereas the analytic mode is slow, effortful, and controllable. Person-perception errors are discussed in terms of these two processing modes. The third section reviews research on motivational biases. This research distinguishes between motivation to reach an accurate conclusions and motivation to reach a conclusion that promotes the self or the ingroup. The chapter reviews research that has examined the mechanisms that underlie the influence of these motives on attribution and person perception.

## References


Ajzen, I. and Fishbein, M. (1975) 'A Bayesian Analysis of the Attribution Process', *Psychological Bulletin*, 8: 267–77.

Arkin, R.M. and Duval, S. (1975) 'Focus of Attention and Causal Attributions of Actors and Observers', *Journal of Experimental Social Psychology*, 11: 427–38.

Butler, R. (2000) 'Making Judgments about Ability: The Role of Implicit Theories of Ability in Moderating Inferences from Temporal and Social Comparison Information', *Journal of Personality and Social Psychology*, 78: 965–78.

Chiu, C., Dweck, C.S., Tong, J.Y., and Fu, J.H. (1997) 'Implicit Theories and Conceptions of Morality', *Journal of Personality and Social Psychology*, 73: 923–40.

Chiu, C., Hong, Y., and Dweck, C.S. (1997) 'Lay Dispositionism and Implicit Theories of Personality', *Journal of Personality and Social Psychology*, 73: 19–30.

Choi, I. and Markus, H.R. (1998) 'Implicit Theories and Causal Attribution East and West'. Unpublished manuscript, University of Michigan.

Choi, I., Nisbett, R.E., and Norenzayan, A. (1999) 'Causal Attribution across Cultures: Variation and Universality', *Psychological Bulletin*, 125: 47–63.

Corneille, O., Leyens, J.P., Yzerbyt, V.Y., and Walther, E. (1999) 'Judgeability Concerns: The Interplay of Information, Applicability, and Accountability in the Overattribution Bias', *Journal of Personality and Social Psychology*, 76: 377–87.

Cousins, S.D. (1989) 'Culture and Self-Perception in Japan and the United States', *Journal of Personality and Social Psychology*, 56: 124–31.

Devine, P.G., Hirt, E.R., and Gehrke, E.M. (1990) 'Diagnostic and Confirmatory Strategies in Trait Hypothesis-Testing', *Journal of Personality and Social Psychology*, 58: 952–63.

Dunning, D. and Sherman, D.A. (1997) 'Stereotypes and Tacit Inference', *Journal of Personality and Social Psychology*, 73: 459–71.

Dweck, C.S., Chiu, C., and Hong, Y. (1995) 'Implicit Theories and Their Role in Judgments and Reactions: A World from Two Perspectives', *Psychological Inquiry*, 6: 267–85.

Dweck, C.S., Hong, Y., and Chiu, C. (1993) 'Implicit Theories: Individual Differences in the Likelihood and Meaning of Dispositional Inference', *Personality and Social Psychology Bulletin*, 19: 633–43.

Dweck, C.S. and Leggett, E.L. (1988) 'A Social-Cognitive Approach to Motivation and Personality', *Psychological Review*, 95: 256–73.

Evett, S.R., Devine, P.G., Hirt, E.R., and Price, J. (1994) 'The Role of the Hypothesis and the Evidence in the Trait Hypothesis Testing Process', *Journal of Experimental Social Psychology*, 30: 456–81.

Fein, S., Hilton, J.L., and Miller, D.T. (1990) 'Suspicion of Ulterior Motivation and the Correspondence Bias', *Journal of Personality and Social Psychology*, 58: 753–64.

Ferguson, T.J., van Roozendaal, J., and Rule, B.G. (1986) 'Informational Basis for Children's Impressions of Others', *Developmental Psychology*, 22: 335–41.

Fiske, S.T. and Taylor, S.E. (1991) *Social Cognition*, 2nd edn. New York: MCGraw-Hill.

Gidron, D., Koehler, D.J., and Tversky, A. (1993) 'Implicit Quantification of Personality Traits', *Personality and Social Psychology Bulletin*, 19: 594–604.

Gilbert, D.T. (1989) 'Thinking Lightly about Others: Automatic Components of the Social Inference Process', in J.S. Ulman and J.A. Bargh (eds), *Unintended Thought*. New York: Guilford, pp. 189–211.

Gilbert, D.T. (1998) 'Ordinary Personology', in D.T. Gilbert, S.T. Fiske, and G. Lindzey (eds), *The Handbook of Social Psychology,* 4th edn. New York: MCGraw-Hill, pp. 89–150.

Gilbert, D.T., Krull, D.S., and Pelham, B.W. (1988a) 'Of Thoughts Unspoken: Social Inference and the Self-Regulation of Behavior', *Journal of Personality and Social Psychology*, 55: 685–94.

Gilbert, D.T. and Malone, P.S. (1995) 'The Correspondence Bias: The What, When, How and Why of Unwarranted Dispositional Inference', *Psychological Bulletin*, 117: 21–38.

Gilbert, D.T., McNulty, S.E., Giuliano, T.A., and Benson, J.E. (1992) 'Blurry Words and Fuzzy Deeds: The Attribution of Obscure Behavior', *Journal of Personality and Social Psychology*, 62: 18–25.

Gilbert, D.T. and Osborne, R.E. (1989) 'Thinking Backward: Some Curable and Incurable Consequences of Cognitive Busyness', *Journal of Personality and Social Psychology*, 57: 940–9.

Gilbert, D.T., Pelham, B.W., and Krull, D.S. (1988b) 'On Cognitive Busyness: When Person Perceivers Meet Persons Perceived', *Journal of Personality and Social Psychology*, 54: 733–40.

Ginossar, Z. and Trope, Y. (1987) 'Problem Solving in Judgment under Uncertainty', *Journal of Personality and Social Psychology*, 52: 464–76.

Harkness, A.R., DeBono, K.G., and Borgida, E. (1985) 'Personal Involvement and Strategies for Making Contingency Judgments: A Stake in the Dating Game Makes a Difference', *Journal of Personality and Social Psychology*, 49: 22–32.

Heider, F. (1958) *The Psychology of Interpersonal Relations*. New York: Wiley.

Higgins, E.T. (1996) 'Knowledge Activation: Accessibility, Applicability, and Salience', in E.T. Higgins and A.W. Kruglanski (eds), *Social Psychology: Handbook of Basic Principles*. New York: Guilford, pp. 133–68.

Higgins, E.T. and King, G. (1981) 'Accessibility of Social Constructs: Information-Processing Consequences of Individual and Contextual Variability', in N. Cantor and J.F. Kihlstrom (eds), *Personality, Cognition and Social Interaction*. Hillsdale, NJ: Erlbaum, pp. 69–121.

Higgins, E.T. and Stangor, C. (1988) 'Context-Driven Social Judgment and Memory: When "Behavior

Engulfs the Field" in Reconstructive Memory', in D. Bar-Tal and A. Kruglanski (eds), *Social Psychology of Knowledge*. Cambridge: Cambridge University Press, pp. 262–98.

Idson, L.C. and Mischel, W. (2001) 'The Personality of Familiar and Significant People: The Lay Perceiver as a Social-Cognitive Theorist', *Journal of Personality and Social Psychology*, 80: 585–96.

Jones, E.E. (1979) 'The Rocky Road from Acts to Dispositions', *American Psychologist*, 34: 107–17.

Jones, E.E. (1990) *Interpersonal Perception*. New York: Macmillan.

Jones, E.E. and Davis, K.E. (1965) 'From Acts to Dispositions: The Attribution Process in Person Perception', in L. Berkowitz (ed.), *Advances in Experimental Social Psychology* (vol. 2). New York: Academic Press, pp. 220–65.

Jones, E.E. and Harris, V.A. (1967) 'The Attribution of Attitudes', *Journal of Experimental Social Psychology*, 3: 1–24.

Jones, E.E. and Nisbett, R.E. (1971) 'The Actor and the Observer: Divergent Perception of the Causes of Behavior', Morristown, NJ: General Learning Press.

Josephson, J. (1977) 'The Child's Use of Situational and Personal Information in Predicting the Behavior of Another'. Unpublished doctoral dissertation, Stanford University.

Kelley, H.H. (1967) 'Attribution Theory in Social Psychology', in D. Levine (ed.), *Nebraska Symposium of Motivation* (vol. 15). Lincoln, NE: University of Nebraska Press, pp. 192–241.

Kelley, H.H. (1972) 'Causal Schemata and the Attribution Process', in E.E. Jones, D.E. Kanouse, H.H. Kelley, R.E. Nisbett, S. Valins, and B. Weiner (eds), *Attribution: Perceiving the Causes of Behavior*. Morristown, NJ: General Learning Press, pp. 151–74.

Kelley, H.H. and Michela, J.L. (1980) 'Attribution Theory and Research', *Annual Review of Psychology*, 31: 457–501.

Kruglanski, A.W. and Mayseless, O. (1988) 'Contextual Effects in Hypothesis Testing: The Role of Competing Alternatives and Epistemic Motivations', *Social Cognition*, 6: 1–20.

Krull, D.S. (1993) 'Does the Grist Change the Mill? The Effect of the Perceiver's Inferential Goal on the Process of Social Inference', *Personality and Social Psychology Bulletin*, 19: 340–8.

Krull, D.S. and Erickson, D.J. (1995) 'Judging Situations: On the Effortful Process of Taking Dispositional Information into Account', *Social Cognition*, 13: 417–38.

Kunda, Z., Sinclair, L., and Griffin, D. (1997) 'Equal Ratings but Separate Meanings: Stereotypes and the Construal of Traits', *Journal of Personality and Social Psychology*, 72: 720–34.

Kunda, Z. and Thagard, P. (1996) 'Forming Impressions from Stereotypes, Traits, and Behaviors: A Parallel-Constraint-Satisfaction Theory', *Psychological Review*, 103: 284–308.

Lee, F. and Hallahan, M. (1998) 'Seeing What We Need to See: Future Expectations and the Primacy of Situational Inferences'. Unpublished manuscript, University of Michigan.

Levy, S.R., Plaks, J.E., and Dweck, C.S. (1999) 'Models of Social Thought: Implicit Theories and Social Understanding', in S. Chaiken and Y. Trope (eds), *Dual-Process Models in Social Psychology*. New York: Guilford Press, pp. 179–202.

Leyens, J.P., Yzerbyt, V., and Corneille, O. (1996) 'The Role of Applicability in the Emergence of the Overattribution Bias', *Journal of Personality and Social Psychology*, 70: 219–29.

Lieberman, M.D., Gaunt, R., Gilbert, D.T., and Trope, Y. (2002) 'Reflexion and Reflection: A Social Cognitive Neuroscience Approach to Attributional Inference', in M. Zanna (ed.), *Advances in Experimental Social Psychology*. New York: Academic Press, pp. 200–50.

Lupfer, M.B., Clark, L.F., and Hutcherson, H.W. (1990) 'Impact of Context on Spontaneous Trait and Situational Attributions', *Journal of Personality and Social Psychology*, 58: 239–49.

Maass, A., Ceccarelli, R., and Rudin, S. (1996) 'Linguistic Intergroup Bias: Evidence for In-Group-Protective Motivation', *Journal of Personality and Social Psychology*, 71: 512–26.

Maass, A., Milesi, A., Zabbini, S., and Stahlberg, D. (1995) 'Linguistic Intergroup Bias: Differential Expectancies or In-Group Protection?', *Journal of Personality and Social Psychology*, 68: 116–26.

Maass, A., Salvi, D., Arcuri, L., and Semin, G.R. (1989) 'Language Use in Intergroup Contexts: The Linguistic Intergroup Bias', *Journal of Personality and Social Psychology*, 57: 981–93.

Markus, H.R. and Kitayama, S. (1991) 'Culture and the Self: Implications for Cognition, Emotion, and Motivation', *Psychological Review*, 98: 224–53.

McArthur, L.Z. and Post, D.L. (1977) 'Figural Emphasis and Person Perception', *Journal of Experimental Social Psychology*, 13: 520–35.

McClure, J. (1998) 'Discounting Causes of Behavior: Are Two Reasons Better than One?', *Journal of Personality and Social Psychology*, 74: 7–20.

Miller, J.G. (1984) 'Culture and the Development of Everyday Social Explanation', *Journal of Personality and Social Psychology*, 46: 961–78.

Miller, D.T. and Ross, M. (1975) 'Self-Serving Biases in Attribution of Causality: Fact or Fiction?', *Psychological Bulletin*, 82: 213–25.

Mischel, W. and Shoda, Y. (1995) 'A Cognitive-Affective System Theory of Personality: Reconceptualizing Situations, Dispositions, Dynamics, and Invariance in Personality Structure', *Psychology Review*, 102: 246–68.

Mischel, W., Shoda, Y., and Mendoza-Denton, R. (2002) 'Situation-Behavior Profiles as a Locus of Consistency in Personality', *Current Directions in Psychological Science*, 11: 50–4.

Morris, M.W. and Larrick, R.P. (1995) 'When One Cause Casts Doubt on Another: A Normative Analysis of Discounting in Causal Attribution', *Psychological Review*, 102: 331–55.

Morris, M.W. and Peng, K. (1994) 'Culture and Cause: American and Chinese Attributions for Social and Physical Events', *Journal of Personality and Social Psychology*, 67: 949–71.

Newman, L.S. and Uleman, J.S. (1989) 'Spontaneous Trait Inference', in J.S. Uleman and J.A. Bargh (eds), *Unintended Thought*. New York: Guilford, pp. 155–88.

Newman, L.S. and Uleman, J.S. (1993) 'When Are You What You Did? Behavior Identification and Dispositional Inference in Person Memory, Attribution, and Social Judgment', *Personality and Social Psychology Bulletin*, 19: 513–25.

Nisbett, R.E. and Ross, L. (1980) *Human Influence: Strategies and Shortcomings*. Englewood Cliffs, NJ: Prentice-Hall.

Osborne, R.E. and Gilbert, D.T. (1992) 'The Preoccupational Hazards of Social Life', *Journal of Personality and Social Psychology*, 62: 219–28.

Read, S.J. and Marcus-Newhall, A. (1993) 'Explanatory Coherence in Social Explanations: A Parallel Distributed Processing Account', *Journal of Personality and Social Psychology*, 65: 429–47.

Read, S.J. and Miller, L.C. (1998) 'On the Dynamic Construction of Meaning: An Interactive Activation and Competition Model of Social Perception', in S.J. Read and L.C. Miller (eds), *Connectionist Models of Social Reasoning and Behavior*. Mahwah, NJ: Erlbaum, pp. 27–86.

Read, S.J. and Montoya, J.A. (1999) 'An Autoassociative Model of Causal Reasoning and Causal Learning: Reply to Van Overwalle's (1998) Critique of Read and Marcus-Newhall (1993)', *Journal of Personality and Social Psychology*, 76: 728–42.

Read, S.J., Vanman, E.J., and Miller, L.C. (1997) 'Connectionism, Parallel Constraint Satisfaction Processes, and Gestalt Principles: (Re)introducing Cognitive Dynamics to Social Psychology', *Personality and Social Psychology Review*, 1: 26–53.

Reeder, G.D. (1985) 'Implicit Relations between Dispositions and Behaviors: Effects on Dispositional Attribution', in J.H. Harvey and G. Weary (eds), *Attribution: Basic Issues and Application*. New York: Academic Press, pp. 87–116.

Reeder, G.D. (1993) 'Trait–Behavior Relations and Dispositional Inference', *Personality and Social Psychology Bulletin*, 19: 586–93.

Reeder, G.D. (1997) 'Dispositional Inferences of Ability: Content and Process', *Journal of Experimental Social Psychology*, 33: 171–89.

Reeder, G.D. and Brewer, M.B. (1979) 'A Schematic Model of Dispositional Attribution in Interpersonal Perception', *Psychological Review*, 86: 61–79.

Reeder, G.D. and Fulks, J.L. (1980) 'When Actions Speak Louder than Words: Implicational Schemata and the Attribution of Ability', *Journal of Experimental Social Psychology*, 16: 33–46.

Reeder, G.D. and Spores, J.M. (1983) 'The Attribution of Morality', *Journal of Personality and Social Psychology*, 44: 736–45.

Rholes, W.S., Newman, L., and Ruble, D. (1990) 'Developmental and Motivational Aspects of Perceiving Persons in Terms of Invariant Dispositions', in E.T. Higgins and R.M. Sorrentino (eds), *Handbook of Motivation and Cognition* (vol. 2). New York: Guilford, pp. 369–407.

Rholes, W.S. and Ruble, D.N. (1984) 'Children's Understanding of Dispositional Characteristics of Others', *Child Development*, 55: 550–60.

Ross, L. (1977) 'The Intuitive Psychologist and his Shortcomings: Distortion in the Attribution Process', in L. Berkowitz (ed.), *Advances in Experimental Social Psychology* (vol. 10). New York: Academic Press, pp. 174–221.

Rothbart, M. and Park, B. (1986) 'On the Confirmability and Disconfirmability of Trait Concepts', *Journal of Personality and Social Psychology*, 50: 131–42.

Ruble, D.N., Feldman, N.S., Higgins, E.T., and Karlovac, M. (1979) 'Locus of Causality and the Use of Information in the Development of Causal Attributions', *Journal of Personality*, 47: 595–614.

Semin, G.R. and Fiedler, K. (1988) 'The Cognitive Functions of Linguistic Categories in Describing Persons: Social Cognition and Language', *Journal of Personality and Social Psychology*, 54: 558–68.

Semin, G. and Fiedler, K. (1992) 'The Inferential Properties of Interpersonal Verbs', in G.R. Semin and K. Fiedler (eds), *Language, Interaction and Social Cognition*. Newbury Park, CA: Sage, pp. 58–78.

Shoda, Y. and Mischel, W. (1993) 'Cognitive Social Approach to Dispositional Inferences: What If the Perceiver Is a Cognitive Social Theorist?', *Personality and Social Psychology Bulletin*, 19: 574–95.

Skowronski, J.J. and Carlston, D.E. (1989) 'Social Judgment and Social Memory: The Role of Cue Diagnosticity in Negativity, Positivity and Extremity Biases', *Journal of Personality and Social Psychology*, 52: 689–99.

Smith, E.R. (1998) 'Mental Representation and Memory', In D.T. Gilbert, S.T. Fiske, and G. Lindzey (eds), *The Handbook of Social Psychology*, 4th edn. New York: MCGraw-Hill, pp. 391–445.

Storms, M.D. (1973) 'Videotape and the Attribution Process: Reversing Actors' and Observers' Points of View', *Journal of Personality and Social Psychology*, 27: 165–75.

Tajfel, H. (1982) *Social Identity and Intergroup Relations*. Cambridge: Cambridge University Press.

Taylor, S. and Fiske, S.T. (1978) 'Salience, Attention, and Attribution: Top of the Head Phenomena', in L. Berkowitz (ed.), *Advances in Experimental Social Psychology* (vol. 11). New York: Academic Press, pp. 249–88.

Tetlock, P.E. (1985) 'Accountability: A Social Check on the Fundamental Attribution Error', *Social Psychology Quarterly*, 48: 227–36.

Tetlock, P.E. (1992) 'The Impact of Accountability on Judgment and Choice: Toward a Social Contingency Model', in M.P. Zanna (ed.), *Advances in Experimental Social Psychology* (vol. 25). San Diego, CA: Academic Press, pp. 331–76.

Todorov, A. and Uleman, J.S. (2002) 'Spontaneous Trait Inferences Are Bound to Actors' Faces: Evidence from a False Recognition Paradigm', *Journal of Personality and Social Psychology*, 83: 1051–65.

Triandis, H.C. (1989) 'The Self and Social Behavior in Differing Cultural Contexts', *Psychological Review*, 96: 506–20.

Trope, Y. (1974) 'Inferential Processes in the Forced Compliance Situation: A Bayesian Analysis', *Journal of Experimental Social Psychology*, 10: 1–16.

Trope, Y. (1986) 'Identification and Inferential Processes in Dispositional Attribution', *Psychological Review*, 93: 239–57.

Trope, Y. (1989) 'The Multiple Roles of Context in Dispositional Judgment', in J.N. Bassili (ed.), *On-line Cognition in Person Perception*. Hillsdale, NJ: Erlbaum, pp. 123–40.

Trope, Y. (1989) 'Levels of Inference in Dispositional Judgment', *Social Cognition*, 7: 296–314.

Trope, Y. (1998) 'Dispositional Bias in Person Perception: A Hypothesis-Testing Perspective', in J. Cooper, J.M. Darley (eds), *Attribution Processes, Person Perception, and Social Interaction: The Legacy of Ned Jones*. Washington, DC: APA Press, pp. 230–55.

Trope, Y. and Alfieri, T. (1997) 'Effortfulness and Flexibility of Dispositional Inference Processes', *Journal of Personality and Social Psychology*, 73: 662–74.

Trope, Y. and Burnstein, E. (1975) 'Processing the Information Contained in Another's Behavior', *Journal of Experimental Social Psychology*, 11: 439–58.

Trope, Y. and Cohen, O. (1989) 'Perceptual and Inferential Determinants of Behavior-Correspondent Attribution', *Journal of Experimental Social Psychology*, 25: 142–58.

Trope, Y., Cohen, O., and Alfieri, T. (1991) 'Behavior Identification as a Mediator of Dispositional Inference', *Journal of Personality and Social Psychology*, 61: 873–83.

Trope, Y., Cohen, O., and Maoz, Y. (1988) 'The Perceptual and Inferential Effects of Situational Inducements on Dispositional Attributions', *Journal of Personality and Social Psychology*, 55: 165–77.

Trope, Y. and Gaunt, R. (1999) 'A Dual-Process Model of Overconfident Attributional Inferences', in S. Chaiken and Y. Trope (eds), *Dual Process Theories in Social Psychology*. New York: Guilford, pp. 161–78.

Trope, Y. and Gaunt, R. (2000) 'Processing Alternative Explanations of Behavior: Correction or Integration?', *Journal of Personality and Social Psychology*, 79: 344–54.

Trope Y. and Higgins, E.T. (1993) 'The What, How, and When of Dispositional Inference: New Questions and Answers', *Personality and Social Psychology Bulletin*, 19: 493–500.

Trope, Y. and Liberman, A. (1993) 'Trait Conceptions in Identification of Behavior and Inferences about Persons', *Personality and Social Psychology Bulletin*, 19: 553–62.

Trope, Y. and Liberman, A. (1996) 'Social Hypothesis-Testing: Cognitive and Motivational Mechanisms', in E.T. Higgins and A.W. Kruglanski (eds), *Social Psychology: Handbook of Basic Principles*. New York: Guilford, pp. 239–70.

Trope, Y. and Mackie, D. (1987) 'Sensitivity to Alternatives in Social Hypothesis-Testing', *Journal of Experimental Social Psychology*, 23: 445–59.

Trope, Y. and Sikron, F. (1992) 'Perceptual and Inferential Mechanism Underlying Trait Attributions', paper presented at the Joint SESP-EASP Meeting. Louvain, Belgium.

Uleman, J.S. (1987) 'Consciousness and Control: The Case of Spontaneous Trait Inference', *Personality and Social Psychology Bulletin*, 13: 337–54.

Uleman, J.S. (1999) 'Spontaneous versus Intentional Inferences in Impression Formation', in S. Chaiken and Y. Trope (eds), *Dual-Process Models in Social Psychology*. New York: Guilford Press, pp. 141–60.

Uleman, J.S. and Moskowitz, G.B. (1994) 'Unintended Effects of Goals on Unintended Inferences', *Journal of Personality and Social Psychology*, 66: 490–501.

Uleman, J.S., Newman, L.S., and Moskowitz, G.B. (1996) 'People as Flexible Interpreters: Evidence and Issues from Spontaneous Trait Inference', in M. Zanna (ed.), *Advances in Experimental Social Psychology* (vol. 28). San Diego, CA: Academic Press, pp. 211–79.

Vonk, R. and Van Knippenberg, A. (1994) 'The Sovereignty of Negative Inferences: Suspicion of Ulterior Motives Does Not Reduce the Negativity Effect', *Social Cognition*, 12: 169–86.

Webster, D.M. (1993) 'Motivated Augmentation and Reduction of the Overattribution Bias', *Journal of Personality and Social Psychology*, 65: 261–71.

Weiner, B. (1979) 'A Theory of Motivation for Some Classroom Experiences', *Journal of Educational Psychology*, 71: 3–25.

Winter, L., Uleman, J.S., and Cunniff, C. (1985) 'How Automatic Are Social Judgments?', *Journal of Personality and Social Psychology*, 49: 904–17.

Wyer, R.S. and Gordon, S.E. (1982) 'The Recall of Information about Persons and Groups', *Journal of Experimental Social Psychology*, 18: 128–64.

Wyer, R.S. and Srull, T.K. (1981) 'Category Accessibility: Some Theoretical and Empirical Issues Concerning the Processing of Social Stimulus Information', in E.T. Higgins, C.P. Herman, and M.P. Zanna (eds), *Social Cognition: The Ontario Symposium*. Hillsdale, NJ: Erlbaum, pp. 161–97.

Ybarra, O. (1999) 'Misanthropic Person Memory when the Need to Self-Enhance is Absent', *Personality and Social Psychology Bulletin*, 25: 261–9.

Ybarra, O. and Stephan, W.G. (1996) 'Misanthropic Person Memory', *Journal of Personality and Social Psychology*, 70: 691–700.

Ybarra, O. and Stephan, W.G. (1999) 'Attributional Orientations and the Prediction of Behavior: The Attribution-Prediction Bias', *Journal of Personality and Social Psychology*, 76: 718–27.

# PART THREE

# INTERPERSONAL PROCESSES

# 9
# Attitude Change

PENNY S. VISSER AND JOEL COOPER

**INTRODUCTION**

Hundreds of times over the course of an average day, people try to change our views. We are bombarded by advertisements extolling the virtues of consumer products. We are urged by politicians to support particular policies. We are cajoled by public-health advocates to adopt favorable attitudes toward exercise and healthy eating. And we are coaxed by friends and family members to bring our views into line with their own. Sometimes these efforts to persuade are explicit and direct, and other times they are subtle and inconspicuous. In this chapter we examine the various processes by which attitude change occurs, exploring how, why, and under what circumstances individuals come to hold positive or negative evaluations of the people, places, and things in their social environment.

It has been more than seventy years since Gordon Allport declared the attitude 'the most distinctive and indispensable concept in contemporary American social psychology' (Allport, 1935: 198). And in the intervening years, interest in the attitude construct has wavered very little. Today, a literature search using 'attitude' as the search term yields nearly 50,000 articles, chapters, books, and dissertations. This longstanding interest in the attitude construct is perhaps not surprising – an extensive literature attests to the fact that attitudes often do, as Allport (1935) suggested, powerfully influence perception, cognition, and behavior, profoundly shaping people's interactions with the social world (for reviews, see Eagly and Chaiken, 1993; Chapter 6, this volume).

Because attitudes have the potential to exert such robust effects, identifying the processes by which attitudes are formed and changed has long been of both practical and theoretical interest. In fact, the modern era of attitude-change research was born of both practical and theoretical concerns. During World War II, Yale social psychologist Carl Hovland took a leave of absence to assist in the war effort, heading the mass-communication program of the US Army's Information and Education Division. One of Hovland's central tasks was to evaluate systematically the effectiveness of a series of indoctrination films designed to change soldiers' attitudes toward the war effort and boost morale among the troops. The hallmark of this work, as well as the work that Hovland did upon returning to Yale after the war, was the experimental isolation of variables within the persuasion context and the assessment of their impact on persuasion (e.g., Hovland, 1957; Hovland et al., 1953; Hovland and Janis, 1959). The seminal work by Hovland and his students profoundly shaped the attitude-change research that followed, and its influence can still be seen in contemporary programs of persuasion research.

In this chapter, we provide a concise overview of the attitude-change literature, reviewing some of the major theories of persuasion and the empirical evidence on which they are based. We begin by reviewing models that focus primarily on attitude change that is brought about through exposure to a persuasive message, paying particular attention to contemporary dual-process models of persuasion. Within the context of these dual-process models, we outline several processes of attitude change that do not involve careful scrutiny of a persuasive message. Finally, we consider the impact of behavior on attitudes, paying particular attention to cognitive-dissonance theory.

### Message-based persuasion

When we think about the process by which attitudes are changed, we typically envision the use of a persuasive message advocating a particular position and providing one or more reasons or arguments in support of the position. The salesperson who wants us to hold a positive attitude toward his or her product, for example, may articulate in great detail the many positive attributes of the product or the favorable consequences that we can anticipate once we own it. Hoping to influence public opinion, advocates of particular public policies often write lengthy editorials outlining the rationale for their positions. And in our informal conversations, we are often exposed to counterattitudinal messages that provide explicit reasons that we should adopt a different attitude. In these situations, we often carefully scrutinize the arguments which are presented in the persuasive message – assessing the logical validity of the arguments and comparing the information contained in the message to other information we have stored in memory. To the extent that we find the arguments to be strong and compelling, we may revise our attitudes about the product, policy, or other attitude object.

Indeed, this is one process by which attitude change can occur. But we do not carefully scrutinize the content of every persuasive message that we encounter. Sometimes we are unable to do so – we may lack the requisite background information to comprehend the message, or we may lack the time or cognitive resources to process it carefully. Other times, we are simply unmotivated to put forth the effort that would be required to attend carefully to the message. One of the most significant advances in the attitude-change literature was the explicit recognition in the early 1980s that attitude change can occur under both of these circumstances – when ability and motivation to process a persuasive message are high or when one or both are lacking – albeit through different processes.

### Dual-process models

Before the 1980s, models of message-based persuasion tended to focus on the deliberate, effortful cognitive processes that underlie attitude change. The *message-learning approach*, for example, posited that the key mechanism of attitude change is learning the content of a persuasive message (e.g., Hovland et al., 1953). Attitude change will occur, according to this perspective, to the extent that a person attends to a persuasive message, comprehends the content of the message, yields to or accepts the message, and retains the content of the message in memory. Research within this tradition sought to identify the features of the persuasion context (such as features of the source of a message, features of the message and recipient, and features of the message itself) that regulate these cognitive processes by providing incentives or disincentives for attending, comprehending, and/or yielding to the message, thereby fostering or inhibiting attitude change (e.g., Hovland and Mandell, 1952; Hovland and Weiss, 1951; Janis and Feshbach, 1953; Kelman and Hovland, 1953).

The *cognitive-response approach* posited a different but similarly deliberate and effortful cognitive process by which attitude change is brought about (e.g., Greenwald, 1968). In response to several failures to find a positive correlation between the extent to which people had learned the content of a persuasive message and the magnitude of attitude change they exhibited (e.g., Miller and Campbell, 1959), the cognitive-response model proposed that attitude change is driven not by message learning but by the generation and retention of one's own idiosyncratic cognitive reactions to a persuasive message.

In this way, the cognitive-response approach ascribed to message recipients a much more active role in the attitude-change process. Instead of simply receiving and accepting a persuasive message, recipients were explicitly posited to engage in 'a silent, internal communication' regarding the content of the message (Greenwald, 1981: 128). According to the cognitive-response perspective, this internal conversation is what mediates the relation between a persuasive message and attitude change. To the extent that a persuasive message elicits positive cognitive responses, attitude change will occur, but a persuasive message that elicits negative cognitive responses will result in no attitude change (or perhaps change in the opposite direction). The focus of research within this tradition, therefore, was on identifying the features of the persuasion context that influenced the volume and valence of people's cognitive responses to a persuasive message (e.g., Brock, 1967; Cacioppo and Petty, 1979a; Harkins and Petty, 1981; Petty and Cacioppo, 1977, 1979a; Petty et al., 1981; Wells and Petty, 1980).

Although these kinds of information-processing models of persuasion stimulated a great deal of productive research and provided a useful framework for investigating the various factors that regulate attitude change, it became increasingly clear during the 1970s that the models were unable to accommodate a growing body of conflicting empirical results. Across studies, for example, features of the persuasion context (for example, source attractiveness) were sometimes shown to increase and other times to decrease persuasion (for a review, see Eagly and Chaiken, 1993). Perhaps more troubling, factors that reduced people's cognitive capacity (thereby disrupting their ability to attend to and carefully process a persuasive message) were sometimes found to *increase* rather than decrease persuasion (e.g., Festinger and Maccoby, 1964).

At roughly the same time in the early 1980s, two dual-process models of attitude change were developed, both of which centered on the notion that the process by which attitude change occurs depends on the degree of cognitive effort that message recipients exert when confronted with a persuasive message. The Elaboration Likelihood Model (ELM) (Petty and Cacioppo, 1981, 1986) and the Heuristic-Systematic Model (HSM) (Chaiken, 1987) provided a reconciliation of the conflicting results of many past attitude-change studies by explicitly positing that a particular feature of the persuasion context (for example, the credibility of the message source, the number of persuasive arguments contained in the message) could have *different* effects on persuasion at different levels of cognitive effort. Furthermore, these models specified that two variables could lead to the same attitude-change outcome, but through different processes, and that the same process could sometimes lead to different outcomes. In a flurry of research during the 1980s, a host of apparent inconsistencies in the literature were shown to be entirely compatible once the underlying processes of attitude change were taken into account. These models, which are similar in most important respects, continue to provide the conceptual framework that guides most contemporary message-based attitude change research.[1]

### *Two routes to persuasion*

At the core of both the ELM and the HSM is the presumption that there are two relatively distinct routes by which persuasion can occur – the central or systematic route, and the peripheral or heuristic route (the ELM and HSM terms for each route, respectively). The central/systematic route to persuasion involves careful scrutiny of the information provided in a persuasive message, including efforts to elaborate the information by relating it to other information stored in memory to assess its merits. If, upon close scrutiny, the arguments presented in a persuasive message are found to be strong and compelling, eliciting predominantly favorable cognitive responses, attitude change through the central/systematic route may occur.

However, as we alluded to earlier, central/systematic processing is cognitively taxing, requiring both the ability and the motivation to process carefully the content of a persuasive message. Both of the dual-process models presume that it is neither possible nor practical for people to scrutinize every persuasive message that they encounter. Instead, people are presumed to be cognitive misers (Taylor, 1981), who selectively deploy their cognitive resources. Unlike the earlier models of message-based persuasion, the dual-process models explicitly posit that attitude change can occur even when minimal cognitive effort is expended.

The HSM refers to this low-effort form of persuasion as the heuristic route, reflecting the notion that when people are unmotivated and/or unable to process the content of a persuasive message, they look for heuristic cues available within the persuasion context that enable them to execute simple decision rules to determine what attitude to adopt. A message that is enthusiastically received by other audience members, for example, may induce attitude change if people rely on a 'consensus implies correctness'heuristic (e.g., Axsom et al., 1987). Similarly, a message that contains many arguments – regardless of the quality of those arguments – may induce attitude change via the heuristic route if people generate the thought, 'if there are so many reasons to support this position, the position is probably valid' (e.g., Petty and Cacioppo, 1984). According to the HSM, heuristics of this sort – culled from past experiences and observations – provide people with resource-conserving cognitive strategies for coping with persuasive messages.

The ELM refers to this as the peripheral route to persuasion and includes in this category all processes of attitude change that do not involve careful processing of a persuasive message. In addition to reliance on heuristic cues, for example, the ELM includes as peripheral processes the establishment of simple associations between an attitude object and positive or negative affect (for example, through classical conditioning), the online generation of simple attributional inferences (for example, 'I signed the petition, so I must really favor the policy'), the relatively nonthoughtful application of balance principles (e.g., 'I like Mary, Mary likes Pepsi, I guess I like Pepsi'), among others.

## Determinants of cognitive effort

According to the ELM, recipients of a persuasive message can be thought of as falling somewhere along an elaboration-likelihood continuum, ranging from very high elaboration likelihood (that is, highly motivated and highly able to process a persuasive message) to very low elaboration likelihood (that is, not at all motivated and/or not able to process the message). Where a person falls on this continuum at any given time depends on both dispositional and situational factors. For example, dispositional factors such as intelligence or expertise in a particular domain can influence a person's ability to process a persuasive message. People also vary in their chronic motivation to process information carefully. For example, people who are high in need for cognition enjoy thinking and, therefore, have a higher baseline level of motivation to process effortfully the content of a persuasive message than do people who are low in need for cognition (Cacioppo and Petty, 1982).

Similarly, situational factors can influence both ability and motivation to process a persuasive message. Tight time constraints, for example, or the introduction of a secondary cognitive task can each reduce a person's ability to scrutinize a persuasive message (e.g., Moore et al., 1986; Petty et al., 1976). And situational factors, such as individual (versus diffuse) responsibility for evaluating an issue or the presence of a clear link between an attitude object and one's own material outcomes, can each increase a person's motivation to process a message carefully (e.g., Petty and Cacioppo, 1979b; Petty et al., 1980).

The HSM represents the determinants of cognitive effort slightly differently. In addition to the basic assumption that people prefer to conserve their cognitive resources whenever possible (which the HSM refers to as the 'least effort principle'), the HSM introduces the 'sufficiency principle'. This principle asserts that when a judgment is required, people have some sense of the level of confidence they would like to have in their judgment, represented as the 'sufficiency threshold'. According to the HSM, the level of cognitive effort that people exert in the persuasion context is a joint function of these two factors: people will put forth as little cognitive effort as is required to achieve the desired level of confidence in their judgment. A discrepancy between one's current level of confidence in a judgment and one's desired level of confidence instigates effortful processing. Thus, if a cursory consideration of the information contained in a persuasive message permits a person to form an attitude with a level of confidence that is equal to or greater than the desired level, he or she will not process the message further. However, if the person's confidence in his or her attitude after just a cursory review of the message is less than the desired level, more effortful processing will ensue.[2]

This feature of the HSM permits more detailed specification of the determinants of cognitive effort. According to the HSM, situational and dispositional factors can affect the amount of cognitive effort that people devote to processing a persuasive message by influencing their desired level of confidence, by influencing their current level of confidence, or both. For example, Chaiken et al. (1989) have suggested that the personal relevance of a persuasive message increases the cognitive effort that people exert by increasing their *desired* level of confidence. Expectancy disconfirmation, on the other hand, appears to increase cognitive effort by decreasing one's *current* level of confidence (e.g., Maheswaran and Chaiken, 1991).

### Assessing elaboration

A number of strategies have been developed to assess the amount and nature of cognitive elaboration in response to a persuasive message. Heeding Hovland's (1951) recommendation that the best way to assess the cognitive processes that give rise to attitude change is to assess directly the thoughts that message recipients generate, some researchers have asked participants simply to list the thoughts that occurred to them as they read a persuasive message (e.g., Petty et al., 1981). Higher elaboration is inferred from a larger number of message-relevant thoughts and a higher correspondence between the valence of people's thoughts and their postmessage attitudes.[3]

Perhaps the most common strategy for assessing the level of cognitive effort that message recipients have exerted (often used in conjunction with thought-listing procedures) involves experimentally manipulating the quality of the arguments contained in a persuasive message in a between-subjects design and assessing the impact of this manipulation on the attitudes that participants express after exposure to the message. Scrutiny of a persuasive message should lead to the adoption of message-congruent attitudes when the message contains strong, compelling arguments but not when it contains weak arguments. In contrast, reliance on low-effort strategies (for example, basing one's attitude on a heuristic cue in the persuasion context) should lead to attitudes that do not differ as a function of argument quality. Differences in the attitudes expressed by people exposed to strong versus to weak arguments, therefore, can be used as an index of the degree to which message recipients carefully scrutinized the content of the persuasive message.

This paradigm has proven tremendously useful for investigating the impact of variables within the persuasion context on attitude change, as well as the processes by which they exert their effects. For example, Mackie and her colleagues have used this paradigm to explore the impact of in-group status of a message source on persuasion (Mackie et al., 1990, 1992; see also van Knippenberg and Wilke, 1992). In one such study, participants were presented with a persuasive message on a topic that was relevant to a group to which participants belonged. The message was attributed to either an in-group member or an out-group member and contained either strong or weak arguments (Mackie et al., 1990). Counterattitudinal messages from an in-group member produced attitude change when the arguments were strong, but not when the arguments were weak. In contrast, counterattitudinal messages from an out-group member produced no attitude change, regardless of argument quality. Mackie et al. (1990) also found greater differentiation in the valence of participants' thoughts (a greater number of favorable responses to strong arguments and a greater number of unfavorable responses to weak arguments) when the message was delivered by an in-group member than when it was delivered by an out-group member. Finally, they found that the valence of participants' thoughts predicted their postmessage attitudes when the message was attributed to an in-group member, but not when it was attributed to an out-group member. All of this led Mackie et al. (1990) to conclude that messages from in-group sources are scrutinized more, a result which can enhance persuasion if the arguments contained within the message are strong.

### Consequences of central/systematic versus peripheral/heuristic route

Both the ELM and the HSM propose that the route by which attitude change occurs has implications for the properties of the new attitude: attitudes changed or formed through the central/systematic route are posited to be more durable and impactful than those changed or formed through the peripheral/heuristic route. And indeed, the existing evidence is generally consistent with this notion. Although much of this evidence is correlational, the few studies that have experimentally manipulated message elaboration reinforce the conclusion that attitudes based on scrutiny of a persuasive message tend to be more persistent over time, more resistant to change and have a greater impact on behavior than attitudes based on cursory processing of a persuasive message (for a review, see Petty et al., 1995).

Petty and Cacioppo (1986) proposed several potential mechanisms of the relation between message elaboration and attitude durability, including increased attitude accessibility, increased accessibility of attitude-supportive information, greater consistency between an attitude and the information on which it is based, and greater confidence in the validity of an attitude (see also Petty and Wegener, 1999). Importantly, Petty and Cacioppo (1986) also noted that greater message elaboration should increase attitude durability only to the extent that elaboration sets into motion the proposed mediating processes. They also acknowledged that low-effort strategies may sometimes instigate these mediating processes, leading to increased attitude durability under some circumstances.

#### *Objective versus biased processing*

Both models acknowledge that in addition to the sheer amount of cognitive effort that is put forth, the processing of a persuasive message can also vary in the degree to which it is objective and balanced as opposed to biased or directional. Objective processing involves an open-minded consideration of the information with no a-priori preference for coming to a particular conclusion or judgment, whereas biased processing involves an implicit or explicit preference or tendency to come to one conclusion or judgment over others. In both models, the presence or absence of bias is posited to be orthogonal to the amount of processing – that is, message recipients can effortfully process a persuasive message in an objective or a biased way, or they can execute low-effort, peripheral processes in an objective or a biased way.

In the HSM, the distinction between objective and biased processing is represented in the specific goals that message recipients are posited to adopt in the persuasion context. Under many circumstances, people are presumed to adopt a *validity-seeking* goal with a primary motivation of holding correct attitudes. This motivation is associated with relatively objective message processing. Under some circumstances, however, people are posited to adopt a *defense*-motivation with a primary goal of forming or maintaining a particular attitude. Under this motivational set, people process a persuasive message with the aim of identifying the merits of information which is consistent with their preferred position and disputing the validity of information that is inconsistent with that position. Finally, in some circumstances, people are posited to adopt an *impression-management* goal with the primary motivation of holding attitudes which are socially acceptable. This motivation presumably leads people to process a message with the aim of identifying the socially appropriate attitude within that context.[4]

The starting assumption of the ELM is that people are motivated to hold correct attitudes, so the default processing strategy is presumed to be objective. Nevertheless, one of the central tenets of the ELM is that people are sometimes biased toward processing a message in predominantly favorable or predominantly unfavorable ways. Rather than spell out specific processing goals that can introduce bias, as the HSM does, the ELM posits more generally that many factors within the persuasion context can lead to biases in the way a persuasive message is processed. For example, being in a good mood can render people more likely to retrieve positive than negative information from memory (e.g., Bower, 1981; Forgas and Bower, 1988), a consequence which may bias their cognitive responses to a persuasive message.[5]

#### *Multiple roles for persuasion variables*

One of the unique features of the ELM is an explicit recognition of several distinct ways in which variables within the persuasion context can affect attitude change. Specifically, the ELM posits that a given variable can serve one of four different roles in the attitude-change process: (1) it can serve as a peripheral 'cue', allowing people to determine what attitude to adopt without scrutinizing the content of the message; (2) it can serve as a persuasive argument, providing substantive information relevant to the attitude object; (3) it can influence the extent of cognitive elaboration; or (4) it can influence the direction of cognitive elaboration, biasing the information processing. And in fact, many of the traditional persuasion variables have been shown to serve multiple roles under different circumstances (see Petty and Wegener, 1998a, for a more complete review).

#### Source variables

For example, when elaboration likelihood is low, the attractiveness of a message source often serves as a persuasive cue – people who are unmotivated and/or unable to process the content of a persuasive message more often adopt the position advocated by an attractive than an unattractive source (e.g., Petty and Cacioppo, 1984). But source attractiveness can also serve as a persuasive argument if attractiveness is relevant to the target attitude object. If a persuasive message advocates a particular beauty product, for example, the attractiveness of the source may be scrutinized for evidence regarding the effectiveness of the product (Petty and Cacioppo, 1984). Finally, source attractiveness may influence either the amount or the direction of thinking. When elaboration likelihood is moderate, people may use source attractiveness to decide how carefully to attend to the persuasive message – they may marshal more cognitive resources to process a message from an attractive source than an unattractive source, for example (e.g., Puckett et al., 1983). Or source attractiveness may bias information processing – people may tend to generate more favorable thoughts in response to a message delivered by an attractive than an unattractive source (Chaiken and Maheswaran, 1994).[6]

Other features of the message source have also been shown to affect attitude change in a variety of ways. Source expertise, for example, often seems to operate as a persuasive cue, increasing attitude change when message recipients are unable (e.g., Kiesler and Mathog, 1968; Wood and Kallgren, 1988) or unmotivated (e.g., Petty et al., 1981) to process the message. But expertise has also been shown to regulate the degree to which recipients scrutinize the content of a persuasive message when elaboration likelihood is moderate (e.g., Moore et al., 1986) and to bias the processing of ambiguous messages (e.g., Chaiken and Maheswaran, 1994). Similarly, source trustworthiness serves as a persuasive cue under some circumstances but regulates the amount of cognitive elaboration under other circumstances (see Priester and Petty, 1995).

#### Message variables

Features of the message have also been shown to influence attitude change through a variety of mechanisms. For example, the length or number of persuasive arguments contained within a message often regulates attitude change at low levels of elaboration likelihood (e.g., Petty and Cacioppo, 1984; Wood et al., 1985), but the quality of those arguments determines attitude change when elaboration likelihood is high (e.g., Petty and Cacioppo, 1984). And the discrepancy between the position advocated in a message and a receiver's initial attitude appears to increase the degree to which the message is scrutinized (e.g., Edwards and Smith, 1996), and it may also bias the way the message is processed (see Zanna, 1993).

#### Recipient variables

The relations between features of the message recipient and attitude-change outcomes and processes have also been widely studied, including demographic characteristics such as gender (e.g., Eagly and Carli, 1981) and age (e.g., Visser and Krosnick, 1998); attitude properties such as accessibility (e.g., Houston and Fazio, 1989; Fabrigar et al., 1998), importance (e.g., Krosnick, 1988), and amount of attitude-relevant knowledge (e.g., Wood et al., 1985); and various personality variables and individual differences, such as self-monitoring (e.g., DeBono and Harnish, 1988; Petty and Wegener, 1998b) and intelligence (e.g., Rhodes and Wood, 1992).

Temporary states have also been shown to affect attitude change. In one set of studies, for example, being in a positive mood led to greater attitude change among participants who were dispositionally (study 1) or situationally (study 2) high *and* low in elaboration, but through different processes (Petty et al., 1993). When elaboration likelihood was high, being in a positive mood increased attitude change by biasing people's cognitive responses to the message. But when elaboration likelihood was low, positive mood served as a peripheral cue, producing an increase in attitude change that was unmediated by the valence of people's thoughts.

### Other peripheral processes

According to the ELM, the various attitude-change processes that have been identified within the attitude literature can be ordered along an elaboration-likelihood continuum based on the level of cognitive effort presumed to underlie them. As such, the ELM has been billed as both a specific theory of the cognitive processes by which attitudes are changed and a more general theoretical framework for organizing other, more specific processes of attitude change (Petty and Cacioppo, 1981, 1986). Many of these processes fall into the category of peripheral routes to attitude change, in that they are not based on effortful elaboration of a persuasive message. These peripheral processes include classical conditioning, operant conditioning, mere exposure, and cognitive balance, among others. We briefly review several of these processes in the sections that follow.

### *Classical conditioning*

Perhaps one of the most purely peripheral processes by which attitudes can be changed is through classical conditioning. Just as Pavlov's dogs came to associate the sound of a bell with the presence of meat powder so that the mere sound of the bell was sufficient to elicit salivation, classical conditioning procedures have been used to elicit positive or negative evaluations of previously neutral attitude objects by repeatedly pairing the neutral objects with liked or disliked stimuli (e.g., Byrne and Clore, 1970; Cacioppo et al., 1992; Insko and Oaks, 1966; Staats and Staats, 1957, 1958). For example, Staats et al. (1962) repeatedly presented participants with relatively neutral words while simultaneously introducing an aversive stimulus (an electric shock or a burst of noise). As expected, when the words were later presented without the aversive stimulus, participants exhibited greater physiological arousal (indexed by galvanic skin response) than they exhibited in response to neutral control words, and they rated the conditioned words significantly more negatively than the control words.

Classical conditioning effects of this sort have been demonstrated with a wide range of initially neutral objects, including words (e.g., Staats et al., 1962), nonsense syllables (e.g., Cacioppo et al., 1992), geometric figures (e.g., Sachs and Byrne, 1970), other people (e.g., Byrne and Clore, 1970; Griffit, 1970), political slogans (e.g., Razran, 1940), and consumer products (e.g., Gorn, 1982), and a wide range of initially liked or disliked stimuli, including electric shocks (e.g., Zanna et al., 1970), liked and disliked music (Gorn, 1982), aversive noise (e.g., Staats et al., 1962), and attitude statements with which one agrees or disagrees (Byrne and Clore, 1970; Sachs and Byrne, 1970). And classically conditioned attitudes have been shown to manifest themselves not only in participants' verbal reports, but in their choices and behaviors as well (e.g., Berkowitz and Knurek, 1969; Gorn, 1982).

Although these effects are quite robust, classical conditioning has been shown to exert more powerful effects for novel than for familiar attitude objects (Cacioppo et al., 1992), among people who are aware of the contingency between the presentation of the initially neutral object and the positive or negative stimulus more than those who are not aware of the contingency (e.g., Sachs and Byrne, 1970), and among people who are low rather than high in elaboration likelihood (e.g., Mackie and Worth, 1990).

### *Operant conditioning*

Attitudes can also be changed through operant conditioning, or the provision of reinforcements to a desired response. And even relatively subtle verbal or nonverbal reinforcements have been shown to influence people's attitudes (for example, saying 'good' or nodding one's head each time a person expresses a particular view; Insko, 1965; Insko and Butzine, 1967; Insko and Cialdini, 1969; Insko and Melson, 1969; Krasner et al., 1965; Verplanck, 1955). In one early demonstration of this effect, Hildum and Brown (1956) conducted a telephone survey in which university students were asked a series of questions about their school's general education policy. A randomly selected subset of the students was verbally reinforced whenever they expressed a view that was favorable toward the policy (that is, the interviewer replied, 'good') and another subset was reinforced whenever they expressed a view that was unfavorable toward the policy. This simple reinforcement was sufficient to increase the frequency with which participants expressed the reinforced view over the course of the interview – those who were reinforced for supporting the policy expressed increasingly supportive views, whereas those who were reinforced for opposing the policy expressed increasingly oppositional views. In a replication and extension of this study, the observed attitude change was shown to persist as much as a week later when students' attitudes were assessed in an entirely unrelated context (Insko, 1965).

### *Mere exposure*

Another nonthoughtful process by which attitudes can be changed involves repeated exposure – simply exposing people to an attitude object repeatedly can cause them to hold more positive attitudes toward the object. In the classic demonstration of this 'mere exposure' effect, Zajonc (1968) briefly exposed participants to novel stimuli (yearbook photographs, ostensible Turkish words, or Chinese characters) either twenty-five times, ten times, five times, twice, once, or not at all. Participants' subsequent ratings of the likability of the person in each photograph or their estimates of the positivity of each Turkish word or Chinese character increased monotonically and quite substantially as frequency of exposure increased. This finding has been replicated with a diverse range of novel attitude objects (such as sounds, geometric shapes, or names) in both experimental and naturalistic settings (for a review, see Bornstein, 1989). Mere exposure effects have even been documented with animals and insects (e.g., Harrison and Fiscaro, 1974; Rajecki, 1973; Zajonc et al., 1973).

### Mechanism of the mere exposure effect

The notion that repeated exposure leads to liking was initially thought to reflect feelings of comfort associated with things that are familiar to us and feelings of discomfort and unease associated with the unfamiliar (e.g., Titchener, 1910). Subsequent research, however, has demonstrated that people need not recognize an object as familiar to demonstrate the mere exposure effect (e.g., Kunst-Wilson and Zajonc, 1980; Wilson, 1979). In fact, repeated *subliminal* presentation of stimuli results in stronger mere exposure effects than repeated exposure of which people are consciously aware (Bornstein, 1989; Bornstein and D'Agostino, 1992).

Bornstein (1989; Bornstein and D'Agostino, 1994) has suggested that, instead of familiarity, mere exposure effects are driven by perceptual fluency or the experience of greater ease of perceiving, encoding, and processing objects that have been encountered before, relative to novel objects. Consistent with this notion, other manipulations of perceptual fluency (for example, longer presentation duration or greater figure/ground contrast) have also been shown to increase liking for previously neutral objects (e.g., Reber et al., 1998). According to Bornstein, people are often unaware of the source of this perceptual fluency and look to contextual cues to explain it. When asked to evaluate an object, people often misattribute the experience of perceptual fluency to liking for the object. Consistent with empirical findings, this misattribution account implies that mere exposure effects should be greater when alternative explanations for the perceptual fluency are absent (for example, when objects have been presented subliminally so that people cannot attribute the processing ease to prior exposure).

Other scholars have posited direct affective accounts for the mere exposure effect rather than cognitively mediated misattribution explanations. For example, Winkielman and his colleagues (Winkielman and Cacioppo, 2001; Winkielman et al., 2003) have developed the hedonic fluency model, which posits that the experience of perceptual fluency itself produces a positive affective response. That is, according to the hedonic fluency model, the affective consequences of repeated exposure are not simply due to misattribution of the (affectively neutral) experience of perceptual fluency, but instead arise directly from the experience of such fluency. And consistent with this reasoning, several studies using physiological measures of affective arousal have demonstrated that increased perceptual fluency elicits an immediate, positive affective response (e.g., Harmon-Jones and Allen, 2001; Winkielman and Cacioppo, 2001).

### *Cognitive balance*

The research of the 1950s and 1960s was heavily influenced by Gestalt notions of consistency. Central to these frameworks was the idea that people strive to maintain consonance among elements (such as beliefs and attitudes) within their cognitive systems. One of the most influential of these consistency-based models was Heider's (1946, 1958) balance theory, which specifies another process by which attitude change can occur in the absence of careful scrutiny of a persuasive message.

Although it can, in principle, be applied to any two or more cognitive elements, balance theory has most often been expressed in terms of the relations between three particular cognitive elements: a reference person (P), another person (O), and an object (X). The relations among these elements are characterized as *sentiment* (liking) relations or *unit* relations (any other, nonevaluative association or bond between elements). These relations can be positive (for example, reference person P likes object X in the case of a sentiment relation; reference person P owns object X as one example of a unit relation) or negative. According to balance theory, these P–O–X triads are balanced when the relations among them are consonant, and they are imbalanced when the relations are dissonant. For example, balance occurs when we agree in terms of our evaluation of an object with others that we like (for example, when we like O, we like X, and O likes X) and when we disagree with others that we dislike (for example, when we dislike O, we like X, and O dislikes X). Imbalance occurs when we disagree in our evaluation of an object with others that we like (for example, we like O, we like X, but O dislikes X), or when we agree with others that we dislike (for example, we dislike O, we like X, and O likes X).

Heider (1946, 1958) suggested that imbalance is psychologically uncomfortable and that people strive to maintain cognitive balance. Consistent with this notion, imbalanced triads have been shown to be rated as less pleasant than balanced triads (e.g., Jordan, 1953) and to produce physiological arousal consistent with discomfort (e.g., Burdick and Burnes,

1958; Tsai and Levenson, 1997). Often, a relatively simple way to restore balance is through attitude change. For example, if a reference person P likes another person O and likes object X, but person O dislikes object X, balance can be restored for person P by adopting a negative attitude toward object X, or by adopting a negative attitude toward person O. Consistent with these priniciples, attitude change in response to cognitive imbalance has been frequently demonstrated (e.g., Davis and Rusbult, 2001; Insko et al., 1974; Insko and Wilson, 1977; Tyler and Sears, 1977).

## Behavioral influences on attitude change

As we have seen, attitudes are affected by the elaboration of persuasive messages, by the heuristic processing of variables within the persuasion context that are peripheral to the central merits of an attitude object and by a host of other low-effort cognitive and affective processes. Another major influence on a person's attitudes is his or her own behavior. We now consider the theoretical positions and empirical evidence suggesting that attitudes are affected by actions.

Perhaps the most influential framework linking behavior and attitude change is Festinger's (1957) theory of cognitive dissonance. Although formulated as a general theory of cognitive consistency, the theory garnered the most attention for its implications for inconsistencies between people's behaviors and their attitudes.

Festinger proposed that cognitive elements (for example, a mental representation of a past behavior and a particular attitude) may be relevant or irrelevant to one another. Furthermore, he proposed that the relations among relevant elements may be either consonant or dissonant. A relationship between a pair of cognitions was considered to be consonant if one cognition followed from the other but was considered to be dissonant if one cognition followed, not from the other member of the pair, but from its obverse. A well-known example posed by Festinger was the pair of cognitions, 'I am standing in the rain' and 'I am not getting wet.' The perception that I am not getting wet clearly does not follow from the cognition that I am standing in the rain, but rather from its obverse. Were that to happen to any of us, we would feel agitated, uncomfortable, and upset. Festinger predicted that dissonant cognitions would cause an unpleasant arousal state, one that people would be motivated to reduce.

Dissonance theory held the promise of having more predictive power than many prior notions of consistency or balance because it postulated that dissonance had a magnitude. Dissonance was predicted to be directly proportional to the magnitude and importance of the cognitions discrepant with the focal cognition (see Mills, 1999) and inversely proportional to the magnitude and importance of the cognitions consistent with the focal cognition. Moreover, unlike previous consistency-based models, the dissonant relationships that Festinger and his students envisioned typically established behavior as the focal cognition and attitudes as the cognitions that changed to reduce the dissonance.

Festinger and Carlsmith's (1959) well-known *induced compliance* study presented a powerful example of the potential for actions to influence attitudes. Research participants were asked to perform a series of tasks which had been designed to be excruciatingly dull and tedious. They were then asked to tell another university student who was waiting to participate in the study that the tasks were fun and enjoyable. Telling another student that the tasks were fun was clearly at variance with the participants' attitudes toward the tasks. The discrepant cognitions were expected to cause the unpleasant tension state of dissonance, and participants were expected to reduce this aversive state in the most direct way available to them: by changing their attitudes toward the tasks to bring them into line with their behavior.

But there was more to Festinger and Carlsmith's (1959) study that helped to propel the theory of cognitive dissonance. The investigators varied the magnitude of dissonance by varying the financial incentive they offered participants to lie to the waiting subject. People who were paid handsomely to lie to the other participant were expected to experience less dissonance because the financial incentive provided a cognition that was consistent with the attitude-discrepant behavior – I said the task was interesting when it was dull, participants would presumably reason, but I had a good reason for doing so. This justification for the attitude-discrepant behavior would reduce the magnitude of dissonance that participants experienced.

In contrast, participants who received a trivial incentive were unable to justify the attitude-discrepant behavior so easily and, therefore, were expected to experience more dissonance. For these participants, one of the most efficient ways to reduce the unpleasant state of dissonance would be to change their attitudes toward the tasks. Indeed, Festinger and Carlsmith (1959) found that participants who were paid $1 to lie to the other subject manifested substantially more attitude change than did participants who were paid $20 to lie to the other subject.

This finding, which has been replicated conceptually dozens of time since the 1950s (see Harmon-Jones and Mills, 1999), was important in a number of ways. It provided a strong test of the notion that people's motivation to change cognitions is a function of the magnitude of the dissonance they experience, it threw down the gauntlet to supporters of various reinforcement theories dominant at the time that would have predicted that the magnitude of incentive should have a positive rather than an inverse relationship to change (Elms and Janis, 1965; Rosenberg, 1965), and it established dissonance as a major theory of attitude change.

### *Types of behaviors that change attitudes*

#### Making a choice

One of the most ubiquitous behaviors in everyday life is the act of choosing. On a daily basis, we decide what to wear, how to travel, what to purchase, and what aspect of our work to pursue. And choosing has consequences. Brehm (1956) was the first to note that one of the potential consequences is the arousal of cognitive dissonance. If we assume at least two attractive alternatives, the act of choosing one action over another necessarily means foregoing all of the attractive qualities of the unchosen alternative and accepting all of the unattractive aspects of the chosen alternative. These consequences are dissonant with the choice, creating the unpleasant arousal that can lead to attitude change. Brehm (1956) showed that one way to reduce this negative arousal is through what he called 'spreading of alternatives', whereby people convince themselves that they like the chosen alternative much more and the unchosen alternative much less. Brehm (1956) found that the closer the items were in initial attractiveness, the more dissonance the choice engendered and the greater the spreading of alternatives after the choice.

The free choice and induced compliance procedures have proven the most robust methods for linking behaviors to attitudes. In recent decades, the paradigms have been used to test a large number of theoretical and practical questions involving the motivational state of dissonance (e.g., Azdia and Joule, 2001; Blanton et al., 1997; Blanton et al., 2001; Brehm and Cohen, 1962; Elliot and Devine, 1994; Festinger, 1964; Galinsky et al., 2000; Harmon-Jones, 2000; Harmon-Jones and Harmon-Jones, 2002; Leippe and Eisenstadt, 1999; Losch and Cacioppo, 1990; Steele and Liu, 1983; Stone, 1999).

#### Acting effortfully

People come to like that for which they suffer. With that prediction, Aronson and Mills (1959) set out to show another fascinating relationship between behaviors and attitudes. Using dissonance theory, they demonstrated that people's attitudes toward a goal or object became more positive to the degree that they behaved effortfully to acquire it. In their well-known study, Aronson and Mills (1959) had participants volunteer to join a discussion group on the psychology of sex. The group discussion, it turned out, was dull and tedious. But in order to join the group, some participants had to engage in an effortful and embarrassing reading of pornographic passages whereas other participants had to perform a relatively easy task before they could join. Consistent with dissonance theory, participants who expended a high amount of effort evaluated the group far more positively than did participants who expended only a small amount of effort. The effortful behavior was inconsistent with the perception of the group as mediocre, so attitudes toward the group were brought into line with the effort. These findings have been replicated with a broad array of effortful behaviors, including receiving a painful electric shock, engaging in highly effortful exercise, or enduring a highly irritating noise (e.g., Axsom, 1984; Axsom and Cooper, 1985; Cooper, 1980; Cooper and Axsom, 1982; Gerard and Mathewson, 1966).

#### Insufficient deterrence

Refraining from a behavior can also cause changes in attitudes. Consider a child who is asked not to play with an attractive toy. Dissonance may arise from the inconsistency between the child's attitude toward the toy and his or her behavior (that is, the child likes the toy, but is not playing with it). The more justification the child has to refrain from playing with the toy, however, the lower the dissonance. Thus, if a caregiver were to tell a child that he or she would be very angry if the child played with a particular toy, the child would have an important cognition consistent with the attitude-inconsistent behavior, reducing dissonance. But when there is insufficient justification for refraining to play with the toy, dissonance will be increased. Indeed, Aronson and Carlsmith (1962) found that children who refrained from playing with an attractive robot when given only a minor admonition not to play with it changed their attitudes by devaluing the toy more than did children who were given a major threat (see also, Freedman, 1965; Zanna et al., 1973).

#### Hypocrisy

Can behavior that is consistent with a person's attitudes also create cognitive dissonance? This twist on dissonance theory was proposed by Aronson and his colleagues (Aronson, 1992; Aronson et al., 1991) and has received considerable support (see Aronson, 1999, for a review). It is not uncommon for people to espouse a position that they have not always lived up to in their past behaviors. For example, someone who tells another never to litter may have thrown a paper on the ground once or twice. Aronson et al. (1991) had college students record a speech to high-school adolescents urging them to use condoms during every sexual encounter. Some of the college students were then asked to think about times that they had failed to use condoms in the past. Becoming mindful of prior acts inconsistent with their speech aroused dissonance in the participants, and, as a result, participants' behavioral intentions to use condoms were strengthened. Actual behavioral changes (for example, the purchase of condoms) have also been demonstrated in response to this type of dissonance arousal (e.g., Dickerson et al., 1992; Stone et al., 1994, 1997).

### *Dissonance and attitude change: a matter of measurement*

It is worth noting that cognitive-dissonance theory is not a theory of attitude change per se. Festinger (1957) introduced cognitive dissonance as a theory of motivation. Tests of the theory have most often focused on the relationship of attitudes to behaviors, but, as we alluded to earlier, the theory is more general than that.

In the dominant experimental paradigm, an inconsistency is created by inducing participants to perform a behavior that is incongruent with an attitude that they hold. Because the behavior has already been performed and cannot be undone, the most efficient way for people to resolve the uncomfortable state of dissonance is to change their discrepant attitude, and the amount of attitude change is taken as an index of the magnitude of dissonance that they experienced. In some situations, however, attitude change is not the most effective way to reduce dissonance. For example, people sometimes bolster their original attitudes (that is, generate additional consonant cognitions) rather than change their attitudes when those attitudes are self-definitional (e.g., Sherman and Gorkin, 1980). Similarly, when people have been induced to behave inconsistently with an attitude that is definitional of a group to which they belong, they sometimes use derogation of the out-group rather than attitude change as a way to reduce their dissonance (e.g., Mackie and Cooper, 1984). Leippe and Eisenstadt (1999) have suggested that when very important self-definitional attitudes are at stake, dissonance reduction may take any of several forms, including an elaborate restructuring of attitudes (Leippe and Elkin, 1992), gathering additional support for one's attitudes (Monteith, 1993), and trivializing the importance of the attitude issue (Simon et al., 1995). Each of these strategies has been used as an index of cognitive dissonance.

More direct measures of cognitive dissonance have also been advocated. For example, Devine et al. (1999) argued for the use of a 'dissonance thermometer', a self-report measure of affective discomfort. And, indeed, Elliot and Devine (1994) showed that psychological discomfort can be reliably measured following counterattitudinal behavior. Not only did participants indissonance-inducing conditions report more emotional discomfort, but also, when invited to express their affect before reporting their attitudes, they no longer showed any attitude change (see also Galinsky et al., 2000; Harmon-Jones, 2000; Losch and Cacioppo, 1990).

### *In search of the motivator*

What purpose does dissonance reduction serve? Festinger (1957) predicated his theory on the assumption that dissonance acts like an aversive motivational state, likening the experience of dissonance to the experience of hunger. According to Festinger, attitude–behavior inconsistency causes an unpleasant state of arousal, and the restoration of consistency is in the service of reducing that arousal. Early, ingenious attempts to implicate arousal demonstrated that dissonance interfered with performance on complex verbal tasks, just as other forms of arousal have been shown to do (Pallak and Pittman, 1972). Furthermore, providing people with an external stimulus to which they could misattribute their unpleasant arousal (for example, a placebo pill they had ingested) was shown to eliminate attitude change following attitude-inconsistent behavior (e.g., Zanna and Cooper, 1974, 1976). Moreover, direct manipulations of arousal (through the use of mild stimulants or sedatives) were shown to regulate attitude change following counterattitudinal behavior – participants who ingested an arousing drug exhibited greater attitude change, whereas those who had ingested a sedative exhibited less change (Cooper et al., 1978). All of these findings indirectly implicated unpleasant arousal as the motivating force behind dissonance.

More direct evidence has generally reinforced this conclusion. For example, Croyle and Cooper (1983) showed that writing a speech contrary to one's opinions had a measurable impact on people's nonspecific skin conductance, a physiological measure of arousal (see also, Elkin and Leippe, 1986; Harmon-Jones et al., 1996; Losch and Cacioppo, 1990). However, psychophysiological evidence of this sort leaves open the question of whether arousal per se motivates dissonance-reducing attitude change, or whether it is the associated unpleasant affect that drives attitude change. Losch and Cacioppo (1990) have argued that, although physiological arousal is a concomitant of dissonance, the true motivating agent is the reduction of negative affect. Further support for the central role of unpleasant, negative affect has been reported by Elliot and Devine (1994) and others (see Devine et al., 1999, for a review).

### *Controversies in dissonance research*

From the earliest years of research on cognitive dissonance, controversies abounded (e.g., Chapanis and Chapanis, 1964; Janis and Gilmore, 1965; Tedeschi et al., 1971). Some scholars have proposed alternative ways of thinking about dissonance in an effort to increase the predictive power of the model. For example, McGregor et al. (1999) have emphasized the importance of considering the simultaneous accessibility of the dissonant cognitions. Sakai (1999) presented a mathematical specification for the magnitude of dissonance, while Schultz and Lepper (1996, 1999) have demonstrated the predictive power of a parallel constraint computational model. Van Overwalle and Jordens (2002) have recently proposed an alternative computational model based on a feed-forward, adaptive connectionist framework that fits some of the more complex empirical findings of research in dissonance theory. Other scholars have more radically reconceptualized cognitive dissonance, in some cases thoroughly recasting the theory. Below, we review some of these models and the lively theoretical and empirical debates that have ensued.

#### Self-perception: inferring attitudes from behavior

One of the earliest and liveliest controversies surrounding cognitive dissonance involved an alternative interpretation of the classic dissonance findings. Specifically, Bem (1967, 1972) proposed that attitude change following attitude-incongruent behavior was not driven by an aversive state of dissonance but by simple self-perception processes. Just as people infer the attitudes of others from the behaviors that those others perform, so, too, according to self-perception theory, do people look to their own behavior for information about what their attitudes must be. When asked to report their attitudes toward an experimental task, for example, people may infer their attitudes from their recent behavior: having told another participant that the experimental task was fun and enjoyable, they may infer that their attitude toward the task is in fact positive.

According to self-perception theory, these kinds of inferences occur unless one's behavior can be unambiguously attributed to some external feature of the situation, in which case, the behavior is seen as uninformative regarding one's attitudes. Bem (1967) argued, therefore, that Festinger and Carlsmith's (1959) findings could easily be explained by self-perception. According to self-perception theory, participants who made a favorable statement about the task for a very small financial incentive used their behavior to infer their attitudes because the behavior could not be easily attributed to an external aspect of the situation. In contrast, participants whose behavior was perceived to be attributable to a very large inducement did not use their behavior as information regarding their attitudes and, thus, did not exhibit attitude change.

Bem's provocative approach stimulated a great deal of debate several decades ago (e.g., Bem, 1967; Bem and McConnell, 1970; Jones et al., 1968). But as evidence began to accumulate that dissonance was indeed an unpleasant state of arousal, self-perception theory began to wane as an explanation for dissonance phenomena. However, self-perception continued to provide important insights into the connection between behaviors and attitudes, especially when attitudes are weak (e.g., Taylor, 1975) and behavior is not markedly discrepant from a person's attitude (Fazio et al., 1977).

In one memorable illustration of self-perception processes, Strack et al. (1988) had participants rate cartoons while holding a pen in their mouth. Some of the participants were instructed to hold the pen with their lips, not allowing the pen to touch their teeth. The consequence of this technique was to put facial muscles in the form of a frown. Other participants held the pen in their teeth, not allowing it to touch their lips. This had the consequence of simulating the formation of a smile. Participants rated the cartoons as funnier when their facial muscles were in the smile position than in the frown position. Considerable research now converges on the notion that people sometimes do look to their own responses for information about how they feel (see Schwarz and Clore, 1996, for a review), a proposition consistent with Bem's theory of self-perception.

#### The New Look Model

In 1984, Cooper and Fazio reviewed the dissonance literature and noted that not all attitude-inconsistent behavior led to attitude change, as Festinger's original theory predicted. Rather, they argued that dissonance occurs when people feel personally responsible for bringing about an unwanted, aversive consequence. According to their New Look Model, people who act in a counterattitudinal fashion first assess whether aversive consequences follow their behavior. An aversive consequence is one that an actor would prefer not to have produced. For example, a participant in the Festinger and Carlsmith (1959) experiment presumably would prefer not to have duped a fellow student into thinking a dull task was going to be interesting. But he or she did exactly that.

In the face of an unwanted consequence of behavior, people infer whether or not they were responsible for the consequence. Responsibility is a function of perceived choice (see Cooper, 1971; Davis and Jones, 1960; Linder et al., 1967) and foreseeability of the consequences (Cooper, 1971; Goethals and Cooper, 1975; Goethals et al., 1979). If people were forced to behave as they did, or if they could not have foreseen the consequences of their actions, then they can feel absolved of responsibility and experience no dissonance. But if they accept responsibility for the aversive consequences of their behavior, the aversive state of dissonance ensues.

Because counterattitudinal behavior frequently leads to consequences that the actor considered aversive, attitude-discrepant behavior typically produces dissonance. However, Scher and Cooper (1989) demonstrated that an attitude-congruent behavior that leads to an unwanted consequence can also produce dissonance, reinforcing the claim that it is the aversive consequences, rather than the inconsistency of the behavior, that is responsible for cognitive dissonance.

The notion that aversive consequences are both necessary (Cooper and Worchel, 1970) and sufficient (Scher and Cooper, 1989) to produce-dissonance remains controversial. Although it is supported by considerable evidence (see Cooper, 1999, for a review), the original version of the theory of cognitive dissonance that focuses on inconsistency rather than behavioral consequences has also received theoretical and empirical support (e.g., Beauvois and Joule, 1999; Harmon-Jones, 2000; Harmon-Jones et al., 1996).

### Self-consistency

Aronson (1968, 1999) was the first to argue that dissonance requires the involvement of the self in order for it to motivate attitude change. In this self-consistency view, Aronson argued that at its core, dissonance was a theory about the self (Aronson, 1999). People strive for consistent views of themselves; thus, when people with reasonably positive self-concepts act in counternormative ways (for example, saying something they do not believe), the behavior challenges their views of themselves as moral and competent human beings. According to the self-consistency account, it is this inconsistency between people's positive views of themselves and the performance of counternormative behavior that sparks the unpleasant state of dissonance and motivates change (and not simply the inconsistency between the behavior and the relevant attitude). An interesting corollary of this perspective is that people who have the most positive views of themselves should be most likely to experience dissonance following an attitude-discrepant act (Aronson and Mettee, 1968), especially if that self-esteem is fragile (Aronson, 1999).

### Self-affirmation

Steele and his colleagues (e.g., Steele, 1988; Steele and Liu, 1983; Steele et al., 1993), in their theory of self-affirmation, agree that the self is crucial for dissonance. They suggest that people are motivated to maintain an overall self-image of adaptive competency and morality, and that behavioral evidence to the contrary is threatening. According to the self-affirmation perspective, negative behaviors are especially threatening to people who already question their general worth (that is, people with low self-esteem). For people who regard themselves positively, self-esteem serves as a resource that mitigates the implications of attitude-discrepant behavior. Unlike the self-consistency perspective, then, the self-affirmation model predicts that cognitive dissonance following a counternormative behavior will be greatest for people low rather than high in self-esteem (see also Tesser, 2000). Consistent with self-affirmation theory, Steele et al. (1993) showed that people with high self-esteem engage in less attitude change following attitude-discrepant behavior than do people with low self-esteem. Furthermore, allowing people to affirm themselves as moral and competent human beings weakens the need to change attitudes following attitude-discrepant behavior (Steele and Liu, 1981, 1983).

### Self-standards model

Stone and Cooper (2001; see also Cooper, 2001; Stone, 1999) proposed that whether the self is involved in the arousal and reduction of dissonance depends on the standard of judgment that is accessible following attitude-discrepant behavior. According to this model, once people have acted, they try to make sense of what they have done. Was their behavior foolish? Did it bring about an unwanted event? Did it compromise their morality? These questions cannot be answered in a vacuum, but rather, the behavior must be compared to some standard of judgment. The interpretation and evaluation of one's behavior depends on the standard of judgment that is accessible at the time. If personal standards are chronically or situationally accessible in memory, the behavior is compared to the person's idiosyncratic expectancies. In short, the self matters. However, if normative standards of judgment are accessible, the behavior is compared to the perception of what most people in the culture believe to be foolish, immoral, or unwanted. In that case, the idiosyncratic self does not matter.

In addition to specifying the conditions under which aspects of the self will regulate cognitive dissonance, the self-standards model also provides an explanation for why self-esteem sometimes serves as a buffer against dissonance (e.g., Steele, 1988) and sometimes provides an expectancy for one's conduct, increasing susceptibility to dissonance (e.g., Aronson, 1968, 1999). To the extent that personal attributes that are *relevant* to the behavior are made salient, the valence of those attributes will determine the expectancy against which one's behavior will be compared. Under these circumstances, positive self-esteem should increase dissonance following a counternormative behavior, because people with positive self-views will hold themselves to a higher standard than do people with negative self-views. However, if the accessible personal attributes are *irrelevant* to the behavior, the positivity of those attributes will serve as a buffer against cognitive dissonance (Aronson et al., 1995; Blanton et al., 1997; Galinsky et al., 2000). For example, Blanton et al. (1997) had students write a speech advocating a reduction in university expenditures for students with disabilities. When personal standards were made accessible by reminding participants of their high degree of compassion (a trait relevant to their behavior), dissonance was increased as evidenced by more attitude change. When the attribute that was made salient was unrelated to the behavior, high standing on the irrelevant trait reduced the magnitude of dissonance.

Similarly, Stone and Cooper (2003) demonstrated that following a high-choice counterattitudinal behavior, priming positive self-attributes which were relevant to the discrepant behavior caused people with high self-esteem to report more attitude change than those with low self-esteem. In contrast, priming positive self-attributes which were irrelevant to the behavior caused people with high self-esteem to report *less* attitude change than those with low self-esteem. Thus, when people's self-views set their expectations for their own behavior, dissonance was increased, but when those self views were not directly relevant to the counterattitudinal behavior they served as a buffer, reducing dissonance.

## Action-orientation

Harmon-Jones and Harmon-Jones (2002; Harmon-Jones, 2000) hold that inconsistency per se is the motivating force behind cognitive dissonance. However, in the action-orientation view, inconsistency is only the proximal cause of dissonance. This model suggests that inconsistency leads to a negative emotive state because it interferes with people's basic need to take an unconflicted action orientation toward the environment (that is, approach versus avoid). Information inconsistent with a decision creates conflict and makes unequivocal action more difficult. The distal motivation for dissonance reduction, therefore, is the need to act unequivocally in the social and physical environment. Consistent with this view, Harmon-Jones and Harmon-Jones (2002) have shown that when people are made to think about the necessity for action, dissonance-produced attitude change increases.

### *Summing up*

Festinger's original version of dissonance theory was designed as a general theory of motivation. The study of rumors, information-seeking, and even gambling behavior all formed major sections of Festinger's original work. However, the impact of dissonance on understanding the relationship between attitudes and behavior has been its most impressive legacy. It has not only provided lively theoretical debates but has also served as an analytic tool in areas ranging from voting behavior (Beasley and Joslyn, 2001) to psychotherapy (Axsom and Cooper, 1985; Cooper and Cooper, 1991). Whether Festinger was completely correct in his analysis of attitude change following behavior or whether newer models of the theory offer greater insight is still a matter of controversy, debate, and continued research.

## Concluding remarks

Every day, we are bombarded by efforts to change our attitudes. Sometimes these efforts are overt. Politicians explicitly try to convince us to support the policies that they advocate by articulating the advantages of these policies; advertisers vigorously try to persuade us that their products or services are preferable to those of their competitors by drawing direct comparisons; and public-health advocates blatantly try to change our views toward exercise and healthy eating by reviewing their various positive consequences. At other times, these efforts are more subtle. Candidates for political office distribute yard signs emblazoned simply with their names in the hopes that repeated exposure will lead to greater liking for the candidate. Advertisements display products in the context of beautiful natural scenery or in the proximity of an attractive model in an effort to establish an association between these positive stimuli and the product. Well-liked spokespeople are chosen to advocate healthy behaviors in hopes that balance principles will lead us to develop positive attitudes toward the behavior.

As we have seen in this chapter, psychologists have devoted a tremendous amount of attention to these and many other processes by which attitude change occurs. Since the pivotal work of Hovland and even before, attitude researchers have continually strived to achieve a fuller understanding of how, why, and under what circumstances individuals come to hold positive or negative evaluations of people, places, and things. And this work, of course, continues today as attitude researchers develop ever more refined models of attitude change and begin to explore the links between this fertile domain and many others within social psychology, including stereotyping and prejudice, social identity, group processes, social neuroscience, and many others. We look forward to the advances that are sure to come from this sort of boundary-crossing pollination of ideas.

## Notes

1 For detailed reviews of the similarities and differences between the ELM and the HSM, see Chaiken et al., 1996; Petty and Wegener, 1998a, 1999.

2 According to the HSM, this holds as long as (1) people have the *ability* systematically to process a message and (2) people perceive that effortfully processing a message will increase their confidence in the attitude they adopt.

3 A number of criticisms have been leveled against the thought-listing technique (for a review, see Eagly and Chaiken, 1993: 293–7), but a diverse set of evidence attests to its usefulness as an index of cognitive elaboration. For example, Cacioppo and his colleagues (1979; Cacioppo and Petty, 1979b, 1981; Cacioppo et al., 1986) have demonstrated that psychophysiological responses associated with extensive cognitive activity correspond quite closely to thought-listing measures of elaboration. Furthermore, thought-listing measures of cognitive elaboration have been shown to vary systematically as a function of direct manipulation of these physiological responses (for example, surreptitiously accelerated heart rate among pacemaker patients), providing further support for the utility of the thought-listing technique (Cacioppo, 1978, 1979).

4 We have focused here on the implications of these goals for systematic processing of a message, but, as we alluded to above, the HSM posits that each of these motivations can be satisfied through systematic *or* heuristic processes.

5 Both models specify that biases in people's response to a persuasive message can result from motivational factors (such as self-presentational concerns) or ability factors (such as a biased store of attitude-relevant information in memory that renders people better *able* to process the attitude-congruent information in a persuasive message than the attitude-incongruent information).

6 This diverse set of findings regarding the impact of source attractiveness on attitude change illustrates an important and sometimes misunderstood feature of the dual-process models: persuasion variables cannot be neatly categorized as 'peripheral' or 'central' because, as we have seen with source attractiveness, the same variable can be carefully scrutinized *or* superficially processed depending on an individual's motivation and ability to process a persuasive message.

**SUMMARY**

The attitude construct has a rich history. For more than seven decades, psychologists have investigated the processes by which people come to hold positive or negative evaluations of the objects and events around them and the processes by which these evaluations are altered. In this chapter, we review the attitude-change literature, examining some of the major theories of persuasion and summarizing the empirical evidence in support of these theories. We begin by considering attitude change that occurs in response to a counterattitudinal persuasive message, paying particular attention to contemporary dual-process models of persuasion. These models specify that attitude change can result from careful scrutiny of a persuasive message or from simpler and less cognitively taxing reliance on salient cues within the persuasion context. We also review several additional processes of attitude change that can occur in the absence of any persuasive message at all. Finally, we consider the impact of behavior on attitudes, reviewing the processes by which acting in a counterattitudinal fashion can induce attitude change. Here we pay particular attention to cognitive-dissonance theory and the various revisions and extensions of this influential theory. This brief review highlights the many and varied ways by which individuals come to hold positive or negative evaluations of the people, places, and things that they encounter.

## References


Allport, G.W. (1935) 'Attitudes', in C. Murchison (ed.), *Handbook of Social Psychology*. Worcester, MA: Clark University Press, pp. 798–884.

Aronson, E. (1968) 'Dissonance Theory: Progress and Problems', in R.P. Abelson, E. Aronson, W.J. McGuire, T.M. Newcomb, M.J. Rosenberg, and P.H. Tannenbaum (eds), *Theories of Cognitive Consistency: A Sourcebook*. Chicago, IL: Rand McNally, pp. 5–27.

Aronson, E. (1992) 'The Return of the Repressed: Dissonance Theory Makes a Comeback', *Psychological Inquiry*, 3: 303–11.

Aronson, E. (1999) 'Dissonance, Hypocrisy, and the Self-Concept', in E. Harmon-Jones and J. Mills (eds), *Cognitive Dissonance: Progress on a Pivotal Theory in Social Psychology*. Washington, DC: American Psychological Association, pp. 103–26.

Aronson, E. and Carlsmith, J.M. (1962) 'Performance Expectancy as a Determinant of Actual Performance', *Journal of Abnormal and Social Psychology*, 65: 178–82.

Aronson, E., Fried, C., and Stone, J. (1991) 'Overcoming Denial and Increasing the Intention to Use Condoms through the Induction of Hypocrisy', *American Journal of Public Health*, 81: 1636–8.

Aronson, E. and Mettee, D. (1968) 'Dishonest Behavior as a Function of Differential Levels of Induced Self-Esteem', *Journal of Personality and Social Psychology*, 9: 121–7.

Aronson, E. and Mills, J. (1959) 'The Effect of Severity of Initiation on Liking for a Group', *Journal of Abnormal and Social Psychology*, 59: 177–81.

Aronson, J., Blanton, H., and Cooper, J. (1995) 'From Dissonance to Disidentification: Selectivity in the Self-Affirmation Process', *Journal of Personality and Social Psychology*, 68: 986–96.

Aronson, J., Cohen, G., and Nail, P.R. (1999) 'Self-Affirmation Theory: An Update and Appraisal', in E. Harmon-Jones and J. Mills (eds), *Cognitive Dissonance: Progress on a Pivotal Theory in Social Psychology*. Washington, DC: American Psychological Association, pp. 127–48.

Axsom, D.K. (1984) 'Anticipated Effort, Dissonance, and Behavior Change'. Unpublished doctoral dissertation, Princeton University.

Axsom, D. (1989) 'Cognitive Dissonance and Behavior Change in Psychotherapy', *Journal of Experimental Social Psychology*, 25: 234–52.

Axsom, D. and Cooper, J. (1985) 'Cognitive Dissonance and Psychotherapy: The Role of Effort Justification in Inducing Weight Loss', *Journal of Experimental Social Psychology*, 21: 149–60.

Axsom, D., Yates, S., and Chaiken, S. (1987) 'Audience Response as a Heuristic Cue in Persuasion', *Journal of Personality and Social Psychology*, 53: 30–40.

Azida, T. and Joule, R.-V. (2001) 'Double Soumission Forcée et Engagement: Le Cas des Comportements Inconsistants', *Revue Internationale de Psychologie Sociale*, 14: 31–55.

Beasley, R.K. and Joslyn, M.R. (2001) 'Cognitive Dissonance and Post-Decision Attitude Change in Six Presidential Elections', *Political Psychology*, 22: 521–40.

Beauvois, J.L. and Joule, R.V. (1999) 'A Radical Point of View on Dissonance Theory', in E. Harmon-Jones and J. Mills (eds), *Cognitive Dissonance: Progress on a Pivotal Theory in Social Psychology*. Washington, DC: Amercian Psychological Association, pp. 43–70.

Bem, D.J. (1967) 'Self-Perception: An Alternate Interpretation of Cognitive Dissonance Phenomena', *Psychological Review*, 74: 183–200.

Bem, D.J. (1972) 'Self-Perception Theory', in L. Berkowitz (ed.), *Advances in Experimental Social Psychology* (vol. 6). New York: Academic Press, pp. 1–62.

Bem, D.J. and McConnell, H.K. (1970) 'Testing the Self-Perception Explanation of Dissonance Phenomena: On the Salience of Premanipulation Attitudes', *Journal of Personality and Social Psychology*, 14: 23–31.

Berkowitz, L. and Knurek, D.A. (1969) 'Label-Mediated Hostility Generalization', *Journal of Personality and Social Psychology*, 13: 200–6.

Blanton, H., Cooper, J., Skurnik, I., and Aronson, J. (1997) 'When Bad Things Happen to Good Feedback: Exacerbating the Need for Self-Justification with Self-Affirmations', *Personality and Social Psychology Bulletin*, 23: 684–92.

Blanton, H., Pelham, B.W., DeHart, T., and Carvallo, M. (2001) 'Overconfidence as Dissonance Reduction', *Journal of Experimental Social Psychology*, 37: 373–85.

Bornstein, R.F. (1989) 'Exposure and Affect: Overview and Meta-Analysis of Research, 1968–1987', *Psychological Bulletin*, 106: 265–89.

Bornstein, R.F. and D'Agostino, P.R. (1992) 'Stimulus Recognition and the Mere Exposure Effect', *Journal of Personality and Social Psychology*, 63: 545–52.

Bornstein, R.F. and D'Agostino, P.R. (1994) 'The Attribution and Discounting of Perceptual Fluency: Preliminary Tests of a Perceptual Fluency/Attributional Model of the Mere Exposure Effect', *Social Cognition*, 12: 103–28.

Bower, G.H. (1981) 'Mood and Memory', *American Psychologist*, 36: 129–48.

Brehm, J.W. (1956) 'Post Decision Changes in the Desirability of Alternatives', *Journal of Abnormal and Social Psychology*, 52: 384–9.

Brehm, J.W. and Cohen, A.R. (1962) *Explorations in Cognitive Dissonance*. New York: Wiley.

Brickman, P., Redfield, J., Harrison, A.A., and Crandall, R. (1972) 'Drive and Predisposition as Factors in the Attitudinal Effects of Mere Exposure', *Journal of Experimental Social Psychology*, 8: 31–44.

Brock, T.C. (1967) 'Communication Discrepancy and Intent to Persuade as Determinants of Counterargument Production', *Journal of Experimental Social Psychology*, 3: 296–309.

Burdick, H.A. and Burnes, A.J. (1958) 'A Test of "Strain toward Symmetry Theories"', *Journal of Abnormal and Social Psychology*, 57: 367–70.

Byrne, D. and Clore, G.L. (1970) 'A Reinforcement Model of Evaluative Responses', *Personality: An International Journal*, 1: 103–28.

Cacioppo, J.T. (1978) 'Heart Rate, Cognitive Response, and Persuasion'. Unpublished doctoral dissertation, Ohio State University.

Cacioppo, J.T. (1979) 'Effects of Exogenous Changes in Heart Rate on Facilitation of Thought and Resistance to Persuasion', *Journal of Personality and Social Psychology*, 37: 489–98.

Cacioppo, J.T., Marshall-Goodell, B.S, Tassinary, L.G., and Petty, R.E. (1992) 'Rudimentary Determinants of Attitudes: Classical Conditioning Is More Effective when Prior Knowledge about the Attitude Stimulus Is Low than High', *Journal of Experimental Social Psychology*, 28: 207–33.

Cacioppo, J.T. and Petty, R.E. (1979a) 'Effects of Message Repetition and Position on Cognitive Response, Recall, and Persuasion', *Journal of Personality and Social Psychology*, 37: 97–109.

Cacioppo, J.T. and Petty, R.E. (1979b) 'Attitudes and Cognitive Response: An Electrophysiological Approach', *Journal of Personality and Social Psychology*, 37: 2181–99.

Cacioppo, J.T. and Petty, R.E. (1981) 'Electromyograms as Measures of Extent and Activity of Information Processing', *American Psychologist*, 36: 441–56.

Cacioppo, J.T. and Petty, R.E. (1982) 'The Need for Cognition', *Journal of Personality and Social Psychology*, 42: 116–31.

Cacioppo, J.T., Petty, R.E., Losch, M.E., and Kim, H.S. (1986) 'Electromyographic Activity over Facial Muscle Regions Can Differentiate the Valence and Intensity of Affective Reactions', *Journal of Personality and Social Psychology*, 50: 260–8.

Chaiken, S. (1987) 'The Heuristic Model of Persuasion', in M.P. Zanna, J.M. Olson, and C.P. Herman (eds), *Social Influence: The Ontario Symposium* (vol. 5). Hillsdale, NJ: Erlbaum, pp. 3–39.

Chaiken, S., Liberman, A., and Eagly, A.H. (1989) 'Heuristic and Systematic Information Processing within and beyond the Persuasion Context', in J.S. Uleman and J.A. Bargh (eds), *Unintended Thought*. New York: Guilford, pp. 212–52.

Chaiken, S. and Maheswaran, D. (1994) 'Heuristic Processing Can Bias Systematic Processing: Effects of Source Credibility, Argument Ambiguity, and Task Importance on Attitude Judgment', *Journal of Personality and Social Psychology*, 66: 460–73.

Chaiken, S., Wood, W. and Eagly, A.H. (1996) 'Principles of Persuasian', in E.T. Higgins and A.W. Kruglarski (eds), *Social Psychology: Handbook of Basic Principles*. New York: Guilford, pp. 702–42.

Chapanis, N.P. and Chapanis, A. (1964) 'Cognitive Dissonance: Five Years Later', *Psychological Bulletin*, 61: 1–22.

Cooper, A. and Cooper, J. (1991) 'How People Change with and without Therapy', in R.C. Curtis and G. Stricker (eds), *How People Change Inside and Outside Therapy*. New York: Plenum, pp. 173–89.

Cooper, J. (1971) 'Personal Responsibility and Dissonance: The Role of Foreseen Consequences', *Journal of Personality and Social Psychology*, 18: 354–63.

Cooper, J. (1980) 'Reducing Fears and Increasing Assertiveness: The Role of Dissonance Reduction', *Journal of Experimental Social Psychology*, 16: 199–213.

Cooper, J. (1999) 'Unwanted Consequences and the Self: In Search of the Motivation for Dissonance Reduction', in E. Harmon-Jones and J. Mills (eds), *Cognitive Dissonance: Progress on a Pivotal Theory in Social Psychology*. Washington, DC: American Psychological Association, pp. 149–74.

Cooper, J. (2001) 'Motivating Cognitive Change: The Self-Standards Model of Dissonance', in J.P. Forgas, K.D. Williams and L. Wheeler (eds), *The Social Mind: Cognitive and Motivational Aspects of Interpersonal Behavior*', Cambridge, MA: Cambridge University Press.

Cooper, J. and Axsom, D. (1982) 'Effort Justification in Psychotherapy', in G. Weary and J.L. Mirels (eds), *Integrations in Clinical and Social Psychology*. New York: Oxford University Press, pp. 214–30.

Cooper, J. and Fazio, R.H. (1984) 'A New Look at Dissonance Theory', in L. Berkowitz (ed.), *Advances in Experimental Social Psychology* (vol. 17). New York: Academic Press, pp. 229–62.

Cooper, J. and Mackie, D. (1983) 'Cognitive Dissonance in an Intergroup Context', *Journal of Personality and Social Psychology*, 44: 536–44.

Cooper, J. and Worchel, S. (1970) 'Role of Undesired Consequences in Arousing Cognitive Dissonance', *Journal of Personality and Social Psychology*, 16: 199–206.

Cooper, J., Zanna, M.P., and Taves, P.A. (1978) 'Arousal as a Necessary Condition for Attitude Change Following Forced Compliance', *Journal of Personality and Social Psychology*, 36: 1101–6.

Croyle, R. and Cooper, J. (1983) 'Dissonance Arousal: Psychological Evidence', *Journal of Personality and Social Psychology*, 45: 782–91.

Davis, K. and Jones, E.E. (1960) 'Changes in Interpersonal Perception as a Means of Reducing Cognitive Dissonance', *Journal of Abnormal and Social Psychology*, 61: 402–10.

Davis, J.L. and Rusbult, C.E. (2001) 'Attitude Alignment in Close Relationships', *Journal of Personality and Social Psychology*, 81: 65–84.

DeBono, K.G. and Harnish, R.J. (1988) 'Source Expertise, Source Attractiveness, and the Processing of Persuasive Information: A Functional Approach', *Journal of Personality and Social Psychology*, 55: 541–6.

Devine, P.G., Tauer, J.M., Barron, K.E., Elliot, A.J., and Vance, K.M. (1999) 'Moving beyond Attitude Change in the Study of Dissonance-Related Processes', in E. Harmon-Jones and J. Mills (eds), *Cognitive Dissonance: Progress on a Pivotal Theory in Social Psychology*. Washington, DC: American Psychological Association, pp. 297–324.

Dickerson, C., Thibodeau, R., Aronson, E., and Miller, D. (1992) 'Using Cognitive Dissonance to Encourage Water Conservation', *Journal of Applied Social Psychology*, 22: 841–54.

Eagly, A.H. and Carli, L.L. (1981) 'Sex of Researchers and Sex-Typed Communications as Determinants of Sex Differences in Influenceability: A Meta-Analysis of Social Influence Studies', *Psychological Bulletin*, 90: 1–20.

Eagly, A.H. and Chaiken, S. (1993) *The Psychology of Attitudes*. Fort Worth, TX: Harcourt, Brace, Janovich.

Edwards, K. and Smith, E.E. (1996) 'A Disconfirmation Bias in the Evaluation of Arguments', *Journal of Personality and Social Psychology*, 71: 5–24.

Elkin, R.A. and Leippe, M.R. (1986) 'Physiological Arousal, Dissonance and Attitude Change: Evidence for a Dissonance-Arousal Link and a "Don't Remind Me" Effect', *Journal of Personality and Social Psychology*, 51: 55–65.

Elliot, A.J. and Devine, P. (1994) 'On the Motivational Nature of Cognitive Dissonance: Dissonance as Psychological Discomfort', *Journal of Personality and Social Psychology*, 67: 382–94.

Elms, A.C. and Janis, I.L. (1965) 'Counter-Norm Attitudes Induced by Consonant Versus Dissonant Conditions of Role Playing', *Journal of Experimental Research in Personality*, 1: 50–60.

Fabrigar, L.R, Priester, J.R., Petty, R.E., and Wegener, D.T. (1998) 'The Impact of Attitude Accessibility on Elaboration of Persuasive Messages', *Personality and Social Psychology Bulletin*, 24: 339–52.

Fazio, R.H., Zanna, M.P. and Cooper, J. (1997) 'Dissonance and Self-Perception: An Integrative View of Each Theory's Proper Domain of Application', *Journal of Experimental Social Psychology*, 13: 464–79.

Festinger, L. (1957) *A Theory of Cognitive Dissonance*. Stanford, CA: Stanford University Press.

Festinger, L. (1964) *Conflict, Decision, and Dissonance*. Stanford, CA: Stanford University Press.

Festinger, L. and Carlsmith, J.M. (1959) 'Cognitive Consequences of Forced Compliance', *Journal of Abnormal and Social Psychology*, 58: 203–10.

Festinger, L. and Maccoby, N. (1964) 'On Resistance to Persuasive Communications', *Journal of Abnormal and Social Psychology*, 68: 359–66.

Forgas, J.P. and Bower, G.H. (1988) 'Affect in Social Judgments', *Australian Journal of Psychology*, 40: 125–45.

Freedman, J. (1965) 'Long-Term Behavioral Effects of Cognitive Dissonance', *Journal of Experimental Social Psychology*, 1: 145–55.

Galinsky, A.D., Stone, J., and Cooper, J. (2000) 'The Reinstatement of Dissonance and Psychological Discomfort Following Failed Affirmation', *European Journal of Social Psychology*, 30: 123–47.

Gerard, H.B. and Mathewson, G. (1966) 'The Effects of Severity of Initiation on Liking for a Group: A Replication', *Journal of Experimental Social Psychology*, 2: 278–87.

Goethals, G.R. and Cooper, J. (1975) 'When Dissonance Is Reduced: The Timing of Self-Justificatory Attitude Change', *Journal of Personality and Social Psychology*, 32: 361–7.

Goethals, G.R., Cooper, J., and Naficy, A. (1979) 'Role of Foreseen, Foreseeable and Unforeseeable Consequences in the Arousal of Cognitive Dissonance', *Journal of Personality and Social Psychology*, 37: 1179–85.

Gorn, G.J. (1982) 'The Effects of Music in Advertising on Choice Behavior: A Classical Conditioning Approach', *Journal of Marketing*, 46: 94–101.

Greenwald, A.G. (1968) 'Cognitive Learning, Cognitive Response to Persuasion, and Attitude Change', in A.G. Greenwald, T.C. Brock, and T.M. Ostrom (eds), *Psychological Foundations of Attitudes*. San Diego, CA: Academic Press, pp. 147–70.

Greenwald, A.G. (1981) 'Cognitive Response Analysis: An Appraisal', in A.G. Greenwald, T.C. Brock, and T.M. Ostrom (eds), *Cognitive Responses in Persuasion*. Hillsdale, NJ: Erlbaum, pp. 127–33.

Griffitt, W. (1970) 'Environmental Effects on Interpersonal Affective Behavior: Ambient Effective Temperature and Attraction', *Journal of Personality and Social Psychology*, 15: 240–4.

Harkins, S.G. and Petty, R.E. (1981) 'The Multiple Source Effect in Persuasion: The Effects of Distraction', *Personality and Social Psychology Bulletin*, 7: 627–35.

Harmon-Jones, E. (2000) 'Cognitive Dissonance and Experienced Negative Affect: Evidence that Dissonance Increases Experienced Negative Affect Even in the Absence of Aversive Consequences', *Personality and Social Psychology Bulletin*, 26: 1490–501.

Harmon-Jones, E. and Allen, J.J.B. (2001) 'The Role of Affect in the Mere Exposure Effect: Evidence from Psychophysiological and Individual Differences Approaches', *Personality and Social Psychology Bulletin*, 27: 889–98.

Harmon-Jones, E. and Allen, J.J.B. (2002) 'The Role of Affect in the Mere Exposure Effect: Evidence from Psychophysiological and Individual Differences Approaches', *Personality and Social Psychology Bulletin*, 27: 889–98.

Harmon-Jones, E., Brehm, J.W., Greenberg, J., Simon, L., and Nelson, D.E. (1996) 'Evidence that the Production of Aversive Consequences Is Not Necessary to Create Cognitive Dissonance', *Journal of Personality and Social Psychology*, 70: 5–16.

Harmon-Jones, E. and Harmon-Jones, C. (2002) 'Testing the Action-Based Model of Cognitive Dissonance: The Effect of Action-Orientation on Post-Decisional Attitudes', *Personality and Social Psychology Bulletin*, 28: 711–23.

Harmon-Jones, E. and Mills, J. (eds) (1999) *Cognitive Dissonance: Progress on a Pivotal Theory in Social Psychology*. Washington, DC: American Psychological Association, pp. 71–99.

Harrison, A.A. and Fiscaro, S.A. (1974) 'Stimulus Familiarity and Alley Illumination as Determinants of

Approach Response Latencies of House Crickets', *Perceptual and Motor Skills*, 39: 147–52.
Heider, F. (1946) 'Attitudes and Cognitive Organization', *Journal of Psychology*, 21: 107–12.
Heider, F. (1958) *The Psychology of Interpersonal Relations*. New York: Wiley.
Hildum, D.C. and Brown, R.W. (1956) 'Verbal Reinforcement and Interviewer Bias', *Journal of Abnormal and Social Psychology*, 53: 108–11.
Houston, D.A. and Fazio, R.H. (1989) 'Biased Processing as a Function of Attitude Accessibility: Making Objective Judgments Subjectively', *Social Cognition*, 7: 51–66.
Hovland, C.I. (1951) 'Human Learning and Retention', in S.S. Stevens (ed.), *Handbook of Experimental Psychology*. New York: Wiley, pp. 613–89.
Hovland, C.I. (1957) *The Order of Presentation in Persuasion*. New Haven, CT: Yale University Press.
Hovland, C.I. and Janis, I.L. (eds) (1959) *Personality and Persuasibility*. New Haven, CT: Yale University Press.
Hovland, C.I., Janis, I.L., and Kelley, H.H. (1953) *Communication and Persuasion: Psychological Studies of Opinion Change*. New Haven, CT: Yale University Press.
Hovland, C.I. and Mandell, W. (1952) 'An Experimental Comparison of Conclusion-Drawing by the Communicator and by the Audience', *Journal of Abnormal and Social Psychology*, 47: 581–8.
Hovland, C.I. and Weiss, W. (1951) 'The Influence of Source Credibility on Communication Effectiveness', *Public Opinion Quarterly*, 15: 635–50.
Insko, C.A. (1965) 'Verbal Reinforcement of Attitude', *Journal of Personality and Social Psychology*, 2: 621–3.
Insko, C.A. and Butzine, K.W. (1967) 'Rapport, Awareness, and Verbal Reinforcement of Attitude', *Journal of Personality and Social Psychology*, 6: 225–8.
Insko, C.A. and Cialdini, R.B. (1969) 'A Test of Three Interpretations of Attitudinal Verbal Reinforcement', *Journal of Personality and Social Psychology*, 12: 333–41.
Insko, C.A. and Melson, W.H. (1969) 'Verbal Reinforcement of Attitude in Laboratory and Nonlaboratory Contexts', *Journal of Personality*, 37: 25–40.
Insko, C.A. and Oakes, W.F. (1966) 'Awareness and the "Conditioning" of Attitudes', *Journal of Personality and Social Psychology*, 4: 487–96.
Insko, C.A., Songer, E., and McGargey, W. (1974) 'Balance Positivity and Agreement in the Jordan Paradigm: A Defense of Balance Theory', *Journal of Personality and Social Psychology*, 10: 53–83.
Insko, C.A. and Wilson, M. (1977) 'Interpersonal Attraction as a Function of Social Interaction', *Journal of Personality and Social Psychology*, 35: 903–11.
Janis, I.L. and Feshbach, S. (1953) 'Effects of Fear-Arousing Communications', *Journal of Abnormal and Social Psychology*, 48: 78–92.
Janis, I.L. and Gilmore, J.B. (1965) 'The Influence of Incentive Conditions on the Success of Role Playing in Modifying Attitudes', *Journal of Personalilty and Social Psychology*, 1: 17–27.
Jones, R.A., Linder, D.E., Kiesler, C.A., Zanna, M.P., and Brehm, J.W. (1968) 'Internal States or External Stimuli: Observers' Judgments of the Dissonance-Self Perception Controversy', *Journal of Experimental Social Psychology*, 4: 247–69.
Jordan, N. (1953) 'Behavioral Forces that Are a Function of Attitude and of Cognitive Organization', *Human Relations*, 6: 273–87.
Kelman, H.C. and Hovland, C.I. (1953) '"Reinstatement" of the Communicator in Delayed Measurement of Opinion Change', *Journal of Abnormal and Social Psychology*, 48: 327–35.
Kiesler, S.B. and Mathog, R. (1968) 'The Distraction Hypothesis in Attitude Change', *Psychological Reports*, 23: 1123–33.
Krasner, L., Knowles, J.B., and Ullman, L.P. (1965) 'Effect of Verbal Conditioning of Attitudes on Subsequent Motor Performance', *Journal of Personality and Social Psychology*, 1: 407–12.
Krosnick, J.A. (1988) 'Attitude Importance and Attitude Change', *Journal of Experimental Social Psychology*, 24: 240–55.
Kunst-Wilson, W.R. and Zajonc, R.B. (1980) 'Affective Discrimination of Stimuli that Cannot Be Recognized', *Science*, 207: 557–8.
Leippe, M.R. and Eisenstadt, D. (1999) 'A Self-Accountability Model of Dissonance Reduction: Multiple Modes on a Continuum of Elaboration', in E. Harmon-Jones and J. Mills (eds), *Cognitive Dissonance: Progress on a Pivotal Theory in Social Psychology.* Washington, DC: American Psychological Association, pp. 201–32.
Leippe, M.R. and Elkin, R.A. (1992) 'Dissonance Reduction and Accountability: Effects of Assessment and Self-Presentational Concern on Mode of Inconsistency Resolution'. Unpublished manuscript, Adelphi University, Garden City, NY.
Linder, D.E., Cooper, J., and Jones, E.E. (1967) 'Decision Freedom as a Determinant of the Role of Incentive Magnitude in Attitude Change', *Journal of Personality and Social Psychology*, 6: 245–54.
Losch, M.E. and Cacioppo, J.T. (1990) 'Cognitive Dissonance May Enhance Sympathetic Tonus, but Attitudes Are Changed to Reduce Negative Affect Rather than Arousal', *Journal of Experimental Social Psychology*, 26: 289–304.
Mackie, D. and Cooper, J. (1984) 'Attitude Polarization: Effects of Group Membership', *Journal of Personality and Social Psychology*, 46: 575–85.
Mackie, D.M., Gastardo-Conaco, M.C., and Skelly, J.J. (1992) 'Knowledge of the Advocated Position and the Processing of In-Group and Out-Group Persuasive Messages', *Personality and Social Psychology Bulletin*, 18: 145–51.
Mackie, D.M. and Worth, L.T., (1990) 'The Impact of Distraction on the Processing of Category-Based and Attribute-Based Evaluations', *Basic and Applied Social Psychology*, 11: 255–71.
Mackie, D.M., Worth, L.T., and Asuncion, A.G. (1990) 'Processing of Persuasive In-Group Messages',

*Journal of Personality and Social Psychology*, 58: 812–22.

Maheswaran, D. and Chaiken, S. (1991) 'Promoting Systematic Processing in Low-Motivation Settings: Effect of Incongruent Information on Processing and Judgment', *Journal of Personality and Social Psychology*, 61: 13–25.

McGregor, I., Newby-Clark, I.R., and Zanna, M.P. (1999) '"Remembering" Dissonance: Simultaneous Accessibility of Inconsistent Cognitive Elements Moderates Epistemic Discomfort', in E. Harmon-Jones and J. Mills (eds), *Cognitive Dissonance: Progress on a Pivotal Theory in Social Psychology*. Washington, DC: American Psychological Association, pp. 325–54.

Miller, N. and Campbell, D.T. (1959) 'Recency and Primacy in Persuasion as a Function of the Timing of Speeches and Measurements', *Journal of Abnormal and Social Psychology*, 59: 1–9.

Mills, J. (1999) 'Historical Note on Festinger's Tests of Dissonance Theory', in E. Harmon-Jones and J. Mills (eds), *Cognitive Dissonance: Progress on a Pivotal Theory in Social Psychology*. Washington, DC: American Psychological Association, pp. 25–42.

Monteith, M.J. (1993) 'Self-Regulation of Prejudiced Responses: Implications for Progress in Prejudice-Reduction Efforts', *Journal of Personality and Social Psychology*, 65: 469–85.

Moore, D.L., Hausknecht, D., and Thamodaran, K. (1986) 'Time Compression, Response Opportunity, and Persuasion', *Journal of Consumer Research*, 13: 85–99.

Newcomb, T.M. (1953) 'An Approach to the Study of Communicative Acts', *Psychological Review*, 60: 393–404.

Newcomb, T.M. (1956) 'The Prediction of Interpersonal Attraction', *American Psychologist*, 11: 575–86.

Pallak, M. and Pittman, T. (1972) 'General Motivation Effects of Dissonance Arousal', *Journal of Personality and Social Psychology*, 21: 349–58.

Petty, R.E. and Cacioppo, J.T. (1977) 'Forewarning, Cognitive Responding, and Resistance to Persuasion', *Journal of Personality and Social Psychology*, 35: 645–55.

Petty, R.E. and Cacioppo, J.T. (1979a) 'Effects of Forewarning of Persuasive Intent and Involvement on Cognitive Responses and Persuasion', *Personality and Social Psychology Bulletin*, 5: 173–6.

Petty, R.E. and Cacioppo, J.T. (1979b) 'Issue Involvement Can Increase or Decrease Persuasion by Enhancing Message-Relevant Cognitive Responses', *Journal of Personality and Social Psychology*, 37: 1915–26.

Petty, R.E. and Cacioppo, J.T. (1981) *Attitudes and Persuasion: Classic and Contemporary Approaches*. Dubuque, IA: Brown.

Petty, R.E. and Cacioppo, J.T. (1984) 'Source Factors and the Elaboration Likelihood Model of Persuasion', in L. Berkowitz (ed.), *Advances in Experimental Social Psychology* (vol. 19). San Diego, CA: Academic Press, pp. 123–205.

Petty, R.E. and Cacioppo, J.T. (1986) *Communication and Persuasion: Central and Peripheral Routes to Attitude Change*. New York: Springer-Verlag.

Petty, R.E., Cacioppo, J.T., and Goldman, R. (1981) 'Personal Involvement as a Determinant of Argument-Based Persuasion', *Journal of Personality and Social Psychology*, 41: 847–55.

Petty, R.E., Cacioppo, J.T., and Heesacker, M. (1981) 'Effects of Rhetorical Questions on Persuasion: A Cognitive Response Analysis', *Journal of Personality and Social Psychology*, 40: 432–40.

Petty, R.E., Harkins, S.G., and Williams, K.D. (1980) 'The Effects of Group Diffusion of Cognitive Effort on Attitudes: An Information-Processing View', *Journal of Personality and Social Psychology*, 38: 81–92.

Petty, R.E., Haugtvedt, C.P., and Smith, S.M. (1995) 'Elaboration as a Determinant of Attitude Strength: Creating Attitudes that Are Persistent, Resistant, and Predictive of Behavior', in R.E. Petty and J.A. Krosnick (eds), *Attitude Strength: Antecedents and Consequences*. Hillsdale, NJ: Erlbaum, pp. 93–130.

Petty, R.E., Schumann, D.W., Richman, S.A., and Strathman, A.J. (1993) 'Positive Mood and Persuasion: Different Roles for Affect Under High- and Low-Elaboration Conditions', *Journal of Personality and Social Psychology*, 64: 5–20.

Petty, R.E. and Wegener, D.T. (1998a) 'Attitude Change: Multiple Roles for Persuasion Variables', in D.T. Gilbert, S.T. Fiske and G. Lindzey (eds), *The Handbook of Social Psychology* (vol. 1), 4th edn. New York: MCGraw-Hill, pp. 323–90.

Petty, R.E. and Wegener, D.T. (1998b) 'Matching versus Mismatching Attitude Functions: Implications for Scrutiny of Persuasive Messages', *Personality and Social Psychology Bulletin*, 24: 227–40.

Petty, R.E. and Wegener, D.T. (1999) 'The Elaboration Likelihood Model: Current Status and Controversies', in S. Chaiken and Y. Trope (eds), *Dual-Process Theories in Social Psychology*. New York: Guilford, pp. 37–72.

Petty, R.E., Wells, G.L., and Brock, T.C. (1976) 'Distraction Can Enhance or Reduce Yielding to Propaganda: Thought Disruption versus Effort Justification', *Journal of Personality and Social Psychology*, 34: 874–84.

Priester, J.R. and Petty, R.E. (1995) 'Source Attributions and Persuasion: Perceived Honesty as a Determinant of Message Scrutiny', *Personality and Social Psychology Bulletin*, 21: 637–54.

Puckett, J.M., Petty, R.E., Cacioppo, J.T., and Fischer, D.L. (1983) 'The Relative Impact of Age and Attractiveness Stereotypes on Persuasion', *Journal of Gerontology*, 38: 340–3.

Rajecki, D.W. (1973) 'Effects of Prenatal Exposure to Auditory and Visual Stimuli on Social Responses in Chicks'. Unpublished doctoral dissertation, University of Michigan, Ann Arbor, MI.

Razran, G.H.S. (1940) 'Conditioned Response Changes in Rating and Appraising Sociopolitical Slogans', *Psychological Bulletin*, 37: 481.

Reber, R., Winkielman, P., and Schwarz, N. (1998) 'Effects of Perceptual Fluency on Affective Judgments', *Psychological Science*, 9: 45–8.

Rhodes, N. and Wood, W. (1992) 'Self-Esteem and Intelligence Affect Influenceability: The Mediating Role of Message Reception', *Psychological Bulletin*, 111: 156–71.

Rosenberg, M.J. (1965) 'When Dissonance Fails: On Eliminating Evaluation Apprehension from Attitude Measurement', *Journal of Personality and Social Psychology*, 1: 28–42.

Sachs, D.H. and Byrne, D. (1970) 'Differential Conditioning of Evaluative Responses to Neutral Stimuli through Association with Attitude Statements', *Journal of Experimental Research in Personality*, 4: 181–5.

Sakai, H. (1999) 'A Multiplicative Power-Function Model of Cognitive Dissonance: Toward an Integrated Theory of Cognition, Emotion, and Behavior after Leon Festinger', in E. Harmon-Jones and J. Mills (eds), *Cognitive Dissonance: Progress on a Pivotal Theory in Social Psychology.* Washington, DC: American Psychological Association, pp. 267–94.

Scher, S.J. and Cooper, J. (1989) 'Motivational Basis of Dissonance: The Singular Role of Behavioral Consequences', *Journal of Personality and Social Psychology*, 56: 899–906.

Schultz, T.R. and Lepper, M.R. (1996) 'Cognitive Dissonance Reduction as Constraint Satisfaction', *Psychological Review*, 103: 219–40.

Schultz, T.R. and Lepper, M.R. (1999) 'Computer Simulation of Cognitive Dissonance Reduction', in E. Harmon-Jones and J. Mills (eds), *Cognitive Dissonance: Progress on a Pivotal Theory in Social Psychology.* Washington, DC: American Psychological Association, pp. 235–65.

Schwarz, N. and Clore, G.L. (1996) 'Feelings and Phenomenal Experiences', in E.T. Higgins and A.W. Kruglanski (eds), *Social Psychology: Handbook of Basic Principles.* New York: Guilford, pp. 433–65.

Sherman, S. and Gorkin, L. (1980) 'Attitude Bolstering when Behavior Is Inconsistent with Central Attitudes', *Journal of Experimental Social Psychology*, 16: 388–403.

Simon, L., Greenberg, J., and Brehm, J. (1995) 'Trivialization: The Forgotten Mode of Dissonance Reduction', *Journal of Personality and Social Psychology*, 68: 247–60.

Staats, A.W. and Staats, C.K. (1957) 'Meaning Established by Classical Conditioning', *Journal of Experimental Psychology*, 54: 74–80.

Staats, A.W. and Staats, C.K. (1958) 'Attitudes Established by Classical Conditioning', *Journal of Abnormal and Social Psychology*, 57: 37–40.

Staats, A.W., Staats, C.K., and Crawford, H.L. (1962) 'First-Order Conditioning of Meaning and the Parallel Conditioning of a GSR', *Journal of General Psychology*, 67: 159–67.

Steele, C.M. (1988) 'The Psychology of Self-Affirmation: Sustaining the Integrity of the Self', in L. Berkowitz (ed.), *Advances in Experimental Social Psychology* (vol. 21). San Diego, CA: Academic Press, pp. 261–302.

Steele, C.M. and Liu, T.J. (1981) 'Making the Dissonant Act Unreflective of Self: Dissonance Avoidance and the Expectancy of a Value-Affirming Response', *Personality and Social Psychology Bulletin*, 7: 393–7.

Steele, C.M. and Liu, T.J. (1983) 'Dissonance Processes as Self-Affirmation', *Journal of Personality and Social Psychology*, 45: 5–19.

Steele, C.M., Spencer, S.J., and Lynch, M. (1993) 'Self-Image Resilience and Dissonance: The Role of Affirmational Resources', *Journal of Personality and Social Psychology*, 64: 885–96.

Stone, J. (1999) 'What Exactly Have I Done? The Role of Self-Attribute Accessibility in Dissonance', in E. Harmon-Jones and J. Mills (eds), *Cognitive Dissonance: Progress on a Pivotal Theory in Social Psychology.* Washington, DC: American Psychological Association, pp. 175–200.

Stone, J., Aronson, E., Crain, A.L., Winslow, M.P., and Fried, C.B. (1994) 'Inducing Hypocrisy as a Means for Encouraging Young Adults to Use Condoms', *Personality and Social Psychology Bulletin*, 20: 116–28.

Stone, J. and Cooper, J. (2001) 'A Self-Standards Model of Cognitive Dissonance', *Journal of Experimental Social Psychology*, 37: 228–43.

Stone, J., and Cooper, J. (2003) 'The Effect of Self-Attribute Relevance on How Self-Esteem Moderates Attitude Change in Dissonance Processes', *Journal of Experimental Social Psychology*, 39: 508–15.

Stone, J., Wiegand, A.W., Cooper, J., and Aronson, E. (1997) 'When Exemplification Fails: Hypocrisy and the Motive for Self-Integrity', *Journal of Personality and Social Psychology*, 72: 54–65.

Strack, F., Martin, L.L., and Stepper, S. (1988) 'Inhibiting and Facilitating Conditions of the Human Smile: A Nonobtrusive Test of the Facial Feedback Hypothesis', *Journal of Personality and Social Psychology*, 54: 768–77.

Taylor, S.E. (1975) 'On Inferring One's Attitudes from One's Behavior: Some Delimiting Conditions', *Journal of Personality and Social Psychology*, 31: 126–31.

Taylor, S.E. (1981) 'The Interface of Cognitive and Social Psychology', in J.H. Harvey (ed.), *Cognition, Social Behavior, and the Environment.* Hillsdale, NJ: Erlbaum, pp. 189–211.

Tedeschi, J.T., Schlenker, B.R., and Bonoma, T.V. (1971) 'Cognitive Dissonance: Private Ratiocination or Public Spectacle?', *American Psychologist*, 26: 685–95.

Tesser, A. (2000). 'On the Confluence of Self-Esteem Maintenance Mechanisms', *Personality and Social Psychology Review*, 4: 290–9.

Titchener, E.B. (1910) *Textbook of Psychology.* New York: Macmillan.

Tsai, J.L. and Levenson, R.W. (1997) 'Cultural Influences of Emotional Responding: Chinese American and European American Dating Couples during Interpersonal Conflict', *Journal of Cross-Cultural Psychology*, 28: 600–25.

Tyler, T.R. and Sears, D.O. (1977) 'Coming to Like Obnoxious People when We Must Live with Them', *Journal of Personality and Social Psychology*, 35: 200–11.

van Knippenberg, D. and Wilke, H. (1992) 'Prototypicality of Arguments and Conformity to Ingroup Norms', *European Journal of Social Psychology*, 22: 141–55.

van Overwelle, F. and Jordens, K. (2002) 'An Adaptive Connectionist Model of Cognitive Dissonance', *Personality and Social Psychology Review*, 6: 204–31.

Verplanck, W.S. (1955) 'The Control of the Content of Conversation: Reinforcement of Statements of Opinion', *Journal of Abnormal and Social Psychology*, 51: 668–76.

Visser, P.S. and Krosnick, J.A. (1998) 'Development of Attitude Strength over the Life Cycle: Surge and Decline', *Journal of Personality and Social Psychology*, 75: 1389–410.

Wells, G.L. and Petty, R.E. (1980) 'The Effects of Overt Head Movements on Persuasion: Compatibility and Incompatibility of Responses', *Basic and Applied Social Psychology*, 1: 219–30.

Wilson, W.R. (1979) 'Feeling More than We Can Know: Exposure Effects without Learning', *Journal of Personality and Social Psychology*, 37: 811–21.

Winkielman, P. and Cacioppo, J.T. (2001) 'Mind at Ease Puts a Smile on the Face: Psychophysiological Evidence that Processing Facilitation Elicits Positive Affect', *Journal of Personality and Social Psychology*, 81: 989–1000.

Winkielman, P., Schwarz, N., Fazendeiro, T., and Reber, R. (2003) 'The Hedonic Marking of Processing Fluency: Implications for Evaluative Judgment', in J. Musch and K.C. Klauer (eds), *The Psychology of Evaluation: Affective Processes in Cognition and Emotion*. Mahwah, NJ: Erlbaum, pp. 189–217.

Wood, W. and Kallgren, C.A. (1988) 'Communicator Attributes and Persuasion: Recipients' Access to Attitude-Relevant Information in Memory', *Personality and Social Psychology Bulletin*, 14: 172–82.

Wood, W., Kallgren, C., and Preisler, R.M. (1985) 'Access to Attitude-Relevant Information in Memory as a Determinant of Persuasion: The Role of Message Attributes', *Journal of Experimental Social Psychology*, 21: 73–85.

Zajonc, R.B. (1968) 'Attitudinal Effects of Mere Exposure', *Journal of Personality and Social Psychology*, 9: 1–27.

Zajonc, R.B., Reimer, D.J., and Hausser, D. (1973) 'Imprinting and the Development of Object Preference in Chicks by Mere Repeated Exposure', *Journal of Comparative and Physiological Psychology*, 83: 434–40.

Zanna, M.P. (1993) 'Message Receptivity: A New Look at the Old Problem of Open- Versus Closed-Mindedness', in A.A. Mitchell (ed.), *Advertising Exposure, Memory, and Choice: Advertising and Consumer Psychology*. Hillsdale, NJ: Erlbaum, pp. 141–62.

Zanna, M.P. and Cooper, J. (1974) 'Dissonance and the Pill: An Attribution Approach to Studying the Arousal Properties of Dissonance', *Journal of Personality and Social Psychology*, 29: 703–9.

Zanna, M.P. and Cooper, J. (1976) 'Dissonance and the Attribution Process', in J.H. Harvey, W.J. Ickes, and R.F. Kidd (eds), *New Directions in Attribution Research* (vol. 1). Hillsdale, NJ: Erlbaum, pp. 199–221.

Zanna, M.P., Kiesler, C.A., and Pilkonis, P.A. (1970) 'Positive and Negative Attitudinal Affect Established by Classical Conditioning', *Journal of Personality and Social Psychology*, 14: 321–8.

Zanna, M.P., Lepper, M.R., and Abelson, R.P. (1973) 'Attentional Mechanisms in Children's Devaluation of a Forbidden Activity in a Forced-Compliance Situation', *Journal of Personality and Social Psychology*, 28: 355–9.

# 10
# Interpersonal Attraction and Intimate Relationships

JULIE FITNESS, GARTH FLETCHER,
AND NICKOLA OVERALL

**INTRODUCTION**

The aim of this chapter is to present a theoretically integrative model of interpersonal attraction and intimate relationships. It argues for the importance of both evolutionary and social cognitive approaches in understanding how relationships work. For example, humans possess evolved motivational mechanisms that enable them to fall in love. However, individuals also learn about falling in (and out of) love throughout their lives, and the lessons they learn influence their thoughts, feelings and responses in their ongoing relationships. This chapter seeks to demonstrate the complementary ways in which evolutionary and social-psychological approaches enrich our understanding of intimate relationship functioning.

Human beings are among the most social animals on the planet. Little wonder, then, that laypersons and scientists alike are strongly motivated to explain, evaluate, predict, and manage intimate relationships. Research relevant to human relationships has taken place for decades across several disciplines, including sociology, anthropology, biology, and, of course, the psychological subdisciplines including clinical psychology, developmental psychology, and cognitive psychology. However, within psychology, the study of human intimate relationships has been dominated by social psychology.

Up to the late 1970s, social psychological research into relationships focused mainly on the factors that attract people to one another at the initial stages of relationship development. This research tended to be atheoretical, and the results read like a laundry list of variables that predict attraction between strangers, including similarity, proximity, physical attractiveness, and so forth. In the 1980s, the psychological zeitgeist moved toward a growing recognition of the complexity inherent in the development, maintenance, and dissolution phases of dyadic romantic relationships, to the point where the study of intimate relationships is now one of the major domains in social psychology.

Over the past decade, social psychological research on intimate relationships has been marked by three major developments. First, there has been an explosion of work concerned with the role that social cognition (beliefs, cognitive processes, etc.) and emotions play in intimate relationships. Second, there has been a burgeoning interest in how attachment processes contribute to the functioning of adult romantic relationships, based on the work of John Bowlby and Mary Ainsworth on infant–caregiver attachment bonds. Third, evolutionary psychology has steadily increased its influence in the area, although not without controversy and opposition. In this chapter, we will focus on these three domains and integrate and explore their connecting threads.

Scientific approaches to the study of intimate relationships can be differentiated according to their goals and to their level of focus. A developmental approach, for example, seeks to understand how different kinds of intimate relationships, including parent–child and sibling relationships, develop across the life span and how such relationships, in turn, influence human development and behavior (Reis et al., 2000). Evolutionary psychology is primarily concerned with understanding the evolutionary origins of human courting, mate selection, sexual behavior, and so forth. Thus, it is concerned with distal causes from the remote past for current human behavioral and cognitive dispositions. A social psychological approach to intimate relationships, in contrast, takes human dispositions, both behavioral and cognitive, as givens, and seeks to model the ways in which such dispositions interact with external contingencies to produce interactive behavior, judgments, and emotions. Thus, social psychology offers much more fine-grained predictions and explanations of specific relationship-related cognitions and behaviors than does evolutionary psychology, and at a very proximal level.

However, it is important to note that evolutionary and social psychological approaches to understanding close relationship phenomena are complementary, rather than mutually exclusive. For example, if we ask why a particular person is attracted to another person, social-cognitive psychologists might argue that people hold cognitive theories about the qualities that are most desirable in potential mates, derived both from their own idiosyncratic learning histories and from socially shared understandings of what is considered attractive within a particular culture. Evolutionary psychology, however, asks questions that social psychologists typically do not ask, such as why people seek physically attractive mates in the first place, or what might be the origin of the characteristic sex differences found in ideal mate standards. Answers for evolutionary psychologists lie in the adaptive advantages that would have accrued to our forebears in the ancestral environment in developing such mate preferences (for reviews of evolutionary approaches to intimate relationships, see Durrant and Ellis, 2005; Fletcher, 2002; and Kenrick and Trost, 2000).

However, although their perspectives are not in competition, evolutionary and social psychological enterprises are not autonomous. Understanding the evolutionary origins of love or mate preferences can help the social psychologist to identify and measure such phenomena, in addition to helping predict how people will feel, think, and behave in contemporary close-relationship contexts. Moreover, an evolutionary approach inspires the social psychologist to ask important questions about the functions of proximal-level cognitive and affective processes – questions, which, as we shall see in this chapter, considerably enhance our ability to understand and explain such processes.

We begin the chapter with a classic topic in the social psychology of relationships: what attracts us to others and how do people select their mates? We proceed to consider the nature and functions of romantic love. We then discuss relationship cognition and the ways in which relationship knowledge structures are causally related to partners' perceptions, judgments, memories, and behaviors. Next, we discuss the nature and function of emotions in intimate relationships, with a particular focus on an inherently relational emotion, romantic jealousy. We conclude by restating the value of adopting an integrative approach that reaches across levels of explanation, while stressing the pivotal role played by social psychology.

## Interpersonal attraction

As noted previously, what attracts one person to another is partly a function of socially shared norms, along with idiosyncratic preferences derived from people's learning histories. At the most fundamental level, however, familiarity plays a crucial role in attraction (Berscheid and Reis, 1998). Whenever people encounter a novel stimulus, their immediate appraisals focus on the extent to which it signals danger; such fast and typically nonconscious appraisals are critical for people's well-being and survival (see Planalp and Fitness, 1999). One way of initially determining the 'goodness' or safety of a stimulus is based on its familiarity (also known as the 'mere exposure' effect; Zajonc, 1968); thus, people's preference for familiar over unfamiliar others is potentially adaptive. However, people are also attracted to complete strangers, so familiarity is not the only factor underpinning interpersonal attraction.

In the 1950s, researchers argued that people are attracted to each other on the basis of complementarity of needs, or, as folklore would put it, 'opposites attract' (Winch et al., 1954). However, there is little support for this proposition (Murstein, 1980); rather, perceived similarity appears to be a much more important criterion (Byrne, 1971; Newcomb, 1961). Recent studies have consistently found that higher perceptions of similarity are associated with increased levels of relationship quality (Acitelli et al., 1993; Hammond and Fletcher, 1991). Interestingly, however, this does not imply that actual similarity is necessarily beneficial for ongoing relationships – researchers have found only weak or nonexistent links between similarity in attitudes or personality traits and perceptions of relationship quality (Acitelli et al., 2001; Karney and Bradbury, 1995; Robins et al., 2000).

Another important determinant of interpersonal attraction involves what Berscheid and Walster (1978) identified as the reciprocity of attraction principle. In general, people are attracted to people who like them and who are responsive to them (see also

Aron et al., 1989). No doubt, people's attraction to admiring others is based partly on familiarity (signaling perceived safety) and perceived similarity (this person is like me); in addition, receiving positive attention from others is rewarding and boosts self-esteem (Myers, 1999). However, there are exceptions to this rule. For example, excessive admiration or flattery may cause a person to suspect the other's motives (Jones, 1964), or a person may simply find the admiring other unattractive and feel embarrassed or even disgusted by his or her attentions (see Baumeister and Wotman, 1992, for an analysis of unrequited love). Moreover, arguing that X likes Y because Y likes X, begs the question as to why Y is attracted to X in the first place.

### *The role of physical appearance*

Although adults frequently admonish children not to 'judge a book by its cover', physical appearance is the most accessible and salient dimension along which people judge others (Sangrador and Yela, 2000). Dion et al. (1972) were among the first to demonstrate people's strong tendencies to attribute positive qualities to physically attractive people and negative qualities to physically unattractive people (supporting the stereotype that 'what is beautiful is good'). Since then, many studies have demonstrated the powerful association between beauty and success in life. Feingold (1992), for example, found that compared with physically unattractive individuals, physically attractive individuals are less socially anxious, more popular, and more sexually experienced (see also Eagly et al., 1991). In a recent meta-analysis, Langlois et al. (2000) found that across cultures, physically attractive individuals had higher status and better social skills and were more successful and mentally healthy than less physically attractive individuals. These associations are likely to be partly a function of the favorable treatment accorded to physically attractive individuals throughout their lives; for example, Langlois et al. found that even young children receive preferential treatment if they are physically attractive.

Physical appearance, then, is an important determinant of attraction across cultures; but do people in different cultures judge physical attractiveness by the same yardstick? Several lines of research suggest that there are universal criteria of physical attractiveness. Ford and Beach (1951) found that across cultures, signs of youth (such as clear skin) and health (such as absence of sores) were reliably regarded as attractive. Similarly, Cunningham et al. (1995) asked people from four ethnic-cultural groups and thirteen countries to rate the facial attractiveness of photographed women of different races and found a high degree of consensus on who was considered to be good-looking, regardless of the judges' exposure to Western standards of beauty. In particular, these researchers found a preference for large, wide-set eyes, a small nose and chin, and prominent cheekbones. According to Cunningham et al., neonate or baby-like facial features such as large eyes suggest youthfulness (see also Berry and McArthur, 1986), whereas prom inent cheekbones are a product of increased hormonal levels during puberty and signal sexual maturity (Enlow, 1990). Accordingly, this particular combination of facial features appears to signal an optimal age for mating.

Another important criterion by which people across cultures judge physical attractiveness is facial symmetry. Researchers have found that people are more attracted to symmetrical than to asymmetrical faces and that people find 'composite' faces (created by computer-morphing several distinctive faces into one, 'average' face) more attractive than individual, distinctive faces (see Langlois et al., 2000). Various explanations have been proposed to account for this preference. For example, from the findings of studies that people rate composite faces as both more attractive and more familiar than the individual faces contributing to the composites (Langlois et al., 1994), Berscheid and Reis (1998) argued that people are attracted to average faces because their apparent familiarity gives people a sense of safety and perceived goodness.

Consistent with evolutionary psychological theory, others have claimed that average or symmetrical faces are perceived as attractive because they are markers of good health and reproductive fitness (the 'good genes' hypothesis; Grammer and Thornhill, 1994). Researchers have found that asymmetry is associated with developmental deviations, lower fertility, slower growth, and poorer survival in many species (Møller and Swaddle, 1997). Moreover, Shackelford and Larsen (1997) found that facial asymmetry was associated with more psychological, affective, and physiological problems in a sample of university students; asymmetrical individuals were also rated as being less healthy in these core dimensions by three independent sets of observers. Rhodes et al. (2001) also found that more extreme perceived averageness and symmetry of individual faces were associated with increases in perceived health. On the basis of these findings, researchers have proposed that symmetry is an 'honest' marker of (at least partly) heritable features such as pathogen-resistance, fitness, and vitality. Given that symmetrical individuals have greater mating success than asymmetrical individuals (see Gangestad and Simpson, 2000), it is plausible that the preference for symmetrical faces evolved because such faces advertise 'good genes'; that is, a healthy immune system and an increased probability of producing healthy offspring (Grammer and Thornhill, 1994).

Of course, physical appearance is not just a function of the face. Singh (1993) reported that in general, men prefer a female body shape characterized by a waist-to-hip ratio (WHR) of about 0.70. Singh argued that this body shape is preferred because, like facial symmetry, it signals youthfulness, good health, and fertility. Indeed, research has shown that the classic hourglass woman's figure (associated with Singh's WHR of .70) is associated with good health and fertility (controlling for age) (Singh and Luis, 1995; Zaadstra et al., 1993). This is not to say, however, that this kind of mate preference is immune from cultural or other ecological factors. For example, Marlowe and Wetsman (2001) found that men in a poor or aging society preferred high WHRs in female figures. These authors argued that this preference for heavier women is adaptive in less developed societies where thinness may indicate illness. In food-rich societies, however, obesity may be a more important marker of poor health than thinness, and men may accordingly prefer a lower WHR.

With respect to what women like about the appearance of men, facial symmetry again appears to be important (Mealey et al., 1999). Other research suggests a role for physical cues suggesting dominance (Sadalla et al., 1987). Collins (2000), for example, found that women preferred deep, rather than high-pitched, men's voices; women also assumed that men with deep voices would be older, heavier, more muscular, and more hairy than higher-voiced men, despite there being no correlations between depth of voice and any male body characteristic except weight. Dabbs (2000) noted that testosterone tends to deepen male voices at puberty. Thus, women may be attracted to deep tones because they associate them with prototypical masculinity and, by implication, dominance. Indeed, Collins noted that voice-overs had to be used for the villains in the film *Star Wars* because although the actors were sufficiently bulky and tall, their voices were not deep enough to be convincing.

Such findings are an important reminder of the role that cultural stereotypes play in people's judgments of physical attractiveness. In addition, there are enormous cross-cultural variations with respect to such appearance-related features as the use of cosmetics and body ornamentation; similarly, ideals of male and female beauty (for example, with respect to weight, hair color, and apparel) have changed dramatically in Western cultures over the years. In short, fads and fashions play a pivotal role in determining attractiveness. However, underlying the vicissitudes of fashion, there exist a raft of universal cues associated with the perception of attractiveness that are (or were) related to reproductive fitness and almost certainly have their origins in our evolutionary past (Berry, 2000; Langlois et al., 2000).

For example, a well-replicated finding is that women prefer the smell of T-shirts which have been worn by men who are more symmetrical (the women have no idea who actually wore the T-shirts). However, the intriguing caveat is that this kind of female preference is only found when the women participants are near ovulation. In this phase of the menstrual cycle, testosterone (which tends to increase sexual desire in women as with men) is generally at its peak of secretion, and women are also most likely to conceive (Gangestad and Simpson, 2000). In the same vein, other research has found that women increasingly prefer more stereotypical male faces (jutting jaws, angular face shape, and craggy eyes) as they near ovulation in the menstrual cycle (Penton-Voak et al., 1999).

It should be noted that although judgments of physical attractiveness may be automatic and deeply rooted in evolutionary adaptations, this does not imply that such judgments operate in encapsulated and splendid isolation from the rest of the intimate-relationship mind. Importantly, and consistent with a fundamental tenet of social psychology, people flexibly alter their cognition and behavior (consciously or unconsciously) in response to such factors as personal goals and the relational or situational context. For example, the country-and-western song by Micky Gilley intones that 'girls get prettier at closing time; they all get to look like film stars'. Inspired by this potential wisdom, Pennebaker et al. (1979) found that, sure enough, as the hours passed and, presumably, options became increasingly limited, both men and women perceived potential mates in bars as more attractive. Further research has replicated the finding for both genders, confirmed that the effect is not simply caused by people steadily becoming inebriated, and has shown that the effect occurs only for those who are not currently involved in an intimate sexual relationship (and who are thus more likely to be monitoring the bar for potential mates) (Gladue and Delaney, 1990; Madey et al., 1996; but see Sprecher et al., 1984, for a failure to replicate the effect).

### Mate selection

Just as familiarity, perceived similarity, reciprocity of liking, and physical attractiveness are important determinants of interpersonal attraction, so each of these factors plays an important role in people's choice of romantic partners. For example, consistent with the mere exposure effect, researchers have found a strong tendency for people to marry people from their own neighborhoods or workplaces. The critical factor here is not so much geographical proximity as 'functional distance', or the extent to which people's paths cross (Myers, 1999). Frequent interactions give individuals the opportunity, not only to become more familiar with one another, but also to explore their potential similarities. Indeed, individuals tend to marry people who are similar to themselves on a number of different dimensions, including height, religion, intelligence, personality, and physical attractiveness (Caspi and Herbener, 1990; Feingold, 1988; Surra, 1990).

Reciprocity also plays an important role in mate selection but not simply with respect to mutual liking. Rather, individuals bring a variety of resources to their relationships, including status, physical attractiveness, love, and material wealth (Foa and Foa, 1980; Murstein, 1980), and every relationship involves an exchange of resources, either in kind (as when partners exchange love) or in value (as when one partner's beauty is exchanged for the other's wealth). In general, researchers have found that partners are happiest when they perceive the allocation of relationship resources is fair and equitable (Sprecher, 1986; Walster et al., 1978). For example, Critelli and Waid (1980) found that individuals who believed their partners were more attractive than themselves tended to report loving them more, presumably to maintain the perception of a fair exchange in the relationship.

With respect to the resources most valued by individuals selecting mates, cross-cultural research has shown that both men and women place an especially high value on kindness, loyalty, and emotional stability (Buss, 1989a). This makes adaptive sense because when we entrust our psychological (and often physical) welfare to another human being, it is important that he or she poses no threat to our safety and can be relied upon to act in a caring and consistent fashion. However, there also exist some well-documented differences between men and women in mate selection. In particular, men tend to place more value on youthfulness and physical attractiveness in a potential mate than women, who tend to give more importance to status and resource acquisition such as education, earning potential, and ambition (Buss and Barnes, 1986; Sprecher et al., 1994). These findings have been replicated across many cultures (Buss, 1989a; Feingold, 1990) and are evident in the personal-advertisement columns of daily newspapers in which men typically offer status and resources to attract women, and women typically offer physical attractiveness and youthfulness to attract men (e.g., Davis, 1990).

One explanation for these robust sex differences involves social conditioning and men's and women's differential access to power (e.g., Murstein, 1980). According to this hypothesis, women's relative powerlessness, compared to men, leads them to seek resources from men that will help them secure status and economic security. Men, however, seek only the rewards of sex in marriage; thus, their main mating criteria involve beauty and physical desirability. Social conditioning and sex-role socialization are theorized to reinforce and maintain these unequal power relations and consequent mating preferences through the generations. One implication of this hypothesis is that women with access to power and wealth of their own should feel and behave like men – that is, they should become less interested in the status of potential mates and more interested in their physical attributes and sexual availability. However, empirical data show that women's sexual preferences actually become more, rather than less, discriminatory as their own wealth and power increase (Ellis, 1992). Of course, women's urges to marry 'up' could still be a product of socialization; however, as Buss and Barnes (1986) noted, this explanation does not address the origins of what appear to be culturally universal sex-role socialization practices and economic power structures.

One standard evolutionary explanation for sex differences in mating preferences is provided by sexual-strategies theory (e.g., Buss and Schmitt, 1993). On the basis of Trivers's (1974) parental-investment theory, sexual-strategy theorists argue that women can produce only a small number of offspring over their lifetimes, and the burdens of pregnancy and child-rearing make each offspring a costly investment. Thus, women need to be highly selective in their approach to mating. In particular, women should be most impressed by a man's status, resources, and willingness to commit to her and her offspring over the long term. Men, however, have the capacity to produce numerous offspring over the course of their lives. Accordingly, men should be motivated to seek multiple mating opportunities, because in this way they acquire additional offspring at low cost. This, in turn, implies that men should be less impressed with a woman's status than with her physical attractiveness (signaling good genes and reproductive fitness; Townsend et al., 1995).

Research evidence supports the theory that men are more interested in sexual variety and multiple short-term relationships than are women (Baumeister et al., 2001; Buss and Schmitt, 1993; Kenrick and Trost, 2000). For example, Clark and Hatfield (1989) conducted studies in 1978 and 1982 in which male and female confederates approached members of the opposite sex on campus at the University of Hawaii and asked them if they would go to bed with them. Approximately 70 percent of the men agreed, whereas none of the women did. This difference was not a function of the attractiveness of the person making the request. When the same individuals softened the request to going out on a date, 50 percent of the women and 53 percent of the men agreed. (Oddly, then, men were more likely to agree to have sex than to go on a date.) Men who declined the offer of sex apologized and explained that they were married or already involved, whereas women responded with outrage or complaints.

Of course, this does not imply that men do not seek and establish long-term partnerships. Indeed, historical and anthropological evidence suggests that most men opt for quality over quantity and commit their resources to a small number of offspring, who are, in turn, likely to survive to adulthood and to pass on their fathers' genes. Moreover, in many cultures, men with high status and ample resources can obtain the best of both worlds by marrying several women, either serially (through repeated divorce and remarriage), or multiply, as in cultures where men are permitted to have several wives at a time. In this way, high-status men achieve sexual variety while also ensuring the survival of their offspring (Wright, 1994). However, if a quality versus quantity trade-off is to be worthwhile for men, they must ensure that they are genetically related to the children in whom they are investing their resources. Accordingly, Buss and Schmitt (1993) reported that men tend to prefer long-term partners who are (or appear to be) more chaste than the women with whom they have sex in short-term relationships, perhaps because men implicitly associate women's premarital chastity with long-term sexual faithfulness.

This observation underscores the point that, like men, women do sometimes engage in short-term mating relationships. One predisposing factor involves an individual-difference characteristic termed sociosexuality (e.g., Simpson and Gangestad, 1992). According to Simpson and Gangestad, individuals with a 'restricted' sociosexual orientation seek emotional commitment before having sex, whereas individuals with an 'unrestricted' orientation are willing to have sex without commitment. Unrestricted sociosexuality has been found to be positively correlated with extraversion and risk-taking behavior, a correlation which may account, in part, for the preference of unrestricted individuals for sexually exciting, short-term relationships. Interestingly, however, Simpson (1987) found that unrestricted women expressed greater anxiety and distress following relationship dissolution than either restricted men or women, or unrestricted men. Townsend et al. (1995) argued that this is because, behavioral tendencies notwithstanding, unrestricted women possess the same emotional-motivational mechanisms as restricted women (that is, they desire long-term emotional commitment). However, because of their personality styles, unrestricted women overestimate their ability to obtain commitment from partners and underestimate the strength of their emotional reactions, including anger, when their partners fail to commit to them.

Cross-cultural research has also demonstrated that in every culture and throughout history, some women engage in extra-pair copulation, often at risk to their safety from spouses or other family members (Greiling and Buss, 2000). In their study of North American women's reported reasons for engaging in extra-pair liaisons, Greiling and Buss found the most important motives involved dissatisfaction with a current partner and the hope of finding a better one, and resource acquisition, including gifts and status-related assets. Both motives make sense with respect to women's reproductive interests; that is, securing the commitment of a man who will invest resources in her and her offspring. However, such brief liaisons may also be attractive to women, who potentially obtain good genes for their offspring from a physically attractive and, by implication, healthy and reproductively successful, partner (Gangestad, 1993; Townsend et al., 1995). In support of this argument, DNA paternity-testing procedures have found some 10–15 percent of children are not, in fact, genetically related to their putative fathers (Baker and Bellis, 1995). This in turn suggests that, like some men, some women may seek the best of both worlds – a committed partner who unwittingly helps to raise a child with better genes than his own; thus, a woman's reproductive fitness may be enhanced at her partner's expense.

It is worth reiterating that individuals typically do not coldly calculate the rewards and costs of short-term versus long-term mating opportunities according to their reproductive interests. Moreover, humans have more than one mating strategy at their disposal, depending on a variety of contextual factors, such as their self-perceived mate value (that is, what they have to offer in a mating or romantic context) and sociocultural norms or regulations about mating. For example, in some cultures, the penalties for women engaging in extra-pair copulations would be too severe to risk. However, although men and women may not typically be consciously aware of the potential costs and benefits associated with mating opportunities or may be unable to take advantage of such opportunities, they do experience related powerful desires and emotions. According to evolutionary theory, such desires and feelings are psychological mechanisms which have evolved over millennia and contributed to human reproductive success. The extent to which such desires and emotions are related to behavior is an open question that social psychology is well placed to examine. We will now examine the role of one such powerful psychological mechanism: romantic love.

## Romantic love

Laypersons (and even some scientists, alas) are prone to claim that romantic love is mysterious and unmeasurable. It is true that love is a complex phenomenon. However, social psychologists (with contributions from other disciplines) have made remarkable progress in defining, measuring, and explaining romantic love (Dion and Dion, 1996; Fletcher, 2002).

One of the richest accounts of the first stage of romantic love was provided by Tennov (1979), who coined the term 'limerence' to describe the process of falling in love. Tennov argued that limerence begins when the target individual becomes figural against a background of generally less interesting, less attractive others. Along with this change in perception comes the tendency to brood and think obsessively about the loved one, to long for reciprocation from him or her, and to regard any of the loved one's flaws as unimportant, or even attractive. Emotionally, limerent lovers swing between ecstasy when their loved ones are responsive and depression when they are not; similarly, they often experience frequent (and debilitating) anxiety over the possibility that they will be rejected.

According to Liebowitz (1983), limerence may be associated with the production of an amphetamine-like chemical called phenylethylamine (PEA), which accounts for its exhilarating (and sometimes paranoid) features (but see Panksepp, 1998, for a more skeptical view). Liebowitz noted that, like speed addicts, so-called love addicts crave the 'rush' of being in love and suffer acute withdrawal when PEA levels decrease – as they inevitably do, typically over a period between 18 months and three years (Tennov, 1979). Fisher (1992) speculated that this decline accounts for the worldwide peak in divorce rates around the fourth year of marriage: after a few years of fading passion, boredom casts its pall and partners begin to wonder what they ever saw in one another.

However, in spite of the inevitable waning of the fires of passion, many couples' relationships develop into a second stage of romantic love, characterized by emotional intimacy, attachment, and deep affection for each other – so-called companionate love (Hatfield, 1988). During this period, sexual activity and obsession with the beloved diminish, and the couple settles into a loving, but less physiologically arousing mode of existence. Partners in the first phase of romantic love typically lose their appetites and spend a great deal of their shared time making love. In contrast, lovers in the latter companionate stage typically relish shared meals, enjoy long hours of joint slumber, and develop an easy-going acceptance and intimacy (Zeifman and Hazan, 2000). This phase of romantic love is theorized to be accompanied by the production of endogenous opioids that elicit feelings of contentment and anxiety reduction (Liebowitz, 1983; Panksepp, 1998). Interestingly, the involvement of these opioids means that disruption to the attachment bond can trigger extreme panic and distress, similar to the withdrawal symptoms suffered by heroin addicts.

Research with mammals has also implicated the role of oxytocin and vasopressin (closely related neuropeptides) in bonding, both in terms of mother–infant and adult–adult relationships. These hormones appear to be present only in the 3 percent of male mammals who are monogamous, expend considerable investment in the offspring, and bond with a female partner (Insel, 2000). In humans also, the same ancient hormones (and hormone receptors in the brain) are present in both men and women, are released by women when giving birth and when breast-feeding and by both men and women during sexual intercourse and after orgasm (Insel, 2000).

According to Zeifman and Hazan (2000), the companionate stage of romantic love may imperceptibly shift to a life-as-usual phase, whereby couples resume their preromance activities and reorient their attention and stimulation, seeking sources outside the relationship. Although partners may cease to experience intense emotions in relation to each other, the relationship is likely to have become profoundly interdependent: in effect, partners have meshed their expectations, behaviors, and goals (Berscheid, 1983). This, in turn, implies that, although partners may perceive their emotionally tranquil relationship to be predictable, they have the capacity to generate powerful emotions in each other simply by behaving in ways that disrupt each other's expectations or goals (such as announcing the relationship is doomed).

### *The functions of romantic love*

During the 1960s and 1970s, a number of theorists argued that romantic love was an exclusively Euro-American phenomenon that did not exist in other cultures (Jankowiak, 1995). Recent research, however, has confirmed that romantic love is, indeed, universally experienced across cultures, although it may not always be tightly linked to the institution of marriage (Shaver et al., 1996). This, in turn, suggests that romantic love has an evolutionary history and has played an adaptive role in human reproductive success. Consistently, current evolutionary thinking holds that the primary adaptive functions of romantic relationships involve sexual reproduction and the provision of mutual support for the successful rearing of offspring (e.g., Kenrick and Trost, 2000). According to this account, the function of the first stage of romantic love, or limerence, is to motivate sexual activity, while the function of the second, companionate stage, is to establish a firm emotional bond between the partners that will motivate them to remain together, at least for enough years to give the children a good chance of making it to adulthood (and passing on the genes of both parents).

At a more proximal level of analysis, attachment theorists have made a pivotal contribution to our understanding of the nature and functions of romantic love. In an influential theoretical analysis and associated program of research, Phillip Shaver and his colleagues have conceptualized adult romantic love in terms of John Bowlby's pioneering (and evolutionary) treatment of attachment systems in humans (e.g., Shaver et al., 1996). Bowlby (1969) argued for the existence of three, basic behavioral systems that bond dyads together: attachment, caregiving, and sex. Thus, Shaver et al. (1996: 93) write that saying 'I love you' can mean any or all of the following.

Love as attachment

- 'I am emotionally dependent on you for happiness, safety, and security;
- I feel anxious and lonely when you're gone, relieved and stronger when you're near.
- I want to be comforted, supported emotionally, and taken care of by you.
- Part of my identity is based on my attachment to you.'

Love as caregiving

- 'I get great pleasure from supporting, caring for, and taking care of you; from facilitating your progress, health, growth, and happiness.
- Part of my identity is based on caring for you, and if you were to disappear I would feel sad, empty, less worthwhile, and perhaps guilty.'

Love as sexual attraction

- 'I am sexually attracted to you and can't get you out of my mind.
- You excite me, "turn me on", make me feel alive, complete with my sense of wholeness.
- I want to see you, devour you, touch you, merge with you, lose myself in you, "get off on you".'

All three behavioral systems are clearly adaptive, because they motivate and reward sexual relations, emotional bonding, and mutual protection – behaviors that contribute to the successful rearing of offspring. Moreover, the parallels between adult-to-adult love and adult-to-child love are exactly what an evolutionary approach would predict. In particular, the attachment and caregiving behavioral/affective systems are ancient, present in all mammals that care for and protect their offspring for long periods of time, and precede the emergence of primates and *Homo sapiens* by millions of years. These two specific affective and behavioral systems clearly increase the odds that vulnerable infants will survive to adulthood. If pair-bonding and love between human adults (or adults of any species) were to emerge as an adaptation, evolution would assuredly tinker with the serviceable attachment networks that were already in place, rather than invent completely different systems. Thus, the basic commitment and intimacy components of adult human love are likely to be derived from the same systems that promote adult–infant bonding.

Another clue to the fundamental nature of the attachment system in humans derives from recent social psychological research (using self-reports) which has examined the underlying dimensions of laypersons' conceptions of love in adult relationships. This research has revealed a remarkably similar tripartite pattern to that postulated by Bowlby; namely, intimacy, commitment, and passion (e.g., Aron and Westbay, 1996; Sternberg, 1986). Tellingly, the social psychologists who have carried out this research have done so without reference to Bowlby's work. Thus, there is a close convergence between laypersons' experiences of, and beliefs about, romantic love, and evolutionary accounts of its nature and function.

Clearly, romantic love plays a crucial role in the development of intimate relationships. However, although affect is pivotal in intimate relationships, cognition also plays a central role. We now turn to this latter topic.

## Relationship cognition

When people are asked how they know whether they are in a good relationship, they normally give responses such as 'I just know' or 'what an interesting question – I've never really thought about it'. If pressed, they might articulate a set of criteria that they believe establishes a good or successful relationship, such as good communication, similarity, good sex life, honesty, humor, and support. One major goal of a cognitive approach to intimate relationships is to answer the same question and to explain how and why people evaluate the state of their relationships. However, the sweep of a cognitive approach is exceptionally broad and deals with every imaginable kind of relationship judgment, from those that occur at the very genesis of the relationship ('looks interesting') to the kind that occur at its end ('This relationship will never work!') to the myriad of mundane judgments that accompany every relationship, every day.

Current research and theorizing on social cognition in intimate relationships is voluminous; thus, we have chosen to present an organizing model that represents an amalgamation of features that have common currency in mainstream cognitive and social psychology (see Figure 10.1). Here is an example to give an intuitive feel for the way the model works:

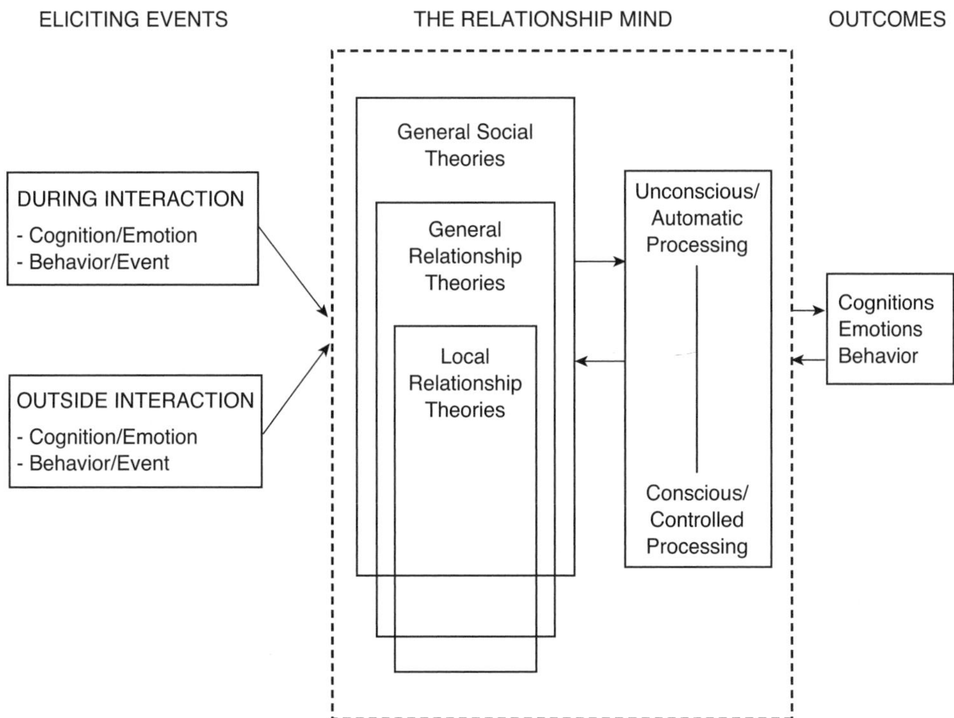


Figure 10.1 Model of the relationship mind

> Joan's partner unexpectedly pays her a compliment (Eliciting Event) which leads her to feel particularly happy (Eliciting Emotion) because she had begun to think her husband was taking her for granted (Local Relationship Theory). She recalls with pleasure the way her husband used to flood her with gifts and romantic notes when they first got together (Conscious Processing) and thinks what a sensitive, loving person he usually is (Cognitive Outcome). Joan decides to make his favorite meal (Behavioral Outcome). Her general belief that intimate relationships need a lot of work to stay successful (General Relationship Theory) and her positive evaluation of her own relationship (Local Relationship Theory) are strengthened (feedback arrow from Outcomes).

Relationship theorists argue that the intimate-relationship mind is split into two basic, but intertwined components: stored relationship theories and online processing. This division is standard in traditional social-cognitive models, although the two components are often termed long-term memory versus short-term or working memory. According to this model, people encode, organize, store, and recall events and behaviors in terms of stored knowledge structures, or schemas, in which details are often lost or blurred. Of course, a small amount of information can be retained in working memory, but this memory store is severely limited both in terms of the amount of information it can retain and in the length of time it remains available. We will now discuss each of these components with reference to the intimate-relationship mind.

### *General social theories*

The topmost category shown in Figure 10.1 (general social theories) is based on the proposition that people hold a variety of rules, beliefs, and so forth that apply generally to both intimate and nonintimate relationships. These include a general folk theory (often termed 'theory of mind') that specifies when and how to attribute beliefs, attitudes, intentions, and personality traits. One important example of such a folk theory involves a much-researched social psychological model called attribution theory, or the rules people use to explain (attribute causes) their own and other people's behavior (Ross and Fletcher, 1985).

Even a minimal level of anecdotal observation is sufficient to suggest that people frequently attempt to understand and explain each other's behaviors, especially in close relationship contexts. This impression is backed up by research. First, people frequently talk about relationships. When Dunbar and Duncan (1997) eavesdropped on people's conversations in public places, they found that talk about personal relationships typically dominated the conversations. Ethnographies of traditional cultures, including hunter/gatherer cultures, also often note that adult sexual relationships are favorite topics of conversation (Haviland, 1977; Shostock, 1981). Second, people often produce causal attributions spontaneously, both in the way they talk about relationships and in the way they think about relationships and relationship events (Fletcher and Fincham, 1991).

However, a central difficulty in developing a scientific theory about the underlying cognitive processes involved is that laypersons use an almost infinite variety of causes and reasons to explain behavior. Attribution theorists have dealt with this problem by hypothesizing that it is not the content of causes that matters so much, as where the putative causes are located along a handful of dimensions including stability, specificity, and locus of attribution. To understand how the standard attribution model works, and what these causal dimensions mean, consider the following example: Mary is unhappy with her marriage and distrusts her husband, Fred. Fred surprises her with a gift of flowers. Mary is likely to explain such an action with causal attributions such as 'Fred is suffering from a rare excess of guilt because he dented my car' or 'Fred has had a rare win on the horses'. In short, Mary writes off Fred's positive behavior with attributions that are unstable, situation-specific, and external to Fred.

Contrast this response with the likely scenario if Fred were to make a cutting remark in response to a polite query about his day. In this case, Mary is likely to make an attribution to Fred's insensitivity, or to his lack of love for her, or to his general bad-tempered personality. Now Mary attributes Fred's negative behavior to stable (ongoing), global (personality-based), internal-to-Fred causes. This entire set of attributions, for both positive and negative behaviors, is clearly bad for the relationship.

Now, imagine that Mary is in a state of marital bliss and Fred surprises her with a gift of flowers. Mary now explains this behavior in a relationship-positive fashion in line with Fred's sensitivity and caring nature (a stable, global, and internal cause). Conversely, a cutting remark by Fred will be attributionally written off with an unstable, specific, and external attribution (for example, had a hard day at work). This set of attributions is clearly good for the relationship.

Not only is the standard attribution model a plausible account, but it is also true. A large body of research across Western cultures using a range of methods, examining relationships both cross-sectionally and longitudinally, and statistically controlling for a range of other variables (such as depression), has revealed solid evidence for this model (for a review, see Fincham, 2001). Strong correlations (typically from 0.30 to 0.60) have typically been found between the positivity of causal attributions and relationship satisfaction. Excessive blame attributed to a relationship partner for relationship problems, or for negative features of the relationship, is especially corrosive (Fletcher and Thomas, 2000).

One important feature of the standard attribution model is that attributions function to maintain existent levels of relationship satisfaction, regardless of the partner's behavior. For example, regardless of whether Fred buys his wife flowers or barks at her, Mary will maintain her existing impression of Fred and her attitude towards the relationship as a function of the way she explains his behaviors. This feature is linked to a central tenet of attribution theories first enunciated by Heider (1958); namely, people have a basic need to sift out and maintain judgments of the dispositional and stable properties of the world, including the social world. Causal attributions are one powerful means by which the relative permanence of any pre-existent belief, attitude, or social-knowledge structure can be maintained, including relationship and partner theories. In this respect, high levels of love and positive partner expectations function like money in a cognitive bank that allows people to ride out bursts of bad behavior from their partner. However, the way in which relationship cognition works also explains why it is so difficult for relationships that have gone sour to be turned around, even when couples are highly motivated to make their relationships work.

### *General relationship theories*

This category (see Figure 10.1) includes constructs such as beliefs, expectations, and ideal standards that concern hypothetical relationships or beliefs about relationships in general. This category is distinct from the first category (general social theories) in that it is more content-loaded and specifically concerned with intimate relationships (see also Baldwin, 1992). Despite an inevitable degree of idiosyncratic content, there is substantial evidence that people's general relationship theories are similar in basic ways. Research within Western cultures, for example, shows that both men and women share similar understandings about the features and meanings of love, commitment, and other relationship emotions (Fehr, 1999; Fitness, 1996), the factors that cause relationships to fail or succeed (Fletcher and Kininmonth, 1992), and the ideal criteria people use in searching for mates (Fletcher et al., 1999).

This class of lay theories also includes attachment working models. According to Bowlby, these are internal cognitive representations that summarize one's previous attachment experiences. Essentially, they comprise beliefs and expectations about the trustworthiness of others and the likely course of close relationships and have important implications for individuals' judgments, emotions, and behaviors in relationship contexts. A considerable body of research suggests these working models revolve around two basic and relatively orthogonal attachment dimensions: secure versus avoidant attachment (a bipolar factor), and ambivalent or anxious attachment (see Brennan et al., 1998; Simpson and Rholes, 1998).

Using a different approach, Bartholomew defined and assessed working models in terms of positive versus negative working models of the self versus others (e.g., Bartholomew and Horowitz, 1991). These four attachment categories are usually labeled as follows: *secure*, indicating a positive model of self and other; *preoccupied*, indicating a negative model of self but a positive model of other; *dismissing*, indicating a positive model of self but a negative model of other; and *fearful*, indicating a negative model of self and other. However, factor-analytic work using these alternative measures has revealed essentially the same two dimensions (secure/avoidance and ambivalence), which, in turn, produce similar attachment style categories to those obtained by the original measures derived directly from Bowlby's work (see Bartholomew and Shaver, 1998).

### Local relationship theories

What do lay local theories of intimate relationships look like? Consider the following representative short account of a participant taken from some research by Fletcher et al. (2000). The participant was asked to describe briefly her current relationship (she had been dating for three months):

> I first met Dan at a party. We seemed to hit it off immediately – he is attractive and outgoing and also seemed to lead an interesting life. We have since developed a rather warm and sweet relationship. He is sensitive and kind, although we have both had our problems with past relationships, and he seems a bit insecure. We do a lot of things together, and we talk about our hopes and dreams. The one problem we do have is getting our schedules together – he likes to spend a lot of time with his friends, which I think is fine (I don't want to have a relationship with someone who is super-dependent on me). But, I think we need some time on our own. I am not sure where the relationship is going, and I am happy keeping it fairly light at the moment, which seems to suit us both.

As this brief but typical account demonstrates, from the time individuals meet a prospective partner, they begin to build theories about each other and the relationship (self vis-à-vis the other). These theories become more complex and integrated over time, with causal connections of various kinds drawn between the elements. Many kinds of judgments will be involved, including personality judgments of the other, relationship-level judgments, and interactions between the relationship and outside situations and other relationships. Within the context of their local relationship theories, people also develop quite elaborate explanations of specific problems or issues that concern them. Moreover, as local relationship theories develop, they also steadily become entwined with self theories. Art and Elaine Aron have documented this point in an extensive program of research, showing how perceptions of the self and the partner influence one another over time (for a review, see Aron et al., 2001). Their research has suggested that as couples become more intimate, they construct an expanded local relationship theory that represents the perceived overlap between the self and the partner.

To understand further how these three levels of cognitive theories are psychologically linked (general social theories, general relationship theories, and local relationship theories), we now discuss the functions of these lay theories.

### The functions of lay relationship theories

Why do people develop relationship theories? The standard social psychological explanation is a functional one; that is, like scientists, people develop relationship theories to serve the goals of explaining (or understanding), predicting, and controlling (or regulating) their relationships. From the time individuals meet a prospective partner, these three goals are activated and remain potent throughout the course of the relationship.

There is good evidence, for example, that attachment working models serve all three basic goals. Collins and Allard (2001) have shown that when securely attached individuals explain partners' negative behavior (such as inattention) they tend to produce charitable, relationship-positive attributions that maintain their beliefs in their partners' essential warmth (such as pressure at work). In contrast, ambivalent individuals tend to adopt a relationship-negative pattern that emphasizes their partners' indifference to their needs. Research has also found that, unlike secure individuals, avoidant individuals expect not to be able to trust their partners, and ambivalent individuals predict (quite realistically) that they will be unable to obtain the kind of deep commitment and intense intimacy they so keenly desire (Morgan and Shaver, 1999).

Attachment models also function to regulate both self and other behaviors in the close relationship context. For example, in a pioneering piece of research, Simpson et al. (1992) revisited Bowlby's hypothesis that the attachment systems should be activated when an individual is under stress. Their study showed that when subject to experimentally induced anxiety, secure women sought support from their partners; avoidant women who were stressed, however, did not seek support, even expressing irritation if their partners offered it. Moreover, secure men offered more emotional and physical support as their partners' anxiety increased, whereas avoidant men became less helpful and again, actually expressed irritation. Finally, in the control group, in which neither partner went through a stress manipulation, partners' attachment styles were not reflected in their behaviors.

Along with attachment working models, another important route by which people explain, predict, and regulate their relationships is through the development and use of relationship quality judgments. Specifically, if people are satisfied with their relationships and trust their partners, they tend, like securely attached individuals, to make charitable attributions for potentially negative partner behaviors. Stored perceptions of relationship quality also provide rapid (albeit superficial) causal attributions for communication difficulties and predictions of relationship longevity.

Recall that we began this section with the question, How do people know whether they are in a good or satisfying relationship? We are finally in a position to advance an answer: people know because they compare their perceptions of their current relationship with their pre-existing ideals, standards, and beliefs concerning what constitutes a good or a bad relationship. In short, individuals integrate and compare their local relationship theories with their general relationship theories (as depicted in Figure 10.1). A series of studies by Fletcher, Simpson, and their colleagues support this view specifically with regard to the ideal standards that people possess (for a review, see Simpson et al., 2001). These researchers have shown that individuals evaluate their current partners and relationships by comparing what they perceive they have against their ideal standards. The more congruent the fit, the happier people are with their intimate relationships and the more likely they are to stay with their partners.

### *Online cognitive processing*

When and how do people think about their close relationships? First, if the general model in Figure 10.1 is correct, online cognitive processing should not normally occur without also activating various stored dispositional constructs that are relevant to the relationship, and these may include aspects of all three knowledge categories (general social theories, general relationship theories, and local relationship theories).

Relationship cognition can be triggered by any event that occurs either inside or outside relationship interaction (see Figure 10.1). Indeed, simply being with one's partner without any interaction may evoke some relationship cognition, as might merely noticing a stranger who resembles one's partner. However relationship cognition is evoked, social psychologists recognize an important distinction between unconscious/automatic cognitive processing and conscious/controlled cognitive processing (Wegner and Bargh, 1998). Unconscious/ automatic processing is typically regarded as relatively fast and effortless, not readily verbalizable, and as relatively undemanding of cognitive capacity. Conversely, conscious/controlled processing is regarded as relatively slow, more readily verbalizable, and demanding of cognitive capacity.

In cognitive-processing terms, many automatic/ unconscious processes can occur simultaneously (or in parallel), whereas conscious/controlled processing tends to occur most efficiently one process at a time (or serially). Moreover, over time, cognitive processes that were initially conscious and controlled may become automated and automatic (such as piano-playing, driving a car, or learning how to please one's partner).

Consider a standard conversation in an intimate dyadic context. Each partner must encode and interpret the barrage of verbal and nonverbal information emanating from the other, while simultaneously controlling the expression of his or her own verbal and nonverbal behavior (including facial expression, eye contact, gestures, and body position) and blending a suite of cognitive, affective, perceptual, and behavioral processes into a smoothly coordinated interaction with the other. Each partner will also be making rapid judgments about the interaction and the other's behavior, guided by stored general and relationship theories and consistent with higher-order goals which will vary from the mundane (for example, Jim wants Mary to take the rubbish out) to the pivotal (Mary is trying to prevent Jim from becoming suspicious about her clandestine affair). The only way such regular interactions could be effectively accomplished is if a large amount of cognitive and perceptual processing is routinely carried out automatically, unconsciously, and simultaneously (in parallel).

The amount and extent of conscious and in-depth analysis of relationship events vary considerably depending on the stage of the relationship, individual differences, and the situational context. In a relationship that has reached a stable plateau and has a long history, complex interactional episodes become overlearned and stereotypical, with very little conscious attention or thought required. This implies that a man can automatically process what his partner is saying, while the TV is on, the baby is crying, and he is reading the newspaper. (An experimental demonstration of this kind of automatic processing was provided by Baldwin et al., 1990.) Nevertheless, research has shown that even in the most automated and well-regulated relationship, two kinds of events will immediately activate conscious cognitive processing (and often, emotion): negative events and unexpected events (Berscheid, 1983; Fletcher and Thomas, 1996).

Note that even when individuals are paying complete attention to their partners and engaging in effortful thinking, their conscious cognition will continue to be (unconsciously) influenced by stored knowledge structures. General relationship theories (for example, ideals and beliefs about what makes a relationship successful) will be silently and constantly at work, subtly influencing online judgments of local relationship events and partner behaviors (see Fletcher et al., 1994). As noted previously, attachment working models, too, will operate as highly accessible relationship theories that unconsciously and automatically influence subsequent emotions, cognitions, and behavioral responses (Collins and Allard, 2001; Mikulincer, 1998).

Having explored the critical role played by cognition in the dynamics of close relationships, we will now turn our focus to emotions. However, as will be seen, cognition is a long way short of being done with.

## Emotion in intimate relationships

Research on emotion is flourishing in every area of psychological inquiry (see Chapter 8). However, it is within intimate relationships that feelings and emotions arguably play their most important roles. In the final section of this chapter, we review social psychological models of the experience and expression of various emotions in intimate relationships. We also discuss the role of emotional experience and expression in adaptive relationship functioning, and conclude with a consideration of a potent relationship-relevant emotion: romantic jealousy.

### *When do people experience emotions in close relationships?*

The seminal model of emotion elicitation in close relationships was proposed by Berscheid (1983) and updated by Berscheid and Ammazzalorso (2001). According to this emotion-in-relationships model (ERM), the greater the number of behavioral interconnections relationship partners share, the more interdependent they are, and, therefore, the greater the potential for interruption when one partner does something unexpected (for example, Fred brings flowers home for Mary), or fails to do something expected (for example, Fred forgets to buy Mary a birthday present). Once an interruption has occurred, the interrupted partner appraises the situation for its relevance (is it important or trivial?) and for the extent to which it is congruent with his or her beliefs, goals, and desires. Fred's surprise gift, for example, may be appraised by Mary as exceeding her expectations but consistent with her general relationship theory about what loving husbands do. According to the model, Mary's positive appraisal of Fred's behavior should elicit physiological arousal and positive, partner-directed emotion. Conversely, Fred's oversight may be appraised by Mary as violating her theory-derived expectations about loving husband behaviors; accordingly, she is likely to experience physiological arousal and negative, partner-directed emotion.

Berscheid's model provides a useful and increasingly well-supported account of how general emotional states are triggered in response to disrupted expectations, but it does not specify how discrete emotions, such as anger, sadness, or guilt, are elicited in response to such disruptions. It is possible, however, to predict discrete emotions once we know how an individual is cognitively appraising an interruptive event along a number of different dimensions, including its causal locus, controllability, predictability, and fairness (e.g., Ellsworth, 1991). In their study of marital emotions, for example, Fitness and Fletcher (1993) found that whereas anger was characterized by cognitive appraisals of partner blame, unfairness, and predictability, hate was characterized by appraisals of relative powerlessness and a perceived lack of control (see also Bradbury and Fincham, 1987).

It is important to note here that the cognition–emotion sequence we have just described is not a simple, linear one. Once elicited via cognitive appraisals, emotions themselves color and shape partners' ongoing perceptions, appraisals, and memories in specific ways, with important implications for relationship judgments and behaviors. Forgas (1994), for example, conducted a study in which people watched sad, happy, or neutral movies (a mood-induction technique); participants then made causal attributions about minor or serious conflicts in their intimate relationships. Forgas found that sad individuals generally inferred more internal, stable, and global causes for conflict than happy individuals, with mood having a much stronger influence on people's explanations for serious than for minor conflicts.

Discrete emotions such as anger and anxiety also have specific effects on people's information processing in the proximal context (e.g., Keltner et al.,

1993; Planalp and Fitness, 1999). For example, just as anger is elicited by cognitive appraisals of unfairness and other blame, so, too, does an angry emotional state prime people more readily to attribute blame and malicious intentions to others. Similarly, anxiety primes vigilance for the probability that threatening events are about to occur. The impact of such emotional states on relationship cognition and behavior may be negative but temporary. However, if they become chronic (as in depression), relationship satisfaction is likely to deteriorate as the unhappy individual consistently expects (and, accordingly, perceives) the worst from his or her partner (see Beach and O'Leary, 1993).

### *The functions of emotions in close relationships*

What purpose do emotions experienced in relationships serve? Within the social psychological literature, there is a growing consensus that a number of evolved, basic emotion systems motivate potentially adaptive behaviors in goal-relevant situations (see Oatley and Jenkins, 1996). Anger, for example, is elicited in response to goal obstruction and provides the impetus to confront and remove the obstruction; fear is elicited in response to perceived danger and motivates escape or avoidance behaviors. Positive emotions such as interest and joy also have functional significance, serving both to motivate and reinforce goal-directed behaviors such as exploration and bonding (Izard, 1991).

Several studies confirm that experiences of different emotions are associated with different motivations or action tendencies (Frijda, 1986). For example, Fitness and Fletcher (1993) found that, consistent with attachment theorists' accounts of the evolved functions of romantic love, spouses' self-reported feelings of love were associated with urges to be physically close to their partners and to express their feelings to them. Similarly, episodes of marital anger were associated with urges to confront the partner and seek redress for an apparent injustice; marital hate, however, was associated with urges to escape from, or reject, the partner. At a fundamental level, both motivations are potentially adaptive with respect to confronting a relationship problem (anger) or avoiding a person who has harmed us (hate) (see also Buss, 1989b; Ellis and Malamuth, 2000). It should be noted, however, that acting mindlessly on the basis of such urges does not always produce adaptive outcomes. Research has shown, for example, that happy spouses are more likely than unhappy spouses to inhibit their angry urges to react defensively during conflict interactions and to respond instead in an accommodating or conciliatory fashion (e.g., Rusbult et al., 1998). These findings underscore the fact that, although emotions serve crucial informational functions about the ongoing state of our needs, their expression must be adaptively managed within close relationship contexts (Fitness, 2006).

It should also be noted that emotional expressions themselves serve potentially important functions in the close-relationship context. Drawing on Darwin (1872), Clark and her colleagues have proposed that emotional expressions serve primarily to communicate partners' needs to one another (e.g., Clark et al., 1996, 2001). For example, expressing sadness communicates a need for comfort, expressing anxiety communicates a need for support, and expressing anger communicates a need for reparative action. Moreover, Clark et al. have argued that, whereas in exchange (for example, workplace) relationships, people may feel uncomfortable or even manipulated by another's expression of negative emotions (see Clark and Taraban, 1991), individuals in communal, or close, relationships expect and welcome their partners' expressions of emotions because they feel responsible for meeting their partners' needs. Similarly, in communal relationships, people expect that their partners will be responsive to their own needs and may feel betrayed when such responsiveness is not forthcoming (e.g., Fitness, 2001).

In line with Clark et al.'s functional argument, research shows that individuals in close relationships generally regard emotional expressiveness as positive and desirable. For example, Huston and Houts (1998) found that emotionally expressive spouses tend to have happier partners. Similarly, more secure attachment styles in intimate relationships are associated with freer expressions of anxiety and sadness (Feeney, 1995, 1999). Happy spouses are also more empathetically aware of their partners' feeling states than unhappy spouses, who are more likely to misunderstand each other's intentions and misidentify each other's emotions. Such misunderstandings have strong, negative impacts on close-relationship functioning and satisfaction (Gottman, 1994; Noller and Ruzzene, 1991).

In summary, both the experience and expression of emotions are integral to the dynamics and functioning of close relationships. One remaining issue, however, concerns the extent to which laypersons understand the nature and function of emotions in relationship contexts and the impact of such understanding on their relationships. We will now briefly review some of the relevant work in this area.

### *Emotion knowledge structures in close relationships*

Previously, we noted that laypersons hold stored theories about close relationships, ranging from general social theories (that embrace social behavior across intimate and nonintimate contexts), to general relationship theories, to relationship theories about local or specific relationships. Lay theoretical knowledge about emotions can also be profitably categorized in terms of the same model (Fitness, 1996; Planalp and Fitness, 1999).

At the most general level, people hold theories about the nature of 'emotional' versus 'nonemotional' stimuli and about the features (such as causes, physiological symptoms, urges, and outcomes) of specific emotions such as anger and happiness. Such lay emotion theories are often referred to as 'scripts' because emotion episodes often involve more than one person and, like dramatic productions, unfold predictably over time (Fitness, 1996). At the next level down of specificity, people hold theories about the causes and features of emotions in relational contexts. For example, people believe that marital episodes of anger are generally caused by unjust or inequitable, partner-caused behaviors (Fehr et al., 1999; Fitness and Fletcher, 1993; Sprecher, 1986). Moreover, as the drama of the angry interaction unfolds between partners, people hold stereotypical beliefs concerning the motivations (such as the urge to yell or scream) and behaviors (such as retaliatory insults and/or apologies) that are likely to occur, depending on the situational context (Fehr et al., 1999; Fitness, 2001).

At the third level of specificity, partners develop local, idiosyncratic theories about how emotions work within their own relationships. Such local lay theories may conflict with general higher-order emotion theories. For example, Mary may hold a general emotion theory that angry spouses are likely to shout at one another, but, within her own relationship, she may typically respond to Fred's anger with tears. He, in turn, may reliably respond to her distress with an apology. In this way, relationship partners can create joint emotion scripts that can become overlearned and 'run off' automatically, with each partner only paying attention when something unexpected happens (Fred continues to shout at Mary, despite her distress).

To date, emotion-script researchers have focused on mapping the structural features of people's emotion theories. Relatively little work has examined the impact of such lay theories on conscious or unconscious information-processing in close-relationship contexts (for an exception, see Clark et al., 1996). In addition, because emotion-script theorists are primarily interested in people's representations of emotions rather than emotions 'proper', there have been few attempts to integrate lay understanding of emotions with the evolutionary and motivational properties of emotions (see Forgas, 1996). However, without such a theoretical integration, we may never fully understand the origins and functioning of emotions in relational contexts.

As previously discussed, one good example of the kind of integrative approach we are arguing for here is romantic love. Another is romantic jealousy, to which we now turn.

### *Romantic jealousy*

Like romantic love, romantic jealousy is a quintessential close-relationship emotion. During the era of 'free love' and open marriage in the 1960s and 1970s, some claimed that romantic jealousy was a culturally specific emotion signaling immaturity and neurosis; many advocated that jealousy could and should be eliminated from the human emotional repertoire (e.g., O'Neill and O'Neill, 1972). Today, however, theorists recognize that romantic jealousy is a natural, universally experienced, and potentially adaptive emotional reaction, triggered by the perception that one is in danger of losing a loved one (and/or associated resources) to a rival (Mathes, 1992).

According to Guerrero and Andersen's (1998) 'componential' model, romantic jealousy is a product of both proximal and distal factors. At the proximal level, a jealousy episode is triggered by the perception of a relational threat, which activates jealousy-related cognitive appraisals and emotions. For example, the jealous individual may feel terror at the thought of abandonment, or depression about perceived self-inadequacy, or rage at his partner's betrayal. These different emotions, in turn, motivate particular kinds of behaviors, such as spying, withdrawal, confrontation, or even murder. Indeed, across all cultures, male sexual jealousy has been identified as the predominant motive for men to kill women (Daly and Wilson, 1988). It should be noted, though, that jealousy can also elicit positive behaviors, such as trying extra hard to please the partner and maintain the relationship (Guerrero and Anderson, 1998).

At the distal level, the kinds of cognitions and emotions people experience in a jealousy-eliciting situation depend on stored relationship theories (including attachment working models), emotion theories (for example, that concerning the appropriateness of jealousy and its likely outcomes), and a variety of other relational, cultural, and evolutionarily driven factors. For example, one of the defining features of the anxious-ambivalent attachment style involves the propensity to experience intense jealousy in response to a perceived relationship threat (e.g., Hazan and Shaver, 1987). Moreover, whereas securely attached individuals are likely to voice jealousy-related concerns to their partners, Guerrero (1998) found that preoccupied individuals, who hold a positive model of others but a negative model of the self, tend to focus on feelings of sadness, fear, inferiority, self-blame, and envy, and to engage in such behaviors as spying, expressing negative emotions to the partner, and clinging to the relationship. In contrast, dismissing individuals, who hold a negative model of others but a positive model of the self, are less likely to experience fear or sadness but are more likely to direct blame and anger toward the rival and to engage in avoidant coping strategies such as denial.

Relational factors are also important in the elicitation and experience of romantic jealousy. For example, emotional dependence in close relationships is positively associated with the reported intensity of jealous feelings (Mathes, 1992). Berscheid and Ammazzalorso (2001) have explained this link by arguing that as relationship partners become increasingly interdependent, they will also become more likely to experience interruption and jealousy-related emotions when a rival appears on the scene (especially one who looks as though they might 'mesh' well with a partner and fulfill their unmet needs). Ironically, then, it is the most intimate relationships that are most vulnerable to the interruptive impact of a rival, especially when few attractive alternatives are available to the threatened partner.

### *The functions of romantic jealousy*

According to evolutionary theorists, romantic jealousy is experienced by individuals in every culture in response to the perception that reproductively relevant resources (including love) are being diverted from a long-term mating relationship to a rival (Buss and Kenrick, 1998). The evolved functions of romantic jealousy, then, are to promote vigilance against such a diversion and to motivate behaviors that will prevent and/or punish its occurrence (some of which may no longer be adaptive in contemporary cultural contexts).

Both men and women are vulnerable to the threat of losing relationship resources and, thus, are equally likely to experience romantic jealousy. However, evolutionary theory suggests that, because of their differing reproductive interests, men and women should experience jealousy in response to different kinds of resource-related threats. Men invest in genetically unrelated offspring at a substantial reproductive cost; thus, men should be more upset by a mate's sexual infidelity (and the subsequent risk of paternity uncertainty) than by her emotional infidelity. Conversely, women should be more upset by an emotional attachment between her partner and a rival, and the consequent diversion of relational and economic resources, than by a mate's sexual infidelity. To test this hypothesis, Buss et al. (1992) asked people to imagine which of two competing scenarios – a mate's sexual or emotional infidelity – would be more upsetting. Confirming the evolutionary hypothesis, they found that women were more upset than men about an imagined emotional infidelity, and men were more upset than women about an imagined sexual infidelity. This finding has been replicated in several countries, including Korea and Japan (Buss et al., 1999).

The evolutionary rationale for Buss et al.'s original study was criticized by DeSteno and Salovey (1996), who argued that the findings might simply be due to differences in how men and women interpret evidence of infidelity. Specifically, they proposed that men find sexual infidelity upsetting because they believe that women who are sexually unfaithful will also be emotionally unfaithful, but not vice versa, and women find emotional infidelity upsetting because they believe it will be associated with sexual infidelity, but not vice versa (the 'double-shot' hypothesis). To control for this possibility, Buss et al. (1999) repeated the study but made the two types of infidelity mutually exclusive; the pattern of results remained the same.

However, these findings do not imply that the evolutionary explanation of sex differences in romantic jealousy is right, and the cognitive/cultural explanation is wrong (or vice versa). Rather, and consistent with our previous argument, the two explanations involve different levels of analysis. That is, stereotypical beliefs about sex differences in sexual activity and emotional commitment are doubtless based on lay observations of people's sexual attitudes and behavior; however, such behavioral sex differences, in turn, may very well be rooted in human biology and genes (see Fletcher, 2002).

## Conclusion

In this chapter, we have reviewed the social psychological research and theorizing concerned with intimate relationships, concentrating on three dominant domains: social cognition and emotion, attachment theory, and evolutionary psychology. We have attempted throughout to explore the interconnecting threads among these three areas and thus illustrate the explanatory gains that can be produced by such an integrative enterprise.

Of course, any genuine science of intimate relationships will represent an amalgamation of many disciplines including anthropology, neuropsychology, developmental psychology, clinical psychology, and so forth. However, understanding the proximal-level workings of the intimate-relationship mind and its connections to interpersonal behavior is the province of the social psychologist, and traditional social-psychological theories and research techniques are ideal tools with which to advance such aims. Any general science of intimate relationships will have such a social-psychological analysis and approach at its heart. Allowing contributions from domains such as evolutionary psychology and attachment theory to inform and enrich social psychological models of intimate relationships holds the promise (fast being realized) of helping us understand both intimate relationships and the basic building blocks of psychology: cognition, affect, and behavior. And this is simply because so much of human cognition, emotion, and behavior is interpersonal in nature.

**SUMMARY**

This chapter begins with a brief overview of scientific approaches to the study of attraction and intimate relationships, with a focus on social psychological and evolutionary psychological theories. It is argued that, rather than being mutually exclusive, these theories are complementary ways of understanding the origins and functions of the intimate relationship mind. The chapter proceeds with an exploration of some key factors in interpersonal attraction, including familiarity, similarity, and physical attractiveness. The chapter then examines the complex topic of mate selection and the differences between men and women in what they look for in short-term and long-term mates. The role of romantic love in motivating sexual intimacy and in establishing a secure bond between relationship partners is also discussed. The next section of the chapter concerns relationship cognition. The emphasis is on the ways in which people's relationship theories and beliefs influence their ongoing perceptions, judgments and memories of relationship events and partner behaviors. This is followed by a discussion of the origins and functions of emotions in close relationships. Finally, romantic jealousy is presented as an example of the explanatory and predictive value of considering both social psychological and evolutionary psychological approaches in the study of intimate relationships.

## References

Acitelli, L.K., Douvan, E., and Veroff, J. (1993) 'Perceptions of Conflict in the First Year of Marriage: How Important Are Similarity and Understanding?', *Journal of Social and Personal Relationships*, 10: 5–19.

Acitelli, L.K., Kenny, D.A., and Weiner, D. (2001) 'The Importance of Similarity and Understanding of Partners' Marital Ideals to Relationship Satisfaction', *Personal Relationships*, 8: 167–85.

Aron, A., Aron, E.N., and Norman, C. (2001) 'Self-Expansion Model of Motivation and Cognition in Close Relationships and Beyond', in G.J.O. Fletcher and M.S. Clark (eds), *Blackwell Handbook of Social Psychology Interpersonal Processes* (vol. 2): Oxford: Blackwell, pp. 478–501.

Aron, A., Dutton, D.G., Aron, E.N., and Iverson, A. (1989) 'Experiences of Falling in Love', *Journal of Social and Personal Relationships*, 6: 243–57.

Aron, A. and Westbay, L. (1996) 'Dimensions of the Prototype of Love', *Journal of Personality and Social Psychology*, 70: 535–51.

Baker, R. and Bellis, M. (1995) *Human Sperm Competition*. New York: Chapman and Hall.

Baldwin, M.W. (1992) 'Relational Schemas and the Processing of Social Information', *Psychological Bulletin*, 112: 461–84.

Baldwin, M.W., Carrell, S.E., and Lopez, D.F. (1990) 'Priming Relationship Schemas: My Advisor and the Pope Are Watching Me from the Back of My Mind', *Journal of Experimental Social Psychology*, 26: 435–54.

Bartholomew, K. and Horowitz, M. (1991) 'Attachment Styles among Young Adults: A Test of a Four Category Model', *Journal of Personality and Social Psychology*, 61: 226–44.

Bartholomew, K. and Shaver, P.R. (1998) 'Methods of Assessing Adult Attachment: Do They Converge?', in J.A. Simpson and W.S. Rholes (eds), *Attachment Theory and Close Relationships*. New York: Guilford, pp. 24–45.

Baumeister, R.F., Catanese, K.R., and Vohs, K.D. (2001) 'Is There a Gender Difference in Strength of Sex Drive? Theoretical Views, Conceptual Distinctions, and a Review of Relevant Evidence', *Personality and Social Psychology Review*, 5: 242–73.

Baumeister, R.F. and Wotman, S. (1992) *Breaking Hearts: The Two Sides of Unrequited Love*. New York: Guilford.

Beach, S.R. and O'Leary, K.D. (1993) 'Dysphoria and Marital Discord: Are Dysphoric Individuals at Risk for Marital Maladjustment?', *Journal of Marital and Family Therapy*, 19: 355–68.

Berry, D.S. (2000) 'Attractiveness, Attraction, and Sexual Selection: Evolutionary Perspectives on the Form and Function of Physical Attractiveness', *Advances in Experimental Social Psychology*, 32: 273–42.

Berry, D.S. and McArthur, L.Z. (1986) 'Perceiving Character in Faces: The Impact of Age-Related Craniofacial Changes on Social Perception', *Psychological Bulletin*, 100: 3–18.

Berscheid, E. (1983) 'Emotion', in H.H. Kelley, E. Berscheid, A. Christensen, J. Harvey, T. Huston, G. Levinger, D. McClintock, L. Peplau, and D. Peterson (eds), *Close Relationships*. San Francisco, CA: Freeman, pp. 110–68.

Berscheid, E. and Ammazzalorso, H. (2001) 'Emotional Experience in Close Relationships', in G.J.O. Fletcher and M. Clark (eds), *Blackwell Handbook of Social Psychology: Interpersonal Processes* (vol. 2): Oxford: Blackwell, pp. 253–78.

Berscheid, E. and Reis, H. (1998) 'Attraction and Close Relationships', in D. Gilbert, S. Fiske and G. Lindzey (eds), *The Handbook of Social Psychology* (vol. 2). Boston, MA: Mcgraw-Hill, pp. 193–281.

Berscheid, E. and Walster, E. (1978) *Interpersonal Attraction*. Reading, MA: Addison-Wesley.

Bowlby, J. (1969) *Attachment and Loss* (vol. 1). New York: Basic Books.

Bradbury, T. and Fincham, F.D. (1987) 'Affect and Cognition in Close Relationships: An Integrative Model', *Cognition and Emotion*, 1: 59–87.

Brennan, K.A., Clark, C.L., and Shaver, P.R. (1998) 'Self-Report Measurement of Adult Attachment: An Integrative Overview', in J.A. Simpson and W.S. Rholes (eds), *Attachment Theory and Close Relationships*. New York: Guilford, pp. 46–76.

Buss, D.M. (1989a) 'Sex Differences in Human Mate Preferences: Evolutionary Hypotheses Tested in 37 Cultures', *Behavioral and Brain Sciences*, 12: 1–49.

Buss, D.M. (1989b) 'Conflict between the Sexes: Strategic Interference and the Evocation of Anger and Upset', *Journal of Personality and Social Psychology*, 56: 735–47.

Buss, D.M. and Barnes, M. (1986) 'Preferences in Human Mate Selection', *Journal of Personality and Social Psychology*, 50: 559–70.

Buss, D.M. and Kenrick, D. (1998) 'Evolutionary Social Psychology', in D. Gilbert, S. Fiske, and G. Lindzey (eds), *The Handbook of Social Psychology* (vol. 2). Boston, MA: McGraw-Hill, pp. 982–1026.

Buss, D., Larsen, R., Westen, D., and Semmelroth, J. (1992) 'Sex Differences in Jealousy: Evolution, Physiology and Psychology', *Psychological Science*, 3: 251–5.

Buss, D.M. and Schmitt, D.P. (1993) 'Sexual Strategies Theory: An Evolutionary Perspective on Human Mating', *Psychological Review*, 100: 204–32.

Buss, D.M., Shackelford, T.K., Kirkpatrick, L.A., Choe, J.C., Kim, H.L., Hasegawa, M., Hasegawa, T., and Bennett, K. (1999) 'Jealousy and the Nature of Beliefs about Infidelity: Tests of the Competing Hypotheses about Sex Differences in the United States, Korea, and Japan', *Personal Relationships*, 6: 125–50.

Byrne, D. (1971) *The Attraction Paradigm*. New York: Academic Press.

Caspi, A. and Herbener, E.S. (1990) 'Continuity and Change: Assortative Marriage and the Consistency of Personality in Adulthood', *Journal of Personality and Social Psychology*, 58: 250–8.

Clark, M.S., Fitness, J., and Brissette, I. (2001) 'Understanding People's Perceptions of Relationships Is Crucial to Understanding Their Emotional Lives', in G.J.O. Fletcher and M. Clark (eds), *Blackwell Handbook of Social Psychology* (vol. 2): *Interpersonal Processes*. Oxford: Blackwell, pp. 252–78.

Clark, M.S., Pataki, S., and Carver, V. (1996) 'Some Thoughts and Findings on Self-Presentation of Emotions in Relationships', in G.J.O. Fletcher and J. Fitness (eds), *Knowledge Structures in Close Relationships', A Social Psychological Approach*. Mahwah, NJ: Erlbaum, pp. 247–74.

Clark, M.S. and Taraban, C.B. (1991) 'Reactions to and Willingness to Express Emotion in Two Types of Relationships', *Journal of Experimental Social Psychology*, 27: 324–36.

Clark, R.D. and Hatfield, E. (1989) 'Gender Differences in Receptivity to Sexual Offers', *Journal of Psychology and Human Sexuality*, 2: 39–55.

Collins, S. (2000) 'Men's Voices and Women's Choices', *Animal Behavior*, 60: 773–80.

Collins, N. and Allard, L. (2001) 'Cognitive Representations of Attachment: The Content and Function of Working Models', in G.J.O. Fletcher and M.S. Clark (eds), *Blackwell Handbook of Social Psychology* (vol. 2): *Interpersonal Processes*. Oxford: Blackwell, pp. 60–85.

Critelli, J.W. and Waid, L.R. (1980) 'Physical Attractiveness, Romantic Love, and Equity Restoration in Dating Relationships', *Journal of Personality Assessment*, 44: 624–9.

Cunningham, M., Roberts, A., Wu, C., Barbee, A., and Druen, P. (1995) '"Their Ideas of Beauty Are, on the Whole, the Same as Ours": Consistency and Variability in the Cross-Cultural Perception of Female Physical Attractiveness', *Journal of Personality and Social Psychology*, 68: 261–79.

Dabbs, J. (2000) *Heroes, Rogues, and Lovers: Testosterone and Behavior*. New York: McGraw-Hill.

Daly, M. and Wilson, M. (1988) *Homicide*. New York: Aldine De Gruyter.

Darwin, C. (1872/1965) *The Expression of the Emotions in Man and Animals*. Chicago,s IL: University of Chicago Press.

Davis, S. (1990) 'Men as Success Objects and Women as Sex Objects: A Study of Personal Advertisements', *Sex Roles*, 23: 43–50.

Desteno, D.A. and Salovey, P. (1996) 'Evolutionary Origins of Sex Differences in Jealousy? Questioning the Fitness of the Model', *Psychological Science*, 7: 367–72.

Dion, K.K., Berscheid, E., and Walster, E. (1972) 'What Is Beautiful Is Good', *Journal of Personality and Social Psychology*, 24: 285–90.

Dion, K.K. and Dion, K.L. (1996) 'Toward Understanding Love', *Personal Relationships*, 3: 1–3.

Dunbar, R.I.M. and Duncan, N.D.C. (1997) 'Human Conversational Behavior', *Human Nature*, 8: 231–46.

Durrant, R. and Ellis, B.J. (2005) 'Evolutionary Psychology', in M. Gallagher and R.J. Nelson (eds),

*Handbook of Psychology* (vol. 3): *Biological Psychology*. New York: Wiley.

Eagly, A.H., Ashmore, R.D., Makhijani, M.G., and Longo, L.C. (1991) 'What Is Beautiful Is Good, but … A Meta-analytic Review of Research on the Physical Attractiveness Stereotype', *Psychological Bulletin*, 110: 109–28.

Ellis, B. (1992) 'The Evolution of Sexual Attraction: Evaluative Mechanisms in Women', in J. Barkow, L. Cosmides, and J. Tooby (eds), *The Adapted Mind: Evolutionary Psychology and the Generation of Culture*. New York: Oxford University Press, pp. 267–88.

Ellis, B.J. and Malamuth, N.M. (2000) 'Love and Anger in Romantic Relationships: A Discrete Systems Model', *Journal of Personality*, 68: 525–56.

Ellsworth, P. (1991) 'Some Implications of Cognitive Appraisal Theories of Emotion', in K.T. Strongman (ed.), *International Review of Studies on Emotion* (vol. 1). Chichester: Wiley, pp. 143–62.

Enlow, D.M. (1990) *Handbook of Facial Growth*, 3rd edn. Philadelphia, PA: Saunders.

Feeney, J.A. (1995) 'Adult Attachment and Emotional Control', *Personal Relationships*, 2: 143–59.

Feeney, J.A. (1999) 'Adult Attachment, Emotional Control, and Marital Satisfaction', *Personal Relationships*, 6: 169–85.

Fehr, B. (1999) 'Laypersons' Perceptions of Commitment', *Journal of Personality and Social Psychology*, 76: 90–103.

Fehr, B., Baldwin, M., Collins, L., Patterson, S., and Benditt, R. (1999) 'Anger in Close Relationships: An Interpersonal Script Analysis', *Personality and Social Psychology Bulletin*, 25: 299–312.

Feingold, A. (1988) 'Matching for Attractiveness in Romantic Partners and Same-Sex Friends: A Meta-Analysis and Theoretical Critique', *Psychological Bulletin*, 104: 226–35.

Feingold, A. (1990) 'Gender Differences in Effect of Physical Attractiveness on Romantic Attraction: A Comparison across Five Research Paradigms', *Journal of Personality and Social Psychology*, 59: 981–93.

Feingold, A. (1992) 'Good-Looking People Are Not What We Think', *Psychological Bulletin*, 111: 304–41.

Fincham, F.D. (2001) 'Attributions in Close Relationships: From Balkanization to Integration', in G.J.O. Fletcher and M.S. Clark (eds), *Blackwell Handbook of Social Psychology* (vol. 2): *Interpersonal Processes*. Oxford: Blackwell, pp. 3–31.

Fisher, H. (1992) *Anatomy of Love: The Natural History of Monogamy, Adultery, and Divorce*. New York: Norton.

Fitness, J. (1996) 'Emotion Knowledge Structures in Close Relationships', in G.J.O. Fletcher and J. Fitness (eds), *Knowledge Structures in Close Relationships: A Social Psychological Approach*. Mahwah, NJ: Erlbaum, pp. 219–45.

Fitness, J. (2001) 'Betrayal, Rejection, Revenge, and Forgiveness: An Interpersonal Script Analysis', in M. Leary (ed)., *Interpersonal Rejection*. New York: Oxford University Press, pp. 73–103.

Fitness, J. (2006) 'The Emotionally Intelligent Marriage', in J. Ciarrochi, J. Forgas, and J. Mayer (eds), *Emotional Intelligence in Everyday Life*, 2nd edn, Philadelphia, PA: Taylor & Francis, pp. 98–112.

Fitness, J. and Fletcher, G.J.O. (1993) 'Love, Hate, Anger, and Jealousy in Close Relationships: A Cognitive Appraisal and Prototype Analysis', *Journal of Personality and Social Psychology*, 65: 942–58.

Fletcher, G.J.O. (2002) *The New Science of Intimate Relationships*. London: Blackwell.

Fletcher, G.J.O. and Fincham, F.D. (1991) 'Attributional Processes in Close Relationships', in G.J.O. Fletcher and F.D. Fincham (eds), *Cognition in Close Relationships*. Hillsdale, NJ: Erlbaum, pp. 6–34.

Fletcher, G.J.O. and Kininmonth, L. (1992) 'Measuring Relationship Beliefs: An Individual Differences Scale', *Journal of Research in Personality*, 26: 371–97.

Fletcher, G.J.O., Rosanowski, J., and Fitness, J. (1994) 'Automatic Processing in Intimate Contexts: The Role of Close-Relationship Beliefs', *Journal of Personality and Social Psychology*, 67: 888–97.

Fletcher, G.J.O., Simpson, J.A., and Thomas, G. (2000) 'Ideals, Perceptions, and Evaluations in Early Relationship Development', *Journal of Personality and Social Psychology*, 79: 933–40.

Fletcher, G.J.O., Simpson, J.A., Thomas, G., and Giles, L. (1999) 'Ideals in Intimate Relationships', *Journal of Personality and Social Psychology*, 76: 72–89.

Fletcher, G.J.O. and Thomas, G. (1996) 'Close Relationship Lay Theories: Their Structure and Function', in G.J.O. Fletcher and J. Fitness (eds), *Knowledge Structures in Close Relationships*. Mahwah, NJ: Erlbaum, pp. 3–24.

Fletcher, G.J.O. and Thomas, G. (2000) 'Behavior and On-Line Cognition in Marital Interaction', *Personal Relationships*, 7: 111–30.

Foa, E.B. and Foa, U.G. (1980) 'Resource Theory: Interpersonal Behavior as Exchange', in K.J. Gergen, M.S. Greenberg, and R.H. Willis (eds), *Social Exchange: Advances in Theory and Research*. New York: Plenum, pp. 77–94.

Ford, C.S. and Beach, F. (1951) *Patterns of Sexual Behavior*. New York: Harper and Row.

Forgas, J.P. (1994) 'Sad and Guilty? Affective Influences on the Explanation of Conflict in Close Relationships', *Journal of Personality and Social Psychology*, 66: 56–68.

Forgas, J.P. (1996) 'The Role of Emotion Scripts and Transient Moods in Relationships: Structural and Functional Perspectives', in G.J.O. Fletcher and J. Fitness (eds), *Knowledge Structures in Close Relationships: A Social Psychological Approach*. Mahwah, NJ: Erlbaum, pp. 275–96.

Frijda, N. (1986) *The Emotions*. Cambridge: Cambridge University Press.

Gangestad, S.W. (1993) 'Sexual Selection and Physical Attractiveness: Implications for Mating Dynamics', *Human Nature*, 4: 205–35.

Gangestad, S.W. and Simpson, J.A. (2000) 'The Evolution of Human Mating: Trade-Offs and Strategic Pluralism', *Behavioral and Brain Sciences*, 23: 573–644.

Gladue, B.A. and Delaney, H.J. (1990) 'Gender Differences in Perception of Attractiveness of Men and Women in Bars', *Personality and Social Psychology Bulletin*, 16: 378–91.

Gottman, J.M. (1994) *What Predicts Divorce? The Relationship between Marital Processes and Marital Outcomes*. Hillsdale, NJ: Erlbaum.

Grammer, K. and Thornhill, R. (1994) 'Human (*Homo sapiens*) Facial Attractiveness and Sexual Selection: The Role of Symmetry and Averageness', *Journal of Comparative Psychology*, 108: 233–42.

Greiling, H. and Buss, D.M. (2000) 'Women's Sexual Strategies: The Hidden Dimension of Extra-Pair Mating', *Personality and Individual Differences*, 28: 929–63.

Guerrero, L.K. (1998) 'Attachment-Style Differences in the Experience and Expression of Romantic Jealousy', *Personal Relationships*, 5: 273–91.

Guerrero, L.K. and Andersen, P. (1998) 'Jealousy Experience and Expression in Romantic Relationships', in P. Andersen and L. Guerrero (eds), *Handbook of Communication and Emotion: Research, Theory, Applications, and Contexts*. New York: Academic Press, pp. 155–88.

Hammond, J.R. and Fletcher, G.J.O. (1991) 'Attachment Styles and Relationship Satisfaction in the Development of Close Relationships', *New Zealand Journal of Psychology*, 20: 56–62.

Hatfield, E. (1988) 'Passionate and Companionate Love', in R. Sternberg and M. Barnes (eds), *The Psychology of Love*. New Haven, CT: Yale University Press, pp. 191–217.

Haviland, J.B. (1977) *Gossip, Reputation and Knowledge in Zinacantan*. Chicago, IL: University of Chicago Press.

Hazan, C. and Shaver, P. (1987) 'Romantic Love Conceptualized as an Attachment Process', *Journal of Personality and Social Psychology*, 52: 511–24.

Heider, F. (1958) *The Psychology of Interpersonal Relations*. New York: Wiley.

Huston, T. and Houts, R. (1998) 'The Psychological Infrastructure of Courtship and Marriage: The Role of Personality and Compatibility in Romantic Relationships', in T. Bradbury (ed.), *The Developmental Course of Marital Dysfunction*. New York: Cambridge University Press, pp. 114–51.

Insel, T.R. (2000) 'Toward a Neurobiology of Attachment', *Review of General Psychology*, 4: 176–85.

Izard, C. (1991) *The Psychology of Human Emotions*. New York: Plenum.

Jankowiak, W. (ed.) (1995) *Romantic Passion: A Universal Experience?* New York: Columbia University Press.

Jones, E.E. (1964) *Ingratiation*. New York: Appleton Century Crofts.

Karney, B.R. and Bradbury, T.N. (1995) 'The Longitudinal Course of Marital Quality and Stability: A Review of Theory, Methods, and Research', *Psychological Bulletin*, 118: 3–34.

Keltner, D., Ellsworth, P., and Edwards, K. (1993) 'Beyond Simple Pessimism: Effects of Sadness and Anger on Social Perception', *Journal of Personality and Social Psychology*, 64: 740–52.

Kenrick, D.T. and Trost, M.R. (2000) 'An Evolutionary Perspective on Human Relationships', in W. Ickes and S. Duck (eds), *The Social Psychology of Personal Relationships*. Chichester: Wiley, pp. 9–36.

Langlois, J., Roggman, L., and Musselman, L. (1994) 'What Is Average and What Is Not Average about Attractive Faces?', *Psychological Science*, 5: 214–20.

Langlois, J., Kalakanis, L., Rubenstein, A., Larson, A., Hallam, M., and Smoot, M. (2000) 'Maxims or Myths of Beauty? A Meta-Analytic and Theoretical Review', *Psychological Bulletin*, 126: 390–423.

Liebowitz, M. (1983) *The Chemistry of Love*. Boston, MA: Little, Brown.

Madey, S.F., Simo, M., Dillworth, D., Kemper, D., Toczynski, A., and Perella, A. (1996) 'They Do Get More Attractive at Closing Time, but Only when You Are Not in a Relationship', *Basic and Applied Social Psychology*, 18: 387–93.

Marlowe, F. and Wetsman, A. (2001) 'Preferred Waist-to-Hip Ratio and Ecology', *Personality and Individual Differences*, 30: 481–9.

Mathes, E. (1992) *Jealousy: The Psychological Data*. New York: University Press of America.

Mealey, L., Bridgestock, R. and Townsend, G. (1999) 'Symmetry and Perceived Facial Attractiveness: A Monozygotic Co-Twin Comparison', *Journal of Personality and Social Psychology*, 76: 151–8.

Mikulincer, M. (1998) 'Attachment Working Models and the Sense of Trust: An Exploration of Interaction Goals and Affect Regulation', *Journal of Personality and Social Psychology*, 74: 1209–24.

Møller, A.P. and Swaddle, J.P. (1997) *Asymmetry, Developmental Stability, and Evolution*. New York: Oxford University Press.

Morgan, H.J. and Shaver, P.R. (1999) 'Attachment Processes and Commitment to Romantic Relationships', in J.M. Adams and W.H. Jones (eds), *Handbook of Interpersonal Commitment and Relationship Stability*. New York: Plenum, pp. 109–24.

Murstein, B.I. (1980) 'Mate Selection in the 1970s', *Journal of Marriage and the Family*, 42: 777–92.

Myers, D. (1999) *Social Psychology*, 6th edn. New York: McGraw-Hill.

Newcomb, T.M. (1961) *The Acquaintance Process*. New York: Holt, Rinehart & Winston.

Noller, P. and Ruzzene, M. (1991) 'Communication in Marriage: The Influence of Affect and Cognition', in G.J.O. Fletcher and F. Fincham (eds), *Cognition in Close Relationships*. Hillsdale, NJ: Erlbaum, pp. 203–34.

Oatley, K. and Jenkins, J. (1996) *Understanding Emotions*. Cambridge: Blackwell.

O'Neill, N. and O'Neill, G. (1972) *Open Marriage*. New York: Avon.

Panksepp, J. (1998) *Affective Neuroscience: The Foundations of Human and Animal Emotions*. New York: Oxford University Press.

Pennebaker, J.W., Dyer, M.A., Caulkins, R.S., Litowitz, D.L., Ackreman, P.L., Anderson, D.B., and Mcgraw, K.M. (1979) 'Don't the Girls Get Prettier at Closing Time? A Country and Western Application to Psychology', *Personality and Social Psychology Bulletin*, 5: 122–5.

Penton-Voak, I.S., Perrett, D.I., Castles, D., Koyabashi, T., Burt, D.M., Murray, L.K., and Minamisawa, R. (1999) 'Female Preference for Male Faces Changes Cyclically', *Nature*, 399: 741–2.

Planalp, S. and Fitness, J. (1999) 'Thinking/Feeling about Social and Personal Relationships', *Journal of Social and Personal Relationships*, 16: 731–50.

Reis, H., Collins, W.A., and Berscheid, E. (2000) 'The Relationship Context of Human Behavior and Development', *Psychological Bulletin*, 126: 844–72.

Rhodes, G., Zebrowitz, L., Clark, A., Kalick, M., Hightower, A., and Mckay, R. (2001) 'Do Facial Averageness and Symmetry Signal Health?', *Evolution and Human Behavior*, 22: 31–46.

Robins, R.W., Caspi, A., and Moffitt, T.E. (2000) 'Two Personalities, One Relationship: Both Partners' Personality Traits Shape the Quality of Their Relationship', *Journal of Personality and Social Psychology*, 79: 251–9.

Ross, M. and Fletcher, G.J.O. (1985) 'Attribution and Social Perception', in G. Lindzey and E. Aronson (eds), *The Handbook of Social Psychology*, 3rd edn. New York: Random House, pp. 73–122.

Rusbult, C.E., Bissonnette, V.L., Arriaga, X.B., and Cox, C.L. (1998) 'Accommodation Processes during the Early Years of Marriage', in T. Bradbury (ed.), *The Developmental Course of Marital Dysfunction*. New York: Cambridge University Press, pp. 74–113.

Sadalla, E.K., Kenrick, D.T., and Vershure, B. (1987) 'Dominance and Heterosexual Attraction', *Journal of Personality and Social Psychology*, 52: 730–8.

Sangrador, J. and Yela, C. (2000) '"What Is Beautiful Is Loved": Physical Attractiveness in Love Relationships in a Representative Sample', *Social Behavior and Personality*, 28: 207–18.

Shackelford, T. and Larsen, R.J. (1997) 'Facial Asymmetry as an Indicator of Psychological, Emotional, and Physiological Distress', *Journal of Personality and Social Psychology*, 72: 456–66.

Shaver, P.R., Morgan, H.J., and Wu, S. (1996) 'Is Love a "Basic" Emotion?', *Personal Relationships*, 3: 81–96.

Shostock, M. (1981) *Nisa: The Life and Words of a !Kung Woman*. London: Allen Lane.

Simpson, J. (1987) 'The Dissolution of Romantic Relationship: Factors Involved in Relationship Stability and Emotional Distress', *Journal of Personality and Social Psychology*, 53: 683–92.

Simpson, J., Fletcher, G.J.O., and Campbell, L. (2001) 'The Structure and Function of Ideal Standards in Close Relationships', in G.J.O. Fletcher and M. Clark (eds), *Blackwell Handbook of Social Psychology* (vol. 2): *Interpersonal Processes*. Oxford: Blackwell, pp. 107–26.

Simpson, J. and Gangestad, S.W. (1992) 'Sociosexuality and Romantic Partner Choice', *Journal of Personality*, 60: 31–51.

Simpson, J. and Rholes, W.S. (eds) (1998) *Attachment Theory and Close Relationships*. New York: Guilford.

Simpson, J.A., Rholes, W.S., and Nelligan, J.S. (1992) 'Support-Seeking and Support-Giving within Couples in an Anxiety-Provoking Situation: The Role of Attachment Styles', *Journal of Personality and Social Psychology*, 62: 434–46.

Singh, D. (1993) 'Adaptive Significance of Female Physical Attractiveness: Role of Waist-to-Hip Ratio', *Journal of Personality and Social Psychology*, 65: 293–307.

Singh, D. and Luis, S. (1995) 'Ethnic and Gender Consensus for the Effect of Waist-to-Hip Ratio on Judgment of Women's Attractiveness', *Human Nature*, 6: 51–65.

Sprecher, S. (1986) 'The Relation between Inequity and Emotion in Close Relationships', *Social Psychological Quarterly*, 49: 309–21.

Sprecher, S., Delamater, J., Neuman, N., Neuman, M., Kahn, P., Orbuch, D., and Mckinney, K. (1984) 'Asking Questions in Bars: The Girls (and Boys) May Not Get Prettier at Closing Time and Other Interesting Results', *Personality and Social Psychology Bulletin*, 10: 482–8.

Sprecher, S., Sullivan, Q., and Hatfield, E. (1994) 'Mate Selection Preferences: Gender Differences Examined in a National Sample', *Journal of Personality and Social Psychology*, 8: 1074–80.

Sternberg, R. (1986) 'A Triangular Theory of Love', *Psychological Review*, 93: 119–35.

Surra, C. (1990) 'Research and Theory on Mate Selection and Premarital Relationships in the 1980s', *Journal of Marriage and the Family*, 52: 844–65.

Tennov, D. (1979) *Love and Limerence*. New York: Stein and Day.

Townsend, J.M., Kline, J., and Wasserman, T. (1995) 'Low-Investment Copulation: Sex Differences in Motivations and Emotional Reactions', *Ethology and Sociobiology*, 16: 25–51.

Trivers, R. (1974) 'Parent–Offspring Conflict', *American Zoology*, 14: 249–64.

Walster, E., Walster, G.W., and Berscheid, E. (1978) *Equity Theory and Research*. Boston, MA: Allyn and Bacon.

Wegner, D.M. and Bargh, J.A. (1998) 'Control and Automaticity in Social Life', in D.T. Gilbert, S.T. Fiske, and G. Lindzey (eds), *The Handbook of Social Psychology*, 4th edn (vol. 1). New York: McGraw-Hill, pp. 446–96.

Winch, R., Ktsanes, T., and Ktsanes, V. (1954) 'The Theory of Complementary Needs in Mate Selection', *American Sociological Review*, 19: 241–9.

Wright, R. (1994) *The Moral Animal*. New York: Pantheon Books.

Zaadstra, B.M., Seidell, J.C., Van Noord, P.A.H., te Velde, E.R., Habbema, J.D.F., Vrieswijk, B., and Karbaat, J. (1993) 'Fat and Female Fecundity: Prospective Study of Effect of Body Fat Distribution on Conception Rates', *British Medical Journal*, 306: 484–7.

Zajonc, R.B. (1968) 'The Attitudinal Effects of Mere Exposure', *Journal of Personality and Social Psychology*, 9: 1–27.

Zeifman, D. and Hazan, C. (2000) 'A Process Model of Adult Attachment Formation', in W. Ickes and S. Duck (eds), *The Social Psychology of Personal Relationships*. Chichester: Wiley, pp. 37–54.

# 11
# Altruism and Helping Behavior

C. DANIEL BATSON, PAUL A.M. VAN LANGE,
NADIA AHMAD, AND DAVID A. LISHNER

**INTRODUCTION**

Why do we help others – when we do? The majority view in psychology (and Western thought) has long been that everything we do for others, no matter how noble, is directed toward the ultimate goal of self-benefit. This view is called universal egoism. A minority view is that even though helping is often motivated by self-benefit, under certain circumstances humans are also capable of altruism – of seeking another person's benefit as an ultimate goal. Social psychologists have entered this egoism–altruism debate, conducting experiments designed to test the competing views. Results of these experiments may surprise you. So may the implications.

We humans spend much of our time and energy helping others. We stay up all night to comfort a friend who has just suffered a broken relationship. We send money to rescue famine victims halfway around the world, or to save whales, or to support public television. We spend millions of hours per week helping as volunteers in hospitals, nursing homes, AIDS hospices, fire departments, rescue squads, shelters, halfway houses, peer-counseling programs, and the like. We stop on a busy highway to help a stranded motorist change a flat tire, or spend an hour in the cold to push a friend's – even a stranger's – car out of a snowdrift.

At times, what people do for others can be truly spectacular. Soldiers have been known to throw themselves on live grenades to protect their comrades. Firemen at the World Trade Center, on September 11, 2001, lost their lives directing others to safety. Mother Teresa dedicated her life to the dying of Calcutta, the poorest of the poor, and brought care and comfort to thousands. Rescuers of Jews in Nazi Europe, such as Miep Gies (1987), who helped hide Anne Frank and her parents, and Oskar Schindler, risked their own lives – and often the lives of their loved ones – day after day for months, even years.

## The question of prosocial motivation: why do people help?

Such examples are heartwarming, even inspiring. For the social psychologist, they are also a puzzle. They raise the question of motives. Clearly, we humans can and do act to benefit others. But why? Why do we spend so much of our time, money, and energy on others? How are we to explain the Mother Teresas, Miep Gieses, Oskar Schindlers, courageous firemen, thousands of volunteers, and billions of charity dollars? Is it really true that other people, however dear, are simply complex objects in our environment – important sources of stimulation and gratification, of facilitation and inhibition – as we each pursue self-interest? Or can we care for others too? If so, for whom – for our immediate family, friends, nation, all humanity? Can we care about moral ideals? Answers to these questions should tell us something about how interconnected we humans really are, about how truly social we are – or are capable of becoming. Behind the question of motives is, then, an even more fundamental question of human nature.

### *A little history*

Long before psychology was born as a separate discipline, philosophers puzzled over prosocial motivation and its implications for human nature, often with insight and wit. The debate has raged for centuries – from Plato and Aristotle, to St Thomas Aquinas, Thomas Hobbes, La Rochefoucauld, Bernard Mandeville, David Hume, Adam Smith, Jeremy Bentham, John Stuart Mill, and Friedrich Nietzsche. Among these philosophers, the majority view – but by no means the unanimous view – is that everything we humans do, including everything we do for others, is always, ultimately, done to benefit ourselves; we are unremitting egoists. La Rochefoucauld put it prosaically: 'The most disinterested love is, after all, but a kind of bargain, in which the dear love of our own selves always proposes to be the gainer some way or other' (1691: Maxim 82).

This majority view in Western philosophy has dominated psychology as well. In his 1975 Presidential Address to the American Psychological Association, Donald Campbell summarized the situation: 'Psychology and psychiatry [...] not only describe man as selfishly motivated, but implicitly or explicitly teach that he ought to be so' (1975: 1104). Universal egoism is the majority view in economics and political science as well (Mansbridge, 1990).

### *A question for the 1960s and 1970s: why don't people help?*

Given this historical context, it is no surprise that when social psychologists became interested in helping behavior in the late 1960s, they were not trying to answer the question of why people help. That motivational question was assumed to be either already clearly answered or clearly unanswerable. They were instead trying to understand why people fail to help when we think they should. Specifically, they were trying to understand why the thirty-eight witnesses to the brutal stabbing and eventual murder of Kitty Genovese in the Kew Gardens neighborhood of Queens, New York, on the night of March 13, 1964, did nothing to help her – not even call the police.

John Darley and Bibb Latané (1968; Latané and Darley, 1970) came up with an ingenious answer to this question. They suggested that once we notice a possible emergency situation, we must make a number of decisions in sequence before we help. First, we must decide that a need exists, then we must decide that it is our personal responsibility to act, and then we must decide that there is something we can do to help. To complicate matters, these decisions are made under pressure; emergencies involve threat, ambiguity, urgency, and stress. The presence of other bystanders can influence this pressure-packed decision sequence at each step, tipping the scales toward inaction.

Is a scream in the night a woman being attacked, or harmless high-spirited play? Uncertain, bystanders may look to others present, seeking cues to help them decide. No one wishes to appear foolishly excited over an event that is not an emergency, so each individual reacts initially with a calm outward demeanor, while observing others' reactions. This creates a state of pluralistic ignorance (Miller and McFarland, 1987) in which everyone decides that since no one else seems upset, the event must not be an emergency (Latané and Darley, 1968; Latané and Rodin, 1969).

Even if one decides that the situation is an emergency, that someone is in dire need of help, the presence of others can still discourage action. To explain how, Darley and Latané (1968) proposed a diffusion of responsibility. If others are available, each individual may feel less personal obligation to come forward and help. One call to the police is as helpful, if not more helpful, than 20 calls. In the Kitty Genovese case, for example, bystanders may have thought that others had also heard the screams and that someone else had already called. Some may have thought, 'Something should be done, but why should I be the one to do it?' Thoughts like these, made possible by awareness of the presence of other bystanders without knowing what the others are doing, diffuses the responsibility to help among all the bystanders present and makes it less likely that any one bystander will help.

Latané and Darley's (1970) answer to the question of why none of the thirty-eight witnesses to the murder of Kitty Genovese helped her has stood up remarkably well to experimental test (see Latané and Nida, 1981, for a review). But neither Darley and Latané's answer, nor the large mountain of subsequent work during the 1970s on situational factors affecting the likelihood of helping, addressed the question of why anyone would *help* Kitty Genovese. The presence of others can lead a bystander to misinterpret the situation or to diffuse responsibility, failing to help when he or she otherwise might have done so (bystanders alone in emergency studies are very likely to help), but the question of what motivates helping when it does occur – and whether helping might ever be motivated by concerns for the other rather than by self-concern – was ruled out of bounds. Darley and Latané (1970: 84) said of this question: it is 'a general one, of enormous social interest and importance, and of a semiphilosophic nature. It probably will never be completely answered by reference to data'. They quickly let it drop.

### *Back to the question of prosocial motives*

As difficult as the question of what motivates helping may be, in the past twenty-five years, a number of social psychologists have begun a serious attempt to provide an answer – by reference to data. These social psychologists have drawn heavily on general theories of motivation, especially those stemming from the work of Sigmund Freud, Clark Hull, and various social-learning theorists (e.g., Bandura, 1977; Dollard and Miller, 1950), but they have been most importantly influenced by the motivational theories of Kurt Lewin. Lewin (1951) thought of motives as goal-directed forces within the life space of the individual, and this is how motives have typically been conceived by the social psychologists seeking to answer the question of what motivates our concern for others.

Thinking of motives as goal-directed forces allows one to distinguish among instrumental goals, ultimate goals, and unintended consequences. An *instrumental goal* is sought as a means to reach some other goal. An *ultimate goal* is sought as an end in itself. An *unintended consequence* is a result of acting to reach a goal but is not itself sought as a goal. Employing these distinctions, it becomes clear that the debate over why people help is a debate over whether benefiting others is an instrumental goal on the way to some self-interested ultimate goal or an ultimate goal in its own right with the self-benefits being unintended consequences.

In the pages that follow, we wish to consider four possible ultimate goals of acting to benefit someone else: self-benefit (*egoism*), benefiting another individual (*altruism*), benefiting a group (*collectivism*), and upholding a moral principle (*principlism*). These goals are not mutually exclusive; any or all might be the ultimate goals of acting to benefit someone.

## Four answers

### *Egoism: benefiting another as a means to benefit oneself*

Humans are clearly capable of benefiting others as a means of benefiting themselves. When the ultimate goal is self-benefit, the motivation is egoistic. This is true no matter how noble or beneficial to others the helping behavior may be.

The list of possible self-benefits that can motivate helping is long. Batson (1995) offered the list in Table 11.1; it includes those self-benefits for which there is clear empirical evidence (see Batson, 1998; Schroeder et al., 1995, for reviews). The list is organized into three general categories, reflecting three fundamental forms of egoistic motivation for benefiting others: (a) to gain material, social, or self-rewards (the entries in Table 11.1 are organized in rough order of material, then social, and then self-rewards); (b) to avoid material, social, and self-punishments (again, in rough order); and (c) to reduce aversive arousal evoked by seeing another in need. In each case, benefiting the other is an instrumental goal which is sought as a means to reach the ultimate goal specified.

Table 11.1 *Possible self-benefits from benefiting another*

| | |
|---|---|
| **1 Material, social, and self-rewards received** | |
| Payment | Praise |
| Gifts | Honor |
| Reciprocity credit | Enhanced self-image |
| Thanks | Mood enhancement (maintenance) |
| Esteem | Empathic joy |
| Heaven | |
| **2 Material, social, and self-punishments avoided** | |
| Fines/imprisonment | Sanctions for norm violation |
| Attack | Shame |
| Censure | Guilt |
| Recrimination | Empathy costs |
| Hell | |
| **3 Aversive-arousal reduction** | |
| Escape distressing situation | |
| Escape discrepant situation | |
| Escape unjust situation | |

### Gaining rewards

Among the rewards that a helper may seek, perhaps the only three that need any explanation are reciprocity credit, mood enhancement (maintenance), and empathic joy.

#### Reciprocity credit

Reciprocity credit is the self-benefit of knowing that the person you have benefited owes you one. Sociologist Alvin Gouldner (1960) identified what he called the 'universal norm of reciprocity' – the norm that for a benefit received an equivalent benefit ought eventually to be returned. After reviewing the evidence, Gouldner concluded that 'a norm of reciprocity is, I suspect, no less universal and important an element of culture than the incest taboo' (1960: 171). Gouldner assumed that this norm was instilled through socialization, although biologist Robert Trivers (1971) has suggested that it may have a genetic base.

Reciprocity credit can lead us to look for an opportunity to help someone from whom we want some reward in the future, as occurs with ingratiation (Jones, 1964). It may also lead at least some of us to help others whom we know cannot reciprocate; we may help them because of belief in generalized reciprocity, a feeling that we get in equal measure to what we give to the world in general (Zuckerman, 1975). Alternatively, the reason for helping someone who cannot reciprocate may be more strategic; it may be a way to enhance our reputation as a caring, helpful person. Building on Trivers's (1971) biological analysis (see also Alexander, 1987), economist Robert Frank (1988) suggested that if you have a reputation for being helpful, others may be more likely to trust and help you. Recent research supports the idea that one's reputation for helpfulness may be an important mechanism for maintaining cooperation in groups when more direct forms of reciprocity are not possible. People are much more likely to contribute resources to another group member when they know that other members of the group will be informed of their action (Milinski et al., 2002; Nowak and Sigmund, 1998).

#### Mood enhancement (maintenance)

Mood enhancement can also be a reason for helping. Cialdini et al. (1973) proposed that we are more likely to help someone when we feel bad because we know that we can give ourselves a pat on the back when we do something nice like helping, and this will make us feel better. Consistent with this *negative-state relief model*, Cialdini et al. found that people who felt bad (that is, were in a negative state) because they had accidentally harmed someone – or had seen another person harm someone – were more likely to volunteer to make telephone calls for a worthy cause than were people who did not feel bad. When, however, people who felt bad had their negative state relieved by receiving praise or a dollar before being given the chance to volunteer, they did *not* help more.

Not only does helping have reward value for a person feeling bad, but it also seems to be rewarding for persons who feel good. Indeed, the effect seems even stronger when people are in a good mood. Alice Isen and her associates have used a number of clever techniques to enhance people's moods – having them succeed at a task, giving them a cookie while they studied in the library and having them find a coin in the return slot of a telephone booth. She found that each of these experiences increased the likelihood of a person's giving help to good causes (Isen, 1970; Isen and Levin, 1972).

What accounts for this pervasive reward value of helping for people in a good mood? One possibility is desire for good-mood maintenance. Seeing another person in need can throw a wet blanket on a good mood, so one helps in order to shed this blanket and maintain the mood (Isen and Levin, 1972; Wegener and Petty, 1994). Isen (1987; Isen et al., 1978) has also suggested a second possibility: being in a good mood may bias one's memory about the positive and negative aspects of various activities, including helping. She suggested that people in a good mood are more likely to recall and attend to positive rather than negative aspects of their lives. Applied to helping, this makes such people more likely to remember and attend to the positive, rewarding features and less likely to attend to the negative features, such as the costs involved (also see Berkowitz, 1987; Clark and Waddell, 1983; Cunningham et al., 1990).

#### Empathic joy

Empathic joy is the vicarious feeling of pleasure one has at seeing the person in need experience relief. As Hoffman (1981: 135) described it, 'When the victim shows visible signs of relief or joy after being helped, the helper may actually feel empathic joy. Having experienced empathic joy, he or she may subsequently be motivated to help in order to experience it again'. At the time Hoffman wrote, there was no empirical evidence for the existence of such a motive; now there is (Batson et al., 1991; Smith et al., 1989). It might seem that a person who feels a high degree of empathy or sympathy for another in need might be especially attuned to and desirous of an opportunity to experience empathic joy, but the evidence suggests otherwise. Batson et al. (1991) found that the desire to experience empathic joy seemed to motivate the helping of individuals induced to feel little empathic concern for a person in need, but not of individuals induced to feel high empathy.

### Avoiding punishments

Probably the only punishments listed in Table 11.1 that need explanation are fines/imprisonment, sanctions for norm violation, and empathy costs.

*Fines/imprisonment* In some countries, especially in Europe, there are Good Samaritan laws. If you fail to offer aid when (a) someone's life is in danger; (b) there is no serious risk for you; and (c) no one better qualified is available, you are liable for a fine or a jail sentence. One reason for these laws is, of course, to motivate people to help in order to avoid these penalties. Another reason is to reduce the possible punishments that one might receive if a sincere attempt to help goes awry. Good Samaritan laws typically include protection from suit should one's attempt to help do harm rather than good. The assumption behind such laws is that people can be encouraged to help by (a) increasing the potential punishments for not helping and (b) reducing the potential punishments for helping.

*Sanctions for norm violation* A number of social norms apply to helping. They dictate that you should help people in need – at least some people under some circumstances – lest you suffer socially administered or self-administered sanctions. One norm already mentioned is the norm of reciprocity. In addition to leading you to expect repayment when you help, this norm dictates that you should help those who help you. Although Gouldner (1960) believed that the norm of reciprocity is universal, he also believed that the pressure on us to help in return depends on the circumstances under which we received help: (a) how badly we needed help; (b) our perception of how much the other person gave us relative to his or her total resources; (c) our perception of the other person's motives for helping (for example, was it a bribe?); and (d) whether the other person helped voluntarily or was pressured into it. Research supports each of Gouldner's beliefs (see, for example, Gergen et al., 1975; Pruitt, 1968; Wilke and Lanzetta, 1970).

A second norm that psychologists have suggested motivates helping is the norm of social responsibility. This norm tells us that we should help a person in need who is dependent upon us – that is, when no one else is available to help and so the person is counting specifically on us. Although such a norm does seem to exist, its effect has been surprisingly difficult to demonstrate. After over a decade of research, Berkowitz (1972: 68, 77) concluded, 'The findings do not provide any clear-cut support for the normative analysis of help-giving. [...] The potency of the conjectured "social responsibility norm" was greatly exaggerated'.

Why has evidence that the norm of social responsibility leads to helping been so hard to find? Darley and Latané (1970) suggested that this norm may be at once too general and too specific. The norm may be too general in that everyone in our society adheres to it. If this is true, the norm cannot account for why one person helps and another does not. The norm may be too specific in that along with it comes a complex pattern of exceptions, situations in which an individual may feel exempt from acting in accordance with the norm. To take an extreme example, if someone is dependent on you for help with what you believe to be an immoral act – such as robbery – you will likely feel no normative pressure to help. Thus, the norm of social responsibility seems to be characterized not simply by a rule that says, 'If someone is dependent on you for help, then help' but by a more complex rule that says, 'If someone is dependent on you for help, then help, *except when* ...' The exceptions will vary for different individuals and different social situations.

Other researchers have suggested that the problem with social norms may lie in our focus of attention. Only when our attention is focused on a particular norm as a standard for our behavior is concern about violating it likely to affect our behavior (Cialdini et al., 1991). Consistent with this suggestion, Gibbons and Wicklund (1982) found that if standards of helpfulness or a sense that one ought to help were salient and so a focus of attention, then also focusing on oneself increased helping. Presumably, being self-focused when the norm was salient highlighted the threat of sanctions for failing to act in line with personal standards. But in the absence of salient standards for helpfulness, Gibbons and Wicklund (1982) found that people who were self-focused were *less* helpful than people who were not self-focused.

Because general social norms such as the norm of social responsibility have limited ability to predict whether a person will help, Shalom Schwartz (1977) suggested a change of focus from general social norms to more specific, personal norms. Paralleling the difficulties encountered by those attempting to use general attitudes to predict specific behaviors (Fazio, 1990), Schwartz argued that general social norms are too abstract to be good predictors of specific helping acts but that personal norms are more predictive. By personal norms, Schwartz meant internalized rules of conduct which are learned from social interaction, rules which vary between individuals within the same society and that function to direct behavior in particular situations.

Applied to helping, a personal norm involves a sense of obligation to perform a *particular* helping act. For example, people may say, either publicly or to themselves, 'I ought to give a pint of blood in the blood drive.' Such statements appear to be far more predictive of whether a person will give blood than are statements of agreement with more general social norms such as the norm of social responsibility. Specific statements such as this are particularly powerful as predictors when one also takes into account extenuating circumstances such as whether the person was in town during the blood drive, had no major scheduling conflicts, and was physically fit to give blood (Zuckerman and Reis, 1978). Of course, at this level of specificity, it is not clear whether the statement about giving blood reflects a sense of personal obligation stemming from an internalized rule of conduct – a personal norm – or simply an intention to act in a particular way.

*Empathy costs* Empathy costs are the discomfort and distress you anticipate feeling because of the empathy you will feel for the person in need as he or she continues to suffer. Piliavin et al. (1981) have suggested that desire to avoid these costs is one source of motivation to help.

### Reducing aversive arousal

The three self-benefits under aversive-arousal reduction in Table 11.1 may be less familiar than the self-benefits under rewards and punishments. The general idea of aversive-arousal reduction is that it is upsetting to see someone else suffer, and people prefer not to be upset. To eliminate this aversive arousal, one option is to relieve the other person's suffering because it is the stimulus causing one's own suffering. Once again, the prosocial aspect of this motivation is instrumental, not ultimate; the ultimate goal is the self-benefit of having one's own discomfort go away.

Why should the suffering of others cause us to suffer? Answers vary. One is that we have learned over the years that when others are suffering, there is a greater chance that we will soon suffer too (St Thomas Aquinas, among others, suggested this). Another answer is that we have a genetic predisposition to be distressed by the distress of others (Hoffman, 1981; Preston and de Waal, 2002). Whatever the source, our aversion to television news showing the mangled body of a victim of terrorism or the hollow stares of starving refugees suggests that we often find the suffering of others aversive. Sometimes this aversion leads us only to look away, cover our ears, or seek distraction, but at other times it may lead us to help.

Each of the three self-benefits under aversive arousal in Table 11.1 is based on the assumption that witnessing another in distress is aversive; yet each specifies a different form of aversive arousal.

*Escaping one's own distress* Most straightforward is the possibility suggested by Piliavin et al. (1981), Hoffman (1981) and Dovidio et al. (1991), among others. They propose that the witness's vicarious distress has much the same character as the victim's distress; both are aversive, and the witness is motivated to escape his or her own distress. One way to escape is to help, because helping terminates the stimulus causing the distress. Of course, running away may enable the witness to escape just as well and at less cost, as long as the principle 'out of sight, out of mind' works.

*Escaping discrepancy* Janusz Reykowski (1982: 361) proposed a quite different source of prosocial motivation, but still one that involves reduction of an aversive tension state: 'The sheer discrepancy between information about the real or possible state of an object and standards of its normal or desirable state will evoke motivation'. Reykowski applied this general psychological principle – which is closely akin to cognitive dissonance (Festinger, 1957) – to prosocial motivation as follows: if a person perceives a discrepancy between the current state and the expected or ideal state of another person (that is, perceives the other to be in need), this will produce cognitive inconsistency and motivation to reduce this uncomfortable inconsistency. Relieving the other's need by helping is one way to remove the inconsistency and escape the discrepant situation. Another, less prosocial way is to change one's perception and decide that the other's suffering is acceptable, even desirable. This has been called 'blaming the victim' (Ryan, 1971).

*Escaping injustice* Melvin Lerner's (1980) just-world hypothesis led him to a similar but more specific view. Lerner argued that virtually all of us have a need to believe that our world is predictable or just, that our efforts and the efforts of others like us will be rewarded. But if one needs to believe in a just world – a world in which people get what they deserve and deserve what they get – then witnessing an innocent victim suffer is likely to be upsetting because it violates this belief. In order to reduce the discomfort produced by this threat, one may help the victim. Once again, however, there is an alternative way to escape the aversive arousal. It is possible to derogate or blame the victim; if the victim is a less deserving person, his or her suffering is more just and less upsetting. Indeed, escaping injustice rather than escaping discrepancy per se is the most common explanation of victim derogation or blame. Consistent with Lerner's analysis, research suggests that if people can easily help in order to relieve the suffering of an innocent victim, they are likely to do so, but if they cannot easily help, they are likely to derogate the victim (Hafer, 2000; Lerner and Simmons, 1966; Mills and Egger, 1972).

### *Altruism: benefiting another as an end in itself*

Both for philosophers through the ages and for behavioral and social scientists today, the most intriguing and the most controversial question raised by helping behavior is whether it provides evidence for altruistic motivation. Is it possible for one person to have another person's welfare as an ultimate goal rather than simply as an instrumental means of reaching the ultimate goal of one or another form of self-benefit?

One rejoinder to the possibility of altruism that needs to be laid to rest at the outset goes like this. Even if it were possible for a person to be motivated to increase another's welfare, such a person would be pleased by attaining this desired goal, so even this apparent altruism would actually be a product of egoism. This argument, based on the general principle of *psychological hedonism*, is, in the words of Edward Tolman's (1923: 203) well-turned epithet, 'more brilliant than cogent'. It has been shown to be flawed by philosophers who have pointed out that it involves a confusion between two different forms of hedonism. The *strong* form of psychological hedonism asserts that attainment of personal pleasure is always the goal of human action; the *weak* form asserts only that goal attainment always brings pleasure. The weak form is not inconsistent with the possibility that the ultimate goal of some action is to benefit another rather than to benefit oneself; the pleasure obtained can be a consequence of reaching the goal without being the goal itself. The strong form of psychological hedonism is inconsistent with the possibility of altruism but to affirm this form of hedonism is simply to assert that altruism does not exist. This is an empirical assertion that may or may not be true, an assertion that begs for the kind of empirical evidence that social-psychological research can provide. (See MacIntyre, 1967; Milo, 1973; Nagel, 1970; Sober and Wilson, 1998, for discussion of these philosophical arguments.)

Advocates of universal egoism argue for the strong form of psychological hedonism. They assert that some self-benefit is always the ultimate goal of helping; benefiting the other is simply an instrumental goal on the way to one or another ultimately self-serving end. They remind us of all the self-benefits of helping, such as those listed in Table 11.1. Advocates of altruism reply that simply to show that self-benefits follow from benefiting someone does not prove that the self-benefits were the ultimate goal. It is at least logically possible that the self-benefits were unintended consequences of reaching the ultimate goal of benefiting the other. If so, then the motivation was altruistic, not egoistic.

Advocates of altruism claim more than logical possibility, of course. They claim that altruistic motivation is an empirical reality, that at least some people under some circumstances act with the ultimate goal of increasing another person's welfare. They claim that people can want another person to be happy and free of distress, not because it is upsetting to them if he or she is not – although it quite likely *is* upsetting – but because they care about the other's welfare as an end in itself.

### The empathy-altruism hypothesis

Over the centuries, the most frequently proposed source of altruistic motivation has been an other-oriented emotional response congruent with the perceived welfare of another person – today usually called empathy (Batson, 1987) or sympathy (Wispé, 1986). If another person is in need, these empathic emotions include sympathy, compassion, tenderness, and the like. The *empathy-altruism hypothesis* claims that these emotions produce motivation with the ultimate goal of benefiting the person for whom the empathy is felt – that is, altruistic motivation. Various forms of this hypothesis have been espoused by Thomas Aquinas, David Hume, Adam Smith, Charles Darwin, Herbert Spencer, and William McDougall, and in contemporary psychology by Hoffman (1975), Krebs (1975), and Batson (1987).

Considerable evidence supports the idea that feeling empathy for a person in need leads to increased helping of that person (Coke et al., 1978; Dovidio et al., 1990; Krebs, 1975; see Batson, 1991; Eisenberg and Miller, 1987, for reviews). To observe an empathy-helping relationship, however, tells one nothing about the nature of the motivation that underlies this relationship. Increasing the other person's welfare could be (a) an ultimate goal, producing self-benefits as unintended consequences; (b) an instrumental goal sought as a means to reach the ultimate goal of gaining one or more self-benefits; or (c) both. That is, the motivation could be altruistic, egoistic, or both.

### Egoistic alternatives to the empathy-altruism hypothesis

Self-benefits in each of the three general classes listed in Table 11.1 can result from helping a person for whom one feels empathy. Such help can (a) reduce one's empathic arousal, which may be experienced as aversive; (b) enable one to avoid possible social and self-punishments for failing to help;

and (c) enable one to gain social and self-rewards for doing what is good and right. The empathy-altruism hypothesis does not deny that these self-benefits of empathy-induced helping exist, but it claims that they are unintended consequences of the empathically aroused helper reaching the ultimate goal of reducing the other's suffering. Proponents of egoistic alternatives to the empathy-altruism hypothesis disagree; they claim that one or more of these self-benefits is the ultimate goal of empathy-induced helping.

*Aversive-arousal reduction* The most frequently proposed egoistic explanation of the empathy-helping relationship is aversive-arousal reduction. This explanation claims that feeling empathy for someone who is suffering is unpleasant, and empathically aroused individuals help in order to benefit themselves by eliminating their empathic feelings. Benefiting the victim is simply a means to this self-serving end.

Over half a dozen experiments have tested the aversive-arousal reduction explanation against the empathy-altruism hypothesis by varying the ease of escaping further exposure to a suffering victim without helping. Because empathic arousal is a result of witnessing the victim's suffering, either terminating this suffering by helping or terminating exposure to it by escaping should reduce one's own aversive arousal. Escape does not, however, enable one to reach the altruistic goal of relieving the victim's distress. Therefore, the aversive-arousal explanation predicts elimination of the empathy-helping relationship when escape is easy; the empathy-altruism hypothesis does not.

In a typical experiment, participants observe a 'worker' whom they believe is reacting badly to a series of uncomfortable electric shocks; they are then given a chance to help the worker by taking the shocks themselves. To manipulate ease of escape, some participants are informed that if they do not help, they will continue observing the worker take the shocks (difficult escape); others are informed that they will observe no more (easy escape). Empathy has been both manipulated and measured.

The results of these experiments have consistently patterned as predicted by the empathy-altruism hypothesis, not the aversive-arousal reduction explanation. Only among individuals experiencing a predominance of personal distress rather than empathy (that is, feeling relatively anxious, upset, distressed, and the like) does the chance for easy escape reduce helping. Individuals experiencing a predominance of empathy are as likely to help when escape is easy as when it is difficult. These results have cast serious doubt on the claim that the motivation underlying the empathy-helping relationship is a desire to reduce the aversive empathic arousal (see Batson, 1991, for a review).

*Empathy-specific punishment* A second egoistic explanation claims that people learn through socialization that additional obligation to help and so additional shame and guilt for failure to help is attendant on feeling empathy for someone in need. As a result, when people feel empathy, they are faced with impending social or self-censure beyond any general punishment associated with not helping. They say to themselves, 'What will others think – or what will I think of myself – if I don't help when I feel like this?' Therefore, they help out of an egoistic desire to avoid these empathy-specific punishments. Once again, experiments designed to test this explanation have consistently failed to support it; results have consistently supported the empathy-altruism hypothesis instead (Batson, 1991).

*Empathy-specific reward* The third major egoistic explanation claims that people learn through socialization that special rewards in the form of praise, honor, and pride are attendant on helping a person for whom they feel empathy. As a result, when people feel empathy, they think of these rewards and help out of an egoistic desire to gain them.

The general form of this explanation has been tested in several experiments and received no support (Batson et al., 1988: Studies 1 and 5; Batson and Weeks, 1996), but two variations have been proposed for which at least some support has been claimed. The best known is the negative-state relief explanation proposed by Cialdini et al. (1987). Cialdini et al. suggested that the empathy experienced when witnessing another person's suffering is a negative affective state – a state of temporary sadness or sorrow – and the person feeling empathy helps in order to relieve this negative state.

Although this egoistic alternative received some initial support (Cialdini et al., 1987; Schaller and Cialdini, 1988), subsequent research has revealed that the initial support may have been due to procedural artifacts. Experiments avoiding these artifacts have not provided support for the negative-state relief explanation; they have instead supported the empathy-altruism hypothesis (Batson et al., 1989; Dovidio et al., 1990; Schroeder et al., 1988). Considering all relevant evidence, it now appears that the motivation evoked by empathy cannot be explained in terms of negative-state relief.

A second interesting variation on an empathy-specific reward explanation was proposed by Smith et al. (1989). They claimed that, rather than helping to gain the rewards of seeing oneself or being seen by others as a helpful person, empathically aroused individuals help in order to feel joy at the needy individual's relief: 'It is proposed that the prospect of empathic joy, conveyed by feedback from the help recipient, is essential to the special tendency of empathic witnesses to help. […] The empathically concerned witness to the distress of others helps in order to be happy' (Smith et al., 1989: 641).

Some early self-report data were supportive of this empathic-joy hypothesis, but more rigorous experimental evidence has failed to provide support. Instead, experimental results have once again consistently supported the empathy-altruism hypothesis (Batson et al., 1991; Smith et al., 1989). The empathic-joy hypothesis, like other versions of the empathy-specific reward explanation, seems unable to account for the empathy-helping relationship.

### A tentative conclusion

Reviewing the empathy-altruism research, as well as recent literature in sociology, economics, political science, and biology, Piliavin and Charng (1990: 27) concluded:

> There appears to be a 'paradigm shift' away from the earlier position that behavior that appears to be altruistic must, under closer scrutiny, be revealed as reflecting egoistic motives. Rather, theory and data now being advanced are more compatible with the view that true altruism – acting with the goal of benefiting another – does exist and is a part of human nature.

Pending new evidence or a plausible new egoistic explanation of the existing evidence, this conclusion seems to reflect accurately our current understanding. It appears that the empathy-altruism hypothesis should – tentatively – be accepted as true.

### Implications of the empathy-altruism hypothesis

If the empathy-altruism hypothesis is true, the implications are wide ranging. Universal egoism – the assumption that all human behavior is ultimately directed toward self-benefit – has long dominated not only psychology but other social and behavioral sciences as well (Campbell, 1975; Hoffman, 1981; Mansbridge, 1990; Wallach and Wallach, 1983). If individuals feeling empathy act, at least in part, with an ultimate goal of increasing the welfare of another, the assumption of universal egoism must be replaced by a more complex view of motivation that allows for altruism as well as egoism. Such a shift in our view of motivation requires, in turn, a revision of our underlying assumptions about human nature and human potential. It implies that we humans may be more social than we have thought: other people can be more to us than sources of information, stimulation, and reward as we each seek our own welfare. We have the potential to care about their welfare as well.

The evidence for the empathy-altruism hypothesis also forces us to face the question of why empathic feelings exist. What evolutionary function do they serve? Admittedly speculative, the most plausible answer relates empathic feelings to parenting among higher mammals, in which offspring live for some time in a very vulnerable state (Bell, 2001; de Waal, 1996; Hoffman, 1981; McDougall, 1908; Zahn-Waxler and Radke-Yarrow, 1990). Were parents not intensely interested in the welfare of their progeny, these species would quickly die out. Empathic feelings for offspring and the resulting altruistic motivation may promote one's reproductive potential, not by increasing the number of offspring but by increasing the chance of their survival.

Clearly, however, empathic feelings extend well beyond one's own children. People can feel empathy for a wide range of individuals (including animals), as long as there is no pre-existing antipathy (Batson, 1991; Krebs, 1975; Shelton and Rogers, 1981). From an evolutionary perspective, this extension is usually attributed to cognitive generalization whereby one 'adopts' others, making it possible to evoke the primitive and fundamental impulse to care for progeny when these adopted others are in need (Batson, 1987; Hoffman, 1981; MacLean, 1973). Such cognitive generalization may be possible because of (a) human cognitive capacity, including symbolic thought (Tomasello, 1999), and (b) the lack of evolutionary advantage for sharp discrimination of empathic feelings in early human small hunter-gatherer bands. In these bands, those in need were often one's children or close kin, and one's own welfare was tightly tied to the welfare even of those who were not close kin (Hoffman, 1981).

The empathy-altruism hypothesis also may have wide-ranging practical implications. Given the power of empathic feelings to evoke altruistic motivation, people may sometimes suppress or avoid these feelings. Loss of the capacity to feel empathy for clients may be a factor, possibly a central one, in the experience of burnout among caseworkers in the helping professions (Maslach, 1982). Aware of the extreme effort involved in helping or the impossibility of helping effectively, these caseworkers – or nurses caring for terminal patients, or even pedestrians confronted by the homeless – may try to avoid feeling empathy in order to avoid the resulting altruistic motivation (Shaw et al., 1994; Stotland et al., 1978). There seems to be, then, an egoistic motive to avoid empathy-induced altruistic motivation.

More positively, experiments have tested the possibility that empathy-induced altruism can be used to improve attitudes toward stigmatized outgroups. Thus far, results look quite encouraging. Inducing empathy has improved racial attitudes, as well as attitudes toward people with AIDS, the homeless, and even convicted murderers and drug dealers (Batson et al., 1997, 2002a; Dovidio et al., 1999; Stephan and Finlay, 1999). Empathy-induced altruism has also been found to increase cooperation in a competitive situation (a prisoner's dilemma) – even when one knows that the person for whom one feels empathy has acted competitively (Batson and Ahmad, 2001; Batson and Moran, 1999).

## Other possible sources of altruistic motivation

Might there be sources of altruistic motivation other than empathic emotion? Several have been proposed, including an 'altruistic personality' (Oliner and Oliner, 1988), principled moral reasoning (Kohlberg, 1976), and internalized prosocial values (Staub, 1974). There is some evidence that each of these potential sources is associated with increased prosocial motivation, but, as yet, it is not clear that this motivation is altruistic. It may be, or it may be an instrumental means to the egoistic ultimate goals of (a) maintaining one's positive self-concept or (b) avoiding guilt (Batson, 1991; Batson et al., 1986; Carlo et al., 1991; Eisenberg et al., 1989). More and better research exploring these possibilities is needed.

If we think even more broadly, beyond the egoism-altruism debate which has been a focus of attention and contention for the past twenty-five years, might there be other forms of prosocial motivation, forms in which the ultimate goal is neither to benefit self nor to benefit another individual? Two seem especially worthy of consideration.

### *Collectivism: benefiting another to benefit a group*

*Collectivism* is motivation to benefit a particular group as a whole. The ultimate goal is not to increase one's own welfare or the welfare of the specific others who are benefited; the ultimate goal is to increase the welfare of the group. Robyn Dawes and his colleagues put it succinctly: 'Not me or thee but we' (Dawes et al., 1988). They suggested that collectivist motivation is a product of group identity (Brewer and Kramer, 1986; Tajfel, 1981; Turner, 1987) and may be especially important in addressing social dilemmas. A *social dilemma* arises when (a) individuals in a group or collective have a choice about how to allocate personally held scarce resources (such as money, time, or energy), and (b) allocation to the group provides more benefit for the group as a whole than does allocation to any single individual (for example, oneself), but allocation to a single individual provides that individual with more benefit than does allocation to the group as a whole (Dawes, 1980). It has often been assumed that when people act to benefit the group in a social dilemma, they are motivated by collectivism.

As with altruism, however, what looks like collectivism may actually be a subtle form of egoism. Perhaps attention to group welfare is simply an expression of enlightened self-interest. After all, if one recognizes that ignoring group needs in a headlong pursuit of self-benefit will only lead to less self-benefit in the long run, then one may decide to benefit the group as a means to maximize overall self-benefit. Appeals to enlightened self-interest are commonly used by politicians and social activists to encourage response to societal needs. They warn of the long-term consequences for us and our children of pollution and squandering natural resources; they remind us that if the plight of the poor becomes too severe, the well-off may face revolution. Such appeals seem to assume that collectivism is simply a form of egoism. Enlightened self-interest also seems to underlie strategies for collective action based on reciprocity, such as tit-for-tat in dyads and small groups (Axelrod, 1984; Komorita and Parks, 1995), or on the implementation of sanction systems that punish those who seek to ride free on the efforts of other group members (Hardin, 1977; Yamagishi, 1986).

There are reasons, however, to think that acting to benefit a group is more than enlightened egoism, at least for some of the people some of the time. People seem to differ in the degree to which they are concerned to (a) do well themselves without regard to others, (b) do well while ensuring that others do well, too, or (c) do well relative to others (McClintock and Liebrand, 1988). These (a) individualistic, (b) prosocial, and (c) competitive value orientations appear to be, at least in part, a product of social interaction experiences (van Lange et al., 1997). Relative to individualists and competitors, those whose dominant value orientation is prosocial have been found to be more concerned with collective outcomes and equality in social dilemmas (van Lange, 1999). Whether this concern is based on an egoistic motive to gain rewards and avoid punishments by adhering to norms for equality or fairness, or on a collectivistic motive to benefit the group as a whole, is not yet clear.

The most direct evidence that collectivism is independent of egoism comes from research by Dawes et al. (1990). They examined the responses of individuals who had been given a choice between allocating money to themselves or to a group, when allocation to oneself maximized individual but not group profit, whereas allocation to the group maximized collective but not individual profit.

Dawes et al. found that if individuals faced with this dilemma made their allocation after discussing it with other members of the group, they gave more to the group than if they had no prior discussion. Moreover, this effect was specific to the in-group with whom the discussion occurred; allocation to an out-group was not enhanced. From this research, Dawes et al. (1990) claimed evidence for collectivist motivation independent of egoism, arguing that their procedure ruled out the two most plausible egoistic explanations: (a) enlightened self-interest (by eliminating the chance for one's behavior to be reciprocated) and (b) socially instilled conscience (which may have been pricked by someone in the discussion mentioning the obligation to share, creating a norm). However, the research on norms reviewed earlier suggests that norms can be more refined than the one Dawes and his coworkers ruled out. We may have a norm that says 'share with your group' rather than a norm that simply says 'share'. So, although Dawes et al.'s (1990) research is important and suggestive, more and better evidence is needed to justify the conclusion that collectivist motivation is not reducible to egoism.

### *Principlism: benefiting another to uphold a moral principle*

Not only have most moral philosophers argued for the importance of a prosocial motive other than egoism, but most since Kant (1724–1804) have shunned altruism and collectivism as well. They reject appeals to altruism, especially empathy-induced altruism, because feelings of empathy, sympathy, and compassion are too fickle and too circumscribed. Empathy is not felt for everyone in need, at least not to the same degree. They reject appeals to collectivism because group interest is bounded by the limits of the group; it not only permits but may even encourage doing harm to those outside the group. Given these problems with altruism and collectivism, moral philosophers have typically advocated prosocial motivation with an ultimate goal of upholding a universal and impartial moral principle, such as justice (Rawls, 1971). We shall call this moral motivation *principlism*.

Is acting with an ultimate goal of upholding a moral principle really possible? When Kant (1785/1898: 23–4) briefly shifted from his analysis of what ought to be to what is, he was ready to admit that even when the concern we show for others appears to be prompted by duty to principle, it may actually be prompted by self-love. The goal of upholding a moral principle may be only an instrumental goal pursued as a means to reach the ultimate goal of self-benefit. If this is true, then principle-based motivation is actually egoistic.

The self-benefits of upholding a moral principle are conspicuous. One can gain the social and self-rewards of being seen and seeing oneself as a good person. One can also avoid the social and self-punishments of shame and guilt for failing to do the right thing. As Freud (1930) suggested, society may inculcate such principles in the young in order to bridle their antisocial impulses by making it in their best personal interest to act morally (see also Campbell, 1975). Alternatively, through internalization (Staub, 1989) or development of moral reasoning (Gilligan, 1982; Kohlberg, 1976), principles may come to be valued in their own right and not simply as instrumental means to self-serving ends.

The issue here is the same we faced with altruism and collectivism. Once again, we need to know the nature of a prosocial motive. Is the desire to uphold justice (or some other moral principle) an instrumental goal on the way to the ultimate goal of self-benefit? If so, then this desire is a subtle and sophisticated form of egoism. Alternatively, is upholding the principle an ultimate goal, with the ensuing self-benefits unintended consequences? If so, then principlism is a fourth type of prosocial motivation, independent of egoism, altruism, and collectivism.

Recent research suggests that behavior that appears to be motivated by a desire to uphold moral principle as an ultimate goal (moral integrity) may instead be an instrumental means to pursue self-benefit. The underlying motive often seems to reflect a desire to appear moral while, if possible, avoiding the cost of actually being moral (moral hypocrisy – Batson et al., 1997a, 1999b, 2002b). Many of us are, it seems, quite adept at moral rationalization. We are good at justifying to ourselves – if not to others – why a situation that benefits us or those we care about does not violate our moral principles. Why, for example, storing our nuclear waste in someone else's backyard is fair. Why terrorist attacks by our side are courageous acts of moral retribution, but terrorist attacks by the other side are atrocities. Why we must obey orders, even if it means killing innocents. The abstractness of most moral principles, and their multiplicity, makes rationalization all too easy (Bandura, 1991; Bersoff, 1999; Staub, 1990).

Pursuing morality as an instrumental goal on the way to self-benefit may, however, be only part of the story. Perhaps upholding a moral principle *can* serve as an ultimate goal, defining a form of motivation independent of egoism. If so, principlism may be an extremely valuable form of prosocial motivation. Motivation to uphold moral principles such as justice may provide a basis for responding to the needs of others that transcends reliance on self-interest or on vested interest in and feeling for the welfare of certain other individuals or groups. This is quite an 'if', but it seems well worth conducting research to find out.

## Toward a general model of prosocial motivation

Staub (1989) and Schwartz (1992) have, for many years, emphasized the importance of values as determinants of prosocial behavior. Batson (1994) has proposed a general model that links prosocial values and motives. The value underlying egoism is enhanced personal welfare; the value underlying altruism is the enhanced welfare of one or more other individuals as individuals; the value underlying collectivism is enhanced group welfare; and the value underlying principlism is upholding a moral principle. Four experiments have provided evidence for the predicted link between empathic emotion – a source of altruistic motivation – and valuing another individual's welfare (Batson et al., 1995c); the other value-motive links await testing.

To entertain the possibility of multiple prosocial motives (egoism, altruism, collectivism, and principlism) based on multiple prosocial values (self, other, group, and principle) begs for a better understanding of cognitive representation of the self–other relationship. Several representations have been proposed. Concern for another's welfare may be a product of the following: (a) a sense of 'we-ness' based on cognitive unit formation or identification with the other's situation (Hornstein, 1982; Lerner, 1982); (b) the self expanding to incorporate the other (Aron and Aron, 1986); (c) empathic feeling for the other, who remains distinct from self (Batson and Shaw, 1991; Jarymowicz, 1992); (d) the self being redefined at a group level, where 'me' and 'thee' become interchangeable parts of a self that is 'we' (Dawes et al., 1988; Turner, 1987); or (e) the self dissolving in devotion to something outside itself, whether another person, a group, or a principle (James, 1910/1982).

Most of these proposals seem plausible; some even seem profound. Yet not all can be true, at least not at the same time. From research to date, it appears that empathic feelings are not a product of self–other merging (Batson et al., 1997c; Cialdini et al., 1997), but the effect on one's self-concept of caring for people, groups, and principles is not, as yet, well understood.

## Conflict and cooperation of prosocial motives

To recognize the range of possible prosocial motives makes available more resources to those seeking to produce a more humane, caring society. At the same time, a multiplicity of prosocial motives complicates matters. These different motives for helping others do not always work in harmony. They can undercut or compete with one another.

Well-intentioned appeals to extended or enlightened self-interest can backfire by undermining other prosocial motives. Providing people with money or other tangible incentives for showing concern may lead people to interpret their motivation as egoistic even when it is not (Batson et al., 1978; Stukas et al., 1999). In this way, the assumption that there is only one answer to the question of why we act for the common good – egoism – may become a self-fulfilling prophecy (Batson et al., 1987). It may lead to what Miller (1999) has called a norm of self-interest, a belief that in many situations people not only will but should pursue their self-interest (for supporting evidence, see Miller and Ratner, 1998; Ratner and Miller, 2001).

Nor do the other three prosocial motives always work in harmony; they can conflict. For example, altruism can – and often does – conflict with collectivism or principlism: we may ignore the larger social good, and we may compromise our principles, not only to benefit ourselves but also to benefit those individuals about whom we especially care (Batson et al., 1995a, 1995b). Indeed, whereas there are clear social sanctions against unbridled self-interest, there are not clear sanctions against altruism. Batson et al. (1999a) found that, at times, altruism can be a greater threat to the common good than is egoism.

Each of the four prosocial motives that we have identified has its strengths. Each also has its weaknesses. The potential for the greatest good may come from strategies that orchestrate prosocial motives so that the strengths of one can overcome weaknesses of another. Strategies that combine appeals to either altruism or collectivism with appeals to prin ciple seem especially promising. For example, think about the principle of justice. Upholding justice is a powerful motive but vulnerable to rationalization; it is easily co-opted. Empathy-induced altruism and collectivism are also powerful motives but limited in scope; they produce partiality, special concern for a particular person or persons or for a particular group. Perhaps if we can lead people to feel empathy for the victims of injustice or to perceive themselves in a common group with them, we can get these motives working together rather than at odds. Desire for justice may provide perspective and reason; empathy-induced altruism or collectivism may provide emotional fire and a force directed specifically toward seeing the victims' suffering end, preventing rationalization. (For a parallel argument, see Blader and Tyler, 2002.)

Something of this sort occurred, we believe, in a number of rescuers of Jews in Nazi Europe. A careful look at data collected by the Oliners and their colleagues (Oliner and Oliner, 1988) suggests that involvement in rescue activity frequently began with concern for a specific individual or individuals, or members of a specific group, for whom compassion was felt – often individuals known previously. This initial involvement subsequently led to further contacts and rescue activity and to a concern for justice that extended well beyond the bounds of the initial empathic concern. Something of this sort also lay at the heart of Gandhi's and Martin Luther King's practice of nonviolent protest. The sight on the television news of a small black child in Birmingham, Alabama, being literally rolled down the street by water from a fire hose under the direction of Police Chief Bull Connor, and the emotions this sight evoked, seemed to do more to arouse a concern for justice than hours of reasoned argument and appeals for equal civil rights.

Something of this sort also can be found in the writing of Jonathan Kozol. Deeply concerned about the 'savage inequalities' in public education between rich and poor communities in the USA, Kozol (1991) does not simply document the inequity. He takes us into the lives of individual children. We come to care deeply for them and, as a result, about the injustice.

## Summary and conclusion

Why do people help others, even at considerable cost to themselves? What does this behavior tell us about the human capacity to care, about the degree of interconnectedness among us, about how social an animal we humans really are? These classic philosophical questions have resurfaced in the behavioral and social sciences in the past several decades. Social psychologists have begun to address the question of the nature of prosocial motivation by drawing on (a) Kurt Lewin's ideas about goal-directed motivation and the resulting distinctions among instrumental goals, ultimate goals, and unintended consequences, and (b) the experimental research methods that have become their trademark over the past fifty years.

Specifically, social-psychological research has, first, added to and documented a long list of self-benefits that may serve as the ultimate goal of egoistic prosocial motives. This list includes material, social, and self-rewards to be obtained; material, social, and self-punishments to be avoided; and three forms of aversive arousal to be reduced.

Social-psychological research has also been used to test the claim that altruistic motives – motives with the ultimate goal of increasing another's welfare – exist which are independent of and irreducible to egoistic motives. The results of the over thirty experiments designed to test the empathy-altruism hypothesis against egoistic alternatives have proved remarkably supportive of that hypothesis, leading to the tentative conclusion that feeling empathy for a person in need produces altruistic motivation to help that person. Sources of altruistic motivation other than empathy have also been proposed, but there is still not compelling research evidence to support these proposals.

Beyond the egoism–altruism debate, two additional forms of prosocial motivation seem especially worthy of consideration: collectivism and principlism. Collectivism – motivation with the ultimate goal of benefiting some group or collective as a whole – has been claimed to result from group identity and to account for prosocial responses to social dilemmas. Principlism – motivation with the ultimate goal of upholding some moral principle – has long been advocated by religious teachers and moral philosophers. Whether either is a separate form of motivation, independent of and irreducible to egoism, is not yet clear. The research done to test the independence of empathy-induced altruism from egoism may serve as a useful model for future research assessing the independent status of collectivism and principlism.

We know more now than a few years ago about why people help others. As a result, we know more about human motivation, and even about human nature. These are substantial gains. Still, many questions remain about the motivational resources we can tap in trying to build a more caring, humane society. Fortunately, the legacy from Lewin – both his rich conceptual framework for understanding motivation and his use of laboratory experiments to isolate and identify complex social motives – places social psychologists in an ideal situation to provide further answers. A lot may rest on their ability to marshal these resources and deliver.

### SUMMARY

Social-psychological research has documented a long list of self-benefits that can serve as the ultimate goal of helping behavior. The list includes material, social, and self-rewards obtained; material, social, and self-punishments avoided; and the reduction of aversive arousal. Social-psychological research has also tested the claim that feeling empathy for a person in need produces altruistic motivation to help that person – motivation with the ultimate goal of increasing that person's welfare – that is independent of and irreducible to self-interested, egoistic motivation. Results of the over thirty experiments designed to test this claim have proved remarkably supportive. Sources of altruistic motivation other than empathy have been proposed, but, as yet, there is not compelling research evidence to support these proposals.

*(Continued)*

*(Continued)*

Two additional forms of prosocial motivation also seem worthy of consideration. Collectivism – motivation with the ultimate goal of benefiting some group or collective as a whole – has been claimed to result from group identity and to account for prosocial responses to social dilemmas. Principlism – motivation with the ultimate goal of upholding some moral principle – has long been advocated by religious teachers and moral philosophers. Whether either of these motives is independent of and irreducible to egoism is not yet clear.

## References


Alexander, R.D. (1987) *The Biology of Moral Systems.* New York: Aldine de Gruyter.

Aron, A. and Aron, E.N. (1986) *Love and the Expansion of Self: Understanding Attraction and Satisfaction.* Washington, DC: Hemisphere.

Axelrod, R. (1984) *The Evolution of Cooperation.* New York: Basic Books.

Bandura, A. (1977) *Social Learning Theory.* Englewood Cliffs, NJ: Prentice-Hall.

Bandura, A. (1991) 'Social Cognitive Theory of Moral Thought and Action', in W.M. Kurtines and W.M. Gewirtz (eds), *Handbook of Moral Behavior and Development.* (vol. 1). *Theory.* Hillsdale, NJ: Erlbaum, pp. 45–103.

Batson, C.D. (1987) 'Prosocial Motivation: Is It Ever Truly Altruistic?', in L. Berkowitz (ed.), *Advances in Experimental Social Psychology* (vol. 20). New York: Academic Press, pp. 65–122.

Batson, C.D. (1991) *The Altruism Question: Toward a Social-Psychological Answer.* Hillsdale, NJ: Erlbaum.

Batson, C.D. (1994) 'Why Act for the Public Good?: Four Answers', *Personality and Social Psychology Bulletin,* 20: 603–10.

Batson, C.D. (1995) 'Prosocial Motivation: Why Do We Help Others?', in A. Tesser (ed.), *Advanced Social Psychology.* New York: McGraw-Hill, pp. 333–81.

Batson, C.D. (1998) 'Altruism and Prosocial Behavior', in D.T. Gilbert, S.T. Fiske, and G. Lindzey (eds), *The Handbook of Social Psychology*, 4th edn (vol. 2). Boston, MA: McGraw-Hill, pp. 282–316.

Batson, C.D. and Ahmad, N. (2001) 'Empathy-Induced Altruism in a Prisoner's Dilemma II: What If the Target of Empathy Has Defected?', *European Journal of Social Psychology*, 31: 25–36.

Batson, C.D., Ahmad, N., Yin, J., Bedell, S.J., Johnson, J.W., Templin, C.M., and Whiteside, A. (1999a) 'Two Threats to the Common Good: Self-Interested Egoism and Empathy-Induced Altruism', *Personality and Social Psychology Bulletin*, 25: 3–16.

Batson, C.D., Batson, J.G., Griffitt, C.A., Barrientos, S., Brandt, J.R., Sprengelmeyer, P., and Bayly, M.J. (1989) 'Negative-State Relief and the Empathy-Altruism Hypothesis', *Journal of Personality and Social Psychology*, 56: 922–33.

Batson, C.D., Batson, J.G., Slingsby, J.K., Harrell, K.L., Peekna, H.M., and Todd, R.M. (1991) 'Empathic Joy and the Empathy-Altruism Hypothesis', *Journal of Personality and Social Psychology*, 61: 413–26.

Batson, C.D., Batson, J.G., Todd, R.M., Brummett, B.H., Shaw, L.L., and Aldeguer, C.M.R. (1995a) 'Empathy and the Collective Good: Caring for One of the Others in a Social Dilemma', *Journal of Personality and Social Psychology*, 68: 619–31.

Batson, C.D., Bolen, M.H., Cross, J.A., and Neuringer-Benefiel, H.E. (1986) 'Where Is the Altruism in the Altruistic Personality?', *Journal of Personality and Social Psychology*, 50: 212–20.

Batson, C.D., Chang, J., Orr, R. and Rowland, J. (2002a) 'Empathy, Attitudes, and Action: Can Feeling for a Member of a Stigmatized Group Motivate One to Help the Group?', *Personality and Social Psychology Bulletin*, 28: 1656–66.

Batson, C.D., Coke, J.S., Jasnoski, M.L., and Hanson, M. (1978) 'Buying Kindness: Effect of an Extrinsic Incentive for Helping on Perceived Altruism', *Personality and Social Psychology Bulletin*, 4: 86–91.

Batson, C.D., Dyck, J.L., Brandt, J.R., Batson, J.G., Powell, A.L., Mcmaster, M.R., and Griffitt, C. (1988) 'Five Studies Testing Two New Egoistic Alternatives to the Empathy-Altruism Hypothesis', *Journal of Personality and Social Psychology*, 55: 52–77.

Batson, C.D., Fultz, J., Schoenrade, P.A., and Paduano, A. (1987) 'Critical Self-Reflection and Self-Perceived Altruism: When Self-Reward Fails', *Journal of Personality and Social Psychology*, 53: 594–602.

Batson, C.D., Klein, T.R., Highberger, L., and Shaw, L.L. (1995b) 'Immorality from Empathy-Induced Altruism: When Compassion and Justice Conflict', *Journal of Personality and Social Psychology*, 68: 1042–54.

Batson, C.D., Kobrynowicz, D., Dinnerstein, J.L., Kampf, H.C., and Wilson, A.D. (1997a) 'In a Very Different Voice: Unmasking Moral Hypocrisy', *Journal of Personality and Social Psychology*, 72: 1335–48.

Batson, C.D. and Moran, T. (1999) 'Empathy-Induced Altruism in a Prisoner's Dilemma', *European Journal of Social Psychology*, 29: 909–24.

Batson, C.D., Polycarpou, M.P., Harmon-Jones, E., Imhoff, H.J., Mitchener, E.C., Bednar, L.L., Klein, T.R., and Highberger, L. (1997b) 'Empathy and Attitudes: Can Feeling for a Member of a Stigmatized Group

Improve Feelings toward the Group?', *Journal of Personality and Social Psychology*, 72: 105–18.

Batson, C.D., Sager, K., Garst, E., Kang, M., Rubchinsky, K., and Dawson, K. (1997c) 'Is Empathy-Induced Helping Due to Self–Other Merging?', *Journal of Personality and Social Psychology*, 73: 495–509.

Batson, C.D. and Shaw, L.L. (1991) 'Evidence for Altruism: Toward a Pluralism of Prosocial Motives', *Psychological Inquiry*, 2: 107–22.

Batson, C.D., Thompson, E.R., and Chen, H. (2002b) 'Moral Hypocrisy: Addressing Some Alternatives', *Journal of Personality and Social Psychology*, 83: 330–9.

Batson, C.D., Thompson, E.R., Seuferling, G., Whitney, H., and Strongman, J. (1999b) 'Moral Hypocrisy: Appearing Moral to Oneself without Being So', *Journal of Personality and Social Psychology*, 77: 525–37.

Batson, C.D., Turk, C.L., Shaw, L.L., and Klein, T.R. (1995c) 'Information Function of Empathic Emotion: Learning that We Value the Other's Welfare', *Journal of Personality and Social Psychology*, 68: 300–13.

Batson, C.D. and Weeks, J.L. (1996) 'Mood Effects of Unsuccessful Helping: Another Test of the Empathy-Altruism Hypothesis', *Personality and Social Psychology Bulletin*, 22: 148–57.

Bell, D.C. (2001) 'Evolution of Parental Caregiving', *Personality and Social Psychology Review*, 5: 216–29.

Berkowitz, L. (1972) 'Social Norms, Feelings, and Other Factors Affecting Helping and Altruism', in L. Berkowitz (ed.), *Advances in Experimental Social Psychology* (vol. 6). New York: Academic Press, pp. 63–108.

Berkowitz, L. (1987) 'Mood, Self-Awareness, and Willingness to Help', *Journal of Personality and Social Psychology*, 52: 721–9.

Bersoff, D.M. (1999) 'Why Good People Sometimes Do Bad Things: Motivated Reasoning and Unethical Behavior', *Personality and Social Psychology Bulletin*, 25: 28–39.

Blader, S.L. and Tyler, T.R. (2002) 'Justice and Empathy: What Motivates People to Help Others?', in M. Ross and D.T. Miller (eds), *The Justice Motive in Everyday Life*. New York: Cambridge University Press, pp. 226–50.

Brewer, M.B. and Kramer, R.M. (1986) 'Choice Behavior in Social Dilemmas: Effects of Social Identity, Group Size, and Decision Framing', *Journal of Personality and Social Psychology*, 50: 543–9.

Campbell, D.T. (1975) 'On the Conflicts Between Biological and Social Evolution and Between Psychology and Moral Tradition', *American Psychologist*, 30: 1103–26.

Carlo, G., Eisenberg, N., Troyer, D., Switzer, G., and Speer, A.L. (1991) 'The Altruistic Personality: In What Contexts Is It Apparent?', *Journal of Personality and Social Psychology*, 61: 450–8.

Cialdini, R.B., Brown, S.L., Lewis, B.P., Luce, C., and Neuberg, S.L. (1997) 'Reinterpreting the Empathy-Altruism Relationship: When One into One Equals Oneness', *Journal of Personality and Social Psychology*, 73: 481–94.

Cialdini, R.B., Darby, B.L., and Vincent, J.E. (1973) 'Transgression and Altruism: A Case for Hedonism', *Journal of Experimental Social Psychology*, 9: 502–16.

Cialdini, R.B., Kallgren, C.A., and Reno, R.R. (1991) 'A Focus Theory of Normative Conduct: A Theoretical Refinement and Reevaluation of the Role of Norms in Human Behavior', in M.P. Zanna (ed.), *Advances in Experimental Social Psychology* (vol. 24). Orlando, FL: Academic Press, pp. 201–34.

Cialdini, R.B., Schaller, M., Houlihan, D., Arps, K., Fultz, J., and Beaman, A.L. (1987) 'Empathy-Based Helping: Is it Selflessly or Selfishly Motivated?', *Journal of Personality and Social Psychology*, 52: 749–58.

Clark, M.S. and Waddell, B.A. (1983) 'Effect of Moods on Thoughts about Helping, Attraction, and Information Acquisition', *Social Psychology Quarterly*, 46: 31–5.

Coke, J.S., Batson, C.D., and McDavis, K. (1978) 'Empathic Mediation of Helping: A Two-Stage Model', *Journal of Personality and Social Psychology*, 36: 752–66.

Cunningham, M.R., Shaffer, D.R., Barbee, A.P., Wolff, P.L., and Kelley, D.J. (1990) 'Separate Processes in the Relation of Elation and Depression to Helping: Social versus Personal Concerns', *Journal of Experimental Social Psychology*, 26: 13–33.

Darley, J.M. and Latané, B. (1968) 'Bystander Intervention in Emergencies: Diffusion of Responsibility', *Journal of Personality and Social Psychology*, 10: 202–14.

Darley, J.M. and Latané, B. (1970) 'Norms and Normative Behavior: Field Studies of Social Interdependence', in J. Macaulay and L. Berkowitz (eds), *Altruism and Helping Behavior*. New York: Academic Press, pp. 83–101.

Dawes, R.M. (1980) 'Social Dilemmas', *Annual Review of Psychology*, 31: 169–93.

Dawes, R., Van De Kragt, A.J.C., and Orbell, J.M. (1988) 'Not Me or Thee but We: The Importance of Group Identity in Eliciting Cooperation in Dilemma Situations: Experimental Manipulations', *Acta Psychological*, 68: 83–97.

Dawes, R., van de Kragt, A.J.C., and Orbell, J.M. (1990) 'Cooperation for the Benefit of Us – Not Me, or My Conscience', in J.J. Mansbridge (ed.), *Beyond Self-Interest*. Chicago, IL: University of Chicago Press, pp. 97–110.

de Waal, F. (1996) *Good Natured: The Origins of Rights and Wrongs in Humans and Other Animals*. Cambridge, MA: Harvard University Press.

Dollard, J. and Miller, N.E. (1950) *Personality and Psychotherapy*. New York: McGraw-Hill.

Dovidio, J.F., Allen, J.L., and Schroeder, D.A. (1990) 'The Specificity of Empathy-Induced Helping: Evidence for Altruistic Motivation', *Journal of Personality and Social Psychology*, 59: 249–60.

Dovidio, J.F. and Gaertner, S.L., and Johnson, J.D. (1999, October) 'New Directions in Prejudice and Prejudice

Reduction: The Role of Cognitive Representations and Affect'. Paper presented at the annual meeting of the Society of Experimental Social Psychology, St Louis.

Dovidio, J.F., Piliavin, J.A., Gaertner, S.L., Schroeder, D.A., and Clark, R.D., III (1991) 'The Arousal:Cost-Reward Model and the Process of Intervention: A Review of the Evidence', in M.S. Clark (ed.), *Prosocial Behavior.* Newbury Park, CA: Sage, pp. 86–118.

Eisenberg, N. and Miller, P. (1987) 'Empathy and Prosocial Behavior', *Psychological Bulletin*, 101: 91–119.

Eisenberg, N., Miller, P.A., Schaller, M., Fabes, R.A., Fultz, J., Shell, R., and Shea, C.L. (1989) 'The Role of Sympathy and Altruistic Personality Traits in Helping: A Re-Examination', *Journal of Personality*, 57: 41–67.

Fazio, R.H. (1990) 'Multiple Processes by Which Attitudes Guide Behavior: The MODE Model as an Integrative Framework', in M.P. Zanna (ed.), *Advances in Experimental Social Psychology* (vol. 23). San Diego, CA: Academic Press, pp. 75–109.

Festinger, L. (1957) *A Theory of Cognitive Dissonance*. Stanford, CA: Stanford University Press.

Frank, R.H. (1988) *Passions within Reason: The Strategic Role of the Emotions*. New York: W.W. Norton.

Freud, S. (1930) *Civilization and Its Discontents* (J. Riviere, trans.). London: Hogarth.

Gergen, K.J., Ellsworth, P., Maslach, C., and Seipel, M. (1975) 'Obligation, Donor Resources, and Reactions to Aid in 3 Cultures', *Journal of Personality and Social Psychology*, 31: 390–400.

Gibbons, F.X. and Wicklund, R.A. (1982) 'Self-Focused Attention and Helping Behavior', *Journal of Personality and Social Psychology*, 43: 462–74.

Gies, M. (1987) *Anne Frank Remembered: The Story of the Woman who Helped to Hide the Frank Family*. New York: Simon & Schuster.

Gilligan, C. (1982) *In a Different Voice: Psychological Theory and Women's Development*. Cambridge, MA: Harvard University Press.

Gouldner, A.W. (1960) 'The Norm of Reciprocity: A Preliminary Statement', *American Sociological Review*, 25: 161–79.

Hafer, C.L. (2000) 'Do Innocent Victims Threaten the Belief in a Just World? Evidence from a Modified Stroop Task', *Journal of Personality and Social Psychology*, 79: 165–73.

Hardin, G. (1977) *The Limits of Altruism: An Ecologist's View of Survival*. Bloomington, IN: Indiana University Press.

Hoffman, M.L. (1975) 'Developmental Synthesis of Affect and Cognition and Its Implications for Altruistic Motivation', *Developmental Psychology*, 11: 607–22.

Hoffman, M.L. (1981) 'Is Altruism Part of Human Nature?', *Journal of Personality and Social Psychology*, 40: 121–37.

Hornstein, H.A. (1982) 'Promotive Tension: Theory and Research', in V. Derlega and J. Grzelak (eds), *Cooperation and Helping Behavior: Theories and Research.* New York: Academic Press, pp. 229–48.

Isen, A.M. (1970) 'Success, Failure, Attention and Reaction to Others: The Warm Glow of Success', *Journal of Personality and Social Psychology*, 15: 294–301.

Isen, A.M. (1987) 'Positive Affect, Cognitive Organization, and Social Behavior', in L. Berkowitz (ed.), *Advances in Experimental Social Psychology* (vol. 20). New York: Academic Press, pp. 203–53.

Isen, A.M. and Levin, P.F. (1972) 'Effect of Feeling Good on Helping: Cookies and Kindness', *Journal of Personality and Social Psychology*, 21: 344–8.

Isen, A.M., Shalker, T.E., Clark, M., and Karp, L. (1978) 'Affect, Accessibility of Material in Memory, and Behavior: A Cognitive Loop?', *Journal of Personality and Social Psychology*, 36: 1–13.

James, W. (1910/1982) 'The Moral Equivalent of War', in F.H. Burkhardt (ed.), *The Works of William James: Essays in Religion and Morality.* Cambridge, MA: Harvard University Press, pp. 162–73.

Jarymowicz, M. (1992) 'Self, We, and Other(s): Schemata, Distinctiveness, and Altruism', in P.M. Oliner, S.P. Oliner, L. Baron, L.A. Blum, D.L. Krebs, and M.Z. Smolenska (eds), *Embracing the Other: Philosophical, Psychological, and Historical Perspectives on Altruism.* New York: New York University Press, pp. 194–212.

Jones, E.E. (1964) *Ingratiation*. New York: Appleton-Century-Crofts.

Kant, I. (1889) *Kant's Critique of Practical Reason and Other Works on the Theory of Ethics*, 4th edn (T.K. Abbott, trans.). New York: Longmans, Green (original work published 1785).

Kohlberg, L. (1976) 'Moral Stages and Moralization: The Cognitive-Developmental Approach', in T. Lickona (ed.), *Moral Development and Behavior: Theory, Research, and Social Issues*. New York: Holt, Rinehart, & Winston, pp. 31–53.

Komorita, S.S. and Parks, C.D. (1995) 'Interpersonal Relations: Mixed-Motive Interaction', *Annual Review of Psychology*, 46: 183–207.

Kozol, J. (1991) *Savage Inequalities: Children in America's Schools*. New York: Crown.

Krebs, D.L. (1975) 'Empathy and Altruism', *Journal of Personality and Social Psychology*, 32: 1134–46.

La Rochefoucauld, F., duc de (1691) *Moral Maxims and Reflections, in Four Parts*. London: Gillyflower, Sare & Everyingham.

Latané, B. and Darley, J.M. (1968) 'Group Inhibition of Bystander Intervention', *Journal of Personality and Social Psychology*, 10: 215–21.

Latané, B. and Darley, J.M. (1970) *The Unresponsive Bystander: Why Doesn't He Help*? New York: Appleton-Century-Crofts.

Latané, B. and Nida, S.A. (1981) 'Ten Years of Research on Group Size and Helping', *Psychological Bulletin*, 89: 308–24.

Latané, B. and Rodin, J.A. (1969) 'A Lady in Distress: Inhibiting Effects of Friends and Strangers on

Bystander Intervention', *Journal of Experimental Social Psychology*, 5: 189–202.

Lerner, M.J. (1980) *The Belief in a Just World: A Fundamental Delusion*. New York: Plenum.

Lerner, M.J. (1982) 'The Justice Motive in Human Relations and the Economic Model of Man: A Radical Analysis of Facts and Fictions', in V.J. Derlega and J. Grzelak (eds), *Cooperation and Helping Behavior: Theories and Research.* New York: Academic Press, pp. 249–78.

Lerner, M.J. and Simmons, C.H. (1966) 'Observer's Reaction to the "Innocent Victim": Compassion or Rejection?', *Journal of Personality and Social Psychology*, 4: 203–10.

Lewin, K. (1951) *Field Theory in Social Science*. New York: Harper.

Maclean, P.D. (1973) *A Triune Concept of the Brain and Behavior*. Toronto: University of Toronto Press.

Mcclintock, C.G. and Liebrand, W.B.G. (1988) 'The Role of Interdependence Structure, Individual Value Orientation and Other's Strategy in Social Decision Making: A Transformational Analysis', *Journal of Personality and Social Psychology*, 55: 396–409.

McDougall, W. (1908) *An Introduction to Social Psychology*. London: Methuen.

MacIntyre, A. (1967) 'Egoism and Altruism', in P. Edwards (ed.), *The Encyclopedia of Philosophy* (vol. 2). New York: Macmillan, pp. 462–6.

Mansbridge, J.J. (ed.) (1990) *Beyond Self-Interest*. Chicago, IL: University of Chicago Press.

Maslach, C. (1982) *Burnout: The Cost of Caring*. Englewood Cliffs, NJ: Prentice-Hall.

Milinski, M., Semmann, D., and Krambeck, H.-J. (2002) 'Reputation Helps Solve the "Tragedy of the Commons"', *Nature*, 415: 424–6.

Miller, D.T. (1999) 'The Norm of Self-Interest', *American Psychologist*, 54: 1053–60.

Miller, D.T. and McFarland, C. (1987) 'Pluralistic Ignorance: When Similarity Is Interpreted as Dissimilarity', *Journal of Personality and Social Psychology*, 53: 298–305.

Miller, D.T. and Ratner, R.K. (1998) 'The Disparity between the Actual and Assumed Power of Self-Interest', *Journal of Personality and Social Psychology*, 74: 53–62.

Mills, J. and Egger, R. (1972) 'Effect on Derogation of a Victim of Choosing to Reduce His Stress', *Journal of Personality and Social Psychology*, 23: 405–8.

Milo, R.D. (ed.) (1973) *Egoism and Altruism*. Belmont, CA: Wadsworth.

Nagel, T. (1970) *The Possibility of Altruism*. Princeton, NJ: Princeton University Press.

Nowak, M.A. and Sigmund, K. (1998) 'Evolution of Indirect Reciprocity by Image Scoring', *Nature*, 393: 573–7.

Oliner, S.P. and Oliner, P.M. (1988) *The Altruistic Personality: Rescuers of Jews in Nazi Europe*. New York: Free Press.

Piliavin, J.A. and Charng, H.-W. (1990) 'Altruism: A Review of Recent Theory and Research', *American Sociological Review*, 16: 27–65.

Piliavin, J.A., Dovidio, J.F., Gaertner, S.L., and Clark, R.D., III (1981) *Emergency Intervention*. New York: Academic Press.

Preston, S.D. and de Waal, F.B.M. (2002) 'Empathy: Its Ultimate and Proximate Bases', *Behavioral and Brain Sciences*, 25: 1–72.

Pruitt, D.G. (1968) 'Reciprocity and Credit Building in a Laboratory Dyad', *Journal of Personality and Social Psychology*, 8: 143–7.

Ratner, R.K. and Miller, D.T. (2001) 'The Norm of Self-Interest and Its Effects on Social Action', *Journal of Personality and Social Psychology*, 81: 5–16.

Rawls, J. (1971) *A Theory of Justice*. Cambridge, MA: Harvard University Press.

Reykowski, J. (1982) 'Motivation of Prosocial Behavior', in V.J. Derlega and J. Grzelak (eds), *Cooperation and Helping Behavior: Theories and Research*. New York: Academic Press, pp. 352–75.

Ryan, W. (1971) *Blaming the Victim*. New York: Random House.

Schaller, M. and Cialdini, R.B. (1988) 'The Economics of Empathic Helping: Support for a Mood-Management Motive', *Journal of Experimental Social Psychology*, 24: 163–81.

Schroeder, D.A., Dovidio, J.F., Sibicky, M.E., Matthews, L.L., and Allen, J.L. (1988) 'Empathy and Helping Behavior: Egoism or Altruism?', *Journal of Experimental Social Psychology*, 24: 333–53.

Schroeder, D.A., Penner, L.A., Dovidio, J.F., and Piliavin, J.A. (1995) *The Psychology of Helping and Altruism: Problems and Puzzles*. New York: McGraw-Hill.

Schwartz, S.H. (1977) 'Normative Influences on Altruism', in L. Berkowitz (ed.), *Advances in Experimental Social Psychology* (vol. 10). New York: Academic Press, pp. 221–79.

Schwartz, S.H. (1992) 'Universals in the Content and Structure of Values: Theoretical Advances and Empirical Tests in 20 Countries', in M.P. Zanna (ed.), *Advances in Experimental Social Psychology* (vol. 25). San Diego, CA: Academic Press, pp. 1–65.

Shaw, L.L., Batson, C.D., and Todd, R.M. (1994) 'Empathy Avoidance: Forestalling Feeling for Another in Order to Escape the Motivational Consequences', *Journal of Personality and Social Psychology*, 67: 879–87.

Shelton, M.L. and Rogers, R.W. (1981) 'Fear-Arousing and Empathy-Arousing Appeals to Help: The Pathos of Persuasion', *Journal of Applied Social Psychology*, 11: 366–78.

Smith, K.D., Keating, J.P., and Stotland, E. (1989) 'Altruism Reconsidered: The Effect of Denying Feedback on a Victim's Status to Empathic Witnesses', *Journal of Personality and Social Psychology*, 57: 641–50.

Sober, E. and Wilson, D.S. (1998) *Unto Others: The Evolution and Psychology of Unselfish Behavior.* Cambridge, MA: Harvard University Press.

Staub, E. (1974) 'Helping a Distressed Person: Social, Personality, and Stimulus Determinants', in

L. Berkowitz (ed.), *Advances in Experimental Social Psychology* (vol. 7). New York: Academic Press, pp. 293–341.

Staub, E. (1989) 'Individual and Societal (Group) Values in a Motivational Perspective and Their Role in Benevolence and Harmdoing', in N. Eisenberg, J. Reykowski, and E. Staub (eds), *Social and Moral Values: Individual and Societal Perspectives*. Hillsdale, NJ: Erlbaum, pp. 45–61.

Staub, E. (1990) 'Moral Exclusion, Personal Goal Theory, and Extreme Destructiveness', *Journal of Social Issues*, 46 (1): 47–64.

Stephan, W.G. and Finlay, K. (1999) 'The Role of Empathy in Improving Intergroup Relations', *Journal of Social Issues*, 55: 729–43.

Stotland, E. (1969) 'Exploratory Investigations of Empathy', in L. Berkowitz (ed.), *Advances in Experimental Social Psychology* (vol. 4). New York: Academic Press, pp. 271–313.

Stotland, E., Mathews, K.E., Sherman, S.E., Hansson, R.O., and Richardson, B.Z. (1978) *Empathy, Fantasy, and Helping*. Beverly Hills, CA: Sage.

Stukas, A.A., Snyder, M., and Clary, E.G. (1999) 'The Effects of "Mandatory Volunteerism" on Intentions to Volunteer', *Psychological Science*, 10: 59–64.

Tajfel, H. (1981) *Human Groups and Social Categories: Studies in Social Psychology*. Cambridge: Cambridge University Press.

Tolman, E.C. (1923) 'The Nature of Instinct', *Psychological Bulletin*, 20: 200–18.

Tomasello, M. (1999) *The Cultural Origins of Human Cognition*. Cambridge, MA: Harvard University Press.

Trivers, R.L. (1971) 'The Evolution of Reciprocal Altruism', *Quarterly Review of Biology*, 46: 35–57.

Turner, J.C. (1987) *Rediscovering the Social Group: A Self-Categorization Theory*. London: Basil Blackwell.

van Lange, P.A.M. (1999) 'The Pursuit of Joint Outcomes and Equality in Outcomes: An Integrative Model of Social Value Orientation', *Journal of Personality and Social Psychology*, 77: 337–49.

van Lange, P.A.M., Otten, W., De Bruin, E.M.N., and Joireman, J.A. (1997) 'Development of Prosocial, Individualistic, and Competitive Orientations: Theory and Preliminary Evidence', *Journal of Personality and Social Psychology*, 73: 733–46.

Wallach, M.A. and Wallach, L. (1983) *Psychology's Sanction for Selfishness: The Error of Egoism in Theory and Therapy*. San Francisco, CA: W.H. Freeman.

Wegener, D.T. and Petty, R.E. (1994) 'Mood Management across Affective States: The Hedonic Contingency Hypothesis', *Journal of Personality and Social Psychology*, 66: 1034–48.

Wilke, H. and Lanzetta, J.T. (1970) 'The Obligation to Help: The Effects of Amount of Prior Help on Subsequent Helping Behavior', *Journal of Experimental Social Psychology*, 6: 483–93.

Wispé, L. (1986) 'The Distinction between Sympathy and Empathy: To Call Forth a Concept a Word Is Needed', *Journal of Personality and Social Psychology*, 50: 314–21.

Yamagishi, T. (1986) 'The Provision of a Sanctioning System as a Public Good', *Journal of Personality and Social Psychology*, 51: 110–16.

Zahn-Waxler, C. and Radke-Yarrow, M. (1990) 'The Origins of Empathic Concern', *Motivation and Emotion*, 14: 107–30.

Zuckerman, M. (1975) 'Belief in a Just World and Altruistic Behavior', *Journal of Personality and Social Psychology*, 31: 972–6.

Zuckerman, M. and Reis, H.T. (1978) 'Comparison of Three Models for Predicting Altruistic Behavior', *Journal of Personality and Social Psychology*, 36: 498–510.

# 12
# Human Aggression: A Social-Cognitive View

CRAIG A. ANDERSON AND L. ROWELL HUESMANN

**INTRODUCTION**

That the modern social world is a violent place is obvious from a glance at any major news source on the web, television, or print media. War in the Middle East and Africa, terrorist bombings, torture, murder, rape, school shootings, and other acts of human aggression are a constant reminder of just how badly we humans sometimes treat each other. This chapter uses a simple yet powerful theory to understand the development and prevalence of modern human aggression. It also suggests how we can change factors underlying different types of human aggression, to reduce their frequency and severity.

Aggressive and violent behavior by one human being toward another is not a new phenomenon. It was prevalent among our hunter/gatherer ancestors 25,000 years ago, among the Greek, Egyptian, and Roman societies 2,000 to 3,000 years ago, among most societies in the past two centuries, and in almost every society today. Periodically, events such as the Holocaust, the Columbine, Colorado school shootings; or the terrorist attack on the World Trade Center on September 11, 2001 make people wonder 'what the world is coming to'; but although technology has made mass violence easier to accomplish, it is doubtful that people are more prone to be violent today than thousands of years ago. In fact, the portion of the world's population who behave violently today is probably lower than in most previous times. Nevertheless, the prevalence of aggressive and violent behavior today is sufficient to make it a social problem worthy of attention around the world.

## Recent trends

### *Frequency of violence*

Measuring societal rates of violence is fraught with difficulties because politics affects definitions and reporting of violence and crime. Homicide rates are usually considered the best measure of societal violence because they are the hardest to distort or hide. Historically, rates of serious interpersonal violence within societies rise and fall over short periods as a function of socioeconomic, demographic, and other factors. For example, the past 100 years of homicide rates in the USA are shown in Figure 12.1 (US Department of Justice, 2001). Rates were highest during the Depression and in the 1980s and early 1990s, and have declined substantially in recent years. Nevertheless, 6.5 homicides per 100,000 people is a serious social problem. Furthermore, though the overall homicide rate has dropped significantly since 1994 (due largely to decreased gun homicides), the assault rate among American youth has steadily remained at unacceptably high levels (Surgeon General, 2001).

### *Cross-national comparisons*

Figure 12.2 displays the 1995 homicide rates for a variety of countries and regions (Maguire and Pastore, 2001). As has been true for most of the past fifty years, the USA has less violence than less developed countries undergoing radical socioeconomic changes, but more homicides than most

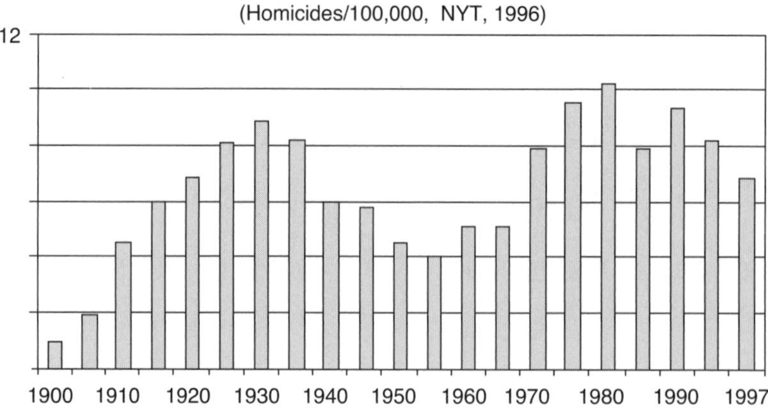


Figure 12.1 A century of murder

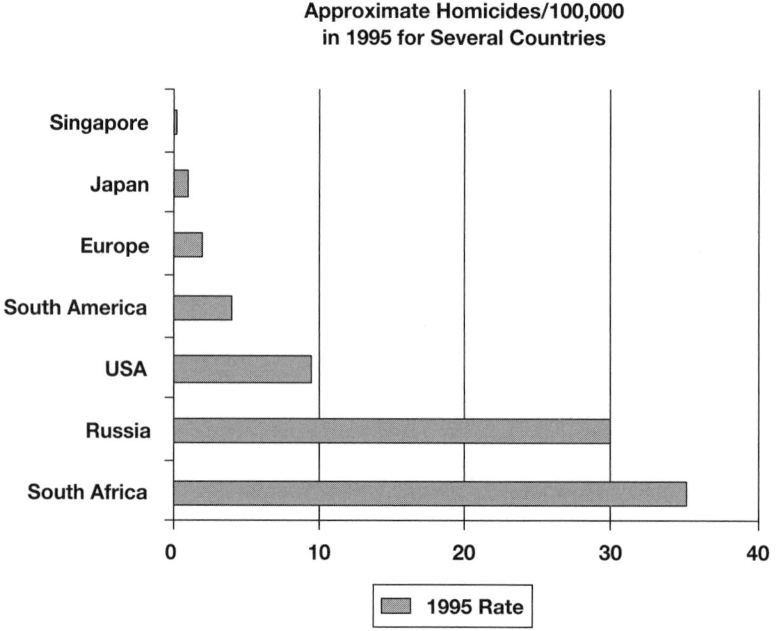


Figure 12.2 Homicide rates in 1995 in selected countries

stable developed countries. However, the picture changes if one considers other measures of violent behavior. Victimization surveys, in which randomly selected representative samples of the population are interviewed, are better measures of nonhomicide types of violence. Rates of aggression and violence reported in victimization surveys are higher than 'officially reported rates' because the political and personal filters are removed from the reporting. For example, in 1991, there were 732 violent crimes per 100,000 population in the USA according to the FBI's Uniform Crime Reports but 2,415 violent crimes per 100,000 population according to the US Department of Justice's (1992) national victimization survey. Few other countries regularly conduct comparable victimization surveys, but they have been done in the UK. These surveys show that, contrary to popular belief, on average, the UK is now more dangerous than the USA. Overall violent crime rates (excluding homicide) are higher in the UK than in the USA (Farrington, 1999) for every violent crime except homicide, which are probably higher in the USA simply because of the easier availability of guns.

### *Multidisciplinarity of research*

The study of aggressive and violent social behavior has attracted a diverse set of researchers. Although our focus is on social psychological theory and research, it would be a mistake to ignore important studies and theories from criminology, psychiatry, biology, and other branches of psychology. Furthermore, we believe that one cannot understand the social psychology of aggressive behavior without placing it in a developmental context of differing social-cognitive processes at different ages (Coie and Dodge, 1998). Aggressive behavior occurs in adults and children, but in different manifestations. An important task in understanding the social psychology of aggression is mapping the relations between adulthood and childhood aggression.

Nonetheless, like most social psychologists, we believe it is valuable to conceive of aggressive behavior (and most human characteristics) as occurring on a continuum. In this chapter, we avoid the less fruitful tendencies of some clinical, psychiatric, and criminological researchers to study aggressive behavior mostly in terms of categories of individuals (for example, conduct disordered or not, aggressive or not, violent or not), or overly restrictive definitions of aggressive behavior (for example, counting only violent crimes as aggression).

## Types of aggression

Scholars from different fields and different eras use different definitions of key concepts. In this section, we identify some key distinctions and recent changes.

### *Aggression versus violence*

Like most psychologists, we define human aggression as *behavior directed toward another individual carried out with the proximate (immediate) intent to cause harm*. Furthermore, the perpetrator must believe that the behavior will harm the target and that the target is motivated to avoid the behavior. Actual harm is not required. (For detailed discussions, see Baron and Richardson, 1994; Berkowitz, 1993; Bushman and Anderson, 2001; Geen, 2001.)

Violence is physical aggression at the extremely high end of the aggression continuum, such as murder and aggravated assault. All violence is aggression, but much aggression is not violence. For example, one child pushing another off a tricycle is aggression, but is not violence. A school shooting is both aggression and violence. Some criminologists and public-health officials use quite different definitions of violence and seem largely uninterested in aggression or the aggression–violence continuum (Surgeon General, 2001). For some, 'violence' requires actual serious physical harm to another person and it must be illegal. Such a definition may be valuable for epidemiological purposes, but for understanding the processes underlying the behavior it is inferior to the social-psychological definition.

### *Physical, verbal, direct, and indirect aggression*

The difference between physical and verbal aggression is obvious. Less obvious is the distinction between direct and indirect aggression that emerged in the late 1980s (Lagerspetz et al., 1988).[1] Indirect aggression is committed outside the presence of the target, such as telling stories and lies behind someone's back to get them in trouble or taking a person's things when they are not there. Direct aggression is committed in the presence of the target. Substantial evidence suggests that females are more likely to engage in indirect forms of aggression, males are more likely to engage in direct physical aggression, and both genders are about equally likely to engage in verbal aggression (Bjorkqvist et al., 1992; Crick and Grotpeter, 1995; Lagerspetz et al., 1988; Lagerspetz and Bjorkqvist, 1992).

### *Dimensions versus categories of aggression*

Traditional discussions of aggression draw a series of dichotomous distinctions between types of aggression. The main dichotomies are affective versus instrumental, impulsive versus premeditated, and proactive versus reactive. These dichotomies are typically conceived in overlapping ways, leading to some confusion. *Affective aggression* (also labeled 'hostile' [Feshbach, 1964], or 'emotional' [Berkowitz, 1993]) is usually conceived as impulsive, thoughtless (that is, unplanned), driven by anger, having the ultimate motive of harming the target, and occurring in reaction to some perceived provocation. *Instrumental aggression*, in contrast, is usually conceived as a premeditated means of obtaining some goal other than harming the victim, being proactive rather than reactive, and resulting from cold calculation rather than hot affect. *Impulsive aggression* is usually conceived as thoughtless (automatic, fast, and without consideration of consequences), reactive, and affect laden. *Premeditated aggression*, in contrast, is usually conceived as thoughtful (deliberative, slow, and instrumental), proactive, and affect-less. Proactive and reactive aggression are frequently used interchangeably with instrumental and affective, but they have slightly different emphases. *Proactive aggression* is usually conceived as occurring without provocation, is thoughtful, and has little or no affect. *Reactive aggression* is a response to a prior

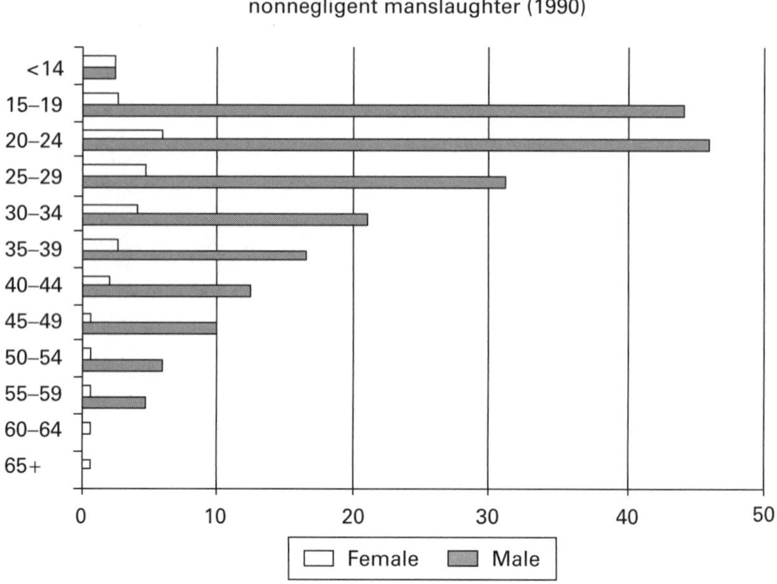


Figure 12.3 Arrest rates for homicide in the USA in 1990

provocation and usually is accompanied by anger (Dodge and Coie, 1987; Pulkkinen, 1996).

When taken too literally, these dichotomies create many conceptual and empirical problems. Apparently instrumental aggression can also contain much hostile affect; some angry outbursts appear to be coldly calculated, some proactive aggression has a distinctly emotional aspect, and instrumental considerations of potential consequences can be made both automatically and without awareness (Anderson and Bushman, 2002a; Bushman and Anderson, 2001). For example, frequent use of aggression to obtain valued goals can become so automated or habitual that it becomes impulsive (Bargh and Pietromonaco, 1982; Schneider and Shiffrin, 1977; Shiffrin and Schneider, 1977).

We believe that it is more useful explicitly to abandon strict dichotomies in favor of a dimensional approach. Any aggressive act can therefore be characterized along each of the following dimensions: degree of hostile or agitated affect present; automaticity; degree to which the primary or ultimate goal is to harm the victim versus benefit the perpetrator; and degree to which consequences were considered. (Intention to harm is still seen as a necessary *proximate* goal of all aggression.) This approach yields a clearer understanding of mixed-motive aggression, quick but consequence-sensitive aggressive acts, and other forms of aggression that have been problematic for traditional dichotomous approaches (Anderson and Bushman, 2002a; Bushman and Anderson, 2001).

### *Situation versus person causes of aggression*

One final dichotomy deserves special attention because of its prevalence throughout modern social and personality psychology as well as historical and modern theories of aggression – the distinction between *personological* and *situational* factors. Personological causes include whatever the person brings to the current situation, factors such as attitudes, beliefs, and behavioral tendencies. Situational causes are features of the present situation that increase (or inhibit) aggression, factors such as an insult, uncomfortable temperature, presence of a weapon, or presence of one's religious leader. Both types may be conceived as *proximate* causal factors, because both are present in the current situation. All social behavior, including aggression, is the result of the convergence of both types of factors. Situational factors (that is, instigators or inhibitors of aggression) and personological factors (that is, propensity or preparedness to aggress) combine in complex ways to determine what type of behavior will emerge. The right situation can provoke most people to behave aggressively, but some people are much more likely to aggress than others.

### Age and gender trends

Regardless of the particular epoch or particular country, age and gender predict the likelihood of different types of aggressive and violent behavior. Figure 12.3 presents US 1990 arrest rates for murder separately by age and gender. Males are much more likely to be violent aggressors at any age, but for both males and females the age effect is dramatic; the highest incidence of violence occurs between fifteen and thirty-five (US Department of Justice, 2001).

#### *Emergence of aggression in early childhood*

Angry affective responses revealed by facial expressions (Ekman and Friesen, 1975) are apparent in most infants before any aggressive behaviors are noticeable, as early as at four to seven months (Stenberg et al., 1983; Stenberg and Campos, 1990). However, aggressive behavior appears shortly afterwards. Provocations by other infants (such as grabbing toys) result in protest and aggressive retaliation by the age of one year (Caplan et al., 1991). Conflict physical aggression is frequent in peer interactions at ages one to three (Loeber and Hay, 1993; Shantz and Shantz, 1985; Tremblay et al., 1996), usually to obtain instrumental goals. Epidemiological studies have shown rates of about 10 percent for peer fighting problems in three-year-olds (Earls, 1980). In the preschool and early elementary years, physical aggression generally decreases while verbal aggression increases (Loeber and Hay, 1997; Tremblay, 2000). For most normal people, the age trend for physical aggression is downward after age three (Tremblay, 2000; Tremblay et al., 1996) as they are socialized out of behaving aggressively.

Some children, however, increase in aggressiveness as they age. Although the toddler years are the period of greatest aggression for most children, the most dangerous years for this subset of individuals (and for society) are late adolescence and early adulthood. Not only are these individuals behaving objectively more aggressively than at earlier ages, but at this age weapons are used more frequently, and the consequences are more severe (Cairns and Cairns, 1994; Verlinden et al., 2000).

Although these generalizations summarize the empirical data accurately, the many different ways one can assess violence and aggression allow for many deviations from this general picture. Grabbing toys, physical fighting, telling lies to get others in trouble, and taking others' things all may show different trajectories. Farrington (1993) proposed that aggressiveness can best be measured by different constructs at different ages; for example, fighting at age eight, vandalism at age twelve, and homicide at age eighteen. Huesmann et al. (1984a) propose that a latent construct of aggressiveness manifests itself in different ways at different ages. Additionally, different contexts may influence the growth of aggression quite differently. For example, Guerra et al. (1995) reported that in high-risk inner-city schools, average aggression by children increases dramatically during the first year of school. Similarly, the prevalence of a gang culture in the child's environment may radically alter the growth curve of aggressive behavior (Goldstein, 1994).

#### *Emergence of gender differences*

Gender differences in aggression are very noticeable by the preschool years (Loeber and Hay, 1997), with boys showing higher levels of physical aggression than girls. However, many girls are physically aggressive at this age, and, on average, girls show levels of verbal and indirect aggression similar to or greater than boys (Crick and Grotpeter, 1995; Rys and Bear, 1997). In later elementary grades and adolescence, gender differences increase. Indirect aggression becomes much greater for girls than boys, physical aggression becomes much greater for boys than girls, and both genders become about equally likely to engage in verbal aggression (Bjorkqvist et al., 1992; Crick and Grotpeter, 1995; Lagerspetz et al., 1988; Lagerspetz and Bjorkqvist, 1992). These gender differences culminate in dramatic differences in physically violent behavior in young adulthood, reflected by the different homicide rates shown in Figure 12.3. Nevertheless, this should not lead one to believe that females are never physically aggressive. Straus (1997) in surveys and Archer (2000) in a meta-analysis have convincingly demonstrated that in aggression between domestic partners, females are slightly *more* likely to use physical aggression against their partners than are males! Although males are more likely to inflict serious injury on their partners, females inflict 35 percent of serious injuries and 44 percent of deaths.

Laboratory studies with college students often yield higher aggression by males, but provocation apparently has a greater effect on aggression than does sex. Bettencourt and Miller's (1996) meta-analysis found that sex differences in aggression practically disappear under high provocation.

Developmental research suggests that many gender differences in aggression result both from different socialization experiences (White, 2001) and from innate physical, neurological, and hormonal differences. We discuss these innate factors in more detail below, but their obvious relevance has led to substantial evolutionary theorizing about the resons for gender differences in aggression (Campbell, 1999; Geary, 1998). For example, Geary et al. (1995)

and Buss and Shackelford (1997a, 1997b) have offered evolutionary reasons for why males are more upset by sexual infidelity of their mates than by emotional infidelity, whereas the opposite pattern occurs for females and for why males are more likely to use violent tactics to retain their mates. Additionally, Malamuth and Heilmann (1998) have proposed a comprehensive evolutionary theory for sexual aggression.

### *Continuity of aggression from childhood to adulthood*

By the preschool and early elementary years, individual differences in the propensity to behave aggressively are apparent (Eron et al., 1971; Huesmann et al., 1984a). Such early differences are highly predictive of later aggressive behavior, even for the eventual offspring of these aggressive children (Farrington, 1982, 1995, 2002; Huesmann et al., 1984a; Huesmann and Moise, 1998; Loeber and Dishion, 1983; Magnusson et al., 1975; Olweus, 1979). Continuity coefficients range from 0.76 for one year to 0.60 for ten years for both males and females (Olweus, 1979). Huesmann et al. (1984a) report twenty-two year disattenuated continuity coefficients of 0.50 for males and 0.35 for females. This is not simply a case of a few highly aggressive children remaining aggressive while others change radically. The continuity occurs all along the range of aggression (Huesmann and Moise, 1998). Of course, many aggressive children become nonviolent adults. However, it is rare for severe, habitual aggressive behavior to appear suddenly in late adolescence or adulthood (Brame et al., 2001).

## Recent theoretical developments

For social psychologists, probably the most notable theoretical development of the 1980s and 1990s was the emergence of social-cognitive models. Social learning and social-cognitive theorists (e.g., Bandura, 1973, 1983, 1986; Mischel, 1973) set the stage for this advance with the view that social behavior moves under the control of internal, self-regulating processes. What is important is the cognitive evaluation (construal) of events taking place in the child's environment, how the child interprets these events, and how competent the child feels in responding in different ways. These cognitions provide a basis for stability of behavior tendencies across a variety of situations, but coupled with frequent situational specificity. Internalized standards for behavior are developed from information conveyed by a variety of sources of social influence, including conditioning and observational learning.

Berkowitz (1989, 1993) added another important dimension with his 'cognitive neoassociationist view' of aversively stimulated aggression. While not disputing the importance of internalized standards, Berkowitz emphasized the importance of enduring associations between affect, cognition, and situational cues. Aversive stimulation produces initially undifferentiated negative affect. However, this negative affect and other situational cues prime a network of cognitive structures that influence the evaluation of the meaning of the negative affect and the aversive stimulus. A person's eventual behavior and emotions depend on this cognitive process.

### *Social-cognitive, information-processing models of aggression*

Three specific information-processing models have emerged from these developments, proposed respectively by Anderson (Anderson et al., 1996; Anderson and Bushman, 2002a; Anderson and Dill, 2000), Dodge (1980, 1986; Crick and Dodge, 1994), and Huesmann (1982, 1986, 1988, 1998). Although varying in their focus, terminology, specificity, and scope, these models all adopt similar premises about the processing of information in social problem-solving, the social-cognitive structures involved, the interacting role of emotions and cognitions, and the interaction of person and situation. These models have provided a coherent way to think theoretically about aggression and have also stimulated substantial research.

These models are based on the assumption that human memory can be represented as a complex associative network of nodes representing cognitive concepts and emotions. Experience leads to the development of links among elemental nodes. Sets of concepts that are strongly interconnected are known as knowledge structures. The activation of a simple node or a more complex knowledge structure at any time is determined by how many links to it have been activated, as well as the strength of associations among the activated links. When total activation is above threshold, the knowledge structure is activated, 'experienced', and used. When a stimulus increases the activation level but does not fully activate the knowledge structure (that is, it is still below threshold), the stimulus is said to have 'primed' the knowledge structure.

Knowledge structures influence perception at multiple levels, from basic visual patterns to complex behavioral sequences. Knowledge structures are used to guide people's interpretations and behavioral responses to their social (and physical) environment. They contain (or are linked to) affective states, behavioral programs, and beliefs (including beliefs about likely consequences), and can become automated with use.

Four macroprocesses in social problem-solving are as follows: (1) encoding and interpretation of environmental cues; (2) generation and selection of goals, behaviors, or scripts to guide behavior; (3) evaluation of the selected script for appropriateness on several dimensions; and (4) behavioral enactment followed by interpretation of the response of others. Emotional state affects these processes and can be changed by the outcome of these processes. Furthermore, because affect can be a part of the knowledge-structure network, current emotions can directly prime specific knowledge structures and thereby influence which schemata are brought to bear on the present situation.

Figure 12.4 displays two simplified types of knowledge structures from an associative network perspective, a general schema about guns, and a behavioral script for retaliation. In general, concepts with similar meanings (such as hurt and harm) and concepts which are frequently activated simultaneously (such as gun and shoot) become strongly associated. In Figure 12.4, thicker lines represent stronger associations and shorter distances represent greater similarity of meaning. The figure also illustrates how network associations can activate particular knowledge structures. For example, if the nodes 'gun', 'kill', 'hurt', and 'harm' are activated, the retaliation script would be strongly primed; a situation that is ambiguous with regard to whether one has been ridiculed would more likely be interpreted as a provocation warranting retaliation.

All of the social-cognitive models agree that aggression results from the way in which person variables and current situational variables combine to influence the individual's present internal state. Sometimes person and situation variables combine interactively, as in K.B. Anderson et al.'s (1998) finding that pain and trait hostility interactively affect aggressive cognitions. Figure 12.5 illustrates this point with the general aggression model schematic. The present internal state then influences a host of appraisal and decision processes (see Anderson and Bushman, 2002a, for more detail). Eventually (sometimes very quickly), an action emerges, which in turn moves the social encounter along to its next cycle.

From the social-cognitive perspective, personality is the sum of a person's knowledge structures (Mischel and Shoda, 1995; Sedikides and Skowronski, 1990). How people construe and

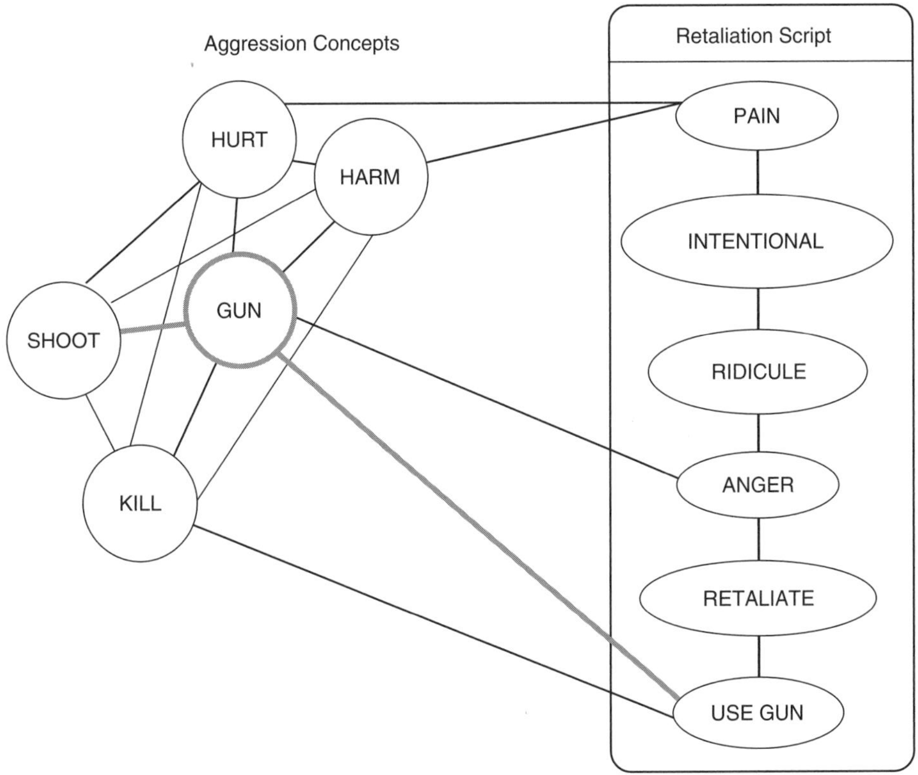


Figure 12.4 Simplified associative network with aggression concepts and a retaliation script (from C.A. Anderson et al., 1998)

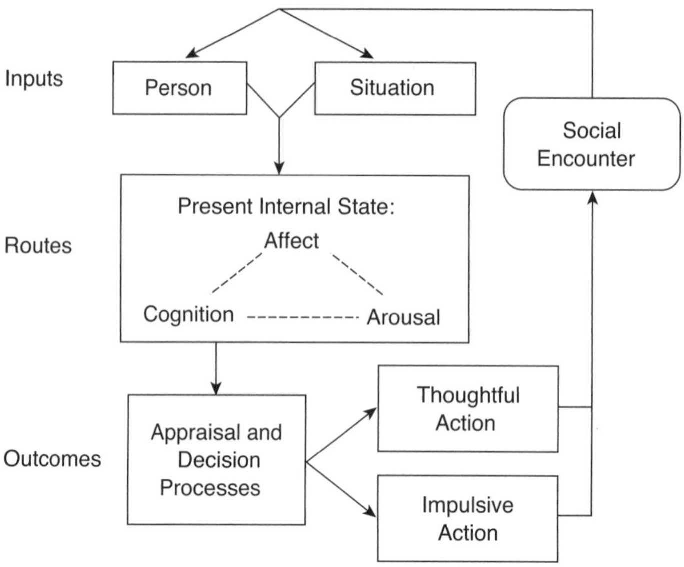


Figure 12.5 The general aggression model episodic processes (from Anderson and Bushman, 2002a)

respond to their world depends upon the particular situational factors in their world and on the knowledge structures they have learned and habitually use. Situational realities impose constraints on how people construe their world, but individual differences in the structure, accessibility, and use of underlying knowledge structures create a range of possible construals. In this view, personality results from the development and construction of knowledge structures, based primarily on life experiences, but including biological influences as well.

Research has shown that the process by which hostile schemas or aggressive scripts – indeed, all types of knowledge structure – are activated is cognitive but can with practice become completely automatic and operate without awareness (Schneider and Shiffrin, 1977; Todorov and Bargh, 2002). One can view each episodic cycle depicted in Figure 12.5 as a learning trial, leading to the development of well-rehearsed (and eventually automatized) knowledge structures of various kinds. The social-cognitive information-processing model implies systematic information-processing, but it does not imply that such processing must be conscious and controlled.

### *Biosocial interactions*

Another important theoretical movement has been toward models that integrate the effects of predisposing biological factors with the effects of environmental social influences. According to the emerging interactionist perspective, inherited biological factors clearly influence the risk of aggression but do not determine aggression (Raine et al., 1997). Raine introduced the term 'biosocial interactions' to refer to the view that biological predispositions manifest themselves through 'interactions' with the social context in which the organism develops. Thus, the effects of biological processes are included in social-cognitive models through their influence on knowledge structures (such as scripts, beliefs, and schemas) and through their influence on affective components.

A related movement is the emergence of more sophisticated evolutionary theorizing about aggression and the recognition of the importance of 'calibration' through learning experiences in the emergence of inherited behavior patterns (e.g., Buss and Shackelford, 1997b; Daly and Wilson, 1994; Malamuth and Heilmann, 1998). Similarly, learning is now viewed by many social-development researchers as a process through which behavioral predispositions are modified as children are socialized via conditioning and observational learning (Huesmann, 1997; Tremblay, 2000).

Along these same lines is the concept of 'preparedness' (Seligman, 1970), the idea from the animal-learning literature that it is easier to link some stimulus–response pairs than others. One well-known example of a 'prepared' connection is food aversions. Preparedness relates to human aggression in two ways. First, certain emotional states and behavioral syndromes appear to be easily linked (e.g., Berkowitz, 1993). Humans appear to develop links easily between frustration, pain and anger, and aggression. Second, biological effects on development of aggressive personality may work by preparing some individuals to learn more easily frustration–anger–aggression linkages and by preparing others to learn more easily the negative consequences of aggression (e.g., Soubrie, 1986).

## Causes of aggression

Research over the past several decades has suggested a wide variety of causes of cyclical increases and decreases in violence, of age trends in violence, and of differences in violence between societies and genders. For example, the increased accessibility of guns (O'Donnell, 1995) global warming (Anderson et al., 1997), different cultural norms about violence (Nisbett and Cohen, 1996),[2] and the widespread exposure to violent entertainment media (Bushman and Huesmann, 2000) all probably contribute to the high level of violence and aggression in modern societies and to differences between societies. However, severe aggressive and violent acts rarely occur unless there is a convergence of multiple, precipitating *situational instigators* and multiple, predisposing *personological characteristics*. No one causal factor by itself can be expected to explain more than a small portion of individual differences in aggressiveness. Nevertheless, accumulating empirical evidence reveals that several fundamental social-psychological processes that operate among all people at all times explain a lot of the individual differences in aggression and violent behavior and how situational factors interact with individual predispositions to increase and decrease aggression and violent tendencies. Aggression is most likely to develop in children who grow up in environments that reinforce aggression, provide aggressive models, frustrate and victimize them and teach them that aggression is acceptable. The acquired scripts, schemas, and beliefs (that is, knowledge structures) are most likely to produce aggression when situational factors instigate aggression.

As noted earlier, and as illustrated in Figure 12.5, two types of proximate causes of aggression interact in the present situational context, *situational instigators* and *personal preparedness* to aggress. In the following sections, we briefly review these two types of causal factors.

There are also two types of *distal* causal factors. These are *environmental* and *biological modifiers* of personal preparedness to aggress. Typically, they exert their influence over a long period of time and operate by increasing proximate factors that facilitate aggression or decreasing proximate factors that inhibit aggression. For example, repeated exposure to media violence can create highly accessible retaliation scripts which are easily activated on future occasions. Of course, some modifiers may operate in both a short-term and a long-term manner. Exposure to a violent movie both primes aggression-related knowledge structures in the immediate situation and constitutes an additional learning trial that teaches the viewer beliefs that will have long-lasting effects.

### *Situational instigators*

#### Aversive conditions

One of the most important classes of instigators is aversive stimulation. Berkowitz (1982, 1993) proposed that any aversive stimulation increases negative affect, which, in turn, increases the likelihood of aggression. Hostile aggression, almost by definition, requires aversive stimulation producing negative affect. However, instrumental aggression may occur without an instigation to negative affect. Yet, instigation of negative affect can also increase instrumental aggression. A large class of stimuli have been found to increase the likelihood of aggression by increasing the negative emotion we label as anger.

*Provocation* is undoubtedly the strongest situational instigator of human aggression (Berkowitz, 1993; Geen, 2001). Provocations include insults, slights, other forms of verbal aggression, physical aggression, interference with one's attempts to attain an important goal – the list is almost endless. But provocation is 'in the eye of the beholder'. Some things which are provoking to one individual are not provoking to another. Indeed, this is one of the key ways in which situational and personological factors interact. For example, certain subcultures develop codes of honor or personal respect that influence aggression by influencing what is considered provocative (Horowitz and Schwartz, 1974; Nisbett and Cohen, 1996), and different individuals react differently to threat (Baumeister and Boden, 1998; Baumeister et al., 1996).

Why is provocation such a robust instigator to aggression? Research suggests that humans obtain gratification from hurting those who provoke them. Baron (1977) varied whether experimental participants received information about whether their aggression was hurting another person. When the target person had not provoked the participant, receiving feedback that their aggression hurt the target reduced participants' aggression. But when the target person had seriously provoked the participant, feedback that the aggression hurt the target led to further increases in aggression. Baron concluded that humans, when provoked, do have a desire to hurt (see also Berkowitz, 1993).

*Frustration* is the classical aversive instigator (Dollard et al., 1939). Frustration can be defined as the blockage of goal attainment. Most frustrations are also viewed as provocations because a person is identified as the agent responsible for goal blockage. Research from several domains supports the early notion that frustration can increase aggression even when the frustrating agent is unknown, or is blameless, or is not the target of subsequent aggression, or is not even another human (Berkowitz, 1993). For example, frustrations that are fully justified increase aggression against the frustrating agent (e.g., Dill and Anderson, 1995) and against a person who was not responsible for the failure to attain the goal (e.g., Geen, 1968). Recent work has shown that displaced aggression, wherein the target of aggression is not the person who caused the initial frustration, is a robust phenomenon (Marcus-Newhall et al., 2000; Pedersen et al., 2000).

*Pain and discomfort* in animals is a strong instigator to aggression even against targets not connected to the pain (Ulrich, 1966). Similarly, research with people has shown that even nonsocial aversive conditions (for example, hot temperatures, loud noises, and unpleasant odors) increase aggression (Baron, 1977; Griffit, 1970; Jones and Bogat, 1978). Acute aversive conditions, such as pain produced by immersing a hand in a bucket of ice water increases aggression (e.g., Berkowitz, 1993; Berkowitz et al., 1981). General discomfort, such as that produced by sitting in a hot or cold room (Anderson et al., 2000) can also increase aggression. Criminological data consistently show that violent crime rates are higher when the temperature is higher (Anderson, 1989), and there is even evidence that general trends in global warming are correlated with trends in aggression (Anderson, 2001; Anderson et al., 1997).

*Bad moods* produce negative affect and thus serve as an instigation to aggression (Berkowitz, 1993). This has been found in clinical studies of children (Pfeffer et al., 1987; Poznanski and Zrull, 1970). Additionally, inductions of depressive moods are accompanied by increases in aggressiveness (Berkowitz and Troccoli, 1990; Miller and Norman, 1979).

*Social stress* can also instigate aggression. Landau (1988) showed that general social stress in Israel is related to levels of violent crime. Guerra et al. (1995) showed that higher levels of life stress among Chicago children was related to increased aggression.

### Priming aggressive cognitions and affect

A second class of situational instigators consists of stimuli that prime aggressive cognitions or negative affective states and, thus, increase the likelihood of aggression. By 'prime', we mean that the stimulus raises the activation level of a relevant knowledge structure, thereby making it more likely to be subsequently activated.

Numerous stimuli can serve as aggression primes. For instance, Berkowitz and LePage (1967) found that the mere presence of a gun (versus a tennis racket) increased the aggression of angered research participants. Later reviews (e.g., Berkowitz and Donnerstein, 1982; Carlson et al., 1990) confirmed the phenomenon in a variety of field and laboratory settings. A recent meta-analysis found that a weapon can prime aggression even without provocation (Bettencourt and Kernahan, 1997). More recent research has found that weapons automatically prime aggressive thoughts (C.A. Anderson et al., 1998). Initially, neutral stimuli may become primes for aggression through learning. Leyens and Fraczek (1983) showed that the color of a room which was associated in the past with aggression could prime later aggression. The immediate increase in aggression after exposure to media violence may also result in part from the priming of aggressive thoughts, feelings, and scripts (Anderson, 1997; Bushman and Huesmann, 2000).

Priming is an automatic process that can occur without conscious awareness. For example, people exposed subliminally to aggressive words subsequently rate a target person as more aggressive (Bargh and Pietromonaco, 1982), presumedly because well-practiced schemata involving aggression were primed. Stereotypes can also operate automatically. Devine (1989) showed that people primed subliminally with nonaggressive words closely related to the African-American culture were relatively more likely to ascribe aggression to a target person. Automatic priming also works on behavioral scripts. Bargh et al. (1996) and Carver et al. (1983) have shown that solving anagram problems whose solutions are aggressive words increases the chances of aggressive (or rude) behavior immediately afterwards, at least if participants are provoked. Chen and Bargh (1997; Bargh et al., 1996) also found that subliminal priming with African-American faces increases aggression.

Because priming activates associative pathways, automatic priming has been used to demonstrate subtle relations between aggression and other concepts. Zubriggen (2000) showed that men for whom sexual words primed power constructs were more likely to have engaged in aggression against women. Bargh et al. (1995) showed that power words primed recognition of sexual words for men who scored high on propensity to be sexually aggressive. Thus, power is an important component of motivation for sexual aggression in many men. Cognitive stereotypes about the aggressiveness of groups of people have also been shown to serve as automatic aggressive primes. For example, Payne (2002) demonstrated that priming people with a picture of an African-American increases the likelihood that they will correctly recognize a degraded picture as a weapon.

### Stimuli that arouse

A third class of situational instigators are those that increase arousal level. There are at least three different ways that arousal can increase aggression. First, high general arousal energizes the dominant behavioral tendency (Berkowitz, 1993). If a person is provoked when arousal is already heightened, heightened aggression can result (Geen and O'Neal, 1969). Second, arousal produced by one stimulus can be 'transferred' or 'misattributed' to another situational instigator by being misperceived as having been generated by it (Zillmann, 1979, 1983). Such misattribution or 'excitation transfer' effects can persist long after the original instigation, mainly because, once the instigation event has been perceived as anger-inducing, the person will remember it as a more serious transgression. Third, high arousal (and very low arousal) may themselves be aversive states, and may therefore increase aggression in the same manner as other aversive stimuli.

### Factors that interfere with aggression inhibition

A fourth class of situational instigators consists of factors that interfere with cognitive processes that normally inhibit aggression.

*High levels of arousal and stress* seem to have such an effect. Attention is narrowed to a few salient cues (Broadbent, 1971; Easterbrook, 1959). Additionally, working memory capacity is reduced, memory search is narrowed, activation of weakly associated schemas becomes less likely, and the activation of the best-connected schemas and scripts becomes more likely (Anderson, 1990; Luria, 1973). Thus, threatening situations such as those containing provocations are likely to cue only aggressive interpretative schema and scripts.

*Alcohol and other drugs* have been linked to increased aggressive and antisocial behavior (Baron and Richardson, 1994; Berkowitz, 1993; Bushman, 1993; Murdoch et al., 1990), including homicide (Parker and Auerhahn, 1999), domestic violence (Wiehe, 1998), and sports violence (Russell, 1993). Some experimental studies suggest that alcohol *causes* an increase in aggressive behavior; however, alcohol's action on the brain mechanisms for aggressive behavior is modulated by genetic predispositions, learned expectations, social restraints, and cultural habits (Miczek et al., 1994: 406–7). The effects of other drugs on aggression are less clear, stimulants, depressants, opiates, and hallucinogens showing different effects in different studies. The body of empirical research on aggression and drugs and alcohol is too complex to disentangle in this chapter. However, the effects of such drugs on aggression appear to be a consequence of three processes: (1) disinhibition of behavior by the physiological effect of alcohol on serotonergic mechanisms (Brain, 1986); (2) cognitive myopia due to physiological effects on social-cognitive processing (Steele and Josephs, 1990; Taylor and Leonard, 1983); and (3) psychological disinhibition due to expectancy beliefs (Lang et al., 1975). One interesting finding from a meta-analytic review (Bushman, 1997) is that aggression-facilitating factors (such as provocation, frustration, and aggressive cues) have a stronger effect on people who are under the influence of certain types of drugs than on people who are not.

## *Personal preparedness*

As described earlier, in the context of social-cognitive models of behavior, personality or 'the self' is viewed as the collection of cognitive structures and emotional tendencies that influence behavior in interactions with situational factors. Personal preparedness for aggression is represented by the extent to which those cognitive and emotional structures support aggression. 'Trait' measures of aggression seem either to assess past aggressiveness (e.g., Buss and Perry, physical aggression subscale, 1992) or assess these emotional and cognitive structures (e.g., Buss and Perry, hostility subscale, 1992; Caprara et al., 1994, 1985). In this section, we focus on research identifying specific elements of these relatively permanent cognitive and emotional structures that influence preparedness for aggression.

### Self-schemas

Contrary to popular belief, low self-esteem is not a good predictor of aggression. Instead, individuals with inflated or unstable high self-esteem are the most prone to anger and are the most aggressive, especially when their high self-image is threatened (Baumeister et al., 1996; Bushman and Baumeister, 1998; Kernis et al., 1989). However, Lee et al. (2002) found that, for people of average self-esteem, negative self-evaluations in a self-esteem-relevant domain instigate prosocial behavior seemingly aimed at counteracting the negative evaluation.

Beliefs about oneself may also influence aggression by influencing script selection and evaluation. Self-schemas provide an internal context within which scripts must be evaluated. Heightened activation of self-schemas decreases the likelihood of aggression when the self-schema is nonaggressive (Carver, 1974), probably by filtering out potential aggressive scripts. Finally, there are theoretical reasons to believe that efficacy-related beliefs should be related to aggression, though the evidence of such associations is not strong (e.g., Bandura, 1977, 1986; McFall, 1982).

### Beliefs and attitudes about appropriateness of aggression

Many beliefs seem to play a role in preparedness to aggress. Huesmann and Guerra (1997) have extensively studied the role of *normative beliefs* about aggression. Such beliefs consist of a person's perception about the appropriateness of aggression in particular contexts. In a study of urban children, they demonstrated that normative beliefs stabilize in the middle-elementary grades for most children. In the early grades, these beliefs were influenced by the children's aggressive behavior, but aggressive behavior was not influenced by the beliefs. However, by the fifth grade, the children's aggressive behavior was influenced by their beliefs, and their behavior had less influence on subsequent beliefs. In another large sample study, Guerra et al. (1995) showed that these beliefs interacted with socioeconomic status and with neighborhood-violence-induced stress. Children from low socioeconomic-status families typically showed greater acceptance of aggression and greater neighborhood-violence stress. In turn, the combination of such stress and beliefs approving of aggression was a potent predictor of subsequent aggression by the child. Huesmann and Moise (2002) have also shown that childhood exposure to media violence predicts adult normative beliefs more approving of aggression, which, in turn, predicts adult aggression.

Other researchers looking at different measures of cognitive approval of aggression have uncovered links to aggression (e.g., Gouze, 1987; Pakaslahti and Keltikangas-Järvinen, 1996; Richards and Dodge, 1982; Slaby and Guerra, 1988). There are also substantial cultural differences in approval of aggression on many such measures. Fraczek (1985) studied youth in Poland and Finland and found different levels of approval of different kinds of aggressive acts (for defense, for gain, etc.). Fujihara et al. (1999) found similar approval levels for physical aggression among youth in Japan, Spain, and the USA, but different attitudes to verbal aggression. In a more recent study of Eastern and Western countries, Ramirez et al. (2001) discovered that verbal irony was considered relatively harmless in Spain, Poland, and the USA, but very aggressive in Japan and Iran. However, individual use of aggression to punish others was judged very acceptable in Japan and Iran, but not very acceptable in Spain, Poland, Finland, and the USA.

Attitudes to violence correlate with both mild and serious forms of aggression among youth and adults (e.g., Anderson et al., forthcoming; Bookwala et al., 1992; Kingery, 1998; Markowitz, 2001). Positive attitudes towards violence in general prepare certain individuals for aggression. More specific positive attitudes to violence against specific groups of people also increase aggression against those people. For example, attitudes to women are related to sexual aggressiveness against women (e.g., Malamuth et al., 1995). K.B. Anderson (1996) has further shown that males prone to aggress against women are not generally aggressive against all people in all situations; rather, they specifically target women (but not men) who have provoked them. Similarly, beliefs about punishment (Hyman, 1995), the need to squash children's challenges to adult authority (Azar and Rohrbeck, 1986), and misconceptions about what children at various ages can do (Azar and Rohrbeck, 1986) all contribute to parental violence towards children.

### Hostile world schemas

There are several ways in which *hostile world schemas* influence aggression. Aggressive individuals tend to perceive hostility in others where there is no hostility; that is, they display a hostile attributional bias (Dodge, 1980; Dodge and Coie, 1987; Dodge and Frame, 1982; Dodge et al., 1990; Graham and Hudley, 1994; Nasby et al., 1979; Slaby and Guerra, 1988; Steinberg and Dodge, 1983). Research on social perception (e.g., Fiske, 1982; Fiske and Taylor, 1991; Schneider, 1991), as well as aggression, suggests that hostile attributional biases are products of well-developed schemas. Dodge and Tomlin (1987) found that aggressive children rely on aggressive self-schemas and stereotypes to infer intent. Dill et al. (1997) found that aggressive college students perceive relatively more aggression in observed dyadic interactions and expect others to behave more aggressively in hypothetical encounters. Zelli and Huesmann (1993) found that college students with greater ingrained persecution beliefs are more likely to perceive hostility when none is present. These hostile cue interpretations can become an automatic cognitive process (Bargh, 1989; Todorov and Bargh, 2002; Winter and Uleman, 1984; Zelli et al., 1995).

### Long-term goals

Long-term, abstract goals influence the preparedness of the individual for aggression. For example, the overriding goal of some gang members is to be respected and feared (Horowitz and Schwartz, 1974; Klein and Maxson, 1989). Such a goal obviously colors one's perceptions of personally involving episodes, values, and beliefs about the appropriateness of various courses of action.

### Scripts

Scripts include many different elements, such as goals, beliefs, and action plans. Research suggests that the most accessible social scripts for aggressive children and adults are aggressive ones. For example, scripts retrieved by more aggressive people to solve hypothetical problems incorporate relatively more physical aggression (Dill et al., 1997; Rubin et al., 1987, 1991; Waas, 1988). Priming by negative intent cues is more likely to activate an aggressive script in aggressive children (Graham and Hudley, 1994). Aggressive children are less likely to generate prosocial scripts to solve social problems (Deluty, 1981; Taylor and Gabriel, 1989), and there is some evidence that, as hypothesized, a narrower search process for a script is associated with more aggression (Shure and Spivac, 1980).

### Other knowledge structures

The social-cognitive approach makes it clear that distinctions between traits, attitudes, beliefs, and goals are not as clear-cut or necessary as traditional textbook treatments of personality and social psychology might suggest. Most can be seen as variations of schematic knowledge structures. The importance of this becomes clearer when considering individual differences that do not fit neatly into one of the standard categories, or when considering the explanatory power of certain types of individual differences. For example, take the well-established finding that trait-aggressiveness, measured by self-reports of past aggressive behaviors, predicts future aggression in both laboratory and field settings. Unless one adopts a very behavioristic attitude, there is little explanatory power in this trait-aggression concept. However, the social-cognitive view suggests that the predictive power results from the fact that there are individual differences in knowledge structures that influence perceptions of intent, construals of appropriate ways of responding, and decisions regarding likely outcomes. These insights have all been borne out, and a deeper level of theorizing and explaining empirical relations results.

Individual differences in susceptibility to the weapons effect provides another useful example. The weapons effect itself is an example of a situational instigator, but recent work has demonstrated that both aggressive thoughts and aggressive behaviors prompted by the image of a weapon depend on both the type of person and the type of weapon (C.A. Anderson et al., 1998; Bartholow et al., forthcoming). Hunters have more extensive knowledge about hunting and assault rifles than nonhunters. Furthermore, hunters display relatively more positive affect, less aggressive thinking, and less aggressive behavior when a hunting rifle is present than when an assault rifle is present, but nonhunters show the opposite pattern. Hunter status is clearly an individual difference variable, one that indexes different life experiences, but it is not a personality trait, attitude, or even a belief. The social-cognitive approach provides a theoretical explanation for how such life experience variables influence the weapons effect, and subsequent studies have confirmed it.

The hunting example provides an excellent transition to our next section on *environmental modifiers*. These environmental variables influence a host of long-term person factors, such as personality traits, attitudes, scripts, and beliefs.

### *Environmental modifiers*

These are environmental factors that exert long-lasting effects by influencing what people learn, what they believe, and characteristic levels of mood. For example, parenting practices, community environments, culture, peers, exposure to violence, and socioeconomic level are all environmental modifiers by this definition. In all of these cases, observational learning plays a major role in the development of various knowledge structures that support aggression.

### Family, community, and cultural environment

Children hear beliefs expressed by parents and peers and observe parental and peer behaviors. From both types of observations, they draw inferences about the acceptability of aggression and violence. Thus, children's aggression beliefs tend to be correlated with those of parents (Huesmann et al., 1984a; Miller, 1991) and peers (Henry et al., 1996).

Whereas peers and family are the proximal influence in the socialization of young children, the community and culture exert influence through them and through direct connections to the child – schools, church, and mass media. Cultural variations in acceptance of aggression under various circumstances appear quite large. For example, K.L. Anderson (1990) has noted how subcultures of urban youth develop their own norms for behavior that emphasize aggression in many situations. In a series of field studies and experiments, Nisbett (1993; Nisbett and Cohen, 1996) has shown how southern-born males have adopted the normative beliefs of what Nisbett calls 'a culture of honor' and behave more aggressively in certain contexts. Cultural effects are also apparent in studies of immigrants. Souweidane and Huesmann (1999) found that the longer Lebanese immigrants were in the USA, the more they 'accepted' violence in general, but they became less accepting of violence by men against women.

Children who grow up observing or experiencing violence around them develop numerous problems (Osofsky, 1995). They behave more violently (Guerra et al., 1995) and are more likely to be physically aggressive against their own children later in life (Widom, 1989). Furthermore, recent research shows that such observations of violence seem to lead to the development of beliefs and scripts supporting aggression (Guerra et al., 2002).

Along these same lines is recent work on genocide and the failure of aggression inhibitions that normally operate in most people. Three research groups have independently identified and discussed how these inhibitions are sometimes overridden (Bandura et al., 1996; Keltner and Robinson, 1996; Staub, 1989, 1998). Most people do not commit extreme acts of violence even if they could do so with little chance of discovery or punishment. Such self-regulation may be due to the fact that people cannot escape the consequences that they apply to themselves. Self-image, self-standards, and sense of self-worth (that is, moral standards) are used in normal self-regulation of behavior. However, there appear to be at least two particularly important mechanisms that allow people to disengage their moral standards – moral justification and dehumanizing the victim. Moral justifications for extreme and mass violence include ‘it is for the person’s own good’, ‘it is for the good of society’, or ‘it is to satisfy the demands of personal honor’. Such justifications can be applied at multiple levels, from child abuse to genocidal war. Dehumanizing the victim operates by making sure that one’s moral standards are simply not applicable. War propaganda fits this mechanism, but people also use this mechanism at an individual level. Potential victims are placed in the ultimate out-group – one that has no human qualities (see also Diener, 1976; Prentice-Dunn and Rogers, 1983).

### Media violence

Observation of violence in the mass media not only stimulates aggressive behavior in the short run by priming aggressive scripts and schemas but also stimulates aggressive behavior in the long run by changing schemas, scripts, and beliefs about aggression. Undoubtedly, more research has been devoted to the influence of the mass media on aggression than to any other aspect of the cultural environment. As many researchers have shown, most recently in a meta-analysis by Anderson and Bushman (2002b), regardless of how one studies the media violence/aggression link, the outcomes are the same – significant, substantial positive relations. This is true for longitudinal studies, cross-sectional correlational studies, field experiments, and laboratory experiments. Figure 12.6 displays the results of this meta-analysis. The effect sizes are substantial by public-health standards (see Rosenthal, 1986). For example, the media violence/aggression relation is larger than the effects of calcium intake on bone density or the effect of condom use on reduced risk of HIV infection (Anderson and Bushman, 2002a). Because this literature is so huge, we highlight only a few points and direct readers to recent reviews of the TV/movie-violence literature (Bushman and Huesmann, 2000) and the video-game violence literature (Anderson, 2002; Anderson and Bushman, 2001).

First, the evidence of a causal connection is now overwhelming and has been strong since at least 1975 (Bushman and Anderson, 2001). The consistency of results regardless of design type, research group, media type, country of study, and control variables makes this one of the strongest research literatures in all of social and behavioral science. Alternative explanations generated by the lay public, media representatives, and professional naysayers have been examined and debunked many times. Yet, the general public seems to not have gotten the message, perhaps because of inaccurate news media reports (Bushman and Anderson, 2001).

Second, though the evidence of causality has been weakest for more extreme types of aggression, even in this restricted domain the overall pattern of results is strong. For ethical reasons, of course, one cannot randomly assign infants to low versus high violence-upbringing, conditions, and then follow them for thirty or more years to obtain measures of homicide and aggravated assault rates. However, the combination of cross-sectional, longitudinal, and intervention studies makes a convincing case for causal effects on even extreme aggressive behaviors, especially when the results of field and laboratory experiments are also considered. For extremely aggressive behaviors, longitudinal studies with children provide the best tests of the plausibility of long-term effects. Only a few have been completed, but the results are quite consistent. In a study initiated in 1960 on 856 youths in New York State, Eron et al. (1972) found that boys’ early childhood viewing of violence on TV was positively related to their aggressive and antisocial behavior ten years later (after graduating from high school), even controlling for initial aggressiveness, social class, education, and other variables (Lefkowitz et al., 1977). A twenty-two-year-follow-up of these same boys revealed that early aggression predicted criminality at age thirty and that early violence viewing was independently related to adult criminality (Huesmann, 1986, 1995).

A more representative longitudinal study was initiated by Huesmann and his colleagues in 1977

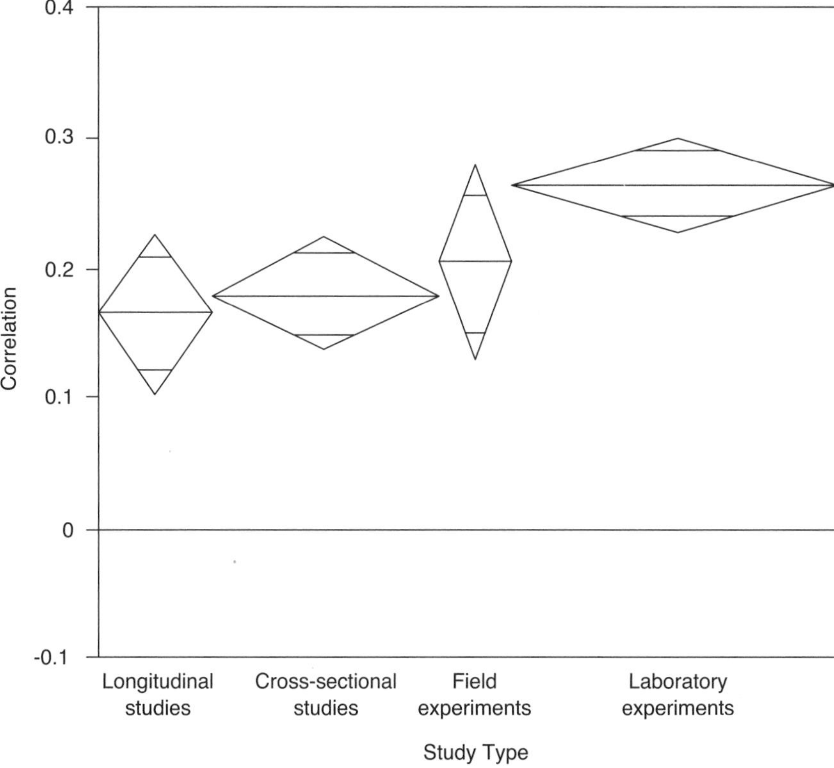


Figure 12.6 Effects of media violence on aggressive behavior (from Anderson and Bushman, 2002b). Diamond widths are proportional to the number of independent Samples. There were 46 longitudinal samples involving 4,975 participants, 86 cross-sectional samples involving 37,341 participants, 28 field experiment samples involving 1,976 participants, and 124 laboratory experiment samples involving 7,305 participants. Red lines indicate the mean effect sizes. Blue lines indicate 95 percent confidence intervals. Note that zero (dashed line, indicating no effect) is excluded from all confidence intervals.

(Huesmann and Eron, 1986; Huesmann et al., 1984b). This three-year longitudinal study of children in five countries also revealed that the television habits of children as young as first-graders also predicted subsequent childhood aggression, even controlling for initial level of aggression. In contrast to earlier longitudinal studies, this effect was obtained *for both boys and girls* even in countries without large amounts of violent programming such as Israel, Finland, and Poland (Huesmann and Eron, 1986). A fifteen-year follow-up of the US children in this cross-national study revealed perhaps the strongest longitudinal effects of all (Huesmann et al., 2003). Both boys and girls who had been high violence viewers in childhood behaved significantly more aggressively in their mid-twenties; for males, this included being convicted of more crimes. Finally, a very recent study by Johnson et al. (2002) showed a significant effect of TV viewing at ages fourteen and twenty-two on aggression in later adulthood. In all of these longitudinal studies, a large number of covariates (such as IQ, social class, parenting practices, and previous level of aggression) were included in analyses and eliminated the possibility that the effects could be due to these 'third' variables.[3]

Third, both short-term and long-term media violence effects are now well understood. Research has found that exposure to media violence influences a host of theoretically important factors. For example, watching violent movie clips increases aggressive thoughts (e.g., Bushman, 1998), as does playing violent video games (e.g., Anderson and Dill, 2000). Exposure to violent media also desensitizes people to later violence, reducing physiological arousal to subsequent violence (e.g., Smith and Donnerstein, 1998; see also our following section on 'Low arousal'). Several studies have found that watching violent music videos increases viewers' acceptance and endorsement of violent behavior and attitudes (Greeson and Williams, 1986; Hansen and Hansen, 1989, 1990). One recent study has examined the effects of exposure to rap music videos on the attitudes of African-American adolescents. It found that participants exposed to violent rap music videos reported greater acceptance of the use of violence and increased probability that they would engage in violent behavior (Johnson et al., 1995). Other research has linked self-reported fantasizing about aggression with peer-nominated aggression (Huesmann and Eron, 1986; Rosenfeld et al., 1982). Furthermore, both Viemero and Paajanen (1992) and Huesmann (Huesmann and Eron, 1986; Huesmann and Moise, 2002) found that viewing of TV violence predicts fantasizing about aggression, which in turn predicts later aggression. These and many other studies reveal that exposure to media violence modifies important aggression-related personological variables.

### Maladaptive families/parenting

Family variables have been linked to the development of life-long aggression (e.g., Patterson et al., 1989). Among the key problems they identified are parental use of poor disciplinary measures and inadequate monitoring of their children's activities. Similarly, Olweus (1995) identified a number of factors conducive to creating bullies: caretakers with indifferent attitudes towards the child, permissiveness for aggression by the child, and physical punishment and other power-assertive disciplinary techniques. Child abuse and neglect are themselves self-perpetuating problems. Abused or neglected children are particularly likely to become abusive and neglectful parents and violent criminals (e.g., Azar and Rohrbeck, 1986; Peterson et al., 1997). Recent prospective studies strongly suggest that corporal punishment of children leads to later increases in aggression against parents, peers, and dating partners (Straus, 2000).

### Extreme social environments

As noted earlier, many social environments foster the development of aggressive personality. Such factors include poverty, living in violent neighborhoods, deviant peers, lack of safe child recreational areas, exposure to media violence, bad parenting, and lack of social support. Growing up in a culture of fear and hate, as in many ethnic-minority communities around the world, may be the most extreme version of an aggression-fostering environment and may well account for generations of ethnic and religious hatreds and genocidal tendencies that occasionally erupt into genocidal wars (Keltner and Robinson, 1996; Staub, 1989, 1998). All of these conditions facilitate the development of hostile interpretative schemata, the priming of existing hostile knowledge structures, and the chronic accessibility of such structures, and these structures may be strongly linked to a particular ethnic or racial out-group. It is easy to see how these factors operate via learning processes (including rewards for aggression), creating well-developed aggressive knowledge structures for perception, interpretation, decision-making, and action. The perceptual knowledge structures modeled and explicitly taught in these contexts guarantee continued mistrust, misunderstanding, and hatred of key out-groups.

### *Biological modifiers*

There is considerable evidence that a number of biological factors play a role in individual differences in preparedness to aggress. The exact mechanisms by which these factors produce aggressive people, in interaction with the person's environment, need additional study. Nonetheless, scholars in this area have already learned much.

### Low arousal

Individuals with lower-than-average baseline levels of arousal seem to be more at risk of behaving aggressively. Rogeness et al. (1990) found that conduct-disordered children had lower baseline heart rates and blood pressure, and Raine (1993) reported low resting heart rates among antisocial children and adolescents. So-called psychopaths have long been known to have lower arousal as measured by EEG (Howard, 1984) or skin conductance (Hare, 1978). Indeed, Moise-Titus (1999) demonstrated that males who show depressed skin conductance and little negative emotion in response to seeing violence report having engaged in more aggression and behave more aggressively in the laboratory. In a longitudinal study, Raine et al. (1990) assessed the heart rate, skin conductance, and EEG patterns of 101 fifteen-year-old boys. Nine years later, they found significant relations between early low baseline arousal on each of the three measures and later criminal status. In a separate study of 5,000 youths, Wadsworth (1976) also found a significant relation between low resting heart rate at age eleven and criminal acts by age twenty-one. Studies assessing arousal through measures of catecholamines (adrenaline or noradrenaline) or cortisol have shown similar relations between low arousal and aggression (Magnusson et al., Virkkunen, 1985).

One social-cognitive interpretation of this effect is that low-arousal individuals are less likely to experience negative affect during evaluation of aggressive scripts. Thus, they are more likely to use the script (Huesmann, 1997). An alternative possibility presumes an optimal arousal level for everyone. Low-arousal individuals may engage in more risky and sensation-producing kinds of behavior, including antisocial and aggressive acts, to increase their arousal. These two interpretations help to make sense of the phenomenon, described earlier, in which stimuli that increase arousal can produce increases in aggression. Individuals with low average levels of arousal may be more likely to seek arousing stimuli or situations that also tend to increase aggression, or they may be less likely to avoid such stimuli or situations.

Some individual differences in baseline arousal are innate, but it appears that learning also plays a role. Researchers have shown that people habituate to repeated exposure to scenes of violence, displaying less emotional reaction (Smith and Donnerstein, 1998). Lazarus et al. (1962) found that skin-conductance responses decreased as the presentation of a violent film continued. Cline et al. (1973) reported that heavy TV viewers showed less skin conductance when they saw a violent film. Thomas et al. (1977) showed a similar effect for children. This *desensitization* process illustrates how a repeated environmental stimulus can act as a modifier of biological processes.

### Low serotonin

Heightened aggressiveness is also related to low levels of the neurotransmitter serotonin (5-HT [5-hydroxytryptamine] or its metabolite 5-HIAA [5-hydroxyindoleacetic acid]). Studies of humans and animals (even invertebrates) have found changes in serotonin levels in individuals who engage in aggressive and violent behavior repeatedly (Miczek et al., 1994). For example, Linnoila and Virkkunen (Linnoila et al., 1983; Virkkunen and Narvanen, 1987; Virkkunen et al., 1989a, 1989b) reported that violent offenders, impulsive criminals, and people who have attempted suicide all have lower levels of serotonin. In other studies of suicide, low serotonin has been shown to be correlated with number of suicide attempts but not with depression (Oreland et al., 1981). Self-ratings of hostility (Rydin et al., 1982) and aggression (Coccaro, 1989; Brown et al., 1979) also correlate with depressed central nervous system (CNS) serotonin. In children, low serotonin has been found to correlate with reported behavior problems (Brown et al., 1985) and with conduct disorder (Stoff et al., 1987). Animal experimental data in which CNS serotonin is manipulated provide causal data consistent with these correlational data (Kantak et al., 1981).

Low serotonin appears to produce an inability to inhibit impulsive responses to provocation or aversive stimulation. For example, in the Linnoila et al. (1983) study, criminals convicted of impulsive violent crimes had lower serotonin than criminals with premeditated crimes. Soubrie (1986) proposed that the CNS serotonergic system's role is to inhibit active responses to external stimuli when passive responses are more appropriate.

### High testosterone

Testosterone may affect aggression in two different ways. Over the long term, it can affect the development of various CNS and bodily structures (such as muscles and height) that change the likelihood and the success rate of aggression. This can be called the organizing effect. In the short run, it may also have an instigating effect on aggression. Though both effects are well established in animals (Book et al., 2002), only the organizing effect is supported by substantial evidence in humans.

Injection studies in animals demonstrate causal links between testosterone and developmental changes that promote aggression (see Brain, 1994, for a review). A few studies with humans in which pregnant woman have been treated with androgens provide causal support for such organizing effects in humans. For example, Reinisch (1981) found that children of mothers treated with progestin to prevent toxemia showed more propensity for physical aggression at about age five than did same-sex siblings who were born when the mother was not being treated.

In animals, the immediate instigating effect of testosterone on aggression has also been clearly demonstrated with injection studies and with observation that naturally occurring cyclical variations in testosterone correspond to variations in aggression (Brain, 1994). However, in humans, the presence of an instigating effect is much more problematic. One of the reasons is that there is also substantial evidence that various behavioral outcomes closely related to aggression affect circulating testosterone levels (Archer, 1988).

Two major meta-analyses (Archer, 1991; Book et al., 2002) have concluded that there is a weak but significant positive correlation (about 0.14) between current level of circulating testosterone and various measures of aggression in humans. Studies investigating whether testosterone levels in humans are affected by certain outcomes (such as dominance, winning, losing, and aggression) also tend to show weak positive effects, but with many exceptions. Laboratory studies of competitions such as reaction-time tasks, video games, or coin-tossing show that male winners usually experience an increase in testosterone (Gladue et al., 1989; Mazur et al., 1997; McCaul et al., 1992). Similar results have occurred in naturalistic studies of judo competitors (Salvador et al., 1987), wrestlers and tennis players (Elias, 1981), and chess players (Mazur et al., 1992). Even the fans of a winning team show increases in testosterone relative to fans of a losing team (Mazur and Booth, 1998).

Taken together, this research strongly suggests a reciprocal influence process for the short-term relation between testosterone and aggression. Higher levels of plasma testosterone probably increase aggression slightly, but the outcome of winning and dominating or losing probably affects testosterone levels just as much. Interestingly, Schaal et al. (1995) report that twelve-year-old boys rated as being 'tough' and 'socially dominating' had the highest levels of testosterone – greater than 'nondominant' boys who scored even higher on aggression.

### Executive functioning deficits

Although heightened aggressiveness has been linked to low IQ (Huesmann et al., 1987; Moffitt and Lynam, 1994; Wilson and Herrnstein, 1985), the reason is not clear. Moffitt and Lyman (1994) argued that a verbal IQ deficit makes it difficult for a child to develop appropriate social problem-solving skills. Pennington and Bennetto (1993) argued that deficits in frontal-lobe executive functioning limit the ways social behaviors can be planned, evaluated, and controlled. Even the direction of the relationship is unclear. Early longitudinal analyses showed that low IQ predicted later delinquency and aggression (Moffitt et al., 1981; West and Farrington, 1973), but the only published sophisticated comparison of directionality showed that, at least after age eight, aggression influenced academic performance more than IQ affected aggression (Huesmann et al., 1987). Of course, it is likely that early IQ and executive-functioning deficits increase the risk of early aggression, which, in turn, interferes with later intellectual development.

### Attention-deficit hyperactivity disorder (ADHD)

Early ADHD is strongly correlated with early aggression (Hinshaw, 1987). ADHD also predicts aggression in adolescence and young adulthood (Farrington et al., 1990; Magnusson, 1987; Moffitt, 1990; Satterfield et al., 1982). Hinshaw (1991; Hinshaw et al., 1992) has shown that pharmacological treatment of ADHD symptoms also lowers concurrent aggression, though it has little effect on long-term aggression.

### Genetic predispositions

It is clear that a substantial number of individual neurophysiological factors are related to aggression. The extent to which these factors are influenced by heredity therefore becomes a relevant question. In animals, the heritability of aggression is well established (see Lagerspetz and Lagerspetz, 1971), and there is some evidence for humans as well. As Dick and Rose (2002: 70) succinctly conclude in their recent review, 'genetic variation contributes to individual differences in virtually all behavioral domains'. A substantial number of twin and adoption studies show some heritability of aggressive or antisocial tendencies (Coie and Dodge, 1998: 35; Miles and Carey, 1997). For example, in Tellegen et al.'s (1988) 'Minnesota' study of twins reared apart, correlations of aggression scores in adulthood were 0.64 for same-sexed dyzygotic twins (DZ) and 0.34 for monozygotic twins (MZ). The Denmark studies of all twins born between 1880 and 1910 found that correlations with criminal registration were 0.74 for MZ twins and 0.46 for DZ twins (Christiansen, 1977; Cloninger and Gottesman, 1987). However, in their meta-analysis of twenty-two twin and adoption studies, Miles and Carey (1997) found two discrepant results. First, shared genetic variance accounted for up to 50 percent of the variance in self- or parent-reported aggression. Second, when aggressiveness was measured by careful observation of laboratory behaviors, the genetic effect disappeared and a strong family-environment effect emerged. Similarly, DiLalla and Gottesman (1991) pointed out that genetic effects are smaller when the criterion measure is prediction of actual behaviors. One must also remember that the likely neurophysiological mechanisms involved act as predisposers to higher risk, and that biosocial interactions are probably important.

## Interventions

For years, it seemed that interventions designed to reduce aggression in highly aggressive people were doomed to failure. Indeed, many of the most popular interventions currently in use have no validity, and some may increase aggression (Surgeon General, 2001).

Social-cognitive theories of aggression provide a plausible explanation for the fact that attempts to change overly aggressive individuals become increasingly less successful as these individuals become older. An admittedly oversimplified explanation is that, with increasing life experiences, one's typical construal of the social world is based on increasingly well-rehearsed and accessible knowledge structures, which are inherently difficult to change. Similarly, this approach accounts for the fact that narrowly based prevention or treatment programs tend not to work, presumably because there are so many ways that maladaptive knowledge structures can be learned and reinforced. Indeed, the most successful interventions are those that address multiple sources of potentially maladaptive learning environments and do so at relatively young ages (e.g., Zigler et al., 1992).

Attempts to treat or rehabilitate violent adults, usually done in the context of prison programs, have led to a general consensus of failure. However, several studies of very time-intensive interventions have yielded some positive effects (e.g., Rice, 1997; Simon, 1998).

Many treatments have been tried with violent juvenile offenders, including such things as boot camps, individual therapy, scared-straight programs, and group therapy; there is little evidence of sustained success for these particular approaches. One problem is that these approaches do not address the wide range of factors that contribute to the development and maintenance of violent behavior. However, treatment can have a significant beneficial impact on violent juvenile offenders (e.g., Simon, 1998; Tate et al., 1995). One promising approach is multisystemic therapy (Borduin, 1999; Henggeler et al., 1998). This family-based approach identifies the major factors contributing to the delinquent and violent behaviors of the particular individual undergoing treatment. Biological, school, work, peer-group, family, and neighborhood factors are examined. Intervention is then tailored to fit the individual constellation of contributing factors. Opportunities to observe and commit further violent and criminal offenses are severely restricted, whereas prosocial behavior opportunities are enhanced and rewarded. The long-term success rate and the cost–benefit ratio of this approach have greatly exceeded other attempts at treating violent juveniles.

Attempts at primary prevention of aggression in youth through school-based interventions also generally yield disappointing results (Surgeon General, 2001) though some successes for social-cognitive interventions have been reported. A large-scale elementary-school-based preventive intervention in the Chicago area involving a social-cognitive curriculum, social-cognitive peer-group training, and a family intervention showed some success, but only for children living in communities that were not severely impoverished (Huesmann, 2000; Metropolitan Area Child Research Group, 2002). Another social-cognitive intervention (Conduct Problems Prevention Research Group, 1999) which followed a smaller set of high-risk children with repeated interventions, also reported some success in reducing aggression, but only in some contexts. More research on long-term effects of social-cognitive primary-prevention interventions is needed before definitive conclusions can be reached on their value.

## Conclusions

Social-cognitive approaches to understanding human aggression have been developing for over thirty years. Current models converge on a common set of theoretical assumptions, largely because those assumptions have proven useful in organizing the vast research literature and in generating new, testable hypotheses concerning the development, persistence, and change of aggression. The general aggression model is itself merely an attempt to unify these many strands into a common framework. It is possible to do so only because of the intensive theoretical work that has gone before and because the underlying concepts have been so valuable, regardless of the specific labels used.

An interesting trend that has emerged in the past decade or so concerns interventions. Gone are the days when aggression scholars had to admit that despite years of work there were no successful ones. The social-cognitive approach itself suggests why many popular approaches have failed and why certain approaches work (Eron et al., 1994).

## Notes

1 Crick and Grotpeter (1995) have renamed (with minor changes) the indirect-aggression construct developed by Lagerspetz and Bjorkqvist (1992) as 'relational aggression'. However, we prefer to use the original label which seems to reflect the kind of aggression more accurately.

2 Though Nisbett and Cohen (1996) present evidence that a culture of honor is positively related to violence, that finding cannot 'explain' the apparent hot-temperature effects on violence (Anderson, 2001; Anderson and Anderson, 1996; Anderson et al., 2000; Berkowitz, 2003).

3 A few longitudinal studies have seemed to produce results at odds with the thesis that media violence causes aggression, but closer inspection of these studies reveals that their results are not discrepant but simply not strongly supportive of the thesis. (For a review, see Huesmann and Miller, 1994.) The most widely cited – NBC's longitudinal study of middle-childhood youth conducted in the 1970s (Milavsky et al., 1982) – reported significant regression coefficients for only two of the fifteen critical tests of the causal theory for boys; however, an additional ten were in the predicted direction. For girls, three of the fifteen critical tests were significant and an additional seven were in the predicted direction. Furthermore, a number of the most aggressive children were dropped from the reported analyses, a fact which may have biased the results against finding significant media-violence effects.

**SUMMARY**

This chapter uses an integrative social-cognitive theory to make sense of the complicated phenomenon of human aggression. It begins by presenting information about patterns of violence across nations, gender, and ages. Violence is best understood as an extreme form of physical aggression which is present in virtually all modern societies. Aggression emerges early in life and is shaped by a confluence of biological (e.g., low serotonin) and environmental factors (e.g., family and media violence) that interactively combine to create each individual's capacity and propensity to use aggressive (or nonaggressive) tactics in response to specific situations. Elements of a person's preparedness to aggress include self-schemas, beliefs and attitudes concerning aggression, hostile world schemas, behavioral scripts, and long-term goals. Preparedness to aggress interacts with situational factors to determine whether aggression results, and if so, the form it takes. Situational factors include aversive conditions (e.g., provocation, frustration, pain), stimuli that prime aggressive thoughts and emotions (e.g., presence of guns, people associated in memory with violence), and factors that increase physiological arousal. Successful interventions require considerable time and effort to change various elements of preparedness to aggress and are more likely to work on younger individuals whose personalities are more malleable.

## References

Anderson, C.A. (1989) 'Temperature and Aggression: Ubiquitous Effects of Heat on the Occurrence of Human Violence', *Psychological Bulletin*, 106: 74–96.

Anderson, C.A. (1997) 'Effects of Violent Movies and Trait Irritability on Hostile Feelings and Aggressive Thoughts', *Aggressive Behavior*, 23: 161–78.

Anderson, C.A. (2001) 'Heat and Violence', *Current Directions in Psychological Science*, 10: 33–8.

Anderson, C.A. (2002) 'Violent Video Games and Aggressive Thoughts, Feelings and Behaviors', in S.L. Calvert, A.B. Jordan and R.R. Cocking (eds), *Children in the Digital Age*. Westport, CT: Praeger Publishers, pp. 101–19.

Anderson, C.A. and Anderson, K.B. (1996) 'Violent Crime Rate Studies in Philosophical Context: A Destructive Testing Approach to Heat and Southern Culture of Violence Effects', *Journal of Personality and Social Psychology*, 70: 740–56.

Anderson, C.A., Anderson, K.B. and Deuser, W.E. (1996) 'Examining an Affective Aggression Framework: Weapon and Temperature Effects on Aggressive Thoughts, Affect and Attitudes', *Personality and Social Psychology Bulletin*, 22: 366–76.

Anderson, C.A., Anderson, K.B., Dorr, N., Deneve, K.M. and Flanagan, M. (2000) 'Temperature and Aggression', in M. Zanna (ed.), *Advances in Experimental Social Psychology* (vol. 32). New York: Academic Press, pp. 63–133.

Anderson, C.A., Benjamin, A.J. and Bartholow, B.D. (1998) 'Does the Gun Pull the Trigger? Automatic Priming Effects of Weapon Pictures and Weapon Names', *Psychological Science*, 9: 308–14.

Anderson, C.A., Benjamin, A.J., Wood, P.K., and Bonacci, A.M. (under review) 'Development and Testing of the Attitudes toward Violence Scale: Evidence for a Four-Factor Model'.

Anderson, C.A. and Bushman, B.J. (2001) 'Effects of Violent Video Games on Aggressive Behavior, Aggressive Cognition, Aggressive Affect, Physiological Arousal and Prosocial Behavior: A Meta-analytic Review of the Scientific Literature', *Psychological Science*, 12: 353–9.

Anderson, C.A. and Bushman, B.J. (2002a) 'Human Aggression', *Annual Review of Psychology*, 53: 27–51.

Anderson, C.A. and Bushman, B.J. (2002b) 'The Effects of Media Violence on Society', *Science*, 295: 2377–8.

Anderson, C.A., Bushman, B.J., and Groom, R.W. (1997) 'Hot Years and Serious and Deadly Assault: Empirical Tests of the Heat Hypothesis', *Journal of Personality and Social Psychology*, 16: 1213–23.

Anderson, C.A. and Dill, K.E. (2000) 'Video Games and Aggressive Thoughts, Feelings and Behavior in the Laboratory and in Life', *Journal of Personality and Social Psychology*, 78: 772–90.

Anderson, K.L. (1990) 'Arousal and the Inverted-U Hypothesis: A Critique of Neiss's "Reconceptualizing Arousal"', *Psychological Bulletin*, 107: 96–100.

Anderson, K.B. (1996) 'Cognitive and Personality Predictors of Male-on-Female Aggression: An Integration of Theoretical Perspectives'. Unpublished dissertation, Columbia, MO.

Anderson, K.B., Anderson, C.A., Dill, K.E., and Deuser, W.E. (1998) 'The Interactive Relations between Trait Hostility, Pain and Aggressive Thoughts', *Aggressive Behavior*, 24: 161–71.

Archer, J. (1988) *The Behavioral Biology of Aggression*. Cambridge: Cambridge University Press.

Archer, J. (1991) 'The Influence of Testosterone on Human Aggression', *British Journal of Psychology*, 82: 1–28.

Archer, J. (2000) 'Sex Differences in Aggression between Heterosexual Partners: A Meta-Analytic Review', *Psychological Bulletin*, 126: 697–702.

Azar, S.T. and Rohrbeck, C.A. (1986) 'Child Abuse and Unrealistic Expectations: Further Validation of the Parent Opinion Questionnaire', *Journal of Consulting and Clinical Psychology*, 54: 867–8.

Bandura, A. (1973) *Aggression: A Social Learning Theory Analysis*. Englewood Cliffs, NJ: Prentice-Hall.

Bandura, A. (1977) *Social Learning Theory*. New York: Prentice-Hall.

Bandura, A. (1983) 'Psychological Mechanism of Aggression', in R.G. Geen and E.I. Donnerstein (eds), *Aggression: Theoretical and Empirical Reviews* (vol. 1). New York: Academic Press, pp. 1–40.

Bandura, A. (1986) *Social Foundations of Thought and Action: A Social-Cognitive Theory*. Englewood Cliffs, NJ: Prentice-Hall.

Bandura, A., Barbaranelli, C., Caprara, G.V., and Pastorelli, C. (1996) 'Mechanisms of Moral Disengagement in the Exercise of Moral Agency', *Journal of Personality and Social Psychology*, 71: 364–74.

Bargh, J.A., (1989) 'Conditional Automaticity: Varieties of Automatic Influence in Social Perception and Cognition', in J.S. Uleman and J.A. Bargh (eds), *Unintended Thought*. New York: Guilford Press.

Bargh, J.A., Chen, M., and Burrows, L. (1996) 'Automaticity of Social Behavior: Direct Effects of Trait Construct and Stereotype Priming on Action', *Journal of Personality and Social Psychology*, 71: 230–44.

Bargh, J.A., Raymond, P., Pryor, J., and Strack, F. (1995) 'Attractiveness of the Underling: An Automatic Power–Sex Association and its Consequences for Sexual Harassment and Aggression', *Journal of Personality and Social Psychology*, 68: 768–81.

Bargh, J.A. and Pietromonaco, P. (1982) 'Automatic Information Processing and Social Perception: The Influence of Trait Information Presented Outside of Conscious Awareness on Impression Formation', *Journal of Personality and Social Psychology*, 43: 437–49.

Baron, R. (1977) *Human Aggression*. New York: Plenum.

Baron, R.A. and Richardson, D.R. (1994) *Human Aggression*, 2nd edn. New York: Plenum Press.

Bartholow, B.D., Anderson, C.A., Benjamin, A.J., and Carnagey, N.L. (under review) *Individual Differences in Knowledge Structures and Priming: The Weapons Priming Effect in Hunters and Nonhunters*.

Baumeister, R.F. and Boden, J.M. (1998) 'Aggression and the Self: High Self-Esteem, Low Self-Control and Ego Threat', in R. Green and E. Donnerstein (eds), *Human Aggression: Theories, Research and Implications for Policy*. New York: Academic Press, pp. 111–37.

Baumeister, R.F., Smart, L., and Boden, J.M. (1996) 'Relation of Threatened Egotism to Violence and Aggression: The Dark Side of High Self-Esteem', *Psychological Review*, 103: 5–33.

Berkowitz, L. (1982) 'Aversive Conditions as Stimuli to Aggression', in L. Berkowitz (ed.), *Advances in Experimental Social Psychology* (vol. 15). New York: Academic Press, pp. 249–88.

Berkowitz, L. (1989) 'Frustration-Aggression Hypothesis: Examination and Reformulation', *Psychological Bulletin*, 106: 59–73.

Berkowitz, L. (1993) *Aggression: Its Causes, Consequences and Control*. New York: MCGraw-Hill.

Berkowitz, L. (2003) 'Affect, Aggression and Antisocial Behavior', in R. Davidson, K. Scherer, and H. Goldsmith (eds), *Handbook of Affective Sciences*, New York: Oxford University Press, pp. 804–23.

Berkowitz, L. and Donnerstein, E. (1982) 'External Validity Is More than Skin Deep: Some Answers to Criticism of Laboratory Experiments', *American Psychologist*, 37: 245–57.

Berkowitz, L., Cochran, S.T., and Embree, M.C. (1981) 'Physical Pain and the Goal of Aversively Stimulated Aggression', *Journal of Personality and Social Psychology*, 40: 687–700.

Berkowitz, L. and LePage, A. (1967) 'Weapons as Aggression-Eliciting Stimuli', *Journal of Personality and Social Psychology*, 7: 202–7.

Berkowitz, L. and Troccoli, B.T. (1990) 'Feelings, Direction of Attention and Expressed Evaluations of Others', *Cognition and Emotion*, 4: 305–25.

Bettencourt, B.A. and Kernahan, C. (1997) 'A Meta-Analysis of Aggression in the Presence of Violent Cues: Effects of Gender Differences and Aversive Provocation', *Aggressive Behavior*, 23: 447–56.

Bettencourt, B.A. and Miller, N. (1996) 'Gender Differences in Aggression as a Function of Provocation: A Meta-Analysis', *Psychological Bulletin*, 119: 422–47.

Bjorkqvist, K., Lagerspetz, K., and Kaukiainen, A. (1992) 'Do Girls Manipulate and Boys Fight? Developmental Trends in Regard to Direct and Indirect Aggression', *Aggressive Behavior*, 18: 117–27.

Book, A.S., Starzyk, K.B., and Quinsey, V.L. (2002) 'The Relationship between Testosterone and Aggression: A Meta-Analysis', *Aggression and Violent Behavior*, 6: 579–99.

Bookwala, J., Frieze, I., Smith, C., and Ryan, K. (1992) 'Predictors of Dating Violence: A Multivariate Analysis', *Violence and Victims*, 7: 297–311.

Borduin, C.M. (1999) 'Multisystemic Treatment of Criminality and Violence in Adolescents', *Journal of the American Academy of Child and Adolescent Psychiatry*, 38: 242–9.

Brain, P.F. (1986) 'Multidisciplinary Examinations of the "Causes" of Crime: The Case of the Link between Alcohol and Violence', *Alcohol and Alcoholism*, 21: 237–40.

Brain, P.F. (1994) 'Hormonal Aspects of Aggression and Violence', in A.J. Reis, Jr. and J.A. Roth (eds), *Understanding and Control of Biobehavioral Influences on Violence* (vol. 2). Washington, DC: National Academy Press, pp. 177–244.

Brame, B., Nagin, D.S., and Tremblay, R.E. (2001) 'Developmental Trajectories of Physical Aggression from School Entry to Late Adolescence', *Journal of Child Psychology and Psychiatry*, 42 (4): 503–12.

Broadbent, D.E. (1971) *Decision and Stress*. London: Academic Press.

Brown, G.L., Goodwin, F.K., Ballenger, J.C., Goyer, P.F., and Major, L.F. (1979) 'Aggression in Humans Correlates with Cerebrospinal Fluid Amine Metabolites', *Psychiatry Research*, 1: 131–9.

Brown, G.L., Klein, W.J., Goyer, P.F., et al. (1985) 'Relationship of Childhood Characteristics of CSF 5–HIAA in Aggressive Adults', presented at Fourth World Congress of Biological Psychiatry (Abstract 216.3), Philadelphia, PA.

Bushman, B.J. (1993) 'Human Aggression while under the Influence of Alcohol and Other Drugs: An Integrative Research Review', *Current Directions in Psychological Science*, 2, 148–52.

Bushman, B.J. (1997) 'Effects of Alcohol on Human Aggression: Validity of Proposed Explanations', in D. Fuller, R. Dietrich, and E. Gottheil (eds), *Recent Developments in Alcoholism: Alcohol and Violence* (vol. 13). New York: Plenum, pp. 227–43.

Bushman, B.J. (1998) 'Priming Effects of Violent Media on the Accessibility of Aggressive Constructs in Memory', *Personality and Social Psychology Bulletin*. 24: 537–45.

Bushman, B.J. and Anderson, C.A. (2001) 'Is It Time to Pull the Plug on the Hostile versus Instrumental Aggression Dichotomy?', *Psychological Review*, 108: 273–9.

Bushman, B.J. and Baumeister, R.F. (1998) 'Threatened Egotism, Narcissism, Self-Esteem and Direct and Displaced Aggression: Does Self-Love or Self-Hate Lead to Violence?', *Journal of Personality and Social Psychology*, 75: 219–29.

Bushman, B.J. and Huesmann, L.R. (2000) 'Effects of Televised Violence on Aggression', in D. Singer and J. Singer (eds), *Handbook of Children and the Media*. Thousand Oaks, CA: Sage, pp. 223–54.

Buss, A.H. and Perry, M.P. (1992) 'The Aggression Questionnaire', *Journal of Personality and Social Psychology*, 63: 452–9.

Buss, D.M. and Shackelford, T.K. (1997a) 'From Vigilance to Violence: Mate Retention Tactics in Married Couples', *Journal of Personality and Social Psychology*, 72: 346–61.

Buss, D.M. and Shackelford, T.K. (1997b) 'Human Aggression in Evolutionary Psychological Perspective', *Clinical Psychology Review*, 17: 605–19.

Cairns, R.B. and Cairns, B.D. (1994) *Lifelines and Risks: Pathways of Youth in Our Time*. New York: Cambridge University Press.

Campbell, A. (1999) 'Staying Alive: Evolution, Culture and Women's Intrasexual Aggression', *Behavioral and Brain Sciences*, 22: 203–52.

Caplan, M., Vespo, J., Pedersen, J., and Hay, D.F. (1991) 'Conflict over Resources in Small Groups of One- and Two-Year-Olds', *Child Development*, 62: 1513–24.

Caprara, G.V., Barbaranelli, C., Pastorelli, C., and Perugini, M. (1994) 'Individual Differences in the Study of Aggression', *Aggressive Behavior*, 20: 291–303.

Caprara, G.V., Cinanni, B., D'Imperio, G., Passerini, S., Renzi, P., and Travaglia, G. (1985) 'Indicators of Impulsive Aggression: Present Status of Research on Irritability and Emotional Susceptibility Scales', *Personality and Individual Differences*, 6: 665–74.

Carlson, M., Marcus-Newhall, A., and Miller, N. (1990) 'Effects of Situational Aggression Cues: A Quantitative Review', *Journal of Personality and Social Psychology*, 58: 622–33.

Carver, C.S. (1974) 'Facilitation of Physical Aggression through Objective Self-Awareness', *Journal of Experimental Social Psychology*, 10: 365–70.

Carver, C., Ganellen, R., Froming, W., and Chambers, W. (1983) 'Modeling: An Analysis in Terms of Category Accessibility', *Journal of Experimental Social Psychology*, 19: 403–21.

Chen, M. and Bargh, J.A. (1997) 'Nonconscious Behavioral Confirmation Processes: The Self-Fulfilling Consequences of Automatic Stereotype Activation', *Journal of Experimental Social Psychology*, 33: 541–60.

Christiansen, K. (1977) 'A Preliminary Study of Criminality among Twins', in S.A. Mednick and K.O. Christiansen (eds), *Biosocial Bases of Criminal Behavior*. New York: Gardner Press, pp. 89–108.

Cline, V.B., Croft, R.G., and Courrier, S. (1973) 'Desensitization of Children to Television Violence', *Journal of Personality and Social Psychology*, 27: 360–5.

Cloninger, C.R. and Gottesman, I.I. (1987) 'Genetic and Environmental Factors in Antisocial Behavior Disorders', in S.A. Mednick, T.E. Moffitt, and S. Stack (eds), *The Causes of Crime: New Biological Approaches*. Cambridge: Cambridge University Press.

Coccaro, E.G. (1989) 'Central Serotonin and Impulsive Aggression', *British Journal of Psychiatry*, 155: 52–62.

Coie, J. and Dodge, K. (1998) 'Aggression and Anti-Social Behavior', in W. Damon and N. Eisenberg (eds), *Handbook of Child Psychology*. New York: Wiley, pp. 779–862.

Conduct Problems Prevention Research Group (1999) 'Initial Impact of the Fast Track Prevention Trial for Conduct Problems. I. The High Risk Sample', *Journal of Consulting and Clinical Psychology*, 67: 631–47.

Crick, N.R. and Dodge, K.A. (1994) 'A Review and Reformulation of Social Information Processing Mechanisms in Children's Adjustment', *Psychological Bulletin*, 115: 74–101.

Crick, N.R. and Grotpeter, J.K. (1995) 'Relational Aggression, Gender and Social-Psychological Adjustment', *Child Development*, 66: 710–22.

Daly, M. and Wilson, M. (1994) 'Evolutionary Psychology of Male Violence', in J. Archer (ed.), *Male Violence*. London: Routledge, pp. 253–88.

Deluty, R.H. (1981) 'Alternative Thinking Ability of Aggressive, Assertive and Submissive Children', *Cognitive Therapy and Research*, 5: 309–12.

Devine, P.G. (1989) 'Stereotypes and Prejudice: Their Automatic and Controlled Components', *Journal of Personality and Social Psychology*, 56: 680–90.

Dick, D.M. and Rose, R.J. (2002) 'Behavior Genetics: What's New? What's Next?', *Current Directions in Psychological Science*, 11 (2): 70–4.

Diener, E. (1976) 'Effects of Prior Destructive Behavior, Anonymity and Group Presence on Deindividuation and Aggression', *Journal of Personality and Social Psychology*, 33: 497–507.

Dilalla, L.F. and Gottesman, I.I. (1991) 'Biological and Genetic Contributions to Violence: Widom's Untold Tale', *Psychological Bulletin*, 109: 125–29.

Dill, J. and Anderson, C.A. (1995) 'Effects of Justified and Unjustified Frustration on Aggression', *Aggressive Behavior*, 21: 359–69.

Dill, K.E., Anderson, C.A., Anderson, K.B., and Deuser, W.E. (1997) 'Effects of Aggressive Personality on Social Expectations and Social Perceptions', *Journal of Research in Personality*, 31: 272–92.

Dodge, K.A. (1980) 'Social Cognition and Children's Aggressive Behavior', *Child Development*, 51: 620–35.

Dodge, K.A. (1986) 'A Social Information Processing Model of Social Competence in Children', in M. Perlmutter (ed.), *The Minnesota Symposium on Child Psychology* (vol. 18). Hillsdale, NJ: Erlbaum, pp. 77–125.

Dodge, K.A. and Coie, J.D. (1987) 'Social Information-Processing Factors in Reactive and Proactive Aggression in Children's Peer Groups', *Journal of Personality and Social Psychology*, 53: 1146–58.

Dodge, K.A. and Frame, C.L. (1982) 'Social Cognitive Biases and Deficits in Aggressive Boys', *Child Development*, 53: 620–35.

Dodge, K.A., Price, J.M., Bachorowski, J.A., and Newman, J.P. (1990) 'Hostile Attributional Biases in Severely Aggressive Adolescents', *Journal of Abnormal Psychology*, 99: 385–92.

Dodge, K.A. and Tomlin, A. (1987) 'Utilization of Self-Schemas as a Mechanism of Attributional Bias in Aggressive Children', *Social Cognition*, 5 (3): pp. 280–300.

Dollard, J., Doob, L.W., Miller, N.E., Mower, O.H., and Sears, R.R. (1939) *Frustration and Aggression*. New Haven, CT: Yale University Press.

Earls, F. (1980) 'The Prevalence of Behavior Problems in 3-Year-Old Children', *Archives of General Psychiatry*, 37: 1153–9.

Easterbrook, J.A. (1959) 'The Effect of Emotion on Cue Utilization and the Organization of Behavior', *Psychological Review*, 66: 183–201.

Ekman, P. and Friesen, W.V. (1975) *Unmasking the Face: A Guide to Recognizing Emotions from Facial Clues*. New York: Prentice-Hall.

Elias, M. (1981) 'Serum Cortisol, Testosterone and Testosterone-Binding Globulin Responses to Competitive Fighting in Human Males', *Aggressive Behavior*, 7: 215–24.

Eron, L.D., Walder, L.O., and Lefkowitz, M.M. (1971) *The Learning of Aggression in Children*. Boston, MA: Little Brown.

Eron, L.D., Gentry, J.H., and Schlegel, P. (1994) *Reason to Hope: A Psychosocial Perspective on Violence and Youth*. Washington, DC: American Psychological Association.

Eron, L.D., Huesmann, L.R., Lefkowitz, M.M., and Walder, L.O. (1972) 'Does T.V. Violence Cause Aggression?', *American Psychologist*, 27: 153–263.

Farrington, D.P. (1982) 'Longitudinal Analyses of Criminal Violence', in M.E. Wolfgang and N.A. Weiner (eds), *Criminal Violence*. Beverly Hills, CA: Sage, pp. 171–200.

Farrington, D.P. (1993) 'Motivations for Conduct Disorder and Delinquency', *Development and Psychopathology*, 5: 225–41.

Farrington, D.P. (1995) 'The Development of Offending and Antisocial Behavior from Childhood: Key Findings from the Cambridge Study in Delinquent Development', *Journal of Child Psychology and Psychiatry*, 36: 1–36.

Farrington, D.P. (1999) *Crime and Justice in the United States and in England and Wales, 1981–1996*. Washington, DC: US Department of Justice, Bureau of Justice Statistics.

Farrington, D.P. (2002) 'Multiple Risk Factors for Multiple Problem Violent Boys', in R. Corrado et al. (eds), *Multi-Problem Violent Youth: A Foundation for Comparative Research on Needs Interventions and Outcomes*. Series 1: Life and Behavioural Sciences (vol. 324). Netherlands: IOS Press, pp. 23–34.

Farrington, D.P., Loeber, R., and Van Kammen, W.B. (1990) 'Long-Term Criminal Outcomes of Hyperactivity-Impulsivity-Attention Deficit and Conduct Problems in Childhood', in L.N. Robins and M. Rutter (eds), *Straight and Devious Pathways from Childhood to Adulthood*. Cambridge: Cambridge University Press, pp. 62–81.

Feshbach, S. (1964) 'The Function of Aggression and the Regulation of Aggressive Drive', *Psychological Review*, 71: 257–72.

Fiske, S.T. (1982) 'Schema-Triggered Affect: Applications to Social Perception', in M.S. Clark and S.T. Fiske (eds), *Affect and Cognition: The 17th Annual Carnegie Symposium on Cognition*. Hillsdale, NJ: Erlbaum, pp. 55–78.

Fiske, S.T. and Taylor, S.E. (1991) *Social Cognition*. New York: MCGraw-Hill.

Fraczek, A. (1985) 'Moral Approval of Aggressive Acts: A Polish-Finnish Comparative Study', *Journal of Cross-Cultural Psychology*, 16: 41–51.

Fujihara, T., Kohyama, T., Andreu, J.M., and Ramirez, M.J. (1999) 'Justification of Interpersonal Aggression in Japanese, American and Spanish Students', *Aggressive Behaviour*, 25 (3): 185–95.

Geary, D.C. (1998) *Male, Female: The Evolution of Human Sex Differences*. Washington, DC: American Psychological Association.

Geary, D.C., Rumsey, M., Bow-Thomas, C.C., and Hoard, M.K. (1995) 'Sexual Jealousy as a Facultative Trait: Evidence from the Pattern of Sex Differences in Adults from China and the United States', *Ethology and Sociobiology*, 16: 355–83.

Geen, R.G. (1968) 'Effects of Frustration, Attack and Prior Training in Aggressiveness upon Aggressive Behavior', *Journal of Personality and Social Psychology*, 27: 389–95.

Geen, R.G. (2001) *Human Aggression.* Philadelphia, PA: Open University Press.

Geen, R.G. and O'Neal, E.C. (1969) 'Activation of Cue-Elicited Aggression by General Arousal', *Journal of Personality and Social Psychology*, 11: 289–92.

Gladue, B.A., Boechler, M., and McCaul, K.D. (1989) 'Hormonal Responses to Competition in Human Males', *Aggressive Behavior*, 17: 313–26.

Goldstein, A.P. (1994) 'Delinquent Gangs', in L.R. Huesmann (ed.), *Aggressive Behavior: Current Perspectives.* Plenum Series in Social/Clinical Psychology. New York: Plenum Press, pp. 255–73.

Gouse, K.R. (1981) 'Attention and Social Problem Solving as Correlates of Aggression in Preschool Males', *Journal of Abnormal Child Psychology*, 15: 181–97.

Graham, S. and Hudley, C. (1994) 'Attributions of Aggressive and Nonaggressive African-American Male Early Adolescents: A Study of Construct Accessibility', *Developmental Psychology*, 30: 365–73.

Greeson, L.E. and Williams, R.A. (1986) 'Social Implications of Music Videos for Youth: An Analysis of the Content and Effects of MTV', *Youth and Society*, 18: 177–89.

Griffitt, W. (1970) 'Environmental Effects on Interpersonal Affective Behavior: Ambient Effective Temperature and Attraction', *Journal of Personality and Social Psychology*, 15: 240–4.

Guerra, N.G., Huesmann, L.R., and Spindler, A.J. (2002) *Community Violence Exposure, Social Cognition and Aggression among Urban Elementary-School Children.* Institute for Social Research, University of Michigan.

Guerra, N.G., Huesmann, L.R., Tolan, P., Van Acker, R., and Eron, L.D. (1995) 'Stressful Events and Individual Beliefs as Correlates of Economic Disadvantage and Aggression among Urban Children', *Journal of Consulting and Clinical Psychology*, 63 (4): 518–28.

Hansen, C.H. and Hansen, R.D. (1989) 'The Content of MTS's Daily Countdown: "Dial MTV" for Sex, Violence and Antisocial Behavior'. Unpublished manuscript.

Hansen, C.H. and Hansen, R.D. (1990) 'Rock Music Videos and Antisocial Behavior', *Basic and Applied Social Psychology*, 11: 357–69.

Hare, R.D. (1978) 'Electrodermal and Cardiovascular Correlates of Psychopathy', in R.D. Hare and D. Schalling (eds), *Psychopathic Behavior: Approaches to Research.* New York: Wiley, pp. 107–44.

Henggeler, S.W., Schoenwald, S.K., Borduin, C.M., Rowland, M.D., and Cunningham, P.B. (1998) *Multisystemic Treatment of Antisocial Behavior in Children and Adolescents*. New York: Guilford.

Henry, D., Guerra, N., Huesmann, R., and Van Acker, R. (1996) 'Normative Influences on Aggression in Urban Elementary School Classrooms'. Manuscript submitted for publication.

Hinshaw, S.P. (1987) 'On the Distinction between Attentional Deficits/Hyperactivity and Conduct Problems/Aggression in Child Psychopathology', *Psychological Bulletin*, 101: 443–63.

Hinshaw, S.P. (1991) 'Stimulant Medication and the Treatment of Aggression in Children with Attentional Deficits', *Journal of Clinical Child Psychology*, 20: 301–12.

Hinshaw, S.P., Heller, T., and Mchale, J.P. (1992) 'Covert Antisocial Behavior in Boys with Attention-Deficit Hyperactivity Disorder: External Validation and Effects of Methylphenidate', *Journal of Consulting and Clinical Psychology*, 60: 274–81.

Horowitz, R. and Schwartz, G. (1974) 'Honor, Normative Ambiguity and Gang Violence', *American Sociological Review*, 39: 238–51.

Howard, R.C. (1984) 'The Clinical EEG and Personality in Mentally Abnormal Offenders', *Psychological Medicine*, 14: 569–80.

Huesmann, L.R. (1982) 'Information Processing Models of Behavior', in N. Hirschberg and L. Humphreys (eds), *Multivariate Applications in the Social Sciences.* Hillsdale, NJ: Erlbaum, pp. 261–88.

Huesmann, L.R. (1986) 'Psychological Processes Promoting the Relation between Exposure to Media Violence and Aggressive Behavior by the Viewer', *Journal of Social Issues*, 42 (3): 125–39.

Huesmann, L.R. (1988) 'An Information Processing Model for the Development of Aggression', *Aggressive Behavior*, 14: 13–24.

Huesmann, L.R. (1995) 'Early Prediction and Prevention of Aggression and Antisocial Behavior', *Aggressive Behavior*, 21 (3): 190.

Huesmann, L.R. (1997) 'Observational Learning of Violent Behavior: Social and Biosocial Processes', in A. Raine, D.P. Farrington, P.O. Brennen, and S.A. Mednick (eds), *The Biosocial Basis of Violence.* New York: Plenum, pp. 69–88.

Huesmann, LR. (1998) 'The Role of Social Information Processing and Cognitive Schemas in the Acquisition and Maintenance of Habitual Aggressive Behavior', in R.G. Geen and E. Donnerstein (eds), *Human Aggression: Theories, Research and Implications for Policy.* New York: Academic Press, pp. 73–109.

Huesmann, L.R. (2000) 'Analysis of a Cognitive-Ecological Program for the Prevention of Violence in Inner-City Youth'. Paper presented at the meetings of the International Society for Research on Aggression, Valencia, Spain.

Huesmann, L.R. and Eron, L.D. (eds) (1986) *Television and the Aggressive Child: A Cross-National Comparison.* Hillsdale, NJ: Erlbaum.

Huesmann, L.R., Eron, L.D., Lefkowitz, M.M., and Walder, L.O. (1984a) 'Stability of Aggression over

Time and Generations', *Developmental Psychology*, 20: 1120–34.

Huesmann, L.R., Eron, L.D., and Yarmel, P.W. (1987) 'Intellectual Functioning and Aggression', *Journal of Personality and Social Psychology*, 52: 232–40.

Huesmann, L.R. and Guerra, N.G. (1997) 'Children's Normative Beliefs about Aggression and Aggressive Behavior', *Journal of Personality and Social Psychology*, 72: 408–19.

Huesmann, L.R., Lagerspetz, K., and Eron, L.D. (1984b) 'Intervening Variables in the Television Violence – Aggression Relation: Evidence from Two Countries', *Developmental Psychology*, 20 (5): 746–75.

Huesmann, L.R. and Miller, L.S. (1994) 'Long-Term Effects of Repeated Exposure to Media Violence in Childhood', in L.R. Huesmann (ed.), *Aggressive Behavior: Current Perspectives*. New York: Plenum, pp. 153–86.

Huesmann, L.R. and Moise, J. (1998) 'The Stability and Continuity of Aggression from Early Childhood to Young Adulthood', in D.J. Flannery and C.R. Huff (eds), *Youth Violence: Prevention, Intervention, and Social Policy*, Washington, DC: American Psychiatric Press, pp. 73–95.

Huesmann, L.R. and Moise-Titus, J. (2002) 'Normative Beliefs, Hostile Schemas and Script Rehearsal as Mediators of the Relation between Childhood Observation of Violence and Adult Aggressive Behavior'. Paper presented at the meetings of the European Society for Social Psychology, San Sebastian, Spain, June.

Huesmann, L.R., Moise J., Podolski, C.P., and Eron, L.D. (2003) 'Longitudinal Relations between Children's Exposure to Television Violence and their Aggressive and Violent Behaviour in Young Adulthood', *Developmental Psychology, 1977–92*: 39, 201–21.

Hyman, I.A. (1995) 'Corporal Punishment, Psychological Maltreatment, Violence and Punitiveness in America: Research, Advocacy and Public Policy', *Applied and Preventive Psychology*, 4: 113–30.

Johnson, J.G., Cohen, P., Smailes, E.M., Kasen, S., and Brook, J.S. (2002) 'Television Viewing and Aggressive Behavior during Adolescence and Adulthood', *Science*, 295: 2468–71.

Johnson, J., Jackson, L., and Gatto, L. (1995) 'Violent Attitudes and Deferred Academic Aspirations: Deleterious Effects of Exposure to Rap Music', *Basic and Applied Social Psychology*, 16: 279–94.

Jones, J. and Bogat, G. (1978) 'Air Pollution and Human Aggression', *Psychological Reports*, 43: 721–2.

Kantak, K.M., Hegstrand, L.R., Eichelman, B. (1981) 'Facilitation of Shock-Induced Fighting Following Intraventricular 5,7-Dehydroxytryptamine and 6-Hydroxydopa', *Psychopharmacology*, 74: 157–60.

Keltner, D. and Robinson, R.J. (1996) 'Extremism, Power and the Imagined Basis of Social Conflict', *Current Directions in Psychological Science*, 5: 101–5.

Kernis, M.H., Grannemann, B.D., and Barclay, L.C. (1989) 'Stability and Level of Self-Esteem as Predictors of Anger Arousal and Hostility', *Journal of Personality and Social Psychology*, 56: 1013–22.

Kingery, P.M. (1998) 'The Adolescent Violence Survey: A Psychometric Analysis', *School Psychology International*, 19: 43–59.

Klein, M.W. and Maxson, C.K. (1989) 'Street Gang Violence', in N. Weiner and M. Wolfgang (eds), *Violent Crime, Violent Criminals*. Newbury Park, CA: Sage, pp. 198–234.

Lagerspetz, K.M. and Bjorkqvist, K. (1992) 'Indirect Aggression in Girls and Boys', in L.R. Huesmann (ed.), *Aggressive Behavior: Current Perspectives*. New York: Plenum, pp. 131–50.

Lagerspetz, K.M., Bjorkqvist, K., and Peltonen, T. (1988) 'Is Indirect Aggression Typical of Females? Gender Differences in Aggressiveness in 11-to 12-Year-Old Children', *Aggressive Behavior*, 14: 403–14.

Lagerspetz, K. and Lagerspetz, K.M.J. (1971) 'Changes in Aggressiveness of Mice Resulting from Selective Breeding, Learning and Social Isolation', *Scandinavian Journal of Psychology*, 12: 241–78.

Landau, S.F. (1988) 'Violent Crime and Its Relation to Subjective Social Stress Indicators: The Case of Israel', *Aggressive Behavior*, 13: 67–85.

Lang, A.R., Goeckner, D.J., Adesso, V.J., and Marlatt, G.A. (1975) 'Effects of Alcohol on Aggression in Male Social Drinkers', *Journal of Abnormal Psychology*, 84: 508–18.

Lazarus, R.S., Speisman, J.C., Mordkoff, A.M., and Davidson, L.A. (1962) 'A Laboratory Study of Psychological Stress Produced by a Motion Picture Film', *Psychological Monographs: General and Applied*, 76 (34).

Lee, S., Huesmann, L.R., Crocker, J. (2002) 'Contingencies of Self-Worth and Aggressive Behavior'. Paper presented at the American Psychological Society, June.

Lefkowitz, M.M., Eron, L.D., Walder, L.O., and Huesmann, L.R. (1977) *Growing Up to Be Violent: A Longitudinal Study of the Development of Aggression.* New York: Pergamon.

Leyens, J.P. and Fraczek, A. (1983) 'Aggression as an Interpersonal Phenomenon', in H. Tajfel (ed.), *The Social Dimension*, (vol. 1). Cambridge: Cambridge University Press, p. 192.

Linnolia, M., Virkkunen, M., Scheinin, M., Nuutila, A., Rimon, R., and Goodwin, F.K. (1983) 'Low Cerebrospinal Fluid 5–Hydroxyindoleacetic Acid Concentration Differentiates Impulsive from Nonimpulsive Violent Behaviour', *Life Science*, 33: 2609–614.

Loeber, R. and Dishion, T.J. (1983) 'Early Predictors of Male Delinquency: A Review', *Psychological Bulletin*, 94: 68–94.

Loeber, R. and Hay, D.F. (1993) 'Developmental Approaches to Aggression and Conduct Problems', in M. Rutter and D.F. Hay (eds), *Development through Life: A Handbook for Clinicians*. Oxford: Blackwell Scientific, pp. 488–516.

Loeber, R. and Hay, D. (1997) 'Key Issues in the Development of Aggression from Childhood to Early

Adulthood', *Annual Review of Psychology*, 48: 371–410.

Luria, A.R. (1973) *The Working Brain*. London: Penguin.

Magnusson, D. (1987) 'Adult Delinquency and Early Conduct and Physiology', in D. Magnusson and A. Ohman (eds), *Psychopathology: An International Perspective*. New York: Academic Press, pp. 221–34.

Magnusson, D., Duner, A., and Zetterblom, G. (1975) *Adjustment: A Longitudinal Study*. Stockholm: Almqvist & Wiksell.

Magnusson, D., Klinteberg, B., and Stattin, H. (1994) 'Juvenile and Persistent Offenders: Behavioral and Physiological Characteristics', in R.D. Ketterlinus (ed.), *Adolescent Problem Behaviors: Issues and Research*. Hillsdale, NJ: Erlbaum, pp. 81–91.

Maguire, K. and Pastore, A.L. (eds) (2001) *Sourcebook of Criminal Justice Statistics*. Available at http://www.albany.edu/sourcebook. Accessed 3/1/2002.

Malamuth, N.M. and Heilmann, M.F. (1998) 'Evolutionary Psychology and Sexual Aggression', in C.H. Crawford and D.L. Krebs (eds), *Handbook of Evolutionary Psychology*. Mahwah, NJ: Erlbaum, pp. 515–42.

Malamuth, N.M., Linz, D., Heavey, C.L., Barnes, G., and Acker, M. (1995) 'Using the Confluence Model of Sexual Aggression to Predict Men's Conflict with Women: a 10-Year Follow-Up Study', *Journal of Personality and Social Psychology*, 69: 353–69.

Marcus-Newhall, A., Pedersen, W.C., Carlson, M., and Miller, N. (2000) 'Displaced Aggression is Alive and Well: A Meta-Analytic Review', *Journal of Personality and Social Psychology*, 78: 670–89.

Markowitz, F.E. (2001) 'Attitudes and Family Violence: Linking Intergenerational and Cultural Theories', *Journal of Family Violence*, 16: 205–18.

Mazur, A. and Booth, A. (1998) 'Testosterone and Dominance in Men', *Behavioral and Brain Sciences*, 21: 353–97.

Mazur, A., Booth, A., and Dabbs Jr., J.M. (1992) 'Testosterone and Chess Competition', *Social Psychology Quarterly*, 55 (1): 70–7.

Mazur, A., Susman, E.J., and Edelbrock, S. (1997) 'Sex Differences in Testosterone Response to a Video Game Contest', *Evolution and Human Behavior*, 18: 317–26.

McCaul, K.D., Gladue, B.A., and Joppa, M. (1992) 'Winning, Losing, Mood and Testosterone', *Hormones and Behavior*, 26: 486–504.

Mcfall, R.M. (1982) 'A Review and Reformulation of the Concept of Social Skills', *Behavioral Assessment*, 4: 1–35.

Metropolitan Area Research Group (Eron, L.D., Huesmann, L.R., Spindler, A., Guerra, N.G., Henry, D., Tolan, P., and Van Acker, R.) (2002) 'A Cognitive/Ecological Approach to Preventing Aggression in Urban Settings: Initial Outcomes for High Risk Children', *Journal of Consulting and Clinical Psychology*, 70 (1): 179–94.

Miczek, K.A., DeBold, J.F., Haney, M., Tidey, J., Vivian, J., and Weerts, E.M. (1994) 'Alcohol, Drugs of Abuse, Aggression and Violence', in A.J. Reiss and J.A. Roth (ed.), *National Research Council: Understanding and Preventing Violence* (vol. 3). *Social Influences*. Washington, DC: National Academy Press, pp. 377–570.

Miczek, K.A., Mirsky, A.F., Carey, G., DeBold, J., and Raine, A. (1994) 'An Overview of Biological Influences on Violent Behavior', in National Research Council, *Understanding and Preventing Violence* (vol. 2). Washington, DC: National Academy Press, pp. 1–20.

Milavsky, J.R., Kessler, R., Stipp, H., and Rubens, W.S. (1982) 'Television and Aggression: Results of a Panel Study', in D. Pearl, L. Bouthilet and J. Lazar (eds), *Television and Behavior: Ten Years of Scientific Progress and Implications for the 80's* (vol. 2). Technical Reviews. Washington, DC: Government Printing Office.

Miles, D.R. and Carey, G. (1997) 'Genetic and Environmental Architecture of Aggression', *Journal of Personality and Social Psychology*, 72: 207–17.

Miller, I. and Norman, W. (1979) 'Learned Helplessness in Humans: A Review and Attribution Theory Model', *Psychological Bulletin*, 86: 93–118.

Miller, L.S. (1991) 'Mothers' and Children's Attitudes about Aggression'. Dissertation abstracts.

Mischel, W. and Shoda, Y. (1995) 'A Cognitive-Affective System Theory of Personality: Reconceptualizing Situations, Dispositions, Dynamics and Invariance in Personality Structure', *Psychological Review*, 102: 246–68.

Mischel, W. (1973) 'Toward a Cognitive Social Learning Reconceptualization of Personality', *Psychological Review*, 80: 252–83.

Moffitt, T.E. (1990) 'Juvenile Delinquency and Attention-Deficit Disorder: Boys' Developmental Trajectories from Age 3 to 15', *Child Development*, 61: 893–910.

Moffitt, T.E. and Lynam, D.R. (1994) 'The Neuropsychology of Conduct Disorder and Delinquency: Implications for Understanding Antisocial Behavior', in D.C. Fowles, P. Sutker, and S.H. Goodman (eds), *Progress in Experimental Personality and Psychopathology Research*. New York: Springer-Verlag, pp. 233–62.

Moffitt, T.E., Gabrielli, W.F., Mednick, S.A., and Schulsinger, F. (1981) 'Socioeconomic Status, IQ and Delinquency', *Journal of Abnormal Psychology*, 90: 152–6.

Moise-Titus, J. (1999) 'The Role of Negative Emotions in the Media Violence–Aggression Relation'. Unpublished doctoral dissertation, University of Michigan, Ann Arbor, MI.

Murdoch, D., Pihl, R.O., and Ross, D. (1990) 'Alcohol and Crimes of Violence: Present Issues', *International Journal of the Addictions*, 25: 1065–81.

Nasby, H., Hayden, B., and DePaulo, B.M. (1979) 'Attributional Bias among Aggressive Boys to Interpret Unambiguous Social Stimuli as Displays of Hostility', *Journal of Abnormal Psychology*, 89: 459–68.

Nisbett, R.E. (1993) 'Violence and U.S. Regional Culture', *American Psychologist*, 48: 441–9.

Nisbett, R.E. and Cohen, D. (1996) *Culture of Honor: The Psychology of Violence in the South*. Boulder, CO: Westview Press.

O'Donnell, C.R. (1995) 'Firearm Deaths among Children and Youth', *American Psychologist*, 50: 771–6.

Olweus, D. (1979) 'Stability of Aggressive Reaction Patterns in Males: A Review', *Psychological Bulletin*, 86: 852–75.

Olweus, D. (1995) 'Bullying or Peer Abuse at School: Facts and Intervention', *Current Directions in Psychological Science*, 4: 196–200.

Oreland, L., Wiberg, A., Asberg, M., Traskman, L., Sjostrand, L., Thoren, P.L., Bertilsson, L., and Tybring, G. (1981) 'Platelet MAO Activity and Monoamine Metabolites in Cerebrospinal Fluid in Depressed and Suicidal Patients and in Health Control', *Psychiatry Research*, 4: 21–9.

Osofsky, J.D. (1995) 'The Effects of Exposure to Violence on Young Children', *American Psychologist*, 50: 782–8.

Pakaslahti, L. and Keltikangas-Jarvinen, L. (1996) 'Social Acceptance and the Relationship between Aggressive Problem-Solving Strategies and Aggressive Behavior in 14-Year-Old Adolescents', *European Journal of Personality*, 10: 249–61.

Parker, R.N. and Auerhahn, K. (1999) 'Drugs, Alcohol and Homicide', in M.D. Smith and M.A. Zahn (eds), *Homicide: A Sourcebook of Social Research*. Thousand Oaks, CA: Sage, pp. 176–91.

Patterson, G.R., Debaryshe, B.D., and Ramsey, E. (1989) 'A Developmental Perspective on Antisocial Behavior', *American Psychologist*, 44: 329–35.

Payne, K. (2002) 'On Losing It: Accessibility and Cognitive Control in Social Situations'. Paper presented at Society for Personality and Social Psychology meetings, Savannah, Georgia, February.

Pedersen, W.C., Gonzales, C., and Miller, N. (2000) 'The Moderating Effect of Trivial Triggering Provocation on Displaced Aggression', *Journal of Personality and Social Psychology*, 78: 913–27.

Pennington, B.F. and Bennetto, L. (1993) 'Main Effects of Transactions in the Neuropsychology of Conduct Disorder. Commentary on "The Neuropsychology of Conduct Disorder"', *Development and Psychopathology*, 5: 153–64.

Peterson, L., Gable, S., Doyle, C., and Ewugman, B. (1997) 'Beyond Parenting Skills: Battling Barriers and Building Bonds to Prevent Child Abuse and Neglect', *Cognitive and Behavioral Practice*, 4: 53–74.

Pfeffer, C.R., Zuckerman, S., Plutchik, R., and Mizruchi, M.S. (1987) 'Assaultive Behavior in Normal Schoolchildren', *Child Psychiatry and Human Development*, 17: 166–76.

Poznanski, E. and Zrull, J.P. (1970) 'Childhood Depression: Clinical Characteristics of Overtly Depressed Children', *Archives of General Psychiatry*, 23: 8–15.

Prentice-Dunn, S. and Rogers, R. (1983) 'Deindividuation in Aggression', in R.G. Geen and E. Donnerstein (eds), *Aggression: Theoretical and Empirical Reviews* (vol. 2). New York: Academic Press, pp. 155–71.

Pulkkinen, L. (1996) 'Proactive and Reactive Aggression in Early Adolescence as Precursors to Anti- and Prosocial Behavior in Young Adults', *Aggressive Behavior*, 22: 241–57.

Raine, A. (1993) *The Psychopathology of Crime: Criminal Behavior as a Clinical Disorder*. San Diego, CA: Academic Press.

Raine, A., Brennen, P.A., Farrington, D.P., and Mednick, S.A. (eds) (1997) *Biosocial Bases of Violence*. London: Plenum.

Raine, A., Venables, P.H., and Williams, M. (1990) 'Relationships between CNS and ANS Measures of Arousal at Age 15 and Criminality at Age 24', *Archives of General Psychiatry*, 47: 1003–7.

Ramirez, J.M., Lagerspetz, K., Fraczek, A., Fujihara, T., Musazahedeh, Z., and Theron, W.H. (2001) 'Difference and Similarities in Moral Approval of Aggressive Acts: A Cross-National Study', *Aggressive Behavior*, 27 (3): 225–6.

Reinisch, J.M. (1981) 'Prenatal Exposure to Synthetic Progestins Increases Potential for Aggression in Humans', *Science*, 211: 1171–3.

Rice, M.E. (1997) 'Violent Offender Research and Implications for the Criminal Justice System', *American Psychologist*, 52: 414–23.

Richard, B.A. and Dodge, K.A. (1982) 'Social Maladjustment and Problem-Solving in School-Aged Children. *Journal of Consulting and Clinical Psychology*, 50: 226–33.

Rogeness, G.A., Cepeda, C., Macedo, C.A., Fischer, C., and Harris, W.R. (1990) 'Differences in Heart Rate and Blood Pressure in Children with Conduct Disorder, Major Depression and Separation Anxiety', *Psychiatry Research*, 33: 199–206.

Rosenfeld, E., Huesmann, L.R., Eron, L.D., and Torney-Purta, J.V. (1982) 'Measuring Patterns of Fantasy Behavior in Children', *Journal of Personality and Social Psychology*, 42: 347–66.

Rosenthal, R. (1986) 'The Social Consequences of Small Effects', *Journal of Social Issues*, 42: 141–54.

Rubin, K.H., Bream, L.A., and Rose-Krasnor, L. (1991) 'Social Problem Solving and Aggression in Childhood', in D.J. Pepler and K.H. Rubin (eds), *The Development and Treatment of Childhood Aggression*. Hillsdale, NJ: Erlbaum, pp. 219–48.

Rubin, K.H., Moller, L., and Emptage, A. (1987) 'The Preschool Behavior Questionnaire: A Useful Index of Behavior Problems in Elementary School-Age Children', *Canadian Journal of Behavioral Science*, 19: 86–100.

Russell, G.W. (1993) *The Social Psychology of Sport*. New York: Springer.

Rydin, E., Schalling, D., and Asberg, M. (1982) 'Rorschach Ratings in Depressed and Suicidal Patients with Low Levels of 5–Hydroxyindoleacetic Acid in Cerebrospinal Fluid', *Psychiatric Research*, 7: 229–43.

Rys, G.S. and Bear, G.G. (1997) 'Relational Aggression and Peer Relations: Gender and Developmental Issues', *Merrill-Palmer Quarterly*, 43: 87–106.

Salvador, A., Simon, V., Suay, F., and Llorens, L. (1987) 'Testosterone and Cortisol Responses to Competitive Fighting in Human Males: A Pilot Study', *Aggressive Behavior*, 13: 9–13.

Satterfield, J.H., Hoppe, C.M., and Schell, A.M. (1982) 'A Prospective Study of Delinquency in 110 Adolescent Boys with Attention Deficit Disorder and 88 Normal Adolescent Boys', *American Journal of Psychiatry*, 139: 795–8.

Schaal, B., Tremblay, R.E., Soussignan, R., and Susman, E.J. (1995) 'Male Testosterone Linked to High Social Dominance but Low Physical Aggression in Early Adolescence'. Unpublished manuscript, University of Montreal.

Schneider, D.J. (1991) 'Social Cognition', *Annual Review of Psychology*, 42, 527–61.

Schneider, W. and Shiffrin, R.M. (1977) 'Controlled and Automatic Human Information Processing: I. Detection, Search and Attention', *Psychological Review*, 84: 1–66.

Sedikides, C. and Skowronski, J.J. (1990) 'Towards Reconciling Personality and Social Psychology: A Construct Accessibility Approach', *Journal of Social Behavior and Personality*, 5: 531–46.

Seligman, M.E.P. (1970) 'On the Generality of the Law of Learning', *Psychological Review*, 77: 406–18.

Shantz, C.U. and Shantz, D.W. (1985) 'Conflict between Children: Social-Cognitive and Sociometric Correlates', *New Directions for Child Development*, 20: 3–21.

Shiffrin, R.M. and Schneider, W. (1977) 'Controlled and Automatic Human Information Processing: II. Perceptual Learning, Automatic Attending and General Theory', *Psychological Review*, 84: 127–90.

Shure, M.B. and Spivack, G. (1980) 'Interpersonal Problem-Solving as a Mediator of Behavioral Adjustment in Preschool and Kindergarten Children', *Journal of Applied Developmental Psychology*, 1: 45–57.

Simon, L.M.J. (1998) 'Does Criminal Offender Treatment Work?', *Applied and Preventive Psychology*, 7: 137–59.

Slaby, R.G. and Guerra, N.G. (1988) 'Cognitive Mediators of Aggression in Adolescent Offenders: I. Assessment', *Developmental Psychology*, 24: 580–8.

Smith, S.L. and Donnerstein, E. (1998) 'Harmful Effects of Exposure to Media Violence: Learning of Aggression Emotional Desensitization, and Fear', in R.G. Geen and E. Donnerstein (eds), *Human Aggression: Theories, Research and Implications for Social Policy.* New York: Academic Press, pp. 167–202.

Soubrie, P. (1986) 'Reconciling the Role of Central Serotoning Neurons in Humans and Animal Behavior', *The Behavioral and Brain Sciences*, 9: 319–64.

Souweidane, V. and Huesmann, L.R. (1999) 'The Influence of American Urban Culture on the Development of Normative Beliefs about Aggression in Middle-Eastern Immigrants', *American Journal of Community Psychology*, 27 (2): 239–54.

Staub, E. (1989) *The Roots of Evil: The Origins of Genocide and Other Group Violence*. New York: Cambridge University Press.

Staub, E. (1998) 'Breaking the Cycle of Genocidal Violence: Healing and Reconciliation', in J. Harvey (ed.), *Perspectives on Loss: A Sourcebook.* Philadelphia, PA: Taylor & Francis, pp. 23–38.

Steele, C.M. and Josephs, R.A. (1990) 'Alcohol Myopia: Its Prized and Dangerous Effects', *American Psychologist*, 45: 921–33.

Steinberg, M.D. and Dodge, K.A. (1983) 'Attributional Bias in Aggressive Boys and Girls', *Journal of Social and Clinical Psychology*, 1: 312–21.

Stenberg, C.R. and Campos, J.J. (1990) 'The Development of Anger and Expressions in Infancy', in N. Stein, B. Leventhal, and T. Trabasso (eds), *Psychological and Biological Approaches to Emotion.* Hillsdale, NJ: Erlbaum.

Stenberg, C., Campos, J. and Emde, R. (1983) 'The Facial Expression of Anger in Seven-Month-Old Infants', *Child Development*, 54: 178–84.

Stoff, D.M., Pollack, L., Vetiell, B., Behar, D., and Bridger, W.H. (1987) 'Reduction of [3H]-Imipramine Binding Sites on Platelets of Conduct-Disordered Children', *Neuropsychopharmacology*, 1: 55–62.

Straus, M.A. (1997) 'Physical Assaults by Women Partners: A Major Social Problem', in M.R. Walsh (ed.), *Women, Men and Gender: Ongoing Debates.* New Haven, CT: Yale University Press, pp. 210–21.

Straus, M.A. (2000) *Beating the Devil out of Them: Corporal Punishment by American Families and Its Effects on Children*, 2nd edn. Somerset, NJ: Transaction Publishers.

Surgeon General (2001) *Youth Violence: A Report of the Surgeon General.* Rockville, MD: US Department of Health and Human Services.

Tate, D.C., Reppucci, N.D., and Mulvey, E.P. (1995) 'Violent Juvenile Delinquents: Treatment Effectiveness and Implications for Future Action', *American Psychologist*, 50: 777–81.

Taylor, A.R. and Gabriel, S.W. (1989) 'Cooperative versus Competitive Game-Playing Strategies of Peer Accepted and Peer Rejected Children in a Goal Conflict Situation'. Paper presented at the biennial meeting of the *Society for Research in Child Development*, Kansas City, MO.

Taylor, S.P. and Leonard, K.E. (1983) 'Alcohol and Human Physical Aggression', in R.G. Green and E. Donnerstein (eds), *Aggression: Theoretical and Empirical Reviews* (vol. 2). New York: Academic Press, pp. 77–101.

Tellegen, A., Lykken, D.T., Bouchard, Jr., T.J., Wilcox, K.J., Segal, N.L., and Rich, S. (1988) 'Personality Similarity in Twins Reared Apart and Together', *Journal of Personality and Social Psychology*, 54: 1031–9.

Thomas, M.H., Horton, R.W., Lippincott, E.C., and Drabman, R.S. (1977) 'Desensitization to Portrayals of Real Life Aggression as a Function of Television Violence', *Journal of Personality and Social Psychology*, 35: 450–8.

Todorov, A. and Bargh, J.A. (2002) 'Automatic Sources of Aggression', *Aggression and Violent Behavior*, 7: 53–68.

Tremblay, R.E. (2000) 'The Development of Aggressive Behavior during Childhood: What Have We Learned in the Past Century?', *International Journal of Behavioral Development*, 24: 129–41.

Tremblay, R.E., Boulerice, B., Harden, P.W., Mcduff, P., Perusse, D., Pihl, R.O., and Zoccolillo, M. (1996) 'Do Children in Canada Become More Aggressive as They Approach Adolescence?', in Human Resources Development Canada (ed.), *Growing up in Canada: National Longitudinal Survey of Children and Youth*. Ottawa: Statistics Canada, pp. 127–37.

US Department of Justice (1992) *A National Crime Victimization Survey Report*, December 1992. Justice Statistics Clearinghouse, National Criminal Justice Reference Service. Box 6000, Rockville, MD, 20850.

US Department of Justice Bureau of Justice Statistics (2001) *Homicide Trends in the United States*. Available at http//:www.ojp.usdoj.gov/bjs/homicide/homtrnd.htm.

Ulrich, R.E. (1966) 'Pain as a Cause of Aggression', *American Zoologist*, 6: 643–62.

Verlinden, S., Herden, M. and Thomas, J. (2000) 'Risk Factors in School Shootings', *Clinical Psychology Review*, 20: 3–56.

Viemero, V. and Paajanen, S. (1992) 'The Role of Fantasies and Dreams in the TV Viewing–Aggression Relationship', *Aggressive Behavior*, 18 (2): 109–16.

Virkkunen, M. (1985) 'Urinary Free Cortisol Secretion in Habitually Violent Offenders', *Acta Psychiatrica Scandinavica*, 72: 40–4.

Virkkunen, M., De Jong, J., Bartko, J., Goodwin, F.K., and Linnolia, M. (1989a) 'Relationship of Psychobiological Variables to Recidivism in Violent Offenders and Impulsive Fire Setters', *Archives of General Psychiatry*, 46: 600–3.

Virkkunen, M., De Jong, J., Bartko, J., and Linnolia, M. (1989b) 'Psychobiological Concomitants of History of Suicide Attempts among Violent Offenders and Impulsive Fire Setters', *Archives of General Psychiatry*, 46: 604–6.

Virkkunen, M. and Narvanen, S. (1987) 'Plasma Insulin, Tryptophan and Serotonin Levels during the Glucose Tolerance Test among Habitually Violent and Impulsive Offenders', *Neuropsychobiology*, 17: 19–23.

Waas, G.A. (1988) 'Social Attributional Biases of Peer-Rejected and Aggressive Children', *Child Development*, 59: 969–92.

Wadsworth, M.E.J. (1976) 'Delinquency, Pulse Rate and Early Emotional Deprivation', *British Journal of Criminology*, 16: 245–56.

West, D.J. and Farrington, D.P. (1973) *Who Becomes Delinquent? Second Report of the Cambridge Study in Delinquent Development*. London: Heinemann.

White, J. W. (2001) 'Gendered Aggression across the Lifespan', in J. Worell (ed.), *Encyclopedia of Women and Gender: Sex Similarities and Differences and the Impact of Society on Gender New York:* Academic Press, pp. 81–93.

Widom, C.S. (1989) 'Does Violence Beget Violence? A Critical Examination of the Literature', *Psychological Bulletin*, 106 (1): 3–28.

Wiehe, V.R. (1998) *Understanding Family Violence*. Thousand Oaks, CA: Sage.

Wilson, J.Q. and Herrnstein, R.J. (1985) *Crime and Human Nature*. New York: Simon & Schuster.

Winter, L. and Uleman, J.S. (1984) 'When Are Social Judgements Made? Evidence for the Spontaneousness of Trait Inference', *Journal of Personality and Social Psychology*, 4: 904–17.

Zelli, A. and Huesmann, L.R. (1993) 'Accuracy of Social Information Processing by Those who Are Aggressive: The Role of Beliefs about a Hostile World'. Prevention Research Center, University of Illinois at Chicago.

Zelli, A., Huesmann, L.R., and Cervone, D.P. (1995) 'Social Inferences in Aggressive Individuals: Evidence for Automatic Processing in the Expression of Hostile Biases', *Aggressive Behavior*, 21: 405–18.

Zigler, E., Taussig, C., and Black, K. (1992) 'Early Childhood Intervention: A Promising Preventative for Juvenile Delinquency', *American Psychologist*, 47: 997–1006.

Zillmann, D. (1979) *Hostility and Aggression*. Hillsdale, NJ: Erlbaum.

Zillmann, D. (1983) 'Arousal and Aggression', in R. Geen and E. Donnerstein (eds), *Aggression: Theoretical and Empirical Reviews* (vol. 1). New York: Academic Press, pp. 75–102.

Zubriggen, E.I. (2000) 'Social Motives and Cognitive Power–Sex Associations: Predictors of Aggressive Sexual Behavior', *Journal of Personality and Social Psychology*, 78: 559–81.

# PART FOUR

# PROCESSES WITHIN GROUPS

# 13
# Social Performance

KIPLING D. WILLIAMS, STEPHEN G. HARKINS, AND STEVE J. KARAU

**INTRODUCTION**

How does the mere presence of others affect our motivation, effort, and performance on tasks? This is a fundamental question of human behavior that social psychologists have grappled with for over 125 years. In this chapter we find the answer to be complex, yet understandable within a common theoretical framework. We review the literature on social facilitation and social loafing. Whereas social facilitation suggests that others motivate us, social loafing suggests that others demotivate us. The link that bridges these two opposing conclusions suggests that it depends upon how we construe the others: are they with us, or against us?

It is probably the case that there are some tasks that humans routinely perform alone. Yet, if one tries to think of such tasks, it becomes abundantly clear that, in fact, they are usually performed alongside or with other people. Essentially, humans play in groups and work in groups. Groups offer individuals a host of functions, from fulfilling needs for belonging, support, and intimacy to the ability to accomplish tasks that sole individuals could not even attempt (Forsyth, 1999). Group play and group work involve a number of layers of social complexity, including social inferences, impression formation, attitudes, stereotypes, affect, attraction, and conflict within and between groups. These layers are dealt with in other chapters of this volume. The bottom layer, however, requires an understanding of the basic psychological effects on the individual of trying to perform tasks with or alongside others.

In this chapter, we use the least restrictive definition of group: two or more people who are working on a task. It has been argued that small groups are no smaller than triads and that dyads are qualitatively different entities (see Moreland et al., 1994); however, a substantial amount of small group phenomena, such as social facilitation and social loafing, have been documented at the dyadic level and appear to operate under the same principles.

We restrict our review to the substantial research efforts on task performance in groups in which the outcome is quantifiable and achieved through effort. The dynamics of group decisions is excluded because it is dealt with elsewhere in this volume (see Chapter 18). We do not examine separately motivation, effort, and performance in groups, as that would prove to be largely repetitive. Thus, we discuss motivation and effort and note when they are not linked positively to performance.

We concentrate our review on two major research efforts: social facilitation and social loafing, although other related phenomena are discussed as well. These two phenomena are perhaps the two oldest lines of research in social psychology, each beginning at the end of the nineteenth century. Hundreds of publications have examined the validity, robustness, generality, and explanations of these two phenomena. On the face of it, they appear to be saying opposite things. Assuming for the moment that we are interested in relatively easy or well-learned tasks, social facilitation refers to the fact that we work harder in groups, and social loafing refers to the fact that we reduce our efforts in groups. Thus, sense must be made of these two old well-researched, yet apparently opposite phenomena. One useful distinction will be how individuals regard the 'others'. Are they with us, or against us? If they are *against* us, as competitors, evaluators, or sources of comparison, we are likely to observe social facilitation; if they are *with* us, sharing the task demands and evaluation, we are likely to observe social loafing.

Finally, as will be apparent by the literature reviewed, each phenomenon has been marked by a distinctly different research agenda that may be related to a very simple characterization: social facilitation is good, and social loafing is bad. Thus, we search for ways to promote social facilitation and thwart social loafing. Because so much of our time is spent working in groups, we would like to find instances in which the presence of others facilitates our motivation and performance. In contrast, it is distressing to think that working in groups portends laziness, so much so that the term 'social loafing', when coined, was referred to as a 'social disease' (Latané et al., 1979: 831). Perhaps as a consequence of these two agendas, research on social facilitation has largely been aimed at explaining *why* it happens. Rarely, if ever, have researchers tried to stop its occurrence. As will be seen, researchers have not devoted much attention to determining the conditions under which social facilitation is most and least likely to emerge. This approach, however, is precisely on what researchers in social loafing have focused: under what conditions can social loafing be eliminated or overcome?

## Social facilitation

### *Early efforts*

The first experiment published in social psychology was prompted by Triplett's (1898: 516) observation that bicyclists consistently posted faster times in paced than unpaced races. In his paper, Triplett listed a number of mechanical and psychological theories that had been advanced to account for these findings. To these factors, Triplett added what he termed 'dynamogenic factors', by which he meant the fact that 'the bodily presence of another rider is a stimulus to the racer in arousing the competitive instinct; that another can thus be the means of releasing or freeing nervous energy for him that he cannot of himself release; and, further, that the sight of movement in that other by perhaps suggesting a higher rate of speed, is also an inspiration to greater effort'.

To test this hypothesis, Triplett built an apparatus consisting of two fishing reels which were placed in a Y-shaped framework. The reels were placed in the open end of the 'Y', and when cranked, they moved bands of twisted silk down the arms to the base and back via a set of pulleys. A trial consisted of turning the crank until a small flag sewed to the respective silk bands had made four circuits of the 4-meter course. The participants, who were children, were asked to perform the task alone on some trials and alongside another child on others. The majority of the children cranked faster when reeling alongside another child than when reeling alone.

This research began a line of work on the effects that the presence of others has on task performance that has continued over 100 years. These effects have been studied in two paradigms. In one, the audience paradigm, the others are present as observers or spectators watching the task performance of the participant. In the other paradigm, coaction, the others are present working on the same task alongside the participant. Because this is a chapter on social productivity, we will focus for the most part on the findings in the coaction paradigm, which may be seen as the 'minimal groups paradigm' of group performance. However, because the presence of audiences and coactors has been found to have the same effects on task performance, and because much of the theoretical development has focused on the audience paradigm, we will refer to that literature as needed.

In Triplett's (1898) work and in much of the work that followed (e.g., Allport, 1920, 1924), it was found that the presence of others enhanced performance, an effect which Allport (1924) termed 'social facilitation'. However, it was also found that the presence of others sometimes debilitated performance, and, in his review, Dashiell (1935) was unable to specify when performance would be facilitated and when debilitated. Matters had not progressed by the 1950s when Asch (1952: 67) observed that what determined whether performance would be facilitated or debilitated remained obscure. He commented, 'The suspicion then arises that the proffered concepts are simply restatements of the quantitative results'. Although this criticism was pointed specifically at Allport's (1924) research, it could just as well have been directed at the whole line of work. After some fifty years of research, there was no convincing refutation of Asch's suspicion.

### *Drive theory*

Perhaps as a result, interest in social facilitation waned until 1965, when Zajonc brought renewed interest to the area with his drive interpretation of social facilitation. In his article, Zajonc surveyed past research on audience (e.g., Bergum and Lehr, 1963; Dashiell, 1930; Pessin, 1933; Travis, 1925) and coaction effects (e.g., Allport, 1920; Gates and Allee, 1933; Travis, 1928), and suggested that these findings could be organized by a simple generalization: the presence of others, as spectators or as coactors, enhances the emission of dominant responses. By dominant response, Zajonc meant the response that was most probable in a participant's task-relevant behavioral repertoire. In the early stages of learning to perform a task, Zajonc argued that this response is likely to be incorrect, but, with practice, correct answers become more probable; that is, they become dominant.

Zajonc (1965) went on to note that Spence (1956) had already established that arousal, activation, or drive results in the enhancement of dominant responses. He then described indirect, but suggestive, evidence supporting the notion that the presence of others increases a person's arousal level. Thus, his resolution suggested that the presence of others produces arousal that enhances the likelihood of the emission of the dominant response. If the task is simple or well learned, the dominant response is likely to be correct and, as a result, performance will be facilitated, but if the task is complex or the appropriate responses are not yet mastered, the dominant response is likely to be incorrect, and performance will be debilitated.

Zajonc's (1965) paper had a galvanizing effect on research in social facilitation. In his review of social facilitation, Guerin (1993) included a cumulative graph of research activity in this area, which showed that following the publication of Triplett's work in 1898, a small number of articles were published each year from 1920 through 1965, but, at this point, the number of articles simply took off. This high rate of activity continued through 1983, the endpoint of the graph. Although other interpretations for facilitation effects were offered (e.g., Blank et al., 1976; Duval and Wicklund, 1972), most of the research conducted during this period focused on this drive account. Zajonc (1965) had suggested that the mere presence of others was sufficient to increase drive, whereas others argued that it was the evaluation and/or competition associated with the others that produced the drive. For example, Cottrell (1968: 104) argued: 'If coaction and performance before an audience usually result in positive or negative outcomes for the individual, then he will quickly come to anticipate these outcomes when he coacts with others or performs before an audience', and Cottrell proposed that it was these associations that produced the drive effects. This proposal led to a whole series of studies in which researchers tried to design experiments to pit these explanations against each other (e.g., Cottrell et al., 1968; Henchy and Glass, 1968; Paulus and Murdoch, 1971).

Whether it was mere presence or evaluation apprehension that produced drive, the drive theory account of social facilitation remained the dominant theory of the time. For example, in 1977, Geen and Gange wrote: 'A review of the literature on social facilitation following Zajonc's advocacy of drive theory as the explanatory principle shows that this theory, in general, provides the most parsimonious explanation of the findings reported over those 12 years' (p. 1283).

### *Alternative approaches to social-facilitation effects*

However, twelve years later, matters had changed. In his review of the facilitation literature since 1977, Geen (1989: 17) concluded, 'today such a confident assertion of the primacy of the drive theoretical approach is not warranted. Instead, several sophisticated alternatives have found considerable support in experimental studies'. Geen (1989) organized these alternative approaches into three classes.

One class of theories included those approaches that continued to rely on the notion that the presence of others increases drive; for example, distraction/conflict (Baron, 1986), evaluation apprehension (Cottrell, 1972), social monitoring (Guerin and Innes, 1982), and compresence (Zajonc, 1980). The second class included those approaches that suggested 'the presence of others creates either explicit or implicit demands on the person to behave in some way' (Geen, 1989: 31); for example, self-presentation (Bond, 1982) and self-awareness (Carver and Scheier, 1981). The third class proposed that the presence of others affects the focus of attention and information processing; for example, Baron's (1986) information-processing view of distraction/conflict.

Moreover, what about the controversy concerning whether mere presence or evaluation apprehension was responsible for social facilitation? It still had not been resolved. Each of the theories that Geen reviewed incorporated mere-presence effects, evaluation-apprehension effects, or both. The 'presence' theories argued as follows: the mere presence of others produces uncertainty that leads to increased drive (Zajonc, 1980); when the behavior of the others cannot be monitored, their presence leads to uncertainty and increased drive (Guerin and Innes, 1982); the presence of others is distracting, triggering attentional conflict and increased drive (Baron, 1986); or the simple presence of others is distracting, producing an attentional overload affecting focus of attention (Baron, 1986).

The 'evaluation' theories argued as follows: we come to learn that the presence of others is associated with evaluation and/or competition, and this association leads to increased drive (Cottrell, 1968, 1972); the possibility of evaluation leads to distraction that increases drive (Baron, 1986); the potential for evaluation makes us self-aware, leading to greater attention to how performance matches some standard (Carver and Scheier, 1981); the prospect of evaluation leads to concerns about self-presentation

(Bond, 1982); or the potential for evaluation affects the focus of attention (Baron, 1986).

### *Tests of mere presence*

Why was this issue not resolved? In his 1935 review, Dashiell noted, 'to get pure "alone" or pure "co-working" (and, we may add, pure "spectator" or pure "competing") situations is extraordinarily difficult' (p. 1115). This difficulty has remained with us to this day. In virtually all social-facilitation experiments, the experimenter could represent a potent source of evaluation in the 'alone' conditions. There has been some recognition of this problem in its most egregious form. For example, Bond and Titus (1983: 271), in a review of social facilitation research, wrote: 'In 96 of 241 studies, the experimenter was in the room with the "alone" subject, and in 52 of these studies, this "alone" subject could see the experimenter!'.

Guerin (1993: 129) raised this issue again in his review of mere-presence effects. After excluding studies 'if they clearly involved group discussion, imitation or the exchange of reinforcements', Guerin was left with 313 studies. After applying the twelve criteria that he judged to be required for a good test of the mere-presence hypothesis, including the removal of the experimenter from the room, he was left with eighteen studies. Of these eighteen, Guerin reports that 'eleven found evidence for mere-presence effects and seven did not' (1993: 137). However, it could be argued that Guerin's criteria were not stringent enough for a reasonable test. Markus (1978: 391) has pointed out: 'In virtually all experiments with humans, the subject in the alone condition is not "phenomenologically" alone even when the experimenter is physically removed and out of sight. That is, he is quite aware of the experimenter and knows that his performance is being recorded, presumably for some present or future evaluation'. Guerin (1993) did not exclude experiments that provided the experimenter with the opportunity to evaluate performance in the alone condition at the conclusion of the session because he felt that eliminating studies on this basis might eliminate all relevant studies.

However, if one wants to test the mere-presence hypothesis, it would appear that the reduction of all sources of evaluation to a minimum is exactly what is required in the 'no evaluation' conditions. Of Guerin's (1993) published studies, only four experiments in which performance was measured meet this more stringent criterion. Two are audience experiments (Markus, 1978; Schmitt et al., 1986), and each of these experiments found evidence consistent with the mere-presence hypothesis.

The other two are coaction experiments (Harkins, 1987) in which participants in 'no evaluation' conditions were led to believe that their performances could not be evaluated by anyone during or after the experiment. In the 2 (alone versus coaction) × 2 (no evaluation versus evaluation) design, mere presence was manipulated by asking participants to work alone, or alongside another person working independently on the same task (coaction). Evaluation was manipulated by arranging the situation so that the participant's performance was either identifiable and could be compared to that of others, or was not identifiable.

Using two different, simple tasks (use-generation and vigilance), Harkins (1987) found main effects for both mere presence and evaluation in this design. Coactors outperformed participants working alone, a 'mere-presence' effect, and participants whose outputs could be evaluated outperformed participants whose outputs could not be, an evaluation effect. It is probably not feasible to eliminate all concerns about the possibility of evaluation when participants know that they are taking part in an experiment. However, by minimizing the apparent opportunities for evaluation, Harkins's (1987) research approached this goal more closely than other coaction experiments in which the most that was done was to remove the experimenter from the room.

Subsequent to Guerin's (1993) review, other attempts have been made to test the mere presence hypothesis. For example, Platania and Moran (2001) asked participants, who were either alone or observed by another student, to make verbal judgments on the relative size of stimulus squares as they were presented on a wall. The authors report that they found that the participants in the audience condition responded with their preferred response numbers (responses with the highest habit strength) more often than participants who were alone. They argued that the 'socially facilitated dominant responses were personal choices (numerical preferences) that could not be construed as either right or wrong and, therefore, were irrelevant to evaluative judgments' (2001: 196). Thomas et al. (2002) exposed participants who were either alone or in a group composed of one real participant and two confederates (coaction) to an experimenter who attempted to make a very favorable or very unfavorable impression on them. After completing a phrase-completion task, the ostensible point of the study, participants were asked to rate the experimenter as part of the departmental research process. These evaluations were anonymous. The experimenter left the room, and the evaluations were placed into envelopes that the participants put in a box full of other envelopes. Consistent with the mere-presence hypothesis, the participants in the coaction condition rated the experimenter who had attempted to make a favorable impression more favorably and the experimenter who had attempted to make a negative impression less favorably than participants who took part alone.

In these experiments, the potential for evaluation is apparently eliminated, and, along with the experiments of Markus (1978) and Schmitt et al. (1986), they provide evidence consistent with the mere-presence hypothesis. However, it must be acknowledged that these studies do not use typical measures of task performance. For example, Markus (1978) measured how long it took participants to don and doff familiar and unfamiliar pieces of clothing while they were getting ready to take part in the experiment. Schmitt et al. (1986) measured how long it took participants to type their name (simple task) and to type their name backward with interspersed ascending digits as a code name (complex task) in preparation for the experiment. Platania and Moran (2001) describe their task as a measure of preference, not as a measure of performance, and Thomas et al. (2002) looked at the participants' evaluation of the experimenter.

However, mere-presence effects have also been reported in experiments that use traditional performance tasks. As noted previously, in his coaction experiments, Harkins (1987) used traditional performance tasks, use-generation and vigilance. More recently, Huguet et al. (1999) used the Stroop color-word task in their research testing the mere-presence hypothesis. They led participants to believe that the computer on which they would be performing the Stroop color-word task had not yet been programmed to record their responses. They were asked to perform the task anyway so that they could give their impressions about this new task at the end of the session. They performed the task alone or in the presence of different types of audiences (that is, inattentive, invisible, or attentive). Huguet et al. (1999) found that Stroop interference (that is, the difference in the time taken to identify the ink colors of incongruent words, such as the word 'red' printed in green ink) and the ink color of control signs (for example, +++ printed in green) was reduced overall in the audience conditions. This finding is consistent with previous research with the Stroop task in which other social manipulations (such as competition) have been shown to reduce Stroop interference (e.g., MacKinnon et al., 1985; Peretti, 1971).

Guerin (1983, 1986, 1993) has proposed that mere-presence effects can be produced, but only when there is some uncertainty about the behavior of the other person present. If the participant can monitor this person's behavior, there will be no mere-presence effects; if this behavior cannot be monitored, there will be. In fact, Huguet et al.'s (1999) audience manipulation was meant to be a test of Guerin's monitoring hypothesis. The authors argue that there would be most uncertainty in the invisible and attentive audience conditions, and it is under these conditions that the authors report their strongest effects. However, examination of the results suggests some effect even for the inattentive audience.

In addition, Guerin (1993) reports two audience experiments (Rajecki et al., 1977; Schmitt et al., 1986) in which mere-presence effects were found despite the fact that monitoring was possible. Harkins (1987) found mere-presence effects in his coaction experiments, even though coaction lends itself to monitorability and should minimize mere-presence effects. Thus, at this point, we would argue that there is evidence for mere-presence effects in the audience and the coaction paradigm, and the jury is still out on Guerin's monitoring hypothesis.

### *Tests of the potential for evaluation*

Having established that mere presence appears to contribute to social-facilitation effects, we must next ask what contribution is the contribution of the potential for evaluation. As noted previously, when Zajonc (1965) proposed his drive explanation, research efforts focused on whether the effects were produced by mere presence *or* by evaluation apprehension. The research that we have reviewed suggests that mere presence is sufficient to produce social-facilitation effects, but it certainly does not suggest that mere presence is *the* explanation. As pointed out by Markus (1981), both factors could contribute to facilitation effects.

In fact, this is the outcome reported in the Harkins (1987) research. In that research, participants worked alone or coacted, and their performances could be evaluated or could not be. For two tasks, Harkins (1987) found main effects for evaluation and presence. This research appears to support an additive model with mere presence and the potential for evaluation, each contributing to the social-facilitation effects on these simple tasks. And it does provide evidence consistent with the mere-presence hypothesis: participants in the coaction/no-evaluation condition outperformed participants in the alone/no-evaluation condition. However, interpretation of the evaluation conditions is problematic.

In the alone/evaluation condition, the experimenter had access to the participants' outputs, and so could evaluate them by comparing them to the performances of previous participants. Because this same opportunity for evaluation existed in the coaction/evaluation condition, it would seem that the improved performance in this condition must be the result of mere presence because the potential for evaluation has been held constant. But, in fact, the potential for evaluation was not held constant. In the alone/evaluation condition, the experimenter could evaluate participants only by comparing their performance to that of their predecessors, but, in the coaction/evaluation condition, there were at least three different ways in which the potential for evaluation could have been increased.

First, participants might feel more evaluation apprehension when they know that the experimenter can compare their performances not only to those of their predecessors but also to those of coactors who are present in the same session (the experimenter account). Second, participants could feel more apprehension in the coaction setting when they know that they themselves can compare their performances to those of participants who are present in the same session (the self-evaluation account). Third, participants could feel more apprehension when they know that their performances can be evaluated by coactors who are present in the same session (the coactor account).

In Harkins's (1987) research, in the alone/evaluation and coaction/evaluation conditions, there was the potential for evaluation by the experimenter, but in the coaction condition, there was also the potential for coactor and self-evaluation. This raises the question of how the effects of these potential sources of evaluation combine. Latané's (1981) theory of social impact would suggest that when a person is the target of social forces emanating from other people, the magnitude of these sources will be a multiplicative function of the strength, immediacy, and number of people present. Thus, as the number of sources is increased, the amount of impact should be increased, resulting in improved performance on a simple task. Of course, social-impact theory would only make clear predictions in those cases in which there is a manipulation of the number of *external* sources (for example, increasing the number of coactors, or coactors plus experimenter). It would not make a clear prediction if one of the sources of evaluations was the self.

In fact, in a series of experiments (Bartis et al., 1988; Harkins, 2000, 2001b, 2001c; Harkins and Szymanski, 1988, 1989; Harkins et al., 2000; Szymanski and Harkins, 1987, 1993; White et al., 1995; for a review, see Harkins, 2001), Harkins and his colleagues have found that, when taken alone, the potential for experimenter and self-evaluation each motivate performance, but when both are possible, concern over the potential for experimenter evaluation supersedes interest in self-evaluation. These findings suggest that the potential for self-evaluation may not contribute to facilitation effects, at least in combination with the potential for experimenter evaluation.

Of course, this research leaves open the possibility that the potential for self-evaluation can contribute to facilitation effects in combination with the potential for evaluation by a coactor. However, Szymanski et al. (2000: Experiment 1) found that concern over the potential for evaluation by a coactor appears to supersede interest in the potential for self-evaluation in just the same way as the potential for evaluation by the experimenter. In a second experiment, Szymanski et al. (2000) tested the coactor account and found that the motivation stemming from the potential for evaluation by the coactor summed with the motivation produced by the potential for evaluation by the experimenter. Thus, consistent with Latané's (1981) theory of social impact, the combination of these sources (experimenter plus coactor) led to better performance than either one taken alone.

Gagné and Zuckerman (1999) also report findings consistent with this analysis. Their participants were led to believe that no one would be able to evaluate their performance on a use-generation task, that the experimenter alone would be able to do so, or that the experimenter and coactors could evaluate them. The linear contrast on these data was significant. That is, the combination of the potential for experimenter and coactor evaluation produced better performance than the potential for experimenter evaluation alone, which produced better performance than when evaluation by no one was possible.

These experiments represent the bare beginning of what will be required to understand the effects of mere presence and the potential for evaluation in the social-facilitation paradigm. In many experiments, researchers leave out conditions that would allow a systematic examination of the effects of evaluation on performance, because these conditions may not bear on the particular question that they are asking. For example, Gagné and Zuckerman (1999) did not include a condition in which there was the potential for coactor evaluation alone. Jackson and Williams (1985) included an alone/evaluation condition along with coaction/evaluation and coaction/no-evaluation conditions, but not an alone/no-evaluation condition. Sanna (1992) included an alone/no-evaluation condition along with coaction/evaluation and coaction/no-evaluation conditions, but no alone/evaluation condition.

In addition, in research in which the potential for evaluation is manipulated, it is not clear what the participants were told or infer about which source or sources would have access to their performances. The haphazard manipulation of this variable may account for the Bond and Titus (1983) finding that evaluation potential had no systematic effects in social facilitation. To tie down these evaluation effects will require a set of experiments that focuses on each of the potential sources of evaluation in the facilitation paradigm individually (for example, experimenter, self, and coactor), and then in combination with the other sources, along with the appropriate tests of mere-presence effects.

### *Theories of social facilitation*

But when this research is completed, we will have learned only how mere presence and evaluation contribute to social-facilitation effects. We are still left with the task of specifying which, if any, of the theories incorporated in Geen's (1989) review can account for facilitation effects. In our view, what is most noteworthy about these accounts is the fact that they do not even agree on whether participants subject to evaluation are working hard on complex tasks, but failing nonetheless (or as a consequence), or are withdrawing effort and failing as a result.

That is, the drive approaches suggest that participants are putting out more effort when they work with coactors, and this increased effort enhances performance on simple tasks (correct answer high in the habit hierarchy), but debilitates performance on complex tasks (correct answer low in the habit hierarchy). Bond's (1982) self-presentation approach suggests that participants are working hard in the presence of coactors, but concern over the embarrassment of potential failure causes cognitive interference. Baron's (1986) focus-of-attention interpretation would suggest that it is not a motivational effect, but a cognitive one. They are working as hard as participants facing easy tasks. The presence of others leads to a narrowing of attention that debilitates performance on complex tasks because these tasks require attention to a wide range of cues.

In contrast to these approaches, Carver and Scheier (1981) suggested that debilitated performance on complex tasks results from the withdrawal of effort. That is, the presence of others makes participants self-aware, leading them to be 'more cognizant of both the level of performance being manifested at the moment and the salient standard' (Geen, 1989: 32). When they find that they have little chance of bringing their performance into alignment with the standard, they stop trying. Thus, there is not even agreement about something as basic as whether people working with coactors perform poorly on complex tasks because they are working hard or are hardly working, or whether the effect is cognitive rather than motivational.

Sanna (1992) has proposed a unified model of social loafing and social facilitation that draws on Bandura's (1986: 780) self-efficacy theory. Sanna argues that 'self-efficacy expectancies develop spontaneously while participants work on easy or difficult tasks'. Sanna suggests that a positive expectancy develops during the course of performance on a simple task, whereas a negative expectancy is produced by performance on a complex one. Of course, the expectancy that one can perform a task well does not mean that one could expect favorable outcomes from this performance. Sanna notes that one must also take into account outcome expectancy. As Sanna (1992: 776) writes, 'What type of social recognition can a participant expect from the experimenter when he or she cannot be individually identified and evaluated? Likely, not much'. Thus, Sanna (1992) predicts that participants who work on a simple task develop high-efficacy expectations, and if they have high-outcome expectancy (experimenter evaluation), they will expect positive evaluation from the experimenter, resulting in improved performance compared to participants with low-outcome expectancies (no experimenter evaluation). However, participants who perform a difficult task develop low-efficacy expectancies, and if they have high-outcome expectancies (experimenter evaluation), they will anticipate negative evaluation from the experimenter, resulting in impaired performance compared to participants with low-outcome expectancies (no experimenter evaluation).

What is not clear from this account is how the expectation of negative evaluation from the experimenter produces the impaired performance. That is, one could imagine that when a person comes to believe that she or he is performing poorly and must soon face the evaluation of the experimenter, if anything, the person would work harder. However, one could simply withdraw effort and give up. And so, we see once again that this account does not clarify what happens during the performance of complex tasks.

Huguet et al. (1999) argue that their findings on the Stroop color-word task support Baron's (1986) focus-of-attention explanation rather than Zajonc's (1965) drive explanation, which relies on the facilitation of dominant responses. Huguet et al. (1999) note that in the Stroop task, the dominant response is to read the color word, which interferes with the correct response, naming the ink color in which the word is printed. As a result, when drive is increased either through an audience or a coaction manipulation, the dominant response version of drive theory would predict that performance should be debilitated. But it is not. Participants perform better in audience or coaction conditions than when alone. This finding is consistent with Baron's (1986) argument that the presence of others can lead to the narrowing of one's focus of attention, and Huguet et al. argue that this reduced focus of attention makes it easier for the participants to respond to the color alone.

These findings would seem to favor a focus-of-attention explanation. However, their findings would be more compelling if the authors could demonstrate that the reduced focus of attention undermines performance when a wider focus of attention is necessary for successful task performance. For example, MacLeod (1991) reports that Stroop interference is reduced when the color word and the color are presented in different locations. In this case, Huguet et al. (1999) would have to predict that the presence of others would debilitate performance, because the reduced focus of attention should be a disadvantage. Findings like this would make their case more compelling.

In addition, despite the authors' claims to the contrary, it is not clear that these findings are inconsistent with Zajonc's dominant-response view. The dominant response is the one that is most likely to be emitted in the given situation. In social-facilitation research that has used 'complex' tasks, the correct answer has not been the one most likely to be given, and the presence of others as coactors or an audience makes it even less likely. But on the Stroop, the correct answer is the most likely one. The error rate in these experiments is extremely low. In what sense is this not the dominant response? The tendency to read the color word may interfere with the emission of this response, but it does not prevent it. And the presence of others simply enhances this dominant response.

Finally, this line of research does not rule out the 'withdrawal of effort' explanation (e.g., Carver and Scheier, 1981). The 'withdrawal' interpretation would suggest that if the participants are in an audience or coactor condition, a few moments after they begin, they will check to see how they are doing. On the Stroop task, they will find that they are doing fine. That is, it may be a little difficult to solve the problems, but they are solvable, and so there is no reason for them to lose heart and to withdraw their effort. Thus, the 'withdrawal-of-effort' explanation would have no difficulty accounting for these finding, even though the authors prefer a different interpretation.

One could argue that the mediating process will emerge from an analysis of the psychophysiology of performance. For example, Blascovich has applied his biopsychological model of challenge and threat to the phenomenon of social facilitation (Blascovich et al., 1999). Blascovich et al. (1999) found the pattern of cardiovascular reactivity associated with challenge when participants performed well-learned tasks in the presence of others, whereas on tasks that were not well-learned (that is, complex), they exhibited the pattern of cardiovascular reactivity associated with threat. In contrast, participants working alone demonstrated no reactivity from baseline, whether the task was well learned or not.

This work identifies precise physiological patterns of cardiovascular reactivity that are associated with the facilitation and debilitation of performance. However, as Blascovich et al. (1999) note, it does not tell us whether the physiological responses are causes, concomitants, or the results of the performance effects. In addition, because the timing period was limited to the first minute of the testing period, we know only that the participants performing the unlearned task in front of the audience were displaying the cardiac pattern associated with threat at that point. We do not know whether these participants continued to exhibit this patterning as the timing period continued, nor do we know whether these participants continued their striving in an effort to perform the task successfully or if they withdrew their efforts. As a result, we are left with the same questions that are left unresolved in the other accounts.

### *Conclusion*

Thus, after more than 100 years of research on social facilitation, we have evidence consistent with the view that both mere presence and the potential for evaluation contribute to social-facilitation effects. However, we know relatively little about how the potential sources of evaluation combine with each other and with the effects of mere presence to produce these effects. We also require further research to identify the mediating process through which evaluation and mere presence have their effects on performance. Perhaps the most striking example of this state of affairs is the fact that there is not even agreement about whether the potential for evaluation on complex tasks results in poor performance because these participants are putting out *more* or *less* effort than participants for whom evaluation is less salient. We would argue that that state of affairs exists, at least in part, because we have focused our efforts at the molar rather than the molecular level of analysis. We are much more likely to be interested in and rewarded for theory construction than for the molecular analysis that is required to learn exactly how these variables affect performance on a given task. Of course, one might think that such an analysis would be an integral part of theory development, but such has not been the case. However, this is exactly what is required. Dashiell (1935: 1115), after noting the difficulty of conducting facilitation research, went on to state: 'But this is no counsel of despair. Before solid findings can be achieved in any science a great amount of grub-work must be done in the way of clarification of problems and trying-out of techniques. Analysis and ever more analysis and classification first!'. Nearly seventy years later, we are still in need of a great deal of 'grub-work'.

## Social loafing

Social-facilitation research demonstrates that the presence of others can affect our individual performance, sometimes enhancing it and sometimes reducing it. But what about situations in which we are working together with other people and our efforts are being combined into a group product? How does actually working with others affect our motivation? More than 100 studies have examined this issue. Although common sense and some social-facilitation theories might suggest that groups should energize and motivate us, much of the research shows the opposite effect and documents a tendency for people to work less hard on a collective task than on an individual or coactive task – a phenomenon known as social loafing. Yet social loafing is not inevitable, and a number of moderating variables have been identified that can reduce or eliminate it. In addition, a handful of recent studies have documented some situations under which motivation gains may actually emerge.

### *Early efforts*

In the 1880s, in what may have been the very first experiments of a social-psychological nature, Ringelmann (cited in Kravitz and Martin, 1986) examined the effects that working together with others has on physical performance, after noticing that oxen pulling in teams did less than expected from how strongly they pulled when pulling alone. Deciding to test his observation on humans (in what may be one of the rare instances that research was conducted with humans to understand the behavior of lower animals!), he asked male volunteers to pull on a rope as hard as they could in groups of varying sizes. As group size increased, group performance was increasingly lower than would be expected from the simple addition of individual performances. As later noted by Steiner (1972), there were two possible causes of this performance decrement – motivation loss and coordination loss. Thus, performance may have suffered because the individuals worked less hard as group size increased (motivation loss), or because the individual group members were not able to coordinate their efforts optimally (for example, pulling while others were adjusting their grip). Process losses have been found to be an important influence on the performance of interacting groups in a variety of situations including brainstorming (for reviews, see Mullen et al., 1991; Paulus et al., 2001) and group discussion (for reviews, see Baron et al., 1992; Hinsz et al., 1997). Because social-loafing researchers are concerned with motivation rather than process loss, it was an important early challenge for researchers to devise methods for separating these two factors.

Nearly 100 years passed before Ingham et al. (1974) replicated Ringelmann's results. Ingham et al. also sought to separate motivation loss from process loss and show that both factors contributed to the overall decrement in group performance. They asked male students to perform a rope-pulling task both in actual groups and in pseudogroups in which blindfolded subjects believed they were pulling along with others but were actually pulling alone. Data from the pseudogroups showed that performance still decreased as group size increased, suggesting that individuals worked less hard on group trials than on individual trials. Although these results were provocative, they were not definitive because group size was inversely related to audience size, leaving open the possibility that effort was facilitated by larger audiences in the individual trials.

Latané et al. (1979) conceptually replicated these results while holding audience size constant. College men were asked to shout and clap as loudly as possible, both individually and with others. They were asked to make noise both in actual groups and in pseudogroups. Blindfolds and headphones that played masking noise were used to prevent detection of the true nature of the pseudogroup trials. Latané et al. found that a substantial portion of the reduced group performance was due to reduced individual effort, distinct from coordination loss and that audience size did not account for these effects. They also coined the term 'social loafing' to describe the demotivating properties of groups.

### *Magnitude and robustness of social loafing*

To date, more than 100 studies have examined the effects of groups on the motivation of individual members. Social loafing has been replicated repeatedly in most of these studies. Both laboratory experiments and field studies have been conducted, employing a wide range of subject populations. Social loafing has been found for a rich variety of widely varying tasks demanding different types of effort. Using Steiner's (1972) classification, most social-loafing studies have focused on tasks that are maximizing, unitary, and additive. In other words, the task is one in which the harder one tries, the more that is accomplished; the inputs are not divisible into smaller subtasks; and participants' contributions are added to form the final total.

Specifically, several researchers have used evaluative tasks, such as providing ratings of advertisements (Williams and Burmont, 1981), essays and poems (Petty et al., 1977), résumés (Erez and Somech, 1996), or clinical therapists (Petty et al., 1980). A variety of cognitive tasks have also been used, such as navigating mazes (Griffith et al., 1989; Jackson and Williams, 1985), remembering information relevant to a mock trial (Henningsen et al., 2000), maintaining one's vigilance for the appearance of signals on a computer (e.g., Harkins and Petty, 1982; Harkins and Szymanksi, 1988, 1989; Smith et al., 2001), or completing classroom educational tasks (North et al., 2000). A wide variety of creative tasks have been studied, including writing songs (Jackson and Padgett, 1982), finding hidden items in a picture (Brickner and Wingard, 1988), and listing thoughts or generating ideas (e.g., Bartis et al., 1988; Brickner et al., 1986; Harkins and Jackson, 1985; Karau and Williams, 1997; Shepperd and Wright, 1989; Williams and Karau, 1991).

Physical tasks have been a popular choice among researchers, including rope-pulling (Ingham et al., 1974; Kugihara, 1999), holding one's arm above a wire for as long as possible (Hertel et al., 2000a; Messé et al., 2002), making noise by shouting or clapping (e.g., Gabrenya et al., 1981, 1983; Hardy and Latané, 1988; Harkins et al., 1980; Jackson and Harkins, 1985; Latané et al., 1979; Shirakashi, 1985), swimming (Everett et al., 1992; Miles and Greenberg, 1993; Sorrentino and Sheppard, 1978; Williams et al., 1989), rowing (Anshel, 1995), folding paper (Kokubo, 1996), and pumping air through a handheld device (Kerr, 1983; Kerr and Bruun, 1983).

Finally, several work-related tasks have been employed, including typing (Karau and Williams, 1997), selling product lines (George, 1995), and completing an in-basket managerial exercise (Earley, 1989). Moreover, although occasionally differences emerge across samples, a number of studies have produced significant social-loafing effects for participants of different ages, genders, and nationalities. The bulk of the available evidence suggests that social loafing is moderate in magnitude and has been fairly consistently replicated across studies conducted in both laboratory and field settings. A meta-analysis of seventy-eight studies by Karau and Williams (1993) found that the magnitude of social loafing was comparable in size to that of a number of prominent social-psychological effects.

### *Classic theoretical accounts*

#### Social-impact theory

Latané (1981) suggested that people could serve as both sources and targets of social influence. He proposed that the amount of such social influence experienced in a group setting is a function of the strength, immediacy, and number of sources and targets present. When a group is working collectively, the demands of a source of social influence to work as hard as possible are diffused across all group members, resulting in diminished social impact and reduced effort. On individual tasks, however, there is no diffusion of the source's social impact, and individuals work hard. Social-impact theory has been very useful in predicting group-size effects. However, researchers in the small-groups realm have neglected the strength and immediacy factors somewhat, and some critics argue that the theory does not explicitly address the psychological processes it describes (e.g., Mullen, 1985).

#### Arousal reduction

Jackson and Williams (1985) offered a drive explanation to accompany a social-impact-theory perspective on social loafing. They argued that the presence of others is not always drive inducing. Instead, the presence of others should be drive inducing only when those others serve as sources of impact (that is, when they are coactors or observers), but should be drive reducing when those others serve as cotargets (that is, when they are coworkers). Jackson and Williams (1985) asked subjects to complete simple and complex computer mazes either alone, coactively, or collectively. For the simple mazes, performance was higher coactively than collectively, but for the complex mazes, performance was higher collectively than collectively. These findings are consistent with the notion that the presence of other coworkers can actually reduce drive, thereby reducing performance on simple tasks (in which the dominant response is likely to be correct) and increasing it on novel, complex tasks (in which the dominant response is likely to be in error).

#### Evaluation potential

Several interpretations rely on the concept of evaluation potential (e.g., Harkins, 1987; Kerr and Bruun, 1983; Williams et al., 1981). These researchers suggest that social loafing occurs because working collectively often makes individual group members' inputs hard to identify and evaluate. Thus, working collectively can allow individuals to 'hide in the crowd' and avoid pulling their weight, and can also lead individuals to feel 'lost in the crowd' such that they cannot receive fair credit or acknowledgment for their hard work. A number of studies by Harkins and colleagues (e.g., Harkins, 1987, 2000; Harkins and Szymanski, 1989; Szymanski and Harkins, 1993; White et al., 1995) have documented that evaluation potential can indeed eliminate social loafing in many situations.

#### Dispensability of effort

Another reason why people may work less hard collectively is because they feel that their inputs are dispensable or unnecessary for the group to perform well. Kerr and colleagues (Kerr, 1983; Kerr and Bruun, 1983) found that individuals tend to reduce their collective efforts when working with a highly capable coworker on a disjunctive task in which the group succeeded if either group member reached a preset performance criterion. These motivation losses occurred when the capable coworker either succeeded regularly or failed regularly on the criterion task over a series of trials. Kerr reasoned that when working with a capable and successful partner, individuals decided not to bother working hard themselves because their partner's hard work would lead the group to succeed regardless, an effect he referred to as 'free riding' (consistent with the label prior researchers have given to the tendency to fail to contribute to a collective good in the social dilemma paradigm [e.g., Albanese and Van Fleet, 1985; Olson, 1965]; for a discussion of similarities and differences between free riding and social loafing, see Williams et al., 1993). These motivation losses emerged even though each group member's contribution was identifiable to themselves, their coworker, and the experimenter. Thus, people may not be willing to work hard on a group task if they feel their efforts will have little impact on the group outcome.

### *An integrative theory: the collective-effort model (CEM)*

Some support has been found for all these classic theories. However, each viewpoint is somewhat limited in scope and focuses on social loafing within a restricted domain. Several researchers have suggested that expectancy-value models may have special value for integrating research on motivation losses (Karau and Williams, 1993; Kerr, 1983; Olson, 1965; Sheppard, 1993). We focus on the collective-effort model (CEM) (Karau and Williams, 1993) due to its recent influence and broad scope, as well as several unique attributes.

The CEM suggests that individuals will be willing to work hard on a collective task only to the degree that they expect their efforts to be instrumental in leading to outcomes that they value personally. Thus, individuals are not likely to work hard if they view the outcomes of the group performance or collective task as trivial, meaningless, or inconsistent with their own desires. Moreover, even when individuals do value the outcomes associated with the collective task, they are still not likely to work hard unless they expect their own efforts to lead to performance that will be instrumental in obtaining those outcomes. A unique feature of the CEM is that it specifies a number of additional contingencies affecting individual motivation that become operative when one is working on collective tasks. In other words, collective tasks introduce a number of unique potential barriers to individual motivation because one's outcomes are affected by factors beyond individual performance – such as the performance of other group members, the relationship between group performance and group outcomes, and the degree to which group outcomes lead to desired individual outcomes.

Regarding what outcomes people value, the CEM suggests that value depends on a variety of factors, including personal beliefs, task meaningfulness, the nature of rewards associated with performance, individual differences in the value attached to collective outcomes, and the extent to which the outcome is relevant to future goals or favorable interactions within the group. Valued outcomes can consist of either objective outcomes, such as pay and rewards, or subjective outcomes such as personal satisfaction and feelings of growth, belonging, or enjoyment. The CEM places special importance on group-level outcomes that have implications for self-evaluation (e.g., Greenwald and Pratkanis, 1984) and social identification (e.g., Hogg, 2002; Hogg and Abrams, 1988). Because group tasks often provide individuals with access to self-evaluation information from a variety of sources, collective settings that provide high levels of self-evaluation information from sources such as oneself, one's coworkers, or one's supervisor, should have greater motivation potential than settings that provide less self-evaluation information or that make it ambiguous or less potent. Such group-level outcomes may have special relevance to individuals due to processes involving belongingness needs (Baumeister and Leary, 1995), social identification (Banaji and Prentice, 1994), and group-level social comparison (Goethals and Darley, 1987).

Thus, the CEM suggests that collective work settings are highly susceptible to social loafing because individuals' outcomes frequently depend less on their own individual efforts when working collectively than when working coactively. According to this perspective, the key to reducing or eliminating social loafing is to reduce or eliminate barriers to individuals' perceptions that their efforts will make a difference in producing outcomes that they value, a challenging proposition indeed for many collective tasks.

The CEM also highlights a number of factors that can moderate social loafing. Because the CEM suggests that individuals will work harder on a collective task when they expect their effort to be instrumental in obtaining valued outcomes, the conditions under which social loafing may be reduced should include situations in which individuals: (a) believe their collective inputs can be evaluated; (b) work in smaller rather than larger groups; (c) view their contributions to the collective task as unique or important rather than redundant or trivial; (d) work on tasks that are meaningful, high in personal involvement, important to respected others, or intrinsically interesting; (e) work in cohesive groups or in situations that activate a salient group identity; (f) expect their coworkers to perform poorly; and (g) have a dispositional tendency to value collective outcomes. Of course, these moderator predictions are made on the basis of holding other variables constant. The CEM suggests that on many group tasks these factors could interact. As just one example, individuals may be willing to work harder when they expect their coworkers to perform poorly, but only if they view the task as somewhat meaningful (Williams and Karau, 1991). Karau and Williams (1993) documented meta-analytically that these logical implications of the CEM account nicely for moderating variables in the extant social-loafing literature.

Finally, the CEM provides some clues as to situations in which motivation gains might emerge such that individuals may actually work harder collectively than individually (motivation gains are discussed later). Specifically, motivation gains should emerge when group members' valued outcomes are more rather than less reliant on their individual inputs when working collectively than when working alone or coactively. Stated differently, according to the CEM, the key to finding motivation gains in groups is to identify group situations in which individuals are likely to attach a high degree of value to group outcomes and in which their own individual efforts are especially important to the attainment of those valued outcomes.

### *Moderators of social loafing*

#### Evaluation

Consistent with the evaluation potential viewpoint introduced earlier, a number of studies have found that social loafing can be reduced or eliminated when individuals' inputs to the collective task can be identified and evaluated (e.g., Harkins, 1987; Harkins and Szymanski, 1988, 1989; Szymanski and Harkins, 1987; White et al., 1995; Williams et al., 1981). This research has demonstrated that when individuals' collective inputs can be evaluated by anyone (including oneself), this alone may be enough to eliminate social loafing in many situations. This research has also shown that two criteria are necessary for evaluation of individual inputs to be possible: (a) the inputs must be known or identifiable; and (b) there must be a standard (personal, social, or objective) with which this output can be compared. Evaluation can also operate at the group level. Harkins and Szymanski (1989) found that providing groups with an objective, group-level performance standard eliminated social loafing.

Although making inputs identifiable may help reduce or eliminate social loafing, it does have some potentially negative implications. For example, electronic monitoring of work performance in laboratory and work settings has been found to reduce perceived control, increase stress, and impair performance on complex tasks (e.g., Aiello, 1993; Davidson and Henderson, 2000; Stanton and Barnes-Farrell, 1996). In addition, evaluation potential from both an external source (Bartis et al., 1988) and from oneself (Szymanski and Harkins, 1992) has been found to undermine performance on creativity tasks.

#### Task features

Consistent with the value component of the CEM, social loafing should be reduced or eliminated when individuals are working on a task that has a high degree of importance, personal relevance, or interest for them. Indeed, several studies have found that social loafing has been reduced or eliminated by designing tasks that are personally involving (Brickner et al., 1986), attractive (Zaccaro, 1984), or associated with either rewards for performing well (Shepperd and Wright, 1989) or punishment for performing poorly (Miles and Greenberg, 1993). Karau and Williams (1993) also found that task meaningfulness reduced the magnitude of social loafing across all of the studies in their meta-analysis. However, it appears that task meaningfulness is not always sufficient, in and of itself, to prevent social loafing. Several studies have found significant social-loafing effects on tasks that were probably at least somewhat meaningful to participants (e.g., George, 1995; Hardy and Latané, 1988; Henningsen et al., 2000; Karau and Williams, 1997; Williams and Karau, 1991). Moreover, it is likely that the influence of task meaningfulness on performance may fade over many days and months of repeated collective effort. Most job-related tasks also have multiple components that vary in meaningfulness, creating plenty of opportunity for social loafing to emerge on the less desirable aspects. Consistent with this reasoning, an interesting study by Hoeksema-van Orden et al. (1998) found that performance deteriorated over time when subjects were asked to work continuously for twenty hours without sleep on a variety of tasks. Performance decrements were held partially in check when subjects worked individually or were provided with individual feedback, but in the group condition social-loafing effects strengthened over time regardless.

The uniqueness of contributions is also important. Harkins and Petty (1982) found that social loafing was most likely to occur on tasks in which there was a chance that one's efforts would duplicate those of other group members, rendering one's own inputs at least partially unnecessary. This finding also held up meta-analytically across studies (Karau and Williams, 1993). These results are consistent both with the CEM and with Kerr's dispensability perspective.

## Group cohesion

Another factor influencing the value attached to the task is the degree to which individuals like, value, or strongly identify with the group they are working for. Several studies have found that social loafing can be eliminated when individuals are working with close friends (Karau and Williams, 1997) or in cohesive groups (Karau and Hart, 1998). The value of the group was also inversely related to social loafing in the Karau and Williams (1993) meta-analysis. These findings suggest that enhancing the importance of the group to the individuals within can reduce social loafing under some conditions. However, future research is needed to determine the potential constraints on these findings and to evaluate the implications of different types of cohesion (cf. Mullen and Copper, 1994; Zaccaro and McCoy, 1988).

Another way to enhance concern with group outcomes is to activate or make salient individuals' social identification with the group. Indeed, group cohesiveness may even reside within individuals in the form of their identification with groups and social categories (e.g., Banaji and Prentice, 1994; Hogg, 1993). Three recent studies by Karau et al. (2002) support this reasoning. They found that social loafing was eliminated when social identification was enhanced or made more salient with regard to one's university affiliation (Study 1) or gender (Studies 2 and 3) and an outgroup comparison was implied.

## Individual differences

The final major class of factors that have been shown to moderate social loafing concern individual differences in the value that people attach to collective outcomes. The CEM suggests that loafing should be reduced or eliminated when individuals attach a high degree of importance to collective tasks. Several factors might influence such perceptions, including personality, gender, and culture.

Regarding personality, the CEM suggests that a number of individual difference variables may tap into the tendency to value collective outcomes, including individualism/collectivism, need for affiliation, Protestant work ethic, and self-monitoring. Individual differences are also likely to affect social loafing via the value attached to specific tasks. Some individual difference constructs affecting task value may include need for cognition, affect intensity, need for control, and need for power. Finally, individual difference variables affecting one's perceptions of expectancy and instrumentality may also influence collective effort. These factors may include self-esteem and locus of control.

Unfortunately, only a few studies have examined personality and social loafing. First, Williams and Karau (1991) found that individuals low in interpersonal trust actually worked harder collectively than coactively on a meaningful task – presumably because they did not trust their partner to work hard enough for the group to succeed, whereas those high or moderate in trust engaged in social loafing. Second, two recent studies found that individuals who viewed themselves as generally superior to others in performance tended to loaf on an easy task (Charbonnier et al., 1998) but tended to work harder collectively than coactively on a challenging task (Huguet et al., 1999). Third, two studies have found that individuals who were high in need for cognition did not loaf when working on tasks that were cognitively engaging (Petty et al., 1985; Smith et al., 2001). Finally, a recent study (Hart et al., 2004) on achievement motivation found that subjects high in achievement motivation did not engage in loafing, whereas subjects low in achievement motivation worked hard if working with a low-ability coworker but loafed if working with a high-ability worker. Taken as a whole, these studies take important first steps and suggest that individuals are less likely to engage in social loafing when their personality leads them to value either collective tasks or specific tasks as intrinsically meaningful. However, there is room for much additional work to isolate the conditions under which specific personality types and situational combinations either enhance or reduce effort.

Regarding gender and culture, a number of analyses have suggested that women often tend to be more group or communally oriented than men (e.g., Anderson and Blanchard, 1982; Bakan, 1966; Carli, 1990; Eagly, 1987). Similarly, Eastern culture is often depicted as group or socially oriented, whereas Western culture is often depicted as individualistic (e.g., Triandis, 1989; Wheeler et al., 1989). Hence, following the logic of the CEM, one might expect social loafing to be less prominent among women or among those in an Eastern culture. The Karau and Williams (1993) meta-analysis provides support for these inferences. They found that although significant levels of social loafing were found within each class of participants within both gender and culture, the effect was smaller for women and for individuals from nations such as Japan, Taiwan, and China. However, gender and culture are both richly complex constructs, and it seems likely that these factors will interact with task and situational variables to influence effort. As just one example of such possible interactions,

Earley (1993) found that individuals from collective cultures worked harder collectively than alone, but only when working with members of their own group.

### Motivation gains in groups

Although intuition may suggest that working in groups should enhance our motivation, the vast majority of studies have found that individuals tend to engage in social loafing when working on collective tasks. However, a number of recent studies have identified some situations in which motivation gains may emerge such that individuals actually work harder collectively than coactively.

#### Social compensation

Research by Williams and Karau (1991) has demonstrated some conditions under which individuals may actually work harder on a collective task than on a coactive task in order to compensate for others in the group who are expected to perform poorly – a phenomenon called *social compensation*. Compensating for others could be done either to maintain the success or viability of the groups or to ensure one's own favorable outcomes related to the group task. Williams and Karau (1991) found support for these ideas in a series of three studies. In each study, participants worked either coactively or collectively on an idea-generation task that was designed to be viewed as meaningful. Expectations of coworker performance were either inferred from interpersonal trust scores (Experiment 1) or were manipulated by a confederate coworker's statement of either effort (Experiment 2) or ability (Experiment 3). In all three studies, participants worked harder coactively than collectively (that is, they loafed) when working with a coworker who was expected to perform well, but actually worked harder collectively than coactively when working with a coworker who was expected to perform poorly.

Several recent studies provide additional support for social compensation (Hart et al., 2001; Karau and Williams, 1997; Plaks and Higgins, 2000; Williams and Sommer, 1997). In one such study, Williams and Sommer (1997) found that female workers who had just been ostracized by their coworkers in an incidental ball-tossing game worked harder collectively than coactively on a subsequent idea-generation task. In a series of four studies, Plaks and Higgins (2000) found that participants worked harder on cognitive tasks when there was a poor fit between the stereotypic strengths of their partner and the requirements for good task performance.

Although social compensation has been documented in several instances of expected poor coworker performance, it probably has important limiting conditions. For example, Williams and Karau (1991: Study 3) found that individuals loafed rather than compensated if the task was low in meaningfulness. Social compensation also might not persist over time unless reciprocated in some form due to concerns over equity or fairness. The effect also may be limited to smaller groups and may not emerge under conditions where compensating for others creates a great deal of negative affect. Consistent with this logic, Hart et al. (2001) found that individuals engaged in social compensation only when their coworker was low in both ability and effort but socially loafed when their coworker was high in ability but was not trying hard (cf. 'the sucker effect' – Kerr, 1983).

#### The Köhler effect

Otto Köhler provided the first published evidence for group motivation gains (1926, 1927). He asked male athletes to perform biceps curls for as long as possible, both individually and in pairs. Note that this is a conjunctive task in the dyad condition, because the first individual to tire determines the dyad's performance. When dyad members were moderately discrepant in their ability levels (that is, neither too similar nor too dissimilar), they performed better as a dyad than would be expected from their individual performances. Stroebe et al. (1996) conceptually replicated the Köhler effect and found that it was the weaker member of the dyad that was responsible for the motivation gain.

Hertel et al. (2000a) made several improvements to the basic paradigm and examined the Köhler effect with an endurance task in which individuals and dyads were asked to hold a bar above a tripwire for as long as possible (both individuals held one end of the bar in the dyad condition). Hertel et al. found evidence for a motivation gain among the weaker member of the dyad, although the ability-discrepancy effect was not found. Messé et al. (2002) once again replicated the basic Köhler motivation-gain effect, and also showed that the ability-discrepancy effect can be found when participants are aware of their coworkers' ability beforehand. Several additional studies have also found support for Köhler's basic motivation gain effect (Hertel et al., 2000b; Lount et al., 2000).

At first glance, the Köhler effect seems to be inconsistent with social compensation. After all, social compensation finds that the more able partner works harder, whereas the Köhler effect finds that the less able partner works harder. On closer examination, however, social compensation and the Köhler effect appear to be two sides of a motivational coin. Specifically, both effects suggest that individuals may work especially hard when instrumentality is very high and the group outcome is highly reliant on their own individual efforts, consistent with the logic of the CEM. When working on an additive task with a poorly performing worker, one must increase personal efforts if the group is to succeed. Similarly, when working on a conjunctive task with a more able coworker, one's own performance will determine the group's success or failure. Both phenomena suggest that individuals may be willing to work harder collectively than individually or coactively if their own efforts are especially important to the success of the group.

### Other possible motivation gains

There are additional hints of possible sources of motivation gains in several studies. First, gender composition may have some motivational properties. Kerr and Sullaway (1983) found that both men and women worked harder than individual controls when working with an opposite-sex partner. Similarly, Kerr and MacCoun (1985) found that men and women worked harder in mixed-sex dyads than individually when they thought their partner was higher in ability. They suggest that self-esteem maintenance comes to the fore when one's partner is very able and is of the opposite sex. Second, Erev et al. (1993) found that dyads that were directly competing with other dyads worked harder than coactive controls, suggesting that social competition might stimulate collective effort. Finally, Matsui et al. (1987) found that group-level goal setting produced higher group than individual effort. Hence, three additional potential sources of motivation gains have been highlighted, but all three are in need of further replication and exploration of causal factors and limiting conditions.

### *Conclusion*

Kerr (2001: 367) states: 'We have seen our field pass through [a sustained, programmatic, and highly productive] stage in work on group motivation losses over the last 25 years [...] In the next 25 years our field can be equally successful in identifying and understanding powerful motivation gain mechanisms, with the promise of substantially improving the performance of work groups and teams'. Although it would be nice to strive for such lofty aims, it appears to us that research has shown motivation gains only when (a) we do not trust our coworkers, (b) coworkers have previously ostracized us, or (c) we do not want to be stigmatized for being responsible for the failure of our team. None of these conditions seem to be the *esprit de corps*-like foundation on which one would hope to base improved group and team performance.

Thus, the available evidence on motivation gains is rather meager compared with what has been uncovered for motivation losses, and does not particularly embody the inspiration that groups are supposed to muster in individuals. Perhaps this is because only recently have psychologists tried to focus their attention on 'positive' psychology, or perhaps individuals are simply not motivated to work as hard on group tasks. It may be that our search for motivation gains is misplaced: rather than looking for increased motivation to work harder in groups, pehaps we should look for motivation to work at all. That is, maybe individuals are more likely to approach or choose tasks in which they can combine their efforts with others. Maybe group tasks are more enjoyable, either because they allow individuals to reduce their efforts while still producing reasonable accomplishments or because they offer the social support and stimulation absent in solo tasks. Whereas being less motivated to work hard in groups may seem to be a drawback to group work, perhaps individuals are more likely to engage in this sort of work and less likely to burn out.

## Social facilitation and social loafing: who are those 'others'?

As should be apparent by now, whereas social facilitation and social loafing do describe opposite motivational tendencies, they need not be regarded as inconsistent or in some sort of empirical battle. There are several studies in which social facilitation and social loafing have been integrated either experimentally (see Gagné and Zuckerman, 1999; Harkins, 1987; Jackson and Williams, 1985), or theoretically (see Geen, 1991; Harkins and Szymanski, 1987; Paulus, 1983). It should be clear that it is overly simplistic to claim that the mere presence of *others* is arousing. Sometimes, the presence of others is arousing (Zajonc, 1965), but other times, being with other people reduces arousal, as noted by Schachter (1959) in his research on fear and affiliation. At present, it appears that the most parsimonious distinction is the way in which the 'others' are regarded. In terms of social impact (Latané, 1981), are the others *sources* or *cotargets*? If the others are primarily standards for comparison, competition, or evaluation, as in the case of coaction, they appear to facilitate our motivation to work harder. If the others are, along with us, a part of a collective performance with whom we share (or can hide behind or with whom our efforts seem lost in) the comparison, competition, or evaluation, they reduce our motivation to work hard. There are, of course, instances in which the same 'others' can be regarded as sources and cotargets, and further investigation is needed to determine how individuals make the distinction in such cases, and how construal of others as both sources and cotargets affects our motivation and performance.

### Final comments

At the beginning of this chapter, we noted that social facilitation and social loafing have enjoyed two productive, yet distinct research agendas. The agenda for social-facilitation research, because it is a relatively desirable group effect, first emphasized its generality and then focused on explaining why the presence of others is arousing or enhances drive. The agenda for social-loafing research also first emphasized its generality, but because it is an undesirable effect, then turned towards eliminating or reversing its effects. While it is not surprising that the societal consequences of a phenomenon will drive different research questions, it may be wise for researchers in social performance to step back and think of what questions they have missed asking because of their socially guided agendas. Might it not be useful to know the conditions under which social facilitation will and will not occur? Put bluntly, if one wanted to stop individuals from being facilitated by others' presence, what steps would have to be taken? Conversely, suppose researchers started asking how we could increase social loafing? Neither of these questions seems natural or worthwhile. Yet, we know that asking questions from only one perspective or one value system will lead to, at best, a limited and biased understanding of the phenomenon. Researchers should try to remove themselves from such obvious blinders, so they can ask questions that may lead to discoveries about both phenomena that will yield a deeper and broader understanding of others' effect on our motivation, effort, and performance.

Despite over 100 years of research on social performance, it is clear that there is still much to be learned. The next generation of research will probably be aimed at supplying the 'grub-work' still necessary to pin down the mechanisms by which others affect individual performance (Harkins, 2006). There will also be a continued search for the existence of motivation gains, perhaps gains that emanate from the positive, rather than the negative, consequences associated with working with others. Finally, we expect to see an interest in other factors that make working in groups worthwhile in the long run, even if social performance is less than optimal in the short run.

**SUMMARY**

We review the literature on two of the oldest and still most prominent phenomena in the field of social performance: social facilitation and social loafing. Both phenomena deal with consequences of other people (as audience members, coactors, or collective partners) and their impact on motivation, effort, and performance. We begin with social facilitation, which can be described as increased effort when one performs in the presence or under the evaluative influence of others. This increased effort can, in some cases, improve performance but in other cases, can debilitate performance. Early efforts were met with inconsistent findings. A drive theory explanation brought coherence and sparked research interest, but also met with controversy concerning why others motivated effort. In the next section, we review social loafing, can be defined as a reduction in motivation and effort as a consequence of performing collectively with others. We review its history and consider the various theories that accounted for portions of its effect. We then discuss the collective-effort model, and a meta-analytical review that provided a theoretical framework and identified important boundary conditions. We discuss instances in which collective effort results in motivation gains, concluding with suggestions for future research.

### References

Aiello, J.R. (1993) 'Computer-Based Work Monitoring: Electronic Surveillance and Its Effects', *Journal of Applied Social Psychology*, 23: 499–507.

Albanese, R. and Van Fleet, D.D. (1985) 'Rational Behavior in Groups: The Free-Riding Tendency', *Academy of Management Review*, 10: 244–55.

Allport, F. (1920) 'The Influence of the Group upon Association and Thought', *Journal of Experimental Psychology*, 3: 159–82.

Allport, F. (1924) *Social Psychology*. New York: Houghton Mifflin.

Anderson, L.R. and Blanchard, P.N. (1982) 'Sex Differences in Task and Social-Emotional Behavior', *Basic and Applied Social Psychology*, 3: 109–39.

Anshel, M.H. (1995) 'Examining Social Loafing among Elite Female Rowers as a Function of Task Duration and Mood', *Journal of Sport Behavior*, 18: 39–49.

Asch, S. (1952) *Social Psychology*. New York: Holt, Rinehart & Winston.

Bakan, D. (1966) *The Duality of Human Existence: An Essay on Psychology and Religion*. Chicago, IL.: Rand McNally.

Banaji, M.R. and Prentice, D.A. (1994) 'The Self in Social Contexts', *Annual Review of Psychology*, 45: 297–332.

Bandura, A. (1986) *Social Foundations of Thought and Action: A Social Cognitive Theory*. Englewood Cliffs, NJ: Prentice Hall.

Baron, R. (1986) 'Distraction-Conflict Theory: Progress and Problems', in L. Berkowitz (ed.), *Advances in Experimental Social Psychology* (vol. 19). New York: Academic Press, pp. 1–40.

Baron, R.S., Kerr, N.L., and Miller, N. (1992) *Group Process, Group Decision, Group Action*. Belmont, CA: Brooks/Cole.

Bartis, S., Szymanski, K., and Harkins, S. (1988) 'Evaluation of Performance: A Two-Edged Knife', *Personality and Social Psychology Bulletin*, 14: 242–51.

Baumeister, R.F. and Leary, M.R. (1995) 'The Need to Belong: Desire for Interpersonal Attachments as a Fundamental Human Motivation', *Psychological Bulletin*, 117: 497–529.

Bergum, B. and Lehr, D. (1963) 'Vigilance Performance as a Function of Paired Monitoring', *Journal of Applied Psychology*, 46: 341–3.

Blank, T., Staff, I., and Shaver, P. (1976) 'Social Facilitation of Word Associations: Further Questions', *Journal of Personality and Social Psychology*, 34: 725–33.

Blascovich, J., Mendes, W., Salomon, K., and Hunter, S. (1999) 'Social "Facilitation" as Challenge and Threat', *Journal of Personality and Social Psychology*, 77: 68–77.

Bond, C. (1982) 'Social Facilitation: A Self-Presentational View', *Journal of Personality and Social Psychology*, 42: 1042–50.

Bond, C. and Titus, J. (1983) 'Social Facilitation: A Meta-analysis of 241 Studies', *Psychological Bulletin*, 94: 265–92.

Brickner, M.A. and Wingard, K. (1988) 'Social Identity and Self-Motivation: Improvements in Productivity'. Unpublished manuscript. Akron, OH: University of Akron.

Brickner, M.A., Harkins, S.G. and Ostrom, T.M. (1986) 'Effects of Personal Involvement: Thought-Provoking Implications for Social Loafing', *Journal of Personality and Social Psychology*, 51: 763–9.

Brockner, J. (1988) *Self-Esteem at Work: Research, Theory and Practice*. Lexington, MA: Lexington Books.

Carli, L.L. (1990) 'Gender, Language and Influence', *Journal of Personality and Social Psychology*, 59: 941–51.

Carver, C. and Scheier, M. (1981) 'The Self-Attention-Induced Feedback Loop and Social Facilitation', *Journal of Experimental Social Psychology*, 17: 545–68.

Charbonnier, E., Huguet, P., Brauer, M., and Monteil, J.M. (1998) 'Social Loafing and Self-Beliefs: Peoples' Collective Effort Depends on the Extent to which They Distinguish Themselves as Better than Others', *Social Behavior and Personality*, 26: 329–40.

Cottrell, N. (1968) 'Performance in the Presence of Other Human Beings: Mere Presence, Audience, and Affiliation Effects', in E. Simmell, R.A. Hoppe, and G. Milton (eds), *Social Facilitation and Imitative Behavior*. New York: Holt, pp. 91–110.

Cottrell, N. (1972) 'Social Facilitation', in C. McClintock (ed.), *Experimental Social Psychology*. New York: Holt, Rinehart & Winston, pp.185–236.

Cottrell, N., Wack, D., Sekerak, G., and Rittle, R. (1968) 'Social Facilitation of Dominant Responses by the Presence of an Audience and the Mere Presence of Others', *Journal of Personality and Social Psychology*, 9: 245–50.

Dashiell, J. (1930) 'An Experimental Analysis of Some Group Effects', *Journal of Abnormal and Social Psychology*, 25: 190–9.

Dashiell, J. (1935) 'Experimental Studies of the Influence of Social Situations on the Behavior of Individual Human Adults', in C. Murchison (ed.), *A Handbook of Social Psychology*. Worcester, MA: Clark University Press, pp. 1097–158.

Davidson, R. and Henderson, R. (2000) 'Electronic Performance Monitoring: A Laboratory Investigation of the Influence of Monitoring and Difficulty on Task Performance, Mood State, and Self-Reported Stress Levels', *Journal of Applied Social Psychology*, 30: 906–20.

Duval, S. and Wicklund, R. (1972) *A Theory of Objective Self-Awareness*. New York: Academic Press.

Eagly, A.H. (1987) *Sex Differences in Social Behavior: A Social-Role Interpretation*. Hillsdale, NJ: Erlbaum.

Earley, P.C. (1989) 'Social Loafing and Collectivism: A Comparison of the United States and the People's Republic of China', *Administrative Science Quarterly*, 34: 565–81.

Earley, P.C. (1993) 'East Meets West Meets Mideast: Further Explorations of Collectivistic and Individualistic Work Groups', *Academy of Management Journal*, 36: 319–48.

Erev, I., Bornstein, G., and Galili, R. (1993) 'Constructive Intergroup Competition as a Solution to the Free Rider Problem: A Field Experiment', *Journal of Experimental Social Psychology*, 29: 463–78.

Erez, M. and Somech, A. (1996) 'In Group Productivity Loss the Rule or the Exception? Effects of Culture and Group-Based Motivation', *Academy of Management Journal*, 39: 1513–37.

Everett, J.J., Smith, R.E., and Williams, K.D. (1992) 'Effects of Team Cohesion and Identifiability on Social Loafing in Relay Swimming Performance', *International Journal of Sport Psychology*, 23: 311–24.

Forsyth, D.R. (1999) *Group Dynamics*, 3rd edn. Belmont, CA: Wadsworth.

Gabrenya, W.K., Jr. Latané, B., and Wang, Y.E. (1981) 'Social Loafing among Chinese Overseas and U.S.

Students'. Paper presented at the Asian Conference of the International Association for Cross-Cultural Psychology, Taipei, Taiwan, August.

Gabrenya, W.K., Jr., Latané, B., and Wang, Y.E. (1983) 'Social Loafing in Cross-Cultural Perspective: Chinese in Taiwan', *Journal of Cross-Cultural Psychology*, 14: 368–84.

Gagné, M. and Zuckerman, M. (1999) 'Performance and Learning Goal Orientations as Moderators of Social Loafing and Social Facilitation', *Small Group Research*, 30: 524–41.

Gates, M. and Allee, W. (1933) 'Conditioned Behavior of Isolated and Grouped Cockroaches on a Simple Maze', *Journal of Comparative Psychology*, 15: 331–58.

Geen, R. (1989) 'Alternative Conceptions of Social Facilitation', in P. Paulus (ed.), *Psychology of Group Influence*. Hillsdale, NJ: Erlbaum, pp. 15–51.

Geen, R.G. (1991) 'Social Motivation', *Annual Review of Psychology*, 42: 377–99.

Geen, R. and Gange, J. (1977) 'Drive Theory of Social Facilitation: Twelve Years of Theory and Research', *Psychological Bulletin*, 84: 1267–88.

George, J.M. (1995) 'Asymmetrical Effects of Rewards and Punishments: The Case of Social Loafing', *Journal of Occupational and Organizational Psychology*, 68: 327–38.

Goethals, G. and Darley, J. (1987) 'Social Comparison Theory: Self-Evaluation and Group Life', in B. Mullen and G. Goethals (eds), *Theories of Group Behavior*. New York: Springer-Verlag, pp. 21–47.

Greenwald, A.G. and Pratkanis, A.R. (1984) 'The Self', in R.S. Wyer and T.K. Srull (eds), *Handbook of Social Cognition*. Hillsdale, NJ: Erlbaum, pp. 129–78.

Griffith, T.L., Fichman, M., and Moreland, R.L. (1989) 'Social Loafing and Social Facilitation: An Empirical Test of the Cognitive-Motivational Model of Performance', *Basic and Applied Social Psychology*, 10: 253–71.

Guerin, B. (1983) 'Social Facilitation and Social Monitoring: A Test of Three Models', *British Journal of Social Psychology*, 22: 203–14.

Guerin, B. (1986) 'Mere Presence Effects in Humans: A Review', *Journal of Experimental Social Psychology*, 22: 38–77.

Guerin, B. (1993) *Social Facilitation*. Cambridge: Cambridge University Press.

Guerin, B. and Innes, J. (1982) 'Social Facilitation and Social Monitoring: A New Look at Zajonc's Mere Presence Hypothesis', *British Journal of Social Psychology*, 7: 81–90.

Hardy, C.J. and Latané, B. (1988) 'Social Loafing in Cheerleaders: Effects of Team Membership and Competition', *Journal of Sport and Exercise Psychology*, 10: 109–14.

Harkins, S. and Szymanski, K. (1987) 'Social Facilitation and Social Loafing: New Wine in Old Bottles', in C. Hendrick (ed.), *Review of Personality and Social Psychology* (vol. 9). Beverly Hills, CA: Sage, pp. 167–88.

Harkins, S. (1987) 'Social Loafing and Social Facilitation', *Journal of Experimental Social Psychology*, 23: 1–18.

Harkins, S.G. (2000) 'The Potency of the Potential for Experimenter and Self-Evaluation in Motivating Vigilance Performance', *Basic and Applied Social Psychology*, 22: 277–89.

Harkins, S. (2001a) 'Social Influence Effects on Task Performance: The Ascendancy of Social Evaluation over Self-Evaluation', in J.P. Forgas and K.D. Williams (eds), *Social Influence: Direct and Indirect Processes*. Philadelphia, PA: Psychology Press, pp. 271–92.

Harkins, S. (2001b) 'The Role of Task Complexity, and Sources and Criteria of Evaluation in Motivating Task Performance', in S. Harkins (ed.), *Multiple Perspectives on the Effects of Evaluation on Performance: Toward an Integration*. Norwell, MA: Kluwer Press, pp. 99–131.

Harkins, S. (2001c) 'The Three-Variable Model: From Occam's Razor to the Black Box', in S. Harkins (ed.), *Multiple Perspectives on the Effects of Evaluation on Performance: Toward an Integration*. Norwell, MA: Kluwer Press, pp. 207–59.

Harkins, S.G. (1987) 'Social Loafing and Social Facilitation', *Journal of Experimental Social Psychology*, 23: 1–18.

Harkins, S.G. (2006) 'Mere Effort as the Mediator of the Evaluation-Performance Relationship', *Journal of Personality and Social Psychology*, 91 436–55.

Harkins, S.G. and Jackson, J.M. (1985) 'The Role of Evaluation in Eliminating Social Loafing', *Personality and Social Psychology Bulletin*, 11: 575–84.

Harkins, S.G., Latané, B., and Williams, K. (1980) 'Social Loafing: Allocating Effort or Taking It Easy?', *Journal of Experimental Social Psychology*, 16: 457–65.

Harkins, S.G. and Petty, R.E. (1982) 'Effects of Task Difficulty and Task Uniqueness on Social Loafing', *Journal of Personality and Social Psychology*, 43: 1214–29.

Harkins, S.G. and Szymanski, K. (1987) 'Social Facilitation and Social Loafing: New Wine in Old Bottles', in C. Hendrick (ed.), *Review of Personality and Social Psychology* (vol. 9). Beverly Hills, CA: Sage, pp. 167–88.

Harkins, S.G. and Szymanski, K. (1988) 'Social Loafing and Self-Evaluation with an Objective Standard', *Journal of Experimental Social Psychology*, 24: 354–65.

Harkins, S.G. and Szymanski, K. (1989) 'Social Loafing and Group Evaluation', *Journal of Personality and Social Psychology*, 56: 934–41.

Harkins, S., White, P., and Utman, C. (2000) 'The Role of Internal and External Sources of Evaluation in Motivating Task Performance', *Personality and Social Psychology Bulletin*, 26: 100–17.

Hart, J.W., Bridgett, D.J., and Karau, S.J. (2001) 'Coworker Ability and Effort as Determinants of Individual Effort on a Collective Task', *Group Dynamics: Theory, Research, and Practice*, 5: 181–90.

Hart, J.W., Karau, S.J., Stasson, M.F., and Kerr, N.A. (2004) 'Achievement Motivation, Expected Coworker

Performance, and Collective Task Motivation: Working Hard or Hardly Working?', *Journal of Applied Social Psychology'*, 34: 984–1000.

Henchy, T. and Glass, D. (1968) 'Evaluation Apprehension and the Social Facilitation of Dominant and Subordinate Responses', *Journal of Personality and Social Psychology*, 10: 446–54.

Henningsen, D.D., Cruz, M.G., and Miller, M.L. (2000) 'Role of Social Loafing in Predeliberation Decision Making', *Group Dynamics: Theory, Research, and Practice*, 4: 168–75.

Hertel, G., Kerr, N.L., and Messé, L.A. (2000a) 'Motivation Gains in Groups: Paradigmatic and Theoretical Advances on the Köhler Effect', *Journal of Personality and Social Psychology*, 79: 580–601.

Hertel, G., Kerr, N.L., Scheffler, M., Geister, S., and Messé, L.A. (2000b) 'Exploring the Kohler Motivation Gain Effect: Impression Management and Spontaneous Goal Setting', *Zeitschrift für Sozialpsychologie*, 31: 204–20.

Hinsz, V.B., Tindale, R.S., and Vollrath, D.A. (1997) 'The Emerging Conceptualization of Groups as Information Processes', *Psychological Bulletin*, 121: 43–64.

Hoeksema-van Orden, C.Y.D., Gaillard, A.W.K., and Buunk, B.P. (1998) 'Social Loafing under Fatigue', *Journal of Personality and Social Psychology*, 75: 1179–90.

Hogg, M.A. (1993) 'Group Cohesiveness: A Critical Review and Some New Directions', *European Review of Social Psychology*, 4: 85–111.

Hogg, M.A. (2002) 'Social Identity', in M. Leary and J. Tangney (eds), *Handbook of Self and Identity.* New York: Guilford, pp. 462–79.

Hogg, M.A. and Abrams, D. (1988) *Social Identifications: A Social Psychology of Intergroup Relations and Group Processes.* London: Routledge.

Huguet, P., Charbonnier, E., and Monteil, J.M. (1999) 'Productivity Loss in Performance Groups: People who See Themselves as Average Do Not Engage in Social Loafing', *Group Dynamics: Theory, Research, and Practice*, 3: 118–31.

Huguet, P., Galvaing, M., Monteil, J., and Dumas, F. (1999) 'Social Presence Effects in the Stroop Task: Further Evidence for an Attentional View of Social Facilitation', *Journal of Personality and Social Psychology*, 77: 1011–25.

Ingham, A.G., Levinger, G., Graves, J., and Peckham, V. (1974) 'The Ringelmann Effect: Studies of Group Size and Group Performance', *Journal of Personality and Social Psychology*, 10: 371–84.

Jackson, J.M. and Harkins, S.G. (1985) 'Equity in Effort: An Explanation of the Social Loafing Effect', *Journal of Personality and Social Psychology*, 49: 1199–206.

Jackson, J.M. and Padgett, V.R. (1982) 'With a Little Help from My Friend: Social Loafing and the Lennon–McCartney Songs', *Personality and Social Psychology Bulletin*, 8: 672–7.

Jackson, J.M. and Williams, K.D. (1985) 'Social Loafing on Difficult Tasks: Working Collectively Can Improve Performance', *Journal of Personality and Social Psychology*, 49: 937–42.

Karau, S.J. and Hart, J.W. (1998) 'Group Cohesiveness and Social Loafing: Effects of a Social Interaction Manipulation on Individual Motivation Within Groups', *Group Dynamics: Theory, Research, and Practice*, 3: 185–91.

Karau, S.J. and Williams, K.D. (1993) 'Social Loafing: A Meta-Analytic Review and Theoretical Integration', *Journal of Personality and Social Psychology*, 65: 681–706.

Karau, S.J. and Williams, K.D. (1997) 'The Effects of Group Cohesiveness on Social Loafing and Social Compensation', *Group Dynamics: Theory, Research, and Practice*, 1: 156–68.

Karau, S.J., Williams, K.D., and Hitlan, R.T. (2002) 'Social Identification and Social Loafing'. Unpublished manuscript.

Kerr, N.L. (1983) 'Motivation Losses in Small Groups: A Social Dilemma Analysis', *Journal of Personality and Social Psychology*, 45: 819–28.

Kerr, N.L. (2001) 'Motivation Gains in Performance Groups: Aspects and Prospects', in J.P. Forgas, K.D. Williams, and L. Wheeler (eds), *The Social Mind: Cognitive and Motivational Aspects of Interpersonal Behavior.* New York: Cambridge University Press, pp. 350–70.

Kerr, N.L. and Bruun, S.E. (1983) 'Dispensability of Member Effort and Group Motivation Losses: Free-Rider Effects', *Journal of Personality and Social Psychology*, 44: 78–94.

Kerr, N.L. and MacCoun, R.J. (1985) 'Role Expectation in Social Dilemmas: Sex Roles and Task Motivation in Groups', *Journal of Personality and Social Psychology*, 49: 1547–56.

Kerr, N.L. and Sullaway, M.E. (1983) 'Group Sex Composition and Member Task Motivation', *Sex Roles*, 9: 403–17.

Köhler, O. (1926) 'Kraftleistungen bei Einzel- und Gruppenarbeit [Physical Performance in Individual and Group Situations]', *Industrielle Psycholtechnik*, 3: 274–82.

Köhler, O. (1927) 'Über Den Gruppenwirkungsgrad der menschlichen Körperarbeit und die Bedingung Optimaler Kollektivkraftreaktion [On Group Efficiency of Physical Labor and the Conditions of Optimal Collective Performance]', *Industrielle Psychotechnik*, 4: 209–26.

Kokubo, T. (1996) 'An Effect of Internal Incentives to Task Performance on Social Loafing', *Japanese Journal of Experimental Social Psychology*, 36: 12–19.

Kravitz, D.A. and Martin, B. (1986) 'Ringelmann Rediscovered: The Original Article', *Journal of Personality and Social Psychology*, 50: 936–41.

Kugihara, N. (1999) 'Gender and Social Loafing in Japan', *Journal of Social Psychology*, 139: 516–26.

Latané, B. (1981) 'The Psychology of Social Impact', *American Psychologist*, 36: 343–56.

Latané, B., Williams, K., and Harkins, S. (1979) 'Many Hands Make Light the Work: The Causes and Consequences of Social Loafing', *Journal of Personality and Social Psychology*, 37: 822–32.

Lount, R.B., Messé, L.A., and Kerr, N.L. (2000) 'Trying Harder for Different Reasons: Conjunctivity and Sex Composition as Bases for Motivation Gains in Performing Groups', *Zeitschrift Für Sozialpsychologie*, 31: 221–30.

MacKinnon, D., Geiselman, E., and Woodward, J. (1985) 'The Effects of Effort on Stroop Interference', *Acta Psychological*, 58: 225–35.

MacLeod, C. (1991) 'Half a Century of Research on the Stroop Effect: An Integrative Review', *Psychological Bulletin*, 109: 163–203.

Markus, H. (1978) 'The Effect of Mere Presence on Social Facilitation: An Unobtrusive Test', *Journal of Experimental Social Psychology*, 14: 389–97.

Markus, H. (1981) 'The Drive for Integration: Some Comment', *Journal of Experimental Social Psychology*, 17: 257–61.

Matsui, T., Kakuyama, T., and Onglatco, M.U. (1987) 'Effects of Goals and Feedback on Performance in Groups', *Journal of Applied Psychology*, 72: 407–15.

Messé, L.A., Hertel, G., Kerr, N.L., Lount, R.B., and Park, E.S. (2002) 'Knowledge of Partner's Ability as a Moderator of Group Motivation Gains: An Exploration of the Kohler Discrepancy Effect', *Journal of Personality and Social Psychology*, 82: 935–46.

Miles, J.A. and Greenberg, J. (1993) 'Using Punishment Threats to Attenuate Social Loafing Effects among Swimmers', *Organizational Behavior and Human Decision Processes*, 56: 246–65.

Moreland, R.L., Hogg, M.A., and Hains, S. (1994) 'Back to the Future: Social Psychological Research on Groups', *Journal of Experimental Social Psychology*, 30: 527–55.

Mullen, B. (1985) 'Strength and Immediacy of Sources: A Meta-Analytic Evaluation of the Forgotten Elements of Social Impact Theory', *Journal of Personality and Social Psychology*, 48: 1458–66.

Mullen, B. and Copper, C. (1994) 'The Relation between Group Cohesiveness and Performance: An Integration', *Psychological Bulletin*, 115: 210–27.

Mullen, B., Johnson, C. and Salas, E. (1991) 'Productivity Loss in Brainstorming Groups: A Meta-Analytic Integration', *Basic and Applied Social Psychology*,12: 3–23.

North, A.C., Linley, A., and Hargreaves, D.J. (2000) 'Social Loafing in a Co-operative Classroom Task', *Educational Psychology*, 20: 389–92.

Olson, M. (1965) *The Logic of Collective Action: Public Goods and the Theory of Groups.* Cambridge, MA: Harvard University Press.

Paulus, P.B. (1983) 'Group Influence on Individual Task Performance', in P.B. Paulus (ed.), *Basic Group Processes*. New York: Springer-Verlag, pp. 97–120.

Paulus, P.B., Larey, T.S., and Dzindolet, M.T. (2001) 'Creativity in Groups and Teams', in M.E. Turner (ed.), *Groups at Work: Theory and Research.* Mahwah, NJ: Erlbaum, pp. 319–38.

Paulus, P. and Murdoch, P. (1971) 'Anticipated Evaluation and Audience Presence in the Enhancement of Dominant Responses', *Journal of Experimental Social Psychology*, 7: 280–91.

Peretti, P. (1971) 'Effects of Noncompetitive, Competitive Instructions, and Sex on Performance in a Color-Word Interference Task', *Journal of Psychology*, 79: 67–70.

Pessin, J. (1933) 'The Comparative Effects of Social and Mechanical Stimulation on Memorizing', *American Journal of Psychology*, 45: 263–70.

Petty, R.E., Cacioppo, J.T., and Kasmer, J.A. (1985) 'Individual Differences in Social Loafing on Cognitive Tasks'. Paper presented at the annual meeting of the Midwestern Psychological Association, Chicago, May.

Petty, R.E., Harkins, S.G., and Williams, K.D. (1980) 'The Effects of Diffusion of Cognitive Effort on Attitudes: An Information Processing View', *Journal of Personality and Social Psychology*, 38: 81–92.

Petty, R.E., Harkins, S.G., Williams, K.D., and Latané, B. (1977) 'The Effects of Group Size on Cognitive Effort and Evaluation', *Personality and Social Psychology Bulletin*, 3: 579–82.

Plaks, J.E. and Higgins, E.T. (2000) 'Pragmatic Use of Stereotyping in Teamwork: Social Loafing and Compensation as a Function of Inferred Partner-Situation Fit', *Journal of Personality and Social Psychology*, 79: 962–74.

Platania, J. and Moran, G. (2001) 'Social Facilitation as a Function of the Mere Presence of Others', *Journal of Social Psychology*, 14: 190–7.

Rajecki, D.W., Ickes, W., Corcoran, C., and Lenerz, K. (1977) 'Social Facilitation of Human Performance: Mere Presence Effects', *Journal of Social Psychology*, 102: 297–310.

Sanna, L. (1992) 'Self-Efficacy Theory: Implications for Social Facilitation and Social Loafing', *Journal of Personality and Social Psychology*, 62: 774–86.

Schachter, S. (1959) *The Psychology of Affiliation.* Stanford, CA: Stanford University Press.

Schmitt, B., Gilovich, T., Goore, N., and Joseph, L. (1986) 'Mere Presence and Social Facilitation: One More Time', *Journal of Experimental Social Psychology*, 22: 242–8.

Shepperd, J.A. (1993) 'Productivity Loss in Performance Groups: A Motivation Analysis', *Psychological Bulletin*, 113: 67–81.

Shepperd, J.A. and Wright, R.A. (1989) 'Individual Contributions to a Collective Effort: An Incentive Analysis', *Personality and Social Psychology Bulletin*, 15: 141–9.

Shirakashi, S. (1985) 'Social Loafing of Japanese Students', *Hiroshina Forum for Psychology*, 10: 35–40.

Smith, B.N., Kerr, N.A., Markus, M.J., and Stasson, M.F. (2001) 'Individual Differences in Social Loafing: Need for Cognition as a Motivator in Collective Performance', *Group Dynamics: Theory, Research, and Practice*, 5: 150–8.

Sorrentino, R.M. and Sheppard, B.H. (1978) 'Effects of Affiliation-Related Motives on Swimmers in Individual versus Group Competition: A Field Experiment', *Journal of Personality and Social Psychology*, 36: 707–14.

Spence, K.W. (1956) *Behavior Theory and Conditioning*. New Haven, CT: Yale University Press.

Stanton, J.M. and Barnes-Farrell, J.L. (1996) 'Effects of Electronic Performance Monitoring on Personal Control, Task Satisfaction and Task Performance', *Journal of Applied Psychology*, 81: 738–45.

Steiner, I.D. (1972) *Group Process and Productivity*. San Diego, CA: Academic Press.

Stroebe, W., Diehl, W., and Abakoumkin, G. (1996) 'Social Compensation and the Köhler Effect: Toward a Theoretical Explanation of Motivation Gains in Group Productivity', in E.H. Witte and J.H. Davis (eds), *Understanding Group Behavior* (vol. 2): *Small Group Processes and Interpersonal Relations*. Mahwah, NJ: Erlbaum, pp. 37–65.

Szymanski, K., Garczynski, J., and Harkins, S. (2000) 'The Contribution of the Potential for Evaluation to Coaction Effects', *Group Processes and Intergroup Relations*, 3: 269–83.

Szymanski, K. and Harkins, S. (1987) 'Social Loafing and Self-Evaluation with a Social Standard', *Journal of Personality and Social Psychology*, 53: 891–7.

Szymanski, K. and Harkins, S.G. (1992) 'Self-Evaluation and Creativity', *Personality and Social Psychology Bulletin*, 18: 259–65.

Szymanski, K. and Harkins, S.G. (1993) 'The Effect of Experimenter Evaluation on Self-Evaluation within the Social Loafing Paradigm', *Journal of Experimental Social Psychology*, 29: 268–86.

Thomas, G., Skitka, L., Christen, S., and Jurgena, M. (2002) 'Social Facilitation and Impression Formation', *Basic and Applied Social Psychology*, 24: 67–70.

Travis, L. (1925) 'The Effect of a Small Audience upon Eye–Hand Coordination', *Journal of Abnormal and Social Psychology*, 20: 142–6.

Travis, L. (1928) 'The Influence of the Group upon the Stutterer's Speed in Free Association', *Journal of Abnormal and Social Psychology*, 23: 45–51.

Triandis, H.C. (1989) 'The Self and Social Behavior in Differing Cultural Contexts', *Psychological Review*, 96: 506–20.

Triplett, N. (1898) 'The Dynamogenic Factors in Pacemaking and Competition', *American Journal of Psychology*, 9: 507–33.

Wheeler, L., Reis, H.T., and Bond, M.H. (1989) 'Collectivism–Individualism in Everyday Social Life: The Middle Kingdom and the Melting Pot', *Journal of Personality and Social Psychology*, 57: 79–86.

White, P.H., Kjelgaard, M.M., and Harkins, S.G. (1995) 'Testing the Contributions of Self-Evaluation to Goal-Setting Effects', *Journal of Personality and Social Psychology*, 69: 69–79.

White, P., Kjelgaard, M., and Harkins, S. (1995) 'Testing the Contribution of Self-Evaluation to Goal Setting Effects Using the Social Loafing Paradigm', *Journal of Personality and Social Psychology*, 69: 69–79.

Williams, K.D. and Burmont, S.C. (1981) 'A Look at Social Loafing in a Cognitive Task: Individual Effort in Advertising Evaluations'. Paper presented at the First Annual Nags Head Conference, Kill Devil Hills, NC, June.

Williams, K., Harkins, S., and Latané, B. (1981) 'Identifiability as a Deterrent to Social Loafing: Two Cheering Experiments', *Journal of Personality and Social Psychology*, 40: 303–11.

Williams, K.D. and Karau, S.J. (1991) 'Social Loafing and Social Compensation: The Effects of Expectations of Coworker Performance', *Journal of Personality and Social Psychology*, 61: 570–81.

Williams, K.D., Karau, S.J., and Bourgeois, M.J. (1993) 'Working on Collective Tasks: Social Loafing and Social Compensation', in M. Hogg and D. Abrams (eds), *Group Motivation: Social Psychological Perspectives*. New York and London: Harvester-Wheatsheaf, pp. 130–48.

Williams, K.D., Nida, S.A., Baca, L.D., and Latané, B. (1989) 'Social Loafing and Swimming: Effects of Identifiability on Individual and Relay Performance of Intercollegiate Swimmers', *Basic and Applied Social Psychology*, 10: 73–81.

Williams, K.D. and Sommer, K.L. (1997) 'Social Ostracism by One's Coworkers: Does Rejection Lead to Loafing or Compensation?', *Personality and Social Psychology Bulletin*, 23: 693–706.

Zaccaro, S.J. (1984) 'Social Loafing: The Role of Task Attractiveness', *Personality and Social Psychology Bulletin*, 10: 99–106.

Zaccaro, S.J. and McCoy, M.C. (1988) 'The Effects of Task and Interpersonal Cohesiveness on Performance of a Disjunctive Group Task', *Journal of Applied Social Psychology*, 18: 837–51.

Zajonc, R. (1965) 'Social Facilitation', *Science*, 149: 269–74.

Zajonc, R. (1980) 'Compresence', in P. Paulus (ed.), *Psychology of Group Influence*. Hillsdale, NJ: Erlbaum, pp. 35–60.

# 14
# Social-Influence Processes of Control and Change: Conformity, Obedience to Authority, and Innovation

ROBIN MARTIN AND MILES HEWSTONE

## INTRODUCTION

Social influence refers to the ways in which the opinions and attitudes of one person affect the opinions and attitudes of another person. Since people are exposed to many attempts to change their attitudes (e.g., via the media, advertisements, political campaigns), the study of social influence is one of the most fundamental areas of social psychological inquiry. This chapter focuses on two forms of social influence that serve the function of either maintaining group norms (social control: conformity and obedience) or changing group norms (social change: minority influence and innovation). However, both forms of social influence can affect peoples' attitudes under different situations.

The study of social influence is one of the most fundamental areas of social-psychological inquiry. Social influence refers to the ways in which the opinions and attitudes of one person affect the opinions and attitudes of another person. Although influence can occur between individuals, it is widely seen to operate in the context of social groups, where group members are continually influencing each other through the dynamic formation and change of group norms. Two forms of social influence can be identified within groups, which serve the function of either maintaining group norms (social control) or changing group norms (social change).

The dominant form of social control is conformity, that is, the processes through which an individual accepts (or complies with) the group's view. Since this line of research examines how a majority can cause an individual to conform to its view, it is often referred to as *majority influence*. Another process of social control is *obedience*, whereby individuals obey (often against their free will) an authority figure. However, in order for group norms to change, there must be processes of social change, which often create conflict and are resisted by group members. Processes of social change typically originate from a small subsection of members of the group, and, therefore, the process is often referred to as *minority influence*. Without active minorities, group opinions would never be challenged, fashions would not change, political campaigns would never succeed, and innovations would be thwarted. Social-influence research has a long tradition in social psychology and the amount of contemporary research, in terms of both published articles and active scholars, appears to be increasing, reflecting a continued interest in the area. The aim of this chapter is to review research relevant to these areas with particular attention to contemporary emphases and developments.

Before proceeding, we need first to consider what the terms 'majority' and 'minority' mean. There are at least three ways to define these terms. First, we might simply resort to the number of people in each group, with the majority group being numerically larger than the minority group. Interestingly, this need not mean that the 'majority' represents most people in the population (that is, over 50 percent), but that it is larger in size than the minority (which, by definition, must always be lower than 50 percent). Second, we can define these terms with reference to normative positions (that is, opinions and beliefs that reflect 'accepted' standards in society). In this dimension, the majority typically holds the normative position and the minority the antinormative or deviant position. Finally, we can refer to the power relationship between the source and recipient of influence; that is, the ability of the former to exert influence over the latter. Majorities are considered to be high in power, whereas minorities are low in power, as they are often discriminated against and marginalized in society. Using these dimensions, one might define a 'majority' as the numerically larger group that holds the normative position and has power over others. In contrast, minorities tend to be numerically small, hold antinormative positions, and lack power over others. We stress that this is a generalized definition and there are exceptions; for example, black people in South Africa during the period of apartheid were the numerically larger group in the population but lacked power.

Our review of the literature revolves around Moscovici's (1976) distinction between the different ways in which people resolve conflict arising from majority influence (conformity) and minority influence (innovation). Conformity is the process of resolution of conflict by deviant group members changing their opinion to that of the majority. Innovation refers to the process of the minority using conflict to bring about change; that is, for majority members to change their opinions to the minority view. In this chapter, we are concerned with two categories of influence process: processes with the aim of ensuring that others adhere to the group position (what might be referred to as 'social control' – conformity and obedience), and processes with the aim of changing the group position (what might be referred to as 'social change' – innovation and active minorities). We should make explicit, however, that the terms 'social control' and 'social change' refer to the *motives* of the source of influence (majority, authority figure versus minority) rather than the outcome of influence. As this review will show, both majority and minority sources can exert influence under different situations.

The above categorization maps neatly onto an observation made in a review of the literature by Martin and Hewstone (2001a) that research on majority and minority influence has progressed through three distinct chronological stages. The first stage of research (pre-1970), conducted mainly in North America, was concerned with the ability of majorities to cause individuals to conform or comply with its view (for reviews, see Allen 1965, 1975; Kent, 1994; Levine and Russo, 1987). The second stage of research (late 1960s–1980), which was dominated by European researchers, concerned the study of active minorities and how these can influence the majority (for reviews, see Maass and Clark, 1984; Maass et al., 1987; Martin and Hewstone, 2001a; Moscovici and Mugny, 1983; Mugny and Pérez, 1991). The final stage of research (1980–present) integrates both the first- and second-stage research traditions, which had until then remained distinct, and compares majority and minority influence within the same research paradigm. The aim of this stage is to examine the underlying processes involved in, and the effects this has upon, different levels of influence.

The chapter is divided into five parts. The first and second parts provide brief reviews of the processes associated with social control (majority influence and obedience) and social change (minority influence), respectively. The third part describes the main theoretical approaches to understanding majority and minority influence. The fourth part considers a number of contemporary developments in the literature, and the final part provides a summary.

## Social control: majority influence, conformity, and obedience

### *Majority influence and conformity*

The first studies of social influence examined the conditions under which an individual yields or conforms to a numerical majority (e.g., Asch, 1951; Crutchfield, 1955 – see Levine, 1999; Leyens and Corneille, 1999, for commentaries on the impact of Asch's research). These studies typically involved objective judgment tasks (such as the length of lines) and exposed participants to the erroneous responses of a numerical majority. Faced with this situation, one might wonder whether naive participants would agree publicly with an obviously incorrect response. Research has consistently shown that they do. Bond and Smith (1996), in a meta-analytic review of 133 studies conducted in seventeen countries with the classic Asch line-judgment paradigm, found robust evidence that individuals conform to the judgments of a numerical majority even when that majority gave the obviously wrong response. However, Bond and Smith found that conformity rates were higher in collectivist than individualistic cultures (see also Kim and Markus, 1999).

The most popular explanation for conformity was based upon the functionalist perspective of small-group behavior derived from work by Festinger (1950, 1954). According to Festinger, there are pressures for uniformity within groups to reach consensus, particularly when there is an explicit group goal. These pressures create a psychological dependency of the individual upon the group. It was argued that individuals are dependent upon others for social approval and verification of opinions and beliefs. In situations where there are no objective means for verification, as is the case for opinions and attitudes, people will use others to verify their opinions (what Festinger refers to as the 'social reality' function – see Turner, 1991, for an alternative analysis). In this sense, the majority is able to satisfy both these needs: first, because people generally wish to belong to majority groups, and, second, because people accept as true, opinions that are widely shared (Jones and Gerard, 1967). Building upon these ideas, Deutsch and Gerard (1955: 629) made a distinction between two social-influence processes underlying conformity: *normative social influence* ('an influence to conform with the positive expectations of others' and *informational social influence* ('an influence to accept information obtained from another as evidence about reality', 1955: 629).

This distinction has shaped much of the subsequent research in this area. It is a dual-process model of conformity that provides a compelling explanation of why group members conform to the majority. People conform to the majority because they believe the majority provides a valid source of evidence about reality (informational influence) and/or because majority membership is desirable and protects against group rejection (normative influence). There is wide-ranging evidence supporting these explanations (see Allen, 1965, 1975, for reviews), showing situations where both normative and informational factors can lead to increased or decreased conformity. For example, there is evidence that increasing the normative 'value' of the group (for example, increasing similarity or attractiveness) increases conformity (Allen, 1965; Deutsch and Gerard, 1955; Lott and Lott, 1961). However, situations in which surveillance by the majority is low (for example, when group members' responses are anonymous to the majority) reduce conformity (Asch, 1956; Deutsch and Gerard, 1955 – see also Abrams et al., 1990). In terms of informational factors, research shows that reducing the majority's credibility as a source of information (for example, making it inconsistent by having defectors from the majority) reduces conformity (Allen, 1975; Asch, 1951; Hoffman et al., 2001). Increasing the majority's ability to act as a valid source of information about reality (for example, increasing group size or increasing task uncertainty) can increase conformity (Bond, 2005; Crutchfield, 1955; Gerard et al., 1968; Wilder, 1977 – see also research on the relationship between task importance and conformity; e.g., Baron et al., 1996).

Contemporary research on conformity has highlighted the importance of self-conception and group identification in conformity (Van Knippenberg and Wilke, 1992; Wood et al., 1997). Another major recent theme has been a greater focus on the cognitive processes involved in conformity. This work includes research on the effects of unconscious priming processes (Epley and Gilovich, 1999), encoding processes in memory (Hoffman et al., 2001), and postconformity change-of-meaning effects (Buehler and Griffin, 1994; Griffin and Buehler, 1993). It is likely that future research is this area will continue to embrace the social-cognitive approach, currently dominant in social psychology and further examine the mediators and consequence of conformity processes.

Consistent findings that conformity rates can be affected by factors that affect normative and informational motives do not, by themselves, demonstrate that there are two separate processes. Indeed, the assumption that there are two influence routes has been routinely questioned (e.g., Kelman, 1958 – see also the critical evaluation by Turner, 1991). Contemporary views have suggested consideration of three motives for conformity based on normative concerns for (i) positive self-evaluations; and (ii) to have good relationships with others; and, based on informational concerns (iii) to have a better understanding of the situation and to reduce uncertainty (e.g., Cialdini and Trost, 1998; Griskevicius, Goldstein, Morftensen, Cialdini and Kenrick 2006, for a review, see Cialdinid and Goldstein, 2004). In this section, we were concerned with how people might comply with a majority even if they did not agree with its position. The next section looks at another form of social control, but here we are concerned with how someone might comply with a person to conduct acts that can clearly cause harm to others. This process is referred to as *obedience*.

### Obedience to authority

The social psychological study of obedience to authority is intimately tied to one figure, Stanley Milgram (1963, 1974; see Sabini and Silver, 1992, for a collection of Milgram's works; for reviews, see Blass, 1992, 1999, 2000; Miller et al., 1995; see also the very good web site dedicated to Stanley Milgram and maintained by Thomas Blass at <http://www. stanleymilgram.com>). The impetus for Milgram's research was to understand why people might engage in horrific atrocities that cause considerable harm to other people. At the time of Milgram's initial research in the early 1960s, Adolf Eichmann, one of the main architects of the Nazi's 'final solution', was being tried for war crimes. Eichmann was identified as one of the main perpetrators of this grotesque crime, and people wanted, perhaps needed, to believe that he was disturbed and that his actions were the act of a madman or, at least, that he was intrinsically evil. To think of him as abnormal was to categorize him as different from 'normal' people, and surely no normal human being would have performed these acts? However, Eichmann did not conveniently fit this view and, if anything, he appeared to be an ordinary person little different from anyone else and claimed that he did not personally have anything against Jews (Arendt, 1965). If Eichmann was not naturally evil, one was left to wonder why he had been involved in these horrendous crimes against humanity. His answer was simply that he was a soldier in a system that expected compliance to authority and that he was obeying orders. Furthermore, since he had obeyed orders, his defense was that he was not responsible for his actions. If Eichmann was 'just following orders', his case opens the potentially disturbing fact that maybe we are all possible of committing horrible acts against others.

History is, unfortunately, littered with many examples of obedience to authority leading to inhumane acts, as in inappropriate military obedience (for example, the My Lai massacre in Vietnam in the 1960s) and genocides (for example, Rwanda and Bosnia in the 1990s) (for more information, see Kelman and Hamilton, 1989; Staub, 1989). The rationale for Milgram's research, which was to examine whether people would obey an authority figure and commit acts which they believed could harm another person, is as valid today as it was when originally conceived in the early 1960s. His initial expectation and that of many others was that the vast majority of people would disobey an authority figure that asked them to harm another person.

To test this hypothesis, Milgram designed a now classic study in which naive participants believed they were administering electric shocks to another participant every time that person made an error on a task. The naive participant was required to increase the level of the shock every time the other participant made an error. If the naive participants made any protests, the experimenter gave a number of planned verbal 'prods' designed to encourage the participant to continue (such as 'The experiment requires you to go on'). As the shock levels increased, the receiver responded with increasingly distressing reactions, including screaming and claiming the shocks were affecting his heart. In fact, the person allocated to receive the shocks was a confederate and acted the role but did not receive any shocks. The main dependent variable was the level of electric shock the naive participant would administer before disobeying the experimenter.

To what extent would normal people obey instructions to take actions that could harm another person? Milgram's findings were unexpected and showed that 65 percent of the participants progressed through all the levels of electric shock – even past levels that could do permanent physical harm to the receiver. Milgram conducted a number of variations on his basic design. These showed that the level of obedience was considerably reduced if the naive participant was made more aware of the consequences of his or her actions; for example, by being able to see the victim's reaction to the shocks or by holding the victim's hand on the plate through which the shocks were administered. Obedience rates increased if other participants (in fact, confederates) also obeyed the experimenter, but decreased if the same participants did not obey the experimenter. Milgram's findings have been replicated across many samples and in different countries with rates of obedience remaining at a consistent level over time (Blass, 1999).

But why did people obey? Milgram offered a number of explanations. First, there are the 'binding' factors between the participant and the experimenter. The participants may have continued administering the electrical shocks because they had entered into a 'contract' to take part in the study, and they wanted to avoid being awkward and spoiling the experiment. In addition, the participants could become so absorbed in the procedure and the technical aspects of the study that they lost sight of the implications of their actions, a complication which might account for why obedience dropped when the participants could 'see' the consequences of their actions. The participants start to think they are acting for the experimenter and, while they might physically be pressing the button to administer the electrical shock, the experimenter would have done this anyway. This is referred to as the *agentic state* in which the person sees him- or herself as an agent for another person, carrying out orders but not being responsible for them – a shift in perceived responsibility that Eichmann and other perpetrators of extreme acts have invoked to explain their behavior.

The reasons for obedience outlined above clearly point to a situational explanation based upon the power associated with the experimenter's role as someone in authority who is controlling the people and events within that situation. By engaging in the experiment, the naive participants had unwittingly entered into a powerful role relationship between themselves (as the follower) and the experimenter (as the leader). The experimenter is perceived as the expert who has done this study many times and knows what he is doing while the participant is unfamiliar with the situation. Consistent with this view was the finding that obedience rates fell considerably when another participant was asked to play the role of the experimenter or when the experimenter left the room and communicated with the naive participant over the telephone. However, the rates of obedience did not fall to zero, showing that the role relationship per se can lead to obedience even if it is not so tightly associated with authority status.

Although Milgram's research has provoked considerable controversy, especially concerning its ethical ramifications (Baumrind, 1964; Miller, 1986), it nonetheless provides one of the best examples of how an authority figure can secure destructive obedience. Other studies of obedience have used different paradigms to confirm the general finding that many people will obey an authority figure and perform acts they know can harm others. For example, nurses have been shown to obey doctors' orders to administer what they know to be harmfully incorrect doses of drugs (Hofling et al., 1966; Krackow and Blass, 1995; Rank and Jacobson, 1977), and interviewers have obeyed their bosses' orders to use interview tactics that they know will ruin interviewees' prospects of getting a job (Meeus and Raaijmakers, 1986, 1995).

Research on obedience shows that, under specific circumstances, people will obey an authority figure and commit acts they would not usually commit. The key to this process are the power and role expectations associated with the authority person that enable such persons to control others and to make them comply with their requests. In the next section, we examine how an individual (or a small number of individuals, such as minorities) can change other people's opinions. The main difference between the processes involved in obedience and minority influence is that the former is based upon power while the latter is not. Indeed, minorities typically lack power over others, and, therefore, one needs to adopt a quite different theoretical framework and employ different explanatory variables in order to understand minority influence.

## Social change: minority influence and innovation

### Minority influence and innovation

Some of the key features of research on conformity were its focus on the ability of the majority to influence the individual and its neglect of whether the individual (or minority) could influence the majority. Perhaps this latter focus was ignored because it contradicted the spirit of the functionalist approach with its emphasis on pressures towards uniformity and dependency as the key psychological mediating process. Therefore, according to the conformity approach, social influence can only flow from those who have the power to create psychological dependency (such as a majority) to those who do not (such as a minority). Deviancy, within the functionalist approach, was seen as dysfunctional and a threat to group harmony; consequently, deviants either conform to the group or face rejection.

In the late 1960s, research by the French social psychologist Serge Moscovici was pivotal in changing people's perspectives on social-influence processes. Moscovici argued that there had been a 'conformity bias' in the literature, with nearly all research focusing upon majority influence, and that this had led to the dominance of the functionalist approach towards social influence, with its reliance on dependency as its explanatory variable (Moscovici and Faucheux, 1972). A major problem for the functionalist approach is that it takes a unilateral perspective on social influence that sees influence flowing only from the majority to the minority. If influence really was like this, it would be difficult to see how groups change, new ideas develop, and innovation might occur. Moscovici illustrated how important it was to examine active minorities by analyzing social movements (such as the ecology and student movements) and case histories of deviants who had a profound impact upon the majority (such as Galileo and Freud).

In his seminal book *Social Influence and Social Change*, Moscovici (1976) argued against the functionalist approach as an explanation of social influence and, instead, proposed what he referred to as a 'genetic' model. At the heart of his approach was the proposition that all attempts at social influence create conflict between the source and the recipient of influence. Of particular importance here, Moscovici argued that minorities can, and often do, create conflict because they challenge the dominate majority view and, in so doing, offer a new and different perspective. Since people wish to avoid conflict, they will often dismiss the minority position – perhaps even attributing its deviancy to some underlying, undesirable psychological dimension (Papastamou, 1986).

However, what happens when the minority refuses to be dismissed – when the minority demonstrates that it is certain and committed to its position, that it will not compromise, and that its members believe that the majority should change to its position? Moscovici argues that by adopting such a style the minority can make the majority reconsider its own beliefs and consider the minority's position as a viable alternative. Moscovici termed this the minority's *behavioral style* and defined it as the 'way in which the behavior is organized and presented [...] to provoke the acceptance or rejection of a judgement [...] the fact that it maintains a well defined point of view and develops it in a coherent manner' (Moscovici et al., 1969: 366; see Maass and Clark, 1984, for a review). Moscovici (1976) identified five key aspects of behavioral style (consistency, investment, autonomy, rigidity, and fairness). By 'standing up' to the majority, the minority shows that it is certain, confident, and committed to its position and will not be easily swayed (see recent work on behavioral style by Buschini, 1998).

To explain why behavioral style is important to minority influence, Moscovici has relied upon Kelley's (1967) attribution theory (for alternative perspectives, see Chaiken and Stangor, 1987; Eagly and Chaiken, 1993; Maass and Clark, 1984). By being consistent, the minority is 'visible' within the group and attracts, or even demands, attention (Schachter, 1951). Response consistency leads to attributions of certainty and confidence, especially when the minority is seen to reject publicly the majority position. Such a style of behavior creates two types of conflict within members of the majority: one cognitive (from an increase in response diversity) and the other social (from threatened interpersonal relations). The majority members resolve this conflict by questioning their own position and considering the minority's position as a valid alternative.

Mugny (1982) extended much of Moscovici's research by examining the impact of minority influence on a range of social attitudes that were the subject of real debate within contemporary Swiss society (for example, pollution, acceptance of foreign workers, and military service). The central thesis of Mugny's work has been to distinguish between behavior directed towards the 'majority norm' and that towards the 'population' which the minority wishes to influence. These considerations led Mugny to distinguish between what Moscovici called behavioral style and what Mugny called negotiating style (Mugny, 1975). The basis of this distinction is the fact that the minority lacks power and the means to exact dependency, and therefore the minority has to negotiate its influence with the majority. Mugny identified two negotiating styles; a rigid style where the minority refuses to compromise on any issue, and a flexible style where the minority is prepared to adapt to the majority position and accept certain compromises. In a series of studies, Mugny was able to show that a minority that uses the flexible style was more likely to influence the majority than one that used the rigid style (for a review, see Mugny, 1982).

Evidence in favor of the 'genetic' model can be drawn from various lines of research. For example, a number of studies have shown that key aspects of the minority's behavioral style are important in determining influence; these include response consistency (Moscovici et al., 1969; Moscovici and Lage, 1976), flexibility (Mugny, 1975; Mugny and Papastamou, 1981), and minority consensus (Arbuthnot and Wayner, 1982; Bray et al., 1982; Moscovici and Lage, 1976; Nemeth et al., 1977). Although there is much evidence to show that key behavioral styles do increase minority influence, and that these lead to perceptions of minority confidence and competence, there is no evidence that these attributions actually mediate influence (see Maass and Clark, 1984, for a critical evaluation).

Although Moscovici's early theorizing about minority influence received some criticisms (e.g., Kelvin, 1979 [reply by Moscovici, 1979]; Levine, 1980; Turner, 1991), it clearly was extremely important for placing the study of active minorities on the research agenda. Moreover, it questioned the functionalist account of influence that viewed social influence as invariably flowing from those with power (majorities) to those without power (minorities) and, instead, showed that influence is a reciprocal, or dialectical, process. As Moscovici (1976) argued, people can be both the source and the recipient of influence.

## Comparing majority and minority influence

At the beginning of this review, we noted that research on social influence has gone through three major stages, with the first two focusing almost exclusively on majority and minority influence, respectively. The next logical step, from a scientific point of view, was to compare majority and minority influence within the *same* paradigm. While intuitively appealing, this change in the focus of the research, as we will see, had major implications for the type of research that was conducted, the key variables examined, and the content of theories that evolved. More specifically, to be able to compare the influence of both sources, it promoted research designs where the same counterattitudinal position was attributed to either a numerical majority or minority.

### *Theoretical approaches to majority and minority influence*

It has been common to categorize the various theoretical approaches to majority and minority influence into those proposing that they are determined by two different processes (dual-process models), or by one process (single-process models) (Maass and Clark, 1984). However, as noted by Martin and Hewstone (2001a), this classification is misleading because of the lack of theoretical clarity between 'process' and 'outcome' and the inability to infer one from the other (see also Kruglanski and Mackie, 1990). According to Martin and Hewstone (2001a), a more useful categorization is to consider whether the models specify *main effects* (that is, specific antecedents, processes, and outcomes exclusive to each source) or *contingency effects* (that is, antecedents, processes, and outcomes nonexclusive to each source but dependent upon one or more contingency factors). This categorization also nicely overlays the chronological order of theoretical development, with contemporary theories generally advocating contingency effects – no doubt reflecting research findings that the outcomes of majority and minority influence are not exclusive to one source. We follow this categorization in our review and describe the various models in terms of their being either main effects or contingency approaches.

### *Main-effects models*

Four major main-effects models have been developed in majority and minority influence: *conversion theory* (Moscovici, 1980), *convergent-divergent theory* (Nemeth, 1986), *mathematical models* (Latané and Wolf, 1981; Tanford and Penrod, 1984), and the *objective-consensus approach* (Mackie, 1987).

#### Conversion theory

Moscovici's (1980, 1985) conversion theory is the dominant theoretical perspective in this area. Moscovici argues that all forms of influence, whether from a majority or minority, result in conflict and that individuals are motivated to reduce that conflict. However, Moscovici argues that people employ different processes, with different outcomes, depending on whether the source of the conflict is a majority or a minority. In the case of majority influence, individuals engage in a *comparison process* whereby they concentrate attention on 'what others say, so as to fit in with their opinions or judgements' (1980: 214). Since identification with a majority is desirable, people conform to the majority position without examining the content of the majority's message in detail. The outcome of majority influence is public compliance with the majority position with little or no private or indirect attitude change. While social comparison might drive majority influence, Moscovici argues it cannot be the case in minority influence, as people typically wish to avoid association with undesirable groups. However, minorities are distinctive, in the sense that they stand out from the majority, and this encourages a *validation process* leading one to 'examine one's own responses, one's own judgments, in order to confirm and validate them […] to see what the minority saw, to understand what it understood' (1980: 215). While minority influence may not lead to public agreement, for fear of being categorized as a minority member (Mugny, 1982), the close examination of the validity of the minority's arguments may bring about attitude conversion on an indirect, latent, or private level.

Moscovici's conversion theory represents a major change from his earlier genetic model. Indeed, the difference is so great that they might usefully be considered as two separate theories. For majority influence, far more emphasis is placed in conversion theory upon the normative value associated with majority-group membership and less upon its ability to act as verifier of information. The change in perspective in minority influence is equally great. Rather than being an attribution account in the genetic model (based upon perceptions derived from the source's behavioral style), conversion theory relies more upon a cognitive explanation (where influence results from the degree of evaluation of the source's message). The behavioral style, which was pivotal in the genetic model (Moscovici, 1976), is seldom mentioned in conversion theory (Moscovici, 1980). Moscovici's accounts of comparison/validation processes appear similar to the normative/informational processes described in the conformity literature (cf. Turner, 1991). The conflict associated with majority influence is resolved by a process of social comparison and public compliance, whereas the conflict associated with minority influence leads to an examination of the content of the message and is resolved by public rejection and private acceptance (what Moscovici terms 'conversion').

What evidence is there to support conversion theory? Interestingly, one might argue that the evidence cited earlier to support his genetic model provides only weak support for conversion theory. For example, research showing that conformity depends upon the majority's being unanimous and having a consistent behavioral style (see Moscovici and Nemeth, 1974) supports conversion theory only if one assumes that such consistency correlates with the increased normative value of belonging to the majority group. One can usefully organize the research according to the following three major hypotheses arising from conversion theory:

1 *The direction-of-attention* hypothesis: majority influence causes people to focus on the relationship between themselves and the source of influence, whereas minority influence causes people to focus on the content of the minority message.
2 *The content-of-thinking* hypothesis: majority influence leads to a superficial examination of the majority's argument, whereas minority influence leads to a detailed evaluation of the minority's arguments.
3 *The differential-influence* hypothesis: majority influence leads to more public/direct influence than private/indirect, whereas minority influence leads to the opposite.

In terms of the direction-of-attention hypothesis, research has shown that majorities encourage individuals to focus attention on the relationship between themselves and members of the majority (interpersonal focus) whereas a minority leads to greater attention being focused on the content of the minority's message (message focus) (e.g., Campbell et al., 1986; Guillon and Personnaz, 1983; Tesser et al., 1983). For the content-of-thinking hypothesis, evidence showing that minorities lead to the generation of more arguments and counterarguments, in an attempt to evaluate the message, than do majorities is mixed. These studies have used a thought-listing technique to elicit participants' elaborations of the message, typical of that developed in cognitive research on persuasion (e.g., Petty and Cacioppo, 1986), and have found results suggesting differences in the quantity and quality of thinking following majority and minority influence (e.g., Alvaro and Crano, 1996; De Dreu and De Vries, 1993, 1996; Maass and Clark, 1983; Mackie, 1987; Martin, 1996; Mucchi-Faina et al., 1991).

A corollary of the content-of-thinking hypothesis is that minority influence leads to more message processing than does majority influence. To examine this hypothesis, researchers have used a technique originally developed in cognitive research on persuasion to determine whether a message has been systematically processed: that is, by manipulating the quality of the arguments in the message (either weak and non-persuasive, or strong and persuasive). If participants are motivated and able to process a message, they should be more persuaded by the strong than the weak message. The results of studies crossing source status and message quality have been mixed, with some supporting conversion theory and some not (e.g., Baker and Petty, 1994; Bohner et al., 1998; Crano and Chen, 1998; De Dreu and De Vries, 1993; Kerr, 2002; Martin and Hewstone, 2003; Ziegler et al., 2004).

Martin and Hewstone (2001b, 2002, 2003) have been able to clarify these inconsistent results by showing that the level of message processing depends upon the processing demands that prevail at the time of message presentation. When the message-processing demands are low, individuals may rely upon a heuristic such as 'consensus equals correctness' and show greater majority than minority influence. When there is a moderate level of processing demands, there tends to be greater message processing in the minority than majority condition. When processing demands are high, there tends to be significant message processing for both a majority and minority source (see Martin et al., in press). These studies show, counter to conversion theory, that both majorities and minorities can lead to message processes under different situations. The results support a contingency approach to majority and minority influence. This is considered below.

Finally, the differential-influence hypothesis has received the most research attention. In a meta-analysis of ninety-seven studies, Wood et al. (1994) made a distinction between influence that was measured in public (where the source is aware of participants' responses) and in private (where the source is unaware of the participants' responses). The private-response category was further divided into direct responses (influence on the same dimension as proposed by the source) or indirect responses (influence on a different, but related, dimension as proposed by the source). Wood et al. (1994: 323) concluded that 'Minority impact was most marked on measures of influence that were private from the source and indirectly related to the content of the appeal and less evident on direct private influence measures and on public measures'. Research has examined majority and minority influence on a number of different response dimensions.

In another review, Maass et al. (1987) identified the following four dimensions:

1 *Time*: influence measured immediately following exposure to the source versus influence measured latter in time (e.g., Crano and Chen, 1998; Moscovici et al., 1981).
2 *Specificity*: influence specific to the message versus influence that goes beyond the message and considers a wider set of issues. This dimension is commonly referred to as 'direct' and 'indirect' influence, respectively (e.g., Alvaro and Crano, 1997; Moscovici et al., 1981; Mugny and Pérez, 1991).
3 *Privacy*: responses which are made in public versus those that are made anonymously and in private (e.g., Maass and Clark, 1983, Martin, 1988a, b).
4 *Awareness*: participants are aware of the connection between source message and influence dimension, versus not being aware of this connection (e.g., Brandstätter et al., 1991; Martin, 1998; Moscovici and Personnaz, 1980, 1991).

## Convergent-divergent theory

The second, major main-effects model of majority and minority influence arises from the convergent-divergent theory proposed by Charlan Nemeth (Nemeth, 1986, 1995). Nemeth proposes that majority and minority influence lead people to engage in different styles of thinking which lead to different outcomes. Nemeth argues that people expect to share the same attitude as the majority and to differ from the minority (the 'false-consensus heuristic', Ross et al., 1977). Therefore, learning that the majority has a different position from oneself creates stress, particularly if one is in the physical presence of the majority. Since stress is known to narrow one's focus of attention (Easterbrook, 1959), Nemeth proposes that majority influence leads to convergent thinking that is characterized by a 'convergence of attention, thought, and the number of alternatives considered' (Nemeth, 1986: 25). However, if minorities do not cause high levels of stress (because it is not surprising that they hold different views), the focus of attention is not restricted and individuals can consider a range of issues, some of which may not have been proposed by the minority. Nemeth refers to minority influence leading to divergent thinking that involves 'a greater consideration of other alternatives, ones that were not proposed but would not have been considered without the influence of the minority' (Nemeth, 1986: 25). Moscovici and Nemeth's theories differ in at least two fundamental ways; with respect to which source leads to most stress (Nemeth – majority; Moscovici – minority) and the proposed relationship between stress and message processing (Nemeth – majority-induced stress restricts message-processing; Moscovici – minority-induced stress increases message-processing).

What is radical about Nemeth's perspective is that it suggests minority influence leads individuals to consider a wider range of alternatives than would have been considered without exposure to the minority. This can result in improved judgments and performance. In short, Nemeth argues that minorities can lead to the detection of new and better ideas and solutions and, in so doing, can increase creativity. It is this prediction, that minority influence can lead to new, original, and often correct solutions, which has received the most research attention.

In testing this hypothesis, researchers have typically employed objective tasks (such as the Stroop test, or identifying anagrams) where it is possible to measure performance objectively and hence compare the results of being exposed to a numerical majority or minority. The results tend to support Nemeth's theory. In tasks where performance benefits from divergent thinking, minority influence has been shown to lead to better performance than majority influence (e.g., Martin and Hewstone, 1999; Nemeth and Kwan, 1987; Nemeth and Wachtler, 1983), but on tasks where performance benefits from convergent thinking, majority influence leads to better performance than minority influence (e.g., Nemeth et al., 1992; Peterson and Nemeth, 1996). Furthermore, minority influence has been shown to lead to the generation of more creative and novel judgments than does majority influence (e.g., Mucchi-Faina et al., 1991; Nemeth and Kwan, 1985; Nemeth and Wachtler, 1983; Volpato et al., 1990; see also Martin, 1996).

Some research has examined more directly the types of thinking following majority and minority influence. For example, minority influence leads to the use of multiple strategies in solving problems, whereas majority influence leads individuals to focus on the majority-endorsed strategy (e.g., Butera et al., 1996; Legrenzi et al., 1991; Nemeth and Kwan, 1987; Peterson and Nemeth, 1996). Finally, minority influence encourages issue-relevant thinking, whereas majority influence leads to message-relevant thinking (e.g., De Dreu and De Vries, 1993; De Dreu et al., 1999; Trost et al., 1992).

Nemeth's theory yields interesting insights into the processes of majority and minority influence and offers the tantalizing hypothesis that minorities can lead to improved performance through stimulating creativity (see also work on devil's advocacy; e.g., Nemeth et al., 2001). However, most of the research has employed simple cognitive tasks, and there have been few tests of the theory with more complex cognitive tasks (but see Martin and Hewstone, 1999). For this reason, it is difficult to evaluate Nemeth's theory against other models of social influence, and it is not known whether the theory will apply to attitudes (Kruglanski and Mackie, 1990). A further problem is that there is little research directly examining the underlying processes, especially showing the predicted link between experienced stress and convergent and divergent thinking.

### Mathematical models

While conversion and convergent-divergent theories specified different processes for majority and minority influence, the mathematical models were explicit attempts to explain these phenomena within a single-process framework.

Latané and Wolf (1981) applied the principles of *social-impact theory* to majority and minority influence (Latané, 1981, 1996). They claim that the level of social impact experienced by the target of influence is determined by three factors, strength (as in status), immediacy (as in physical closeness), and number (that, is, how many people hold that position). The greater the social impact, the greater is the level of influence. However, the relationship between these three factors and their impact upon the target is not linear but is governed by a number of mathematical principles. For example, the relationship between source numbers and social impact follows a power function with an exponential value of less than one. This predicts that the addition of each person to the source group increases the social impact of the group by a factor less than the addition of the immediately preceding person to the source group.

Support for these predictions comes from two lines of research. First, studies have shown that social-impact theory variables, in particular the number of members of the source, were better predictors of social influence than aspects of the source's behavioral style, such as response consistency (e.g., Hart et al., 1999; Latané et al., 1995; Wolf, 1985; Wolf and Latané, 1983). Second, meta-analyses have confirmed that the findings of various studies can be predicted by applying the mathematical principles to the three main contributors to social impact (Latané and Wolf, 1981).

Soon after social-impact theory was published, another mathematical model of majority and minority influence was proposed by Tanford and Penrod (1984), called the *social-impact model*. Like social-impact theory, the social-impact model proposed a mathematical relationship between source size and influence, although it proposed different mathematical relationships governing the amount of influence. Like social-impact-theory, the social-impact model has not generated research testing its predictions with respect to minority influence (see Clark, 1998, for an exception).

The mathematical models of the social-impact theory and the social-impact model are both single-process models as they suggest that majority and minority influence are determined by the same set of variables. Martin and Hewstone (2001a) identified three main concerns regarding these models. First, these models are very descriptive, and, since they focus exclusively on the characteristics of the source of influence, they do not provide an understanding of the underlying psychological process (see also Maass and Clark, 1984). While these models may be able to predict *when* influence occurs they say little about *why* it occurs. As Latané (1981: 343) himself notes, social-impact theory 'does not say when social impact will occur or detail the exact mechanisms whereby social impact is transmitted. It does not purport to 'explain' the operation of any number of particular social processes'.

The second concern is that these models place substantial emphasis upon the role of source size in determining influence, yet the concept of source size simply refers to the absolute number of people holding a position, without consideration of factors such as the perceived independence of the positions (see Wilder, 1977, for a critique of this approach). Finally, these models do not consider the influence of the source beyond the public or direct level, and therefore, they cannot explain the private and indirect influence often observed with minority influence. It is for these reasons, and probably many others, that mathematical models have lost favor in understanding majority and minority influence. Currently, little research attention is directed towards them.

### The objective-consensus approach

The objective-consensus approach (Mackie, 1987; see also De Dreu et al., 1999; De Vries et al., 1996) to understanding majority and minority influence has developed from the cognitive-response approach to persuasion (which is discussed later). In contrast to conversion theory, this approach proposes that people are more likely to process a majority than a minority message. Two reasons are given for this. The first relies upon the notion of informational influence, discussed earlier, and proposes that people believe the majority view is valid. If people believe their opinion is different from the majority, they will process the majority's arguments to try to understand the discrepancy – the majority view reflects reality in the sense that 'several pairs of eyes are better than one'.

The second factor relies upon the 'false-consensus heuristic' discussed in relation to Nemeth's theory. If the majority breaks the consensus heuristic (for example, occupies a counterattitudinal position), people are motivated to analyze majority arguments in an attempt to understand this discrepancy. By contrast, exposure to a counterattitudinal minority is consistent with the consensus heuristic, and, therefore, it is not surprising; consequently, one is less likely to process the minority's message. Baker and Petty (1994) suggest additional reasons why a majority might lead to greater message processing. For example, message recipients may assume that majority-endorsed positions are more likely to become adopted than minority-endorsed positions, and, therefore, they believe it would be more important to process the majority's arguments.

In the objective-consensus approach, it is difficult to determine the causal process for majority and minority influence. The approach suggests that counterattitudinal majorities are surprising (because they hold different views) and therefore people will process majority arguments to reconcile this difference. The causal process is as follows: unexpected source/position $\rightarrow$ surprise $\rightarrow$ message processing $\rightarrow$ understand opinion difference. Counterattitudinal minorities are expected, and not surprising; therefore, people are unlikely to process the minority's message. This clearly differs from conversion theory; majority influence relies upon informational aspects and not on the normative value of majority group membership, whereas minority influence results in minority rejection. Why surprise should lead to systematic message-processing rather than heuristic acceptance of the message (see Erb et al., 1998) is unclear, yet both responses seem equally likely.

It should be recognized that the objective-consensus approach is a relatively new perspective; consequently, there has been little empirical research testing its main predictions. Recent work by Carsten De Dreu and colleagues has integrated the central theme of the objective-consensus approach with elements of Nemeth's theory to develop an integrative model with some supporting evidence (see De Dreu et al., 1999; De Vries et al., 1996). As yet, however, there is relatively little evidence for its main proposition that majorities promote more message-processing than minorities, and that this leads to greater private attitude acceptance (see Mackie, 1987). Indeed, both meta-analytic review (Wood et al., 1994) and the research cited above in support of conversion theory strongly support the reverse, that minorities lead to greater private and indirect attitude change.

### *Contingency approaches*

In this section, we outline three contingency models that specify that the outcomes of majority and minority influence are determined by one or more contingency factors; *conflict-elaboration theory* (Pérez and Mugny, 1996), the *context/comparison model* (Crano and Alvaro, 1998), and *self-categorization theory* (David and Turner, 1996).

#### Conflict-elaboration theory

The third major theoretical framework for analyzing majority and minority influence is conflict-elaboration theory, as proposed by Gabriel Mugny, Juan Pérez, and their colleagues (Mugny et al., 1995; Pérez and Mugny, 1996: for empirical tests of the model, see Brandstätter et al., 1991; Butera et al., 1996; Butera and Mugny, 1995; Pérez et al., 1991; Quiamzade et al., 2000; Sanchez-Mazas et al., 1993). The model is similar to conversion theory, in proposing that divergence from a source of influence causes conflict (with the level of conflict proportional to the divergence) and that the resulting psychological processes arising from that conflict depend on whether it originates from a majority or minority source. However, unlike conversion theory, which focuses on conflict *resolution*, this approach considers conflict *elaboration*, a process that 'refers to the way people give meaning to this divergence' (Mugny et al., 1995: 161). Like the previous theoretical model, this approach focuses more on the consequences of these processes, leaving the underlying psychological processes themselves rather vague.

Unlike conversion theory and convergent-divergent theory, which specify main-effects models (exclusive processes and outcome for each source), conflict-elaboration theory specifies a contingency approach. The nature of the conflict elaboration and the types of influence depend on the nature of the task and the nature of the source introducing the divergence. Two contingency variables are associated with the nature of the task. The first concerns the *relevance of making an error*. If the task is objective with a clearly correct response (with all other responses being wrong), the cost to the individual of an error is high, whereas if the task is one where objectively correct responses cannot be determined, the cost of making an error is low. The second dimension concerns whether the responses are *socially anchoring*. If the response defines the individual within a particular group membership, it is socially anchoring, but if the response does not define an individual in terms of a particular social category, the task is not socially anchoring. These two dimensions yield four social situations, each of which is associated with different psychological processes involved in conflict elaboration.

Conflict-elaboration theory is an attempt to explain many social-influence phenomena, across many social situations, within a single theoretical framework. One of these quadrants is particularly relevant to the present discussion, as it is synonymous with the typical majority and minority influence-research scenario (this involves subjective tasks that are socially anchoring). The conflict associated with a source in this situation is determined by the meaning attached to it in terms of in-group or out-group membership. When the source is the in-group, as one may assume a majority would be, normative influence would be increased, and conformity to the majority position will occur with little need to consider the content of the majority message. This is similar to Moscovici's description of a comparison process for majority influence. When the source is an out-group such as a minority and, thereby, associated with negative connotations, agreement would be threatening to self-image, and an identification conflict arises. Private and indirect influence can occur through a process of dissociation between social comparison and validation, whereby targets of influence resolve the intergroup conflict, because 'Only then can subjects focus their attention on the content of the minority position' (Mugny et al., 1995: 166). The conflict-elaboration theory proposes hypotheses similar to those of Moscovici, suggesting that a majority source leads to minimal processing of its message while a minority source can lead to detailed consideration of its message especially when social-comparison processes are weak.

#### The context/comparison model

The context/comparison model (Crano, 2001; Crano and Alvaro, 1998) identifies several contingency factors that determine the processes underlying majority and minority influence. Two processes are important in determining whether there is direct or indirect influence: message elaboration and source derogation.

If the message concerns *weak or unvested attitudes*, an in-group minority can be persuasive because it is perceived by majority members as being distinctive, and this leads to message elaboration. If the minority is part of the in-group, it is unlikely to be derogated by the majority because the attitude dimension has little implication for in-group membership. Majorities, however, are unlikely to lead to much influence because the majority is not distinctive and, therefore, does not trigger message elaboration. If the message concerns *vested or central attitudes*, targets of in-group minority influence are reluctant to be identified with the minority position, yet there is a reluctance to derogate other in-group members. This leads to what Crano and Alvaro (1998) term the 'leniency contract', which allows the target to elaborate upon the in-group minority's message without source derogation, 'open-mindedly, with little defensiveness or hostility' (Crano and Alvaro, 1998: 180), and this can lead to indirect attitude change. In the case of out-group minorities, however, source derogation results in little direct or indirect influence. Because the message relates to important group-relevant dimensions, there can be compliance without message elaboration leading to influence on both a public or direct level.

Research supporting the context/comparison model comes from various studies by Crano and colleagues (e.g., Alvaro and Crano, 1997; Crano and Chen, 1998; Crano and Hannula-Bral, 1994). One area that needs more attention and clearer theoretical elaboration is the causal psychological processes involved. The model proposes various mediating factors (such as source distinctiveness, majority-group acceptance, and identification), and future research could usefully identify when these operate. Moreover, the distinction between weak and central attitudes is an important one, as there has been surprisingly little research examining the role of the topic on majority and minority influence.

### Self-categorization theory

Self-categorization theory has been developd by John Turner and his colleagues (Turner, 1991; Turner et al., 1987) as the cognitive aspect of the more general social-identity perspective in social psychology (e.g., Hogg, 2002). The fundamental assertion of self-categorization theory is that only those who are similar to self (on dimensions relevant to influence) can be the agents of influence. This is because similar others provide consensual validation for one's opinions whereas dissimilar others do not. Indeed, the very fact that dissimilar others are different (or 'out-group') can be a basis for explaining, and dismissing, the difference in opinions. Self-categorization theory does not claim that similar others always have influence, as individuals may resist change by recategorizing themselves, the group, and the relevance of the influence topic or by acting upon the source to change their opinions.

David and Turner (1996, 1999, 2001) have applied self-categorization theory to majority and minority influence. They suggest that a minority will have influence only if it is defined as the target's in-group. The categorization of the minority as different from self reduces its influence. According to self-categorization theory, indirect influence occurs when there is a shift in perspective from intragroup to intergroup. In the intergroup perspective, individuals perceive the minority in a wider context and begin to see the minority as 'part of "us" rather than "them", basically on our side, standing for basic values that "we" all share' (Turner, 1991: 171). In this case, the minority can lead to an indirect change without its being apparent on the direct level.

Self-categorization theory is a single-process theory, proposing that majority and minority influence are affected by the same process. However, since the outcomes of this process are determined by the in-group/out-group status of the source, we have considered it as a contingency model. Evidence for self-categorization theory comes from research by David and Turner (1996; 1999), who found majority compliance and minority conversion only when the source of influence was categorized as similar to the target of influence (which is consistent with conversion theory). When the source was characterized as being dissimilar to the target of influence, there was no direct or indirect influence. However, there is mixed evidence concerning self-categorization theory's claim that only in-group minorities lead to indirect attitude change. There is much evidence to show that, in fact, out-group minorities can have considerable indirect influence (e.g., Aebischer et al., 1984; Martin, 1988a, 1988b; Mugny et al., 1984; Pérez and Mugny, 1987; for a review, see Pérez and Mugny, 1998). Furthermore, research on majority–minority influence conducted within the self-categorization theory framework has failed to show that self-categorization is the mediating process (for an exception, see Gordijn et al., 2001).

## Contemporary developments and themes: the cognitive-response era

Perhaps the most significant development within the area of majority and minority influence has been the application of concepts and methodologies derived from the cognitive-response approach to persuasion. This approach focuses on how people's cognitions affect their acceptance (or rejection) of persuasive arguments. The extent to which a message encourages people to generate thoughts that are consistent with that message determines whether they will be influenced by it. In contrast, if a message leads people to generate thoughts counter to the message (or neutral ones or none at all), their attitudes will not be affected by the message. Attitude change is therefore linked to the extent to which a message results in the generation of message-congruent thoughts.

The cognitive-response approach has led to the development of models of persuasion (Eagly and Chaiken, 1993; Petty and Cacioppo, 1986) that can potentially provide a more detailed cognitive analysis of attitude change than the above theories of majority and minority influence. Both the elaboration-likelihood model (ELM) (Petty and Wegner, 1999) and the heuristic/systematic model (HSM) (Chen and Chaiken, 1999) distinguish two strategies of information-processing in persuasion settings. Central-route persuasion (ELM) or systematic processing (HSM) entails thinking carefully about persuasive arguments and other issue-related information. Alternatively, attitudes may be changed by peripheral-route persuasion (ELM) or heuristic processing (HSM), whereby systematic processing is minimal, and persuasion occurs due to some cue(s) in the persuasion environment (such as status of source) or use of simple heuristics (for example, 'the majority is always right'). These different routes to persuasion lead to different outcomes. Attitudes formed through systematic processing are 'strong' (Krosnick et al., 1993) in terms of being more resistant to counterpersuasion, persistent over time, and predictive of behavior than attitudes formed via nonsystematic processing (Petty, 1995). Maass and Clark (1983) were the first to draw a parallel between Moscovici's concepts of comparison/validation and the nonsystematic/systematic processing strategies proposed in models of persuasion. If this analogy is valid, one would expect majority and minority influence to lead to attitudes varying in attitude 'strength'.

The application of methodologies developed within the cognitive-response approach has offered new ways to examine the processes involved in majority and minority influence. The most obvious has been the application of thought-listing methodologies to examine people's cognitions. This is now widely used in the majority- and minority-influence literature. Several other research techniques have also been applied, as in research manipulating message quality (that is, 'strong' versus 'weak' messages) to identify which source condition is associated with systematic processing (see research quoted concerning conversion theory's direction-of-attention hypothesis above; Martin and Hewstone, 2003), the use of orientating tasks to manipulate processing demands (De Dreu et al., 1999; Martin and Hewstone, 2001b; Sanchez-Mazas et al., 1997), and the use of attitude-resistance paradigms to examine strength of attitude change (Martin et al., in press).

It is clear that the impact of the cognitive-response approach will continue to grow with the potential to offer greater insights into the processes of majority and minority influence. However, we must raise one potential concern, which has been echoed in several places in this chapter, that this approach reinforces an informationprocessing approach to understanding social influence. Such an approach, by virtue of its methodologies, places much emphasis upon cognitive processes to the neglect of normative issues.

### Some recent research developments

As the review above demonstrates, research on majority and majority influence is burgeoning. This growth is organized around a number of themes that we believe are likely to continue to develop.

The first concerns renewed interest in the *structural aspects* of majority and minority influence, such as the size of the majority and minority (e.g., Gardikiotis et al., 2005; Gordijn et al., 2002; Martin et al., 2002; Zdaniuk and Levine, 1996), majority/minority composition, and changing from one source group to another (e.g., Clark, 2001; Prislin et al., 2000, 2002). This research is leading to a debate over the role of consensus information for majority- and minority-group membership (e.g., Erb and Bohner, 2001). In addition, research is examining the social representation of majorities and minorities (e.g., Brandin et al., 1998; Gardikiotis et al., 2004; Laurens and Viaud, 2000) and the role of both cultural factors and norms (e.g., Kim and Markus, 1999; Ng and Van Dyne, 2001a, 2001b). Research continues to examine the *different levels of influence* as summarized above. However, research is increasingly focusing on the cognitive implications of influence in terms of strategies people adopt when being influenced (e.g., Laughlin, 1992), the reasons people give for changing their attitudes (e.g., Laurens and Masson, 1996), and the consequences of attitude change for the structure of attitudes (e.g., Alvaro and Crano, 1997; Gruenfeld et al., 1998; Mucchi-Faina, 2000). The trend for a more 'fine-grained' cognitive analysis of social-influence processes is one we believe is likely to be a major growth area. This will be facilitated by the use of new methodologies to clarify attitude structures, such as multidimensional scaling (Alvaro and Crano, 1997) and argument-coding schemes (Meyers et al., 2000).

The final main development concerns more *applied research and situational awareness* of the effects of majority and minority influence. Several commentators have pointed to the lack of applied research in this area and noted that most research uses what Maass and Clark (1984: 434) referred to as groups that 'are constituted for no other reason than a one-shot experiment'. Although there have not been any field experiments that directly test majority and minority influence (probably for ethical reasons), contemporary research is making many advances in applying the findings of basic research to real-life issues and/or to more ecologically valid situations. These include:

1 group interaction (e.g., Prislin and Christensen, 2005; Smith et al., 1996, 2001; Van Dyne and Saavedra, 1996);
2 real-life minority movements (e.g., Kelly, 1990; Pascaline et al., 1998; Petrillo, 1994) and political groups (e.g., Gaffie, 1992; Levine and Kaarbo, 2001; Smith and Diven, 2002);
3 group decision-making (e.g., Brodbeck et al., 2002; Fischer, 1997; McLeod et al., 1997; Meyers et al., 2000);
4 changing smoking behaviors (e.g., Falomir-Picastor, Butera, and Mugny, 2002; Joule et al., 1988);
5 organizational settings (e.g., De Dreu and Beersma, 2001; De Dreu and De Vries, 1997; De Dreu and West, 2001; De Rosa and Smith, 1998; Nemeth and Staw, 1989).

## Summary and concluding remarks

This chapter has summarized research examining a number of social-influence processes that aim either to control and maintain the group norm (majority influence and obedience to authority) or to change the group norm (minority influence). In dividing these processes into social control and social change, we again emphasize that this distinction reflects the source of motives to influence other people and not the outcomes of influence. As this review shows, both majorities and minorities can bring about change in people's attitudes, albeit under different circumstances.

We have taken a chronological approach that reflects the progression of research through three distinct stages; studies examining exclusively majority or minority influence and, finally, research that examines both majority and minority influence within the same paradigm. These chronological stages also reflect contrasting methodological and theoretical differences. For example, research on majority influence was strongly influenced by the functionalist model with its emphasis on psychological dependency as the explanatory variable. By contrast, research on minority influence was framed within an attribution approach, with influence being determined by the minority's behavioral style (in particular, consistency). Finally, research examining both majority and minority influence has been conducted within the social-ognition tradition with emphasis upon the role of information-processing strategies upon social influence.

The difference in research foci has, no doubt, affected the style of research and the causal models that they inspire. Early research on majority and, in particular, minority influence was inspired by real-life issues (see, for example, the opening pages of Moscovici and Nemeth, 1974), and these concerns contributed to the development of the research program. This led to separate research traditions, each of which reflected the different situational factors inherent in each form of influence. Studies of majority influence were designed to emphasize dependency (for example, by an implied or actual majority present, or by surveillance), while research on minority influence was designed to capture the minority's behavioral style (for example, by manipulating response repetition).

Contemporary studies of majority and minority influence use the typical attitude-change paradigm with its emphasis upon information-processing. Majority and minority status are defined in purely numerical terms, and participants receive the same (usually counterattitudinal) message in order to allow comparisons between the different sources of influence. Generally, these studies strip the social situation to a minimum with no contact between source and recipient of influence. Integrating the majority and minority research traditions has compromised the distinctive aspects that were associated with each and reduced the research agenda to the examination of informational aspects with scant regard to normative issues that had been pivotal in initial theorizing in both areas. This leads us to suggest that contemporary research, by its design and emphasis on informational aspects, is distorting theoretical developments. Future research needs to address this issue and use a variety of paradigms to examine both informational and normative aspects of influence. Concepts such as 'dependency' and 'behavioral style', which were crucial to early theore tical advances, are almost completely overlooked in contemporary work – mainly, we believe, because they do not fit the current vogue for information-processing paradigms and theories.

Our next observation concerns the way in which the various theories of majority and minority influence are categorized and compared. It has been typical to group them into whether they propose that majority and minority influence are caused by different processes or by the same process – originally, termed 'dual-process' and 'single-process' models by Maass and Clark (1983). This led to the common question of whether majority and minority influence is caused by two processes or one? (e.g., Turner, 1991). We have avoided this comparison for a number of reasons. First, we believe the methodological and theoretical distinction between 'process' and 'outcome' is so obscured in this research that it is often difficult to establish the integrity of the causal process (see Kruglanski and Mackie, 1990). Very few studies are designed to test mediating models, and most measure intervening variables out of causal order, such as some time after influence has occurred (see Wood et al., 1996). Second, contemporary research suggests that no set of outcomes is exclusively associated with each source and that each can lead to similar levels and types of influence. Instead of using the single versus dual-process model distinction, we have used a main versus contingency-effects categorization system for, we believe, the first time to summarize the literature. This system allows a more appropriate comparison of the theories.

Following from the above, we would also welcome more research examining the causal processes involved in majority and minority influence. Extrapolating from variations of dependent variables is not, by itself, sufficient unless there is clear evidence that these were determined by theoretically relevant mediating variables. Some researchers have risen to this challenge by using regression procedures to conduct mediational analyses to test the role of various mediators in determining influence (e.g., Baker and Petty, 1994; Erb et al., 1998; Gordijn et al., 2001; Martin et al., 2002). However, more can be done in this respect, such as the use of structural equation modeling to examine the relationship between antecedents, mediating factors, and outcomes of influence. We believe that this will provide a much better understanding of majority and minority influence as well as more exacting testing of the various theoretical models.

**SUMMARY**

This chapter summarises research examining a number of social-influence processes that aim to change peoples' attitudes and behaviors. The processes are divided into two categories: those that aim to control and maintain the group norm (social control) or to change the group norm (social change). The dominant form of social control is conformity, that is, the processes through which an individual accepts (or complies with) the group's view. Since this research examines how a majority can cause an individual to conform to its view, it is often referred to as majority influence. A different process of social control is obedience, whereby individuals obey (often against their free will) an authority figure. Since groups strive to maintain their group norm, attempts to induce social change often create conflict, and this is resisted by group members. Since social change typically originates from a small subsection of the group, this is often referred to as minority influence. While the chapter presents research on social control and change in separate sections, groups are continually experiencing processes of social control and change and both forms of influence can affect group member's attitudes under different circumstances.

## References

Abrams, D., Wetherell, M., Cochrane, S., Hogg, M.A., and Turner, J. (1990) 'Knowing What to Think by Knowing Who You Are: Self-Categorization and the Nature of Norm Formation, Conformity and Group Polarization', *British Journal of Social Psychology*, 29: 97–119.

Aebischer, V., Hewstone, M., and Henderson, M. (1984) 'Minority Influence and Musical Preference: Innovation by Conversion Not Coercion', *European Journal of Social Psychology*, 14: 23–33.

Allen, V.L. (1965) 'Situational Factors in Conformity', in L. Berkowitz (ed.), *Advances in Experimental Social Psychology* (vol. 2). San Diego, CA: Academic Press, pp. 133–75.

Allen, V.L. (1975) 'Social Support for Nonconformity', in L. Berkowitz (ed.), *Advances in Experimental Social Psychology* (vol. 8). New York: Academic Press, pp. 1–43.

Alvaro, E.M. and Crano, W.D. (1997) 'Indirect Minority Influence: Evidence for Leniency in Source Evaluation and Counterargumentation', *Journal of Personality and Social Psychology*, 72: 949–64.

Arbuthnot, J., Wayner, M. (1982) 'Minority Influence: Effects of Size, Conversion and Sex', *Journal of Psychology*, 111: 285–95.

Arendt, H. (1965) *Eichmann in Jerusalem: A Report on the Banality of Evil.* New York: Viking Press.

Asch, S.E. (1951) 'Effects of Group Pressure upon the Modification and Distortion of Judgments', in H. Guetzhow (ed.), *Groups, Leadership, and Men.* Pittsburgh, PA: Carnegie Press, pp. 177–90.

Asch, S.E. (1956) 'Studies of Independence and Conformity: A Minority of One against a Unanimous Majority', *Psychological Monographs: General and Applied*, Whole No. 416.

Baker, S.M. and Petty, R.E. (1994) 'Majority and Minority Influence: Source-Position Imbalance as a Determinant of Message Scrutiny', *Journal of Personality and Social Psychology*, 67: 5–19.

Baron, R.S., Vandello, J.A., and Brunsman, B. (1996) 'The Forgotten Variable in Conformity Research: Impact of Task Importance on Social Influence', *Journal of Personality and Social Psychology*, 71: 915–27.

Baumrind, D. (1964) 'Some Thoughts on the Ethics of Research after Reading Milgram's "Behavioral Study of Obedience"', *American Psychologist*, 19: 421–3.

Blass, T. (1992) 'The Social Psychology of Stanley Milgram', in M. Zanna (ed.), *Advances in Experimental Social Psychology* (vol. 25). San Diego, CA: Academic Press, pp. 227–329.

Blass, T. (1999) 'The Milgram Paradigm after 35 Years: Some Things We Now Know about Obedience to Authority', *Journal of Applied Social Psychology*, 29: 955–78.

Blass, T. (ed.) (2000) *Obedience to Authority: Current Perspectives on the Milgram Paradigm*. Mahwah, NJ: Erlbaum.

Bohner, G., Frank, S., and Erb, H.P. (1998) 'Heuristic Processing of Distinctiveness Information in Minority and Majority Influence', *European Journal of Social Psychology*, 28: 855–60.

Bond, R. (2005) 'Group Size and Conformity', *Group Processes and Intergroup Relations*, 8: 331–54.

Bond, R. and Smith, P.B. (1996) 'Culture and Conformity: A Meta-Analysis of Studies Using Asch's (1952b, 1956) Line Judgment Task', *Psychological Bulletin*, 119: 111–37.

Brandin, P., Choulot, S., and Gaffie, B. (1998) 'Étude Expérimentale de la Transformation de Deux Représentations en Réseau', *Cahiers Internationaux de Psychologie Sociale*, 37: 97–121.

Brandstätter, V., Ellmers, N., Gaviria, E., Giosue, F., Huguet, P., Kroon, M., Morchain, P., Pujal, M., Rubini, M., Mugny, G., and Pérez, J.A. (1991) 'Indirect Majority and Minority Influence: An Exploratory Study', *European Journal of Social Psychology*, 21: 199–211.

Bray, R.M., Johnson, D., and Chilstrom, J.T. (1982) 'Social Influence by Group Members with Minority Opinions: A Comparison of Hollander and Moscovici', *Journal of Personality and Social Psychology*, 43: 78–88.

Brodbeck, F.C., Kerschreiter, R., Mojzisch, A., Frey, D., and Schulz-Hardt, S. (2002) 'The Dissemination of Critical, Unshared Information in Decision-Making Groups: The Effects of Pre-Discussion Dissent', *European Journal of Social Psychology*, 32: 35–56.

Buehler, R. and Griffin, D. (1994) 'Change of Meaning Effects in Conformity and Dissent: Observing Construal Processes over Time', *Journal of Personality and Social Psychology*, 67: 984–96.

Buschini, F. (1998) L'Impact de Messages aux Styles d'Expression Positif ou Negatif en Fonction du Statut Minoritaire ou Majoritaire de la Source d'Influence', *Cahiers Internationaux de Psychologie Sociale*, 39: 9–22.

Butera, F. and Mugny, G. (1995) 'Conflict between Incompetencies and Influence of a Low-Expertise Source in Hypothesis Testing', *European Journal of Social Psychology*, 25: 457–62.

Butera, F., Mugny, G., Legrenzi, P., and Pérez, J.A. (1996) 'Majority and Minority Influence, Task Representation and Inductive Reasoning', *British Journal of Social Psychology*, 35: 123–36.

Campbell, J.D., Tesser, A. and Fairey, P.J. (1986) 'Conformity and Attention to the Stimulus: Some Temporal and Contextual Dynamics', *Journal of Personality and Social Psychology*, 51: 315–24.

Chaiken, S. and Stangor, C. (1987) 'Attitudes and Attitude Change', *Annual Review of Psychology*, 38: 575–630.

Chen, S. and Chaiken, S. (1999) 'The Heuristic-Systematic Model in Its Broader Context', in S. Chaiken and Y. Trope (eds), *Dual-Process Theories in Social Psychology*. New York: Guilford Press, pp. 73–96.

Cialdinid, R.B. and Goldstein, N.J. (2004) 'Social Influence: Compliance and Conformity', *Annual Review of Psychology*, 55: 591–621.

Cialdini, R.B. and Trost, M.R. (1998) 'Social Influence: Social Norms, Conformity, and Compliance', in D.T. Gilbert, S.T. Fiske and G. Lindzey (eds), *The Handbook of Social Psychology*, 4th edn. (vol. 2). New York: Mcgraw-Hill, pp. 151–92.

Clark, R.D., III (1998) 'Minority Influence: The Role of the Rate of Majority Defection and Persuasive Arguments', *European Journal of Social Psychology*, 28: 787–96.

Clark, R.D., III (2001) 'Effects of Majority Defection and Multiple Minority Sources on Minority Influence', *Group Dynamics*, 5: 57–62.

Crano, W.D. (2001) 'Social Influence, Social Identity, and Ingroup Leniency', in C.K.W. De Dreu and N.K. De Vries (eds), *Group Consensus and Innovation*. Oxford: Blackwell, pp. 122–43.

Crano, W.D. and Alvaro, E.M. (1998) 'The Context/Comparison Model of Social Influence: Mechanisms, Structure, and Linkages that Underlie Indirect Attitude Change', in W. Stroebe and M. Hewstone (eds), *European Review of Social Psychology* (vol. 8). Chichester: Wiley, pp. 175–202.

Crano, W.D. and Chen, X. (1998) 'The Leniency Contract and Persistence of Majority and Minority Influence', *Journal of Personality and Social Psychology*, 74: 1437–50.

Crano, W.D. and Hannula-Bral, K.A. (1994) 'Context/Categorization Model of Social Influence: Minority and Majority Influence in the Formation of a Novel Response Norm', *Journal of Experimental Social Psychology*, 30: 247–76.

Crutchfield, R.S. (1955) 'Conformity and Character', *American Psychologist*, 10: 191–8.

David, B. and Turner, J.C. (1996) 'Studies in Self-Categorization and Minority Conversion: Is Being a Member of the Outgroup an Advantage?', *British Journal of Social Psychology*, 35: 179–99.

David, B. and Turner, J.C. (1999) 'Studies in Self-Categorization and Minority Conversion: The Ingroup Minority in Intragroup and Intergroup Contexts', *British Journal of Social Psychology*, 38: 115–34.

David, B. and Turner, J.C. (2001) 'Majority and Minority Influence: A Single Process Self-Categorization Analysis', in C.K.W. De Dreu and N.K. De Vries (eds), *Group Consensus and Innovation*. Oxford: Blackwell, pp. 91–121.

De Dreu, C.K.W. and Beersma, B. (2001) 'Minority Influence in Organizations: Its Origins and Implications for Learning and Group Performance', in C.K.W. De Dreu and N.K. De Vries (eds), *Group Consensus and Innovation*. Oxford: Blackwell, pp. 258–83.

De Dreu, C.K.W. and De Vries, N.K. (1993) 'Numerical Support, Information Processing and Attitude Change', *European Journal of Social Psychology*, 23: 647–63.

De Dreu, C.K.W. and De Vries, N.K. (1996) 'Differential Processing and Attitude Change Following Majority and Minority Arguments', *British Journal of Social Psychology*, 35: 77–90.

De Dreu, C.K.W. and De Vries, N.K. (1997) 'Minority Dissent in Organizations', in C.K.W. De Dreu and E. Van de Vliert (eds), *Using Conflict in Organizations*. London: Sage, pp. 72–86.

De Dreu, C.K.W., De Vries, N.K., Gordijn, E., and Schuurman, M. (1999) 'Convergent and Divergent Processing of Majority and Minority Arguments: Effects on Focal and Related Attitudes', *European Journal of Social Psychology*, 29: 329–48.

De Dreu, C.K.W. and West, M.A. (2001) 'Minority Dissent and Team Innovation: The Importance of Participation in Decision Making', *Journal of Applied Psychology*, 86: 1191–201.

De Rosa, A.S. and Smith, A.H. (1998) 'Représentations Sociales Polémiques et Styles d'Influence Minoritaire, la Communication Publicitaire de Benetton', *Bulletin de Psychologie*, 51: 399–416.

Deutsch, M. and Gerard, H.G. (1955) 'A Study of Normative and Informational Social Influence upon Individual Judgment', *Journal of Abnormal and Social Psychology*, 51: 629–36.

De Vries, N.K., De Dreu, C.K.W., Gordijn, E., and Schuurman, M. (1996) 'Majority and Minority Influence: A Dual Interpretation', in W. Stroebe and M. Hewstone (eds), *European Review of Social Psychology* (vol. 7). Chichester: Wiley, pp. 145–72.

Eagly, A.H. and Chaiken, S. (1993) *The Psychology of Attitudes*. Fort Worth, TX: Harcourt Brace Jovanovich.

Easterbrook, J.A. (1959) 'The Effect of Emotion on the Utilization and the Organization of Behavior', *Psychological Review*, 66: 183–201.

Epley, N. and Gilovich, T. (1999) 'Just Going Along: Nonconscious Priming and Conformity to Social Pressure', *Journal of Experimental Social Psychology*, 35: 578–89.

Erb, H.P. and Bohner, G. (2001) 'Mere Consensus Effects in Minority and Majority Influence', in C.K.W. De Dreu and N.K. De Vries (eds), *Group Consensus and Innovation*. Oxford: Blackwell, pp. 40–59.

Erb, H.P., Bohner, G., Schmaelzle, K., and Rank, S. (1998) 'Beyond Conflict and Discrepancy: Cognitive Bias in Minority and Majority Influence', *Personality and Social Psychology Bulletin*, 24: 620–33.

Falomir-Picastor, J.M., Butera, F., and Mugny, G. (2002) 'Persuasive Constraint and Expert versus Non-Expert Influence in Intention to Quit Smoking', *European Journal of Social Psychology*, 32: 209–22.

Festinger, L. (1950) 'Informal Social Communication', *Psychological Review*, 57: 271–82.

Festinger, L. (1954) 'A Theory of Social Comparison Processes', *Human Relations*, 7: 337–60.

Fischer, L.J. (1997) 'Processus d'Influence dans la Situation de Médiation et Modéle de la Conversion Minoritaire', *Cahiers Internationaux de Psychologie Sociale*, 35: 12–29.

Gaffie, B. (1991) 'Quelques Régulations Orthodoxes Lors d'Une Confrontation Idéologique avec des Minorites', *Revue Internationale de Psychologie Sociale*, 4: 145–70.

Gaffie, B. (1992) 'The Processes of Minority Influence in an Ideological Confrontation', *Political Psychology*, 13: 407–27.

Gardikiotis, A., Martin, R., and Hewstone, M. (2004) 'The Representation of Majorities and Minorities in the British Press: A Content Analytic Approach', *European Journal of Social Psychology*, 34: 637–46.

Gardikiotis, A., Martin, R., and Hewstone, M. (2005) 'Group Consensus in Social Influence: Type of Consensus Information as a Moderator of Majority and Minority Influence', *Personality and Social Psychology Bulletin*, 31: 1163–1174.

Gerard, H.B., Wilhelmy, R.A., and Connolley, E.S. (1968) 'Conformity and Group Size', *Journal of Personality and Social Psychology*, 8: 79–82.

Gordijn, E., De Vries, N.K., and De Vries, C.K.W. (2002) 'Minority Influence on Focal and Related Attitudes: Change in Size, Attributions and Information Processing', *Personality and Social Psychology Bulletin*', 28: 1315–26.

Gordijn, E., Postmes, T., and De Vries, N.K. (2001) 'Devil's Advocate or Advocate of Oneself: Effects of Numerical Support on Pro- and Counterattitudinal Self-Persuasion', *Personality and Social Psychology Bulletin*, 27: 395–407.

Griffin, D. and Buehler, R. (1993) 'Role of Construal Processes in Conformity and Dissent', *Journal of Personality and Social Psychology*, 65: 657–69.

Griskevicius, V., Goldstein, N.J., Mortensen, C.R., Cialdini, R.B., and Kenrick, D.T. (2006) 'Going Along versus Going Alone: When Fundamental Motives Facilitate Strategic (Non)conformity', *Journal of Personality and Social Psychology*', 91: 281–94.

Gruenfeld, D.H., Thomas-Hunt, M.C., and Kim, P.H. (1998) 'Cognitive Flexibility, Communication Strategy, and Integrative Complexity in Groups: Public Versus Private Reactions to Majority and Minority Status', *Journal of Experimental Social Psychology*, 34: 202–26.

Guillon, M. and Personnaz, B. (1983) 'Analyse de la Dynamique des Représentations des Conflits

Minoritaire et Majoritaire', *Cahiers de Psychologie Cognitive*, 3: 65–87.

Hart, J.W., Stasson, M.F., and Karau, S.J. (1999) 'Effects of Source Expertise and Physical Distance on Minority Influence', *Group Dynamics*, 3: 81–92.

Hoffman, H.G., Granhag, P.A., See, S.T.K., and Loftus, E.F. (2001) 'Social Influences on Reality-Monitoring Decisions', *Memory and Cognition*, 29: 394–404.

Hofling, C.K., Brotzman, E., Dairymple, S., Graves, N., and Pierce, C.M. (1966) 'An Experimental Study in Nurse–Physician Relationships', *Journal of Nervous and Mental Disease*, 143: 171–80.

Hogg, M.A. (2002) 'Social Identity', in M.R. Leary and J.P. Tangney (eds), *Handbook of Self and Identity.* New York: Guilford, pp. 462–79.

Jones, E.E. and Gerard, H.B. (1967) *Foundations of Social Psychology*. New York: Wiley.

Joule, R.V., Mugny, G., and Pérez, J.A. (1988) 'When a Compliance without Pressure Strategy Fails Due to a Minority Dissenter. A Case of "Behavioral Conversion"', *European Journal of Social Psychology*, 18: 531–5.

Kelley, H.H. (1967) 'Attribution Theory in Social Psychology', in D. Levine (ed.), *Nebraska Symposium on Motivation*. Lincoln, NE: University of Nebraska Press, pp. 192–241.

Kelly, C. (1990) 'Social Identity and Levels of Influence: When a Political Minority Fails', *British Journal of Social Psychology*, 29: 289–301.

Kelman, H.C. (1958) 'Compliance, Identification, and Internalization: Three Processes of Attitude Change', *Journal of Conflict Resolution*, 2: 51–60.

Kelman, H.C. and Hamilton, V.L. (1989) *Crimes of Obedience: Toward a Social Psychology of Authority and Responsibility*. New Haven, CT: Yale University Press.

Kelvin, P. (1979) 'Review of Moscovici (1976) "Social Influence and Social Change"', *European Journal of Social Psychology*, 9: 441–6.

Kent, M.V. (1994) 'Conformity', in A.P. Hare and H.H. Blumberg (eds), *Small Group Research: A Hand book*. Norwood, NJ: Ablex, pp. 107–37.

Kerr, N. (2002) 'When Is a Minority a Minority? Active vs. Passive Minority Advocacy and Social Influence', *European Journal of Social Psychology*, 32: 471–83.

Kim, H. and Markus, H.R. (1999) 'Deviance or Uniqueness, Harmony or Conformity? A Cultural Analysis', *Journal of Personality and Social Psychology*, 77: 785–800.

Krackow, A. and Blass, T. (1995) 'When Nurses Obey or Defy Inappropriate Physician Orders: Attributional Differences', *Journal of Social Behavior and Personality*, 10: 585–94.

Krosnick, J.A., Boninger, D.S., Chuang, Y.C., Berent, M.K., and Carnot, C. (1993) 'Attitude Strength: One Construct or Many Related Constructs?', *Journal of Personality and Social Psychology*, 65: 1132–51.

Kruglanski, A.W. and Mackie, D.M. (1990) 'Majority and Minority Influence: A Judgmental Process Analysis', in W. Stroebe and M. Hewstone (eds), *European Review of Social Psychology* (vol. 1). Chichester: Wiley, pp. 229–61.

Latané, B. (1981) 'The Psychology of Social Impact', *American Psychologist*, 36: 343–56.

Latané, B. (1996) 'Strength from Weakness: The Fate of Opinion Minorities in Spatially Distributed Groups', in E.H. Witte and J.H. Davis (eds), *Understanding Group Behavior* (vol. 1). *Consensual Action by Small Groups.* Mahwah, NJ: Erlbaum, pp. 193–219.

Latané, B., Liu, J.H., Nowak, A., Bonvento, M., and Zheng, L. (1995) 'Distance Matters: Physical Space and Social Impact', *Personality and Social Psychology Bulletin*, 21: 795–805.

Latané, B. and Wolf, S. (1981) 'The Social Impact of Majorities and Minorities', *Psychological Review*, 88: 438–53.

Laughlin, P.R. (1992) 'Influence and Performance in Simultaneous Collective and Individual Induction', *Organizational Behavior and Human Decision Processes*, 51: 447–70.

Laurens, S. and Masson, E. (1996) 'Critique du Sens Commun et Changement Social: Le Rôle des Minorités', *Cahiers Internationaux de Psychologie Sociale*, 32: 13–32.

Laurens, S. and Viaud, J. (2000) 'Influence Minoritaire Versus Majoritaire sur la Representation de la Distribution des Opinions d'Autrui', *Cahiers Internationaux de Psychologie Sociale*, 46: 26–33.

Legrenzi, P., Butera, F., Mugny, G., and Pérez, J.A. (1991) 'Majority and Minority Influence in Inductive Reason ing: A Preliminary Study', *European Journal of Social Psychology*, 21: 359–63.

Levine, J.M. (1980) 'Reaction to Opinion Deviance in Small Groups', in P.B. Paulus (ed.), *Psychology of Group Influence.* Hillsdale, NJ: Erlbaum, pp. 375–429.

Levine, J.M. (1999) 'Solomon Asch's Legacy for Group Research', *Personality and Social Psychology Review*, 3: 358–64.

Levine, J.M. and Kaarbo, J. (2001) 'Minority Influence in Political Decision-Making Groups', in C.K.W. De Dreu and N.K. De Vries (eds), *Group Consensus and Innovation*. Oxford: Blackwell, pp. 229–57.

Levine, J.M. and Russo, E.M. (1987) 'Majority and Minority Influence', in C. Hendrick (ed.), *Group Processes: Review of Personality and Social Psychology* (vol. 8). Newbury Park, CA: Sage, pp. 13–54.

Leyens, J.P. and Corneille, O. (1999) 'Asch's Social Psychology: Not as Social as You May Think', *Personality and Social Psychology Review*, 3: 345–57.

Lott, A.J. and Lott, B.E. (1961) 'Group Cohesiveness, Communication Level, and Conformity', *Journal of Abnormal and Social Psychology*, 62: 408–12.

Maass, A. and Clark, R.D., III (1983) 'Internalization versus Compliance: Differential Processes Underlying Minority Influence and Conformity', *European Journal of Social Psychology*, 13: 197–215.

Maass, A. and Clark, R.D., III (1984) 'Hidden Impact of Minorities: Fifteen Years of Minority Influence Research', *Psychological Bulletin*, 95: 428–50.

Maass, A., West, S., and Cialdini, R.B. (1987) 'Minority Influence and Conversion', in C. Hendrick (ed.), *Group Processes: Review of Personality and Social Psychology* (vol. 8). Newbury Park, CA: Sage, pp. 55–79.

Mackie, D.M. (1987) 'Systematic and Nonsystematic Processing of Majority and Minority Persuasive Communications', *Journal of Personality and Social Psychology*, 53: 41–52.

Martin, R. (1988a) 'Ingroup and Outgroup Minorities: Differential Impact upon Public and Private Responses', *European Journal of Social Psychology*, 18: 39–52.

Martin, R. (1988b) 'Minority Influence and Social Categorization: A Replication', *European Journal of Social Psychology*, 18: 369–73.

Martin, R. (1996) 'Minority Influence and Argument Generation', *British Journal of Social Psychology*, 35: 91–103.

Martin, R. (1998) 'Majority and Minority Influence Using the Afterimage Paradigm: A Series of Attempted Replications', *Journal of Experimental Social Psychology*, 34: 1–26.

Martin, R., Gardikiotis, A., and Hewstone, M. (2002) 'Levels of Consensus and Majority and Minority Influence', *European Journal of Social Psychology*, 32: 645–65.

Martin, R. and Hewstone, M. (1999) 'Minority Influence and Optimal Problem-Solving', *European Journal of Social Psychology*, 29: 825–32.

Martin, R. and Hewstone, M. (2001a) 'Conformity and Independence in Groups: Majorities and Minorities', in M.A. Hogg and R.S. Tindale (eds), *Blackwell Handbook of Social Psychology* (vol. 1): *Group Processes*. Oxford: Blackwell, pp. 209–34.

Martin, R. and Hewstone, M. (2001b) 'Determinants and Consequences of Cognitive Processes in Majority and Minority Influence', in J. Forgas and K. Williams (eds), *Social Influence: Direct and Indirect Processes*. Philadelphia, PA: Psychology Press, pp. 315–30.

Martin, R. and Hewstone, M. (2003) 'Majority versus Minority Influence: When, Not Whether, Source Status Instigates Heuristic or Systematic Processing', *European Journal of Social Psychology*: 33: 313–30.

Martin, R., Hewstone, M., and Martin, P.Y. (2003) 'Resistance to Persuasive Messages as a Function of Majority and Minority Source Status', *Journal of Experimental Social Psychology*, 39: 585–93.

Martin, R., Hewstone, M. and Martin, P.Y. (in press) 'Systematic and Heuristic Processing of Majority- and Minority-Endorsed Messages: The Effects of Varying Outcome Relevance and "Levels of Orientation" on Attitude and Message Processing', *Personality and Social Psychology Bulletin*.

McLeod, P.L., Baron, R.S., Marti, M.W., and Yoon, K. (1997) 'The Eyes Have It: Minority Influence in Face-to-Face and Computer-Mediated Group Discussion', *Journal of Applied Psychology*, 82: 706–18.

Meeus, W.H.J. and Raaijmakers, Q.A.W. (1986) 'Administrative Obedience: Carrying out Orders to Use Psychological-Administrative Violence', *European Journal of Social Psychology*, 16: 311–24.

Meeus, W.H.J. and Raaijmakers, Q.A.W. (1995) 'Obedience in Modern Society: The Utrecht Studies', *Journal of Social Issues*, 51: 155–75.

Meyers, R.A., Brashers, D.E., and Hanner, J. (2000) 'Majority-Minority Influence: Identifying Argumentative Patterns and Predicting Argument-Outcome Links', *Journal of Communication*, 50: 3–30.

Milgram, S. (1963) 'Behavioral Study of Obedience', *Journal of Abnormal and Social Psychology*, 67: 371–8.

Milgram, S. (1974) *Obedience to Authority: An Experimental View*. New York: Harper & Row.

Miller, A.G. (1986) *The Obedience Experiments: A Case Study of Controversy in Social Science*. New York: Praeger.

Miller, A.G., Collins, B.E., and Brief, D.E. (eds) (1995) *Perspectives on Obedience to Authority: The Legacy of the Milgram Experiments*, *Journal of Social Issues*, 51 (3).

Moscovici, S. (1976) *Social Influence and Social Change*. London: Academic Press.

Moscovici, S. (1979) 'Rejoinder to Kelvin's (1979) Review of Moscovici (1976) "Social Influence and Social Change"', *European Journal of Social Psychology*, 9: 446–51.

Moscovici, S. (1980) 'Toward a Theory of Conversion Behavior', in L. Berkowitz (ed.), *Advances in Experimental Social Psychology* (vol. 13). New York: Academic Press, pp. 209–39.

Moscovici, S. (1985) 'Social Influence and Conformity', in G. Lindsey and E. Aronson (eds), *The Handbook of Social Psychology*, 3rd edn (vol. 2). New York: Random House, pp. 347–412.

Moscovici, S. and Faucheux, C. (1972) 'Social Influence, Conformity Bias and the Study of Active Minorities', in L. Berkowitz (ed.), *Advances in Experimental Social Psychology* (vol. 6). New York: Academic Press, pp. 149–202.

Moscovici, S. and Lage, E. (1976) 'Studies in Social Influence. III: Majority versus Minority Influence in a Group', *European Journal of Social Psychology*, 6: 149–74.

Moscovici, S., Lage, E., and Naffrechoux, M. (1969) 'Influence of a Consistent Minority on the Responses of a Majority in a Color Perception Task', *Sociometry*, 32: 365–80.

Moscovici, S. and Mugny, G. (1983) 'Minority Influence', in P.B. Paulhus (ed.), *Basic Group* Processes. New York: Springer-Verlag, pp. 41–64.

Moscovici, S., Mugny, G., and Papastamou, S. (1981) '"Sleeper Effect" et/ou Éffet Minoritaire? Étude Théorique et Expérimentale de L'Influence Sociale à Retardement', *Cahiers de Psychologie Cognitive*, 1: 199–221.

Moscovici, S. and Nemeth, C. (1974) 'Social Influence. II: Minority Influence', in C. Nemeth (ed.), *Social Psychology: Classic and Contemporary Integrations*. Chicago, IL: Rand Mcnally, pp. 217–49.

Moscovici, S. and Personnaz, B. (1980) 'Studies in Social Influence. V. Minority Influence and Conversion Behavior in a Perceptual Task', *Journal of Experimental Social Psychology*, 16: 270–82.

Moscovici, S. and Personnaz, B. (1991) 'Studies in Social Influence. VI. Is Lenin Orange or Red? Imagery and 'Social Influence', *European Journal of Social Psychology*, 21: 101–18.

Mucchi-Faina, A. (2000) 'Minority Influence and Ambivalence', *Revue Internationale de Psychologie Sociale*, 13: 65–87.

Mucchi-Faina, A., Maass, A., and Volpato, C. (1991) 'Social Influence: The Role of Originality', *European Journal of Social Psychology*, 21: 183–97.

Mugny, G. (1975) 'Negotiations, Image of the Other and the Process of Minority Influence', *European Journal of Social Psychology*, 5: 209–28.

Mugny, G. (1982) *The Power of Minorities*. London: Academic Press.

Mugny, G., Butera, F., Sanchez-Mazas, M., and Pérez, J.A. (1995) 'Judgements in Conflict: The Conflict Elaboration Theory of Social Influence', in B. Boothe, R. Hirsig, A. Helminger, B. Meier, and R. Volkart (eds), *Perception-Evaluation-Interpretation*. Göttingen: Hogrefe and Huber, pp. 160–8.

Mugny, G., Kaiser, C., Papastamou, S., and Pérez, J.A. (1984) 'Intergroup Relations, Identification and Social Influence', *British Journal of Social Psychology*, 23: 317–22.

Mugny, G. and Papastamou, S. (1981) 'When Rigidity Does Not Fail: Individualization and Psychologization as Resistances to the Diffusion of Minority Innovations', *European Journal of Social Psychology*, 10: 43–62.

Mugny, G. and Pérez, J. (1991) *The Social Psychology of Minority Influence*. Cambridge: Cambridge University Press.

Nemeth, C. (1986) 'Differential Contributions of Majority and Minority Influence', *Psychological Review*, 93: 23–32.

Nemeth, C. (1995) 'Dissent as Driving Cognition, Attitudes and Judgements', *Social Cognition*, 13: 273–91.

Nemeth, C.J., Brown, K., and Rogers, J. (2001) 'Devil's Advocate versus Authentic Dissent: Stimulating Quantity and Quality', *European Journal of Social Psychology*, 31: 707–20.

Nemeth, C.J. and Kwan, J. (1985) 'Originality of Word Associations as a Function of Majority and Minority Influence', *Social Psychology Quarterly*, 48: 277–82.

Nemeth, C.J. and Kwan, J. (1987) 'Minority Influence, Divergent Thinking and Detection of Correct Solutions', *Journal of Applied Social Psychology*, 17: 788–99.

Nemeth, C., Mosier, K., and Chiles, C. (1992) 'When Convergent Thought Improves Performance: Majority vs. Minority Influence', *Personality and Social Psychology Bulletin*, 18: 139–44.

Nemeth, C.J. and Staw, B.M. (1989) 'The Tradeoffs of Social Control and Innovation in Groups and Organizations', in L. Berkowitz (ed.), *Advances in Experimental Social Psychology* (vol. 22). New York: Academic Press, pp. 175–209.

Nemeth, C.J. and Wachtler, J. (1983) 'Creative Problem Solving as a Result of Majority vs Minority Influence', *European Journal of Social Psychology*, 13: 45–55.

Nemeth, C.J., Wachtler, J., and Endicott J. (1977) 'Increasing the Size of the Minority: Some Gains and Some Losses', *European Journal of Social Psychology*, 7: 15–27.

Ng, K.Y. and Van Dyne, L. (2001a) 'Culture and Minority Influence: Effects on Persuasion and Originality', in C.K.W. De Dreu and N.K. De Vries (eds), *Group Consensus and Innovation*. Oxford: Blackwell, pp. 284–306.

Ng, K.Y. and Van Dyne, L. (2001b) 'Individualism–Collectivism as a Boundary Condition for Effectiveness of Minority Influence in Decision Making', *Organizational Behavior and Human Decision Processes*, 84: 198–225.

Papastamou, S. (1986) 'Psychologization and Processes of Minority and Majority Influence', *European Journal of Social Psychology*, 16: 165–80.

Pérez, J.A. and Mugny, G. (1987) 'Paradoxical Effects of Categorization in Minority Influence: When Being an Outgroup Is an Advantage', *European Journal of Social Psychology*, 17: 157–69.

Pérez, J.A. and Mugny, G. (1996) 'The Conflict Elaboration Theory of Social influence', in E.H. Witte and J.H. Davis (eds), *Understanding Group Behavior: Small Group Processes and Interpersonal Relations* (vol. 2). Hillsdale, NJ: Erlbaum, pp. 191–210.

Pérez, J.A. and Mugny, G. (1998) 'Categorization and Social Influence', in S. Worchel and J.M. Francisco (eds), *Social Identity: International Perspectives*. London: Sage, pp. 142–53.

Pérez, J.A., Mugny, G., Butera, F., Kaiser, C., and Roux, P. (1991) 'Integrazione tra Influenza Magioritaria e Minoritaria: Conversione, Consenso e Uniformità', *Ricerche di Psicologia*, 4: 75–102.

Peterson, R. and Nemeth, C.J. (1996) 'Focus versus Flexibility: Majority and Minority Influence Can Both Improve Performance', *Personality and Social Psychology Bulletin*, 22: 14–23.

Petrillo, G. (1994) 'Collective Movements and Minority Influence: The Processes of Social Influence beyond the Confines of Experimental Groups', in S. Moscovici, A. Mucchi-Faina, and A. Maass (eds), *Minority Influence*. Chicago, IL: Nelson-Hall, pp. 209–30.

Petty, R.E. (1995) 'Attitude Change', in A. Tesser (ed.), *Advanced Social Psychology*. New York: McGraw-Hill, pp. 195–255.

Petty, R.E. and Cacioppo, J.T. (1986) *Communication and Persuasion: Central and Peripheral Routes to Attitude Change*. New York: Springer-Verlag.

Petty, R.E. and Wegner, D.T. (1999) 'The Elaboration Likelihood Model: Current Status and Controversies', in S. Chaiken and Y. Trope (eds), *Dual-Process Theories in Social Psychology*. New York: Guilford, pp. 37–72.

Prislin, R., Brewer, M., and Wilson, D.J. (2002) 'Changing Majority and Minority Positions within a Group versus an Aggregate', *Personality and Social Psychology Bulletin*, 28: 640–7.

Prislin, R. and Christensen, P.N. (2005) 'Social Change in the Aftermath of Successful Minority Influence', *European Review of Social Psychology*, 16: 43–73.

Prislin, R., Limbert, W.M., and Bauer, E. (2000) 'From Majority to Minority and Vice Versa: The Asymmetrical Effects of Losing and Gaining Majority Positions within a Group', *Journal of Personality and Social Psychology*, 79: 385–97.

Quiamzade, A., Tomei, A., and Butera, F. (2000) 'Informational Dependence and Informational Constraint: Social Comparison and Social Influences in an Anagram Resolution Task', *Revue Internationale de Psychologie Sociale*, 13: 123–50.

Rank, S.G. and Jacobson, C.K. (1977) 'Hospital Nurses' Compliance with Medication Overdose Orders: A Failure to Replicate', *Journal of Health and Social Behavior*, 18: 188–93.

Ross, L., Greene, D., and House, P. (1977) 'The "False Consensus Effect": An Egocentric Bias in Social Perception and Attribution Processes', *Journal of Experimental Social Psychology*, 13: 279–301.

Sabini, J. and Silver, M. (eds) (1992) *The Individual in a Social World: Essays and Experiments*, 2nd edn. New York: Mcgraw-Hill.

Sanchez-Mazas, M., Mugny, G., and Falomir, J.M. (1997) 'Minority Influence and Intergroup Relations: Social Comparison and Validation Processes in the Context of Xenophobia in Switzerland', *Swiss Journal of Psychology*, 56: 182–92.

Sanchez-Mazas, M., Pérez, J.A., Navarro, E., Mugny, G., and Jovanovic, J. (1993) 'De la Paralysie Intragroupe au Conflit Normatif: Études sur l'Avortement, la Contraception et la Xénophobie', in J.A. Pérez and G. Mugny (eds), *Influences Sociales: La Théorie de l'élaboration du Conflit*. Neuchâtel, Switzerland: Delachaux & Niestlé, pp. 121–43.

Schachter, S. (1951) 'Deviation, Rejection, and Communication', *Journal of Abnormal and Social Psychology*, 46: 190–207.

Smith, C.M. and Diven, P.J. (2002) 'Minority Influence and Political Interest Groups', in V.C. Ottati and R.S. Tindale (eds), *The Social Psychology of Politics: Social Psychological Applications to Social Issues*. New York: Kluwer Academic, pp. 175–92.

Smith, C.M, Tindale, R.S., and Anderson, E.M. (2001) 'The Impact of Shared Representations on Minority Influence in Freely Interacting Groups', in C.K.W. De Dreu and N.K. De Vries (eds), *Group Consensus and Innovation*. Oxford: Blackwell, pp. 183–200.

Smith, C.M., Tindale, R.S., and Dugoni, B.L. (1996) 'Minority and Majority Influence in Freely Interacting Groups: Qualitative versus Quantitative Differences', *British Journal of Social Psychology*, 35: 137–49.

Staub, E. (1989) *The Roots of Evil: The Origins of Genocide and Other Group Violence*. Cambridge: Cambridge University Press.

Tanford, S. and Penrod, S. (1984) 'Social Influence Model: A Formal Integration of Research on Majority and Minority Influence Processes', *Psychological Bulletin*, 95: 189–225.

Tesser, A., Campbell, J., and Mickler, S. (1983) 'The Role of Social Pressure, Attention to the Stimulus, and Self-Doubt in Conformity', *European Journal of Social Psychology*, 13: 217–33.

Trost, M.R., Maass, A., and Kenrick, D.T. (1992) 'Minority Influence: Personal Relevance Biases Cognitive Processes and Reverses Private Acceptance', *Journal of Experimental Social Psychology*, 28: 234–54.

Turner, J.C. (1991) *Social Influence*. Milton Keynes: Open University Press.

Turner, J.C., Hogg, M.A., Oakes, P.J., Reicher, S.D., and Wetherell, M.S. (1987) *Rediscovering the Social Group: A Self-Categorization Theory*. Oxford: Blackwell.

Van Dyne, L. and Saavedra, R. (1996) 'A Naturalistic Minority Influence Experiment: Effects of Divergent Thinking, Conflict and Originality in Work-Groups', *British Journal of Social Psychology*, 35: 151–67.

Van Knippenberg, D. and Wilke, H. (1992) 'Prototypicality of Arguments and Conformity to Ingroup Norms', *European Journal of Social Psychology*, 22: 141–55.

Volpato, C., Maass, A., Mucchi-Faina, A., and Vitti, E. (1990) 'Minority Influence and Social Categorization', *European Journal of Social Psychology*, 20: 119–32.

Wilder, D.A. (1977) 'Perceptions of Groups, Size of Opposition, and Influence', *Journal of Experimental Social Psychology*, 13: 253–68.

Wolf, S. (1985) 'Manifest and Latent Influence of Majorities and Minorities', *Journal of Personality and Social Psychology*, 48: 899–908.

Wolf, S. and Latané, B. (1983) 'Majority and Minority Influence on Restaurant Preferences', *Journal of Personality and Social Psychology*, 45: 282–92.

Wood, W., Christensen, P.N., Hebl, M.R., and Rothgerber, H. (1997) 'Conformity to Sex-Typed Norms, Affect, and the Self-Concept', *Journal of Personality and Social Psychology*, 73: 523–35.

Wood, W., Lundgren, S., Ouellette, J.A., Busceme, S., and Blackstone, T. (1994) 'Minority Influence: A Meta-Analytic Review of Social Influence Processes', *Psychological Bulletin*, 115: 323–45.

Wood, W., Pool, G.J., Leck, K., and Purvis, D. (1996) 'Self-Definition, Defensive Processing, and Influence: The Normative Impact of Majority and Minority Groups', *Journal of Personality and Social Psychology*, 71: 1181–93.

Zdaniuk, B. and Levine, J.M. (1996) 'Anticipated Interaction and Thought Generation: The Role of Faction Size', *British Journal of Social Psychology*, 35: 201–18.

Ziegler, R., Diehl, M., Zigon, R. and Fett, T. (2004) 'Source Consistency, Distinctiveness, and Consensus: The Three Dimensions of the Kelley ANOVA Model in Persuasion', *Personality and Social Psychology Bulletin*, 30: 352–64.

# PART FIVE

# INTERGROUP PROCESSES AND SOCIETY

# 15
# Intergroup Behavior and Social Identity

MICHAEL A. HOGG AND DOMINIC ABRAMS

**INTRODUCTION**

Our sense of who we are, our identity, is profoundly influenced by the groups in society that we belong to. Man or woman, Syrian or Israeli, Latino or African American, Muslim or Hindu, academic or politician – these are (social) identities which are grounded in social groups and defined by the normative properties of such groups and the nature of the relations between one's ingroup and relevant outgroups. Intergroup behavior and self-definition are inextricable – each influencing one another. In this chapter, we discuss intergroup behavior (prejudice, discrimination, stigma, disadvantage, social conflict and harmony, and so forth) and its relationship to self-conception and social identity.

Intergroup behavior refers to how people in groups perceive, think about, feel about, act towards, and relate to people in other groups. This behavior is psychologically tied to social identity, that is, people's cognitive representation of themselves and of other people as social category or group members. It is also tied to how people view the relations between groups. Intergroup behavior and social identity may be social psychologically inextricable. Social identity processes generate intergroup behaviors, and intergroup behavior influences the nature of relations between groups and thus the form and content of social identity.

In this chapter, we provide an overview of what social psychology has learned about intergroup behavior, intergroup relations, and social identity, and about their interrelationship. This is a very large literature that can encompass the study of the cognitive bases of perception, attitudes, motivation and emotion, social disadvantage and justice, bargaining and negotiation, international relations, intercultural relations, and issues of ideology and social representation. In short, the study of intergroup relations is inextricable from other domains of social psychology (Mackie and Smith, 1998). Our coverage is, by necessity, selective, and, therefore, we focus primarily on personality, self-conception, social identity, cognitive processes, motivation, goals, stereotypes, prejudice, disadvantage, stigma, collective action, conflict, and harmony. This chapter connects with, but does not replicate, other chapters in this handbook – in particular Chapter 4 on stereotyping and Chapter 16 on prejudice and discrimination.

## Self-conception, group membership, and intergroup behavior

Our first task is to define what we mean by 'intergroup behavior'. But in order to do this, we need to define what we mean by a group. Although there are many controversies and debates about how to define the social group (for example, compare Allport, 1924; Arrow et al., 2000; Tajfel and Turner, 1986; Taylor and Brown, 1979), we adopt the basically cognitive definition of the social group that underpins the social-identity perspective (for recent overviews, see Hogg, 2001a, 2003, 2006). Hence, in this chapter, there is a tight link between intergroup behavior, intergroup relations, and social identity. A group exists psychologically when two or more people define and evaluate themselves in terms of the defining and often prescriptive properties of a common self-inclusive category. However, it should be recognized that group life also involves social interaction, interdependent goals, and so forth. For example, Brown (2000: 3) suggests that 'a group exists when two or more people define themselves as members of it and when its existence is recognized by at least one other'. The idea that groups exist *in relation* to some social context is entirely consistent with Sherif's classic and relatively widely accepted definition of intergroup relations and intergroup behavior:

> Intergroup relations refer to relations between two or more groups and their respective members. Whenever individuals belonging to one group interact, collectively or individually, with another group or its members in terms of their group identifications we have an instance of intergroup behavior. (Sherif, 1962: 5)

What this definition implies is that we can count a wide range of behaviors as instances of intergroup behavior. These might include a football match, negotiation between representatives of different companies, summit meetings between nations, street fights between ethnic groups, racial ethnophaulisms, discriminatory comments made by one person about a member of a different group, and so forth. Intergroup behavior can span international, interethnic, interfamily, and interteam phenomena. Indeed, two individuals can be engaged in an exchange purely in terms of their memberships of different social categories, and so even this apparently interpersonal activity can be an instance of intergroup behavior.

## Personality and individual differences

Intergroup behavior tends to be competitive and ethnocentric. In intergroup contexts, people generally behave so as to gain or maintain an advantage for their own group over other groups in terms of resources, status, prestige, and so forth (e.g., Brewer and Campbell, 1976). Sumner described this beautifully when he defined ethnocentrism as:

> a view of things in which one's own group is the center of everything, and all others are scaled and rated with reference to it. [...] Each group nourishes its own pride and vanity, boasts itself superior, exalts its own divinities, and looks with contempt on outsiders. Each group thinks its own folkways the only right one. [...] Ethnocentrism leads a people to exaggerate and intensify everything in their own folkways which is peculiar and which differentiates them from others. (Sumner, 1906: 13)

Although intergroup relations are intrinsically ethnocentric, relations between groups can vary widely in the form and extremity of ethnocentrism – from harmless generalized images, tolerance, and friendly rivalry to entrenched hatred, intolerance, and violent conflict.

Because the latter form of intergroup behavior can be responsible for appalling injustices and inhumanities, the study of intergroup behavior has tended to focus on these extreme forms. Social psychologists, like many other people, have wondered whether there may be something 'wrong' with people who behave in this way – perhaps these people have dysfunctional personalities that are, perhaps, innate or tied to early childhood experiences, predisposing them to be extremely ethnocentric and intolerant. This perspective has produced one of social psychology's major and enduring theories of prejudice and intergroup conflict – Adorno et al.'s (1950) authoritarian personality syndrome (see also Titus and Hollander, 1957).

Adorno and colleagues adopted a psychodynamic framework to argue that early childhood rearing practices that are harsh, disciplinarian, and emotionally manipulative, produce people who are obsessed by status and authority, intolerant of ambiguity and uncertainty, and hostile and aggressive toward weaker others. These people have an authoritarian personality that predisposes them to extreme forms of intergroup behavior. Research on the authoritarian personality confirms the existence of such a syndrome but does not provide good evidence for its origins in early child-rearing or for its relationship to prejudice and discrimination. People who do not have an authoritarian personality can be prejudiced, and people who do have an authoritarian personality can be free of prejudice. From his classic study of authoritarianism and racism in South Africa and the USA, Pettigrew (1958) concluded that prejudice is less related to personality than it is to socialization within a culture of prejudice that legitimizes prejudice as the background to everyday life. This perspective is now widely accepted by social psychologists who study prejudice and intergroup relations (Billig, 1976; Reynolds et al., 2001).

Nevertheless, social psychologists have an enduring tendency to develop explanations of extreme and pathological behaviors, such as prejudice, in terms of extreme individuals who have extreme and perhaps pathological personalities. The notion of authoritarianism continues to be popular but with an emphasis on people's tendency to submit to in-group conventions and authority and to punish in-group deviants (Duckitt, 1989). Indeed, Altemeyer (1994) reports a series of studies demonstrating that right-wing authoritarianism is reliably associated with various forms of prejudice, and that right-wing authoritarians are quite resilient against attempts to challenge their values. In contrast to the psychodynamic explanation offered by Adorno et al. (1950), Altemeyer favors the view that social processes resulting in a combination of fearfulness and self-righteousness underpin right-wing authoritarians' stronger commitment to in-groups and intolerance of out-groups. In turn, right-wing authoritarians selectively expose themselves to a social circle that reinforces these perceptions.

Another 'individual-differences' explanation of prejudice is Rokeach's (1960) idea that some people have a dogmatic and closed-minded personality that predisposes them to ethnocentrism, intergroup intolerance, and prejudice. This distinction between dogmatic and closed-minded people relates to a entire catalog of similar individual differences that are less explicitly tied to explanations of prejudice – for example, need for structure and closure versus fear of invalidity (Kruglanski, 2004; Kruglanski and Webster, 1996), uncertainty orientation (Sorrentino and Roney, 1999), attributional complexity (Fletcher et al., 1986), need for cognition (Cacioppo and Petty, 1982), cognitive complexity (Crockett, 1965), self-concept clarity (Campbell et al., 1996), self-complexity (Linville, 1987), and self-compartmentalization (Showers, 1992).

Recently, Sidanius and Pratto and their associates have described a relatively sophisticated, but nonetheless 'individual-differences', analysis of exploitative power-based intergroup relations – called social-dominance theory (e.g., Pratto, 1999; Pratto et al., 1994; Sidanius and Pratto, 1999). Social-dominance theory explains the extent to which people accept or reject societal ideologies or myths that legitimize hierarchy and discrimination, or that legitimize equality and fairness. People who desire their own group to be dominant and superior to out-groups have a high social-dominance orientation that encourages them to reject egalitarian ideologies and to accept myths that legitimize hierarchy and discrimination. These kinds of people are more inclined to be prejudiced than are people who have a low social-dominance orientation. Moreover, as people become better educated, a high social-dominance orientation provides a basis for a more sophisticated brand of prejudice in which racism becomes more strongly associated with political conservatism (Sidanius et al., 1996).

Recent research on prejudice tends to focus on the subtle ways in which prejudice is often expressed when social norms and conventions outlaw prejudice. These *modern* forms of prejudice are discussed later in this chapter; however, it is worth noting here that this research has also produced a number of scales to measure individual differences. For example, there is the *modern racism scale* (e.g., McConahay, 1986) which identifies people who believe that there is actually very little racism in the USA and that black anger and societal support for black people are, therefore, unwarranted. There is also a scale that differentiates people in terms of how ambivalent their feelings are towards black people (see Katz et al., 1986). In the area of attitudes towards women, Swim et al. (1995) have developed a neosexism scale that differentiates between old-fashioned and modern sexists, and Glick and Fiske (1996) have developed an ambivalent sexism scale that differentiates between 'hostile' and 'benevolent' sexism.

As noted above, social psychologists emphasize an account of prejudice that focuses on socialization and cognitive processes, and the role of a culture of prejudice. This is because pure personality and individual-differences explanations of prejudice leave the context specificity and situational and temporal variability of prejudice poorly explained. Prejudices can change in form and strength rather faster than personality (that is, enduring properties of the individual that are largely uninfluenced by context) would be expected to change.

Although personality is traditionally conceptualized as an enduring disposition or stable set of traits that resides *within* individuals and causes behavior, other conceptualizations of individual differences take a more interactionist, situational, or functional perspective (see Snyder and Cantor, 1998): for example, the view that enduring regularities in a person's behavior may occur because the social context remains invariant. From this perspective, a prejudiced personality is one that is formed and fixed in place by a particular social context but also plays itself out in different contexts. Only enduring and radical contextual changes would modify personality. These more modern perspectives on personality that focus on an interaction between personality and social context are more versatile and can, to some extent, accommodate more modern approaches to the study of self-conception and its relationship to intergroup behavior. But one wonders if the interaction is actually between enduring contextual influences (for example, one's culture), and immediate situational influences (for example, an intergroup atrocity) – in which case, the notion of personality may be redundant. Increasingly, the measurement of individual differences is used to capture variations, within a particular context, in social attitudes or endorsement of different cultural values. These differences may have many different origins (such as, cultural, historical, and situational) and are not necessarily assumed to be stable across situations.

## Goal relations and interdependence

In contrast to those who emphasize personality and individual differences as an explanation of intergroup behavior – a bottom-up analysis – are those who emphasize the goal relations between groups or individuals – a top-down analysis. A champion of this perspective is Sherif, who maintained that 'we cannot extrapolate from the properties of individuals to the characteristics of group situations' (Sherif, 1962: 5). Building on Campbell's (e.g., Campbell, 1965) observation that much intergroup behavior reflects real or even rational competition between groups over scarce resources, Sherif proposed a *realistic conflict* or interdependence theory of intergroup relations. This was predicated on the belief that behavior is driven by goals and by people's perceptions of their relationship to one another with respect to achieving goals. If two groups have the same goal (such as prosperity), but the goal is such that one group can gain only at the expense of the other (there is a zero-sum goal relationship, with mutually exclusive goals, and negative interdependence between groups), intergroup relations will be competitive and lacking in harmony. If two groups have the same goal, and the goal is such that it can be achieved only if both groups work together (there is a non-zero-sum goal relationship, with a superordinate goal, and positive interdependence between groups), intergroup relations will be cooperative and harmonious. At the interpersonal level, mutually exclusive goals lead to interpersonal conflict and group dissolution, whereas superordinate goals lead to interpersonal harmony, group formation, and group cohesion.

This idea was initially tested by Sherif and his associates in a series of classic field experiments at boys' camps in the USA (see Sherif, 1958, 1966; Sherif et al., 1961; Sherif and Sherif, 1953). In these studies, Sherif varied goal relations between individuals and between groups and was able to create cohesive groups, intergroup conflict and hostility, and to some extent intergroup harmony. Variants of the boys'-camp paradigm have been used by other researchers (Fisher, 1990). For example, Blake and Mouton (1961) ran two-week studies with more than 1,000 business executives on management-training programs (also see Blake et al., 1964), and others have replicated Sherif's studies in different cultures (e.g., Andreeva, 1984; Diab, 1970). Because realistic-conflict theory is a top-down analysis of intergroup relations, it is metatheoretically consistent with more sociological analyses of social behavior. Not surprisingly, it has a substantial legacy in research that traces ethnic and race relations to perceived intergroup threat and to competition over scarce resources (e.g., Bobo, 1999; Bobo and Hutchings, 1996).

The idea that goal relations determine the complexion of intergroup behavior continues to be a powerful theme in social psychology – for example, in the work of Morton Deutsch (1949, 1973), in the field research of Brewer and Campbell (1976), in the research of Insko and associates on the individual–group discontinuity effect (Insko et al., 1992), and in the work of Rabbie on his behavioral interdependence model (e.g., Rabbie et al., 1989).

Insko and colleagues (Insko et al., 1992) argue that there is a discontinuity between interpersonal and intergroup behavior. In intergroup contexts, people are generally significantly more competitive and more oriented toward relative rather than absolute gain. This is because people have a general schema in which they distrust the out-group and assume the out-group will be competitive (motives driven by fear and greed prevail), and, therefore, people need to protect the in-group by being highly competitive themselves. One limitation of this analysis is that competitive intergroup behavior can occur even when people have indisputable evidence that the out-group will behave in a fair and noncompetitive manner (e.g., Diehl, 1989). This suggests that some motive other than fear or greed may underlie competitive intergroup behavior.

In a related vein, Rabbie and his colleagues (e.g., Rabbie et al., 1989) attribute intergroup competitiveness and discrimination to self-interest. In intergroup contexts, people believe that their own treatment (for example, reward allocation) is more heavily dependent on the behavior of fellow in-group members than out-group members. Self-interest ensures that people are fairer to in-group than out-group members. This generates the in-group favoritism and intergroup discrimination that characterize intergroup behavior. One limitation of this analysis comes from Diehl's (1989) research, mentioned above. Even when people have incontrovertible evidence that both in-group and out-group members will treat them fairly, they still show in-group bias. Much of the debate over the validity of Rabbie's behavioral interdependence model centers on the extent to which self-interest is or is not present in specific studies, and on what level of *self* is being referred to; individual self and personal identity or collective self and social identity – see Turner and Bourhis's (1996) commentary and critique.

Interdependence or realistic conflict approaches to intergroup behavior see conflict arising from situations where other groups threaten in-group goal achievement. There is, however, another form of threat. Out-group actions, or even the existence of an out-group, can pose a threat to the prestige or distinctiveness of one's own group and one's identity as a member of that group. This is a cognitive self-conceptual threat that can provoke a range of actions designed to protect the status of the group and the integrity of the group's boundaries. Some of these reactions include unfavorable reactions towards marginal or deviant in-group members (e.g., Marques et al., 2001a), increased pressures towards in-group uniformity and homogeneity (e.g., Branscombe et al., 1993; Jetten et al., 1997), and adoption of strategies designed to consolidate or improve the group's status (e.g., Ellemers, 1993).

Goals and goal relations play a critical role in intergroup behavior, and are an important component of social psychological explanations of intergroup relations. There is little doubt that groups that can see themselves only as competing over a zero-sum resource are likely to have conflictual intergroup relations, and that this relationship could be improved if those groups could view themselves only as having superordinate goals or non-zero-sum goal relations. There are, however, some general limitations to an analysis of intergroup behavior that focuses exclusively on goal relations and realistic conflict between groups. Most significant is probably the fact that research shows negative goal interdependence not to be sufficient to produce competitive intergroup behavior. It is often the case that negative goal interdependence produces competitive intergroup behavior only among people who identify more strongly with their group (Turner, 1981). For example, Struch and Schwartz (1989) found, among religious groups in Israel, a significant correlation between intergroup hostility and perceived conflict of interests only among those people who strongly identified with their religious group.

## Social categorization

The idea that in-group identification or belonging may directly produce competitive intergroup behavior, in the absence of competitive goal relations, can be taken further. The mere recognition that different social categories exist, and the feeling that one belongs to one of them may be sufficient. The very existence of separate categories may generate competitive behaviors automatically (cf. Otten, 2003). After all, social categorization is the foundation of intergroup behavior – behavior *between* groups can occur only if the social world can be categorized into separate groups (see Ehrlich, 1973; Hogg, 2001a).

### *Minimal groups*

This idea was investigated in a series of *minimal-group* experiments originally conducted in the late 1960s (e.g., Tajfel, 1970; Tajfel et al., 1971), but now replicated countless times (see Diehl, 1990). Minimal-group studies are laboratory experiments in which people are categorized into two groups, ostensibly either randomly or on the basis of some trivial criterion. They then allocate resources (often only points) between anonymous members of their group and anonymous members of the out-group, and complete various other measures about their feelings about themselves, their group, and the other group. The groups have no prior history and no future, there is no interaction, there is no material gain for individuals from membership, and people do not know who is in their group or in the other group. The robust finding from these experiments is that, relative to people who are not explicitly categorized, people who are categorized discriminate in favor of their group, show evaluative in-group bias (ethnocentrism), and indicate that they feel a sense of belonging to their group, and similarity to and liking for their anonymous fellow in-group members.

From the minimal-group studies, it seemed that competitive intergroup behavior might be an intrinsic feature of the mere existence of a social categorization into in-group and out-group. Competitive goal relations might accentuate the effect or serve as a criterion for the existence of categories, but there is clearly a deeper social-cognitive dynamic at play. This finding and its conceptual implications were a key catalyst for the development of social-identity theory, described below. Subsequent research has identified a number of factors that moderate the minimal intergroup discrimination effect (see below).

### *Automatic schema activation*

People cognitively represent physical or social categories as schemas that describe the attributes of the category and the relationships among those attributes. Category schemas vary from concrete exemplars of the category to abstract fuzzy sets of loosely related attributes (prototypes) (e.g., Rosch, 1978). Categories themselves vary in entitativity – the degree to which they have the properties of a tightly organized, distinctive, and cohesive, unitary construct (e.g., Hamilton and Sherman, 1996).

Social-cognition researchers describe how perceptual cues, particularly distinctive visual cues (Zebrowitz, 1996), cause us to categorize people and to imbue them with the properties that are described by our schema of that group (e.g., Fiske and Taylor, 1991; Hamilton and Sherman, 1994). The entire process can be deliberate, but, in general, it is automatic. Stereotyping of out-group members may be largely an automatic categorization-contingent process that we have little control over (Bargh, 1994; Devine, 1989; Greenwald and Banaji, 1995). It even occurs where the groups are only minimally defined (e.g., Ashburn-Nardo et al., 2001). Other research suggests that the process may be moderated by a number of factors, including the extent to which someone is prejudiced (e.g., Lepore and Brown, 1997; Monteith et al., 2001).

One controversial line of investigation suggests that if people consciously think about the automatic category-stereotype link, ostensibly to disrupt the automaticity of stereotyping, the process paradoxically strengthens the link and increases automatic stereotype activation (Macrae et al., 1994). Although conscious stereotype suppression may not always be as effective as one initially might suppose, other research suggests that people may nevertheless be able to learn how to control automatic stereotype activation and use through practice and efforts at deautomatization (Monteith and Voils, 2001).

### *Accentuation and illusory correlation effects*

Another effect of social categorization is that it causes us perceptually to accentuate similarities among members of the same category and differences between categories. This appears to be a general consequence of categorization (Tajfel, 1959), but one that is asymmetrical because we tend to see out-groups as more homogeneous than in-groups (e.g., Judd and Park, 1988; Quattrone, 1986) irrespective of whether our own group is lower or higher in status than the out-group (Brauer, 2001). A popular explanation for this asymmetry is that we are more familiar with the in-group and therefore have more individuating information about in-group than out-group members (Linville et al., 1989). Other research has questioned this explanation (e.g., Jones et al., 1981), Simon and Brown (1987) showing that relative homogeneity effects may be influenced by strategic considerations. For example, active minorities often consider themselves to be relatively more homogeneous than the majority out-group – this is clearly quite functional, as such groups need to be consistent, consensual, and unified in order to survive and have a chance at initiating social change. Research on minority influence shows that active minorities need to be synchronically and diachronically consistent in order to be able to change the attitudes of the majority (e.g., Maass and Clark, 1984; Moscovici, 1980; Mugny, 1982).

Related to the accentuation effect is the illusory correlation effect (e.g., Hamilton and Gifford, 1976), in which people associate distinctive or rare behaviors with distinctive or rare categories – thus laying a foundation for erroneously correlating negative attributes, which are often subjectively rare, with minority groups. Subsequent research suggests that although illusory correlation, as an automatic associative bias, may well underpin intergroup evaluative biases (such as stereotypes) in information-poor contexts, stereotyping is more often highly functional in providing a self-evaluative advantage for one's own group and thus oneself (e.g., Oakes et al., 1994).

## Self and social identity

Social categorization segments the social world into groups and cognitively represents such groups in terms of schemas, usually in the form of prototypes. Social categorization profoundly affects person perception, but also, as shown by the minimal group studies described above, influences how we behave. To explore fully the relationship between social categorization and the entire array of behaviors we associate with groups and intergroup relations, we need to invoke the self-concept. After all, when we categorize other people, perhaps we also categorize self. The self provides an anchor for judgments and reactions to the in-group, and indeed the in-group becomes a part of the self (Cadinu and Rothbart, 1996; Otten, 2003; Smith and Henry, 1996). The link between social categorization, self-conception, and group and intergroup behavior is most fully explored by the social-identity perspective (e.g., Hogg and Abrams, 1988; Tajfel and Turner, 1986; Turner et al., 1987) – for recent overviews, see Abrams and Hogg (2001) and Hogg (2001a, 2003, 2006). The social-identity perspective has a number of integrated conceptual components – for example, a focus on the structure of self and identity (e.g., Abrams, 1996; Turner, 1982), a focus on social-comparison processes (see Hogg, 2000a), a focus on self-enhancement motivation (e.g., Abrams and Hogg, 1988), a focus on uncertainty-reduction motivation (Hogg, 2000b, 2007), a focus on social-influence processes (see Turner, 1991), a focus on the role of beliefs about intergroup relations (Tajfel and Turner, 1986), and a focus on the generative role of the categorization process (Turner et al., 1987).

The social-identity perspective argues that people define and evaluate themselves in terms of the groups to which they belong – groups provide people with a collective self-concept, a social identity, and people have as many social identities as the groups to which they feel they belong. Social identity is clearly differentiated from personal identity, which is tied to interpersonal relationships and idiosyncratic personal traits (see Hogg, 2001c; Hogg and Williams, 2000; cf. Brewer and Gardner, 1996). Because social identities define, prescribe, and evaluate who one is and how one should think, feel, and act, people have a strong desire to establish or maintain the evaluative superiority of their own group over relevant other groups – there is an intergroup struggle for evaluatively positive group distinctiveness.

This struggle is, however, tempered by people's understanding of the nature of the relations between their group and relevant out-groups – their social belief systems. In particular, people pay attention to status differences and the stability and legitimacy of such differences, to the permeability of intergroup boundaries and thus the possibility of passing psychologically from one group to another, and to the existence of achievable alternatives to the status quo (Ellemers et al., 1999). When there are opportunities for individuals to move between groups of differing status, members of low-status groups are likely to seize these opportunities (van Knippenberg and Ellemers, 1993), but members of high-status groups are likely to be motivated to preserve their group membership (Ellemers et al., 1992). Moreover, members of high-status groups are generally more likely to show in-group bias on status-relevant dimensions, but members of lower-status groups are likely to show in-group bias on status-irrelevant dimensions (Mullen et al., 1992). Thus, the evidence suggests that groups and their members act strategically (Abrams, 1994b) to sustain positive social identity, within the bounds of what is possible and legitimate (we describe responses to illegitimate intergroup status relations below). When the power or status of a dominant group is under threat, perhaps because it is in a numerical minority, it is particularly likely to respond with acts of prejudice or discrimination against the subordinate group (Sachdev and Bourhis, 1991).

For social-identity theory, group behaviors (conformity, stereotyping, ethnocentrism, in-group favoritism, intergroup discrimination, in-group cohesion, etc.), as distinct from interpersonal behaviors, occur when social identity is the salient basis of self-conceptualization, and the content of group behavior rests on the specific social identity that is salient. Social identity is context specific insofar as different social identities are salient in different social contexts, and the same social identity may take a different form as a function of contextual demands (Abrams, 1992, 1996; Oakes et al., 1994).

Social-identity processes are cognitively generated by social categorization of self and others. People represent groups as prototypes – multidimensional fuzzy sets of attributes that describe and prescribe perceptions, thoughts, feelings, and actions that define the in-group and distinguish it from relevant out-groups. The configuration of a prototype is governed by the metacontrast principle. Prototypes form and are modified in a given social comparative context to maximize differences between categories but also to minimize differences within categories – they optimize the ratio of intercategory differences to intracategory differences, and thus maximize entitativity (Hogg, 2006). The cognitive-perceptual system selects, and forms prototypes around, attributes that identify similarities among people in the same group, and differences between people from different groups.

Social categorization perceptually assimilates people to the relevant in-group or out-group prototype and causes people to be viewed not as unique individual people, but through the lens of category membership – a process referred to as *depersonalization*. Depersonalization simply refers to a change in the basis of perception. It does not, in itself, have the negative connotations of terms such as *deindividuation*, which refers to loss of identity and its automatic link to irresponsible and antisocial behaviors (e.g., Zimbardo, 1970), or *dehumanization* (e.g., Haslam, 2006), which refers to the perception and treatment of other people as essentially nonhuman (e.g., Leyens et al., 2000). Applied to self, social categorization has the same effect as the categorization of other people – it transforms self-conception so that people feel like group members, and it depersonalizes attitudes, feelings, and behaviors such that they conform to the in-group prototype. Thus, self-categorization is the fundamental requirement for conformity, normative behavior, and the rest of the constellation of group and intergroup behaviors.

The social-identity perspective has made a great impact on the social psychology of intergroup relations and has also contributed significantly to a revival of research on group processes in general (see Abrams and Hogg, 1998; Moreland et al., 1994). Some of the most recent developments in social-identity research are covered in recently edited books, for example, Abrams and Hogg (1999), Capozza and Brown (2000), Ellemers et al. (1999), Hogg and Terry (2001), Postmes and Jetten (2006), and Worchel et al. (1998).

## Motivation and affect

### *Motivation*

Why do people engage in intergroup behavior? To answer this question, we actually need to ask the more fundamental question of what motivates people to identify with groups in the first place and then what motivates specific forms of intergroup behavior. One answer is in terms of specific goals that people or groups may want to achieve – goals that can be achieved only by interpersonal or intergroup cooperative interaction (superordinate goals), or goals that are mutually exclusive and can be achieved only by interpersonal or intergroup competition. Functional theories of intergroup relations, such as that proposed by Sherif (e.g., 1958) fall in this camp (see above).

Personality approaches such as Adorno et al.'s (1950) authoritarian personality or Rokeach's (1960) dogmatic personality treat people's need to compartmentalize their social world as a core aspect of authoritarianism or dogmatism. Authoritarian or dogmatic people are therefore motivated to discriminate starkly between groups, and, in the case of authoritarianism, to displace negative feelings onto lower-status out-groups (see above). Theories of why people affiliate in the first place have produced a range of motives, of which social-reality testing through social comparison is an important one (e.g., Festinger, 1954) – people come together with similar others to obtain validation from individual others for their perceptions, attitudes, and feelings. Terror management is another motive for affiliation (e.g., Greenberg et al., 1997) – people affiliate with others because they fear death. Baumeister and Leary (1995) argue that people simply have a fundamental need to belong that underpins the existence of groups and the way in which groups struggle against one another for survival – the consequences of not belonging, or of being ostracized can be quite extreme (Williams, 2001). Finally, there is a plethora of motivational accounts for why people construe themselves in particular ways (see Sedikides and Strube, 1997).

Social-categorization research tends to focus on contextual factors that cause us to categorize ourselves and others in particular ways, and on the consequences of categorizing in that way. One very fundamental motive for social categorization, which also underpins categorization more generally, is a need to structure our subjective environment in contextually meaningful ways that reduce uncertainty and allow us to predict people's behavior, plan our own actions, and locate ourselves relative to other people (e.g., Abrams and Hogg, 2001; Hogg, 2000b, 2001b, 2007). People are more likely to identify with groups when they are faced by self-conceptual uncertainty – for example, Schmitt and Branscombe (2001) found that men whose male prototypicality had been challenged felt more threatened and behaved in ways that reaffirmed their male identity. When uncertainty is very high, people may seek out totalist groups that are highly orthodox, have simple and consensual prototypes, high entitativity, and strong, charismatic leaders, and engage in extreme forms of intergroup behavior (e.g., Hogg, 2004, 2005).

This analysis allows us to understand why disadvantaged groups may acquiesce in their position rather than struggle for change – change may improve status, but it will also introduce uncertainty (also see Jost and Banaji, 1994; Jost and Burgess, 2000; Jost and Kramer, 2002). It also allows us to understand why groups whose distinctiveness is threatened may sometimes react in ways that are aimed, not so much at improving status as raising entitativity and cohesion in order to provide a secure and clear social identity (e.g., Hamilton and Sherman, 1996). One way this may be achieved is through control over deviant group members (e.g., Marques and Páez, 1994). For example, Marques et al. (2001b) conducted three experiments to show that in-group deviants were generally derogated more strongly when in-group identity was threatened in various ways relating to in-group normative consensus and consistency. Schmitt and Branscombe (2001) found that highly identified men showed greater differential liking for high than low male prototypical men, when they themselves had their male prototypicality challenged than not challenged. However, groups are not always threatened by diversity or nonconformity. For example, Abrams et al. (2000) showed that deviance is tolerated or even welcomed by group members if it does not lend legitimacy to out-group norms. Conversely, deviant out-group members are evaluated positively if they lend legitimacy to in-group norms.

Another powerful intergroup motive is self-enhancement. According to social-identity theory, intergroup behavior is motivated by a struggle between groups to promote or protect their evaluatively positive distinctiveness from one another, and thus secure a relatively favorable social identity. People engage in this struggle because, at the individual level, group membership mediates self-evaluation via social identity, and people tend to be motivated to feel good about themselves – to have a positive sense of self-esteem (e.g., Sedikides and Strube, 1997). In intergroup contexts, self-esteem may motivate social-identity processes, but how this is pursued is significantly affected by social conventions, social-belief systems, and cultural differences (see Abrams and Hogg, 1988; Heine et al., 1999; Long and Spears, 1997; Rubin and Hewstone, 1998). An alternative view is that self-esteem may not motivate intergroup behavior, but, rather, act as a psychological monitor, or 'sociometer', of satisfaction of other motives to do with social connectedness and belonging (e.g., Leary et al., 1995).

What is the optimal level of distinctiveness among people? According to some researchers, the individual self is motivationally primary when it comes to reactions to threat and opportunities for self-enhancement (Gaertner et al., 1999, 2002). However, according to Brewer's (1991) theory of optimal distinctiveness, people simultaneously strive to be the same as other people (assimilation/inclusiveness) and different from other people (differentiation/uniqueness). Because these are contrasting human motives, the equilibrium state is one of optimal distinctiveness. Oversatisfaction of one motive engages the contrasting motive to reinstate optimal distinctiveness. For example, Pickett and Brewer (2001) conducted an experiment in which they aroused assimilation and differentiation needs by threatening intragroup standing and intergroup distinctiveness. As predicted, they found, relative to controls, heightened perceptions of in-group and out-group homogeneity, greater perceived in-group stereotypicality, and a tendency to be more restrictive in defining in-group membership. These behaviors enhance intragroup assimilation and intergroup contrast, and serve the need for increased inclusion within the in-group and the need for increased intergroup distinctiveness.

Group size may have a role to play in optimal distinctiveness. Large groups tend to make people feel insufficiently distinctive, whereas very small groups tend to make people feel too distinctive. Optimal distinctiveness is, therefore, best satisfied by intergroup contexts in which the in-group is not overly large – there is sufficient intergroup and intragroup distinctiveness to balance in-group assimilation. For example, from a survey of political affiliations of over 4,000 eighteen- to twenty-one-year-olds in the UK, Abrams (1994a) found greater identification with smaller (minority) political parties (such as the Scottish Nationalist Party) than with larger majority parties. Abrams argued that minority parties might attract members through their capacity to provide a meaningful and distinctive social identity.

Generally speaking, there is good evidence that threats to group integrity or group valence, and thus to self-conception and self-evaluation, motivate protective reactions. For example, we can distinguish between four different types of social identity threat that can be experienced – categorization threat, distinctiveness threat, threats to the value of social identity, and acceptance threat (e.g., Branscombe et al., 1999). Depending on the type of threat, people's strength of identification with the group, and on the available material and psychological resources, protective reactions can manifest themselves as intergroup conflict, 'backlash', more subtle forms of intergroup behavior, or as dis-identification (e.g., Branscombe et al., 1993; Ethier and Deaux, 1994). For example, self-affirmation theory (Steele, 1988) describes how people whose identity in one domain is evaluatively threatened engage in practices that publicly affirm a favorable identity in another domain.

### *Affect*

Perhaps due to the success of social-cognition and social-categorization perspectives on intergroup relations, there has been a tendency for social psychologists to underemphasize the affective aspect of intergroup behavior. This is problematic, given that the most troublesome aspects of intergroup behavior are precisely those that involve strong emotions, and powerful affect. Not only do people often have negative stereotypes and feelings towards out-groups, but they often experience anxiety and discomfort about interacting with stigmatized out-groups. This anxiety can stem directly from (anticipated) negative outcomes such as embarrassment, rejection, and ridicule (Stephan and Stephan, 1985) and, more indirectly, from worry about how to behave and about possibly betraying deep-seated negative feelings (e.g., Katz et al., 1986). Trying hard to suppress negative out-group feelings or to hide their expression can be particularly stressful (Devine, 1989; Monteith, 1993). Where deep-seated negative out-group feelings clash with a cherished egalitarian, nonprejudiced, value system, prejudice can take a form that Gaertner and Dovidio (1986) call *aversive prejudice* (see below) – prejudice sometimes inadvertently leaks out in unconventional and convoluted ways.

There has been a recent resurgence of interest in affective aspects of intergroup behavior (Mackie and Smith, 2002) that focuses mainly on intergroup emotions (Mackie et al., 2000; Smith, 1993, 1999). For example, Smith (1993) argues that in intergroup contexts where social identity is salient, people interpret events in terms of whether they benefit or harm the in-group rather than the self, and these appraisals dictate emotional and behavioral reactions to the events. Prejudice is, thus, a context- and appraisal-specific social emotion. So, for example, whether one feels anger, fear, or contempt towards an out-group has been shown to depend on strength of in-group identification, and perceptions of the strength of the in-group relative to the out-group (Mackie et al., 2000).

Another example of intergroup emotion research is research on collective guilt. Branscombe et al. (2002) examine how a dominant group experiences collective guilt if members identify strongly with the group, the identity is central to self-conception, and members believe that the group's position of superiority is illegitimate because it rests on the group's violation of a moral value that the group adheres to. The pivotal factor here is the recognition of status illegitimacy. Doosje et al. (1998) report an experiment in which they were able to elicit group-based guilt that was quite separate from personal guilt. They also report a field study in which low-identified group members acknowledged the negative aspects of their own nation's history and felt more guilt than high identifiers, when both negative and positive aspects of their nation's history were made salient. Because positive aspects of history were salient, unlike in the Branscombe et al. (2002) study, high identifiers were not confronted with having to recognize the illegitimacy of their group's status, and thus they did not experience collective guilt.

Much of the analysis of intergroup affect and emotion rests on the notion of depersonalization that underpins the social-identity perspective (described above). People in salient groups feel other people's emotions as their own because self-categorization merges self and other via prototype-based depersonalization – people experience, or include, the other as part of the self (e.g., Tropp and Wright, 2001; Wright et al., 2002). In this way, intergroup feelings (which are often negative) can readily become powerfully consensual collective intergroup feelings. Similarly, positive in-group feelings can change into consensual positive regard and in-group solidarity (e.g., Hogg, 1993).

## Intergroup attitudes and prejudice

### *Stereotyping and prejudice*

Earlier, we saw how categories are cognitively represented as schemas or prototypes, and that the link between category cues, categorization, and prototype-based perception of self and others is relatively automatic – the process of stereotyping that we normally associate with out-group perceptions and prejudice. However, stereotypes, although held by individuals who apply them to out-groups, need to be understood more broadly as widely shared intergroup attitudes (Tajfel, 1981) that act as theories (e.g., von Hippel et al., 1995) or social representations (see Farr and Moscovici, 1984) of the attributes of other groups. Tajfel (1981), in particular, makes a strong case for the various social functions that stereotypes serve. For example, he explains how stereotypes may emerge to justify actions that have been committed or planned by one group against another group. If one group exploits another group, it may be useful to justify this action by developing a stereotype of the out-group as unsophisticated and dependent. In this way, the world appears a just place in which bad things happen to bad people, and good things to good people (e.g., Lerner and Miller, 1978). Indeed, the out-group may be subjected to infrahumanization, a perception that they do not share the more subtle emotions associated with humanness (Leyens et al., 2001). Stereotypes become more extreme and more resistant to change under conditions of intergroup conflict.

### *Subtle and modern forms of prejudice*

Stereotypes are not simply shared intergroup attitudes, but are intergroup attitudes that take their form from the wider sociohistorical context in which a specific intergroup relationship exists. They are also affected by the wider normative and legislative environment in which intergroup relations exist. So, for example, racist attitudes may assume different forms depending on whether the normative environment is one that suppresses overt racism or one that supports overt racism. In addition, we have already seen how people may have ambivalent intergroup feelings that cause anxiety and discomfort. A number of researchers have investigated these ideas and developed theories of modern or subtle forms of prejudice – the focus is mainly on racism in the USA, but there is some research on sexism (Glick and Fiske, 1996; Swim et al., 1995) and homophobia (Haddock et al., 1993).

Theories of modern or subtle forms of prejudice come in a number of forms – for example, symbolic racism (Kinder and Sears, 1981), aversive racism (Gaertner and Dovidio, 1986), and ambivalent racism (e.g., Katz et al., 1986) and ambivalent sexism (Glick and Fiske, 1996). There is, however, a common analysis underlying these theories (e.g., Dovidio and Gaertner, 1996, 1998; McConahay, 1986). In Western societies, there is a long history of racism that produces deep-seated racial prejudice, fears, and suspicions. However, there is also a tradition of tolerance and egalitarianism that in recent years has become enshrined by social norms and by legislation to suppress racist behavior. For many people, therefore, there is an uncomfortable psychological conflict between two sets of contrasting attitudes. People tend to resolve the conflict by avoiding the racial out-group, avoiding the issue of race, denying the existence of disadvantage, opposing preferential treatment, and so forth. In many sectors of society, this 'modern' form has replaced overt forms of racism.

The different theories of modern prejudice have different emphases. Symbolic racism (Kinder and Sears, 1981) focuses on the way that racist attitudes can be concealed behind espousal of traditional values (such as fairness) and policy preferences (such as opposition to affirmative action) that appear only incidentally to disadvantage black people. Ambivalent racism (e.g., Katz et al., 1986) focuses on the way that whites' conflicted feelings about blacks are grounded in fundamental value systems (egalitarianism, humanism, and the work ethic). The ambivalence often produces extreme responses – disproportionate praise of black altruism, and disproportionate condemnation of black incompetence. Aversive racism (e.g., Gaertner and Dovidio, 1986) focuses on the way that egalitarians cannot admit their racism to themselves – they avoid behaving in an overtly racist manner. However, when racist behavior has an obvious nonracial explanation or when situational norms are weak or confusing, aversive racists can behave in a racist manner without damaging their nonracist self-image.

### *Social explanation*

Stereotyping also has an attribution dimension (Hewstone and Jaspars, 1982). Pettigrew (1979) draws on classic attribution theory, in particular Ross's (1977) fundamental attribution error (people overattribute others' behavior to dispositions – and their own behavior to the situation) to describe what he calls the ultimate attribution error. The ultimate attribution error is a group-level attribution in which people behave ethnocentrically. Good acts are attributed dispositionally if performed by an in-group member and situationally if performed by an out-group member, and vice versa for bad acts. Research conducted in India (Taylor and Jaggi, 1974) and Malaysia (Hewstone and Ward, 1985) certainly supports this analysis.

A particularly disturbing aspect of intergroup attributions is the tendency to attribute unfavorable out-group attributes to underlying dispositions or essences. This is a process that transforms intergroup attitudes into immutable properties or essences of out-groups and their members (see Medin and Ortony, 1989). Miller and Prentice

(1999) argue that intergroup perceptions that rest on such essentialism create insurmountable category divides than can make it extremely difficult to improve intergroup relations – they cite examples drawn from the Balkans, Northern Ireland, and the Middle East.

## Discrimination

Intergroup relations are not just about attitudes and explanations. They are, as we have already seen, about how one group behaves towards another group. The main behavioral feature of intergroup relations is discrimination, which can range from relatively innocuous in-group favoritism, through name-calling and verbal abuse, to systematic intergroup violence and genocide. A key question is what is the relationship between intergroup attitudes and intergroup behavior – a question that is part of the broader attitude–behavior issue.

Attitude–behavior research reveals that people's attitudes and their behavior do not often correspond very closely (see Eagly and Chaiken, 1993). For example, LaPiere's (1934) classic study of attitudes towards Chinese-Americans revealed that although a young Chinese-American couple was hardly ever denied service at hotels and restaurants across the USA, almost all those same establishments subsequently expressed the strong anti-Chinese sentiment that they would not serve Chinese people. The research was conducted mainly in the western USA where, at the time, anti-Chinese sentiment was strongest. As we have seen above, unfavorable intergroup attitudes can be well concealed when a normative environment exists that proscribes prejudice or that mutates it into modern forms (Crosby et al., 1980).

Because the absence of overt discrimination may not indicate the absence of underlying negative intergroup sentiments, a great challenge for social psychology is to be able to detect prejudice in environments in which the expression of prejudice is normatively (and often legally) prohibited. The key seems to be to use unobtrusive measures – if people do not know they are being observed or measured, they are more likely to behave in accordance with their attitudes (Crosby et al., 1980). Other methods involve the careful analysis of the subtext of what people say in natural conversation (e.g., van Dijk, 1987) or the analysis of behaviors that people have little or no conscious control over (e.g., Brauer et al., 2000; Dovidio et al., 1997; Fazio et al., 1986; Maass, 1999; Maass et al., 2000, Vanman et al., 1997).

Discriminatory behavior is, however, rather easy to obtain in minimal group studies (Tajfel, 1970), probably because the groups have no history, and thus no social norms exist to proscribe discrimination against minimal groups. This research has sometimes been interpreted as leading to the rather gloomy prognosis for humanity that, all things being equal, social categorization per se leads to discrimination. Fortunately, this inference is not completely accurate. Social categorization may be a necessary condition for intergroup discrimination, but it is not sufficient. A series of minimal group experiments by Hogg (2000b) has shown that people need to internalize the social categorization as a context-specific self-definition – people need to self-categorize in order to engage in minimal intergroup discrimination. This research shows that people identify with a minimal categorization if they are in a state of subjective uncertainty. More generally, Hogg (2000b, 2007) argues that subjective uncertainty reduction is an important motivation for self-categorization and social-identity processes. Other minimal group research has shown that whether people discriminate or not is influenced by the available dimension of discrimination. For example, there is a positive–negative asymmetry effect (Otten et al., 1996; Wenzel and Mummendey, 1996) in which people discriminate against out-groups when they are giving rewards. People do not discriminate when they are giving punishments, unless their group is under threat by being disadvantaged or being in a minority position.

We should also remind ourselves that 'real' groups exist in a sociohistorical context that contains wider societal norms that prescribe, proscribe, or direct discriminatory behavior. Furthermore, people have social belief systems relating to status stability and legitimacy, intergroup permeability, and realistic alternatives to the status quo (e.g., Ellemers, 1993; Hinkle and Brown, 1990; Jetten et al., 2002; Tajfel and Turner, 1986). In the pursuit of positive social identity, these beliefs influence the form that intergroup behavior takes.

Although discrimination is often viewed unfavorably from the perspective of liberal democratic societies, and from the perspective of dominant groups who experience collective guilt (Branscombe et al., 2002; see above), in-groups generally view discrimination positively – discrimination indicates in-group loyalty and commitment. People seem prepared to accept and even praise unfair or unjust practices when they are directed towards out-groups. However, the story is very different when such behavior is directed toward the in-group (cf. Hornsey, 2005; Hornsey et al., 2002). Tyler and his colleagues (e.g., Tyler et al., 1996) provide evidence that people in groups are not overly concerned about having less than fellow group members (distributive inequality), but they are very concerned about being treated fairly (procedural justice). In-group procedural fairness signifies respect, and is an important influence on members' sense of belonging and, thus, the extent to which they bond with the group.

One implication of Tyler's analysis is that intergroup discrimination can serve a strategic function. The primary audience for discriminatory behavior may be the in-group – people may overtly discriminate against an out-group in order to bolster their own in-group credentials and standing. For instance, jingoistic rhetoric and overt out-group discrimination on the part of leaders may serve this function (e.g., Rabbie and Bekkers, 1978; Reicher and Hopkins, 1986), as may the publicly verifiable nature of delinquent behavior (Emler and Reicher, 1995). Leaders may also, under some circumstances, behave in ways that represent relatively extreme intergroup behavior. For example, according to the social-identity analysis of leadership (e.g., Hogg, 2001d; Hogg and van Knippenberg, 2003), as people identify more strongly with a group – for example, in a charged intergroup context or under conditions of threat or uncertainty – effective leadership becomes increasingly influenced by group prototypicality. Highly prototypical members are more likely to be endorsed as leaders, and leaders, particularly those who feel that they are not sufficiently prototypical, may overtly behave in a highly prototypical manner, which includes pronounced in-group favoritism and intergroup discrimination, in order to affirm their membership credentials.

## Stigma and disadvantage

The power and status inequalities that almost always exist between groups in society have far-reaching consequences, and are in many ways the essential problem of intergroup relations. If intergroup relations were characterized by groups of equal status and power, disadvantage and all that flows from it would not be present. As it is, intergroup relations are almost always associated with differential status, power, prestige, resources, and so forth. Dominant, majority groups do well out of this arrangement, and their members generally experience a positive sense of identity and esteem. Subordinate, minority groups do not do so well, and their members can carry a stigma that has quite profound effects on self-conception. 'Stigmatized individuals possess (or are believed to possess) some attribute, or characteristic, that conveys a social identity that is devalued in a particular social context' (Crocker et al., 1998: 505). Stigmas can be visible (race) or concealable (sexual orientation), and can vary in perceived controllability (race has low controllability, whereas obesity has high controllability). Stigma visibility and perceived controllability affect the extent and form of prejudice or discrimination that a member of a stigmatized group suffers. For example, Crandall (1994) has shown that fat people attract strong negative reactions in contemporary Western cultures not only because obesity is highly stigmatized, but also because people believe obesity is controllable.

Because stigmatized groups know exactly the negative stereotypes that others have of them, they experience what Steele and Aronson (1995) have called stereotype threat. Stigmatized individuals are aware that others may judge and treat them stereotypically, and thus, on tasks that really matter to them, they worry that through their behavior they may confirm the stereotypes. This worry can interfere with and thus impair task performance. Stigmatized people can also suffer attributional ambiguity – continually wondering whether it is prejudice that drives people's treatment of them (Crocker and Major, 1989). Stigmatized groups suffer material and social disadvantage, and can find that their goals and aspirations are continually frustrated relative to other groups. A sense of reduced efficacy and motivation can eventually set in, and rather than fight for change, groups can sometimes acquiesce in these conditions – some groups can prefer disadvantage to the uncertainties and dangers of engaging in a struggle for social change (e.g., Jost and Kramer, 2002). By the language of Higgins's (1998) regulatory focus theory, groups may change their regulatory focus from a focus on promotion – in this case, a proactive struggle to banish stigma – to a focus on prevention – in this case, a reactive attempt to minimize stigma.

In general, although some stigmatized individuals are vulnerable to low self-esteem, diminished life satisfaction, and, in some cases, depression, most members of stigmatized groups are able to weather the assaults and maintain a positive self-image (Crocker and Major, 1989, 1994). One way in which this is accomplished is by denying personal disadvantage. Although stigmatized groups are clearly disadvantaged, members of those groups often deny any personal experience of discrimination (e.g., Major, 1994; Taylor et al., 1994). For example, Crosby (1982, 1984) found that employed women who were clearly discriminated against with respect to pay rarely indicated that they personally had experienced sex discrimination.

## Collective action and social protest

Although disadvantaged or stigmatized groups have an impressive armory of protective or avoidant strategies to redirect energy from direct intergroup conflict, this is not always effective. When deprivation is very acute and a recipe for effective social change is available, disadvantaged groups will eagerly challenge the status quo by political means, or through social protest or other collective behaviors, including demonstrations, riots, and uprisings.

### *Crowds and riots*

According to theories that focus on frustration and relative deprivation, disadvantaged groups will engage in protest only when they actually experience acute frustration. For example, Berkowitz (1972) offered a detailed analysis of how riots may occur. He suggested that in addition to a sense of frustration there needed to be three other conditions:

1 aversive environmental circumstances that would amplify chronic frustration, such as heat and overcrowding;
2 aggressive environmental cues that would introduce a social learning component, such as armed police;
3 a social presence that would engage a social facilitation process, such as many people assembled in the streets.

Berkowitz emphasized the automatic, emotional, and impulsive aspects of collective behavior – he is famous for his 'long, hot summer' analysis of the late-1960s urban race riots in the USA that mainly occurred during heat waves.

Reicher (1984, 2001) provides a quite different analysis of the crowd. He adopts a social-identity perspective to argue that crowd behavior is a set of deliberate and logical actions that are directly related to the goals and objectives of the group that defines the social identity of the crowd. The apparent volatility of crowd behavior is less extreme than media reports lead one to believe, occurs within limits set by the crowd's identity, and reflects a search for situation-specific behaviors that are consistent with the wider identity of the group.

### *Collective action and social change*

Although disadvantage, particularly acute disadvantage, can translate into riots and demonstrations, it also, of course, sponsors enduring campaigns for social change, campaigns that can last decades or even centuries. Relative deprivation researchers (e.g., Davis, 1959; see Walker and Pettigrew, 1984) suggest that disadvantage translates into social action when people suddenly become aware that their expectations and attainments have parted company; in particular, when there is a sudden drop in attainments against a background of rising expectations (Davies, 1969; Gurr, 1970). These conditions have been invoked to explain the rise of anti-Semitism in 1930s Europe, the respective French and Russian revolutions of 1789 and 1917, the American Civil War of the 1860s, and the Black Power movement of the 1960s.

However, as explained earlier, although collective action and social protest are aimed at improvements in social standing, minority groups often avoid collective action because of the specter of self-conceptual and wider uncertainty that such behavior raises (e.g., Hogg, 2000b, 2007). Instead, groups often engage in behaviors designed to justify the existing social order (e.g., Jost and Kramer, 2002).

Runciman (1966) introduced an important distinction between fraternalistic (intergroup) relative deprivation (a feeling that one's own group is deprived relative to relevant other groups), and egoistic (interpersonal) relative deprivation (a feeling that oneself is deprived relative to specific other individuals). It is the former that appears to be associated with social protest, whereas the latter is more likely to be associated with acquiescence and depression. For example, racist attitudes in the USA and Britain may be more extreme among skilled blue-collar people than any other group, because this group is most vulnerable to competition from other groups (such as immigrants) and thus feels most threatened and fraternalistically most deprived (Vanneman and Pettigrew, 1972; see Esses et al., 1998). Walker and Mann (1987) provide a similar analysis of reactions to unemployment among unemployed Australians.

According to social-identity theory, disadvantaged groups engage in direct competition with the dominant group if they perceive intergroup boundaries to be impermeable, if they perceive their lower status to be illegitimate and unstable, and if they can conceive of a new status quo that is achievable (see Ellemers, 1993; Hogg and Abrams, 1988; Kelly and Breinlinger, 1996; Tajfel and Turner, 1986). This analysis attributes protest by disadvantaged groups to a conjunction of social-cognitive factors and social belief systems and ideologies. For example, according to research by Wright et al. (1990), if members of a disadvantaged group believe that entry to an advantaged group is open, even only slightly open (only a token percentage of people can pass), they shun collective action and instead individually try to gain entry to the advantaged group. Collective action is most likely to be taken when entry to the advantaged group is closed, and then it is taken only by those who believe they were closest to entry, because they feel the strongest sense of relative deprivation. Collective action is only likely to be extreme (riots and uprisings) when socially acceptable normative means (peaceful protest and lobbying) are unavailable.

There is clear evidence that social protest is motivated by social identification (Abrams and

Randsley de Moura, 2002; Ellemers et al., 1997). For example, Mummendey et al. (1999) found that (low-status) East Germans who perceived the East–West boundary as less permeable identified more strongly as East German and were more likely to endorse collective strategies for change.

### *Social protest and active minorities*

The study of social protest is the study of how individual discontents or grievances are transformed into collective action: how and why do sympathizers become mobilized as activists or participants (e.g., Klandermans, 1997; Reicher, 2001). Klandermans (1997) argues that mobilization is a facet of the attitude–behavior relationship – sympathizers hold sympathetic attitudes towards an issue, yet these attitudes do not readily translate into behavior. Participation also resembles a social dilemma. Protest is generally *for* a social good (such as equality) or *against* a social ill (such as oppression), and as success benefits everyone irrespective of participation but failure harms participants more, it is tempting to 'free ride' — to remain a sympathizer rather than become a participant. Social protest can, however, only be fully understood in its wider intergroup context, where there is a clash of ideas and ideologies between groups, and there is politicized and strategic articulation with other more or less sympathetic organizations. Simon et al. (1998; Stürmer and Simon, 2004) proposed that the three expectancy value motives from Klandermans's model (goal, social, and reward) and social identity all contribute to protest. This idea was supported in field studies of both gay and elderly people's protest movements. Moreover, people's beliefs about their collective efficacy or control may moderate engagement in protest behavior (Abrams and Randsley de Moura, 2002, Abrams et al., 1999).

Social protest is often engaged in by minorities who actively try to change majority attitudes and practices. Research on minority influence suggests that majority and minority groups have access to different influence resources and may actually influence through different processes (e.g., Maass and Clark, 1984; Wood et al., 1994). Active minorities need to adopt a particular behavioral style to influence members of a majority group (Mugny, 1982). They need to present a consistent and consensual message, they need to be seen to have made some sacrifice for their cause, they need to be seen to be acting out of principle, and they need to be seen by the majority to be, to some extent, in-group members. This behavioral style, particularly consistency, creates cognitive conflict in the mind of majority members between majority and minority views – majority members are not immediately influenced but experience a sudden conversion to the minority point of view at a later time. Consistent minorities have latent, deep-seated influence over majorities that produces a sudden and enduring conversion effect (Moscovici, 1980; Nemeth, 1986). Minorities that are inconsistent have little impact because their message is easily disregarded. Majorities are taken for granted, and people simply comply with their views without internalizing them or undergoing any deep-seated cognitive change.

Intergroup influence can also involve attitude polarization (e.g., Abrams et al., 1990; Mackie, 1986). One or both groups extremitize their normative attitudes to distance themselves further from an out-group or from people not in the in-group. This is particularly likely to occur where groups are in competition, and members identify strongly with their in-group and thus internalize the group norm as their own attitude. From the social-identity perspective, the underlying process is self-categorization and depersonalization (e.g., Turner, 1991). In a salient intergroup context, people construct in-group and out-group prototypes according to the principle of metacontrast, which maximizes the entitativity of the in-group by representing in-group prototypical similarities and accentuating intergroup prototypical distinctiveness – thus producing a polarized prototype. Self-categorization assimilates the self to the in-group prototype and thus produces conformity and in-group normative attitudes, feelings, and behavior.

## Social harmony among groups

### *Intergroup contact*

The goal of most intergroup-relations researchers is to understand intergroup relations sufficiently to know, and perhaps advise, how to improve these relations and build social harmony. To this end, a prevalent belief is that close and pleasant interpersonal contact between people from different groups is probably the best way to achieve social harmony – the contact hypothesis (Allport, 1954; see also Amir, 1969; Cook, 1985; Hewstone and Brown, 1986; Miller and Brewer, 1984). The idea that appropriate intergroup contact could improve intergroup relations was a central plank in the policy put in place in the USA in 1954 to improve race relations by desegregating the school system. The later practice of 'busing' children in and out of racially homogeneous school districts was partly aimed at increasing interracial contact (Schofield, 1991). For contact to be effective, it needs to be prolonged and cooperative, it needs to occur within an official and institutional climate that strongly encourages integration, and it needs to be between equal-status groups. These conditions are nigh impossible to satisfy; therefore, contact is notoriously ineffective at changing intergroup attitudes or improving intergroup relations. After all, charged intergroup relations are often associated with groups that are very different – contact simply confirms one's worst fears (Bochner, 1982). In addition, as we have seen above (e.g., Sherif, 1958), intergroup conflict may rest upon real conflicts of interest over scarce resources. Until perceived or actual goal relations are changed, contact will simply provide a forum for conflict, particularly where there is a wide cultural divide between groups that is grounded in a long history of fierce conflict, vicious atrocities, and so forth (Prentice and Miller, 1999).

One specific problem is that there can be substantial anxiety associated with intergroup contact, an effect, which, of course, renders the interaction relatively aversive (Stephan and Stephan, 1985). Intergroup anxiety is a state in which people worry about negative psychological and behavioral consequences for the self and negative evaluations of the self by both in-group and out-group, as a consequence of intergroup contact. Intergroup anxiety arises out of past experience of contact, intergroup beliefs (stereotypes), and the degree of normative structure of the contact situation. It affects intergroup behavior – intergroup anxiety can produce intergroup avoidance and stereotype-confirming perceptions, evaluations, and feelings.

Contact which is not associated with intergroup anxiety can be pleasant; indeed sufficiently pleasant to encourage the development of enduring friendships across group boundaries (Pettigrew, 1998). However, being close friends with people from another group does not guarantee that one has positive attitudes towards that group as a whole (but see Wright et al., 1997). Close friendships between members of different groups often do not improve generalized intergroup images. People may like each other as individuals, but they still harbor negative attitudes towards the other group as a whole.

One way to get around this problem is to encourage people in contact situations to *decategorize* themselves and treat each other as unique individuals, or to *recategorize* themselves as members of a shared superordinate identity. Research by Gaertner, Dovidio, and their colleagues (e.g., Gaertner et al., 1989, 1993) shows that both strategies reduce intergroup discrimination, but by diferent routes: recategorization improves out-group attitudes, whereas decategorization worsens in-group attitudes.

One problem with recategorization is that it can, particularly in nonlaboratory contexts, represent a threat to the distinctiveness and associated social identities of the separate groups that are being encouraged to recategorize themselves as a single entity. For instance, many organizational mergers fail for precisely these reasons (e.g., Terry et al., 2001). This problem surfaces at the cultural level in the relative ineffectiveness of assimilationist strategies to forge a single harmonious cultural or national identity out of many cultural groups. Social harmony may be better served by a multicultural strategy that avoids the distinctiveness threat raised by assimilation (see Hornsey and Hogg, 2000; Prentice and Miller, 1999). Hornsey and Hogg (2000; see also Hogg and Hornsey, 2006) suggest that the knack is for the superordinate identity to affirm subgroup distinctiveness at the same time as configuring relations between subgroups as role relations in which subgroups are distinct entities working together 'on the same team'. A degree of dual, subgroup–superordinate group identification may be necessary.

Since recategorization has a tendency to backfire, perhaps improved generalized intergroup attitudes and relations are more likely to emerge from contact that is framed in intergroup terms. But the problem here, as we have already seen, is that intergroup contact is often sufficiently stressful to render it unpleasant or even hostile. It can be very difficult to produce pleasant intergroup contact, which is a prerequisite for improved generalized images. More generally, it is very difficult to create enduring pluralistic contexts where people identify at the subgroup and at the superordinate group level simultaneously, and thus do not experience identity threat and do not interact in a hostile intergroup manner, but do view each other in group terms that permit generalization.

The main aim of contact is for pleasant interaction to change enduring intergroup images; that is, the aim is for generalization to occur through the accumulation of favorable out-group information (bookkeeping), or through a sudden encounter with counterstereotypical information (conversion), or through the development of a more textured out-group representation (subtyping) (Weber and Crocker, 1983). Research (e.g., Wilder, 1984) shows that people who have pleasant contact with an out-group member that is clearly viewed as being representative or stereotypical of the out-group, do develop improved attitudes towards the out-group as a whole. But, generally speaking, the relationship between intergroup contact and enduring social harmony is an enormously complex one which involves a large number of interacting variables (e.g., Islam and Hewstone, 1993).

Pettigrew (1998) recently incorporated much of the previous research into a developmental model. He proposed that the generation of affective ties, in-group reappraisal, changing behavior, and learning about the out-group mediate between intergroup contact and subsequent intergroup attitudes. Moreover, although decategorization may be important at the early stages of contact, once potential intergroup anxiety is allayed, it is important for intergroup distinctiveness to be maintained. Ultimately, it is beneficial for group members to share a recategorized superordinate group membership in which common aims and goals are understood.

### *Diversity*

Intergroup contact is actually extremely prevalent. For example, most people work or study in organizations and groups that are sociodemographically diverse in race, gender, ethnicity, religion, and so forth. Such groups act as a crucible in which intergroup relations are played out. Social-identity-based research tends to show that because roles within such groups tend to correlate with category membership, intergroup relations are highly salient (e.g., Brewer, 1996; Brewer et al., 1999). If such relations are hostile in the wider society, the interactive group accentuates that behavior. Better relations are achieved by cross-cutting roles with category membership (see also Vescio et al., 1999).

This can, however, be difficult to implement, because of the human tendency to assign leadership roles automatically to people who belong to high-status social categories. According to expectation-states theory and status-characteristics theory (e.g., Berger et al., 1977, 1985; Ridgeway, 2001), influence within an interactive group is a function of the extent to which a person possesses characteristics that suit him or her to effective task performance (that is, specific status characteristics), and possesses characteristics that categorize him or her as a member of a high-status sociodemographic group (that is, diffuse status characteristics).

### *Schism*

Another reason why social harmony can be difficult to maintain is the tendency for groups to fragment into warring factions. We have already seen, above, how attempts to bring groups together can pose an identity threat that reinforces intergroup divisions, particularly where deep cultural divides already exist. But existing groups can also split asunder. In their analysis of schisms, Sani and Reicher (1998, 1999, 2000; see also Reicher and Hopkins, 2001) describe the way that identity threat, self-conceptual uncertainty, and a sense of self-conceptual impermanence and instability can arise in groups whose defining properties are suddenly changed. The change can be brought about by the actions of a subgroup or a leadership clique. Under these circumstances, members either can try to re-establish the group's identity or split into a separate subgroup that is in conflict with the rest of the group. A schism is most likely to occur if the group isseen not to tolerate dissent and is instead likely to marginalize dissenting individuals.

## Concluding comments

In this chapter, we have given an overview of the social psychology of intergroup behavior and social identity. By necessity, we have sacrificed some detail in preference for inclusiveness, though the coverage should not be considered encyclopedic. For further or different recent coverage of the social psychology of intergroup behavior, see Brewer and Brown (1998), Brown and Gaertner (2001), Hogg and Abrams (2001b), and Mackie and Smith (1998). The social-identity approach has recently been overviewed by Abrams and Hogg (2001) and by Hogg (2001a, 2003, 2006).

At the social-psychological level, intergroup behavior hinges on some very basic social-cognitive processes. Social categorization segments the world of people into groups and represents groups schematically, mainly in terms of prototypes. Prototypes of groups are generally shared by people within a group (that is, they are social stereotypes) – they describe and prescribe perceptions, attitudes, behaviors, and feelings that define one group and clearly differentiate that group from other groups. The social-categorization process strives to maximize entitativity by maximizing the ratio of intergroup differences to intragroup differences on all relevant dimensions. The link between category cues, social categorization, and stereotyping is generally very fast and relatively automatic.

People define themselves in terms of the groups they belong to – they derive their social identity from group memberships. Because of this, intergroup relations are characterized by a struggle over status and prestige – membership in a prestigious, high-status group reflects well on self-conception, but membership of a low-status group is a stigma that is often associated with disadvantage. People are, however, very creative in avoiding the self-evaluative consequences of stigma. Intergroup relations are underpinned by people's need to feel positive about themselves (self-enhancement) and by their need to feel certain about themselves, their place in the world, and how they relate to other people (uncertainty reduction). These motives guide intergroup behavior, but they are moderated by strategic intergroup considerations that rest on people's understanding of the nature of the relations between groups, in terms of the stability and legitimacy of intergroup status differences, the permeability of group boundaries, the goal relations between groups, and so forth.

The relationship between intergroup attitudes and intergroup behavior is a manifestation of the wider issue of attitude–behavior relations – prejudice does not always express itself very obviously in discrimination, and oppressed minorities do not always engage in minority influence, social protest, and collective action.

Finally, because intergroup relations are intrinsically competitive and ethnocentric, improvement can be difficult and slow. Intergroup contact and diversity improve relations only under very restricted conditions, and attempts to merge groups often backfire because of the identity threat that is usually present. Schisms within existing groups can readily arise to produce new intergroup conflicts. Conditions that respect group differences and affirm identity but reconfigure intergroup relations within a superordinate identity are most promising.

**SUMMARY**

This chapter examines how intergroup relations configure our sense of who we are as group members, our social identity, and how social-identity processes in turn influence or generate group and intergroup behaviors. This perspective on how people in different groups behave towards and think about one another has, over the past thirty-five years, had a dramatic and wide-ranging impact on social psychology. Its focus on social categorization, collective self-conception, and associated motivational and social influence processes has contributed to our understanding of a wide range of intergroup phenomena – most of which are discussed in this chapter. We discuss prejudice as a reflection of intergroup relations not individual personality, and intergroup conflict as a struggle over identity not scarce resources. We discuss how categorization sows the seeds of ethnocentrism and discrimination, and how self-enhancement, optimal distinctiveness and uncertainty reduction motivate group behaviors. Emotions are shared among group members, and people feel anxious about outgroups and hold stereotypical attitudes whose expression in language or discrimination is influenced by group and societal norms. Members of disadvantaged groups are, however, remarkably adept at protecting themselves from stigma. We discuss the role of social identity in crowd behavior, social protest and minority-induced social change, and discuss difficulties in improving intergroup relations and creating tolerance through intergroup contact.

## References

Abrams, D. (1992) 'Processes of Social Identification', in G. Breakwell (ed.), *The Social Psychology of the Self-Concept*. London: Academic Press/Surrey University Press, pp. 57–100.

Abrams, D. (1994a) 'Political Distinctiveness: An Identity Optimising Approach', *European Journal of Social Psychology*, 24: 357–65.

Abrams, D. (1994b) 'Social Self-Regulation', *Personality and Social Psychology Bulletin*, 20: 473–84.

Abrams, D. (1996) 'Social Identity, Self as Structure and Self as Process', in W.P. Robinson (ed.), *Social Groups and Identities: Developing the Legacy of Henri Tajfel.* London: Butterworth Heinemann, pp. 143–68.

Abrams, D., Hinkle, S.W., and Tomlins, M. (1999) 'Leaving Hong Kong? The Roles of Attitude, Subjective Norm, Perceived Control, Social Identity and Relative Deprivation', *International Journal of Intercultural Relations*, 23: 319–38.

Abrams, D. and Hogg, M.A. (1988) 'Comments on the Motivational Status of Self-Esteem in Social Identity and Intergroup Discrimination', *European Journal of Social Psychology*, 18: 317–34.

Abrams, D. and Hogg, M.A. (1998) 'Prospects for Research in Group Processes and Intergroup Relations', *Group Processes and Intergroup Relations*, 1: 7–20.

Abrams, D. and Hogg, M.A. (eds) (1999) *Social Identity and Social Cognition*. Oxford: Blackwell.

Abrams, D. and Hogg, M.A. (2001) 'Collective Identity: Group Membership and Self-Conception', in M.A. Hogg and R.S. Tindale (eds), *Blackwell Handbook of Social Psychology: Group Processes*. Oxford: Blackwell, pp. 425–60.

Abrams, D., Marques, J.M., Bown, N.J., and Henson, M. (2000) 'Pro-Norm and Anti-Norm Deviance within In-Groups and Out-Groups', *Journal of Personality and Social Psychology*, 78: 906–12.

Abrams, D. and Randsley de Moura, G. (2002) 'The Psychology of Collective Political Protest', in V.C. Ottati, R.S. Tindale, J. Edwards, F.B. Bryant, L.Health, D.C. O'Connell, Y. Suarez-Balzacar, and E.J. Posavac (eds), *The Social Psychology of Politics*. New York: Kluwer Academic/Plenum.

Abrams, D., Wetherell, M.S., Cochrane, S., Hogg, M.A., and Turner, J.C. (1990) 'Knowing What to Think by Knowing Who You Are: Self-Categorization and the Nature of Norm Formation, Conformity, and Group Polarization', *British Journal of Social Psychology*, 29: 97–119.

Adorno, T.W., Frenkel-Brunswik, E., Levinson, D.J., and Sanford, R.M. (1950) *The Authoritarian Personality*. New York: Harper.

Allport, F.H. (1924) *Social Psychology*. Boston, MA: Houghton-Mifflin.

Allport, G.W. (1954) *The Nature of Prejudice*. Reading, MA: Addison-Wesley.

Altemeyer, B. (1994) 'Reducing Prejudice in Right-Wing Authoritarians', in M.P. Zanna and J.M. Olsen (eds), *The Psychology of Prejudice: The Ontario Symposium*. Hillsdale, NJ: Erlbaum, pp. 131–48.

Amir, Y. (1969) 'Contact Hypothesis in Ethnic Relations', *Psychological Bulletin*, 71: 319–42.

Andreeva, G. (1984) 'Cognitive Processes in Developing Groups', in L.H. Strickland (ed.), *Directions in Soviet Social Psychology*. New York: Springer, pp. 67–82.

Arrow, H., McGrath, J.E., and Berdahl, J.L. (2000) *Small Groups as Complex Systems: Formation, Coordination, Development, and Adaptation*. Thousand Oaks, CA: Sage.

Ashburn-Nardo, L., Voils, C.I., and Monteith, M.J. (2001) 'Implicit Associations as the Seeds of Intergroup Bias: How Easily Do They Take Root', *Journal of Personality and Social Psychology*, 81: 789–99.

Bargh, J.A. (1994) 'The Four Horsemen of Automaticity: Awareness, Intention, Efficiency, and Control in Social Cognition', in R.S. Wyer, Jr. and T.K. Srull (eds), *Handbook of Social Cognition*, 2nd edn (vol. 1). Hillsdale, NJ: Erlbaum, pp. 1–40.

Baumeister, R.F. and Leary, M.R. (1995) 'The Need to Belong: Desire for Interpersonal Attachments as a Fundamental Human Motivation', *Psychological Bulletin*, 117: 497–529.

Berger, J., Fisek, M.H., Norman, R.Z., and Zelditch, M. Jr. (1977) *Status Characteristics and Social Interaction*. New York: Elsevier.

Berger, J., Wagner, D., and Zelditch, M. Jr. (1985) 'Expectation States Theory: Review and Assessment', in J. Berger and M. Zelditch, Jr. (eds), *Status, Rewards and Influence*. San Francisco, CA: Jossey-Bass, pp. 1–72.

Berkowitz, L. (1972) 'Frustrations, Comparisons, and Other Sources of Emotion Arousal as Contributors to Social Unrest', *Journal of Social Issues*, 28: 77–91.

Billig, M. (1976) *Social Psychology and Intergroup Relations*. London: Academic Press.

Blake, R.R. and Mouton, J.S. (1961) 'Reactions to Intergroup Competition under Win/Lose Conditions', *Management Science*, 7: 420–35.

Blake, R.R., Shepard, H.A., and Mouton, J.S. (1964) *Managing Intergroup Conflict in Industry*. Houston, TX: Gulf Publishing.

Bobo, L. (1999) 'Prejudice as Group Position: Microfoundations of a Sociological Approach to Racism and Race Relations', *Journal of Social Issues*, 55: 445–72.

Bobo, L. and Hutchings, V.L. (1996) 'Perceptions of Racial Group Competition: Extending Blumer's Theory of Group Position to a Multiracial Social Context', *American Sociological Review*, 61: 951–72.

Bochner, S. (1982) 'The Social Psychology of Cross-Cultural Relations', in S. Bochner (ed.), *Cultures in Contact: Studies in Cross-Cultural Interaction*. Oxford: Pergamon.

Branscombe, N.R., Doosje, B., and McGarty, C. (2002) 'Antecedents and Consequences of Collective Guilt', in D.M. Mackie and E.R. Smith (eds), *From Prejudice to Intergroup Emotions: Differentiated Reactions to Social Groups*', New York: Psychology Press, pp. 49–61.

Branscombe, N.R., Ellemers, N., Spears, R., and Doosje, B. (1999) 'The Context and Content of Social Identity Threat', in N. Ellemers, R. Spears, and B. Doosje (eds), *Social Identity: Context, Commitment, Content*. Oxford: Blackwell, pp. 35–58.

Branscombe, N.R., Wann, D.L., Noel, J.G., and Coleman, J. (1993) 'In-Group or Out-Group Extremity: Importance of the Threatened Social Identity', *Personality and Social Psychology Bulletin*, 19: 381–8.

Brauer, M. (2001) 'Intergroup Perception in the Social Context: The Effects of Social Status and Group Membership on Perceived Out-Group Homogeneity and Ethnocentrism', *Journal of Experimental Social Psychology*, 37: 15–31.

Brauer, M., Wasel, W., and Niedenthal, P. (2000) 'Implicit and Explicit Components of Prejudice', *Review of General Psychology*, 4: 79–101.

Brewer, M.B. (1991) 'The Social Self: On Being the Same and Different at the Same Time', *Personality and Social Psychology Bulletin*, 17: 475–82.

Brewer, M.B. (1996) 'Managing Diversity: The Role of Social Identities', in S. Jackson and M. Ruderman (eds), *Diversity in Work Teams*. Washington, DC: American Psychological Association, pp. 47–68.

Brewer, M.B. and Brown, R.J. (1998) 'Intergroup Relations', in D.T. Gilbert, S.T. Fiske, and G. Lindzey (eds), *The Handbook of Social Psychology*, 4th edn (vol. 2). New York: MCGraw-Hill, pp. 554–94.

Brewer, M.B. and Campbell, D.T. (1976) *Ethnocentrism and Intergroup Attitudes: East African Evidence*. New York: Sage.

Brewer, M.B. and Gardner, W. (1996) 'Who Is This "We"? Levels of Collective Identity and Self Representations', *Journal of Personality and Social Psychology*, 71: 83–93.

Brewer, M.B., Von Hippel, W., and Gooden, M.P. (1999) 'Diversity and Organizational Identity: The Problem of Entrée after Entry', in D.A. Prentice and D.T. Miller (eds), *Cultural Divides: Understanding and Overcoming Group Conflict*. New York: Russell Sage Foundation, pp. 337–63.

Brown, R.J. (2000) *Group Processes*, 2nd edn. Oxford: Blackwell.

Brown, R.J. and Gaertner, S. (eds) (2001) *Blackwell Handbook of Social Psychology: Intergroup Processes*. Oxford: Blackwell.

Cacioppo, J.T. and Petty, R.E. (1982) 'The Need for Cognition', *Journal of Personality and Social Psychology*, 42: 116–31.

Cadinu, M.R. and Rothbart, M. (1996) 'Self-Anchoring and Differentiation Processes in the Minimal Group Setting', *Journal of Personality and Social Psychology*, 70: 661–77.

Campbell, D.T. (1965) 'Ethnocentric and Other Altruistic Motives', in D. Levine (ed.), *Nebraska Symposium on Motivation*. Lincoln, NE: University of Nebraska Press, pp. 283–311.

Campbell, J.D., Trapnell, P.D., Heine, S.J., Katz, I.M., Lavalle, L.F., and Lehman, D.R. (1996) 'Self-Concept Clarity: Measurement, Personality Correlates, and Cultural Boundaries', *Journal of Personality and Social Psychology*, 70: 141–56.

Capozza, D. and Brown, R.J. (eds) (2000) *Social Identity Processes*. London: Sage.

Cook, S.W. (1985) 'Experimenting on Social Issues: The Case of School Desegregation', *American Psychologist*, 40: 452–60.

Crandall, C.S. (1994) 'Prejudice against Fat People: Ideology and Self-Interest', *Journal of Personality and Social Psychology*, 66: 882–94.

Crocker, J. and Major, B. (1989) 'Social Stigma and Self-Esteem: The Self-Protective Properties of Stigma', *Psychological Review*, 96: 608–30.

Crocker, J. and Major, B. (1994) 'Reactions to Stigma: The Moderating Role of Justifications', in M.P. Zanna and J.M. Olson (eds), *The Psychology of Prejudice: The Ontario Symposium* (vol. 7). Hillsdale, NJ: Erlbaum, pp. 289–314.

Crocker, J., Major, B., and Steele, C. (1998) 'Social Stigma', in D.T. Gilbert, S.T. Fiske, and G. Lindzey (eds), *The Handbook of Social Psychology*, 4th edn (vol. 2). New York: MCGraw-Hill, pp. 504–53

Crockett, W.H. (1965) 'Cognitive Complexity and Impression Formation', in B.A. Maher (ed.), *Progress in Experimental Personality Research* (vol. 2). New York: Academic Press, pp. 47–90.

Crosby, F. (1982) *Relative Deprivation and Working Women*. New York: Oxford University Press.

Crosby, F. (1984) 'The Denial of Personal Discrimination', *American Behavioral Scientist*, 27: 371–86.

Crosby, F. Bromley, S. and Saxe, L. (1980) 'Recent Unobtrusive Studies of Black and White Discrimination and Prejudice: A Literature Review', *Psychological Bulletin*, 87: 546–63.

Davies, J.C. (1969) 'The J-Curve of Rising and Declining Satisfaction as a Cause of Some Great Revolutions and a Contained Rebellion', in H.D. Graham and T.R. Gurr (eds), *The History of Violence in America: Historical and Comparative Perspectives*. New York: Praeger, pp. 690–730.

Davis, J.A. (1959) 'A Formal Interpretation of the Theory of Relative Deprivation', *Sociometry*, 22: 280–96.

Deutsch, M. (1949) 'A Theory of Cooperation and Competition', *Human Relations*, 2: 129–52.

Deutsch, M. (1973) *The Resolution of Conflict*. New Haven, CT: Yale University Press.

Devine, P.G. (1989) 'Stereotypes and Prejudice: Their Automatic and Controlled Components', *Journal of Personality and Social Psychology*, 56: 5–18.

Diab, L.N. (1970) 'A Study of Intragroup and Intergroup Relations among Experimentally Produced Small Groups', *Genetic Psychology Monographs*, 82: 49–82.

Diehl, M. (1989) 'Justice and Discrimination between Minimal Groups: The Limits of Equity', *British Journal of Social Psychology*, 28: 227–38.

Diehl, M. (1990) 'The Minimal Group Paradigm: Theoretical Explanations and Empirical Findings', *European Review of Social Psychology*, 1: 263–92.

Doosje, B., Branscombe, N.R., Spears, R., and Manstead, A.S.R. (1998) 'Guilty by Association: When One's Group Has a Negative History', *Journal of Personality and Social Psychology*, 75: 872–86.

Dovidio, J.F. and Gaertner, S.L. (1996) 'Affirmative Action, Unintentional Racial Biases, and Intergroup Relations', *Journal of Social Issues*, 52 (4): 51–75.

Dovidio, J.F. and Gaertner, S.L. (1998) 'On the Nature of Contemporary Prejudice: The Causes, Consequences, and Challenges of Aversive Racism', in J.L. Eberhardt and S.T. Fiske (eds), *Confronting Prejudice: The Problem and the Response*. Thousand Oaks, CA: Sage, pp. 3–32.

Dovidio, J.F., Kawakami, K. Johnson, C., Johnson, B., and Howard, A., (1997) 'On the Nature of Prejudice: Automatic and Controlled Processes', *Journal of Experimental Social Psychology*, 33: 510–40.

Duckitt, J. (1989) 'Authoritarianism and Group Identification: A New View of an Old Construct', *Political Psychology*, 10: 63–84.

Eagly, A.H. and Chaiken, S. (1993) *The Psychology of Attitudes*. San Diego, CA: Harcourt Brace Jovanovich.

Ehrlich, H.J. (1973) *The Social Psychology of Prejudice*. New York: Wiley.

Ellemers, N. (1993) 'The Influence of Socio-Structural Variables on Identity Management Strategies', *European Review of Social Psychology*, 4: 27–57.

Ellemers, N., Doojse, B., van Knippenberg, A., and Wilke, H. (1992) 'Status Protection in High Status Minority Groups', *European Journal of Social Psychology*, 22: 123–40.

Ellemers, N., Spears, R., and Doojse, B. (1997) 'Sticking Together or Falling Apart: In-group Identification as a Psychological Determinant of Group Commitment versus Individual Mobility', *Journal of Personality and Social Psychology*, 72: 617–26.

Ellemers, N., Spears, R. and Doosje, B. (eds) (1999) *Social Identity*. Oxford: Blackwell.

Emler, N. and Reicher, S.D. (1995) *Adolescence and Delinquency: The Collective Management of Reputation*. Oxford: Blackwell.

Esses, V.M., Jackson, L.M., and Armstrong, T.L. (1998) 'Intergroup Competition and Attitudes towards Immigrants and Immigration: An Instrumental Model of Group Conflict', *Journal of Social Issues*, 54: 699–724.

Ethier, K.A. and Deaux, K. (1994) 'Negotiating Social Identity when Contexts Change: Maintaining Identification and Responding to Threat', *Journal of Personality and Social Psychology*, 67: 243–51.

Farr, R.M. and Moscovici, S. (eds) (1984) *Social Representations*. Cambridge: Cambridge University Press.

Fazio, R.H., Sanbonmatsu, D.M., Powell, M.C., and Kardes, F.R. (1986) 'On the Automatic Activation of Attitudes', *Journal of Personality and Social Psychology*, 50: 229–38.

Festinger, L. (1954) 'A Theory of Social Comparison Processes', *Human Relations*, 7: 117–40.

Fisher, R.J. (1990) *The Social Psychology of Intergroup and International Conflict Resolution*. New York: Springer-Verlag.

Fiske, S.T. and Taylor, S.E. (1991) *Social Cognition*, 2nd edn. New York: MCGraw-Hill.

Fletcher, G.J.O., Danilovics, P., Fernandez, G., Peterson, D., and Reeder, G.D. (1986) 'Attributional Complexity: An Individual Differences Measure', *Journal of Personality and Social Psychology*, 51: 875–84.

Gaertner, L., Sedikides, C., and Graetz, K. (1999) 'In Search of Self-Definition: Motivational Primacy of the Individual Self, Motivational Primacy of the Collective Self, or Contextual Primacy?', *Journal of Personality and Social Psychology*, 76: 5–18.

Gaertner, L., Sedikides, C., Vevea, J.L., and Iuzzini, J. (2002) the "I", 'The "We", and the "When": A Meta-Analysis of Motivational Primacy in Self-Definition', *Journal of Personality and Social Psychology*, 83: 574–91.

Gaertner, S.L. and Dovidio, J.F. (1986) 'The Aversive Form of Racism', in J.F. Dovidio and S.L. Gaertner (eds), *Prejudice, Discrimination, and Racism*. San Diego, CA: Academic Press, pp. 61–89.

Gaertner, S.L., Dovidio, J.F., Anastasio, P.A., Bachman, B.A., and Rust, M.C. (1993) 'Reducing Intergroup Bias: The Common Ingroup Identity Model', *European Review of Social Psychology*, 4: 1–26.

Gaertner, S.L., Mann, J., Murrell, A., and Dovidio, J.F. (1989) 'Reducing Intergroup Bias: The Benefits of Recategorization', *Journal of Personality and Social Psychology*, 57: 239–49.

Glick, P. and Fiske, S.T. (1996) 'The Ambivalent Sexism Inventory: Differentiating Hostile and Benevolent Sexism', *Journal of Personality and Social Psychology*, 70: 491–512.

Greenberg, J., Solomon, S., and Pyszczynski, T. (1997) 'Terror Management Theory of Self-Esteem and Cultural Worldviews: Empirical Assessments and Conceptual Refinements', in M. Zanna (ed.), *Advances in Experimental Social Psychology* (vol. 29). Orlando, FL: Academic Press, pp. 61–139.

Greenwald, A.G. and Banaji, M.R. (1995) 'Implicit Social Cognition: Attitudes, Self-Esteem, and Stereotypes', *Psychological Review*, 102: 4–27.

Gurr, T.R. (1970) *Why Men Rebel*. Princeton, NJ: Princeton University Press.

Haddock, G., Zanna, M.P., and Esses, V.M. (1993) 'Assessing the Structure of Prejudicial Attitudes: The Case of Attitudes toward Homosexuals', *Journal of Personality and Social Psychology*, 65: 1105–18.

Hamilton, D.L. and Gifford, R.K. (1976) 'Illusory Correlation in Interpersonal Person Perception: A Cognitive Basis of Stereotypic Judgments', *Journal of Experimental Social Psychology*, 12: 392–407.

Hamilton, D.L. and Sherman, J.W. (1994) 'Stereotypes', in R.S. Wyer, Jr and T.K. Srull (eds), *Handbook of Social Cognition* (vol. 2). Hillsdale, NJ: Erlbaumm, pp. 1–68.

Hamilton, D.L. and Sherman, S.J. (1996) 'Perceiving Persons and Groups', *Psychological Review*, 103: 336–55.

Haslam, N. (2006) 'Dehumanization: An Integrative Review', *Personality and Social Psychology Review*, 10: 252–64.

Heine, S.J., Lehman, D.R., Markus, H.R., and Kitayama, S. (1999) 'Is There a Universal Need for Positive Self-Regard?', *Psychological Review*, 106: 766–94.

Hewstone, M. and Jaspars, J.M.F. (1982) 'Intergroup Relations and Attribution Processes', in H. Tajfel (ed.), *Social Identity and Intergroup Relations*. Cambridge: Cambridge University Press, pp. 99–133.

Hewstone. M. and Brown, R.J. (eds) (1986) *Contact and Conflict in Intergroup Encounters*. Oxford: Blackwell.

Hewstone, M. and Ward, C. (1985) 'Ethnocentrism and Causal Attribution in Southeast Asia', *Journal of Personality and Social Psychology*, 48: 614–23.

Higgins, E.T. (1998) 'Promotion and Prevention: Regulatory Focus as a Motivational Principle', in M.P. Zanna (ed.), *Advances in Experimental Social Psychology* (vol. 30). New York: Academic Press, pp. 1–46.

Hinkle, S.W. and Brown, R.J. (1990) 'Intergroup Comparisons and Social Identity: Some Links and Lacunae', in D. Abrams and M.A. Hogg (eds), *Social Identity Theory: Constructive and Critical Advances*. London: Harvester Wheatsheaf, pp. 48–70.

Hogg, M.A. (1993) 'Group Cohesiveness: A Critical Review and Some New Directions', *European Review of Social Psychology*, 4: 85–111.

Hogg, M.A. (2000a) 'Social Identity and Social Comparison', in J. Suls and L. Wheeler (eds), *Handbook of Social Comparison: Theory and Research*. New York: Kluwer/Plenum, pp. 401–21.

Hogg, M.A. (2000b) 'Subjective Uncertainty Reduction through Self-Categorization: A Motivational Theory of Social Identity Processes', *European Review of Social Psychology*, 11: 223–55.

Hogg, M.A. (2001a) 'Social Categorization, Depersonalization, and Group Behavior', in M.A. Hogg and R.S. Tindale (eds), *Blackwell Handbook of Social Psychology: Group Processes*. Oxford: Blackwell, pp. 56–85.

Hogg, M.A. (2001b) 'Self-Categorization and Subjective Uncertainty Resolution: Cognitive and Motivational Facets of Social Identity and Group Membership', in J.P. Forgas, K.D. Williams, and L. Wheeler (eds), *The Social Mind: Cognitive and Motivational Aspects of Interpersonal Behavior*. New York: Cambridge University Press, pp. 323–49.

Hogg, M.A. (2001c) 'Social Identity and the Sovereignty of the Group: A Psychology of Belonging', in C. Sedikides and M.B. Brewer (eds), *Individual Self, Relational Self, and Collective Self: Partners, Opponents, or Strangers*. Philadelphia, PA: Psychology Press, pp. 123–43.

Hogg, M.A. (2001d) 'A Social Identity Theory of Leadership', *Personality and Social Psychology Review*, 5: 184–200.

Hogg, M.A. (2003) 'Social Identity', in M.R. Leary and J.P. Tangney (eds), *Handbook of Self and Identity*. New York: Guilford, pp. 462–79.

Hogg, M.A. (2004) 'Uncertainty and Extremism: Identification with High Entitativity Groups under Conditions of Uncertainty', in V. Yzerbyt, C.M. Judd, and O. Corneille (eds), *The Psychology of Group Perception: Perceived Variability, Entitativity, and Essentialism*. New York: Psychology Press, pp. 401–18.

Hogg, M.A. (2005) 'Uncertainty, Social Identity, and Ideology', in S.R. Thye and E.J. Lawler (eds), *Advances in Group Processes* (Vol. 22). San Diego, CA: Elsevier, pp. 203–29.

Hogg, M.A. (2006) 'Social Identity Theory', in P.J. Burke (ed.), *Contemporary Social Psychological Theories*. Palo Alto, CA: Stanford University Press, pp. 111–36.

Hogg, M.A. (2007) 'Uncertainty-Identity Theory', in M.P. Zanna (ed.), *Advances in Experimental Social Psychology* (Vol. 39, pp. 69–126). San Diego, CA: Academic Press.

Hogg, M.A. and Abrams, D. (1988) *Social Identifications: A Social Psychology of Intergroup Relations and Group Processes*. London: Routledge.

Hogg, M.A. and Abrams, D. (2001a) 'Intergroup Relations: An Overview', in M.A. Hogg and D. Abrams (eds), *Intergroup Relations: Essential Readings*. Philadelphia, PA: Psychology Press, pp. 1–14.

Hogg, M.A. and Abrams, D. (eds) (2001b) *Intergroup Relations: Essential Readings*. Philadelphia, PA: Psychology Press.

Hogg, M.A. and Hornsey, M.J. (2006) 'Self-Concept Threat and Differentiation Within Groups', in R.J. Crisp and M. Hewstone (eds), *Multiple Social Categorization: Processes, Models, and Applications*, New York: Psychology Press, pp. 112–35.

Hogg, M.A. and Terry, D.J. (eds) (2001) *Social Identity Processes in Organizational Contexts*. Philadelphia, PA: Psychology Press.

Hogg, M.A., and van Knippenberg, D. (2003) 'Social Identity and Leadership Processes in Groups', in M.P. Zanna (ed.), *Advances in Experimental Social Psychology* (Vol. 35). San Diego, CA: Academic Press, pp. 1–52.

Hogg, M.A. and Williams, K.D. (2000) 'From I to We: Social Identity and the Collective Self', *Group Dynamics: Theory, Research, and Practice*, 4: 81–97.

Hornsey, M.J. (2005) 'Why Being Right Is Not Enough: Predicting Defensiveness in the Face of Group Criticism', *European Review of Social Psychology*, 16: 301–334.

Hornsey, M.J. and Hogg, M.A. (2000) 'Assimilation and Diversity: An Integrative Model of Subgroup Relations', *Personality and Social Psychology Review*, 4: 143–56.

Hornsey, M.J., Oppes, T., and Svensson, A. (2002) '"It's OK if We Say It, but You Can't": Responses to Intergroup and Intragroup Criticism', *European Journal of Social Psychology*, 32: 293–307.

Insko, C.A., Schopler, J., Kennedy, J.F., Dahl, K.R., Graetz, K.A., and Drigotas, S.M. (1992) 'Individual–Group Discontinuity from the Differing Perspectives of Campbell's Realistic Group Conflict Theory and Tajfel and Turner's Social Identity Theory', *Social Psychology Quarterly*, 55: 272–91.

Islam, M. and Hewstone, M. (1993) 'Intergroup Attributions and Affective Consequences in Majority and Minority Groups', *Journal of Personality and Social Psychology*, 65: 936–50.

Jetten, J., Spears, R., and Manstead, A.S.R. (1997) 'Identity Threat and Prototypicality: Combined Effects on Intergroup Discrimination and Collective Self-Esteem', *European Journal of Social Psychology*, 27: 635–57.

Jetten, J., Postmes, T., and McAuliffe, B.J. (2002) '"We're All Individuals": Group Norms of Individualism and Collectivism, Levels of Identification, and Identity Threat', *European Journal of Social Psychology*, 32: 189–207.

Jones, E.E., Wood, G.C., and Quattrone, G.A. (1981) 'Perceived Variability of Personal Characteristics in Ingroups and Outgroups: The Role of Knowledge and Evaluation', *Personality and Social Psychology Bulletin*, 7: 523–8.

Jost, J.T. and Banaji, M.R. (1994) 'The Role of Stereotyping in System-Justification and the Production of False Consciousness', *British Journal of Social Psychology*, 33: 1–27.

Jost, J.T. and Burgess, D. (2000) 'Attitudinal Ambivalence and the Conflict Between Group and System Justification Motives in Low Status Groups', *Personality and Social Psychology Bulletin*, 26: 293–305.

Jost, J.T. and Kramer, R.M. (2002) 'The System Justification Motive in Intergroup Relations', in D.M. Mackie and E.R. Smith (eds), *From Prejudice to Intergroup Emotions: Differentiated Reactions to Social Groups*', New York: Psychology Press, pp. 227–45.

Judd, C.M. and Park, B. (1988) 'Out-Group Homogeneity: Judgments of Variability at the Individual and Group Levels', *Journal of Personality and Social Psychology*, 54: 778–88.

Katz, I., Wackenhut, J., and Hass, R.G. (1986) 'Racial Ambivalence, Value Duality, and Behavior', in J.F. Dovidio and S.L. Gaertner (eds), *Prejudice, Discrimination, and Racism*. San Diego, CA: Academic Press, pp. 35–60.

Kelly, C. and Breinlinger, S. (1996) *The Social Psychology of Collective Action: Identity, Injustice and Gender*. London: Taylor & Francis.

Kinder, D.R. and Sears, D.O. (1981) 'Prejudice and Politics: Symbolic Racism versus Racial Threats to the Good Life', *Journal of Personality and Social Psychology*, 40: 414–31.

Klandermans, B. (1997) *The Social Psychology of Protest*. Oxford: Blackwell.

Kruglanski, A.W. (2004) *The Psychology of Closed Mindedness*. New York: Psychology Press.

Kruglanski, A.W. and Webster, D.M. (1996) 'Motivated Closing of the Mind: "Seizing" and "Freezing"', *Psychological Review*, 103: 263–83.

LaPiere, R.T. (1934) 'Attitudes vs Actions', *Social Forces*, 13: 230–7.

Leary, M.R., Tambor, E.S., Terdal, S.K., and Downs, D.L. (1995) 'Self-Esteem as an Interpersonal Monitor: The Sociometer Hypothesis', *Journal of Personality and Social Psychology*, 68: 518–30.

Lepore, L. and Brown, R. (1997) 'Category and Stereotype Activation: Is Prejudice Inevitable?', *Journal of Personality and Social Psychology*, 72: 275–87.

Lerner, M.J. and Miller, D.T. (1978) 'Just-World Research and the Attribution Process: Looking Back and Ahead', *Psychological Bulletin*, 85: 1030–51.

Leyens, J.-P., Paladino, P.M., Rodriguez-Torres, R., Vaes, J., Demoulin, S., Rodriguez-Perez, A., and Gaunt, R. (2000) 'The Emotional Side of Prejudice: The Attribution of Secondary Emotions to Ingroups and Outgroups', *Personality and Social Psychology Review*, 4: 186–97.

Leyens, J.Ph., Rodriguez, A.P., Rodriguez, R.T., Gaunt, R., Paladino, M.P., and Vaes, J. and Demoulin, S. (2001) 'Psychological Essentialism and the Differential Attribution of Uniquely Human Emotions to Ingroups and Outgroups', *European Journal of Social Psychology*, 31: 395–411.

Linville, P.W. (1987) 'Self-Complexity as a Buffer Against Stress-Related Illness and Depression', *Journal of Personality and Social Psychology*, 52: 663–76.

Linville, P.W., Fischer, G.W., and Salovey, P. (1989) 'Perceived Distributions of the Characteristics of In-Group and Out-Group Members: Empirical Evidence and a Computer Simulation', *Journal of Personality and Social Psychology*, 57: 165–88.

Long, K. and Spears, R. (1997) 'The Self-Esteem Hypothesis Revisited: Differentiation and the Dis-affected', in R. Spears, P.J. Oakes, N. Ellemers, and S.A. Haslam (eds), *The Social Psychology of Stereotyping and Group Life*. Oxford: Blackwell, pp. 296–317.

Maass, A. (1999) 'Linguistic Intergroup Bias: Stereotype-Perpetuation Through Language', in M.P. Zanna (ed.), *Advances in Experimental Social Psychology* (Vol. 31). San Diego, CA: Academic Press, pp. 79–121.

Maass, A. Castelli, L., and Acuri, L. (2000) 'Measuring Prejudice: Implicit Versus Explicit Techniques', in D. Capozza and R.J. Brown (eds), *Social Identity Processes*. London: Sage, pp. 96–116.

Maass, A. and Clark, R.D. III (1984) 'Hidden Impact of Minorities: Fifteen Years of Minority Influence Research', *Psychological Bulletin*, 95: 428–50.

Mackie, D.M. (1986) 'Social Identification Effects in Group Polarization', *Journal of Personality and Social Psychology*, 50: 720–8.

Mackie, D.M., Devos, T., and Smith, E.R. (2000) 'Intergroup Emotions: Explaining Offensive Action Tendencies in an Intergroup Context', *Journal of Personality and Social Psychology*, 79: 602–16.

Mackie, D.M. and Smith, E.R. (1998) 'Intergroup Relations: Insights from a Theoretically Integrative Approach', *Psychological Review*, 105: 499–529.

Mackie, D.M. and Smith, E.R. (eds) (2002) *From Prejudice to Intergroup Emotions: Differentiated Reactions to Social Groups*. New York: Psychology Press.

Macrae, N., Bodenhausen, G.V., Milne, A.B., and Jetten, J. (1994) 'Out of Mind but Back in Sight: Stereotypes on the Rebound', *Journal of Personality and Social Psychology*, 67: 808–17.

Major, B. (1994) 'From Social Inequality to Personal Entitlement: The Role of Social Comparisons, Legitimacy Appraisals and Group Memberships', in M.P. Zanna (ed.), *Advances in Experimental Social Psychology* (Vol. 26). San Diego, CA: Academic Press, pp. 293–355.

Marques, J.M., Abrams, D., Páez, D., and Hogg, M.A. (2001a) 'Social Categorization, Social Identification, and Rejection of Deviant Group Members', in M.A. Hogg and R.S. Tindale, (eds), *Blackwell Handbook of Social Psychology: Group Processes*. Oxford: Blackwell, pp. 400–24.

Marques, J.M., Abrams, D., and Serodio, R.G. (2001b) 'Being Better by Being Right: Subjective Group Dynamics and Derogation of In-Group Deviants When Generic Norms Are Undermined', *Journal of Personality and Social Psychology*, 81: 436–47.

Marques, J.M. and Páez, D. (1994) 'The Black Sheep Effect: Social Categorization, Rejection of Ingroup Deviates, and Perception of Group Variability', *European Review of Social Psychology*, 5: 37–68.

McConahay, J.G. (1986) 'Modern Racism, Ambivalence, and the Modern Racism Scale', in J.F. Dovidio and S.L. Gaertner (eds), *Prejudice, Discrimination, and Racism*. New York: Academic Press, pp. 91–125.

Medin, D.L. and Ortony, A. (1989) 'Psychological Essentialism', in S. Vosnaidou and A. Ortony (eds), *Similarity and Analogical Reasoning*. Cambridge: Cambridge University Press, pp. 179–95.

Miller, D.T. and Prentice, D.A. (1999) 'Some Consequences of a Belief in Group Essence: The Category Divide Hypothesis', in D.A. Prentice and D.T. Miller (eds), *Cultural Divides: Understanding and Overcoming Group Conflict*. New York: Russell Sage Foundation, pp. 213–38.

Miller, N. and Brewer, M.B. (eds) (1984) *Groups in Contact: The Psychology of Desegregation*. New York: Academic Press.

Monteith, M.J. (1993) 'Self-Regulation of Prejudiced Responses: Implications for Progress in Prejudice Reduction Efforts', *Journal of Personality and Social Psychology*, 65: 469–85.

Monteith, M.J. and Voils, C.I. (2001) 'Exerting Control over Prejudiced Responses', in G.B. Moskowitz (ed.), *Cognitive Social Psychology: The Princeton Symposium on the Legacy and Future of Social Cognition*. Mahwah, NJ: Erlbaum, pp. 375–88.

Monteith, M.J., Voils, C.I., and Ashburn-Nardo, L. (2001) 'Taking a Look Underground: Detecting, Interpreting, and Reacting to Implicit Racial Biases', *Social Cognition*, 19: 395–417.

Moreland, R.L., Hogg, M.A., and Hains, S.C. (1994) 'Back to the Future: Social Psychological Research on Groups', *Journal of Experimental Social Psychology*, 30: 527–55.

Moscovici, S. (1980) 'Toward a Theory of Conversion Behavior', in L. Berkowitz (ed.), *Advances in Experimental Social Psychology* (Vol. 13). New York: Academic Press, pp. 202–39.

Mugny, G. (1982) *The Power of Minorities*. London: Academic Press.

Mullen, B., Brown, R.J., and Smith, C. (1992) 'Ingroup Bias as a Function of Salience, Relevance and Status: An Integration', *European Journal of Social Psychology*, 22: 103–22.

Mummendey, A., Kessler, T., Klink, M., and Mielkle, R. (1999) 'Strategies to Cope with Negative Social Identity: Predications by Social Identity Theory and Relative Deprivation Theory', *Journal of Personality and Social Psychology*, 76: 229–45.

Nemeth, C. (1986) 'Differential Contributions of Majority and Minority Influence', *Psychological Review*, 93: 23–32.

Oakes, P.J., Haslam, S.A., and Turner, J.C. (1994) *Stereotyping and Social Reality*. Oxford: Blackwell.

Otten, S. (2003) '"Me and Us" or "Us and Them"? – The Self as a Heuristic for Defining Minimal Ingroups', *European Review of Social Psychology*, 13: 1–33.

Otten, S., Mummendey, A., and Blanz, M. (1996) 'Intergroup Discrimination in Positive and Negative Outcome Allocations: Impact of Stimulus Valence, Relative Group Status and Relative Group Size', *Personality and Social Psychology Bulletin*, 22: 568–81.

Pettigrew, T.F. (1958) 'Personality and Sociocultural Factors in Intergroup Attitudes: A Cross-National Comparison', *Journal of Conflict Resolution*, 2: 29–42.

Pettigrew, T.F. (1979) 'The Ultimate Attribution Error: Extending Allport's Cognitive Analysis of Prejudice', *Personality and Social Psychology Bulletin*, 5: 461–76.

Pettigrew, T.F. (1998) 'Intergroup Contact Theory', *Annual Review of Psychology*, 49: 65–85.

Pickett, C.L. and Brewer, M.B. (2001) 'Assimilation and Differentiation Needs as Motivational Determinants of Perceived In-Group and Out-Group Homogeneity', *Journal of Experimental Social Psychology*, 37: 341–8.

Postmes T., and Jetten J. (eds), *Individuality and the Group: Advances in Social Identity*. London: Sage.

Pratto, F. (1999) 'The Puzzle of Continuing Group Inequality: Piecing Together Psychological, Social and Cultural Forces in Social Dominance Theory', in M.P. Zanna (ed.), *Advances in Experimental Social Psychology* (Vol. 31). New York: Academic Press, pp. 191–263.

Pratto, F., Sidanius, J., Stallworth, L.M., and Malle, B.F. (1994) 'Social Dominance Orientation: A Personality Variable Predicting Social and Political Attitudes', *Journal of Personality and Social Psychology*, 67: 741–63.

Prentice, D.A. and Miller, D.T. (eds) (1999) *Cultural Divides: Understanding and Overcoming Group Conflict*. New York: Russell Sage Foundation.

Quattrone, G.A. (1986) 'On the Perception of a Group's Variability', in S. Worchel and W. Austin (eds), *The Psychology of Intergroup Relations* (Vol. 2). New York: Nelson-Hall, pp. 25–48.

Rabbie, J.M. and Bekkers, F. (1978) 'Threatened Leadership and Intergroup Competition', *European Journal of Social Psychology*, 8: 9–20.

Rabbie, J.M., Schot, J.C., and Visser, L. (1989) 'Social Identity Theory: A Conceptual and Empirical Critique from the Perspective of a Behavioural Interaction Model', *European Journal of Social Psychology*, 19: 171–202.

Reicher, S.D. (1984) 'The St Pauls' Riot: An Explanation of the Limits of Crowd Action in Terms of a Social Identity Model', *European Journal of Social Psychology*, 14: 1–21.

Reicher, S.D. (2001) 'The Psychology of Crowd Dynamics', in M.A. Hogg and R.S. Tindale (eds), *Blackwell Handbook of Social Psychology: Group Processes*. Oxford: Blackwell, pp. 182–208.

Reicher, S.D. and Hopkins, N. (1986) 'Seeking Influence through Characterising Self-Categories: An Analysis of Anti-Abortionist Rhetoric', *British Journal of Social Psychology*, 35: 297–311.

Reicher, S.D. and Hopkins, N. (2001) *Self and Nation*. London: Sage.

Reynolds, K.J., Turner, J.C., Haslam, S.A., and Ryan, M.K. (2001) 'The Role of Personality and Group Factors in Explaining Prejudice', *Journal of Experimental Social Psychology*, 37: 427–34.

Ridgeway, C.L. (2001) 'Social Status and Group Structure', in M.A. Hogg and R.S. Tindale (eds), *Blackwell Handbook of Social Psychology: Group Processes*. Oxford: Blackwell, pp. 352–75.

Rokeach, M. (ed.) (1960) *The Open and Closed Mind*. New York: Basic Books.

Rosch, E. (1978) 'Principles of Categorization', in E. Rosch and B.B. Lloyd (eds), *Cognition and Categorization*. Hillsdale, NJ: Erlbaum, pp. 27–48.

Ross, L. (1977) 'The Intuitive Psychologist and His Shortcomings', in L. Berkowitz (ed.), *Advances in*

*Experimental Social Psychology* (vol. 10). New York: Academic Press, pp. 174–220.

Rubin, M. and Hewstone, M. (1998) 'Social Identity Theory's Self-Esteem Hypothesis: A Review and Some Suggestions for Clarification', *Personality and Social Psychology Review*, 2: 40–62.

Runciman, W.G. (1966) *Relative Deprivation and Social Justice*. London: Routledge & Kegan Paul.

Sachdev, I. and Bourhis, R.Y. (1991) 'Power and Status Differentials in Minority and Majority Group Relations', *European Journal of Social Psychology*, 21: 1–24.

Sani, F. and Reicher, S.D. (1998) 'When Consensus Fails: An Analysis of the Schism within the Italian Communist Party (1991)', *European Journal of Social Psychology*, 28: 623–45.

Sani, F. and Reicher, S.D. (1999) 'Identity, Argument and Schisms: Two Longitudinal Studies of the Split in the Church of England over the Ordination of Women to the Priesthood', *Group Processes and Intergroup Relations*, 2: 279–300.

Sani, F. and Reicher, S.D. (2000) 'Contested Identities and Schisms in Groups: Opposing the Ordination of Women as Priests in the Church of England', *British Journal of Social Psychology*, 39: 95–112.

Schmitt, M.T. and Branscombe, N.R. (2001) 'The Good, the Bad, and the Manly: Threats to One's Prototypicality and Evaluations of Fellow In-Group Members', *Journal of Experimental Social Psychology*, 37: 510–17.

Schofield, J.W. (1991) 'School Desegregation and Intergroup Relations: A Review of the Literature', in G. Grant (ed.), *Review of Research in Education* (vol. 17). Washington, DC: American Education Research Association, pp. 335–409.

Sedikides, C. and Strube, M.J. (1997) 'Self-Evaluation: To Thine Own Self Be Good, to Thine Own Self Be Sure, to Thine Own Self Be True, and to Thine Own Self Be Better', in M.P. Zanna (ed.), *Advances in Experimental Social Psychology* (Vol. 29). New York: Academic Press, pp. 209–96.

Sherif, M. (1958) 'Superordinate Goals in the Reduction of Intergroup Conflicts', *American Journal of Sociology*, 63: 349–56.

Sherif, M. (ed.) (1962) *Intergroup Relations and Leadership*. New York: Wiley.

Sherif, M. (1966) *In Common Predicament: Social Psychology of Intergroup Conflict and Cooperation*. Boston, MA: Houghton-Mifflin.

Sherif, M., Harvey, O.J., White, B.J., Hood, W., and Sherif, C. (1961) *Intergroup Conflict and Cooperation: The Robbers Cave Experiment*. Norman, OK: University of Oklahoma Institute of Intergroup Relations.

Sherif, M. and Sherif, C.W. (1953) *Groups in Harmony and Tension: An Integration of Studies in Intergroup Behavior*. New York: Harper & Row.

Showers, C. (1992) 'Compartmentalization of Positive and Negative Self-Knowledge: Keeping Bad Apples out of the Bunch', *Journal of Personality and Social Psychology*, 62: 1036–49.

Sidanius, J. and Pratto, F. (1999) *Social Dominance: An Intergroup Theory of Social Hierarchy and Oppression*. New York: Cambridge University Press.

Sidanius, J., Pratto, F., and Bobo, L. (1996) 'Racism, Conservatism, Affirmative Action, and Intellectual Sophistication: A Matter of Principled Conservatism or Group Dominance?', *Journal of Personality and Social Psychology*, 70: 476–90.

Simon, B. and Brown, R.J. (1987) 'Perceived Intragroup Homogeneity in Minority–Majority Contexts', *Journal of Personality and Social Psychology*, 53: 703–11.

Simon, B., Loewy, M., Sturmer, S., Weber, U., Freytang, P., Habig, C., Kampmeier, C., and Spahlinger, P. (1998) 'Collective Identification and Social Movement Participation', *Journal of Personality and Social Psychology*, 74: 646–58.

Smith, E.R. (1993) 'Social Identity and Emotions: Toward New Conceptualizations of Prejudice', in D.M. Mackie and D.L. Hamilton (eds), *Affect, Cognition, and Stereotyping: Interactive Processes in Group Perception*. San Diego, CA: Academic Press, pp. 297–315.

Smith, E.R. (1999) 'Affective and Cognitive Implications of a Group Becoming Part of the Self: New Models of Prejudice and of the Self-Concept', in D. Abrams and M.A. Hogg (eds), *Social Identity and Social Cognition*. Oxford: Blackwell, pp. 183–96.

Smith, E.R. and Henry, S. (1996) 'An In-Group Becomes Part of the Self: Response Time Evidence', *Personality and Social Psychology Bulletin*, 25: 873–82.

Snyder, M. and Cantor, N. (1998) 'Understanding Personality and Social Behavior: A Functionalist Strategy', in D.T. Gilbert, S.T. Fiske, and G. Lindzey (eds), *The Handbook of Social Psychology*, 4th edn. (Vol. 1). New York: MCGraw-Hill, pp. 635–79.

Sorrentino, R.M. and Roney, C.J.R. (1999) *The Uncertain Mind: Individual Differences in Facing the Unknown*. Philadelphia, PA: Psychology Press.

Steele, C.M. (1988) 'The Psychology of Self-Affirmation: Sustaining the Integrity of the Self', *Advances in Experimental Social Psychology*, 21: 261–302.

Steele, C.M. and Aronson, J. (1995) 'Stereotype Vulnerability and the Intellectual Test Performance of African-Americans', *Journal of Personality and Social Psychology*, 69: 797–811.

Stephan, W.G. and Stephan, C.W. (1985) 'Intergroup Anxiety' *Journal of Social Issues*, 41: 157–75.

Struch, N. and Schwartz, S.H. (1989) 'Intergroup Aggression: Its Predictors and Distinctiveness from In-Group Bias', *Journal of Personality and Social Psychology*, 56: 364–73.

Stürmer, S. and Simon, B. (2004) 'Collective Action: Towards a Dual-Pathway Model', *European Review of Social Psychology*, 15: 59–99.

Sumner, W.G. (1906) *Folkways*. Boston, MA: Ginn.

Swim, J.K., Aikin, K.J., Hall, W.S., and Hunter, B.A. (1995) 'Sexism and Racism: Old-Fashioned and

Modern Prejudices', *Journal of Personality and Social Psychology*, 68: 199–214.

Tajfel, H. (1959) 'Quantitative Judgement in Social Perception', *British Journal of Psychology*, 50: 16–29.

Tajfel, H. (1970) 'Experiments in Intergroup Discrimination', *Scientific American*, 223: 96–102.

Tajfel, H. (1981) 'Social Stereotypes and Social Groups', in J.C. Turner and H. Giles (eds), *Intergroup Behaviour*. Oxford: Blackwell, pp. 144–67.

Tajfel, H., Billig, M., Bundy R.P., and Flament, C. (1971) 'Social Categorization and Intergroup Behaviour', *European Journal of Social Psychology*, 1: 149–77.

Tajfel, H. and Turner, J.C. (1986) 'The Social Identity Theory of Intergroup Behavior', in S. Worchel and W. Austin (eds), *Psychology of Intergroup Relations*. Chicago: Nelson-Hall, pp. 7–24.

Taylor, D.M. and Brown, R.J. (1979) 'Towards a More Social Social Psychology', *British Journal of Social and Clinical Psychology*, 18: 173–79.

Taylor, D.M. and Jaggi, V. (1974) 'Ethnocentrism and Causal Attribution in a S. Indian Context', *Journal of Cross-Cultural Psychology*, 5: 162–71.

Taylor, D.M., Wright, S.C., and Porter, L.E. (1994) 'Dimensions of Perceived Discrimination: The Personal/Group Discrimination Discrepancy', in M.P. Zanna and J.M. Olson (eds), *The Psychology of Prejudice: The Ontario Symposium* (vol. 7). Hillsdale, NJ: Erlbaum, pp. 233–55.

Terry, D.J., Carey, C.J., and Callan, V.J. (2001) 'Employee Adjustment to an Organizational Merger: An Intergroup Perspective', *Personality and Social Psychology Bulletin*, 27: 267–80.

Titus, H.E. and Hollander, E.P. (1957) 'The California F-Scale in Psychological Research (1950–1955)', *Psychological Bulletin*, 54: 47–74.

Tropp, L.R. and Wright, S.C. (2001) 'Ingroup Identification as Inclusion of Ingroup in the Self', *Personality and Social Psychology Bulletin*, 27: 585–600.

Turner, J.C. (1981) 'The Experimental Social Psychology of Intergroup Behaviour', in J.C. Turner and H. Giles (eds), *Intergroup Behaviour*. Oxford: Blackwell, pp. 66–101.

Turner, J.C. (1982) 'Towards a Cognitive Redefinition of the Social Group', in H. Tajfel (ed.), *Social Identity and Intergroup Relations*. Cambridge: Cambridge University Press, pp. 15–40.

Turner, J.C. (1991) *Social Influence*. Milton Keynes, UK: Open University Press.

Turner, J.C. and Bourhis, R.Y. (1996) 'Social Identity, Interdependence and the Social Group. A Reply to Rabbie et al.', in W.P. Robinson (ed.), *Social Groups and Identities: Developing the Legacy of Henri Tajfel*. Oxford: Butterworth–Heinemann, pp. 25–63.

Turner, J.C., Hogg, M.A., Oakes, P.J., Reicher, S.D., and Wetherell, M.S. (1987) *Rediscovering the Social Group: A Self-Categorization Theory*. Oxford: Blackwell.

Tyler, T.R., DeGoey, P., and Smith, H. (1996) 'Understanding Why the Justice of Group Procedures Matters: A Test of the Psychological Dynamics of the Group-Value Model', *Journal of Personality and Social Psychology*, 70: 913–30.

Van Dijk, T.A. (1987) *Communicating Racism: Ethnic Prejudice in Thought and Talk*. Newburg Park, CA: Sage.

van Knippenberg, A. and Ellemers, N. (1993) 'Strategies in Intergroup Relations', in M.A. Hogg and D. Abrams (eds), *Group Motivation: Social Psychological Perspectives*. London: Harvester Wheatsheaf. pp 17–32.

Vanman, E.J., Paul, B.Y, Ito, T.A., and Miller, N. (1997) 'The Modern Face of Prejudice and Structural Features That Moderate the Effect of Cooperation on Affect', *Journal of Personality and Social Psychology*, 73: 841–959.

Vanneman, R.D. and Pettigrew, T.F. (1972) 'Race and Relative Deprivation in the Urban United States', *Race*, 13: 461–86.

Vescio, T.K., Hewstone, M., Crisp, R.J., and Rubin, J.M. (1999) 'Perceiving and Responding to Multiple Categorizable Individuals: Cognitive Processes and Affective Intergroup Bias', in D. Abrams and M.A. Hogg (eds), *Social Identity and Social Cognition*. Oxford: Blackwell, pp. 111–40.

von Hippel, W., Sekaquaptewa, D., and Vargas, P. (1995) 'On the Role of Encoding Processes in Stereotype Maintenance', in L. Berkowitz (ed.), *Advances in Experimental Social Psychology* (vol. 27). New York: Academic Press, pp. 177–254.

Walker, I. and Mann, L. (1987) 'Unemployment, Relative Deprivation, and Social Protest', *Personality and Social Psychology Bulletin*, 13: 275–83.

Walker, I. and Pettigrew, T.F. (1984) 'Relative Deprivation Theory: An Overview and Conceptual Critique', *British Journal of Social Psychology*, 23: 301–10.

Weber, R. and Crocker, J. (1983) 'Cognitive Processes in the Revision of Stereotypic Beliefs', *Journal of Personality and Social Psychology*, 45: 961–77.

Wenzel, M. and Mummendey, A. (1996) 'Positive–Negative Asymmetry of Social Discrimination: A Normative Analysis of Differential Evaluations of Ingroup and Outgroup on Positive and Negative Attributes', *British Journal of Social Psychology*, 35: 493–507.

Wilder, D.A. (1984) 'Intergroup Contact: The Typical Member and the Exception to the Rule', *Journal of Experimental Social Psychology*, 20: 177–94.

Williams, K.D. (2001) *Ostracism: The Power of Silence*. New York: Guilford.

Wood, W., Lundgren, S., Ouellette, J.A., Busceme, S., and Blackstone, T. (1994) 'Minority Influence: A Meta-Analytic Review of Social Influence Processes', *Psychological Bulletin*, 115: 323–45.

Worchel, S., Morales, J.F., Páez, D., and Deschamps, J.-C. (eds) (1998) *Social Identity: International Perspectives*. London: Sage.

Wright, S.C., Aron, A., McLaughlin-Volpe, T., and Ropp, S.A. (1997) 'The Extended Contact Effect: Knowledge of Cross-Group Friendships and Prejudice', *Journal of Personality and Social Psychology*, 73: 73–90.

Wright, S.C., Aron, A. and Tropp, L.R. (2002) 'Including Others (and groups) in the Self: Self-Expansion and Intergroup Relations', in J.P. Forgas and K.D. Williams (eds), *The Social Self: Cognitive, Interpersonal and Intergroup Perspectives*. New York: Psychology Press, pp. 343–63.

Wright, S.C., Taylor, D.M., and Moghaddam, F.M. (1990) 'Responding to Membership in a Disadvantaged Group', *Journal of Personality and Social Psychology*, 58: 994–1003.

Zebrowitz, L.A. (1996) 'Physical Appearance as a Basis of Stereotyping', in C.N. Macrae, C. Stangor, and M. Hewstone, (eds), *Stereotypes and Stereotyping*. New York: Guilford, pp. 79–120.

Zimbardo, P.G. (1970) 'The Human Choice: Individuation, Reason, and Order Versus Deindividuation, Impulse, and Chaos', in W.J. Arnold and D. Levine (eds), *Nebraska Symposium on Motivation 1969* (vol. 17). Lincoln, NE: University of Nebraska Press, pp. 237–307.

# 16
# The Social Psychology of Cultural Diversity: Social Stereotyping, Prejudice, and Discrimination

STEPHEN C. WRIGHT AND DONALD M. TAYLOR

**INTRODUCTION**

Current fears of conflict between ethnic, religious and social groups makes understanding the forces that shape and sustain our attitudes about groups both topical and essential. This chapter examines our thoughts about (stereotypes), feelings towards, and evaluations of (prejudice) groups. What is absolutely clear is that these processes are not simply about irrational dislike and unfair mistreatment of members of other groups. Certainly, stereotypes and prejudice are a critical part of the story when relations between groups go wrong. However, they are also essential to group harmony and positive social change. In fact, they are the very basis of group life.

Interaction among different cultural, national, and religious groups has always been an integral part of human social life. Dramatically, however, patterns of immigration, emigration, and the explosion in the refugee population, not to mention travel as well as recent changes in the social mobility of members of traditionally disadvantaged groups, and efforts to reduce segregation, have led to unprecedented group-based diversity in many societies. Those who 'celebrate diversity' see in this an opportunity for innovation and societal growth. However, the rise of ultranationalistic, right-wing organizations makes it clear that diversity is not without its opponents. Nonetheless, concerns about people's thoughts, feelings, judgments, and actions towards members of other groups have become highly relevant to the day-to-day lives of an increasing percentage of the world's population.

Concern for the suffering created by intolerance, hatred, and discrimination has always played a major role in motivating social-psychological work in intergroup relations. Thus, it is not surprising that our present unprecedented diversity coincides with a proliferation of research and theory on the role that group memberships play in our thoughts, feelings, and actions. Managing the relations between groups in a complex, diverse society has become one of our truly great challenges. It is certainly not the intention of this chapter to provide definitive answers to the many challenges posed by societal diversity; however, we do attempt to describe some of what social psychological work on stereotyping, prejudice, and discrimination has contributed to our understanding of the experiences of both societally advantaged and disadvantaged groups.

## Stereotypes, prejudice, and related concepts: defining terms

Although stereotypes were first described as 'pictures in the head' by Lippmann in 1922, Sumner's

(1906) earlier discussion of ethnocentrisms clearly presages the concept. Prejudice, as a construct, has been around for considerably longer. Over the years, numerous definitions and conceptualizations of the terms have been offered. Moreover, the recent rapid proliferation of research and theory has introduced many new terms and led to wide variability in the conceptualization of stereotypes and prejudice. There are lively debates about the benefits of one perspective over the other and about the connections and relationships between perspectives. These debates reveal the intellectual excitement that pervades the field, and have led to some conceptual refinement and to a more detailed understanding of this complex problem. However, they can also leave us confused about what we are talking about. At times, it seems that we may be 'talking past each other' because we have different definitions or understandings of the terms we are using. Thus, it is worthwhile to consider definitions seriously.

We begin our analysis with a careful description of terms. *Stereotypes*, for our purposes, are primarily cognitive and are defined as *the beliefs, shared by members of one group, about the shared characteristics of another group. Prejudice* is *a socially shared judgment or evaluation of the group including the feelings (affect) associated with that judgment.* These are distinct but obviously related concepts, and we will revisit the relationship between stereotypes and prejudice later. However, we will also consider stereotypes and prejudices together as associated components of a more overriding orientation or predisposition towards the group that we will label *intergroup attitudes* (see Esses et al., 1993). We need to draw attention to a number of points about these definitions that we believe to be pivotal, including the evaluative overtones, their socially shared feature, and their relationship to intergroup relations.

### The valence of stereotypes and prejudice

None of our definitions contain information about the evaluative direction of the beliefs, judgments, or orientations. Many definitions of stereotypes and prejudice reflect the strong link that these concepts have had to the study of ethnic and racial groups. This link resulted in a near exclusive focus on derogatory characterizations and feelings directed at out-group members. Thus, most definitions of stereotypes and prejudice have been limited to negative thoughts and feelings. Recently, however, there is a growing recognition that while intergroup conflict and in-group bias may be common, it is useful to consider the processes of categorization and stereotyping as normal and even adaptive (see Chapter 15, this volume; Fiske, 1998; Oakes, 2001; Tajfel, 1981; Taylor and Moghaddam, 1994). Much of the credit for this goes to the introduction and subsequent development of social-identity and self-categorization theories (Tajfel and Turner, 1979; Turner et al., 1987). Despite a continued overwhelming focus on their negative side (see Oakes, 2001; Oakes and Haslam, 2001), most social-psychological accounts now recognize that stereotypes need not be negative, maladaptive, faulty, or irrational.

Prejudice, however, has not faired so well. Many definitions still imply that prejudice is 'unfair', 'unjustified', or 'irrational'. Most definitions maintain the idea of antipathy, containing phrases such as 'negative feelings', 'negative attitudes', and 'derogatory social attitudes' (noteworthy exceptions, Brewer and Kramer, 1985; Tajfel, 1982). However, we believe that there is much to be gained by suspending our own evaluation of prejudice as well. Our judgments and feelings about an out-group can be neutral or, indeed, positive, and, to date, social psychology has seemed uninterested and thus unable to account for these cases. Nor do we agree with those who recognize that out-group evaluations and feelings can be positive, but dismiss favorable out-group orientations as unimportant and unworthy of attention (e.g., Brown, 1995). If one of the goals of our discipline is to promote intergroup harmony, would it not be useful to recognize that harmony may be as much the result of positive judgments of and emotions towards the out-group, as conflict is about negative judgments and emotions?

In addition, while our focus has tended to be on attitudes about an out-group, it is clear that we also hold beliefs and make judgments about our in-groups. However, while the concept of in-group stereotypes (self-stereotypes) has become part of the modern social-psychology parlance (see Chapter 15), the evaluation and emotional reactions towards one's own group are seldom considered in association with attitudes towards the out-group. Concepts such as ethnocentrism or in-group derogation are seldom considered relevant to discussions of 'prejudice'.

Certainly, our analysis of stereotyping and prejudice will be dominated by discussions of the negative side simply because this has been the focus of the vast majority of social-psychological inquiry. There is simply more to report about this side. However, on occasion, we will provide a more balanced approach.

### Stereotypes and prejudice as social phenomena

Our definition of stereotypes and prejudices portrays them as group-based thoughts and feeling. Thus, our focus here is on the ways in which these particular thoughts and feelings are uniquely *social* phenomena.

### Stereotypes and prejudice involve depersonalization

First and foremost, the target of stereotypes and prejudice is a social category. Thus, stereotypes and prejudice involve a depersonalized view of the other (see Chapter 15); members of the target group are seen not as individual persons, but as representatives of the category. Thus, stereotypes and prejudices are held about groups and are applied to individuals not as unique individuals, but rather as interchangeable exemplars of the category.

### Stereotypes and prejudice are socially shared

Stereotypes and prejudices clearly reside in the heads of individuals (see Chapter 4) and there are certainly idiosyncratic differences in the specific content of individual people's beliefs about a given social group (see Esses et al., 1993). However, the most important intergroup attitudes are those that are shared widely by members of a society (Gardner, 1973; Lalonde and Gardner, 1989; Moscovici, 1981; Taylor, 1981; Taylor and Moghaddam, 1994; see also Claire and Fiske, 1998). Intergroup attitudes gain their importance and potency because these beliefs are not only well known (Devine, 1989) but are shared within, and at times across, social groups (Banaji and Greenwald, 1994; Haslam et al., 2002). In this way, stereotypes and prejudice become part of our shared understanding of who 'we' and 'they' are.

Of course, there are individual differences in people's beliefs about groups and even consensually shared intergroup attitudes change. Conversely, there is considerable agreement and consistency, not only across people but also across time (Gilbert, 1951; Karlins et al., 1969). This consistency results, in part, because the content of stereotypes and the judgments of relevant groups become embedded in the culture of the society (see Allport, 1954). This cultural 'knowledge' becomes institutionalized in the norms and practices of a society (Jones, 1996; Pettigrew, 1958, 1991), and is transferred to others through the usual socialization channels – parents, schools, books, the media, and other social institutions. Intergroup attitudes become embedded in language (see Giles, 1977; LeCouteur and Augoustinos, 2001; Ng and Bradac, 1993), not only in the things we say but more subtly in the patterns and style of our communications (e.g., DePaulo and Coleman, 1986; Maass and Arcuri, 1992; Wenneker et al., 2005).

In addition, intergroup attitudes are perpetuated and spread through daily cross-group interactions between individuals. Ridgeway's (e.g., 2001; Ridgeway and Balkwell, 1997) theory and research describe how real group differences in status and power lead to shared expectations about individual group members. These expectations structure daily cross-group interactions between individuals, and repeated participation in these interactions both confirms and strengthens the initial beliefs and transmits them to others through their participation in the interactions. Thus, daily participation in 'normal' social life both solidifies and transmits intergroup attitudes.

While the socially shared nature of intergroup attitudes was a key component of social psychology's early investigations (see Brigham, 1971; Katz and Braly, 1933), it has often been ignored and even denied. The 'social' roots became lost as interest turned sharply to the study of individual cognitive processes (e.g., Hamilton et al., 1994; see also Stangor and Schaller, 1996; Taylor and Moghaddam, 1994). However, if stereotypes were simply the idiosyncratic beliefs of individuals, they would represent relatively unimportant societal phenomena (see Haslam et al., 2002). It is precisely because intergroup attitudes come to be consensually shared that they form the basis for conflict or cooperation between groups. Thus, our definition of both stereotypes and prejudice includes the term 'socially shared', and our analysis focuses on their collective or consensual nature.

### Stereotypes and prejudice are intimately connected to intergroup relations

The third sense in which intergroup attitudes can be understood to be group-based phenomena is their direct connection to intergroup relations. Stereotype content and group evaluations emerge rather directly from the nature of the relationship between the relevant groups. This idea has been a key element of the most influential perspectives in intergroup relations (e.g., Allport, 1954; Brewer and Campbell, 1976; Sherif, 1966; Tajfel and Turner, 1979), and is basic to a number of more recent influential models (e.g., Esses, et al., 2005; Eagly, 1987; Glick and Fiske; 2001a; Jost and Banaji, 1994; Major, 1994; Turner et al., 1987). Stated simply, we might expect that when intergroup relations are harmonious and cooperative, we are likely to see the out-group as having traits, beliefs, and attitudes that are compatible (although not identical) to those of our in-group. If, however, there is intergroup conflict, we are more likely to construct a view of the out-group that is decidedly negative.

Once formed, intergroup attitudes are by no means benign. They provide prescriptions for our interactions with out-group members. That is, when category memberships are salient, people's individual interactions with out-group members will be determined by their stereotypes and prejudices. Because these attitudes are widely shared, there will be considerable consistency in cross-group interactions (e.g., Oakes et al., 1994; Reynolds and Turner, 2001; see also Claire and Fiske, 1998). Thus, in our simplified example, once we see the out-group as having complementary traits and evaluate them positively, we are likely to initiate cooperative, friendly interactions with out-group members. If we describe the out-group as having undesirable traits, we are likely to avoid out-group members or initiate competitive or even hostile interactions.

### *Summary*

We believe this lengthy discussion of definitions goes beyond simply making the reader aware of what we mean by stereotypes and prejudice, to illuminate some of the controversies in this area. Our definitions are quite different from those of others who focus primarily, or exclusively, on the intrapersonal processes associated with perceptions of groups. Our focus is on the *social* nature of stereotypes and prejudice; how they serve as socially shared (collective) representations of groups, how they are guided by the existing intergroup relationship and how they assist in structuring and perpetuating that relationship. In addition, our definitions give full recognition of the possibility of intergroup harmony by removing the exclusive focus on derogatory characteristics and negative evaluations found in most definitions.

## Stereotypes and prejudice as the product of intergroup relations

Stereotypes and prejudice owe much of their content and intensity to the nature of the extant relationship between the groups. Initially, we presented this idea simply with the characterization that intergroup harmony would be associated with positive intergroup attitudes and conflict with negative attitudes. In fact, the association is more complex. In this section, we consider some of the contextual factors that can influence the content, strength, and valence of intergroup attitudes.

## Stereotypes as explanations

One key function of social groups is they provide structure to, and explanation for, the events in our world (e.g., Chapter 15, this volume; Hogg, 2000; McGarty et al., 2002). In order to serve this function, group members must be seen to share attributes that explain their common behaviors and the treatment they receive from others (Oakes et al., 1994; Tajfel, 1981). Thus, real group differences (often the result of socioeconomic factors) provide the foundation or 'soil' for stereotype content. For example, low-status groups are often described as 'lazy', 'stupid', or 'evil'. These characterizations provide an explanation for their low status as well as for the poor treatment they receive from others.

This general idea is consistent with earlier 'grain of truth' theories (Allport, 1954; Brewer and Campbell, 1976). However, social identity and self-categorization theorists (e.g., Oakes et al., 1994; Tajfel, 1981; Turner and Reynolds, 2001) have described this relationship in greater detail and have argued that the relationship between intergroup perceptions and intergroup attitudes is very much like other forms of social knowledge. Thus, intergroup attitudes are no more or less rational than any other inferences that we make about our world. In addition, social-identity approaches have focused on the importance of present situational constraints as well as the broad consistent patterns of intergroup relations in determining the specific stereotypes that are brought to mind in a particular cross-group interaction. That is, it is not only the broader socioeconomic relationship that determines whether an out-group member will be characterized as lazy, stupid, or evil. It is also the current social context. If the context is one in which motivation and hard work are at issue (hiring for a manual labor job), laziness might come to mind and result in a decision not to hire a member of the low-status group. However, if the current context involves a decision about who should receive special attention at airport security, the stereotype of evil might be most salient. To the degree that intergroup attitudes represent our efforts to explain the social world, the specific stereotypes that are brought to mind in a given interaction should be those that are the most useful in guiding our ongoing interaction (see Biernat and Crandall, 1994).

Therefore, the breadth of available intergroup attitudes is, in part, determined by the nature of the intergroup relationship. From this available pool, specific stereotypes and prejudices are brought to mind when the current context makes them relevant, and when they provide some degree of explanation and prescriptions for the particular cross-group interaction. While we may find it distasteful that low-status groups are characterized as lazy or evil, these characterizations are not entirely arbitrary. They provide meaning for the perceiver and prescriptions for his or her actions. This is not to suggest that these characterizations are 'objectively true'. It may not be that the target group is, in fact, less energetic or less moral than the in-group.[1] The point is that these characterizations provide psychologically meaningful explanations for the perceivers' observations of the relative status and treatment of the out-group (or the in-group, in the case of self-stereotyping).

### Entitativity

A number of lines of research have extended this basic view of stereotypes to describe further the role of explanation in intergroup attitudes. For example, attributions to the character of the group, such as describing them as lazy, stupid, or evil, are more likely to be made and are made with more confidence when the group is perceived to have high entitativity (Campbell, 1958; Yzerbyt et al., 2004); that is, to be a bounded unit whole rather than a loosely associated aggregate (Yzerbyt and Rogier, 2001). Thus, it is worth considering what aspects of social reality will encourage a perception of group entitativity.

While entitativity strictly refers to the extent to which a group appears to have the quality of a unit entity, these perceptions can be particularly strong with they are based on the belief that the group members share some 'essential' or biological characteristic – categories such as 'race' or gender are very likely to attract these strong dispositional attributions (Hoffman and Hurst, 1990; Rothbart and Taylor, 1992; Yzerbyt et al., 1997). It may be that groups with greater apparent structure and organization (Hamilton et al., 1998), numerically smaller groups (Mullen, 1991), and minority rather than majority groups (Brewer et al., 1995) will be more readily seen as highly entitative. Finally, when the individual has observed a greater number of cases or when there appears to be greater group homogeneity in relevant attributes (Doosje et al., 1995), it is more reasonable to make more confident generalizations about the fundamental character of the group and its members.

### Roles

Eagly (1987) also evokes the concept of stereotypes as explanations as part of social-role theory (see also Eagly and Wood, 1991). Gender stereotypes are described as deriving from the differential distribution of men and women in particular social roles, roles requiring different specific behaviors. Observers confuse the groups with the roles, thus attributing to women characteristics of nurturance and warmth as a result of their greater representation in the role of homemaker and attributing to men traits of competence and agency because of their overrepresentation in professional and worker roles (Diekman and Eagly, 2000).

Certainly, there remains a great deal of room for individual interpretation, bias, and error (Chapter 4), and the present needs or motives of the particular individual affect intergroup attitude processes (e.g., Sinclair and Kunda, 1999). However, the point here is that intergroup attitudes are not entirely arbitrary. They often reflect direct observations of the 'real' inter-group relationships and represent interpretations of the actions and treatment of the relevant groups. In this sense, the development and utilization of inter-group attitudes is directly influenced by 'reality constrains' (Bourhis et al., 1997; Ellemers et al., 1997b; Spears et al., 2001).

#### *Intergroup attitudes as justification*

While the idea of intergroup attitudes as explanations for the social world is itself an invitation for concern for disadvantaged groups, there is an even more significant concern. In many cases, simple explanation is replaced by justification. Thus, intergroup attitudes serve not only to clarify the position of the groups, but also to justify their status and treatment (Eberhardt and Randall, 1997; Fiske, 1993a; Goodwin et al., 2000; Hoffman and Hurst, 1990; Jost and Banaji, 1994; Tajfel, 1981). Attributing laziness, stupidity, or evil to low-status groups not only explains their disadvantage, but also serves as a justification for their continuing victimization.

This justification function of intergroup attitudes may be motivated by basic psychological motives, including consistency motives (see Crandall and Beasley, 2001), the need for predictability and control, the avoidance of aversive feelings of subjective uncertainty (Hogg, 2000; Hogg and Abrams, 1993), and the need to see one's world as just. Lerner (1980) suggested that, in order to feel reassured about their own position, perceivers justify the occurrence of misfortune by putting some responsibility on the sufferer. This idea has been applied to groups to explain the derogatory intergroup attitudes often directed at groups that suffer as a result of their low status in the social hierarchy (see Major and Schmader, 2001; Sidanius and Pratto, 1999).

### Realistic-conflict theory

This general view of stereotypes and prejudices as justification is also consistent with realistic conflict theory (Sherif, 1966). Here the focus is on the role of material interests. Intergroup attitudes are posited to be the product of the economic relationship between the groups. Real competition over scarce resources leads to hostile and antagonistic interactions that then serve as the basis for negative descriptions and evaluations of the out-group. Sherif's classic 'robber's cave' study, involving two groups of eleven-year-old boys in a specially designed and monitored summer camp experience, clearly demonstrated the importance of the structural relationship between groups in determining the actions and attitudes of the group members (see Taylor and Moghaddam, 1994, for review). This study and numerous replications and extensions (see Platow and Hunter, 2001, for a summary) demonstrated that, rather than being insensitive to reality, stereotyping and prejudice, while often exaggerated, reflect the reality of the in-group's relationship with the out-group.

Research on realistic-group-conflict theory also demonstrates that intergroup attitudes become more extreme and more resistant to change as the conflict between groups becomes more intense and protracted (see also Tajfel, 1981). As more of the group's resources are invested and as the group's self-definition becomes increasingly tied to the conflict, it becomes increasingly important that the characterizations of the in-group and out-group provide justification for the increasingly hostile interactions. This process of hardening of intergroup attitudes provides a partial explanation for the tendency for competitive conflicts to escalate (Pruitt, 1989).

Sherif (1966) also clearly recognized the possibility of intergroup harmony and positive intergroup attitudes in proposing the concept of superordinate goals – mutually beneficial outcomes whose achievement required the joint cooperative participation of both groups. The idea is that cooperative interdependence between groups leads to accommodating interactions and to the generation of complimentary evaluations of the out-group and its members. Dozens of studies have tested both the robustness and the limitations of the concept of superordinate goals (see Taylor and Moghaddam, 1994; Platow and Hunter, 2001, for a recent summary).[2] However, the primary point here is that both positive and negative intergroup attitudes result from efforts to explain and justify the in-group's and the out-group's cooperative or hostile actions.

### Systems justification

As this example illustrates, the justification process affects not only out-group representations but also our stereotypes and evaluations of the in-group. Members of high-status groups tend to represent their in-group in very positive terms. Beyond their obvious ego-enhancing benefit, these positive in-group characterizations provide legitimization of our high-status position and justification for continued in-group favoritism. Similarly, low-status group members may be convinced to accept the unflattering characterizations and evaluations of their in-group as a means of justifying their low status and poorer treatment (see Jost and Banaji, 1994; Mlicki and Ellemers, 1996; Sidanius et al., 2001; Sidanius and Pratto, 1999). Jost et al. (2001) consider how high-status group members can meet their motivation for self-enhancement, enhancement of the in-group and justification of the social system simultaneously by generating positive in-group characterizations and negative out-group characterizations. For low-status groups, these three motives are in conflict. This conflict provides a potential explanation for some of the important negative psychological consequences of disadvantaged-group status (we will revisit this and related issues later in the chapter). Nonetheless, Jost et al. show that under some circumstances the need to justify the broader social system can lead disadvantaged groups to show out-group favoritism and to accept the negative characterization of the in-group.

### *Group-based emotions*

Another recent perspective on prejudice also points to the importance of assessments of the intergroup relationship as a determinant of one's emotional response to the out-group. Smith, Mackie, and colleagues (Mackie et al., 2000; Smith, 1993; Smith and Ho, 2002) propose a model of prejudice as 'group-based emotion' and show that appraisals of the threat posed by the out-group and of the ability of the in-group to respond determine whether the individual will feel anger, disgust, fear, or contempt towards the out-group. The individual's understanding of the relationship between the two groups, in terms of threat and power, determines the in-group's emotional response to the out-group. Thus, when an out-group is perceived to threaten the interests of the in-group and the in-group is perceived not to have the necessary resources to defend itself, prejudice will involve feelings of fear and disgust. However, prejudice will involve feelings of anger and hatred when the in-group is threatened but is perceived to have adequate resources to answer the threat. Compared to traditional approaches to prejudice, which focus primarily on the affective direction (positive or negative) of the evaluation, this approach provides valuable specificity in predicting the actual content of emotional responses (see also Alexander et al., 1999; 2005) to the out-group. In addition, it shares the view that prejudice is directly determined by assessments of the intergroup context.

Complementary work on the group-based emotions among high-status groups has shown that appraisals of the legitimacy of the in-group's advantaged position and of the in-group's culpability in causing and enforcing the out-group's inferior position are critical determinants of feelings of collective guilt (Leach et al., 2002). Branscombe et al. (2000) conclude that collective guilt results when social identity is salient and the person believes the in-group is responsible for violating important standards. Feelings of collective guilt should lower the appraisal of the in-group, improve the appraisal of the out-group and increase willingness to compensate the out-group (see also Iyer et al., 2003). Again, we see that the specific appraisal of the intergroup relationship (in terms of status, legitimacy, and in-group responsibility) determines the specific content and the general valence of the intergroup attitudes.

## Stereotypes and prejudice solidify and maintain intergroup relations

### *Distinguishing between stereotypes and prejudice*

So far, we have been considering stereotypes and prejudice jointly as components of intergroup attitudes. However, it is also very useful to distinguish between the two concepts. While social psychology's 'cognitive revolution' in the 1970s and 1980s led to near exclusive focus on 'cold' cognitive stereotyping (see Fiske, 1998), there was a decided swing in the 1990s back to a focus on the 'hot' affect of prejudice (e.g., Mackie and Hamilton, 1993). The general view now is that affect rather than cognition accounts for the lion's share of the important effects in intergroup relations (see Dovidio et al., 1996; Dijker, 1987; Esses and Dovidio, 2002; Esses et al., 1993; Jackson et al., 1996; Pettigrew, 1998b; Smith, 1993; Stangor et al., 1991; Tropp and Pettigrew, 2005). While the relative importance of stereotypes and affect probably depends on the target group and the local social context, it appears that in many (perhaps most) circumstances, affective measures of prejudice outperform cognitive measures of stereotyping in predicting the general attitude towards the out-group and discriminatory behavior.

It is also important to recognize that while the two are clearly related, the stereotype content does not necessarily imply the direction of the evaluation or the specific affective response. Most stereotypes can be interpreted as either positive or negative. For example, Smith and Ho (2002) report that non-Asian participants' stereotyping of Asian-Americans as 'intelligent' and 'diligent' led some to evaluate Asians positively and to feel admiration and respect, while others evaluated these same characteristics negatively and expressed feelings of hostility, resentment, and threat.

Virtually any trait lends itself to multiple construals and to positive or negative interpretations. This point was made painfully apparent in a comparison of two 'handbills' posted in Vancouver. The first was posted in the early 1900s. It warned Canadians to 'beware the yellow peril' and described how Chinese immigrants were undermining the Canadian economy because they would work for a 'coolie's' wages. The basic message was that the Chinese were undesirable because they were *too poor*. The second handbill posted in the early 1990s was more subtle, but it similarly warned that Chinese immigration was undermining the Canadian economy. According to this handbill, Chinese immigrants were buying up businesses and property and their willingness to pay inflated prices was playing havoc with real-estate markets and local businesses. The basic message was that the Chinese were undesirable because they were *too rich*.

### *Intergroup relations and cross-group agreement about stereotypes and prejudice*

This distinction between content (stereotypes) and affective (prejudice) evaluation is also important in understanding how intergroup attitudes, once formed, can help solidify and maintain the current state of intergroup relations. In an initial model of the influence of intergroup attitudes on intergroup relations, Taylor (1981; Taylor and Moghaddam, 1994) recognized that identical stereotype content could be judged either positively or negatively. With this understanding, one can predict the nature of intergroup relations from the pattern of stereotypes and evaluations by considering:

1 the degree to which the two groups agree about the content of their own and the other's attributes – that is, the degree to which each group's self-stereotypes match the stereotypes held by the other group about them;
2 the valence of the evaluation of in-group and out-group stereotypes – that is, whether each group values (or devalues) the attributes ascribed to the in-group and the out-group.

Implicit in this model is a view that is overlooked in most discussions of stereotypes and prejudice that described prejudice almost exclusively as having to do with out-group evaluations. A discussion of cross-group consensus about stereotype content and group evaluation requires the recognition that group members accept, endorse, and act in accordance with stereotypes and evaluations of *their own group* (Leyens et al., 1994; Oakes et al., 1994). It is usually the case that positively valenced assessments of the in-group are most easily endorsed – we easily accept views of our group that are a source of pride – although this need not always be the case.

Thus, the model holds that intergroup relations will be characterized by conflict in two situations. First, conflict results from cross-group disagreement about each other's stereotypes. That is, conflict arises when group A sees group B as possessing attributes that group B does not agree are characteristic of their group, and/or group B sees group A as possessing attributes that group A does not agree are characteristic of their group. In this case, the conflict is over the content of the group representation, and the struggle is to convince the out-group that we are not as they see us. Examples of this type of intergroup conflict abound. For example, efforts to reduce racial conflict in the USA often involve attempts to change the stereotypes that European-Americans hold to be more consistent with the self-stereotypes of African-Americans and other ethnic minorities. The concepts of cultural sensitivity and intercultural training (Brislin and Yoshida, 1994) are predicated on the idea that cross-cultural conflict is less likely if understanding of the out-group is consistent with their self-conception.

In the second case, intergroup conflict arises when there is consensus across groups about the content of each group's character (that is, self-stereotypes match the stereotypes held by the other group), but there is disagreement about the valence of the evaluation of these characteristics. Here, while groups see their own characteristic as admirable, the out-group views these same traits negatively. The struggle here is to convince the out-group to see our attributes in a more positive light. An example of this might be the 'Black is beautiful' movement in the USA, or the 'French immersion education' movement in Canada. The intention was to change the perception of the attribute so it was respected and valued by both white and black Americans or by both French and English Canadians.

Intergroup harmony can also arise in two contexts. The first involves legitimized intergroup inequality, where there is agreement across groups about both the content and the evaluation of group attributes. However, the consensus is that the attributes of one group – the dominant group – are positively valued and the attributes of the other group – the subordinate group – are not. Here we have the legitimized consensual domination described by system-justification (Jost et al., 2001) and social-dominance (Sidanius and Pratto, 1999) theories. The negative characterizations of the subordinate group and the positive characterization of the dominant group serve the dominant group well, and there is little reason for them to object to the existing perceptions. In addition, when the pressures to accept the dominant perspective are strong, subordinate group members acquiesce, accepting their relatively negative characterization (see also Jackman, 1994; Major, 1994; Major and Schmader, 2001; Martin, 1986). As long as the cross-group consensus remains, there will be continued domination of one group by the other in a highly stable (nonconflictive) group hierarchy.

In the other case of intergroup harmony, the two groups agree about the content of each other's attributes and evaluate both the in-group and out-group attributes positively. That is, there is mutual respect for the consensually shared stereotypes of each group. This configuration of intergroup attitudes may seem optimistic given social psychology's consistent focus on intergroup conflict. However, this conceptualization of intergroup relations is at the core of concepts such as 'pluralism' 'multiculturalism', and 'diversity' (see Flowers and Davidov, 2006) that serve as the basis for widely supported programs such as multicultural education (e.g., Banks 1997; Stephan and Stephan 2001), intercultural training (e.g., Brislin and Yoshida, 1994), and diversity training (e.g., Hollister et al., 1993; Rudman et al., 2001) (see also Aboud and Levy, 2000; Oskamp and Jones, 2000). Kramer and Carnevale (2001) discuss ways to create 'sustained trust in intergroup negotiations'. Many of the strategies they describe clearly recognize that the two groups can maintain and express distinct identities while still coming to hold a positive (trusting) orientation towards each other.

In summary, the match or mismatch between the content of in-group and out-group stereotypes and/or the match or mismatch of the evaluation of those stereotypes can influence the nature of the general intergroup relations. A mismatch between our self-stereotypes and the out-group's stereotypes about our group, or a mismatch in the perceived valence of the groups' attributes can lead to intergroup conflict. Intergroup harmony is associated with cross-group matches. In addition, in the case of matching, the content of the stereotypes and the valence of evaluation are implicated in the degree to which the intergroup relations will be characterized by subordination and domination or by more equal, mutually respectful relations.

### *The self-fulfilling prophecy*

There are other ways in which intergroup attitudes help to maintain the relations between groups that are less dependent on the self-stereotypes of the target group. One involves the self-fulfilling impact of stereotypes and prejudice. A series of studies on 'behavioral confirmation' or 'the self-fulfilling prophecy' have clearly demonstrated that a perceiver's attitudes about an out-group can lead him or her to interact with members of that group in such a way as to elicit behaviors that confirm their expectations (e.g., Smith et al., 1999; Snyder and Swann, 1978; Snyder et al., 1977; Zanna and Pack, 1975; see Snyder, 1992, for a review).

In a classic study by Word et al. (1974), white interviewers' negative expectations about black people led them to be generally less comfortable, less intimate, and less supportive with a black than a white interviewee. A second part of the study showed that these subtle changes in the interviewer's behavior resulted in poorer performance by the interviewee. Thus, the white perceiver's negative prejudices led him to interact with the black person in such as way as to elicit responses that confirmed his negative expectations. When these individual interactions are repeated over and over across many interaction pairs and across time (see Claire and Fiske, 1998), this process can help to solidify the broader societal inequality between the groups.

### *Stereotype threat*

Recently, led by the work of Claude Steele and his colleagues (see Steele, 1998; Steele et al., 2002), an important extension has been made to our understanding of the subtlety and power of stereotypes to affect targets of negatively charged stereotypes. Because stereotypes and prejudice are part of our cultural knowledge (see Devine, 1989), and the content and evaluation of these characterizations are well known to members of the target group (Steele and Aronson, 1995), anxiety that one might be treated on the basis of these stereotypes or that one might confirm these stereotypes places additional pressures on members of the targeted group. This heightened pressure can interfere with their performance on the relevant task. Thus, the stereotype-threatened person performs more poorly on the task, perhaps confirming the stereotyped expectation.

For example, in a series of experiments, Steele and Aronson (1995) demonstrated that African-American university students are well aware of stereotypes about the intellectual inferiority of black people and that knowledge that others also know these stereotypes leads black students to be concerned that, should they perform poorly on a task that is diagnostic of intelligence, they will be seen to have confirmed the stereotype. Thus, when presented with an 'intelligence test', African-American students face the additional pressures associated with these fears, and this additional pressure interferes with their performance. The result is that African-American students perform more poorly than they would have in the absences of the stereotype threat.

Numerous studies have replicated this finding and extended it to other societal groups and other stereotype content, such as women and mathematical ability (e.g., Spencer et al., 1999), low socio-economic status and intelligence (Croizet and Claire, 1998), the elderly and memory (Levy, 1996), Latino women and mathematical ability (Gonzales et al., 2002), women and negotiation skills (Kray etal., 2001), and black and white men in the context of athletic performance (Stone et al., 1999). In each case, making either the relevant group identity or the specific negative stereotype salient led to poorer performance.

There are a number of aspects of this general finding that are of particular importance. First, stereotype threat is contextually dependent. That is, members of target groups are not chronically under threat (and thus chronically underperforming). Rather, it only occurs in contexts where the stereotype is relevant to performance and where the relevant group identity is salient. It is also most likely to occur when the performance requirements are quite demanding (for example, the test is hard). In addition, in order to experience stereotype threat, the persons must be 'domain identified'. That is, they must care about their performance in that domain. People whose self-esteem is not attached to their performance in that domain will be unaffected by stereotype threats. In fact, domain disidentification – reducing the degree to which one's identity is attached to the relevant domain (or to the threatening feedback in that domain) – has been proposed as one coping strategy for those who face chronic stereotype threat (see Major and Schmader, 1998; Steele et al., 2002).

The importance of context is made very clear in research by Stone et al. (1999). Using a ten-hole minigolf game, they demonstrated stereotype threat effects for both black and white athletes. As predicted, white athletes underperformed when the game was described as testing 'natural athletic ability' (priming a negative stereotype about white athletes), and black athletes underperformed when the game was described as testing 'sports strategic intelligence' (priming a negative stereotype about black athletes). Thus, stereotype threat can be experienced by members of any group, but only when the context makes salient a well-known negative in-group stereotype.

However, this does not mean that stereotype threat is an uncommon experience for members of devalued groups. For the African-American students at Stanford University who served as the participants in Steele and Aronson's studies, their numerical distinctiveness on campus is a frequent reminder of their ethnic group membership (Lord and Saenz, 1985; Pettigrew and Martin, 1987), and intellectual ability may appear relevant to many of their daily activities (such as classes and tests). Consequently, these students may well face a steady diet of threatening experiences. In fact, stereotype threat is a much more common occurrence for members of societally disadvantaged groups because the negative stereotypes about these groups tend to be more negative, more numerous, and more global in their application. It is also likely that situational cues that strengthen the target's concern that stereotyping is going to occur will increase the threat. Steele et al. (2002) propose that stereotype threat will be greatest when there are cues that the present environment is 'culturally centered', that is, that it is dominated by a cultural orientation other than one's own.

While we will discuss other ways that stereotypes and prejudices affect disadvantaged group members later in the chapter, we describe the work on stereotype threat here to point out the enormous power of consensual stereotypes. Unlike the systems-justification effects, stereotype threat does not require that disadvantaged group members accept the negative stereotype of their group. In fact, it is strong objections to the stereotype that motivate the desire not to confirm it. In addition, unlike the self-fulfilling prophecy, which requires discriminatory behavior by the out-group member, stereotype threat does not require any direct discrimination. The mere knowledge that others know the stereotype is enough to produce performance deficits. This point was made rather dramatically in one of Steele and Aronson's (1995) original studies. They found that simply asking black students to indicate their race on an information sheet prior to taking an 'intelligence test' raised stereotype threat and impaired performance.

### *Institutional discrimination*

Finally, intergroup attitudes become institutionalized so that discriminatory practices become part of the structure of societal institutions (Pettigrew, 1985). Not only does this institutionalization serve to sustain intergroup attitudes by encouraging (even mandating) attitude-consistent behavior, but it also can render these original attitudes unnecessary for continued discrimination. That is, once in place, these institutional practices can maintain group-based inequality even if the attitudes change to become more egalitarian (see Pettigrew, 1998b). Thus, past negative intergroup attitudes have residual effects on intergroup relations that maintain the relative status of the groups even after these initial attitudes have been replaced by ones that are much more positive.

## Complexity in intergroup attitudes: modern, aversive, and ambivalent prejudice

A number of recent theories have made apparent the need for an even more complex view of intergroup attitudes. Not only can the content of the stereotype and the affective evaluation vary somewhat independently, it appears that intergroup attitudes are often much more conflicted, ambivalent, and complicated than we may first think (e.g., Fiske, 1998; MacDonald and Zanna, 1998; Operario and Fiske, 2001). Often intergroup attitudes are associated with conflicting feelings and contain a combination of positive and negative characterizations, evaluations, and emotions (see also Kay and Jost, 2003).

In view of the rather convincing evidence that blatant expressions of negative prejudice towards ethnic minorities, and African-Americans in particular, have declined steadily in America (see Dovidio et al., 1996), a number of theories of 'contemporary' racism have emerged: *symbolic* and *modern racism* (e.g., McConahay, 1986; Sears, 1988), *ambivalent racism* (e.g., Katz and Glass, 1979; Katz and Hass, 1988), and *subtle racism* (e.g., Pettigrew and Meertens, 1995). We are unable here to explore fully the details of each of these perspectives. However, all three distinguish between two forms of prejudice. One (usually described as 'old-fashioned') is overt, blatant, and hostile, involving clearly negative and derogatory characterizations of the out-group. The second (usually considered more contemporary) is more subtle, often containing conflicting cognitions and affect towards the out-group, and often camouflaged with rationalizations and ideologies that justify avoidance and support of discriminatory practices (see Augoustinos and Walker, 1998; Brown, 1995; Walker, 2001). In addition, all three perspectives hold that the contemporary form of prejudice is much more pervasive than the 'old-fashioned' form and that it now accounts for most current discrimination.

### *Aversive racism*

Another influential account of contemporary prejudice is Gaertner and Dovidio's (e.g., 1986, 2005) model of *aversive racism*. This view holds that many (perhaps most) white Americans firmly endorse egalitarian principles and see themselves as nonprejudiced. They express support for racial equality, condemn overt expressions of prejudice, and are very concerned about appearing nonprejudiced. However, aversive racists also harbor negative attitudes and emotions (fears) about African-Americans. These negative evaluations are actively dissociated from their nonprejudiced self-representation and, thus, are often below the level of conscious awareness. However, these unconscious feelings can have important influences on the aversive racist's behavior. Aversive racists find cross-group interactions uncomfortable, even stressful, and subsequently find reasons to avoid interactions with the out-group. While they will appear completely nonprejudiced when they are aware that their actions could be seen to demonstrate bias or prejudice, when their actions appear to be unrelated to race, or when discriminatory actions can be reasonably explained away, they show clear discrimination against out-group members (for reviews, see; Gaertner and Dovidio, 2000; 2005 see also Crosby et al., 1980).

One way that aversive racism leads to discrimination involves the tendency of aversive racists to support the status quo. While blatant racists support policies that directly limit the rights and opportunities of the out-group, aversive racists object to these obviously racist initiatives. However, when it comes to policies that would remove existing barriers, or improve opportunities for the out-group, aversive racists tend to support the status quo. Thus, aversive racism has been implicated in opposition to programs such as affirmative action (Dovidio et al., 1989; Murrell et al., 1994).

This view of contemporary racism is consistent with the present analysis of the role of the broader intergroup relations in determining intergroup attitudes and actions. The negative unconscious orientation is the result of centuries of blatant discrimination and a lingering negative representation of the out-group, and the strong egalitarian self-concept is the result of endorsing the modern cultural imperatives of fairness, justice and racial equality.

The aversive-racism perspective also points to the importance of subconscious or 'implicit' processes in intergroup attitudes. This idea that important elements of intergroup cognitions and emotions reside below our conscious awareness, but nonetheless can have important implications for our overt thoughts and actions, has attracted a great deal of attention in recent years (see Brauer et al., 2000; Dovidio et al., 2001). While the measurement and meaning of implicit prejudice remain sources of lively debate (e.g., Arkes and Tetlock, 2004; Blanton and Jaccard, 2006), there is growing evidence that implicit prejudices can have interesting and important influences on intergroup behavior and that these influences are not necessarily identical to those found for explicit prejudice (e.g., Banaji et al., 2004; Dasgupta and Rivera, 2006; Dovidio et al., 2002, Florak et al., 2001; Hugenberg and Bodenhausen, 2003; McConnell and Liebold, 2001; Towles-Schwen and Fazio, 2003).

### *Ambivalent sexism*

Recent work by Glick, Fiske, and their colleagues (see Glick and Fiske, 2001a, for a review) has demonstrated that attitudes toward women contain a combination of both highly positive, socially valued attributes (for example, warm and nurturant) as well as negative undesirable traits (for example, incompetent). In addition, the near universal domination of women by men requires not only hostile negative representations of women that legitimize their subjugation, but also benevolent positive representations of women that assist in keeping women dependent upon men.

Domination and protection are combined to produce a paternalistic relationship where women are characterized as less competent, but highly valued, and men are thus obligated to protect but also control women. In addition, gender differentiation and enforcement of gender roles combine hostility and benevolence. They describe women as less able to make important decisions and hold positions of authority and power, while 'awarding' women traits (such as warmth and kindness) and activities (such as child-rearing) that are highly valued. In fact, in a head-to-head comparison, men and women agree that 'women's traits' are at least as positive as 'men's traits', leading to what Eagly and Mladinic (1993) call the 'women are wonderful' phenomenon. Finally, heterosexual intimacy also involves ambivalence, including the hostile view of women as seductress and possessors of the power to withhold sex (the *femme fatale*) and the benevolent view of women as partners in passionate, intimate, and fairy-tale-like romance.

Glick and Fiske (2001a, 2001b; Fiske et al., 1999) extend their approach to describe a general model of intergroup relations based on the idea that group stereotypes fall along two dimensions: competence and warmth (see also Allport, 1954; Eagly, 1987). These two dimensions combine to produce four possible combinations of stereotype content: two that involve consistency in terms of the evaluative direction and two that are ambivalent. Groups which are judged as both competent and warm (such as doctors and teachers) are 'admired', and groups which are judged both incompetent and not warm (such as poor black people or welfare recipients) are the target of 'contemptuous prejudice'. Groups such as traditional women and the elderly, who are seen as warm but not competent, are the target of 'paternalistic prejudice', and groups such as Jews and Asians, who are characterized as competent but not warm, are the target of 'envious prejudice'.

Glick and Fiske (2001a) further propose that the type of prejudice results directly from the structural relations between the two groups along two dimensions: their relative status and the nature of their relationship with the in-group (competitive or cooperative). Relatively high-status groups will be seen as competent, and low-status groups will be seen as incompetent. Cooperation with the in-group will be rewarded with attributions of warmth, while competition will lead to the attribution that the group is not warm. Thus, 'admiration' is reserved for high-status cooperative out-groups, 'envious prejudice' for high-status competitive out-groups, 'paternalistic prejudice' for low-status cooperative out-groups, and 'contemptuous prejudice' for low-status competitive out-groups.

Finally, Glick and Fiske (2001a) argue that while contemptuous prejudice (the entirely negative view of the out-group) may seem the most problematic form of prejudice, this may not be the case. Paternalistic prejudice can be used to justify long-term subordination of low-status groups and even colonialism and slavery (see Jackman, 1994). In addition, envious prejudice places economically successful minorities at particular risk of 'justified' aggression, as in the Nazi belief in a Jewish conspiracy (see Glick, 2002) or the view of many

European-Americans of the competent but overly competitive and untrustworthy Asian (see Smith and Ho, 2002).

The ambivalent sexism model is consistent with several main points made in this chapter. First it focuses on the functional relationship between the groups as the agent of consensual group stereotypes and prejudice evaluations. Second, it recognizes the possibility that out-groups can be characterized entirely positively in the case of admiration and partially positively in the two cases of ambivalent prejudices.

Finally, the ambivalent sexism model focuses on two dimensions of intergroup relations that have received considerable attention as mediators of intergroup attitudes and intergroup behavior – competitive versus cooperative relations, and relative group status. We have already discussed the dimension of cooperation and competition in reference to Sherif (1966) and realistic-conflict theory. However, this theory has been criticized (see Taylor and Moghaddam, 1994) for failing to represent adequately the second importance dimension of status differences. A dominant feature of most real-world intergroup relations is inequality of resources, status, and power, and stratification into relatively advantaged and disadvantaged groups. In the next section, we consider the importance of status in intergroup relations with a brief discussion of the impact of relative advantage, but with greater attention to the experiences and actions of members of low-status groups.

## Intergroup status differences

The study of stereotyping and prejudice has focused almost exclusively on members of relatively advantaged (dominant) groups. However, most of this research has not focused on the advantaged group engaged in a dynamic relationship with a disadvantaged group. The prejudiced person is considered with relatively little reference to the target. When we instead take an explicitly *intergroup* focus, we begin to consider how the actions of both the disadvantaged and advantaged groups are determined by their relationship and their perceptions of the in-group in comparison to the out-group.

Social-identity theory (Tajfel and Turner, 1979; see also Hogg and Abrams, 1988) holds that in-group behavior is, at least in part, motivated by the desire to hold a positively valued and distinctive social identity. Thus, we wish to belong to social groups that are recognizably different from other groups and that hold a relatively high-status position. Two points are important here. First, membership in a high-status group is desirable, and membership in a low-status group is generally undesirable. Second, a group's status is determined by intergroup comparisons. Thus, members of advantaged groups should be motivated to maintain their superior position, and disadvantaged groups should be motivated to improve their relative position. However, despite their similar motives, their differing status leads to interesting asymmetries in their behaviors.

### *Power and advantaged/disadvantaged group asymmetry*

Simon and his colleagues (Simon et al., 2001) describe an asymmetry they label 'mindful minorities and mindless majorities'. Advantaged group members, because of their superior status, pay little attention to the intergroup relationship (Azzi, 1992; Leach et al., 2002). They are less likely than disadvantaged group members to recognize their group membership or to identify spontaneously with the in-group (Mullen, 1991). This stems, in part, from the usual confound that powerful groups tend also to be the numerical majority. Thus, defining themselves in terms of their group membership is simply less descriptive. However, it also results because their social identity is 'unmarked' (see Leach et al., 2002). They are, after all, the 'default'.

However, this does not mean that members of the advantaged group are less likely to engage in intergroup behavior. Their relative obliviousness to group membership seems to apply primarily to the in-group (Simon, 1993). Members of a powerful group need not attend to the individual characteristics, needs, or desires of subordinate group members. Thus, they are likely to see the disadvantaged group in highly categorical terms (Fiske, 1993b; Fiske and Depret, 1996). In addition, members of powerful groups have little motivation to monitor or inhibit their expressions of prejudice and discrimination (Operario and Fiske, 1998). However, the most extreme prejudice and discrimination result when powerful groups perceive a disadvantaged group as threatening their high-status position. Advantaged-group members tend strongly to endorse the legitimizing myths that support the status quo. Thus, the disadvantaged group's attempt to undermine their position not only threatens their material advantage, but is also seen as inappropriate, unjust, or even immoral. The resulting indignation leads to emotions such as anger, outrage, and disgust (see Smith, 1993).

Members of disadvantaged groups, however, must remain much more aware of the intergroup relationship and attend more carefully to the actions and interests of advantaged-group members (Azzi, 1992). Often, low status implies material dependency on high-status group members or threats of physical force. Therefore, low-status group members must adapt their actions to meet the desires of advantaged-group members in order to ensure the continued supply of needed resources or to avoid provoking a violent response (Operario and Fiske, 1998). Thus, it is not surprising that, for the most part, research shows that high-status groups show greater in-group favoritism in resource allocation (see Mullen et al., 1992; Sachdev and Bourhis, 1991).

### *Facing disadvantage*

For much of its history, the social-psychological study of prejudice and discrimination focused on the source rather than the target (noteworthy exceptions: Jones et al., 1984; Tajfel and Turner, 1979). Recently, however, there has been a dramatic shift, and the disadvantaged perspective has become a major focus, producing a number of collections and reviews (e.g., Branscombe and Ellemers, 1998; Crocker et al., 1998; Crocker and Quinn, 2001; Ellemers and Barreto, 2001; Heatherton et al., 2000; Major et al., 2002; Oyserman and Swim, 2001; Swim and Stangor, 1998). There are numerous lines of research in this area (for example, stereotype threat considered earlier). However, we consider briefly two basic questions:

1 When do people notice the discrimination and prejudice and what are the consequences of that recognition?
2 How do people respond to membership in a disadvantaged group?

#### Recognizing discrimination or not

Expressions of prejudice and discrimination remain a common experience for disadvantaged-group members. Often they are subtle and veiled, creating a situation of 'attributional ambiguity' (Crocker and Major, 1989), in which the target must decide whether the act was really discrimination or not. This raises the questions: When do attributions to discrimination occur? and What is the result of noticing or failing to notice discrimination?

The answers to these questions turn out to be anything but simple, as demonstrated by the two competing dominant theoretical perspectives on this issue (see Major et al., 2002). The vigilance perspective proposes that disadvantaged-group members become 'hypersensitive' to signs of prejudice (Allport, 1954; Feldman-Barrett and Swim, 1998). While there are a number of accounts of vigilance, a key focus of this position has been Crocker and Major's (1989) claim that attributions to discrimination can buffer self-esteem when a disadvantaged-group member receives negative feedback. Blaming prejudice for one's negative treatment is less damaging to one's self-esteem than blaming flaws in one's character. Major, Crocker, and colleagues (see Major et al., 2002) have amassed considerable evidence supporting this claim. Under a variety of circumstances, members of stigmatized groups recognize discrimination, and this can have buffering effects on their personal self-esteem.

The alternative perspective holds that disadvantaged-group members tend to be less aware of discrimination than perhaps they ought to be; that they minimize the degree to which they experience discrimination. Crosby (1984) found that while working women were objectively disadvantaged relative to their male counterparts and were well aware of discrimination against women in general, they perceived little or no discrimination directed at themselves. Crosby labeled this 'the denial of personal discrimination'. Subsequently, Taylor et al. (1990) showed that, while the word 'denial' was probably overly emphatic – members of many groups recognize personal discrimination – there is a robust tendency for people to see themselves as less discriminated against than their group as a whole. The cause of this effect, labeled the 'personal/group-discrimination discrepancy' (Taylor et al., 1990), has been the source of debate (e.g., Dion and Kawakami, 1996; Postmes et al., 1999; Taylor et al., 1996; Zanna et al., 1987). However, we share Olson and his colleagues' (Olson and Hafer, 2001; Olson et al., 1995; Quinn et al., 1999) conclusion that this phenomenon is overdetermined and results from a number of cognitive and motivational processes, one of which is the minimization of personal discrimination (Taylor et al., 1994). The minimization hypothesis is also supported by other research findings and theoretical perspectives too plentiful to review here (e.g., Crocker et al., 1993; Crosby and Ropp, 2002; Glick and Fiske, 2001a; Jost and Banaji, 1994; Kaiser and Miller, 2001a; Ruggiero and Taylor, 1995, 1997; Stangor et al., 2002). However, it seems clear that, under some circumstances, members of disadvantaged groups fail to recognize discrimination against them or fail to label these acts as discrimination.

Our view is that, rather than arguing the relative merits of these two perspectives, we should recognize that both vigilance and minimization occur. We propose that one explanation for the variance in this behavior involves the combined impact of the level of identity made salient by the current context (e.g., Schmitt and Branscombe, 2002) and the individual's current goals and motives (Taylor et al., 1994), including relationship concerns (Crosby, 1984). For example, consider a female student who is being evaluated by a stranger on an individual performance task (the usual scenario in an attributional ambiguity paradigm). She is likely to have an individual performance goal and to be thinking of herself as an individual (personal identity salient). If she has any relationship concerns, they probably involve impressing the experimenter with whom she is interacting, not the unseen evaluator. Under these circumstances, attributing a poor evaluation to the judge's prejudice makes sense. It allows her to suspend judgment on her performance goals, to save face with her primary audience (cf., Kaiser and Miller, 2001b), and to protect the currently salient element of her self-esteem, her personal self-esteem.

However, consider another scenario involving consistent mild discrimination (sexism perhaps) perpetrated by a close other. The discrimination probably involves sexist comments, harassment, jokes, or an expectation of traditional gender-role adherence, and has little to do with performance evaluation. Maintaining or enhancing the interpersonal relationship (individual identity salient) may be very important (strong relationship goal). Under these circumstances, minimization is likely. The interaction is highly interpersonal, and the relationship goals make labeling one's partner a sexist very costly.

In a final scenario, imagine a woman who is strongly identified with her minority-ethnic group. She has just attended a rally protesting the end of affirmative action (group identity highly salient). One of the speakers argued that affirmative action is necessary to fight continuing ethnic discrimination. On her way home, a white male gruffly mutters something to her, but she cannot hear the content. Under these circumstances, she is very likely to make an attribution to prejudice, not to buffer her personal self-esteem, but to affirm her present understanding of the world and to legitimize her struggle for ethnic equality (Wright and Tropp, 2002). This attribution may even enhance collective self-esteem by affirming her group's worldview and the legitimacy of their actions.

The general point is that making attributions to discrimination, or avoiding them, probably results from a variety of interrelated motives, goals, and identity issues.[3] The question should not be whether disadvantaged-group members notice, minimize, or exaggerate the discrimination they face, but, rather, how these processes are influenced by the current context and personal and collective motives.

## Behavior: individual mobility or collective action

Given that 'privileged groups rarely give up their privileges without strong resistance', according to Martin Luther King, Jr., the stability of the intergroup hierarchy depends principally on the actions of the disadvantaged. Lalonde and Cameron (1994) review a number of efforts to conceptualize the range of possible actions available to disadvantaged-group members. Most of these frameworks distinguished between *individual* and *collective action*. Individual action is intended to improve one's personal conditions, and collective action is designed to improve the position of one's entire group. Wright et al. (1990a) also distinguish between *normative* actions, which conform to the norms of the social system, and *nonnormative action,* which violates existing social rules, and point out that disadvantaged-group members may take no action to alter the status quo (see Martin, 1986).

From the perspective of advancing social change and creating greater intergroup equality, collective (perhaps collective nonnormative) action is the most effective strategy (see Wright, 2001a for a review). In fact, there is some evidence that individual action, while perhaps raising one's personal status, can legitimize and reinforce existing intergroup inequalities (Ellemers, 2001; Wright, 2001b). Thus, perhaps the most interesting question is, 'When will disadvantaged-group members take collective action instead of pursuing their individual interests or doing nothing?'

The choice to act collectively rather than individually hinges first on identification with the disadvantaged in-group (Branscombe and Ellemers, 1998; Ellemers et al., 1997a; Simon, 1998; Simon and Klandermans, 2001; Stürmer and Simon, 2004; Wright and Tropp, 2002). In-group identification refers to the degree to which one's group identity is an important element of the self (see Tropp and Wright, 2001). While both high and low identifiers are likely to be unhappy when facing discrimination, low identifiers are likely to be unhappy because they are being treated on the basis of their group membership and will distance themselves from the disadvantaged group (take individual action). High identifiers are more likely to be angry that their group is being treated poorly and will consider collective action to reduce group-based discrimination (Branscombe and Ellemers, 1998).

Next, members of the disadvantaged group must assess (a) the permeability of intergroup boundaries; (b) the legitimacy; and (c) the stability of the intergroup context; and (d) the availability of normative channels for change (see Tajfel and Turner, 1979; Wright, 2001a). Wright (1997, 2001b) has argued, in a manner consistent with Tajfel (1982), that boundary permeability may be the primary assessment in determining disadvantaged-group behavior (see also Taylor and McKirnan, 1984). This assessment involves the degree to which the advantaged group is open or closed to qualified members of the disadvantaged group.

Perceiving boundary permeability leads to dissociation from the disadvantaged in-group, and a preference for individual actions. Conversely, perceiving boundary impermeability leads to increased in-group identification, motivation to improve the in-group's position, and collective action (Ellemers, 1993; Lalonde and Silverman, 1994; Wright and Taylor, 1998; Wright et al., 1990a, 1990b).

While most studies have characterized boundary permeability as a dichotomous distinction between an 'open' and a 'closed' condition, Wright (e.g., 2001b) has argued that in contemporary North American society (and many other intergroup contexts), group boundaries are restricted such that a small number of disadvantaged-group members are accepted into advantaged positions, while access is systematically blocked for the rest of the group (see also Pettigrew and Martin, 1987) – a context labeled 'tokenism'. In several experiments, Wright and his colleagues (Wright, 1997; Wright and Taylor, 1998; Wright et al., 1990a) have shown that, while closed intergroup contexts produce strong endorsement of nonnormative collective action, when as few as 2 percent of the qualified members of the disadvantaged group are allowed access to advantaged positions, individual actions become the response of choice. The slightest hint of permeability appears to undermine interest in collective action. There is some evidence that tokenism may have this effect by focusing attention on personal identities and encouraging interpersonal comparisons with the successful tokens. However, there is also evidence that tokenism obfuscates assessments of legitimacy and stability.

When disadvantaged-group members cannot (or will not) abandon the disadvantaged group, individual action is no longer an option. They must choose between collective action and inaction. Now, collective action depends upon the perception that the in-group's low status is illegitimate. Feelings of illegitimacy arise from the sense that one's group is deprived of something to which they are entitled (Major, 1994), and provide the motivation and justification for potentially costly and dangerous nonnormative collective actions (Abrams, 1990; Grant and Brown, 1995).

However, feelings of illegitimacy alone seldom produce collective action. Disadvantaged-group members must believe that there is enough instability in the social system that change in the status of the in-group is possible, and they must believe that the in-group has the necessary resources or abilities to effect change. When perceived illegitimacy and instability are combined, collective action becomes likely. Normative actions usually involve considerably less risk and are the preferred choice. However, if normative channels are unavailable or prove unsuccessful, or if the level of discontent is extremely high, collective nonnormative action will result.

Simon and Klandermans (2001) introduce the concept of 'politicized collective identity', adding the need to label clearly the out-group as the enemy (see also Wright and Tropp, 2002) and a sense of oneself as involved in the general political process, to the requirement for collective political participation. This conception of collective action, while similar to other analyses, places it much more firmly in the political and societal context.

Given the near universality of intergroup inequality, it is perhaps surprising that protest and rebellion are relatively uncommon events. However, the infrequency of nonnormative collective action hints at the many obstacles that can derail the processes necessary to motivate this form of behavior.

## Reducing prejudice

From the disadvantaged group's perspective, recognizing collective mistreatment, delegitimizing the existing unequal relationship, and taking collective action are the primary solutions to intergroup inequality. However, social psychology's focus on the advantaged group has made prejudice reduction the primary goal. In this section, we consider how, despite their persistence, intergroup attitudes can undergo significant change. Recently, more social psychologists have set aside traditional concerns about promoting applications of their research (see Pettigrew, 2001), and a number of recent reviews, collections, and books review strategies for reducing prejudice and discrimination (e.g., Aboud and Levy, 1999; Brewer and Gaertner, 2001; Eberhardt and Fiske, 1998; Gaertner and Dovidio, 2000; Oskamp, 2000; Stephan and Stephan, 2001).

Often changes in intergroup attitudes result from dramatic changes in intergroup relations. The huge increases in prejudice among North Americans towards the Japanese and Germans during the 1940s and the relatively positive view of these groups held today is easily understood in terms of the broader relationship between nations – wartime enemies versus peacetime allies. The idea that structural change should precede attitudinal change has had its champions (see Pettigrew, 1998b). However, the vast majority of social-psychological research has emphasized changing the attitudes of individuals – reducing prejudice one person at a time.

While a complete discussion of the many strategies proposed to accomplish this is clearly not possible, it may be observed first that most efforts to change individual intergroup attitudes involve either 'education', 'interaction', or both. Based on the perceived role of ignorance in prejudice, education programs usually involve teaching people about the out-group or attempts to convince them to endorse diversity and tolerance (see Stephan and Stephan, 2001 for a review). Interaction involves putting people into contact with out-group members, usually in a controlled situation. Some programs, such as service learning, combine both interaction with the out-group group and education (see Stukas and Dunlap, 2002).

However, the most enduring and influential social psychological perspective on intergroup attitude change has been the intergroup-contact hypothesis (Allport, 1954; Williams, 1947). The basic premise is that interaction between members of different groups, under specified conditions, can lead to more positive intergroup attitudes. Recognizing that simply bringing groups together is just as likely to produce conflict that will reinforce existing prejudice, Allport's original model focused on the conditions necessary for contact to lead to reduction of prejudice. This basic idea has inspired a great deal of research, and there is relatively strong support for Allport's contention that cooperation, shared goals, equal status, and the support of local authorities and norms are important preconditions to positive attitude change (see Brewer and Gaertner, 2001; Brown and Hewstone, 2005; Dovidio et al., 2003; Gaertner and Dovidio, 2000; Pettigrew, 1998a; Pettigrew and Tropp, 2006; Wright et al., 2005 for reviews).

Unfortunately, almost forty years of effort focused on the necessary conditions has resulted in little attention to specifying the processes that produce attitude change (Pettigrew, 1986). However, thanks primarily to insights derived from social-identity theory (Brewer and Miller, 1984; Hewstone and Brown, 1986), the contact hypothesis has experienced something of a renaissance. The search for a process model involves, first, determining what happens during cross-group contact that leads individuals to hold a positive view of their out-group partner, and, second, determining how that positive view of the individual generalizes to alter attitudes towards the out-group as a whole. When what happens during cross-group contact was considered, much attention was given to stereotype disconfirmation (see Stephan and Stephan, 1984; Triandis, 1972). Interaction with an out-group member who disconfirmed negative stereotypes should serve to undermine these negative beliefs. While there is some evidence for this, effects are comparatively small and inconsistent (see Pettigrew, 1998a; Rothbart and John, 1985). The largest positive effects of contact appear to involve affect and evaluation. Warmth, liking, empathy, and respect for the out-group member (Batson et al., 1997; Pettigrew and Tropp, 2006) and the reduction of anxiety (see Hewstone, 2003; Stephan and Stephan, 1985) seem to be key.

Consistent with this focus on positive affect, several researchers (e.g., Herek and Capitanio, 1996; Wright et al., 2002, 2005) have focused on cross-group friendships as the relationship most likely to produce positive attitude change. Using a large international European sample, Pettigrew (1997) demonstrated that having an out-group friendship predicted lower levels of subtle and blatant prejudice, greater support for pro-out-group policies, and even positive attitudes towards other unrelated out-groups. Having an out-group coworker or neighbor produced much smaller effects (see also Hamberger and Hewstone, 1997). In fact, interpersonal closeness appears to be able to produce 'extended contact effects' (Wright et al., 1997). That is, simply knowing about an in-group member who shares a close relationship with an out-group member can improve attitudes towards that out-group (see also Cameron and Rutland, 2006; Liebkind and McAlister, 1999).

Recently, Wright, Aron, and their colleagues (Aron and McLaughlin-Volpe, 2001; Wright et al., 1997, 2002, 2005) have proposed that the notion of *including the other in the self* provides a potential process model to explain how intergroup friendships lead to intergroup attitude change. The idea is that when two people become close, aspects of the other are included in the self. That is, close others begin to function as part of oneself (Aron and Aron, 1996), and regard held for oneself is extended to them. When the close other is a member of an out-group and social identities (group memberships) are salient, the other's social identity may also be included in the self. Thus, through the close friend, the out-group is included in the self and is then accorded some of the benefits usually accorded to the self (that is, positive biases in attribution and resource allocation, feelings of empathy, shared pride, etc.).

However, most of the recent debate on a process model of intergroup contact has focused on three alternative models. Brewer and Miller's (1984) *decategorization model* proposes that intergroup bias will be most effectively reduced when personal, rather than social, identities are salient. This assertion is consistent with evidence showing:

1 that social-identity salience heightens intergroup differentiation, stereotyping, and in-group bias (see Mullen et al., 1992);
2 that expectations for intergroup interactions can involve greater distrust than interpersonal interactions (Insko and Schopler, 1998);
3 that interactions across groups can be fraught with anxiety (Britt et al., 1996; Stephan and Stephan, 1985).

Thus, Brewer and Miller proposed that positive 'personalized' interactions will lead to greater differentiation of out-group members and to a reduction in the availability and utility of the category distinction.

In apparent contradiction, Hewstone and Brown's (1986) *mutual-differentiation model* proposes that generalization from the individual to the out-group requires that group categories be salient during the interactions. If individuals interact entirely at the level of personal identities, the outcomes should have no effect on group-based attitudes. Support for the categorization approach comes from (a) research on stereotype change showing that viewing positive out-group models who are *typical*, compared to a typical, of the out-group produces greater attitude change (e.g., Wilder, 1984; Wilder et al., 1996); and (b) direct evidence of the value of group salience on generalized intergroup-contact effects (e.g., Brown et al., 1999). In fact, Brown et al. (1999) criticize the evidence for the decategorization model (e.g., Bettencourt et al., 1992; Miller et al., 1985), claiming that category memberships were probable quite salient even in their decategorized conditions.

Gaertner, Dovidio, and their colleagues have proposed a third alternative, the *common-in-group-identity model* (see Gaertner and Dovidio, 2000, for a review). They argue that intergroup bias is reduced when the members of the two groups come to view themselves as members of one superordinate category, and they provide considerable evidence for the utility of this model.

While each model takes a different approach to the issues of categorization and attitude change, a number of authors have suggested combining models. Some (Gaertner et al., 2000; Pettigrew, 1998a; Wright, 1995) have proposed a longitudinal approach in which two or three models are combined sequentially. Others (e.g., Brewer and Gaertner, 2001) have called for dual-identity models or hybrid models. There remains considerable work to be done to test these many suggestions, but the growing number of theoretical innovations demonstrate that our understanding of intergroup contact and its application to real-world problems is evolving quickly. Perhaps Brewer and Brown (1998: 583) are correct in their assessment that 'in the long run, cooperative contact seems to be the key to improving intergroup relations and changing the social psychological processes that underlie prejudice and discrimination'.

## Summary and conclusions

A review chapter is by nature selective, and we have attempted to focus on the social nature of stereotypes and prejudice. We have considered their close relationship with the broader intergroup relationship, describing some of the ways that the functional and structural relationships between the groups determine the beliefs and evaluations that each group makes. Stereotypes and prejudices provide explanations and justification for the status and treatment of groups and their members. Recent work on group-based emotions further demonstrates the importance of the intergroup relationship in determining the valence and content of our beliefs about and emotional responses to the out-group.

It is also clear that stereotypes and prejudices, once formed, serve to solidify and structure intergroup behavior and the broader intergroup relationship. The pattern of cross-group consensus or disagreement about the content and evaluation of group characteristics supports either harmony or conflict and helps to produce and maintain intergroup inequality or genuine respect. The self-fulfilling nature of intergroup attitudes, stereotype threat, and institutional discrimination are all examples of ways that stereotypes and prejudice perpetuate present intergroup relations.

Theories such as aversive racism and ambivalent sexism have helped to bring into focus the complexity of intergroup attitudes and, along with a number of other related theories, provide numerous new avenues for research and application. Similarly, the strong, relatively recent focus on the targets of prejudice and discrimination has yielded a broad range of insights into this side of the equation. It may provide the basis for extending and strengthening social-identity theory's conception of prejudice and discrimination as a dynamic interactive process between advantaged and disadvantaged groups.

There is also good reason for hope that social psychology will be able to play a more effective role in tackling societal problems associated with the negative side of stereotypes and prejudice, by providing strategies to reduce negative prejudice and encourage collective action on behalf of the disadvantaged group. While the study of stereotypes and prejudice has a long tradition in social psychology, the discipline has responded to the current dramatic increase in societal diversity with a profusion of interest and an enthusiasm for innovation and application that ensure that stereotypes and prejudice will continue to be central themes.

## Notes

1 There is considerable debate over the issue of stereotype accuracy and what is meant by 'objective reality' (see Judd and Park, 1993; Lee et al., 1995). Space constraints do not allow a full discussion here.

2 Gaertner et al. (2000) provide an interesting analysis of this concept and revisit Sherif's original study to consider it in light of more recent theorizing on the role of categorization in intergroup attitudes and behavior (see also Gaertner and Dovidio, 2000).

3 Major et al. (2002) also call for a more complex view of this phenomenon, but they present a somewhat different theoretical model, and their conclusions are more decidedly in favor of a vigilance model.

**SUMMARY**

The chapter begins with reflections on the definitions of stereotype, prejudice, and related concepts. Our definitions may differ from some found elsewhere, and this discussion is meant to go beyond simply explaining what we mean by stereotypes and prejudice, but also to illuminate some of the controversies in this area. The discussion then turns to ways in which stereotypes and prejudice emerge from the existing relationships between groups; how they are directly connected to the structural and historical realities of those groups. Stereotypes and prejudice often serve as explanations and justifications for differences in group status and power. At the same time, once formed, they can serve as anchors maintaining and strengthening group inequality through processes like systems justification, the self-fulfilling prophecy, stereotype threat, and institutional discrimination. It is also clear that intergroup attitudes are not simple. Some of the complexities are described in theories of aversive racism and ambivalent sexism. Social psychologists have also examined how the targets of negative intergroup attitudes and discrimination respond; how and when people will label mistreatment as 'discrimination' and when this will lead to collective action and social change. Finally, we consider the evidence for how and why contact across groups can reduce prejudice.

## References

Aboud, F.E. and Levy, S.R. (eds) (1999) 'Reducing Racial Prejudice, Discrimination, and Stereotyping: Translating Research into Programs', *Journal of Social Issues*, 55 (4).

Aboud, F.E. and Levy, S.R. (2000) 'Interventions to Reduce Prejudice and Discrimination in Children and Adolescents', in S. Oskamp (ed.), *Reducing Prejudice and Discrimination: Social Psychological Perspectives.* Mahwah, NJ: Erlbaum, pp. 269–93.

Abrams, D. (1990) *Political Identity: Relative Deprivation, Social Identity, and the Case of Scottish Nationalism.* Economic and Social Research Council 16–19 Initiative Occasional Paper No. 24. Social Statistics Research Unit, City University, London.

Alexander, M.G., Brewer, M.B., and Hermann, R.K. (1999) 'Images and Affect: A Functional Analysis of Out-Group Stereotypes', *Journal of Personality and Social Psychology*, 77: 78–93.

Alexander, M., Brewer, M., and Livingston, R. (2005) 'Putting Stereotype Content in Context: Image Theory and Interethnic Stereotypes', *Personality and Social Psychology Bulletin*, 31 (6): 781–94.

Allport, G.W. (1954) *The Nature of Prejudice*. Reading, MA: Addison-Wesley.

Arkes, H.R., and Tetlock, P.E. (2004) 'Attributions of Implicit Prejudice, or "Would Jesse Jackson 'Fail' the Implicit Association Test?" *Psychological Inquiry*, 15: 257–79.

Aron, A. and Aron, E.N. (1996) 'Self and Self-Expansion in Relationships', in G.J.O. Fletcher and J. Fitness (eds), *Knowledge Structures in Close Relationships: A Social Psychological Approach.* Mahwah, NJ: Erlbaum, pp. 325–44.

Aron, A. and McLaughlin-Volpe, T. (2001) 'Including Others in the Self: Extensions to Own and Partner's Group Memberships', in C. Sedikides and M.B. Brewer (eds), *Individual Self, Relational Self, and Collective Self: Partners, Opponents, or Strangers?* Philadelphia, PA: Psychology Press, pp. 89–108.

Augoustinos, M. and Walker, I. (1998) 'The Construction of Stereotypes within Social Psychology: From Social Cognition to Ideology', *Theory and Psychology*, 8: 629–52.

Azzi, A.E. (1992) 'Procedural Justice and the Allocation of Power in Intergroup Relations: Studies in the United States and South Africa', *Personality and Social Psychology Bulletin*, 18: 736–47.

Banaji, M.R. and Greenwald, A.G. (1994) 'Implicit Stereotypes and Unconscious Prejudice', in M.P. Zanna and J.M. Olson (eds), *The Psychology of Prejudice: The Ontario Symposium* (vol. 7). Hillsdale, NJ: Erlbaum, pp. 55–76.

Banaji, M.R., Nosek, B.A. and Greenwald, A.G. (2004) 'No Place for Nostalgia in Science: A Response to Arkes and Tetlock', *Psychological Inquiry*, 15 (4): 279–310.

Banks, J.A. (1997) *Educating Citizens in a Multicultural Society.* New York: Teachers College Press.

Batson, C.D., Polycarpou, M.P., Harmon-Jones, E., Imhoff, H.J., Mitchener, E.C., Bednar, L.L., Klein, T.R., and Highberger, L. (1997) 'Empathy and Attitudes: Can Feelings for a Member of a Stigmatized Group Improve Feelings Towards the Group?', *Journal of Personality and Social Psychology*, 72: 105–18.

Bettencourt, B.A., Brewer, M.B., Croak, M.R., and Miller, N. (1992) 'Cooperation and the Reduction of Intergroup Bias: The Role of Reward Structure and Social Orientation', *Journal of Experimental Social Psychology*, 28: 301–19.

Biernat, M. and Crandall, C.S. (1994) 'Stereotyping and Contact with Social Groups: Measurement and Conceptual Issues', *European Journal of Social Psychology*, 24: 659–77.

Blanton, H. and Jaccard, J. (2006) 'Arbitrary Metrics in Psychology', *American Psychologist*, 61 (1): 27–41.

Bourhis, R.Y., Turner, J.C., and Gagnon, A. (1997) 'Interdependence, Social Identity and Discrimination', in R. Spears, P. Oakes, N. Ellemers, and S.A. Haslam (eds), *The Social Psychology of Stereotyping and Group Life*. Oxford: Blackwell, pp. 273–95.

Branscombe, N.R., Doosje, B., and McGarty, C. (2002) 'Antecedents and Consequences of Collective Guilt', in D.M. Mackie and E.R. Smith (eds), *From Prejudice to Intergroup Emotions: Differentiated Reactions to Social Groups*', Philadelphia, PA: Psychology Press.

Branscombe, N.R. and Ellemers, N. (1998) 'Coping with Group-Based Discrimination: Individualistic Versus Group-Level Strategies', in J.K. Swim and C. Stangor (eds), *Prejudice: The Target's Perspective*. San Diego, CA: Academic Press, pp. 243–66.

Branscombe, N.R., Schmitt M.T., and Harvey, R.D. (1999) 'Perceiving Pervasive Discrimination Among African Americans: Implications for Group Identification and Well-Being', *Journal of Personality and Social Psychology*, 77: 135–49.

Brauer, M., Wasel, W. and Niedenthal, P. (2000) 'Implicit and Explicit Components of Prejudice', *Review of General Psychology*, 4: 79–101.

Brewer, M.B. and Brown, R.J. (1998) 'Intergroup Relations', in D.T. Gilbert and S.T. Fiske (eds), *The Handbook of Social Psychology*, 4th edn (vol. 2). Boston, MA: MCGraw-Hill, pp. 554–94.

Brewer, M.B. and Campbell, D.T. (1976) *Ethnocentrism and Intergroup Attitudes: East African Evidence*. New York: Sage.

Brewer, M.B. and Gaertner, S.L. (2001) 'Towards Reduction of Prejudice: Intergroup Contact and Social Categorization', in R. Brown and S. Gaertner (eds), *Blackwell Handbook of Social Psychology* (vol. 4). *Intergroup Processes*. Oxford: Blackwell Press. pp. 451–72.

Brewer, M.B. and Kramer, R.M. (1985) 'The Psychology of Intergroup Attitudes and Behavior', *Annual Review of Psychology*, 36: 219–44.

Brewer, M.B. and Miller, N. (1984) 'Beyond the Contact Hypothesis: Theoretical Perspectives On Desegregation', in N. Miller and M.B. Brewer (eds), *Groups in Contact: The Psychology of Desegregation*. New York: Academic Press, pp. 281–302.

Brewer, M.B., Weber, J.G., and Carini, B. (1995) 'Person Memory in Intergroup Contexts: Categorization Versus Individuation', *Journal of Personality and Social Psychology*, 69: 29–40.

Brigham, J.C. (1971) 'Ethnic Stereotypes', *Psychological Bulletin*, 76: 15–38.

Brislin, R.W. and Yoshida, T. (eds) (1994) *Intercultural Communication Training: An Introduction*. Thousand Oaks, CA: Sage.

Britt, T.W. Boniecki, K.A., Vescio, T.K., and Biernat, M. (1996) 'Intergroup Anxiety: A Person X Situation Approach', *Personality and Social Psychology Bulletin*, 22: 1177–88.

Brown, R. (1995) *Prejudice: Its Social Psychology*. Oxford: Blackwell.

Brown, R. and Hewstone, M. (2005) 'An Integrative Theory of Intergroup Contact', in M. Zanna (ed.), *Advances in Experimental Social Psychology* (Vol. 37). San Diego, CA: Elsevier Academic Press, pp. 255–343.

Brown, R., Vivian, J., and Hewstone, M. (1999) 'Changing Attitudes through Intergroup Contact: The Effects of Group Membership Salience', *European Journal of Social Psychology*, 29: 741–64.

Cameron, L. and Rutland, A. (2006) 'Extended Contact through Story Reading in School: Reducing Children's Prejudice toward the Disabled', *Journal of Social Issues*, 62 (3): 469–88.

Campbell, D.T. (1958) 'Common Fate, Similarity, and Other Indices of the Status of Aggregates of Persons as Social Entities', *Behavioral Science*, 3: 14–25.

Claire, T. and Fiske, S.T. (1998) 'A Systemic View of Behavioral Confirmation: Counterpoint to the Individualist View', in C. Sedikides, J. Schopler, and C.A. Insko, (eds), *Intergroup Cognition and Intergroup Behavior*. Mahwah, NJ: Erlbaum, pp. 205–31.

Cook, S.W. (1984) 'Cooperative Interaction in Multiethnic Contexts', in N. Miller and M.B. Brewer (eds), *Groups in Contact: The Psychology of Desegregation*. London: Academic Press, pp. 155–85.

Crandall, C.S. and Beasley, R.K. (2001) 'A Perceptual Theory of Legitimacy: Politics, Prejudice, Social Institutions, and Moral Value', in J.T. Jost and B. Major (eds), *The Psychology of Legitimacy: Emerging Perspectives on Ideology, Justice, and Intergroup Relations*. New York: Cambridge University Press, pp. 77–102.

Crocker, J., Cornwell, B. and Major, B. (1993) 'The Stigma of Overweight: Affective Consequences of Attributional Ambiguity', *Journal of Personality and Social Psychology*, 64: 60–70.

Crocker, J. and Major, B. (1989) 'Social Stigma and Self-Esteem: The Self-Protective Properties of Stigma', *Psychological Review*, 96: 608–30.

Crocker, J., Major, B., and Steele, C. (1998) 'Social Stigma', in D.T. Gilbert, S.T. Fiske, and G. Lindsey (eds), *The Handbook of Social Psychology*, 4th edn (Vol. 2). Boston, MA: MCGraw-Hill, pp. 504–53.

Crocker, J. and Quinn, D.M. (2001) 'Psychological Consequences of Devalued Identities', in R. Brown and S. Gaertner (eds), *Blackwell Handbook of Social Psychology* (Vol. 4). *Intergroup Processes*. Oxford: Blackwell Press, pp. 238–57.

Croizet, J.-C. and Claire, T. (1998) 'Extending the Concept of Stereotype and Threat to Social Class: The Intellectual Underperformance of Students From Low Socioeconomic Backgrounds', *Personality and Social Psychology Bulletin*, 24: 588–94.

Crosby, F. (1984) 'The Denial of Personal Discrimination', *American Behavioral Scientist*, 27: 371–86.

Crosby, F., Bromley, S., and Saxe, L. (1980) 'Recent Unobtrusive Studies of Black and White Discrimination and Prejudice: A Literature Review', *Psychological Bulletin*, 87: 546–63.

Crosby, F. and Ropp, S.A. (2002) 'Awakening to Discrimination', in M. Ross and D.T. Miller (eds),

*The Justice Motive in Everyday Life*. New York: Cambridge University Press.

Dasgupta, N. and Rivera, L.M. (2006) 'From Automatic Antigay Prejudice to Behavior: The Moderating Role of Conscious Beliefs about Gender and Behavioral Control', *Journal of Personality and Social Psychology*, 91 (2): 268–80.

DePaulo, B.M. and Coleman, L.M. (1986) 'Talking to Children, Foreigners, and Retarded Adults', *Journal of Personality and Social Psychology*, 51: 945–59.

Devine, P.G. (1989) 'Stereotypes and Prejudice: Their Automatic and Controlled Components', *Journal of Personality and Social Psychology*, 56: 5–18.

Devine, P.G. and Elliot, A.J. (1995) 'Are Racial Stereotypes Really Fading? The Princeton Trilogy Revisited', *Personality and Social Psychology Bulletin*, 21: 1139–50.

Diekman, A.B. and Eagly, A.H. (2000) 'Stereotypes as Dynamic Constructs: Women and Men of the Past, Present, and Future', *Personality and Social Psychology Bulletin*, 26 (10): 1171–88.

Dijker, A.J. (1987) 'Emotional Reactions to Ethnic Minorities', *European Journal of Social Psychology*, 17: 305–25.

Dion, K.L. and Kawakami, K. (1996) 'Ethnicity and Perceived Discrimination in Toronto: Another Look at the Personal/Group Discrimination Discrepancy', *Canadian Journal of Behavioural Science*, 28: 203–13.

Doosje, B., Spears, R., and Koomen, W. (1995) 'When Bad Isn't All Bad: Strategic Use of Sample Information in Generalization and Stereotyping', *Journal of Personality and Social Psychology*, 69: 642–55.

Dovidio, J.F., Brigham, J.C., Johnson, B.T., and Gaertner, S.L. (1996) 'Stereotyping, Prejudice and Discrimination: Another Look', in C.N. Macrae, C. Stangor, and M. Hewstone (eds), *Stereotypes and Stereotyping*. New York: Guilford Press, pp. 276–319.

Dovidio, J.F., Gaertner, S.L. and Kawakami, K. (2003) 'Intergroup Contact: The Past, Present, and the Future', *Group Processes & Intergroup Relations*, 6 (1): 5–20.

Dovidio, J.F., Kawakami, K., and Beach, K.R. (2001) 'Implicit and Explicit Attitudes: Examination of the Relationship Between Measures of Intergroup Bias', in R. Brown and S. Gaertner (eds), *Blackwell Handbook of Social Psychology* (Vol. 4). *Intergroup Processes*. Oxford: Blackwell, pp. 175–97.

Dovidio, J.F., Kawakami, K., and Gaertner, S.L. (2002) 'Implicit and Explicit Prejudice and Interracial Interaction', *Journal of Personality and Social Psychology*, 82: 62–8.

Dovidio, J.F., Mann J., and Gaertner, S.L. (1989) 'Resistance to Affirmative Action: The Implications of Aversive Racism', in F. Blanchard and F. Crosby (eds), *Affirmative Action in Perspective*. New York: Springer-Verlag, pp. 83–102.

Eagly, A.H. (1987) *Sex Differences in Social Behavior: A Social-Role Interpretation*. Hillsdale, NJ: Erlbaum.

Eagly, A.H. and Mladinic, A. (1993) 'Are People Prejudiced Against Women? Some Answers from Research on Attitudes, Gender Stereotypes and Judgments of Competence', in W. Stroebe and M. Hewstone (eds), *European Review of Social Psychology* (Vol. 5). New York: Wiley, pp. 1–35.

Eagly, A.H. and Wood, W. (1999) 'The Origins of Sex Differences in Human Behavior: Evolved Dispositions Versus Social Roles', *American Psychologist*, 54: 408–23.

Eberhardt, J.L. and Fiske, S.T. (eds) (1989) *Confronting Racism: The Problem and the Response*. Thousand Oaks, CA: Sage.

Eberhardt, J.L. and Randall, J.L. (1997) 'The Essential Notion of Race', *Psychological Science*, 8: 198–203.

Ellemers, N. (1993) 'The Influence of Socio-Structural Variables on Identity Management Strategies', in W. Stroebe and M. Hewstone (eds), *European Review of Social Psychology* (Vol. 4). Chichester: Wiley. pp. 27–57.

Ellemers, N. (2001) 'Individual Upward Mobility and the Perceived Legitimacy of Intergroup Relations', in J.T. Jost and B. Major (eds), *The Psychology of Legitimacy: Emerging Perspectives on Ideology, Justice, and Intergroup Relations*. Cambridge University Press, pp. 205–22.

Ellemers, N. and Barreto, M. (2001) 'The Impact of Relative Group Status: Affective, Perceptual and Behavioral Consequences', in R. Brown and S. Gaertner (eds), *Blackwell Handbook of Social Psychology*. (Vol. 4). *Intergroup Processes*. Oxford: Blackwell, pp. 324–43.

Ellemers, N., Spears, R., and Doosje, B. (1997a) 'Sticking Together or Falling Apart: In-Group Identification as a Psychological Determinant of Group Commitment Versus Individual Mobility', *Journal of Personality and Social Psychology*, 72: 617–26.

Ellemers, N., Van Rijswijk, W., Roefs, M., and Simons, C. (1997b) 'Bias in Intergroup Perceptions: Balancing Group Identity with Social Reality', *Personality and Social Psychology Bulletin*, 23: 186–98.

Esses, V.M. and Dovidio, J.F. (2002) 'The Role of Emotions in Determining Willingness to Engage in Intergroup Contact', *Personality and Social Psychology Bulletin*, 28 (9): 1202–14.

Esses, V.M., Haddock, G., and Zanna, M.P. (1993) 'Values, Stereotypes, and Emotions as Determinants of Intergroup Attitudes', in D.M. Mackie and D. Lewis Hamilton (eds), *Affect, Cognition, and Stereotyping: Interactive Processes in Group Perception*. San Diego, CA: Academic Press, pp. 137–66.

Esses, V.M., Jackson, L.M., Dovidio, J.F. and Hodson, G. (2005) 'Instrumental Relations among Groups: Group Competition, Conflict, and Prejudice', in J.F. Dovidio, P. Glick and L.A. Rudman (eds), *On the Nature of Prejudice: Fifty Years after Allport*. Malden, MA: Blackwell Publishing, pp. 227–43.

Feldman-Barrett, L. and Swim, J.K. (1998) 'Appraisals of Prejudice and Discrimination', in J.K. Swim and C. Stangor (eds), *Prejudice: The Target's Perspective*. San Diego, CA: Academic Press, pp. 12–37.

Fiske, S.T. (1993a) 'Social Cognition and Social Perception', *Annual Review of Psychology*, 44: 155–94.

Fiske, S.T. (1993b) 'Controlling Other People: The Impact of Power on Stereotyping', *American Psychologist*, 48: 621–8.

Fiske, S.T. (1998) 'Prejudice, Stereotyping, and Discrimination', in D.T. Gilbert, S.T. Fiske, and G. Lindzey (eds), *The Handbook of Social Psychology*, 4th edn. New York: MCGraw-Hill, pp. 357–411.

Fiske, S.T. and Depret, E. (1996) 'Control, Interdependence and Power: Understanding Social Cognition and Its Social Context', in W. Stroebe and M. Hewstone (eds), *European Review of Social Psychology* (Vol. 7). Chichester: Wiley.

Fiske, S.T., Xu, J., Cuddy, A.J.C., and Glick, P. (1999) 'Respect Versus Liking: Status and Interdependence Underlie Ambivalent Stereotypes', *Journal of Social Issues*, 55: 473–89.

Florack, A., Scarabis M. and Bless, H. (2001) 'When Do Associations Matter?: The Use of Implicit Associations toward Ethnic Groups in Person Judgments', *Journal of Experimental Social Psychology*, 37: 518–24

Fowers, B.J. and Davidov, B.J. (2006) 'The Virtue of Multiculturalism: Personal Transformation, Character, and Openness to the Other', *American Psychologist*, 61(6): 581–94.

Gaertner, S.L. and Dovidio, J.F. (1986) 'The Aversive Form of Racism', in J.F. Dovidio and S.L. Gaertner (eds), *Prejudice, Discrimination, and Racism*. San Diego, CA: Academic Press, pp. 61–89.

Gaertner, S.L. and Dovidio, J.F. (2000) *Reducing Intergroup Bias: The Common Ingroup Identity Model*. Philadelphia, PA: Psychology Press.

Gaertner, S.L. and Dovidio, J.F. (2005) 'Understanding and Addressing Contemporary Racism: From Aversive Racism to the Common Ingroup Identity Model', *Journal of Social Issues*, 61 (3): 615–39.

Gaertner, S.L., Dovidio, J.F., Banker, B.S., Houlette, M., Johnson, K.M., and McGlynn, E.A. (2000) 'Reducing Intergroup Conflict: From Superordinate Goals to Decategorization, Recategorization, and Mutual Differentiation', *Group Dynamics*, 4: 98–114.

Gardner, R.C. (1973) 'Ethnic Stereotypes: The Traditional Approach, a New Look', *Canadian Psychologist*, 14: 133–48.

Gilbert, G.M. (1951) 'Stereotype Persistence and Change Among College Students', *Journal of Abnormal and Social Psychology*, 46: 245–54.

Giles, H. (ed.) (1977) *Language, Ethnicity, and Intergroup Relations*. London: Academic Press.

Glick, P. (in press) 'Sacrificial Lambs Dressed in Wolves' Clothing: Envious Prejudice, Ideology, and the Scapegoating of the Jews', in L.S. Newman and R. Erber (eds), *What Social Psychology Can Tell Us about the Holocaust*. New York: Oxford University Press.

Glick, P. and Fiske, S.T. (2001a) 'Ambivalent Sexism', in M.P. Zanna (ed.), *Advances in Experimental Social Psychology* (Vol. 33). San Diego, CA: Academic Press, pp. 115–88.

Glick, P. and Fiske, S.T. (2001b) 'Ambivalent Stereotypes as Legitimizing Ideologies: Differentiating Paternalistic and Resentful Prejudice', in J.T. Jost and B. Major (eds), *The Psychology of Legitimacy: Emerging Perspectives on Ideology, Justice, and Intergroup Relations*. New York: Cambridge University Press. pp. 278–306.

Gonzales, P.M., Blanton, H., and Williams, K.J. (2002) 'The Effects of Stereotype Threat and Double-Minority Status on the Test Performance of Latino Women', *Personality and Social Psychology Bulletin*, 28: 659–70.

Goodwin, S.A., Gubin, A., Fiske, S.T., and Yzerbyt, V.Y. (2000) 'Power Can Bias Impression Processes: Stereotyping Subordinates by Default and by Design', *Group Processes and Intergroup Relations*, 3: 227–56.

Grant, P.R. and Brown, R. (1995) 'From Ethnocentrism to Collective Protest: Responses to Relative Deprivation and Threats to Social Identity', *Social Psychology Quarterly*, 58: 195–211.

Hamberger, J. and Hewstone, M. (1997) 'Inter-Ethnic Contact as a Predictor of Blatant and Subtle Prejudice: Tests of a Model in Four West European Nations', *British Journal of Social Psychology*, 36: 173–90.

Hamilton, D.L. and Sherman, S.J. (1996) 'Perceiving Persons and Groups', *Psychological Review*, 103: 336–55.

Hamilton, D.L., Sherman, S.J., and Lickel, B. (1998) 'Perceiving Social Groups: The Importance of the Entitativity Continuum', in C. Sedikides, J. Schopler, and C.A. Insko (eds), *Intergroup Cognition and Intergroup Behavior*. Mahwah, NJ: Erlbaum, pp. 47–74.

Hamilton, D.L., Stroessner, S.J., and Driscoll, D.M. (1994) 'Social Cognition and the Study of Stereotyping', in P.G. Devine and D.L. Hamilton (eds), *Social Cognition: Impact on Social Psychology*. San Diego, CA: Academic Press, pp. 291–321.

Haslam, S.A., Turner, J.C., Oakes, P.J., Reynolds, K.J. and Doosje, B. (2002) 'From Personal Pictures in the Head to Collective Tools in the World: How Shared Stereotypes Allow Groups to Represent and Change Social Reality', in C. McGarty, V.Y. Yzerbyt and R. Spears, (eds), *Stereotypes as Explanations: The Formation of Meaningful Beliefs about Social Groups*. New York: Cambridge University Press, pp. 157–85.

Heatherton, T.F., Kleck, R.E., Hebl, M.R., and Hull, J.G. (eds) (2000) *The Social Psychology of Stigma*. New York: Guilford.

Herek, G.M. and Capitanio, J.P. (1996) 'Some of My Best Friends: Intergroup Contact, Concealable Stigma, and Heterosexuals' Attitudes towards Gay Men and Lesbians', *Personality and Social Psychology Bulletin*, 22: 412–24.

Hewstone, M. (2003) 'Intergroup Contact: Panacea for Prejudice?' *Psychologist*, 16 (7): 352–55.

Hewstone, M. and Brown, R. (1986) 'Contact Is Not Enough: An Intergroup Perspective on the "Contact

Hypothesis', in M. Hewstone and R. Brown (eds), *Contact and Conflict in Intergroup Encounters. Social Psychology and Society*. Oxford: Blackwell, pp. 1–44.

Hoffman, C. and Hurst, N. (1990) 'Gender Stereotypes: Perception or Rationalization?', *Journal of Personality and Social Psychology*, 58: 197–208.

Hogg, M.A. (2000) 'Subjective Uncertainty Reduction through Self-Categorization: A Motivational Theory of Social Identity Processes', *European Review of Social Psychology*, 11: 223–55.

Hogg, M.A. and Abrams, D. (1988) *Social Identification: A Social Psychology of Intergroup Relations and Group Processes*, New York: Routledge.

Hogg, M.A. and Abrams, D. (1993) 'Towards a Single-Process Uncertainty-Reduction Model of Social Motivation in Groups', in M.A. Hogg and D. Abrams (eds), *Group Motivation: Social Psychological Perspectives*. London: Harvester Wheatsheaf, pp. 173–90.

Hollister, L., Day, N.E., and Jesiatis, P.T. (1993) 'Diversity Programs: Key to Competitiveness or Just Another Fad', *Organizational Development Journal*, 11 (4): 49–59.

Hugenberg K. and Bodenhausen G.V. (2003) 'Facing Prejudice: Implicit Prejudice and the Perception of Facial Threat', *Psychological Science*, 14: 640–3.

Insko, C.A. and Schopler, J. (1998) 'Differential Distrust of Groups and Individuals', in C. Sedikides, J. Schopler, and C.A. Insko (eds), *Intergroup Cognition and Intergroup Behavior*. Mahwah, NJ: Erlbaum. pp. 75–107.

Iyer, A., Leach, C.W., and Crosby, F.J. (2003) 'White Guilt and Racial Compensation: The Benefits and Limits of Self-Focus', *Personality and Social Psychology Bulletin*, 29 (1): 117–29.

Jackman, M.R. (1994) *The Velvet Glove: Paternalism and Conflict in Gender, Class, and Race Relations*. Berkeley, CA: University of California Press.

Jackson, L.A., Hodge, C.N., Gerard, D.A., Ingram, J.M., Ervin, K.S., and Sheppard, L.A. (1996) 'Cognition, Affect, and Behavior in the Prediction of Group Attitudes', *Personality and Social Psychology Bulletin*, 22: 306–16.

Jones, E.E., Farina, A., Hastorf, A.H., Markus, H., Miller, D.T., and Scott, R.A. (1984) *Social Stigma: The Psychology of Marked Relationships*. New York: Freeman.

Jones, J.M. (1996) *Prejudice and Racism*, 2nd edn. New York: MCGraw-Hill.

Jost, J.T. and Banaji, M.R. (1994) 'The Role of Stereotyping in System-Justification and the Production of False-Consciousness', *British Journal of Social Psychology*, 33: 1–27.

Jost, J.T., Burgess, D., and Mosso, C. (2001) 'Conflicts of Legitimation among Self, Group, and System: The Integrative Potential of System-Justification Theory', in J.T. Jost and B. Major (eds), *The Psychology of Legitimacy: Emerging Perspectives on Ideology, Justice, and Intergroup Relations*. New York: Cambridge University Press, pp. 363–88.

Judd, C.M. and Park, B. (1993) 'Definition and Assessment of Accuracy in Social Stereotypes', *Psychological Review*, 100: 109–28.

Jussim, L., McCauley, C.R., and Lee, Y. (1995) 'Why Study Stereotype Accuracy and Inaccuracy?', in Y. Lee, L. Jussim, and C.R. McCauley (eds), *Stereotype Accuracy*. Washington DC: American Psychological Association, pp. 3–27.

Kaiser, C.R. and Miller, C.T. (2001a) 'Reacting to Impending Discrimination: Compensation for Prejudice and Attributions to Discrimination', *Personality and Social Psychology Bulletin*, 27: 1357–67.

Kaiser, C.R. and Miller, C.T. (2001b) 'Stop Complaining! The Social Costs of Making Attributions to Discrimination', *Personality and Social Psychology Bulletin*, 27: 254–63.

Karlins, M., Coffman, T.L., and Walters, G. (1969) 'On the Fading of Social Stereotypes: Studies in Three Generations of College Students', *Journal of Personality and Social Psychology*, 13: 1–16.

Katz, D. and Braly, K. (1933) 'Racial Stereotypes of One Hundred College Students', *Journal of Abnormal and Social Psychology*, 28: 280–90.

Katz, I. and Glass, D.C. (1979) 'An Ambivalence-Amplification Theory of Behavior Towards the Stigmatized', in W.G. Austin and S. Worchel (eds), *The Social Psychology of intergroup relations*. Monterey, CA: Brooks/Cole, pp. 55–70.

Katz, I. and Hass, R.G. (1988) 'Racial Ambivalence and American Value Conflict: Correlational and Priming Studies of Dual Cognitive Structures', *Journal of Personality and Social Psychology*, 55: 893–905.

Kay, A.C. and Jost, J.T. (2003) 'Complementary Justice: Effects of "Poor but Happy" and "Poor but Honest" Stereotype Exemplars on System Justification and Implicit Activation of the Justice Motive', *Journal of Personality and Social Psychology*, 85 (5): 823–37.

Kramer, R.M. and Carnevale, P.J. (2001) 'Trust and Intergroup Negotiations', in R. Brown and S. Gaertner (eds), *Blackwell Handbook of Social Psychology* (Vol. 4). *Intergroup Processes*. Oxford: Blackwell, pp. 431–50.

Kray, L.J., Thompson, L., and Galinsky, A. (2001) 'Battle of the Sexes: Gender Stereotype Confirmation and Reactance in Negotiations', *Journal of Personality and Social Psychology*, 80: 942–58.

Lalonde, R.N. and Cameron, J.E. (1994) 'Behavioral Responses to Discrimination: A Focus on Action', in M.P. Zanna and J.M. Olson (eds), *The Psychology of Prejudice: The Ontario Symposium* (Vol. 7). Hillsdale, NJ: Erlbaum, pp. 257–88.

Lalonde, R.N. and Gardner, R.C. (1989) 'An Intergroup Perspective on Stereotype Organization and Processing', *British Journal of Social Psychology*, 28: 289–303.

Lalonde, R.N. and Silverman, R.A. (1994) 'Behavioral Preferences in Response to Social Injustice: The Effects of Group Permeability and Social Identity Salience', *Journal of Personality and Social Psychology*, 66: 78–85.

Leach, C.W., Snider, N., and Iyer, A. (2002) '"Poisoning the Consciences of the Fortunate": The Experience of Relative Advantage and Support for Social Equality', in I. Walker and H. Smith (eds), *Relative Deprivation: Specification, Development, and Integration*. Cambridge: Cambridge University Press, pp. 136–63.

LeCouteur, A. and Augoustinos, M. (2001) 'The Language of Prejudice and Racism', in M. Augoustinos and K.J. Reynolds (eds), *Understanding Prejudice, Racism, and Social Conflict*. London: Sage, pp. 215–30.

Lee, Y.-T., Jussim, L.J., and McCauley, C.R. (eds) (1995) *Stereotype Accuracy: Toward Appreciating Group Differences*. Washington, DC: American Psychological Association.

Lerner, M.J. (1980) *The Belief in a Just World*. New York: Plenum.

Levy, B. (1996) 'Improving Memory in Old Age Through Implicit Self-Stereotyping', *Journal of Personality and Social Psychology*, 71: 1092–1107.

Leyens, J.-Ph., Yzerbyt, V., and Schadron, G. (1992) 'Stereotypes and Social Judgeability', in W. Stroebe and M. Hewstone (eds), *European Review of Social Psychology* (vol. 3). Chichester: Wiley, pp. 91–120.

Liebkind, K. and McAlister, A.L. (1999) 'Extending Contact through Peer Modeling to Promote Tolerance in Finland', *European Journal of Social Psychology*, 29: 765–80.

Lippmann, W. (1922) *Public Opinion*. New York: Harcourt Brace.

Lord, C.G. and Saenz, D.S. (1985) 'Memory Deficits and Memory Surfeits: Differential Cognitive Consequences of Tokenism for Token and Observers', *Journal of Personality and Social Psychology*, 49: 918–26.

Maass, A. and Arcuri, L. (1992) 'The Role of Language in the Persistence of Stereotypes', in G.R. Semin and K. Fiedler (eds), *Language, Interaction and Social Cognition*. Thousand Oaks, CA: Sage. pp. 129–43.

MacDonald, T.K. and Zanna, M.P. (1998) 'Cross-Dimension Ambivalence toward Social Groups: Can Ambivalence Affect Intentions to Hire Feminists?', *Personality and Social Psychology Bulletin*, 24: 427–41.

Mackie, D.M., Devos, T., and Smith, E.R. (2000) 'Intergroup Emotions: Explaining offensive Action Tendencies in an Intergroup Context', *Journal of Personality and Social Psychology*, 79: 602–16.

Mackie, D.M. and Hamilton, D.L. (eds) (1993) *Affect, Cognition, and Stereotyping: Interactive Processes in Group Perception*. San Diego, CA: Academic Press.

Major, B. (1994) 'From Social Inequality to Personal Entitlement: The Role of Social Comparisons, Legitimacy Appraisals, and Group Membership', *Advances in Experimental Social Psychology*, 26: 293–355.

Major, B. and Crocker, J. (1993) 'Social Stigma: The Consequences of Attributional Ambiguity', in D.M. Mackie and D.L. Hamilton (eds), *Affect, Cognition, and Stereotyping: Interactive Processes in Group Perception*. San Diego, CA: Academic Press, pp. 345–70.

Major, B., Quinton, W.J., and McCoy, S.K. (2002) 'Antecedents and Consequences of Attributions to Discrimination: Theoretical and Empirical Advances', in M.P. Zanna (ed.), *Advances in Experimental Social Psychology* (Vol. 34). San Diego, CA: Academic Press, pp. 251–330.

Major, B. and Schmader, T. (1998) 'Coping with Stigma through Psychological Disengagement', in J.K. Swim and C. Stangor (eds), *Prejudice: The Target's Perspective*. San Diego, CA: Academic Press, pp. 219–42.

Major, B. and Schmader, T. (2001) 'Legitimacy and the Construal of Social Disadvantage', in J.T. Jost and B. Major (eds), *The Psychology of Legitimacy: Emerging Perspectives on Ideology Justice and Intergroup Relations*. Cambridge: Cambridge University Press, pp. 176–204.

Martin, J. (1986) 'The Tolerance of Injustice', in J.M. Olson, C.P. Herman, and M.P. Zanna (eds), *Relative Deprivation and Social Comparison: The Ontario Symposium* (Vol. 4). Mahwah, NJ: Erlbaum, pp. 217–42.

McConahay, J.B. (1986) 'Modern Racism, Ambivalence and the Modern Racism Scale', in J.F. Dovidio and S.L. Gaertner (eds), *Prejudice, Discrimination and Racism*. Orlando, FL: Academic Press, pp. 91–125.

McConnell, A.R. and Liebold, J.M. (2001) 'Relations between the Implicit Association Test, Explicit Racial Attitudes, and Discriminatory Behavior', *Journal of Experimental Social Psychology*, 37: 435–42.

McGarty, C., Yzerbyt, V.Y., and Spears, R. (2002) *Stereotypes as Explanations: The Formation of Meaningful Bliefs about Social Groups*. Cambridge: Cambridge University Press.

Miller, N., Brewer, M.B., and Edwards, K. (1985) 'Cooperative Interaction in Desegregated Settings: A Laboratory Analogue', *Journal of Social Issues*, 41: 63–80.

Mlicki, P.P. and Ellemers, N. (1996) 'Being Different or Being Better? National Stereotypes and Identifications of Polish and Dutch Students', *European Journal of Social Psychology*, 26: 97–114.

Moscovici, S. (1981) 'On Social Representation', in J. Forgas (ed.), *Social Cognition*. London: Academic Press, pp. 181–209.

Mullen, B. (1991) 'Group Composition, Salience, and Cognitive Representations: The Phenomenology of Being in a Group', *Journal of Experimental Social Psychology*, 27: 297–323.

Mullen, B., Brown, R., and Smith, C. (1992) 'Intergroup Bias as a Function of Salience, Relevance, and Status: An Integration', *European Journal of Social Psychology*, 22: 103–22.

Murrell, A.J., Dietz-Uhler, B.L., Dovidio, J.F., Gaertner, S.L., and Drout, E. (1994) 'Aversive Racism and Resistance to Affirmative Action: Perceptions of Justice Are Not Necessarily Color Blind', *Basic and Applied Social Psychology*, 15: 71–86.

Ng, S.H. (1982) 'Power and Intergroup Discrimination', in H. Tajfel (ed.), *Social Identity and Intergroup*

*Relations*. London: Cardiff University Press, pp. 179–206.

Ng, S.H. and Bradac, J.J. (1993) *Power in Language: Verbal Communication and Social Influence*. Thousand Oaks, CA: Sage.

Oakes, P. (2001) 'The Root of All Evil in Intergroup Relations? Unearthing the Categorization Process', in R. Brown and S. Gaertner (eds), *Blackwell Handbook of Social Psychology* (Vol. 4). *Intergroup Processes*. Oxford: Blackwell Press, pp. 3–21.

Oakes, P.J. and Haslam, S.A. (2001) 'Distortion v. Meaning: Categorization on Trial for Inciting Intergroup Hatred', in M. Augoustinos and K.J. Reynolds (eds), *Understanding Prejudice, Racism, and Social Conflict*. London: Sage, pp. 179–94.

Oakes, P.J., Haslam, S.A., and Turner, J.C. (1994) *Stereotyping and Social Reality*. Oxford: Blackwell.

Olson, J. and Hafer, C.L. (2001) 'Tolerance of Personal Deprivation', in J.T. Jost and B. Major (eds), *The Psychology of Legitimacy: Emerging Perspectives on Ideology, Justice, and Intergroup Relations*. New York: Cambridge University Press, pp. 157–75.

Olson, J.M., Roese, N.J., Meen, J., and Robertson, D.J. (1995) 'The Preconditions and Consequences of Relative Deprivation: Two Field Studies', *Journal of Applied Social Psychology*, 25: 944–64.

Operario, D. and Fiske, S.T. (1998) 'Racism Equals Power Plus Prejudice: A Social Psychological Equation for Racial Oppression', in J.L. Eberhardt and S.T. Fiske (eds), *Confronting Racism: The Problem and the Response*. Thousand Oaks, CA: Sage, pp. 33–53.

Operario, D. and Fiske, S.T. (2001) 'Stereotypes: Content, Structure, Process, and Context', in R. Brown and S. Gaertner (eds), *Blackwell Handbook of Social Psychology* (Vol. 4). *Intergroup Processes*. Oxford: Blackwell Press, pp. 22–44.

Oskamp, S. (ed.) (2000) *Reducing Prejudice and Discrimination: Social Psychological Perspectives*. Mahwah, NJ: Erlbaum.

Oskamp, S. and Jones, J.M. (2000) 'Promising Practice in Reducing Prejudice: A Report from the President's Initiative on Race', in S. Oskamp (ed.), *Reducing Prejudice and Discrimination: Social Psychological Perspectives*. Mahwah, NJ: Erlbaum, pp. 319–34.

Oyserman, D. and Swim, J.K. (eds) (2001) 'Stigma: An Insider's Perspective', *Journal of Social Issues*, 57 (1):

Pettigrew, T.F. (1958) 'Personality and Sociocultural Factors in Intergroup Attitudes: A Cross-National Comparison', *Journal of Conflict Resolution*, 2: 29–42.

Pettigrew, T.F. (1985) 'New Black-White Patterns: How Best to Conceptualize Them?', *Annual Review of Sociology*, 11: 329–46.

Pettigrew, T.F. (1986) 'The Intergroup Contact Hypothesis Reconsidered', in M. Hewstone and R. Brown (eds), *Contact and Conflict in Intergroup Encounters*. New York: Blackwell, pp. 169–95.

Pettigrew, T.F. (1991) 'Normative Theory in Intergroup Relations: Explaining Both Harmony and Conflict', *Psychology and Developing Societies*, 3: 3–16.

Pettigrew, T.F. (1997) 'Generalized Intergroup Contact Effects on Prejudice', *Personality and Social Psychology Bulletin*, 23: 173–85.

Pettigrew, T.F. (1998a) 'Intergroup Contact Theory', *Annual Review of Psychology*, 49: 65–85.

Pettigrew, T.F. (1998b) 'Prejudice and Discrimination on the College Campus', in J.L. Eberhardt and S.T. Fiske (eds), *Confronting Racism: The Problem and the Response*. Thousand Oaks, CA: Sage, pp. 263–79.

Pettigrew, T.F. (2001) 'Intergroup Relations in National and International Relations', in R. Brown and S. Gaertner (eds), *Blackwell Handbook of Social Psychology* (Vol. 4). *Intergroup Processes*. Oxford: Blackwell, pp. 514–32.

Pettigrew, T.F. and Martin, J. (1987) 'Shaping the Organizational Context for Black American Inclusion', *Journal of Social Issues*, 43: 41–78.

Pettigrew, T.F. and Meertens, R.W. (1995) 'Subtle and Blatant Prejudice in Western Europe', *European Journal of Social Psychology*, 25: 57–75.

Pettigrew, T.F. and Tropp, L.R. (2006) 'A Meta-Analytic Test of Intergroup Contact Theory', *Journal of Personality and Social Psychology*, 90 (5): 751–83.

Platow, M.J. and Hunter, J. (2001) 'Realistic Intergroup Conflict: Prejudice, Power, and Protest', in M. Augoustinos and K.J. Reynolds (eds), *Understanding Prejudice, Racism, and Social Conflict*. London: Sage, pp. 195–212.

Postmes, T., Branscombe, N.R., Spears, R., and Young, H. (1999) 'Personal and Group Judgments of Discrimination and Privilege: Resolving the Discrepancy', *Journal of Personality and Social Psychology*, 76: 320–38.

Pruitt, D.G. (1989) 'Social Conflict', in D.T. Gilbert, S.T. Fiske, and G. Lindzey (eds), *The Handbook of Social Psychology*, 4th edn. New York: MCGraw-Hill, pp. 470–503.

Quinn, K.A., Roese, N.J., Pennington, G.L., and Olson, J.M. (1999) 'The Personal/Group Discrimination Discre pancy: The Role of Informational Complexity', *Personality and Social Psychology Bulletin*, 25: 1430–40.

Reynolds, K.J. and Turner, J.C. (2001) 'Prejudice as a Group Process: The Role of Social Identity', in M. Augoustinos and K.J. Reynolds (eds), *Understanding Prejudice, Racism, and Social Conflict*. London: Sage, pp. 159–78.

Ridgeway, C.L. (2001) 'The Emergence of Status Beliefs: From Structural Inequality to Legitimizing Ideology', in J.T. Jost and B. Major (eds), *The Psychology of Legitimacy: Emerging Perspectives on Ideology, Justice, and Intergroup Relations*. Cambridge University Press, pp. 257–77.

Ridgeway, C.L. and Balkwell, J.W. (1997) 'Group Processes and the Diffusion of Status Beliefs', *Social Psychology Quarterly*, 60: 14–31.

Rothbart, M. and John, O.P. (1985) 'Social Categorization and Behavioral Episodes: A Cognitive Analysis of the Effects of Intergroup Contact', *Journal of Social Issues*, 41: 81–104.

Rothbart, M. and Taylor, M. (1992) 'Category Labels and Social Reality: Do We View Social Categories as Natural Kinds?', in G.R. Semin and K. Fiedler (eds), *Language, Interaction and Social Cognition*. Thousand Oaks, CA: Sage, pp. 11–36.

Rudman, L.A., Ashmore, R.D., and Gary, M.L. (2001) '"Unlearning" Automatic Biases: The Malleability of Implicit Prejudice and Stereotypes', *Journal of Personality and Social Psychology*, 81 (5): 856–68.

Ruggiero, K.M. and Taylor, D.M. (1995) 'Coping with Discrimination: How Disadvantaged Group Members Perceive the Discrimination that Confronts Them', *Journal of Personality and Social Psychology*, 68: 826–38.

Ruggiero, K.M. and Taylor, D.M. (1997) 'Why Minority Group Members Perceive or Do Not Perceive the Discrimination that Confronts Them: The Role of Self-Esteem and Social Support', *Journal of Personality and Social Psychology*, 72: 373–89.

Sachdev, I. and Bourhis, R.Y. (1991) 'Power and Status Differentials in Minority and Majority Group Relations', *European Journal of Social Psychology*, 21: 1–24.

Schmitt, M.T. and Branscombe, N.R. (2002) 'The Causal Loci of Attributions to Prejudice', *Personality and Social Psychology Bulletin*, 28: 620–8.

Sears, D.O. (1988) 'Symbolic Racism', in P.A. Katz and D.A. Taylor (eds), *Eliminating Racism: Profiles in Controversy*. New York: Plenum Press, pp. 53–84.

Sherif, M. (1966) *Group Conflict and Co-operation: Their Social Psychology*. London: Routledge & Kegan Paul.

Sidanius, J., Levin, S., Federico, C.M., and Pratto, F. (2001) 'Legitimizing Ideologies: The Social Dominance Approach', in J.T. Jost and B. Major (eds), *The Psychology of Legitimacy: Emerging Perspectives on Ideology, Justice, and Intergroup Relations*. New York: Cambridge University Press, pp. 307–31.

Sidanius, J. and Pratto, F. (1999) *Social Dominance: An Intergroup Theory of Social Hierarchy and Oppression*. Cambridge: Cambridge University Press.

Simon, B. (1993) 'On the Asymmetry in the Cognitive Construal of Ingroup and Outgroup: A Model of Egocentric Social Categorization', *European Journal of Social Psychology*, 23: 131–47.

Simon, B. (1998) 'Individuals, Groups, and Social Change: On the Relationship Between Individual and Collective Self-Interpretations and Collective Action', in C. Sedikides, J. Schopler, and C.A. Insko (eds), *Intergroup Cognition and Intergroup Behavior*. Mahwah, NJ: Erlbaum, pp. 257–82.

Simon, B., Aufderheide, B. and Kampmeier, C. (2001) 'The Social Psychology of Minority–Majority Relations', in R. Brown and S. Gaertner (eds), *Blackwell Handbook of Social Psychology* (Vol. 4). *Intergroup Processes*. Oxford: Blackwell Press, pp. 303–23.

Simon, B. and Klandermans, B. (2001) 'Politicized Collective Identity: A Social Psychological Analysis', *American Psychologist*, 56: 319–31.

Sinclair, L. and Kunda, Z. (1999) 'Reactions to a Black Professional: Motivated Inhibition and Activation of Conflicting Stereotypes', *Journal of Personality and Social Psychology*, 77: 885–904.

Smith, A.E., Jussim, L., and Eccles, J. (1999) 'Do Self-Fulfilling Prophecies Accumulate, Dissipate, or Remain Stable over Time?', *Journal of Personality and Social Psychology*, 77: 548–65.

Smith, E.R. (1993) 'Social Identity and Social Emotions: Toward New Conceptualizations of Prejudice', in D.M. Mackie and D.L. Hamilton (eds), *Affect, Cognition, and Stereotyping: Interactive Processes in Group Perception*. San Diego, CA : Academic Press. pp. 297–315.

Smith, E.R. and Ho, C. (2002) 'Prejudice as Intergroup Emotion: Integrating Relative Deprivation and Social Comparison Explanations of Prejudice', in I. Walker and H. Smith (eds), *Relative Deprivation: Specification, Development, and Integration*. Cambridge: Cambridge University Press, pp. 332–48.

Snyder, M. (1992) 'Motivational Foundations of Behavioral Confirmation', in Zanna, M.P. (ed.), *Advances in Experimental Social Psychology* (Vol. 25). San Diego, CA: Academic Press, pp. 67–114.

Snyder, M. and Swann, W.B., Jr. (1978) 'Behavioral Confirmation in Social Interaction: From Social Perception to Social Reality', *Journal of Experimental Social Psychology*, 14: 148–62.

Snyder, M., Tanke, E.D., and Berscheid, E. (1977) 'Social Perception and Interpersonal Behavior: On the Self-Fulfilling Nature of Social Stereotypes', *Journal of Personality and Social Psychology*, 35: 656–66.

Spears, R., Jetten, J., and Doosje, B. (2001) 'The (Il)legitimacy of Ingroup Bias: From Social Reality to Social Resistance', in J.T. Jost and B. Major (eds), *The Psychology of Legitimacy: Emerging Perspectives on Ideology Justice and Intergroup Relations*. Cambridge: Cambridge University Press, pp. 332–62.

Spencer, S.J., Steele, C.M., and Quinn, D.M. (1999) 'Stereotype Threat and Women's Math Performance', *Journal of Experimental Social Psychology*, 35: 4–28.

Stangor, C. and Schaller, M. (1996) 'Stereotypes as Individual and Collective Representations', in C.N. Macrae, C. Stangor, and M. Hewstone (eds), *Stereotypes and Stereotyping*. New York: Guilford, pp. 3–40.

Stangor, C., Sullivan, L.A., and Ford, T.E. (1991) 'Affective and Cognitive Determinants of Prejudice', *Social Cognition*, 9: 359–80.

Stangor, C., Swim, J.K., Van Allen, K.L., and Sechrist, G.B. (2002) 'Reporting Discrimination in Public and Private Contexts', *Journal of Personality and Social Psychology*, 82: 69–74.

Steele, C.M. (1998) 'A Threat in the Air: How Stereotypes Shape Intellectual Identity and Performance', in J.L. Eberhardt and S.T. Fiske (eds), *Confronting Racism: The Problem and the Response*. Thousand Oaks, CA: Sage, pp. 202–33.

Steele, C.M. and Aronson, J. (1995) 'Stereotype Vulnerability and the Intellectual Test Performance of

African-Americans', *Journal of Personality and Social Psychology*, 69: 797–811.

Steele, C.M., Spencer, S., and Aronson, J. (2002) 'Stereotype Threat', in M.P. Zanna, (ed.), *Advances in Experimental Social Psychology* (Vol. 34). San Diego, CA: Academic Press, pp. 379–440.

Stephan, W.G. and Stephan, C. (1984) 'The Role of Ignorance in Intergroup Relations', in N. Miller and M.B. Brewer (eds), *Groups in Contact: The Psychology of Desegregation.* New York: Academic Press, pp. 229–56.

Stephan, W.G. and Stephan, C. (1985) 'Intergroup Anxiety', *Journal of Social Issues*, 41: 157–76.

Stephan, W.G. and Stephan, C. (2001) *Improving Intergroup Relations.* Thousand Oaks, CA: Sage.

Stone, J., Lynch, C.I., Sjomeling, M., and Darley, J.M. (1999) 'Stereotype Threat Effects on Black and White Athletic Performance', *Journal of Personality and Social Psychology*, 77: 1213–27.

Stukas, A.A. and Dunlap, M.R. (eds) (2002) 'Community Involvement, Service-Learning, and Social Activism', *Journal of Social Issues*, 58 (3).

Stürmer, S. and Simon, B. (2004) 'Collective Action: Towards a Dual-Pathway Model', in W. Stroebe and M. Hewstone (eds), *European Review of Social Psychology* (Vol. 15). Hove: Psychology Press, pp. 59–99.

Sumner, W.G. (1906) *Folkways.* Boston, MA: Ginn.

Swim, J.K. and Stangor, C. (eds) (1998) *Prejudice: The Target's Perspective.* San Diego, CA: Academic Press.

Tajfel, H. (1981) *Human Groups and Social Categories: Studies in Social Psychology.* London: Cambridge University Press.

Tajfel, H. (1982) *Social Identity and Intergroup Relations.* Cambridge: Cambridge University Press.

Tajfel, H. and Turner, J.C. (1979) 'An Integrative Theory of Intergroup Conflict', in W.G. Austin and S. Worchel (eds), *The Social Psychology of Intergroup Relations.* Monterey, CA: Brooks/Cole, pp. 33–48.

Taylor, D.M. (1981) 'Stereotypes and Intergroup Relations', in R.C. Gardner and R. Kalin (eds), *A Canadian Social Psychology of Ethnic Relations.* Toronto, ON: Methuen, pp. 151–71.

Taylor, D.M. and McKirnan, D.J. (1984) 'A Five Stage Model of Intergroup Relations', *British Journal of Social Psychology*, 23: 291–300.

Taylor, D.M. and Moghaddam, F.M. (1994). *Theories of Intergroup Relations: International and Social Psychological Perspectives*, 2nd edn. Westport, CT: Preager.

Taylor, D.M., Ruggiero, K.M., and Louis, W.R. (1996) 'Personal/Group Discrimination Discrepancy: Towards a Two-Factor Explanation', *Canadian Journal of Behavioural Science*, 28: 193–202.

Taylor, D.M., Wright, S.C., Moghaddam, F.M., and Lalonde, R.N. (1990) 'The Personal/Group Discrimination Discrepancy: Perceiving My Group, but Not Myself, to Be a Target for Discrimination', *Personality and Social Psychology Bulletin*, 16 (2): 254–62.

Taylor, D.M., Wright, S.C., and Porter, L.E. (1994) 'Dimensions of Perceived Discrimination: The Personal/Group Discrimination Discrepancy', in M.P. Zanna and J.M. Olson (eds), *The Psychology of Prejudice: The Ontario Symposium* (vol. 7). Hillsdale, NJ: Erlbaum, pp. 233–55.

Towles-Schwen, T. and Fazio, R.H. (2003) 'Choosing Social Situations: The Relation between Automatically Activated Racial Attitudes and Anticipated Comfort Interacting with African Americans', *Personality and Social Psychology Bulletin*, 29 (2): 170–82.

Triandis, H.C. (1972) *The Analysis of Subjective Culture.* New York: Wiley.

Tropp, L.R. and Pettigrew, T.F. (2005) 'Differential Relationships between Intergroup Contact and Affective and Cognitive Dimensions of Prejudice', *Personality and Social Psychology Bulletin*, 31 (8): 1145–58.

Tropp, L.R. and Wright, S.C. (1999) 'Ingroup Identification and Relative Deprivation: An Examination across Multiple Social Comparison', *European Journal of Social Psychology*, 29: 707–24.

Tropp, L.R. and Wright, S.C. (2001) 'Ingroup Identification as Inclusion of Ingroup in the Self', *Personality and Social Psychology Bulletin*, 27: 585–600.

Turner, J.C., Hogg, M.A., Oakes, P.J., Reicher, S.D., and Wetherell, M.S. (1987) *Rediscovering The Social Group: A Self-Categorization Theory.* New York: Blackwell.

Turner, J.C. and Reynolds, K.J. (2001) 'The Social Identity Perspective in Intergroup Relations: Theories, Themes, and Controversies', in R.J. Brown and S. Gaertner (eds), *Blackwell Handbook of Social Psychology: Intergroup Processes* (vol. 4). Oxford: Blackwell, pp. 133–52.

Walker, I. (2001) 'The Changing Nature of Racism: From Old to New?', in M. Augoustinos and K.J. Reynolds (eds), *Understanding Prejudice, Racism, and Social Conflict.* London: Sage, pp. 24–42.

Wenneker, C.P.J., Wigboldus, D.H.J. and Spears, R. (2005) 'Biased Language Use in Stereotype Maintenance: The Role of Encoding and Goals', *Journal of Personality and Social Psychology*, 89 (4): 504–16.

Wilder, D.A. (1984) 'Intergroup Contact: The Typical Member and the Exception to the Rule', *Journal of Experimental Social Psychology*, 20: 177–94.

Wilder, D.A., Simon, A.F., and Faith, M. (1996) 'Enhancing the Impact of Counterstereotypic Information: Dispositional Attributions for Deviance', *Journal of Personality and Social Psychology*, 71: 276–87.

Williams, R.M., Jr. (1947) *The Reduction of Intergroup Tensions.* New York: Social Science Research Council.

Word, C.G., Zanna, M.P., and Cooper, J. (1974) 'The Nonverbal Mediation of Self-Fulfilling Prophecies in Interracial Interaction', *Journal of Experimental Social Psychology*, 10: 109–20.

Wright, S.C. (1995) 'The Impact of Cross-Group Friendships on Intergroup Attitudes: An Intergroup

Conflict Simulation'. Paper presented at the annual meeting of the Society for Experimental Social Psychology, Washington, DC, October.

Wright, S.C. (1997) 'Ambiguity, Social Influence and Collective Action: Generating Collective Protest in Response to Tokenism', *Personality and Social Psychology Bulletin*, 23: 1277–90.

Wright, S.C. (2001a) 'Strategic Collective Action: Social Psychology and Social Change', in R. Brown and S. Gaertner (eds), *Blackwell Handbook of Social Psychology* (Vol. 4). *Intergroup Processes.* Oxford: Blackwell, pp. 409–30.

Wright, S.C. (2001b) 'Restricted Intergroup Boundaries: Tokenism, Ambiguity and the Tolerance of Injustice', in J. Jost and B. Major (eds), *The Psychology of Legiti macy: Emerging Perspectives on Ideology, Justice, and Intergroup Relations.* Cambridge University Press. pp. 223–54.

Wright, S.C., Aron, A., McLaughlin-Volpe, T., and Ropp, S.A. (1997) 'The Extended Contact Effect: Knowledge of Cross-Group Friendships and Prejudice', *Journal of Personality and Social Psychology*, 73: 73–90.

Wright, S.C., Aron, A., and Tropp, L.R. (2002) 'Including Others (and their Groups) in the Self: Self-Expansion and Intergroup Relations', in J.P. Forgas and K. Williams (eds), *The Social Self: Cognitive, Interpersonal and Intergroup Perspectives.* Philadelphia, PA: Psychology Press, pp. 343–63.

Wright, S.C., Brody, S.M. and Aron, A. (2005) 'Intergroup Contact: Still Our Best Hope for Improving Intergroup Relations', in C.S. Crandall and M. Schaller, (eds) *Social Psychology of prejudice: Historical and Contemporary Issues.* Seattle, WA: Lewinian Press, pp. 115–42.

Wright, S.C., Brody, S.M., and Stout, A. (2000) 'The Avoidance of Contact: One Explanation for Attitude/Contact Inconsistencies'. Paper presented at the annual conference of the Society for Experimental Social Psychology, Atlanta, GA.

Wright, S.C. and Taylor, D.M. (1998) 'Responding to Tokenism: Individual Action in the Face of Collective Injustice', *European Journal of Social Psychology*, 28: 647–67.

Wright, S.C., Taylor, D.M., and Moghaddam, F.M. (1990a) 'Responding to Membership in a Disadvantaged Group: From Acceptance to Collective Action', *Journal of Personality and Social Psychology*, 58: 994–1003.

Wright, S.C., Taylor, D.M., and Moghaddam, F.M. (1990b) 'The Relationship of Perceptions and Emotions to Behavior in the Face of Collective Inequality', *Social Justice Research*, 4: 229–50.

Wright, S.C. and Tropp, L. (2002) 'Collective Action in Response to Disadvantage: Intergroup Perceptions, Social Identification and Social Change', in I. Walker and H. Smith (eds), *Relative Deprivation: Specification, Development, and Integration.* Cambridge: Cambridge University Press, pp. 200–36.

Yzerbyt, V.Y., Judd, C.M., and Corneille, O. (eds) (2004) *The Psychology of Group Perception: Perceived Variability, Entitativity, and Essentialism.* Hove: Psychology Press.

Yzerbyt, V.Y., Rocher, S., and Schadron, G. (1997) 'Stereotypes as Explanations: A Subjective Essentialistic View of Group Perception', in R. Spears, P. Oakes, N. Ellemers, and S.A. Haslam (eds), *The Social Psychology of Stereotyping and Group Life.* Oxford: Blackwell, pp. 20–50.

Yzerbyt, V. and Rogier, A. (2001) 'Blame It on the Group: Entitativity, Subjective Essentialism, and Social Attribution', in J.T. Jost and B. Major (eds), *The Psychology of Legitimacy: Emerging Perspectives on Ideology, Justice, and Intergroup Relations.* New York: Cambridge University Press, pp. 103–34.

Zanna, M.P., Crosby, F., and Loewenstein, G. (1987) 'Male Reference Groups and Discontent Among Female Professionals', in B.A. Gutek and L. Larwood (eds), *Women's Career Development.* Newbury Park, CA: Sage, pp. 28–41.

Zanna, M.P. and Pack, S.J. (1975) 'On the Self-Fulfilling Nature of Apparent Sex Differences in Behavior', *Journal of Experimental Social Psychology*, 11: 583–91.

# Index